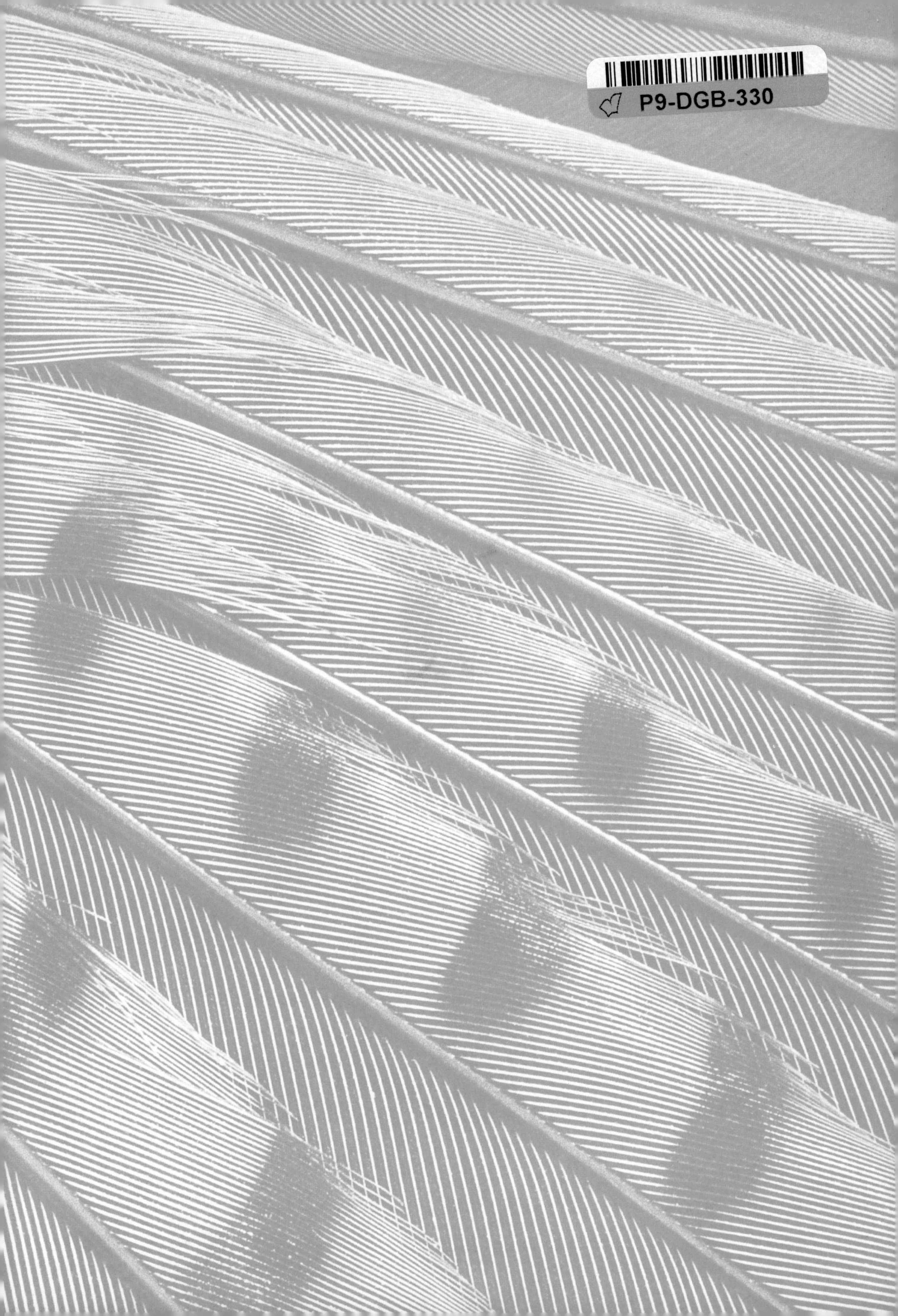
P9-DGB-330

BIRDS of CANADA

BIRDS of CANADA

CONSULTANT EDITOR
David M. Bird, Ph.D.
Director, Avian Science and Conservation Centre
McGill University

DK

DORLING KINDERSLEY

DORLING KINDERSLEY

Senior Art Editors
Caroline Hill, Ina Stradins

Senior Editor
Angeles Gavira Guerrero

Canadian Editor
Barbara Campbell

Project Editor
Nathan Joyce

Designers
Sonia Barbate, Helen McTeer

Editors
Jamie Ambrose, Lori Baird, Tamlyn Calitz, Marcus Hardy, Patrick Newman, Siobhan O'Connor, David Summers, Miezan van Zyl, Rebecca Warren

Design Assistant
Becky Tennant

Editorial Assistants
Elizabeth Munsey, Jaime Tenreiro

Creative Technical Support
John Goldsmid

Production Editor
Maria Elia

Production Controller
Rita Sinha

Jacket Designer
Mark Cavanagh

Illustrators
John Cox, Andrew Mackay

Picture Editor
Neil Fletcher

Picture Researchers
Laura Barwick, Will Jones

Managing Art Editor
Phil Ormerod

Managing Editor
Sarah Larter

Publishing Manager
Liz Wheeler

Art Director
Bryn Walls

Publisher
Jonathan Metcalf

DK INDIA

Senior Editor
Ankush Saikia

Editor
Garima Sharma

Project Designer
Mahua Sharma

DTP Co-ordinator
Balwant Singh

Senior DTP Designer
Harish Aggarwal

DTP Designers
Dheeraj Arora
Tarun Sharma

Editorial Manager
Glenda Fernandes

Art Director
Shefali Upadhyay

Head of Publishing
Aparna Sharma

AMERICAN MUSEUM OF NATURAL HISTORY

Editor-in-chief
François Vuilleumier

Project Coordinators
Caitlin Roxby, Molly Leff

First Edition, 2010

Dorling Kindersley is represented in Canada by:
Tourmaline Editions Inc.
662 King Street West, Suite 304
Toronto, Ontario M5V 1M7

11 12 10 9 8 7 6 5 4 3 2

176389—March 2010

Library and Archives Canada Cataloguing in Publication

Birds of Canada/Canadian consultant: David M. Bird; Editor-in-chief: François Vuilleumier. -- Canadian ed.
Includes index.
ISBN 978-1-55363-120-0
1. Birds--Canada--Identification.
2. Bird watching--Canada--Guidebooks.
I. Bird, David M. (David Michael), 1949-
II. Vuilleumier, François, 1938-
QL685.B58 2010
598.072'3471
C2009-904375-0
Printed and bound in China by Toppan, China

Discover more at
www.dk.com

CONTRIBUTORS

David M. Bird
Nicholas L. Block
Peter Capainolo
Matthew Cormons
Malcolm Coulter
Joseph DiCostanzo
Shawneen Finnegan
Neil Fletcher
Ted Floyd
Jeff Groth
Paul Hess
Brian Hiller
Rob Hume
Thomas Brodie Johnson
Kevin T. Karlson
Stephen Kress
William Moskoff
Bill Pranty
Michael L. P. Retter
Noah Strycker
Paul Sweet
Rodger Titman
Elissa Wolfson

Map Editor Paul Lehman

Project Coordinator Joseph DiCostanzo

CONTENTS

HOW THIS BOOK WORKS

This guide covers just over 600 Canadian bird species. The species are organized into three sections: the first profiles common Canadian species, with each given full-page treatment; the second covers rarer birds in quarter-page entries; the third section consists of a list of rare visitors.

▽ COMMON SPECIES

The main section of the book features the 435 most commonly seen bird species in the Canadian region. Each entry is clear and detailed, following the same easy-to-access structure.

▽ INTRODUCTION

The species are organized conventionally by order, family, and genus. Related birds appear together, preceded by a group introduction. The book follows the American Ornithologists' Union's most recent checklist of North American birds.

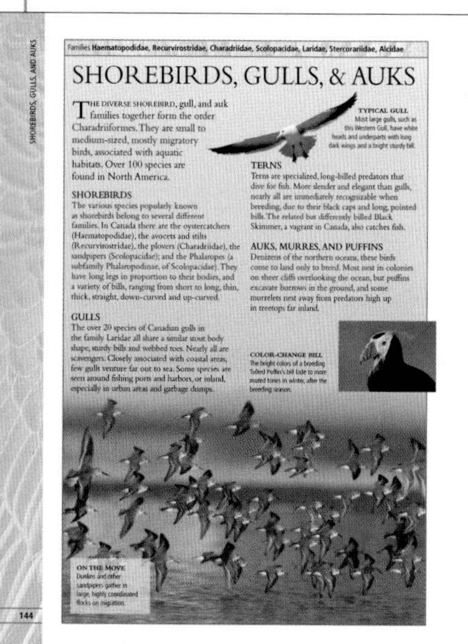

SHOREBIRDS, GULLS, AND AUKS

Families **Haematopodidae, Recurvirostridae, Charadriidae, Scolopacidae, Laridae, Stercorariidae, Alcidae**

SHOREBIRDS, GULLS, & AUKS

THE DIVERSE SHOREBIRD, gull, and auk families together form the order Charadriiformes. They are small to medium-sized, mostly migratory birds, associated with aquatic habitats. Over 100 species are found in North America.

SHOREBIRDS
The various species popularly known as shorebirds belong to several different families. In Canada there are the oystercatchers (Haematopodidae), the avocets and stilts (Recurvirostridae), the plovers (Charadriidae), the sandpipers (Scolopacidae); and the Phalaropes (a subfamily Phalaropodinae, of Scolopacidae). They have long legs in proportion to their bodies, and a variety of bills, ranging from short to long, thin, thick, straight, down-curved and up-curved.

GULLS
The over 20 species of Canadian gulls in the family Laridae all share a similar stout body shape, sturdy bills and webbed toes. Nearly all are scavengers. Closely associated with coastal areas, few gulls venture far out to sea. Some species are seen around fishing ports and harbors, or inland, especially in urban areas and garbage dumps.

TYPICAL GULL
Most large gulls, such as this Western Gull, have white heads and underparts with long dark wings and a bright sturdy bill.

TERNS
Terns are specialized, long-billed predators that dive for fish. More slender and elegant than gulls, nearly all are immediately recognizable when breeding, due to their black caps and long, pointed bills. The related but differently billed Black Skimmer, a vagrant in Canada, also catches fish.

AUKS, MURRES, AND PUFFINS
Denizens of the northern oceans, these birds come to land only to breed. Most nest in colonies on sheer cliffs overlooking the ocean, but puffins excavate burrows in the ground, and some murrelets nest away from predators high up in treetops far inland.

COLOR-CHANGE BILL
The bright colors of a breeding Tufted Puffin's bill fade to more muted tones in winter, after the breeding season.

ON THE MOVE
Dunlins and other sandpipers gather in large, highly coordinated flocks on migration.

144

MAPS

In this book, North America is the region from the southern tip of Florida and the US–Mexico border to the Canadian High Arctic. Each profile includes a map showing the range of the species, with colors reflecting seasonal movements.

KEY

- Resident all year
- Summer distribution
- Winter distribution
- Seen on migration

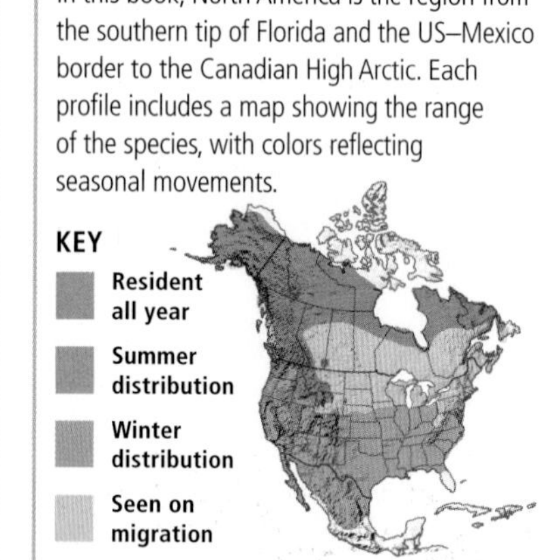

GROUP NAME
The common name of the group the species belongs to is at the top of each page.

COMMON NAME

IN FLIGHT
Illustrations show the bird in flight, from above and/or below —differences of season, age, or sex are not always visible.

DESCRIPTION
Conveys the main features and essential character of the species including:

VOICE
A description of the species' calls and songs, given phonetically where possible.

NESTING
The type of nest and its usual location; the number of eggs in a clutch; the number of broods in a year; the breeding season.

FEEDING
How, where, and what the species feeds on.

SIMILAR SPECIES
Similar-looking species are identified and key differences pointed out.

LENGTH, WINGSPAN, AND WEIGHT
Length is tip of tail to tip of bill; measurements are averages or ranges.

SOCIAL
The social unit the species is usually found in.

LIFESPAN
The average or maximum life expectancy.

STATUS
The conservation status of the species; the symbol (p) means the data available can only suggest a provisional status.

Order **Charadriiformes**	Family **Laridae**

California Gull

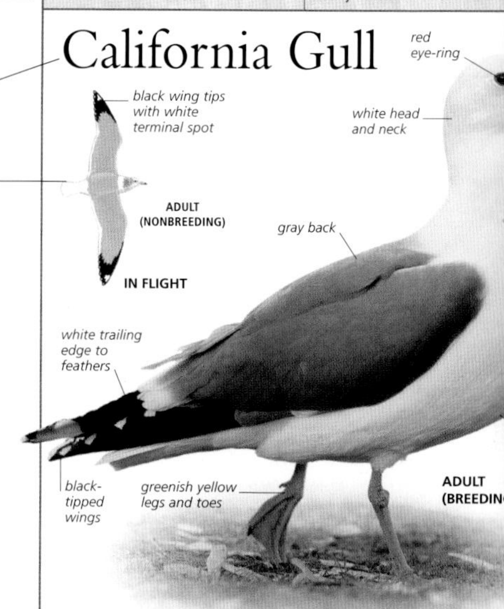
red eye-ring
black wing tips with white terminal spot
white head and neck
ADULT (NONBREEDING)
IN FLIGHT
gray back
white trailing edge to feathers
black-tipped wings
greenish yellow legs and toes
ADULT (BREEDING

Slightly smaller than the Herring Gull, the medium-sized California Gull has a darker back and longer wings. In breeding plumage, it can also be distinguished by the black and red coloration on its bill and its greenish yellow legs. In winter and on young birds, dark streaks are prominent on the nape of the neck. A common interior gull, it is honored by a large, gilded statue in Salt Lake City that commemorates the birds rescue of the settlers' crops from a plague of grasshoppers in 1848.

VOICE Call a repeated *kee-yah, kee-yah, kee-yah.*
NESTING Shallow scrape, lined with feathers, bones, and vegetation, usually on islands; 2–3 eggs; 1 brood; May–July.
FEEDING Forages around lakes for insects, mollusks; hovers over cherry trees dislodging fruits with its wings.

SIMILAR SPECIES

HERRING GULL ☼
see p.198
paler back
pink legs
larger body
HERRING GULL ❄
see p.198
heavy streaking on head
paler back

Length **17½–20in (45–51cm)**	Wingspan **4–4½ft (1.2–1.4m)**
Social **Colonies**	Lifespan **Up to 30 years**

SYMBOLS

♂ Male	Spring
♀ Female	☼ Summer
Juvenile	Autumn
Immature	❄ Winter

MAPS
See panel, left. The occurrence caption describes the bird's preferred habitats and range within the North American region.

CLASSIFICATION
The top band of each entry provides the scientific order, family, and species names (see glossary, pp. 498-500 for full definitions of these terms).

COLOR BAND
The information bands at the top and bottom of each entry are color-coded for each family.

◁ RARE SPECIES

Thirty less common birds are presented on pp. 483–490. Arranged in the same group order used in the main section, these entries consist of one clear photograph of the species accompanied by a description of the bird.

Species *Larus californicus*
SHOREBIRDS, GULLS, AND AUKS
black line and red spot on bill
brownish mottling on head and neck
IMMATURE (2ND WINTER)
gray legs
IMMATURE (3RD SUMMER)
dark streaks on nape of neck
ADULT (NONBREEDING)

PHOTOGRAPHS
These illustrate the species in different views and plumage variations. Significant differences relating to age, sex, and season (breeding/nonbreeding) are shown and the images labelled accordingly; if there is no variation, the images have no label. Unless stated otherwise, the bird shown is an adult.

FLIGHT PATTERNS
This feature illustrates and briefly describes the way the species flies. See panel below.

VAGRANTS ▷

Very rare visitors and peripheral bird species are listed at the back of the book with a brief description, including where the species is from.

VAGRANTS

THE LIST THAT FOLLOWS, ALTHOUGH not exhaustive, consists of species that occur only very rarely in Canada. Vagrants to Canada arrive from both the Northern and Southern Hemispheres—Europe, Russia, and eastern Asia as well as South America, Africa, and Oceania. The US and Canada are well placed to receive birds that drift off course from eastern Asia and Siberia, crossing the Pacific, and from Europe, crossing the Atlantic. Western Alaska has a particularly high concentration of vagrants because the western tip forms a series of islands, the Aleutians, that reach almost all the way across the Bering Sea to Russia. Some of these birds find their way to Canada's west coast.

The occurrence of vagrant species is classified by the American Birding Association as rare, casual, or accidental depending on how often they have been seen, and this terminology is used in the comment section on each species. Rare species are seen every year, but in low numbers. Casual visitors have been seen in Canada at least half a dozen times, including three sightings in the last 30 years. Accidental species have been recorded in Canada no more than five times.

COMMON NAME	SCIENTIFIC NAME	SCIENTIFIC/FAMILY NAME	DESCRIPTION
Waterfowl			
Black-bellied Whistling Duck	*Dendrocygna autumnalis*	Anatidae/Waterfowl	Casual visitor to Ontario
Fulvous Whistling Duck	*Dendrocygna bicolor*	Anatidae/Waterfowl	Casual visitor across Canada
Taiga Bean-Goose	*Anser fabalis*	Anatidae/Waterfowl	Rare visitor to Maritimes
Pink-footed Goose	*Anser brachyrhynchus*	Anatidae/Waterfowl	Accidental in southern Quebec
Emperor Goose	*Chen canagica*	Anatidae/Waterfowl	Accidental on southern British Columbia coast
Barnacle Goose	*Branta leucopsis*	Anatidae/Waterfowl	Accidental in southern Quebec, Baffin Island, Ontario, and Maritimes
Graylag Goose	*Anser anser*	Anatidae/Waterfowl	Accidental off the coast of Newfoundland and Labrador
Common Pochard	*Aythya ferina*	Anatidae/Waterfowl	Accidental in southern Quebec
Tufted Duck	*Aythya fuligula*	Anatidae/Waterfowl	Accidental in British Columbia, southern Ontario, and southern Quebec
Spectacled Eider	*Somateria fischeri*	Anatidae/Waterfowl	Accidental in northern British Columbia
Smew	*Mergellus albellus*	Anatidae/Waterfowl	Accidental in British Columbia, Ontario, and Quebec
Albatrosses, Petrels, and Shearwaters			
Laysan Albatross	*Phoebastria immutabilis*	Diomedeidae/Albatrosses	Rare visitor to Pacific coast
Short-tailed Albatross	*Phoebastria albatrus*	Diomedeidae/Albatrosses	Accidental in northern British Columbia
Yellow-nosed Albatross	*Thalassarche chlororhynchos*	Diomedeidae/Albatrosses	Casual visitor off Maritime coast
Black-browed Albatross	*Thalassarche melanophris*	Diomedeidae/Albatrosses	Casual visitor off Maritime coast
Fea's Petrel	*Pterodroma feae*	Procellariidae/Petrels and Shearwaters	Accidental off Nova Scotia coast

491

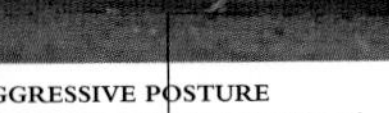

LIGHT: strong and direct, but somewhat stiff, with deep wing beats.

AGGRESSIVE POSTURE
This California Gull is displaying signs of aggression—possibly against another bird.

OCCURRENCE
Breeds at scattered locations across interior western Canada and the US. Some of the largest colonies are on the highly saline Mono Lake and the Great Salt Lake; winters along the Pacific Coast from British Columbia to Mexico; strays increasingly reported in the East.

Weight **18–35oz (0.5–1kg)**

Status **Secure**

191

HABITAT/BEHAVIOR
Additional photographs reveal the species in its typical habitat or show the bird exhibiting typical behavior.

FLIGHT PATTERNS

Simple line diagrams are used to illustrate eight basic flight patterns.

wingbeats

Woodpecker-like: bursts of wingbeats between deeply undulating glides.

Finch-like: light, bouncy action with flurries of wingbeats between deep, undulating glides.

Grouse-like: bursts of wing beats between short, straight glides.

Hawk-like: straight, with several quick, deep beats between short, flat glides.

Gull-like: continually flapping, with slow, steady wingbeats.

Duck-like: continually flapping, with fast wingbeats.

Kite-like: deep, slow wingbeats between soaring glides.

Swallow-like: swooping, with bursts of wingbeats between glides.

EVOLUTION

Ornithologists agree that birds evolved from dinosaurs about 150 million years ago, but there is still debate about the dinosaur group from which they descended. Around 10,000 species of birds exist today, living in many different kinds of habitats across the world, from desert to Arctic tundra.

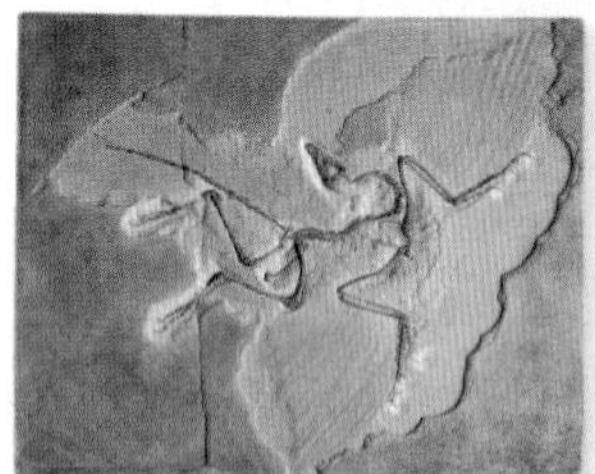

MISSING LINK?
Archaeopteryx, shown here as a 145-million-year-old fossil, had dinosaur-like teeth, but birdlike feathers.

SPECIATION

What are species and how do they evolve? Species are biological entities. When two species of a genus overlap they rarely interbreed and produce hybrids. The North American Flicker has an eastern (yellow-shafted) and a western (red-shafted) form; after the discovery that these two forms interbreed in the Great Plains, the flickers are now considered one species. In other cases, a previously single species, such as the Blue Grouse, has been divided into the Dusky Grouse and the Sooty Grouse. Such examples illustrate how species evolve, first by geographic separation, followed in time by overlap. This process can take millions of years.

BIRD GENEALOGY

The diagram below is called a phylogeny, and shows how selected groups of birds are related to each other. The timescale at the top of the diagram is derived from both fossil and DNA evidence, which allows ornithologists to estimate when different lineages of birds diverged. The names of groups shown in bold are those living in Canada.

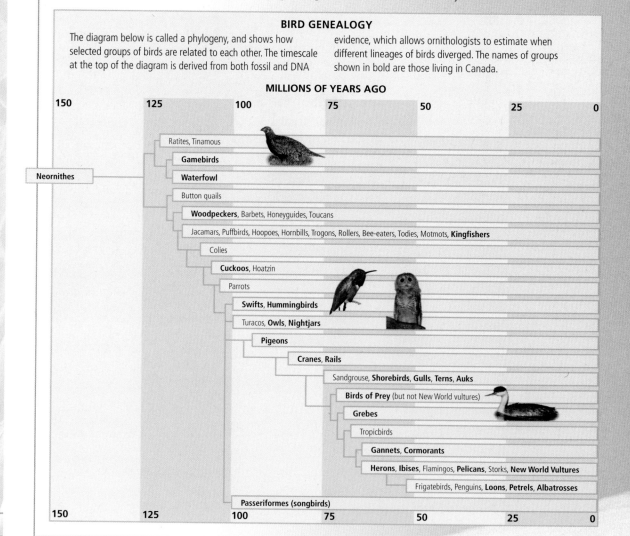

MILLIONS OF YEARS AGO

150 125 100 75 50 25 0

Neornithes

- Ratites, Tinamous
- **Gamebirds**
- **Waterfowl**
- Button quails
- **Woodpeckers**, Barbets, Honeyguides, Toucans
- Jacamars, Puffbirds, Hoopoes, Hornbills, Trogons, Rollers, Bee-eaters, Todies, Motmots, **Kingfishers**
- Colies
- **Cuckoos**, Hoatzin
- Parrots
- **Swifts**, **Hummingbirds**
- Turacos, **Owls**, **Nightjars**
- **Pigeons**
- **Cranes**, **Rails**
- Sandgrouse, **Shorebirds**, **Gulls**, **Terns**, **Auks**
- **Birds of Prey** (but not New World vultures)
- **Grebes**
- Tropicbirds
- **Gannets**, **Cormorants**
- **Herons**, **Ibises**, Flamingos, **Pelicans**, Storks, **New World Vultures**
- Frigatebirds, Penguins, **Loons**, **Petrels**, **Albatrosses**
- **Passeriformes (songbirds)**

150 125 100 75 50 25 0

BLENDING IN
This magnificent species is diurnal, unlike most other owls, which are nocturnal. The Snowy Owl breeds in the Arctic tundra and if the ground is covered with snow, it blends in perfectly.

CONVERGENCE

The evolutionary process during which birds of two distantly related groups develop similarities is called convergence. Carrion-eating birds of prey are one example. Old World vultures belong to the hawk family (Accipitridae), while New World vultures are more closely related to storks. However, both groups are characterized by hooked bills, bare heads, and weak talons.

PARALLEL EVOLUTION
The African longclaws (family Motacillidae) and North American meadowlarks (family Icteridae) show convergence in plumage color and pattern.

CAPE LONGCLAW

WESTERN MEADOWLARK

EXTINCTION

During the last 150 years, North America has lost the Passenger Pigeon, the Great Auk, the Carolina Parakeet, the Labrador Duck, and the Eskimo Curlew. Humans either hunted them out of existence or destroyed their habitat. Some species that seemed doomed have had a reprieve. Thanks to a breeding and release program, the Whooping Crane still makes its annual migration from Canada to the US.

OVERHUNTING
The Passenger Pigeon was eradicated as a result of relentless hunting.

CLASSIFYING BIRDS

All past and present animal life is named and categorized into groups. Classifications reflect the genealogical relationships among groups, based on traits such as color, bones, or DNA. Birds make up the class "Aves," which includes "orders;" each "order" is made up of one or more "families." "Genus" is a subdivision of "family," which contains one or more "species." A species is a unique group of similar organisms that interbreed and produce fertile offspring. Some species have distinct populations, which are known as subspecies.

Class
Aves (Birds)
Order
Passeriformes (songbirds)
Family
Parulidae (wood-warblers)
Genus
Dendroica
Species
Dendroica castanea
Dendroica palmarum
Dendroica tigrina
Subspecies
D. p. palmarum

ANATOMY AND FLIGHT

IN SPITE OF THEIR EXTERNAL DIVERSITY, birds are remarkably similar internally. To allow flight, birds require a skeleton that is both rigid and light. Rigidity is achieved by the fusion of some bones, especially the lower vertebrae, while lightness is maintained by having hollow limb bones. These are connected to air sacs, which, in turn, are connected to the bird's lungs.

"hand"
"forearm"
neck vertebrae
bill
furcula
fused tail vertebrae
keeled sternum

SKELETON
Avian skeletal features include the furcula (wishbone), the keeled sternum (breastbone), and the fused tail vertebrae.

FLIGHT ADAPTATIONS

For birds to be able to fly, they need light and rigid bones, a lightweight skull, and hollow wing and leg bones. In addition, pouch-like air sacs are connected to hollow bones, which reduce a bird's weight. The air sacs also function as a cooling system, which birds need because they have a high metabolic rate. The breast muscles, which are crucial for flight, attach to the keeled sternum (breastbone).

secondaries
tail feathers
uppertail coverts
rump
tertials
scapulars
primaries

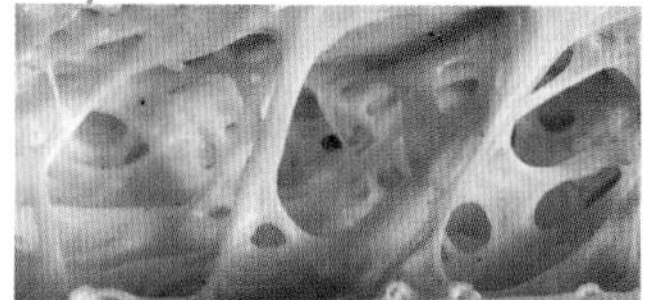

BIRD BONE STRUCTURE
Most bird bones, except those of penguins and other flightless birds, are hollow, which reduces their weight. A honeycomb of internal struts makes the bones remarkably strong.

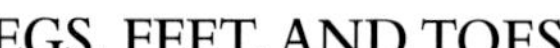

LEGS, FEET, AND TOES

When you look at a bird's leg, you do not see its thigh, which is inside the body cavity, but the leg from the knee down. When we talk about a bird's feet we really mean its toes. The shin is a fused tibia and fibula. This fused bone plus the heel are known as the "tarso-metatarsus."

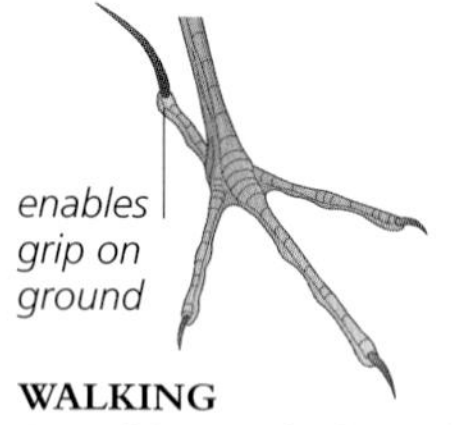
enables grip on ground

WALKING
Ground-foraging birds usually have a long hind claw.

enables strong grip on branches

CLIMBING
Most climbers have two toes forward and two backward.

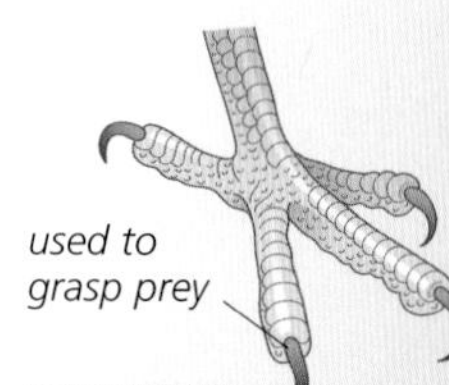
webbing provides thrust in water

SWIMMING
Water-loving birds have webbing between their toes.

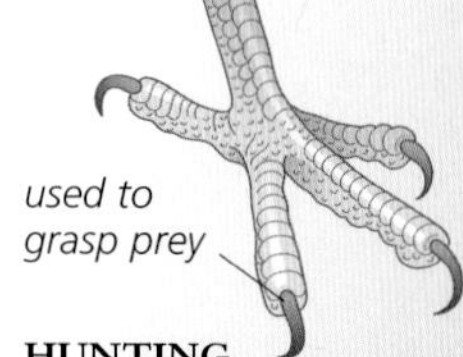
used to grasp prey

HUNTING
Birds of prey have powerful toes and strong, sharp claws.

axillaries
breast
bill
undertail coverts
belly
toes

UNDERPARTS
Underwing coverts have a regular pattern of overlapping rows. Short feathers cover the head, breast, belly, and flanks. In most birds, the toes are unfeathered.

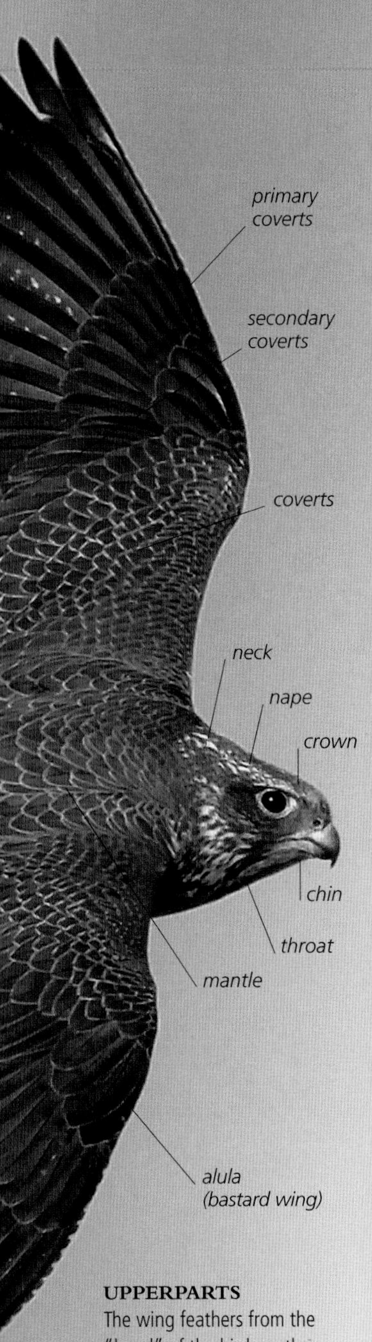
primary coverts
secondary coverts
coverts
neck
nape
crown
chin
throat
mantle
alula (bastard wing)

UPPERPARTS
The wing feathers from the "hand" of the bird are the primaries and those on the "forearm" are the secondaries. Each set has its accompanying row of coverts. The tertials are adjacent to the secondaries.

FEATHERS

All birds, by definition, have feathers. These remarkable structures, which are modified scales, serve two main functions: insulation and flight. Special muscles allow birds to raise their feathers or to flatten them against the body. In cold weather, fluffed-out feathers keep an insulating layer of air between the skin and the outside. This insulating capacity is why humans often find wearing loose-fitting "down" jackets so effective against the cold. The first feathers that chicks have after hatching are down feathers. The rigidity of the flight feathers helps to create a supporting surface that birds use to generate thrust and lift.

TYPES OF FEATHERS
Birds have three main kinds of feathers: down, contour, and flight feathers. The rigid axis of all feathers is called the "rachis."

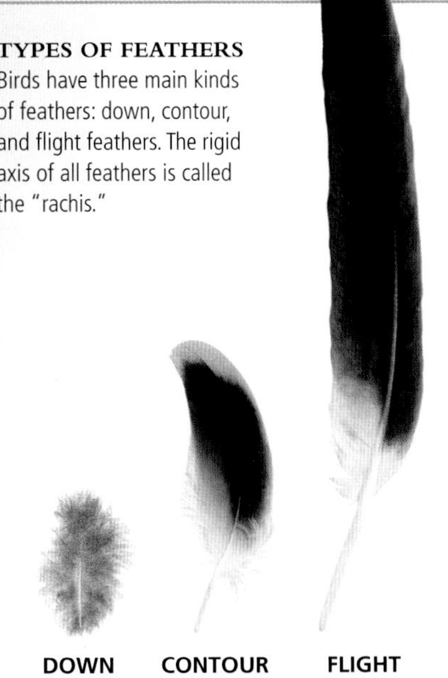
DOWN FEATHER
CONTOUR FEATHER
FLIGHT FEATHER

WING FUNCTIONS

Flapping, soaring, gliding, and hovering are among the ways birds can use their wings. They also exhibit colors or patterns as part of territorial and courtship displays. Several birds, such as herons, open their wings like an umbrella when foraging in water for fish. An important aspect of wings is their relationship to a bird's weight. The ratio of a bird's wing area to weight is called wing loading, but this may also be affected by wing shape. An eagle has a large wing area to weight ratio, which means it has lower wing loading, whereas a swallow has a small wing area to weight ratio, and therefore high wing loading. This means that the slow, soaring eagle is capable of much more energy-efficient flight than the fast, agile swallow.

LONG AND BROAD
The broad, long, rectangular wings of an eagle allow it to soar. The outstretched alulae (bastard wings) give it extra lift.

POINTED
Broad at their base and tapering toward a point, and bent at the wrist, a swallow's wings enable fast flight and sharp turns.

SHORT AND ROUND
Short, broad, and round wings enable warblers to move between perches and to migrate long distances.

WING AERODYNAMICS

The supporting surface of a bird's wing enables it to takeoff and stay aloft. Propulsion and lift are linked in birds—which use their wings for both—unlike in airplanes in which these two functions are separate. Large and heavy birds, like swans, flap their wings energetically to create propulsion, and need a long, watery runway before they can fly off. The Golden Eagle can take off from a cliff with little or no wing flapping, but the Turkey Vulture hops up from carrion then flaps vigorously and finally uses air flowing across its wings to soar. This diagram shows how air flow affects lift.

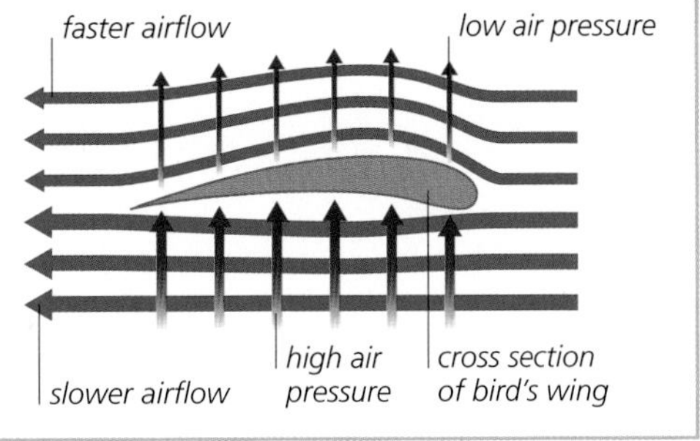
faster airflow
low air pressure
slower airflow
high air pressure
cross section of bird's wing

MIGRATION

Until recently, the mechanics, or the "how" of migration was poorly understood. Today, however, ornithologists know that birds use a variety of cues including visual and magnetic, whether they migrate by day or by night. Birds do not leave northern breeding areas because of the winter cold, but because day-length is getting shorter and food scarcer.

NIGHT MIGRANTS
During migration, ornithologists can point a telescope on the moon and count the birds that cross its surface.

REFUELING
Red Knots make a stop on their long journey to eat horseshoe crab eggs.

INSTINCTIVE MOVE

Even though many birds use visual cues and landmarks during their migration, for example birds of prey flying along the Appalachians, "instinctive" behavior must control much of how and where they move. Instinct is a loose term that is hard to define, but ornithologists generally understand it as a genetically programmed activity. They assume that natural selection has molded a behavior as complex as migration by acting on birds' DNA; this hypothesis is reasonable but hard to prove. Nevertheless, it would seem to be the only explanation why many juvenile shorebirds leave their breeding grounds after their parents and yet find their way to their final destination.

NAVIGATION

One of the most puzzling aspects of migration is understanding how birds make their way from their breeding grounds to their destination. Ornithologists have devised experiments to determine how the different components of a navigation system work. For example, if visual landmarks are hidden by fog, a faint sun can give birds a directional clue; if heavy clouds hide the sun, then the birds' magnetic compass may be used to ascertain their direction.

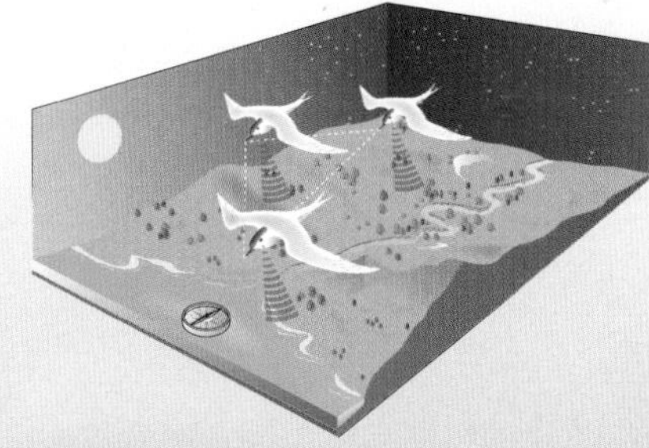

FINDING THE WAY
Birds coordinate information their brains receive from the sun, moon, stars, landmarks, and magnetite, or iron oxide, and use it as a compass.

OVERLAND FLIERS
Sandhill Cranes migrate over hills and mountains from their Arctic tundra breeding grounds to the marshes of the Platte River in the midwestern US.

GLOBETROTTERS

Some bird species in Canada are year-round residents, although a few individuals of these species move away from where they hatched at some time in the year. However, a large number of Canadian species are migratory. A few species breed in Labrador, but winter in the Gulf of the Caribbean. Others breed in the Canadian Arctic Archipelago, fly over land and the Pacific Ocean, and spend the winter at sea off the coast of Peru. Many songbirds fly from Canada's boreal forests to Mexico and northern South America. The most amazing globetrotters, such as the Red Knot, fly all the way to Tierra del Fuego, making only a few stops along the way after their short breeding season in the Arctic tundra. The return journeys of some of these travelers are not over the same route—instead, their entire trip is elliptical in shape.

EPIC JOURNEY
The Arctic Tern is a notorious long-distance migrant, breeding in northern regions and wintering in the pack ice of Antarctica after flying a round-trip distance of about 25,000 miles (40,000km).

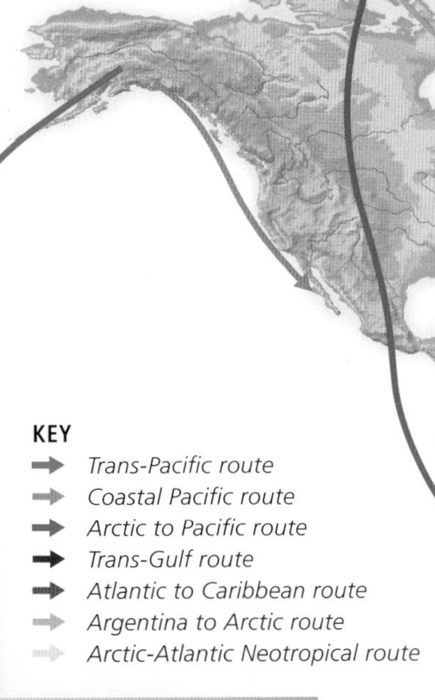

KEY
- *Trans-Pacific route*
- *Coastal Pacific route*
- *Arctic to Pacific route*
- *Trans-Gulf route*
- *Atlantic to Caribbean route*
- *Argentina to Arctic route*
- *Arctic-Atlantic Neotropical route*

NEOTROPICAL MIGRANT
Many wood-warblers, such as this Blackpoll Warbler breed in boreal forests, before migrating to their wintering grounds in the Caribbean, or Central or South America.

MIGRATION ROUTES
The map above shows the range of migration routes that some North American species take to and from their breeding grounds.

V-FORMATION
Geese and other large waterfowl fly in a v-formation. The leader falls back and is replaced by another individual, saving energy for all the birds.

PARTIAL MIGRANT

The American Robin is a good example of a partial migrant, a species in which the birds of some populations are resident whereas others migrate out of their breeding range. Most Canadian populations of the American Robin fly south, US populations are largely resident, and quite a few from either population spend the winter in the Southwest, Florida, or Mexico.

KEY
- *Breeding distribution*
- *Resident all year*
- *Nonbreeding distribution*

COURTSHIP AND MATING

Whether monogamous or not, males and females need to mate for their species to perpetuate itself. With most species, the male plays the dominant role of advertising a territory to potential mates using vocal or visual displays. Females then select a male and if the two respond positively to each other, a period of courtship follows ending in mating. The next step is nest building, egg laying and rearing the young.

DANCING CRANES
During courtship, Sandhill Cranes perform spectacular dances, the two birds of a pair leaping into the air with wings opened and legs splayed.

DISPLAYS

Mutual attraction between the sexes starts with some sort of display, usually performed by the male. These displays can take a number of forms, from flashing dazzling breeding plumage, conducting elaborate dancing rituals, performing complex songs, offering food or nesting material, or actually building a nest. Some birds, such as grebes have fascinatingly intricate ceremonies, in which both male and female simultaneously perform the same movements.

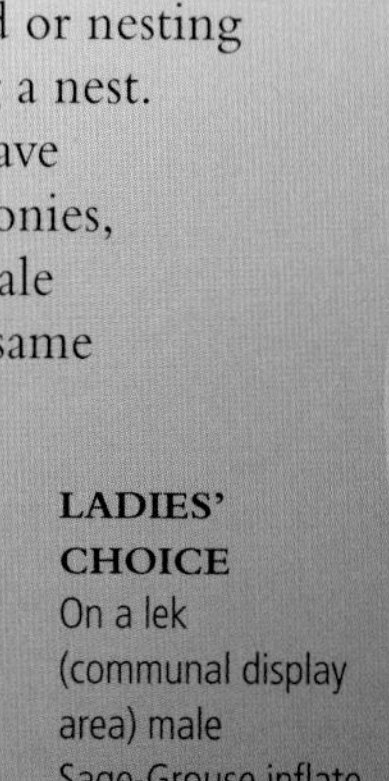

WELCOME HOME
Northern Gannets greet their mates throughout the breeding season by rubbing bills together and opening their wings.

LADIES' CHOICE
On a lek (communal display area) male Sage-Grouse inflate chest pouches while females flock around them and select a mate.

COURTSHIP FEEDING

In some species, males offer food to their mate to maintain the pair-bond. The male Common Tern routinely brings small fish to a mate in a nesting colony, spreading his wings and tail until she accepts the fish.

MAINTAINING RELATIONS
A male Northern Cardinal offers food to the female, which is a way of reinforcing their pair bond.

BREEDING

After mating, a nest is made, often by the female, where she lays from one to a dozen eggs. Not all birds make nests. Nightjars, for example lay their eggs directly on the ground. In many species incubation doesn't start until the female has laid all the eggs. Incubation, again usually done by the female, varies from about twelve days to about 45 days. Songbirds ranging from the temperate zone to the Arctic show a range in clutch size with more eggs produced in the North than in the South. The breeding process can fail at any stage, for example a predator can eat the eggs or the chicks. Some birds will nest again but others give up breeding for the season.

MATING
Mating is usually brief, and typically takes place on a perch or on the ground, but a few species like swifts and swallows mate in the air. This male Black Tern balances himself by opening his wings.

POLYGAMY
This Winter Wren collects nesting material for one of the several nests he will build.

MUTUAL PREENING
Many species of albatross, like these Black-footed Albatrosses from the Pacific, preen each other, with one bird softly nibbling the feathers on the other's head.

MONOGAMOUS BONDS
Some birds, such as Snow Geese, remain paired for life after establishing a bond.

SINGLE FATHER

A male Red-necked Phalarope incubates eggs in the Arctic tundra. Phalaropes are well known for their reversal of breeding roles. The female, who is the larger and more colorful of the two sexes, aggressively competes for males, and after mating with several of them, plays no role in nest building, incubation, or caring for chicks, but tends to her territory instead. Although the chicks can feed by themselves immediately after hatching, they remain with a male before growing feathers and living on their own.

NESTS AND EGGS

MOST BIRD SPECIES BUILD THEIR OWN NEST, which is a necessary container for their eggs. Exceptions include cowbirds, which lay their eggs in other species' nests. Nest-building is often done by the female alone, but in some species the male may help or even build it himself. Eggs are incubated either by females alone, or by males or females, depending on the species. Egg shells are hard enough to sustain the weight of incubating parents, yet soft enough for a chick to break its way out. Eggs, consisting of 60 percent water, contain a fatty yolk for nourishment of the embryo as well as sugars and proteins.

NEST TYPES

In addition to the four types shown below, nests range from a simple scrape in the ground with a few added pebbles to an elaborate woven basket-like structure. Plant matter forms basic nest material. This includes twigs, grass stems, bark, lichens, mosses, plant down, and rootlets. Some birds add mud to their nest for strength. Others incorporate animal hair or feathers to improve its softness and insulation. Female eider ducks pluck down feathers from their belly. Some birds include bits of plastic or threads in their nests. Many birds make their nest or lay their eggs deep inside the empty burrows of other animals. Burrowing Owls nest in prairie dog burrows, where they coexist with the rodents.

UNTIDY NEST
Huge stick nests, built on top of dead trees, are the hallmark of Ospreys. They also use custom-made nesting platforms erected by humans specifically for them.

EGG CUP
A clutch of three blue robin's eggs rest in a cup lined with grass stems. Robins build their nests either in shrubs or trees.

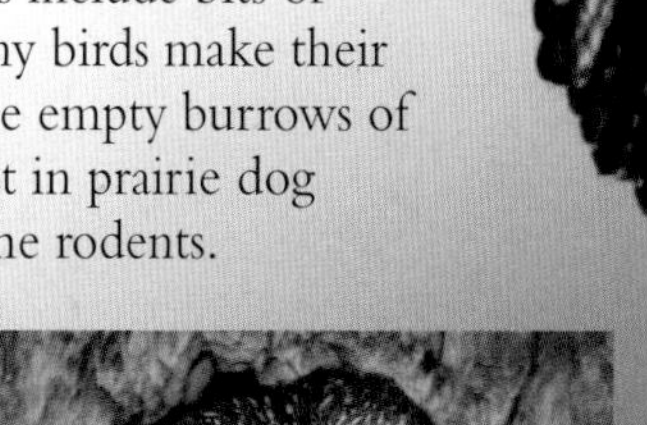

NATURAL CAVITY
This Northern Saw-whet Owl is nesting at the bottom of a cavity in a tree that has probably been excavated by a woodpecker.

NEST BOX
Cavity-nesting bluebirds have been affected by habitat loss, and compete with other birds for nest sites, which may include human-made structures.

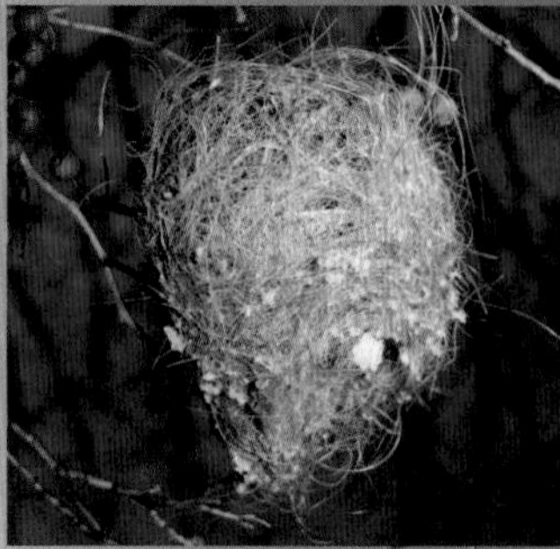

COMPLEX WEAVE
New World orioles weave intricate nests from dried grass stems and other plant material, and hang them from the tip of branches, often high up in trees.

EGG SHAPES

There are six basic egg shapes among birds, as illustrated to the right. The most common egg shapes are longitudinal or elliptical. Murres lay pear-shaped eggs, an adaptation for nesting on the narrow ledges of sea cliffs; if an egg rolls, it does so in a tight circle and remains on the ledge. Spherical eggs with irregular red blotches are characteristic of birds of prey. Pigeons and doves lay white oval eggs, usually two per clutch. The eggs of many songbirds, including sparrows and buntings, are conical and have a variety of dark markings on a pale background.

NEAT ARRANGEMENT
Many shorebirds, such as plovers and sandpipers, lay four conical eggs with the narrow ends pointed in toward each other.

COLOR AND SHAPE
Birds' eggs vary widely in terms of shape, colors, and markings. The American Robin's egg on the left is a beautiful blue.

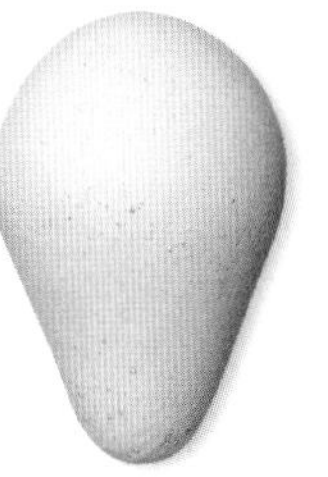

PEAR SHAPED LONGITUDINAL ELLIPTICAL

OVAL CONICAL SPHERICAL

HATCHING CONDITION

After a period of incubation, which varies from species to species, chicks break the eggshell, some of them using an egg tooth, a special bill feature that falls off after hatching. After a long and exhausting struggle, the chick eventually tumbles out of the shell fragments. The transition from the watery medium inside the egg to the air outside is a tremendous physiological switch. Once free of their shell, the hatchlings recover from the exertion and either beg food from their parents or feed on their own.

FOOD DELIVERY
Tern chicks, although able to move around, cannot catch the fish they need to survive and must rely on their parents to provide food until they can fly.

PARENTAL GUIDANCE
Birds of prey, such as these Snowy Owl owlets, need their parents to care for them longer than some other bird species, and do not leave the nest until their feathers are sufficiently developed for their first flight.

FAST FEEDER
Coots, gallinules, and rails hatch with a complete covering of down and can feed themselves immediately after birth.

BROOD PARASITISM

Neither cowbirds in the New World nor cuckoos in the Old World make a nest. Female cowbirds deposit up to 20 eggs in the nests of several other species. If the foster parents accept the foreign egg, they will feed the chick of the parasite until it fledges. In the picture below, a tiny wood-warbler feeds its adopted chick, a huge cowbird hatchling that has overgrown the nest.

IDENTIFICATION

Some species are easy to identify, but in many cases, species identification is tricky. In Canada, a notoriously difficult group in terms of identification is the wood-warblers, especially in the fall, when most species have similar greenish or yellowish plumage.

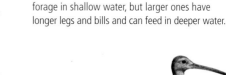

GEOGRAPHIC RANGE

Each species of bird in Canada lives in a particular area that is called its geographic range. Some species have a restricted range; for example, the Whooping Crane breeds only in Wood Buffalo National Park in Alberta and the Northwest Territories. Other species, such as the Red-tailed Hawk, range from coast to coast and from northern Canada to Mexico. Species with a broad range usually breed in a variety of vegetation types, while species with narrow ranges often have a specialized habitat; Northern Gannet's is steep rocky shores.

bright blue wings

white belly

chestnut flanks

BLUEBIRD VARIATIONS
Species of the genus *Sialia*, such as the Mountain Bluebird above and the Eastern Bluebird below, are easy to identify.

SIZE AND WEIGHT

From hummingbird to Tundra Swan and from extra-light to heavy, such is the range of sizes and weights found among the bird species of Canada. Size can be measured in several ways, for example the length of a bird from bill-tip to tail-tip, or its wingspan. Size can also be estimated for a given bird in relationship with another that is familiar. For example, the less familiar Bicknells' Thrush can be compared with the well-known American Robin.

SIZE MATTERS
Smaller shorebirds, with shorter legs and bills, forage in shallow water, but larger ones have longer legs and bills and can feed in deeper water.

SEMIPALMATED SANDPIPER

LESSER YELLOWLEGS

HUDSONIAN GODWIT

LONG-BILLED CURLEW

GENERAL SHAPE

Just as birds come in all sizes, their body shapes vary, but size and shape are not necessarily correlated. In the dense reed beds in which it lives, the American Bittern's long and thin body blends in with stems. The round-bodied Sedge Wren hops in shrubby vegetation or near the ground where slimness is not an advantage. In dense forest canopy, the slender and long-tailed Yellow-billed Cuckoo can maneuver easily. Mourning Doves inhabit rather open habitats and their plumpness is irrelevant when it comes to their living space.

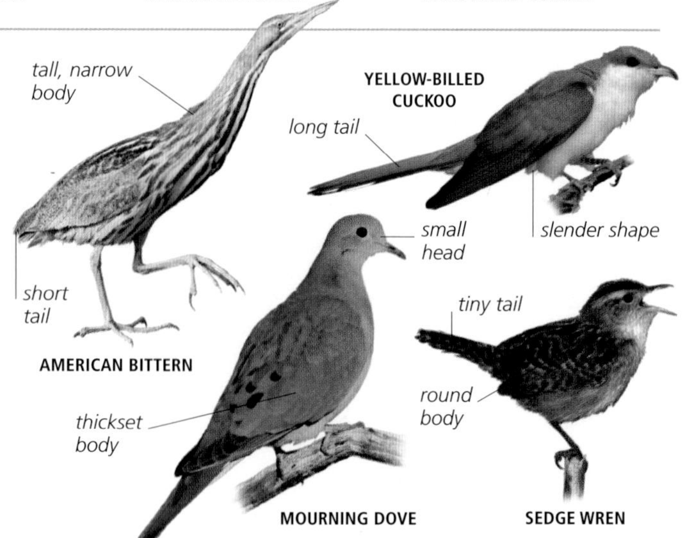
tall, narrow body
short tail
AMERICAN BITTERN
YELLOW-BILLED CUCKOO
long tail
slender shape
small head
thickset body
MOURNING DOVE
tiny tail
round body
SEDGE WREN

BILL SHAPE

These images show a range of bill shapes and sizes relative to the bird's head size. In general, bill form, including length or thickness, corresponds to the kinds of food a birds consumes. With its pointed bill, the Mountain Chickadee picks tiny insects from crevices in tree bark. At another extreme, dowitchers probe mud with their long thin bills, feeling for worms. The avocet swishes its bill back and forth in briny water in search of shrimp.

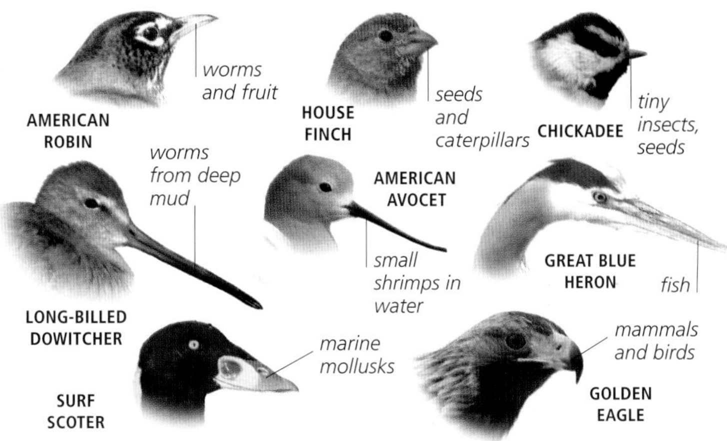
AMERICAN ROBIN
worms and fruit
HOUSE FINCH
seeds and caterpillars
CHICKADEE
tiny insects, seeds
LONG-BILLED DOWITCHER
worms from deep mud
AMERICAN AVOCET
small shrimps in water
GREAT BLUE HERON
fish
SURF SCOTER
marine mollusks
GOLDEN EAGLE
mammals and birds

WING SHAPE

Birds' wing shapes are correlated with their flight style. The long, round-tipped wings of the Red-tailed Hawk are perfect for soaring, while the tiny wings of hummingbirds are exactly what is needed to hover in front of flowers and then to back away after a meal of nectar. When flushed, quails flutter with their round wings and quickly drop down.

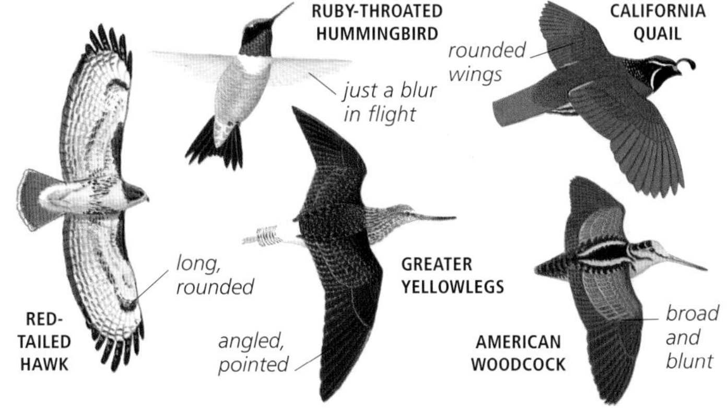
RUBY-THROATED HUMMINGBIRD
just a blur in flight
CALIFORNIA QUAIL
rounded wings
RED-TAILED HAWK
long, rounded
GREATER YELLOWLEGS
angled, pointed
AMERICAN WOODCOCK
broad and blunt

TAIL SHAPE

It is not clear why some songbirds, like the American Goldfinch, have a notched tail while other similar sized birds do not. Tail shapes vary as much as wing shapes, but are not so easily linked to a function. Irrespective of shape, tails are needed for balance. In some birds, tail shape, color, and pattern are used in courtship displays or in defensive displays when threatened.

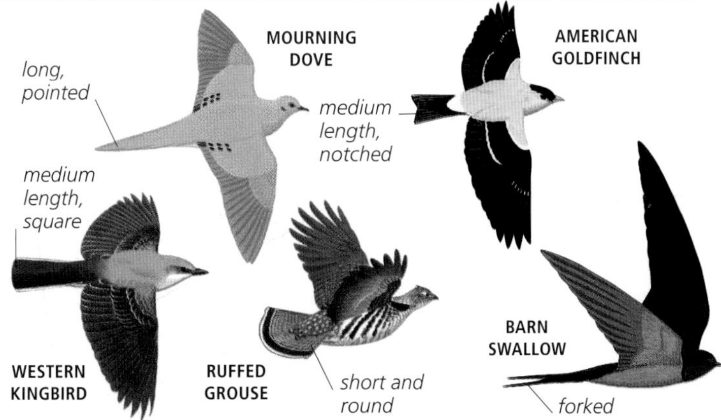
MOURNING DOVE
long, pointed
AMERICAN GOLDFINCH
medium length, notched
WESTERN KINGBIRD
medium length, square
RUFFED GROUSE
short and round
BARN SWALLOW
forked

COLORS AND MARKINGS

Melanin and carotenoid pigments determine color. Gray and brown birds have melanin (under hormonal influence), yellow and red ones carotenoid (derived from food). Flamingos are pink because they eat carotenoid-rich crustaceans. Diversity in color and markings also results from scattering of white light by feathers (producing blue colors) and optical interference (iridescence) due to the structural properties of some feathers.

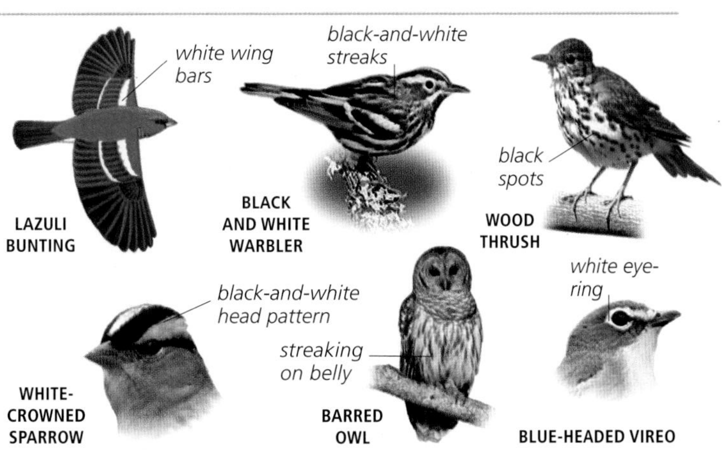
LAZULI BUNTING
white wing bars
BLACK AND WHITE WARBLER
black-and-white streaks
WOOD THRUSH
black spots
WHITE-CROWNED SPARROW
black-and-white head pattern
BARRED OWL
streaking on belly
BLUE-HEADED VIREO
white eye-ring

SPECIES GUIDE

Families **Phasianidae, Odontophoridae**

GAMEBIRDS

THIS DIVERSE AND ADAPTABLE group of birds thrives in habitats ranging from hot desert to frozen tundra. Gamebirds spend most of the time on the ground, springing loudly into the air when alarmed.

QUAILS

Among the most terrestrial of all gamebirds, quails are also renowned for their great sociability, often forming large family groups, or "coveys," of up to 100 birds. The five species found in western North America each live in a specific habitat or at a particular elevation, but the single species found in the East, the Northern Bobwhite, ranges over a variety of habitats.

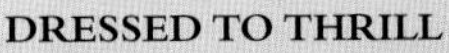

DRESSED TO THRILL
With its striking plumage, the California Quail is one of the most widespread quails of western North America.

GROUSE

The most numerous and widespread of gamebirds, the 12 different species of grouse can be divided into three groups based on their preferred habitats. Forest grouse include the Ruffed Grouse in the East, the Spruce Grouse in the North, and the Sooty Grouse and Dusky Grouse in the West. Prairie grouse, including the Sharp-tailed Grouse, are found throughout the middle of the continent. All three tundra and mountaintop grouse or Ptarmigan are found in the extreme North and the Rockies. Grouse often possess patterns that match their surroundings, providing camouflage from enemies both animal and human.

GRASSLAND GROUSE
The aptly named Sharp-tailed Grouse is locally common in western prairies, strutting in search of grasshoppers.

PHEASANTS & PARTRIDGES

These Eurasian gamebirds were introduced into North America in the 19th and 20th centuries to provide additional targets for recreational hunters. While some introductions failed, species such as the colorful Ring-necked Pheasant adapted well and now thrive in established populations.

SNOW BIRD
The Rock Ptarmigan's white winter plumage camouflages it against the snow, helping to hide it from predators.

Order **Galliformes**	Family **Odontophoridae**	Species ***Callipepla californica***

California Quail

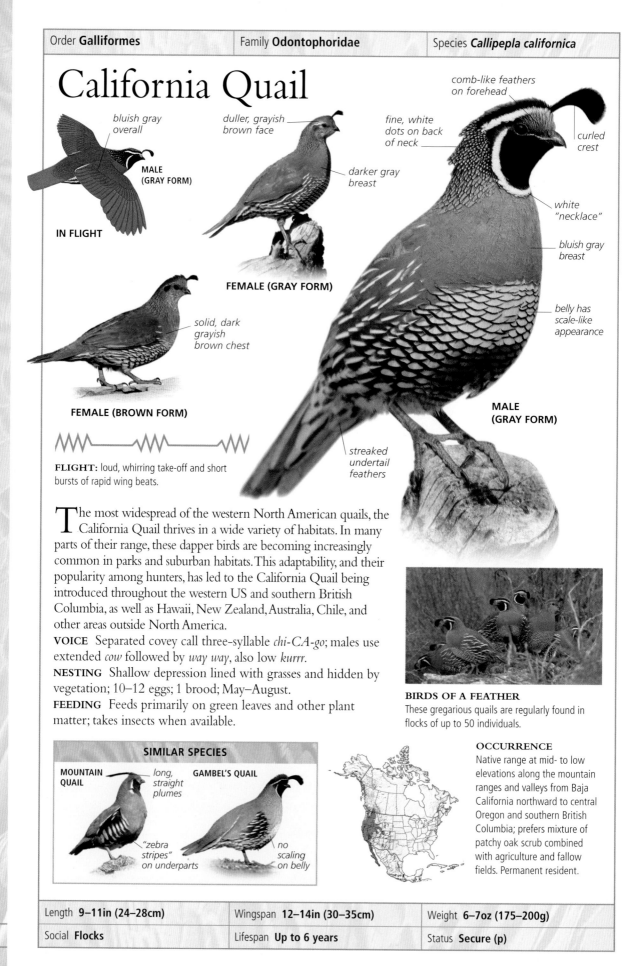

bluish gray overall

MALE (GRAY FORM)

IN FLIGHT

duller, grayish brown face

darker gray breast

FEMALE (GRAY FORM)

solid, dark grayish brown chest

FEMALE (BROWN FORM)

comb-like feathers on forehead

fine, white dots on back of neck

curled crest

white "necklace"

bluish gray breast

belly has scale-like appearance

MALE (GRAY FORM)

streaked undertail feathers

FLIGHT: loud, whirring take-off and short bursts of rapid wing beats.

The most widespread of the western North American quails, the California Quail thrives in a wide variety of habitats. In many parts of their range, these dapper birds are becoming increasingly common in parks and suburban habitats. This adaptability, and their popularity among hunters, has led to the California Quail being introduced throughout the western US and southern British Columbia, as well as Hawaii, New Zealand, Australia, Chile, and other areas outside North America.

VOICE Separated covey call three-syllable *chi-CA-go*; males use extended *cow* followed by *way way*, also low *kurrr*.

NESTING Shallow depression lined with grasses and hidden by vegetation; 10–12 eggs; 1 brood; May–August.

FEEDING Feeds primarily on green leaves and other plant matter; takes insects when available.

BIRDS OF A FEATHER
These gregarious quails are regularly found in flocks of up to 50 individuals.

SIMILAR SPECIES
MOUNTAIN QUAIL
long, straight plumes
"zebra stripes" on underparts
GAMBEL'S QUAIL
no scaling on belly

OCCURRENCE
Native range at mid- to low elevations along the mountain ranges and valleys from Baja California northward to central Oregon and southern British Columbia; prefers mixture of patchy oak scrub combined with agriculture and fallow fields. Permanent resident.

Length **9–11in (24–28cm)**	Wingspan **12–14in (30–35cm)**	Weight **6–7oz (175–200g)**
Social **Flocks**	Lifespan **Up to 6 years**	Status **Secure (p)**

Order **Galliformes**	Family **Odontophoridae**	Species ***Colinus virginianus***

Northern Bobwhite

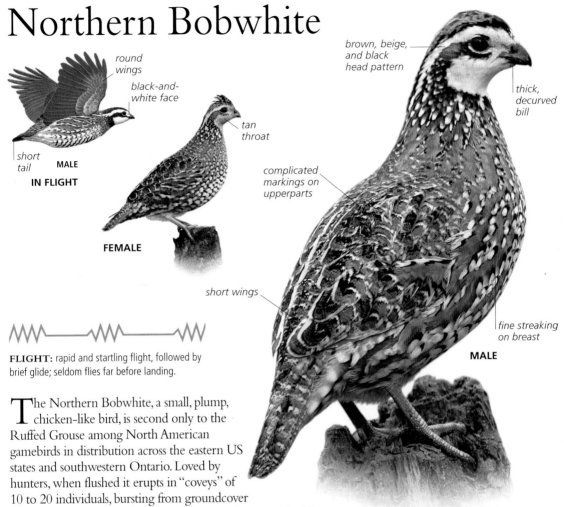

round wings
black-and-white face
short tail
MALE
IN FLIGHT

tan throat
FEMALE

brown, beige, and black head pattern
thick, decurved bill
complicated markings on upperparts
short wings
fine streaking on breast
MALE

FLIGHT: rapid and startling flight, followed by brief glide; seldom flies far before landing.

The Northern Bobwhite, a small, plump, chicken-like bird, is second only to the Ruffed Grouse among North American gamebirds in distribution across the eastern US states and southwestern Ontario. Loved by hunters, when flushed it erupts in "coveys" of 10 to 20 individuals, bursting from groundcover and dispersing in many directions. Large numbers are raised in captivity and released to supplement wild populations for hunting.

VOICE Characteristic *bob-WHITE* or *bob-bob-WHITE* whistled by males in breeding season; call to reunite flock includes *hoi-lee* and *hoi* following dispersal.

NESTING Shallow depression lined with plant matter, located on ground within sight of an opening; 10–15 eggs; sometimes multiple broods per season; January–March.

FEEDING Forages for wide variety of plant matter (seeds, buds, leaves), and insects, snails, and spiders, depending on the season.

COVEY LIFE
Male, female, and immature Northern Bobwhites live together in tight flocks called coveys.

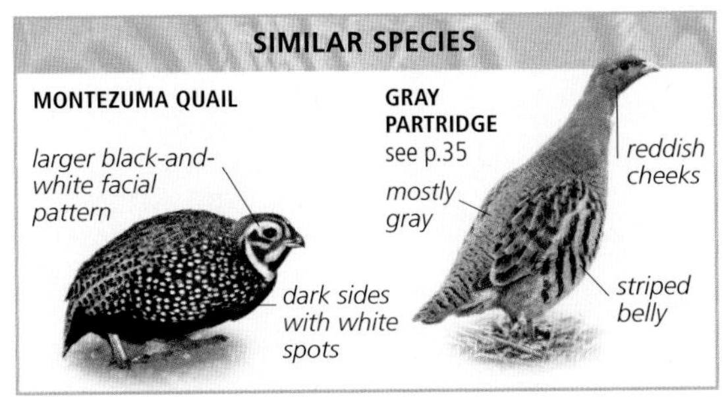
SIMILAR SPECIES
MONTEZUMA QUAIL
larger black-and-white facial pattern
dark sides with white spots
GRAY PARTRIDGE
see p.35
mostly gray
reddish cheeks
striped belly

OCCURRENCE
Widely distributed but only locally common in much of the eastern US and southwestern Ontario, and in Mexico, southward to Guatemala. Most often associated with agricultural fields, it thrives in a patchwork of mixed young forests, fields, and brushy hedges. A permanent resident.

Length **8–10in (20–25cm)**	Wingspan **11–14in (28–35cm)**	Weight **6oz (175g)**
Social **Small flocks**	Lifespan **Up to 6 years**	Status **Declining**

Order **Galliformes**	Family **Phasianidae**	Species ***Meleagris gallopavo***

Wild Turkey

MALE (EAST)

IN FLIGHT

rusty tail with black band

black-and-white barred wings

tail fanned in display

humped back

no feathers on head

long legs

IMMATURE

unfeathered blue-and-red head

large red wattles

hair-like "beard" on breast

dark overall

iridescent bronze-and-purplish body

FEMALE

dark body, with bronze iridescence

MALE (WEST)

Once proposed by Benjamin Franklin as the national emblem of the US, the Wild Turkey—the largest gamebird in North America—was eliminated from most of its original range by the early 1900s due to over-hunting and habitat destruction. Since then, habitat restoration and the subsequent reintroduction of Wild Turkeys has been very successful.

VOICE Well-known gobble, given by males especially during courtship; female makes various yelps, clucks, and purrs, based on mood and threat level.

NESTING Scrape on ground lined with grass; placed against or under protective cover; 10–15 eggs; 1 brood; March–June.

FEEDING Omnivorous, it scratches in leaf litter on forest floor for acorns and other food, mostly vegetation; also takes plants and insects from agricultural fields.

FLIGHT: after running, leaps into the air with loud, rapid wing beats, then glides.

COLLECTIVE DISPLAY
Once the population expands into new areas, numerous males will be seen displaying together.

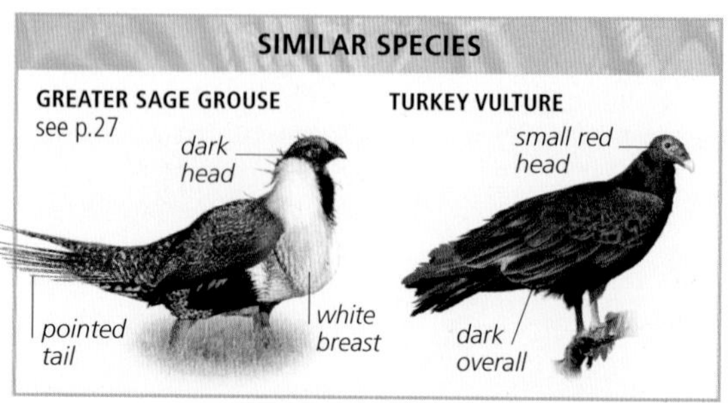
SIMILAR SPECIES
GREATER SAGE GROUSE
see p.27
dark head
pointed tail
white breast
TURKEY VULTURE
small red head
dark overall

OCCURRENCE
Found in mixed mature woodlands, fields with agricultural crops; also in various grasslands, close to swamps, but adaptable and increasingly common in suburban and urban habitats. Quite widespread, but patchily distributed across the US and southern Canada.

Length **2¾–4ft (0.9–1.2m)**	Wingspan **4–5ft (1.2–1.5m)**	Weight **10–24lb (4.5–11kg)**
Social **Flocks**	Lifespan **Up to 9 years**	Status **Secure**

Order **Galliformes**	Family **Phasianidae**	Species ***Bonasa umbellus***

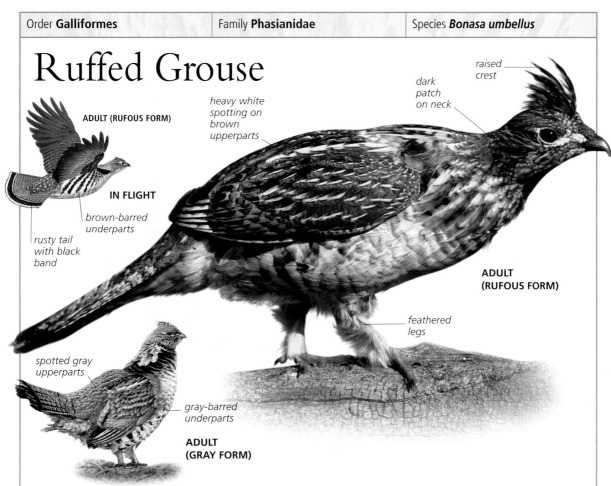

Ruffed Grouse

ADULT (RUFOUS FORM)

IN FLIGHT

brown-barred underparts

rusty tail with black band

heavy white spotting on brown upperparts

dark patch on neck

raised crest

ADULT (RUFOUS FORM)

feathered legs

spotted gray upperparts

gray-barred underparts

ADULT (GRAY FORM)

The Ruffed Grouse is perhaps the most widespread gamebird in North America. There are two color forms, rufous and gray, both allowing the birds to remain camouflaged and undetected on the forest floor, until they eventually burst into the air in an explosion of whirring wings. The male is well known for his extraordinary wing beating or "drumming" display, which he performs year-round, but most frequently in the spring.

VOICE Hissing notes, and soft *purrt, purrt, purrt* when alarmed, by both sexes; males "drumming" display when heard from distance resembles small engine starting, *thump…thump…thump...thump… thump…thuthuthuth.*

NESTING Shallow, leaf-lined bowl set against a tree trunk, rock or fallen log in forest; 6–14 eggs; 1 brood; March–June.

FEEDING Forages on ground for leaves, buds, and fruit; occasionally insects.

FLIGHT: an explosive take-off, usually at close range, glides for a short distance before landing.

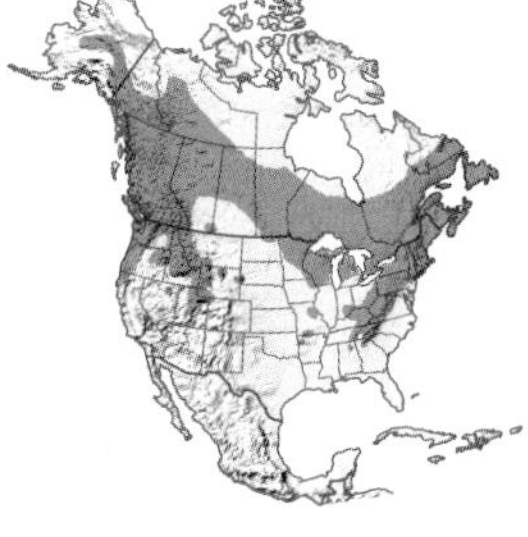

OCCURRENCE
Found in young, mixed habitat forests throughout northern US and Canada. Southern edge of range extends along higher elevations of the Appalachians and middle levels of the Rocky Mountains, if suitable habitat is available.

WARM RED
The rufous form of the Ruffed Grouse is more common in hotter parts of the continent.

SIMILAR SPECIES

SPRUCE GROUSE ♀
smaller overall; see p.26

DUSKY GROUSE
see p.28

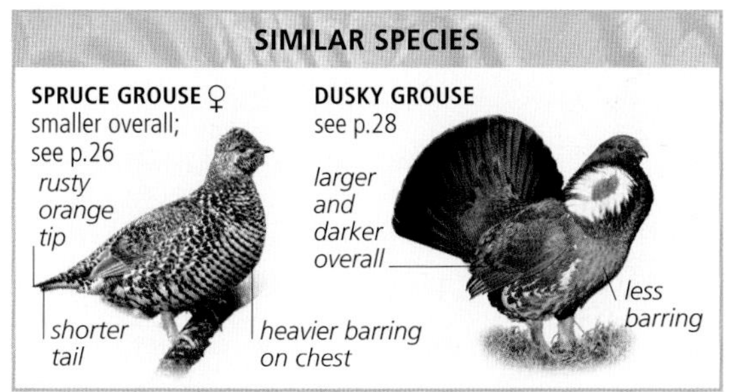

rusty orange tip
shorter tail
heavier barring on chest
larger and darker overall
less barring

Length **17–20in (43–51cm)**	Wingspan **20–23in (51–58cm)**	Weight **20–22oz (575–625g)**
Social **Solitary/Small flocks**	Lifespan **Up to 10 years**	Status **Secure**

Order **Galliformes**	Family **Phasianidae**	Species ***Falcipennis canadensis***

Spruce Grouse

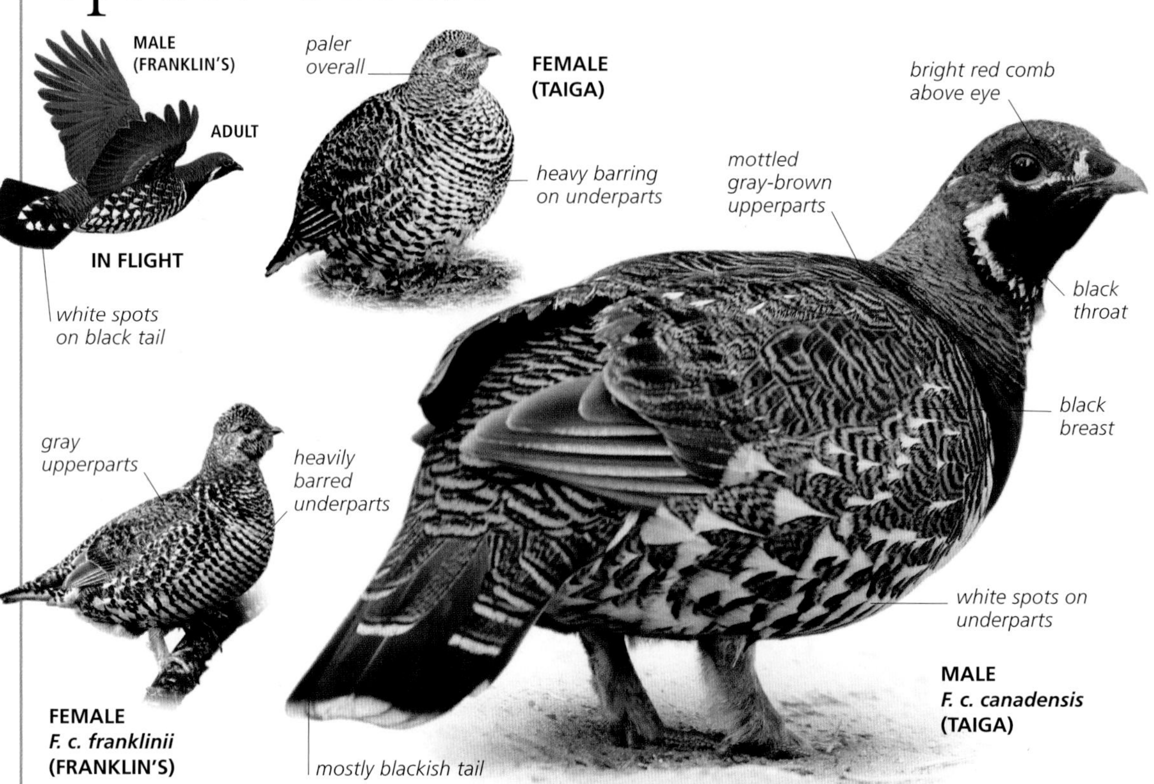
MALE (FRANKLIN'S)
ADULT
IN FLIGHT
white spots on black tail
paler overall
FEMALE (TAIGA)
heavy barring on underparts
bright red comb above eye
mottled gray-brown upperparts
black throat
black breast
white spots on underparts
gray upperparts
heavily barred underparts
FEMALE
F. c. franklinii
(FRANKLIN'S)
mostly blackish tail
MALE
F. c. canadensis
(TAIGA)

Perhaps because of the remoteness of their habitat and lack of human contact, Spruce Grouse are not afraid of humans. This lack of wariness when approached has earned them the name "fool hens." Their specialized diet of pine needles causes the intestinal tract to expand in order to accommodate a larger volume of food to compensate for its low nutritional value. There are two different subspecies of Spruce Grouse (*F. c. canadensis and F. c. franklinii*), both of which have red and gray forms.

VOICE Mostly silent; males clap their wings during courtship display; females often utter long cackle at dawn and dusk.

NESTING Lined with moss, leaves, feathers; often at base of tree; naturally low area in forest floor 4–6 eggs; 1 brood; May–July.

FEEDING Feeds mostly on pine but also spruce needles; will eat insects, leaves, fruits, and seeds when available.

FLIGHT: generally avoids flying; when disturbed, bursts into flight on whirring wings. rapid beats.

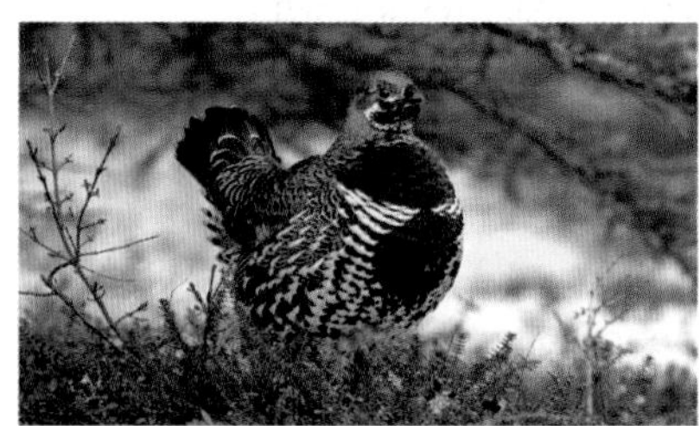

RUFOUS BAND
The male "Taiga" subspecies displays the thin rufous band on the tip of his tail.

SIMILAR SPECIES

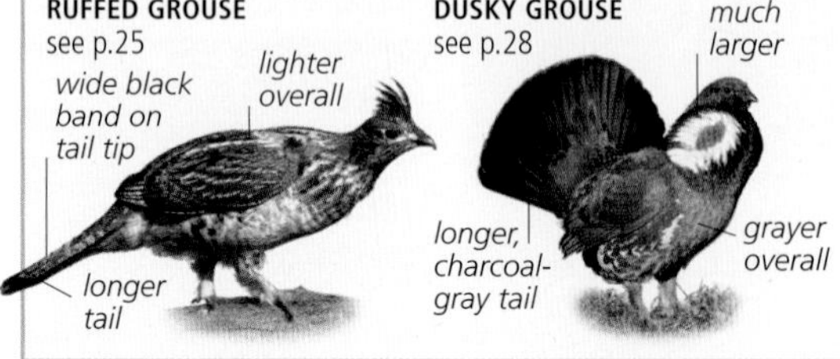
RUFFED GROUSE
see p.25
wide black band on tail tip
lighter overall
longer tail
DUSKY GROUSE
see p.28
much larger
longer, charcoal-gray tail
grayer overall

OCCURRENCE
Present year-round in forests dominated by conifers, including Jack, Lodgepole, Spruce, Red Spruce, Black Spruce, Balsam Fir, Subalpine Fir, Hemlock, and Cedar. Found from western Alaska to the Atlantic Coast.

Length **14–17in (36–43cm)**	Wingspan **21–23in (53–58cm)**	Weight **16oz (450g)**
Social **Solitary**	Lifespan **Up to 10 years**	Status **Secure**

Order **Galliformes**	Family **Phasianidae**	Species ***Centrocercus urophasianus***

Greater Sage Grouse

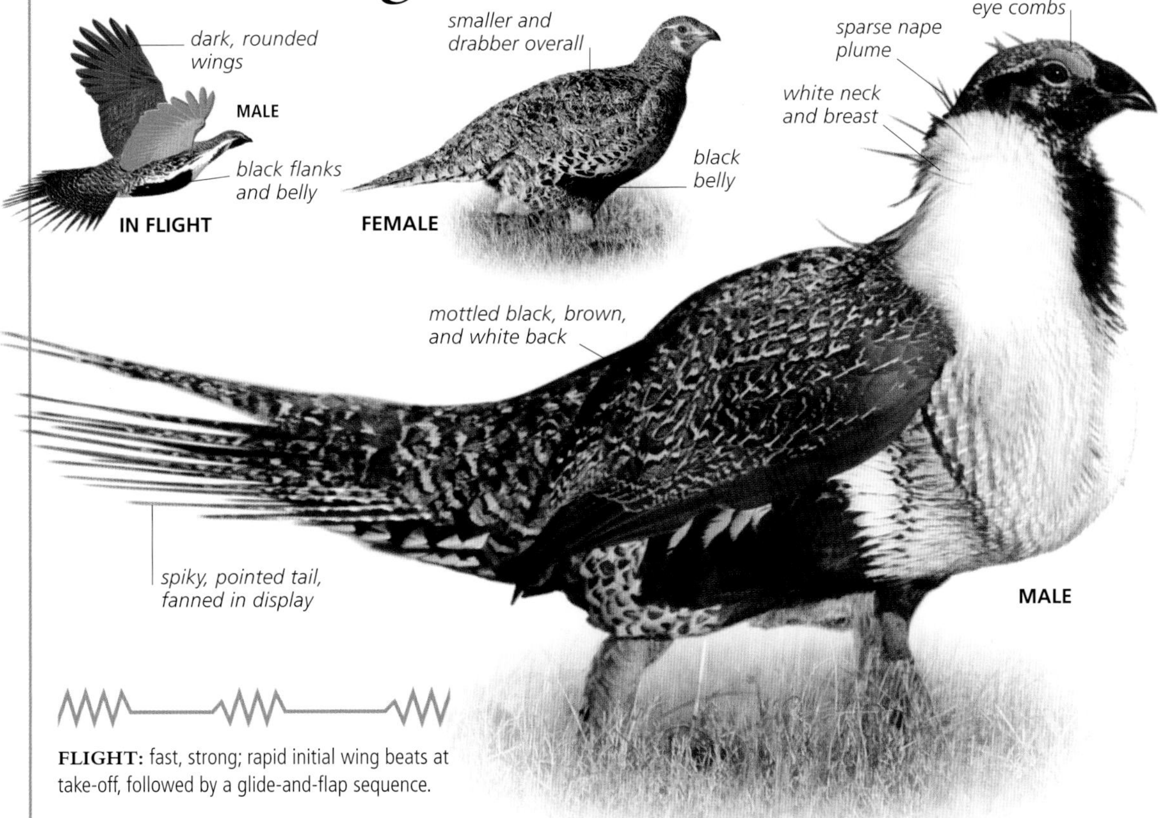

dark, rounded wings

MALE

black flanks and belly

IN FLIGHT

smaller and drabber overall

black belly

FEMALE

dark head, with dull yellowish eye combs

sparse nape plume

white neck and breast

mottled black, brown, and white back

spiky, pointed tail, fanned in display

MALE

FLIGHT: fast, strong; rapid initial wing beats at take-off, followed by a glide-and-flap sequence.

The Greater Sage Grouse is by far the largest native North American grouse. Each spring, the males gather on communal sites, known as leks, where they compete for females with spectacular courtship displays. As many as 40 males may gather at a lek for these events. Once widespread, Greater Sage Grouse populations have declined, as human encroachment on sagebrush habitats has increased.

VOICE Clucks repeatedly when flushed; male makes odd popping sounds with throat sacs when displaying.

NESTING Depression scraped into soil next to protective cover of grass or sagebrush branches; 6–10 eggs; 1 brood; March–May.

FEEDING Eats mainly on sagebrush leaves; also eats insects, fruit, flowers, and succulent green plants when available.

IMPRESSIVE SHOW
The male's courtship display is remarkable—he inflates his air sacs, fans his tail and struts around.

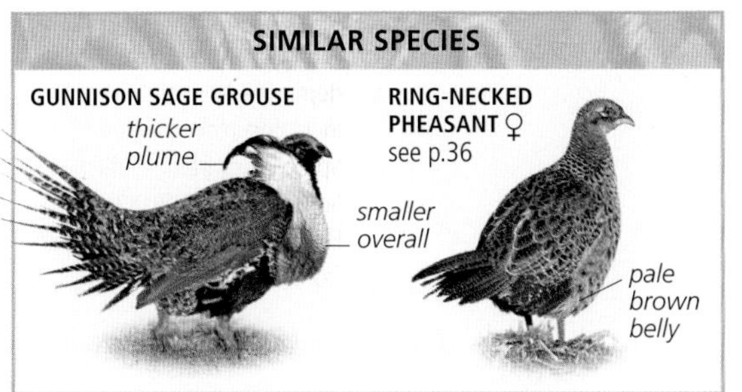
SIMILAR SPECIES
GUNNISON SAGE GROUSE
thicker plume
RING-NECKED PHEASANT ♀
see p.36
smaller overall
pale brown belly

OCCURRENCE
In North America its present distribution is a fraction of its formerly large range in the vast sagebrush plains of the West. In Canada, it is found only in the southern prairies. Breeds in a variety of habitats, the ideal being composed of several sagebrush species of varying heights.

Length **19½–30in (50–76cm)**	Wingspan **32–39in (81–99cm)**	Weight **2½–6½lb (1–3kg)**
Social **Flocks**	Lifespan **Up to 6 years**	Status **Vulnerable**

Order **Galliformes**	Family **Phasianidae**	Species ***Dendragapus obscurus***

Dusky Grouse

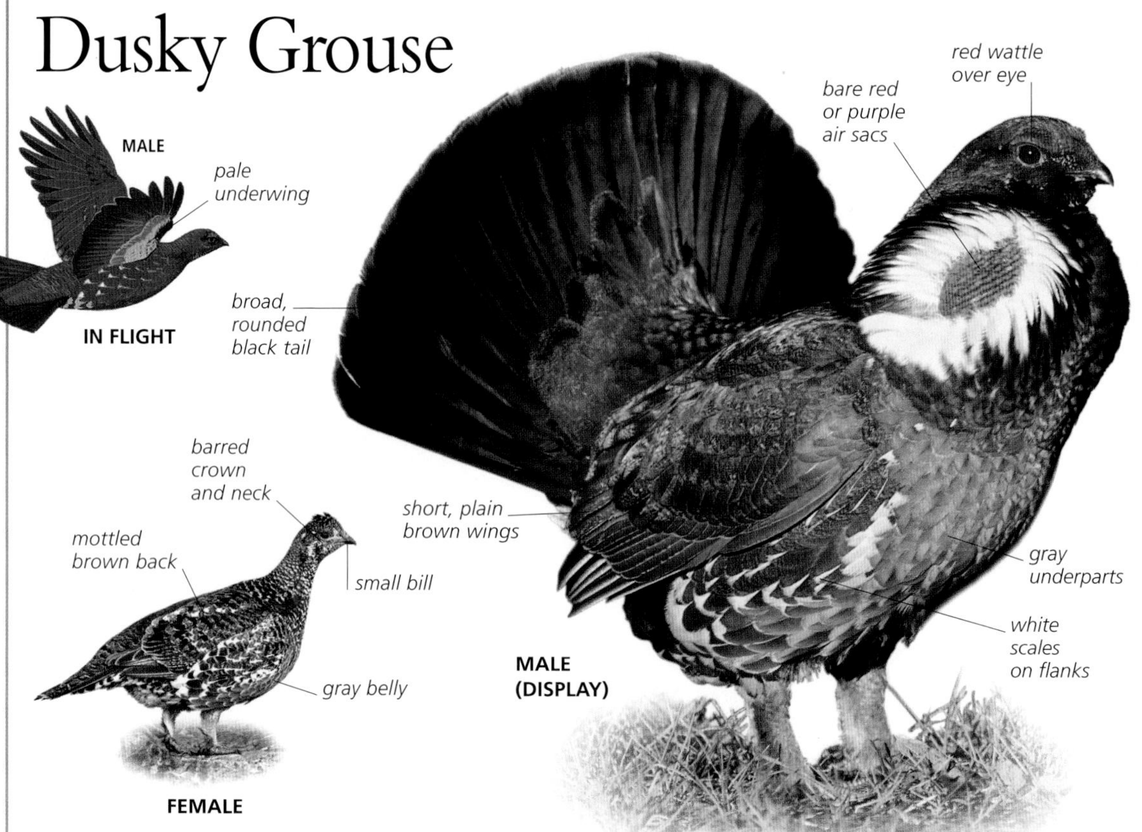
MALE
pale underwing
IN FLIGHT
broad, rounded black tail
red wattle over eye
bare red or purple air sacs
barred crown and neck
mottled brown back
small bill
short, plain brown wings
gray underparts
white scales on flanks
gray belly
MALE (DISPLAY)
FEMALE

Once considered a Blue Grouse subspecies, the Dusky Grouse was recently reclassified as a species in its own right, distinct from the Sooty Grouse. Male Dusky Grouse can be identified by their courtship displays, which are primarily ground-based and quieter than those of the Dusky Grouse, and by their reddish purple air sacs. The Dusky Grouse also has a plainer tail, lacking the grayer tip of the Sooty, and its chicks are more gray than brown.

VOICE A series of five soft hoots; also a hiss, growl, and cluck; females emit a whinnying cry.

NESTING Shallow scrape, usually lined with dead grass, leaves, or other plants, located under shrubs, against rocks or logs; 7–10 eggs; 1 brood; March–May.

FEEDING Feeds on leaves, flowers, fruit, also some insects; evergreen needles, buds, and cones in season.

FLIGHT: loud, short-distance flight with rapid wing beats before gliding to the ground.

FREEZING FOR SAFETY
This female Dusky Grouse stands still as a statue, relying on camouflage, not flight, for protection.

SIMILAR SPECIES

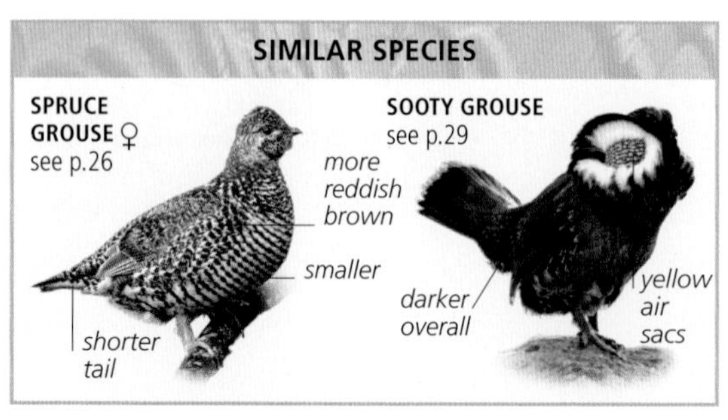
SPRUCE GROUSE ♀
see p.26
more reddish brown
smaller
shorter tail
SOOTY GROUSE
see p.29
darker overall
yellow air sacs

OCCURRENCE
Found in the northern, central Rocky Mountains in Canada and US in high or mid-altitude open forests and shrublands. Typically uses older, denser, mixed or evergreen forests at higher elevations in winter, more open-country, lighter forests at lower elevations in summer.

Length **16–20in (41–51cm)**	Wingspan **25–28in (64–71cm)**	Weight **2½–2¾lb (1.1–1.3kg)**
Social **Solitary/Winter flocks**	Lifespan **Up to 14 years**	Status **Localized**

Order **Galliformes**	Family **Phasianidae**	Species ***Dendragapus fuliginosus***

Sooty Grouse

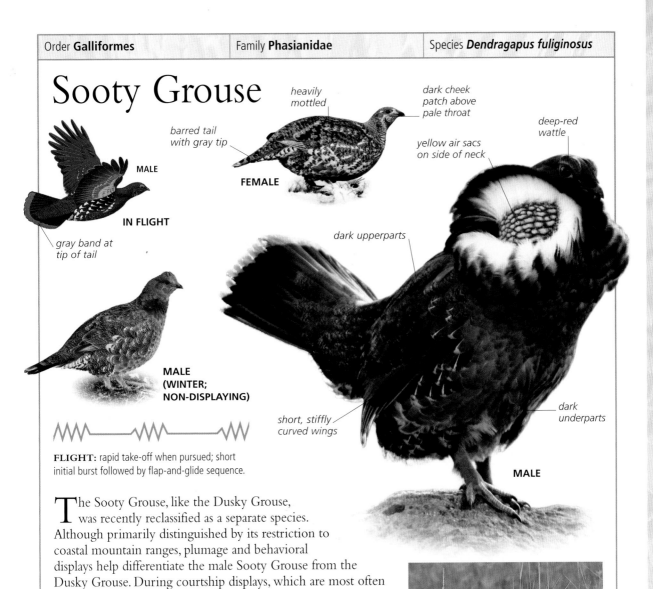

heavily mottled

dark cheek patch above pale throat

deep-red wattle

barred tail with gray tip

yellow air sacs on side of neck

MALE

FEMALE

IN FLIGHT

gray band at tip of tail

dark upperparts

MALE (WINTER; NON-DISPLAYING)

short, stiffly curved wings

dark underparts

MALE

FLIGHT: rapid take-off when pursued; short initial burst followed by flap-and-glide sequence.

The Sooty Grouse, like the Dusky Grouse, was recently reclassified as a separate species. Although primarily distinguished by its restriction to coastal mountain ranges, plumage and behavioral displays help differentiate the male Sooty Grouse from the Dusky Grouse. During courtship displays, which are most often performed in trees, the male Sooty Grouse shows rough, yellow air sacs. Females and chicks have a browner overall appearance to their plumage than those of the Dusky Grouse.

VOICE Loud six-syllable hooting; also growl, hiss, cluck, *purrr*.

NESTING Shallow depression lined with dead vegetation, usually under small pine trees; 5–8 eggs; 1 brood; March–May.

FEEDING Feeds primarily on evergreen needles, especially Douglas Fir; will take leaves, grasses, fruit, and insects when seasonally available.

CAUTIOUS PEEK
Female Sooty Grouse disturbed on the ground peer up through grasses to check for danger.

SIMILAR SPECIES

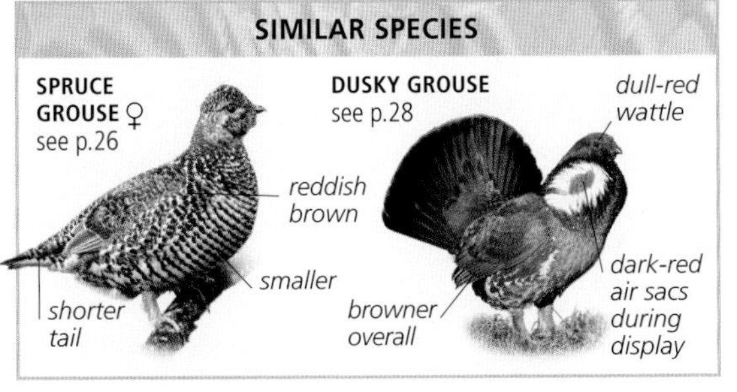
SPRUCE GROUSE ♀
see p.26
reddish brown
smaller
shorter tail
DUSKY GROUSE
see p.28
dull-red wattle
browner overall
dark-red air sacs during display

OCCURRENCE
Found west of the Rocky Mountains in Canada and the US, from sea level to the timberline. Breeds at lower elevations in open areas with grassland, forest clearings, and shrubs, and moves up into thicker evergreen forests at higher elevations in winter.

Length **16–20in (41–51cm)**	Wingspan **25–28in (64–71cm)**	Weight **2½–2¾lb (1.1–1.3g)**
Social **Solitary/Winter flocks**	Lifespan **Up to 14 years**	Status **Secure**

Order **Galliformes**	Family **Phasianidae**	Species ***Tympanuchus phasianellus***

Sharp-tailed Grouse

ADULT
mottled wings
IN FLIGHT
pale, wedge-shaped tail, with protruding central feathers
long central tail feather
white tail with two long, mottled center feathers
MALE
brown wings with white dots
tan eyebrow
naked pink skin
heavily mottled brown, white, and black upperparts
white underside, with dark brown arrowheads along flanks

FLIGHT: flushes from hiding on rapid wing beats to flight speed, then onto glide-flap-glide sequence.

The most widespread species of its genus, the Sharp-tailed Grouse is able to adapt to the greatest variety of habitats. It is not migratory, but undertakes seasonal movements between grassland summer habitats and woodland winter habitats. Elements of this grouse's spectacular courtship display have been incorporated into the culture and dance of Native American people, including foot stomping and tail feather rattling. The Sharp-tailed Grouse is the provincial bird of Saskatchewan.

VOICE Male calls a variety of unusual clucks, cooing, barks, and gobbles during courtship; females cluck with different intonations.

NESTING Shallow depression lined with plant matter close at hand as well as some feathers from female, usually near overhead cover; 10–12 eggs; 1 brood; March–May.

FEEDING Forages primarily for seeds, leaves, buds, and fruit; also takes insects and flowers when available.

PRAIRIE DANCER
The courtship dance of the Sharp-tailed Grouse heralds the arrival of spring to the grasslands.

SIMILAR SPECIES

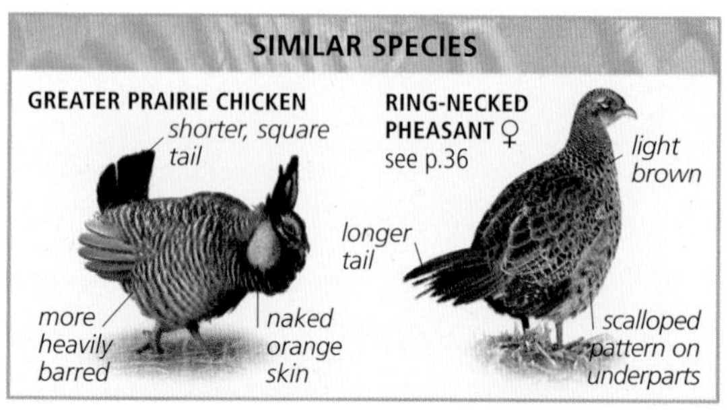
GREATER PRAIRIE CHICKEN
shorter, square tail
more heavily barred
naked orange skin
RING-NECKED PHEASANT ♀
see p.36
longer tail
light brown
scalloped pattern on underparts

OCCURRENCE
Has a northern and western distribution in North America, from Alaska (isolated population) southward across Canada to northern prairie states. Prefers a mixture of fallow and active agricultural fields combined with brushy forest edges and woodlots along river beds.

Length **15–19in (38–48cm)**	Wingspan **23–26in (58–66cm)**	Weight **26–34oz (750–950g)**
Social **Flocks**	Lifespan **Up to 7 years**	Status **Declining (p)**

Order **Galliformes**	Family **Phasianidae**	Species ***Lagopus leucura***

White-tailed Ptarmigan

all-white overall

ADULT (WINTER)

IN FLIGHT

lichen-like coloration and patterning

FEMALE (SUMMER)

red naked skin over eye

small, black bill

ADULT (WINTER)

varied breeding plumage is turning white with molting feathers

MALE (LATE SUMMER)

The smallest and most southerly of the three North American ptarmigans, the White-tailed Ptarmigan's native range is still largely intact. In the winter, its almost completely white plumage—unique among the gamebird species—blends it in perfectly to its icy mountainous home. Its plumage is one of several adaptations to the inhospitable environment it inhabits. The feathers on its feet increase the surface area in contact with the ground, and so help to prevent the bird from sinking into the snow.

VOICE Males emit various cackling clucks, *cuk-cuk-cuuuk* during display; females cluck, purr, and growl softly.

NESTING Scrape in ground lined with plants and feathers; 4–8 eggs; 1 brood; May–June.

FEEDING Feeds heavily on willows, eating mostly leaves, buds, and twigs; insects when nesting.

FLIGHT: rarely flies unless pursued; flush on explosive wing beats, then flap-and-glide sequence.

WHITE ON WHITE
Immobile on white snow, the male blends in superbly with the wintry surroundings.

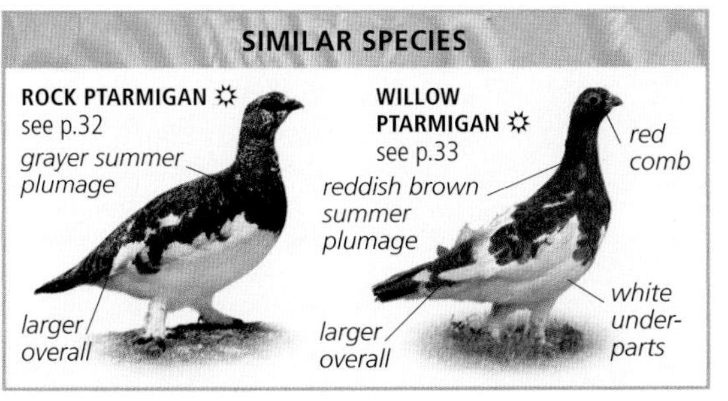
SIMILAR SPECIES
ROCK PTARMIGAN ☼
see p.32
grayer summer plumage
larger overall
WILLOW PTARMIGAN ☼
see p.33
red comb
reddish brown summer plumage
white under-parts
larger overall

OCCURRENCE
Has a more restricted distribution than Rock and Willow Ptarmigans, occurring from Alaska and the Yukon south to Idaho and Montana; small isolated populations exist in Colorado and New Hampshire. Associated with willow stands above tree-line; also meadows and evergreen stand mixtures.

Length **12in (30–31cm)**	Wingspan **20–22in (51–56cm)**	Weight **12–16oz (350–450g)**
Social **Large flocks**	Lifespan **Up to 15 years**	Status **Secure**

Order **Galliformes**	Family **Phasianidae**	Species ***Lagopus muta***

Rock Ptarmigan

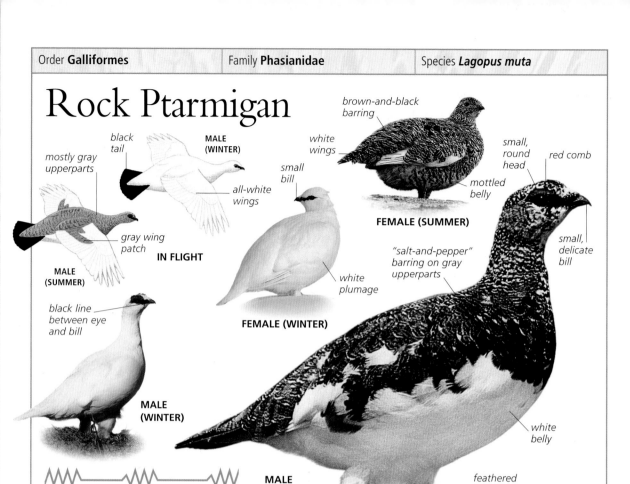

mostly gray upperparts
black tail
MALE (WINTER)
all-white wings
gray wing patch
IN FLIGHT
MALE (SUMMER)
small bill
white plumage
FEMALE (WINTER)
brown-and-black barring
white wings
mottled belly
FEMALE (SUMMER)
small, round head
red comb
small, delicate bill
"salt-and-pepper" barring on gray upperparts
black line between eye and bill
MALE (WINTER)
white belly
feathered feet
MALE (SUMMER)

FLIGHT: bursts into flight with rapid wing beats, followed by gliding and shallow flapping.

The Rock Ptarmigan is the most northerly of the three ptarmigan species found in North America. Although some birds make a short migration to more southern wintering grounds, many remain on their breeding grounds year-round. This species is well known for its distinctive seasonal variation in plumage, which helps to camouflage it against its surroundings. The Rock Ptarmigan is the official bird of Nunavut Territory.

VOICE Quiet; male call a raspy *krrrh*, also growls and clucks.

NESTING Small scrape or natural depression, lined with plant matter, often away from cover; 8–10 eggs; 1 brood; April–June.

FEEDING Feeds on buds, seeds, flowers, and leaves, especially birch and willow; eats insects in summer.

IN BETWEEN PLUMAGE
Various transitional plumage patterns can be seen on the Rock Ptarmigan in spring and fall.

SIMILAR SPECIES

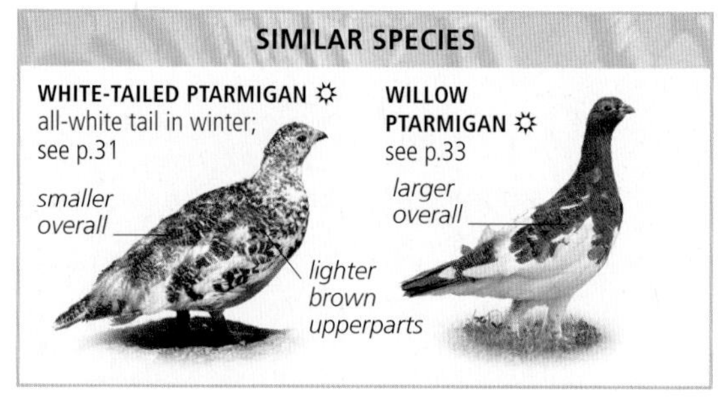

WHITE-TAILED PTARMIGAN ☼
all-white tail in winter;
see p.31

smaller overall
lighter brown upperparts

WILLOW PTARMIGAN ☼
see p.33

larger overall

OCCURRENCE
Prefers dry, rocky tundra and shrubby ridge tops; will use edges of open meadows and dense evergreen stands along fairly high-elevation rivers and streams during winter. Occurs throughout the Northern Hemisphere in Arctic tundra from Iceland to Kamçhatka in far east Russia.

Length **12½–15½in (32–40cm)**	Wingspan **19½–23½in (50–60cm)**	Weight **16–23oz (450–650g)**
Social **Winter flocks**	Lifespan **Up to 8 years**	Status **Secure**

Order **Galliformes**	Family **Phasianidae**	Species ***Lagopus lagopus***

Willow Ptarmigan

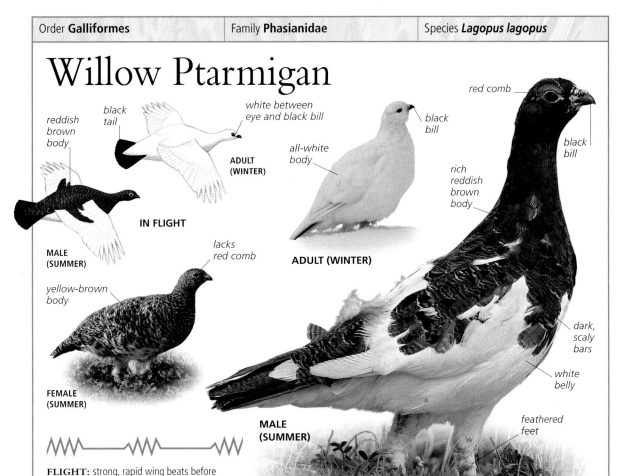

reddish brown body
black tail
white between eye and black bill
ADULT (WINTER)
IN FLIGHT
MALE (SUMMER)
black bill
all-white body
ADULT (WINTER)
red comb
black bill
rich reddish brown body
lacks red comb
yellow-brown body
FEMALE (SUMMER)
dark, scaly bars
white belly
feathered feet
MALE (SUMMER)

FLIGHT: strong, rapid wing beats before gliding; prefers to walk.

The most common of the three ptarmigan species, the Willow Ptarmigan also undertakes the longest migration of the group. The Willow Ptarmigan is an unusual gamebird species, as male and female remain bonded throughout the chick-rearing process, in which the male is an active participant. The "Red Grouse" of British moors is a subspecies (*L. l. scotius*) of the Willow Ptarmigan.

VOICE Variety of purrs, clucks, hissing, meowing noises; *Kow-Kow-Kow* call given before flushing, possibly alerting others.

NESTING Shallow bowl scraped in soil, lined with plant matter, protected by overhead cover; 8–10 eggs; 1 brood; March–May.

FEEDING Mostly eats buds, stems, and seeds, but also flowers, insects, and leaves when available.

PERFECT BLEND-IN
Its reddish brown upperparts camouflage this summer ptarmigan in the shrubby areas it inhabits.

SIMILAR SPECIES
WHITE-TAILED PTARMIGAN
see p.31
browner plumage
smaller overall
ROCK PTARMIGAN
see p.32
grayer plumage
darker

OCCURRENCE
Prefers tundra, in Arctic, sub-Arctic and sub-alpine regions. Thrives in willow thickets along low, moist river corridors; also in the low woodlands of the sub-Arctic tundra.

Length **14–17½in (35–44cm)**	Wingspan **22–24in (56–61cm)**	Weight **15–28oz (425–800g)**
Social **Winter flocks**	Lifespan **Up to 9 years**	Status **Secure**

Order **Galliformes**	Family **Phasianidae**	Species ***Alectoris chukar***

Chukar

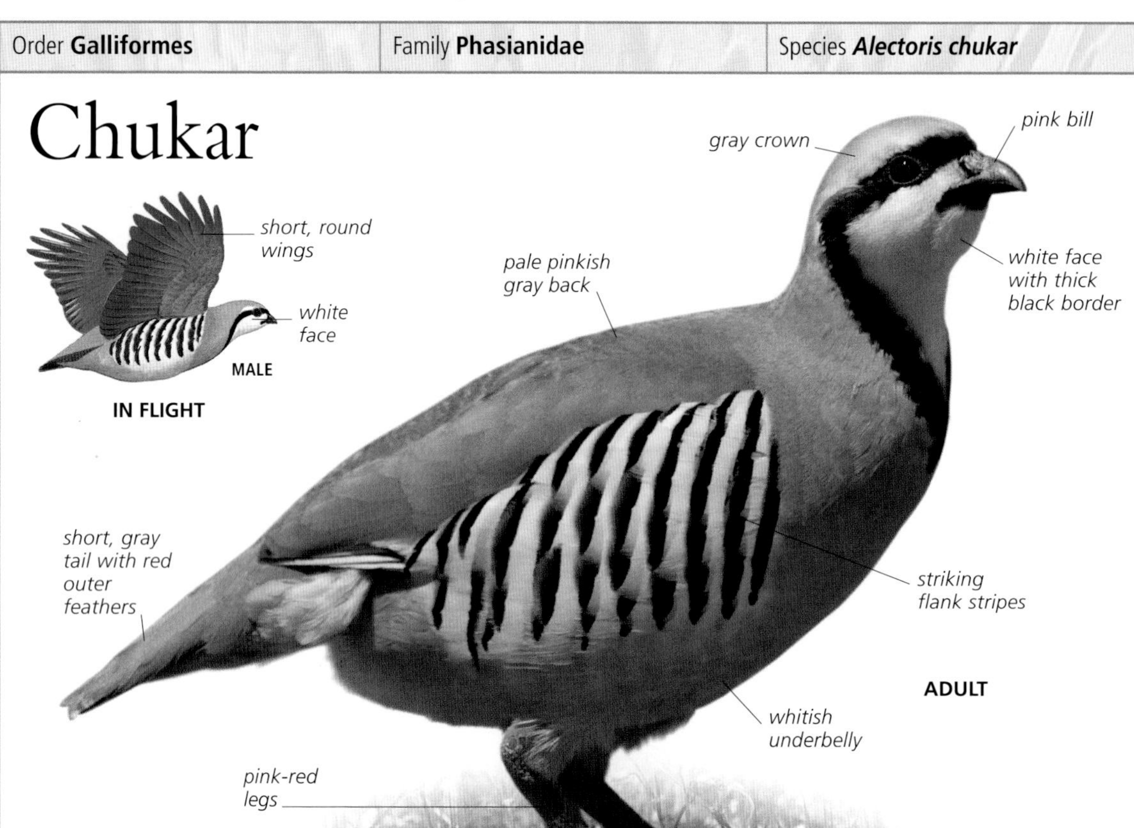
short, round wings
white face
MALE
IN FLIGHT
gray crown
pink bill
pale pinkish gray back
white face with thick black border
short, gray tail with red outer feathers
striking flank stripes
ADULT
whitish underbelly
pink-red legs

A native of Eurasia, from eastern Europe to China, the Chukar was brought to North America in the early 1890s. In the mid-20th century, nearly a million birds were released in more than 40 US states and six Canadian provinces, after the Chukar became popular as a game bird. While most introductions failed, the species did succeed in some areas, especially on steep mountain slopes in the West. Chukars form large communal groups, or crèches, of up to 100 young birds, with 10–12 adults overseeing them.

VOICE When flushed, a thin whistled *peee*, then a series of squeals *pittoo-pittoo-pittoo*; *chukka-chuka-chuka-chuka* reunites flushed or dispersed covey.

NESTING Shallow scrape lined with nearby dead vegetation, well-concealed among shrubs and rocks on hillside; 7–12 eggs; 1 brood; March–May.

FEEDING Eats mainly seeds from various grasses and green succulent plants; berries; also eats insects.

FLIGHT: explosive takeoff from cover, usually heading downslope when flushed.

SIMILAR SPECIES
MOUNTAIN QUAIL
long, thin, straight head plume
brown face
brown flanks edged with black and white
GRAY PARTRIDGE
see p.35
lighter gray body
rusty-orange face
dark chestnut bars on flanks

MAKING AN EFFORT Perched on a rock, this Chukar calls loudly, stretching its neck to increase vocal capacity.

OCCURRENCE Introduced to the West, released for shooting in the East; found on wide open areas and steep slopes at high elevation, up to 2,500m (8,200ft), with a mix of deep, brushy canyons and hillsides of loose rocks and boulders, sparse bush, low woody shrubs, grasses and aromatic herbs.

Length **13½–15in (34–38cm)**	Wingspan **19–22in (48–56cm)**	Weight **18–23oz (500–650g)**
Social **Family groups**	Lifespan **Up to 3 years**	Status **Secure**

Order **Galliformes**	Family **Phasianidae**	Species ***Perdix perdix***

Gray Partridge

ADULT

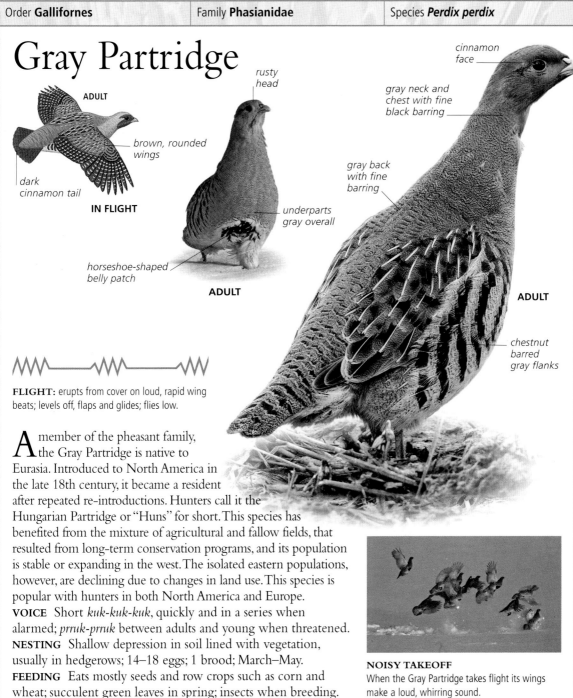

brown, rounded wings

dark cinnamon tail

IN FLIGHT

rusty head

underparts gray overall

horseshoe-shaped belly patch

ADULT

cinnamon face

gray neck and chest with fine black barring

gray back with fine barring

ADULT

chestnut barred gray flanks

FLIGHT: erupts from cover on loud, rapid wing beats; levels off, flaps and glides; flies low.

A member of the pheasant family, the Gray Partridge is native to Eurasia. Introduced to North America in the late 18th century, it became a resident after repeated re-introductions. Hunters call it the Hungarian Partridge or "Huns" for short. This species has benefited from the mixture of agricultural and fallow fields, that resulted from long-term conservation programs, and its population is stable or expanding in the west. The isolated eastern populations, however, are declining due to changes in land use. This species is popular with hunters in both North America and Europe.

VOICE Short *kuk-kuk-kuk*, quickly and in a series when alarmed; *prruk-prruk* between adults and young when threatened.

NESTING Shallow depression in soil lined with vegetation, usually in hedgerows; 14–18 eggs; 1 brood; March–May.

FEEDING Eats mostly seeds and row crops such as corn and wheat; succulent green leaves in spring; insects when breeding.

NOISY TAKEOFF
When the Gray Partridge takes flight its wings make a loud, whirring sound.

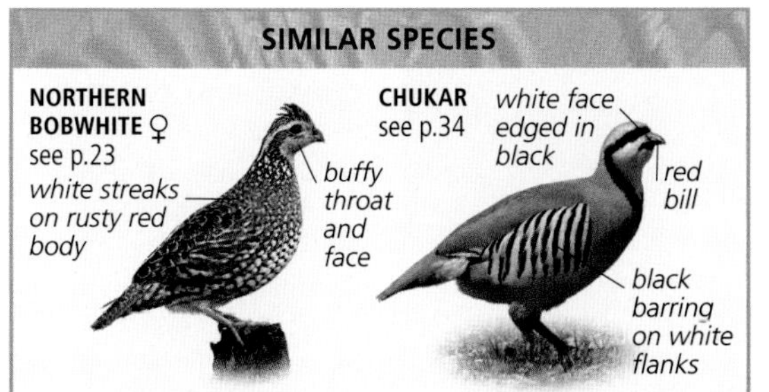
SIMILAR SPECIES
NORTHERN BOBWHITE ♀
see p.23
white streaks on rusty red body
buffy throat and face
CHUKAR
see p.34
white face edged in black
red bill
black barring on white flanks

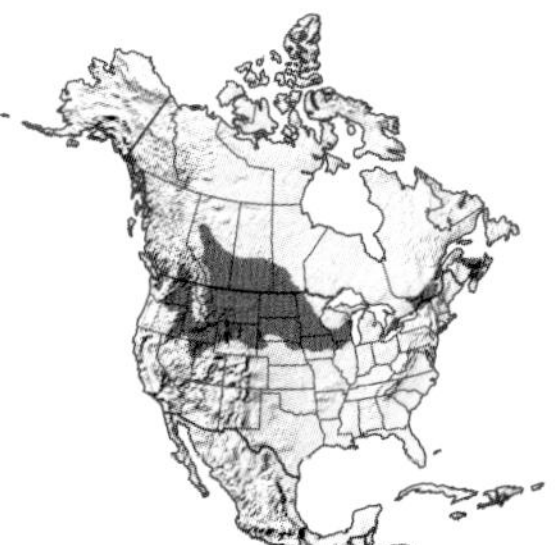

OCCURRENCE
Primarily agricultural fields of crops including corn, wheat, and oats, as well as associated hedgerows and fallow grasslands. Most birds are nonmigratory, but there is some movement by eastern birds after breeding.

Length **11–13in (28–33cm)**	Wingspan **17–20in (43–51cm)**	Weight **12–18oz (350–500g)**
Social **Family groups**	Lifespan **Up to 4 years**	Status **Secure**

Order **Galliformes**	Family **Phasianidae**	Species ***Phasianus colchicus***

Ring-necked Pheasant

long tail
MALE
pale rump
short, round wings
pointed tail
FEMALE
IN FLIGHT
green-black head
orange-copper flanks
MALE (DARK FORM)
pale brown body
bold black markings
FEMALE
iridescent ear tufts
white neck ring
red face wattles
iridescent bronze sheen
long, pointed tail
barred underparts
MALE

FLIGHT: bursts vertically from cover on loud rapid wing beats; levels off, flaps, then glides.

A native of Asia, the variable-looking Ring-necked Pheasant was originally introduced in North America for recreational hunting purposes, and is now widely distributed across North America. Birds released after being bred in captivity are used to supplement natural reproduction for hunting purposes. In the wild, several females may lay eggs in the same nest—a phenomenon called "egg-dumping." There is a less common dark form, which can be distinguished principally because it lacks the distinctive white band around the neck.

VOICE Male emits a loud, raucous, explosive double note, *Karrk-KORK*, followed by loud wing-flapping; both sexes cackle when flushed.

NESTING Shallow bowl composed of grasses, usually on ground in tall grass or among low shrubs; 7–15 eggs; 1 brood; March–June.

FEEDING Feeds on corn and other grain, seeds, fruit, row crops, grass, leaves and shoots; eats insects when available.

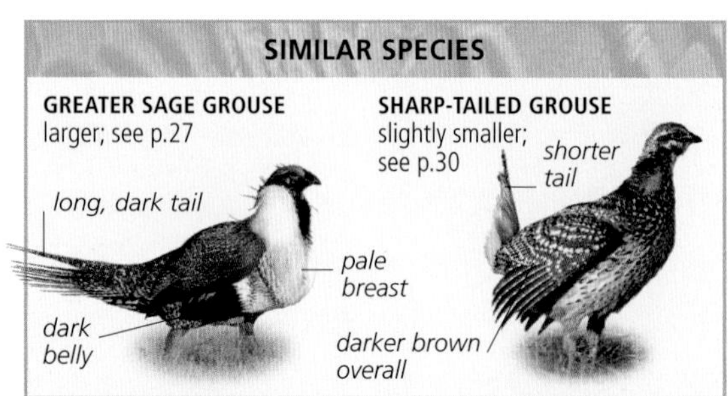
SIMILAR SPECIES
GREATER SAGE GROUSE
larger; see p.27
long, dark tail
pale breast
dark belly
SHARP-TAILED GROUSE
slightly smaller; see p.30
shorter tail
darker brown overall

FLUSHED OUT
The Ring-necked Pheasant is a powerful flier when alarmed or flushed out of its cover.

OCCURRENCE
Widespread across southern Canada and the US; prefers mixture of active agricultural crops (especially corn fields), fallow fields, and hedgerows; also cattail marshes and wooded river bottoms. The Ring-necked Pheasant is native to Asia from the Caucasus east to China.

Length **19½–28in (50–70cm)**	Wingspan **30–34in (76–86cm)**	Weight **1¼–6½lb (0.5–3kg)**
Social **Solitary/Flocks**	Lifespan **Up to 4 years**	Status **Secure**

WATERFOWL

RECENT SCIENTIFIC studies indicate that waterfowl are closely related to gamebirds. Most species molt all their flight feathers at once after breeding, making them flightless for several weeks until they grow new ones.

GEESE

Ornithologists group geese and swans together into the subfamily Anserinae. Intermediate in body size and neck length between swans and ducks, geese are more terrestrial than either, often being seen grazing on dry land. Like swans, geese pair for life. They are also highly social, and most species are migratory, flying south for the winter in large flocks.

SWANS

Swans are essentially large, long-necked geese. Their heavier weight makes them ungainly on land, and they tend to be more aquatic than their smaller relatives. On water, however, they are extremely graceful. When feeding, a swan stretches its long neck to reach water plants at the bottom, submerging up to half its body as it does so. The Trumpeter Swan is North America's largest native waterfowl, growing up to to 5ft (1.5m) long, and weighing up to 25lb (12kg).

DUCKS

Classified in their own subfamily, called the Anatinae, ducks are more varied than swans or geese, with many more species. They are loosely grouped by their feeding habits. Dabblers, or puddle ducks, such as the Mallard, teals, and wigeons, eat plants and other edible matter like snails. They feed by upending on the surface of shallow water. By contrast, diving ducks, a group that includes scaups, scoters, eiders, mergansers, and the Ruddy Duck, dive deep underwater for their food.

INSTANT TAKEOFF
Puddle ducks like the Mallard can shoot out of the water and into the air.

GAGGLING GEESE
Gregarious Snow Geese form large, noisy flocks during migration and on winter feeding grounds.

Order **Anseriformes**	Family **Anatidae**	Species ***Anser albifrons***

Greater White-fronted Goose

gray wing feathers
ADULT
white rump band
IN FLIGHT
white tip to tail
white flank streak
brownish gray head
pink bill with white base
darker chocolate-brown upperparts
larger body
longer legs, bill, and neck
A. a gambeli (TULE)
bright orange legs
MALE
A. a. frontalis (TUNDRA)
brown underparts with black bands
dull yellowish orange bill
no belly barring
JUVENILE

The Greater White-fronted Goose is the most widespread goose in the Northern Hemisphere. It is easily distinguished by its black-barred belly and the patch of white at the base of its bill. There are five subspecies, two of which are most commonly seen in North America. The "Tundra" (*A. a. frontalis*), makes up the largest population, breeding across northwestern Canada and western Alaska. The "Tule" (*A. a. gambeli*), while the largest in stature, occurs in the fewest numbers, and is restricted in range to northwest Canada.

VOICE Laugh-like *klow-yo* or *klew-yo-yo;* very musical in a flock.
NESTING Bowl-shaped nest made of plant material, lined with down, constructed near water; 3–7 eggs; 1 brood; May–August.
FEEDING Eats sedges, grasses, berries, and plants on both land and water in summer; feeds on grasses, seeds, and grains in winter.

FLIGHT: strong, direct flight; flies alone, in multiple lines, or in a V-formation.

FLIGHT FORMATIONS
This heavy-bodied, powerful flier can often be seen in tightly packed flocks.

SIMILAR SPECIES

CANADA GOOSE
see p.41

black head, neck, and bill
white chin strap

HEAVY GRAZER
Grass is the major component of this goose's diet.

OCCURRENCE
Different habitats are utilized, both for breeding and wintering. Nesting areas include tundra ponds and lakes, dry rocky fields, and grassy slopes in Alaska and northern Canada. In winter, coastal marshes, inland wetlands, agricultural fields, and refuges are used along Pacific Coast, southern US, and Mexico.

Length **25–32in (64–81cm)**	Wingspan **4¼–5¼ft (1.3–1.6m)**	Weight **4–6½lb (1.8–3kg)**
Social **Flocks**	Lifespan **Up to 22 years**	Status **Secure**

Order **Anseriformes**	Family **Anatidae**	Species ***Chen caerulescens***

Snow Goose

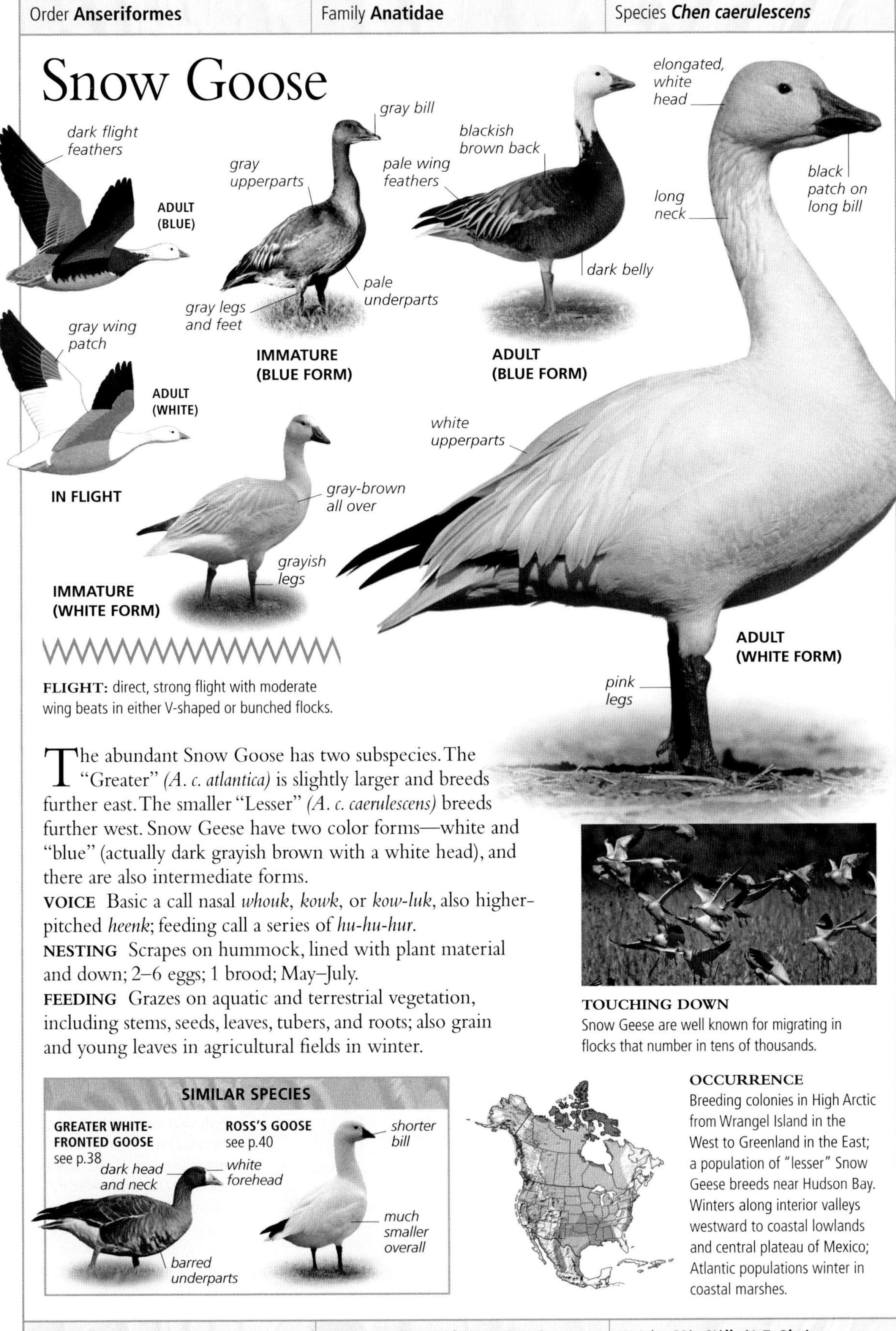
dark flight feathers
ADULT (BLUE)
gray wing patch
ADULT (WHITE)
IN FLIGHT
gray bill
gray upperparts
gray legs and feet
pale underparts
IMMATURE (BLUE FORM)
blackish brown back
pale wing feathers
dark belly
ADULT (BLUE FORM)
elongated, white head
black patch on long bill
long neck
white upperparts
gray-brown all over
grayish legs
IMMATURE (WHITE FORM)
pink legs
ADULT (WHITE FORM)

FLIGHT: direct, strong flight with moderate wing beats in either V-shaped or bunched flocks.

The abundant Snow Goose has two subspecies. The "Greater" *(A. c. atlantica)* is slightly larger and breeds further east. The smaller "Lesser" *(A. c. caerulescens)* breeds further west. Snow Geese have two color forms—white and "blue" (actually dark grayish brown with a white head), and there are also intermediate forms.

VOICE Basic a call nasal *whouk, kowk,* or *kow-luk,* also higher-pitched *heenk*; feeding call a series of *hu-hu-hur.*

NESTING Scrapes on hummock, lined with plant material and down; 2–6 eggs; 1 brood; May–July.

FEEDING Grazes on aquatic and terrestrial vegetation, including stems, seeds, leaves, tubers, and roots; also grain and young leaves in agricultural fields in winter.

TOUCHING DOWN
Snow Geese are well known for migrating in flocks that number in tens of thousands.

SIMILAR SPECIES

GREATER WHITE-FRONTED GOOSE see p.38
dark head and neck
barred underparts

ROSS'S GOOSE see p.40
white forehead
shorter bill
much smaller overall

OCCURRENCE
Breeding colonies in High Arctic from Wrangel Island in the West to Greenland in the East; a population of "lesser" Snow Geese breeds near Hudson Bay. Winters along interior valleys westward to coastal lowlands and central plateau of Mexico; Atlantic populations winter in coastal marshes.

Length **27–33in (69–83cm)**	Wingspan **4¼–5½ft (1.3–1.7m)**	Weight **3¾–6½lb (1.7–3kg)**
Social **Flocks**	Lifespan **Up to 27 years**	Status **Secure**

Order **Anseriformes**	Family **Anatidae**	Species ***Chen rossii***

Ross's Goose

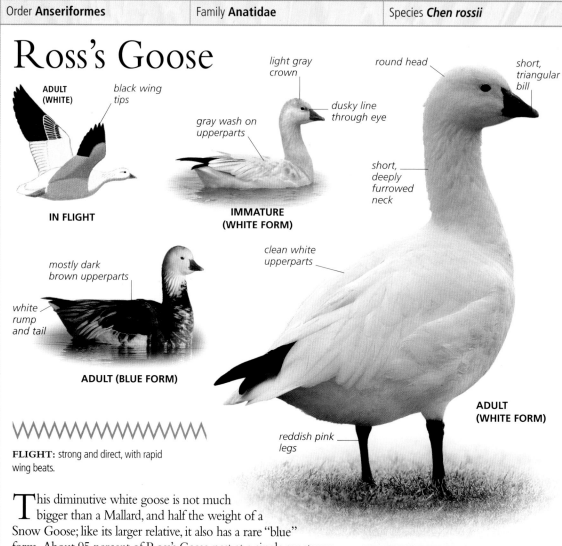

ADULT (WHITE)
black wing tips

IN FLIGHT

light gray crown
dusky line through eye
gray wash on upperparts

IMMATURE (WHITE FORM)

round head
short, triangular bill
short, deeply furrowed neck
clean white upperparts
reddish pink legs

ADULT (WHITE FORM)

mostly dark brown upperparts
white rump and tail

ADULT (BLUE FORM)

FLIGHT: strong and direct, with rapid wing beats.

This diminutive white goose is not much bigger than a Mallard, and half the weight of a Snow Goose; like its larger relative, it also has a rare "blue" form. About 95 percent of Ross's Geese nest at a single sanctuary in Arctic Canada, the rest breed along Hudson Bay and at several island locations. Hunting reduced the population to just 6,000 in the early 1950s, but the species has rebounded substantially, becoming more common along the East Coast as numbers improve.

VOICE Call a *keek keek keeek*, higher-pitched than Snow Goose; also a harsh, low *kork* or *kowk*; quiet when feeding.

NESTING Plant materials placed on ground, usually in colonies with Lesser Snow Geese; 3–5 eggs; 1 brood; June–August.

FEEDING Grazes on grasses, sedges, and small grains.

TRAVELING IN FAMILIES
Family groups migrate thousands of miles together, usually from northern Canada to central California.

SIMILAR SPECIES

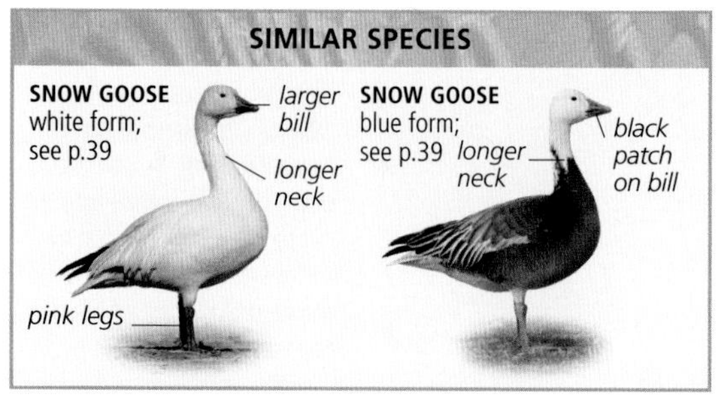
SNOW GOOSE
white form;
see p.39
larger bill
longer neck
pink legs
SNOW GOOSE
blue form;
see p.39
longer neck
black patch on bill

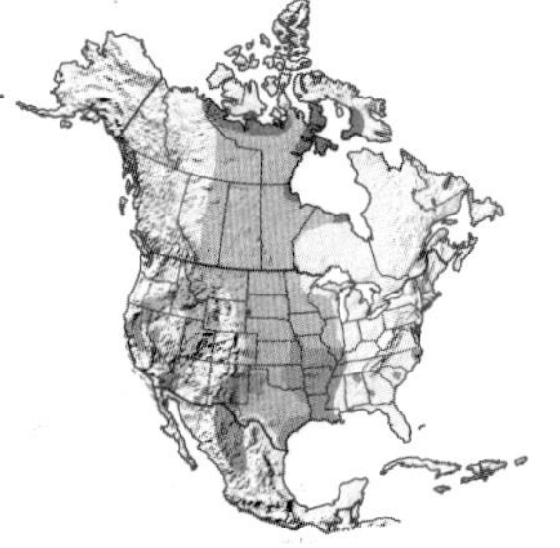

OCCURRENCE
Breeding grounds are amidst tundra in a number of scattered, High Arctic locations. Main wintering areas in California. On the wintering grounds, it feeds in agricultural fields, and also grasslands. Roosts overnight in several types of wetlands.

Length **22½–25in (57–64cm)**	Wingspan **3¼ft (1.1m)**	Weight **1¾–4½lb (0.85–2kg)**
Social **Flocks**	Lifespan **Up to 21 years**	Status **Localized**

Order **Anseriformes**	Family **Anatidae**	Species ***Branta canadensis***

Canada Goose

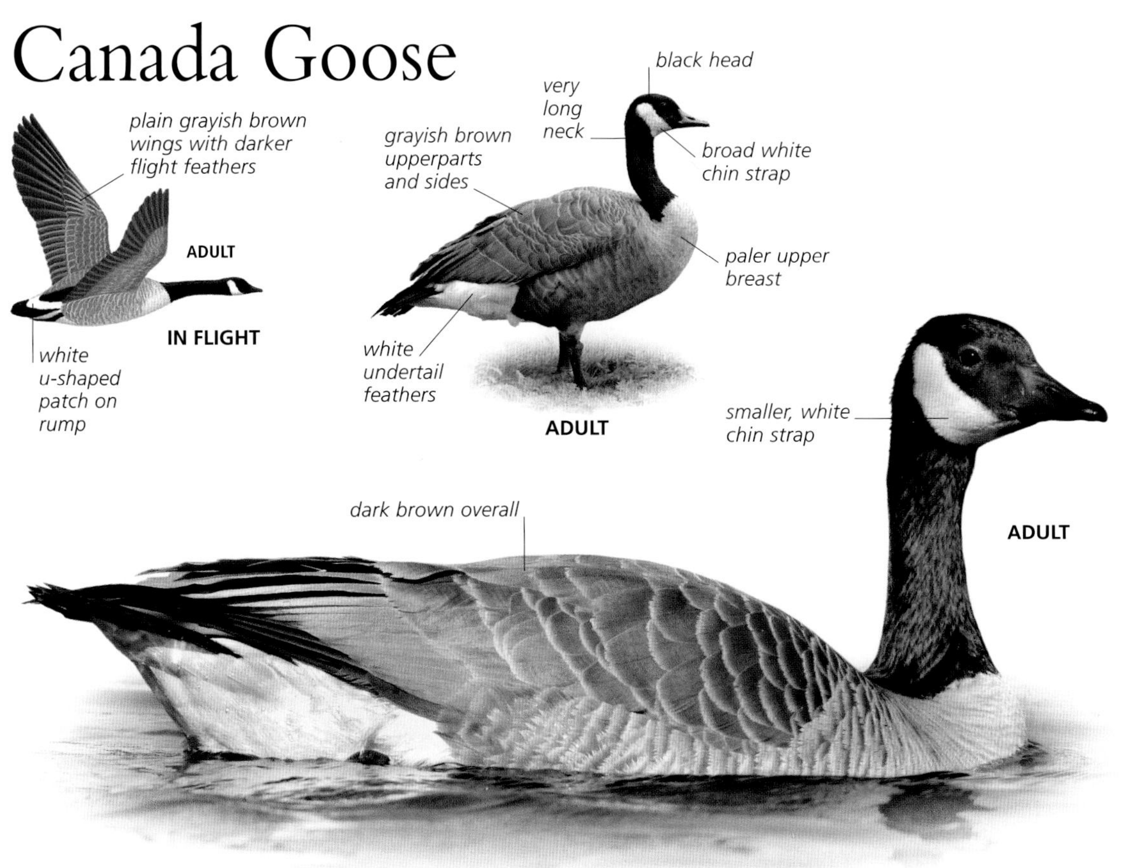
plain grayish brown wings with darker flight feathers
ADULT
IN FLIGHT
white u-shaped patch on rump
black head
very long neck
grayish brown upperparts and sides
broad white chin strap
paler upper breast
white undertail feathers
ADULT
smaller, white chin strap
dark brown overall
ADULT

The Canada Goose is the most common, widespread, and familiar goose in North America. Given its colossal range, it is not surprising that the Canada Goose has much geographic variation, and 12 subspecies have been recognized. With the exception of the Cackling Goose, from which it has recently been separated, it is difficult to confuse it, with its distinctive white chin strap, black head and neck, and grayish brown body, with any other species of goose. It is a monogamous species, and once pairs are formed, they stay together for life.

VOICE Male call *honk* or *bark*; females have higher pitched *hrink*.

NESTING Scrape lined with available plant matter and down, near water; 1–2 broods; 2–12 eggs; May–August.

FEEDING Grazes on grasses, sedges, leaves, seeds, agricultural crops and berries; also insects.

FLIGHT: strong and direct with fairly slow, deep wing beats; often flies in V-formation.

TRICK OF THE LIGHT
A low sun can play tricks—these birds are actually pale grayish underneath.

SIMILAR SPECIES

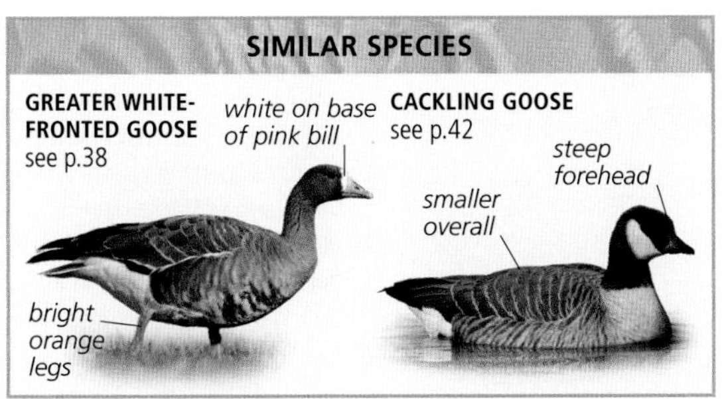
GREATER WHITE-FRONTED GOOSE
see p.38
white on base of pink bill
bright orange legs
CACKLING GOOSE
see p.42
steep forehead
smaller overall

OCCURRENCE
Variety of inland breeding habitats near water, including grassy urban areas, marshes, prairie, parkland, coastal temperate forest, northern coniferous forest, and Arctic tundra. Winters in agricultural fields, mudflats, saltwater marshes, lakes, and rivers.

Length **2¼–3½ft (0.7–1.1m)**	Wingspan **4¼–5½ft (1.3–1.7m)**	Weight **6½–9¾lb (3–4.4kg)**
Social **Flocks**	Lifespan **Up to 25 years**	Status **Secure**

Order **Anseriformes**	Family **Anatidae**	Species ***Branta hutchinsii***

Cackling Goose

plain grayish brown wings
ADULT
small, black head
white u-shaped patch on rump
IN FLIGHT
broad, white neck ring
black line separates white chin strap
darker breast
ADULT
B. h. leucopareia
dark brown breast
ADULT
B. h. minima
small stubby bill
white chin strap
no black under chin
pale breast
black tail
ADULT
B. h. hutchinsii

The Cackling Goose has recently been split from the Canada Goose; it can be distinguished from the latter by its short stubby bill, steep forehead, and short neck. There are four subspecies of Cackling Goose, which vary in breast color, ranging from dark on *C. h. minima,* fairly dark on *C. h. leucopareia*, and pale on *C. h. hutchinsii.* The Cackling Goose is much smaller than all subspecies of Canada Goose, except the "Lesser" Canada Goose, which has a longer neck and a less sloped forehead.

VOICE Male call a *honk* or *bark*; females have higher pitched *hrink;* also high-pitched yelps.

NESTING Scrape lined with available plant matter and down; 2–8 eggs; 1 brood; May–August.

FEEDING Consumes plants in summer; in winter, grazes on grass livestock and dairy pastures; also in agricultural fields.

FLIGHT: strong with rapid wing beats; flies in bunched V–formations.

LITTLE GEESE
Cackling Geese are tiny when seen together with the larger Canada Goose.

SIMILAR SPECIES

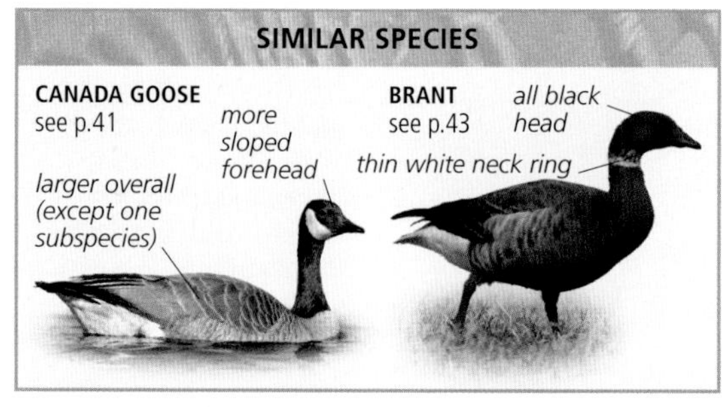
CANADA GOOSE
see p.41
more sloped forehead
larger overall (except one subspecies)
BRANT
see p.43
all black head
thin white neck ring

OCCURRENCE
At the northernmost fringe of the Canada Goose's range, in the tundra, it breeds on rocky tundra slopes from the Aleutians east to Baffin Island and Hudson Bay. Winters from British Columbia to California, also central US, Texas, and New Mexico in pastures and agricultural fields.

Length **21½–30in (55–75cm)**	Wingspan **4¼–5ft (1.3–1.5m)**	Weight **2–6½lb (0.9–3kg)**
Social **Flocks**	Lifespan **Unknown**	Status **Secure**

Order **Anseriformes**	Family **Anatidae**	Species ***Branta bernicla***

Brant

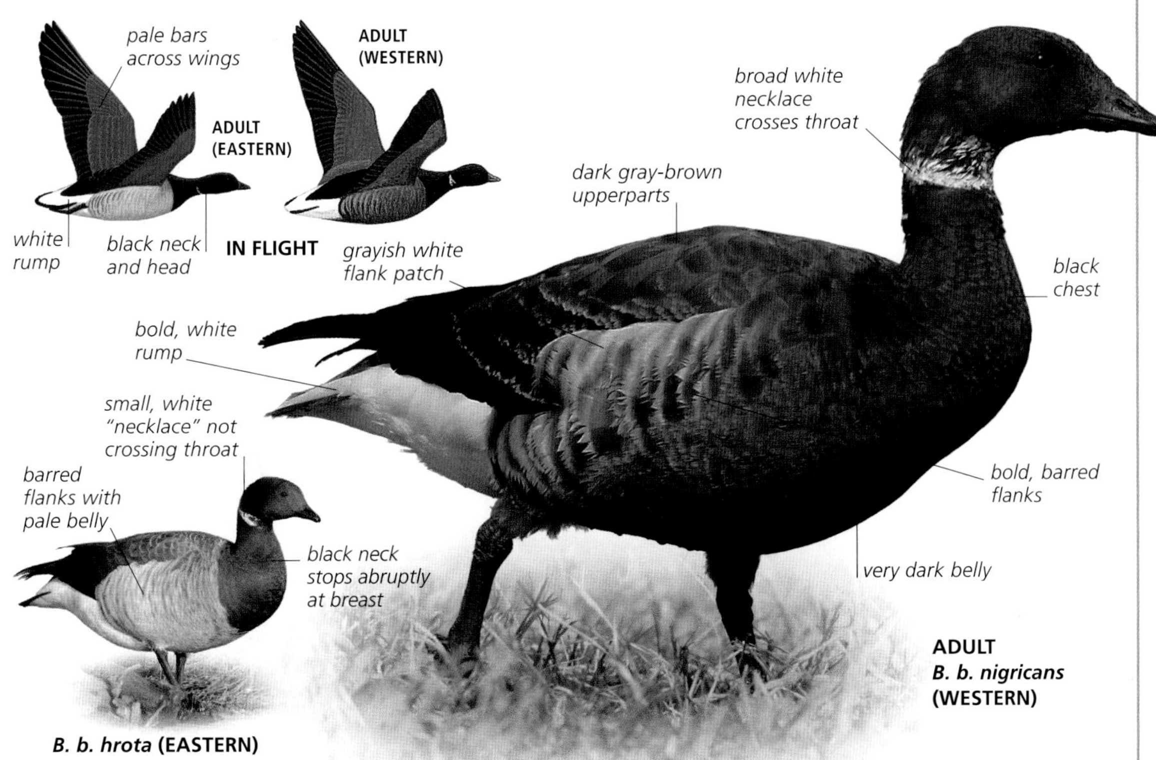

pale bars across wings
ADULT (EASTERN)
ADULT (WESTERN)
white rump
black neck and head
IN FLIGHT
grayish white flank patch
dark gray-brown upperparts
broad white necklace crosses throat
black chest
bold, white rump
small, white "necklace" not crossing throat
barred flanks with pale belly
black neck stops abruptly at breast
bold, barred flanks
very dark belly
ADULT
B. b. nigricans
(WESTERN)
B. b. hrota (EASTERN)

A small-billed, dark, stocky sea goose, the Brant winters on both the east and west coasts of North America. There are two subspecies named in North America—the pale-bellied "Atlantic" Brant (*B. b. hrota*), found in the east, and the darker "Black" Brant (*B. b. nigricans*), found in the west; an intermediate gray-bellied form, not yet named, breeds in the Canadian archipelago and winters in Boundary Bay, British Columbia. Unlike other North American geese, the Brant feeds mainly on eelgrass in winter.

VOICE Nasal *cruk*, harsh-sounding in tone; rolling series of *cut cut cut cronk*, with an upward inflection at end.

NESTING Scrape lined with grass, plant matter, and down on islands or gravel spits; 3–5 eggs; 1 brood; May–July.

FEEDING Eats grass and sedges when nesting; eelgrass in winter; also green algae, salt marsh plants, and mollusks.

FLIGHT: rapid and strong; low, irregular flight formations.

GRASSY MEAL
In winter, Brants forage almost exclusively on eelgrass between the high and low tide marks.

SIMILAR SPECIES

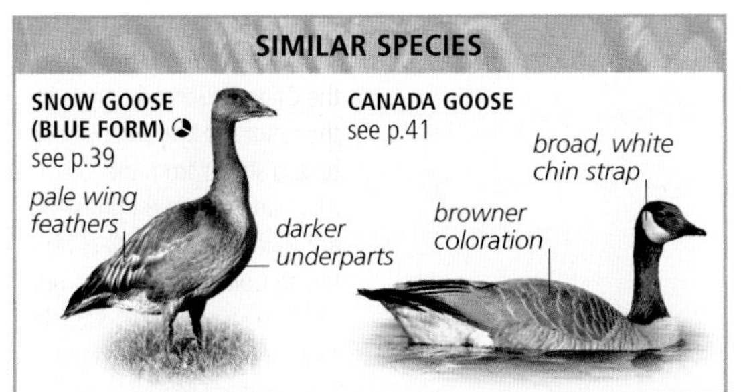

SNOW GOOSE (BLUE FORM)
see p.39
pale wing feathers
darker underparts
CANADA GOOSE
see p.41
broad, white chin strap
browner coloration

OCCURRENCE
Breeds in colonies in northern Canada and Alaska, and winters along both Pacific and Atlantic coasts. The western breeding population of the Brant ("Black") winters from the Aleutian Islands to northern Mexico, while the pale-bellied form ("Atlantic") is restricted in range to the East Coast.

Length **22–26in (56–66cm)**	Wingspan **3½–4ft (1.1–1.2m)**	Weight **2½–4lb (1–1.8kg)**
Social **Flocks**	Lifespan **Up to 25 years**	Status **Secure**

Order **Anseriformes**	Family **Anatidae**	Species ***Cygnus olor***

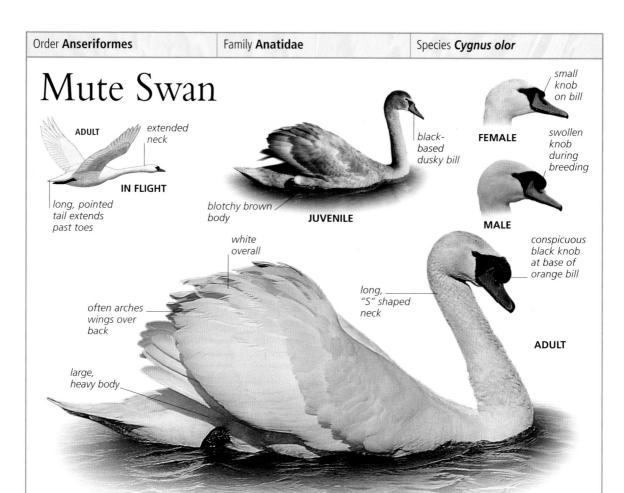

Mute Swan

ADULT

extended neck

IN FLIGHT

long, pointed tail extends past toes

black-based dusky bill

blotchy brown body

JUVENILE

small knob on bill

FEMALE

swollen knob during breeding

MALE

white overall

conspicuous black knob at base of orange bill

long, "S" shaped neck

often arches wings over back

ADULT

large, heavy body

One of the heaviest birds in North America, the Mute Swan was introduced from Europe due to its graceful appearance on water, if not on land, and easy domestication. However, this is an extremely territorial and aggressive bird. When threatened, it points its bill downwards, arches its wings, hisses, and then attacks. Displacement of native waterfowl species and overgrazing by this species have led to efforts to reduce its numbers in North America.

VOICE Not mute; hisses, grunts, snorts, and snores; during courtship, trumpets, although more quietly than other swans.

NESTING Platform nest of plant materials, built on ground near water; 4–8 eggs; 1–2 broods; March–October.

FEEDING Dabbles, dips, and upends, mainly for underwater plants, but occasionally for small creatures too.

FLIGHT: strong, steady wing beats; creating a distinctive whirring and throbbing sound.

FORMATION FLYING

Groups of Mute Swans will sometimes fly in a line, and at other times, as here, they will arrange themselves in a "V" formation.

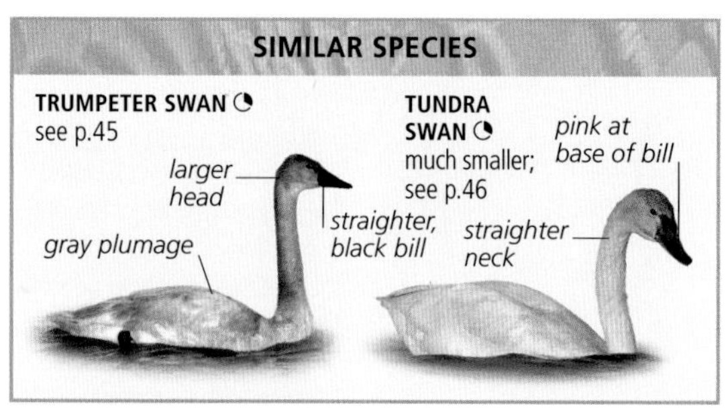
SIMILAR SPECIES
TRUMPETER SWAN ◔
see p.45
larger head
gray plumage
straighter, black bill
TUNDRA SWAN ◔
much smaller; see p.46
pink at base of bill
straighter neck

OCCURRENCE

Bulk of population is found along the Atlantic Coast from Maine to North Carolina; smaller populations around the Great Lakes and southern British Columbia. Breeds and lives year-round on sluggish rivers, ponds, or lakes, preferring still water with emergent vegetation.

Length **4–5ft (1.2–1.5m)**	Wingspan **6½–7½ft (2–2.3m)**	Weight **12–32lb (5.5–14.5kg)**
Social **Pairs/Family groups**	Lifespan **Up to 21 years**	Status **Localized**

Order **Anseriformes**	Family **Anatidae**	Species ***Cygnus buccinator***

Trumpeter Swan

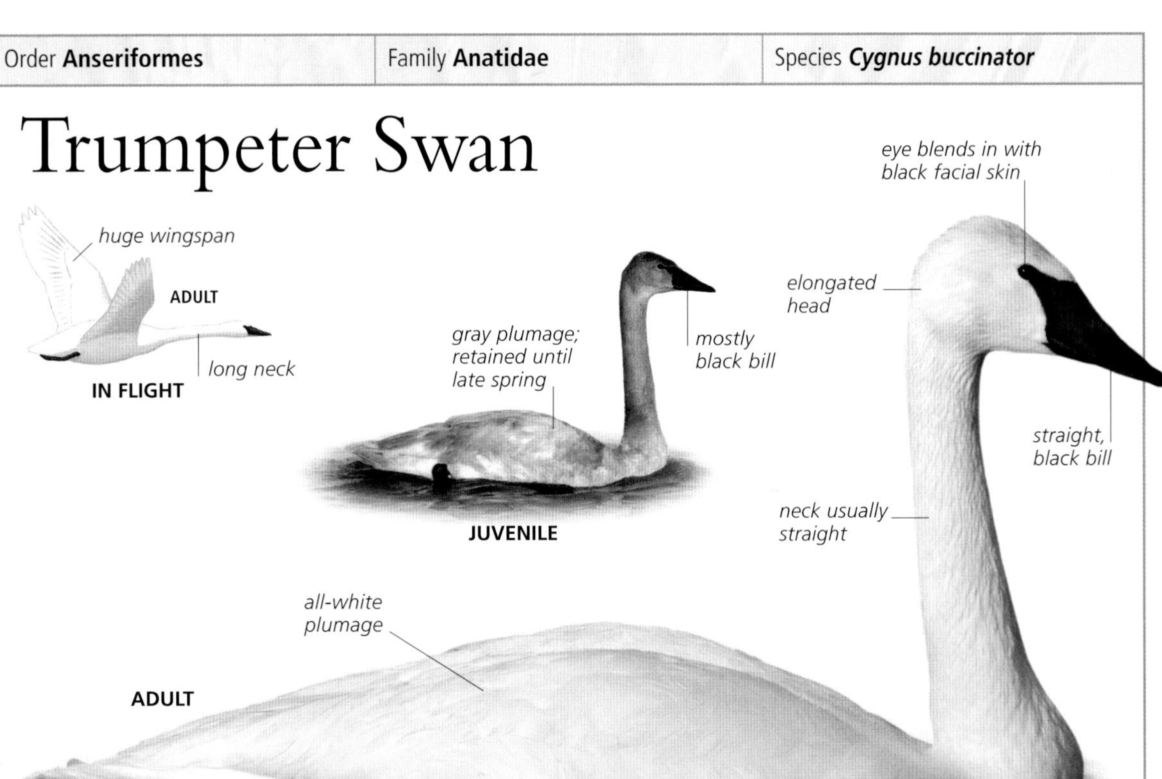
huge wingspan
ADULT
long neck
IN FLIGHT
gray plumage; retained until late spring
mostly black bill
JUVENILE
eye blends in with black facial skin
elongated head
straight, black bill
neck usually straight
all-white plumage
ADULT

North America's quintessential swan and heaviest waterfowl, the Trumpeter Swan is a magnificent sight to behold. This species has made a remarkable comeback after numbers were severely reduced by hunting in the 1600-1800s; by the mid-1930s, fewer than a hundred were known to exist. Active reintroduction efforts were made in the upper Midwest and Ontario to re-establish the species to its former breeding range. The Trumpeter Swan's characteristic far-reaching call is usually the best way to identify it.

VOICE Call nasal, resonant *oh-OH* reminiscent of French horn.

NESTING Large mound made of plant matter on raised areas near or in freshwater; 3–6 eggs; 1 brood; April–September.

FEEDING Eats algae and aquatic plants, including moss, at or below the surface; feeds on grain in pastures and fields.

FLIGHT: slow, heavy, ponderous wing beats; "runs" on water's surface when taking off.

RUSTY STAINING
Trumpeter Swans often have rufous-stained heads and necks due to probing in iron-rich mud.

SIMILAR SPECIES

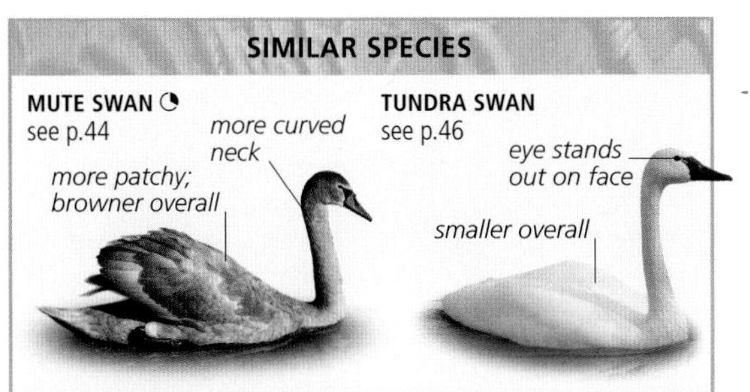
MUTE SWAN
see p.44
more curved neck
more patchy; browner overall

TUNDRA SWAN
see p.46
eye stands out on face
smaller overall

OCCURRENCE
Alaskan and northern Canadian breeders go south to winter; others remain year round at local places such as Yellowstone National Park. Found on freshwater lakes and marshes with plenty of vegetation on which to feed. Also found on estuaries in winter.

Length **4¼–5ft (1.3–1.5m)**	Wingspan **6½ft (2m)**	Weight **17–28lb (7.5–12.5kg)**
Social **Flocks**	Lifespan **Up to 24 years**	Status **Secure**

Order **Anseriformes**	Family **Anatidae**	Species ***Cygnus columbianus***

Tundra Swan

ADULT

small head and bill

dark legs

IN FLIGHT

fairly thick neck

dull grayish body

dirty pink bill

JUVENILE

eye stands out from face at close range

yellow facial skin next to eye

large yellow bill patch

BEWICK'S SWAN

all-white plumage

ADULT

Nesting in the Arctic tundra, this well-named species is North America's most widespread and smallest swan. Two populations exist, with one wintering in the West, and the other along the East Coast. The Tundra Swan can be confused with the Trumpeter Swan, but their different calls immediately distinguish the two species. When they are silent, weight and bill structure are the best way to tell them apart. In Eurasia, this species is known as Bewick's Swan and possesses a larger yellow patch at the base of its bill.

VOICE Clear, high-pitched yodelling *whoo-hooo* calls mixed with garbles, yelping, and barking sounds.

NESTING Mound-shaped nest made of plant matter near water; 3–6 eggs; 1 brood; May–September.

FEEDING Eats aquatic vegetation, insects, mollusks; also grain.

FLIGHT: flight pattern like that of other swans but with slightly faster wing beats.

LARGE WINTER FLOCKS
Its size, white plumage, and flocking habits make the Tundra Swan a conspicuous species.

SIMILAR SPECIES

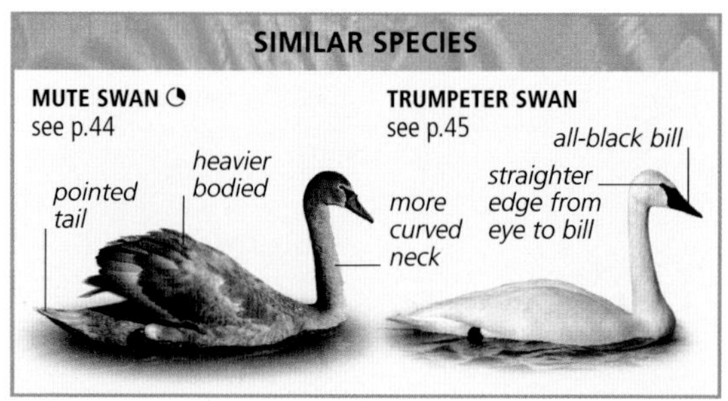
MUTE SWAN ◔
see p.44
pointed tail
heavier bodied
TRUMPETER SWAN
see p.45
all-black bill
straighter edge from eye to bill
more curved neck

OCCURRENCE
Nests around lakes and pools in northern tundra from the Aleutians to the Yukon, and east to northwest Quebec. Winters in southern British Columbia, western US, and mid-Atlantic states, mostly New Jersey to south Carolina. Winter habitat includes shallow coastal bays, ponds, and lakes.

Length **4–5ft (1.2–1.5m)**	Wingspan **6¼–7¼ft (1.9–2.2m)**	Weight **12–18lb (5.5–8kg)**
Social **Flocks**	Lifespan **Up to 21 years**	Status **Secure**

Order **Anseriformes**	Family **Anatidae**	Species ***Aix sponsa***

Wood Duck

blue wing patch
long wings
MALE
head held high
IN FLIGHT
bold, tear-shaped eye-ring
smaller crest
brownish breast
white-edged feathers
FEMALE
subdued facial pattern
brown eye
grayish bill
IMMATURE
red eye
complex, white facial markings
helmet-like head profile
burgundy flanks
black tip of bill
long, dark tail
white-flecked maroon breast appears black at a distance
MALE
white, vertical breast stripe

The male Wood Duck is perhaps the most striking of all North American ducks. With its bright plumage, red eye and bill, and its long sleek crest that gives its head a helmet-shaped profile, the male is unmistakable. It is related to the Mandarin Duck of Asia. The Wood Duck is very dependent on mature swampy forestland, and is typically found on swamps, shallow lakes, ponds, and park settings that are surrounded by trees. Although it adapts to human activity, it is quite shy. When swimming, the Wood Duck can be seen jerking its head front to back. Of all waterfowl, this is the only species that regularly raises two broods each season.

VOICE Male gives a wheezy upslurred whistle *zweeet*; female's call a double-note, rising *oh-eek oh-eek*.

NESTING Nests in natural tree cavities or nest boxes in close proximity to water; 10–13 eggs; 2 broods; April–August.

FEEDING Forages for seeds, tree fruits, and small acorns; also spiders, insects, and crustaceans.

FLIGHT: rapid flight with deep wing beats; flies with head up; leaps straight off the water.

PLAIN BELLY
Wings raised, a male reveals one of the only plain areas of its plumage—its pale belly and undertail.

SIMILAR SPECIES
BUFFLEHEAD ♀
see p.69
white on cheek
shorter neck
shorter tail
HOODED MERGANSER ♀
narrower wings; see p.72
no eye-ring
long, tan crest

OCCURRENCE
Usually found throughout the year, along rivers, streams, and creeks, in swamps, and marshy areas. Has a preference for permanent bodies of water. If good aquatic feeding areas are unavailable, the Wood Duck feeds in open areas, including agricultural fields.

Length **18½–21½in (47–54cm)**	Wingspan **26–29in (66–73cm)**	Weight **16–30oz (450–850g)**
Social **Small flocks**	Lifespan **Up to 18 years**	Status **Secure**

Order **Anseriformes**	Family **Anatidae**	Species ***Anas strepera***

Gadwall

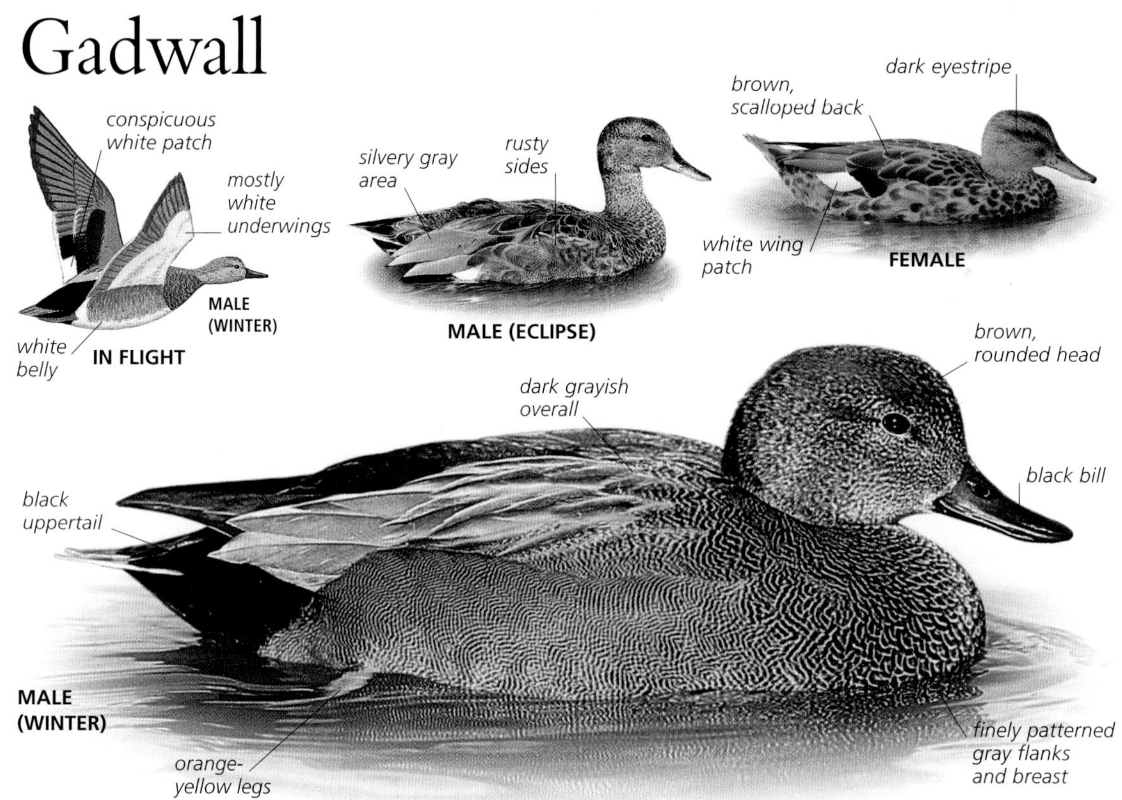

conspicuous white patch
mostly white underwings
MALE (WINTER)
white belly
IN FLIGHT
silvery gray area
rusty sides
MALE (ECLIPSE)
brown, scalloped back
dark eyestripe
white wing patch
FEMALE
brown, rounded head
dark grayish overall
black bill
black uppertail
MALE (WINTER)
orange-yellow legs
finely patterned gray flanks and breast

Although the Gadwall's appearance is somewhat somber, many birders consider this duck one of North America's most elegant species because of the subtlety of its plumage. Despite being common and widespread, Gadwalls are often overlooked because of their retiring behavior and relatively quiet vocalizations. This dabbling duck is slightly smaller and more delicate than the Mallard, yet female Gadwalls are often mistaken for female Mallards. Gadwalls associate with other species, especially in winter.

VOICE Low, raspy *meep* or *reb* given in quick succession; female *quack* similar to that of female Mallard, but higher-pitched and more nasal; high-pitched *peep*, or *pe-peep*; both sexes give *tickety-tickety-tickety* chatter while feeding.

NESTING Bowl nest made of plant material in a scrape; 8–12 eggs; 1 brood; April–August.

FEEDING Dabbles on the surface or below for seeds, aquatic vegetation, and invertebrates, including mollusks and insects.

FLIGHT: direct flight with fast wing beats; leaps straight off the water.

BROOD ON THE MOVE
Females lead their ducklings from their nest to a brood-rearing habitat that provides cover and ample food for the ducklings to forage.

SIMILAR SPECIES

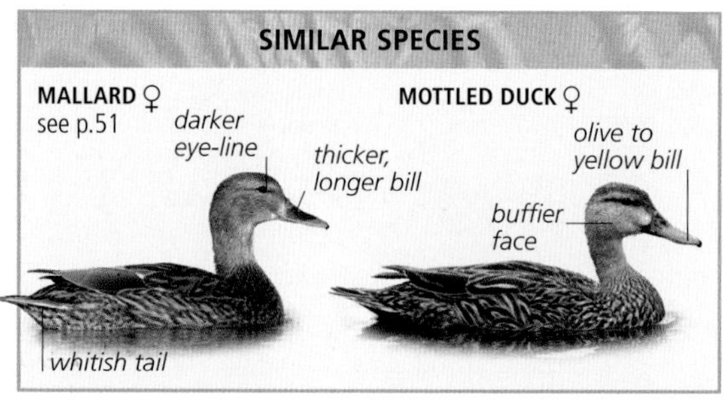

MALLARD ♀
see p.51
darker eye-line
thicker, longer bill
whitish tail
MOTTLED DUCK ♀
olive to yellow bill
buffier face

OCCURRENCE
From the western prairie pothole country of Canada and the northern US, the Gadwall's range has expanded as it has adapted to man-made bodies of water, such as reservoirs and ponds. In winter, mostly found on lakes, marshes, and along rivers.

Length **18–22½in (46–57cm)**	Wingspan **33in (84cm)**	Weight **18–45oz (500–1,250g)**
Social **Winter flocks**	Lifespan **Up to 19 years**	Status **Secure**

Order **Anseriformes**	Family **Anatidae**	Species ***Anas americana***

American Wigeon

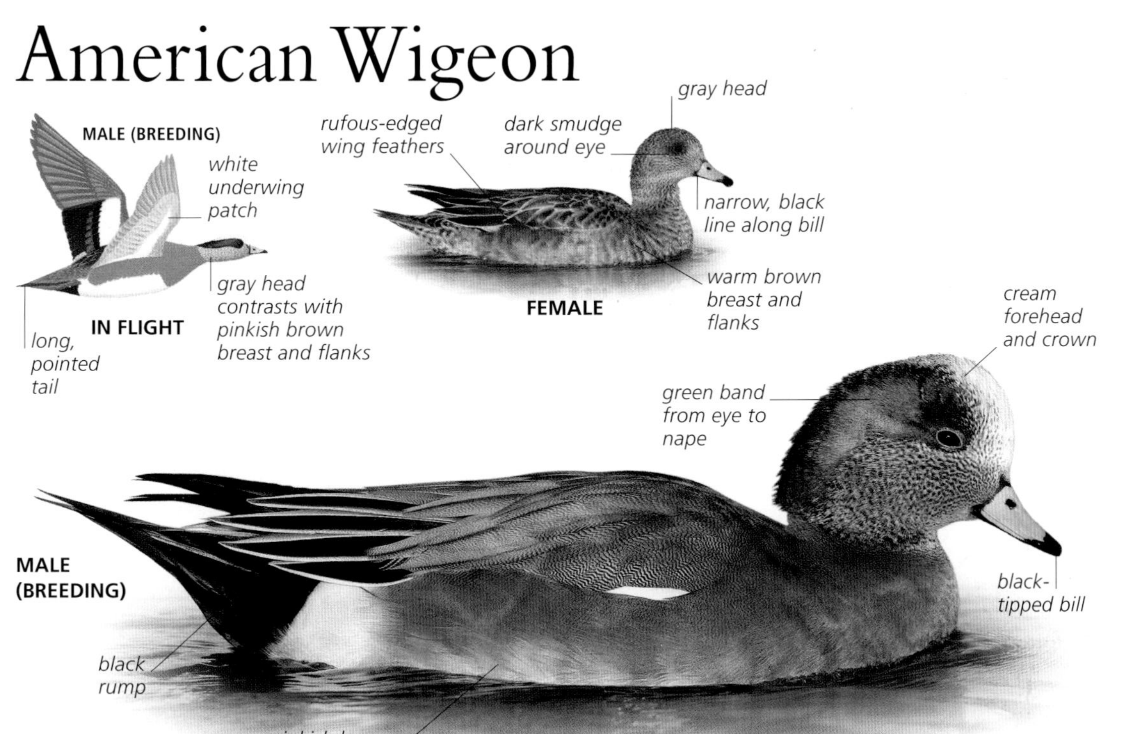

MALE (BREEDING)
white underwing patch
IN FLIGHT
long, pointed tail
gray head contrasts with pinkish brown breast and flanks
rufous-edged wing feathers
dark smudge around eye
gray head
narrow, black line along bill
warm brown breast and flanks
FEMALE
cream forehead and crown
green band from eye to nape
black-tipped bill
MALE (BREEDING)
black rump
pinkish brown flanks

Often found in mixed flocks with other ducks, the American Wigeon is a common and widespread, medium-sized dabbling duck. This bird is an opportunist that loiters around other diving ducks and coots, feeding on the vegetation they dislodge. It is more social during migration and in the nonbreeding season than when breeding.

VOICE Slow and fast whistles; male's most common call a slow, high-pitched, wheezy, three-syllable *whew-whew-whew*, with middle note loudest; also, a faster *whee* whistle.

NESTING Depression lined with plant material and down, usually in tall grass away from water; 5–10 eggs; 1 brood; May–August.

FEEDING Grazes on grass, clover, algae, and, in agricultural fields; feeds on many seeds, insects, mollusks, and crustaceans during the breeding season.

FLIGHT: rapid, fairly deep wing beats; leaps almost vertically off the water.

COMING IN FOR LANDING
This male's cream-colored forehead is clearly visible, as is the sharp contrast between the white belly, and the pinkish breast and flanks.

FLAPPING WINGS
This bird has a white patch on its underwing, while the Eurasian Wigeon has a gray patch.

SIMILAR SPECIES

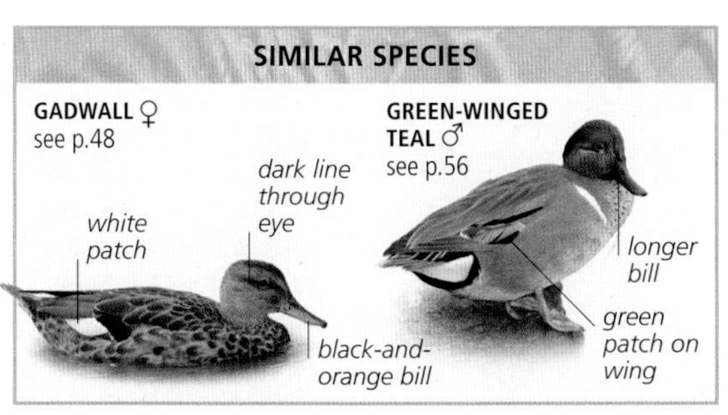

GADWALL ♀
see p.48
white patch
dark line through eye
black-and-orange bill
GREEN-WINGED TEAL ♂
see p.56
longer bill
green patch on wing

OCCURRENCE
The northernmost breeder of the dabbling ducks, occurs from Alaska to the Maritimes. Prefers pothole and grassland habitats; found almost anywhere near water in winter. Winters south to northern South America and the Caribbean, in freshwater and coastal bay habitats.

Length **17½–23in (45–58cm)**	Wingspan **33in (84cm)**	Weight **1⅛–3lb (0.5–1.3kg)**
Social **Flocks**	Lifespan **Up to 21 years**	Status **Secure**

Order **Anseriformes**	Family **Anatidae**	Species ***Anas rubripes***

American Black Duck

rich violet patch
white underwing
MALE
dark tail
IN FLIGHT
heavily streaked head and neck
olive bill
cinnamon-edged flank feathers
FEMALE
pale head
dark cap
narrow, dark eye-line
greenish yellow bill
dark body
MALE

The American Black Duck, a large dabbling duck, is closely related to the Mallard. In the past, the two species were separated by different habitat preferences—the American Black Duck preferring forested locations, and the Mallard favoring more open habitats. Over the years, these habitats became less distinct as the East was deforested and trees were planted in the Midwest. As a result, there are now many hybrids between the two species. It has also been argued that the introduction of Mallards to various areas in the East has further increased interbreeding. The American Black Duck breeds throughout a wide area in the northern part of its range. When breeding, males can be seen chasing away other males to maintain their territories.

VOICE Male's call a reedy *raeb*, given once or twice; female *quack* sounds very similar to Mallard.

NESTING Scrape lined with plant material and down, usually on ground or close to water; 4–10 eggs; 1 brood; March–September.

FEEDING An omnivore, the American Black Duck eats plant leaves and stems, roots, seeds, grains, fruit, aquatic plants, fish, and amphibians.

FLIGHT: fast, shallow, and regular; often flies in groups.

DARK PLUMAGE
This species is the darkest of all the Mallard-type ducks that occur in North America.

SIMILAR SPECIES

MALLARD ♀
see p.51

MOTTLED DUCK ♀

orange bill
whitish tail
paler body
mottled brown upperparts
unstreaked face

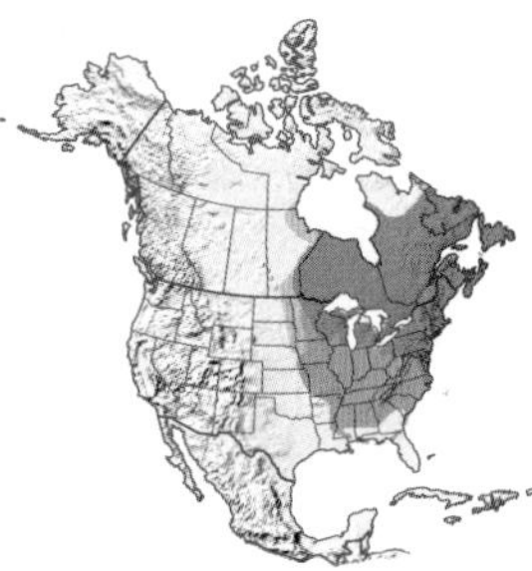

OCCURRENCE
Nests in eastern Canada and adjacent areas of the US in a variety of habitats including northerly and mixed hardwood forest, wooded uplands, bogs, salt- and freshwater marshes, and on islands. Resident in the central part of its range, but large numbers winter in saltwater marshes.

Length **21½–23in (54–59cm)**	Wingspan **35–37in (88–95cm)**	Weight **1½–3½lb (0.7–1.6kg)**
Social **Flocks**	Lifespan **Up to 26 years**	Status **Secure**

Order **Anseriformes**	Family **Anatidae**	Species ***Anas platyrhynchos***

Mallard

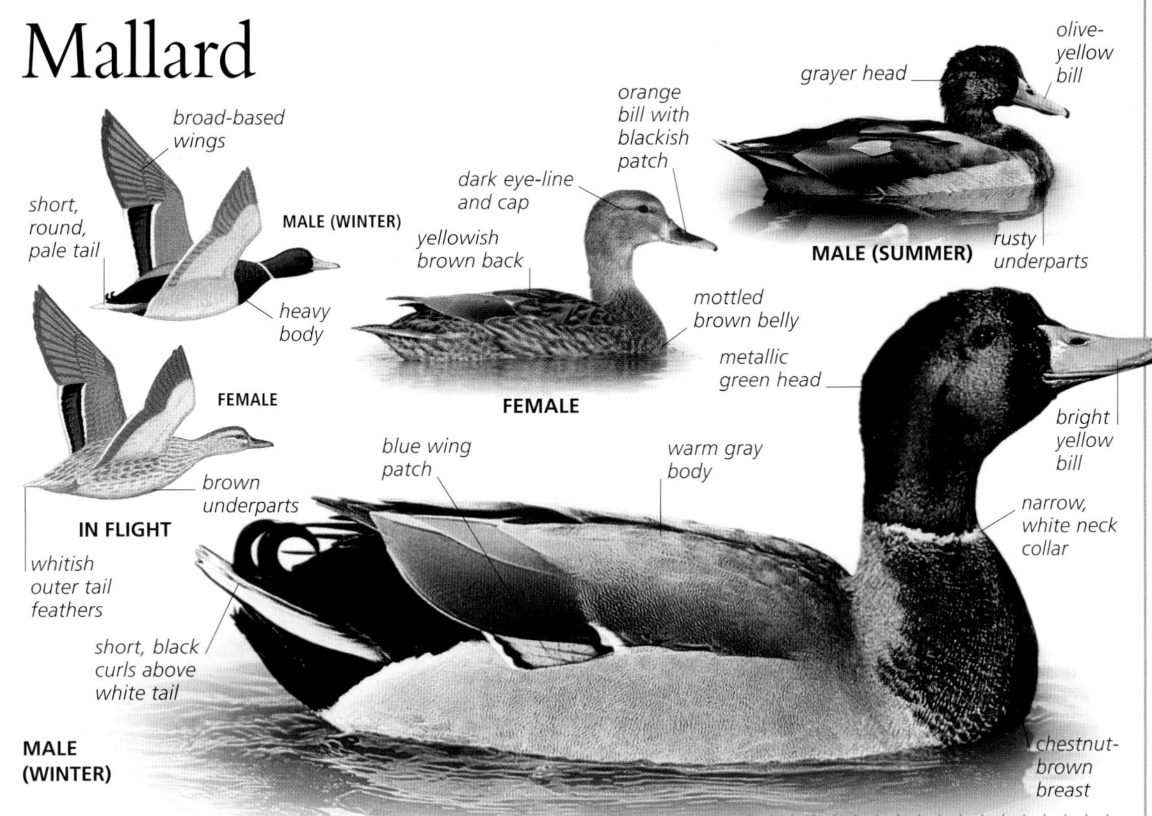
broad-based wings
short, round, pale tail
MALE (WINTER)
heavy body
FEMALE
IN FLIGHT
brown underparts
whitish outer tail feathers
dark eye-line and cap
yellowish brown back
orange bill with blackish patch
mottled brown belly
FEMALE
grayer head
olive-yellow bill
MALE (SUMMER)
rusty underparts
metallic green head
bright yellow bill
blue wing patch
warm gray body
narrow, white neck collar
short, black curls above white tail
MALE (WINTER)
chestnut-brown breast

The Mallard is perhaps the most familiar of all ducks, and occurs in the wild all across the Northern Hemisphere. It is the ancestor of most domestic ducks, and hybrids between the wild and domestic forms are frequently seen in city lakes and ponds, often with patches of white on the breast. Mating is generally a violent affair, but outside the breeding season the wild species is strongly migratory and gregarious, sometimes forming large flocks that may join with other species.

VOICE Male's call a quiet raspy *raab*; during courtship a high-pitched whistle; female call a *quack* or repeated in series.

NESTING Scrape lined with plant matter, usually near water, often on floating vegetation; 6–15 eggs; 1 brood; February–September.

FEEDING Feeds omnivorously on insects, crustaceans, mollusks, and earthworms when breeding; otherwise largely vegetarian; takes seeds, acorns, agricultural crops, aquatic vegetation, and bread.

FLIGHT: fast, shallow, and regular; often flies in groups.

STICKING TOGETHER
The mother leads her ducklings to water soon after they hatch. She looks after them until they can fend for themselves.

SIMILAR SPECIES

GADWALL ♀ see p.48

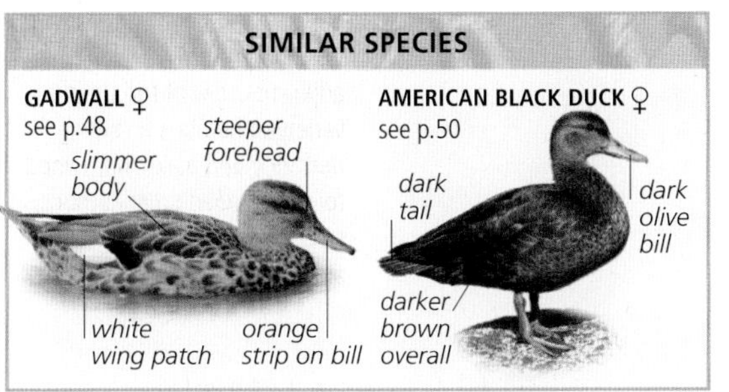
steeper forehead
slimmer body
white wing patch
orange strip on bill

AMERICAN BLACK DUCK ♀ see p.50

dark tail
dark olive bill
darker brown overall

OCCURRENCE
Occurs throughout the region, choosing shallow water in natural wetlands, such as marshes, prairie potholes, ponds, and ditches; can also be found in man-made habitats such as city parks and reservoirs, preferring more open habitats in winter.

Length **19½–26in (50–65cm)**	Wingspan **32–37in (82–95cm)**	Weight **1⅞–3lb (0.9–1.4kg)**
Social **Flocks**	Lifespan **Up to 29 years**	Status **Secure**

Order **Anseriformes**	Family **Anatidae**	Species ***Anas discors***

Blue-winged Teal

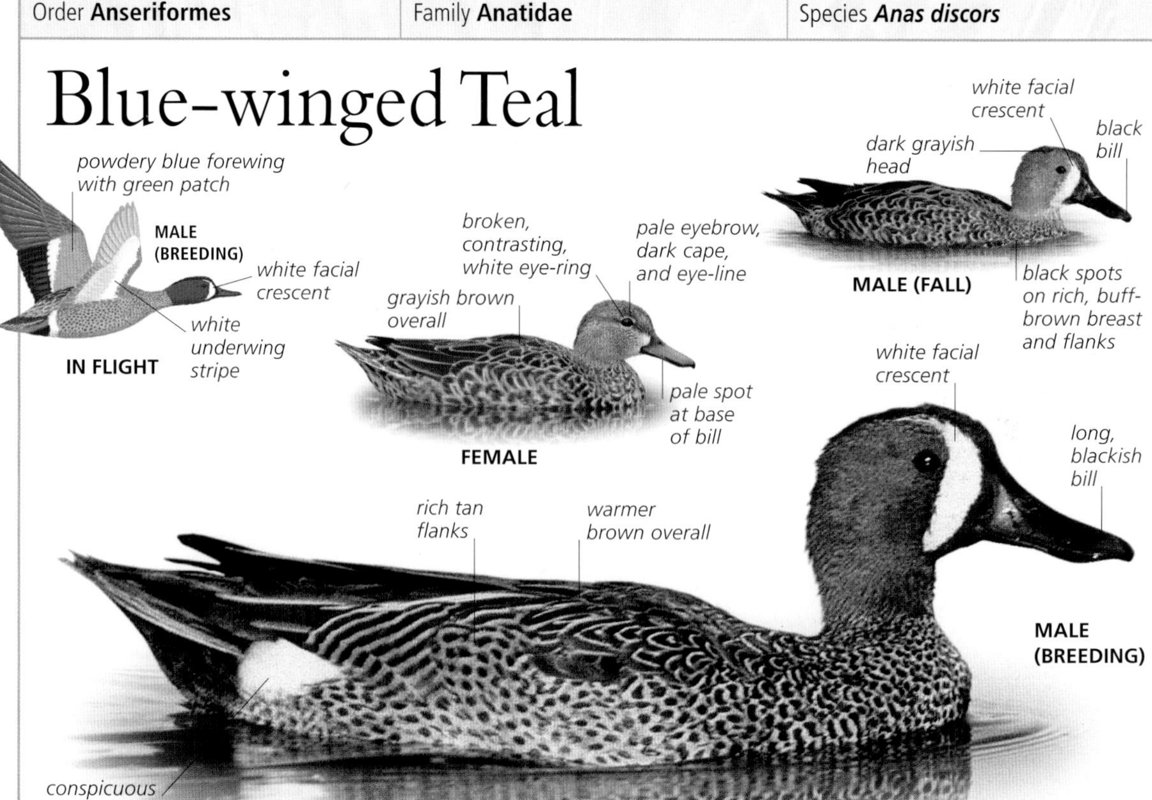

powdery blue forewing with green patch
MALE (BREEDING)
white facial crescent
white underwing stripe
IN FLIGHT
broken, contrasting, white eye-ring
pale eyebrow, dark cape, and eye-line
grayish brown overall
pale spot at base of bill
FEMALE
white facial crescent
dark grayish head
black bill
MALE (FALL)
black spots on rich, buff-brown breast and flanks
white facial crescent
long, blackish bill
rich tan flanks
warmer brown overall
MALE (BREEDING)
conspicuous white patch

This small dabbling duck is a common and widespread North American breeding species. With a bold white crescent between bill and eye on its otherwise slate-gray head and neck, the male Blue-winged Teal is quite distinctive. The Blue-winged and Cinnamon Teals, along with the Northern Shoveler, constitute the three "blue-winged" ducks; this is a feature that is conspicuous when the birds are flying. The Cinnamon and the Blue-winged Teals are almost identical genetically and interbreed to form hybrids. The Blue-winged Teal winters mostly south of the US and migrates north in spring.

VOICE Male a high-pitched, raspy *peew* or low-pitched *paay* during courtship; female a loud single *quack*.

NESTING Bowl-shaped depression lined with grasses, close to water's edge, in meadows; 6–14 eggs; 1 brood; April–September.

FEEDING Eats seeds of a variety of plants; feeds heavily on insect larvae, crustaceans, and snails, when breeding.

FLIGHT: fast, twisting flight; flies in compact, small groups.

OUTSTRETCHED WING
Wing stretch behavior shows the white feathers between the blue forewing and green rearwing.

OCCURRENCE
Nests across North America, with highest numbers in the prairie and parkland regions of the midcontinent. Prefers shallow ponds or marshes during nesting; freshwater to brackish water and (less so) saltwater marshes during migration. In winter, prefers saline environments, including mangroves.

SIMILAR SPECIES

CINNAMON TEAL ♀
see p.53
plain face
warmer brown
streaked rump

GREEN-WINGED TEAL ♀
see p.56
different wing pattern
smaller, more compact body
smaller bill

Length **14½–16in (37–41cm)**	Wingspan **23½–25in (60–64cm)**	Weight **11–18oz (300–500g)**
Social **Flocks**	Lifespan **Up to 17 years**	Status **Secure**

Order **Anseriformes**	Family **Anatidae**	Species ***Anas cyanoptera***

Cinnamon Teal

powdery blue forewing
MALE
IN FLIGHT
white underwing stripe
warm brown, upperparts with rust tinge
plain face pattern
shoveler-like bill
FEMALE
dull yellow legs
solid cinnamon color
conspicuous orange to red eye
long, spoon-shaped, black bill
MALE

True to his name, the male Cinnamon Teal is unmistakable in its overall rusty brown color and blazing red eyes. A fairly small duck, the Cinnamon Teal is the only North American dabbling duck species that does not breed in the Great Plains and prairies of the midcontinent. Most of its population winters in the coastal marshes and interior wetlands of Mexico. The Cinnamon Teal is common in southwestern Canada and western US, and even seen in tiny roadside pools. Closely related to both the Northern Shoveler and Blue-winged Teal, the Cinnamon Teal's wing pattern is indistinguishable from that of the latter.

VOICE Male a snuffled *chuk chuk chuk*; female a loud single *quack* and soft *gack gack gack ga*.

NESTING Shallow depression lined with grass near water; 4–16 eggs; 1 brood; March–September.

FEEDING Feeds on seeds of many plant species; adds aquatic insects, crustaceans, and snails, when breeding; omnivorous.

FLIGHT: rapid wing beats; very agile, making sharp turns.

FLOCKING TOGETHER
The cinnamon-colored males and tan females are often found in flocks.

SIMILAR SPECIES

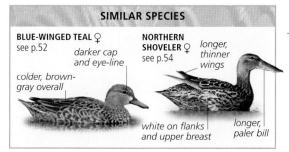

BLUE-WINGED TEAL ♀ see p.52
darker cap and eye-line; colder, brown-gray overall

NORTHERN SHOVELER ♀ see p.54
longer, thinner wings; white on flanks and upper breast; longer, paler bill

OCCURRENCE
Found in freshwater and brackish habitats of various sizes, such as marshes, reservoirs, flooded fields, ponds, ditches, and stock ponds. In the southern part of its wintering range, can also be found in tidal estuaries, salt marshes, and mangrove forests. Widespread in Central and South America.

Length **14–17in (36–43cm)**	Wingspan **22in (56cm)**	Weight **10–17oz (275–475g)**
Social **Winter flocks**	Lifespan **Up to 12 years**	Status **Secure**

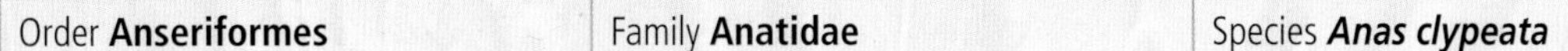

Order **Anseriformes**	Family **Anatidae**	Species ***Anas clypeata***

Northern Shoveler

grayish blue wing patch
whitish tail
IN FLIGHT
long bill
FEMALE
pale blue wing patch
heavy fronted
MALE
dark, narrow eye-line
brown overall
dusky olive-gray to orange bill
pale-edged, brown flank feathers
FEMALE
yellow eye
large, dark spatula-shaped bill
dark green head
MALE
white breast
chestnut belly and flanks
black-and-white rump

The Northern Shoveler is a common, medium-sized, dabbling duck found in North America and Eurasia. It is monogamous—pairs remain together longer than any other dabbler species. Its distinctive long bill is highly specialized; it is wider at the tip and contains thin, comb-like structures (called "lamellae") along the sides, used to filter food items from the water. Shovelers often form tight feeding groups, swimming close together as they sieve the water for prey.

VOICE Male call a nasal, muffled *thuk thuk…thuk thuk*; also a loud, nasal *paaaay*; female call a variety of *quacks*, singly or in a series of 4–5 descending notes.

NESTING Scrape lined with plant matter and down, in short plants, near water; 6–19 eggs; 1 brood; May–August.

FEEDING Forages for seeds; filters small crustaceans and mollusks out of the water.

FLIGHT: strong direct flight; male's wings make a rattling noise when taking off.

UPSIDE DOWN FEEDER
This male upends to feed below the water's surface, revealing his orange legs.

FILTER FEEDING
Their bills open, these ducks sieve small invertebrates from the water.

SIMILAR SPECIES

MALLARD ♀ larger; see p.51

CINNAMON TEAL ♀ see p.53

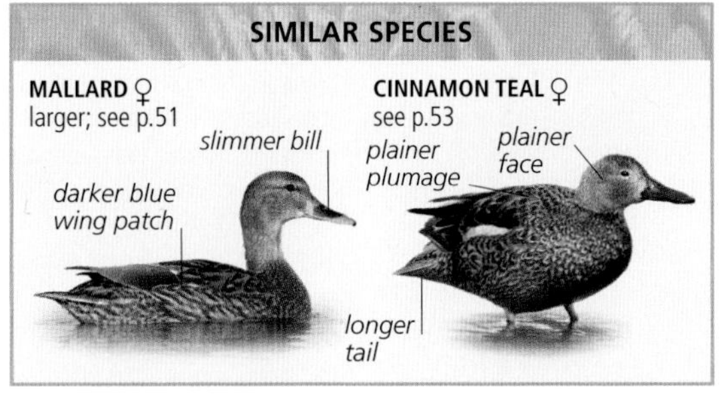
slimmer bill
darker blue wing patch
plainer plumage
plainer face
longer tail

OCCURRENCE
Widespread across North America, south of the tundra. Breeds in a variety of wetlands, in edges of shallow pools with nearby tall and short grasslands. Occurs in fresh- and saltmarshes, ponds, and other shallow bodies of water in winter; does not feed on land.

Length **17½–20in (44–51cm)**	Wingspan **27–33in (69–84cm)**	Weight **14–29oz (400–825g)**
Social **Flocks**	Lifespan **Up to 18 years**	Status **Secure**

Order **Anseriformes**	Family **Anatidae**	Species ***Anas acuta***

Northern Pintail

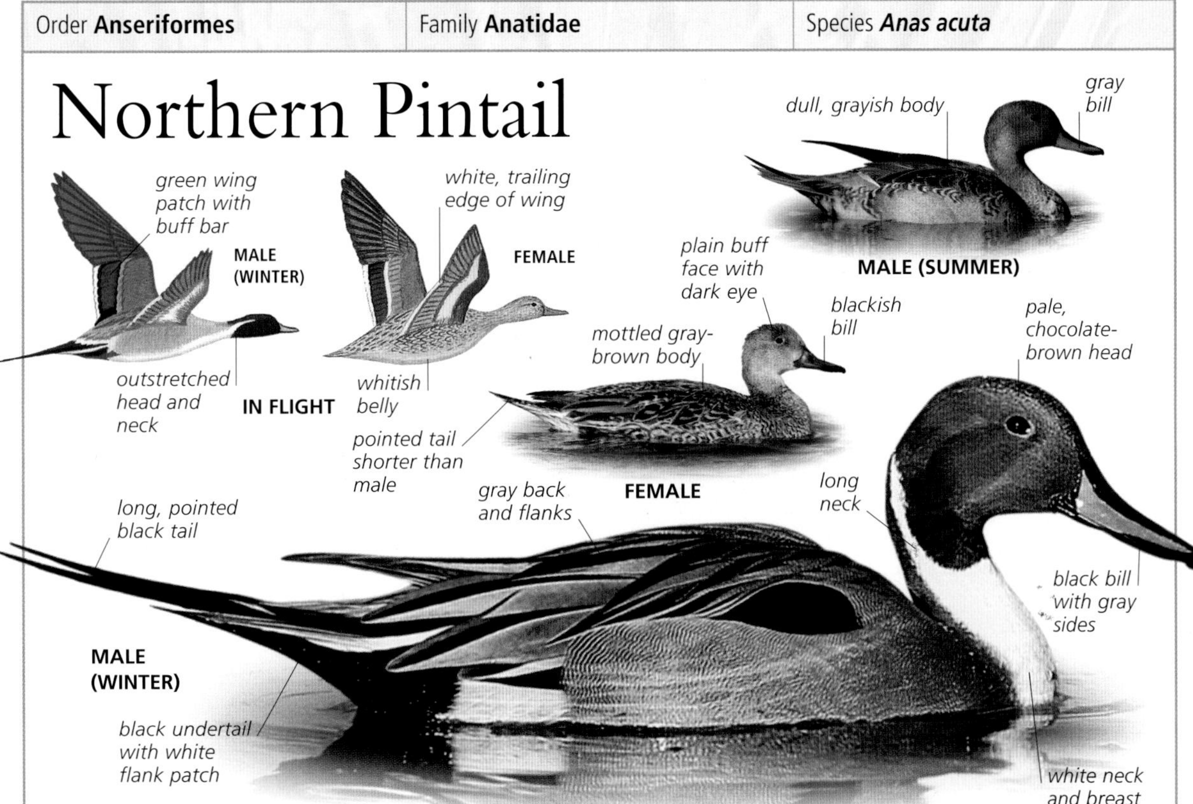

green wing patch with buff bar
MALE (WINTER)
outstretched head and neck
IN FLIGHT
white, trailing edge of wing
FEMALE
whitish belly
dull, grayish body
gray bill
MALE (SUMMER)
plain buff face with dark eye
blackish bill
mottled gray-brown body
pale, chocolate-brown head
pointed tail shorter than male
FEMALE
long, pointed black tail
gray back and flanks
long neck
black bill with gray sides
MALE (WINTER)
black undertail with white flank patch
white neck and breast

An elegant, long-necked dabbler, the Northern Pintail has extremely distinctive marking and a very long tail—in fact, the longest tail to be found on any freshwater duck. One of the earliest breeders in the year, these ducks begin nesting soon after the ice thaws. Northern Pintails were once one of the most abundant prairie breeding ducks. However, in recent decades, droughts, combined with the reduction of habitat on both their wintering and breeding grounds, have resulted in a significant decline in their population.

VOICE Male call a high-pitched rolling *prrreep prrreep;* lower-pitched wheezy *wheeeee*, which gets louder then drops off; female call a quiet, harsh *quack* or *kuk* singularly or as short series; also a loud *gaak*, often repeated.

NESTING Scrape lined with plant materials and down, usually in short grass, brush, or even in the open; 3–12 eggs; 1 brood; April–August.

FEEDING Feeds on grains, rice, seeds, aquatic weeds, insect larvae, crustaceans, and snails.

FLIGHT: fast, direct flight; can be very acrobatic in the air.

FEEDING TIME
Even when tipping up to feed, these pintails can be identified by their long, black, pointed tails.

SIMILAR SPECIES

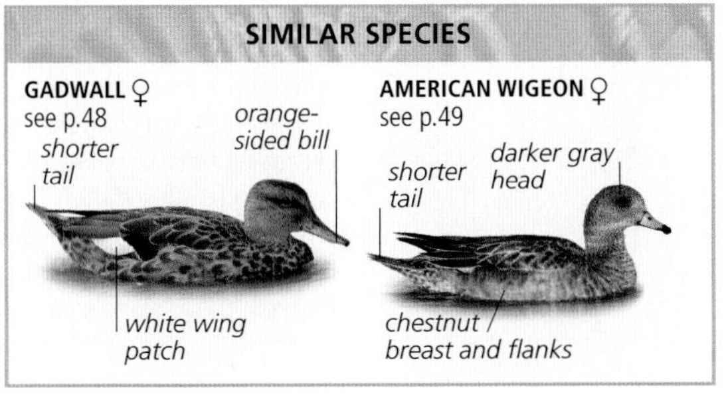

GADWALL ♀
see p.48
shorter tail
orange-sided bill
white wing patch
AMERICAN WIGEON ♀
see p.49
shorter tail
darker gray head
chestnut breast and flanks

OCCURRENCE
Widely distributed in North America; breeding in open country in shallow wetlands or meadows in mountainous forest regions. Found in tidal wetlands and saltwater habitats in migration and winter; dry harvested and flooded agricultural fields in autumn and winter.

Length **20–30in (51–76cm)**	Wingspan **35in (89cm)**	Weight **18–44oz (500–1250g)**
Social **Flocks**	Lifespan **Up to 21 years**	Status **Declining**

Order **Anseriformes**	Family **Anatidae**	Species ***Anas crecca***

Green-winged Teal

MALE

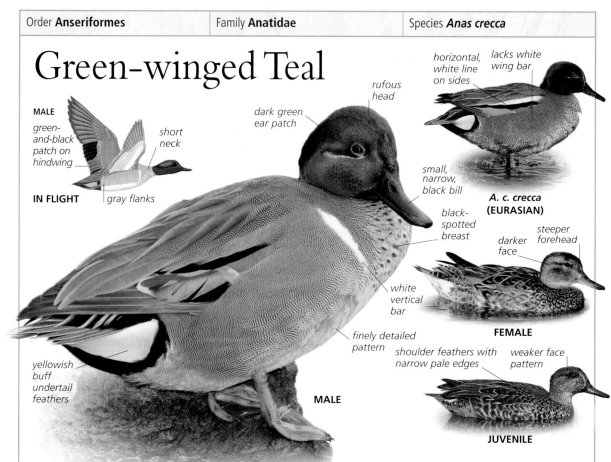

green-and-black patch on hindwing

short neck

gray flanks

IN FLIGHT

dark green ear patch

rufous head

small, narrow, black bill

black-spotted breast

white vertical bar

finely detailed pattern

yellowish buff undertail feathers

MALE

horizontal, white line on sides

lacks white wing bar

***A. c. crecca* (EURASIAN)**

darker face

steeper forehead

FEMALE

shoulder feathers with narrow pale edges

weaker face pattern

JUVENILE

The Green-winged Teal, the smallest North American dabbling duck, is slightly smaller than the Blue-winged and Cinnamon Teals, and lacks their blue wing patch. Its population is increasing, apparently because it breeds in more pristine habitats, and farther north, than the prairie ducks. The species has three subspecies, *A. c. crecca* (Eurasia), *A. c. carolinensis* (North America), and *A. c. nimia* (Aleutian Islands). *Carolinensis* males have a conspicuous vertical white bar, whereas Eurasian *crecca* males do not.

VOICE Male call a high-pitched, slightly rolling *crick crick*, similar to cricket; female a call quiet *quack*.

NESTING Shallow scrape on ground lined with nearby vegetation, often placed in dense vegetation near water; 6–9 eggs; 1 brood; April–September.

FEEDING Eats seeds, aquatic insects, crustaceans, and mollusks year-round; also feeds in grain fields in winter.

FLIGHT: fast flight; often flying in twisting, tight groups reminiscent of shorebird flocks.

SINGLE PARENT
The female duck is deserted by her partner during incubation, so she must provide all parental care.

SIMILAR SPECIES

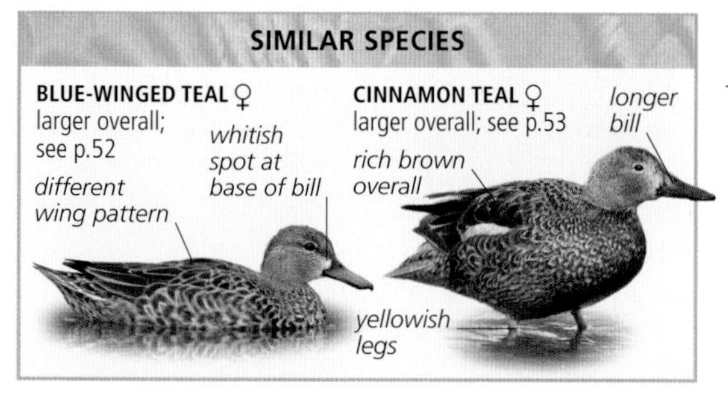
BLUE-WINGED TEAL ♀
larger overall; see p.52
whitish spot at base of bill
different wing pattern
CINNAMON TEAL ♀
larger overall; see p.53
longer bill
rich brown overall
yellowish legs

OCCURRENCE
Breeds north of the tree line in Alaska and Canada—around ponds in forest and deciduous woodlands. Prefers shallow wetlands with vegetation. In winter and migration, inland marshes, sloughs, agricultural fields, and coastal marshes. Winters south of the Caribbean and in southern Mexico.

Length **12–15½in (31–39cm)**	Wingspan **20½–23in (52–59cm)**	Weight **7–16oz (200–450g)**
Social **Flocks**	Lifespan **Up to 20 years**	Status **Secure**

Order **Anseriformes**	Family **Anatidae**	Species ***Aythya valisineria***

Canvasback

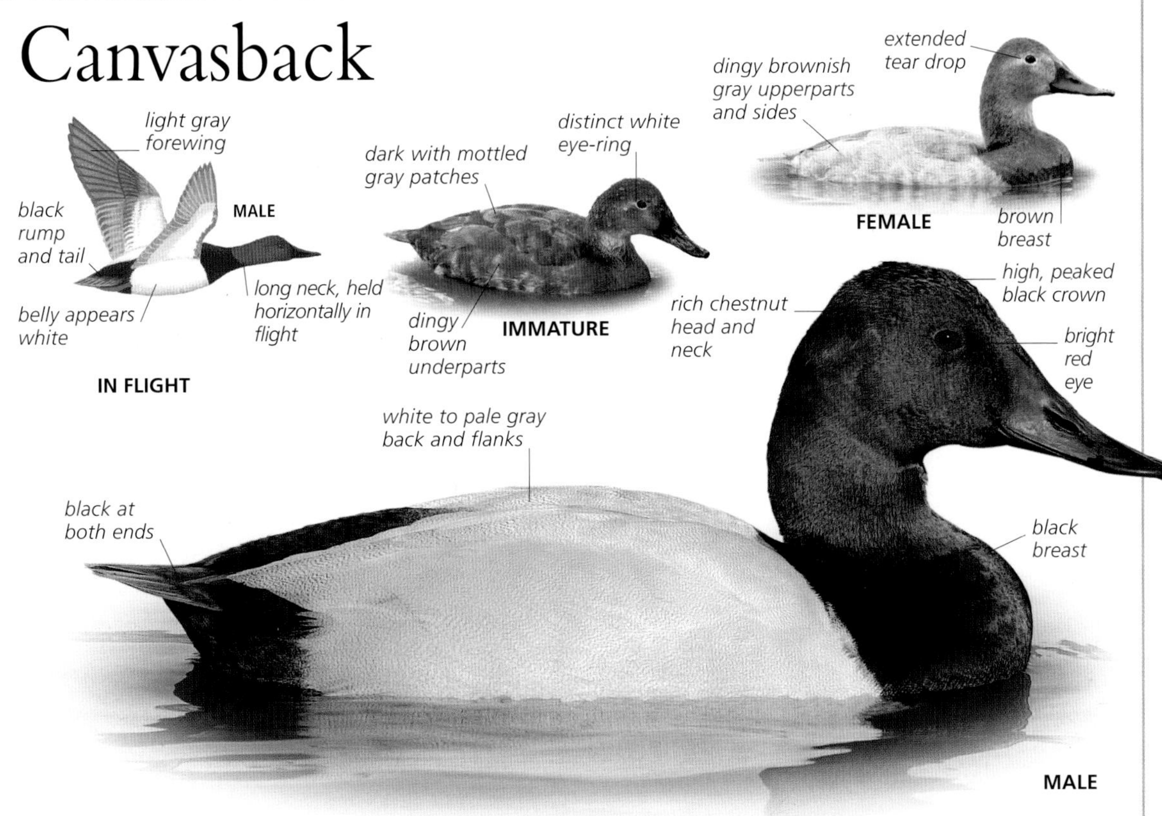
light gray forewing
black rump and tail
MALE
belly appears white
long neck, held horizontally in flight
IN FLIGHT
dark with mottled gray patches
distinct white eye-ring
dingy brown underparts
IMMATURE
dingy brownish gray upperparts and sides
extended tear drop
FEMALE
brown breast
high, peaked black crown
rich chestnut head and neck
bright red eye
white to pale gray back and flanks
black at both ends
black breast
MALE

A large, elegant, long-billed diving duck, the Canvasback is a bird of prairie pothole country. Its specialized diet of aquatic plants has resulted in a smaller population than other ducks. With legs set toward the rear, it is an accomplished swimmer and diver, and is rarely seen on land. Weather conditions and brood parasitism by Redheads determine how successful the Canvasback's nesting is from year to year.

VOICE Mostly silent except during courtship when males make soft *cooing* noises; females emit a grating *krrrrr krrrrrr krrrrr*; females give loud *quack* when taking off; during winter, both sexes make soft wheezing series of *rrrr rrrr rrrr* sounds.

NESTING Platform over water built of woven vegetation; occasionally on shore; 8–11 eggs; 1 brood; April–September.

FEEDING Mainly eats aquatic tubers, buds, root stalks, and shoots, particularly those of wild celery; also eats snails when preferred plants are unavailable.

FLIGHT: direct strong flight; one of the fastest ducks; forms V-shaped flocks.

DEEP WATER
Canvasbacks prefer deeper-bodied waters that support the aquatic vegetation they eat.

SIMILAR SPECIES

REDHEAD ♂
see p.58
shorter gray, black-tipped bill
yellow eye
LESSER SCAUP ♂
see p.61
yellow eye
darker gray on back
smaller overall

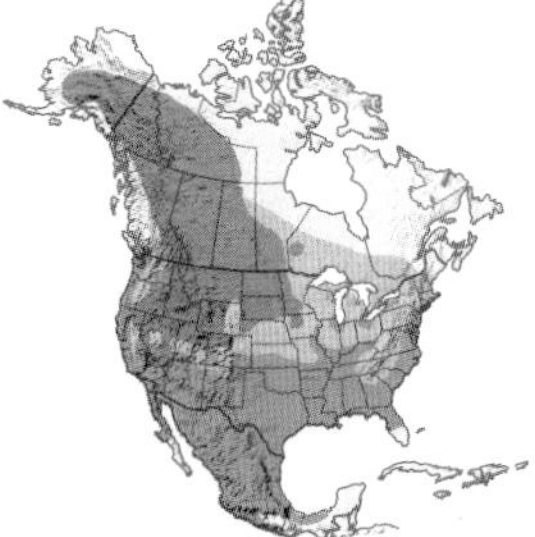

OCCURRENCE
Found in potholes, marshes, and ponds in prairie parkland, tundra; northerly forests preferred where their favorite foods grow. Winters in large numbers in large bays and lakes, and deltas, with smaller numbers scattered across North America and Mexico.

Length **19–22in (48–56cm)**	Wingspan **31–35in (79–89cm)**	Weight **1¾–3½lb (0.8–1.6kg)**
Social **Flocks**	Lifespan **Up to 22 years**	Status **Secure**

Order **Anseriformes**	Family **Anatidae**	Species ***Aythya americana***

Redhead

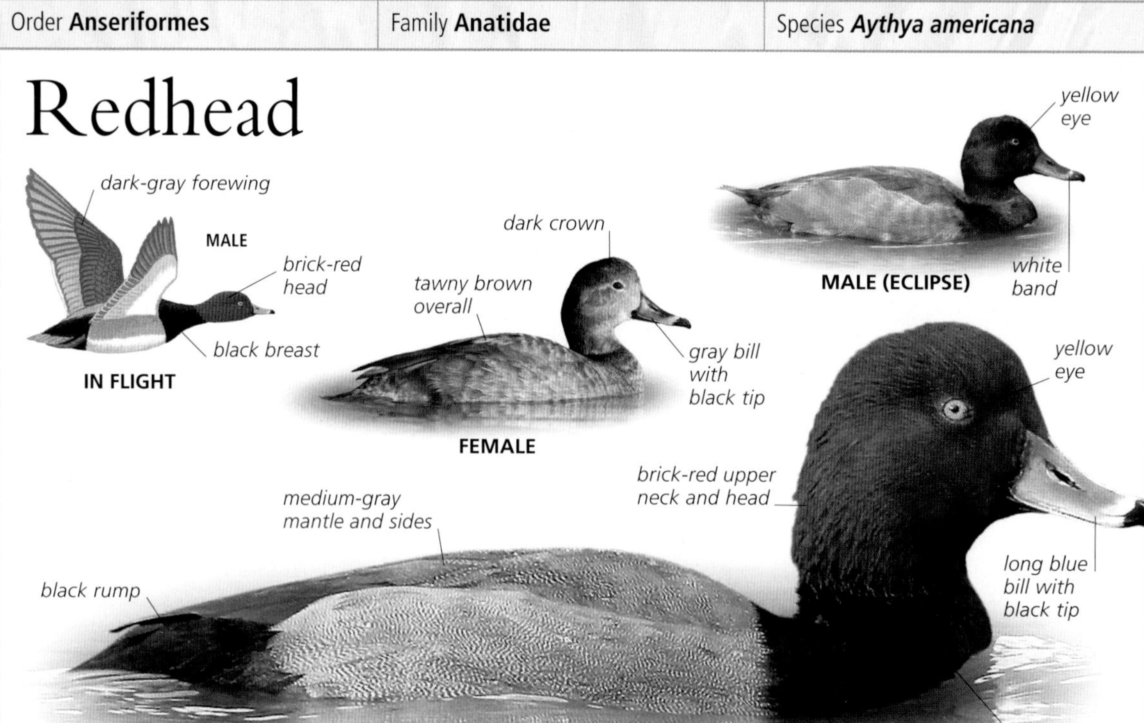
dark-gray forewing
MALE
brick-red head
black breast
IN FLIGHT
dark crown
tawny brown overall
gray bill with black tip
FEMALE
yellow eye
white band
MALE (ECLIPSE)
yellow eye
brick-red upper neck and head
medium-gray mantle and sides
long blue bill with black tip
black rump
black lower neck
MALE

The Redhead, a medium-sized diving duck belonging to the Pochard group, is native only to North America. Only when seen up close is it apparent that the male's seemingly gray upperparts and flanks are actually white, with dense, black, wavy markings. The Redhead often feeds at night and forages mostly around dusk and dawn, drifting during the day. It parasitizes other duck nests more than any other duck species, particularly those of the Canvasback and even other Redheads.

VOICE Male courtship call a wheezy rising then falling *whee ough*, also *meow*; female call a low, raspy *kurr kurr kurr*.

NESTING Weaves solid nest over water in dense vegetation such as cattails, lined with down; 7–14 eggs; 1 brood; May–September.

FEEDING Omniverous; feeds on aquatic plants, seeds, tubers, algae, insects, spiders, fish eggs, snails, and insect larvae; diet is variable depending on location.

FLIGHT: direct flight; runs on water prior to takeoff.

MALE DISPLAY
This male is performing a spectacular courtship display called a head throw, while remaining otherwise completely still on the water.

EASY IDENTIFICATION
The long blue bill with a whitish band and black tip is clearly visible in males.

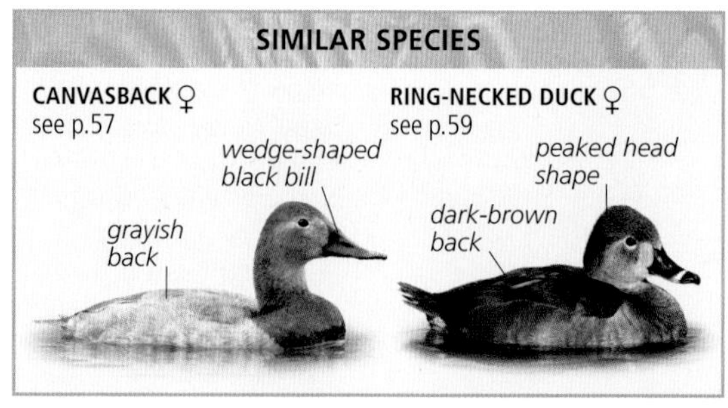
SIMILAR SPECIES
CANVASBACK ♀
see p.57
wedge-shaped black bill
grayish back
RING-NECKED DUCK ♀
see p.59
peaked head shape
dark-brown back

OCCURRENCE
Breeds in shallow wetlands across the Great Basin and Prairie Pothole region, very densely in certain marsh habitats. The bulk of the population winters in coastal lagoons along the Atlantic Coast and the Gulf of Mexico.

Length **17–21in (43–53cm)**	Wingspan **30–31in (75–79cm)**	Weight **1⅜–3¼lbs (0.6–1.5kg)**
Social **Flocks**	Lifespan **Up to 21 years**	Status **Secure**

Order **Anseriformes**	Family **Anatidae**	Species ***Aythya collaris***

Ring-necked Duck

dark forewing
MALE
bold white underwing
IN FLIGHT
dark brown back
bold white eye-ring
white band on bill
FEMALE
tall, peaked head
gray bill with white band at base
yellow eye
thin chestnut ring
rounded gray sides
black neck and breast
MALE

A resident of freshwater ponds and lakes, the Ring-necked Duck is a fairly common medium-sized diving duck. A more descriptive and suitable name might have been Ring-billed Duck as the bold white band on the bill tip is easy to see whereas the thin chestnut ring around the neck can be very difficult to observe. The tall, pointed head is quite distinctive, peaking at the rear of the crown. When it sits on the water, this bird typically holds its head high.

VOICE Male normally silent; female makes low *kerp kerp* call.

NESTING Floating nest built in dense aquatic vegetation, often in marshes; 6–14 eggs; 1 brood; May–August.

FEEDING Feeds in water at all times, either by diving, tipping up, or dabbling for aquatic plant tubers and seeds; also eats aquatic invertebrates such as clams and snails.

FLIGHT: strong flier with deep, rapid wing beats; flight somewhat erratic.

UNIQUE BILL
A white outline around the base of the bill and the white band on the bill are unique markings.

FLAPPING WINGS
Bold white wing linings are apparent when the Ring-necked Duck flaps its wings.

SIMILAR SPECIES

LESSER SCAUP ♂
see p.61
rounded head
wavy-patterned gray mantle

TUFTED DUCK ♂
see p.491
crested tufts
white sides

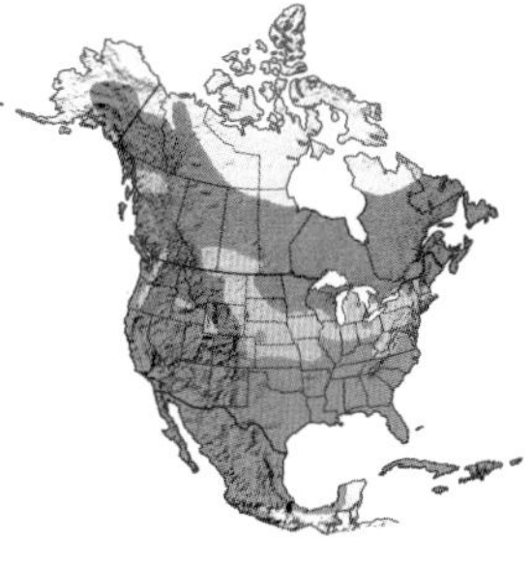

OCCURRENCE
Breeds across Canada, south of the Arctic zone, in shallow freshwater marshes and bogs; sporadically in the western US. Winters in freshwater and brackish habitats such as swamps, lakes, estuaries, reservoirs, and flooded fields. Migrants are found in the Midwest near stands of wild rice.

Length **15–18in (38–46cm)**	Wingspan **24–25in (62–63cm)**	Weight **1⅛–2lbs (500–900g)**
Social **Flocks**	Lifespan **Up to 20 years**	Status **Secure**

Order **Anseriformes**	Family **Anatidae**	Species ***Aythya marila***

Greater Scaup

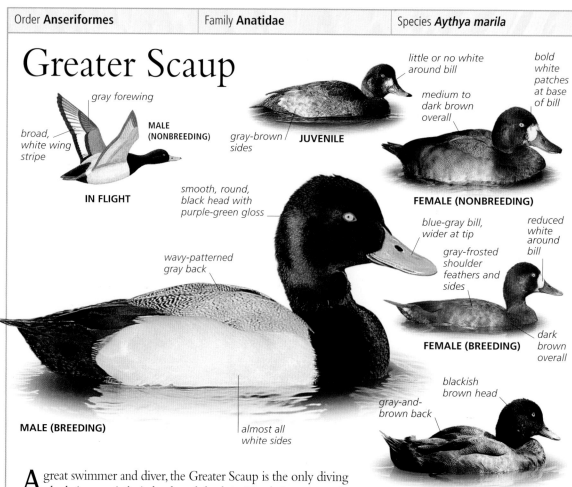

gray forewing
broad, white wing stripe
MALE (NONBREEDING)
IN FLIGHT

little or no white around bill
gray-brown sides
JUVENILE

bold white patches at base of bill
medium to dark brown overall
FEMALE (NONBREEDING)

smooth, round, black head with purple-green gloss
wavy-patterned gray back
almost all white sides
MALE (BREEDING)

blue-gray bill, wider at tip
reduced white around bill
gray-frosted shoulder feathers and sides
dark brown overall
FEMALE (BREEDING)

blackish brown head
gray-and-brown back
MALE (ECLIPSE)

A great swimmer and diver, the Greater Scaup is the only diving duck (genus *Aythya*) that breeds both in North America and Eurasia. Due to its more restricted coastal breeding and wintering habitat preference, it is far less numerous in North America than its close relative, the Lesser Scaup. The Greater Scaup forms large, often sexually segregated flocks outside the breeding season. If both scaup species are present together, they will also segregate within the flocks according to species. Correct identification is difficult.

VOICE During courtship, male call a soft, fast, wheezy *week week wheew*; female gives a series of growled monotone *arrrr* notes.

NESTING Simple depression lined with grasses and down, nest sites need to have dense cover of vegetation from previous year; 6–10 eggs; 1 brood; May–September.

FEEDING Dives for aquatic plants, seeds, insects, crustaceans, snails, shrimp, and bivalves.

FLIGHT: strong, fast, and agile; flocks shift and twist during prolonged flight.

FOND OF FLOCKING
Male Greater Scaups, with distinct black and white markings, flock together on the water.

SIMILAR SPECIES

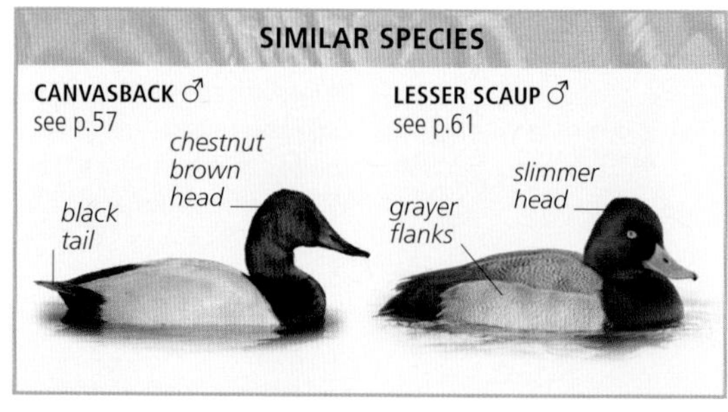
CANVASBACK ♂
see p.57
chestnut brown head
black tail
LESSER SCAUP ♂
see p.61
slimmer head
grayer flanks

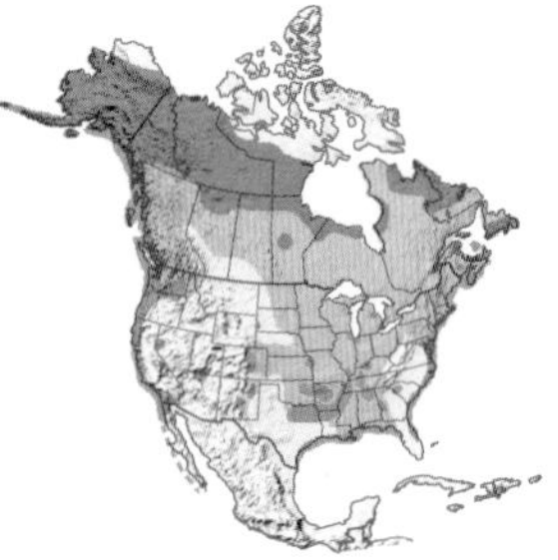

OCCURRENCE
Majority breed in western coastal Alaska on tundra wetlands; also in lower densities in northwest and eastern Canada. Almost all birds winter offshore, along the Atlantic and Pacific coasts, or on the Great Lakes due to increased food availability. Small groups found inland and midcontinent, on unfrozen water bodies.

Length **15–22in (38–56cm)**	Wingspan **28–31in (72–79cm)**	Weight **1¼–3lb (0.6–1.4kg)**
Social **Flocks**	Lifespan **Up to 22 years**	Status **Declining**

Order **Anseriformes**	Family **Anatidae**	Species ***Aythya affinis***

Lesser Scaup

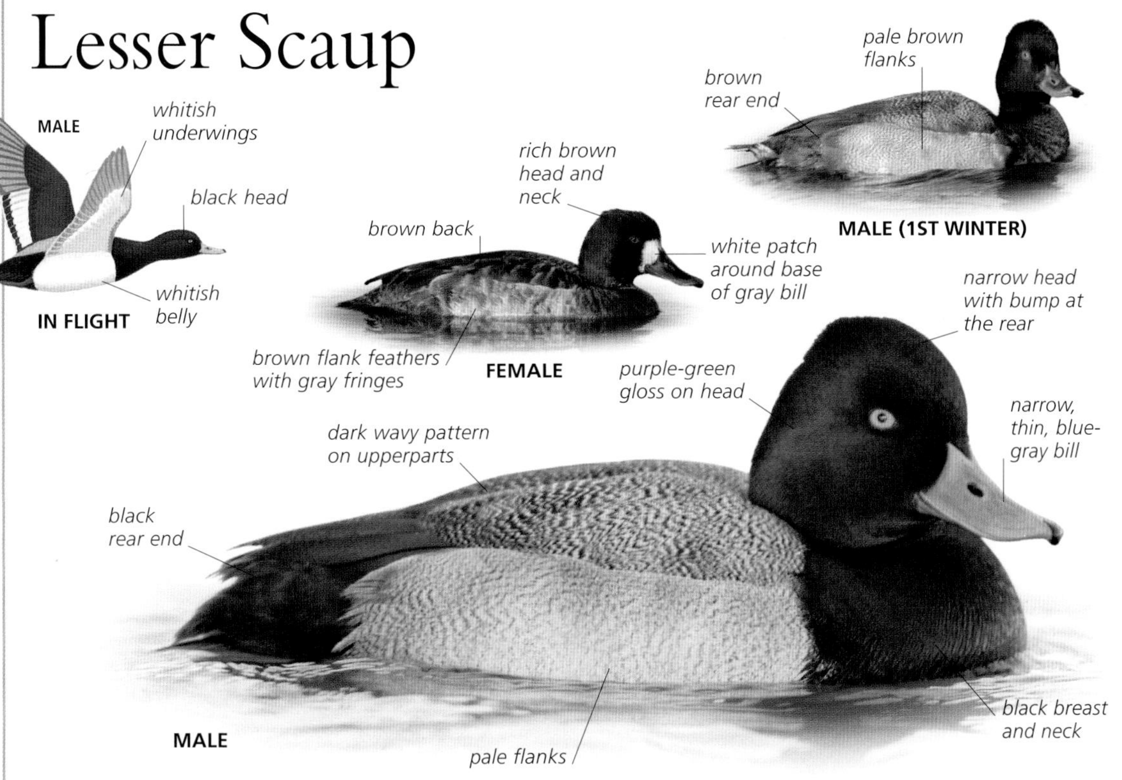
MALE
whitish underwings
black head
whitish belly
IN FLIGHT
rich brown head and neck
brown back
white patch around base of gray bill
brown flank feathers with gray fringes
FEMALE
pale brown flanks
brown rear end
MALE (1ST WINTER)
narrow head with bump at the rear
purple-green gloss on head
narrow, thin, blue-gray bill
dark wavy pattern on upperparts
black rear end
black breast and neck
pale flanks
MALE

The Lesser Scaup, far more numerous than its somewhat larger relative (their size and weight ranges overlap), is also the most abundant diving duck in North America. The two species are very similar in appearance and are best identified by shape. Identification must be done cautiously as head shape changes with position. For example, the crown feathers are flattened just before diving in both species; thus, scaups are best identified when they are not moving.
VOICE Males mostly silent except during courtship when they make a wheezy *wheeow wheeow wheeow* sound; females give repetitive series of grating *garrrf garrrf garrrf* notes.
NESTING Nest built in tall vegetation or under shrubs, sometimes far from water, also on islands and mats of floating vegetation; 8–11 eggs; 1 brood; May–September.
FEEDING Feeds mainly on leeches, crustaceans, mollusks, aquatic insects, and aquatic plants and seeds.

FLIGHT: rapid, direct flight; can jump off water more easily than other diving ducks.

PREENING SCAUP
Ducks are meticulous preeners, and the Lesser Scaup is no exception.

SIMILAR SPECIES

RING-NECKED DUCK ♀ see p.59
GREATER SCAUP ♀ see p.60

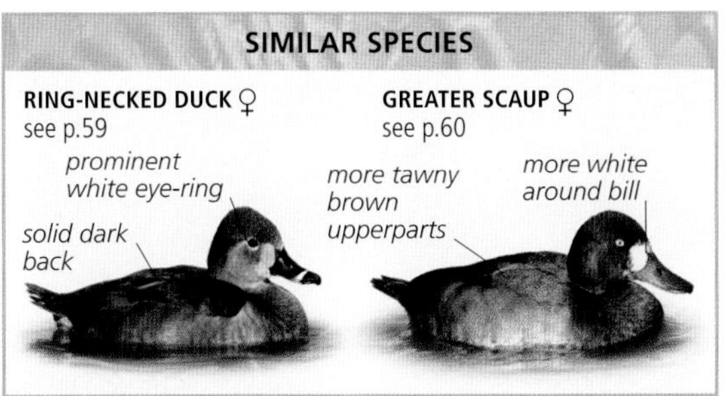
prominent white eye-ring
solid dark back
more tawny brown upperparts
more white around bill

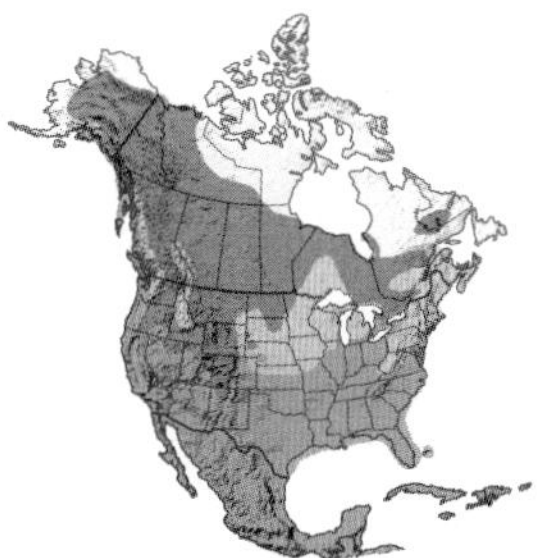

OCCURRENCE
Breeds inland from Alaska to eastern Canada in open northern forests and forest tundra, most farther north. Winters in the Caribbean, southern US, and south to northern South America. Majority winter along coasts; others winter inland on lakes and reservoirs.

Length **15½–17½in (39–45cm)**	Wingspan **27–31in (68–78cm)**	Weight **1–2¾lb (0.45–1.2kg)**
Social **Flocks**	Lifespan **Up to 18 years**	Status **Secure**

Order **Anseriformes**	Family **Anatidae**	Species ***Somateria spectabilis***

King Eider

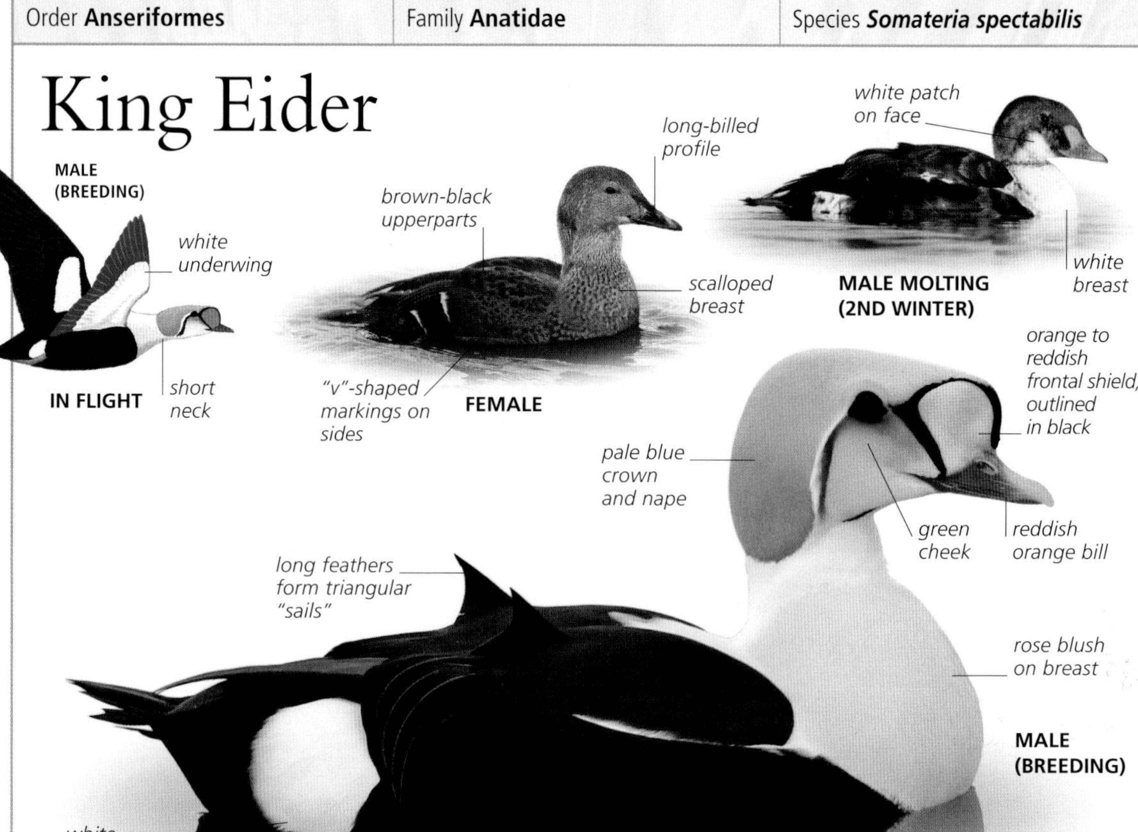
MALE (BREEDING)
white underwing
IN FLIGHT
short neck
brown-black upperparts
long-billed profile
scalloped breast
"v"-shaped markings on sides
FEMALE
white patch on face
MALE MOLTING (2ND WINTER)
white breast
orange to reddish frontal shield, outlined in black
pale blue crown and nape
green cheek
reddish orange bill
long feathers form triangular "sails"
rose blush on breast
MALE (BREEDING)
white flank patch
black underparts

The scientific name of the King Eider, *spectabilis*, means "worth seeing," and its gaudy marking and coloring around the head and bill make it hard to mistake. Females resemble the somewhat larger and paler Common Eider. The female King Eider has a more rounded head, more compact body, and a longer bill than the male. King Eiders may dive down to 180ft (55m) when foraging.

VOICE Courting males give a repeated series of low, rolled dove-like *arrrooooo* calls, each rising, then falling, followed by softer *cooos*; females give grunts and croaks.

NESTING Slight depression in tundra lined with nearby vegetation and down; 4–7 eggs; 1 brood; June–September.

FEEDING Dives for mollusks; other food items include crustaceans, starfish, and when breeding, insects and plants.

FLIGHT: direct and rapid flight; migrates in long lines, abreast in a broad front, or in clusters.

GROUP FLIGHT
Migratory King Eiders move in large groups to their northern breeding habitats.

SIMILAR SPECIES

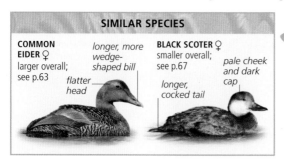

COMMON EIDER ♀ larger overall; see p.63
longer, more wedge-shaped bill
flatter head

BLACK SCOTER ♀ smaller overall; see p.67
longer, cocked tail
pale cheek and dark cap

OCCURRENCE
Nests along coasts and farther inland than Spectacled or Steller's Eiders in the high Arctic, on a variety of habitats; around low marshes, lakes, and islands; prefers well-drained areas. During winter, found mostly along the southern edge of the ice pack, in coastal waters up to 66ft (20m) deep.

Length **18½–25in (47–64cm)**	Wingspan **37in (94cm)**	Weight **2¾–4¾lb (1.2–2.1kg)**
Social **Flocks**	Lifespan **Up to 15 years**	Status **Secure**

Order **Anseriformes**	Family **Anatidae**	Species ***Somateria mollissima***

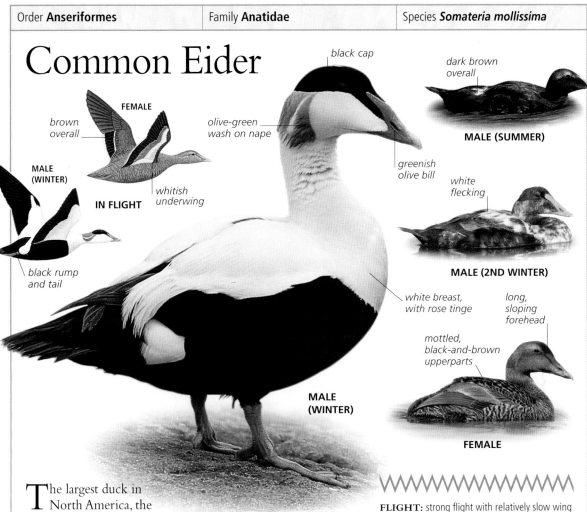

Common Eider

FEMALE
brown overall
MALE (WINTER)
IN FLIGHT
whitish underwing
black rump and tail
black cap
olive-green wash on nape
greenish olive bill
white breast, with rose tinge
MALE (WINTER)
dark brown overall
MALE (SUMMER)
white flecking
MALE (2ND WINTER)
long, sloping forehead
mottled, black-and-brown upperparts
FEMALE

The largest duck in North America, the Common Eider, is also the most numerous, widespread, and variable of the eiders. Four of its seven subspecies occur in North America, and vary in the markings and color of their heads and bills. Male Common Eiders also have considerable seasonal plumage changes, and do not aquire their adult plumage until the third year.

VOICE Repeated hoarse, grating notes *korr-korr-korr;* male's owl-like *ah-WOO-ooo*; female's low, gutteral notes *krrrr-krrrr-krrrr.*

NESTING Depression on ground lined with down and plant matter, often near water; 2–7 eggs; 1 brood; June–September.

FEEDING Forages in open water and areas of shallow water; dives in synchronized flocks for mollusks and crustaceans, but consumes its larger prey above the surface.

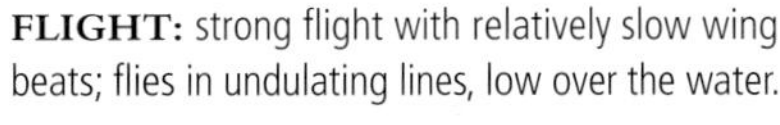

FLIGHT: strong flight with relatively slow wing beats; flies in undulating lines, low over the water.

BROODING FEMALE
Females line their nests with down plucked from their bellies, and cover the eggs with their bodies.

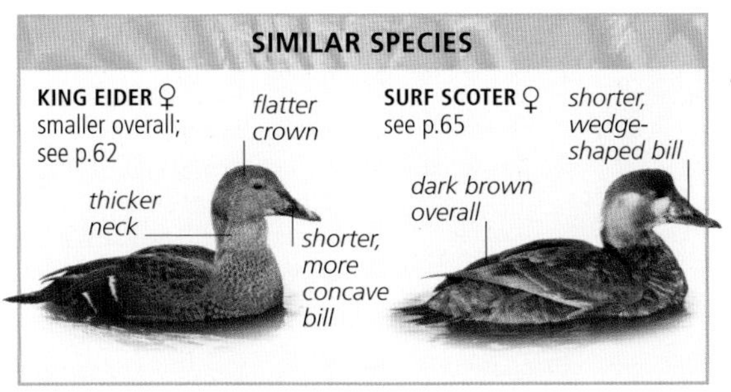
SIMILAR SPECIES
KING EIDER ♀
smaller overall; see p.62
flatter crown
thicker neck
shorter, more concave bill
SURF SCOTER ♀
see p.65
shorter, wedge-shaped bill
dark brown overall

OCCURRENCE
Arctic breeder on coastal islands, peninsulas, seldom along freshwater lakes and deltas near coast. One population is sedentary in the Hudson and James Bays region. Other populations winter in the Bering Sea, Hudson Bay, north British Columbia, Gulf of St. Lawrence, and along the Atlantic Coast.

Length **19½–28in (50–71cm)**	Wingspan **31–42in (80–108cm)**	Weight **2¾–5¾lb (1.2–2.6kg)**
Social **Flocks/Colonies**	Lifespan **Up to 21 years**	Status **Secure**

Order **Anseriformes**	Family **Anatidae**	Species ***Histrionicus histrionicus***

Harlequin Duck

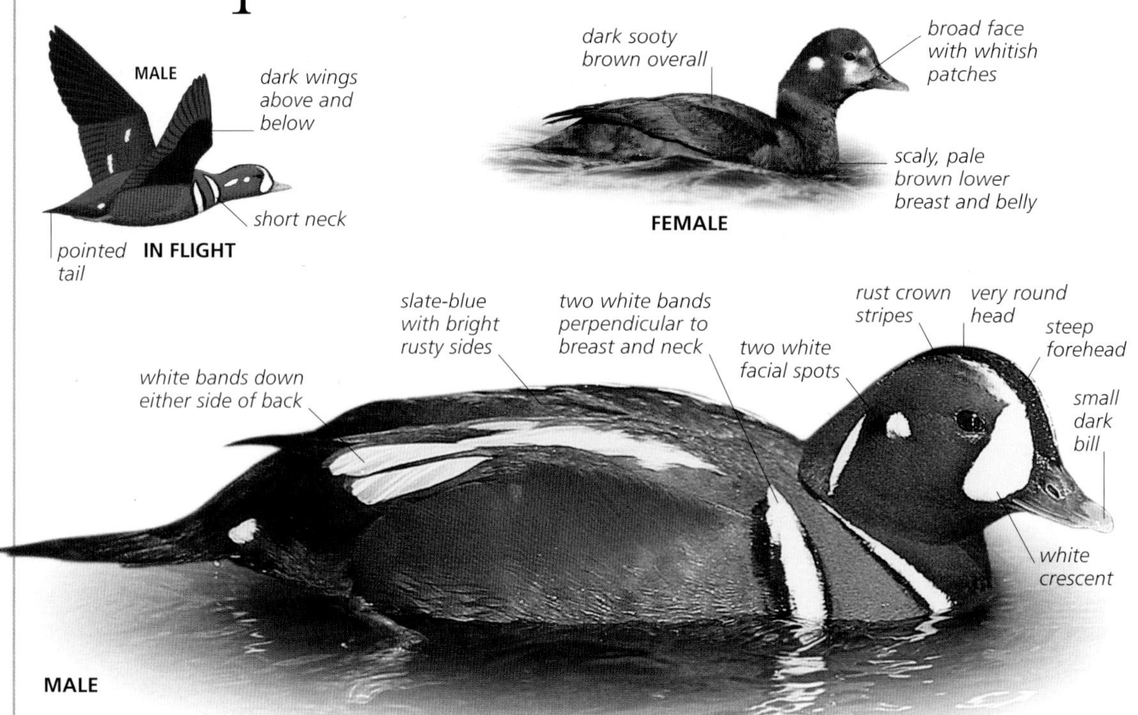

MALE
dark wings above and below
short neck
pointed tail
IN FLIGHT
dark sooty brown overall
broad face with whitish patches
scaly, pale brown lower breast and belly
FEMALE
slate-blue with bright rusty sides
two white bands perpendicular to breast and neck
rust crown stripes
very round head
steep forehead
two white facial spots
white bands down either side of back
small dark bill
white crescent
MALE

This small, hardy duck is a superbly skillful swimmer, diving to forage on the bottom of turbulent streams for its favorite insect prey. Despite the male's unmistakable plumage at close range, it looks very dark from a distance. With head and long tail held high, it can be found among crashing waves, alongside larger and bigger-billed Surf and White-winged Scoters, who feed in the same habitat.

VOICE Male a high-pitched squeak earning it the nickname "sea mice"; female's call a raspy *ekekekekekek*.

NESTING Nests near water under vegetation or base of tree; also tree cavities; 3–9 eggs; 1 brood; April–September.

FEEDING Dives for insects and their larvae, and fish roe when breeding; in winter, eats mollusks, crustaceans, crabs, snails, fish roe, and barnacles.

FLIGHT: rapid and regular wing beats; usually flies low over water, in pairs or small groups.

MALE GROUPS
After the breeding season, many males may gather and forage together.

PAIR IN FLIGHT
Note the crisp white markings on the slate-blue male in flight.

SIMILAR SPECIES

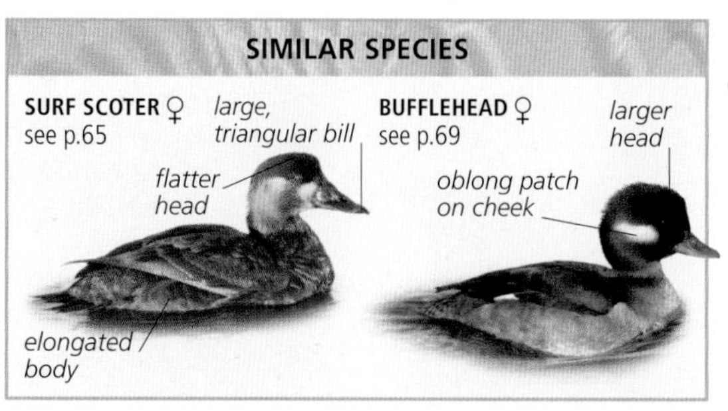

SURF SCOTER ♀
see p.65
large, triangular bill
flatter head
elongated body
BUFFLEHEAD ♀
see p.69
larger head
oblong patch on cheek

OCCURRENCE
Breeds near rushing coastal, mountain, or subalpine streams. During winter, found in small groups or mixed in with other sea ducks close to the shore, particularly along shallow rocky shorelines, jetties, rocky beaches, and headlands.

Length **13–21½in (33–54cm)**	Wingspan **22–26in (56–66cm)**	Weight **18–26oz (500–750g)**
Social **Small flocks**	Lifespan **Unknown**	Status **Secure**

Order **Anseriformes**	Family **Anatidae**	Species ***Melanitta perspicillata***

Surf Scoter

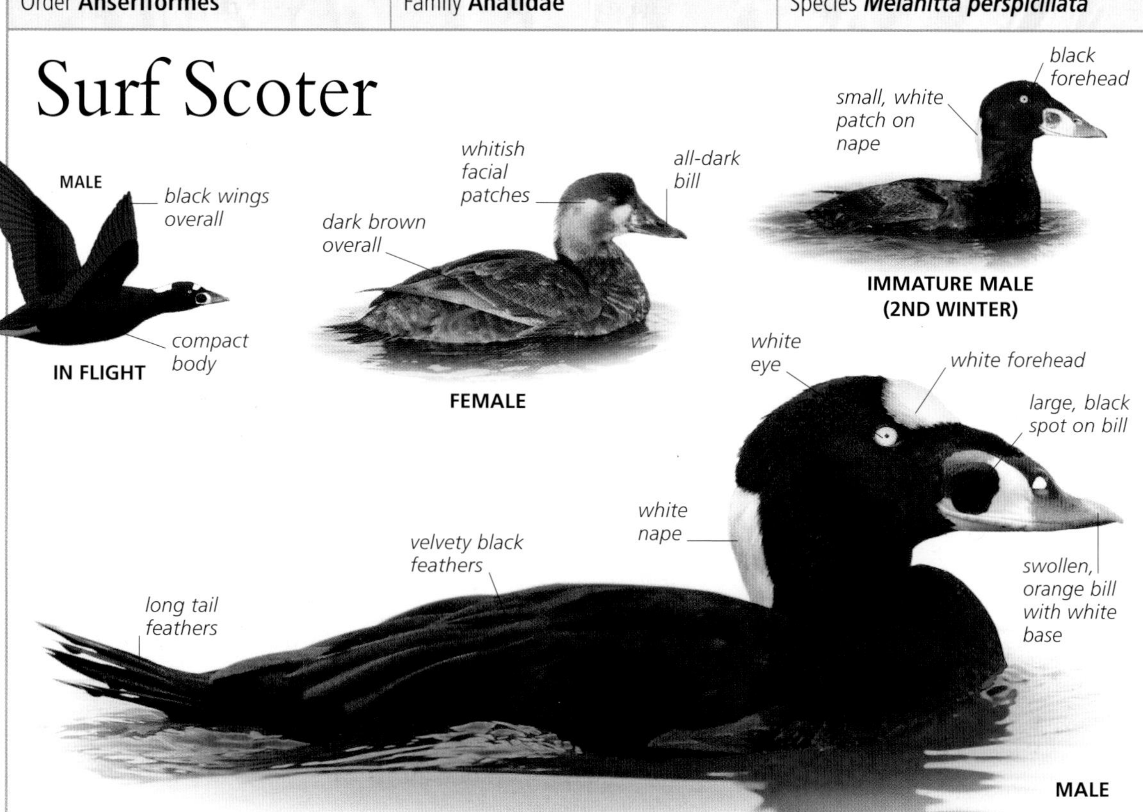
MALE
black wings overall
compact body
IN FLIGHT
whitish facial patches
all-dark bill
dark brown overall
FEMALE
black forehead
small, white patch on nape
IMMATURE MALE (2ND WINTER)
white eye
white forehead
large, black spot on bill
white nape
velvety black feathers
long tail feathers
swollen, orange bill with white base
MALE

Surf Scoters, one of three species of scoters living in North America, migrate up and down both coasts, often with the other species. They take their name from the way they dive for mollusks on the sea floor, in shallow coastal waters, through heavy surf. Groups often dive and resurface in unison. Black and Surf Scoters can be difficult to tell apart as both have all-black wings. The underside of the Surf Scoter's wings are uniform black, whereas the Black Scoter has gray flight feathers, which contrast with the black underwing feathers.

VOICE Normally silent; courting male's variety of calls includes liquid gurgled *puk-puk*, bubbled whistles, and low croaks; female call a harsh *crahh,* reminiscent of a crow.

NESTING Ground nest lined with down and vegetation on brushy tundra, often under low branches of a conifer tree; 5–10 eggs; 1 brood; May–September.

FEEDING Dives for mollusks and other aquatic invertebrates.

FLIGHT: strong wing beats; flies in bunched up groups; male's wings hum or whistle in flight.

DISTINGUISHING FEATURES
The white forehead and bright orange bill, in addition to its red-orange legs and feet, identify male Surf Scoters.

SIMILAR SPECIES

GREATER SCAUP ♀
see p.60

WHITE-WINGED SCOTER ♀
see p.66

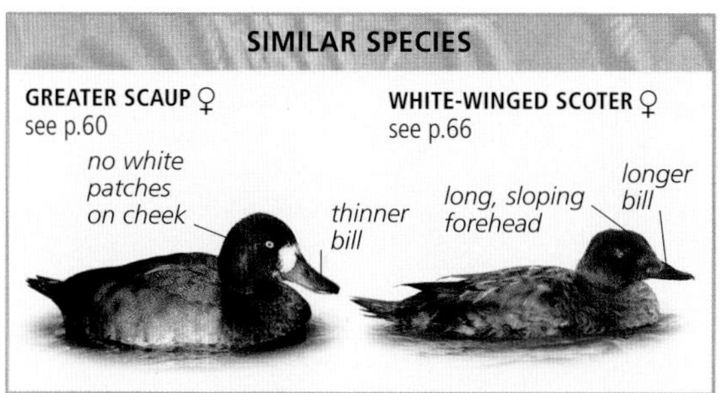
no white patches on cheek
thinner bill
long, sloping forehead
longer bill

OCCURRENCE
Nests on lake islands in forested regions of interior Alaska and northern Canada. Nonbreeders in summer and adults in winter are strictly coastal, with numbers decreasing from north to south along the Pacific coast. In the East, most overwinter in the mid-Atlantic coast region.

Length **19–23½in (48–60cm)**	Wingspan **30in (77cm)**	Weight **1¾–2¾lb (0.8–1.2kg)**
Social **Flocks/Pairs**	Lifespan **Unknown**	Status **Secure**

Order **Anseriformes**	Family **Anatidae**	Species ***Melanitta fusca***

White-winged Scoter

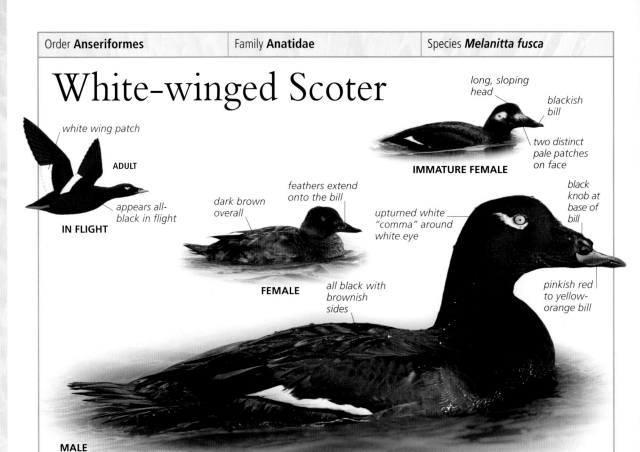

white wing patch
ADULT
appears all-black in flight
IN FLIGHT

long, sloping head
blackish bill
two distinct pale patches on face
IMMATURE FEMALE

dark brown overall
feathers extend onto the bill
FEMALE

upturned white "comma" around white eye
black knob at base of bill
pinkish red to yellow-orange bill
all black with brownish sides
MALE

The White-winged Scoter is the largest of the three scoters. When visible, the white wing patch makes identification easy. Females are quite similar to immature male and female Surf Scoters and can be identified by head shape, extent of bill feathering, and shape of white areas on the face. When diving, this scoter leaps forward and up, arching its neck, and opens its wings when entering the water. Underwater, White-winged Scoters open their wings to propel and stabilize themselves.

VOICE Mostly silent; courting males emit a whistling note; female call a growly *karr*.

NESTING Depression lined with twigs and down in dense thickets, often far from water; 8–9 eggs; 1 brood; June–September.

FEEDING Dives for mollusks and crustaceans; sometimes eats fish and aquatic plants.

FLIGHT: direct with rapid wing beats; flies low over the water in small groups.

WHITE FLASH IN FLIGHT
Scoters often migrate or feed in mixed flocks. The white wing patches are striking in flight.

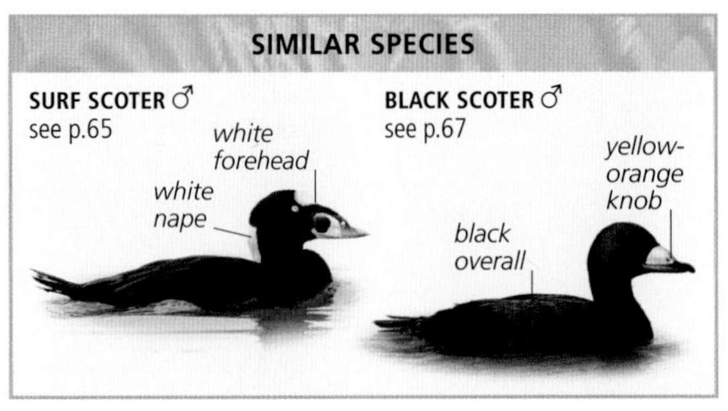
SIMILAR SPECIES
SURF SCOTER ♂
see p.65
white forehead
white nape
BLACK SCOTER ♂
see p.67
yellow-orange knob
black overall

OCCURRENCE
Majority breed in dense colonies in interior Alaska and western Canada on large freshwater or brackish lakes or ponds, sometimes on saltwater lakes. Winters along both coasts, large bays, inlets, and estuaries. Rarely winters inland, except on the Great Lakes.

Length **19–23in (48–58cm)**	Wingspan **31in (80cm)**	Weight **2¾–4¾lb (0.9–1.9kg)**
Social **Flocks/Colonies**	Lifespan **Up to 18 years**	Status **Secure**

Order **Anseriformes**	Family **Anatidae**	Species ***Melanitta nigra***

Black Scoter

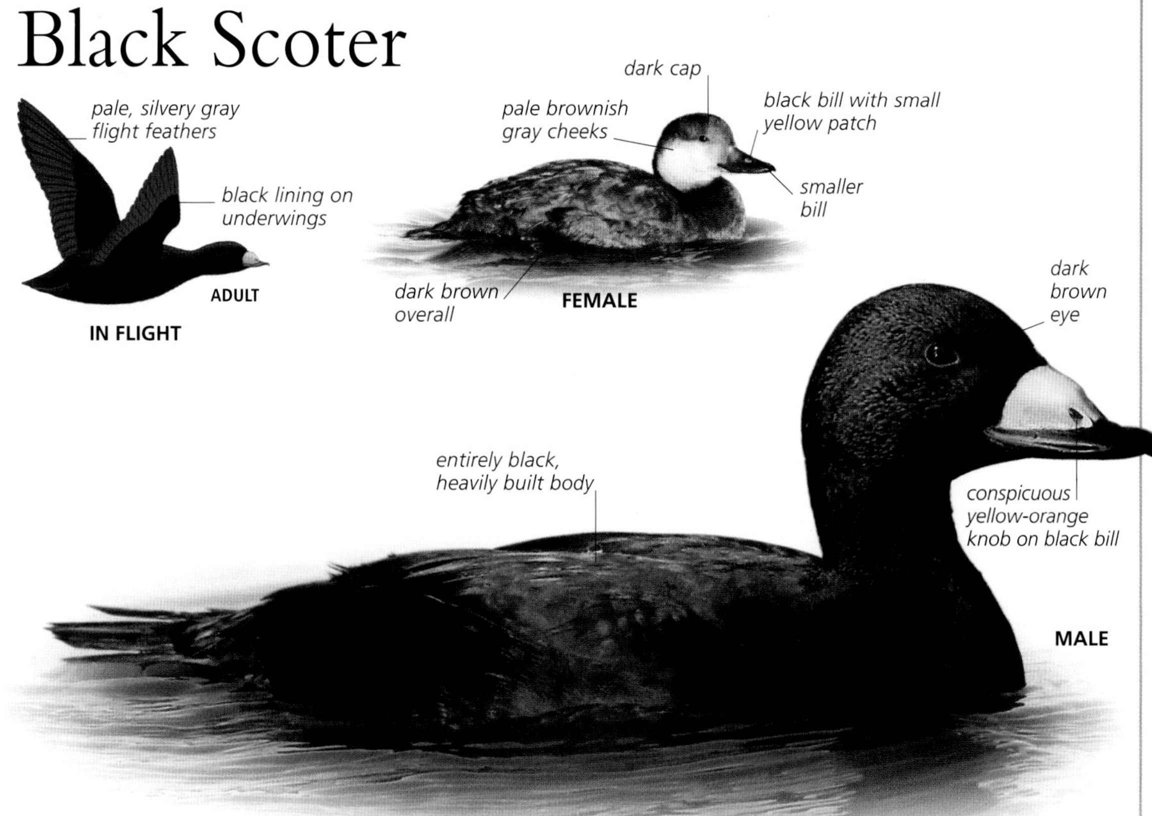
pale, silvery gray flight feathers
black lining on underwings
ADULT
IN FLIGHT
dark cap
pale brownish gray cheeks
black bill with small yellow patch
smaller bill
dark brown overall
FEMALE
dark brown eye
entirely black, heavily built body
conspicuous yellow-orange knob on black bill
MALE

Black Scoters, the most vocal of the scoters, are medium-sized sea ducks that winter along both coasts of North America. Riding high on the waves, they form dense flocks, often segregated by gender. While swimming, the Black Scoter sometimes flaps its wings and while doing so drops its neck low down, unlike the other two scoters. This scoter breeds in two widely separated sub-Arctic breeding areas and is one of the least studied ducks in North America. The Eurasian subspecies, known as the Common Scoter, has much less orange on its bill with a smaller knob at the base.

VOICE Male call a high-whistled *peeew*; female a low raspy *kraaa*.

NESTING Depression lined with grass and down, often in tall grass on tundra; 5–10 eggs; 1 brood; May–September.

FEEDING Dives in saltwater for mollusks, crustaceans, and plant matter; feeds on aquatic insects and freshwater mussels.

FLIGHT: strong wing beats; male's wings make whistling sound during takeoff.

YELLOW BILL
Male Black Scoters are distinctive with their black plumage and yellow bill-knob.

SIMILAR SPECIES

SURF SCOTER ♀ see p.65

WHITE-WINGED SCOTER ♀ see p.66

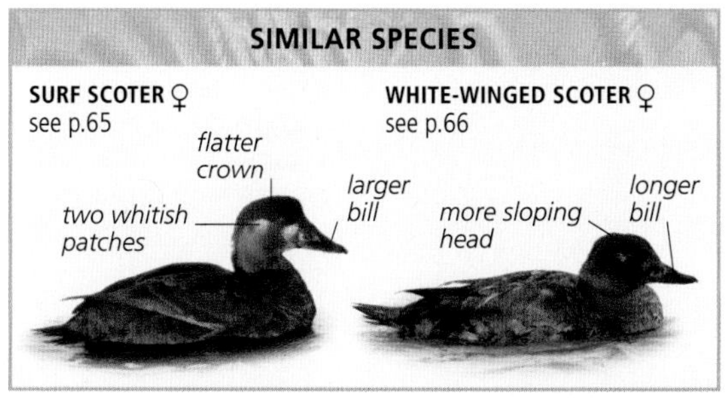
flatter crown
two whitish patches
larger bill
more sloping head
longer bill

OCCURRENCE
Breeding habitat is somewhat varied, but is generally close to fairly shallow, small lakes. Winters along both coasts. Populations wintering farther north prefer water over cobbles, gravel, or offshore ledges, whereas in southern locations, sandier habitats are chosen.

Length **17–21in (43–53cm)**	Wingspan **31–35in (79–90cm)**	Weight **1¾–2¾lb (0.8–1.2kg)**
Social **Flocks**	Lifespan **Unknown**	Status **Declining**

Order **Anseriformes**	Family **Anatidae**	Species ***Clangula hyemalis***

Long-tailed Duck

MALE (WINTER)
chunky body
IN FLIGHT
FEMALE (WINTER)
short tail
whitish underparts
mostly dark brown back, flanks, head, and breast
small, dark bill
FEMALE (SUMMER)
smudgy face pattern
JUVENILE (WINTER)
blackish head, neck, and breast
gray face
MALE (SUMMER)
dark back
brown breastband
FEMALE (WINTER)
white head
white eye-ring
large, brown spot on side of head
white shoulder feathers
all-dark wings
pinkish band on bill
long dark tail
black breastband
MALE (WINTER)

The Long-tailed Duck, which used to be called the Oldsquaw is a small, pudgy sea duck. The male has two extremely long tail feathers, which are often held up in the air like a pennant. The male's loud calls are quite musical, and, when heard from a flock, have a chorus-like quality, hence the name *Clangula*, which is Latin for "loud." The Long-tailed Duck is capable of diving for a prolonged period of time, and can reach depths of 200ft (60m), making it one of the deepest diving ducks. Its three-part molt is more complex than that of other ducks.

VOICE Male call a *ang-ang-eeeooo* with yodelling quality; female barking *urk* or *uk* alarm call.

NESTING Shallow depression in ground lined with plant matter; 6–9 eggs; 1 brood; May–September.

FEEDING Dives to bottom of freshwater or saltwater habitats for mollusks, crustaceans, insects, fish, and roe.

FLIGHT: flies low over the water, somewhat erratically, with fast, fluttering wing beats.

UNMISTAKABLE MALE
In winter, dark wings, a white body with black breast-band, and a long tail make this male unmistakable.

SIMILAR SPECIES

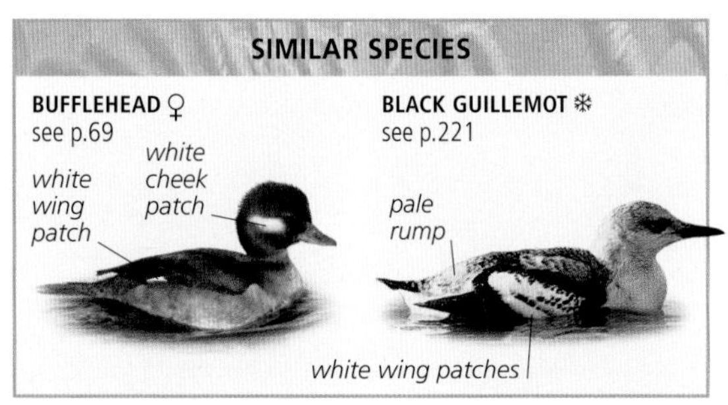
BUFFLEHEAD ♀
see p.69
white wing patch
white cheek patch
BLACK GUILLEMOT ❄
see p.221
pale rump
white wing patches

OCCURRENCE
Breeds in Arctic and sub-Arctic, nesting in small groups on islands and peninsulas on lakes, less commonly on tundra and freshwater ponds on islands. Winters mostly along rocky coasts and headlands, protected bays, or on large freshwater lakes.

Length **14–23in (35–58cm)**	Wingspan **28in (72cm)**	Weight **18–39oz (500–1,100g)**
Social **Flocks**	Lifespan **Up to 22 years**	Status **Secure**

Order **Anseriformes**	Family **Anatidae**	Species ***Bucephala albeola***

Bufflehead

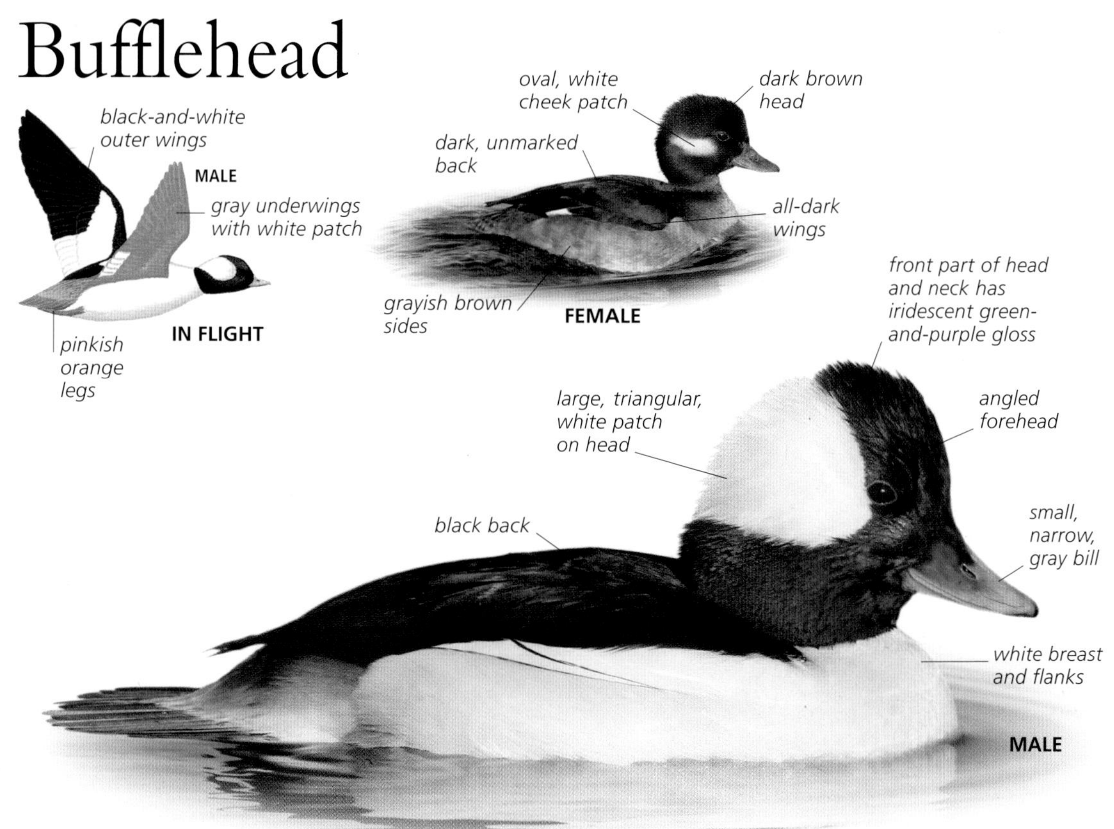
black-and-white outer wings
MALE
gray underwings with white patch
IN FLIGHT
pinkish orange legs
oval, white cheek patch
dark brown head
dark, unmarked back
all-dark wings
grayish brown sides
FEMALE
front part of head and neck has iridescent green-and-purple gloss
large, triangular, white patch on head
angled forehead
black back
small, narrow, gray bill
white breast and flanks
MALE

The smallest diving duck in North America, the Bufflehead is a close relative of the Common and Barrow's Goldeneye. Males make a bold statement with their striking head pattern. In flight, males resemble the larger Common Goldeneye, yet the large white area on their head makes them easy to distinguish. The Common Goldeneye's wings create a whirring sound in flight whereas the Bufflehead's do not. The northern limit of the Bufflehead's breeding range corresponds to that of the Northern Flicker, as the ducks usually nest in abandoned Flicker cavities.

VOICE Male a low growl or squeal; chattering during breeding; female mostly silent except during courtship or calling to chicks.

NESTING Cavity nester, no nesting material added, near water; 7–9 eggs; 1 brood; April–September.

FEEDING Dives for aquatic invertebrates: usually insects in freshwater, mollusks and crustaceans in saltwater; also eats seeds.

FLIGHT: very rapid wing beats; no flight sound, unlike Goldeneyes.

IMMEDIATE TAKE OFF
Unlike other diving ducks, the small, compact Bufflehead can take off almost vertically.

SIMILAR SPECIES

HOODED MERGANSER ♂ see p.72

RUDDY DUCK ♂❄ see p.75

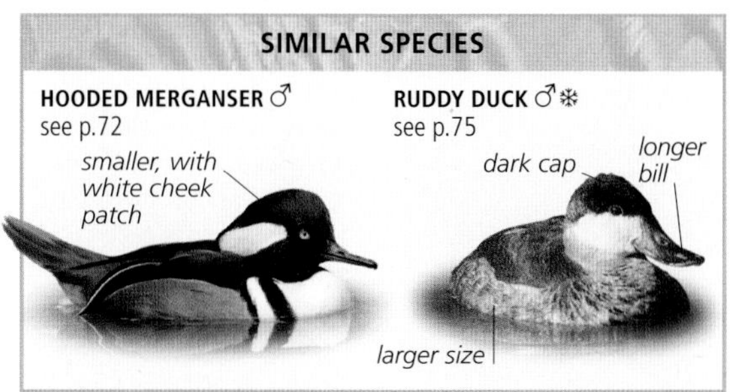
smaller, with white cheek patch
dark cap
longer bill
larger size

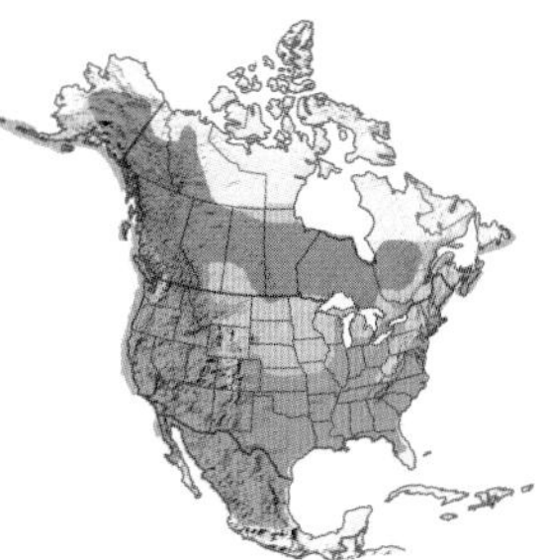

OCCURRENCE
Breeds in forest from Alaska to eastern Canada, in woodlands near small lakes and permanent ponds, where young are raised. Winters largely along the Pacific and Atlantic Coasts with lower densities scattered across the continent, south to northern Mexico, and in Bermuda.

Length **12½–15½in (32–39cm)**	Wingspan **21½–24in (54–61cm)**	Weight **10–18oz (275–500g)**
Social **Flocks**	Lifespan **Up to 15 years**	Status **Secure**

Order **Anseriformes**	Family **Anatidae**	Species ***Bucephala clangula***

Common Goldeneye

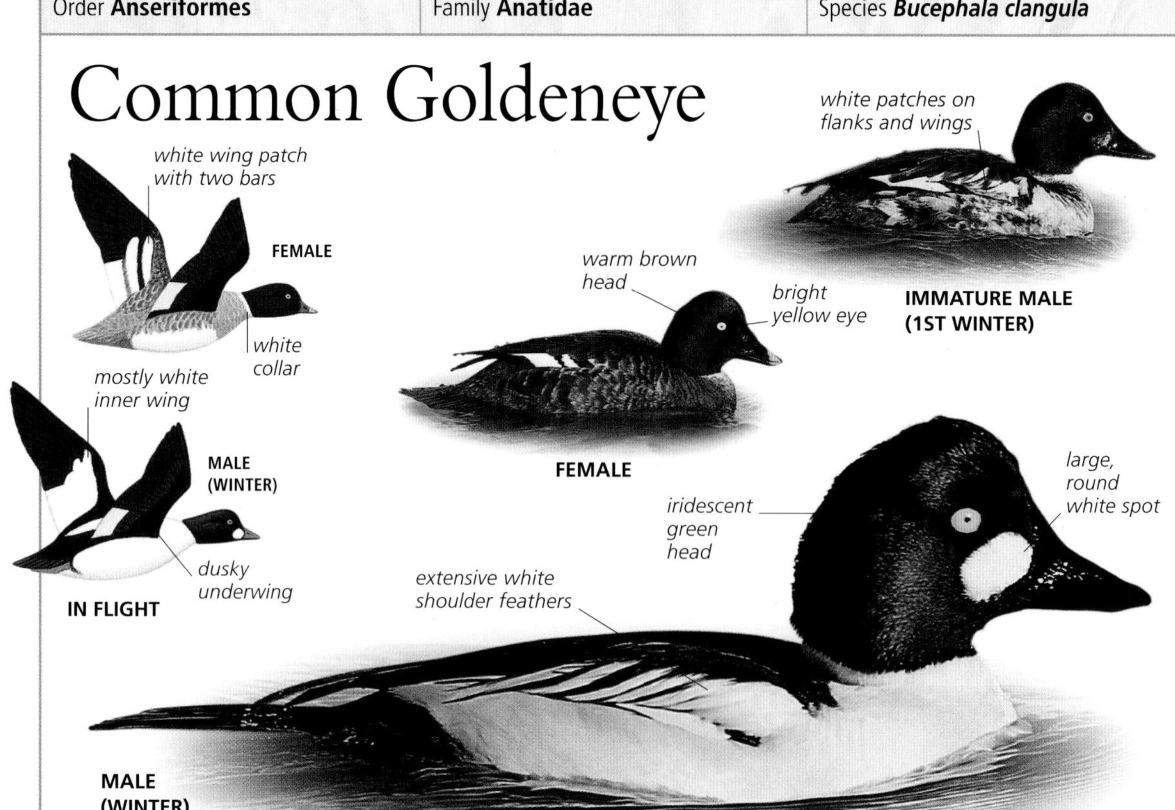
white wing patch with two bars
FEMALE
white collar
mostly white inner wing
MALE (WINTER)
dusky underwing
IN FLIGHT
warm brown head
bright yellow eye
FEMALE
white patches on flanks and wings
IMMATURE MALE (1ST WINTER)
iridescent green head
large, round white spot
extensive white shoulder feathers
MALE (WINTER)

Common Goldeneyes closely resemble Barrow's Goldeneyes. Found in North America and Eurasia, this is a medium-sized, compact, diving duck. It is aggressive and very competitive with members of its own species, as well as other cavity-nesting ducks. It regularly lays eggs in the nests of other species—a behavior that is almost parasitic. Before diving, the Common Goldeneye flattens its feathers in preparation for underwater foraging. The female's head shape changes according to her posture.

VOICE Courting males make a faint *peent* call; females a harsh *gack* or repeated *cuk* calls.

NESTING Cavity nester in holes made by other birds, including Pileated Woodpeckers, in broken branches or hollow trees; also commonly uses nest boxes; 4–13 eggs; 1 brood; April–September.

FEEDING Dives during breeding season for insects; in winter, mollusks and crustaceans; sometimes eats fish and plant matter.

FLIGHT: rapid with fast wing beats; male's wings make a tinkling sound in flight.

MALE TAKING OFF
Quite a long takeoff, involving energetically running on the water, leaves a trail of spray.

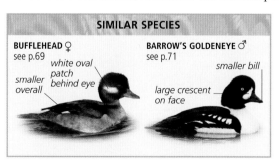

SIMILAR SPECIES

BUFFLEHEAD ♀ see p.69
white oval patch behind eye; smaller overall

BARROW'S GOLDENEYE ♂ see p.71
smaller bill; large crescent on face

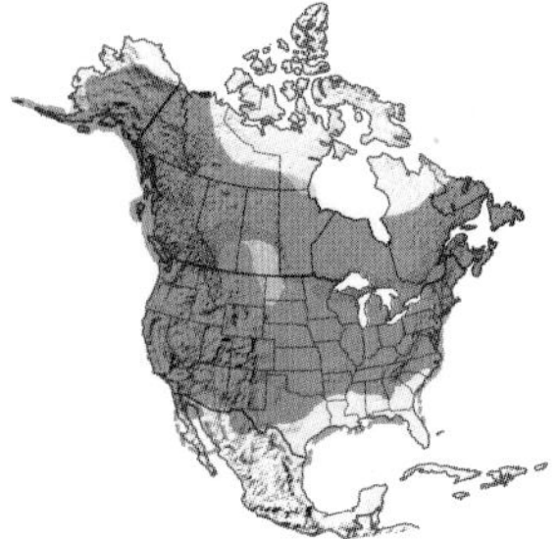

OCCURRENCE
Breeds along wetlands, lakes, and rivers with clear water in northern forests, where large trees provide appropriate nest cavities. Winters across continent, with highest densities located from north New England to the mid-Atlantic on coastal bays and in the West from coastal southeast Alaska to British Columbia.

Length **15½–20in (40–51cm)**	Wingspan **30–33in (77–83cm)**	Weight **19–44oz (550–1,300g)**
Social **Flocks**	Lifespan **Up to 15 years**	Status **Secure**

Order **Anseriformes**	Family **Anatidae**	Species ***Bucephala islandica***

Barrow's Goldeneye

white wing patch
MALE
dark underwings
IN FLIGHT
narrow, white wing patch
FEMALE (BREEDING)
darker brown head
steep forehead
small, yellow bill
black head with purple gloss
sloping crown
grayish brown wing feathers
white neck
IMMATURE MALE (1ST WINTER)
white "piano key" markings on sides
bold, white facial crescent
MALE

Barrow's Goldeneye is a slightly larger, darker version of the Common Goldeneye. Although the female can be identified by its different head structure and bill color, the bill color varies seasonally and geographically. Eastern Barrow's have blacker bills with less yellow, and western populations have entirely yellow bills, which darken in summer. During the breeding season, the majority of Barrow's Goldeneyes are found in mountainous regions of northwest North America.

VOICE Males normally silent; courting males grunt *ka-KAA*; females *cuc* call, slightly higher pitched than Common Goldeneye.

NESTING Tree cavity in holes formed by Pileated Woodpeckers, often broken limbs or hollow trees; also uses nest boxes; 6–12 eggs; 1 brood; April–September.

FEEDING Dives in summer for insects, some fish, and roe; in winter, mainly mollusks and crustaceans; some plant matter.

FLIGHT: rapid flight with fast, deep wing beats; flies near water surface on short flights.

COURTING DISPLAY
A male thrusts his head back and gives a guttural call. His feet then kick back, driving him forward.

SIMILAR SPECIES

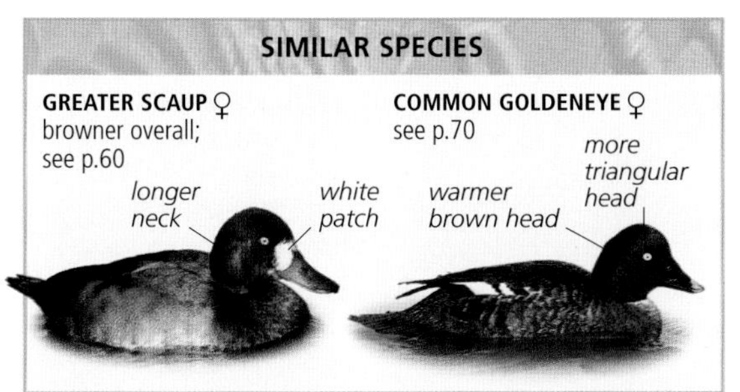
GREATER SCAUP ♀
browner overall;
see p.60
longer neck
white patch
COMMON GOLDENEYE ♀
see p.70
warmer brown head
more triangular head

OCCURRENCE
Winters along the Pacific Coast between southeast Alaska and Washington, with small populations in east Canada. Smaller numbers found inland from the lower Colorado River to Yellowstone National Park. Eastern population is localized in winter with the highest count in St. Lawrence estuary.

Length **17–19in (43–48cm)**	Wingspan **28–30in (71–76cm)**	Weight **17–46oz (475–1,300g)**
Social **Flocks**	Lifespan **Up to 18 years**	Status **Secure**

Order **Anseriformes**	Family **Anatidae**	Species ***Lophodytes cucullatus***

Hooded Merganser

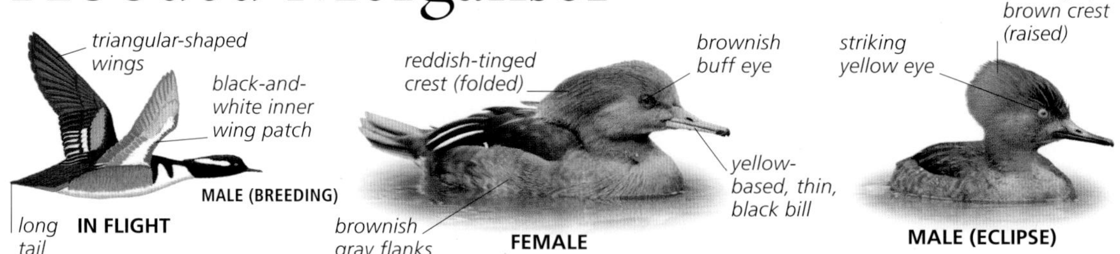

triangular-shaped wings
black-and-white inner wing patch
MALE (BREEDING)
long tail
IN FLIGHT
reddish-tinged crest (folded)
brownish buff eye
yellow-based, thin, black bill
brownish gray flanks
FEMALE
striking yellow eye
small, gray-brown crest (raised)
MALE (ECLIPSE)

longish tail, often raised
crested black-and-white head (crest not raised)
yellow eye
thin, black, serrated bill
black back
white breast
MALE (BREEDING)
warm brown flanks
bold vertical bars

This dapper, miniature fish-eater is the smallest of the three mergansers. Both male and female Hooded Mergansers have crests that they can raise or flatten. When the male raises his crest, the thin horizontal white stripe turns into a gorgeous white fan, surrounded by black. Although easily identified when swimming, the Hooded Merganser and the Wood Duck can be confused when seen in flight since they both are fairly small with bushy heads and long tails.

VOICE Normally silent; during courtship, males produce a low, growly, descending *pah-hwaaaaa*, reminiscent of a frog; females give a soft *rrrep*.

NESTING Cavity nester; nest lined with down feathers in a tree or box close to or over water; 6–15 eggs; 1 brood; February–June.

FEEDING Dives for fish, aquatic insects, and crayfish, preferably in clear and shallow fresh waters, but also in brackish waters.

FLIGHT: low, fast, and direct; shallow wing beats; quiet whirring noise produced by wings.

FANHEAD SPECTACULAR
The male's magnificent black-and-white fan of a crest is like a beacon in the late afternoon light.

SIMILAR SPECIES

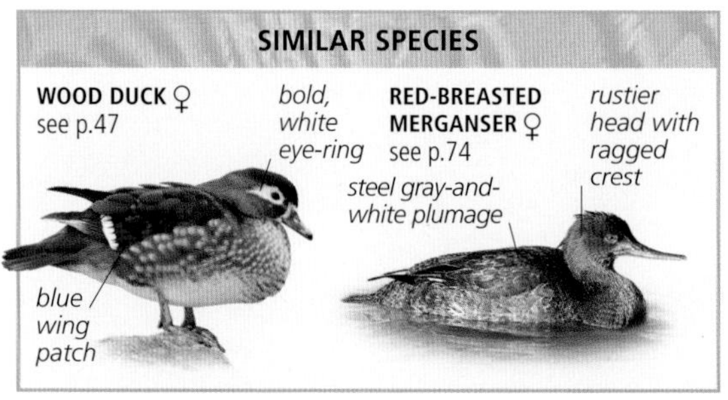

WOOD DUCK ♀
see p.47
bold, white eye-ring
blue wing patch
RED-BREASTED MERGANSER ♀
see p.74
rustier head with ragged crest
steel gray-and-white plumage

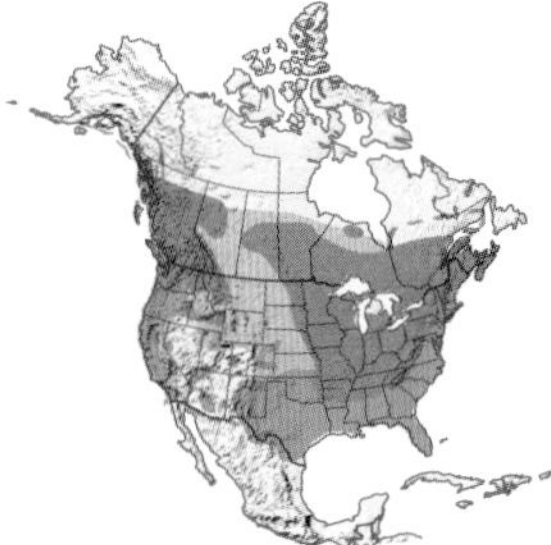

OCCURRENCE
Prefers forested small ponds, marshes, or slow-moving streams during the breeding season. During winter, occurs in shallow water in both fresh- and saltwater bays, estuaries, rivers, streams, ponds, freshwater marshes, and flooded sloughs.

Length **15½–19½in (40–49cm)**	Wingspan **23½–26in (60–66cm)**	Weight **16–31oz (450–875g)**
Social **Small flocks**	Lifespan **Unknown**	Status **Secure**

Order **Anseriformes**	Family **Anatidae**	Species ***Mergus merganser***

Common Merganser

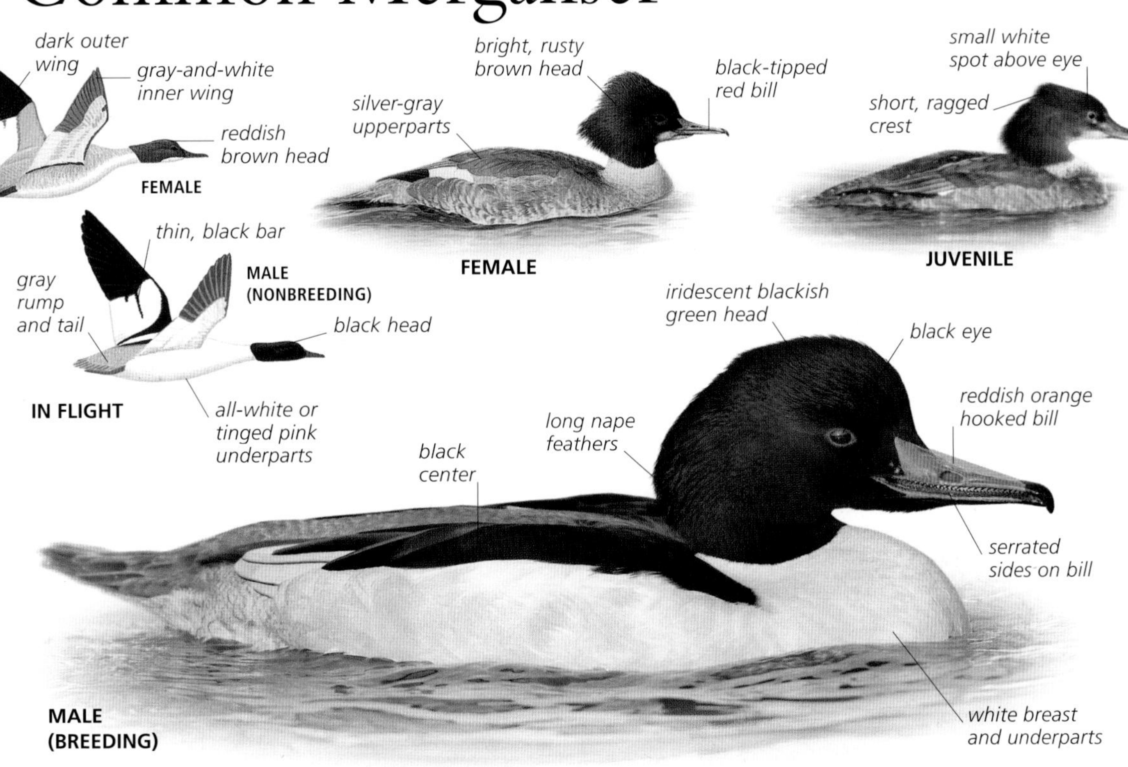
dark outer wing
gray-and-white inner wing
reddish brown head
FEMALE
thin, black bar
gray rump and tail
MALE (NONBREEDING)
black head
IN FLIGHT
all-white or tinged pink underparts
bright, rusty brown head
silver-gray upperparts
black-tipped red bill
FEMALE
small white spot above eye
short, ragged crest
JUVENILE
iridescent blackish green head
black eye
reddish orange hooked bill
long nape feathers
black center
serrated sides on bill
white breast and underparts
MALE (BREEDING)

The largest of the three merganser species in North America, the Common Merganser is called a Goosander in the UK. This large fish-eater is common and widespread, particularly in the northern portion of its range. It is often found in big flocks on lakes or smaller groups along rivers. It spends most of its time on the water, using its serrated bill to catch fish underwater.

VOICE Mostly silent, except when alarmed or during courtship; females give a low-pitched harsh *karr* or *gruk*, the latter also given in series; during courtship, males emit a high-pitched, bell-like note and other twangy notes; alarm call a hoarse *grrr* or *wak*.

NESTING Cavity nester sometimes high in trees; uses nest boxes, nests on ground; 6–17 eggs; 1 brood; April–September.

FEEDING Eats mostly fish (especially fond of trout and salmon, but also carp and catfish), aquatic invertebrates, frogs, small mammals, birds, and plants.

FLIGHT: fast with shallow wing beats; often flying low over the water.

FEEDING ON THE MOVE
This female Common Merganser is trying to swallow, head-first, a rather large fish.

SIMILAR SPECIES

COMMON GOLDENEYE ♂ see p.70

RED-BREASTED MERGANSER ♀ see p.74

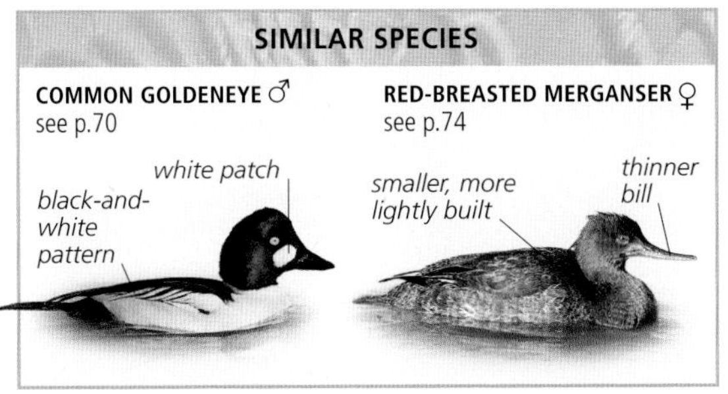
white patch
black-and-white pattern
smaller, more lightly built
thinner bill

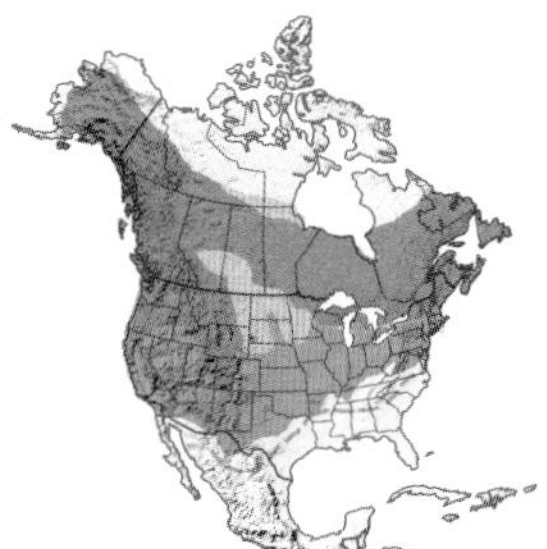

OCCURRENCE
Breeds in the northerly forests from Alaska to Newfoundland; winters south to north central Mexico. Being very hardy, it will winter farther north than most other waterfowl as long as water remains open. Prefers fresh- to saltwater locations.

Length **21½–28in (54–71cm)**	Wingspan **34in (86cm)**	Weight **1¾–4¾lb (0.8–2.1kg)**
Social **Flocks**	Lifespan **Up to 13 years**	Status **Secure**

Order **Anseriformes**	Family **Anatidae**	Species ***Mergus serrator***

Red-breasted Merganser

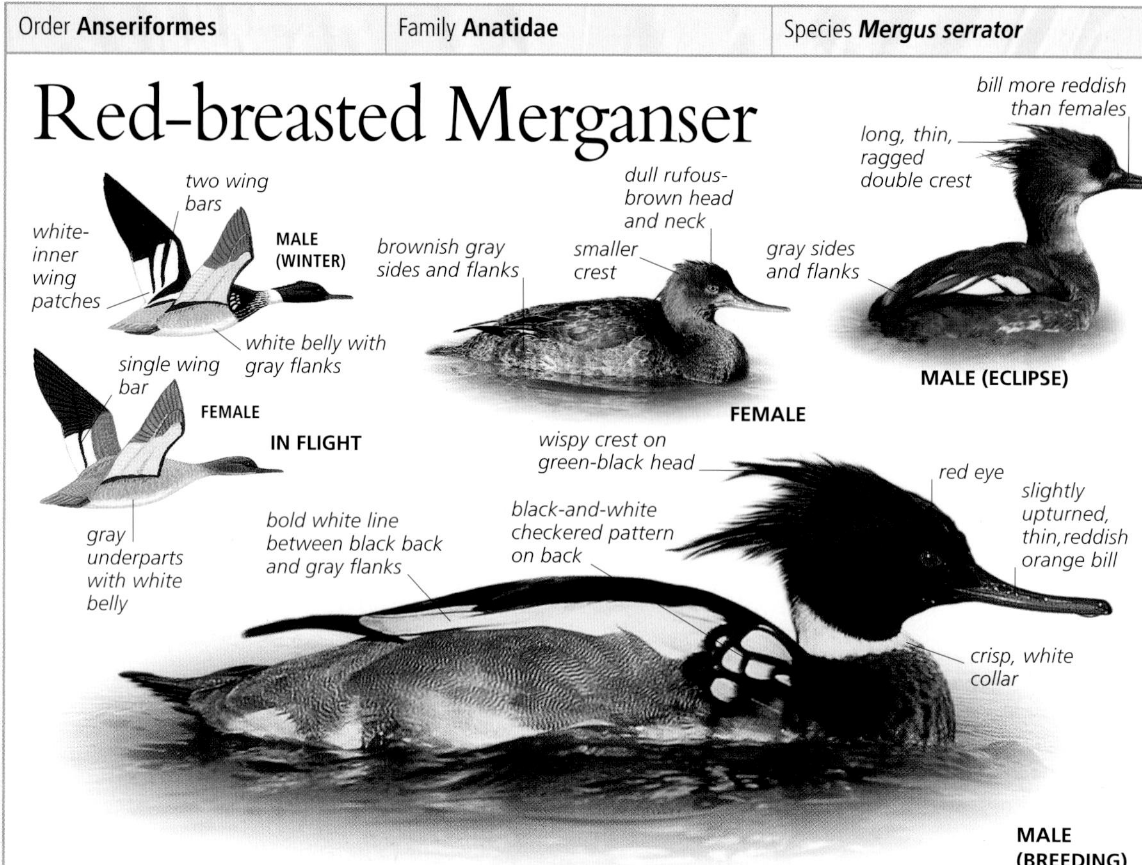
two wing bars
white-inner wing patches
MALE (WINTER)
white belly with gray flanks
single wing bar
FEMALE
IN FLIGHT
gray underparts with white belly
brownish gray sides and flanks
smaller crest
dull rufous-brown head and neck
FEMALE
bill more reddish than females
long, thin, ragged double crest
gray sides and flanks
MALE (ECLIPSE)
wispy crest on green-black head
red eye
slightly upturned, thin, reddish orange bill
bold white line between black back and gray flanks
black-and-white checkered pattern on back
crisp, white collar
MALE (BREEDING)

The Red-breasted Merganser, like the other saw-billed mergansers, is an elegant fish-eating duck. Both sexes are easily recognized by their long, sparse, somewhat ragged-looking double crest. Red-breasted Mergansers are smaller than Common Mergansers, but much larger than the Hooded. The Red-breasted Merganser, unlike the other two mergansers, nests on the ground, in loose colonies, often among gulls and terns, and is protected by its neighbors.

VOICE During courtship males make a raucous *yeow-yeow* call; females emit a raspy *krrr-krrr.*

NESTING Shallow depression on ground lined with down and plant material, near water; 5–11 eggs; 1 brood; May–July.

FEEDING Dives for small fish such as herring and minnows; also salmon eggs; at times flocks coordinate and drive fish together.

FLIGHT: fast flying duck with very rapid, regular, and shallow flapping.

KEEPING CLOSE
Red-breasted Mergansers are gregarious at all times of year, often feeding in loose flocks.

SIMILAR SPECIES

HOODED MERGANSER ♀
see p.72

COMMON MERGANSER ♀
see p.73

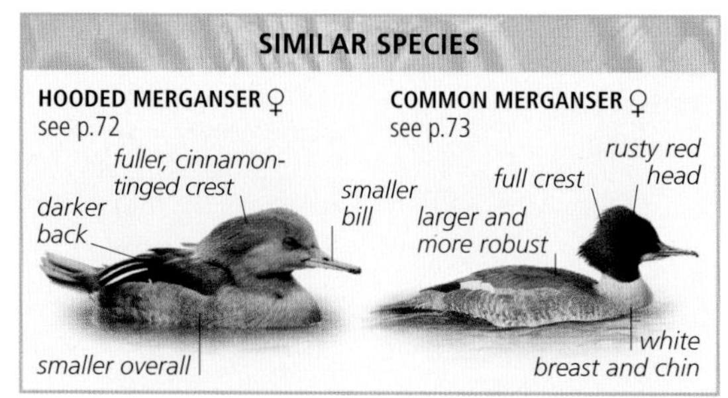
fuller, cinnamon-tinged crest
darker back
smaller overall
smaller bill
full crest
rusty red head
larger and more robust
white breast and chin

OCCURRENCE
Most northerly range of all the mergansers, nests across Arctic and sub-Arctic regions, tundra and northerly forests, along coasts, inland lakes, river banks, marsh edges, and coastal islands. Winters farther south than other mergansers, mostly in protected bays, estuaries, or on the Great Lakes.

Length **20–25in (51–64cm)**	Wingspan **26–29in (66–74cm)**	Weight **1¾–2¾lb (0.8–1.3kg)**
Social **Flocks/Colonies**	Lifespan **Up to 9 years**	Status **Secure**

Order **Anseriformes**	Family **Anatidae**	Species ***Oxyura jamaicensis***

Ruddy Duck

broad, short wings with whitish wing linings
pale belly
MALE (BREEDING) IN FLIGHT

dull gray-brown two-tone body
duller head
blackish bill
MALE (NONBREEDING)

arched dark line on cheek
brownish upperparts
dark bill
paler flanks
FEMALE

black cap and nape
bright blue bill, slightly knobby at base
large head
rich cinnamon body and neck
large, white cheek patches
long tail, often erect
MALE (BREEDING)

Small and stiff-tailed, the Ruddy Duck is comical in both its appearance and behavior. Both sexes often hold their tail in a cocked position, especially when sleeping. During courtship displays, the male points its long tail skyward while rapidly thumping its electric blue bill against its chest, ending the performance with an odd, bubbling sound. In another display, males make a popping sound by slapping their feet on the water's surface. Large feet, on legs set far back on its body, make the Ruddy Duck an excellent swimmer and diver; however, on land it is perhaps one of the most awkward of diving ducks. Females are known to push themselves along instead of walking.

VOICE Females give a nasal *raanh* and high pitched *eeek*; males vocally silent, but make popping noises with feet.

NESTING Platform, bowl-shaped nest built over water in thick emergent vegetation, rarely on land; 6–10 eggs; 1 brood; May–September.

FEEDING Dives for aquatic insects, larvae, crustaceans, and other invertebrates, particularly when breeding; during winter, also eats plants.

FLIGHT: rapid and direct, with fast wing beats; not very agile in flight, which seems labored.

HEAVY HEAD
A female "sitting" on the water streamlines her body ready to dive, making her look large-headed.

SIMILAR SPECIES

MASKED DUCK ♂

black tip to bill
black face
ruddy-colored back with black streaks

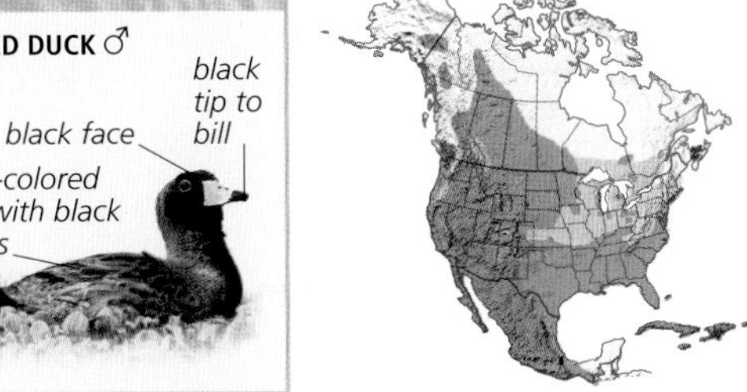

OCCURRENCE
Breeds in the prairie pothole region in wetland habitats; marshes, ponds, reservoirs, and other open shallow water with emergent vegetation and open areas. Majority winter on freshwater habitats from ponds to large lakes; smaller numbers found on brackish coastal marshes, bays, and estuaries.

Length **14–17in (35–43cm)**	Wingspan **22–24in (56–62cm)**	Weight **11–30oz (300–850g)**
Social **Flocks**	Lifespan **Up to 13 years**	Status **Secure**

Family **Gaviidae**

LOONS

WORLDWIDE THERE ARE ONLY five species of loon, comprising a single genus (*Gavia*), a single family (the Gaviidae), and a single order (the Gaviiformes). The five species are limited to the Northern Hemisphere, where they are found in both northern North America and northern Eurasia. One feature of loons is that their legs are positioned so far to the rear of their body that they must shuffle on their bellies when they go from water to land. Not surprisingly, therefore, loons are almost entirely aquatic birds. In summer they are found on rivers, lakes, and ponds, where they nest close to the water's edge. After breeding, they occur along coasts, often after flying hundreds of miles away from their freshwater breeding grounds.

Excellent swimmers and divers, loons are unusual among birds in that their bones are less hollow than those of other groups. Consequently, they can expel air from their lungs and compress their body feathers until they slowly sink beneath the surface. They can remain submerged like this for several minutes. A loon's wings are relatively small in proportion to its body weight. This means that they have to run a long way across the surface of the water, flapping energetically, before they can get airborne. Once in the air they keep on flapping and can fly at up to 60mph (95kmh).

LOON RANGER
The Common Loon has a wider range than any other in North America, as its name suggests.

FLIGHT SHAPE
The humped back and drooping neck of this Red-throated Loon are typical of a loon in flight.

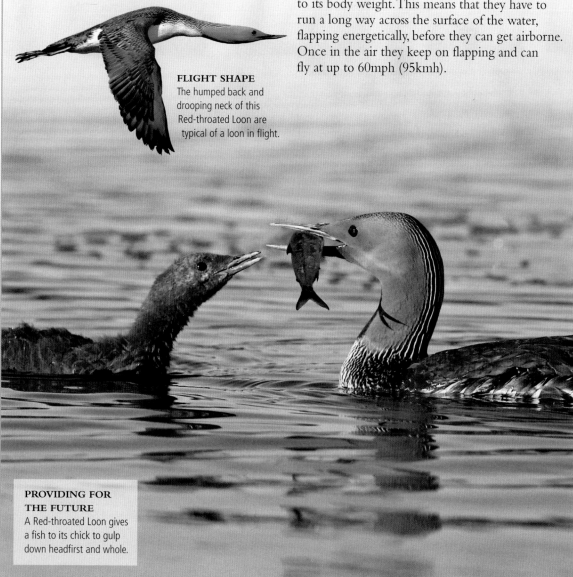

PROVIDING FOR THE FUTURE
A Red-throated Loon gives a fish to its chick to gulp down headfirst and whole.

Order **Gaviiformes**	Family **Gaviidae**	Species ***Gavia stellata***

Red-throated Loon

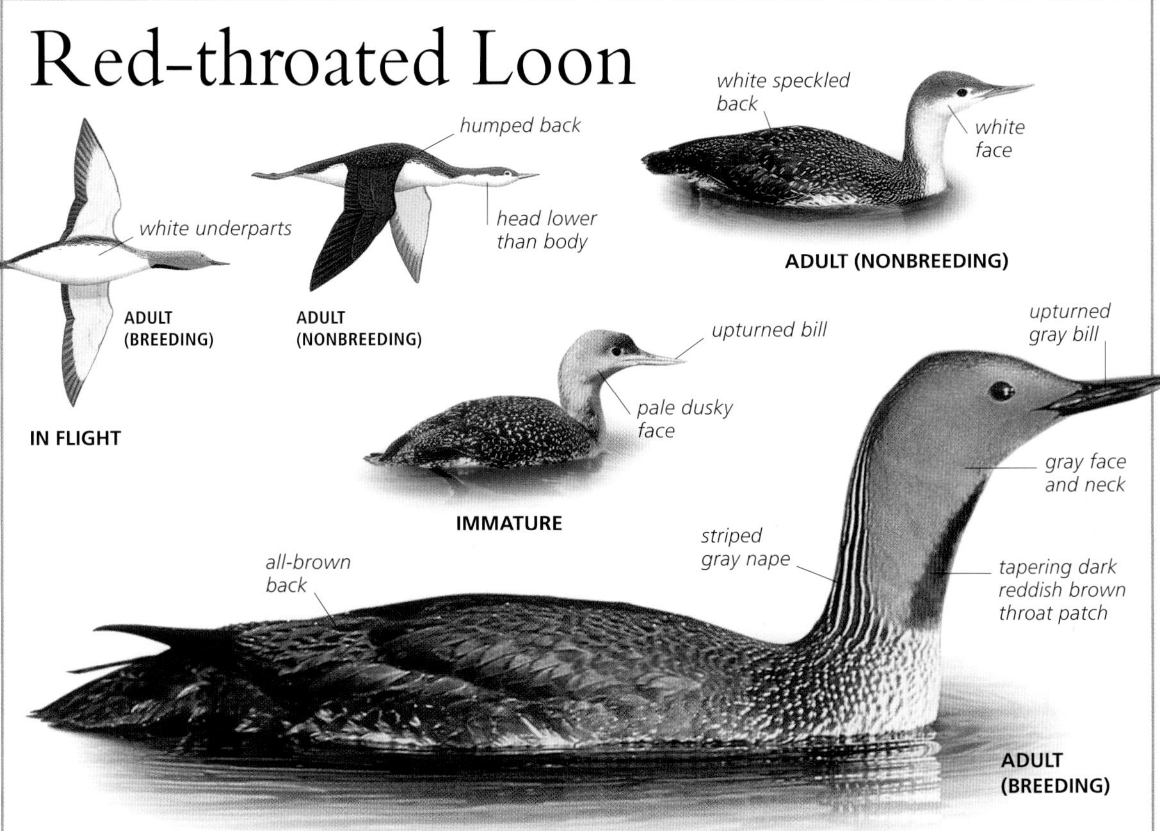
white underparts
ADULT (BREEDING)
IN FLIGHT
humped back
head lower than body
ADULT (NONBREEDING)
white speckled back
white face
ADULT (NONBREEDING)
upturned bill
pale dusky face
IMMATURE
upturned gray bill
gray face and neck
striped gray nape
tapering dark reddish brown throat patch
all-brown back
ADULT (BREEDING)

Even when seen from a distance, this elegant loon is almost unmistakable, with a pale, slim body, upward tilted head, and a thin, upturned bill. Unlike other Loons, the Red-throated Loon can leap straight into the air from both land and water, although most of the time it needs a "runway." The Red-throated Loon has an elaborate breeding ritual—side by side, a pair of birds races upright across the surface of water. Downy chicks climb onto the parents back only when very young.

VOICE High gull-like or even cat-like wail and low goose-like growl; vocal on breeding grounds, otherwise silent.

NESTING Scrape with mud and vegetation added during incubation, placed at water's edge in coastal and lake bays, shallow ponds, often at high altitudes; 2 eggs; 1 brood; April–July.

FEEDING Mainly eats fish; also spiders, crustaceans, and mollusks; flies long distances from shallow ponds when food is scarce.

FLIGHT: very direct; fast, with constant wing beats; head held lower than other loons.

TAKING OFF
While this bird is using the water's surface to take off, it can leap directly into flight from water and land.

SIMILAR SPECIES

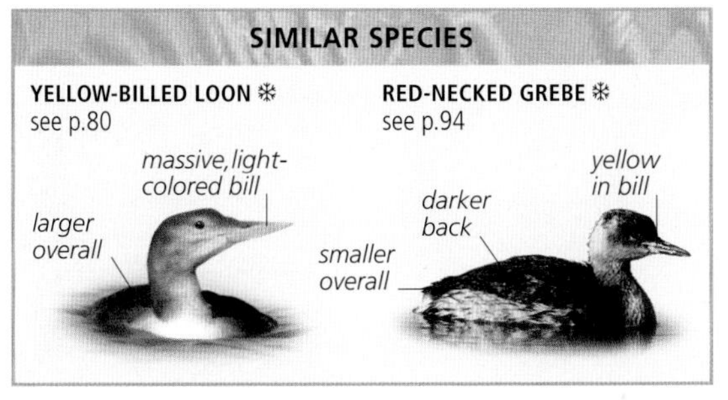
YELLOW-BILLED LOON ❄
see p.80
massive, light-colored bill
larger overall
RED-NECKED GREBE ❄
see p.94
yellow in bill
darker back
smaller overall

OCCURRENCE
Lives in open areas within northern boreal forest, muskeg, and tundra; in Canadian Arctic Archipelago, sometimes in areas almost devoid of vegetation. Winters on the Great Lakes, and both coasts southwards to Florida and northern Mexico.

Length **24–27in (61–69cm)**	Wingspan **3½ft (1.1m)**	Weight **3¼lb (1.5kg)**
Social **Solitary/Loose flocks**	Lifespan **Up to 23 years**	Status **Declining**

Order **Gaviiformes**	Family **Gaviidae**	Species ***Gavia pacifica***

Pacific Loon

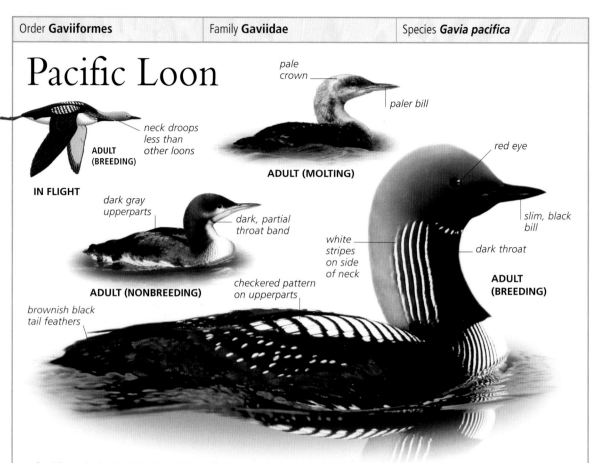

pale crown
paler bill
neck droops less than other loons
ADULT (BREEDING)
IN FLIGHT
ADULT (MOLTING)
red eye
slim, black bill
dark throat
white stripes on side of neck
ADULT (BREEDING)
dark gray upperparts
dark, partial throat band
ADULT (NONBREEDING)
checkered pattern on upperparts
brownish black tail feathers

Although the Pacific Loon's breeding range is about a third of that of the Common Loon, it is believed to be the most abundant loon species in North America. It shares its habitat in northern Alaska with the nearly identical, but slightly larger and darker Arctic Loon. It is a conspicuous migrant along the Pacific Coast in spring, but disappears to its remote breeding grounds in summer. The Pacific Loon is an expert diver and swimmer, capable of remaining underwater for sustained periods of time, usually in pursuit of fish. However, on its terrestrial nesting site, its chicks are vulnerable to a number of mammalian predators.

VOICE Deep barking *kowk*; high-pitched wail, croaks, and growls when breeding; makes a yelping noise when diving.

NESTING Simple scrape in flat area close to water, vegetation and mud added during incubation; 1–2 eggs; June–July.

FEEDING Eats fish, aquatic insects, and mollusks in breeding lake or nearby waters; may dip or dive, depending on the depth.

FLIGHT: swift and direct with constant wing beats; humped back, but head in line with body.

LEVEL GROUND
As loons cannot take off from land, nest sites need to be on flat land close to the water.

SIMILAR SPECIES

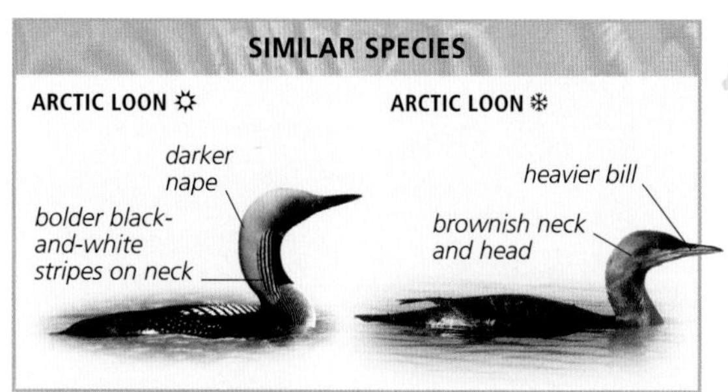
ARCTIC LOON ☼
darker nape
bolder black-and-white stripes on neck
ARCTIC LOON ❄
heavier bill
brownish neck and head

OCCURRENCE
Breeds across Arctic and sub-Arctic North America, from Alaska and northern Canadian provinces to Hudson Bay and on some of the islands of the Canadian Arctic; tundra lakes and muskeg. Small numbers in Great Lakes and along East coast from Quebec to Florida. Vagrant elsewhere.

Length **23–29in (58–74cm)**	Wingspan **2¾–4¼ft (0.9–1.3m)**	Weight **2½–5½lb (1–2.5kg)**
Social **Flocks**	Lifespan **Up to 25 years**	Status **Secure**

Order **Gaviiformes**	Family **Gaviidae**	Species ***Gavia immer***

Common Loon

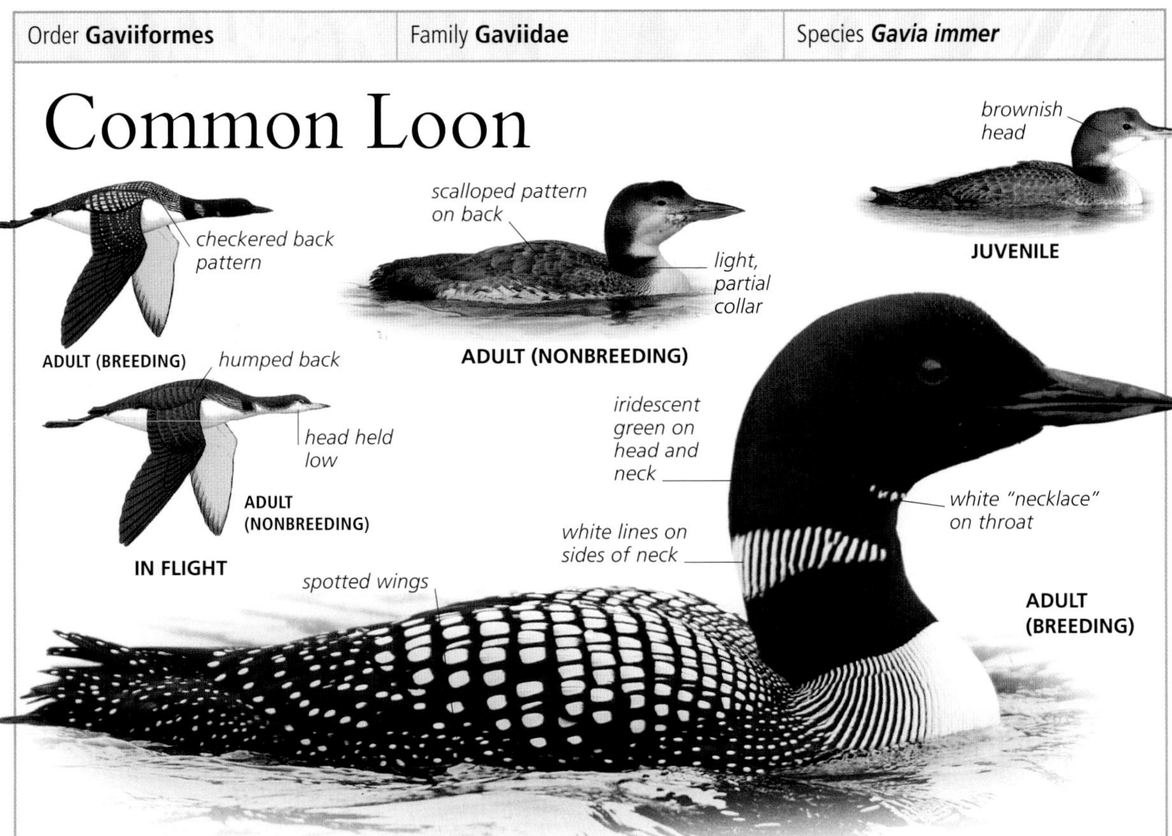
brownish head
JUVENILE
scalloped pattern on back
light, partial collar
ADULT (NONBREEDING)
checkered back pattern
ADULT (BREEDING)
humped back
head held low
ADULT (NONBREEDING)
IN FLIGHT
iridescent green on head and neck
white "necklace" on throat
white lines on sides of neck
spotted wings
ADULT (BREEDING)

The Common Loon has the largest range of all loons in North America and is the only species to nest in a few of the northern states. It is slightly smaller than the Yellow-billed Loon but larger than the other three loons. It can remain underwater for well over 10 minutes, although it usually stays submerged for 40 seconds to 2 minutes while fishing, or a few more minutes if it is being pursued. Evidence shows that, occasionally, it interbreeds with its closest relative, the Yellow-billed Loon, in addition to the Arctic and Pacific Loons. The Common Loon is the provincial bird of Ontario.

VOICE Most recognized call a 3–10 note falsetto yodel, rising, then fading; other calls similar in quality.

NESTING Simple scrape in large mound of vegetation, a few feet from open water; 2 eggs; 1 brood; April–June.

FEEDING Feeds primarily on fish underwater; also eats crustaceans, mollusks, amphibians, leeches, insects, and aquatic plants.

FLIGHT: fast, direct, with constant wing beats; head and neck held just above belly.

COZY RIDE
Downy Common Loon chicks climb up the backs of male and female adults for a safe ride.

BATHING RITUAL
Common Loons often shake their wings after bathing.

SIMILAR SPECIES

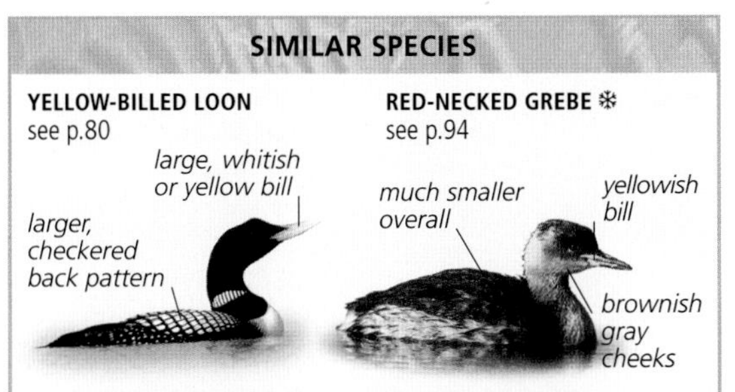
YELLOW-BILLED LOON
see p.80
large, whitish or yellow bill
larger, checkered back pattern
RED-NECKED GREBE ❄
see p.94
much smaller overall
yellowish bill
brownish gray cheeks

OCCURRENCE
Breeds across North America, Canada, and south to northern US. Winters on large ice-free lakes in Canada and the US, and along the Pacific and Atlantic Coasts, south to Baja California and Florida.

Length **26–36in (66–91cm)**	Wingspan **4¼–5ft (1.3–1.5m)**	Weight **4½–18lb (2–8kg)**
Social **Family groups**	Lifespan **Up to 30 years**	Status **Vulnerable**

Order **Gaviiformes**	Family **Gaviidae**	Species ***Gavia adamsii***

Yellow-billed Loon

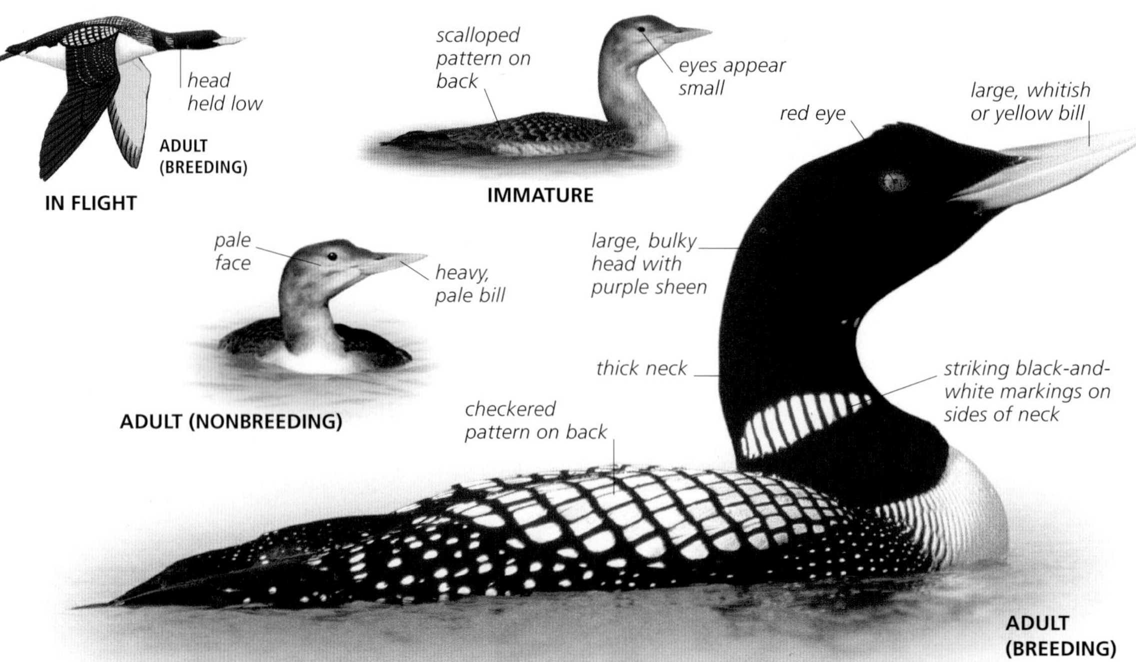
head
held low
ADULT
(BREEDING)
IN FLIGHT
scalloped
pattern on
back
eyes appear
small
IMMATURE
red eye
large, whitish
or yellow bill
pale
face
heavy,
pale bill
ADULT (NONBREEDING)
large, bulky
head with
purple sheen
thick neck
striking black-and-
white markings on
sides of neck
checkered
pattern on back
ADULT
(BREEDING)

The largest of the loons, the Yellow-billed Loon has the most restricted range and smallest global population. About three quarters of the estimated 16,000 birds live in North America. It makes the most of the short nesting season, arriving at its breeding grounds already paired and breeding immediately, although extensive ice formation can prevent it from breeding in some years. Yellow-billed Loons have more rugged proportions than other loons; their feet, for example, extend further away from their bodies.

VOICE Tremulous call much like Common Loon's, but louder, harsher, and even more "mournful"; yodels, wails, and "laughs" also part of repertoire.

NESTING Depression in mass of mud and vegetation, on shores of tundra lakes and ponds, and on river islands at high altitudes; 1–2 eggs; 1 brood; June–July.

FEEDING Dives underwater to catch small fish; also eats crustaceans, worms, and some vegetation.

FLIGHT: rapid and direct; head and neck held lower than body.

BOLDLY PATTERNED
The adult Yellow-billed Loon is strikingly patterned, like a checkerboard.

SIMILAR SPECIES

COMMON LOON ❄ see p.79
dark crown and pale cheeks; heavy, dark bill

RED-NECKED GREBE ❄ see p.94
shorter bill, yellowish at base; smaller overall

OCCURRENCE
Breeds from extreme northern edge of Alaska to eastern Northwest Territories and Nunavut. Also breeds in northern Siberia. Winters along the Pacific Coast of Alaska and British Columbia, and has been sighted in a number of US states.

Length **30–36in (77–92cm)**	Wingspan **4–5ft (1.2–1.5m)**	Weight **8¾–14lb (4–6.5kg)**
Social **Solitary/Pairs/Family groups**	Lifespan **Up to 30 years**	Status **Vulnerable**

TUBENOSES

THE TUBENOSES ARE DIVIDED into several families, but all are characterized by the tubular nostrils for which the order is named. These nostrils help to get rid of excess salt, and may enhance their sense of smell.

FLAP AND GLIDE
Shearwaters alternate stiff-winged flapping with gliding just over the ocean's surface.

ALBATROSSES

The long, narrow wings of albatrosses (family Diomedeidae) are perfectly suited for tackling the strong, constant winds which prevail on the southern oceans that form their main habitat. While they are expert gliders, albatrosses cannot takeoff from the ground without sufficient wing to give them lift.

SHEARWATERS

Shearwaters and gadfly petrels (family Procellariidae) are smaller than albatrosses. Like their larger relatives they are excellent gliders, but their lighter weight and proportionately shorter wings mean that they use more powered flight than Albatrosses. They range over all the world's oceans. With its far more numerous islands, the Pacific Ocean is home to a greater variety of these seabirds than the Atlantic. During and after storms are the best times to look for these birds, as this is when they have been drifting away from the deep sea due to wind and waves.

STORM-PETRELS

The smallest tubenoses in North American waters, the storm-petrels (family Hydrobatidae) are also the most agile fliers. They often patter or "dance" as they fly low to the surface of the ocean in search of small fish, squid, and crustaceans. Storm-petrels spend most of their lives flying over the open sea, only visiting land in the breeding season, when they form huge colonies.

HOOKED BILL
In addition to the tubular nostrils all tubenoses have strongly hooked bills.

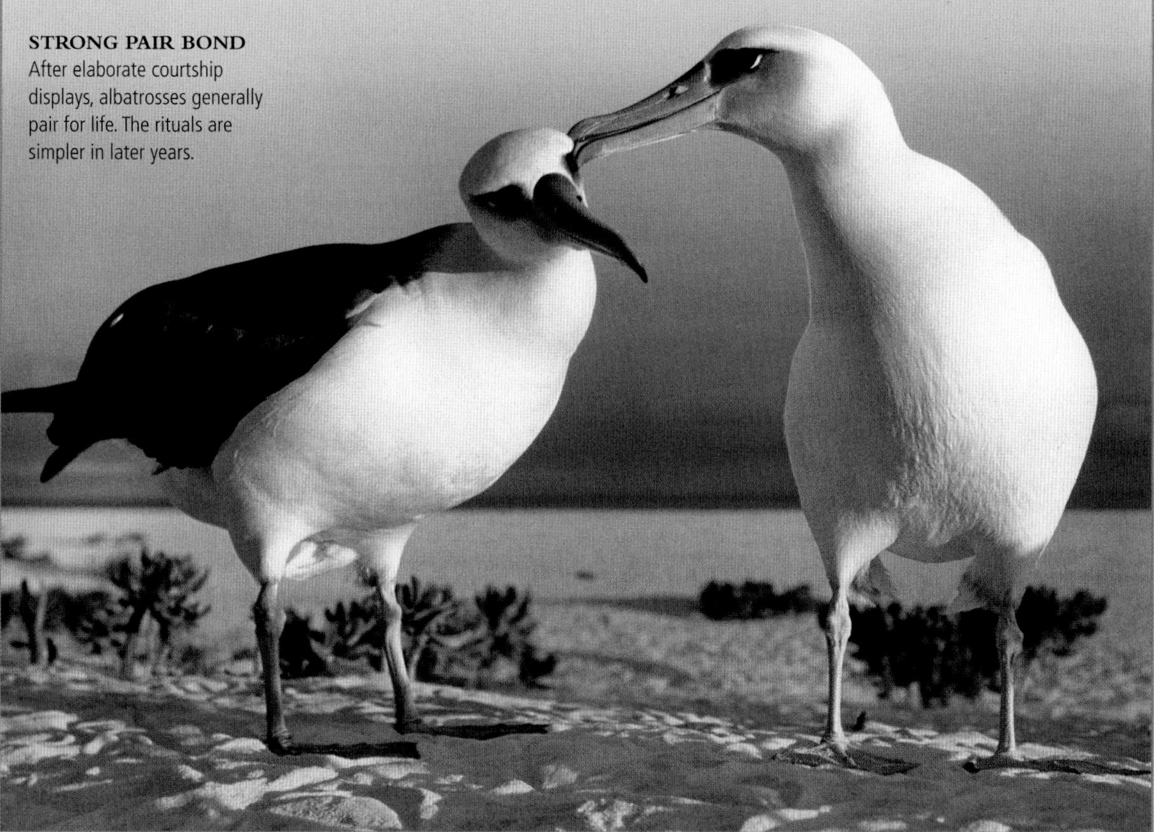

STRONG PAIR BOND
After elaborate courtship displays, albatrosses generally pair for life. The rituals are simpler in later years.

Order **Procellariiformes**	Family **Diomedeidae**	Species ***Phoebastria nigripes***

Black-footed Albatross

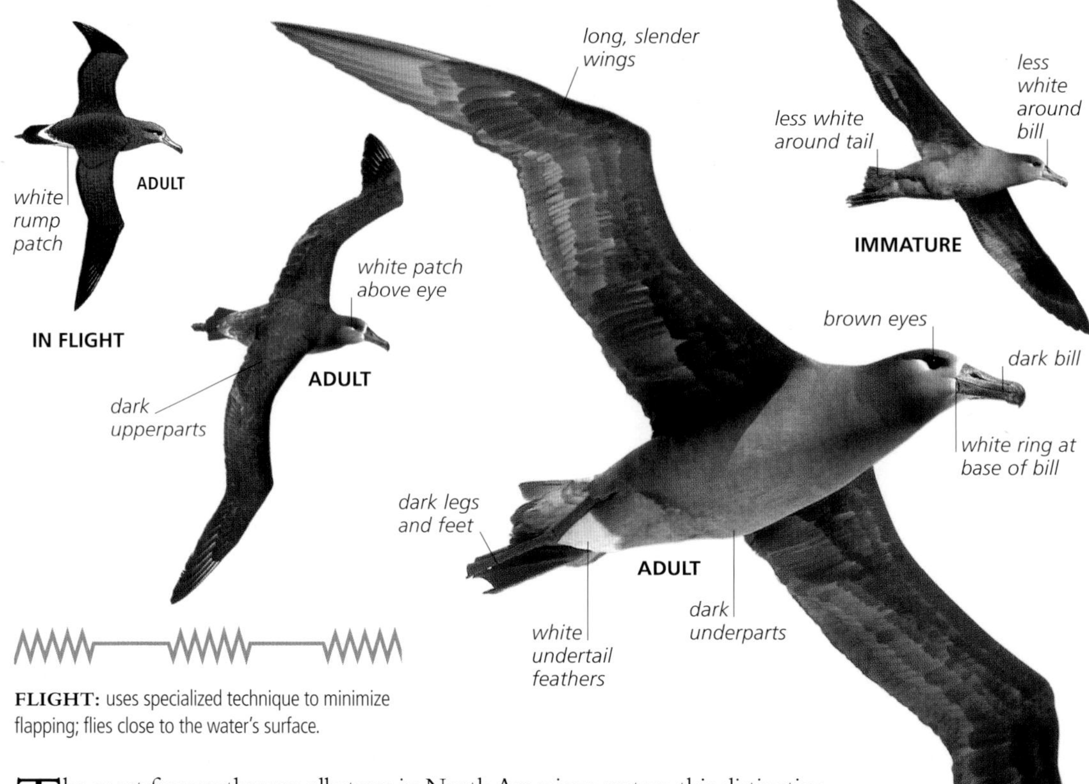
long, slender wings
less white around tail
less white around bill
IMMATURE
white rump patch
ADULT
IN FLIGHT
white patch above eye
ADULT
dark upperparts
brown eyes
dark bill
white ring at base of bill
dark legs and feet
ADULT
dark underparts
white undertail feathers

FLIGHT: uses specialized technique to minimize flapping; flies close to the water's surface.

The most frequently seen albatross in North American waters, this distinctive all-dark bird breeds mainly on the Hawaiian Islands, and regularly visits the Pacific Coast during the nonbreeding season. Unfortunately, a tendency to scavenge around fishing boats results in this and other species of albatross being drowned when they are accidentally hooked on long lines or tangled in drift nets—a major conservation concern for this particular species.

VOICE Generally silent outside the breeding season, but utters weak squeals while scavenging; variety of noises made during courtship.

NESTING Shallow depression in ground on higher reaches of sandy beaches; 1 egg; 1 brood; October–June.

FEEDING Dives for fish and squid, and picks floating masses of fish eggs from the ocean's surface with its bill.

TAKING OFF
Like other albatross species, the big-winged Black-footed Albatross takes off from water by running across the surface, heading into the wind.

SIMILAR SPECIES

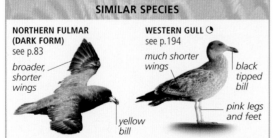

NORTHERN FULMAR (DARK FORM)
see p.83
broader, shorter wings
yellow bill

WESTERN GULL ◔
see p.194
much shorter wings
black tipped bill
pink legs and feet

OCCURRENCE
Breeds on sandy beaches, almost exclusively on remote, uninhabited islands in Hawaii; during the nonbreeding season, the Black-footed Albatross disperses across the whole northern Pacific Ocean.

Length **25–29in (64–74cm)**	Wingspan **6¼–7¼ft (1.9–2.2m)**	Weight **6¼lb (2.8kg)**
Social **Solitary/Flocks**	Lifespan **Up to 28 years**	Status **Endangered**

Order **Procellariiformes**	Family **Procellariidae**	Species ***Fulmarus glacialis***

Northern Fulmar

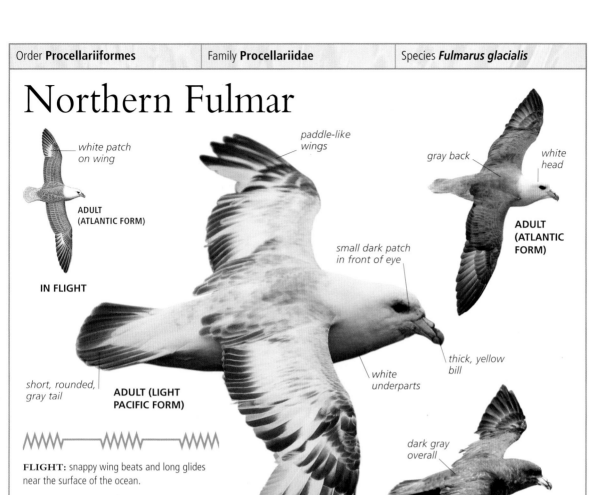

white patch on wing

ADULT (ATLANTIC FORM)

IN FLIGHT

paddle-like wings

small dark patch in front of eye

thick, yellow bill

white underparts

short, rounded, gray tail

ADULT (LIGHT PACIFIC FORM)

gray back

white head

ADULT (ATLANTIC FORM)

dark gray overall

ADULT (DARK PACIFIC FORM)

FLIGHT: snappy wing beats and long glides near the surface of the ocean.

Possessing paddle-shaped wings and distinctive color patterns ranging from almost all-white to all-gray, the Northern Fulmar is among the most common seabirds in places like the Bering Sea. It breeds at high latitudes, then disperses south to offshore waters on both coasts of the continent. The Northern Fulmar can often be seen in large mixed flocks containing albatrosses, shearwaters, and petrels. Fulmars often follow boats, eager to pounce on the offal thrown overboard by fishermen.

VOICE Mostly silent at sea; occasionally utters cackles and grunts.

NESTING Scrape in rock or soil on edge of cliff; 1 egg; 1 brood; May–October.

FEEDING Picks fish and offal from the surface of the ocean; also dives underwater to catch fish.

FEEDING FRENZY
Large numbers of Northern Fulmars compete for the offal discarded by fishing trawlers.

SIMILAR SPECIES

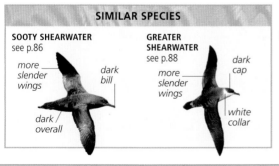

SOOTY SHEARWATER see p.86
more slender wings; *dark bill*; *dark overall*

GREATER SHEARWATER see p.88
more slender wings; *dark cap*; *white collar*

OCCURRENCE
Breeds on remote, high, coastal cliffs in Alaska and northern Canada; winters at sea in offshore Pacific and Atlantic waters, generally farther north than most other seabirds. Breeds in Europe, to Greenland, Svalbard; also parts of Russia.

Length **17½–19½in (45–50cm)**	Wingspan **3¼–3½ft (1–1.1m)**	Weight **16–35oz (0.45–1kg)**
Social **Flocks**	Lifespan **Up to 50 years**	Status **Secure**

Order **Procellariiformes**	Family **Procellariidae**	Species ***Calonectris diomedea***

Cory's Shearwater

long, pointed wings

pale rump

ADULT

IN FLIGHT

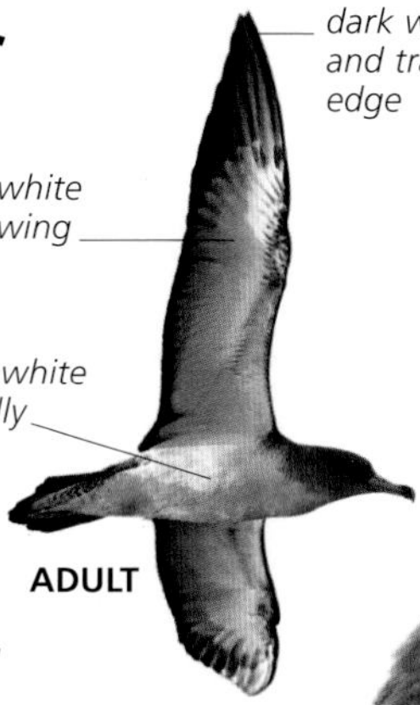

dark wingtip and trailing edge

clean white underwing

all white belly

ADULT

grayish head and chin

yellow bill with dark tip

scalloped pattern

ADULT

white breast, with sooty-gray sides

Close studies of a group of Cory's Shearwaters off the Atlantic coast suggest the presence of two forms. The more common form, *C. d. borealis*, nests in the eastern Atlantic and is chunkier, with less white in the wing from below. The other form, *C. d. diomedea*, breeds in the Mediterranean, has a more slender build (including a thinner bill), and has more extensive white under the wing. Cory's Shearwater has a distinctive, relatively languid flight style that is different from the other shearwaters regularly found in North American waters.

VOICE Mostly silent at sea; descending, lamb-like bleating.

NESTING Nests in burrow or rocky crevice; 1 egg; 1 brood; May–September.

FEEDING Dives into water or picks at surface for small schooling fish, and marine invertebrates such as squid.

FLIGHT: slow, deliberate wing beats interspersed with long glides; often arcs strongly on bent wings.

LAZY FLIERS

In calm weather Cory's Shearwaters look heavy and fly low, swooping higher in strong winds.

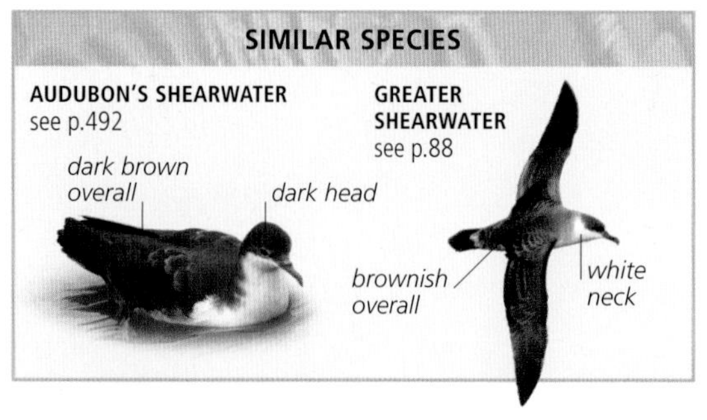
SIMILAR SPECIES
AUDUBON'S SHEARWATER
see p.492
dark brown overall
dark head
GREATER SHEARWATER
see p.88
brownish overall
white neck

OCCURRENCE

This species breeds in the Mediterranean and on islands of the eastern Atlantic, including the Azores, the Salvages, Madeira, and the Canaries. When nonbreeding, Cory's Shearwaters disperse widely over the Atlantic Ocean, including off the east coast of Canada.

Length **18in (46cm)**	Wingspan **3½ft (1.1m)**	Weight **28oz (800g)**
Social **Flocks**	Lifespan **Unknown**	Status **Secure**

Order **Procellariiformes**	Family **Procellariidae**	Species ***Puffinus puffinus***

Manx Shearwater

black edge of wing

IN FLIGHT

white undertail feathers

snow white underparts

very dark brownish black upperparts

head is black above, white below

long, thin, hooked bill

long, pointed wings

crisp white underwings

dark upperwings

small head

short tail

dark, hooked bill

white throat

Most shearwaters are little known because of their nocturnal and oceanic ways, but the Manx is an exception. It is common in the British Isles, and ornithologists have been studying it there for decades. Long-term banding programs revealed one bird that flew over 3,000 miles (4,800km) from Massachusetts to its nesting burrow in Wales in just 12½ days, and another that was captured 56 years after it was first banded, making its accumulated migration-only mileage around 600,000 miles (1,000,000km).

VOICE Usually silent at sea, but at breeding sites, produces loud and raucous series of cries, *kah-kah-kah-kah-kah-HOWW*.

NESTING In burrow, in peaty soil, or rocky crevice; 1 egg; 1 brood; April–October.

FEEDING Dives into water, often with open wings and stays underwater, or picks at surface for small schooling fish and squid.

FLIGHT: rapid, stiff wing beats interspersed with glides; arcs high in strong winds.

PITTER-PATTER

Unlike gulls, shearwaters have to patter along the surface with their feet to achieve lift-off speed.

SIMILAR SPECIES

BLACK-VENTED SHEARWATER
see p.492

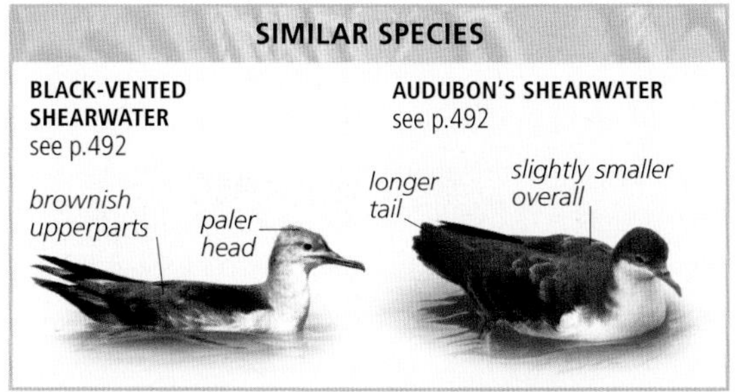
brownish upperparts
paler head

AUDUBON'S SHEARWATER
see p.492

longer tail
slightly smaller overall

OCCURRENCE

Breeds on many islands in eastern North Atlantic; restricted to islands off Newfoundland in North America. Regularly occurs off US east coast as far south as Florida. Rare in Gulf of Mexico and off the West Coast. Rarely seen from shore; cold-water shearwater.

Length **13½in (34cm)**	Wingspan **33in (83cm)**	Weight **14–20oz (400–575g)**
Social **Migrant flocks**	Lifespan **Up to 55 years**	Status **Secure**

Order **Procellariiformes**	Family **Procellariidae**	Species ***Puffinus griseus***

Sooty Shearwater

ADULT
all-dark underparts
IN FLIGHT

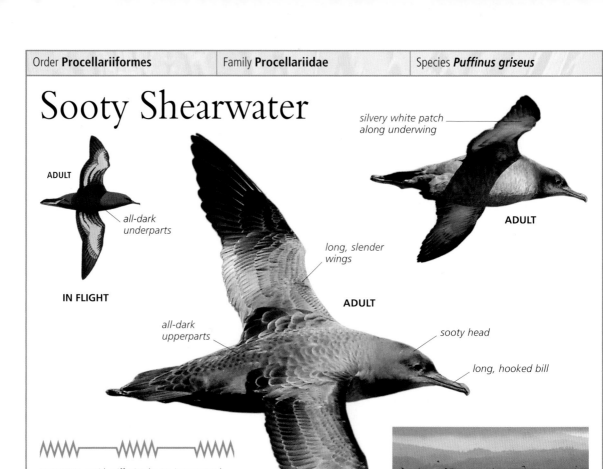

silvery white patch along underwing
ADULT

long, slender wings
ADULT
all-dark upperparts
sooty head
long, hooked bill

FLIGHT: rapid, stiff wing beats, interspersed with glides; arcs up highly in strong winds.

Sooty Shearwaters are extremely long-distance migrants, with both Atlantic and Pacific populations undergoing lengthy circular migrations. Pacific birds in particular travel as far as 300 miles (480km) per day and an extraordinary 45,000 miles (72,500km) or more per year. Huge flocks of this species are often seen off the coast of California. It is fairly easy to identify off the East Coast of North America, as it is the only all-dark shearwater found there.

VOICE Silent at sea; occasionally gives varied, agitated vocalizations when feeding,very loud calls at breeding colonies.

NESTING In burrow or rocky crevice; 1 egg; 1 brood; October–May.

FEEDING Dives and picks at surface for small schooling fish and mollusks such as squid.

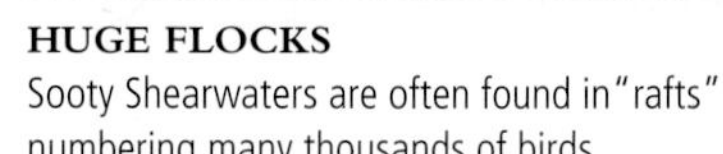

HUGE FLOCKS
Sooty Shearwaters are often found in"rafts" numbering many thousands of birds.

TUBENOSE
Shearwaters are tubenoses, so-called for the salt-excreting tubes on their bills.

SIMILAR SPECIES

SHORT-TAILED SHEARWATER
see p.492
dark upperparts
dark cap
pale throat

GREATER SHEARWATER
see p.88
white tail band
shorter bill
white collar

OCCURRENCE
Sooty Shearwaters breed on islands in the southern Ocean and nearby waters, some colonies number thousands of pairs. Postbreeding movements take them north into the Pacific and Atlantic Ocean, on 8-shaped migrations.

Length **18in (46cm)**	Wingspan **3ft 3in (1m)**	Weight **27oz (775g)**
Social **Flocks**	Lifespan **Unknown**	Status **Secure**

Order **Procellariiformes**	Family **Procellariidae**	Species ***Puffinus creatopus***

Pink-footed Shearwater

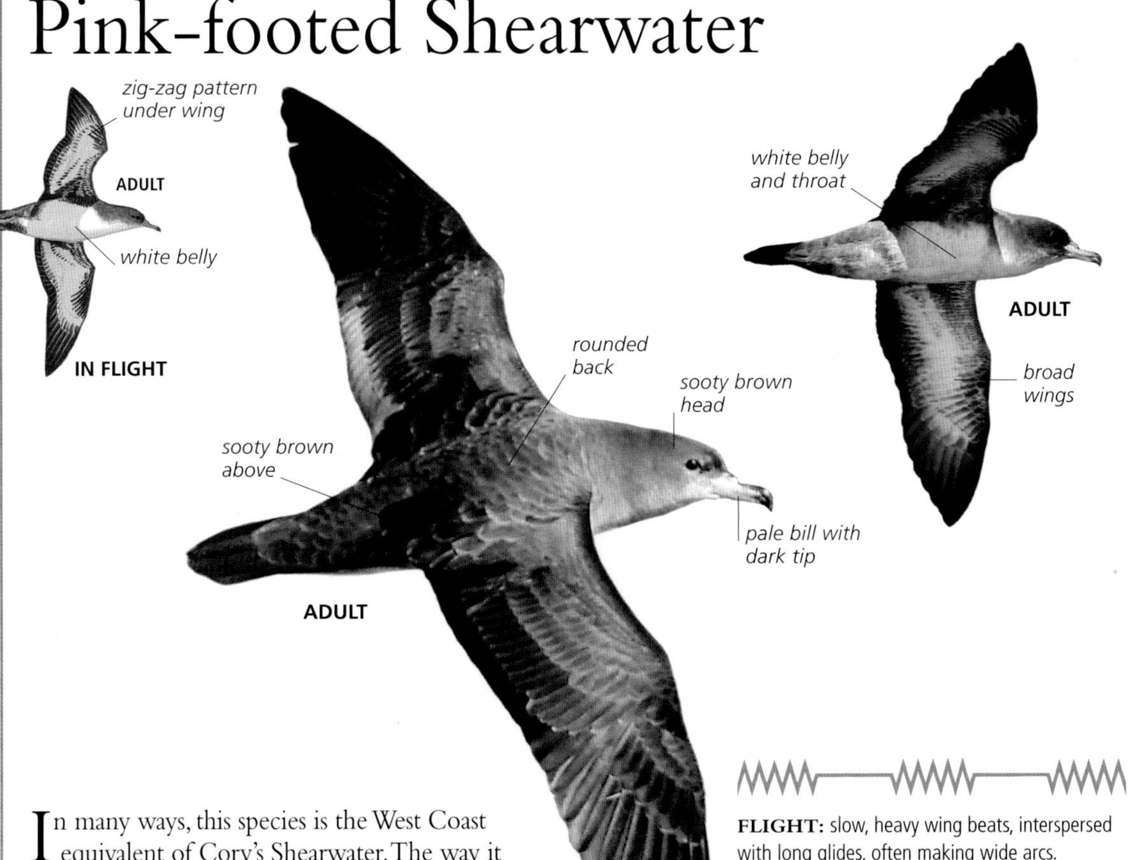
zig-zag pattern under wing
ADULT
white belly
IN FLIGHT
sooty brown above
rounded back
sooty brown head
pale bill with dark tip
ADULT
white belly and throat
ADULT
broad wings

In many ways, this species is the West Coast equivalent of Cory's Shearwater. The way it holds its wings (angled at the "wrist"), its size, and its flight style are all reminiscent of Cory's. Though Pink-footed Shearwaters are fairly variable in plumage, they are always rather dull, with little color variation. This plumage pattern is similar to that of the Black-vented Shearwater, and as both species are found off the Pacific coast in fall and spring identification is difficult. However, the Pink-footed Shearwater can be distinguished by its larger size and distinctly pinkish bill.

VOICE Usually silent at sea, but may produce a horse-like whinny when feeding with other sea birds.

NESTING Burrows in peat; 1 egg; 1 brood; October–March.

FEEDING Like other shearwaters, makes shallow dives to catch squid, octopus, and fish.

FLIGHT: slow, heavy wing beats, interspersed with long glides, often making wide arcs.

PINK FEET
This Pink-footed Shearwater, ready to alight on the water, shows off its pink legs and feet.

SIMILAR SPECIES

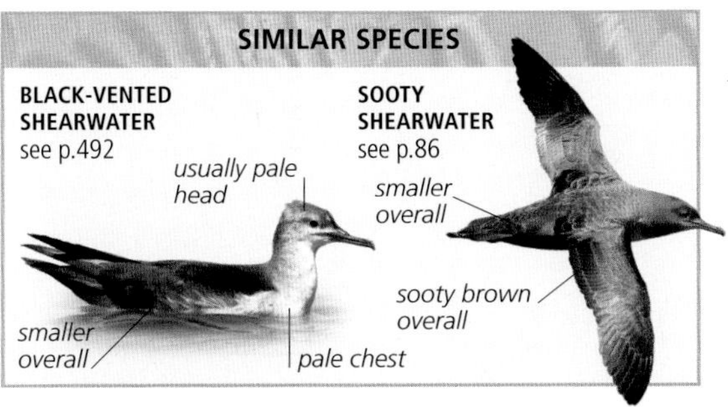
BLACK-VENTED SHEARWATER
see p.492
usually pale head
smaller overall
pale chest
SOOTY SHEARWATER
see p.86
smaller overall
sooty brown overall

OCCURRENCE
Breeds on a few islands off Chile, including Juan Fernandez. Spends its winter (North American summer) off the coasts of the Americas, reaching as far north as British Columbia and southern Alaska. Found closer to shore than other shearwaters. On Juan Fernandez, population reduced by predation of introduced rats.

Length **19in (48cm)**	Wingspan **3½ft (1.1m)**	Weight **26oz (725g)**
Social **Flocks**	Lifespan **Unknown**	Status **Vulnerable**

Order **Procellariiformes**	Family **Procellariidae**	Species ***Puffinus gravis***

Greater Shearwater

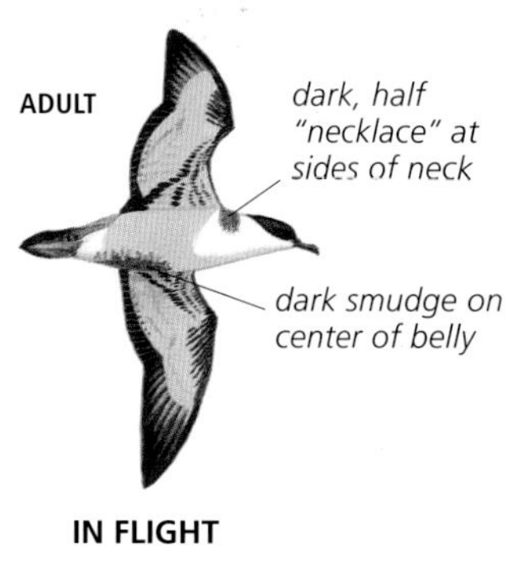
ADULT
dark, half "necklace" at sides of neck
dark smudge on center of belly
IN FLIGHT

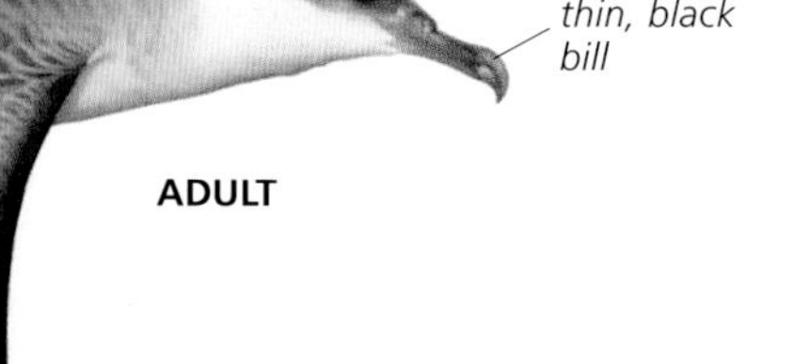
darker outer wing feathers
brownish upperwings
white collar
dark cap
thin, white band on rump
thin, black bill
ADULT

A common species in North Atlantic waters, from northern Canada to Florida, the Greater Shearwater is similar in size to Cory's Shearwater and the birds scavenge together for scraps around fishing boats. However, their plumages and flight styles are quite different. While Cory's Shearwater has slow, labored wing beats, and glides high on broad, bowed, swept-back wings, Greater Shearwaters keep low, flapping hurriedly between glides on straight, narrow wings. The brown smudges on the belly (not always visible) and paler underwings of the Greater Shearwater also help distinguish the species.

VOICE Silent at sea; descending, lamb-like bleating at breeding sites.

NESTING Digs deep burrow in peaty or boggy soil; 1 egg; 1 brood; September–March.

FEEDING Feeds either from the surface, picking up items such as fish and squid, or makes shallow dives with open wings.

FLIGHT: fast, stiff wing beats interspersed with gliding; arcs high in windy conditions.

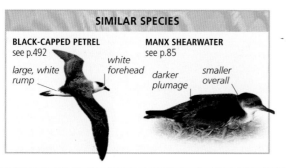

WHITE COLLAR
The Greater Shearwater's white collar is highly visible between its black cap and sooty back.

SIMILAR SPECIES

BLACK-CAPPED PETREL see p.492
large, white rump; white forehead

MANX SHEARWATER see p.85
darker plumage; smaller overall

OCCURRENCE
Nests on just a few islands in the middle of the South Atlantic. Total population probably well over 200 million. Postbreeding birds make a very long 8-shaped migration around the Atantic, spending late July–September in North Atlantic waters, usually offshore.

Length **18in (46cm)**	Wingspan **3½ft (1.1m)**	Weight **30oz (850g)**
Social **Flocks**	Lifespan **At least 25 years**	Status **Secure**

Order **Procellariiformes**	Family **Hydrobatidae**	Species ***Oceanites oceanicus***

Wilson's Storm-Petrel

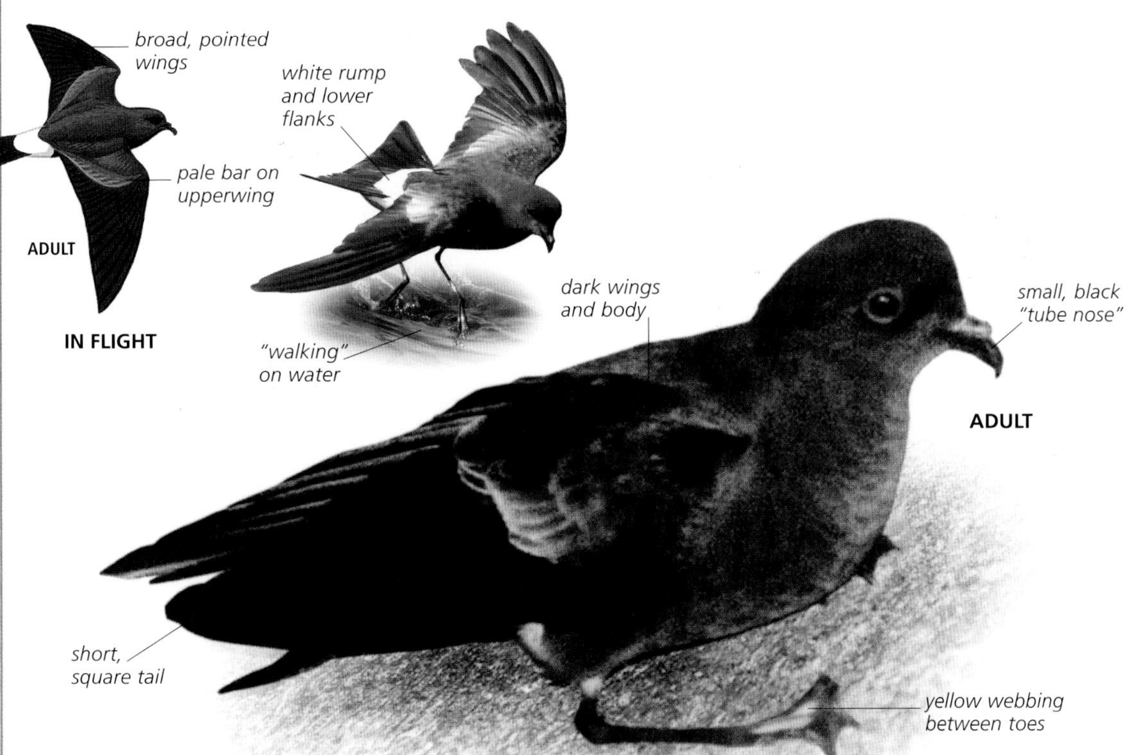

broad, pointed wings
white rump and lower flanks
pale bar on upperwing
ADULT
IN FLIGHT
"walking" on water
dark wings and body
small, black "tube nose"
ADULT
short, square tail
yellow webbing between toes

Named after Alexander Wilson, often called the "father of North American ornithology," Wilson's Storm-Petrel is the quintessential small oceanic petrel. It is an extremely abundant species and breeds in the many millions on the Antarctic Peninsula and islands in Antarctica. After breeding, many move north to spend the summer off the Atlantic coast of North America. Here, they are a familiar sight to fishermen and birders at sea. By August they can be seen lingering, but by October they have flown south.

VOICE At sea, soft rasping notes; at breeding sites a variety of *coos*, *churrs*, and twitters during the night.

NESTING Mostly in rock crevices; also burrows where there is peaty soil; 1 egg; 1 brood; November–March.

FEEDING Patters on the water's surface, legs extended, picking up tiny crustaceans; also carrion, droplets of oil.

FLIGHT: flutters, low to ocean's surface, often "stalling" to drop to the surface and glean food.

FEEDING FLOCK
While flying, this bird "walks" on water, simultaneously picking food from the surface.

SIMILAR SPECIES

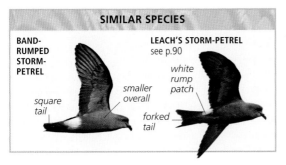

BAND-RUMPED STORM-PETREL
square tail
smaller overall

LEACH'S STORM-PETREL
see p.90
white rump patch
forked tail

OCCURRENCE
Breeds on the Antarctic Peninsula, many sub-Antarctic islands, and islands in the Cape Horn Archipelago. April–September or October, moves north, and is abundant off the coasts of Atlantic Canada and the US in July–September. With inshore winds, can often be seen from land.

Length **6¾in (17cm)**	Wingspan **16in (41cm)**	Weight **1 1/16–1 7/16oz (30–40g)**
Social **Flocks**	Lifespan **Up to 10 years**	Status **Secure**

Order **Procellariiformes**	Family **Hydrobatidae**	Species ***Oceanodroma leucorhoa***

Leach's Storm-Petrel

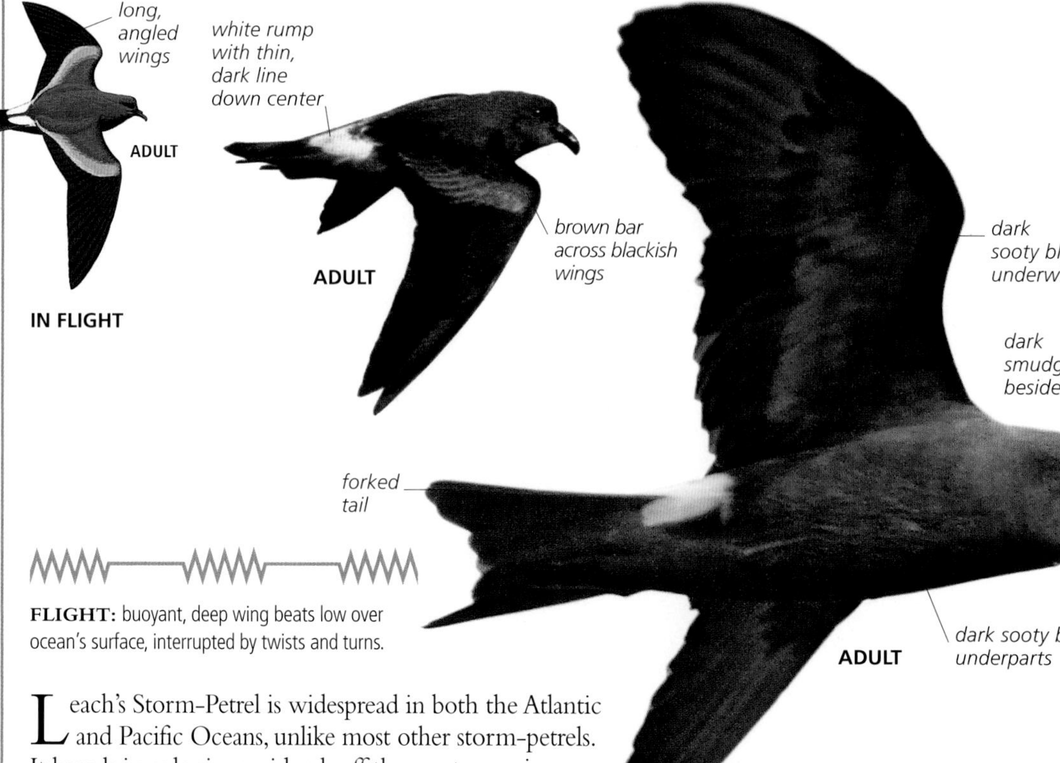
long, angled wings
ADULT
IN FLIGHT
white rump with thin, dark line down center
ADULT
brown bar across blackish wings
dark sooty black underwings
dark smudge beside eye
forked tail
ADULT
dark sooty brown underparts

FLIGHT: buoyant, deep wing beats low over ocean's surface, interrupted by twists and turns.

Leach's Storm-Petrel is widespread in both the Atlantic and Pacific Oceans, unlike most other storm-petrels. It breeds in colonies on islands off the coasts, coming to land at night and feeding offshore during the day, often many miles from the colony. This wide-ranging storm-petrel has both geographical and individual variation; most populations show a white rump, but others have a dark rump that is the same color as the rest of the body. Leach's Storm-Petrel can be distinguished from the similar Band-rumped Storm-Petrel by its notched tail and swooping flight.

VOICE At nesting sites, often from burrows, calls are long series of soft purring and chattering sounds.

NESTING Underground burrow on island free of predators such as rats; 1 egg; 1 brood; May–November.

FEEDING Gleans small crustaceans and small fish from the water's surface while in flight.

BALANCING ACT
Leach's Storm-Petrel will often balance itself with its wings while walking.

SIMILAR SPECIES

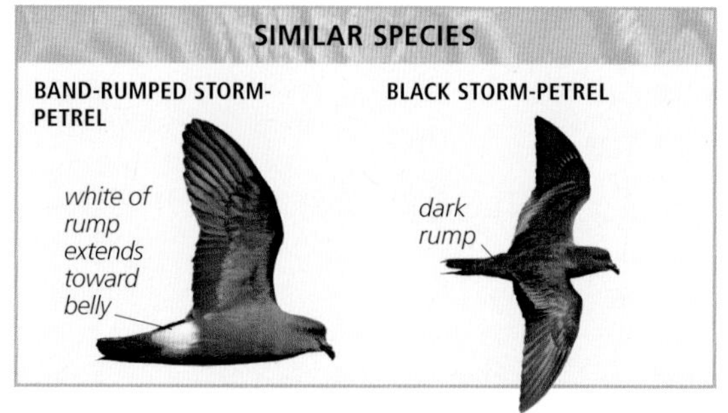
BAND-RUMPED STORM-PETREL
white of rump extends toward belly
BLACK STORM-PETREL
dark rump

OCCURRENCE
Breeds on islands in the Pacific Ocean from Alaska and the Aleutian Islands south to California; in the Atlantic Ocean, from Newfoundland to Maine. After breeding, it wanders widely on both oceans, keeping well out of sight of land.

Length **7–8½in (18–22cm)**	Wingspan **17½–19in (45–48cm)**	Weight **1$\frac{9}{16}$–1¾oz (45–50g)**
Social **Colonies**	Lifespan **Up to 36 years**	Status **Secure**

Order **Procellariiformes**	Family **Hydrobatidae**	Species ***Oceanodroma furcata***

Fork-tailed Storm-Petrel

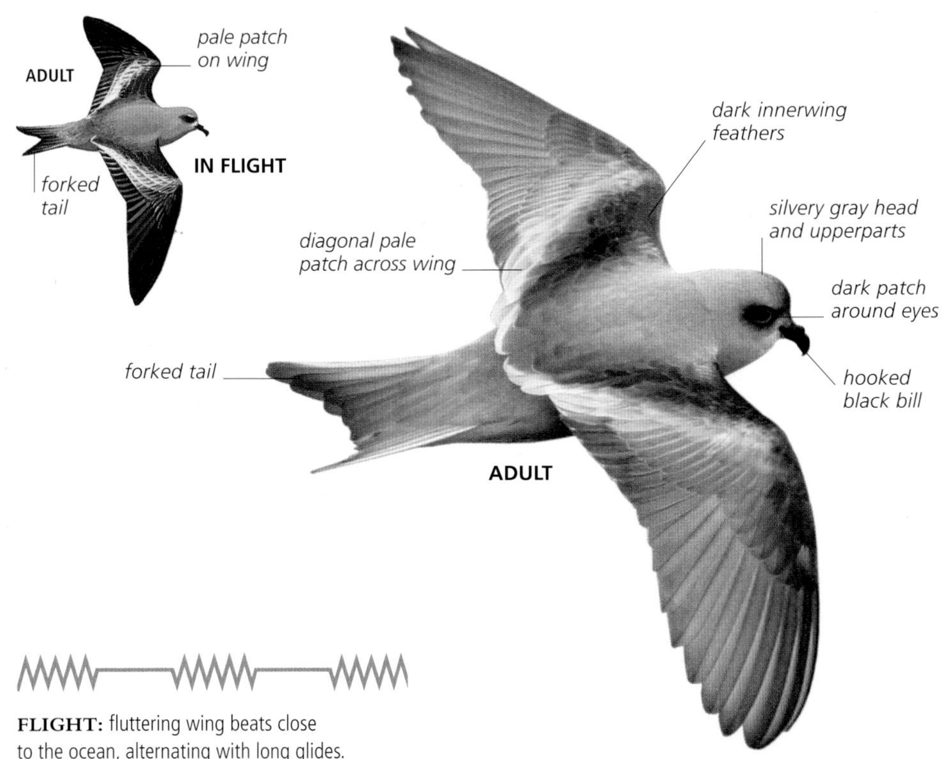

pale patch on wing
ADULT
IN FLIGHT
forked tail
dark innerwing feathers
silvery gray head and upperparts
diagonal pale patch across wing
dark patch around eyes
forked tail
hooked black bill
ADULT

FLIGHT: fluttering wing beats close to the ocean, alternating with long glides.

The Fork-tailed Storm-Petrel is one of the most distinctive of all storm-petrels in North American waters, with its ghostly silvery gray plumage, and forked tail. It is the most northerly breeding storm-petrel in the North Pacific, nesting all the way north to the Aleutian Islands. It incubates its eggs at lower temperatures than other petrels do, and its chicks can be left alone between feeding for a longer time—apparently an adaptation to northern conditions. Its chicks can also lower their body temperature, thereby conserving energy.

VOICE Silent at sea; various purring sounds at colonies.

NESTING Underground burrow on offshore island; 1 egg; 1 brood; March–November.

FEEDING Plucks shrimps, squids, and small fish from the surface of the ocean.

AERIAL SURVEY
Flying low over the ocean, the Fork-tailed Storm-Petrel looks out for fish below.

SIMILAR SPECIES

LEACH'S STORM-PETREL
see p.90

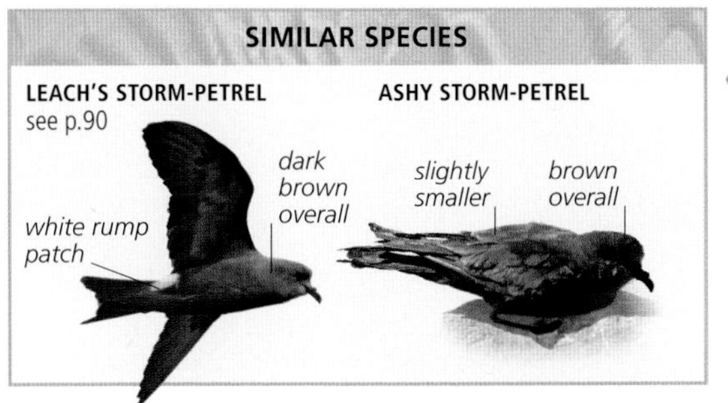

dark brown overall
white rump patch

ASHY STORM-PETREL

slightly smaller
brown overall

OCCURRENCE
Breeds in colonies on offshore rocky islands from California northward to Alaska, mostly to the Aleutian Islands, and south to islands off British Columbia; also Washington and Oregon. Post-breeding dispersal takes birds to the Bering Sea and to offshore waters of California.

Length **8in (20cm)**	Wingspan **18in (46cm)**	Weight **2oz (55g)**
Social **Colonies**	Lifespan **At least 14 years**	Status **Secure**

Family **Podicipedidae**

GREBES

GREBES RESEMBLE LOONS and share many of their aquatic habits, but anatomical and molecular features show that they are actually unrelated; and they are placed in a different order: the Podicipediformes. Grebe bodies are streamlined, offering little resistance when diving and swimming. Underwater their primary means of propulsion is the sideways motion of their lobed toes. The legs are placed far back on the body, which greatly aids the bird when swimming above or below the surface. Grebes have short tails, and their trailing legs and toes serve as rudders when they fly. The position of the legs makes it impossible, however, for grebes to stand upright for long or easily walk on land. Thus, even when breeding they are tied to water; and their nests are usually partially floating platforms, built on beds of water plants. Grebes' toes have broad lobes that splay when the bird thrusts forward through the water with its feet. They dive to catch fish with a short, forward arching spring. Unusually among birds, they swallow feathers, supposedly to trap fish bones and protect their stomachs, then periodically disgorge them. Like loons, grebes can control their buoyancy by exhaling air and compressing their plumage so that they sink quietly below the surface. They are strong fliers, and migratory.

PIED BILL
The black-and-white bill pattern clearly distinguishes this bird as the Pied-billed Grebe.

A FINE DISPLAY
This Horned Grebe reveals the colorful plumes on its head, as part of its elaborate courtship display.

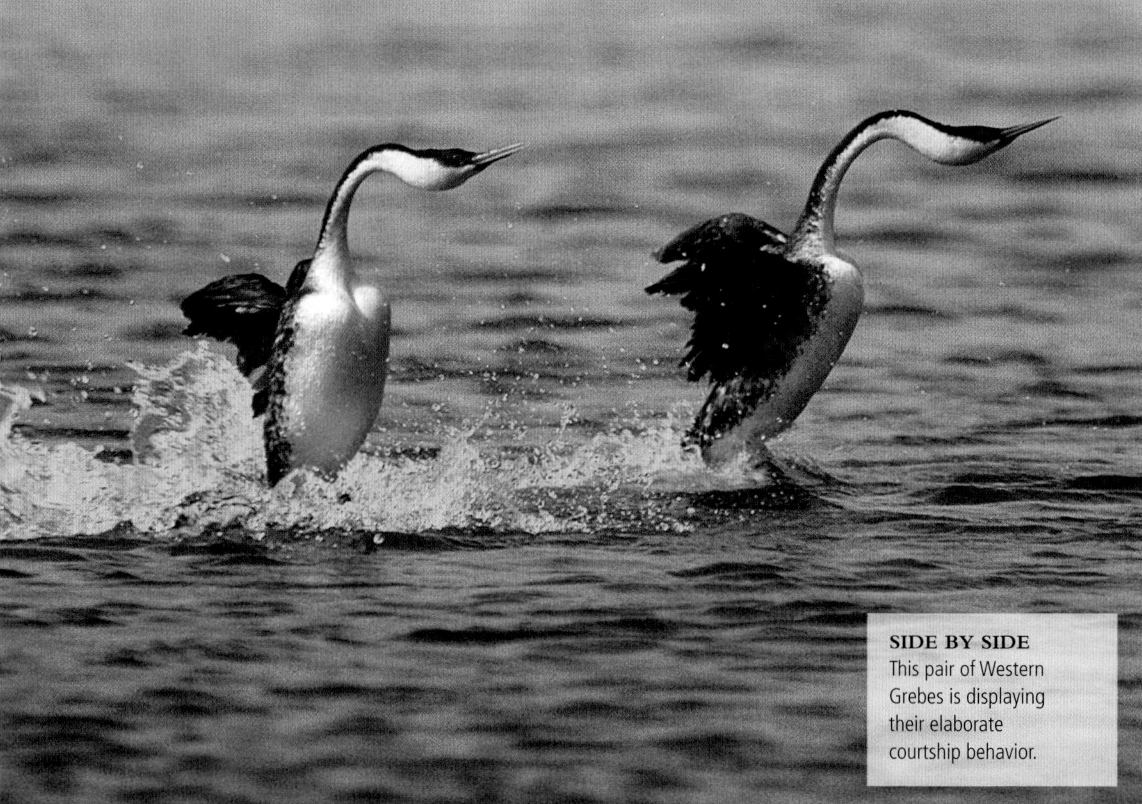

SIDE BY SIDE
This pair of Western Grebes is displaying their elaborate courtship behavior.

Order **Podicipediformes**	Family **Podicipedidae**	Species ***Podilymbus podiceps***

Pied-billed Grebe

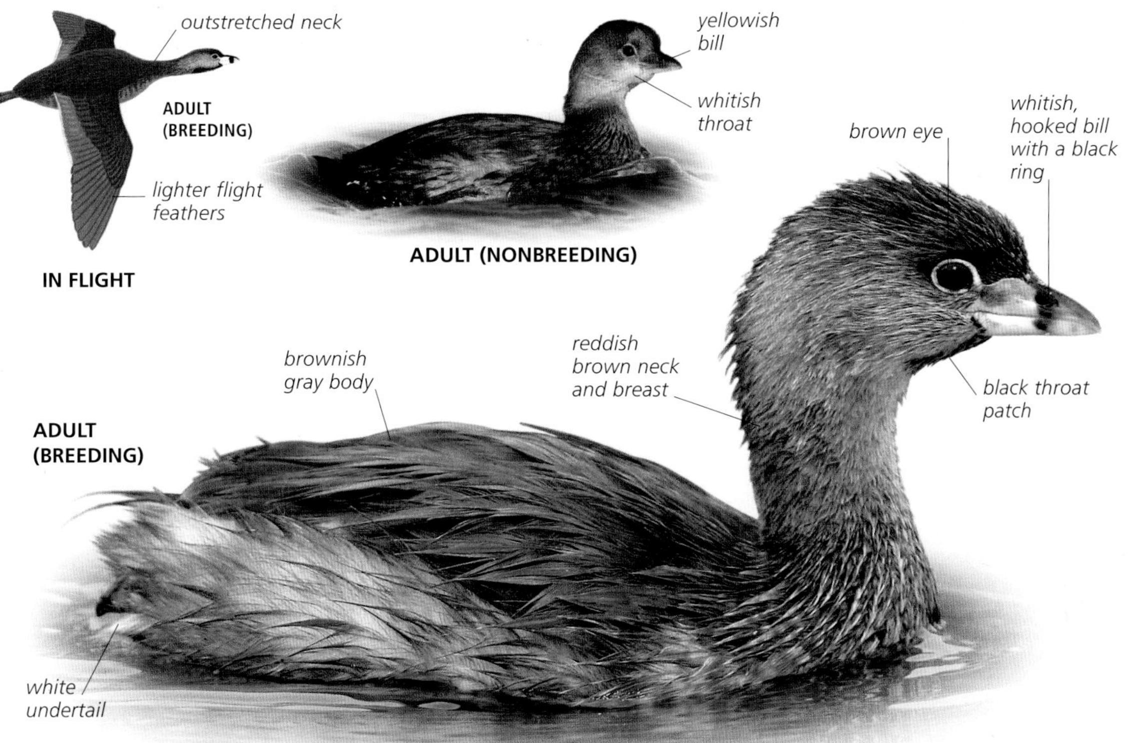
outstretched neck
ADULT (BREEDING)
lighter flight feathers
IN FLIGHT
yellowish bill
whitish throat
ADULT (NONBREEDING)
brown eye
whitish, hooked bill with a black ring
black throat patch
reddish brown neck and breast
brownish gray body
ADULT (BREEDING)
white undertail

The widest ranging of the North American grebes, the Pied-billed Grebe is tolerant of highly populated areas and is often seen breeding on lakes and ponds across North America. It is a powerful swimmer and can remain submerged for 16–30 seconds when it dives. In contrast to some of the elaborate displays from other grebe species, its courtship ritual is more vocal than visual and a pair usually duet-call in the mating season. Migration, conducted at night, is delayed until its breeding area ices up and food becomes scarce. The Pied-billed Grebe is capable of sustained flights of over 2,000 miles (3,200km).

VOICE Various grunts and wails; in spring, call a cuckoo-like repeated gobble *kup-kup-Kaow-Kaow-kaow*, gradually speeding up.

NESTING Floating nest of partially decayed plants and clipped leaves, attached to emergent vegetation in marshes and quiet waters; 4–7 eggs; 2 broods; April–October.

FEEDING Dives to catch a variety of crustaceans, fish, amphibians, insects, and other invertebrates; also picks prey from emergent vegetation, or catches them mid-air.

FLIGHT: strong, direct flight with rapid wing beats, but rarely seen.

BACK OFF
When alarmed, a Pied-billed Grebe will flap its wings in a defensive display.

SIMILAR SPECIES

LEAST GREBE ☼

smaller bill
yellow eye
darker body

OCCURRENCE
Breeds on a variety of water bodies, including coastal brackish ponds, seasonal ponds, marshes, and even sewage ponds. Winters in the breeding area if food and open water are available, otherwise chooses still waters resembling its breeding habitat.

Length **12–15in (31–38cm)**	Wingspan **18–24in (46–62cm)**	Weight **13–17oz (375–475g)**
Social **Family groups**	Lifespan **At least 3 years**	Status **Vulnerable**

Order **Podicipediformes**	Family **Podicipedidae**	Species ***Podiceps grisegena***

Red-necked Grebe

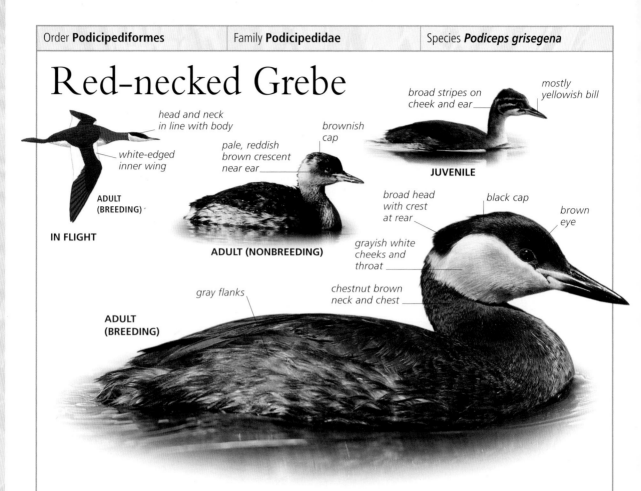

head and neck in line with body

white-edged inner wing

ADULT (BREEDING)

IN FLIGHT

pale, reddish brown crescent near ear

brownish cap

ADULT (NONBREEDING)

broad stripes on cheek and ear

mostly yellowish bill

JUVENILE

broad head with crest at rear

black cap

brown eye

grayish white cheeks and throat

chestnut brown neck and chest

gray flanks

ADULT (BREEDING)

The Red-necked Grebe is smaller than Western and Clark's Grebes, but larger than the other North American grebes. It migrates over short to medium distances and spends the winter along both coasts, where large flocks may be seen during the day. It runs along the water's surface to become airborne, although it rarely flies. This grebe doesn't come ashore often; it stands erect, but walks awkwardly, and prefers to sink to its breast and shuffle along.

VOICE Nasal, gull-like call on breeding grounds, evolves into bray, ends with whinny; also honks, rattles, hisses, purrs, and ticks.

NESTING Compact, buoyant mound of decayed and fresh vegetation in sheltered, shallow marshes and lakes, or artificial wetlands; 4–5 eggs; 1 brood; May–July.

FEEDING An opportunistic hunter, eats fish, crustaceans, aquatic insects, worms, mollusks, salamanders, and tadpoles.

FLIGHT: fast, direct, wing beats, with head and outstretched neck mostly level with line of body.

COURTSHIP DISPLAY
This courting pair face each other, with outstreched necks and raised chests.

SIMILAR SPECIES

RED-THROATED LOON ❄
see p.77

white spots on back
white neck
no yellow on bill

HORNED GREBE ❄
see p.95

reddish eye
paler neck

OCCURRENCE
Breeds from northern prairies and forests, almost to the tree line in the northwest; limited to suitable interior bodies of water such as large marshes and small lakes. Winters primarily in estuaries, inlets, bays, and offshore shallows along Atlantic and Pacific Coasts; can also be found on the Great Lakes.

Length **16½–22in (42–56cm)**	Wingspan **24–35in (61–88cm)**	Weight **1¾–3½lb (0.8–1.6kg)**
Social **Pairs/Loose flocks**	Lifespan **Up to 6 years**	Status **Vulnerable**

Order **Podicipediformes**	Family **Podicipedidae**	Species ***Podiceps auritus***

Horned Grebe

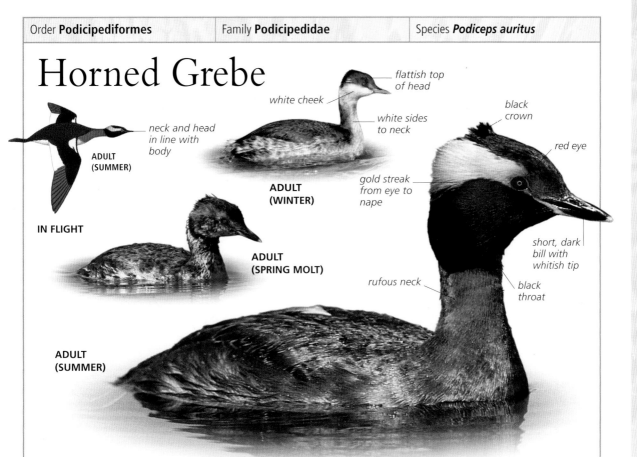

neck and head in line with body

ADULT (SUMMER)

IN FLIGHT

white cheek

flattish top of head

white sides to neck

ADULT (WINTER)

ADULT (SPRING MOLT)

black crown

red eye

gold streak from eye to nape

short, dark bill with whitish tip

rufous neck

black throat

ADULT (SUMMER)

The timing of the Horned Grebe's migration depends largely on the weather—this species may not leave until its breeding grounds get iced over, nor does it arrive before the ice melts. Its breeding behavior is well documented since it is approachable on nesting grounds and has an elaborate breeding ritual. This grebe's so-called "horns" are in fact yellowish feather patches located behind its eyes, which it can raise at will.

VOICE At least 10 calls, but descending *aaanrrh* call most common in winter, ends in trill; muted conversational calls when birds are in groups.

NESTING Floating, soggy nest, hidden in vegetation, in small ponds and lake inlets; 3–9 eggs; 1 brood; May–July.

FEEDING Dives in open water or forages among plants, mainly for small crustaceans and insects, but also leeches, mollusks, amphibians, fish, and some vegetation.

FLIGHT: strong, rapid wing beats; runs on water to become airborne; rarely takes off from land.

HITCHING A RIDE
In common with other grebes, Horned Grebe chicks often ride on the back of a swimming parent.

SIMILAR SPECIES

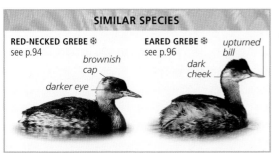

RED-NECKED GREBE ❄
see p.94
brownish cap
darker eye

EARED GREBE ❄
see p.96
upturned bill
dark cheek

OCCURRENCE
Breeds in small freshwater, even slightly brackish, ponds and marshes, including man-made ponds. Prefers areas with open water and patches of sedges, cattails, and other wetland vegetation in any ecosystem. Winters on saltwater close to shore; also on large bodies of freshwater.

Length **12–15in (30–38cm)**	Wingspan **18–24in (46–62cm)**	Weight **11–20oz (300–575g)**
Social **Pairs/Loose flocks/Colonies**	Lifespan **Up to 5 years**	Status **Declining**

Order **Podicipediformes**	Family **Podicipedidae**	Species ***Podiceps nigricollis***

Eared Grebe

white patch on wing
ADULT (SUMMER)
out-stretched neck
dusky white flanks
IN FLIGHT
darker flanks
browner plumage
JUVENILE
dusky cheek
upturned bill
grayish neck
ADULT (WINTER)
black crest
red eye
large, wispy gold patch behind red eye
thin, upturned bill
dark back
black neck
rufous breast and sides
ADULT (SUMMER)

The most abundant grebe in North America, the Eared Grebe is quite remarkable in terms of physiology. After breeding, it undergoes a complex and drastic reorganization of body-fat stores, along with changes in muscle, heart, and digestive organ mass to prepare it for fall migration. All of this increases the bird's energy reserves and body mass, but renders it flightless. It may have the longest periods of flightlessness of any flying bird—up to 10 months.

VOICE Various trills during courtship, including squeaky, rising *poo-eep*; sharp *chirp* when alarmed; usually silent at other times.

NESTING Sodden nest of decayed bottom plants anchored in thinly spaced reeds or submerged vegetation in shallow water of marshes, ponds, and lakes; 1 brood; 1–8 eggs; May–July.

FEEDING Forages underwater for small crustaceans and aquatic insects; also small fish and mollusks; consumes worms in winter.

FLIGHT: flies with neck out-stretched, held at a low angle; rarely flies except during migration.

SALTY WATER
The Eared Grebe prefers salty water at all times except when breeding.

SIMILAR SPECIES

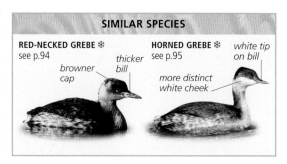

RED-NECKED GREBE ❄ see p.94
browner cap
thicker bill

HORNED GREBE ❄ see p.95
white tip on bill
more distinct white cheek

OCCURRENCE
Breeds in marshes, shallow lakes, and ponds in the four western provinces. After breeding, many birds seek highly saline, slow-to-freeze waters, such as Mono Lake, where their favorite foods thrive—brine shrimp and alkali flies. Winters in coastal bays of Pacific coast and is a vagrant on the Atlantic coast.

Length **12–14in (30–35cm)**	Wingspan **22½–24in (57–62cm)**	Weight **7–26oz (200–725g)**
Social **Flocks**	Lifespan **Up to 12 years**	Status **Secure**

Order **Podicipediformes**	Family **Podicepedidae**	Species ***Aechmophorus occidentalis***

Western Grebe

black nape stripe
ADULT
whitish band on dark wing
IN FLIGHT
dark patch around eyes
light gray back
light white-gray neck
CHICK
black crown extends below eye
distinctive red eye
long, slender, slightly upturned greenish yellow bill
black nape stripe
dark gray back
ADULT
brilliant white throat, breast, and belly

Western and Clark's Grebes are strictly North American species. They share much of their breeding habitat and elaborate mating rituals, and were, until 1985, classified as different color forms of a single species. Interbreeding is uncommon, perhaps because of slight differences in calls, bill colors, and facial patterns. Although hybrids are rare, they appear to be fertile, and produce chicks of their own. Female Western Grebes are smaller than males and have smaller, thinner, slightly upturned bills. The Western Grebe dives more frequently than Clark's, and remains submerged for about 30 seconds.

VOICE Nine calls, each with a specific purpose, such as alarm, begging, and mating calls; advertising call a harsh, rolling two-noted *krrrikk krrreek.*

NESTING Floating pile of available plants, attached to thick growth of submerged vegetation; occasionally constructed on land; 2–3 eggs; 1 brood; May–July.

FEEDING Mainly catches a wide variety of freshwater or saltwater fish; also crustaceans, worms, occasionally insects.

FLIGHT: fast and direct with rapid wing beats; neck extended with feet stretched out behind.

SELF-DEFENSE
The posture of this the Western Grebe shows it is ready to defend itself when threatened.

SIMILAR SPECIES

CLARK'S GREBE
see p.98

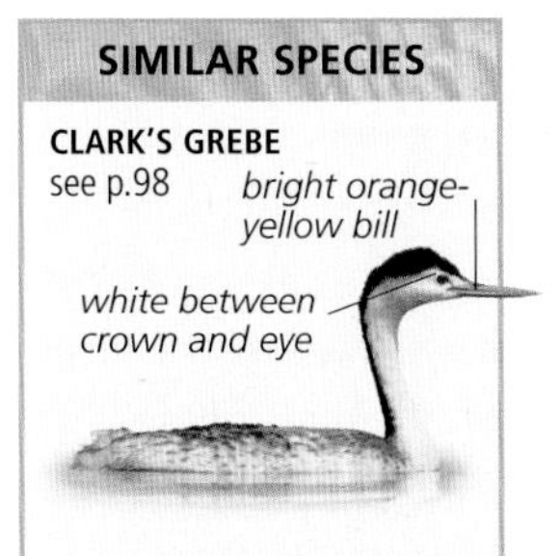
bright orange-yellow bill
white between crown and eye

HIGHLY SOCIAL
Western Grebes, much like Clark's Grebes, are highly gregarious in all seasons.

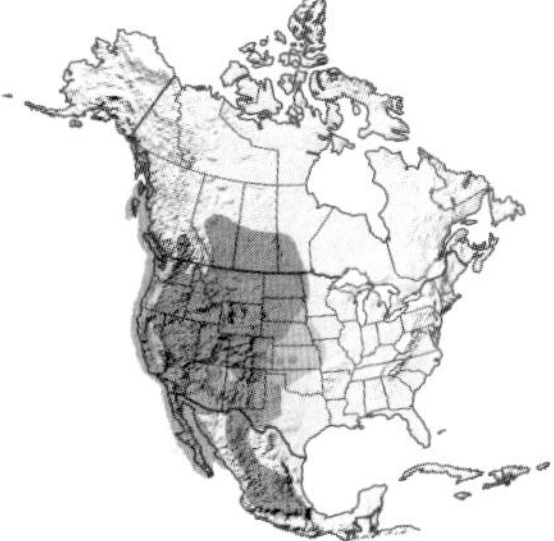

OCCURRENCE
Western North America, breeds from southern Canada to Mexico, in freshwater lakes and marshes with open water and emergent vegetation; rarely on tidewater marshes; also man-made marshes and artificial habitats. Winters along Pacific Coast, in bays and estuaries in the southwest US and Mexico.

Length **21½–30in (55–75cm)**	Wingspan **30–39in (76–100cm)**	Weight **1¾–4lb (0.8–1.8kg)**
Social **Flocks**	Lifespan **At least 15 years**	Status **Declining**

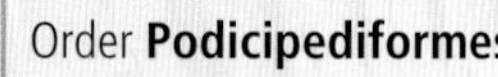

Order **Podicipediformes**	Family **Podicipedidae**	Species ***Aechmophorus clarkii***

Clark's Grebe

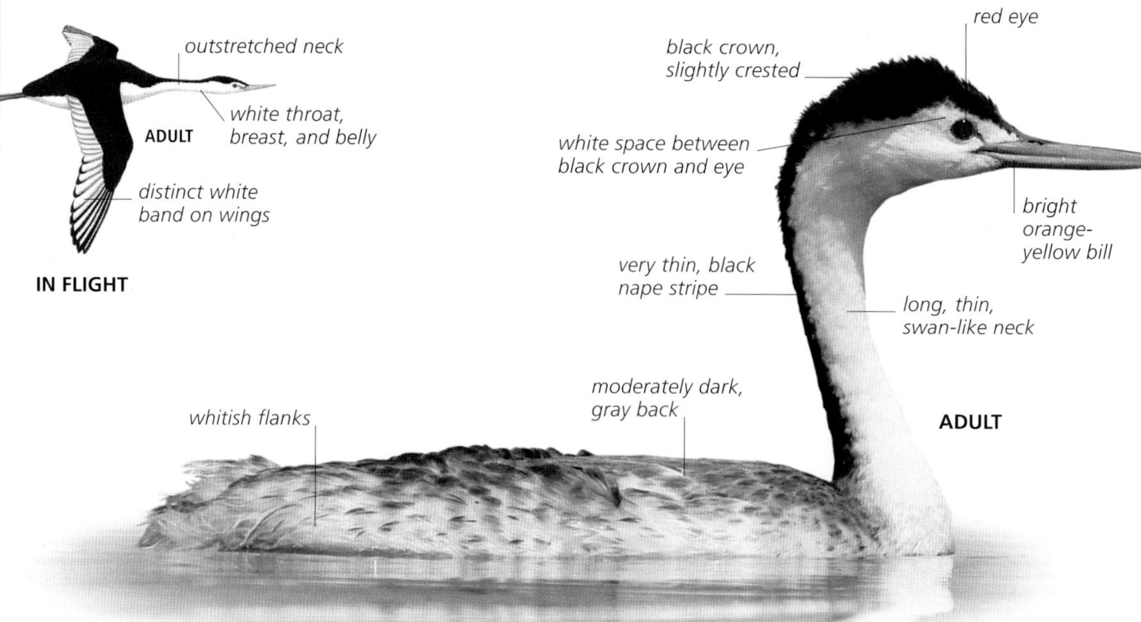
outstretched neck
white throat, breast, and belly
ADULT
distinct white band on wings
IN FLIGHT
red eye
black crown, slightly crested
white space between black crown and eye
bright orange-yellow bill
very thin, black nape stripe
long, thin, swan-like neck
moderately dark, gray back
whitish flanks
ADULT

Clark's and Western grebes are closely related and very difficult to distinguish. They rarely fly except when migrating at night. Both species seldom come to land, where their movement is awkward because their legs and toes are located so far back, although they have been reported to run upright rapidly. Their flight muscles suffer wastage after their arrival on the breeding grounds, which also inhibits their ability to travel, but during the incubation period adults may feed several miles from the colony by following continuous water trails.

VOICE Variety of different calls, including a harsh, reedy, grating, two-syllable, single, rising *kree-eekt* advertising call.

NESTING Floating pile of available plants, attached to thick growth of submerged vegetation; occasionally constructed on land; 2–3 eggs; 1 brood; May-July.

FEEDING Mainly catches saltwater or freshwater fish; also crustaceans.

FLIGHT: swift and direct with quick wing beats; neck extended with feet trailing.

HOW TO SWALLOW?
It is not unusual for grebes to catch large fish; they crush the head first before swallowing.

FORAGING IN DEEP WATER
Clark's Grebe has a distinctive white S-shaped neck and black crown.

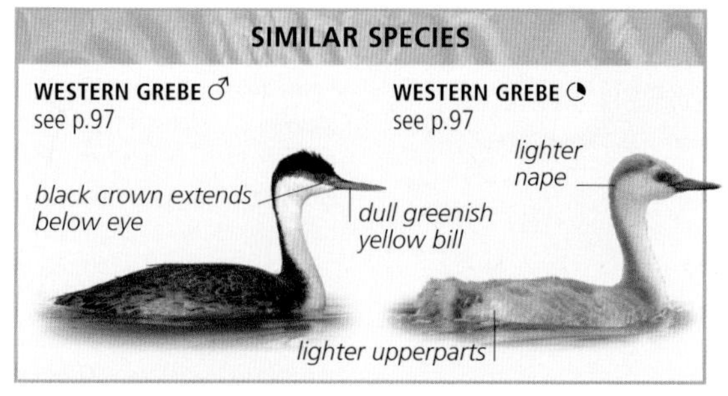
SIMILAR SPECIES
WESTERN GREBE ♂
see p.97
WESTERN GREBE ◔
see p.97
black crown extends below eye
dull greenish yellow bill
lighter nape
lighter upperparts

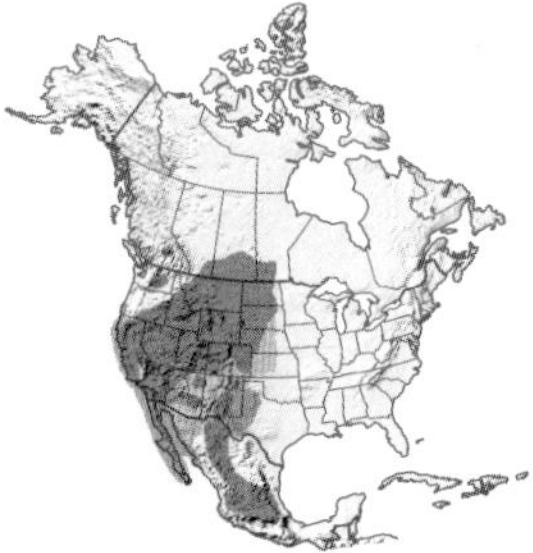

OCCURRENCE
Breeds in freshwater lakes and marshes with open water bordered by emergent vegetation; rarely tidewater marshes; has been nesting in man-made Lake Havasu marshes since 1960s. Winters along Pacific Coast, and in bays and estuaries in the southwest US and Mexico.

Length **21½–30in (55–75cm)**	Wingspan **32in (82cm)**	Weight **1½–3¾lb (0.7–1.7kg)**
Social **Flocks**	Lifespan **At least 15 years**	Status **Declining**

IBISES & HERONS

THESE ARE LARGE, WATER and wetland birds that have long legs and look rather similar, but have different habits. They eat fish and other aquatic prey as well as plants. Most breed in colonies.

IBISES

Birds of the waterside or dry land, ibises (Threskiornithidae) are characterized by rounded bodies, medium-long legs and strong feet that allow an easy, long-striding walk, short tails, rounded wings, and small, often bare, heads on curved necks, merging into long, curved bills. Gregarious birds, they fly in long lines or "V" formation. Ibises feed mostly on insects, worms, small mollusks, and crustaceans, probing for them in the water and wet mud.

EYE-CATCHING IBIS
The White-faced Ibis, a vagrant in Canada, has a distinctive white patch around its eye in the breeding season.

BITTERNS, HERONS, AND EGRETS

These are mostly waterside birds (Ardeidae) with long, slender toes, broad, rounded wings, very short tails, forward-facing eyes, and dagger-shaped bills. Bitterns and night-herons have a shawl of smooth, dense neck feathers, while an egret's long, slender neck is tightly feathered, with an obvious "kink" that allows a lightning-fast stab for prey. Bitterns, herons, and egrets fly with their legs trailing and their necks coiled back into their shoulders. Some make obvious bulky treetop nests and feed in the open, while others, especially bitterns, nest and feed secretively. In fact, often the only clue to a bittern's presence in a dense reedbed is the haunting, booming call it makes to keep in touch with its mate.

EVER ALERT
The Green Heron stalks fish by watching and waiting patiently until prey is near.

DANCING ON AIR
The Great Egret's courtship display often involves spreading its wings and leaping in a kind of aerial dance.

Order **Ciconiiformes**	Family **Threskiornithidae**	Species ***Plegadis falcinellus***

Glossy Ibis

outstretched neck
trailing legs
ADULT (BREEDING)
IN FLIGHT

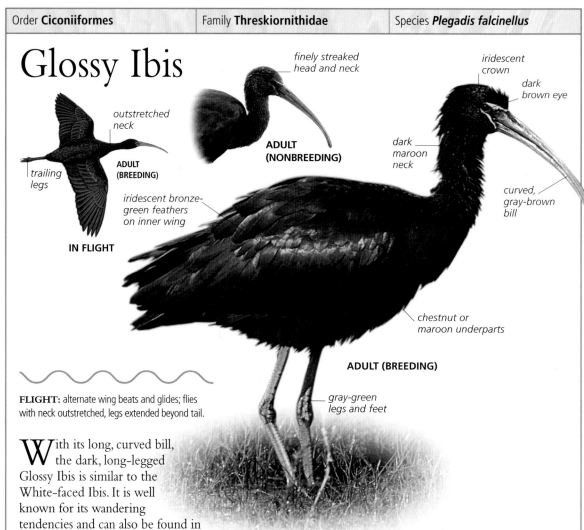

finely streaked head and neck
ADULT (NONBREEDING)

iridescent crown
dark brown eye
dark maroon neck
curved, gray-brown bill
iridescent bronze-green feathers on inner wing
chestnut or maroon underparts
ADULT (BREEDING)
gray-green legs and feet

FLIGHT: alternate wing beats and glides; flies with neck outstretched, legs extended beyond tail.

With its long, curved bill, the dark, long-legged Glossy Ibis is similar to the White-faced Ibis. It is well known for its wandering tendencies and can also be found in southern Europe, Asia, Australia, and Africa. Despite being found in the US in the mid-19th century, the Glossy Ibis was not discovered nesting in Florida until 1886. Confined to Florida until the mid-20th century, it then started spreading northward, eventually as far as southern Ontario and across into Nova Scotia.

VOICE Crow-like croak; subdued nasal chatter in flocks; mostly silent.

NESTING Platform of twigs and reeds in trees, shrubs, or reeds, on ground or over water; 3–4 eggs; 1 brood; April–July.

FEEDING Forages by feel, puts bill in soil and mud to catch prey, including snails, insects, leeches, frogs, and crayfish.

MARSH FEEDER
The Glossy Ibis regularly feeds in shallow pools and along the waterways of coastal marshes.

SIMILAR SPECIES

WHITE-FACED IBIS see p.492

BLACK-CROWNED NIGHT-HERON ◔ see p.103

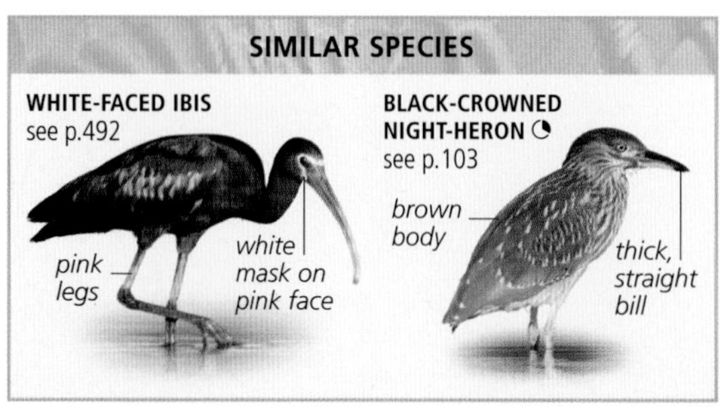
pink legs
white mask on pink face
brown body
thick, straight bill

OCCURRENCE
Common from New England south to Florida but has spread north into the eastern provinces. Occurs in brackish and freshwater marshes and in flooded or plowed fields; feeds with other waders in inland freshwater wetlands as well as coastal lagoons and estuaries.

Length **23in (59cm)**	Wingspan **36in (92cm)**	Weight **13oz (375g)**
Social **Flocks/Colonies**	Lifespan **15–20 years**	Status **Secure (p)**

Order **Ciconiiformes**	Family **Ardeidae**	Species ***Botaurus lentiginosus***

American Bittern

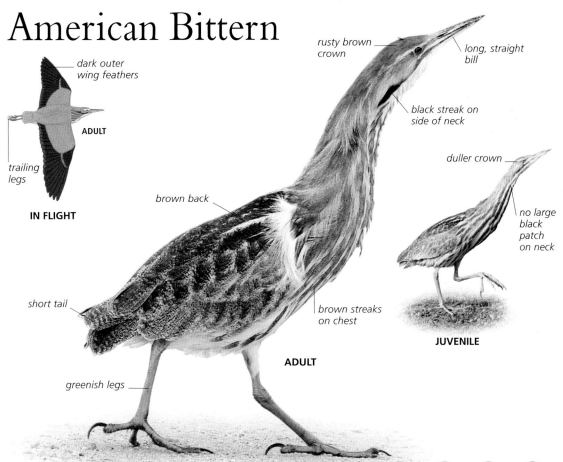

dark outer wing feathers

ADULT

trailing legs

IN FLIGHT

rusty brown crown

long, straight bill

black streak on side of neck

brown back

short tail

brown streaks on chest

greenish legs

ADULT

duller crown

no large black patch on neck

JUVENILE

The American Bittern's camouflaged plumage and secretive behavior help it to blend into the thick vegetation of its freshwater wetland habitat. It is heard much more often than it is seen; its call is unmistakable and has given rise to many evocative colloquial names, such as "thunder pumper."

FLIGHT: steady, deep, slightly stiff wing beats; usually flies relatively low and direct.

VOICE Deep, resonant *pump-er-unk, pump-er-unk*; calls mainly at dawn, dusk, and night time, but also during the day in the early mating season.

NESTING Platform or mound constructed of available marsh vegetation, usually over shallow water; 2–7 eggs; 1 brood; April–August.

FEEDING Stands still or moves slowly, then strikes downward with bill to catch prey; eats fish, insects, crustaceans, snakes, amphibians, and small mammals.

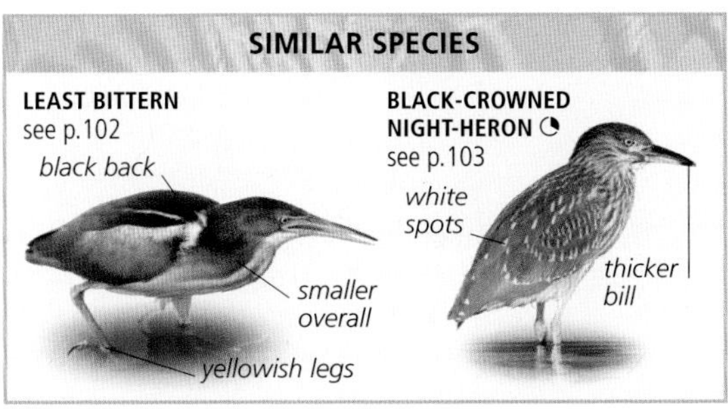
SIMILAR SPECIES
LEAST BITTERN
see p.102
black back
smaller overall
yellowish legs
BLACK-CROWNED NIGHT-HERON
see p.103
white spots
thicker bill

LOOKING UP
Bitterns are secretive birds, but can occasionally be found walking slowly through reeds.

OCCURRENCE
Breeds in heavily vegetated freshwater wetlands across the northern US and southern Canada; also occasionally in estuarine wetlands; winters in southern and coastal wetlands where temperatures stay above freezing; can appear in any wetland habitat during migration.

Length **23½–31in (60–80cm)**	Wingspan **3½–4¼ft (1.1–1.3m)**	Weight **13–20oz (375–575g)**
Social **Solitary**	Lifespan **At least 8 years**	Status **Declining**

Order **Ciconiiformes**	Family **Ardeidae**	Species ***Ixobrychus exilis***

Least Bittern

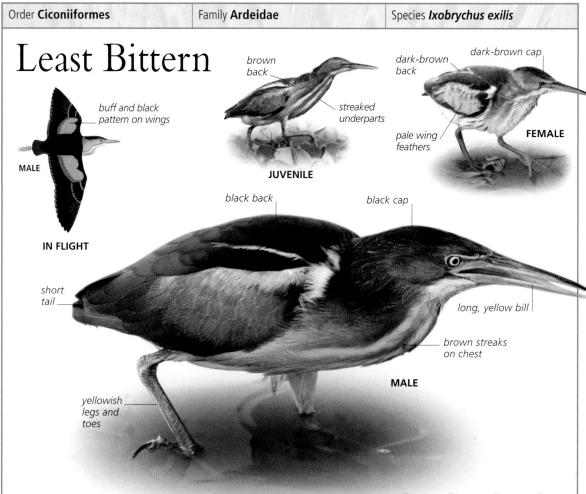

buff and black pattern on wings
MALE
IN FLIGHT
brown back
streaked underparts
JUVENILE
dark-brown back
dark-brown cap
pale wing feathers
FEMALE
black back
black cap
short tail
long, yellow bill
brown streaks on chest
yellowish legs and toes
MALE

The smallest heron in North America, the Least Bittern is also one of the most colorful, but its secretive nature makes it easy to overlook in its densely vegetated marsh habitat. A dark color form, which was originally described in the 1800s as a separate species named Cory's Bittern, has rarely been reported in recent decades.

VOICE Soft *ku, ku, ku, ku, ku* display call; year-round, a loud *kak, kak, kak.*

NESTING Platform of marsh vegetation with sticks and stems added, usually within 30ft (9m) of open water; 2–7 eggs; 1 brood; April–August.

FEEDING Feeds on small fish, insects including dragonflies; also crustaceans; clings quietly to vegetation before striking prey, or stalks slowly.

FLIGHT: rapid wing beats; weak, direct flight; flies low, around top of vegetation.

REED CREEPER
With its small, thin body, this species easily creeps through dense reeds in search of prey.

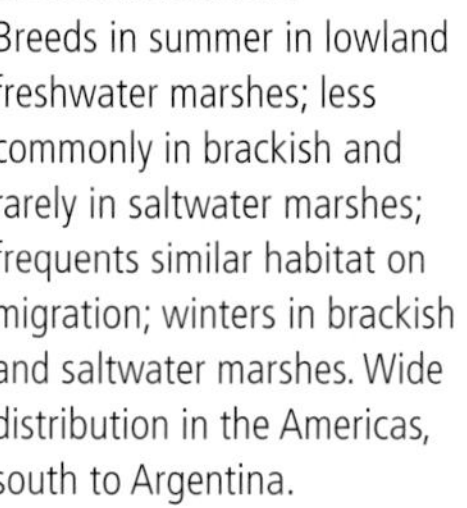

OCCURRENCE
Breeds in summer in lowland freshwater marshes; less commonly in brackish and rarely in saltwater marshes; frequents similar habitat on migration; winters in brackish and saltwater marshes. Wide distribution in the Americas, south to Argentina.

SIMILAR SPECIES

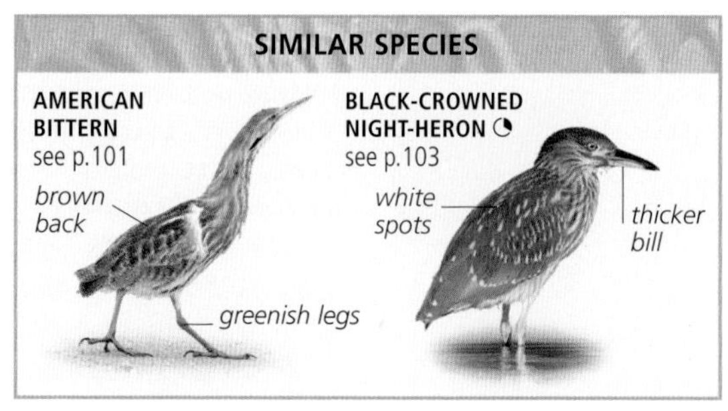
AMERICAN BITTERN
see p.101
brown back
greenish legs
BLACK-CROWNED NIGHT-HERON
see p.103
white spots
thicker bill

Length **11–14in (28–36cm)**	Wingspan **15½–18in (40–46cm)**	Weight **2⅝–3⅜oz (75–95g)**
Social **Solitary/Small flocks**	Lifespan **Unknown**	Status **Secure**

Order **Ciconiiformes**	Family **Ardeidae**	Species ***Nycticorax nycticorax***

Black-crowned Night-Heron

gray wings
heavily speckled back and wings
ADULT
JUVENILE
broad, rounded wings
IN FLIGHT

long, white head plumes
black back
white spots on brown back
pale lower bill
JUVENILE
black crown
short, thick bill
short neck
yellow legs; red in spring
ADULT

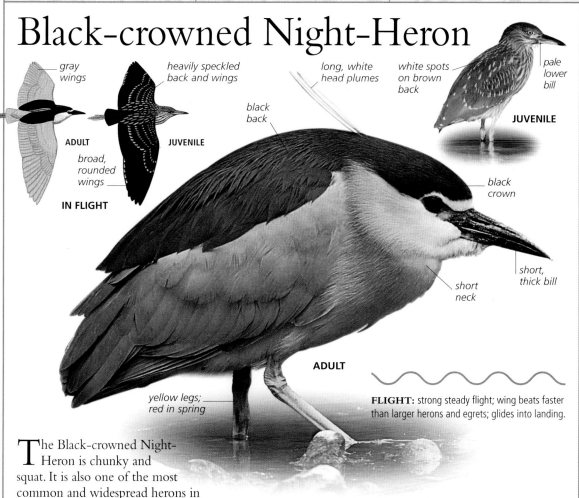

FLIGHT: strong steady flight; wing beats faster than larger herons and egrets; glides into landing.

The Black-crowned Night-Heron is chunky and squat. It is also one of the most common and widespread herons in North America and in the world. But because, as its name suggests, it is mainly active at twilight and at night, many people have never seen one. However, its distinctive barking call can be heard at night—even at the center of large cities.

VOICE Loud, distinctive *quark* or *wok*, often given in flight and around colonies.

NESTING Large stick nests built usually 20–40ft (6–12m) up in trees; 3–5 eggs; 1 brood; November–August.

FEEDING Feeds primarily on aquatic animals, such as fish, crustaceans, insects, and mollusks; also eggs and chicks of colonial birds, such as egrets, ibises, and terns.

LONG PLUMES
In breeding plumage, the plumes of the male of this species are longer than the female's.

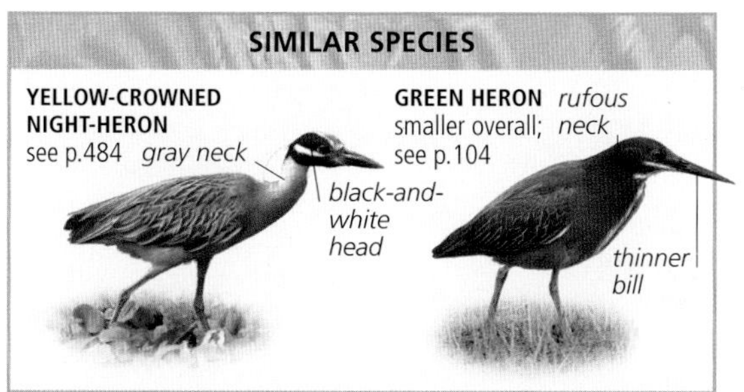
SIMILAR SPECIES
YELLOW-CROWNED NIGHT-HERON
see p.484
gray neck
black-and-white head
GREEN HERON
smaller overall;
see p.104
rufous neck
thinner bill

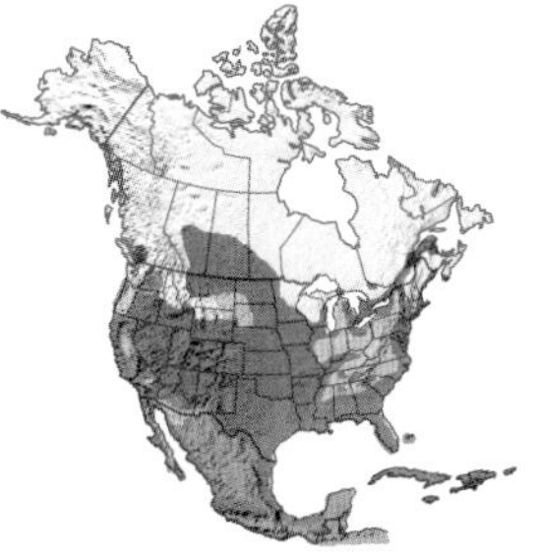

OCCURRENCE
Widespread; can be found wherever there are waterbodies, such as lakes, ponds, streams; generally absent from higher elevations. Colonies often on islands or in marshes; colony sites may be used for decades. In winter, found in areas where water remains open.

Length **23–26in (58–65cm)**	Wingspan **3½–4ft (1.1–1.2m)**	Weight **1½–2½lb (0.7–1kg)**
Social **Colonies**	Lifespan **Up to 21 years**	Status **Secure**

Order **Ciconiiformes**	Family **Ardeidae**	Species ***Butorides virescens***

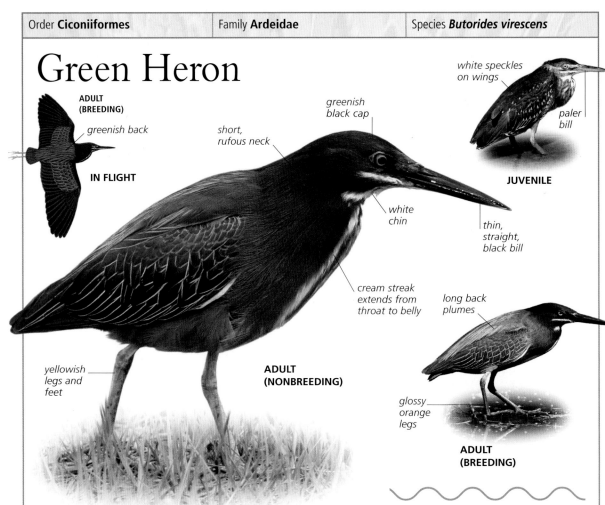

Green Heron

ADULT (BREEDING)

greenish back

IN FLIGHT

short, rufous neck

greenish black cap

white speckles on wings

paler bill

JUVENILE

white chin

thin, straight, black bill

cream streak extends from throat to belly

long back plumes

yellowish legs and feet

ADULT (NONBREEDING)

glossy orange legs

ADULT (BREEDING)

A small, solitary, and secretive bird of dense thicketed wetlands, the Green Heron can be difficult to observe. This dark, crested heron is most often seen flying away from a perceived threat, emitting a loud squawk. While the Green Heron of North and Central America has now been recognized as a separate species, it was earlier grouped with the Green-backed Heron (*B. striatus*), which is found in the tropics and subtropics throughout the world.

VOICE Squawking *keow* when flying from disturbance.

NESTING Nest of twigs often in bushes or trees, often over water but also on land; 1–2 broods; 3–5 eggs; March–July.

FEEDING Stands quietly on the shore or in shallow water and strikes quickly; mainly fish, but also frogs, insects, and spiders.

FLIGHT: direct, a bit plodding, and usually over short distances.

READY TO STRIKE
Green Herons usually catch their prey by lunging forward and downward with their whole body.

SIMILAR SPECIES

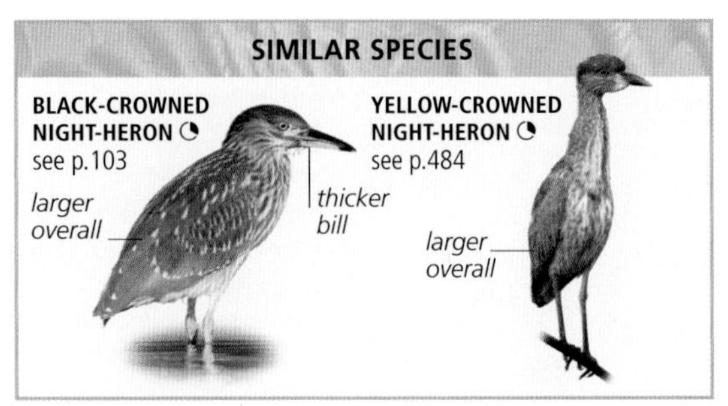
BLACK-CROWNED NIGHT-HERON
see p.103
larger overall
thicker bill
YELLOW-CROWNED NIGHT-HERON
see p.484
larger overall

OCCURRENCE
An inhabitant of swampy thickets, but occasionally dry land close to water across much of North America, but missing in the plains, the Rocky Mountains, and the western deserts that do not provide appropriate wetlands. Winters in coastal wetlands.

Length **14½–15½in (37–39cm)**	Wingspan **25–27in (63–68cm)**	Weight **7–9oz (200–250g)**
Social **Solitary/Pairs/Small flocks**	Lifespan **Up to 10 years**	Status **Secure**

Order **Ciconiiformes**	Family **Ardeidae**	Species ***Bubulcus ibis***

Cattle Egret

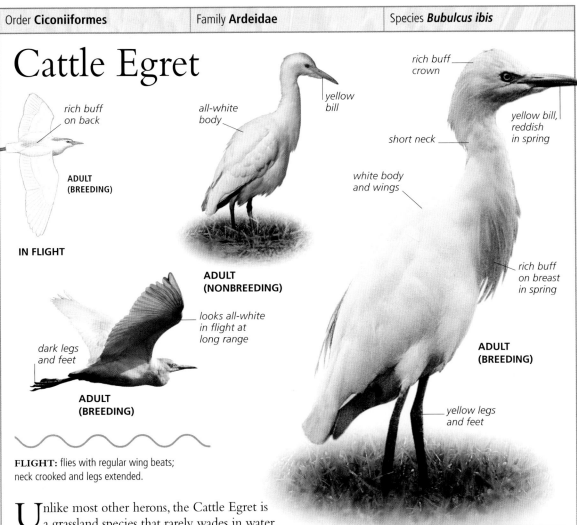

rich buff on back

ADULT (BREEDING)

IN FLIGHT

all-white body

yellow bill

ADULT (NONBREEDING)

rich buff crown

yellow bill, reddish in spring

short neck

white body and wings

rich buff on breast in spring

ADULT (BREEDING)

yellow legs and feet

looks all-white in flight at long range

dark legs and feet

ADULT (BREEDING)

FLIGHT: flies with regular wing beats; neck crooked and legs extended.

Unlike most other herons, the Cattle Egret is a grassland species that rarely wades in water, and is often seen with livestock, feeding on the insects disturbed by their feet. It is thought to have originated in the shortgrass prairies of Africa and is now found worldwide. It was first seen in Florida in 1941, but expanded rapidly and has now bred in over 40 US states and up into the southern provinces of Canada.

VOICE Generally silent; vocal at the nest: *rick-rack* common.

NESTING Nest of branches or plants placed in trees over ground; also in trees or shrubs over water; 2–5 eggs; 1 brood; March–October.

FEEDING Eats in groups, consumes insects, spiders as well as larger animals such as frogs; insects stirred up in grasslands by cattle.

VOCAL BREEDERS
This bird almost never calls away from a breeding colony, but is vocal near its nests.

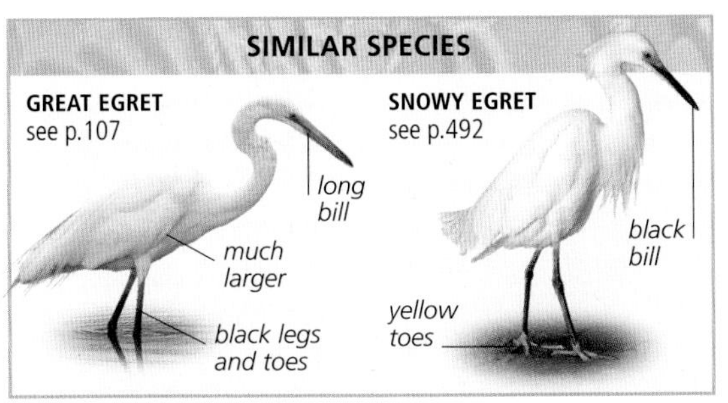
SIMILAR SPECIES
GREAT EGRET
see p.107
long bill
much larger
black legs and toes
SNOWY EGRET
see p.492
black bill
yellow toes

OCCURRENCE
Since the 1940s, it has expanded to many habitats in much of North America, primarily in grasslands and prairies, but also wetland areas. In tropical regions, the Cattle Egrets flock around the cattle feeding in shallow wetlands.

Length **20in (51cm)**	Wingspan **31in (78cm)**	Weight **13oz (375g)**
Social **Colonies**	Lifespan **Up to 17 years**	Status **Secure**

Order **Ciconiiformes**	Family **Ardeidae**	Species ***Ardea herodias***

Great Blue Heron

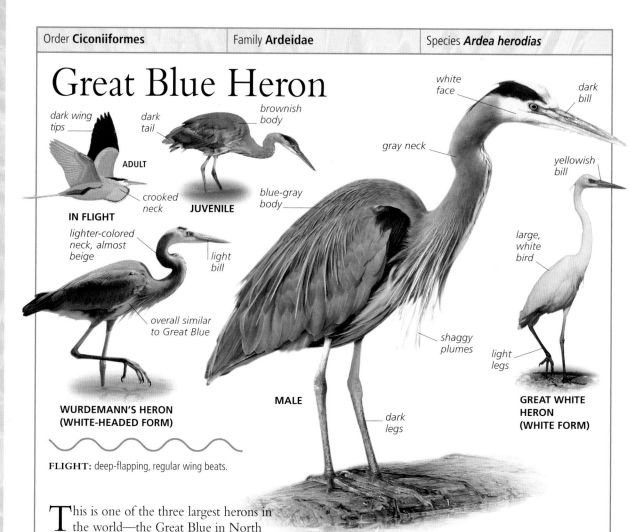

dark wing tips
ADULT
crooked neck
IN FLIGHT
dark tail
brownish body
JUVENILE
lighter-colored neck, almost beige
light bill
overall similar to Great Blue
WURDEMANN'S HERON (WHITE-HEADED FORM)
white face
dark bill
gray neck
blue-gray body
shaggy plumes
dark legs
MALE
yellowish bill
large, white bird
light legs
GREAT WHITE HERON (WHITE FORM)

FLIGHT: deep-flapping, regular wing beats.

This is one of the three largest herons in the world—the Great Blue in North America, the Gray in Eurasia, and the Cocoi in South America—all of which are all interrelated, but classified separately. The Great Blue Heron is a common inhabitant of a variety of North American waterbodies, from marshes to swamps, as well as along sea coasts. Its majestic, deliberate flight is a highly wonderful sight to behold.

VOICE Mostly silent; gives a loud, barking squawk or *crank* in breeding colonies or when disturbed.

NESTING Nest of twigs and branches; usually in colonies, but also singly; in trees, often over water, but also over ground; 2–4 eggs; 1–2 broods; February–August.

FEEDING Catches prey with quick jab of bill; primarily fish.

LOFTY ABODE
Great Blue Herons nest in small colonies in trees, and often roost in them.

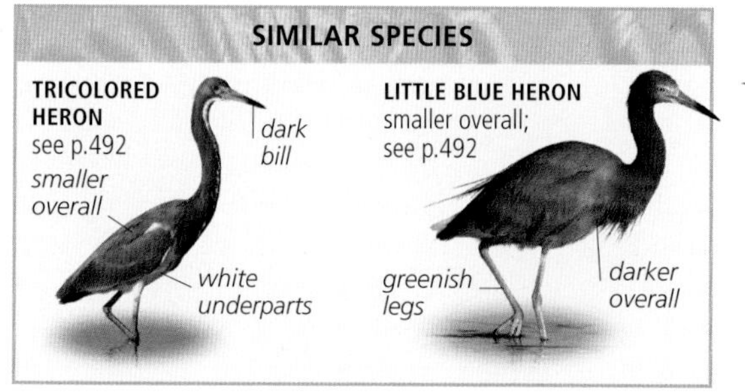
SIMILAR SPECIES
TRICOLORED HERON
see p.492
dark bill
smaller overall
white underparts
LITTLE BLUE HERON
smaller overall;
see p.492
greenish legs
darker overall

OCCURRENCE
Across southern Canada and the US in wetlands, such as marshes, lake edges, and along rivers and swamps; also in marine habitats, especially tidal grass flats. The Great White Heron is primarily found in marine habitats.

Length **2¾–4¼ft (0.9–1.3m)**	Wingspan **5¼–6½ft (1.6–2m)**	Weight **4¾–5½lb (2.1–2.5kg)**
Social **Solitary/Flocks**	Lifespan **Up to 20 years**	Status **Secure**

Order **Ciconiiformes**	Family **Ardeidae**	Species ***Ardea alba***

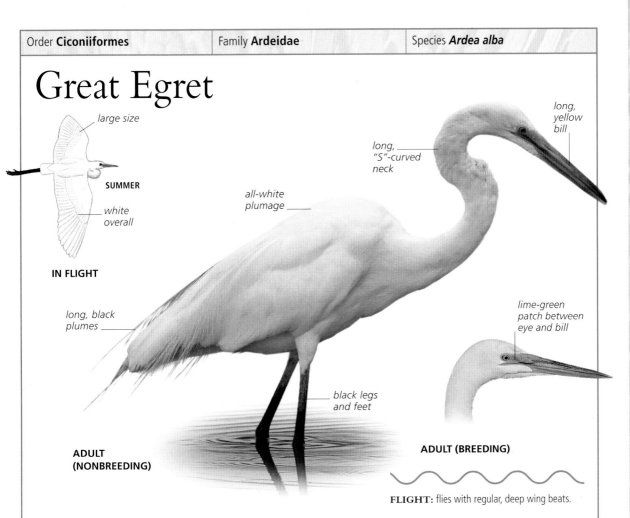

Great Egret

large size

SUMMER

white overall

IN FLIGHT

long, yellow bill

long, "S"-curved neck

all-white plumage

long, black plumes

black legs and feet

ADULT (NONBREEDING)

lime-green patch between eye and bill

ADULT (BREEDING)

FLIGHT: flies with regular, deep wing beats.

This large white heron is found on every continent except Antarctica. When feeding, the Great Egret would apparently rather forage alone than in flocks—it maintains space around itself, and will defend a territory of 10ft (3m) in diameter from other wading birds. This territory "moves" with the bird as it feeds. In years of scarce food supplies, a chick may kill a sibling, permitting the survival of at least one bird.

VOICE Largely vocal during courtship and breeding; otherwise, *kraak* or *cuk-cuk-cuk* when disturbed or in a combative encounter.

NESTING Nest of twigs in trees, over land or water; 2–4 eggs; 1 brood; March–July.

FEEDING Catches prey with quick thrust of bill; feeds on aquatic prey, primarily fish, also crustaceans.

TREE PERCHES

Great Egrets nest in trees and regularly perch in them when not feeding.

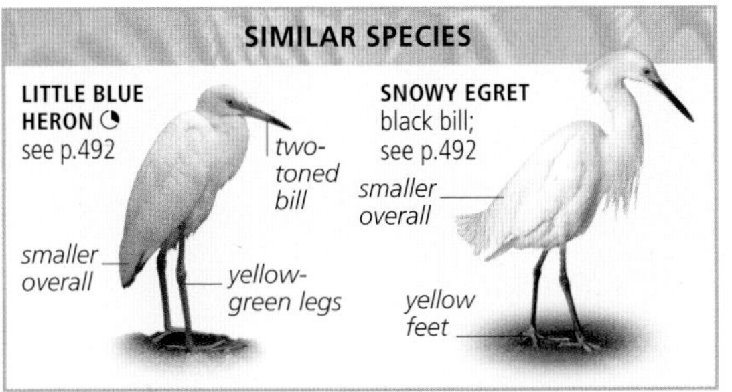
SIMILAR SPECIES
LITTLE BLUE HERON
see p.492
two-toned bill
smaller overall
yellow-green legs
SNOWY EGRET
black bill;
see p.492
smaller overall
yellow feet

OCCURRENCE

Breeds in trees over water or on islands; forages in almost all types of freshwater and marine wetlands from marshes and ponds to rivers. Migratory over much of its North American range; more southerly populations resident. Distance migrated depends on severity of winter.

Length **3¼ft (1m)**	Wingspan **6ft (1.8m)**	Weight **1¾–3¼ft (0.8–1.5kg)**
Social **Solitary**	Lifespan **Up to 25 years**	Status **Secure**

Families **Pelecanidae, Sulidae, Phalacrocoracidae**

PELICANS & RELATIVES

PELICANS AND THEIR relatives belong to an order of large to huge fish-eating birds, Pelecaniformes, with four toes connected by leathery webs, and with fleshy, elastic pouches beneath their bills.

PELICANS

The pelican family includes seven large species, two of which—the American White Pelican and the Brown Pelican—are North American. All pelicans are buoyant swimmers and excellent fliers, capable of great lift on their long, broad wings with wing feathers spread. Flocks can be seen soaring to great heights on migration and when flying to feeding grounds. They feed by sweeping with open bills for fish, often cooperatively, or by plunging from a height to scoop up fish and water in their large, flexible bill pouches.

CORMORANTS

With 36 species worldwide, these are medium to large waterbirds, some marine, others freshwater, with broad, long wings, rounded tails, short, strong legs and hook-tipped bills often tilted upward when swimming. In flight, the neck is extended but noticeably kinked. When hunting for fish, cormorants dive from the surface of the water, rolling smoothly under or with a noticeable forward leap, and then swim underwater with closed wings, using their webbed toes for propulsion. Most are dark birds, apart from some distinctive facial patterns on areas of bare skin which become more colorful in spring. Most cormorants nest on cliff ledges, although some prefer trees; others are happy to use both cliffs and trees. There is one flightless cormorant species in the Galápagos.

DARK PLUMAGE
Grooming for this Double-crested Cormorant includes spreading its wings to dry them in the sun.

WATER BIRD
Webbed feet help Brown Pelicans, a vagrant species in Canada, negotiate water with ease.

Order **Pelecaniformes**	Family **Pelecanidae**	Species ***Pelecanus erythrorhynchos***

American White Pelican

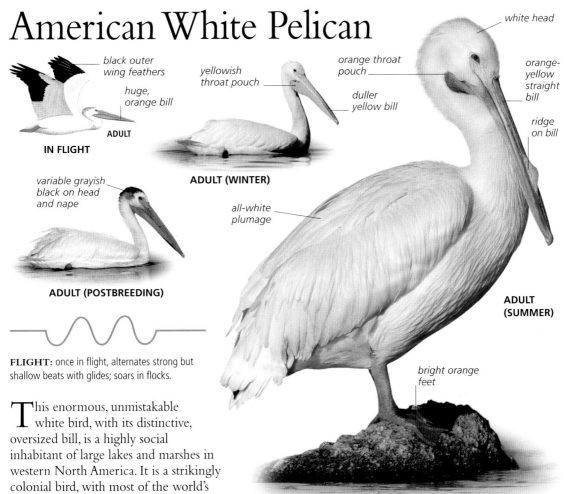

black outer wing feathers
huge, orange bill
ADULT
IN FLIGHT

yellowish throat pouch
duller yellow bill
ADULT (WINTER)

variable grayish black on head and nape
ADULT (POSTBREEDING)

white head
orange throat pouch
orange-yellow straight bill
ridge on bill
all-white plumage
bright orange feet
ADULT (SUMMER)

FLIGHT: once in flight, alternates strong but shallow beats with glides; soars in flocks.

This enormous, unmistakable white bird, with its distinctive, oversized bill, is a highly social inhabitant of large lakes and marshes in western North America. It is a strikingly colonial bird, with most of the world's population being concentrated in just a handful of large colonies in isolated wetland complexes in deserts and prairies. The American White Pelican forms foraging flocks, which beat their wings in coordinated movements to drive fish into shallow water, where they can be caught more easily.

VOICE Usually silent except around nesting colonies; around the nest, young and adults exchange various grunts and hisses.

NESTING Depression in the ground, both sexes incubate; 1–2 eggs; 1 brood; April–August.

FEEDING Mainly gulps down small fish, occasionally eats small amphibians, and crayfish.

LARGE COLONIES
The White Pelican is highly social and is usually seen feeding or roosting in large groups.

SIMILAR SPECIES

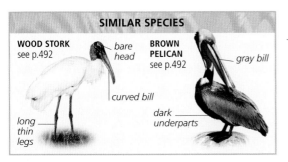

WOOD STORK
see p.492
bare head
curved bill
long thin legs

BROWN PELICAN
see p.492
gray bill
dark underparts

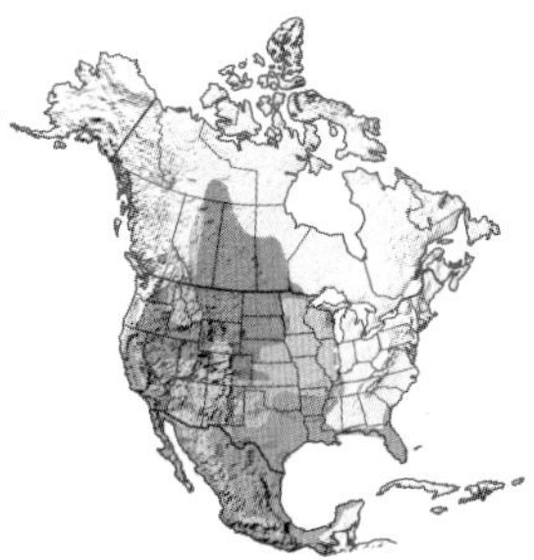

OCCURRENCE
Breeds on islands in freshwater lakes in south-central Canada, mountainous areas of the western US, and in coastal northeast Mexico; an early spring migrant, often returning to breeding grounds in early March. Winters in coastal regions from California and Texas to Mexico and Central America.

Length **4¼–5½ft (1.3–1.7m)**	Wingspan **7¾–9½ft (2.4–2.9m)**	Weight **12–20lb (5.5–9kg)**
Social **Colonies**	Lifespan **Up to 26 years**	Status **Vulnerable**

Order **Pelecaniformes**	Family **Sulidae**	Species ***Morus bassanus***

Northern Gannet

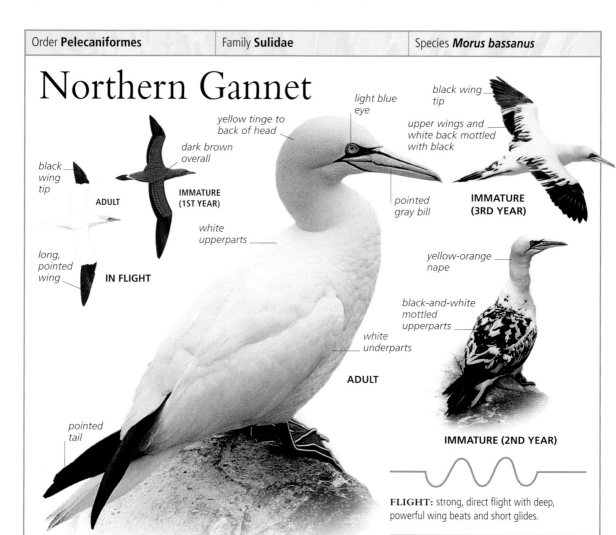

black wing tip
ADULT
dark brown overall
IMMATURE (1ST YEAR)
long, pointed wing
IN FLIGHT
yellow tinge to back of head
light blue eye
pointed gray bill
white upperparts
white underparts
pointed tail
ADULT
black wing tip
upper wings and white back mottled with black
IMMATURE (3RD YEAR)
yellow-orange nape
black-and-white mottled upperparts
IMMATURE (2ND YEAR)

FLIGHT: strong, direct flight with deep, powerful wing beats and short glides.

The Northern Gannet is known for its spectacular headfirst dives during frantic, voracious foraging in flocks of hundreds to thousands for surface-schooling fish. This bird nests in just six locations in northeastern Canada. The Northern Gannet was the first species to have its total world population estimated, at 83,000 birds in 1939. Numbers have since increased.

VOICE Loud landing call by both sexes *arrrr*, *arrah*, or *urrah rah rah*; hollow groan *oh-ah* uttered during take-off; *krok* call at sea.

NESTING Large pile of mud, seaweed, and rubbish, glued with guano, on bare rock or soil; 1 egg; 1 brood; April–November.

FEEDING Plunge-dives headfirst into water and often swims underwater to catch fish; eats mackerel, herring, capelin, and cod.

NESTING SITE
Northern Gannets prefer to nest in huge, noisy colonies on isolated rocky slopes or cliffs.

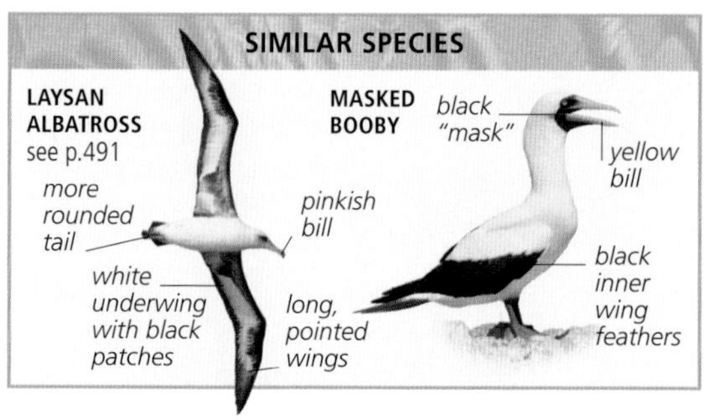
SIMILAR SPECIES
LAYSAN ALBATROSS
see p.491
more rounded tail
white underwing with black patches
pinkish bill
long, pointed wings
MASKED BOOBY
black "mask"
yellow bill
black inner wing feathers

OCCURRENCE
Breeds on isolated rock stacks, on small uninhabited islands in the eastern North Atlantic, or on steep, inaccessible cliffs in marine areas of northeast North America; during migration and in winter, can be found in the waters of the continental shelf of the Gulf and Atlantic coast.

Length **2¾–3½ft (0.8–1.1m)**	Wingspan **5½ft (1.7m)**	Weight **5–8lb (2.2–3.6kg)**
Social **Flocks**	Lifespan **Up to 20 years**	Status **Localized**

Order **Pelecaniformes**	Family **Phalacrocoracidae**	Species ***Phalacrocorax penicillatus***

Brandt's Cormorant

black overall

ADULT (BREEDING)

outstretched neck

IN FLIGHT

no facial whiskers

lacks blue chin

relatively short tail

ADULT (NONBREEDING)

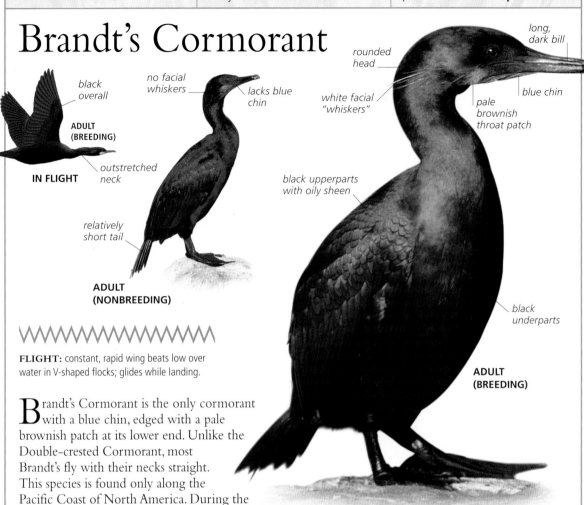

long, dark bill

rounded head

white facial "whiskers"

blue chin

pale brownish throat patch

black upperparts with oily sheen

black underparts

ADULT (BREEDING)

FLIGHT: constant, rapid wing beats low over water in V-shaped flocks; glides while landing.

Brandt's Cormorant is the only cormorant with a blue chin, edged with a pale brownish patch at its lower end. Unlike the Double-crested Cormorant, most Brandt's fly with their necks straight. This species is found only along the Pacific Coast of North America. During the breeding season, it depends heavily on food from the nutrient-rich upwellings of the California Current. Named after a German who was the director of the zoological museum in St. Petersburg, Russia, this species is at risk from commercial fishing, pollution, and recreational disturbance.

VOICE Emits croaks, growls, gargles and coughing sounds.

NESTING Circular, drum-shaped nest of grass, moss, weeds, seaweed, sticks, and rubbish, on gentle slopes of islands or ledges on cliffs; 1–6 eggs; 1 brood; April–August.

FEEDING Dives and chases after surface- and bottom-dwelling fish; grasps fish in bill, crushes it, and swallows it head-first.

DRYING OUT
Like all cormorants, this species stretches its wings to drain its soggy feathers after diving for fish.

SIMILAR SPECIES

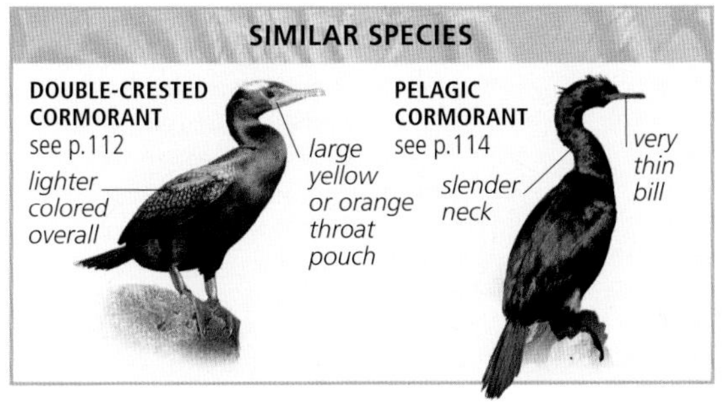
DOUBLE-CRESTED CORMORANT
lighter colored overall
large yellow or orange throat pouch

DOUBLE-CRESTED CORMORANT see p.112

PELAGIC CORMORANT
slender neck
very thin bill

PELAGIC CORMORANT see p.114

OCCURRENCE
Breeding colonies are found on offshore or near-shore islands or on mainland promontories on the Pacific coast of North America occasionally found in inshore lagoons; winters in sheltered inlets and other protected waters or on open ocean within 1 mile (1.6km) of land.

Length **28–31in (70–79cm)**	Wingspan **3½ft (1.1m)**	Weight **3–6lb (1.4–2.7kg)**
Social **Flocks/Colonies**	Lifespan **Up to 18 years**	Status **Secure**

Order **Pelecaniformes**	Family **Phalacrocoracidae**	Species ***Phalacrocorax auritus***

Double-crested Cormorant

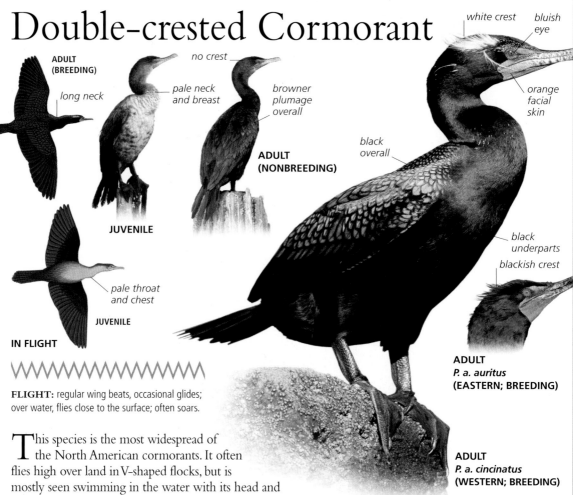

ADULT (BREEDING)
long neck
pale neck and breast
JUVENILE
no crest
browner plumage overall
ADULT (NONBREEDING)
white crest
bluish eye
orange facial skin
black overall
black underparts
ADULT ***P. a. auritus*** **(EASTERN; BREEDING)**
blackish crest
ADULT ***P. a. cincinatus*** **(WESTERN; BREEDING)**
pale throat and chest
JUVENILE
IN FLIGHT

FLIGHT: regular wing beats, occasional glides; over water, flies close to the surface; often soars.

This species is the most widespread of the North American cormorants. It often flies high over land in V-shaped flocks, but is mostly seen swimming in the water with its head and neck visible, or resting on trees and rocks, sometimes with its wings spread. While fishing, it dives from the surface of the water and chases fish underwater, using its webbed toes for propulsion.

VOICE Deep gruntlike calls while nesting, roosting, and fishing; *t-t-t-t* call before taking off and *urg-urg-urg* before landing; prolonged *arr-r-r-r-r-t-t* while mating, and *eh-hr* as threat.

NESTING Nests of twigs and sticks, seaweed, and trash, lined with grass; built on ground, cliffs, or in trees usually in colonies; 3-5 eggs; 1 brood; April–August.

FEEDING Pursues slow-moving or schooling fish; feeds on insects, crustaceans, amphibians, and, rarely, on voles and snakes.

DRYING OFF
Like all cormorants, the Double-crested usually perches with wings spread, to dry its feathers.

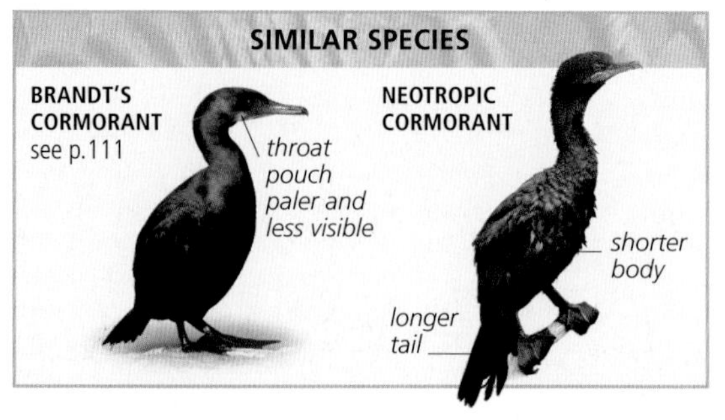
SIMILAR SPECIES
BRANDT'S CORMORANT
see p.111
throat pouch paler and less visible
NEOTROPIC CORMORANT
shorter body
longer tail

OCCURRENCE
Breeds in a wide range of aquatic habitats, including ponds, artificial and natural lakes, slow-moving rivers, estuaries, lagoons, and seashores; winters on coastlines and sandbars in coastal inlets; roosts near catfish farms in some areas.

Length **28–35in (70–90cm)**	Wingspan **3½–4ft (1.1–1.2m)**	Weight **2¾–5½lb (1.2–2.5kg)**
Social **Flocks**	Lifespan **Up to 18 years**	Status **Secure**

Order **Pelecaniformes**	Family **Phalacrocoracidae**	Species ***Phalacrocorax carbo***

Great Cormorant

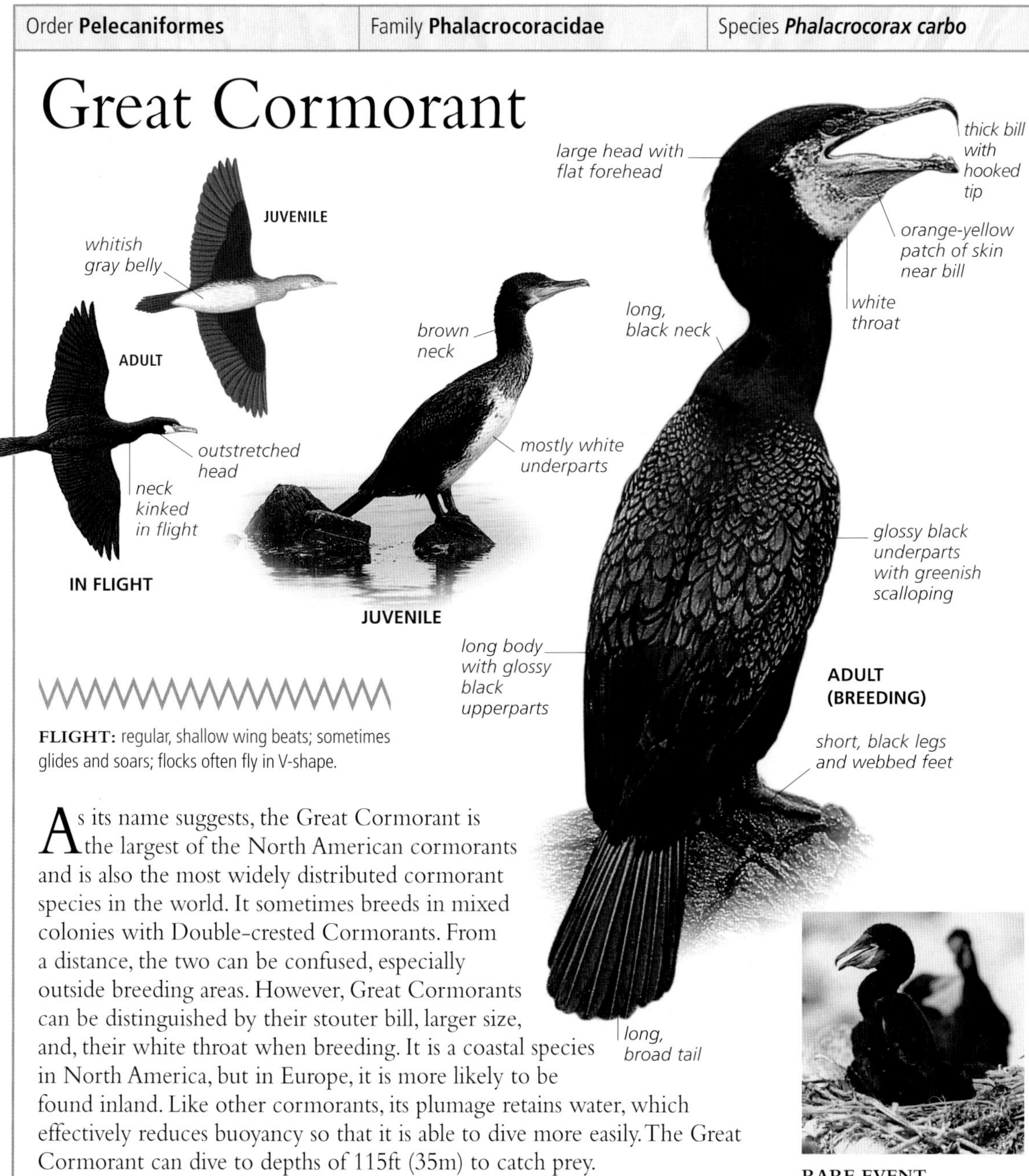

JUVENILE
whitish gray belly
ADULT
outstretched head
neck kinked in flight
IN FLIGHT
brown neck
mostly white underparts
JUVENILE
large head with flat forehead
thick bill with hooked tip
orange-yellow patch of skin near bill
white throat
long, black neck
glossy black underparts with greenish scalloping
long body with glossy black upperparts
ADULT (BREEDING)
short, black legs and webbed feet
long, broad tail

FLIGHT: regular, shallow wing beats; sometimes glides and soars; flocks often fly in V-shape.

As its name suggests, the Great Cormorant is the largest of the North American cormorants and is also the most widely distributed cormorant species in the world. It sometimes breeds in mixed colonies with Double-crested Cormorants. From a distance, the two can be confused, especially outside breeding areas. However, Great Cormorants can be distinguished by their stouter bill, larger size, and, their white throat when breeding. It is a coastal species in North America, but in Europe, it is more likely to be found inland. Like other cormorants, its plumage retains water, which effectively reduces buoyancy so that it is able to dive more easily. The Great Cormorant can dive to depths of 115ft (35m) to catch prey.

VOICE Deep, guttural calls at nesting and roosting site; otherwise silent.

NESTING Mound of seaweed, sticks, and debris added to previous year's nest, built on cliff ledges and flat tops of rocks above high-water mark on islands; 3–5 eggs; 1 brood; April–August.

FEEDING Dives to pursue fish and small crustaceans; smaller prey swallowed underwater, while larger prey brought to surface.

SIMILAR SPECIES

DOUBLE-CRESTED CORMORANT see p.112
thinner bill
black throat

RARE EVENT
Great Cormorants usually nest on sea cliffs; tree breeding is rare in North America.

OCCURRENCE
Breeds on cliff ledges of islands along rocky coasts, in northeast US and Maritimes of Canada; feeds in protected inshore waters. Winters in shallow coastal waters similar to breeding habitat, but not restricted to rocky shoreline; winter habitat extends to the Carolinas in the US.

Length **33–35in (84–90cm)**	Wingspan **4¼–5¼ft (1.3–1.6m)**	Weight **5¾–8¼lb (2.6–3.7kg)**
Social **Colonies**	Lifespan **Up to 14 years**	Status **Secure**

Order **Pelecaniformes**	Family **Phalacrocoracidae**	Species ***Phalacrocorax pelagicus***

Pelagic Cormorant

outstretched head and tail level in flight
small head
ADULT
IN FLIGHT

all-dark face
thin, pale bill
blackish breast and belly
brownish bronze upperparts
IMMATURE

tufts on crown and nape
red patch at base of bill
thin, dark bill with blunt or hooked end
glossy purple tinge on neck
long, thin neck with white flecks
glossy green to greenish bronze on upperparts
iridescent greenish black underparts
ADULT (BREEDING)
long, blackish tail
white patch on flank

FLIGHT: rapid with regular, steady wing beats; glides before landing.

The Pelagic Cormorant is the smallest cormorant species in North America. Although a marine bird, its English (and scientific) name, *pelagicus*, meaning "oceanic," is misleading because this bird mostly inhabits inshore waters. This bird is most visible at its roosting sites, where it spends much of its time drying its feathers. The Pelagic Cormorant has not been well studied, because it is more solitary than the other cormorant species in North America; however, like all cormorants, it is threatened by the disturbance of its nesting colonies, oil spills, entanglement in fishing nets, and pollution.

VOICE Female two-note call *igh-ugh*, similar to ticking grandfather clock; male call note *purring* or *arr-arr-arr;* both utter croaks, hisses, and low groans.

NESTING Saucer-shaped nest of grass, seaweed, sticks, feathers, and marine debris, cemented to cliff face with guano; 3–5 eggs; 1 brood; May–October.

FEEDING Dives from water's surface for any medium-sized fish, and also invertebrates, such as shrimps, worms, and hermit crabs.

SITTING LOW
Pelagic Cormorants sit low in the water with only their head, neck, and back visible.

SIMILAR SPECIES

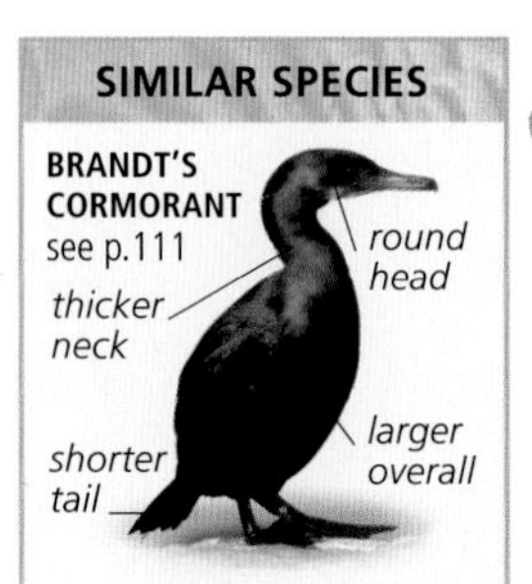
BRANDT'S CORMORANT
see p.111
round head
thicker neck
larger overall
shorter tail

OCCURRENCE
Found in rocky habitat on outer coast, shallow bays, inlets, estuaries, harbors, and lagoons; nesting colonies found on steep cliffs on forested and grassy islands, and on rocky promontories along the shoreline; also seen on built structures such as wharf pilings, bridges, and harbor buoys.

Length **20–30in (51–76cm)**	Wingspan **3¼–4ft (1–1.2m)**	Weight **2¾–5¼lb (1.3–2.4kg)**
Social **Solitary/Pairs**	Lifespan **Up to 17 years**	Status **Secure**

BIRDS OF PREY

THE DEFINING FEATURES of birds of prey, or raptors, but not vultures, are strong feet with sharp talons for catching and holding prey, and a powerful, hooked bill for tearing the catch to pieces.

VULTURES

Of the seven New World species of vulture, only one occurs in Canada: the smaller Turkey Vulture, which has an acute sense of smell that enables it to detect carrion hidden from sight beneath the forest canopy. Now nesting in abandoned farmhouses, this vulture can stay in the air for hours on end, using the lift provided by updrafts to minimize the energy spent on wing flapping.

WEAK TOOL
In spite of its sharp beak, the Turkey Vulture cannot always break the skin of carcasses.

FALCONS

Ranging in size from the diminutive Merlin, with northern breeding habitats, to the large, powerful Gyrfalcon, which nests in the Arctic, this group also includes the American Kestrel, the Prairie Falcon, and perhaps the best-known raptor of all—the fast-diving Peregrine Falcon. Falcon prey ranges from insects to large mammals and birds.

EAGLES AND HAWKS

This group covers a wide range of raptors of varying sizes, from the the iconic Bald Eagle and the majestic Golden Eagle to smaller birds, such as the Northern Harrier, and various hawks and kites. These birds use a wide range of hunting methods. Forest-dwelling hawks, for example, rely on speed and stealth to pounce on small birds among the trees in a sudden, short dash. The Osprey, by contrast, hovers over water until it sees a fish below, then dives steeply, pulling up at the last moment to pluck its prey clean out of the water with its talons.

DOUBLE SHOT
When there are lots of fish running in a tight school, the Osprey has the strength and skill to catch two with one dive.

Order **Ciconiiformes**	Family **Cathartidae**	Species ***Cathartes aura***

Turkey Vulture

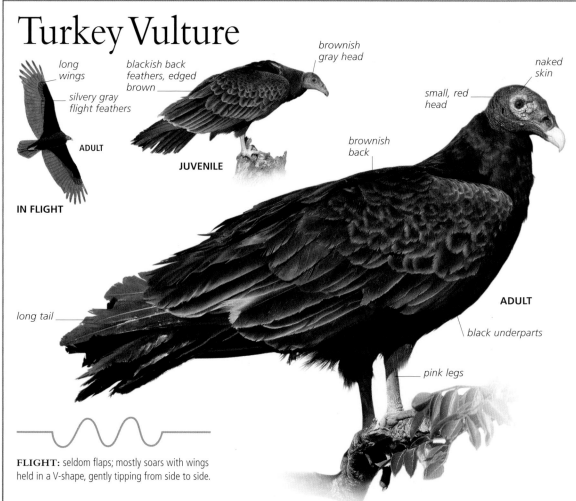

long wings
silvery gray flight feathers
ADULT
IN FLIGHT

blackish back feathers, edged brown
brownish gray head
JUVENILE

naked skin
small, red head
brownish back
long tail
ADULT
black underparts
pink legs

FLIGHT: seldom flaps; mostly soars with wings held in a V-shape, gently tipping from side to side.

The most widely distributed vulture in North America, the Turkey Vulture is found in most of the US and has expanded its range into southern Canada. It possesses a better sense of smell than the Black Vulture, which often follows it and displaces it from carcasses. The Turkey Vulture's habit of defecating down its legs, which it shares with the Wood Stork, may serve to cool it or to kill bacteria with its ammonia content.

VOICE Silent, but will hiss at intruders; also grunts.

NESTING Dark recesses, such as under large rocks or stumps, on rocky ledges in caves, and crevices, in mammal burrows and hollow logs, and abandoned buildings; 1–3 eggs; 1 brood; March–August.

FEEDING Feeds on a wide range of wild and domestic carrion, mostly mammals, also birds, reptiles, amphibians, and fish; occasionally takes live prey such as nestlings or trapped birds.

SOAKING UP THE SUN
Turkey Vultures often spread their wings to sun themselves and increase their body temperature.

SIMILAR SPECIES

BLACK VULTURE
see p.492
all-black body
shorter tail

OCCURRENCE
Generally forages and migrates over mixed farmland and forest; prefers to nest in forested or partly forested hillsides offering hidden ground protected from disturbance; roosts in large trees such as cottonwoods, on rocky outcrops, and on power line transmission towers; some winter in urban areas and near landfills.

Length **25–32in (64–81cm)**	Wingspan **5½–6ft (1.7–1.8m)**	Weight **4½lb (2kg)**
Social **Flocks**	Lifespan **At least 17 years**	Status **Secure**

Order **Falconiformes**	Family **Falconidae**	Species ***Falco sparverius***

American Kestrel

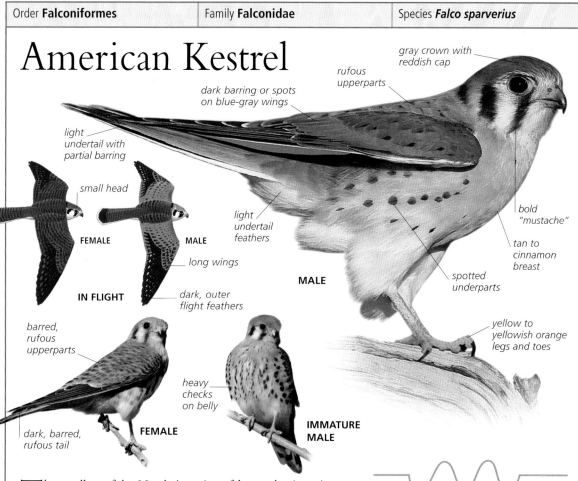

gray crown with reddish cap
rufous upperparts
dark barring or spots on blue-gray wings
light undertail with partial barring
small head
FEMALE
MALE
light undertail feathers
bold "mustache"
tan to cinnamon breast
long wings
MALE
spotted underparts
IN FLIGHT
dark, outer flight feathers
barred, rufous upperparts
yellow to yellowish orange legs and toes
heavy checks on belly
dark, barred, rufous tail
FEMALE
IMMATURE MALE

The smallest of the North American falcons, the American Kestrel features long pointed wings, a "tooth and notch" bill structure, and the dark brown eyes typical of falcons, though kestrels have shorter toes than other falcons. This may be due to the fact that kestrels often dive into long grass to capture insects and small mammals, which would be more difficult with long, thin toes. Male and female American Kestrels show differences in plumage, and also in size.

VOICE Common call a high-pitched *killy-killy-killy*.

NESTING Natural cavities, crevices, holes in dead trees, woodpeckers' holes, crevices in barns, manmade nest boxes if constructed and located properly; 4–5 eggs; 1 brood; April–June.

FEEDING Plunges for grasshoppers and crickets in spring and summer; small birds and mice in fall and winter; lizards and snakes.

FLIGHT: delicate and almost mothlike; may hover in one place for long, searching for prey.

HIGH FLIER

A male American Kestrel hovers over a field, its sharp eyes scanning the ground for insects and rodents.

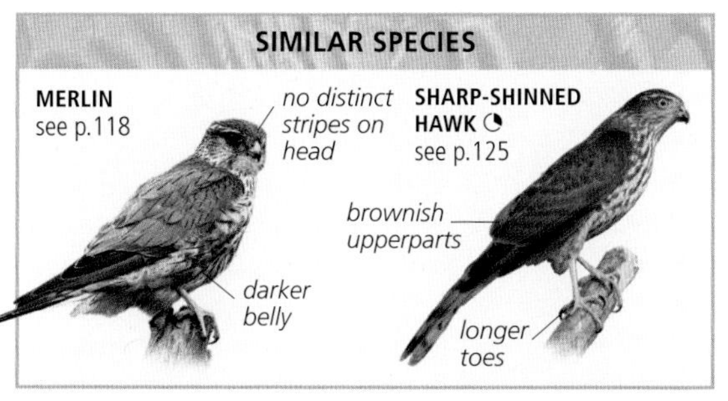
SIMILAR SPECIES
MERLIN
see p.118
no distinct stripes on head
SHARP-SHINNED HAWK
see p.125
brownish upperparts
darker belly
longer toes

OCCURRENCE

From near the northern tree line in Alaska and Canada south, east, and west throughout most of North America. Occurs also in Central and South America. Habitat ranges from semi-open tree groves to grasslands, cultivated and fallow farmland, and open desert.

Length **9in (23cm)**	Wingspan **22in (56cm)**	Weight **3½–4oz (100–125g)**
Social **Family groups**	Lifespan **10–15 years**	Status **Secure**

Order **Falconiformes**	Family **Falconidae**	Species ***Falco columbarius***

Merlin

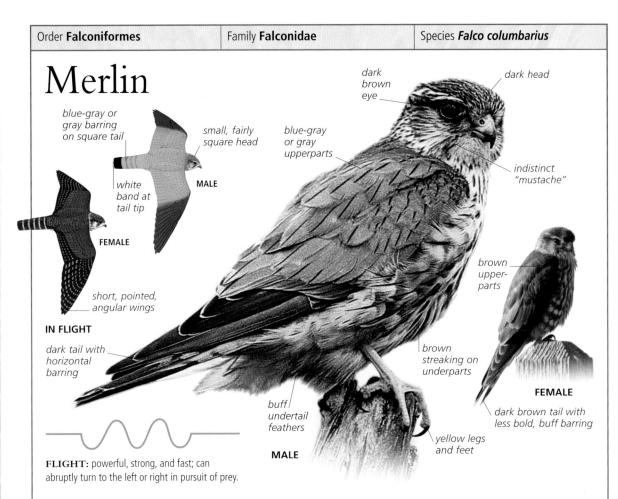

blue-gray or gray barring on square tail

small, fairly square head

white band at tail tip

MALE

FEMALE

short, pointed, angular wings

IN FLIGHT

dark brown eye

dark head

blue-gray or gray upperparts

indistinct "mustache"

brown upper-parts

dark tail with horizontal barring

brown streaking on underparts

FEMALE

buff undertail feathers

dark brown tail with less bold, buff barring

yellow legs and feet

MALE

FLIGHT: powerful, strong, and fast; can abruptly turn to the left or right in pursuit of prey.

Merlins are small, fast-flying falcons that were formerly known as "pigeon hawks," because their shape and flight are similar to those strong fliers. Merlins can overtake and capture a wide variety of prey. They can turn on a dime, and use their long, thin toes, typical of falcons, to pluck birds from the air after launching a direct attack. Males are smaller than females, and different in color. Both males and females show geographical color variations.

VOICE Male call a high-pitched *ki-ki-ki-ki*; female call a low-pitched *kek-ek-ek-ek-ek*.

NESTING Small scrapes on ground in open country, or abandoned nests of other species, such as crows, in forested areas; 4–6 eggs; 1 brood; April–June.

FEEDING Catches small birds in midair, and occasionally birds as large as doves; also feeds on small mammals, including bats.

ABOUT TO ROUSE

An adult female Merlin sits on a moss-covered rock, about to "rouse," or fluff out and shake her feathers.

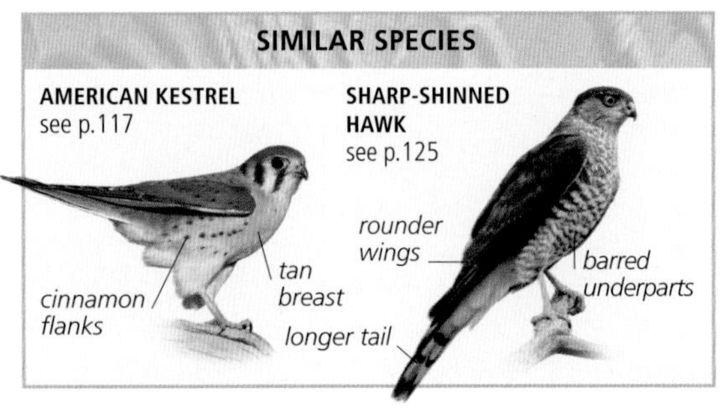
SIMILAR SPECIES
AMERICAN KESTREL
see p.117
SHARP-SHINNED HAWK
see p.125
rounder wings
tan breast
barred underparts
cinnamon flanks
longer tail

OCCURRENCE

Breeds from northern Alaska and the Pacific Northwest across Canada to Newfoundland. Winters mostly in western states down into Mexico. Merlins can be seen hunting along coastlines, over marshlands and open fields, and in desert areas.

Length **10in (25cm)**	Wingspan **24in (61cm)**	Weight **5–7oz (150–200g)**
Social **Pairs/Family groups**	Lifespan **10–15 years**	Status **Secure**

Order **Falconiformes** | Family **Falconidae** | Species ***Falco rusticolus***

Gyrfalcon

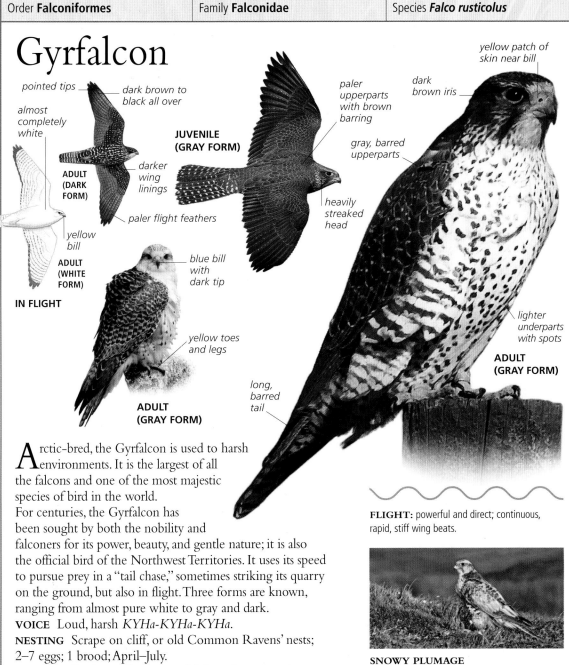

pointed tips
dark brown to black all over
almost completely white
ADULT (DARK FORM)
darker wing linings
paler flight feathers
yellow bill
ADULT (WHITE FORM)
IN FLIGHT

JUVENILE (GRAY FORM)
paler upperparts with brown barring
heavily streaked head

blue bill with dark tip
yellow toes and legs
ADULT (GRAY FORM)

yellow patch of skin near bill
dark brown iris
gray, barred upperparts
lighter underparts with spots
long, barred tail
ADULT (GRAY FORM)

Arctic-bred, the Gyrfalcon is used to harsh environments. It is the largest of all the falcons and one of the most majestic species of bird in the world. For centuries, the Gyrfalcon has been sought by both the nobility and falconers for its power, beauty, and gentle nature; it is also the official bird of the Northwest Territories. It uses its speed to pursue prey in a "tail chase," sometimes striking its quarry on the ground, but also in flight. Three forms are known, ranging from almost pure white to gray and dark.

VOICE Loud, harsh *KYHa-KYHa-KYHa.*

NESTING Scrape on cliff, or old Common Ravens' nests; 2–7 eggs; 1 brood; April–July.

FEEDING Feeds mostly on large birds such as ptarmigan, pigeons, grouse; may also hunt mammals, such as lemmings.

FLIGHT: powerful and direct; continuous, rapid, stiff wing beats.

SNOWY PLUMAGE
A Gyrfalcon stands on an Arctic hillside. From a distance, it might be mistaken for a patch of snow.

SIMILAR SPECIES

PRAIRIE FALCON light, brown-spotted underparts; see p.120
light, sandy brown upperparts

PEREGRINE FALCON see p.121
dark "hood" on head
smaller overall
light, barred underparts

OCCURRENCE
Found in Arctic North America. Sometimes found in northern regions of the US. A truly Arctic species found in the most barren regions of the tundra, high mountains and foothills of the tundra, and Arctic and sub-Arctic evergreen forests and woodlands. Not common outside its breeding range.

Length **22in (56cm)**	Wingspan **4ft (1.2m)**	Weight **2¾–4lb (1.2–1.8kg)**
Social **Solitary/Pairs**	Lifespan **15–30 years**	Status **Localized**

Order **Falconiformes**	Family **Falconidae**	Species ***Falco mexicanus***

Prairie Falcon

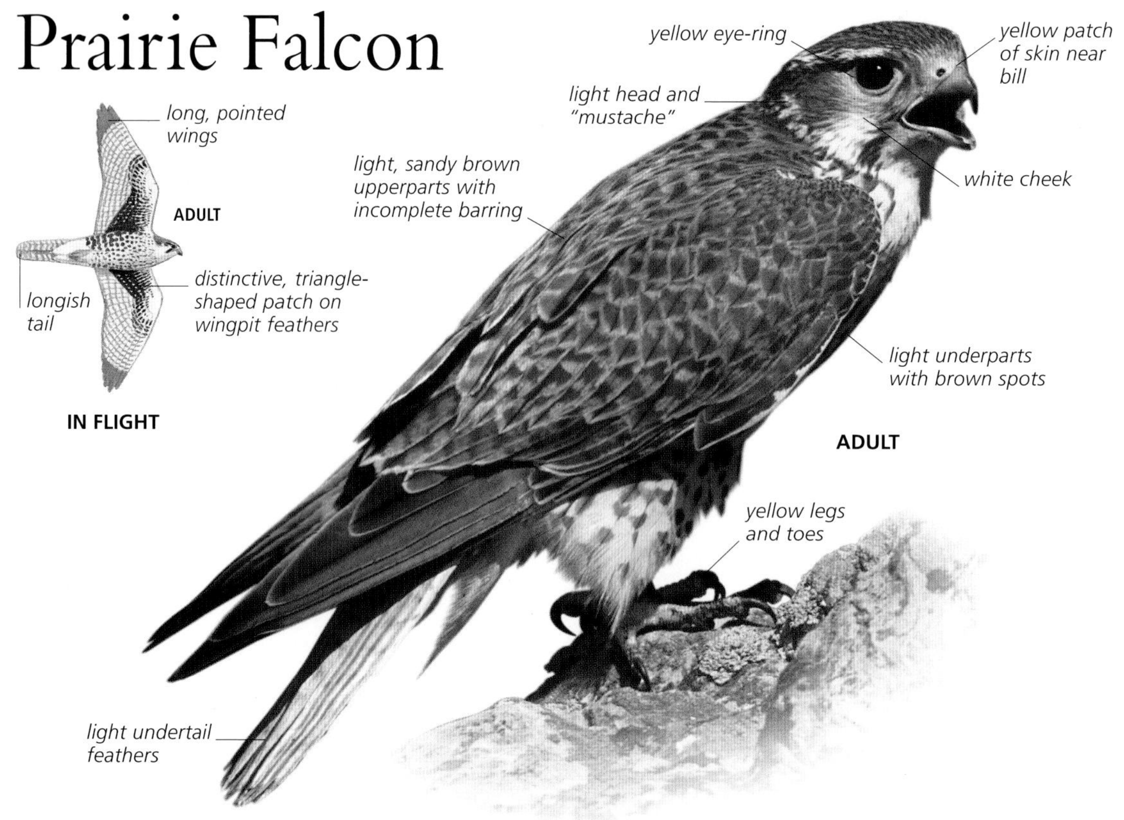
long, pointed wings
ADULT
longish tail
distinctive, triangle-shaped patch on wingpit feathers
IN FLIGHT
yellow eye-ring
yellow patch of skin near bill
light head and "mustache"
light, sandy brown upperparts with incomplete barring
white cheek
light underparts with brown spots
ADULT
yellow legs and toes
light undertail feathers

Prairie Falcons are light-colored, buoyant residents of the arid regions of North America. They blend in well with their surroundings (cliff faces and dry grass), where they are invisible to their prey. Prairie Falcons chase their prey close to the ground and do not often dive or "stoop" on prey from a great height. Ground squirrels are important prey items in some areas, and breeding is often linked with the squirrels' emergence. The sexes are very similar in coloration, though juveniles have a streaked rather than spotted breast. The underwing pattern with almost black feathers in the "wingpits" is distinctive; no other North American falcon shows this mark.

VOICE Repeated shrill *kik-kik-kik-kik-kik.*

NESTING Slight, shallow scrapes, almost always located on high cliff ledges or bluffs; 3–6 eggs; 1 brood; March–July.

FEEDING Feeds on small to medium-sized birds and small mammals, such as ground squirrels.

FLIGHT: fast flight; capable of soaring and diving; usually chases prey low above the ground.

STRIKING MUSTACHE
An inquisitive Prairie Falcon stares at the camera. The white cheek is obvious from this angle.

SIMILAR SPECIES

MERLIN
see p.118
smaller overall
heavily streaked underparts
PEREGRINE FALCON
see p.121
darker head
streaked underparts
yellow or bluish gray legs and toes

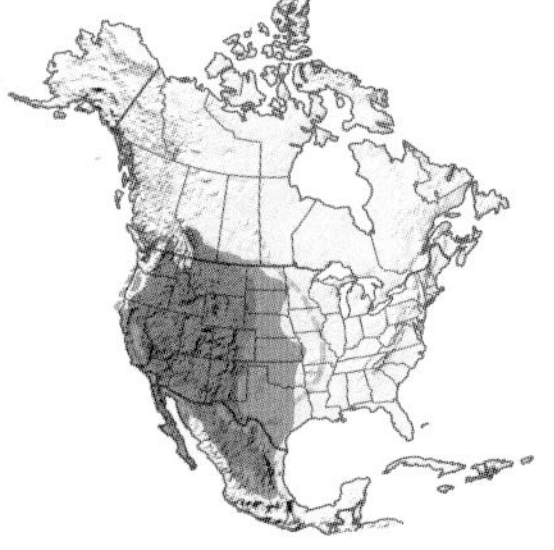

OCCURRENCE
Interior North America, from central British Columbia east to western North Dakota and south to southern California, and Mexico, Arizona, northern Texas. Found in open plains, prairies, and grasslands, dotted with buttes or cliffs. A partial migrant, it moves east of its breeding range in winter.

Length **16in (41cm)**	Wingspan **3¼ft (1m)**	Weight **22–30oz (625–850g)**
Social **Solitary/Pairs**	Lifespan **10–20 years**	Status **Localized**

Order **Falconiformes**	Family **Falconidae**	Species ***Falco peregrinus***

Peregrine Falcon

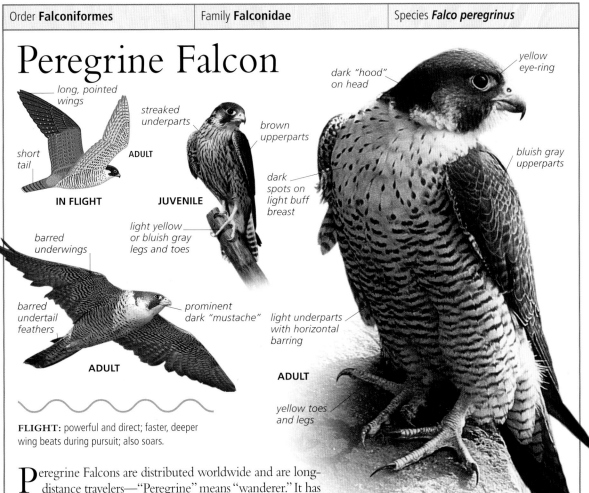

long, pointed wings
short tail
ADULT
IN FLIGHT

streaked underparts
brown upperparts
JUVENILE
light yellow or bluish gray legs and toes

barred underwings
barred undertail feathers
prominent dark "mustache"
ADULT

dark "hood" on head
yellow eye-ring
bluish gray upperparts
dark spots on light buff breast
light underparts with horizontal barring
ADULT
yellow toes and legs

FLIGHT: powerful and direct; faster, deeper wing beats during pursuit; also soars.

Peregrine Falcons are distributed worldwide and are long-distance travelers—"Peregrine" means "wanderer." It has been shown to dive from great heights at speeds of up to 200mph (320kmph)—a technique known as "stooping." Like all true falcons, this species has a pointed "tooth" on its upper beak and a "notch" on the lower one, and it instinctively bites the neck of captured prey to kill it. From the 1950s–1980s, its breeding ability was reduced by the insecticide DDT, which resulted in thin eggshells that could easily be crushed by the parent. Peregrines were then bred in captivity, and later released into the wild. Their status is now secure.

VOICE Sharp *hek-hek-hek* when alarmed.

NESTING Shallow scrape on cliff or building (nest sites are used year after year); 2–5 eggs; 1 brood; March–June.

FEEDING Dives on prey—birds of various sizes in flight; now feeds on pigeons in cities.

PARENTAL CARE
An adult Peregrine gently feeds a hatchling bits of meat; the remaining egg is likely to hatch soon.

SIMILAR SPECIES

GYRFALCON see p.119
larger and stockier
longer tail
less defined "hood"

PRAIRIE FALCON see p.120
lighter head color
light sandy brown upperparts

OCCURRENCE
A variety of habitats across northern North America, ranging from open valleys to cities with tall buildings. Peregrines prefer to inhabit cliffs along sea coasts, in addition to inland mountain ranges, but also occur in open country such as scrubland and salt marshes.

Length **16in (41cm)**	Wingspan **3¼–3½ft (1–1.1m)**	Weight **22–35oz (620–1000g)**
Social **Solitary/Pairs**	Lifespan **15–20 years**	Status **Secure**

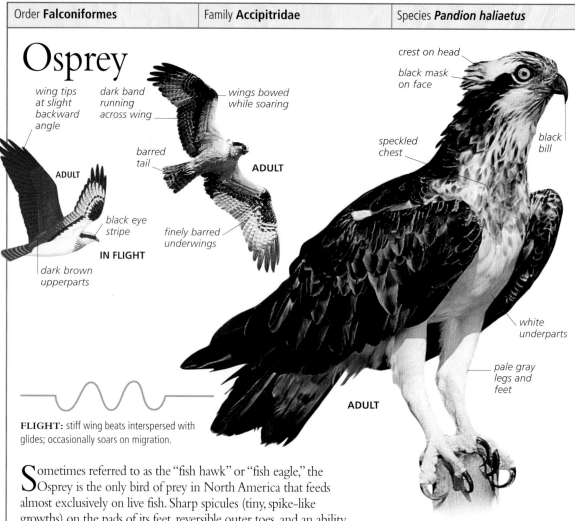

Order **Falconiformes**	Family **Accipitridae**	Species ***Pandion haliaetus***

Osprey

wing tips at slight backward angle

dark band running across wing

wings bowed while soaring

barred tail

ADULT

ADULT

black eye stripe

IN FLIGHT

dark brown upperparts

finely barred underwings

crest on head

black mask on face

speckled chest

black bill

white underparts

pale gray legs and feet

ADULT

FLIGHT: stiff wing beats interspersed with glides; occasionally soars on migration.

Sometimes referred to as the "fish hawk" or "fish eagle," the Osprey is the only bird of prey in North America that feeds almost exclusively on live fish. Sharp spicules (tiny, spike-like growths) on the pads of its feet, reversible outer toes, and an ability to lock its talons in place enable it to hold onto slippery fish. Some populations declined between the 1950s and 1980s due to the use of dangerous pesticides. However, the ban on use of these chemicals, along with availability of artificial nest sites and a tolerance of nearby human activity has allowed the Osprey to return to its former numbers. The Osprey is the provincial bird of Nova Scotia.

VOICE Slow, whistled notes, falling in pitch: *tiooop, tioooop, tiooop*; also screams by displaying male.

NESTING Twig nest on tree, cliff, rock pinnacles, boulders, ground; 1–4 eggs; 1 brood; March–August.

FEEDING Dives to catch fish up to top 3ft (90cm) of water.

IMPROVING AERODYNAMICS

Once caught a fish is held with its head pointing forward reducing drag as the bird flies.

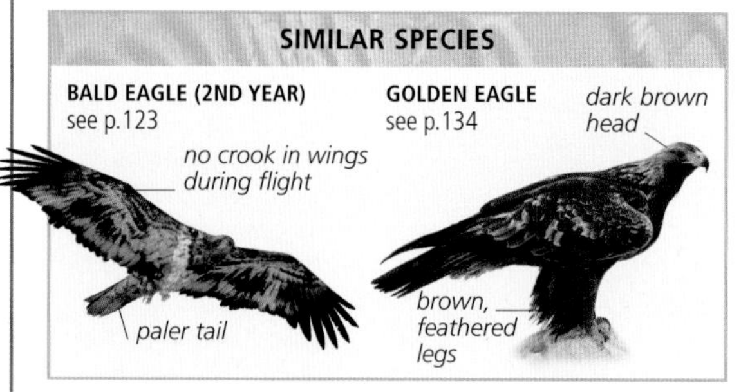
SIMILAR SPECIES
BALD EAGLE (2ND YEAR)
see p.123
no crook in wings during flight
paler tail
GOLDEN EAGLE
see p.134
dark brown head
brown, feathered legs

OCCURRENCE

Breeds in a wide variety of habitats: northern forests, near shallow reservoirs, along freshwater rivers and large lakes, estuaries and salt marshes, coastal deserts and desert saltflat lagoons. Migrates through and winters in similar habitats.

Length **21–23in (53–58cm)**	Wingspan **5–6ft (1.5–1.8m)**	Weight **3–4½lb (1.4–2kg)**
Social **Solitary/Pairs**	Lifespan **Up to 25 years**	Status **Secure**

Order **Falconiformes**	Family **Accipitridae**	Species ***Haliaeetus leucocephalus***

Bald Eagle

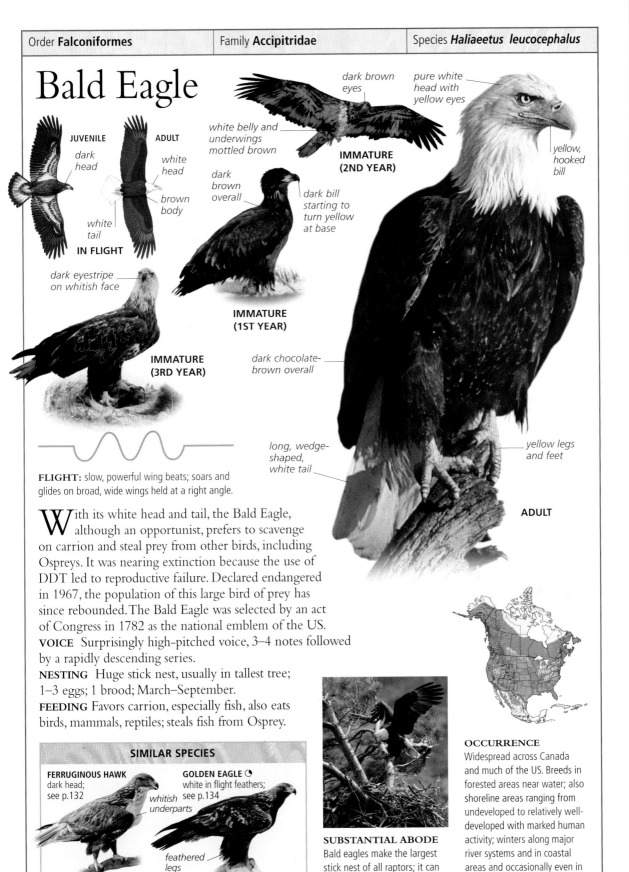

JUVENILE
dark head
white tail
ADULT
white head
brown body
IN FLIGHT

white belly and underwings mottled brown
dark brown eyes
IMMATURE (2ND YEAR)

dark brown overall
dark bill starting to turn yellow at base
IMMATURE (1ST YEAR)

dark eyestripe on whitish face
IMMATURE (3RD YEAR)

pure white head with yellow eyes
yellow, hooked bill
dark chocolate-brown overall
long, wedge-shaped, white tail
yellow legs and feet
ADULT

FLIGHT: slow, powerful wing beats; soars and glides on broad, wide wings held at a right angle.

With its white head and tail, the Bald Eagle, although an opportunist, prefers to scavenge on carrion and steal prey from other birds, including Ospreys. It was nearing extinction because the use of DDT led to reproductive failure. Declared endangered in 1967, the population of this large bird of prey has since rebounded. The Bald Eagle was selected by an act of Congress in 1782 as the national emblem of the US.

VOICE Surprisingly high-pitched voice, 3–4 notes followed by a rapidly descending series.

NESTING Huge stick nest, usually in tallest tree; 1–3 eggs; 1 brood; March–September.

FEEDING Favors carrion, especially fish, also eats birds, mammals, reptiles; steals fish from Osprey.

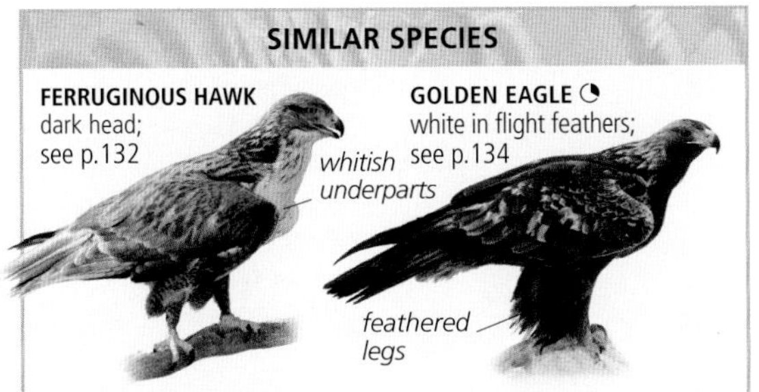
SIMILAR SPECIES
FERRUGINOUS HAWK
dark head;
see p.132
whitish underparts
GOLDEN EAGLE ◔
white in flight feathers;
see p.134
feathered legs

SUBSTANTIAL ABODE
Bald eagles make the largest stick nest of all raptors; it can weigh up to two tons.

OCCURRENCE
Widespread across Canada and much of the US. Breeds in forested areas near water; also shoreline areas ranging from undeveloped to relatively well-developed with marked human activity; winters along major river systems and in coastal areas and occasionally even in arid regions of southwest US.

Length **28–38in (71–96cm)**	Wingspan **6½ft (2m)**	Weight **6½–14lb (3–6.5kg)**
Social **Solitary/Pairs**	Lifespan **Up to 28 years**	Status **Secure**

Order **Falconiformes**	Family **Accipitridae**	Species ***Circus cyaneus***

Northern Harrier

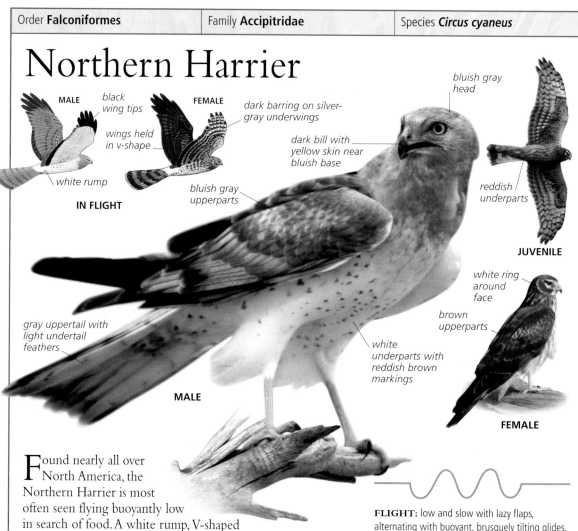

MALE
black wing tips
white rump
FEMALE
wings held in v-shape
dark barring on silver-gray underwings
IN FLIGHT
bluish gray upperparts
dark bill with yellow skin near bluish base
bluish gray head
reddish underparts
JUVENILE
white ring around face
brown upperparts
gray uppertail with light undertail feathers
white underparts with reddish brown markings
MALE
FEMALE

Found nearly all over North America, the Northern Harrier is most often seen flying buoyantly low in search of food. A white rump, V-shaped wings, and tilting flight make this species easily identifiable. The blue-gray males are quite different to the dark-brown females. The bird's most recognizable characteristic is its owl-like face, which contains stiff feathers to help channel in sounds from prey. Northern Harriers are highly migratory throughout their range.

VOICE Call given by both sexes in rapid succession at nest: *kek* becomes more high-pitched when intruders are spotted.

NESTING Platform of sticks on ground in open, wet field; 4–6 eggs; 1 brood; April–September.

FEEDING Mostly hunts rodents like mice and muskrats; also birds, frogs, reptiles; occasionally takes larger prey such as rabbits.

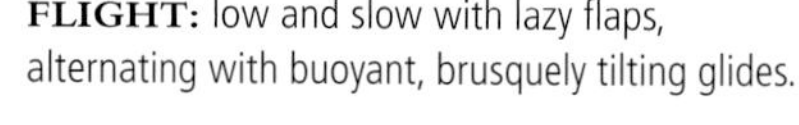

FLIGHT: low and slow with lazy flaps, alternating with buoyant, brusquely tilting glides.

WATERY DWELLING
To avoid predators, Northern Harriers prefer to raise their young on wet sites in tall, dense vegetation.

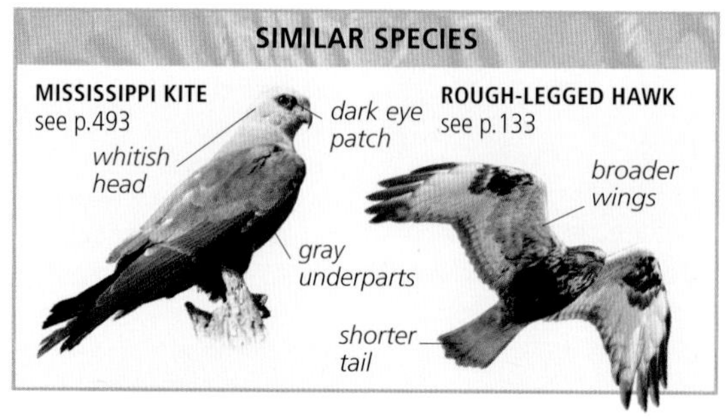
SIMILAR SPECIES
MISSISSIPPI KITE
see p.493
whitish head
dark eye patch
gray underparts
ROUGH-LEGGED HAWK
see p.133
broader wings
shorter tail

OCCURRENCE
Breeds in a variety of open wetlands: marshes, meadows, pastures, fallow fields across most of North America; winters in open habitats like deserts, coastal sand dunes, cropland, grasslands, marshy, and riverside areas.

Length **18–20in (46–51cm)**	Wingspan **3½–4ft (1.1m–1.2m)**	Weight **11–26oz (300–750g)**
Social **Solitary/Pairs/Colonies**	Lifespan **Up to 16 years**	Status **Secure**

Order **Falconiformes**	Family **Accipitridae**	Species ***Accipiter striatus***

Sharp-shinned Hawk

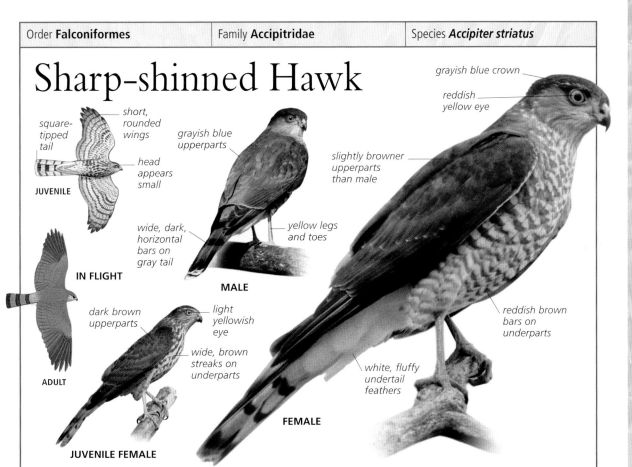

grayish blue crown
reddish yellow eye
square-tipped tail
short, rounded wings
head appears small
JUVENILE
grayish blue upperparts
slightly browner upperparts than male
wide, dark, horizontal bars on gray tail
yellow legs and toes
IN FLIGHT
ADULT
MALE
dark brown upperparts
light yellowish eye
wide, brown streaks on underparts
reddish brown bars on underparts
white, fluffy undertail feathers
JUVENILE FEMALE
FEMALE

This small and swift hawk is quite adept at capturing birds, occasionally even taking species larger than itself. The Sharp-shinned Hawk's short, rounded wings and long tail allow it to make abrupt turns and lightning-fast dashes in thick woods and dense shrubby terrain. With needle-like talons, long, spindle-thin legs, and long toes, this hawk is well adapted to snatching birds in flight. The prey is plucked before being consumed or fed to the nestlings.

VOICE High-pitched, repeated *kiu kiu kiu* call; sometimes makes squealing sound when disturbed at nest.

NESTING Sturdy nest of sticks lined with twigs or pieces of bark; sometimes an old crow or squirrel nest; 3–4 eggs; 1 brood; March–June.

FEEDING Catches small birds, such as sparrows and wood-warblers, on the wing, or takes them unaware while perched.

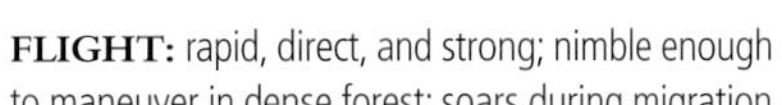

FLIGHT: rapid, direct, and strong; nimble enough to maneuver in dense forest; soars during migration.

HUNTING BIRDS
A Sharp-shinned Hawk pauses on the ground with a freshly captured sparrow in its talons.

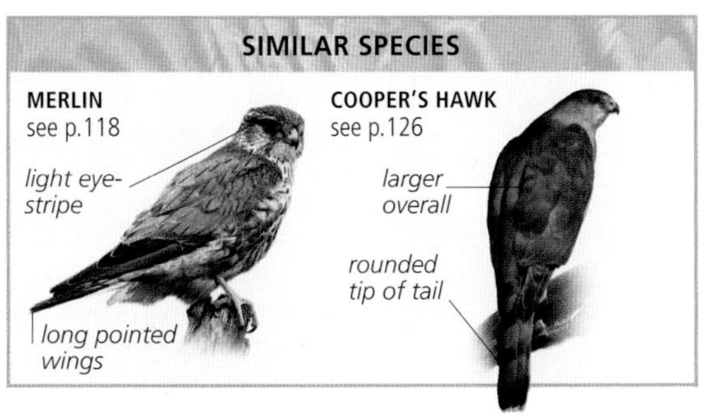
SIMILAR SPECIES
MERLIN
see p.118
light eye-stripe
long pointed wings
COOPER'S HAWK
see p.126
larger overall
rounded tip of tail

OCCURRENCE
Deep coniferous forests and mixed hardwood–conifer woodlands across North America from the tree limit in northern Canada to the Gulf states. During fall migration sometimes seen in flocks of hundreds of individuals. Winters in Central America from Guatemala to Panama.

Length **11in (28 cm)**	Wingspan **23in (58cm)**	Weight **3½–6oz (100–175g)**
Social **Solitary/Flocks**	Lifespan **At least 10 years**	Status **Secure**

Order **Falconiformes**	Family **Accipitridae**	Species ***Accipiter cooperii***

Cooper's Hawk

broad, rounded wings
JUVENILE
long, barred tail with rounded tip
IN FLIGHT

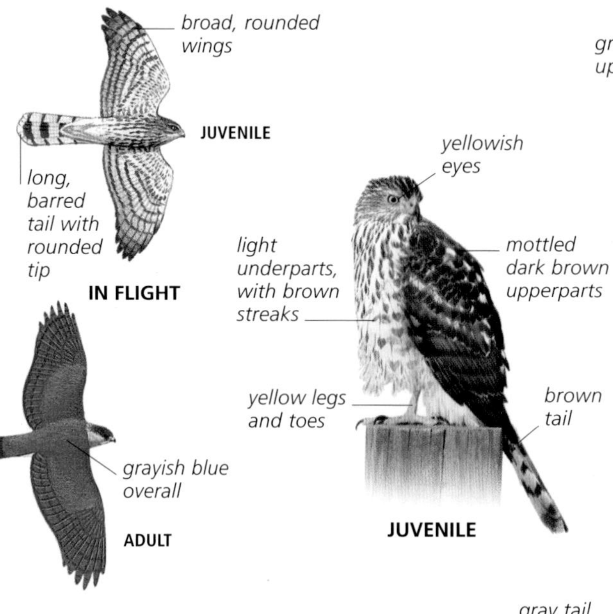
grayish blue overall
ADULT
yellowish eyes
light underparts, with brown streaks
mottled dark brown upperparts
yellow legs and toes
brown tail
JUVENILE
dark crown
reddish eye
grayish blue upperparts
ADULT
gray tail with wide, dark bands
white band at tip of tail

FLIGHT: fast with rapid wing beats interspersed with glides; sometimes soars.

A secretive and inconspicuous bird, Cooper's Hawk, was named by Charles Bonaparte, nephew of French Emperor Napoleon Bonaparte, for William C. Cooper, a noted New York naturalist. It is a typical woodland hawk, capable of quickly maneuvering through dense vegetation. Although it prefers to stay close to cover, it will venture out in search of food. Should a human approach the nest of a Cooper's Hawk, the brooding adult will quietly glide down and away from the nest tree rather than attack the intruder.

VOICE Most common call a staccato *ca-ca-ca-ca*; other vocalizations include as many as 40 different calls.

NESTING Medium-sized, stick nest, usually in a large deciduous tree; 4–5 eggs; 1 brood; April–May.

FEEDING Catches birds, such as robins and blackbirds; larger females can capture grouse; also eats chipmunks, small squirrels, and even bats.

DENSE BARRING
This hawk has characteristic fine, reddish brown, horizontal barring on its undersides.

SIMILAR SPECIES

NORTHERN HARRIER ♀
see p.124
larger overall
whitish underparts
SHARP-SHINNED HAWK
see p.125
square-tipped tail
much smaller head

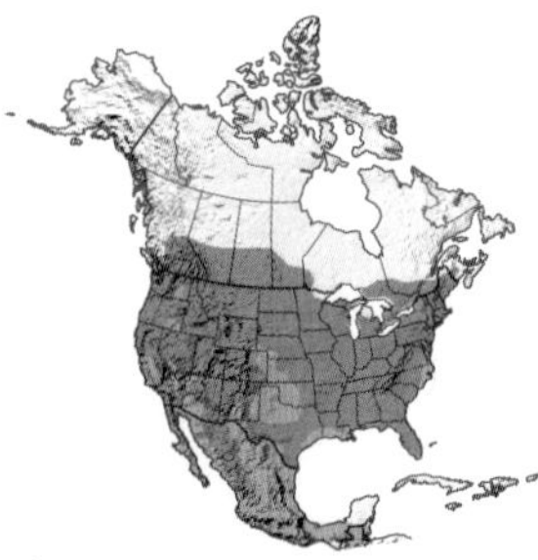

OCCURRENCE
Breeds in woodlands across northern North America, southern Canada, and the northern US, south to Florida, Texas, and northwestern Mexico. Likes mature deciduous forests with leaf cover, and also roosts in conifers. Winters in southwestern US and Mexico.

Length **15½–17½in (40–45cm)**	Wingspan **28–34in (70–86cm)**	Weight **13–19oz (375–525g)**
Social **Solitary/Pairs**	Lifespan **At least 10 years**	Status **Secure**

Order **Falconiformes**	Family **Accipitridae**	Species ***Accipiter gentilis***

Northern Goshawk

fairly short, rounded wings

ADULT

long tail

barred underwings

JUVENILE

brown bars on tail

IN FLIGHT

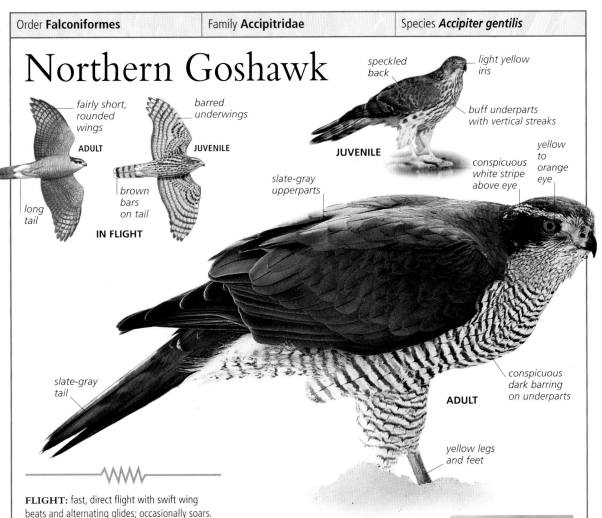

speckled back

light yellow iris

buff underparts with vertical streaks

JUVENILE

slate-gray upperparts

conspicuous white stripe above eye

yellow to orange eye

slate-gray tail

conspicuous dark barring on underparts

ADULT

yellow legs and feet

FLIGHT: fast, direct flight with swift wing beats and alternating glides; occasionally soars.

The powerful and agile Northern Goshawk is secretive by nature and not easily observed, even in regions where it is common. It has few natural enemies, but will defend its territories, nests, and young fiercely, by repeatedly diving and screaming at intruders that get too close. Spring hikers and turkey-hunters occasionally discover Northern Goshawks by wandering into their territory and being driven off by the angry occupants.

VOICE Loud, high-pitched *gek-gek-gek* when agitated.

NESTING Large stick structures lined with bark and plant matter in the mid- to lower region of tree; 1–3 eggs; 1 brood; May–June.

FEEDING Sits and waits on perch before diving rapidly; preys on birds as large as grouse and pheasants; also mammals, including hares and squirrels.

OCCASIONAL SOARER
A juvenile Northern Goshawk takes advantage of a thermal, soaring over its territory.

SIMILAR SPECIES

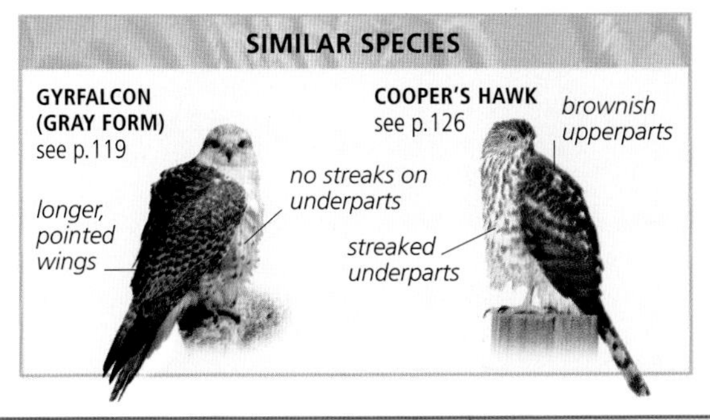
GYRFALCON (GRAY FORM)
see p.119
longer, pointed wings
no streaks on underparts
COOPER'S HAWK
see p.126
brownish upperparts
streaked underparts

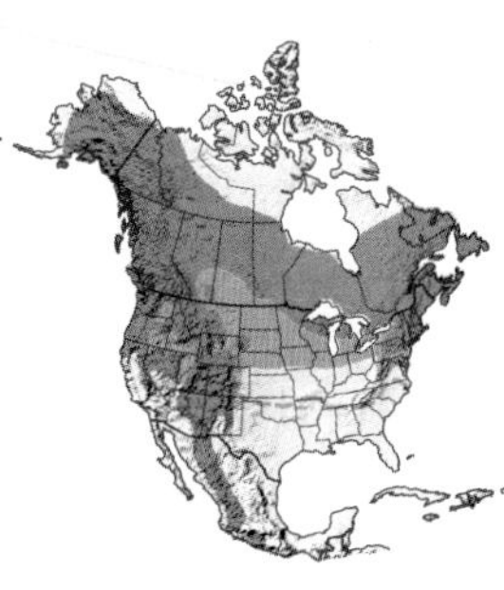

OCCURRENCE
Breeds in deep deciduous, coniferous, and mixed woodlands in northern North America, from the tundra–taiga border south to California, northern Mexico, and Pennsylvania in the eastern US, absent from east central US. The Northern Goshawk is widespread in northern Eurasia.

Length **21in (53cm)**	Wingspan **3½ft (1.1m)**	Weight **2–3lb (0.9–1.4kg)**
Social **Solitary/Pairs**	Lifespan **Up to 20 years**	Status **Secure**

Order **Falconiformes**	Family **Accipitridae**	Species ***Buteo lineatus***

Red-shouldered Hawk

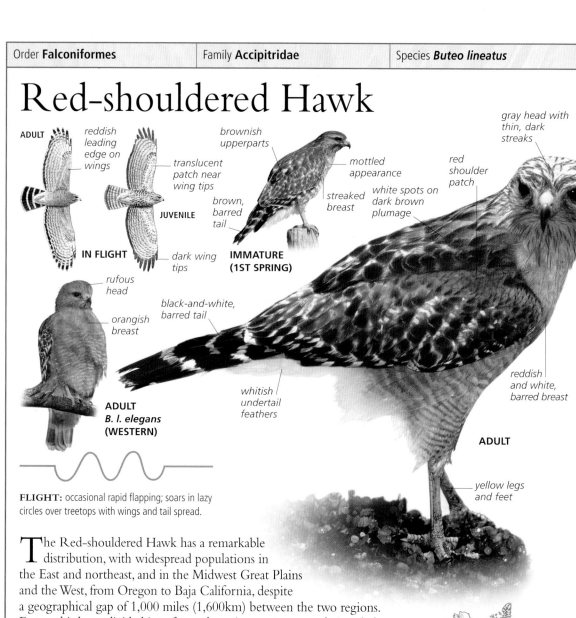

ADULT
reddish leading edge on wings
translucent patch near wing tips
JUVENILE
IN FLIGHT
dark wing tips
brownish upperparts
mottled appearance
streaked breast
brown, barred tail
IMMATURE (1ST SPRING)
gray head with thin, dark streaks
red shoulder patch
white spots on dark brown plumage
rufous head
orangish breast
black-and-white, barred tail
whitish undertail feathers
reddish and white, barred breast
ADULT *B. l. elegans* (WESTERN)
ADULT
yellow legs and feet

FLIGHT: occasional rapid flapping; soars in lazy circles over treetops with wings and tail spread.

The Red-shouldered Hawk has a remarkable distribution, with widespread populations in the East and northeast, and in the Midwest Great Plains and the West, from Oregon to Baja California, despite a geographical gap of 1,000 miles (1,600km) between the two regions. Eastern birds are divided into four subspecies; western populations belong to the subspecies *B. l. elegans.* The red shoulder patches are not always evident, but the striped tail and translucent "windows" in the wings are easily identifiable.

VOICE Call a whistled *kee-aah,* accented on first syllable, descending on second.

NESTING Platform of sticks, dried leaves, bark, moss, and lichens in trees not far from water; 3–4 eggs; 1 brood; March–July.

FEEDING Catches mice, chipmunks, and voles; also snakes, toads, frogs, crayfish, and small birds.

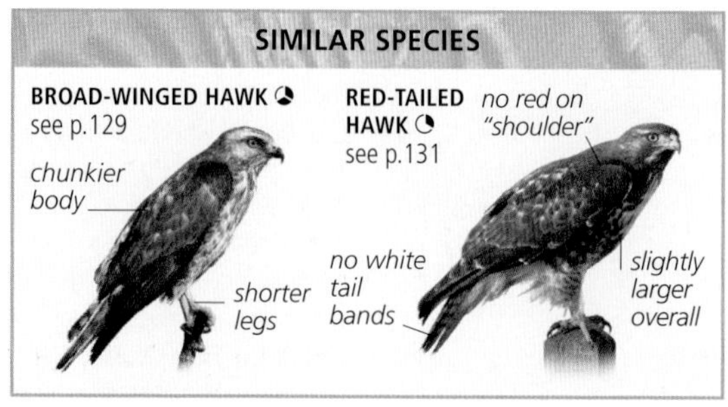
SIMILAR SPECIES
BROAD-WINGED HAWK
see p.129
chunkier body
shorter legs
RED-TAILED HAWK
see p.131
no red on "shoulder"
no white tail bands
slightly larger overall

CHESTNUT WING When seen from below, the reddish forewing of this adult hawk is clearly visible.

OCCURRENCE
Eastern populations breed in woodlands and forest, deciduous or mixed, whereas those in the West occur in oak woodlands and eucalyptus groves. In Florida, this species also lives in mangroves. Eastern birds migrate to Mexico.

Length **17–24in (43–61cm)**	Wingspan **3–3½ft (0.9–1.1m)**	Weight **17–27oz (475–775g)**
Social **Solitary/Flocks**	Lifespan **Up to 18 years**	Status **Declining (p)**

Order **Falconiformes**	Family **Accipitridae**	Species ***Buteo platypterus***

Broad-winged Hawk

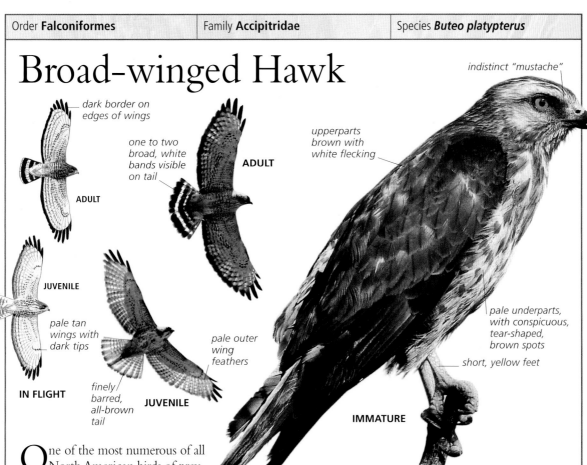

dark border on edges of wings
ADULT
one to two broad, white bands visible on tail
ADULT
JUVENILE
pale tan wings with dark tips
IN FLIGHT
finely barred, all-brown tail
JUVENILE
pale outer wing feathers
upperparts brown with white flecking
indistinct "mustache"
pale underparts, with conspicuous, tear-shaped, brown spots
short, yellow feet
IMMATURE

One of the most numerous of all North American birds of prey, the Broad-winged Hawk migrates in huge flocks or "kettles," with thousands of birds gliding on rising thermals. Some birds winter in Florida, but the majority average about 70 miles (110km) a day to log more than 4,000 miles (6,500km) before ending up in Brazil, Bolivia, and even some of the Caribbean islands. Compared to its two cousins, the Red-shouldered and Red-tailed Hawks, the Broad-winged Hawk is slightly smaller, but stockier. Adults are easily identified by a broad, white-and-black band on their tails. Broad-winged Hawks have two color forms, the light one being more common than the dark, sooty brown one.

VOICE High-pitched *peeoweee* call, first note shorter and higher-pitched.

NESTING Platform of fresh twigs or dead sticks, often on old squirrel, hawk, or crow nest in tree; 2–3 eggs; 1 brood; April–August.

FEEDING Eats small mammals, toads, frogs, snakes, grouse chicks, insects, and spiders; crabs in winter.

FLIGHT: circles above forest canopy with wings and tail spread; short flights from branch to branch.

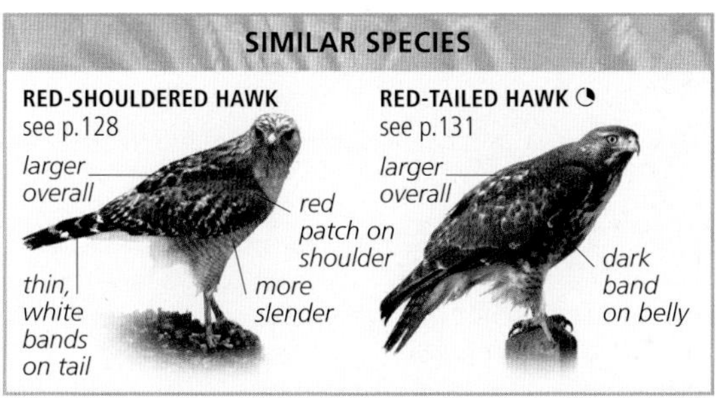
SIMILAR SPECIES
RED-SHOULDERED HAWK
see p.128
larger overall
red patch on shoulder
thin, white bands on tail
more slender
RED-TAILED HAWK
see p.131
larger overall
dark band on belly

WATCHING FOR PREY
From an elevated perch, this hawk scans for vertebrate prey such as rodents.

OCCURRENCE
Breeds across Canada (but not the Rockies) and in the eastern US (not west of the 100th meridien), in forested areas with deciduous, conifers, and mixed trees, with clearings and water nearby. Concentrations of migrants can be seen at bottlenecks such as the Isthmus of Tehuantepec and Panama.

Length **13–17in (33–43cm)**	Wingspan **32–39in (81–100cm)**	Weight **10–19oz (275–550g)**
Social **Flocks**	Lifespan **Up to 14 years**	Status **Secure**

Order **Falconiformes**	Family **Accipitridae**	Species ***Buteo swainsoni***

Swainson's Hawk

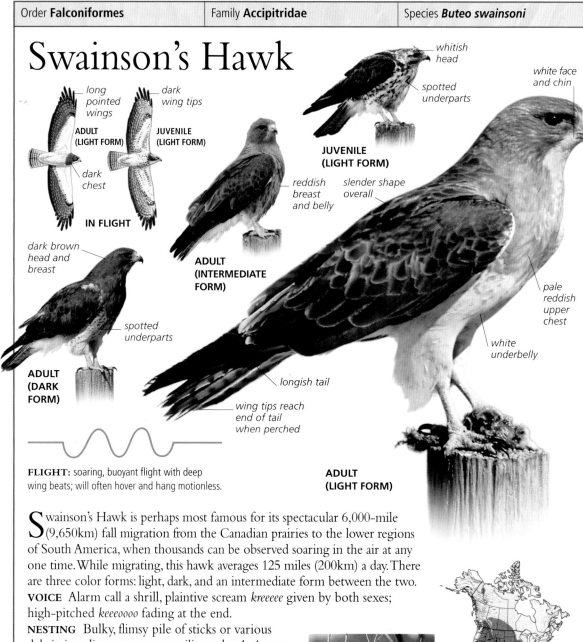

long pointed wings · *dark wing tips*

ADULT (LIGHT FORM) · **JUVENILE (LIGHT FORM)**

dark chest

IN FLIGHT

whitish head · *spotted underparts*

JUVENILE (LIGHT FORM)

reddish breast and belly

ADULT (INTERMEDIATE FORM)

dark brown head and breast · *spotted underparts*

ADULT (DARK FORM)

white face and chin · *slender shape overall* · *pale reddish upper chest* · *white underbelly* · *longish tail* · *wing tips reach end of tail when perched*

ADULT (LIGHT FORM)

FLIGHT: soaring, buoyant flight with deep wing beats; will often hover and hang motionless.

Swainson's Hawk is perhaps most famous for its spectacular 6,000-mile (9,650km) fall migration from the Canadian prairies to the lower regions of South America, when thousands can be observed soaring in the air at any one time. While migrating, this hawk averages 125 miles (200km) a day. There are three color forms: light, dark, and an intermediate form between the two.

VOICE Alarm call a shrill, plaintive scream *kreeeee* given by both sexes; high-pitched *keeeoooo* fading at the end.

NESTING Bulky, flimsy pile of sticks or various debris, in solitary tree or on utility poles; 1–4 eggs; 1 brood; April–July.

FEEDING Eats ground squirrels, pocket gophers, mice, voles, bats, rabbits; also snakes, lizards, songbirds.

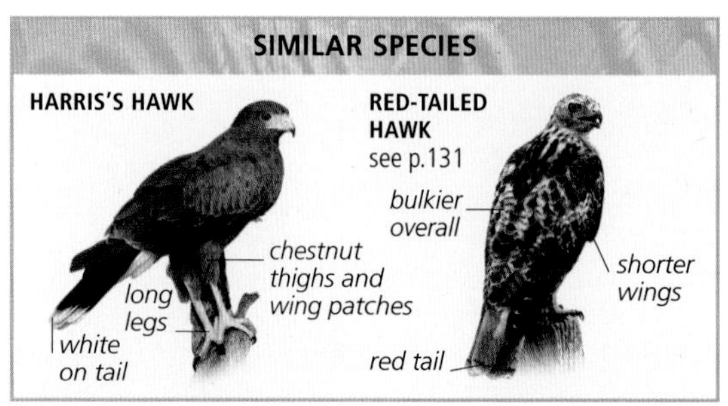
SIMILAR SPECIES
HARRIS'S HAWK
chestnut thighs and wing patches
long legs
white on tail
RED-TAILED HAWK
see p.131
bulkier overall
shorter wings
red tail

ON THE LOOKOUT
This slim, elegant species will perch before diving for its prey.

OCCURRENCE
Breeds in scattered trees along streams; found in areas of open woodland, sparse shrubland, grasslands, and agricultural land; winters in native Argentinian grassland, and in harvested fields where grasshoppers are found abundantly.

Length **19–22in (48–56cm)**	Wingspan **4½ft (1.4m)**	Weight **1½–3lb (0.7–1.4kg)**
Social **Solitary/Pairs/Flocks**	Lifespan **Up to 19 years**	Status **Declining (p)**

Order **Falconiformes**	Family **Accipitridae**	Species ***Buteo jamaicensis***

Red-tailed Hawk

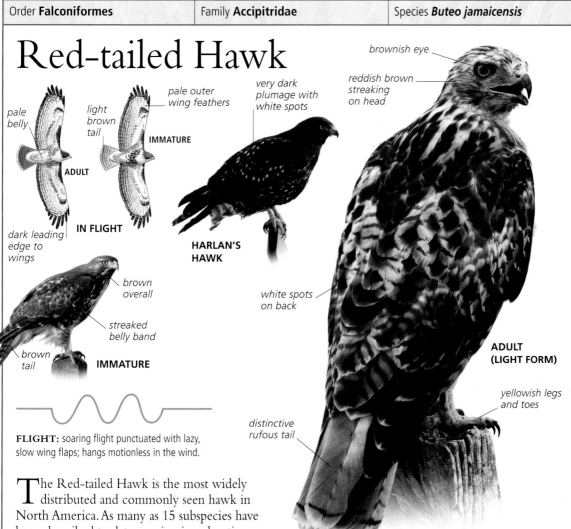

pale belly
light brown tail
pale outer wing feathers
IMMATURE
ADULT
IN FLIGHT
dark leading edge to wings
very dark plumage with white spots
HARLAN'S HAWK
brownish eye
reddish brown streaking on head
brown overall
streaked belly band
brown tail
IMMATURE
white spots on back
ADULT (LIGHT FORM)
yellowish legs and toes
distinctive rufous tail

FLIGHT: soaring flight punctuated with lazy, slow wing flaps; hangs motionless in the wind.

The Red-tailed Hawk is the most widely distributed and commonly seen hawk in North America. As many as 15 subspecies have been described to date, varying in coloration, tail markings, and size. The very dark Harlan's Hawk, which breeds in Alaska and northwestern Canada, is so distinctive that it was at one time thought of as a separate species, but recent research suggests otherwise. While it occasionally stoops on prey, the Red-tailed Hawk usually adopts a sit-and-wait approach.

VOICE Call *kee-eee-arrr* that rises then descends over a period of 2–3 seconds.

NESTING Large platform of sticks, twigs on top of tall tree, cliff, building, ledge, or billboard; 2 eggs; 1 brood; February–September.

FEEDING Captures small mammals, such as voles, mice, rats; birds including pheasant, quail; small reptiles; carrion also eaten.

FLYING HIGH
A Red-tailed Hawk soaring over an open field is a very common sight in North America.

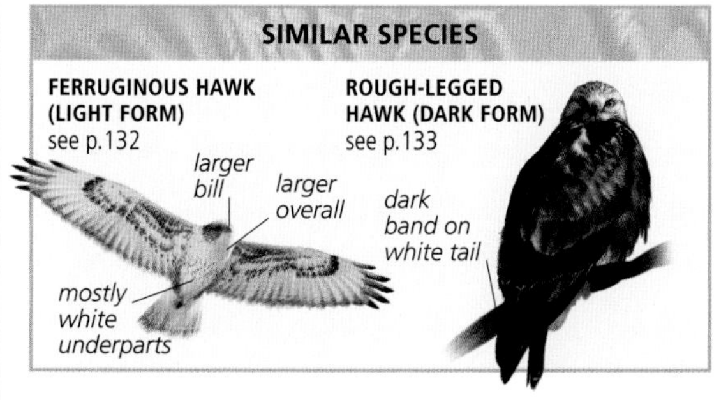
SIMILAR SPECIES
FERRUGINOUS HAWK (LIGHT FORM)
see p.132
larger bill
larger overall
mostly white underparts
ROUGH-LEGGED HAWK (DARK FORM)
see p.133
dark band on white tail

OCCURRENCE
Breeds, forages in open areas in wide range of habitats and altitudes: scrub desert, grasslands, agricultural fields and pastures, coniferous and deciduous woodland, and tropical rainforest. Prefers areas with tall perch sites; can be found in suburban woodlots.

Length **18–26in (46–65cm)**	Wingspan **3½–4¼ft (1.1–1.3m)**	Weight **1½–3¼lb (0.7–1.5kg)**
Social **Solitary/Pairs**	Lifespan **Up to 21 years**	Status **Secure**

Order **Falconiformes**	Family **Accipitridae**	Species ***Buteo regalis***

Ferruginous Hawk

dark chocolate brown

ADULT (DARK FORM)

brown and white contrast on wings

ADULT (LIGHT FORM)

IN FLIGHT

relatively long pointed wings

ADULT (LIGHT FORM)

white undertail

large bill

dark brown overall

JUVENILE (DARK FORM)

reddish tinge to tail

all-white underparts

ADULT (LIGHT FORM)

dark spots on belly

JUVENILE (LIGHT FORM)

fully feathered legs

FLIGHT: slow, deep wing beats alternating with lazy glides; soars high with thermals.

This inhabitant of open country is the largest North American hawk. Its Latin name *regalis* means kingly, and its English name refers to its rusty coloring. It is a versatile nester: it builds its stick nests on cliffs or nearly level ground, trees, and manmade structures like farm buildings. Regrettably, its preference for prairie dogs, which are declining because of habitat loss, shooting, and pesticide use, threatens Ferruginous Hawk populations.

VOICE Screaming *Kree-aa* or *kaah, kaah* during courtship; quieter, lower-pitched, longer alarm call.

NESTING Large stick nest of old sagebrush stems, sticks, and various debris, lined with bark strips; 2–4 eggs; March–August.

FEEDING Hunts mainly rabbits, hares, ground squirrels, and prairie dogs; rarely fledgling birds, amphibians, and reptiles.

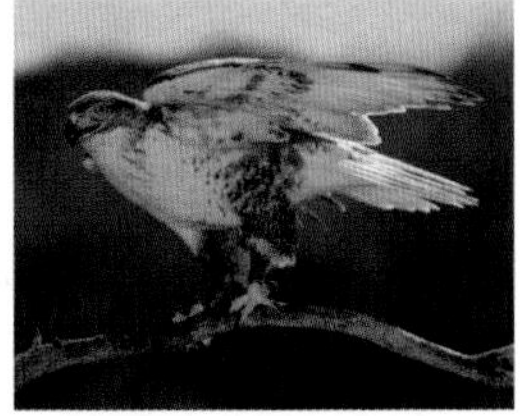

PERCHED HUNTER
The Ferruginous Hawk usually hunts from a perch such as a rock or a branch.

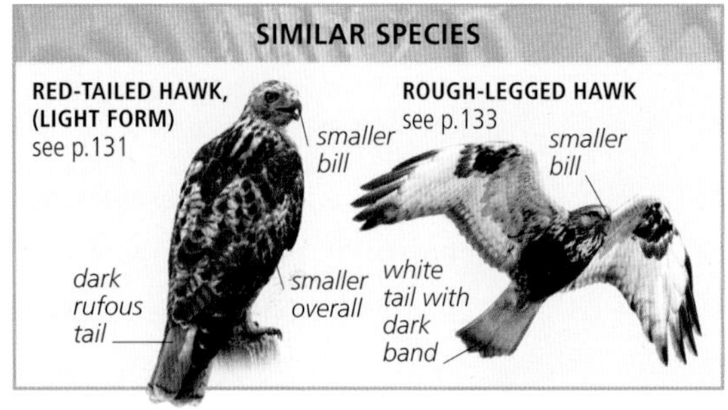
SIMILAR SPECIES
RED-TAILED HAWK, (LIGHT FORM)
see p.131
smaller bill
dark rufous tail
smaller overall
ROUGH-LEGGED HAWK
see p.133
smaller bill
white tail with dark band

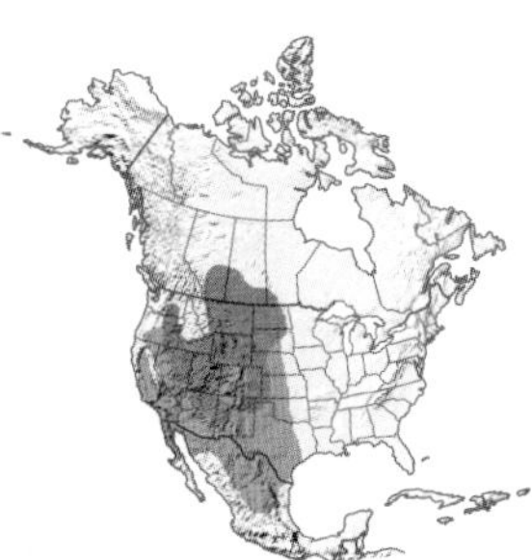

OCCURRENCE
In western North America, breeds in low-elevation grasslands interrupted by cliffs or isolated trees for nesting; winters across southwestern US and Mexico in open terrain ranging from grassland to desert.

Length **22–27in (56–69cm)**	Wingspan **4¼–4½ft (1.3–1.4m)**	Weight **2½–4½lb (1–2kg)**
Social **Solitary/Pairs**	Lifespan **Up to 20 years**	Status **Secure**

Order **Falconiformes**	Family **Accipitridae**	Species ***Buteo lagopus***

Rough-legged Hawk

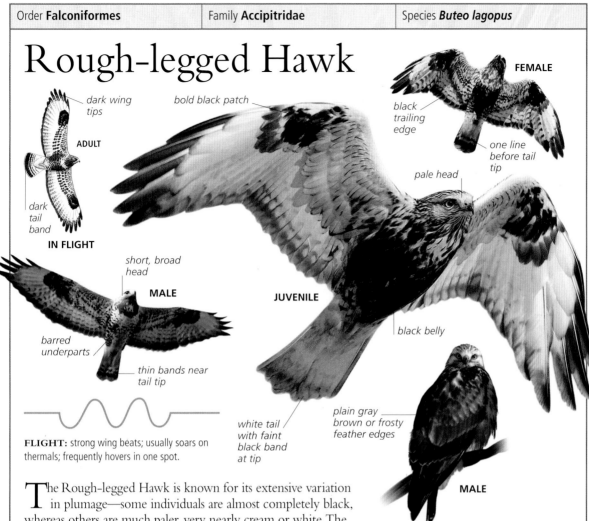

dark wing tips
ADULT
dark tail band
IN FLIGHT
bold black patch
FEMALE
black trailing edge
one line before tail tip
pale head
short, broad head
MALE
JUVENILE
barred underparts
thin bands near tail tip
black belly
white tail with faint black band at tip
plain gray brown or frosty feather edges
MALE

FLIGHT: strong wing beats; usually soars on thermals; frequently hovers in one spot.

The Rough-legged Hawk is known for its extensive variation in plumage—some individuals are almost completely black, whereas others are much paler, very nearly cream or white. The year to year fluctuation in numbers of breeding pairs in a given region strongly suggest that this species is nomadic, moving about as a response to the availiability of its rodent prey.

VOICE Wintering birds silent; breeding birds utter loud, cat-like mewing or thin whistles, slurred downward when alarmed.

NESTING Bulky mass of sticks, lined with grasses, sedges, feathers and fur from prey, constructed on cliff ledge; 2–6 eggs; 1 brood; April–August.

FEEDING Hovers in one spot over fields in search of prey; lemmings and voles in spring and summer; mice and shrews in winters; variety of birds, ground squirrels, and rabbits year-round.

ABUNDANT FOOD SUPPLY
When small mammals are abundant, these hawks produce large broods on cliff ledges in the tundra.

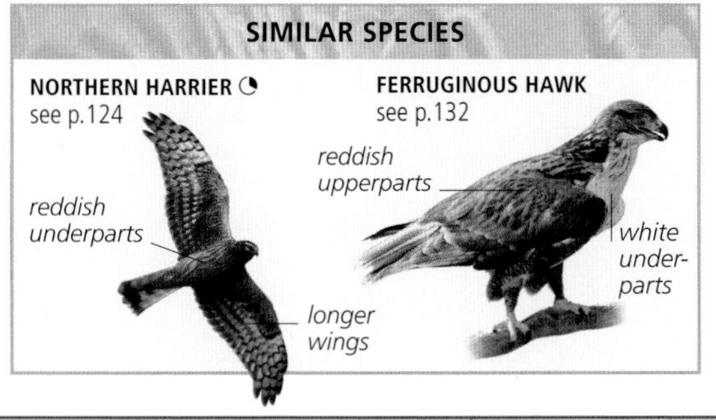
SIMILAR SPECIES
NORTHERN HARRIER
see p.124
reddish underparts
longer wings
FERRUGINOUS HAWK
see p.132
reddish upperparts
white under-parts

OCCURRENCE
Breeds in rough, open country with low crags and cliffs, in high subarctic and Arctic regions; found on the edge of extensive forest or forest clearings, and in treeless tundra, uplands, and alpine habitats. Winters in open areas with fields, marshes, and rough grasslands.

Length **19–20in (48–51cm)**	Wingspan **4¼–4½ft (1.3–1.4m)**	Weight **1½–3lb (0.7–1.4kg)**
Social **Solitary**	Lifespan **Up to 18 years**	Status **Secure**

Order **Falconiformes**	Family **Accipitridae**	Species ***Aquila chrysaetos***

Golden Eagle

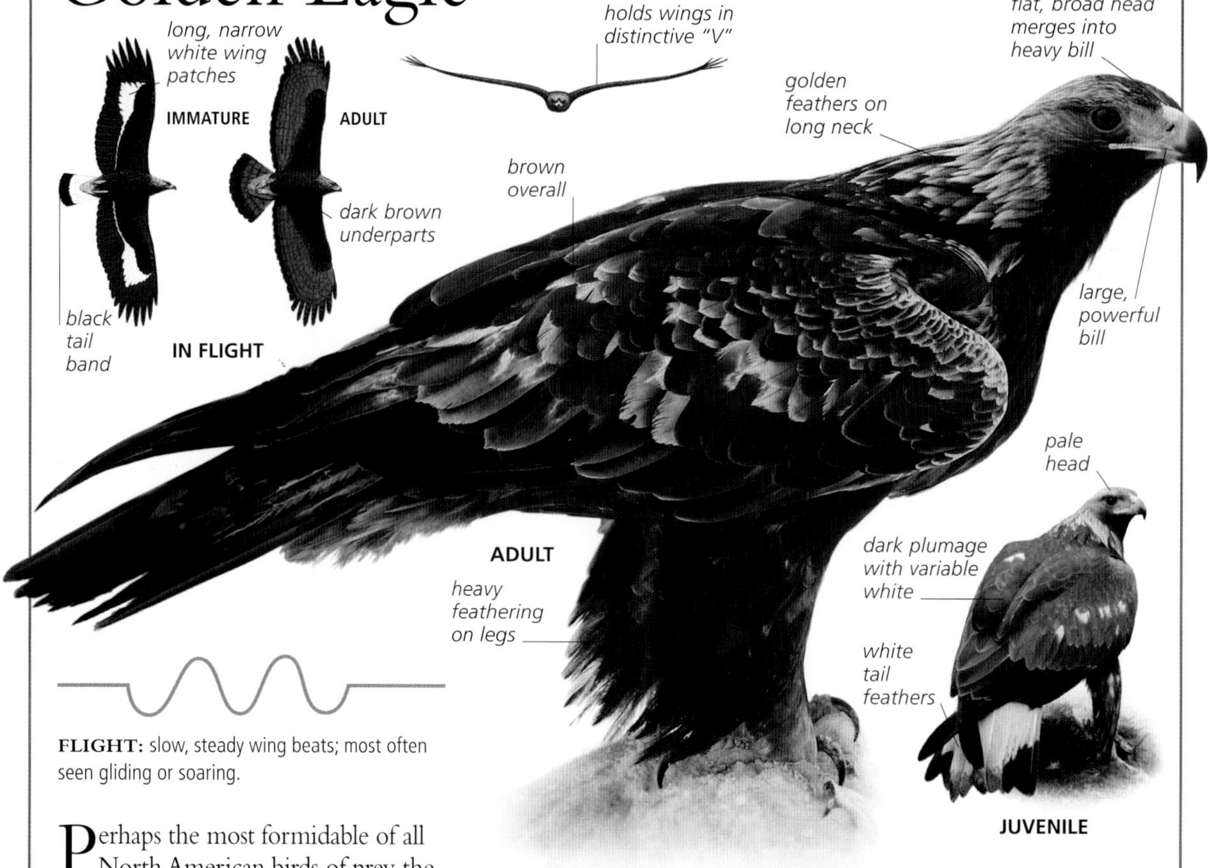

long, narrow white wing patches
IMMATURE
ADULT
black tail band
dark brown underparts
IN FLIGHT
holds wings in distinctive "V"
brown overall
golden feathers on long neck
flat, broad head merges into heavy bill
large, powerful bill
ADULT
heavy feathering on legs
pale head
dark plumage with variable white
white tail feathers
JUVENILE

FLIGHT: slow, steady wing beats; most often seen gliding or soaring.

Perhaps the most formidable of all North American birds of prey, the Golden Eagle is found mostly in the western part of the continent. It defends large territories ranging from 8–12 square miles (20–30 square kilometers), containing up to 14 nests. Although it appears sluggish, it is amazingly swift and agile, and employs a variety of hunting techniques to catch specific prey. Shot and poisoned by ranchers and trappers, it is unfortunately also faced with dwindling habitat and food sources due to human development.

VOICE Mostly silent, but breeding adults yelp and mew.

NESTING Large pile of sticks and vegetation on cliffs, in trees, and on manmade structures; 1–3 eggs; 1 brood; April–August.

FEEDING Eats mammals, such as hares, rabbits, ground squirrels, prairie dogs, marmots, foxes, and coyotes; also birds.

POWER AND STRENGTH
The Golden Eagle symbolizes all birds of prey, with its sharp talons, hooked bill, and large size.

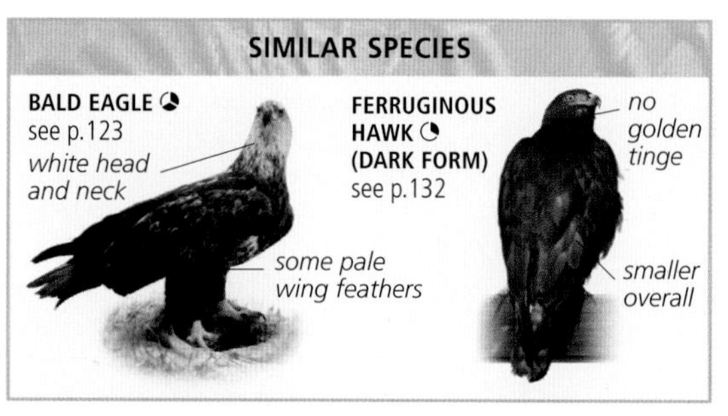
SIMILAR SPECIES
BALD EAGLE
see p.123
white head and neck
some pale wing feathers
FERRUGINOUS HAWK
(DARK FORM)
see p.132
no golden tinge
smaller overall

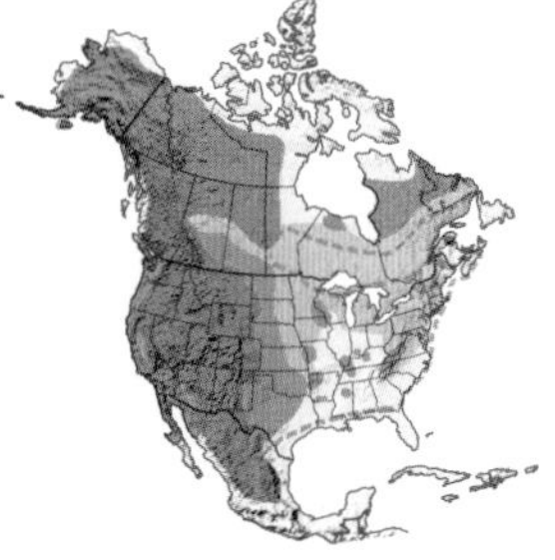

OCCURRENCE
In North America occurs mostly in grasslands, wetlands, and rocky areas; breeds south to Mexico, in open and semi-open habitats from sea level to 12,000ft (3,500m) including tundra, shrublands, grasslands, coniferous forests, farmland, areas close to streams or rivers; winters in open habitat.

Length **28–33in (70–84cm)**	Wingspan **6–7¼in (1.8–2.2m)**	Weight **6½–13lb (3–6kg)**
Social **Solitary/Pairs**	Lifespan **Up to 39 years**	Status **Declining (p)**

Family **Rallidae**

RAILS

THE RALLIDAE, OR RAIL family is a diverse group of small to medium-sized marsh birds. In Canada, rallids, as they are known collectively, are represented by three rails, a gallinule, and a coot. Rails and crakes inhabit dense marshland and are secretive, solitary, and inconspicuous, whereas coots and gallinules are seen on open water. Rallids are chicken-like birds with stubby tails and short, rounded wings. The rails of genus *Rallus* have drab, camouflage coloring, and are long-legged, long-billed, and narrow-bodied. The smaller crakes are similar, but with shorter necks and stout, stubby bills. Both rails and crakes walk and run on the ground in marsh vegetation, but can swim well. Colorful gallinules include the Common Moorhen and the rare Purple Gallinule. Rallids look like weak flyers, but many migrate great distances at night. None has a specialized diet; their food includes insects, small crabs, slugs, snails, and plant matter. Rallids nest in pairs, the birds keep in close contact by calling loudly and clearly.

THIN AS A RAIL
This marsh-dwelling Virginia Rail's narrow body enables it to slip easily through reed beds.

LIGHT ON ITS TOES
Common Moorhens can easily walk on floating vegetation because of their long toes.

Family **Gruidae**

CRANES

CRANES ARE LARGE WADING BIRDS, superficially similar to storks and to the larger herons and egrets. However, several anatomical differences place them in a different family (Gruidae), within a different order (Gruiformes). The two North American species of cranes have much lighter bills than storks. Typically, too, long inner wing feathers form a "bustle" on a standing crane, giving it a different profile than a heron. Additionally, cranes fly with their necks straight out, rather than in the tight S-curve regularly seen in similar-sized herons.

The Whooping Crane is the tallest bird in North America, standing nearly 5ft (1.5m) high.

CRANE RALLY
Large numbers of Sandhill Cranes gather on feeding grounds in winter, groups arriving in V-formation.

Order **Gruiformes**	Family **Rallidae**	Species ***Coturnicops noveboracensis***

Yellow Rail

dangling legs
white patch on inner wing feathers
ADULT
IN FLIGHT

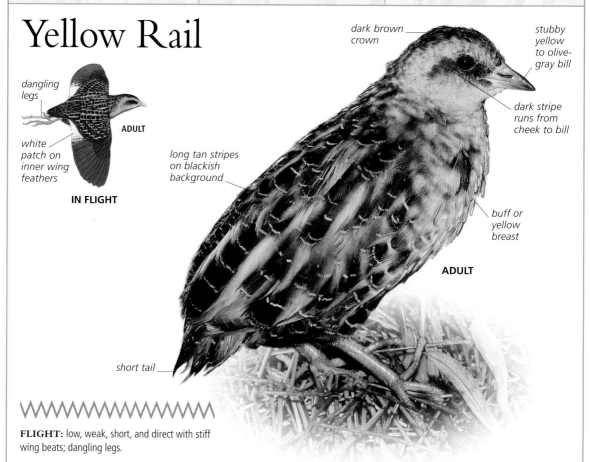

dark brown crown
stubby yellow to olive-gray bill
dark stripe runs from cheek to bill
long tan stripes on blackish background
buff or yellow breast
ADULT
short tail

FLIGHT: low, weak, short, and direct with stiff wing beats; dangling legs.

Although widespread, the diminutive, secretive, nocturnal Yellow Rail is extremely difficult to observe in its dense, damp, grassy habitat, and is detected mainly by its voice. The Yellow Rail, whose Latin name of *noveboracensis* means "New Yorker," has a small head, almost no neck, a stubby bill, a plump, almost tail-less body, and short legs. The bill of the male turns yellow in the breeding season; for the rest of the year, it is olive-gray like the female's. Although the Yellow Rail tends to dart for cover when disturbed, when it does fly, it reveals a distinctive white patch on its inner wing.

VOICE Two clicking calls followed by three more given by males, usually at night, reminiscent of two pebbles being struck together; also descending cackles, quiet croaking, and soft clucking.

NESTING Small cup of grasses and sedges, on the ground or in a plant tuft above water, concealed by overhanging vegetation; 8–10 eggs; 1 brood; May–June.

FEEDING Plucks seeds, aquatic insects, various small crustaceans, and mollusks (primarily small freshwater snails) from vegetation or ground; forages on the marsh surface or in shallow water, hidden by grass.

SIMILAR SPECIES
SORA
see p.139
black streaks on brown upperparts
gray underparts

CURIOUS LISTENER
Imitating the "tick" calls of the Yellow Rail is often an effective way to lure it out into the open.

OCCURRENCE
Breeds in brackish and freshwater marshes and wet sedge meadows in Canada and the north central US; there is an isolated breeding population in Oregon. Winters predominantly in coastal marshes along the eastern seaboard.

Length **7¼in (18.5cm)**	Wingspan **11in (28cm)**	Weight **1¾oz (50g)**
Social **Pairs**	Lifespan **Unknown**	Status **Secure**

Order **Gruiformes**	Family **Rallidae**	Species ***Rallus elegans***

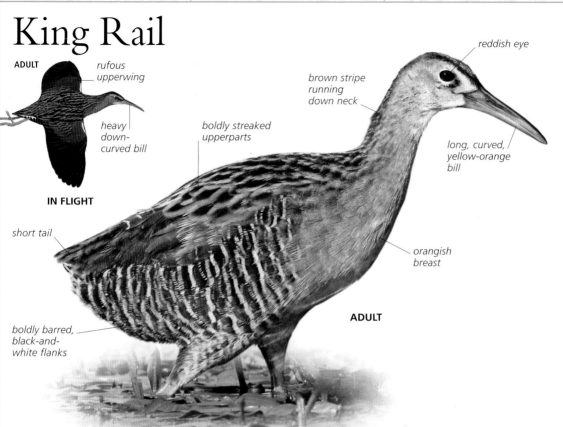

King Rail

ADULT

rufous upperwing

heavy down-curved bill

IN FLIGHT

reddish eye

brown stripe running down neck

boldly streaked upperparts

long, curved, yellow-orange bill

short tail

orangish breast

ADULT

boldly barred, black-and-white flanks

This chicken-like marsh bird is the freshwater version of the Clapper Rail. These two species are known to interbreed where their ranges overlap. A scattered and localized breeder across eastern North America, the King Rail depends on extensive freshwater marsh habitats with tall, emergent reeds and cattails. Concealed by this vegetation, the King Rail is rarely seen and is most often detected by its distinctive calls.

VOICE Male call similar to Clapper Rail but lower; emits a loud *kik kik kik* during breeding season.

NESTING Cup of vegetation, often hidden by bent stems that form a canopy; 6–12 eggs; 2 broods; February–August.

FEEDING Forages in concealed locations for insects, snails, spiders, and crustaceans such as shrimps, crabs, and barnacles; also fish, frogs, and seeds.

FLIGHT: somewhat clumsy and labored; legs dangling; prefers to run.

LARGEST RAIL
Easily confused with the closely related Clapper Rail, this is the largest North American rail.

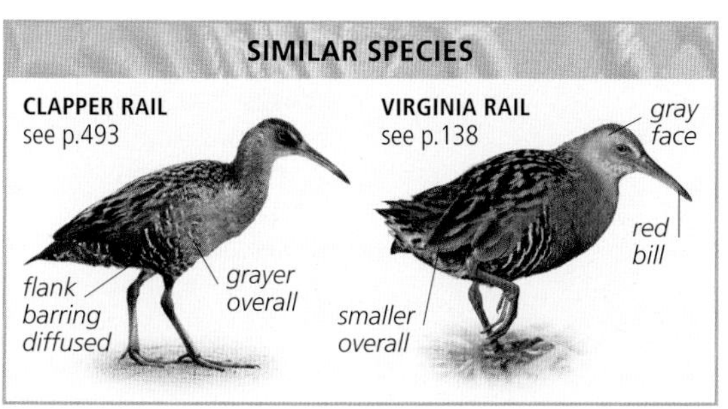
SIMILAR SPECIES
CLAPPER RAIL
see p.493
flank barring diffused
grayer overall
VIRGINIA RAIL
see p.138
gray face
red bill
smaller overall

OCCURRENCE
Mostly breeds in freshwater marshes in the eastern US and in extreme southern Ontario. Also found throughout the year along the southern coast of the US, including Florida, and in central Mexico and Cuba.

Length **15in (38cm)**	Wingspan **20in (51cm)**	Weight **13oz (375g)**
Social **Pairs**	Lifespan **Unknown**	Status **Localized**

Order **Gruiformes**	Family **Rallidae**	Species ***Rallus limicola***

Virginia Rail

rufous upperwing
ADULT (BREEDING)
dark outer wing feathers
IN FLIGHT
streaked black and brown upperparts
gray cheeks
curved, red bill
reddish brown breast
white undertail
black-and-white barring on flanks
diffused streaking
dark bill
dark, blotchy breast
ADULT (NONBREEDING)
reddish legs and toes
ADULT (BREEDING)

A smaller version of the King Rail, this freshwater marsh dweller is similar to its other relatives, more often heard than seen. Distributed in a wide range, the Virginia Rail spends most of its time in thick, reedy vegetation, which it pushes using its "rail thin" body and flexible vertebrae. Although it spends most of its life walking, it can swim and even dive to escape danger. The Virginia Rail is a partial migrant that leaves its northern breeding grounds in winter.

VOICE Series of pig-like grunting *oinks* that start loud and sharp, becoming steadily softer; also emits a series of double notes *ka-dik ka-dik*.

NESTING Substantial cup of plant material, concealed by bent-over stems; 5–12 eggs; 1–2 broods; April–July.

FEEDING Actively stalks prey or may wait and dive into water; primarily eats snails, insects, and spiders, but may also eat seeds.

FLIGHT: weak and struggling with outstretched neck and legs trailing behind.

HARD TO SPOT
The secretive Virginia Rail is difficult to spot in its reedy habitat.

SIMILAR SPECIES

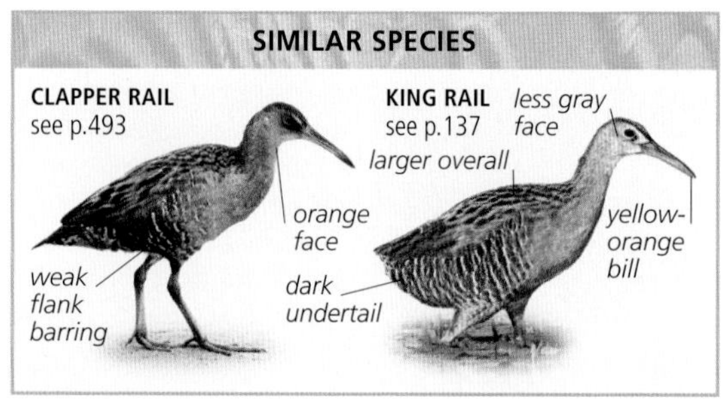

CLAPPER RAIL
see p.493
orange face
weak flank barring
KING RAIL
see p.137
less gray face
larger overall
yellow-orange bill
dark undertail

OCCURRENCE
Breeds in freshwater habitats across North America, though is found throughout the year along the West Coast of the US. In winter, moves to saltwater and freshwater marshes in the southern US, including Florida, and in northern and central Mexico.

Length **9½in (24cm)**	Wingspan **13in (33cm)**	Weight **3oz (85g)**
Social **Pairs**	Lifespan **Unknown**	Status **Secure**

Order **Gruiformes**	Family **Rallidae**	Species ***Porzana carolina***

Sora

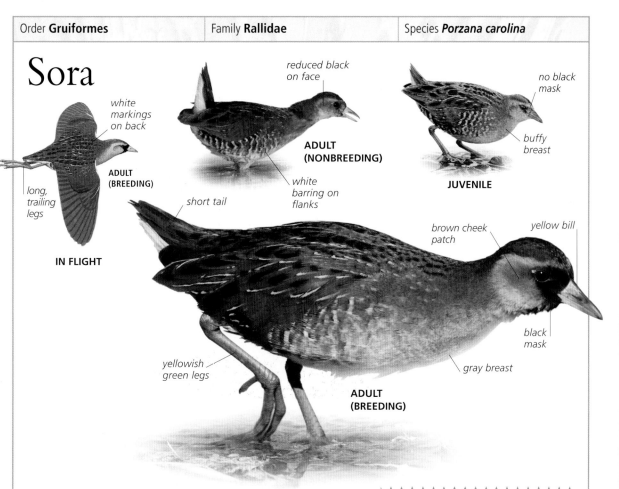

white markings on back
ADULT (BREEDING)
long, trailing legs
IN FLIGHT

reduced black on face
ADULT (NONBREEDING)
white barring on flanks

no black mask
buffy breast
JUVENILE

short tail
brown cheek patch
yellow bill
black mask
yellowish green legs
gray breast
ADULT (BREEDING)

Despite being the most widely distributed rail in North America, the Sora is rarely seen. It breeds in freshwater marshes and migrates hundreds of miles south in winter regardless of its weak and hesitant flight. It swims well, with a characteristic head-bobbing action. The Sora can be spotted walking at the edge of emergent vegetation—its yellow bill and black mask distinguish it from other rails.

VOICE Call a long, high, and loud, descending, horse-like whinny *ko-wee-hee-hee-hee-hee*; has an upslurred whistle.

NESTING Loosely woven basket of marsh vegetation suspended above water or positioned in clumps of vegetation on the water's surface; 8–11 eggs; 1 brood; May–June.

FEEDING Rakes vegetation with feet or pulls with bill in search of seeds of wetland plants, insects, spiders, and snails.

FLIGHT: appears weak, yet strenuous; wing beats hurried and constant.

CHICKEN-LIKE WALK
A rare sight, the Sora walks chicken-like through a marsh, its body in a low crouch.

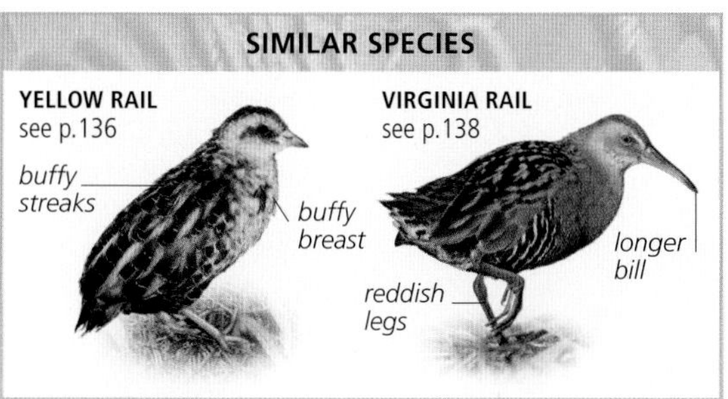
SIMILAR SPECIES
YELLOW RAIL
see p.136
buffy streaks
buffy breast
VIRGINIA RAIL
see p.138
longer bill
reddish legs

OCCURRENCE
Breeds in freshwater marshes with emergent vegetation across most of temperate North America; rarely in salt marshes along the Atlantic Coast. Winters in freshwater, saltwater, and brackish marshes with spartina grass from the southern US to northern South America.

Length **8½in (22cm)**	Wingspan **14in (36cm)**	Weight **2⅝oz (75g)**
Social **Solitary**	Lifespan **Unknown**	Status **Secure**

Order **Gruiformes**	Family **Rallidae**	Species ***Gallinula chloropus***

Common Moorhen

ADULT (BREEDING)

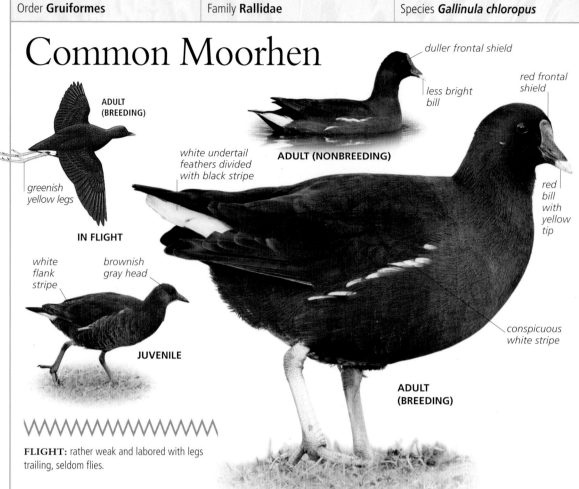

greenish yellow legs

IN FLIGHT

duller frontal shield

less bright bill

ADULT (NONBREEDING)

white undertail feathers divided with black stripe

red frontal shield

red bill with yellow tip

white flank stripe

brownish gray head

JUVENILE

conspicuous white stripe

ADULT (BREEDING)

FLIGHT: rather weak and labored with legs trailing, seldom flies.

The Common Moorhen is fairly widespread in the eastern US and southeastern Canada, although its distribution is more patchy in the western states. It has similarities in behavior and habitat to both the true rails and coots. Equally at home on land and water, its long toes allow it to walk easily over floating vegetation and soft mud. When walking or swimming, the Common Moorhen nervously jerks its short tail, revealing its white undertail feathers, and bobs its head.

VOICE A variety of hen-like clucks and cackles, including an exlosive *krrooo*.

NESTING Bulky platform of aquatic vegetation with growing plants pulled over to conceal it, or close to water; 5–11 eggs, 1–3 broods; May–August, maybe year round in Florida.

FEEDING Forages mainly on aquatic and terrestrial plants and aquatic vegetation; also eats snails, spiders, and insects.

DUAL HABITAT
A walker and a swimmer, the Moorhen is equally at home on land and in water.

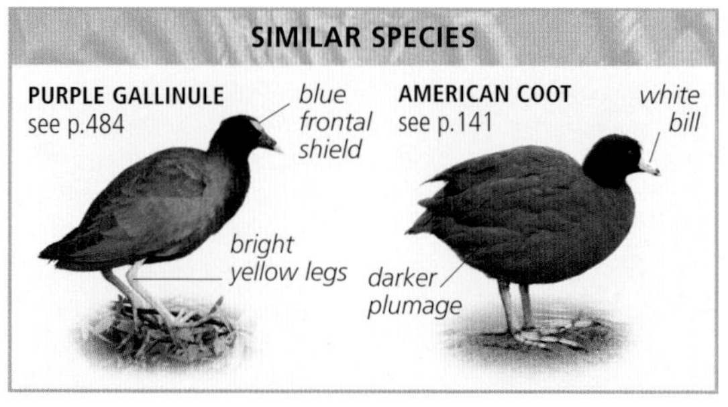
SIMILAR SPECIES
PURPLE GALLINULE
see p.484
blue frontal shield
bright yellow legs
AMERICAN COOT
see p.141
white bill
darker plumage

OCCURRENCE
Breeds in freshwater habitats in the eastern US and Canada; more localized in the West. Winters in warmer areas with open water, such as southern California and Mexico. Also found in Central and South America.

Length **14in (36cm)**	Wingspan **21in (53cm)**	Weight **11oz (325g)**
Social **Pairs**	Lifespan **Up to 10 years**	Status **Secure**

Order **Gruiformes**	Family **Rallidae**	Species ***Fulica americana***

American Coot

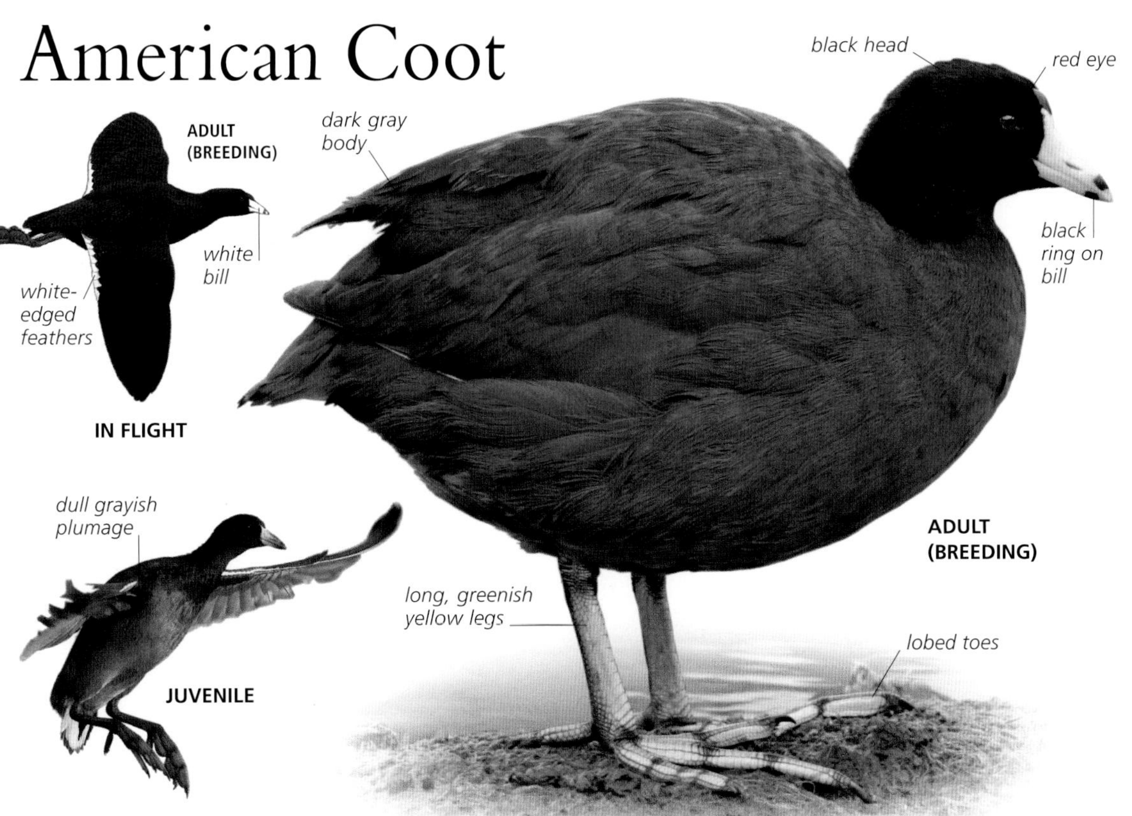
ADULT
(BREEDING)
dark gray
body
black head
red eye
black
ring on
bill
white
bill
white-
edged
feathers
IN FLIGHT
dull grayish
plumage
JUVENILE
long, greenish
yellow legs
lobed toes
ADULT
(BREEDING)

This duck-like species of rail is the most abundant and widely distributed of North American rails. Its lobed toes make it well adapted to swimming and diving, but somewhat of an impediment on land. Its flight is clumsy; it becomes airborne with difficulty, running along the water surface before taking off. American Coots form large flocks on open water in winter, often associating with ducks—an unusual trait for a member of the rail family.

VOICE Various raucous clucks, grunts, and croaks and an explosive *keek*.

NESTING Bulky cup of plant material placed in aquatic vegetation on or near water; 5–15 eggs; 1–2 broods; April–July.

FEEDING Forages on or under shallow water and feeds on land; primarily herbivorous, but also eats snails, insects, spiders, tadpoles, fish, and even carrion.

FLIGHT: low and labored; runs for quite a long distance to take off.

SWIMMING AWAY
The red-headed, baldish looking American Coot chicks leave the nest a day after hatching.

SIMILAR SPECIES

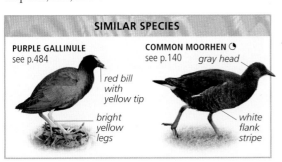

PURPLE GALLINULE see p.484
red bill with yellow tip; bright yellow legs

COMMON MOORHEN ◔ see p.140
gray head; white flank stripe

OCCURRENCE
Breeds in open water habitats west of the Appalachians and in Florida. Moves from the northern parts of its range in winter to the southeastern US, where open water persists; also migrates to western and southern Mexico.

Length **15½in (40cm)**	Wingspan **24in (61cm)**	Weight **16oz (450g)**
Social **Flocks**	Lifespan **Up to 22 years**	Status **Secure**

Order **Gruiformes**	Family **Gruidae**	Species ***Grus canadensis***

Sandhill Crane

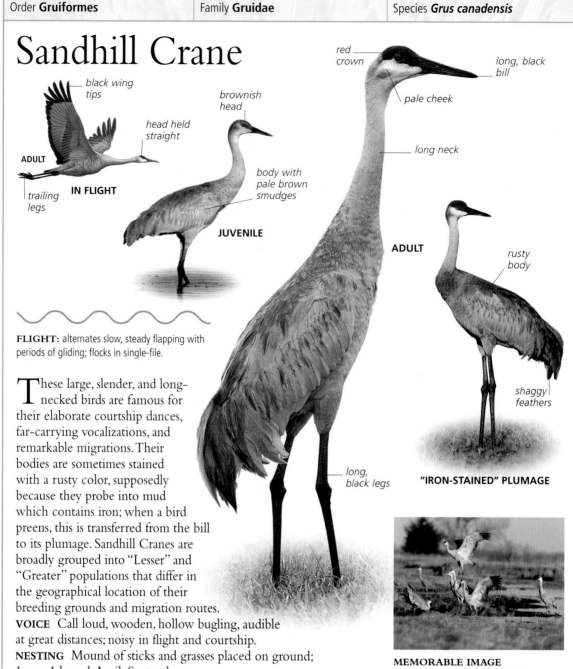

black wing tips
head held straight
ADULT
trailing legs
IN FLIGHT

brownish head
body with pale brown smudges
JUVENILE

red crown
long, black bill
pale cheek
long neck
ADULT
long, black legs

rusty body
shaggy feathers
"IRON-STAINED" PLUMAGE

FLIGHT: alternates slow, steady flapping with periods of gliding; flocks in single-file.

These large, slender, and long-necked birds are famous for their elaborate courtship dances, far-carrying vocalizations, and remarkable migrations. Their bodies are sometimes stained with a rusty color, supposedly because they probe into mud which contains iron; when a bird preens, this is transferred from the bill to its plumage. Sandhill Cranes are broadly grouped into "Lesser" and "Greater" populations that differ in the geographical location of their breeding grounds and migration routes.

VOICE Call loud, wooden, hollow bugling, audible at great distances; noisy in flight and courtship.

NESTING Mound of sticks and grasses placed on ground; 1 egg; 1 brood; April–September.

FEEDING Eats shoots, grain; also aquatic mollusks and insects.

MEMORABLE IMAGE
Its long neck, large wings, and distinctive red crown make it difficult to mistake.

SIMILAR SPECIES

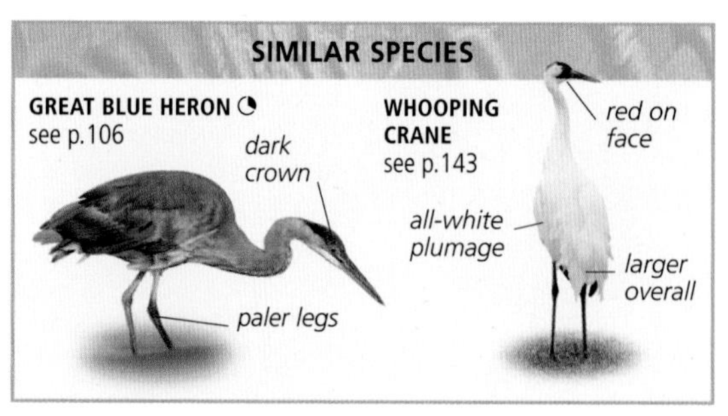
GREAT BLUE HERON
see p.106
dark crown
paler legs
WHOOPING CRANE
see p.143
red on face
all-white plumage
larger overall

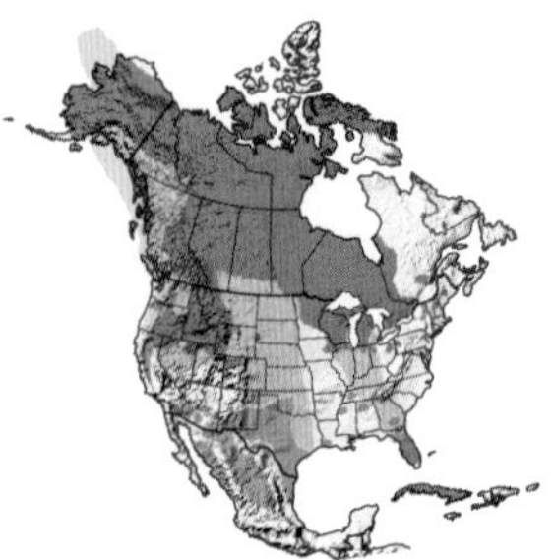

OCCURRENCE
Breeds in muskeg, tundra, and forest clearings across northwestern North America, east to Quebec and the Great Lakes; large wintering and migratory flocks often densely packed, roosting in or near marshes. Winters south to northern Mexico.

Length **2¾–4ft (0.8–1.2m)**	Wingspan **6–7½ft (1.8–2.3m)**	Weight **7¾–11lb (3.5–5kg)**
Social **Flocks**	Lifespan **Up to 25 years**	Status **Secure**

Order **Gruiformes**	Family **Gruidae**	Species ***Grus americana***

Whooping Crane

black wingtips
ADULT
head held straight
IN FLIGHT
trailing legs

very dark red "mask"
long, dark bill
long neck
ADULT
white overall
gray-black legs

brownish head
scattered brown feathers
JUVENILE

FLIGHT: slow and powerful wing beats; appears imposingly large in flight.

The colossal and majestic Whooping Crane is one of the most compelling success stories for endangered bird species in Canada. Thanks to an ambitious campaign of habitat protection, captive breeding and release, and public education, the species has rebounded from just a few dozen birds in the mid-20th century to hundreds of individuals in the early 21st century. However, it still remains endangered, because it reproduces slowly in a restricted range and additional intervention measures are required to help this fragile species continue its recovery.

VOICE Piercing and trumpeting, *kerloo!* and *kerleeyew*, audible from afar; bugling calls during courtship dances.

NESTING Mound of vegetation placed on ground; 2 eggs; 1 brood; April–August.

FEEDING Gleans animal and plant matter, such as frogs, mollusks, berries, and seeds, from the ground.

STATELY PROGRESS
Whooping Cranes move slowly and steadily through the shallows searching for prey.

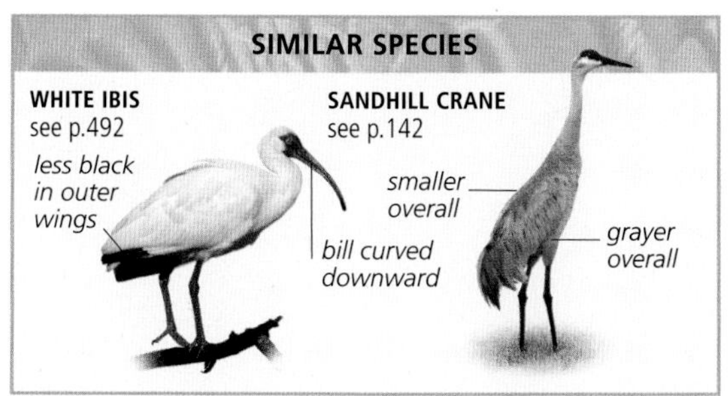
SIMILAR SPECIES
WHITE IBIS
see p.492
less black in outer wings
bill curved downward
SANDHILL CRANE
see p.142
smaller overall
grayer overall

PREPARING TO LAND
The Whooping Crane brakes by opening its outer wing feathers to let air flow through.

OCCURRENCE
Breeds in marshy country with scattered ponds and prairies in a very small region of Canada; birds migrate along a narrow route to winter in coastal estuaries in Texas; on migration, uses both agricultural fields and marshland. Small numbers of migrants found with large numbers of Sandhill Cranes.

Length **4–4½ft (1.2–1.4m)**	Wingspan **7¼ft (2.2m)**	Weight **15–18lb (7–8kg)**
Social **Solitary/Pairs**	Lifespan **Up to 30 years**	Status **Endangered**

Families **Haematopodidae, Recurvirostridae, Charadriidae, Scolopacidae, Laridae, Stercorariidae, Alcidae**

SHOREBIRDS, GULLS, & AUKS

THE DIVERSE SHOREBIRD, gull, and auk families together form the order Charadriiformes. They are small to medium-sized, mostly migratory birds, associated with aquatic habitats. Over 100 species are found in North America.

TYPICAL GULL
Most large gulls, such as this Western Gull, have white heads and underparts with long dark wings and a bright sturdy bill.

SHOREBIRDS

The various species popularly known as shorebirds belong to several different families. In Canada there are the oystercatchers (Haematopodidae), the avocets and stilts (Recurvirostridae), the plovers (Charadriidae), the sandpipers (Scolopacidae); and the Phalaropes (a subfamily Phalaropodinae, of Scolopacidae). They have long legs in proportion to their bodies, and a variety of bills, ranging from short to long, thin, thick, straight, down-curved and up-curved.

GULLS

The over 20 species of Canadian gulls in the family Laridae all share a similar stout body shape, sturdy bills and webbed toes. Nearly all are scavengers. Closely associated with coastal areas, few gulls venture far out to sea. Some species are seen around fishing ports and harbors, or inland, especially in urban areas and garbage dumps.

TERNS

Terns are specialized, long-billed predators that dive for fish. More slender and elegant than gulls, nearly all are immediately recognizable when breeding, due to their black caps and long, pointed bills. The related but differently billed Black Skimmer, a vagrant in Canada, also catches fish.

AUKS, MURRES, AND PUFFINS

Denizens of the northern oceans, these birds come to land only to breed. Most nest in colonies on sheer cliffs overlooking the ocean, but puffins excavate burrows in the ground, and some murrelets nest away from predators high up in treetops far inland.

COLOR-CHANGE BILL
The bright colors of a breeding Tufted Puffin's bill fade to more muted tones in winter, after the breeding season.

ON THE MOVE
Dunlins and other sandpipers gather in large, highly coordinated flocks on migration.

Order **Charadriiformes**	Family **Haematopodidae**	Species ***Haematopus bachmani***

Black Oystercatcher

ADULT

long, orange-red bill

broad, powerful wings

IN FLIGHT

dark brown to black body

bright yellow eye

orange-red eye-ring

ADULT

thick, pink legs

dull orange eye-ring

dark eye

dark tip of bill

JUVENILE

This large, striking oystercatcher shares the typical round-bodied, hunch-backed, and squat-necked shape of other oystercatchers, as well as their typically thick legs and bill. But it is instantly obvious because of its all-dark plumage, making the pale eyes and colorful bill all the more conspicuous. It is restricted to rocky coasts, where it feeds in pairs or family groups, using well-defined territories in summer. In winter, the birds gather in larger flocks where they are numerous, sometimes in hundreds, where mussels are abundant. These are noisy, demonstrative birds, and always entertaining to watch.

VOICE Flight call a loud, whistled *wheeu*, with emphasis on first part of call; alarm call sharper *wheep*; courtship and posturing calls a series of whistles based on flight call, accelerating into descending piping calls.

NESTING Simple scrape just above high-tide line, often lined with broken shells and pebbles; 1–3 eggs; 1 brood; May–June.

FEEDING Feeds on slightly submerged shellfish beds; diet includes mollusks, particularly mussels and limpets; also eats a variety of crustaceans, such as crabs and barnacles; oysters are rarely consumed.

FLIGHT: strong, powerful flight with shallow wing beats.

MUSSEL LOVER
The Black Oystercatcher can often be spotted walking along mussel beds at low tide.

SIMILAR SPECIES

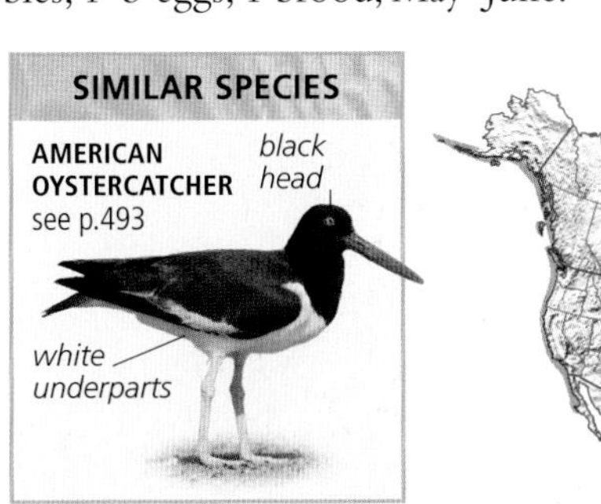
AMERICAN OYSTERCATCHER
see p.493
black head
white underparts

OCCURRENCE
Feeds in the area between the high and low tide marks on rocky shores of western North America, from Alaska southward to Baja California. Breeds just above high tide line on rocky headlands or sand, shell, and gravel beaches. In winter, also found on rocky jetties in southern part of range.

Length **16½–18½in (42–47cm)**	Wingspan **30–34in (77–86cm)**	Weight **18–25oz (500–700g)**
Social **Pairs/Flocks**	Lifespan **10–15 years**	Status **Secure**

Order **Charadriiformes**	Family **Recurvirostridae**	Species ***Himantopus mexicanus***

Black-necked Stilt

long, angular, black wings
ADULT
no white spot above red eye
long, slender neck
IN FLIGHT
scaly appearance
less contrasting head pattern than adult
shorter, stubbier bill
JUVENILE
white spot above red eye
black mask encircles eye
black upperparts
long, needle-like black bill
slender, tapered body
white underparts
MALE
long, bright pink legs
brownish wash to back
duller legs than male
FEMALE

This tall, slender, elegant, and black-and-white shorebird is a familiar sight at ponds and lagoons in the western and southern US and in the southern Canadian prairies. Even among the shorebirds, it is remarkably long-legged, at times almost grotesquely so: in flight, it often crosses its trailing feet as if for extra control and support. Breeding takes place in small colonies, with several pairs sharing the same site. In winter, these tall birds are often seen in small flocks of about 25 individuals. These small groups feed quietly in sheltered areas, but they aggressively drive visitors away with their raucous calls, dog-like yips, and noisy communal protests. The increased use of pesticides and loss of wetland habitat could cause a decline in its numbers in the future.

VOICE Flight and alarm call a loud, continuous poodle-like *yip-yip-yip*, given in a long series when alarmed.

NESTING Simple scrape lined with grass in soft soil; 4 eggs; 1 brood; April–May.

FEEDING Walks slowly in shallow water, picking food off surface; diet includes tadpoles, shrimps, snails, flies, worms, clams, small fish, and frogs.

FLIGHT: direct, but somewhat awkward due to long, trailing legs; deep wing beats.

FRIENDLY BUNCH
Black-necked Stilts are gregarious by nature, and often roost together in shallow water.

OCCURRENCE
Breeds around marshes, shallow grassy ponds, lake margins, and manmade waterbodies, such as reservoirs; uses similar habitats during migration and winter, as well as shallow lagoons, flooded fields, and mangrove swamps. Southern birds migrate locally only.

Length **14–15½in (35–39cm)**	Wingspan **29–32in (73–81cm)**	Weight **4–8oz (125–225g)**
Social **Small flocks**	Lifespan **Up to 19 years**	Status **Secure**

Order **Charadriiformes**	Family **Recurvirostridae**	Species ***Recurvirostra americana***

American Avocet

striking black-and-white pattern

ADULT (BREEDING)

IN FLIGHT

white eye-ring

dark eye

cinnamon-colored head

long, thin, upturned bill

bold shoulder feathers

cinnamon-colored neck

white underparts

FEMALE

long, bluish legs

less upturned bill

MALE

no cinnamon color on head and neck

white plumage

ADULT (NONBREEDING)

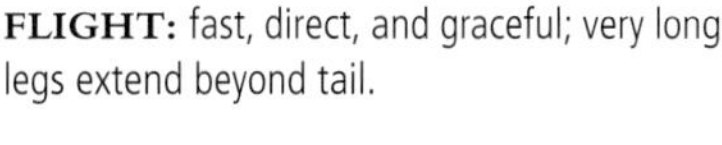

FLIGHT: fast, direct, and graceful; very long legs extend beyond tail.

With its long, thin, and upturned bill, this graceful, long-legged shorebird is unmistakable when foraging. When it takes off, its striking plumage pattern is clearly visible. It is the only one of the four avocet species in the world that changes plumage when breeding. Breeding birds have a cinnamon head and neck, and bold, patterns on their black-and-white wings and upperparts. The American Avocet forms large flocks during migration and in winter.

VOICE Flight call a variable melodic *kleet*, loud and repetitive, given when alarmed and by foraging birds.

NESTING Simple scrape in shallow depression; 4 eggs; 1 brood; May–June.

FEEDING Uses specialized bill to probe, scythe, or jab a variety of aquatic invertebrates, small fish, and seeds; walks steadily in belly-deep water to chase its prey.

FORAGING FLOCK
These birds walk through shallow water in flocks searching mainly for insects and crustaceans.

TRICKY BALANCE
During mating, the male supports himself with raised wings as the female extends her neck.

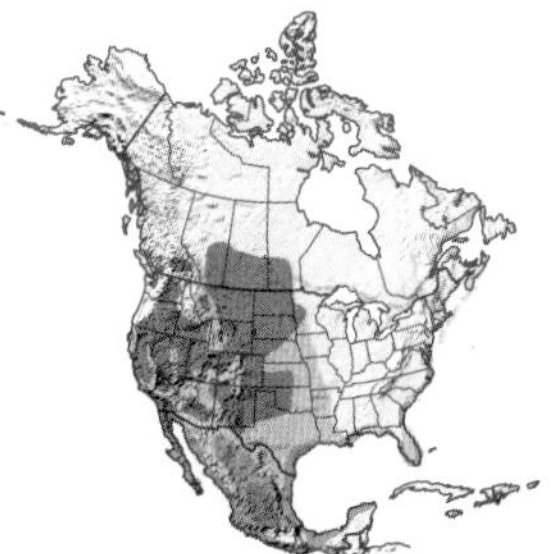

OCCURRENCE
Breeds in temporary wetlands, in dry to arid regions. During migration and in winter, found in shallow water habitats, including ponds, reservoirs, fresh- and saltwater marshes, tidal mudflats, and lagoons. Each year, flock of 10,000 birds winters at Bolivar Flats, Texas. Regular East Coast visitor.

Length **17–18½in (43–47cm)**	Wingspan **29–32in (74–81cm)**	Weight **10–12oz (275–350g)**
Social **Large flocks**	Lifespan **Up to 9 years**	Status **Secure**

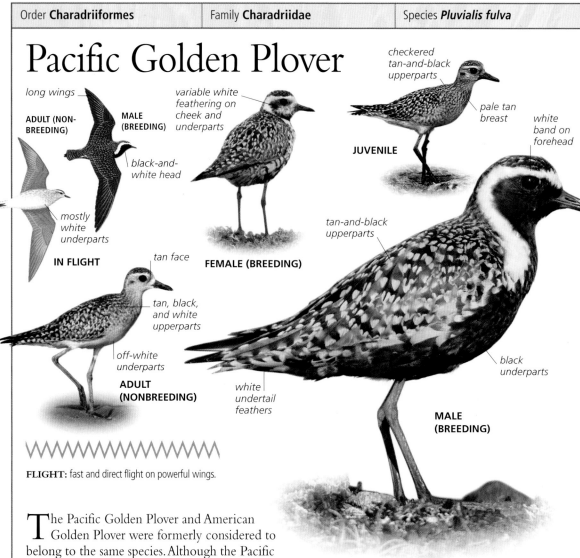

Order **Charadriiformes**	Family **Charadriidae**	Species ***Pluvialis fulva***

Pacific Golden Plover

long wings

ADULT (NON-BREEDING)

MALE (BREEDING)

black-and-white head

mostly white underparts

IN FLIGHT

variable white feathering on cheek and underparts

FEMALE (BREEDING)

checkered tan-and-black upperparts

pale tan breast

JUVENILE

white band on forehead

tan-and-black upperparts

tan face

tan, black, and white upperparts

off-white underparts

ADULT (NONBREEDING)

white undertail feathers

black underparts

MALE (BREEDING)

FLIGHT: fast and direct flight on powerful wings.

The Pacific Golden Plover and American Golden Plover were formerly considered to belong to the same species. Although the Pacific Golden Plover frequents grassy habitats, it is also regularly encountered in coastal habitats as it migrates over the ocean to wintering grounds on remote South Pacific Islands. The species nests in the tundra of the Arctic, but it can adapt to human-altered environments away from the breeding grounds.

VOICE Flight call a clearly two-syllabled *chu-EEt*, with emphasis on second note; breeding song a clear, haunting, low whistle *pEE-prr-EE*.

NESTING Shallow depression lined with lichens on densely vegetated tundra; 4 eggs; 1 brood; May–July.

FEEDING Forages in run and stop manner on grasshoppers, beetles, wireworms; also eats spiders, small mollusks, crustaceans, small fish, berries, and seeds.

SIMILAR SPECIES

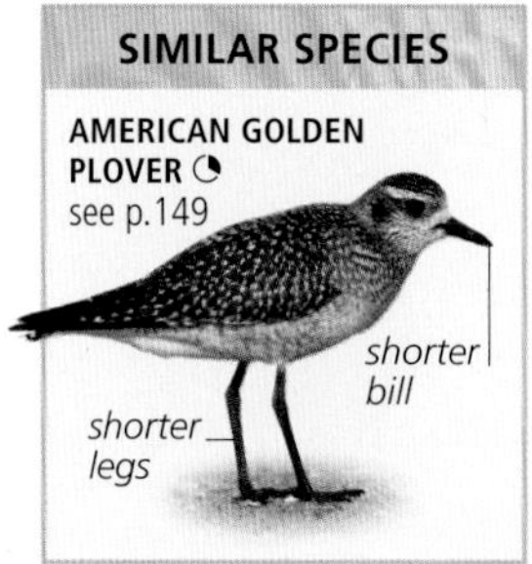
AMERICAN GOLDEN PLOVER
see p.149
shorter bill
shorter legs

FLEDGLING
Vulnerable to predators, the downy chick is camouflaged well in its tundra habitat.

OCCURRENCE
Nests primarily on Arctic and sub-Arctic tundra; in migration and winter, found in a wide variety of habitats, including prairies, pastures, mudflats, shorelines, mangroves, parks, tiny lawns and gardens in urban areas, and roadsides. About 12 percent of the world's population nests in Alaska.

Length **9–10½in (23–27cm)**	Wingspan **21–24in (53–61cm)**	Weight **3½–7oz (100–200g)**
Social **Solitary/Small flocks**	Lifespan **Up to 7 years**	Status **Localized**

Order **Charadriiformes**	Family **Charadriidae**	Species ***Pluvialis dominica***

American Golden Plover

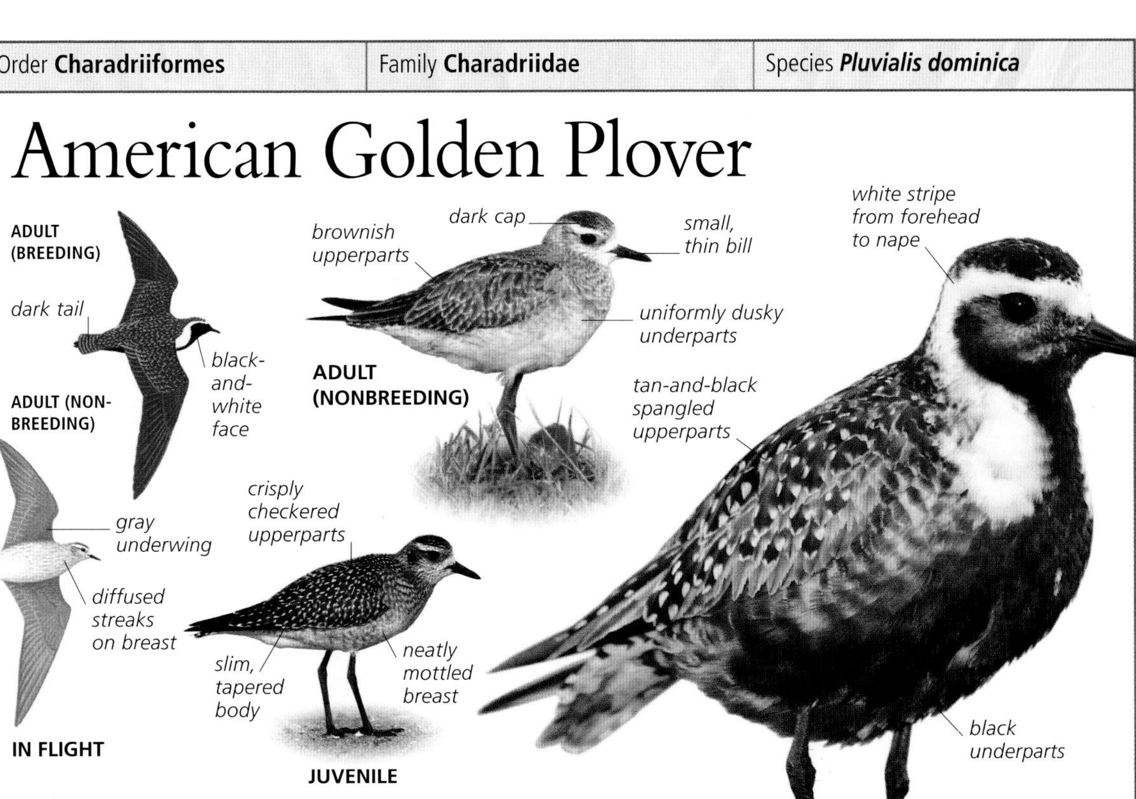
ADULT (BREEDING)
dark tail
black-and-white face
ADULT (NON-BREEDING)
gray underwing
diffused streaks on breast
IN FLIGHT
brownish upperparts
dark cap
small, thin bill
uniformly dusky underparts
ADULT (NONBREEDING)
crisply checkered upperparts
slim, tapered body
neatly mottled breast
JUVENILE
white stripe from forehead to nape
tan-and-black spangled upperparts
black underparts
black legs
ADULT (BREEDING)

FLIGHT: strong, fast, powerful flight on deep wing beats.

This long-distance migrant is seen in North America only during its lengthy spring and fall journeys to and from its high Arctic breeding grounds and wintering locations in southern South America. An elegant, slender, yet large plover, it prefers inland grassy habitats and plowed fields to coastal mudflats. The American Golden Plover's annual migration route includes a feeding stop at Labrador, then a 1,550–1,860 miles (2,500–3,000km) flight over the Atlantic Ocean to South America.

VOICE Flight call a whistled two-note *queE-dle*, or *klee-u*, with second note shorter and lower pitched; male flight song a strong, melodious whistled *kid-eek*, or *kid-EEp*.

NESTING Shallow depression lined with lichens in dry, open tundra; 4 eggs; 1 brood; May–July.

FEEDING Forages in run, pause, and pluck sequence on insects, mollusks, crustaceans, and worms; also berries and seeds.

DISTRACTION TECHNIQUE
This breeding American Golden Plover is feigning an injury to its wing to draw predators away from its eggs or chicks in its nest.

SIMILAR SPECIES

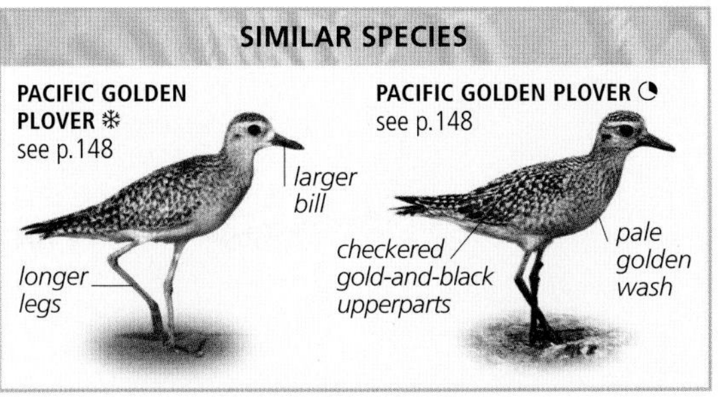
PACIFIC GOLDEN PLOVER ❄
see p.148
larger bill
longer legs
PACIFIC GOLDEN PLOVER ◔
see p.148
checkered gold-and-black upperparts
pale golden wash

OCCURRENCE
Breeds in Arctic tundra habitats. In migration, it occurs in prairies, tilled farmlands, golf courses, pastures, airports; also mudflats, shorelines, and beaches. In spring, seen in Texas and Great Plains; in fall, uncommon in northeast Maritimes and New England; scarce along the Pacific Coast.

Length **9½–11in (24–28cm)**	Wingspan **23–28in (59–72cm)**	Weight **4–7oz (125–200g)**
Social **Solitary/Small flocks**	Lifespan **Unknown**	Status **Secure**

Order **Charadriiformes**	Family **Charadriidae**	Species ***Pluvialis squatarola***

Black-bellied Plover

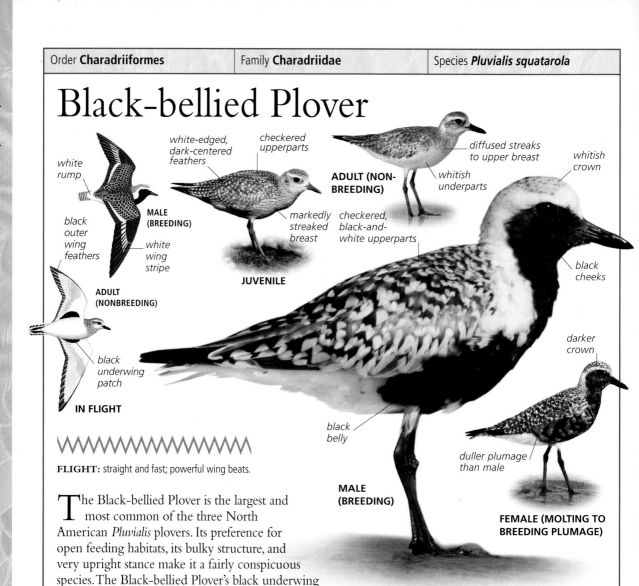

white rump
black outer wing feathers
white wing stripe
MALE (BREEDING)

ADULT (NONBREEDING)
black underwing patch
IN FLIGHT

white-edged, dark-centered feathers
checkered upperparts
markedly streaked breast
JUVENILE

diffused streaks to upper breast
whitish underparts
ADULT (NON-BREEDING)

whitish crown
checkered, black-and-white upperparts
black cheeks
black belly
MALE (BREEDING)

darker crown
duller plumage than male
FEMALE (MOLTING TO BREEDING PLUMAGE)

FLIGHT: straight and fast; powerful wing beats.

The Black-bellied Plover is the largest and most common of the three North American *Pluvialis* plovers. Its preference for open feeding habitats, its bulky structure, and very upright stance make it a fairly conspicuous species. The Black-bellied Plover's black underwing patches, visible in flight, are present in both its breeding and nonbreeding plumages and distinguish it from the other *Pluvialis* plovers.

VOICE Typical call a three-syllabled, clear, plaintive, whistled *whEE-er-eee*, with middle note lower; flight song of male during breeding softer, with accent on second syllable.

NESTING Shallow depression lined with mosses and lichens in moist to dry lowland tundra; 1–5 eggs; 1 brood; May–July.

FEEDING Forages mainly along coasts in typical plover style: run, pause, and pluck; eats insects, worms, bivalves, and crustaceans.

CASUAL WADING
The Black-bellied Plover wades in shallow water but does most of its foraging in mudflats.

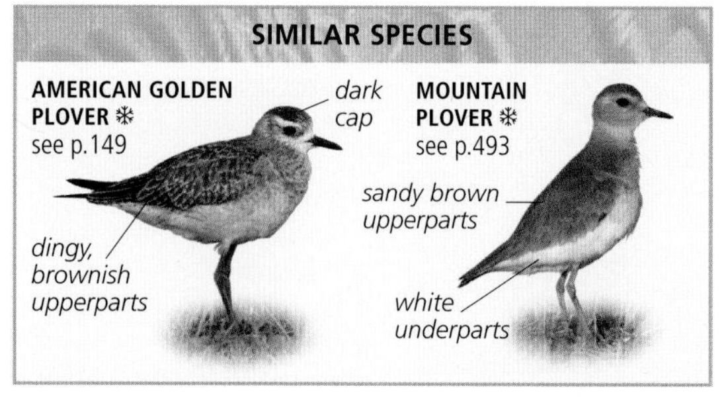
SIMILAR SPECIES
AMERICAN GOLDEN PLOVER ❄
see p.149
dark cap
dingy, brownish upperparts
MOUNTAIN PLOVER ❄
see p.493
sandy brown upperparts
white underparts

OCCURRENCE
Breeds in High Arctic habitats from western Russia across the Bering Sea to Alaska, and east to Baffin Island; winters primarily in coastal areas from southern Canada and US, south to southern South America. Found inland during migration. Migrates south all the way to South America.

Length **10½–12in (27–30cm)**	Wingspan **29–32in (73–81cm)**	Weight **5–9oz (150–250g)**
Social **Flocks**	Lifespan **Up to 12 years**	Status **Secure**

Order **Charadriiformes**	Family **Charadriidae**	Species ***Charadrius semipalmatus***

Semipalmated Plover

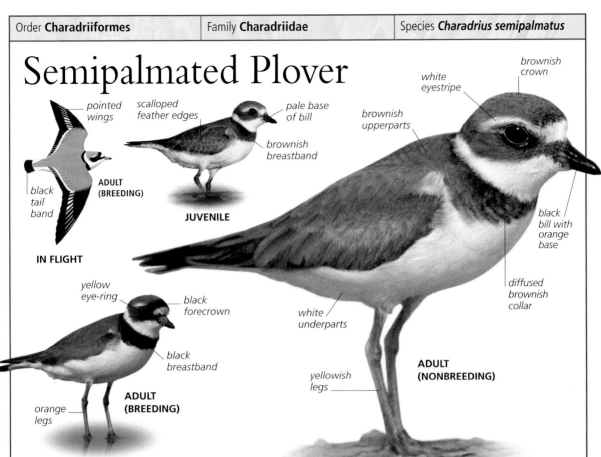

pointed wings
black tail band
ADULT (BREEDING)
IN FLIGHT

scalloped feather edges
pale base of bill
brownish breastband
JUVENILE

yellow eye-ring
black forecrown
black breastband
orange legs
ADULT (BREEDING)

white eyestripe
brownish crown
brownish upperparts
black bill with orange base
diffused brownish collar
white underparts
yellowish legs
ADULT (NONBREEDING)

Similar in appearance to the Eurasian Common Ringed Plover, the Semipalmated Plover is a small bird with a tapered shape. It is a familiar sight in a wide variety of habitats during migration and in winter, when these birds gather in loose flocks. A casual walk down a sandy beach between fall and spring might awaken up to 100 Semipalmated Plovers, sleeping in slight depressions in the sand, though flocks of up to 1,000 birds may also be encountered.

VOICE Flight call a whistled abrupt *chu-WEEp*, with soft emphasis on second syllable; courtship display song quick version of flight call followed by rough *r-r-r-r-r-r-r*, ending with a slurred, descending *yelp*.

NESTING Simple scrape on bare or slightly vegetated ground in Arctic tundra; 3–4 eggs; 1 brood; May–June.

FEEDING Forages in typical plover style: run, pause, and pluck; eats aquatic mollusks, crustaceans, flies, beetles, and spiders.

FLIGHT: straight, fast; with fluttering wing beats.

BY SIGHT AND TOUCH
Semipalmated Plovers locate prey by sight or through the sensitive soles of their feet.

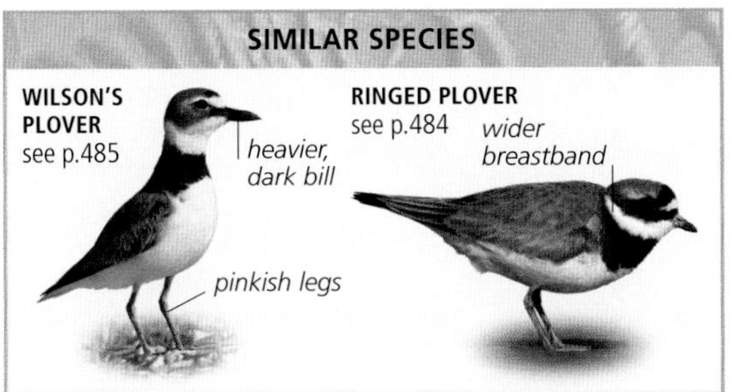
SIMILAR SPECIES
WILSON'S PLOVER
see p.485
heavier, dark bill
pinkish legs
RINGED PLOVER
see p.484
wider breastband

OCCURRENCE
Breeding habitat is Arctic or sub-Arctic tundra well-drained gravel, shale, or other sparsely vegetated ground. During migration, mudflats, saltwater marshes, lake edges, tidal areas, and flooded fields. During winter, coastal or near coastal habitats.

Length **6¾–7½in (17–19cm)**	Wingspan **17–20½in (43–52cm)**	Weight **1 1/16–2½oz (30–70g)**
Social **Solitary/Flocks**	Lifespan **Up to 6 years**	Status **Secure**

Order **Charadriiformes**	Family **Charadriidae**	Species ***Charadrius vociferus***

Killdeer

long wings
white wing bar
ADULT
reddish orange tail and rump
IN FLIGHT
red eye-ring
brownish crown
black collar encircling neck
brownish upperparts
small, thin, black bill
rufous wash to back and wings
MALE
long tail
second neck band crosses upper breast
white underparts
pinkish legs, sometimes with yellowish tinge

FLIGHT: fast, twisting flight with fluid wing beats.

This loud and vocal shorebird is the most widespread plover in North America, nesting in all southern Canadian provinces and across the US. The Killdeer's piercing call carries for long distances, sometimes causing other birds to fly away in fear of imminent danger. These birds often nest near human habitation, allowing a close observation of their vigilant parental nature with young chicks.

VOICE Flight call a rising, drawn out *deeee*; alarm call a loud, penetrating *dee-ee*, given repetitively; agitated birds also give series of *dee* notes, followed by rising trill.

NESTING Scrape on ground, sometimes in slight depression; 4 eggs; 1 brood (north), 2–3 broods (south); March–July.

FEEDING Forages in typical plover style: run, pause, and pick; eats a variety of invertebrates such as worms, snails, grasshoppers, and beetles; also small vertebrates and seeds.

CLEVER MANEUVER
The Killdeer lures intruders away from its nest with a "broken wing" display.

SIMILAR SPECIES

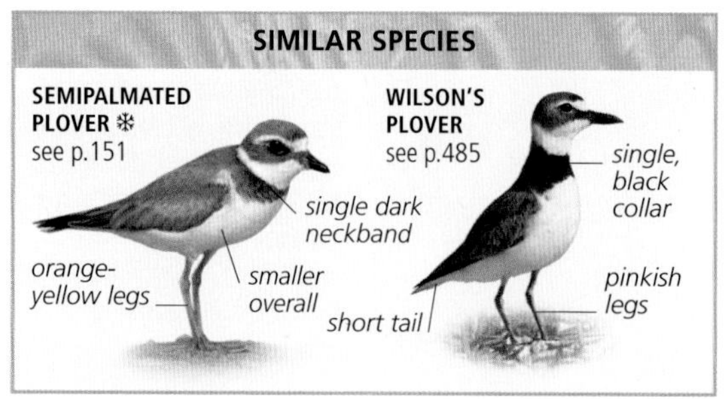
SEMIPALMATED PLOVER ❄
see p.151
single dark neckband
orange-yellow legs
smaller overall
WILSON'S PLOVER
see p.485
single, black collar
short tail
pinkish legs

OCCURRENCE
Widespread across Canada and the US, the Killdeer occurs in a wide variety of habitats. These include shorelines, mudflats, lake and river edges, sparsely grassy fields and pastures, golf courses, roadsides, parking lots, flat rooftops, driveways, and other terrestrial habitats.

Length **9–10in (23–26cm)**	Wingspan **23–25in (58–63cm)**	Weight **2¼–3⅛ oz (65–90g)**
Social **Small flocks**	Lifespan **Up to 10 years**	Status **Secure**

Order **Charadriiformes**	Family **Charadriidae**	Species ***Charadrius melodus***

Piping Plover

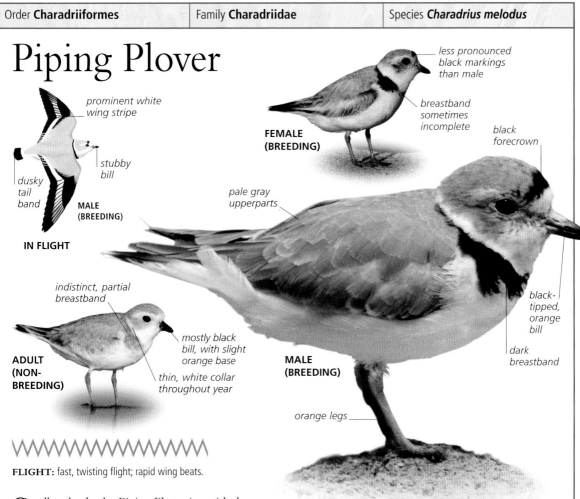

prominent white wing stripe
stubby bill
dusky tail band
MALE (BREEDING)
IN FLIGHT

less pronounced black markings than male
breastband sometimes incomplete
FEMALE (BREEDING)

black forecrown
pale gray upperparts
black-tipped, orange bill
dark breastband
MALE (BREEDING)
orange legs

indistinct, partial breastband
mostly black bill, with slight orange base
thin, white collar throughout year
ADULT (NON-BREEDING)

FLIGHT: fast, twisting flight; rapid wing beats.

Small and pale, the Piping Plover is at risk due to eroding coastlines, human disturbance, and predation by foxes, raccoons, and cats. With its pale gray back, it is well camouflaged along beaches or in dunes, but conservation measures, such as fencing off nesting beaches and control of predators, are necessary to restore populations. Two subspecies of the Piping Plover are recognized; one nests on the Atlantic Coast, and the other inland.

VOICE Clear, whistled *peep* call in flight; quiet *peep-lo* during courtship and contact; high-pitched *pipe-pipe-pipe* song.

NESTING Shallow scrape in sand, gravel, dunes, or salt flats; 4 eggs; 1 brood; April–May.

FEEDING Typical run, pause, and pluck plover feeding style; diet includes marine worms, insects, and mollusks.

VULNERABLE NESTS
The fragile nature of their preferred nesting sites has led to this species becoming endangered.

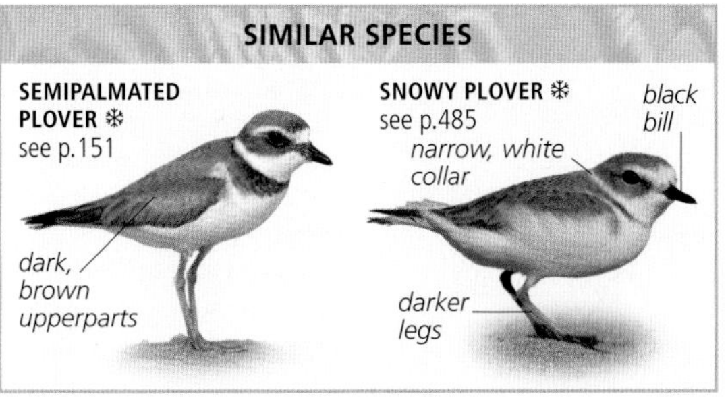
SIMILAR SPECIES
SEMIPALMATED PLOVER ❄
see p.151
dark, brown upperparts
SNOWY PLOVER ❄
see p.485
narrow, white collar
black bill
darker legs

OCCURRENCE
Found along beaches, in saline sandflats, and adjacent mudflats; during winter, found exclusively along the Atlantic and Gulf Coasts, sandflats, and mudflats. Inland subspecies nests on sand or gravel beaches adjacent to large lakes, rivers, and saline lakes.

Length **6½–7in (17–18cm)**	Wingspan **18–18½in (45–47cm)**	Weight **1⅝–2⅜oz (45–65g)**
Social **Small flocks**	Lifespan **Up to 11 years**	Status **Vulnerable**

Order **Charadriiformes**	Family **Scolopacidae**	Species ***Scolopax minor***

American Woodcock

two pale bands across back
long bill
plump body
short, rusty tail
ADULT
IN FLIGHT
large, black eye
long bill, wide at base with slightly drooping tip
black, gray, and buff upperparts
ADULT
rich orange-buff underparts
round, plump body
short, rusty tail
pinkish legs and feet

FLIGHT: twisting, slow and clumsy; wings twitter when flushed.

This forest-dwelling member of the sandpiper family bears little resemblance in behavior to its water-favoring relatives, but slightly resembles Wilson's Snipe and the dowitchers. Although widespread, the American Woodcock is very secretive and seldom seen, except during its twilight courtship displays. It is largely nocturnal, and feeds in mature fields or woodlands. Its noisy, repetitive display flights are a welcome sign of spring in northern breeding areas.

VOICE Low, nasal *peen* call by male during dawn and dusk display; variety of chirping and twittering sounds given by male in display flight, made by air passing through narrow outer wing feathers.

NESTING Shallow depression in existing leaf and twig litter in young, mixed growth woodlands; 4 eggs; 1 brood; January (southern populations) and April (northern populations).

FEEDING Probes deep in damp soil or mud; mostly for earthworms, but also insects, snails, and some plants.

STAYING PUT
A foraging American Woodcock "caught" in an open field will freeze before it flies off.

SIMILAR SPECIES

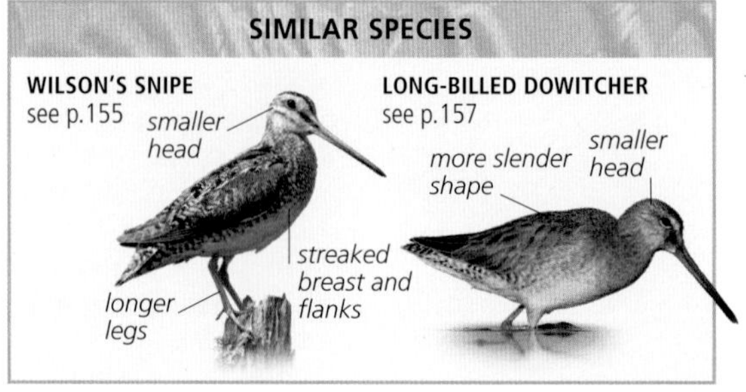
WILSON'S SNIPE
see p.155
smaller head
longer legs
streaked breast and flanks
LONG-BILLED DOWITCHER
see p.157
more slender shape
smaller head

OCCURRENCE
Breeds from southern Canada to southeastern US states, in damp, second growth forest, overgrown fields and bogs. In winter, found in similar habitat; also found along marsh edges, swamps, and damp, grassy roadsides in Texas and Florida in the southern US.

Length **10–12in (25–31cm)**	Wingspan **16–20in (41–51cm)**	Weight **4–7oz (125–200g)**
Social **Solitary**	Lifespan **Up to 9 years**	Status **Secure**

Order **Charadriiformes**	Family **Scolopacidae**	Species ***Gallinago delicata***

Wilson's Snipe

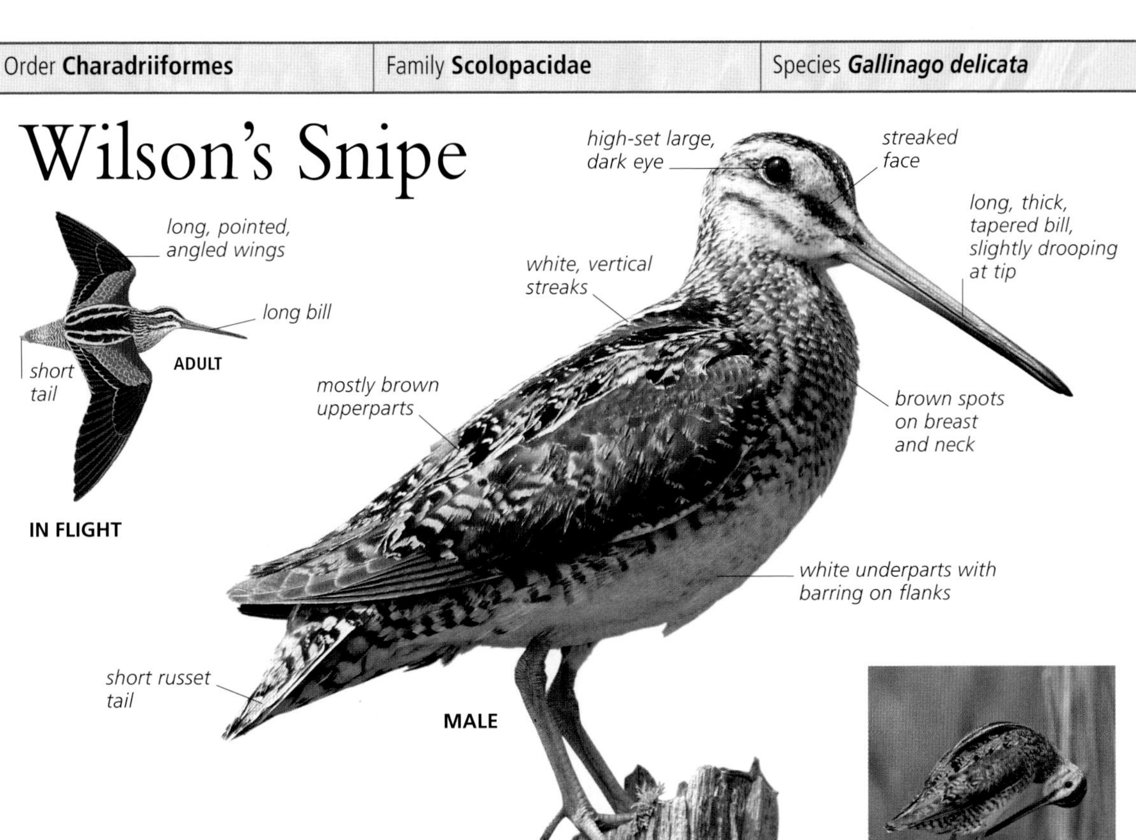

long, pointed, angled wings
long bill
short tail
ADULT
IN FLIGHT
high-set large, dark eye
streaked face
long, thick, tapered bill, slightly drooping at tip
white, vertical streaks
mostly brown upperparts
brown spots on breast and neck
white underparts with barring on flanks
short russet tail
MALE

FLIGHT: extremely fast and zig-zagging, rapid wing beats; erratic-looking changes of direction.

Also known as the Common Snipe, this secretive and well camouflaged member of the sandpiper family has an unsettled taxonomic history, but is now classified individually. On its breeding grounds Wilson's Snipe produces rather eerie sounds during its aerial, mainly nocturnal, display flights. The birds fly up silently from the ground, then, from about 330 feet (100m) up, they descend quickly, with their tail feathers spread, producing a unique, loud and vibrating sound through modified feathers.

VOICE Alarm and overhead flight call raspy *kraitsch*; perched and low flying breeding birds give repetitive, monotonous *kup-kup-kup-kup* in alarm or aggression; distinctive whistling sound during territorial displays.

NESTING Elaborate woven nest lined with fine grass on ground, sedge, or moss; 4 eggs; 1 brood; May–June.

FEEDING Forages in mud or shallow water; probes deep into subsoil; diet includes mostly insect larvae, but also crustaceans, earthworms, and mollusks.

RUSSET TAIL
Wilson's Snipe's russet colored tail is usually hard to see, but it is evident on this preening bird.

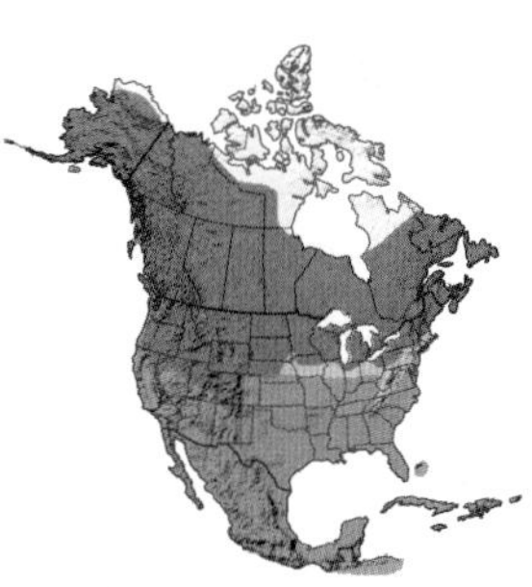

OCCURRENCE
Widespread from Alaska to Quebec and Labrador south of the tundra zone; breeds in a variety of wetlands, including marshes, bogs, and open areas with rich soil. Winters further south, where it prefers damp areas with vegetative cover, such as marshes, wet fields, and other bodies of water.

SIMILAR SPECIES

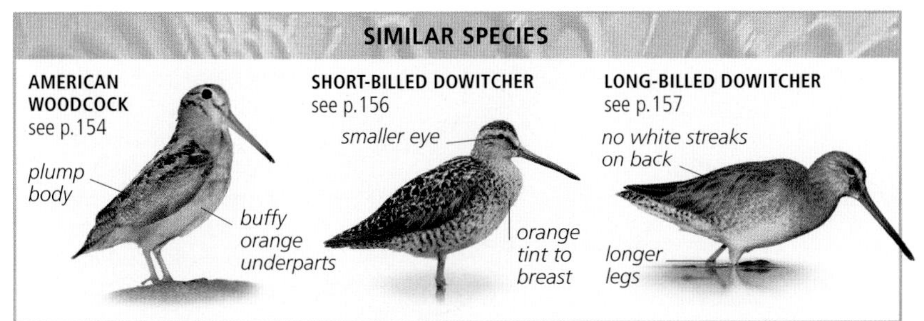

AMERICAN WOODCOCK
see p.154
plump body
buffy orange underparts
SHORT-BILLED DOWITCHER
see p.156
smaller eye
orange tint to breast
LONG-BILLED DOWITCHER
see p.157
no white streaks on back
longer legs

Length **10–11in (25–28cm)**	Wingspan **17–19in (43–48cm)**	Weight **2⅞–5oz (80–150g)**
Social **Solitary**	Lifespan **Up to 10 years**	Status **Secure**

Order **Charadriiformes**	Family **Scolopacidae**	Species ***Limnodromus griseus***

Short-billed Dowitcher

white slash from rump to mid-back

long, pointed wings

ADULT (BREEDING)

IN FLIGHT

orange-fringed feathers

flanks less heavily streaked

JUVENILE

orange wash to face, neck, breast, and underparts

long, stout bill

variable spotting on upper breast

dark-centered upperpart feathers

ADULT *L. g. griseus*

streaked flanks

greenish yellow legs

slightly larger bill

ADULT *L. g. hendersoni*

plain gray upperparts

white belly

ADULT (NONBREEDING)

FLIGHT: swift, powerful with quick wing beats.

The Short-billed Dowitcher is a common visitor along the Atlantic, Gulf, and Pacific Coasts. Its remote and bug-infested breeding areas in northern bogs have hindered the study of its breeding behavior until recent years. There are three subspecies (*L. g. griseus, L. g. hendersoni,* and *L. g. caurinus,*) which differ in plumage, size, and respective breeding areas. Recent knowledge about shape and structure has helped ornithologists distinguish the Short-billed from the Long-billed Dowitcher.

VOICE Flight call low, plaintive *tu-tu-tu*, 3–4 notes; flight song *tu-tu, tu-tu, toodle-ee, tu-tu*, ending with low *anh-anh-anh*.

NESTING Simple depression, typically in sedge hummock; 4 eggs; 1 brood; May–June.

FEEDING Probes in "sewing machine" feeding style with water up to belly for aquatic mollusks, crustaceans, and insects.

ORANGE UNDERPARTS
In complete breeding plumage, the Short-billed Dowitcher is orange, even in late afternoon light.

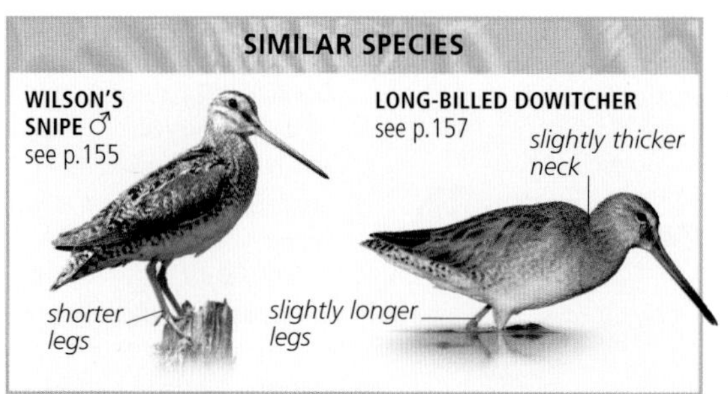
SIMILAR SPECIES
WILSON'S SNIPE ♂
see p.155
shorter legs
LONG-BILLED DOWITCHER
see p.157
slightly thicker neck
slightly longer legs

OCCURRENCE
Breeds mostly in sedge meadows or bogs with interspersed spruce and tamaracks between subarctic tundra and boreal forest. Migrates south to Central and South America, preferring coastal mudflats, salt marshes or adjacent freshwater pools.

Length **9–10in (23–25cm)**	Wingspan **18–20in (46–51cm)**	Weight **2½–5½oz (70–155g)**
Social **Pairs/Flocks**	Lifespan **Up to 20 years**	Status **Secure (p)**

Order **Charadriiformes**	Family **Scolopacidae**	Species ***Limnodromus scolopaceus***

Long-billed Dowitcher

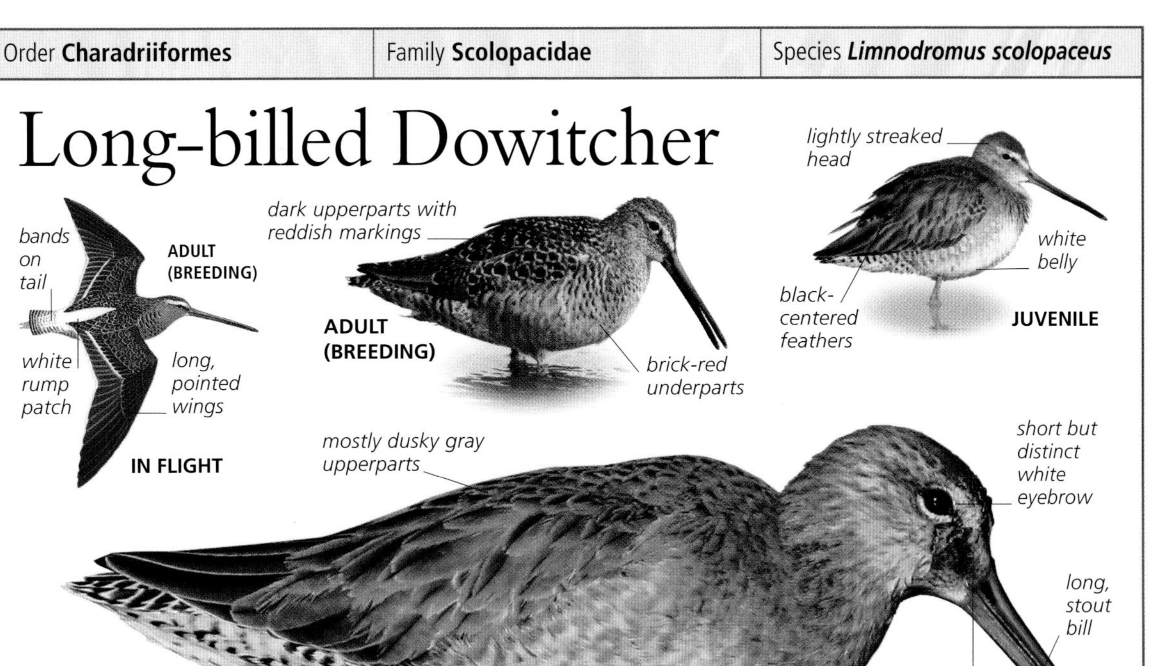
bands on tail
ADULT (BREEDING)
white rump patch
long, pointed wings
IN FLIGHT
dark upperparts with reddish markings
ADULT (BREEDING)
brick-red underparts
lightly streaked head
white belly
black-centered feathers
JUVENILE
mostly dusky gray upperparts
short but distinct white eyebrow
long, stout bill
dark patch between eye and bill
variable dark barring on flanks
white belly
ADULT (NONBREEDING)

It was not until 1950 that museum and field studies identified two seperate species of dowitcher in North America. The Long-billed Dowitcher is usually slightly larger, longer-legged, and heavier in the chest and neck than the Short-billed Dowitcher. The breeding ranges of the two species are separate, but their migration and en route stop-over areas overlap. The Long-billed Dowitcher is usually found in freshwater wetlands, and in the fall most of its population occurs west of the Mississippi River.

VOICE Flight and alarm call sharp, whistled *keek*, given singly or in series when agitated; song buzzy *pipipipipipi-chi-drrr.*

NESTING Deep sedge or grass-lined depression in sedge or grass; 4 eggs; 1 brood; May–June.

FEEDING Probes wet ground with "sewing-machine" motion for spiders, snails, worms, insects, and seeds.

FLIGHT: swift, direct flier with fast, powerful wing beats.

TOUCHY FEELY
Sensitive touch-receptors at the tip of the bird's bill enable it to feel in the mud for food.

SIMILAR SPECIES

WILSON'S SNIPE see p.155
pale, central crown stripe
shorter legs

SHORT-BILLED DOWITCHER see p.156
slightly smaller overall
orangish underparts

OCCURRENCE
Breeds in wet, grassy meadows or coastal sedge tundra near freshwater pools. Migrates to Mexico and Central America, south to Panama, when found in freshwater habitats, including ponds, flooded fields, lake shores, also sheltered lagoons, salt marsh pools, and tidal mudflats.

Length **9½–10in (24–26cm)**	Wingspan **18–20½in (46–52cm)**	Weight **3–4oz (85–125g)**
Social **Pairs/Flocks**	Lifespan **Unknown**	Status **Secure**

Order **Charadriiformes**	Family **Scolopacidae**	Species ***Limosa haemastica***

Hudsonian Godwit

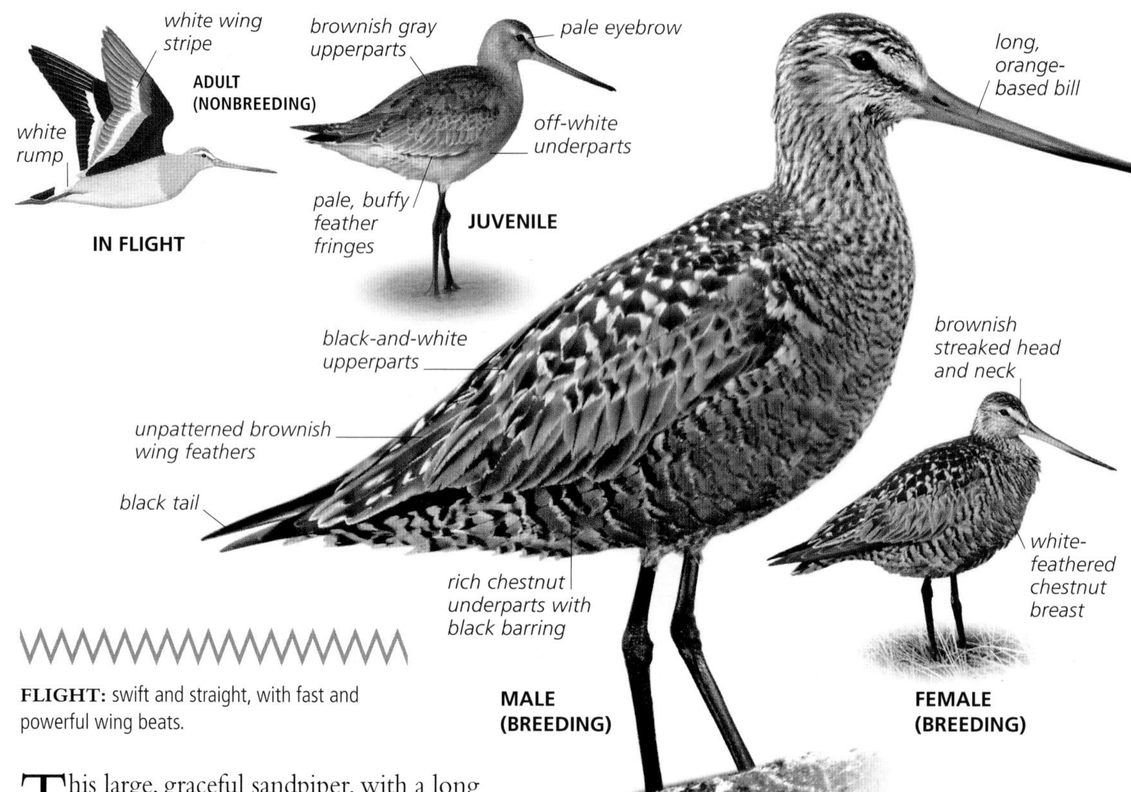
white wing stripe
ADULT (NONBREEDING)
white rump
IN FLIGHT
brownish gray upperparts
pale eyebrow
off-white underparts
pale, buffy feather fringes
JUVENILE
long, orange-based bill
black-and-white upperparts
unpatterned brownish wing feathers
black tail
brownish streaked head and neck
white-feathered chestnut breast
rich chestnut underparts with black barring
MALE (BREEDING)
FEMALE (BREEDING)

FLIGHT: swift and straight, with fast and powerful wing beats.

This large, graceful sandpiper, with a long and slightly upturned bill, undertakes a remarkable annual migration from its tundra breeding grounds in Alaska and Canada all the way to extreme southern South America, a distance probably close to 10,000 miles (16,000km) in one direction, with very few stopovers. The number of breeding birds is unknown, but counts in Tierra del Fuego indicate totals of perhaps 30,000 to 40,000 birds, all found in two areas of tidal mudflats. Between the far North and the far South, North American stops are few, and only in the spring, along a central route mid-continent. Hudsonian Godwits spend six months wintering, two months breeding, and four flying between the two locations.

VOICE Flight call emphatic *peed-wid*; also high *peet* or *kwee*; display song *to-wida to-wida to-wida, or to-wit, to-wit, to-wit.*

NESTING Saucer-shaped depression on dry hummock or tussocks under cover; 4 eggs; 1 brood; May–July.

FEEDING Probes in mud for insects, insect grubs, worms, crustaceans and mollusks; also eats plant tubers in fall.

LONG-HAUL BIRD
Hudsonian Godwits only make a few stops on their long flights to and from South America.

SIMILAR SPECIES

BAR-TAILED GODWIT ◔ see p.493

more streaks
shorter legs
longer bill

OCCURRENCE
Breeds in the High Arctic, in sedge meadows and bogs in scattered tundra; scarce along the Atlantic Coast in fall near coastal freshwater reservoirs; but locally common in flooded rice fields, pastures, and reservoirs in spring. Winters in extreme southern Chile and Argentina.

Length **14–16in (35–41cm)**	Wingspan **27–31in (68–78cm)**	Weight **7–12oz (200–350g)**
Social **Flocks**	Lifespan **Up to 29 years**	Status **Declining**

Order **Charadriiformes**	Family **Scolopacidae**	Species ***Limosa fedoa***

Marbled Godwit

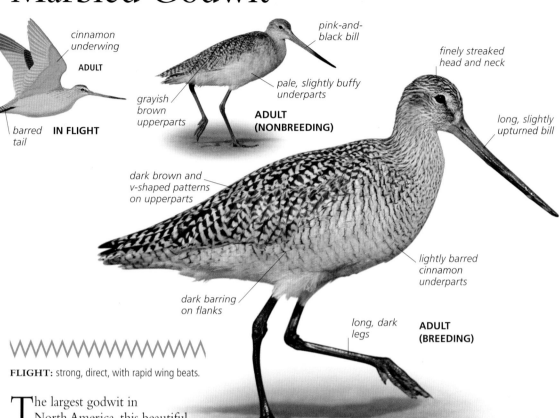

cinnamon underwing
ADULT
barred tail
IN FLIGHT

pink-and-black bill
pale, slightly buffy underparts
grayish brown upperparts
ADULT (NONBREEDING)

finely streaked head and neck
long, slightly upturned bill
dark brown and v-shaped patterns on upperparts
lightly barred cinnamon underparts
dark barring on flanks
long, dark legs
ADULT (BREEDING)

FLIGHT: strong, direct, with rapid wing beats.

The largest godwit in North America, this beautiful, cinnamon-buff shorebird is a familiar sight at its coastal wintering areas. Its distinctive brown-and-cinnamon plumage and the fact that it chooses open habitats, such as mudflats and floodplains, to feed and roost, make the Marbled Godwit a conspicuous species. A monogamous bird, the Marbled Godwit is also long-lived—the oldest bird recorded was 29 years old.

VOICE Call a nasal *ah-ahk*, and single *ahk*; breeding call, *goddWhit*, *wik-wik*; other calls include *rack-a, karatica*, *ratica*, *ratica*.

NESTING Depression in short grass in Alaska; also nests on vegetation in water; 4 eggs; 1 brood; May–July.

FEEDING Probes mudflats, beaches, short grass for insects, especially grasshoppers; also crustaceans, mollusks, and small fish.

EASILY RECOGNIZED
Its large size and buffy to cinnamon color make this godwit a very distinctive shorebird.

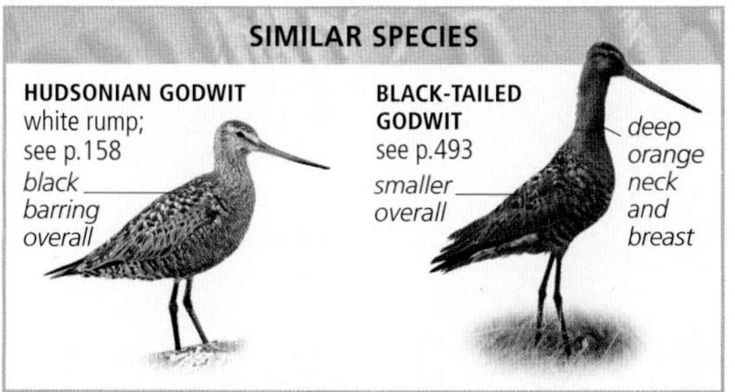
SIMILAR SPECIES
HUDSONIAN GODWIT
white rump;
see p.158
black barring overall
BLACK-TAILED GODWIT
see p.493
smaller overall
deep orange neck and breast

OCCURRENCE
Breeds in the grassy marshes of the Great Plains. During migration and in winter, prefers sandy beaches and coastal mudflats with adjoining meadows or savannas in California and the Gulf of Mexico. Also seen on inland wetlands and lake edges.

Length **16½–19in (42–48cm)**	Wingspan **28–32in (70–81cm)**	Weight **10–16oz (275–450g)**
Social **Winter flocks**	Lifespan **Up to 29 years**	Status **Secure**

Order **Charadriiformes**	Family **Scolopacidae**	Species ***Numenius phaeopus***

Whimbrel

long, pointed wings

ADULT

all-dark rump

coarsely streaked face, neck, and breast

IN FLIGHT

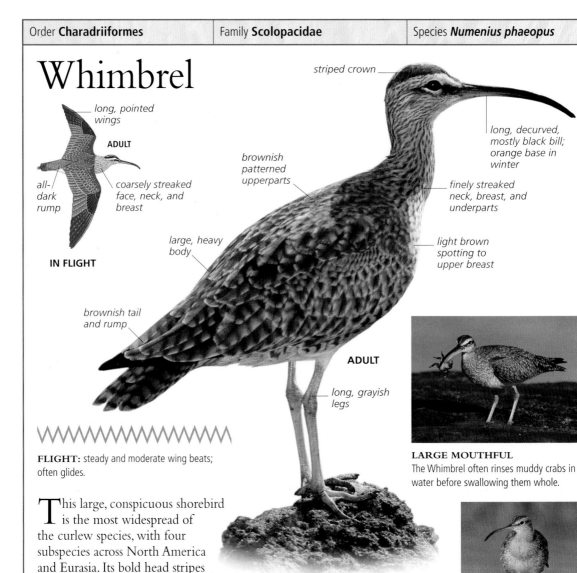

striped crown

long, decurved, mostly black bill; orange base in winter

brownish patterned upperparts

finely streaked neck, breast, and underparts

large, heavy body

light brown spotting to upper breast

brownish tail and rump

ADULT

long, grayish legs

FLIGHT: steady and moderate wing beats; often glides.

LARGE MOUTHFUL
The Whimbrel often rinses muddy crabs in water before swallowing them whole.

This large, conspicuous shorebird is the most widespread of the curlew species, with four subspecies across North America and Eurasia. Its bold head stripes and clearly streaked face, neck, and breast make the species distinctive. The Whimbrel's fairly long, decurved bill allows it to probe into fiddler crab burrows, a favorite food item.

VOICE Characteristic call is a loud, staccato *pi-pi-pi-pi-pi*; flight song a series of haunting melodious whistles, followed by long trill.

NESTING Depression in hummock, mound, grass, sedge, or gravel; 4 eggs; 1 brood; May–August.

FEEDING Probes for crabs, in addition to worms, mollusks, and fish; also eats insects and berries.

UP CLOSE
A close look at the Whimbrel shows this bird's beautiful, fine patterning.

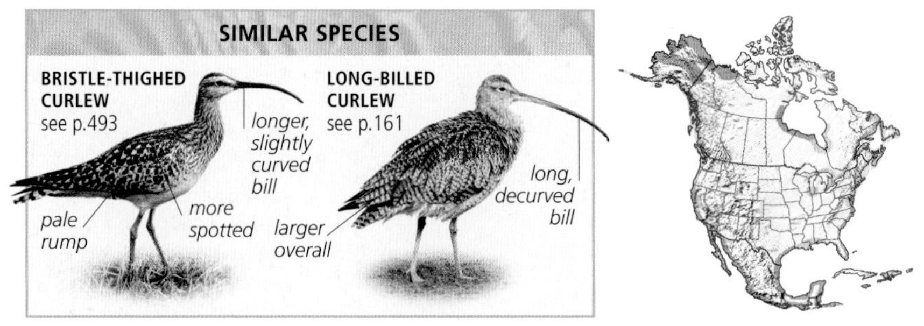
SIMILAR SPECIES
BRISTLE-THIGHED CURLEW
see p.493
longer, slightly curved bill
pale rump
more spotted
LONG-BILLED CURLEW
see p.161
long, decurved bill
larger overall

OCCURRENCE
Several populations breed in northern, sub-Arctic, and low-Arctic regions of North America; during migration and in winter, found mostly in coastal marshes, tidal creeks, flats, and mangroves; also at inland Salton Sea, California. Winters along rocky coasts in South America.

Length **15½–16½in (39–42cm)**	Wingspan **30–35in (76–89cm)**	Weight **11–18oz (300–500g)**
Social **Flocks**	Lifespan **Up to 19 years**	Status **Secure**

Order **Charadriiformes**	Family **Scolopacidae**	Species ***Numenius americanus***

Long-billed Curlew

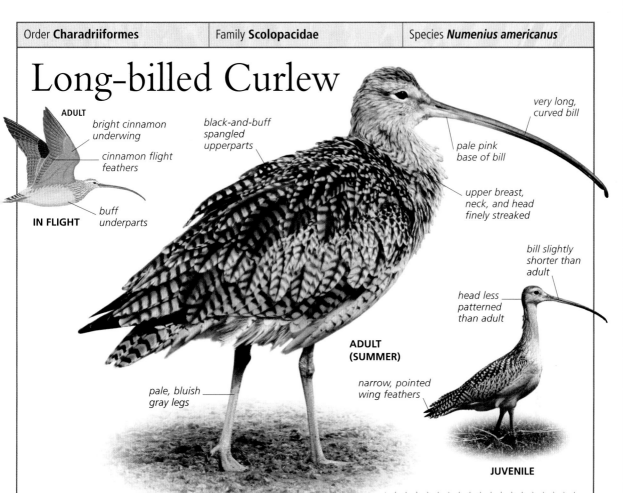

ADULT
bright cinnamon underwing
cinnamon flight feathers
buff underparts
IN FLIGHT

black-and-buff spangled upperparts
very long, curved bill
pale pink base of bill
upper breast, neck, and head finely streaked
pale, bluish gray legs
ADULT (SUMMER)

bill slightly shorter than adult
head less patterned than adult
narrow, pointed wing feathers
JUVENILE

The Long-billed Curlew has the southernmost breeding range and northernmost wintering range of the four North American curlews. It is also one of nine species of birds that are endemic to the grasslands of the Great Plains. Its large size and tame behavior on its wintering grounds in North America add to its mystique. The curvature of its bill is adapted to probe for food in soft mud and sand.

VOICE Flight call a 2-note *cur-LUoo*, often accompanied by rapid *qui-pi-pi-pi-pi*; flight song consists of haunting whistles, trills *werr-EEEer.*

NESTING Shallow depression in sparsely vegetated prairie habitat; 4 eggs; 1 brood; April–May.

FEEDING Picks insects on the surface or probes in soft mud for insects, crustaceans, mollusks, and worms; also eats fish.

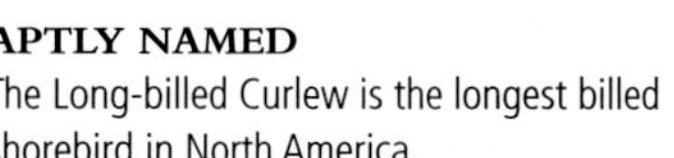

FLIGHT: graceful and strong series of flaps alternating with a glide.

APTLY NAMED
The Long-billed Curlew is the longest billed shorebird in North America.

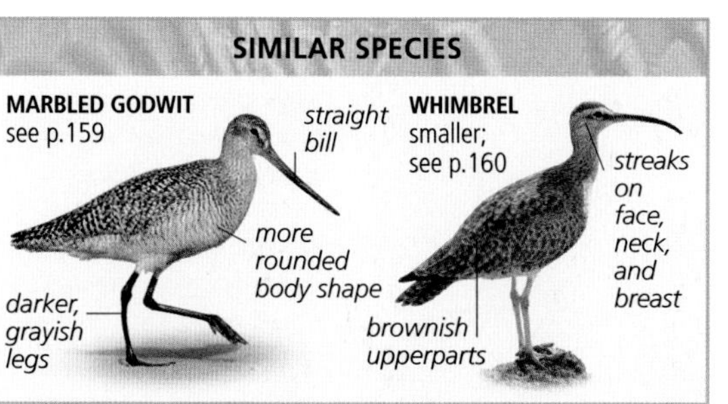
SIMILAR SPECIES
MARBLED GODWIT
see p.159
straight bill
more rounded body shape
darker, grayish legs
WHIMBREL
smaller;
see p.160
streaks on face, neck, and breast
brownish upperparts

OCCURRENCE
Breeds in prairies, short grass and mixed-grass habitats of the Great Basin and Great Plains. Winters in wet pastures, marshes, beaches, and tidal mudflats primarily of California, Texas, and Mexico, with some stragglers occurring in Florida. Generally not a "shorebird" found along shores.

Length **20–26in (51–65cm)**	Wingspan **30–39in (75–100cm)**	Weight **16–28oz (450–800g)**
Social **Solitary/Winter flocks**	Lifespan **At least 8 years**	Status **Vulnerable**

Order **Charadriiformes**	Family **Scolopacidae**	Species ***Bartramia longicauda***

Upland Sandpiper

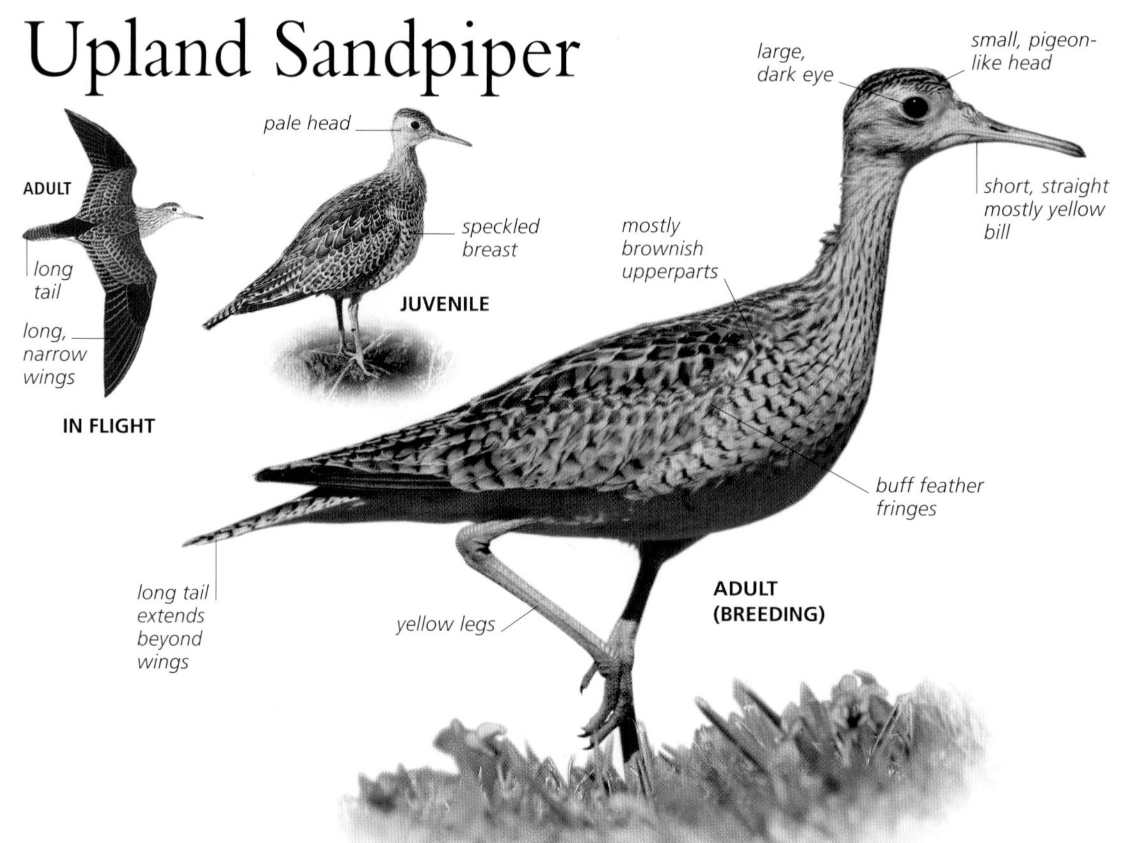
ADULT
long tail
long, narrow wings
IN FLIGHT
pale head
speckled breast
JUVENILE
large, dark eye
small, pigeon-like head
short, straight mostly yellow bill
mostly brownish upperparts
buff feather fringes
long tail extends beyond wings
yellow legs
ADULT (BREEDING)

Unlike other sandpipers, this graceful bird spends most of its life away from water in grassy habitats. The Upland Sandpiper's coloration helps it camouflage itself in the grasslands, especially while nesting on the ground. It is well known for landing on fence posts and raising its wings while giving its tremulous, whistling call. The bird is currently listed as endangered in many of its breeding states due to the disappearance of its grassland habitat.

VOICE Flight call a low *qui-pi-pi-pi*; song consists of gurgling notes followed by long, descending "wolf whistle" *whoooolееееее, wheeeloooоо-ooooo.*

NESTING Simple depression in ground among grass clumps; 4 eggs; 1 brood; May.

FEEDING Feeds with head-bobbing motion on adult and larval insects, spiders, worms, centipedes; occasionally seeds.

FLIGHT: strong and swift; rapid, fluttering flight in breeding display.

DRY GROUND WADER
A true grassland species, the Upland Sandpiper is rarely found away from these habitats.

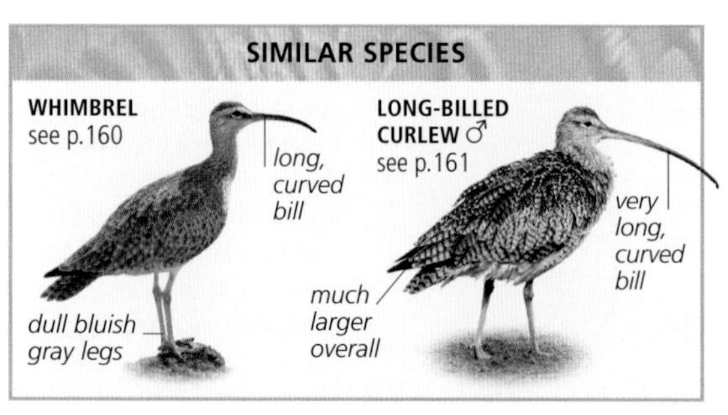
SIMILAR SPECIES
WHIMBREL
see p.160
long, curved bill
dull bluish gray legs
LONG-BILLED CURLEW ♂
see p.161
very long, curved bill
much larger overall

OCCURRENCE
Breeds in native tallgrass or mixed-grass prairies. Airports make up large portion of its breeding habitat in the northeast US. During migration and in winter it prefers shortgrass habitats such as grazed pastures, turf farms, cultivated fields.

Length **11–12½in (28–32cm)**	Wingspan **25–27in (64–68cm)**	Weight **4–7oz (150–200g)**
Social **Migrant flocks**	Lifespan **Unknown**	Status **Declining**

Order **Charadriiformes**	Family **Scolopacidae**	Species ***Tringa melanoleuca***

Greater Yellowlegs

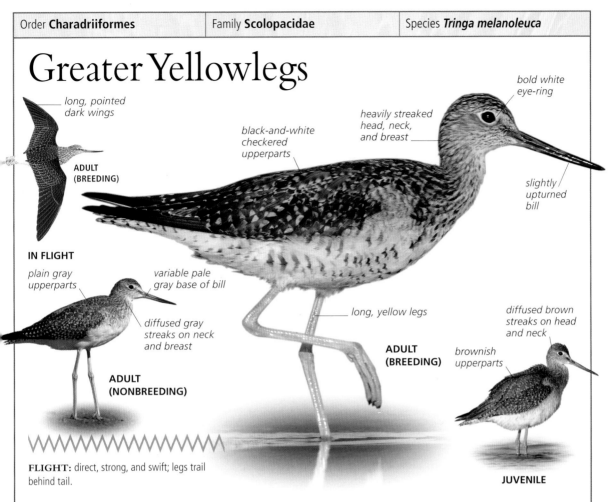

long, pointed dark wings

ADULT (BREEDING)

IN FLIGHT

black-and-white checkered upperparts

heavily streaked head, neck, and breast

bold white eye-ring

slightly upturned bill

plain gray upperparts

variable pale gray base of bill

diffused gray streaks on neck and breast

ADULT (NONBREEDING)

long, yellow legs

ADULT (BREEDING)

diffused brown streaks on head and neck

brownish upperparts

JUVENILE

FLIGHT: direct, strong, and swift; legs trail behind tail.

This fairly large shorebird often runs frantically in many directions while pursuing small prey. It is one of the first northbound spring shorebird migrants, and one of the first to return south in late June or early July. Its plumage, a mixture of brown, black, and white checkered upperparts, and streaked underparts, is more streaked during the breeding season.

VOICE Call a loud, penetrating *tew-tew-tew*; agitated birds make repetitive *keu* notes; song a continuous *too-whee.*

NESTING Simple scrape in moss or peat, usually close to water; 4 eggs; 1 brood; May–June.

FEEDING Picks water surface and mud for small aquatic and terrestrial crustaceans and worms; also eats small fish, frogs, seeds, and berries.

EFFECTIVE METHOD
The Greater Yellowlegs often catches small fish by sweeping its bill sideways through water.

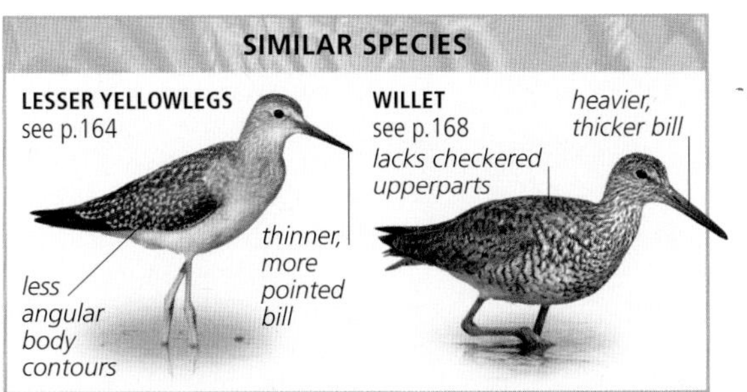
SIMILAR SPECIES
LESSER YELLOWLEGS
see p.164
thinner, more pointed bill
less angular body contours
WILLET
see p.168
heavier, thicker bill
lacks checkered upperparts

OCCURRENCE
Breeds in openings in northerly forests with bogs and wet meadows, a habitat called muskegs. In migration and winter, uses a wide variety of shallow water habitats, including freshwater and saltwater marshes, reservoirs, and tidal mudflats.

Length **11½–13in (29–33cm)**	Wingspan **28–29in (70–74cm)**	Weight **4–8oz (125–225g)**
Social **Solitary/Flocks**	Lifespan **Unknown**	Status **Secure**

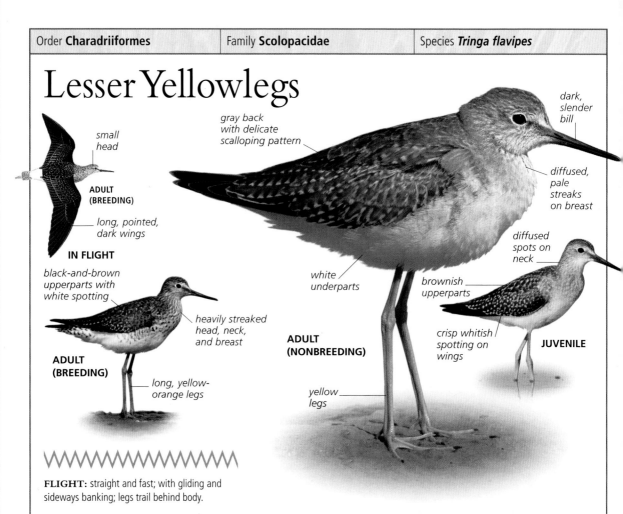

Order **Charadriiformes**	Family **Scolopacidae**	Species ***Tringa flavipes***

Lesser Yellowlegs

small head

ADULT (BREEDING)

long, pointed, dark wings

IN FLIGHT

gray back with delicate scalloping pattern

dark, slender bill

diffused, pale streaks on breast

diffused spots on neck

black-and-brown upperparts with white spotting

white underparts

brownish upperparts

heavily streaked head, neck, and breast

ADULT (NONBREEDING)

crisp whitish spotting on wings

JUVENILE

ADULT (BREEDING)

long, yellow-orange legs

yellow legs

FLIGHT: straight and fast; with gliding and sideways banking; legs trail behind body.

With its smaller head, thinner bill, and smoother body shape, the Lesser Yellowlegs has a more elegant profile than the Greater Yellowlegs. It prefers smaller, freshwater, or brackish pools to open saltwater habitats, and it walks quickly and methodically while feeding. Although this species is a solitary feeder, it is often seen in small to large loose flocks in migration and winter.

VOICE Low, whistled *tu*, or *tu-tu* call; series of *tu* or *cuw* notes when agitated; display song a *pill-e-wee, pill-e-wee, pill-e-wee.*

NESTING Depression in ground or moss, lined with grass and leaves; 4 eggs; 1 brood; May–June.

FEEDING Eats a wide variety of aquatic and terrestrial insects, mollusks, and crustaceans, especially flies and beetles; also seeds.

BALANCING ACT

The Lesser Yellowlegs uses its long, raised wings for balance while feeding in soft mud.

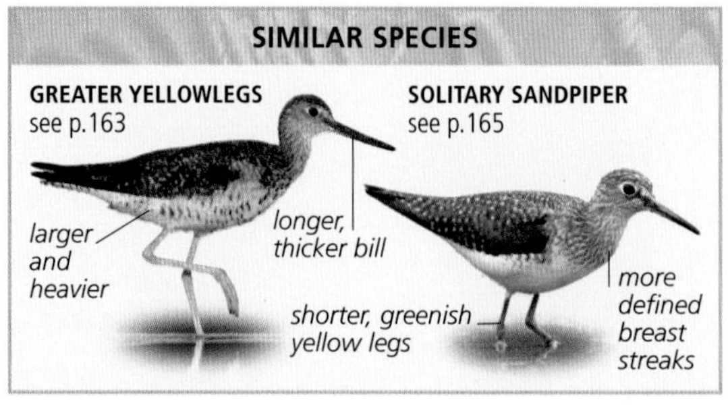
SIMILAR SPECIES
GREATER YELLOWLEGS
see p.163
SOLITARY SANDPIPER
see p.165
larger and heavier
longer, thicker bill
shorter, greenish yellow legs
more defined breast streaks

OCCURRENCE

Breeds in northerly forest with clearings, and where forest meets tundra. In migration and in winter, uses wide variety of shallow wetlands, including flooded pastures and agricultural fields, swamps, lake and river shores, tidal creeks, and brackish mudflats. Winters from Mexico to Argentina.

Length **9–10in (23–25cm)**	Wingspan **23–25in (58–64cm)**	Weight **2–3⅜oz (55–95g)**
Social **Flocks**	Lifespan **Unknown**	Status **Secure**

Order **Charadriiformes**	Family **Scolopacidae**	Species ***Tringa solitaria***

Solitary Sandpiper

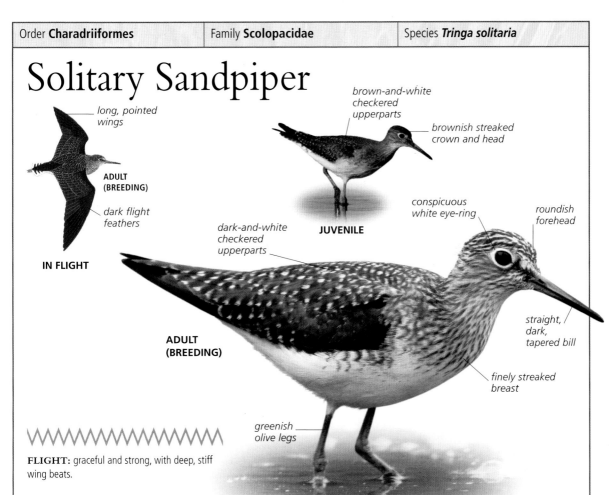

long, pointed wings

ADULT (BREEDING)

dark flight feathers

IN FLIGHT

brown-and-white checkered upperparts

brownish streaked crown and head

JUVENILE

conspicuous white eye-ring

roundish forehead

dark-and-white checkered upperparts

straight, dark, tapered bill

ADULT (BREEDING)

finely streaked breast

greenish olive legs

FLIGHT: graceful and strong, with deep, stiff wing beats.

Alexander Wilson described this species in 1813, naming it, quite appropriately, "Solitary." This Sandpiper seldom associates with other shorebirds as it moves nervously along margins of wetlands. When feeding, the Solitary Sandpiper constantly bobs its head like the Spotted Sandpiper. When disturbed, the Solitary Sandpiper often flies directly upward, and when landing, it keeps its wings upright briefly, flashing the white underneath, before carefully folding them to its body.

VOICE Flight and alarm call a high-pitched *weet-weet-weet* or *pit*; display song a *pit-pit-pit-pit*; *kik-kik-kik*.

NESTING Abandoned nests in trees (a unique behavior for a North American shorebird); 4 eggs; 1 brood; May–June.

FEEDING Eats insects, small crustaceans, snails, and small frogs.

LONE RANGER

This sandpiper is often solitary and is found in quiet, sheltered habitats and along river shores.

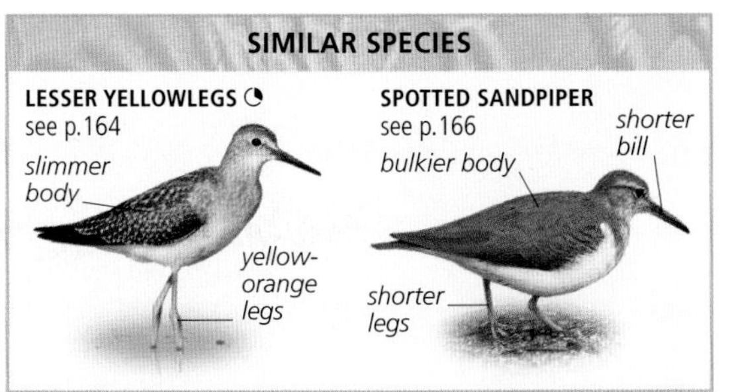
SIMILAR SPECIES
LESSER YELLOWLEGS
see p.164
slimmer body
yellow-orange legs
SPOTTED SANDPIPER
see p.166
bulkier body
shorter bill
shorter legs

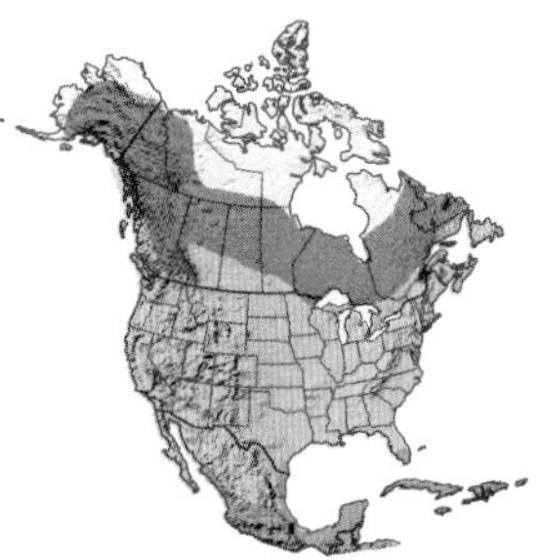

OCCURRENCE

Breeds primarily in bogs in northern forests; in winter and during migration, occurs in sheltered pools or muddy areas near forests. Winters from Mexico down to South America, sometimes in tiny pools at high alitude in the Andes; also riverbanks, streams, rain pools, and ditches.

Length **7½–9in (19–23cm)**	Wingspan **22–23in (56–59cm)**	Weight **$1\frac{1}{16}$–$2\frac{1}{4}$oz (30–65g)**
Social **Solitary/Small flocks**	Lifespan **Unknown**	Status **Secure**

Order **Charadriiformes**	Family **Scolopacidae**	Species ***Actitis macularius***

Spotted Sandpiper

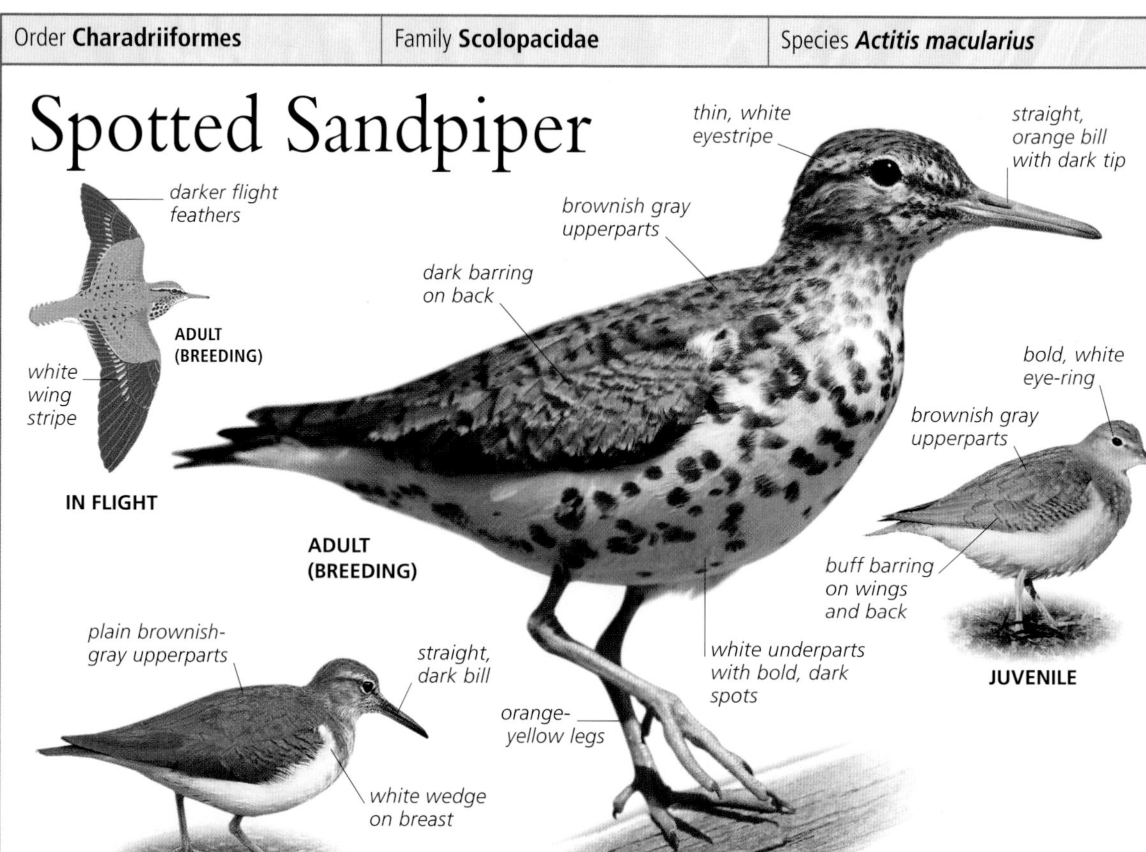
darker flight feathers
ADULT (BREEDING)
white wing stripe
IN FLIGHT
thin, white eyestripe
straight, orange bill with dark tip
brownish gray upperparts
dark barring on back
ADULT (BREEDING)
bold, white eye-ring
brownish gray upperparts
buff barring on wings and back
JUVENILE
white underparts with bold, dark spots
plain brownish-gray upperparts
straight, dark bill
orange-yellow legs
white wedge on breast
ADULT (NONBREEDING)

One of only two species of the genus *Actitis*, from the Latin meaning "a coastal inhabitant," this small, short-legged sandpiper is the most widespread shorebird in North America. It is characterized by its quick walking pace, its habit of constantly teetering and bobbing its tail, and its unique style of flying low over water. Spotted Sandpipers have an unusual mating behavior, in which the females take on an aggressive role, defending territories and mating with three or more males per season.

VOICE Call a clear, ringing note *tee-tee-tee-tee*; flight song a monotonous *cree-cree-cree*.

NESTING Nest cup shaded by or scrape built under herbaceous vegetation; 3 eggs; 1–3 broods; May–June.

FEEDING Eats many items, including adult and larval insects, mollusks, small crabs, and worms.

FLIGHT: mostly shallow, rapidly, stiffly fluttering wing beats, usually low above water.

BEHAVIORAL QUIRKS
This sandpiper "teeters," raising and lowering its tail while walking along the water's edge.

SIMILAR SPECIES

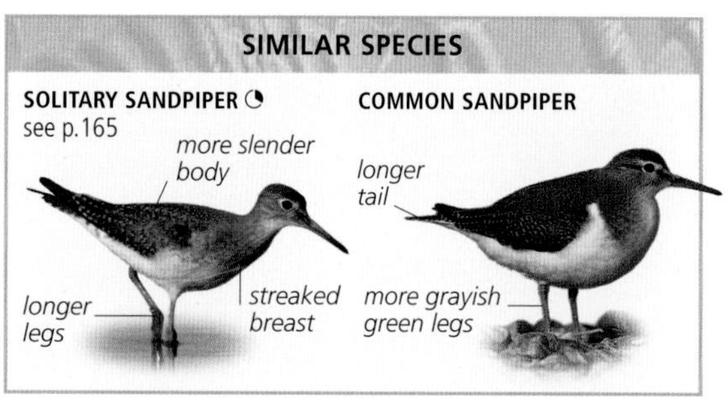
SOLITARY SANDPIPER
see p.165
more slender body
longer legs
streaked breast
COMMON SANDPIPER
longer tail
more grayish green legs

OCCURRENCE
Breeds across North America in a wide variety of grassy, brushy, forested habitats near water, but not High Arctic tundra. During migration and in winter found in habitats near freshwater, including lake shores, rivers, streams, beaches, sewage ponds, ditches, seawalls, sometimes estuaries.

Length **7¼–8in (18.5–20cm)**	Wingspan **15–16in (38–41cm)**	Weight **1⁹⁄₁₆–1¾oz (45–50g)**
Social **Small flocks**	Lifespan **Up to 12 years**	Status **Secure**

Order **Charadriiformes**	Family **Scolopacidae**	Species ***Tringa incana***

Wandering Tattler

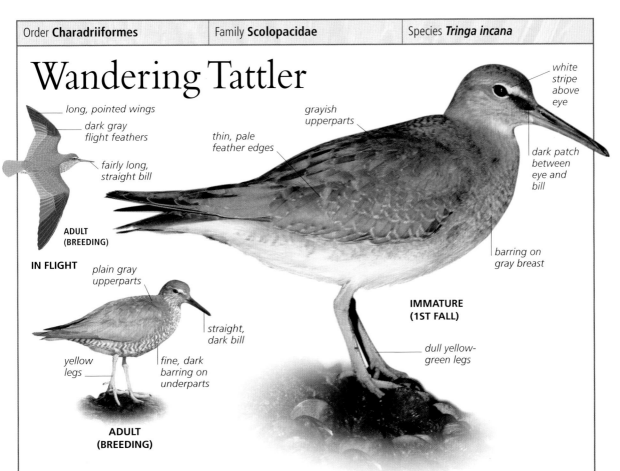

long, pointed wings
dark gray flight feathers
fairly long, straight bill
ADULT (BREEDING)
IN FLIGHT

plain gray upperparts
straight, dark bill
yellow legs
fine, dark barring on underparts
ADULT (BREEDING)

grayish upperparts
thin, pale feather edges
white stripe above eye
dark patch between eye and bill
barring on gray breast
dull yellow-green legs
IMMATURE (1ST FALL)

While "Wandering" refers to this species' widespread annual migration, "Tattler" highlights the loud nature of its calls and songs, which it makes in its mountain breeding haunts in Alaska and western Canada. There is still much to learn about this mostly solitary species, including its remote wintering range, especially given its small world population numbers (10–25,000 birds). Seen singly or occasionally in small groups on the rocky Pacific Coast shoreline from late summer to spring, this enigmatic species is often overlooked.

VOICE Flight call a ringing, trilled *didididididi*; song a sharp, 3–4 note whistle *treea-treea-treea-tree*.

NESTING Depression on rocks in mountain tundra; 4 eggs; 1 brood; May–July.

FEEDING Picks worms, mollusks, and crustaceans from intertidal habitats; also eats insects, sand fleas, and fish.

FLIGHT: swift and direct, can also be buoyant, may dip, soar, nose-dive, and glide.

DISTINCTIVE WALKING
This bird may be seen walking with a teetering motion on rocky shores away from breeding habitats.

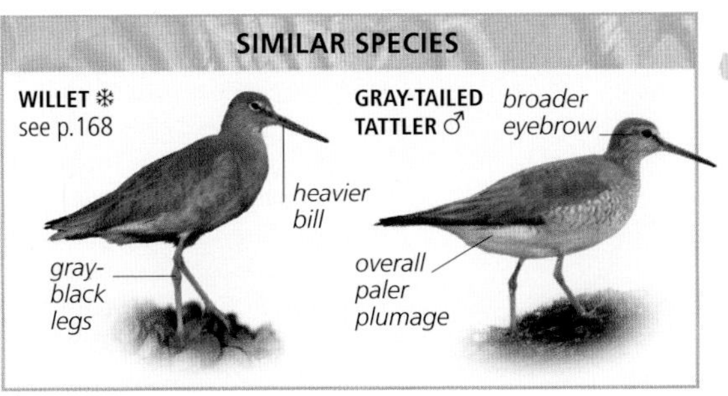
SIMILAR SPECIES
WILLET ❄
see p.168
heavier bill
gray-black legs
GRAY-TAILED TATTLER ♂
broader eyebrow
overall paler plumage

OCCURRENCE
Breeds in shrubby mountainous western Arctic tundra close to water bodies formed as a result of melting glaciers. During migration and winter, uses rocky coastlines, particularly in the area between the high and low tide marks; also reefs, jetties, and piers.

Length **10½–12in (27–30cm)**	Wingspan **20–22in (51–56cm)**	Weight **3½–5oz (100–150g)**
Social **Solitary/Pairs**	Lifespan **Unknown**	Status **Secure**

Order **Charadriiformes**	Family **Scolopacidae**	Species ***Tringa semipalmata***

Willet

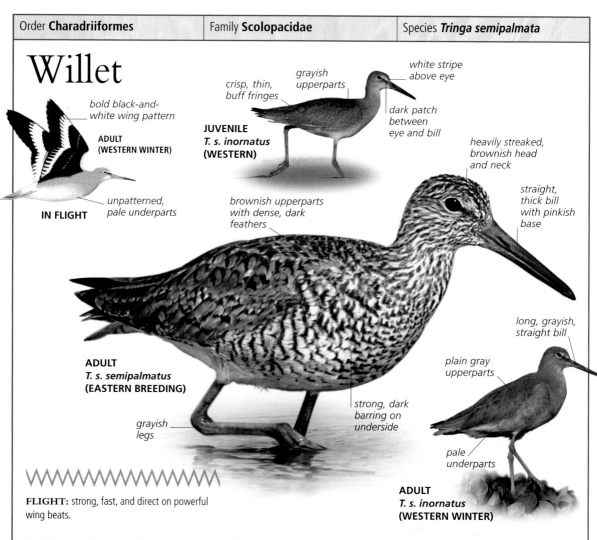

bold black-and-white wing pattern

ADULT (WESTERN WINTER)

unpatterned, pale underparts

IN FLIGHT

crisp, thin, buff fringes

grayish upperparts

white stripe above eye

dark patch between eye and bill

JUVENILE *T. s. inornatus* (WESTERN)

heavily streaked, brownish head and neck

straight, thick bill with pinkish base

brownish upperparts with dense, dark feathers

ADULT *T. s. semipalmatus* (EASTERN BREEDING)

grayish legs

strong, dark barring on underside

long, grayish, straight bill

plain gray upperparts

pale underparts

ADULT *T. s. inornatus* (WESTERN WINTER)

FLIGHT: strong, fast, and direct on powerful wing beats.

The two distinct subspecies of the Willet, Eastern (*T. s. semipalmatus*) and Western (*T. s. inornatus*), differ in breeding habit, plumage coloration, vocalizations, and migratory habits. The Eastern Willet leaves North America from September to March; whereas the Western Willet winters along southern North American shorelines south to South America.

VOICE Flight call a loud *kyah-yah*; alarm call a sharp, repeated *kleep*; song an urgent, rapid *pill-will-willet.*

NESTING Depression in vegetated dunes, wetlands, prairies, or salt marshes; 4 eggs; 1 brood; April–June.

FEEDING Picks, probes, or swishes for crustaceans such as fiddler and mole crabs, aquatic insects, marine worms, small mollusks, and fish.

EXPOSED PERCH
Willets roost on exposed perches at breeding grounds.

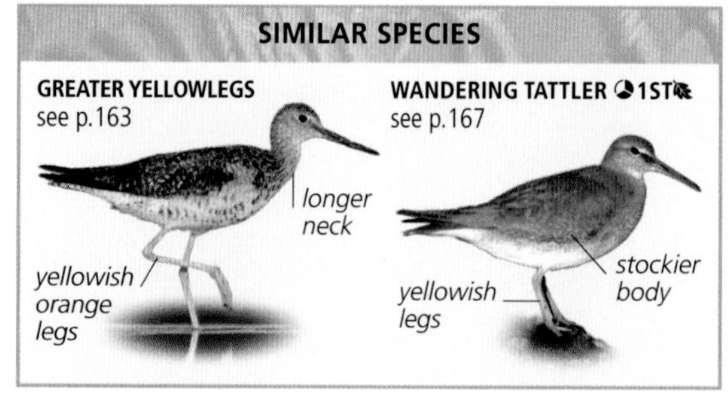
SIMILAR SPECIES
GREATER YELLOWLEGS
see p.163
longer neck
yellowish orange legs
WANDERING TATTLER 1ST
see p.167
stockier body
yellowish legs

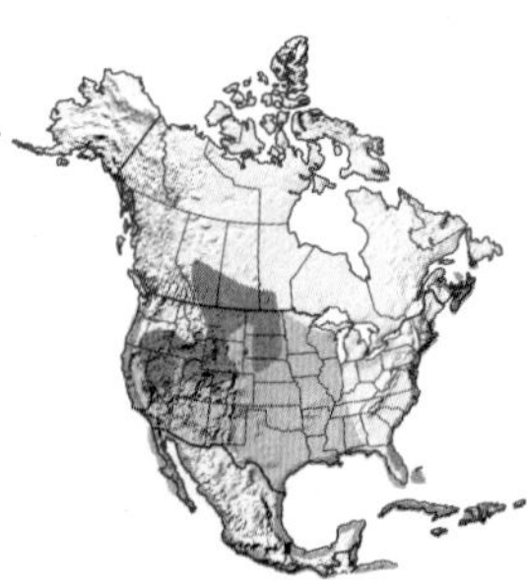

OCCURRENCE
Eastern subspecies breeds in coastal saltwater habitats: salt marshes, barrier islands, beaches, mangroves; winters in similar habitats. Western subspecies breeds near sparsely vegetated prairie wetlands or adjacent semiarid grasslands; winters in coastal regions.

Length **12½–16½in (32–42cm)**	Wingspan **21½–28½in (54–72cm)**	Weight **7–12oz (200–350g)**
Social **Flocks**	Lifespan **Up to 10 years**	Status **Secure**

Order **Charadriiformes**	Family **Scolopacidae**	Species ***Arenaria interpres***

Ruddy Turnstone

bold red patches on back and wings

ADULT (BREEDING)

dark flight feathers

IN FLIGHT

black-and-white head and breast pattern

short, dark, chisel-like bill

brownish head markings

variably streaked, whitish face

brownish upperparts

black breast

ADULT (NONBREEDING)

bright white underparts, at all ages

white-edged, dark feathers

ADULT (BREEDING)

short, orange legs

orange legs

JUVENILE (FALL)

This tame, medium-sized, and stocky sandpiper with a chisel-shaped bill is a common visitor along the shorelines of North and South America. On its high-Arctic breeding grounds, it is bold and aggressive and is able to drive off predators as large as the Glaucous Gull and Parasitic Jaeger. The Ruddy Turnstone was given its name due to its reddish back color and because of its habit of flipping and overturning items like mollusk shells and pebbles, or digging in the sand and looking for small crustaceans and other marine invertebrates. Two subspecies live in Arctic North America: *A. i. interpres* in northeast Canada and *A. i. morinellas* elsewhere in Canada and Alaska.

VOICE Rapid chatter on breeding ground: *TIT-wooo TIT-woooRITititititit*; flight call a low, rapid *kut-a-kut*.

NESTING Simple scrape lined with lichens and grasses in dry, open areas; 4 eggs; 1 brood; June.

FEEDING Forages along shoreline for crustaceans, insects, including beetles, spiders; also eats plants.

FLIGHT: swift and strong flight, with quick wing beats.

WINTER GATHERINGS
Ruddy Turnstones often congregate in large winter flocks on rocky shorelines.

SIMILAR SPECIES

BLACK TURNSTONE
see p.170

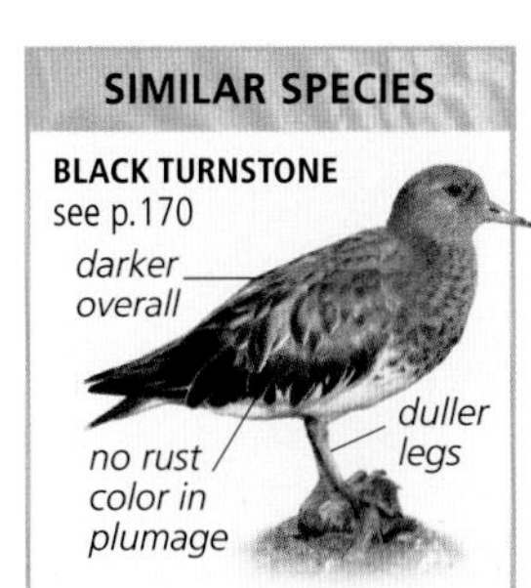
darker overall
no rust color in plumage
duller legs

OCCURRENCE
Breeds in high Arctic: wide-open, barren, and grassy habitats and rocky coasts, usually near water. In winter, on sandy or gravel beaches and rocky shorelines, from northern California to South America, and from northern Massachusetts south along Atlantic and Gulf Coasts.

Length **8–10½in (20–27cm)**	Wingspan **20–22½in (51–57cm)**	Weight **3½–7oz (100–200g)**
Social **Flocks**	Lifespan **Up to 7 years**	Status **Secure**

Order **Charadriiformes**	Family **Scolopacidae**	Species ***Arenaria melanocephala***

Black Turnstone

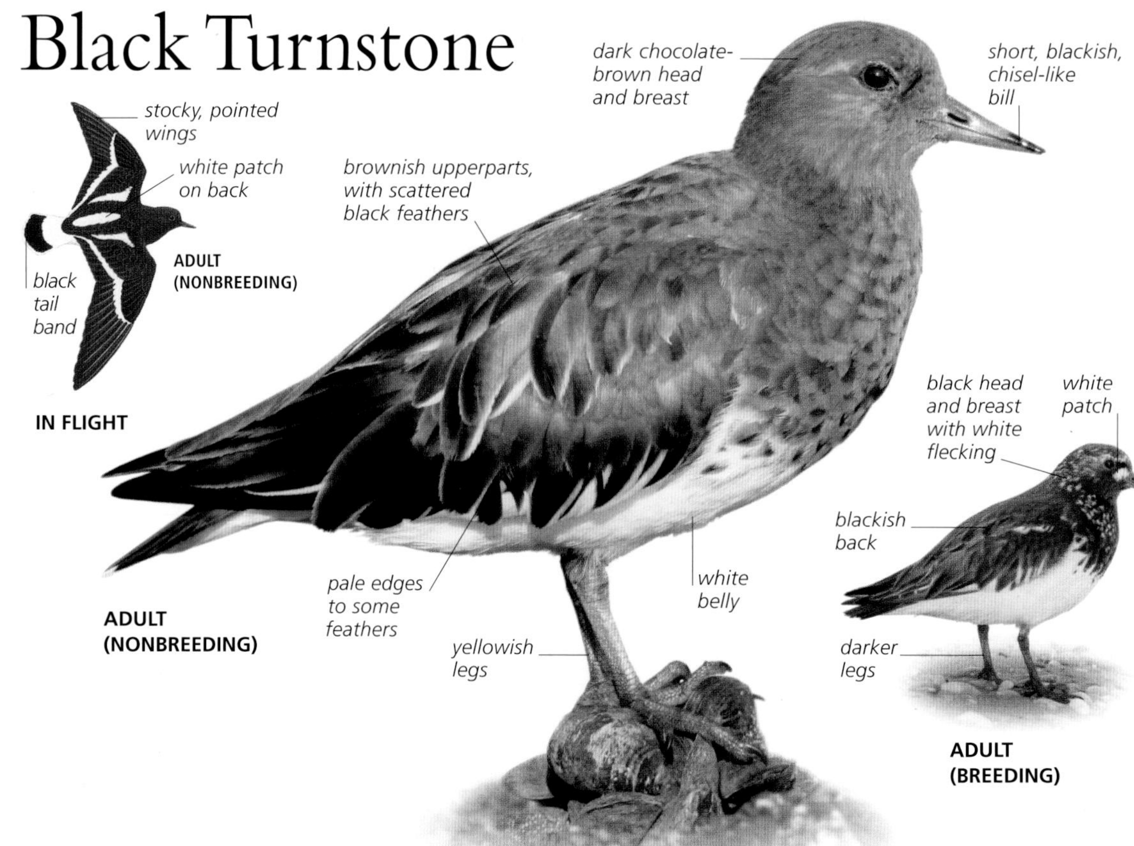
stocky, pointed wings
white patch on back
black tail band
ADULT (NONBREEDING)
IN FLIGHT
brownish upperparts, with scattered black feathers
dark chocolate-brown head and breast
short, blackish, chisel-like bill
black head and breast with white flecking
white patch
blackish back
darker legs
ADULT (BREEDING)
white belly
pale edges to some feathers
yellowish legs
ADULT (NONBREEDING)

The Black Turnstone is found along the entire North American Pacific coastline in winter, from Kodiak Island, Alaska, to the Gulf of California. Highly dependent on rocky shorelines, the zebralike but cryptic plumage of this species blends in well, and it becomes almost invisible when it forages or roosts on dark, rocky surfaces. Although the Black Turnstone flips stones and beach litter in search of food, it uses its chisel-like bill to pry loose or crack tougher prey, particularly mussles and barnacles. On its breeding grounds, this species is a vocal and aggressive defender of the nesting community, even physically attacking predators such as jaegars.

VOICE Flight call a *breerp*, often continued as rapid chattering; variety of trills, purrs, and a *tu-whit* call.

NESTING Hollow depression in tundra; 4 eggs; 1 brood; May–June.

FEEDING Eats invertebrates such as mussels, barnacles, limpets, snails, and crabs, also seeds, small bird eggs, and carrion.

FLIGHT: swift and direct, with strong, shallow wing beats.

CRACKING IT
Black Turnstones use their chisel-shaped bills to break open barnacles on rocks.

SIMILAR SPECIES

RUDDY TURNSTONE
see p.169

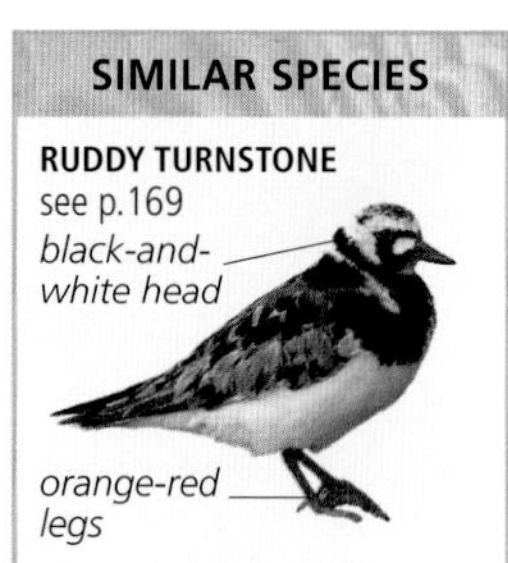
black-and-white head
orange-red legs

OCCURRENCE
Breeds in tundra of western Alaska; also inland along rivers and lakes. It is strictly coastal during migration and winter where it is found in the tidal zone of rocky shorelines, on sand and gravel beaches, mudflats, and rocky jetties of the West Coast, south to Baja, California.

Length **8½–10½in (22–27cm)**	Wingspan **20–22½in (51–57cm)**	Weight **3⅛–6oz (90–175g)**
Social **Flocks**	Lifespan **At least 4 years**	Status **Secure**

Order **Charadriiformes**	Family **Scolopacidae**	Species ***Aphriza virgata***

Surfbird

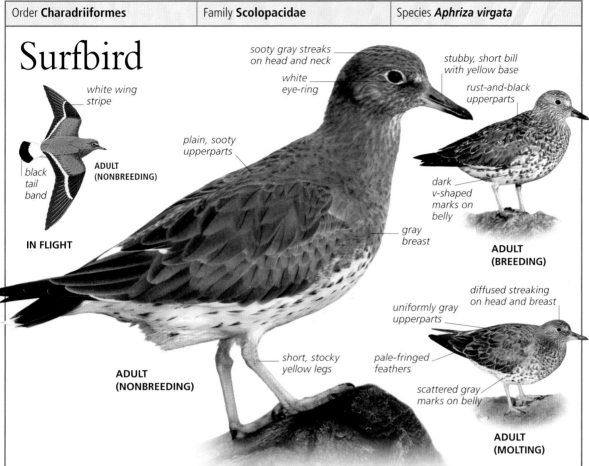

white wing stripe

black tail band

ADULT (NONBREEDING)

IN FLIGHT

sooty gray streaks on head and neck

white eye-ring

plain, sooty upperparts

stubby, short bill with yellow base

rust-and-black upperparts

dark v-shaped marks on belly

gray breast

ADULT (BREEDING)

diffused streaking on head and breast

uniformly gray upperparts

pale-fringed feathers

scattered gray marks on belly

short, stocky yellow legs

ADULT (NONBREEDING)

ADULT (MOLTING)

The chunky, stubby-billed Surfbird has a dual lifestyle—it breeds in the high mountain tundra of Alaska and the Yukon and then migrates to the rocky Pacific coasts of both North and South America. Some individuals migrate as far as southern Chile, a round trip of about 19,000 miles (30,500km) each year. This remarkable wintering range is among the largest of all North American shorebirds. The extent of the rust color on the upperparts of breeding Surfbirds is variable.

VOICE Flight call a soft *whiff-if-if*; feeding flocks soft, chattering *whiks*; display call *kree, kree…ki-drr ki-drr*, and *quoy quoy quoy*.

NESTING Shallow lined depression on vegetated or bare ground; 4 eggs; 1 brood; May–June.

FEEDING Eats mainly insects, especially beetles; also aquatic mollusks and crustaceans, such as mussels and barnacles.

FLIGHT: swift and direct, with strong, powerful wing beats.

COASTAL PROXIMITY
Except when breeding, Surfbirds spend their lives along rocky intertidal shores.

SIMILAR SPECIES

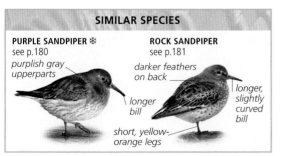

PURPLE SANDPIPER ❄
see p.180
purplish gray upperparts
longer bill
short, yellow-orange legs

ROCK SANDPIPER
see p.181
darker feathers on back
longer, slightly curved bill

OCCURRENCE
Breeds in low to high-elevation steep, rocky slopes of ridges and mountains; the rest of the year it spends exclusively on rocky Pacific coastlines, typically within 6½ft (2m) of the high-tide line (the narrowest range of all North American shorebirds).

Length **9½–10½in (24–27cm)**	Wingspan **25–27in (63–68cm)**	Weight **4–8oz (125–225g)**
Social **Small flocks**	Lifespan **Unknown**	Status **Secure**

Order **Charadriiformes**	Family **Scolopacidae**	Species ***Calidris canutus***

Red Knot

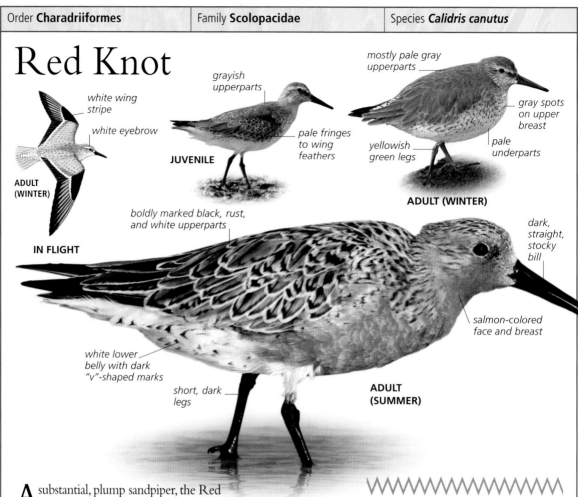

white wing stripe
white eyebrow
ADULT (WINTER)
IN FLIGHT

grayish upperparts
pale fringes to wing feathers
JUVENILE

mostly pale gray upperparts
gray spots on upper breast
yellowish green legs
pale underparts
ADULT (WINTER)

boldly marked black, rust, and white upperparts
dark, straight, stocky bill
salmon-colored face and breast
white lower belly with dark "v"-shaped marks
short, dark legs
ADULT (SUMMER)

A substantial, plump sandpiper, the Red Knot is the largest North American shorebird in the genus *Calidris*. There are two North American subspecies—*C. c. rufa* and *C. c. roselaari*. Noted for its extraordinary long-distance migration, *C. c. rufa* flies about 9,300 miles (15,000km) between its high-Arctic breeding grounds and wintering area in South America, especially in Tierra del Fuego, at the tip of South America. Recent declines have occurred in this population, attributed to over-harvesting of horseshoe crab eggs—its critical food source. With the population of *C. c. rufa* having declined from over 100,000 birds in the mid-1980s to below 15,000 today, the Red Knot is now listed as endangered in New Jersey, and faces possible extinction.

VOICE Flight call a soft *kuEEt* or *kuup*; display song *eerie por-meeee por-meeee*, followed by *por-por por-por.*

NESTING Simple scrape in grassy or barren tundra, often lined; 4 eggs; 1 brood; June.

FEEDING Probes mud or sand for insects, plant material, small mollusks, crustaceans, especially small snails, worms, and other invertebrates.

FLIGHT: powerful, swift, direct flight with rapid wing beats.

STAGING AREAS
Red Knots form colossal flocks during migration and on their wintering grounds.

SIMILAR SPECIES

BLACK-BELLIED PLOVER
see p.150

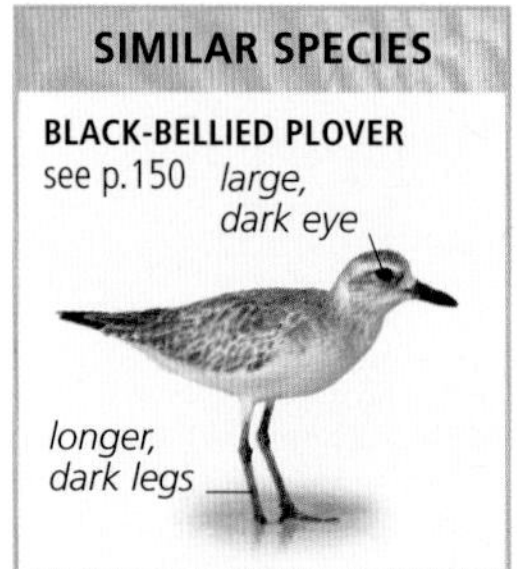
large, dark eye
longer, dark legs

OCCURRENCE
Breeds in flat, barren tundra in high-Arctic islands and peninsulas. Mostly coastal during migration and winter, preferring sandbars, beaches, and tidal flats, where it congregates in huge flocks.

Length **9–10in (23–25cm)**	Wingspan **23–24in (58–61cm)**	Weight **3⅜–8oz (95–225g)**
Social **Large flocks**	Lifespan **Unknown**	Status **Declining**

Order **Charadriiformes**	Family **Scolopacidae**	Species ***Calidris alba***

Sanderling

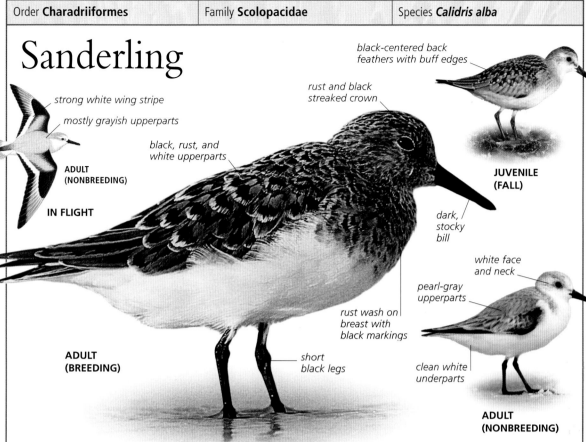

strong white wing stripe

mostly grayish upperparts

ADULT (NONBREEDING)

IN FLIGHT

black, rust, and white upperparts

rust and black streaked crown

black-centered back feathers with buff edges

JUVENILE (FALL)

dark, stocky bill

white face and neck

pearl-gray upperparts

rust wash on breast with black markings

ADULT (BREEDING)

short black legs

clean white underparts

ADULT (NONBREEDING)

The Sanderling is probably the best-known shorebird in the world. It breeds in some of the most remote, high-Arctic habitats, from Greenland to Siberia, but occupies just about every temperate and tropical shoreline in the Americas when not breeding. Indeed, its wintering range spans both American coasts, from Canada to Argentina. Feeding in flocks, it is a common sight in winter on sandy beaches. In many places, though, the bird is declining rapidly, with pollution of the sea and shore, and the disturbance caused by people using beaches for various recreational purposes, the main causes.

VOICE Flight call squeaky *pweet*, threat call *sew-sew-sew*; display song harsh, buzzy notes and chattering *cher-cher-cher*.

NESTING Small, shallow depression on dry, stony ground; 4 eggs; 1–3 broods; June–July.

FEEDING Probes along the surf-line in sand for insects, small crustaceans, small mollusks, and worms.

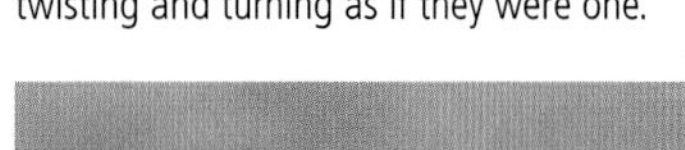

FLIGHT: rapid, free-form; birds in flocks twisting and turning as if they were one.

CHASING THE WAVES

The sanderling scampers after retreating waves to pick up any small creatures stranded by the sea.

SIMILAR SPECIES

SEMIPALMATED SANDPIPER ☼ see p.174

less contrasting upperparts

paler throat and breast

WESTERN SANDPIPER see p.175

prominent eyebrow

tapering bill

OCCURRENCE

Breeds in barren high-Arctic coastal tundra of northernmost Canada, including the islands, north to Ellesmere Island. During winter months and on migration, found along all North American coastlines, but especially sandy beaches; inland migrants found along lake and river edges.

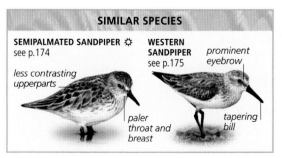

Length **7½–8in (19–20cm)**	Wingspan **16–18in (41–46cm)**	Weight **1⁷⁄₁₆–3½oz (40–100g)**
Social **Small flocks**	Lifespan **Up to 10 years**	Status **Declining**

Order **Charadriiformes**	Family **Scolopacidae**	Species ***Calidris pusilla***

Semipalmated Sandpiper

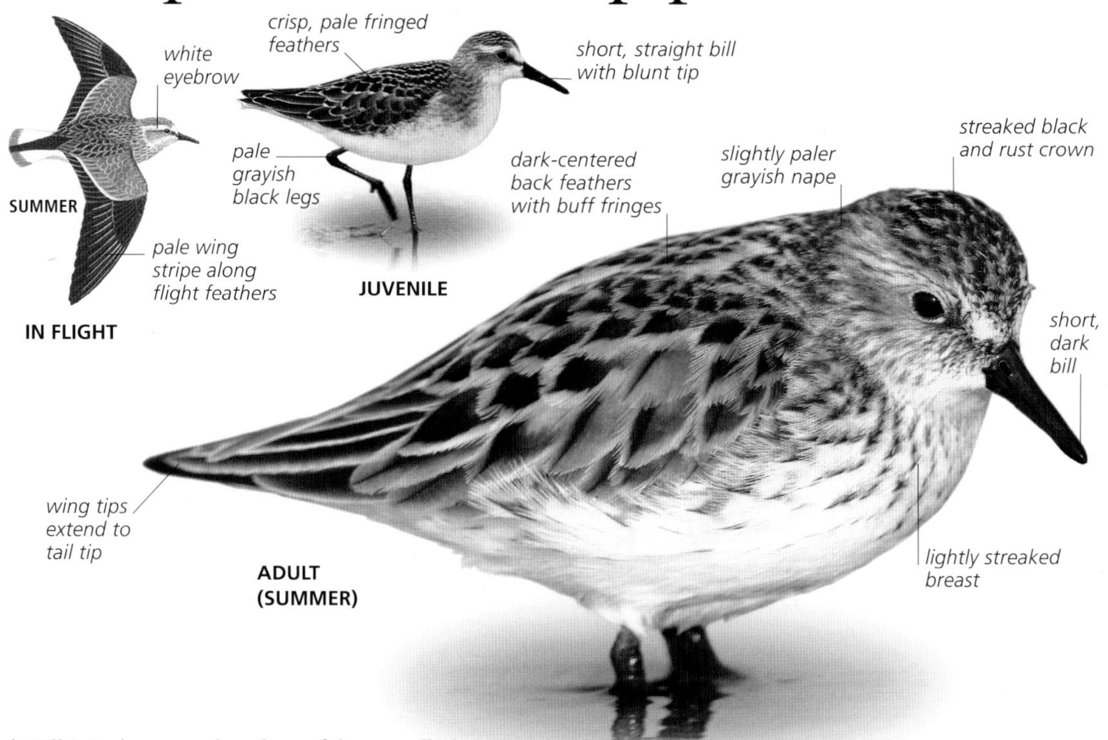

white eyebrow
SUMMER
pale wing stripe along flight feathers
IN FLIGHT
crisp, pale fringed feathers
short, straight bill with blunt tip
pale grayish black legs
JUVENILE
dark-centered back feathers with buff fringes
slightly paler grayish nape
streaked black and rust crown
short, dark bill
wing tips extend to tail tip
ADULT (SUMMER)
lightly streaked breast

This is the most abundant of the so-called "peep" *Calidiris* sandpipers, breeding in Canada's Arctic tundra. Flocks of up to 300,000 birds gather on migration staging areas. As a species, though, it can be hard to identify, due to plumage variation between juveniles and breeding adults, and a bill that varies markedly in size and shape from west to east. Semipalmated sandpipers from northeasterly breeding grounds may fly nonstop to their South American wintering grounds in the fall.

VOICE Flight call *chrrk* or higher, sharper *chit*; display song monotonous, droning trill, often repeated for minutes at a time.

NESTING Shallow, lined scrape in short grass habitat; 4 eggs; 1 brood; May–June.

FEEDING Probes mud for aquatic and terrestrial invertebrates such as mollusks, worms, and spiders.

FLIGHT: fast and direct on narrow, pointed, wings; flies in large flocks in winter.

SLEEPING TOGETHER
Semipalmated Sandpipers form large feeding or resting flocks on migration and in winter.

OCCURRENCE
Breeds in Arctic and sub-Arctic tundra habitats near water; in Alaska, on outer coastal plain. Migrants occur in shallow fresh- or saltwater and open muddy areas with little vegetation, such as intertidal flats or lake shores. Winters in Central and South America, south to Brazil and Peru.

SIMILAR SPECIES

SANDERLING
see p.173

WESTERN SANDPIPER ❄
see p.175

LEAST SANDPIPER ❄
see p.176

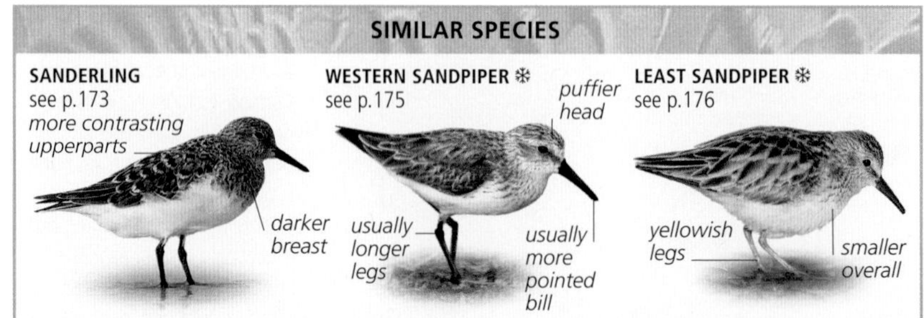

more contrasting upperparts
darker breast
puffier head
usually longer legs
usually more pointed bill
yellowish legs
smaller overall

Length **5¼–6in (13.5–15cm)**	Wingspan **13½–15in (34–38cm)**	Weight **½–1⁷⁄₁₆oz (14–40g)**
Social **Large flocks**	Lifespan **Up to 12 years**	Status **Secure**

Order **Charadriiformes**	Family **Scolopacidae**	Species ***Calidris mauri***

Western Sandpiper

mostly uniform brown or grayish upperparts

grayish, streaked crown, nape, and face

reddish-edged upper shoulder feathers

JUVENILE

white tail

ADULT

dusky tail band

narrow, white wing stripe

long, narrow, pointed wing

IN FLIGHT

dark patch between eyes and bill

white belly

partial grayish, streaked collar

ADULT (NONBREEDING)

bright, rusty cap and cheek patch

grayish, streaked nape and neck

medium-length black legs

ADULT (BREEDING)

Despite its restricted breeding range in western Alaska, the Western Sandpiper is one of the most common shorebirds in the Western Hemisphere. During its spring migration spectacularly large flocks are seen at several Pacific coast locations: at the mudflats of Roberts Bank in British Columbia, around two million Western Sandpipers stop on their way to their tundra breeding grounds to fatten up and refuel for the last hop northward. Many of these migrate over relatively short distances to winter along US coastlines, so the timing of their molt in fall is earlier than that of the similar Semipalmated Sandpiper, which migrates later in winter.

VOICE Flight call loud *chir-eep*; flushed birds make *sirp* call, or *chir-ir-ip*; song *tweer, tweer, tweer*, followed by descending trill.

NESTING Shallow depression on drained Arctic and sub-Arctic tundra; 4 eggs; 1 brood; May–June.

FEEDING Probes mud for insect larvae, crustaceans, and worms.

FLIGHT: direct, rapid flight on narrow, pointed wings; in large flocks.

FORAGING FOR FOOD
The Western Sandpiper feels for hidden prey with the touch-sensitive tip of its bill.

SIMILAR SPECIES

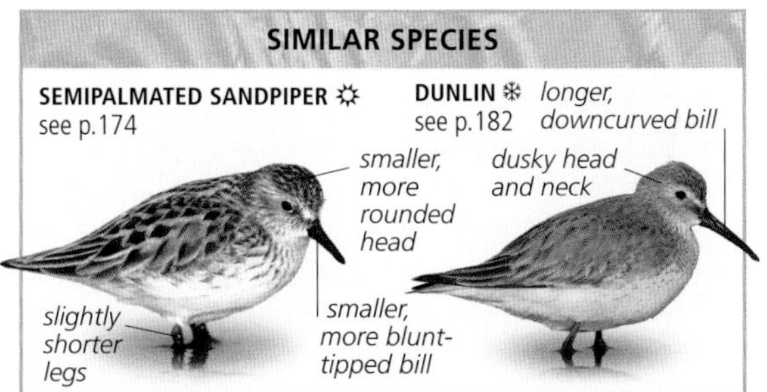
SEMIPALMATED SANDPIPER
see p.174
DUNLIN
see p.182
longer, downcurved bill
smaller, more rounded head
dusky head and neck
slightly shorter legs
smaller, more blunt-tipped bill

OCCURRENCE
Breeds in wet sedge, grassy habitats with well-drained microhabitats; in migration and in winter, prefers shallow freshwater or saltwater habitats with open muddy or sandy areas and little vegetation, such as intertidal mudflats and lake shores.

Length **5½–6½in (14–16cm)**	Wingspan **14–15in (35–38cm)**	Weight **11/16–1¼oz (19–35g)**
Social **Flocks**	Lifespan **Up to 9 years**	Status **Secure**

Order **Charadriiformes**	Family **Scolopacidae**	Species ***Calidris minutilla***

Least Sandpiper

ADULT

faint tail band

IN FLIGHT

buff to rust fringed inner wing

dark patch between eye and bill

JUVENILE

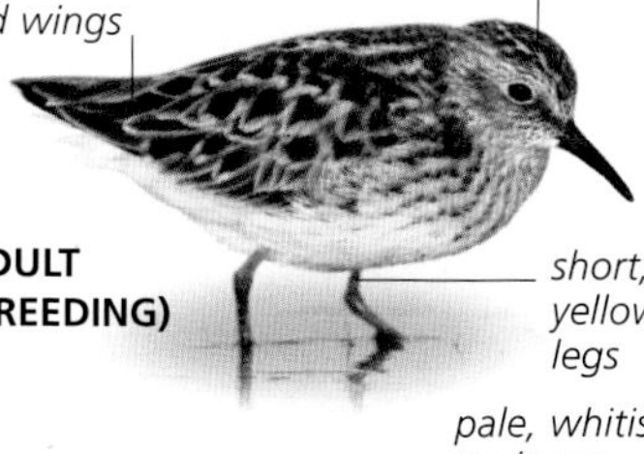

short tail and wings

small, rounded head

ADULT (BREEDING)

short, yellowish legs

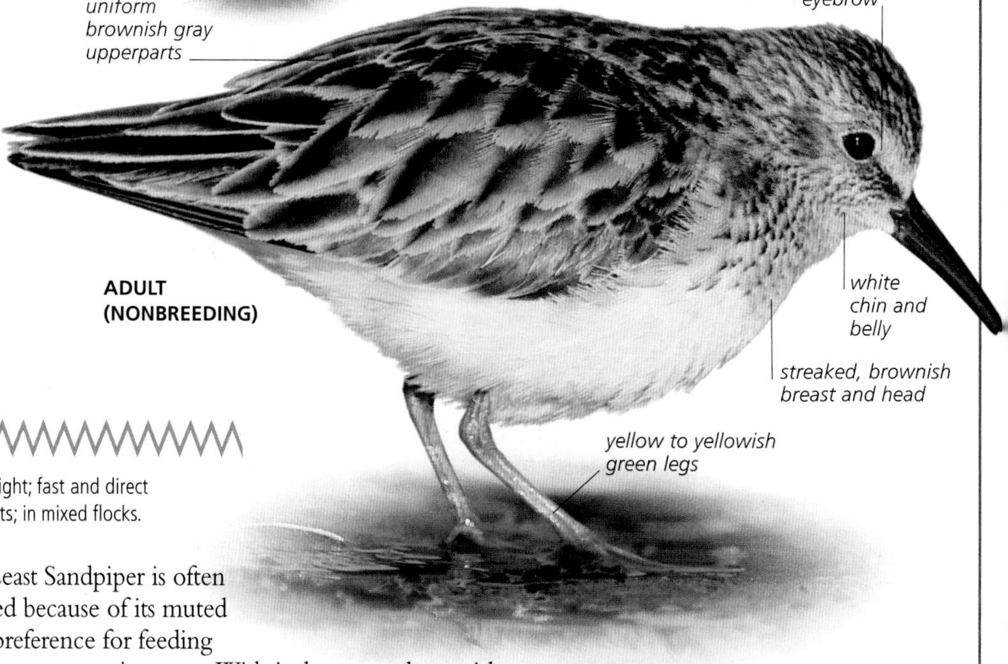

pale, whitish eyebrow

uniform brownish gray upperparts

ADULT (NONBREEDING)

white chin and belly

streaked, brownish breast and head

yellow to yellowish green legs

FLIGHT: level flight; fast and direct on quick wing beats; in mixed flocks.

The little Least Sandpiper is often overlooked because of its muted plumage and preference for feeding unobtrusively near vegetative cover. With its brown or brownish gray plumage, the Least Sandpiper virtually disappears in the landscape when feeding crouched down on wet margins of water bodies. The bird is often found in small to medium flocks, members of which typically are nervous when foraging, and frequently burst into flight, only to alight a short way off.

VOICE Its flight call, *kreeeep*, rises in pitch, often repeated two-syllable *kree-eep*; display call trilled *b-reeee*, *b-reeee*, *b-reeee*.

NESTING Depression in open, sub-Arctic habitat near water; 4 eggs; 1 brood; May–June.

FEEDING Forages for variety of small terrestrial and aquatic prey, especially sand fleas, mollusks, and flies.

FLOCK IN FLIGHT
The narrow pointed wings of the Least Sandpiper allow it to fly fast and level.

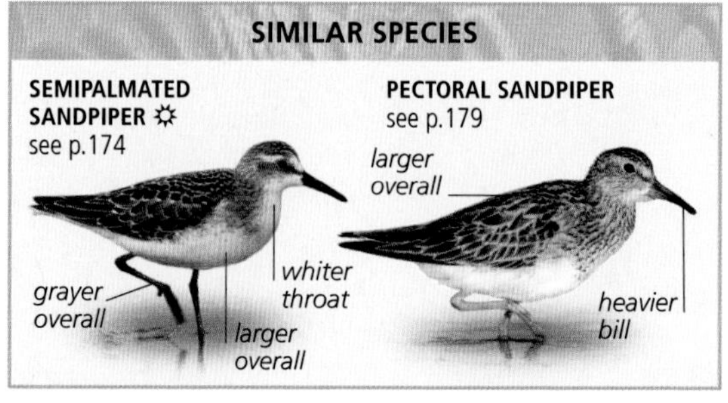
SIMILAR SPECIES
SEMIPALMATED SANDPIPER ☼
see p.174
PECTORAL SANDPIPER
see p.179
larger overall
white throat
grayer overall
larger overall
heavier bill

OCCURRENCE
Breeds in wet low-Arctic areas from Alaska and the Yukon to Quebec and Newfoundland. During migration and in winter, uses muddy areas such as lake shores, riverbanks, flooded fields, and tidal flats. Winters from southern North America south to Peru and Brazil.

Length **4¾in (12cm)**	Wingspan **13–14in (33–35cm)**	Weight **5/16–1oz (9–27g)**
Social **Flocks**	Lifespan **Up to 16 years**	Status **Secure**

Order **Charadriiformes**	Family **Scolopacidae**	Species ***Calidris fuscicollis***

White-rumped Sandpiper

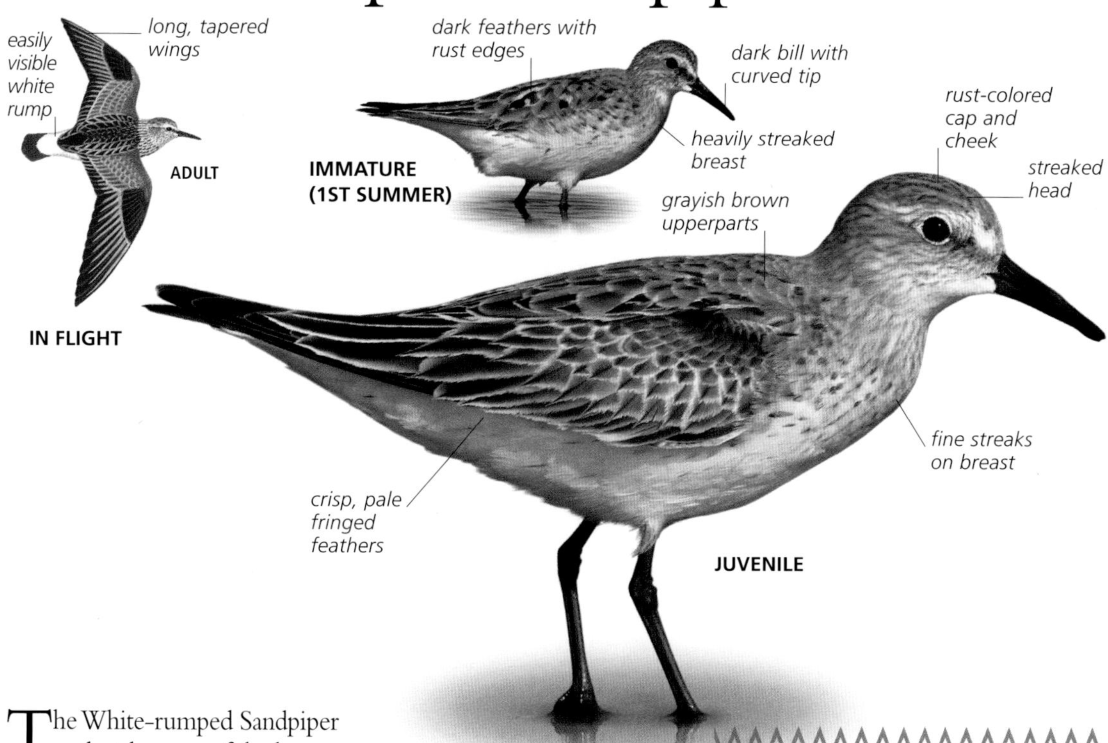
easily visible white rump
long, tapered wings
ADULT
IN FLIGHT
dark feathers with rust edges
IMMATURE (1ST SUMMER)
dark bill with curved tip
heavily streaked breast
rust-colored cap and cheek
streaked head
grayish brown upperparts
fine streaks on breast
crisp, pale fringed feathers
JUVENILE

The White-rumped Sandpiper undertakes one of the longest migrations of any bird in the Western Hemisphere. From its High Arctic breeding grounds in Alaska and Canada, it migrates in several long jumps to extreme southern South America—about 9,000–12,000 miles (14,500–19,300km), twice a year. Almost the entire population migrates through the central US and Canada in spring, with several stopovers, which are critical to the success of its journey. While associating with other shorebird species during migration and winter, it can be overlooked in the crowd. Its insect-like call and white rump aid identification.

VOICE Call a very high-pitched, insect-like *tzeet*; flight song an insect-like, high-pitched, rattling buzz, interspersed with grunts.

NESTING Shallow depression in usually wet but well-vegetated tundra; 4 eggs; 1 brood; June.

FEEDING Picks and probes for insects, spiders, earthworms, and marine worms; also some plant matter.

FLIGHT: fast, strong, and direct flight with deep wing beats.

WING POWER
Long narrow wings enable this species to migrate to and from the Arctic and Tiera del Fuego.

SIMILAR SPECIES

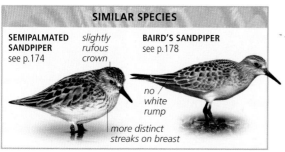

SEMIPALMATED SANDPIPER see p.174
slightly rufous crown
more distinct streaks on breast

BAIRD'S SANDPIPER see p.178
no white rump

OCCURRENCE
Breeds in wet but well-vegetated tundra, usually near ponds, lakes, or streams. In migration and winter, grassy areas: flooded fields, grassy lake margins, rivers, ponds, grassy margins of tidal mudflats, and roadside ditches. On wintering grounds, often associates with Baird's Sandpiper.

Length **6–6¾in (15–17cm)**	Wingspan **16–18in (41–46cm)**	Weight **⅞–1¾oz (25–50g)**
Social **Flocks**	Lifespan **Unknown**	Status **Secure**

Order **Charadriiformes**	Family **Scolopacidae**	Species ***Calidris bairdii***

Baird's Sandpiper

long, pointed wings
finely streaked head
ADULT
IN FLIGHT
blackish upperparts with silver-edged feathers
dark patch between eye and bill
straight, fine-tipped dark bill
clean, white underparts
ADULT
indistinct, pale eye-line
streaked back
scalloped look to upperparts
wings extend beyond tail
buff, finely streaked upper breast
JUVENILE
blackish legs

FLIGHT: strong and direct, with deep, quick wing beats.

Baird's Sandpiper is less well known than the other North American *Calidris* sandpipers. It was described in 1861, later than its relatives, by the famous North American ornithologist Elliott Cowes, a former surgeon in the US Army, in honor of Spencer Fullerton Baird. Both men were founding members of the AOU (the American Ornithologists' Union). From its High Arctic, tundra habitat, Baird's Sandpiper moves across North America and the Western USA, into South America, and all the way to Tierra del Fuego, a remarkable biannual journey of 6,000–9,000 miles (9,700–14,500km).

VOICE Flight call a low, dry *preep*; song on Arctic breeding ground: *brraay, bray, bray*, followed by *hee-aaw, hee-aaw, hee-aaw*.

NESTING Shallow depression in coastal or upland tundra; 4 eggs; 1 brood; June.

FEEDING Picks and probes for insects and larvae; also spiders and pond crustaceans.

FEEDING IN FLOCKS
Flocks of this sandpiper rush about in search of food in shallow water and muddy areas.

SIMILAR SPECIES

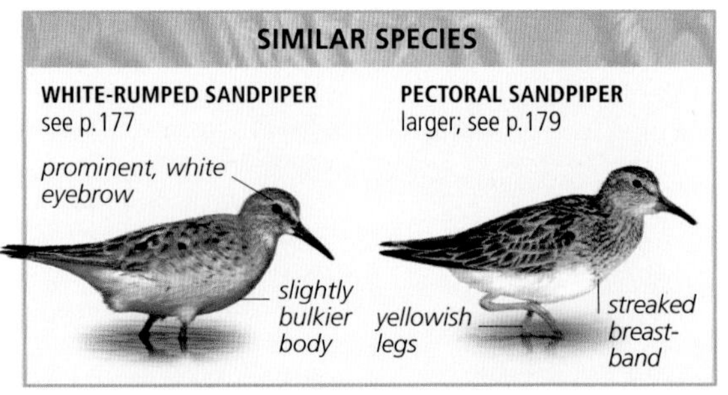

WHITE-RUMPED SANDPIPER
see p.177
prominent, white eyebrow
slightly bulkier body
PECTORAL SANDPIPER
larger; see p.179
yellowish legs
streaked breast-band

OCCURRENCE
Breeds in tundra habitats of High Arctic Alaska and Canada. During migration and winter, inland freshwater habitats: lake and river margins, wet pastures, rice fields; also tidal flats at coastal locations. In winter, common in the high Andes of South America, and sometimes all the way to Tierra del Fuego.

Length **5¾–7¼in (14.5–18.5cm)**	Wingspan **16–18½in (41–47cm)**	Weight **1¹⁄₁₆–2oz (30–55g)**
Social **Flocks**	Lifespan **Unknown**	Status **Secure**

Order **Charadriiformes**	Family **Scolopacidae**	Species ***Calidris melanotos***

Pectoral Sandpiper

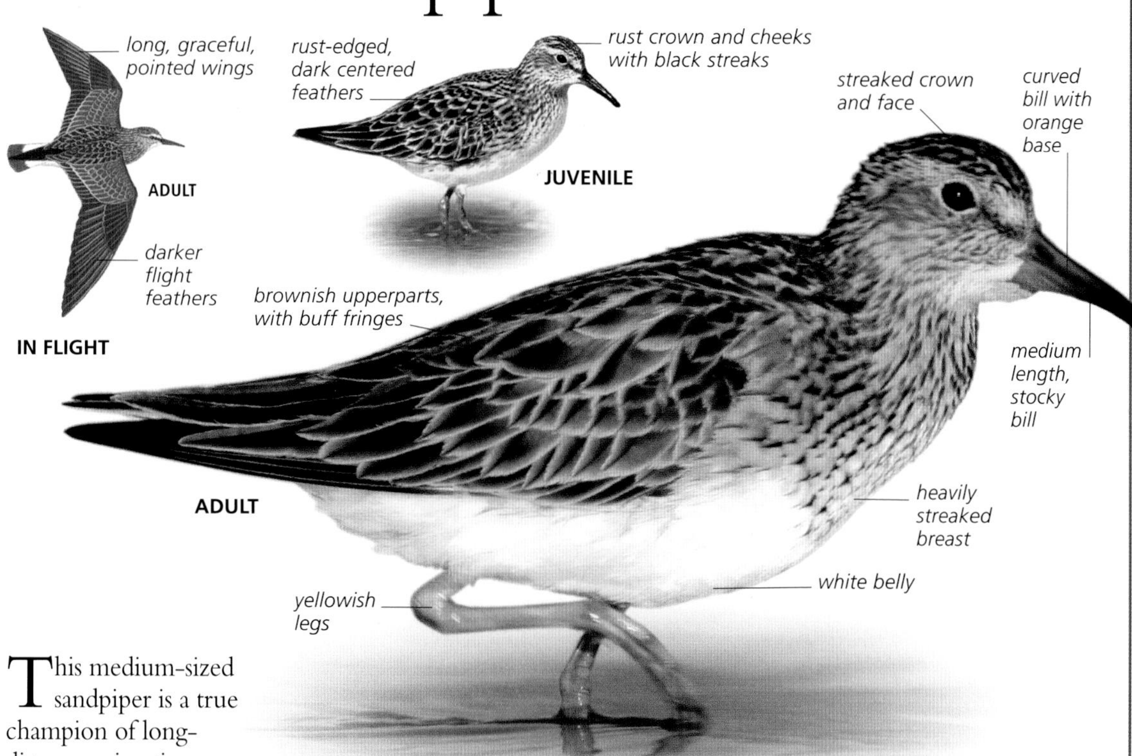
long, graceful, pointed wings
ADULT
darker flight feathers
IN FLIGHT
rust-edged, dark centered feathers
rust crown and cheeks with black streaks
JUVENILE
streaked crown and face
curved bill with orange base
brownish upperparts, with buff fringes
medium length, stocky bill
ADULT
heavily streaked breast
white belly
yellowish legs

This medium-sized sandpiper is a true champion of long-distance migration. From their breeding grounds in the high-Arctic to their wintering grounds on the pampas of southern South America, some birds travel up to 30,000 miles (48,000km) each year. The Pectoral Sandpiper is a promiscuous breeder, with males keeping harems of females in guarded territories. Males mate with as many females as they can attract with a display that includes a deep, booming call, and flights, but take no part in nest duties. Males migrate earlier than females, with both sexes prefer wet, grassy habitats during migration and in winter.

VOICE Flight call low, trilled *chrrk*; display song deep, hollow, hooting: *whoop, whoop, whoop*.

NESTING Shallow depression on ridges in moist to wet sedge tundra; 4 eggs; 1 brood; June.

FEEDING Probes or jabs mud for larvae, and forages for insects and spiders on tundra.

FLIGHT: fast and direct, with rapid, powerful wing beats; flocks zig-zag when flushed.

LONG JOURNEYS
This species migrates long distances to arrive in southern South American for the winter.

OCCURRENCE
In North America, breeds in northern Alaska, northern Yukon, Northern Territories, and some islands of the Canadian Arctic Archipelago, in wet, grassy tundra, especially near coasts. On migration and in winter favors wet pastures, the grassy margins of ponds and lakes, and saltmarshes.

SIMILAR SPECIES

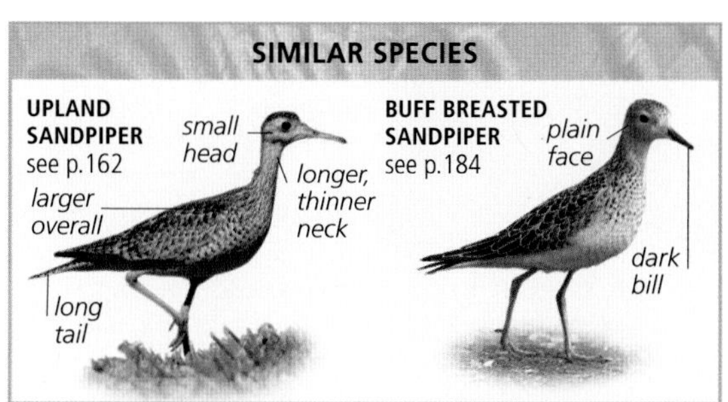
UPLAND SANDPIPER
see p.162
small head
longer, thinner neck
larger overall
long tail
BUFF BREASTED SANDPIPER
see p.184
plain face
dark bill

Length **7½–9in (19–23cm)**	Wingspan **16½–19½in (42–49cm)**	Weight **1¾–4oz (50–125g)**
Social **Migrant flocks**	Lifespan **Up to 4½ years**	Status **Secure**

Order **Charadriiformes**	Family **Scolopacidae**	Species ***Calidris maritima***

Purple Sandpiper

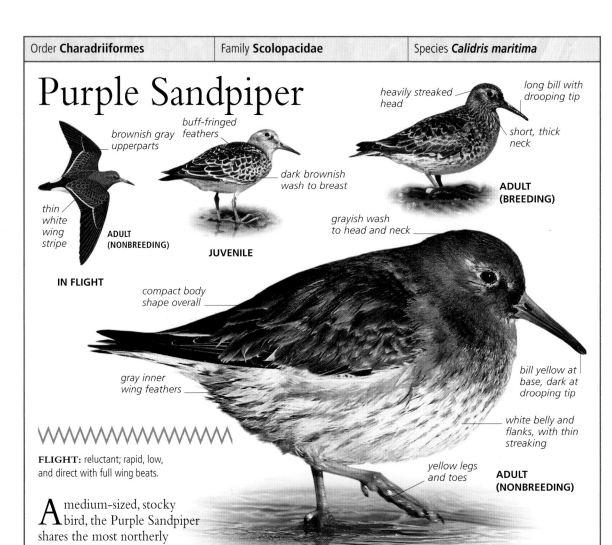

brownish gray upperparts
thin white wing stripe
ADULT (NONBREEDING)
IN FLIGHT

buff-fringed feathers
dark brownish wash to breast
JUVENILE

heavily streaked head
long bill with drooping tip
short, thick neck
ADULT (BREEDING)

grayish wash to head and neck
compact body shape overall
gray inner wing feathers
bill yellow at base, dark at drooping tip
white belly and flanks, with thin streaking
yellow legs and toes
ADULT (NONBREEDING)

FLIGHT: reluctant; rapid, low, and direct with full wing beats.

A medium-sized, stocky bird, the Purple Sandpiper shares the most northerly wintering distribution of all North American shorebirds with its close relative, the Rock Sandpiper. The dark plumage and low, squat body of the Purple Sandpiper often disguise its presence on dark tidal rocks, until a crashing wave causes a previously invisibvle flock to explode into flight.

VOICE Flight call low *kweesh*; when disturbed, *eh-eh-eh*; breeding *kwi-ti-ti-ti-bli-bli-bli* followed by *dooree-dooree-dooree*.

NESTING Simple lined scrape in high-alpine-like or barren low-lying Arctic tundra; 4 eggs; 1 brood; June.

FEEDING Feeds on various invertebrates, including crustaceans, snails, insects, spiders, and worms.

OCCURRENCE
On breeding grounds, found on barren Arctic and alpine tundra habitats in the Canadian Arctic Archipelago. On migration and in winter, predominantly found on rocky, wave-pounded shores on the eastern seaboard.

SIMILAR SPECIES

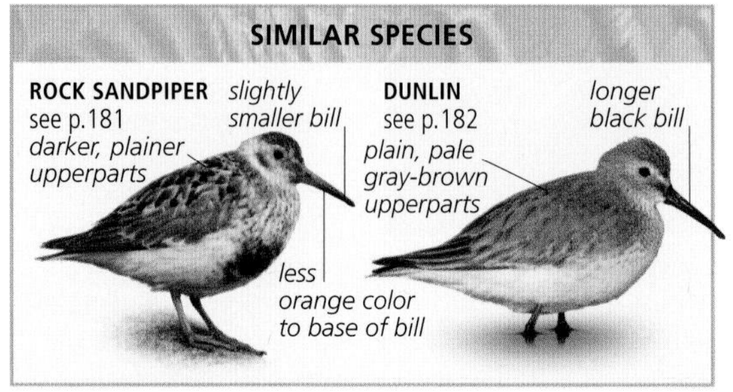
ROCK SANDPIPER
see p.181
slightly smaller bill
darker, plainer upperparts
less orange color to base of bill
DUNLIN
see p.182
longer black bill
plain, pale gray-brown upperparts

WINTER EXPOSURE
The Purple Sandpiper winters mainly on exposed rocky shores along the eastern seaboard.

Length **8–8½in (20–21cm)**	Wingspan **16½–18½in (42–47cm)**	Weight **1¾–3½oz (50–100g)**
Social **Small flocks**	Lifespan **Up to 20 years**	Status **Declining**

Order **Charadriiformes**	Family **Scolopacidae**	Species ***Calidris ptilocnemis***

Rock Sandpiper

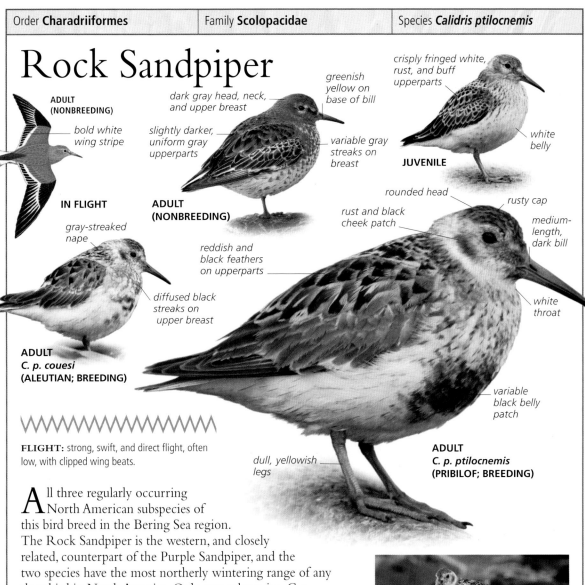

ADULT (NONBREEDING)
bold white wing stripe
IN FLIGHT
dark gray head, neck, and upper breast
greenish yellow on base of bill
slightly darker, uniform gray upperparts
variable gray streaks on breast
ADULT (NONBREEDING)
crisply fringed white, rust, and buff upperparts
white belly
JUVENILE
gray-streaked nape
diffused black streaks on upper breast
ADULT
C. p. couesi
(ALEUTIAN; BREEDING)
rounded head
rusty cap
rust and black cheek patch
medium-length, dark bill
reddish and black feathers on upperparts
white throat
variable black belly patch
dull, yellowish legs
ADULT
C. p. ptilocnemis
(PRIBILOF; BREEDING)

FLIGHT: strong, swift, and direct flight, often low, with clipped wing beats.

All three regularly occurring North American subspecies of this bird breed in the Bering Sea region. The Rock Sandpiper is the western, and closely related, counterpart of the Purple Sandpiper, and the two species have the most northerly wintering range of any shorebird in North America. Only one subspecies, *C. p. tschuktschorum*, migrates to the Pacific coast of North America.

VOICE Call short squeaking *chreet*, *cheet*, or *cheerrt*; song *di-jerr, di-jerr, di-jerr* and more melodic *quida-se-quida-we-quida*.

NESTING Simple scrape in coastal lowland and mountain tundra; 4 eggs; 1 brood; May–June.

FEEDING Probes for clams and snails in seaweed; in breeding season eats mainly land insects, especially beetles.

CLOSE ENCOUNTER
The Rock Sandpiper is not easily frightened, allowing it to be clearly identified.

SIMILAR SPECIES

SURFBIRD
see p.171
short, stout bill
PURPLE SANDPIPER
see p.180
longer bill
spotted underparts
dark-centered shoulder feathers

OCCURRENCE
Breeds in Arctic lowland coastal heath tundra or mountain tundra. On migration and in winter can be found in a variety of habitats including rocky headlands, gravel beaches, mudflats, and sandflats, but perhaps commonest along rocky shores south to southern California.

Length **7¼–9½in (18.5–24cm)**	Wingspan **13–18½in (33–47cm)**	Weight **2½–4oz (70–125g)**
Social **Large flocks**	Lifespan **Unknown**	Status **Secure**

Order **Charadriiformes**	Family **Scolopacidae**	Species ***Calidris alpina***

Dunlin

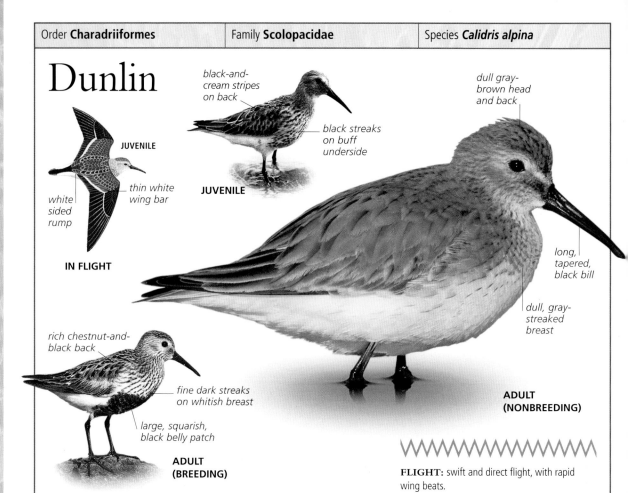

black-and-cream stripes on back
black streaks on buff underside
JUVENILE
dull gray-brown head and back
JUVENILE
thin white wing bar
white sided rump
IN FLIGHT
long, tapered, black bill
dull, gray-streaked breast
ADULT (NONBREEDING)
rich chestnut-and-black back
fine dark streaks on whitish breast
large, squarish, black belly patch
ADULT (BREEDING)

FLIGHT: swift and direct flight, with rapid wing beats.

The Dunlin is one of the most abundant and widespread of North America's shorebirds, but of the ten officially recognized subspecies, only three breed in North America: *C. a. arcticola*, *C. a. pacifica*, and *C. a. hudsonia*. The Dunlin is unmistakable in its striking, red-backed, black-bellied breeding plumage. In winter it sports much drabber colors, but more than makes up for this by gathering in spectacular flocks of many thousands of birds on its favorite, coastal mudflats.

VOICE Call accented trill, *drurr-drurr*, that rises slightly, then descends; flight call *jeeezp*; song *wrraah-wrraah*.

NESTING Simple cup lined with grasses, leaves, and lichens in moist to wet tundra; 4 eggs; 1 brood; June–July.

FEEDING Probes for marine, freshwater, terrestrial invertebrates: clams, worms, insect larvae, crustaceans; also plants and small fish.

OLD RED BACK
The Dunlin was once known as the Red-backed Sandpiper due to its distinct breeding plumage.

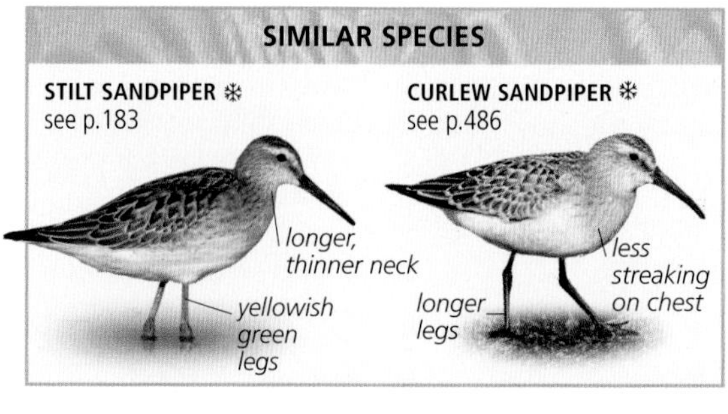
SIMILAR SPECIES
STILT SANDPIPER
see p.183
longer, thinner neck
yellowish green legs
CURLEW SANDPIPER
see p.486
less streaking on chest
longer legs

OCCURRENCE
Breeds in Arctic and sub-Arctic moist, wet tundra, often near ponds, with drier islands for nest sites. In migration and winter, prefers coastal areas with extensive mudflats and sandy beaches; also feeds in flooded fields and seasonal inland wetlands.

Length **6½–8½in (16–22cm)**	Wingspan **12½–17½in (32–44cm)**	Weight **1$\frac{9}{16}$–2¼oz (45–65g)**
Social **Large flocks**	Lifespan **Up to 24 years**	Status **Declining**

Order **Charadriiformes**	Family **Scolopacidae**	Species ***Calidris himantopus***

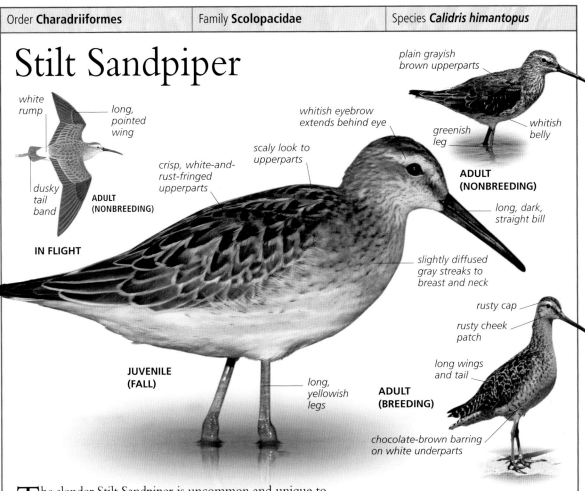

Stilt Sandpiper

white rump

long, pointed wing

dusky tail band

ADULT (NONBREEDING)

IN FLIGHT

crisp, white-and-rust-fringed upperparts

scaly look to upperparts

whitish eyebrow extends behind eye

plain grayish brown upperparts

greenish leg

whitish belly

ADULT (NONBREEDING)

long, dark, straight bill

slightly diffused gray streaks to breast and neck

JUVENILE (FALL)

long, yellowish legs

rusty cap

rusty cheek patch

long wings and tail

ADULT (BREEDING)

chocolate-brown barring on white underparts

The slender Stilt Sandpiper is uncommon and unique to North America, where it breeds in several small areas of northern tundra. It favors shallow, freshwater habitats, where it feeds in a distinctive style, walking slowly through belly-deep water with its neck outstretched and bill pointed downward. It either picks at the surface, or submerges itself, keeping its tail raised up all the while. During migration it forms dense, rapidly moving flocks that sometimes include other sandpiper species.

VOICE Flight or alarm call low, muffled *chuf*; also *krrit* and sharp *kew-it*; display call *xxree-xxree-xxree-xxree-ee-haw, ee-haw.*

NESTING Shallow depression on raised knolls or ridges in tundra; 4 eggs; 1 brood; June.

FEEDING Eats mostly adult and larval insects; also some snails, mollusks, and seeds.

FLIGHT: fast and direct, with rapid beats of its long wings.

SIMILAR SPECIES

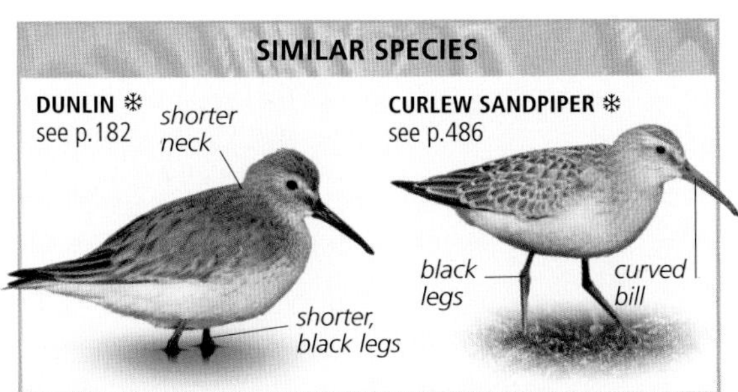

DUNLIN ❄
see p.182
shorter neck
shorter, black legs
CURLEW SANDPIPER ❄
see p.486
black legs
curved bill

PALE BELOW

Wading through shallow water, this Stilt Sandpiper displays its whitish underparts.

OCCURRENCE

Breeds in moist to wet coastal tundra on well-drained, raised knolls or ridges in Alaska, Yukon, and northwestern territories and Hudson Bay. During migration and in winter, prefers freshwater habitats, such as flooded fields, marsh pools, reservoirs, and sheltered lagoons to tidal mudflats.

Length **8–9in (20–23cm)**	Wingspan **17–18½in (43–47cm)**	Weight **1¾–2⅛oz (50–60g)**
Social **Pairs/Flocks**	Lifespan **At least 3 years**	Status **Secure**

Order **Charadriiformes**	Family **Scolopacidae**	Species ***Tryngites subruficollis***

Buff-breasted Sandpiper

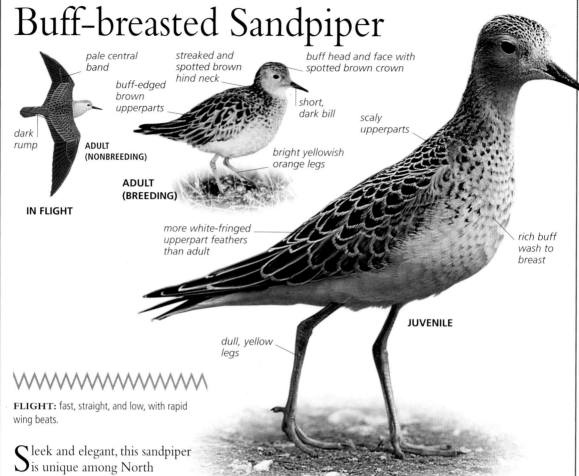

pale central band

dark rump

ADULT (NONBREEDING)

IN FLIGHT

streaked and spotted brown hind neck

buff-edged brown upperparts

buff head and face with spotted brown crown

short, dark bill

bright yellowish orange legs

ADULT (BREEDING)

scaly upperparts

more white-fringed upperpart feathers than adult

rich buff wash to breast

JUVENILE

dull, yellow legs

FLIGHT: fast, straight, and low, with rapid wing beats.

Sleek and elegant, this sandpiper is unique among North American shorebirds in terms of its mating system. On the ground in the Arctic, each male flashes his white underwings to attract females for mating. After mating, the female leaves to perform all nest duties alone, while the male continues to display and mate with other females. Once nesting is over, the Buff-breasted Sandpiper migrates an astonishing 16,000 miles (26,000km) from its breeding grounds to winter in temperate South America.

VOICE Flight call soft, short *gert*, or longer, rising *grriit.*

NESTING Simple depression on well-drained moss or grass hummock; 4 eggs; 1 brood; June.

FEEDING Forages on land for insects, insect larvae, and spiders; occasionally eats seeds.

LANDLUBBER
The Buff-breasted Sandpiper is very much a shorebird of dry land, it doesn't swim or dive.

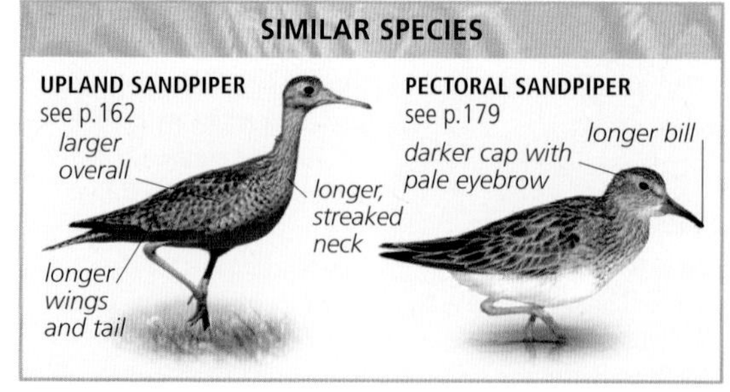
SIMILAR SPECIES
UPLAND SANDPIPER
see p.162
larger overall
longer, streaked neck
longer wings and tail
PECTORAL SANDPIPER
see p.179
darker cap with pale eyebrow
longer bill

OCCURRENCE
Breeds in moist to wet, grassy or sedge coastal tundra; during migration, favors short grass areas such as pastures, sod farms, meadows, rice fields, or agricultural areas. Winters in the pampas region of South America in short, wet grass habitats.

Length **$7\frac{1}{4}$–8in (18.5–20cm)**	Wingspan **17–$18\frac{1}{2}$in (43–47cm)**	Weight **$1\frac{7}{16}$–$3\frac{3}{8}$oz (40–95g)**
Social **Large flocks**	Lifespan **Unknown**	Status **Declining**

Order **Charadriiformes**	Family **Scolopacidae**	Species ***Phalaropus tricolor***

Wilson's Phalarope

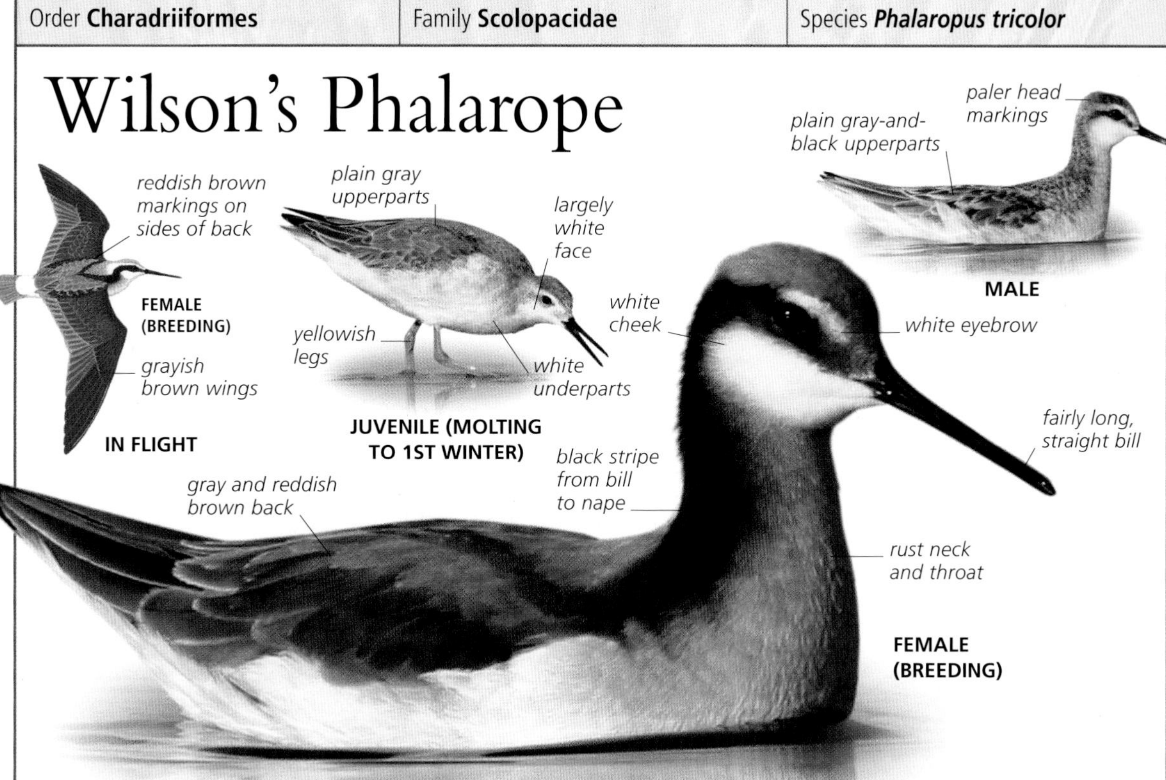
reddish brown markings on sides of back
FEMALE (BREEDING)
grayish brown wings
IN FLIGHT
plain gray upperparts
largely white face
yellowish legs
white underparts
JUVENILE (MOLTING TO 1ST WINTER)
plain gray-and-black upperparts
paler head markings
MALE
white cheek
white eyebrow
fairly long, straight bill
black stripe from bill to nape
gray and reddish brown back
rust neck and throat
FEMALE (BREEDING)

A truly American phalarope, Wilson's is the largest of the three phalarope species. Unlike its two relatives, it does not breed in the Arctic, but in the shallow wetlands of western North America, and winters mainly in continental habitats of Bolivia and Argentina instead of in the ocean. This species can be found employing the feeding technique of spinning in shallow water to churn up adult and larval insects, or running in various directions on muddy wetland edges with its head held low to the ground while chasing and picking up insects. This bird is quite tolerant of humans on its breeding grounds, but this attitude changes immediately before migration, as it has gained weight and its movement is sluggish.

VOICE Flight call a low, nasal *werpf*; also higher, repetitive *emf, emf, emf, emf*, or *luk, luk, luk*.

NESTING Simple scrape lined with grass; 4 eggs; 1 brood; May–June.

FEEDING Eats brine shrimp, various insects, and insect larvae.

FLIGHT: fast and direct with quick wing beats.

ODD ONE OUT
Unlike its two essentially oceanic cousins, Wilson's Phalarope is also found in freshwater habitats.

SIMILAR SPECIES

LESSER YELLOWLEGS see p.164
darker, spotted back
streaked head and neck

RED-NECKED PHALAROPE see p.186
black cheek patch
shorter bill

OCCURRENCE
Breeds in shallow, grassy wetlands of interior North America; during migration and winter, occurs in salty lakes and saline ponds as well as inland waterbodies. In winter, tens of thousands can be seen in the middle of Titicaca Lake in Bolivia.

Length **8½–9½in (22–24cm)**	Wingspan **15½–17in (39–43cm)**	Weight **1¼–3oz (35–85g)**
Social **Large flocks**	Lifespan **Up to 10 years**	Status **Secure**

Order **Charadriiformes**	Family **Scolopacidae**	Species ***Phalaropus lobatus***

Red-necked Phalarope

pointed wings
narrow, white wing stripe
FEMALE (BREEDING)
IN FLIGHT
dark cap and cheek patch
black back with dull, white lines
JUVENILE (WORN PLUMAGE)
dark upperparts with buff stripes
JUVENILE
dark gray crown and face
white throat
dark upperparts with buff or rust feather edges
needle-like, dark bill
rust neck and upper breast
FEMALE (BREEDING)
white underparts with dusky streaked flanks

This aquatic sandpiper spends much of its life in deep ocean waters feeding on tiny plankton; each year, after nine months at sea, it comes to nest in the Arctic. Its Latin name *lobatus* reflects the morphology of its feet, which are webbed (lobed). Both the Red-necked Phalarope and the Red Phalarope are oceanic birds that are found in large flocks or "rafts" far from shore. However, both species are occasionally found swimming inland, in freshwater habitats. Like the other two phalaropes, the Red-necked has a fascinating and unusual reversal of typical sex roles. The female is more brightly colored and slightly larger than the male; she will also pursue the male, compete savagely for him, and will migrate shortly after laying her eggs.

VOICE Flight call a hard, squeaky *pwit* or *kit*; on breeding grounds, vocalizations include variations of flight call notes.

NESTING Depression in wet sedge or grass; 3–4 eggs; 1–2 broods; May–June.

FEEDING Eats plankton; also insects, brine shrimp, and mollusks.

FLIGHT: fast and direct, with rapid wing beats.

SINGLE FATHER
Male phalaropes perform all nesting and rearing duties after the female lays the eggs.

SIMILAR SPECIES

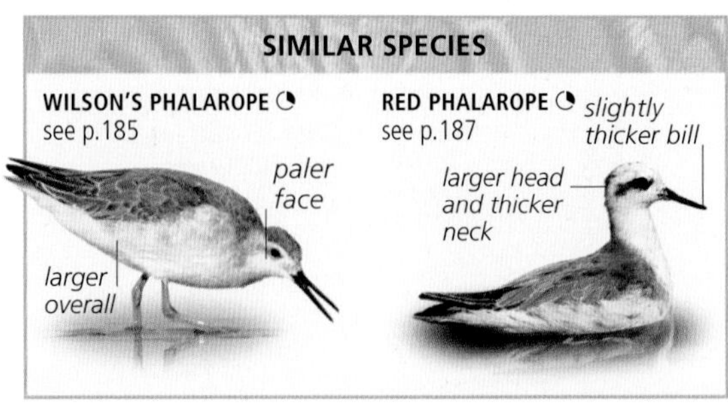
WILSON'S PHALAROPE
see p.185
paler face
larger overall
RED PHALAROPE
see p.187
slightly thicker bill
larger head and thicker neck

OCCURRENCE
Breeds in wet tundra, on raised ridges, or hummocks, but during migration and in winter, occurs far out to sea and away from shores, although sometimes found in a number of freshwater habitats.

Length **7–7½in (18–19cm)**	Wingspan **12½–16in (32–41cm)**	Weight **1 1/16–1 9/16oz (30–45g)**
Social **Flocks**	Lifespan **Unknown**	Status **Secure**

Order **Charadriiformes**	Family **Scolopacidae**	Species ***Phalaropus fulicarius***

Red Phalarope

bold white wing bar
white rump with black line in center, and white edges
broad, pointed wings
FEMALE (BREEDING)
IN FLIGHT
buff feather fringes
scalloped upperparts
dull rust crown with black streaks
brick-red underparts; paler than female
MALE (BREEDING)
black cheek patch and nape
mostly gray upperparts
white neck and head
white underparts
ADULT (NONBREEDING)
bold white cheek patch
black crown
tan-fringed feathers on upperparts
stout, yellow bill with black tip
deep brick-red neck, throat, and underparts
FEMALE (BREEDING)

The Red Phalarope spends over ten months each year over deep ocean waters. It also migrates across the ocean, which explains why few birds of this species are ever seen inland. Many Red Phalaropes winter in tropical waters, with concentrations in the Humboldt Current off Peru and Chile, and in the Benguela current off southwestern Africa. During migration over Alaskan waters, flocks of Red Phalaropes feed on crustaceans in the mud plumes that are created by the foraging of gray and bowhead whales on the ocean floor.

VOICE Flight call a sharp *psip* or *pseet*, often in rapid succession; alarm call a drawn-out, 2-syllabled *sweet*.

NESTING Depression on ridge or hummock in coastal sedge; 3–4 eggs; 1 brood; June.

FEEDING Plucks prey from sea; marine crustaceans, fish eggs, larval fish; adult or larval insects.

FLIGHT: direct with rapid wing beats, birds in flocks often synchronize.

DIFFERENT COLOR
In nonbreeding plumage, phalaropes are gray and white.

NO TIES
After breeding, female Red Phalaropes leave the male and play no role in raising young.

SIMILAR SPECIES

WILSON'S PHALAROPE more terrestrial; see p.185

RED-NECKED PHALAROPE see p.186

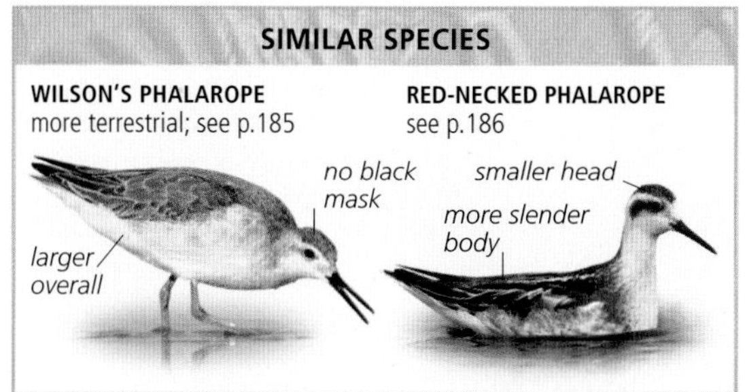
no black mask
larger overall
smaller head
more slender body

OCCURRENCE
Breeds in coastal Arctic tundra; during migration and in winter, occurs in deep ocean waters; small numbers are seen near the shore in coastal California in fall and winter. The Red Phalarope is rare inland.

Length **8–8½in (20–22cm)**	Wingspan **16–17½in (41–44cm)**	Weight **1¼–2⅝oz (35–75g)**
Social **Large flocks**	Lifespan **Unknown**	Status **Secure**

Order **Charadriiformes**	Family **Laridae**	Species ***Larus heermanni***

Heermann's Gull

ADULT (BREEDING)

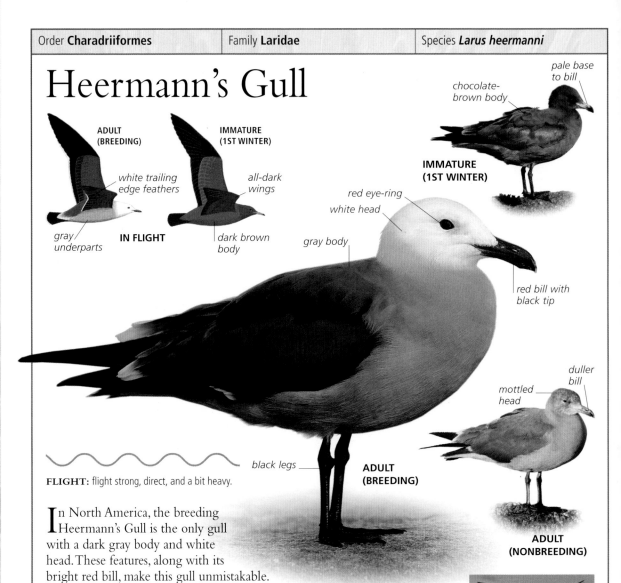

white trailing edge feathers

gray underparts

IN FLIGHT

IMMATURE (1ST WINTER)

all-dark wings

dark brown body

pale base to bill

chocolate-brown body

IMMATURE (1ST WINTER)

red eye-ring

white head

gray body

red bill with black tip

duller bill

mottled head

black legs

ADULT (BREEDING)

ADULT (NONBREEDING)

FLIGHT: flight strong, direct, and a bit heavy.

In North America, the breeding Heermann's Gull is the only gull with a dark gray body and white head. These features, along with its bright red bill, make this gull unmistakable. In nonbreeding plumage, the head is mottled dark and the bill is black-tipped. Juveniles are generally dark brown, with pale patches at the base of their bills. These gulls have black legs in all plumages, unlike any other North American gull, except the Black-legged Kittiwake.

VOICE Nasal *caw* or *cow-awk* call; not very vocal away from breeding grounds.

NESTING Depression lined with dead grass or twigs in sand, small rocks, or grass; usually nests with terns; 1–3 eggs; 1 brood; March–July.

FEEDING Feeds on fish, crustaceans, mollusks, squid, and lizards; in breeding colonies, takes eggs of terns and gulls; also scavenges.

WHITE EDGES

The white trailing edge of the wing and the white tip of the tail are obvious in flight.

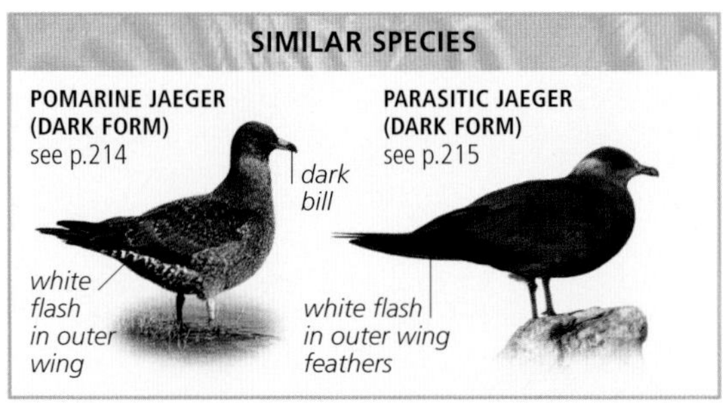
SIMILAR SPECIES
POMARINE JAEGER (DARK FORM)
see p.214
dark bill
white flash in outer wing
PARASITIC JAEGER (DARK FORM)
see p.215
white flash in outer wing feathers

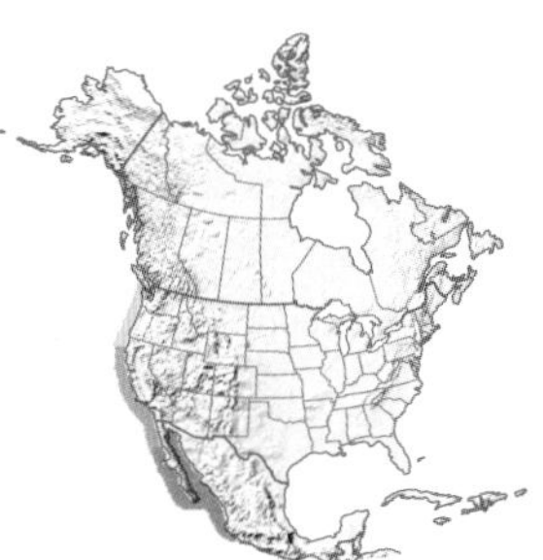

OCCURRENCE

A truly western North American gull, it nests on islands off Baja California; over 90 percent of the world's population nests on Isla Raza; occasionally in California; after breeding spreads north along coast to British Columbia, uncommon north of Monterey; rare inland and accidental elsewhere.

Length **18–21in (46–53cm)**	Wingspan **4¼ft (1.3m)**	Weight **13–23oz (375–650g)**
Social **Colonies**	Lifespan **Up to 13 years**	Status **Secure**

Order **Charadriiformes**	Family **Laridae**	Species ***Larus canus***

Mew Gull

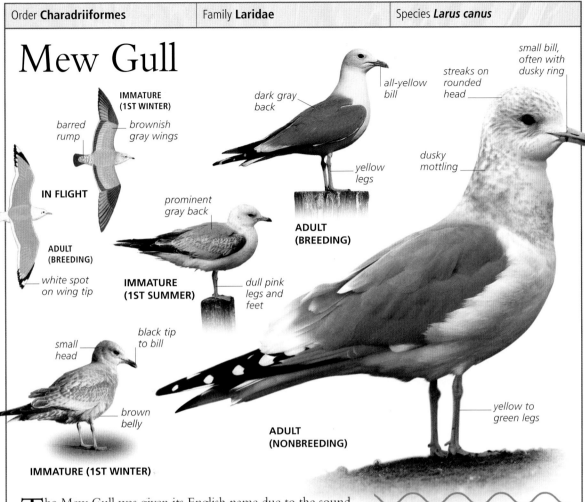

IMMATURE (1ST WINTER)
barred rump
brownish gray wings
IN FLIGHT
ADULT (BREEDING)
white spot on wing tip
prominent gray back
IMMATURE (1ST SUMMER)
dull pink legs and feet
dark gray back
all-yellow bill
yellow legs
ADULT (BREEDING)
small bill, often with dusky ring
streaks on rounded head
dusky mottling
small head
black tip to bill
brown belly
IMMATURE (1ST WINTER)
yellow to green legs
ADULT (NONBREEDING)

The Mew Gull was given its English name due to the sound of its call. Its small bill and rounded head give it a rather dove-like profile. It can be confused with the widespread Ring-billed Gull, which it resembles in all plumages. Some taxonomists split the Mew Gull into four species—the European "Common Gull" (*L. c. canus*), the northeast Asian species (*L. c. heinei*), the "Kamchatka Gull" (*L. c. kamtschatschensis*), and the North American "Short-billed Gull" (*L. c. brachyrhynchus*).

VOICE Shrill mewing calls; higher pitched than other gulls.

NESTING Platform of mainly dry vegetation in trees or on ground; 1–5 eggs; 1 brood; May–August.

FEEDING Eats aquatic crustaceans and mollusks, insects, fish, bird eggs, chicks; scavenges trash and steals food from other birds.

FLIGHT: wing beats faster than larger, similar-looking gulls.

PLAIN YELLOW BILL
Although back color and bill size vary in different forms, all adult Mew Gulls have plain yellow bills.

SIMILAR SPECIES

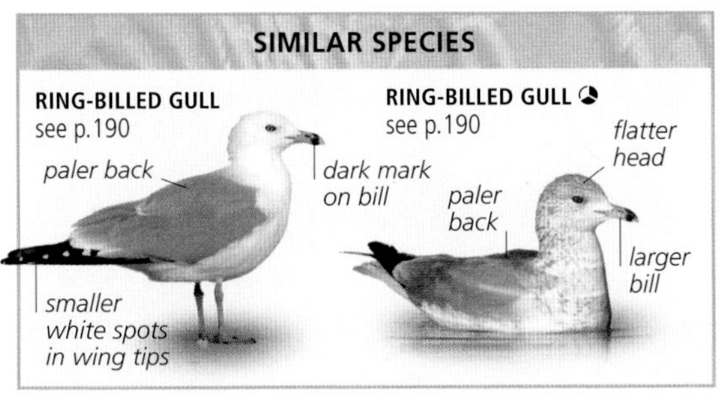
RING-BILLED GULL
see p.190
paler back
dark mark on bill
smaller white spots in wing tips
RING-BILLED GULL
see p.190
flatter head
paler back
larger bill

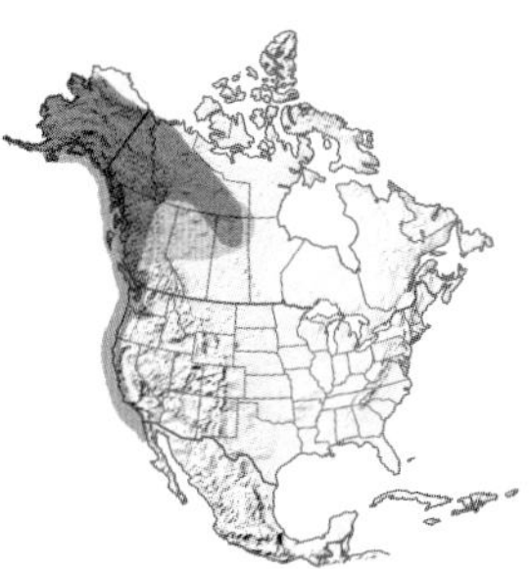

OCCURRENCE
Breeds in Alaska and northwest Canada south along coast into British Columbia; winters along the Pacific Coast south to Baja California and inland on major river systems. Casual to accidental across the continent to Atlantic Coast.

Length **15–16in (38–41cm)**	Wingspan **3ft 3in–4ft (1–1.2m)**	Weight **13–18oz (375–500g)**
Social **Pairs/Colonies**	Lifespan **Up to 24 years**	Status **Secure**

Order **Charadriiformes**	Family **Laridae**	Species ***Larus delawarensis***

Ring-billed Gull

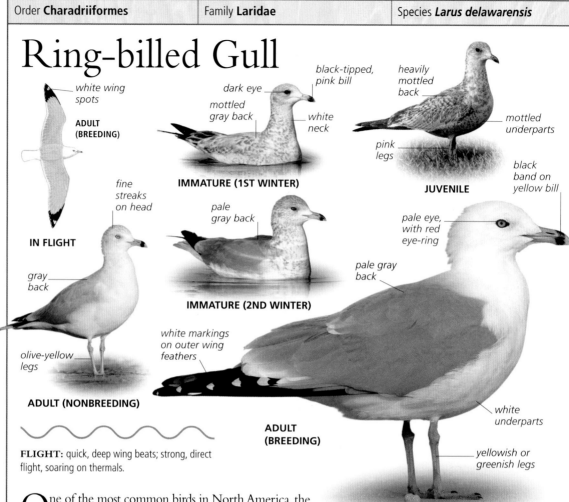

white wing spots
ADULT (BREEDING)
IN FLIGHT

dark eye
black-tipped, pink bill
mottled gray back
white neck
IMMATURE (1ST WINTER)

heavily mottled back
mottled underparts
pink legs
JUVENILE

fine streaks on head
gray back
olive-yellow legs
ADULT (NONBREEDING)

pale gray back
IMMATURE (2ND WINTER)

black band on yellow bill
pale eye, with red eye-ring
pale gray back
white markings on outer wing feathers
white underparts
yellowish or greenish legs
ADULT (BREEDING)

FLIGHT: quick, deep wing beats; strong, direct flight, soaring on thermals.

One of the most common birds in North America, the medium-sized Ring-billed Gull is distinguished by the black band on its yellow bill. From the mid-19th to the early 20th century, population numbers crashed due to hunting and habitat loss. Protection allowed the species to make a spectacular comeback, and in the 1990s, there were an estimated 3–4 million birds. It can often be seen scavenging in parking lots at malls.

VOICE Call a slightly nasal and whiny *kee-ow* or *meee-ow*; series of 4–6 *kyaw* notes, higher pitched than Herring Gull.

NESTING Shallow cup of plant matter on ground in open areas, usually near low vegetation; 1–5 eggs; 1 brood; April–August.

FEEDING Picks food while walking; also dips and plunges in water; eats small fish, insects, grain, small rodents; also scavenges.

BLACK WING MARKING
The sharply demarcated black wing tips are prominent from both above and below.

SIMILAR SPECIES
MEW GULL
see p.189
darker mantle
round head
small bill
MEW GULL 1ST
see p.189
less distinct streaks
round head
small bill

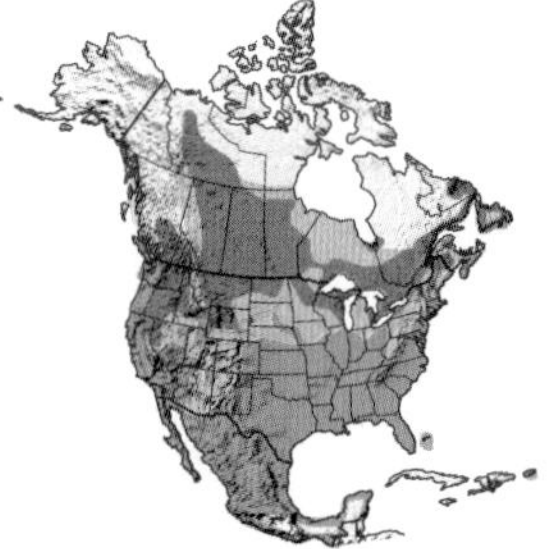

OCCURRENCE
Breeds in freshwater habitats in the interior of the continent. In winter, switches to mostly saltwater areas and along both the East and West Coasts; also along major river systems and reservoirs. Found year-round near the southern Great Lakes.

Length **17–21½in (43–54cm)**	Wingspan **4–5ft (1.2–1.5m)**	Weight **11–25oz (300–700g)**
Social **Colonies**	Lifespan **Up to 32 years**	Status **Secure**

Order **Charadriiformes**	Family **Laridae**	Species ***Larus californicus***

California Gull

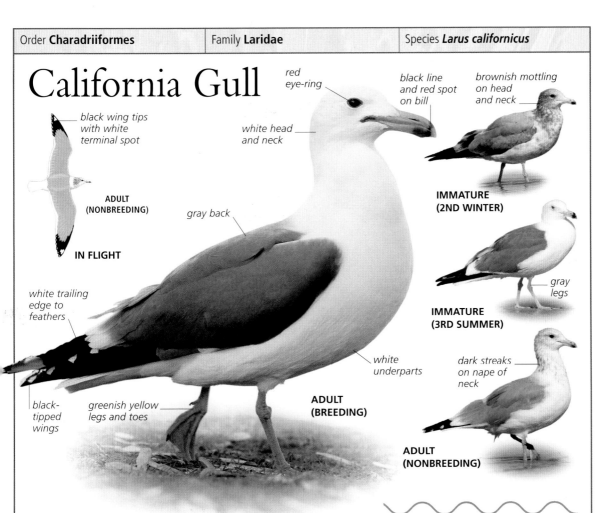

red eye-ring
black line and red spot on bill
brownish mottling on head and neck
black wing tips with white terminal spot
white head and neck
ADULT (NONBREEDING)
IN FLIGHT
gray back
IMMATURE (2ND WINTER)
gray legs
white trailing edge to feathers
IMMATURE (3RD SUMMER)
white underparts
dark streaks on nape of neck
black-tipped wings
greenish yellow legs and toes
ADULT (BREEDING)
ADULT (NONBREEDING)

Slightly smaller than the Herring Gull, the medium-sized California Gull has a darker back and longer wings. In breeding plumage, it can also be distinguished by the black and red coloration on its bill and its greenish yellow legs. In winter and on young birds, dark streaks are prominent on the nape of the neck. A common interior gull, it is honored by a large, gilded statue in Salt Lake City that commemorates the birds' rescue of the settlers' crops from a plague of grasshoppers in 1848.

VOICE Call a repeated *kee-yah, kee-yah, kee-yah.*

NESTING Shallow scrape, lined with feathers, bones, and vegetation, usually on islands; 2–3 eggs; 1 brood; May–July.

FEEDING Forages around lakes for insects, mollusks; hovers over cherry trees dislodging fruits with its wings.

FLIGHT: strong and direct, but somewhat stiff, with deep wing beats.

AGGRESSIVE POSTURE
This California Gull is displaying signs of aggression—possibly against another bird.

SIMILAR SPECIES
HERRING GULL ☼
see p.198
paler back
pink legs
larger body
HERRING GULL ❄
see p.198
heavy streaking on head
paler back

OCCURRENCE
Breeds at scattered locations across interior western Canada and the US. Some of the largest colonies are on the highly saline Mono Lake and the Great Salt Lake; winters along the Pacific Coast from British Columbia to Mexico; strays increasingly reported in the East.

Length **17½–20in (45–51cm)**	Wingspan **4–4½ft (1.2–1.4m)**	Weight **18–35oz (0.5–1kg)**
Social **Colonies**	Lifespan **Up to 30 years**	Status **Secure**

Order **Charadriiformes**	Family **Laridae**	Species ***Larus marinus***

Great Black-backed Gull

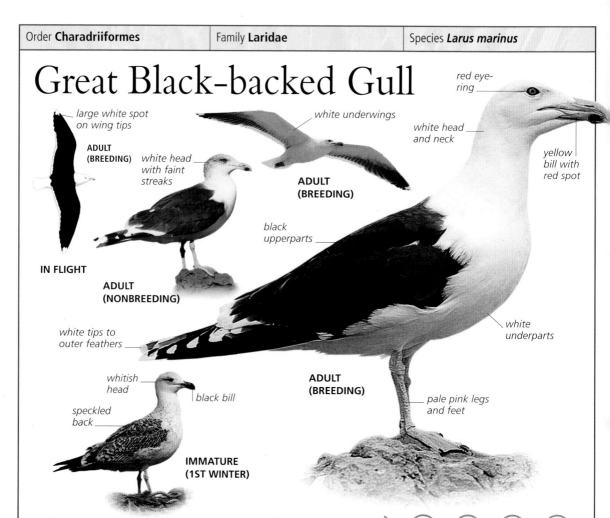

large white spot on wing tips
IN FLIGHT
ADULT (BREEDING)
white head with faint streaks
ADULT (NONBREEDING)
white underwings
ADULT (BREEDING)
red eye-ring
white head and neck
yellow bill with red spot
black upperparts
white tips to outer feathers
white underparts
pale pink legs and feet
ADULT (BREEDING)
whitish head
black bill
speckled back
IMMATURE (1ST WINTER)

The largest gull in North America, the Great Black-backed Gull is known for its bullying dispostion. In breeding colonies, it is especially aggressive in the morning and early evening, and after chicks hatch; adults dive at ground predators and strike them with their wings and feet. Other birds benefit from this forceful behavior, for example eiders nesting in Great Black-backed Gull colonies suffer a low rate of nest predation.

VOICE Low, growling flight call, often repeated, low-pitched *heyaa...heyaa...heyaa...heyaa*, similar to the Herring Gull.

NESTING Shallow bowl on ground, lined with vegetation, feathers, and trash; 2–3 eggs; 1 brood; April–August.

FEEDING Scavenges and hunts fish, marine invertebrates, small mammals, eggs, chicks, adult seabirds, and waterfowl.

FLIGHT: heavy lumbering with deep wing beats.

SOLITARY BIRDS
While all gulls are social animals, the Great Black-breasted Gull is the most solitary.

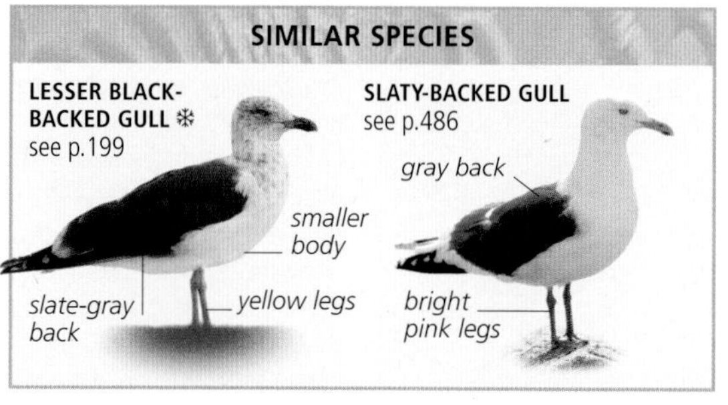
SIMILAR SPECIES
LESSER BLACK-BACKED GULL ❄
see p.199
smaller body
slate-gray back
yellow legs
SLATY-BACKED GULL
see p.486
gray back
bright pink legs

OCCURRENCE
Breeds on natural and artificial islands, barrier beaches, salt marshes, sand dunes; during winter, found along the coast, near shore water, major rivers, landfills, and harbors; in all seasons, often found together with Herring Gulls and Ring-billed Gulls. Also occurs also in Europe.

Length **28–31in (71–79cm)**	Wingspan **5–5¼ft (1.5–1.6m)**	Weight **2¾–4½lb (1.3–2kg)**
Social **Pairs/Colonies**	Lifespan **Up to 27 years**	Status **Secure**

Order **Charadriiformes**	Family **Laridae**	Species ***Larus glaucescens***

Glaucous-winged Gull

pale tan overall
IMMATURE (1ST WINTER)
string of white spots in outer feathers
ADULT (BREEDING)
IN FLIGHT
uniform gray-brown plumage
light brown tail
IMMATURE (1ST WINTER)
gray mantle
pale base of dark bill
IMMATURE (2ND WINTER)
white head
thick bill
pale gray mantle
very faint to dark markings on head and neck
pale blue-gray wings
ADULT (NONBREEDING)
ADULT (BREEDING)
white underparts
pale pink legs

The Glaucous-winged Gull, the most common large gull on the north Pacific coast, is found around towns and cities, even nesting on the roofs of shorefront buildings. This species commonly interbreeds with Western Gulls in the southern part of its range, and with Herring and Glaucous Gulls in the north, producing intermediate birds that are more difficult to identify.

VOICE Call a slow, deep *aah-aah-aah*; many types of calls heard around colonies; voice lower pitched than Herring Gull.

NESTING Scrape surrounded by ring of torn up grass or other vegetation; forms colonies usually on small, low islands; 2–3 eggs; 1 brood; May–August.

FEEDING Snatches fish, aquatic mollusks, and crustaceans while walking, swimming, or diving; also scavenges carrion and trash.

FLIGHT: strong and graceful; shallow wing beats; also soars.

PALE WINGS
The Glaucous-winged Gull is named for its delicate, pale, bluish gray wings.

SIMILAR SPECIES
GLAUCOUS GULL ❄
see p.195
larger and paler body
white wing tips
THAYER'S GULL
see p.197
small bill
dark wing tips
pink legs
smaller body

OCCURRENCE
Breeds along coast of northwest Oregon northward to the Bering Sea coast of Alaska; winters within its breeding range and southward, to Gulf of California; primarily a coastal and offshore gull (farther offshore in winter); it is very rare inland and accidental to central North America.

Length **23–24in (58–62cm)**	Wingspan **4½–5ft (1.4–1.5m)**	Weight **2–2¾lb (0.9–1.3kg)**
Social **Colonies**	Lifespan **Up to 32 years**	Status **Secure**

Order **Charadriiformes**	Family **Laridae**	Species ***Larus occidentalis***

Western Gull

black wing tip with white edges
ADULT
L. o. wymani
(BREEDING)
dark gray wings
IN FLIGHT

white head
orange eye-ring
large, yellow beak with red spot
slate-gray mantle
broad, white trailing edge feathers
pinkish legs
ADULT
L. o. wymani
(BREEDING)

paler gray back
ADULT
L. o. occidentalis

uniform brown back
JUVENILE

brownish gray mantle
IMMATURE (1ST WINTER)

dusky head
dark gray mantle
IMMATURE (2ND WINTER)

The Western Gull is the only dark-backed gull found regularly within its normal range and habitat. However, identification is complicated due to two subspecies: the paler *occidentalis* in the north, and the darker *wymani* in the south. Western Gulls interbreed with Glaucous-winged Gulls, producing confusing hybrids. The total population of these gulls is small, and the small number of nesting colonies makes conservation a concern.

VOICE Shrill, repeated *heyaa...heyaa...heyaa* similar to Herring Gull, but lower in pitch, harsher; very vocal at breeding sites.

NESTING Scrape filled with vegetation, usually next to bush or rock; 3–4 eggs; 1 brood; April–August.

FEEDING Eats crabs, squid, insects, fish, bird eggs, and chicks; also eats sea lion pups; scavenges.

FLIGHT: strong, slow with heavy wing beats; also commonly soars.

DARK UNDERWINGS
The undersides of the outer wing feathers are much darker in this bird than in similar species.

SIMILAR SPECIES
YELLOW-FOOTED GULL
darker back
yellow legs
SLATY-BACKED GULL
see p.486
thinner bill

OCCURRENCE
Nests on offshore islands along West Coast; about one third of the total population breeds on Southeast Farallon Island, west of San Francisco; nonbreeders and wintering birds occur along the coast and in major bays and estuaries southward to Baja California; very rare inland or far offshore.

Length **22–26in (56–66cm)**	Wingspan **4¼–4½ft (1.3–1.4m)**	Weight **1¾–2¾lb (0.8–1.2kg)**
Social **Colonies**	Lifespan **Up to 28 years**	Status **Secure**

Order **Charadriiformes**	Family **Laridae**	Species ***Larus hyperboreus***

Glaucous Gull

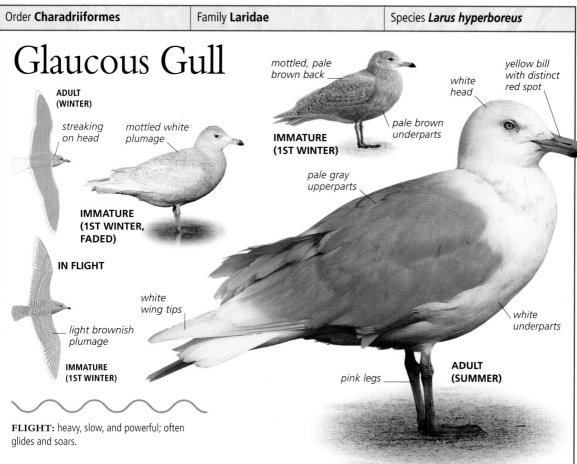

ADULT (WINTER)
streaking on head
mottled white plumage
IMMATURE (1ST WINTER, FADED)
mottled, pale brown back
pale brown underparts
IMMATURE (1ST WINTER)
white head
yellow bill with distinct red spot
pale gray upperparts
IN FLIGHT
white wing tips
light brownish plumage
IMMATURE (1ST WINTER)
white underparts
pink legs
ADULT (SUMMER)

FLIGHT: heavy, slow, and powerful; often glides and soars.

The Glaucous Gull is the largest of the "white-winged" gulls. Its large, pale shape is immediately apparent in a group of gulls as it appears like a large white spectre among its smaller, darker cousins. In the southern part of its US winter range, pale immatures are encountered more frequently than adults. In the Arctic, successful pairs of Glaucous Gulls maintain the bonds with their mates for years, often returning to the same nest site year after year.

VOICE Similar to that of the Herring Gull, but slightly harsher and deeper; hoarse, nasal *ku-ku-ku*.

NESTING Shallow cup lined with vegetation on ground, at edge of tundra pools, on cliffs and ledges and islands; 1–3 eggs; 1 brood; May–July.

FEEDING Eats fish, crustaceans, mollusks; also eggs and chicks of waterfowl, small seabirds, and small mammals.

NORTHERN VISITOR
This large gull is an uncommon visitor over most of North America during the winter months.

SIMILAR SPECIES
GLAUCOUS-WINGED GULL
see p.193
dusky wing tips
ICELAND GULL
see p.196
much smaller bill
much smaller overall

OCCURRENCE
Breeds along the high-Arctic coast, rarely inland; winters along northern Atlantic and Pacific coasts and the Great Lakes; frequently seen at Niagara Falls. Strays, usually immatures, can occur inland anywhere where concentrations of gulls are found, such as trash sites dumps.

Length **26–30in (65–75cm)**	Wingspan **5–6ft (1.5–1.8m)**	Weight **2¾–6lb (1.2–2.7kg)**
Social **Colonies**	Lifespan **Up to 21 years**	Status **Secure**

Order **Charadriiformes**	Family **Laridae**	Species ***Larus glaucoides***

Iceland Gull

gray wing tips

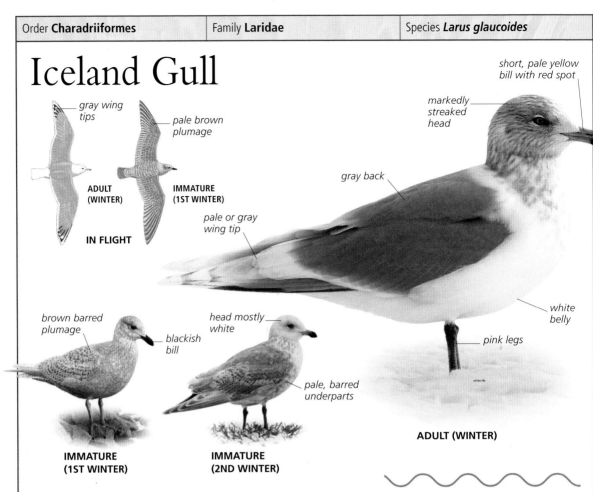

pale brown plumage

ADULT (WINTER)

IMMATURE (1ST WINTER)

IN FLIGHT

short, pale yellow bill with red spot

markedly streaked head

gray back

pale or gray wing tip

white belly

pink legs

ADULT (WINTER)

brown barred plumage

blackish bill

head mostly white

pale, barred underparts

IMMATURE (1ST WINTER)

IMMATURE (2ND WINTER)

The Iceland Gull is the smallest "white-winged" gull. Similar to the larger Glaucous Gull, it is a common sight in winter, and immatures are seen more often than adults. North American breeding birds have gray wing tips, and have been considered a separate species called the "Kumlien's Gull." The subspecies *L. g. glaucoides* is distinguishable as it possesses white wing tips; it breeds in Greenland, and winters in Greenland and Iceland, but a few birds travel to the western North Atlantic.

VOICE Call a *clew, clew, clew* or *kak-kak-kak*; vocal around breeding colonies; virtually silent on wintering grounds.

NESTING Loose nest of moss, vegetation, and feathers, usually on narrow rock ledge; 2–3 eggs; 1 brood; May–August.

FEEDING Grabs small fish from surface while in flight; also eats small fish, crustaceans, mollusks, carrion, and garbage.

FLIGHT: light and graceful; wings long in proportion to body.

WING TIP COLOR VARIATION
Some adult Iceland Gulls found in North America have wing tips that are almost pure white.

SIMILAR SPECIES

GLAUCOUS GULL
see p.195
much larger body
larger bill
white wing tips
THAYER'S GULL
see p.197
dark eye
slightly larger and darker overall

OCCURRENCE
Uncommon far from sea coast; usually nests on ledges on vertical cliffs overlooking the sea; winters where it finds regions of open water in frozen seas and along coast. A few wander to open water areas in the interior, such as the Great Lakes and major rivers; Niagara Falls.

Length **20½–23½in (52–60cm)**	Wingspan **4½–5ft (1.4–1.5m)**	Weight **21–39oz (600–1,100g)**
Social **Colonies**	Lifespan **Up to 33 years**	Status **Secure**

Order **Charadriiformes**	Family **Laridae**	Species ***Larus thayeri***

Thayer's Gull

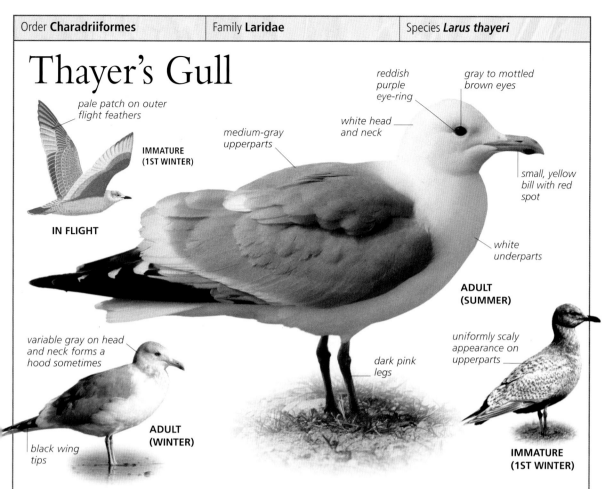

pale patch on outer flight feathers

IMMATURE (1ST WINTER)

IN FLIGHT

medium-gray upperparts

reddish purple eye-ring

gray to mottled brown eyes

white head and neck

small, yellow bill with red spot

white underparts

ADULT (SUMMER)

variable gray on head and neck forms a hood sometimes

dark pink legs

uniformly scaly appearance on upperparts

ADULT (WINTER)

black wing tips

IMMATURE (1ST WINTER)

The classification of Thayer's Gull as a species is still slightly puzzling. After it was described in 1915, it was classified as a subspecies of the Herring Gull, but in the 1970s, it was considered a full species. Although it is still usually treated as a separate species, many authorities now consider the Thayer's Gull to be a subspecies of the Iceland Gull. When standing with the Herring and Iceland Gulls, this bird is difficult to identify. Positive identification is complicated further by the existence of hybrid gulls of various parentages.

VOICE Mewing squeals, like herring gulls familiar *kee-yow*; calls more on breeding grounds than on wintering grounds.

NESTING On cliff ledges; 2–3 eggs; 1 brood; May–August.

FEEDING Picks fish, mollusks, and crustaceans from the water's surface; swallows food while in flight.

FLIGHT: steady and direct, but wing beat varies greatly with wind conditions.

TWO-TONED WINGS
Immature birds have two-toned wings, with a prominent pale patch on the outer flight feathers.

SIMILAR SPECIES

GLAUCOUS-WINGED GULL
see p.193
much larger body
pale wing tips
ICELAND GULL
see p.196
usually pale eye
slightly darker mantle

OCCURRENCE
Nests on cliff ledges of fiords facing the Canadian High Arctic. Winter movements not fully understood; occurs mainly along the Pacific Coast, but is also found across the interior and along the East Coast.

Length **22½–25in (57–64cm)**	Wingspan **4¼–5ft (1.3–1.5m)**	Weight **25–39oz (700–1,100g)**
Social **Colonies**	Lifespan **Unknown**	Status **Secure (p)**

Order **Charadriiformes**	Family **Laridae**	Species ***Larus argentatus***

Herring Gull

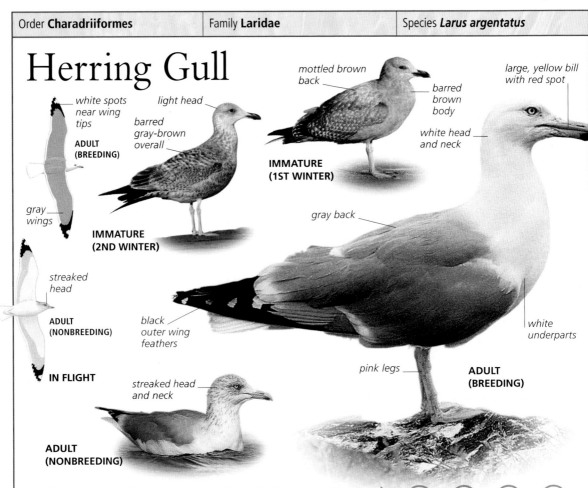

white spots near wing tips
light head
barred gray-brown overall
ADULT (BREEDING)
gray wings
IMMATURE (2ND WINTER)
mottled brown back
barred brown body
IMMATURE (1ST WINTER)
large, yellow bill with red spot
white head and neck
gray back
streaked head
ADULT (NONBREEDING)
black outer wing feathers
white underparts
IN FLIGHT
pink legs
ADULT (BREEDING)
streaked head and neck
ADULT (NONBREEDING)

The Herring Gull is the archetypal, large "white-headed" gull that nearly all other gulls are compared with. When people mention "seagulls" they usually refer to the Herring Gull. The term "seagull" is actually misleading because the Herring Gull, like most other gulls, does not commonly go far out to sea—it is a bird of near-shore waters, coasts, lakes, rivers, and inland waterways. Now very common, the Herring Gull was nearly wiped out in the late 19th and early 20th century by plumage hunters and egg collectors.

VOICE Typical call a high-pitched, shrill, repeated *heyaa… heyaa…heyaa…heyaa*; vocal throughout the year.

NESTING Shallow bowl on ground lined with feathers, vegetation, detritus; 2–4 eggs; 1 brood; April–August.

FEEDING Eats fish, crustaceans, mollusks, worms; eggs and chicks of other seabirds; scavenges carrion, garbage; steals from other birds.

FLIGHT: steady, regular, slow wing beats; also commonly soars and glides.

MASTER SCAVENGER
A common sight near any water body, the Herring Gull is an expert scavenger of carrion and trash.

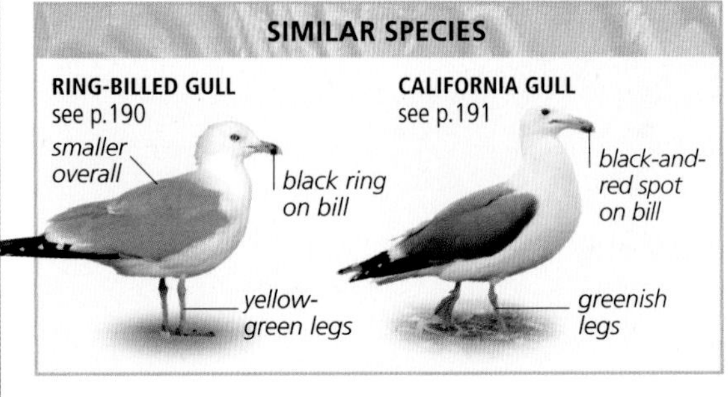
SIMILAR SPECIES
RING-BILLED GULL
see p.190
smaller overall
black ring on bill
yellow-green legs
CALIFORNIA GULL
see p.191
black-and-red spot on bill
greenish legs

OCCURRENCE
Found throughout North America along coasts and inland on lakes, rivers, and reservoirs; also frequents garbage dumps. Breeds in northeastern US and across Canada. Migrates southward across much of the continent to winter in coastal areas and along lakes and major rivers.

Length **22–26in (56–66cm)**	Wingspan **4–5ft (1.2–1.5m)**	Weight **28–42oz (800–1200g)**
Social **Colonies**	Lifespan **At least 35 years**	Status **Secure**

Order **Charadriiformes**	Family **Laridae**	Species ***Larus fuscus***

Lesser Black-backed Gull

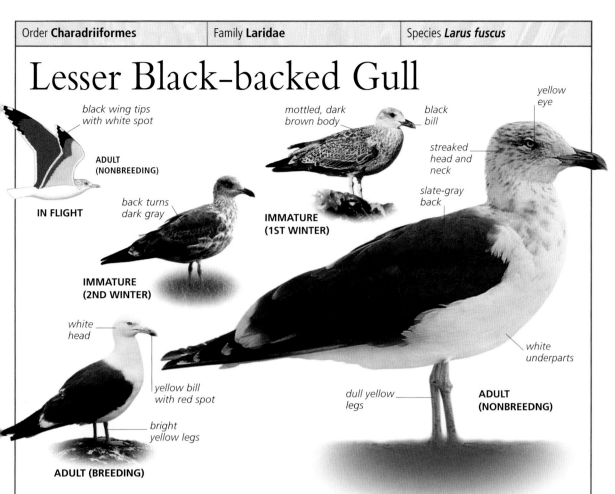

black wing tips with white spot

ADULT (NONBREEDING)

IN FLIGHT

back turns dark gray

IMMATURE (2ND WINTER)

mottled, dark brown body

black bill

IMMATURE (1ST WINTER)

yellow eye

streaked head and neck

slate-gray back

white underparts

dull yellow legs

ADULT (NONBREEDNG)

white head

yellow bill with red spot

bright yellow legs

ADULT (BREEDING)

This European visitor was first discovered in North America on the New Jersey coast on September 9, 1934 and in New York City a few months later. In recent decades, it has become an annual winter visitor. Nearly all the Lesser Black-backed Gulls found in North America are of the Icelandic and western European subspecies *L. f. graellsii*, with a slate-gray back. Another European subspecies, with a much darker back, has rarely been reported in North America, but it is probably only a matter of time before it nests here.

VOICE A *kyow…yow…yow…yow* call, similar to that of Herring Gull; also a deeper and throaty, repeated *gah-gah-gah-gah*.

NESTING Scrape on ground lined with dry lichens, dry grass, and feathers; 3 eggs; 1 brood; April–September.

FEEDING Eats mollusks, crustaceans, and various insects; also scavenges carrion and garbage.

FLIGHT: powerful and direct; regular wing beats; long wings make it appear graceful.

OCCURRENCE
Regular and increasingly common winter visitor to eastern North America, usually along the coast, but also in the interior; wherever gulls commonly concentrate such as harbors, lakeshores, landfills, and around fishing boats.

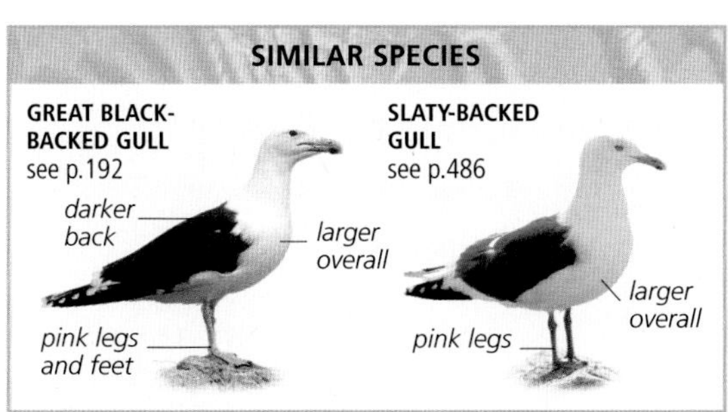
SIMILAR SPECIES
GREAT BLACK-BACKED GULL
see p.192
darker back
larger overall
pink legs and feet
SLATY-BACKED GULL
see p.486
larger overall
pink legs

EXCITING FIND
In recent years, gull enthusiasts and birdwatchers have found these birds visiting from Europe.

Length **20½–26in (52–67cm)**	Wingspan **4¼–5ft (1.3–1.5m)**	Weight **22–35oz (625–1000g)**
Social **Colonies**	Lifespan **Up to 26 years**	Status **Secure**

Order **Charadriiformes**	Family **Laridae**	Species ***Chroicocephalus ridibundus***

Black-headed Gull

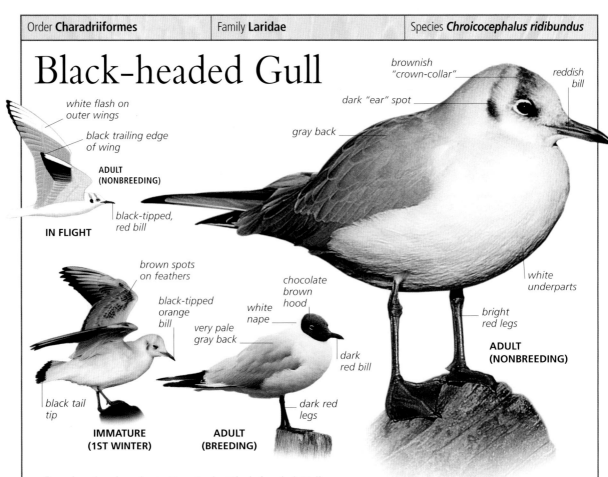

white flash on outer wings
black trailing edge of wing
ADULT (NONBREEDING)
black-tipped, red bill
IN FLIGHT

brownish "crown-collar"
reddish bill
dark "ear" spot
gray back
white underparts
bright red legs
ADULT (NONBREEDING)

brown spots on feathers
black-tipped orange bill
black tail tip
IMMATURE (1ST WINTER)

chocolate brown hood
white nape
very pale gray back
dark red bill
dark red legs
ADULT (BREEDING)

An abundant breeder in Eurasia, the Black-headed Gull colonized North America in the 20th century. It was first seen in the 1920s, not long after nests were discovered in Iceland in 1911. It has become common in Newfoundland after being found nesting there in 1977, and has nested as far south as Cape Cod. However, it has not spread far to the West and remains an infrequent visitor or stray over most of the continent.

VOICE Loud laughing (its French name is Laughing Gull) or a chattering *kek kek keeaar*; very vocal at breeding sites.

NESTING Loose mass of vegetation, on ground or on top of other vegetation; may be a large mound in wet areas; 2–3 eggs; 1 brood; April–August.

FEEDING Picks insects, small crustaceans, and mollusks off water's surface while flying or hovering; eats some vegetation; also forages in plowed farm fields; raids garbage dumps.

FLIGHT: graceful, light, and buoyant; agile.

BEAUTIFUL BREEDING PLUMAGE
Most American birders never see the elegant summer plumage of the Black-headed Gull.

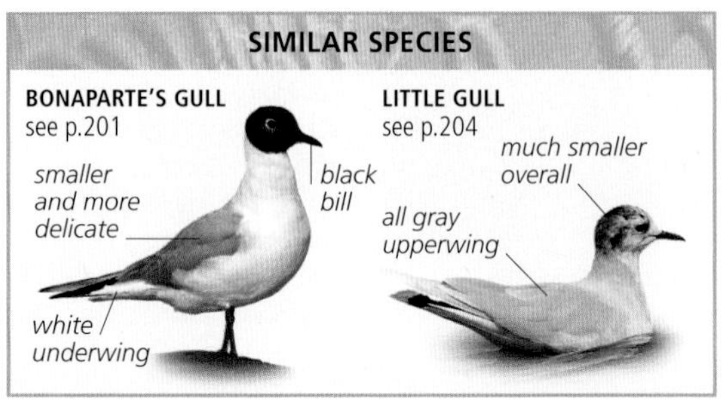
SIMILAR SPECIES
BONAPARTE'S GULL
see p.201
smaller and more delicate
black bill
white underwing
LITTLE GULL
see p.204
much smaller overall
all gray upperwing

OCCURRENCE
Rare breeder in northeastern North America; singles or a few individuals may be found along the coast, often with Bonaparte's Gulls, at harbors, inlets, bays, rivers, lakes, sewage outlets, or garbage dumps; strays may occur anywhere. One of the most common European gulls.

Length **13½–14½in (34–37cm)**	Wingspan **3ft 3in–3½ft (1–1.1m)**	Weight **7–14oz (200–400g)**
Social **Colonies**	Lifespan **Up to 18 years**	Status **Localized**

Order **Charadriiformes**	Family **Laridae**	Species ***Chroicocephalus philadelphia***

Bonaparte's Gull

black wing tips
ADULT (NONBREEDING)
white flash on outer wings
IN FLIGHT
blackish "ear" spot
white head
gray neck
ADULT (NONBREEDING)
black hood
short bill
gray back and wings
gray back
brown patches on wing
IMMATURE (1ST WINTER)
white wedge on wing
ADULT (BREEDING)
orange-red legs
white underparts with rosy glow when breeding

Lighter and more delicate than the other North American gulls, Bonaparte's Gull is commonly distinguished in winter by the blackish smudge behind each eye and the large, white wing patch. It is one of North America's most common and widespread gulls. In 1989, for example, more than 120,000 were estimated to have occured in one harbor near Cleveland, Ohio. This species was named after the 19th century French ornithologist Charles Lucien Bonaparte (nephew of Napoleon).

FLIGHT: graceful, light, and agile; rapid wing beats; can be mistaken for a tern in flight.

VOICE Harsh *keek, keek*; can be vocal in feeding flocks, *kew, kew, kew.*
NESTING Stick nest of twigs, branches, tree bark, lined with mosses or lichens; usually in conifers 5–20ft (1.5–6m) above ground; also in rushes over water; 1–4 eggs; 1 brood; May–July.
FEEDING Catches insects in flight on breeding grounds; picks crustaceans, mollusks, and small fish from water's surface; also plunge-dives.

TERN-LIKE GULL
Bonaparte's Gulls are very social and, flying in flocks, these pale, delicate birds look like terns.

WHITE UNDERWINGS
In all plumages, Bonaparte's Gull have white underwings, unlike other similar small gulls.

SIMILAR SPECIES

BLACK-HEADED GULL
see p.200
dark outer wing feathers
red bill
larger overall

LITTLE GULL
see p.204
smaller overall
uniform gray upperwing

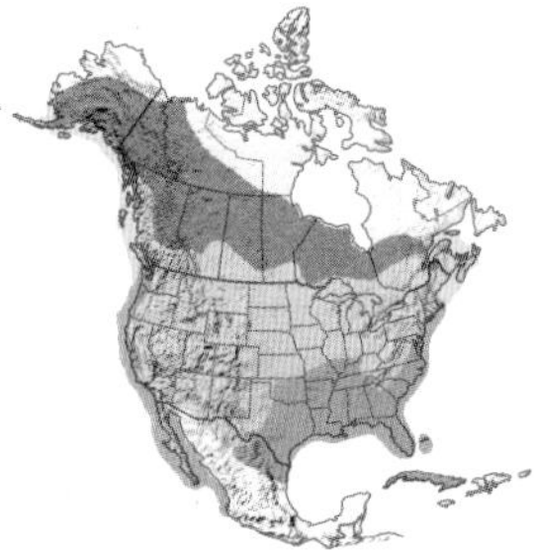

OCCURRENCE
During breeding season, found in northern forest zone, in lakes, ponds, or bogs; on migration, may be found anywhere where there is water: ponds, lakes, sewage pools, or rivers. Winters on Great Lakes and along the coast; often found in large numbers at coastal inlets.

Length **11–12in (28–30cm)**	Wingspan **35in–3ft 3in (90–100cm)**	Weight **6–8oz (175–225g)**
Social **Flocks**	Lifespan **Up to 18 years**	Status **Secure**

Order **Charadriiformes**	Family **Laridae**	Species ***Leucophaeus atricilla***

Laughing Gull

dark gray wings
ADULT (WINTER)
IN FLIGHT
brown wing feathers
white forehead
IMMATURE (1ST WINTER)
broken white eye-ring
black head
long, slightly drooped bill
white neck
dark gray back
black wing tips
long, dark legs
white underparts
ADULT (BREEDING)
gray nape
ADULT (WINTER)

The distinctive call of the Laughing Gull is a familiar sound in spring and summer along the East Coast. Already abundant when the Europeans arrived in North America, it was greatly reduced in the 19th century by egg collectors and the millinery trade. Its numbers increased in the 1920s, following protection, but declined again due to competition with larger gulls from the North. With the closing of landfills however, the Laughing Gull population has recovered.

VOICE Typical call strident laugh, *ha...ha...ha...ha...ha*; very vocal in breeding season; quiet in winter.

NESTING Mass of grass on dry land with heavy vegetation, sand, rocks, and salt marshes; 2–4 eggs, 1 brood; April–July.

FEEDING Picks from surface while walking and swimming; feeds on various invertebrates: insects, earthworms, squid, crabs, crab eggs, and larvae; also eats small fish, garbage, and berries.

FLIGHT: strong and direct; graceful for a gull; agile enough to catch flying insects.

DARK WING TIPS
Unlike many gulls, the Laughing Gull usually shows little or no white in the wing tips.

SIMILAR SPECIES

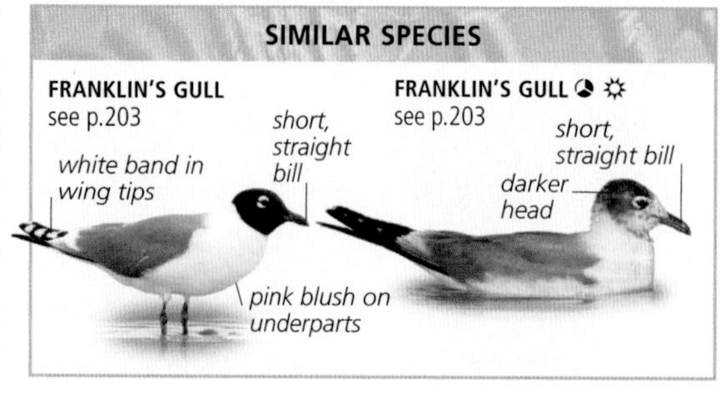
FRANKLIN'S GULL
see p.203
white band in wing tips
short, straight bill
pink blush on underparts
FRANKLIN'S GULL
see p.203
short, straight bill
darker head

OCCURRENCE
During breeding season usually found near saltwater. Post-breeders and juveniles wander widely; strays can turn up anywhere. Rare in winter in the Northeast. Small numbers once nested at the Salton Sea but only a visitor there for the last 50 years.

Length **15½–18in (39–46cm)**	Wingspan **3¼–4ft (1–1.2m)**	Weight **7–13oz (200–375g)**
Social **Colonial**	Lifespan **Up to 20 years**	Status **Secure**

Order **Charadriiformes**	Family **Laridae**	Species ***Leucophaeus pipixcan***

Franklin's Gull

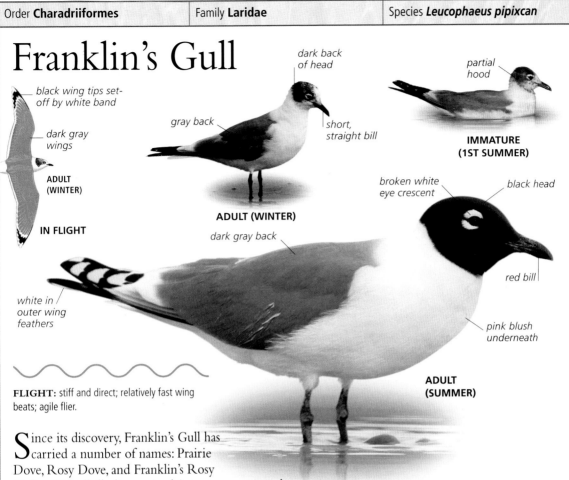

black wing tips set-off by white band

dark gray wings

ADULT (WINTER)

IN FLIGHT

dark back of head

gray back

short, straight bill

ADULT (WINTER)

partial hood

IMMATURE (1ST SUMMER)

broken white eye crescent

black head

dark gray back

red bill

white in outer wing feathers

pink blush underneath

ADULT (SUMMER)

FLIGHT: stiff and direct; relatively fast wing beats; agile flier.

Since its discovery, Franklin's Gull has carried a number of names: Prairie Dove, Rosy Dove, and Franklin's Rosy Gull—"Dove" alluding to its dainty appearance and "rosy" to the pink blush of its undersides. Its official name honors British Arctic explorer, John Franklin, on whose first expedition, the bird was discovered in 1823. Unlike other gulls, this species has two complete molts each year. As a result, its plumage usually looks fresh and it rarely has the scruffy look of some other gulls.

VOICE Nasal *weeh-a, weeh-a*; shrill *kuk kuk kuk kuk*; extremely vocal around breeding colonies.

NESTING Floating mass of bulrushes or other plants; material added as nest sinks; 2–4 eggs; 1 brood; April–July.

FEEDING Feeds mainly on earthworms and insects during breeding and some seeds, taken while walking or flying; opportunistic feeder during migration and winter.

PROMINENT EYES
In all plumages, Franklin's Gull has much more prominent white eye-crescents than similar species.

SIMILAR SPECIES

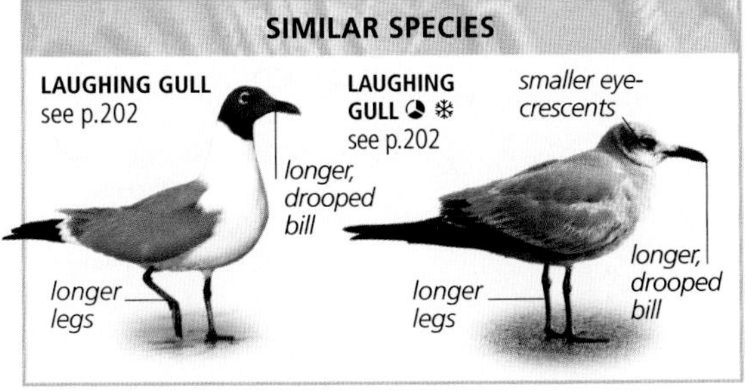
LAUGHING GULL
see p.202
longer, drooped bill
longer legs
LAUGHING GULL
see p.202
smaller eye-crescents
longer legs
longer, drooped bill

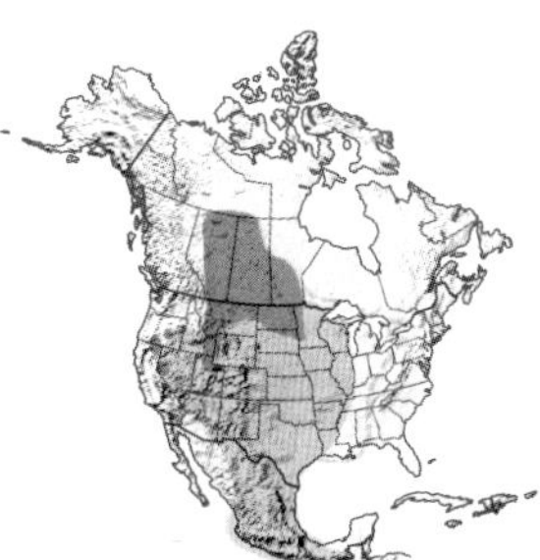

OCCURRENCE
In summer, a bird of the high prairies; always nests over water. On migration often found in agricultural areas; large numbers frequent plowed fields or follows plows. Winters mainly along the Pacific Coast of South America.

Length **12½–14in (32–36cm)**	Wingspan **33in–3ft 1in (85–95cm)**	Weight **8–11oz (225–325g)**
Social **Colonial**	Lifespan **At least 10 years**	Status **Secure**

Order **Charadriiformes**	Family **Laridae**	Species ***Hydrocoloeus minutus***

Little Gull

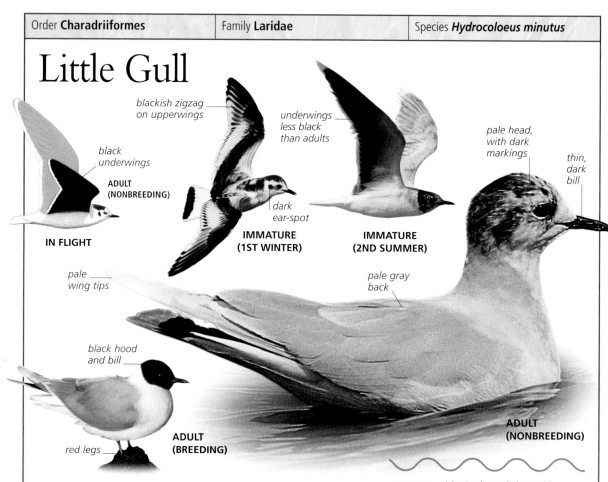

black underwings
ADULT (NONBREEDING)
IN FLIGHT
blackish zigzag on upperwings
dark ear-spot
IMMATURE (1ST WINTER)
underwings less black than adults
IMMATURE (2ND SUMMER)
pale head, with dark markings
thin, dark bill
pale wing tips
pale gray back
black hood and bill
red legs
ADULT (BREEDING)
ADULT (NONBREEDING)

FLIGHT: quick wing beats; light, nimble, and agile.

A Eurasian species distributed from the Baltic to China, the Little Gull is the smallest gull in the world. Whether it is a recent immigrant to North America or has actually been here, unnoticed, in small numbers for many years remains a mystery. It was first recorded in North America in the early 1800s, but a nest was not found until 1962, in Ontario, Canada. Known nesting areas are still few, but winter numbers have been increasing steadily in recent decades.

VOICE Nasal *kek, kek, kek, kek*, reminiscent of a small tern.
NESTING Thick, floating mass of dry cattails, reeds, or other vegetation, in marshes and ponds; 3 eggs; 1 brood; May–August.
FEEDING Seizes prey from water's surface, while swimming or plunge-diving; typical prey includes flying insects, aquatic invertebrates such as shrimps, and small fish.

SIMPLE ELEGANCE
Its long, pale gray wings with a thin white border place this bird among the most elegant of gulls.

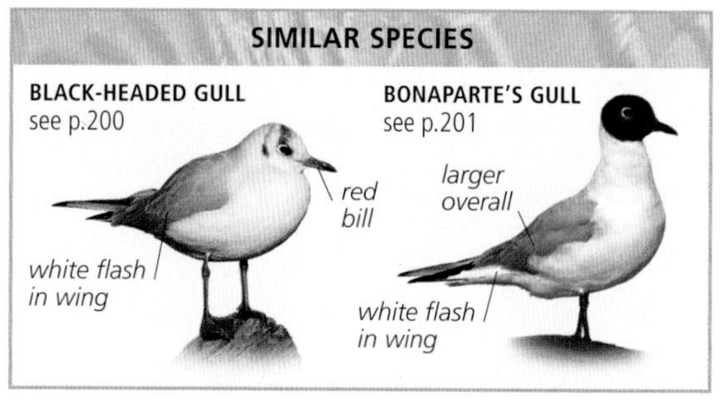
SIMILAR SPECIES
BLACK-HEADED GULL
see p.200
red bill
white flash in wing
BONAPARTE'S GULL
see p.201
larger overall
white flash in wing

OCCURRENCE
Breeds in extensive freshwater marshes in Hudson Bay and Great Lakes region, but the full extent of its breeding range in North America is unknown; can appear almost anywhere while migrating. Winters primarily along sea coasts, at sewage outfalls; often with groups of Bonaparte's Gulls.

Length **10–12in (25–30cm)**	Wingspan **23½–26in (60–65cm)**	Weight **3½–5oz (100–150g)**
Social **Colonies**	Lifespan **Up to 6 years**	Status **Secure**

Order **Charadriiformes**	Family **Laridae**	Species ***Xema sabini***

Sabine's Gull

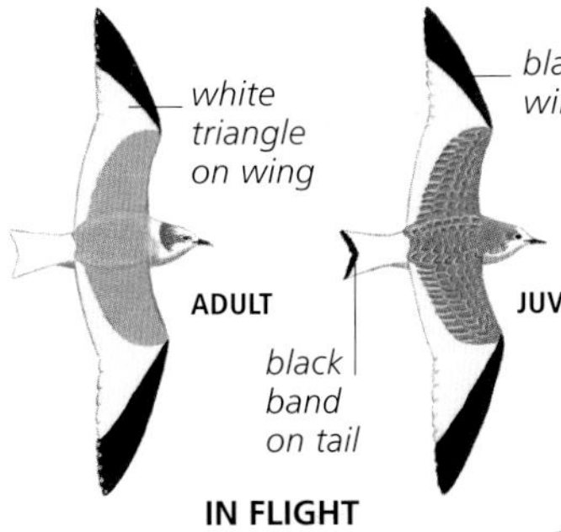

white triangle on wing
black outer wing feathers
ADULT
JUVENILE
black band on tail
IN FLIGHT

gray hood
red eye-ring
black border
yellow-tipped black bill
gray back
white underparts
black legs
ADULT (BREEDING)

barring on gray-brown back
black bill
JUVENILE

This strikingly patterned gull was discovered in Greenland by the English scientist Edward Sabine during John Ross's search for the Northwest Passage in 1818 (it was described in 1819). The distinctive wing pattern and notched tail make it unmistakable in all plumages—only juvenile kittiwakes are superficially similar. Previously thought to be related to the larger, but similarly patterned, Swallow-tailed Gull of the Galapagos, recent research indicates that Sabine's Gull is more closely related to the Ivory Gull. This species breeds in the Arctic and winters at sea, off the coasts of the Americas (south to Peru) and Africa (south to the Cape region).

VOICE Raucous, harsh *kyeer, kyeer, kyeer*; tern-like.

NESTING Shallow depression in marsh or tundra vegetation usually near water, lined with grass or unlined; 3–4 eggs; 1 brood; May–August.

FEEDING Catches aquatic insects from the water surface while swimming, wading, or flying during breeding season; winter diet mainly includes crustaceans, small fish, and plankton.

FLIGHT: wing beats shallow and stiff; tern-like, buoyant.

STRIKING WING PATTERN
Juvenile Sabine's Gulls have a muted version of the distinctive triangular wing pattern seen in the adults.

SIMILAR SPECIES

BLACK-LEGGED KITTIWAKE ◔
see p.206

partial black collar
black wing bar

OCCURRENCE
In the summer, breeds near the Arctic coast and on wet tundra in freshwater and brackish habitats, but also occurs near saltwater. Winters far off-shore in tropical and subtropical waters; widespread in Pacific and Atlantic oceans on migration.

Length **13–14in (33–36 cm)**	Wingspan **35in–3ft 3in (90–100cm)**	Weight **5–9oz (150–250g)**
Social **Colonies**	Lifespan **At least 8 years**	Status **Secure**

Order **Charadriiformes**	Family **Laridae**	Species ***Rissa tridactyla***

Black-legged Kittiwake

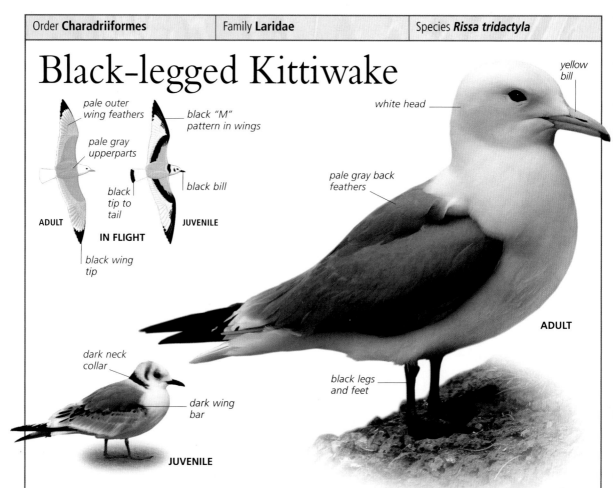

pale outer wing feathers
pale gray upperparts
black "M" pattern in wings
black bill
black tip to tail
black wing tip
ADULT **IN FLIGHT** **JUVENILE**

white head
yellow bill
pale gray back feathers
black legs and feet
ADULT

dark neck collar
dark wing bar
JUVENILE

A kittiwake nesting colony is an impressive sight, with sometimes thousands of birds lined up along steep cliff ledges overlooking the sea. The ledges are often so narrow that the birds' tails stick out over the edge. Kittiwakes have sharper claws than other gulls, probably to give them a better grip on their ledges. In the late 20th century, the Black-legged Kittiwake population expanded greatly in the Canadian maritime provinces, with numbers doubling in the Gulf of St. Lawrence.

VOICE Repeated, nasal *kit-ti-wake, kit-ti-wake* call; vocal near nesting cliffs; usually silent in winter.

NESTING Mound of mud and vegetation on narrow cliff ledge; 1–3 eggs; 1 brood; April–August.

FEEDING Snatches small marine fish and invertebrates from the surface, or dives just below the water's surface; feeds in flocks.

FLIGHT: very stiff-winged; rapid, shallow wing beats; overall more buoyant than most gulls.

LIVING ON THE EDGE
Young and adult kittiwakes pack together tightly on their precariously narrow cliff ledges.

SIMILAR SPECIES

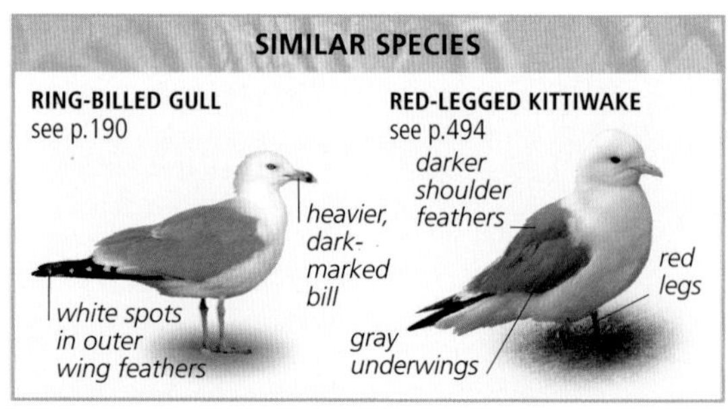
RING-BILLED GULL
see p.190
heavier, dark-marked bill
white spots in outer wing feathers
RED-LEGGED KITTIWAKE
see p.494
darker shoulder feathers
red legs
gray underwings

OCCURRENCE
Rarely seen far from the ocean; common in summer around sea cliffs, with ledges suitable for nesting, and nearby offshore waters; winters at sea; most likely to be seen from land during and after storms; strays have appeared throughout the interior.

Length **15–16in (38–41cm)**	Wingspan **3ft 1in–4ft (0.95m–1.2m)**	Weight **11–18oz (300–500g)**
Social **Colonies**	Lifespan **Up to 26 years**	Status **Secure**

Order **Charadriiformes**	Family **Laridae**	Species ***Hydroprogne caspia***

Caspian Tern

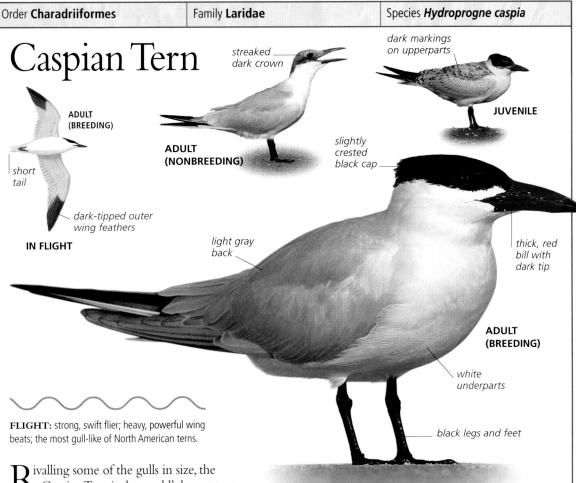

streaked dark crown

dark markings on upperparts

JUVENILE

ADULT (BREEDING)

ADULT (NONBREEDING)

short tail

slightly crested black cap

dark-tipped outer wing feathers

IN FLIGHT

light gray back

thick, red bill with dark tip

ADULT (BREEDING)

white underparts

black legs and feet

FLIGHT: strong, swift flier; heavy, powerful wing beats; the most gull-like of North American terns.

Rivalling some of the gulls in size, the Caspian Tern is the world's largest tern. Unlike other "black-capped" terns, it never has a completely white forehead, even in winter. In non-breeding plumage, the cap is very heavily streaked. The Caspian Tern is known for its predatory habits, stealing prey from other seabirds, as well as snatching eggs from, and hunting the chicks of, other gulls and terns. It is aggressive in defending its nesting territory, giving hoarse alarm calls, and rhythmically opening and closing its beak in a threatening display to intruders.

VOICE Hoarse, deep *kraaa, kraaa*; also barks at intruders; male's wings vibrate loudly in courtship flight.

NESTING Shallow scrape on ground; 2–3 eggs; 1 brood; May–August.

FEEDING Plunges into water to snatch fish, barnacles, and snails.

AGRESSIVE BIRDS

The Caspian Tern is one of the most aggressive terns, though actual physical contact is rare.

SIMILAR SPECIES

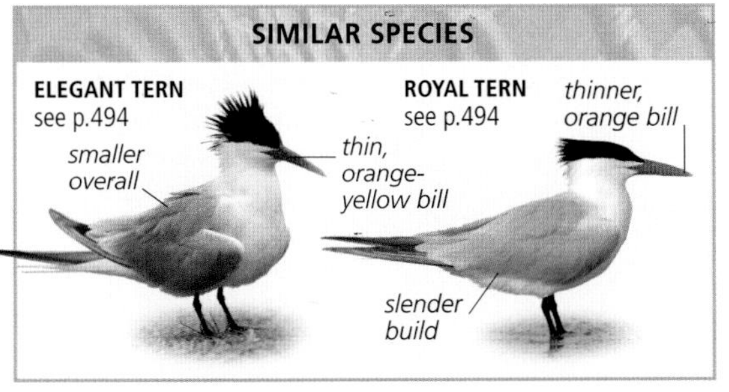
ELEGANT TERN
see p.494
smaller overall
thin, orange-yellow bill
ROYAL TERN
see p.494
thinner, orange bill
slender build

OCCURRENCE

Found in a variety of aquatic habitats, freshwater and marine; rare offshore; breeds on interior lakes, salt marsh, and on coastal barrier islands; winters on and near the coast. May be seen on marshes and wetlands during migration.

Length **18½–21½in (47–54cm)**	Wingspan **4¼–5ft (1.3–1.5m)**	Weight **19–27oz (525–775g)**
Social **Colonies/Pairs**	Lifespan **Up to 30 years**	Status **Declining**

Order **Charadriiformes**	Family **Laridae**	Species ***Sterna dougallii***

Roseate Tern

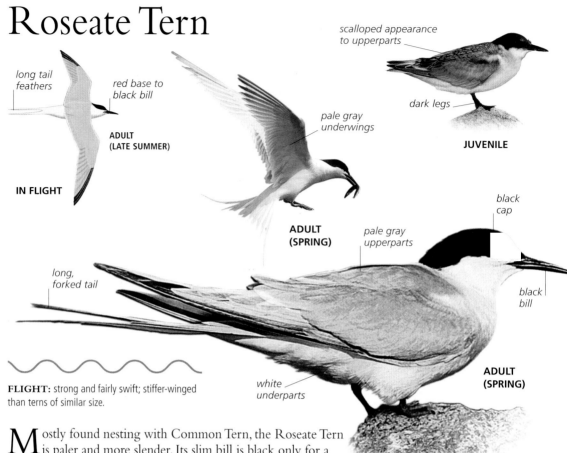

long tail feathers
red base to black bill
ADULT (LATE SUMMER)
IN FLIGHT
pale gray underwings
ADULT (SPRING)
scalloped appearance to upperparts
dark legs
JUVENILE
black cap
pale gray upperparts
long, forked tail
black bill
white underparts
ADULT (SPRING)

FLIGHT: strong and fairly swift; stiffer-winged than terns of similar size.

Mostly found nesting with Common Tern, the Roseate Tern is paler and more slender. Its slim bill is black only for a short time in the spring before turning at least half red during the nesting season. At breeding colonies, these terns engage in distinctive courtship flights, with pairs gliding down from hundreds of feet in the air, swaying side to side with each other. Some birds nest as trios—two females and a male—all taking part in incubating the eggs and raising the young.

VOICE Most common calls *keek* or *ki-rik* given in flight and around nesting colony.

NESTING Simple scrape, often under vegetation or large rocks; adds twigs and dry grass during incubation; 1–3 eggs; 1 brood; May–August.

FEEDING Catches small fish with its bill by diving from a height of 3–20ft (1–6m); carries whole fish to young.

GRACEFUL COURTSHIP
Roseate Tern pairs engage in elegant, graceful courtship displays before mating.

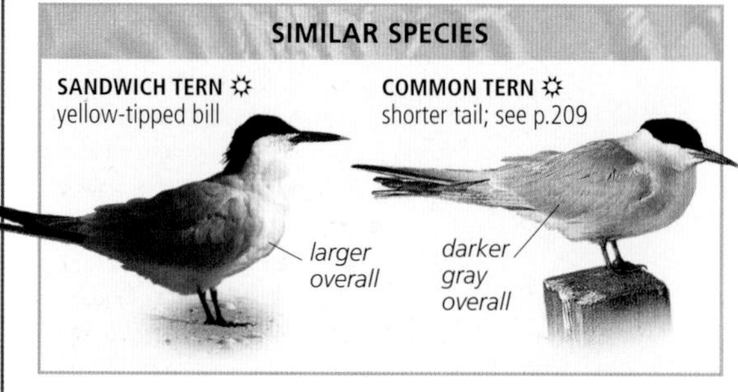
SIMILAR SPECIES
SANDWICH TERN ☼
yellow-tipped bill
larger overall
COMMON TERN ☼
shorter tail; see p.209
darker gray overall

OCCURRENCE
Breeds almost exclusively in coastal areas in the Northeast from Long Island, New York, to Nova Scotia, with another small population in the outer Florida Keys. Typically nests on beaches and off-shore islands. Not often seen far from breeding sites.

Length **13–16in (33–41cm)**	Wingspan **28in (70cm)**	Weight **3–5oz (85–150g)**
Social **Colonies**	Lifespan **Up to 26 years**	Status **Endangered**

Order **Charadriiformes**	Family **Laridae**	Species ***Sterna hirundo***

Common Tern

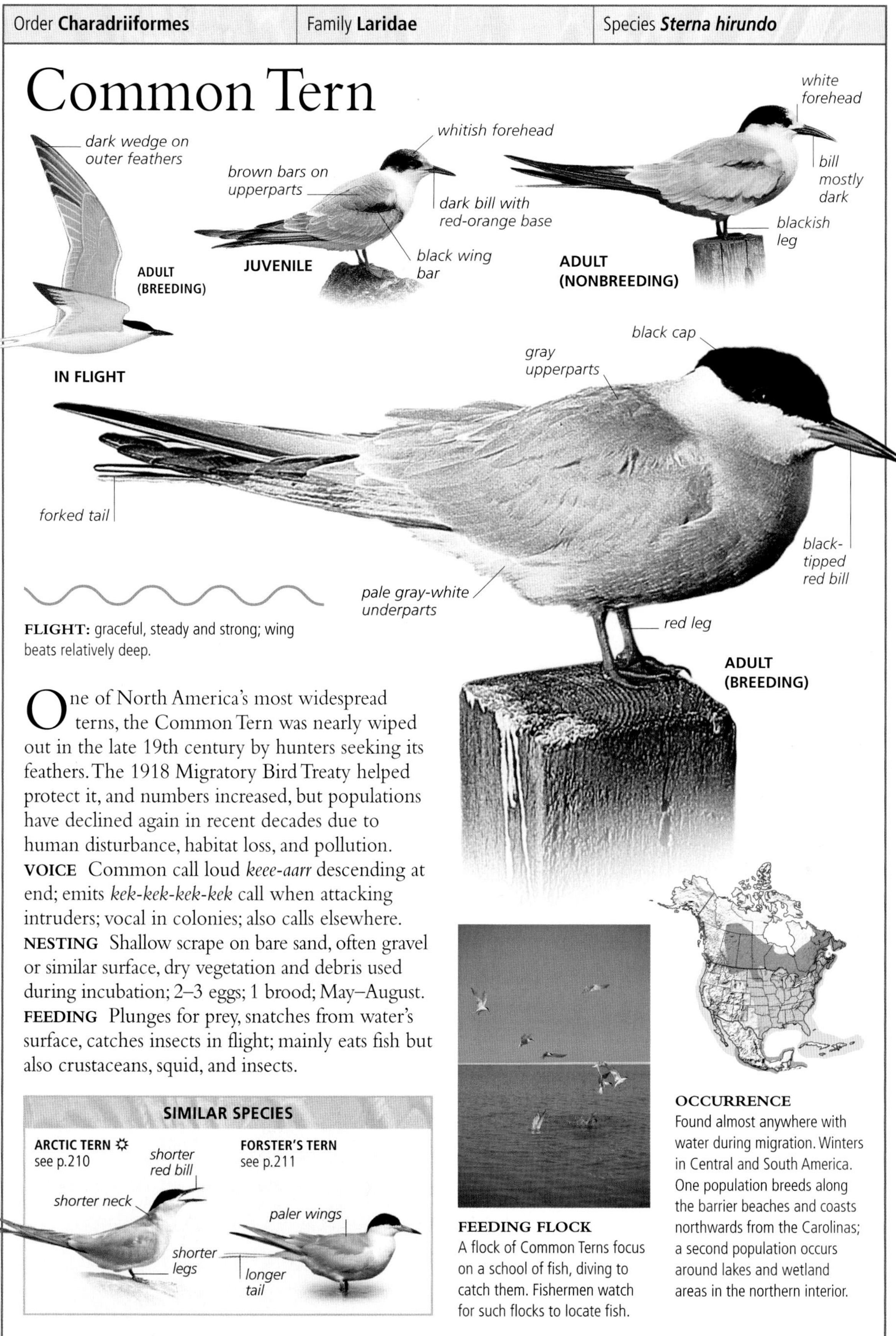

dark wedge on outer feathers
ADULT (BREEDING)
IN FLIGHT
brown bars on upperparts
whitish forehead
dark bill with red-orange base
black wing bar
JUVENILE
white forehead
bill mostly dark
blackish leg
ADULT (NONBREEDING)
black cap
gray upperparts
forked tail
black-tipped red bill
pale gray-white underparts
red leg
ADULT (BREEDING)

FLIGHT: graceful, steady and strong; wing beats relatively deep.

One of North America's most widespread terns, the Common Tern was nearly wiped out in the late 19th century by hunters seeking its feathers. The 1918 Migratory Bird Treaty helped protect it, and numbers increased, but populations have declined again in recent decades due to human disturbance, habitat loss, and pollution.

VOICE Common call loud *keee-aarr* descending at end; emits *kek-kek-kek-kek* call when attacking intruders; vocal in colonies; also calls elsewhere.

NESTING Shallow scrape on bare sand, often gravel or similar surface, dry vegetation and debris used during incubation; 2–3 eggs; 1 brood; May–August.

FEEDING Plunges for prey, snatches from water's surface, catches insects in flight; mainly eats fish but also crustaceans, squid, and insects.

FEEDING FLOCK
A flock of Common Terns focus on a school of fish, diving to catch them. Fishermen watch for such flocks to locate fish.

OCCURRENCE
Found almost anywhere with water during migration. Winters in Central and South America. One population breeds along the barrier beaches and coasts northwards from the Carolinas; a second population occurs around lakes and wetland areas in the northern interior.

SIMILAR SPECIES

ARCTIC TERN ☼ see p.210
shorter red bill; shorter neck; shorter legs

FORSTER'S TERN see p.211
paler wings; longer tail

Length **12–14in (31–35cm)**	Wingspan **30–31in (75–80cm)**	Weight **3⅜–5oz (95–150g)**
Social **Colonies**	Lifespan **Up to 26 years**	Status **Declining**

Order **Charadriiformes**	Family **Laridae**	Species ***Sterna paradisaea***

Arctic Tern

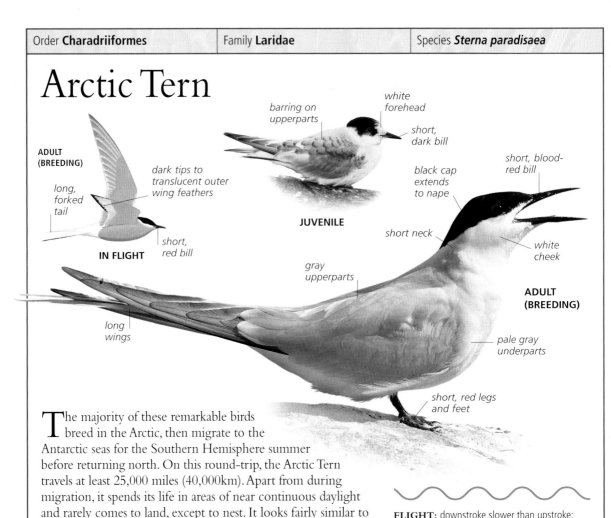

ADULT (BREEDING)
long, forked tail
dark tips to translucent outer wing feathers
short, red bill
IN FLIGHT

barring on upperparts
white forehead
short, dark bill
JUVENILE

black cap extends to nape
short, blood-red bill
short neck
white cheek
gray upperparts
ADULT (BREEDING)
long wings
pale gray underparts
short, red legs and feet

The majority of these remarkable birds breed in the Arctic, then migrate to the Antarctic seas for the Southern Hemisphere summer before returning north. On this round-trip, the Arctic Tern travels at least 25,000 miles (40,000km). Apart from during migration, it spends its life in areas of near continuous daylight and rarely comes to land, except to nest. It looks fairly similar to the Common Tern, but the former has a comparatively smaller bill, shorter legs, and a shorter neck.

VOICE Descending *keeyaar* call; nearly all calls similar to Common Tern, but higher-pitched and harsher.

NESTING Shallow scrape on bare ground or low vegetation in open areas; 2 eggs; 1 brood; May–August.

FEEDING Mostly plunge-dives for small fish and crustaceans, including crabs and shrimps; will also take prey from surface, sometimes catches insects in flight.

FLIGHT: downstroke slower than upstroke; buoyant and elegant with regular wing beats.

FEEDING THE YOUNG
Both parents feed chicks—males bring more food than females, especially right after hatching.

TRANSLUCENT FEATHERS
The translucent outer wing feathers of the Arctic Tern are evident on these two flying birds.

SIMILAR SPECIES

COMMON TERN ☼ see p.209
longer neck
longer bill
longer legs

FORSTER'S TERN see p.211
longer, orange bill
longer legs

OCCURRENCE
Breeds in far North, mostly in open, unforested areas near water and along the coast; generally migrates far off-shore. Spends more time away from land than other northern terns. Winters on edge of pack ice in Antarctica.

Length **11–15½in (28–39cm)**	Wingspan **26–30in (65–75cm)**	Weight **3⅛–4oz (90–125g)**
Social **Colonies**	Lifespan **Up to 34 years**	Status **Vulnerable**

Order **Charadriiformes**	Family **Laridae**	Species ***Sterna forsteri***

Forster's Tern

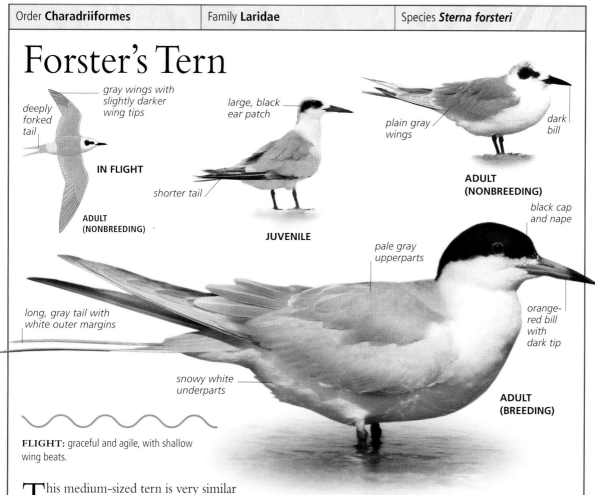

deeply forked tail

gray wings with slightly darker wing tips

IN FLIGHT

ADULT (NONBREEDING)

large, black ear patch

shorter tail

JUVENILE

plain gray wings

dark bill

ADULT (NONBREEDING)

black cap and nape

pale gray upperparts

long, gray tail with white outer margins

orange-red bill with dark tip

snowy white underparts

ADULT (BREEDING)

FLIGHT: graceful and agile, with shallow wing beats.

This medium-sized tern is very similar in appearance to the Common Tern. The features that differentiate it from the Common Tern are its lighter outer wing feathers and longer tail. Early naturalists could not tell the two species apart until 1834 when English botanist Thomas Nuttall made the distinction. He named this tern after Johann Reinhold Forster, a naturalist who accompanied the English explorer Captain Cook on his epic second voyage (1772-75).

VOICE Harsh, descending *kyerr*; more nasal than Common Tern.

NESTING Shallow scrape in mud or sand, but occasionally nests on top of muskrat lodge or on old grebe nest; sometimes constructs raft of floating vegetation; 2–3 eggs; 1 brood; May–August.

FEEDING Catches fish and crustaceans with shallow plunge-diving, often only head submerges; also catches insects in flight.

BLACK EARS
With its black ear patch, Forster's Tern is more distinctive in nonbreeding than breeding plumage.

SIMILAR SPECIES

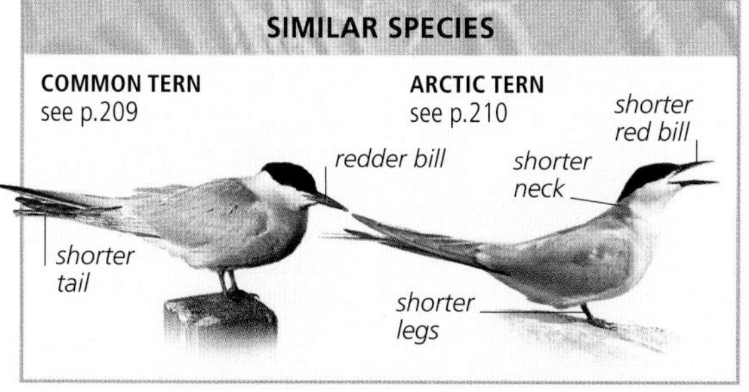
COMMON TERN
see p.209
redder bill
shorter tail
ARCTIC TERN
see p.210
shorter red bill
shorter neck
shorter legs

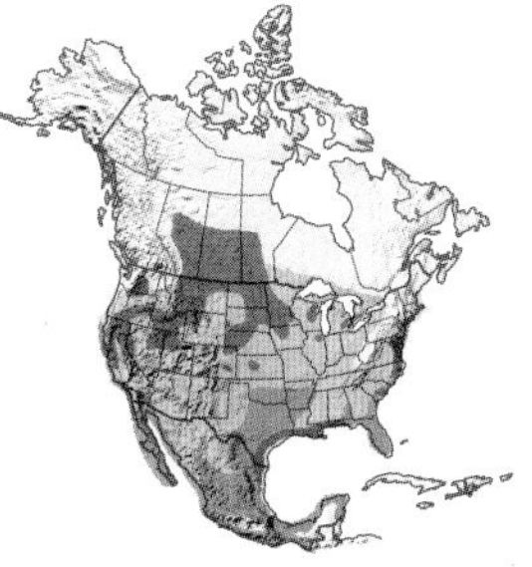

OCCURRENCE
Breeds in prairie provinces and southern Ontario, in freshwater and saltwater marshes with large stretches of open water. Winters on both coasts and across southern US states, unlike the Common Tern, which primarily winters in South America.

Length **13–14in (33–36cm)**	Wingspan **29–32in (73–82cm)**	Weight **4–7oz (125–190g)**
Social **Colonies**	Lifespan **Up to 16 years**	Status **Secure**

Order **Charadriiformes**	Family **Laridae**	Species ***Chlidonias niger***

Black Tern

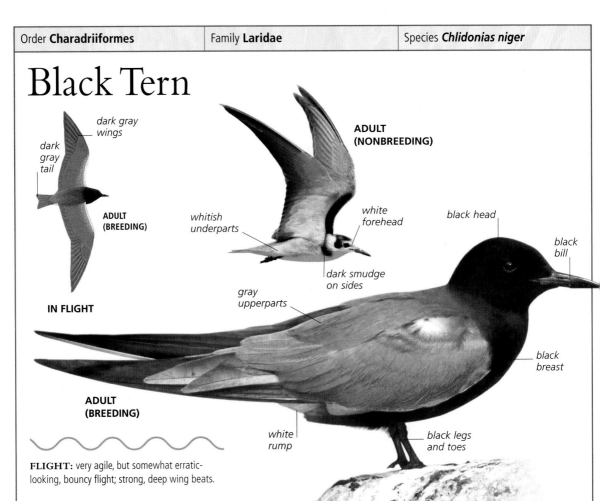

dark gray wings

dark gray tail

ADULT (BREEDING)

IN FLIGHT

ADULT (NONBREEDING)

whitish underparts

white forehead

dark smudge on sides

black head

black bill

gray upperparts

black breast

ADULT (BREEDING)

white rump

black legs and toes

FLIGHT: very agile, but somewhat erratic-looking, bouncy flight; strong, deep wing beats.

The Black Tern is a small, elegant, marsh-dwelling tern that undergoes a remarkable change in appearance from summer to winter—more so than any other regularly occurring North American tern. The Black Tern's breeding plumage can cause the bird to be confused with the closely related White-winged Tern, which is an accidental visitor to North America. The Black Tern's nonbreeding plumage is much paler than its breeding plumage—the head turns white with irregular black streaks, and the neck, breast, and belly become whitish gray.

VOICE Call nasal and harsh *krik*, *kip*, or *kik*; most vocal during breeding, but calls throughout the year.

NESTING Shallow cup on top of floating mass of vegetation, sometimes on top of muskrat lodges; usually 3 eggs; 1 brood; May–August.

FEEDING Picks prey off water's surface or vegetation; rarely plunge dives; in summer, feeds on mainly insects, caught from the air or ground, also freshwater fish; in winter, eats mainly small sea fish.

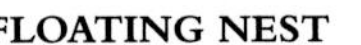

FLOATING NEST
A floating nest is a dry place to lay eggs and raise chicks in a watery environment.

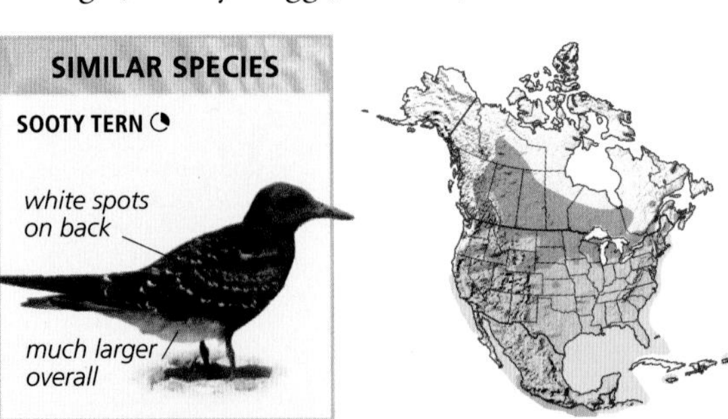

SIMILAR SPECIES

SOOTY TERN

white spots on back

much larger overall

OCCURRENCE
Freshwater marshes in summer, but nonbreeding plumaged birds—probably young—occasionally seen along the coast. During migration, can be found almost anywhere near water. Winters in the marine coastal waters of Central and South America.

Length **9–10in (23–26cm)**	Wingspan **25–35in (63–88cm)**	Weight **1¾–2½ oz (50–70g)**
Social **Colonies**	Lifespan **Up to 9 years**	Status **Vulnerable**

Order **Charadriiformes**	Family **Stercorariidae**	Species ***Stercorarius maccormicki***

South Polar Skua

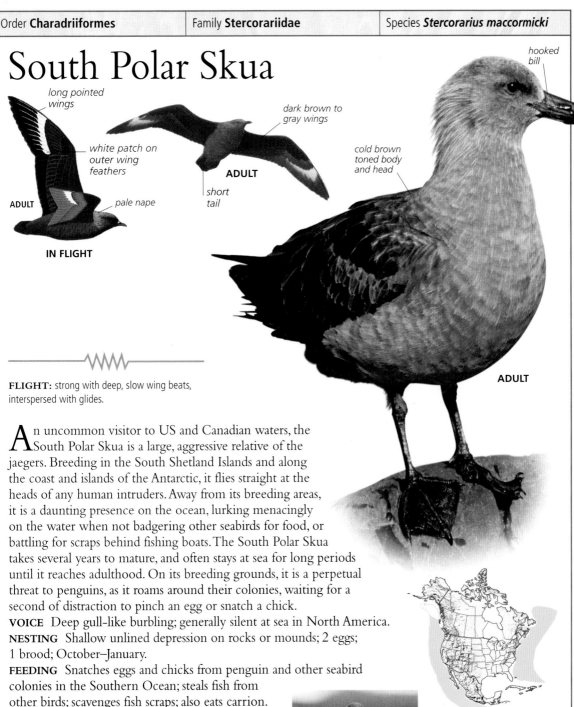

long pointed wings

white patch on outer wing feathers

ADULT

pale nape

IN FLIGHT

dark brown to gray wings

ADULT

short tail

hooked bill

cold brown toned body and head

ADULT

FLIGHT: strong with deep, slow wing beats, interspersed with glides.

An uncommon visitor to US and Canadian waters, the South Polar Skua is a large, aggressive relative of the jaegers. Breeding in the South Shetland Islands and along the coast and islands of the Antarctic, it flies straight at the heads of any human intruders. Away from its breeding areas, it is a daunting presence on the ocean, lurking menacingly on the water when not badgering other seabirds for food, or battling for scraps behind fishing boats. The South Polar Skua takes several years to mature, and often stays at sea for long periods until it reaches adulthood. On its breeding grounds, it is a perpetual threat to penguins, as it roams around their colonies, waiting for a second of distraction to pinch an egg or snatch a chick.

VOICE Deep gull-like burbling; generally silent at sea in North America.

NESTING Shallow unlined depression on rocks or mounds; 2 eggs; 1 brood; October–January.

FEEDING Snatches eggs and chicks from penguin and other seabird colonies in the Southern Ocean; steals fish from other birds; scavenges fish scraps; also eats carrion.

SIMILAR SPECIES

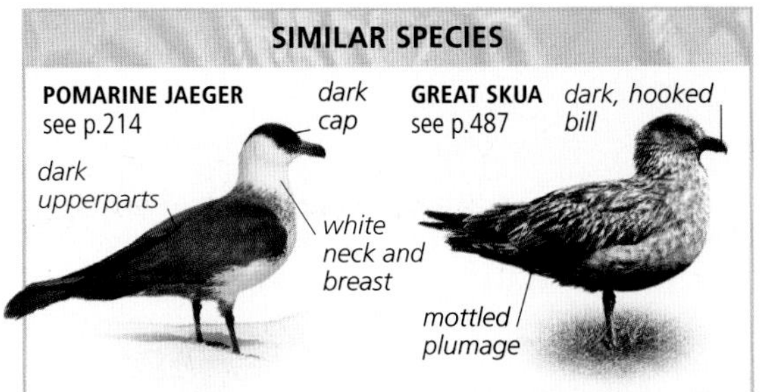
POMARINE JAEGER
see p.214
dark cap
dark upperparts
white neck and breast
GREAT SKUA
see p.487
dark, hooked bill
mottled plumage

ANTARCTIC PIRATE
A strong hooked bill, thick legs, and stocky body help this skua prosper by bullying other birds.

OCCURRENCE
A scarce visitor to seas on both sides of the North American continent, spending southern winters (northern summer) in the North Atlantic and Pacific. It is most numerous in spring and in the fall in the Pacific, and in spring in the Atlantic, usually far offshore.

Length **21in (53cm)**	Wingspan **4¼ft (1.3m)**	Weight **2½lb (1kg)**
Social **Solitary**	Lifespan **Unknown**	Status **Secure**

Order **Charadriiformes**	Family **Stercorariidae**	Species ***Stercorarius pomarinus***

Pomarine Jaeger

ADULT (BREEDING: PALE FORM)

prominent white "flash" in feathers

ADULT (NONBREEDING; PALE FORM)

barred flanks

dusky breastband

JUVENILE (FALL; DARK FORM)

all-dark body

deep, barrel breast

ADULT (DARK FORM)

white wing flash

dark overall

blunt tail spike

IN FLIGHT

ADULT (BREEDING; PALE FORM)

blackish cap

pale based, thick bill

cream cheeks

gray-brown back

dusky breast-band

twisted, spoon-like central tail feathers

The intimidating Pomarine Jaeger uses its size and strength to overpower larger seabirds, such as gulls and shearwaters, in order to steal their food. Thought to be nomadic during the breeding season, it only nests opportunistically, when populations of lemmings are at their peak to provide food for its young. Although larger and more powerful than the Parasitic Jaeger, the Pomarine Jaeger is not as acrobatic in the air and is readily driven away from breeding territories by the more dynamic Parasitic Jaeger. Interestingly, research suggests that the Pomerine Jaeger is actually more closely related to the large skuas—such as the Great and South Polar Skuas—than to other jaegers.

VOICE Nasal *cow-cow-cow* and various sharp, low whistles.

NESTING Shallow unlined depression on a rise or hummock in open tundra; 2 eggs; 1 brood; June–August.

FEEDING Hunts lemmings and other rodents; eats fish or scavenges refuse from fishing boats during nonbreeding season; often steals fish from other seabirds, such as gulls.

FLIGHT: powerful, deep, quick wing beats, with glides; rapid twists and turns in pursuit of prey.

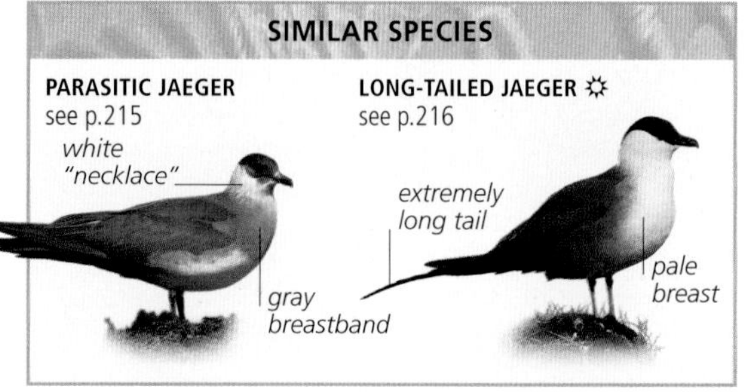
SIMILAR SPECIES
PARASITIC JAEGER
see p.215
white "necklace"
gray breastband
LONG-TAILED JAEGER ☼
see p.216
extremely long tail
pale breast

OBVIOUS FEATURE
The twisted, spoon-like central tail feathers are clearly visible when the Pomerine Jaeger flies.

OCCURRENCE
Breeds on open tundra in the Canadian Arctic. Migrates north in spring and south in fall, along coasts and also far offshore. Most often seen when brought close to land by gales. Storm-driven birds very occasionally found inland. More commonly seen on West Coast than East Coast; winters far out at sea.

Length **17–20in (43–51cm)**	Wingspan **4ft (1.2m)**	Weight **23–26oz (650–750g)**
Social **Solitary**	Lifespan **Unknown**	Status **Secure**

Order **Charadriiformes**	Family **Stercorariidae**	Species ***Stercorarius parasiticus***

Parasitic Jaeger

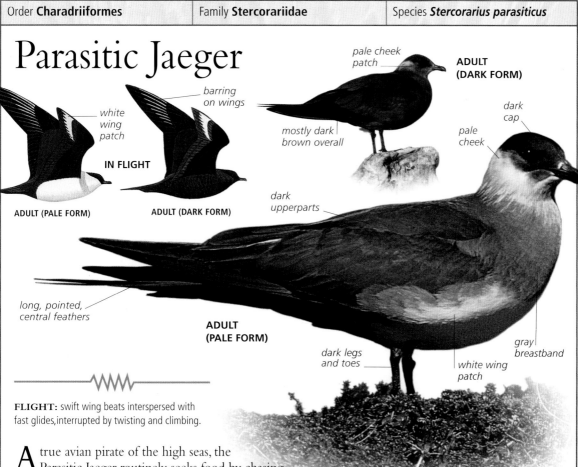

white wing patch
barring on wings
IN FLIGHT
ADULT (PALE FORM)
ADULT (DARK FORM)
pale cheek patch
ADULT (DARK FORM)
mostly dark brown overall
dark cap
pale cheek
dark upperparts
long, pointed, central feathers
ADULT (PALE FORM)
dark legs and toes
white wing patch
gray breastband

FLIGHT: swift wing beats interspersed with fast glides,interrupted by twisting and climbing.

A true avian pirate of the high seas, the Parasitic Jaeger routinely seeks food by chasing, bullying, and forcing other seabirds to drop or regurgitate fish or other food they have caught. Unlike most jaegers, the Parasitic Jaeger is adaptable in its feeding habits so that it can forage and raise its young under a wide range of environmental conditions. Breeding on the Arctic tundra, it migrates to offshore areas during the nonbreeding season.

VOICE Variety of terrier-like yelps and soft squeals, often during interactions with other jaegers or predators, usually around nesting territories.

NESTING Shallow unlined depression on a rise or hummock in open tundra; 2 eggs; 1 brood; May–August.

FEEDING Steals fish and other aquatic prey from gulls and terns; catches small birds, eats eggs, or hunts small rodents on breeding grounds.

PARASITIC PIRATE
This Parasitic Jaeger is harrying a gull by pecking at it, to make it disgorge its hard-won meal.

SIMILAR SPECIES

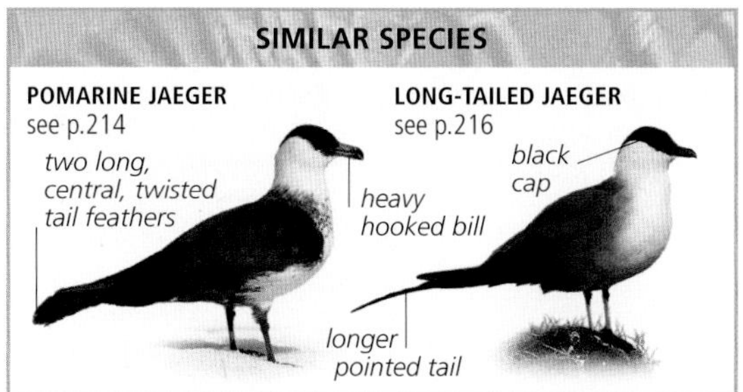
POMARINE JAEGER
see p.214
two long, central, twisted tail feathers
heavy hooked bill
LONG-TAILED JAEGER
see p.216
black cap
longer pointed tail

OCCURRENCE
Breeds on tundra in northern Canada and Alaska (breeds farther south than other jaegers); during migration and in winter, uses both nearshore and offshore waters; rarely found inland in the US outside the breeding season.

Length **16–18½in (41–47cm)**	Wingspan **3ft 3in–3½ ft (1–1.1m)**	Weight **13–18oz (375–500g)**
Social **Solitary/Small flocks**	Lifespan **Up to 18 years**	Status **Secure**

Order **Charadriiformes**	Family **Stercorariidae**	Species ***Stercorarius longicaudus***

Long-tailed Jaeger

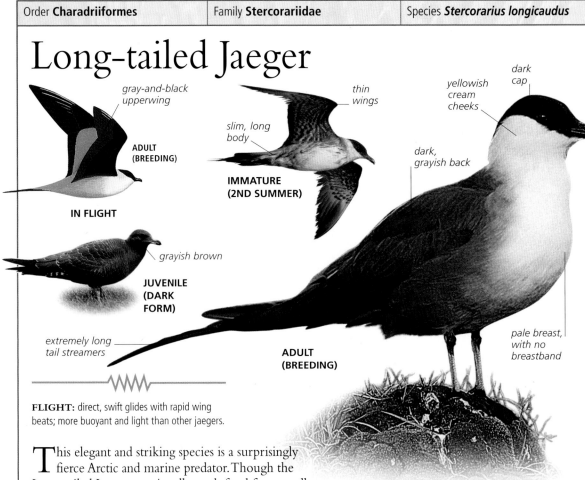

gray-and-black upperwing

ADULT (BREEDING)

IN FLIGHT

thin wings

slim, long body

IMMATURE (2ND SUMMER)

dark cap

yellowish cream cheeks

dark, grayish back

grayish brown

JUVENILE (DARK FORM)

extremely long tail streamers

ADULT (BREEDING)

pale breast, with no breastband

FLIGHT: direct, swift glides with rapid wing beats; more buoyant and light than other jaegers.

This elegant and striking species is a surprisingly fierce Arctic and marine predator. Though the Long-tailed Jaeger occasionally steals food from small gulls and terns, it is much less proficient at such piracy than its larger relatives, and usually hunts for its own food. Indeed, the Long-tailed Jaeger is so dependent on there being an abundance of lemmings in the Arctic that in years when lemming numbers dip low, the bird may not even attempt to nest, because there would not be enough lemmings with which to feed its chicks.

VOICE Calls include a chorus of *kreek*, a loud *kreer* warning call, whistles, and high-pitched, sharp clicks.

NESTING Shallow, unlined depression on a rise or hummock in open tundra; 2 eggs; 1 brood; May–August.

FEEDING Hunts lemmings on tundra breeding grounds; takes fish, beetles, and mayflies from water surface; occasionally steals small fish from terns.

DEFENSIVE MOVES
This species protects its territory with angry calls, aggressive swoops, and distraction displays.

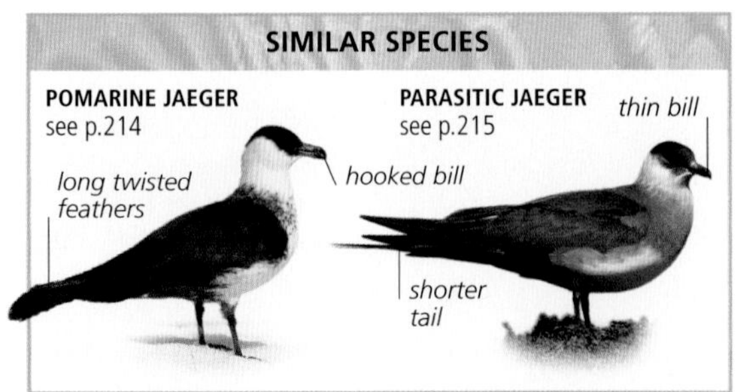
SIMILAR SPECIES
POMARINE JAEGER
see p.214
long twisted feathers
PARASITIC JAEGER
see p.215
thin bill
hooked bill
shorter tail

OCCURRENCE
Breeds on tundra in northern Canada and Alaska—generally the most northern breeding jaeger; on migration and in winter uses mostly offshore waters; very rarely seen inland in winter.

Length **19–21in (48–53cm)**	Wingspan **3½ft (1.1m)**	Weight **10–11oz (275–300g)**
Social **Solitary/Flocks**	Lifespan **Up to 8 years**	Status **Secure**

Order **Charadriiformes**	Family **Alcidae**	Species ***Alle alle***

Dovekie

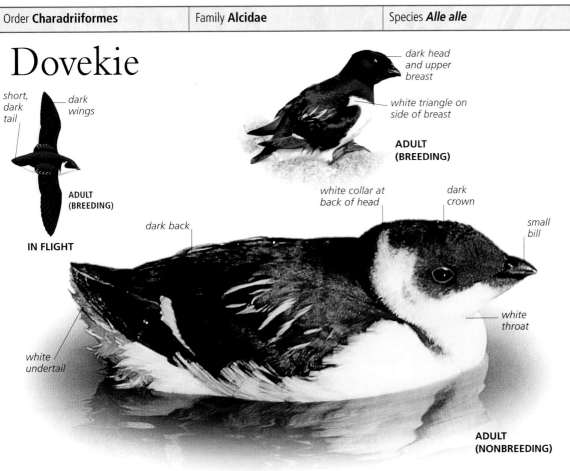

short, dark tail
dark wings
ADULT (BREEDING)
IN FLIGHT

dark head and upper breast
white triangle on side of breast
ADULT (BREEDING)

white collar at back of head
dark crown
small bill
dark back
white throat
white undertail
ADULT (NONBREEDING)

Also known widely as the Little Auk, the stocky and diminutive black-and-white Dovekie is a bird of the High Arctic. Most Dovekies breed in Greenland in large, noisy, crowded colonies (the largest one containing 15–20 million birds), but some breed in northeastern Canada, and others on a few islands in the Bering Sea off Alaska. On their breeding grounds, both adult and immature Dovekies are hunted ruthlessly by Glaucous Gulls, as well as mammalian predators, such as the Arctic Fox. Vast numbers of Dovekies winter on the Low Arctic waters off the northeastern North American seaboard, in immense flocks. Occasionally, severe onshore gales cause entire flocks to become stranded along the East Coast of North America.

VOICE Variety of calls at breeding colony, including high-pitched trilling that rises and falls; silent at sea.

NESTING Pebble nest in crack or crevice in boulder field or rocky outcrop; 1 egg; 1 brood; April–August.

FEEDING Mostly picks tiny crustaceans from just below the sea's surface.

FLIGHT: rapid, whirring wing beats; flies in flocks low over the water's surface.

SOCIABLE LITTLE AUK
After initial squabbles over nest sites, Dovekies in breeding colonies become highly sociable.

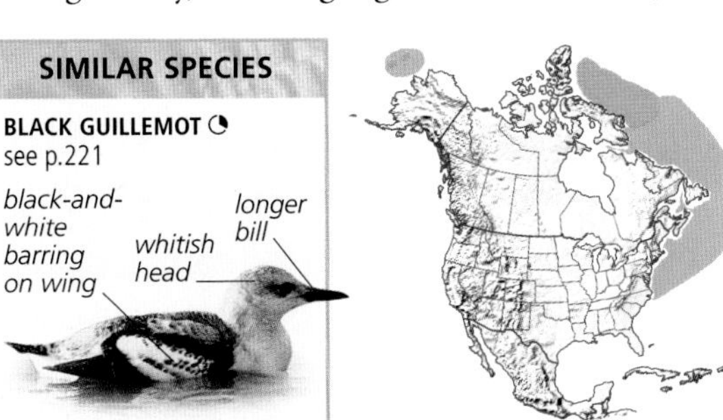
SIMILAR SPECIES
BLACK GUILLEMOT
see p.221
black-and-white barring on wing
whitish head
longer bill

OCCURRENCE
Breeds on islands inside the Arctic Circle; in Greenland, mostly, but also in northeastern Canada and the Bering Sea. Many birds remain just south of the Arctic pack ice throughout the winter; others fly south to winter off the northeastern seaboard of North America.

Length **8½in (21cm)**	Wingspan **15in (38cm)**	Weight **6oz (175g)**
Social **Colonies**	Lifespan **Unknown**	Status **Secure**

Order **Charadriiformes**	Family **Alcidae**	Species ***Uria lomvia***

Thick-billed Murre

ADULT
(BREEDING)
hunched
in flight
IN FLIGHT
short,
black tail
reduced or absent
white line on bill
more extensive
white on throat
ADULT
(NONBREEDING)
brownish black
sides of head
white breast
and underparts
white line
along bill
all-blackish
upperparts
ADULT
(BREEDING)

FLIGHT: near the water surface with strong, rapid wing beats.

Large and robust, the Thick-billed Murre is one of the most abundant seabirds in the whole of the Northern Hemisphere. Its dense, coastal cliff breeding colonies can be made up of around a million birds each. Chicks leave the colony when they are only about 25 percent of the adult's weight. Their growth is completed at sea, while being fed by the male parent alone. The Thick-billed Murre can dive to a remarkable 600ft (180m) to catch fish and squid.

VOICE Roaring, groaning, insistent sounding *aoorrr*; lower-pitched than the Common Murre.

NESTING Rocky coast or narrow sea cliff ledge in dense colony; 1 egg; 1 brood; March–September.

FEEDING Cod, herring, capelin, and sand lance in summer; also crustaceans, worms, and squid.

SIMILAR SPECIES

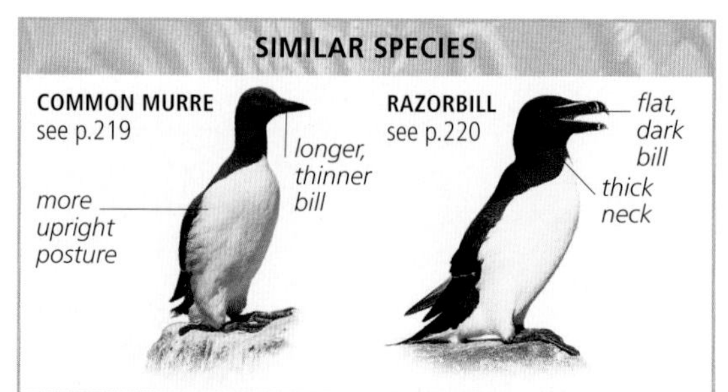
COMMON MURRE
see p.219
longer,
thinner
bill
more
upright
posture
RAZORBILL
see p.220
flat,
dark
bill
thick
neck

CLIFF HANGER
Thick-billed Murres breed in dense colonies on steep cliffs, often in very remote areas.

OCCURRENCE
Breeds on rocky shorelines, using the same nest each year. Winters at sea, spending extended periods of time on very cold, deep, and often remote ocean waters and pack ice edges or openings.

Length **18in (46cm)**	Wingspan **28in (70cm)**	Weight **34oz (975g)**
Social **Colonies**	Lifespan **At least 25 years**	Status **Secure**

Order **Charadriiformes**	Family **Alcidae**	Species ***Uria aalge***

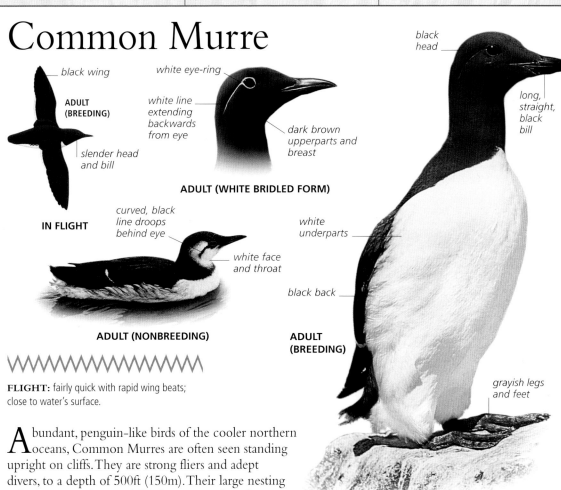

Common Murre

black wing

ADULT (BREEDING)

slender head and bill

IN FLIGHT

white eye-ring

white line extending backwards from eye

dark brown upperparts and breast

ADULT (WHITE BRIDLED FORM)

curved, black line droops behind eye

white face and throat

ADULT (NONBREEDING)

black head

long, straight, black bill

white underparts

black back

ADULT (BREEDING)

grayish legs and feet

FLIGHT: fairly quick with rapid wing beats; close to water's surface.

Abundant, penguin-like birds of the cooler northern oceans, Common Murres are often seen standing upright on cliffs. They are strong fliers and adept divers, to a depth of 500ft (150m). Their large nesting colonies, on rocky sea cliff ledges, are so densely packed that incubating adults may touch each other on both sides. Common Murre eggs are pointed at one end—when pushed, they roll around in a circle, reducing the risk of rolling off the nesting ledge. It has been suggested that unique egg markings may help adults recognize their own eggs.

VOICE Low-pitched, descending call given from cliffs or water, reminiscent of trumpeting elephant.

NESTING Directly on bare rock near shore, on wide cliff ledge, or large crevice; 1 egg; 1 brood; May-July.

FEEDING Pursues small schooling fish, such as herring, sand lance, and haddock; also crustaceans, marine worms, and squid.

BREEDING COLONY
Crowded together, Common Murres are not territorial but will defend a personal space.

SIMILAR SPECIES

THICK-BILLED MURRE
see p.218
thick, pale line between eye and bill

RAZORBILL ☼
see p.220
bill with white bar near tip

OCCURRENCE
Breeds close to rocky shorelines, nesting on coastal cliff ledges or flat rocks on top of sea stacks on both East and West coasts. Found further offshore during nonbreeding season, spending extended periods on the open ocean and in large bays. Winters at sea.

Length **17½in (44cm)**	Wingspan **26in (65cm)**	Weight **35oz (1000g)**
Social **Colonies**	Lifespan **At least 40 years**	Status **Localized**

Order **Charadriiformes**	Family **Alcidae**	Species ***Alca torda***

Razorbill

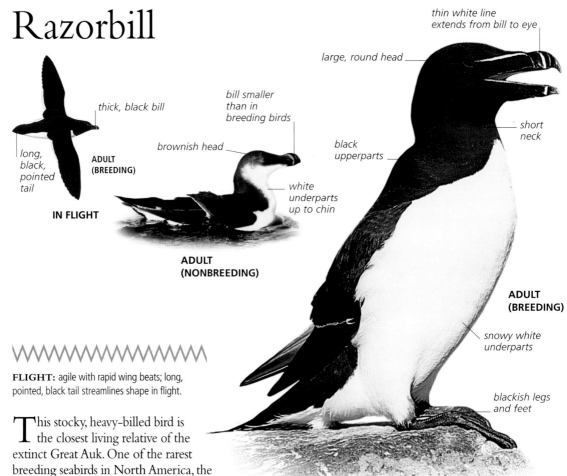

thin white line extends from bill to eye

large, round head

thick, black bill

bill smaller than in breeding birds

long, black, pointed tail

ADULT (BREEDING)

IN FLIGHT

brownish head

white underparts up to chin

ADULT (NONBREEDING)

black upperparts

short neck

ADULT (BREEDING)

snowy white underparts

blackish legs and feet

FLIGHT: agile with rapid wing beats; long, pointed, black tail streamlines shape in flight.

This stocky, heavy-billed bird is the closest living relative of the extinct Great Auk. One of the rarest breeding seabirds in North America, the Razorbill is a strong flier and more agile in flight than many related species. Razorbills typically feed at depths of about 20ft (6m), but are sometimes known to dive to depths of more than 450ft (140m). On shore, Razorbills walk upright like penguins. They carry small fish at once to their chick, later male razorbills escort their flightless young to the sea to feed.

VOICE Deep, guttural, resonant croak, *hey al.*

NESTING Enclosed sites often built in crevices, among boulders, or in abandoned burrows; 1 egg; 1 brood; May-July.

FEEDING Dives for schooling fish, including capelin, herring, and sand lance; also consumes marine worms and crustaceans; sometimes steals fish from other auks.

IN FLIGHT
The razorbill flaps its wings constantly in flight as they are too small for the bird to glide.

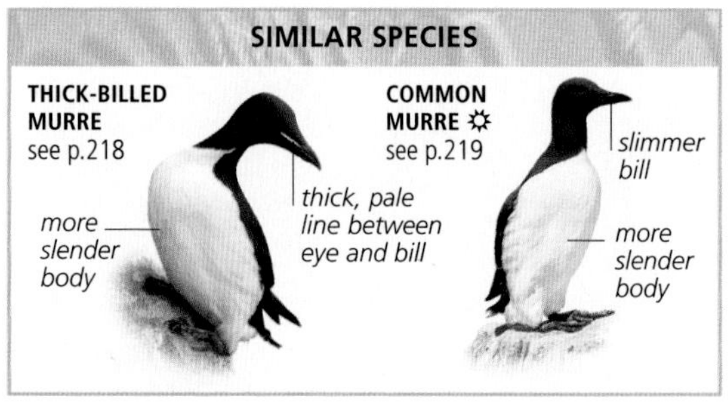
SIMILAR SPECIES
THICK-BILLED MURRE
see p.218
more slender body
thick, pale line between eye and bill
COMMON MURRE ☼
see p.219
slimmer bill
more slender body

OCCURRENCE
Breeds on rocky islands and shorelines, or steep mainland cliffs in northeast North America, most of the world's population breeds in Iceland. Winters south of breeding range on ice-free coastal waters reaching New Jersey and Virginia. Forages in cool, shallower water, near shore.

Length **17in (43cm)**	Wingspan **26in (65cm)**	Weight **26oz (725g)**
Social **Colonies**	Lifespan **At least 30 years**	Status **Localized**

Order **Charadriiformes**	Family **Alcidae**	Species ***Cepphus grylle***

Black Guillemot

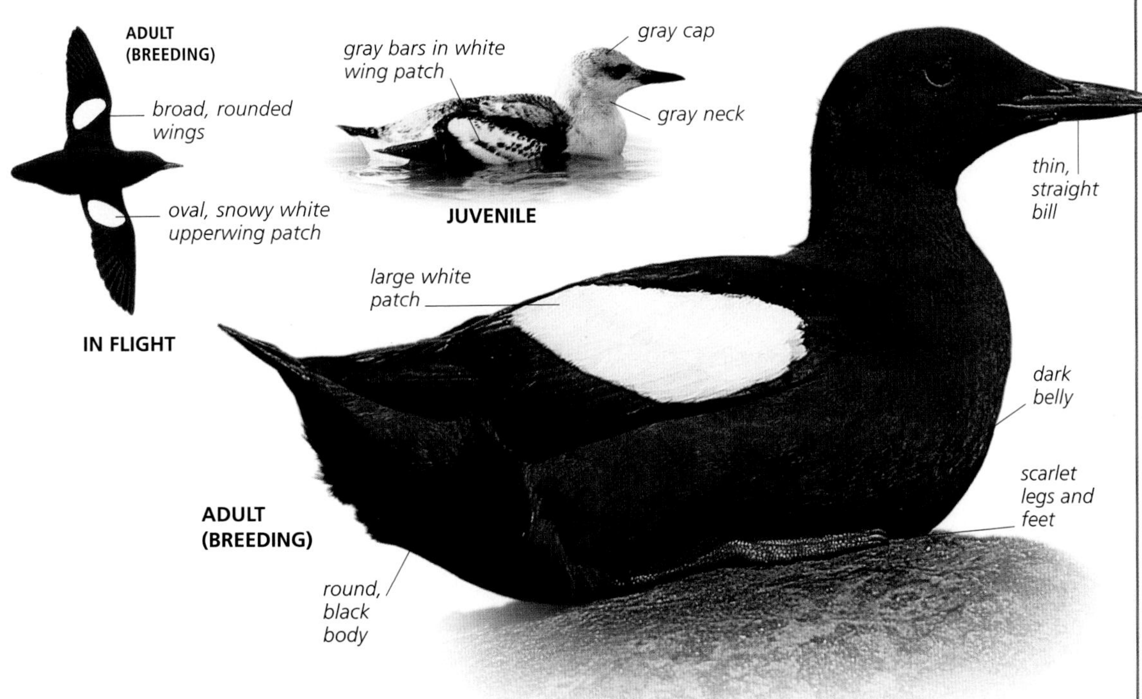
ADULT (BREEDING)
broad, rounded wings
oval, snowy white upperwing patch
IN FLIGHT
gray bars in white wing patch
gray cap
gray neck
JUVENILE
thin, straight bill
large white patch
dark belly
scarlet legs and feet
ADULT (BREEDING)
round, black body

Black Guillemots, also known as "sea pigeons," are medium-sized auks with distinctive black plumage and white wing patches. Their striking scarlet legs and mouth lining help attract a mate during the breeding season. Like the other two species of the *Cepphus* genus, Black Guillemots prefer shallow, inshore waters to the open ocean. They winter near the shore, sometimes moving into the mouths of rivers.

VOICE Very high-pitched whistles and squeaks given on land and water near nesting habitat that resonate like an echo.

NESTING Shallow scrape in soil or pebbles within cave or crevice, site may be reused; 1–2 eggs; 1 brood; May–August.

FEEDING Dives under water near shore to hunt small, bottom-dwelling fish, such as rock eels, sand lance, and sculpin; propels down to depths of 59ft (18m) using partly opened wings, webbed feet as a rudder; feeds close to nesting islands.

FLIGHT: flies low over the water with very rapid wing beats.

FOOD FOR CHICKS
The birds carry food for the chicks in their bills and often pause near the nest before dashing home.

SIMILAR SPECIES

DOVEKIE ❄
see p.217
smaller

dark back
white patch behind eye

PIGEON GUILLEMOT ☼
dusky underwings in flight; see p.222

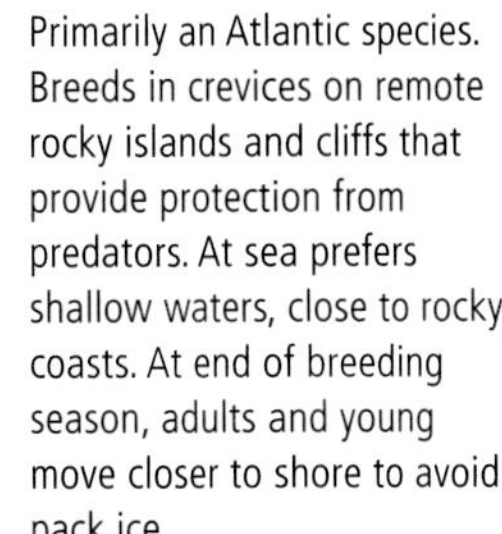
black bar on white wing patch

OCCURRENCE
Primarily an Atlantic species. Breeds in crevices on remote rocky islands and cliffs that provide protection from predators. At sea prefers shallow waters, close to rocky coasts. At end of breeding season, adults and young move closer to shore to avoid pack ice.

Length **13in (33cm)**	Wingspan **21in (53cm)**	Weight **15oz (425g)**
Social **Colonies**	Lifespan **At least 20 years**	Status **Localized**

Order **Charadriiformes**	Family **Alcidae**	Species ***Cepphus columba***

Pigeon Guillemot

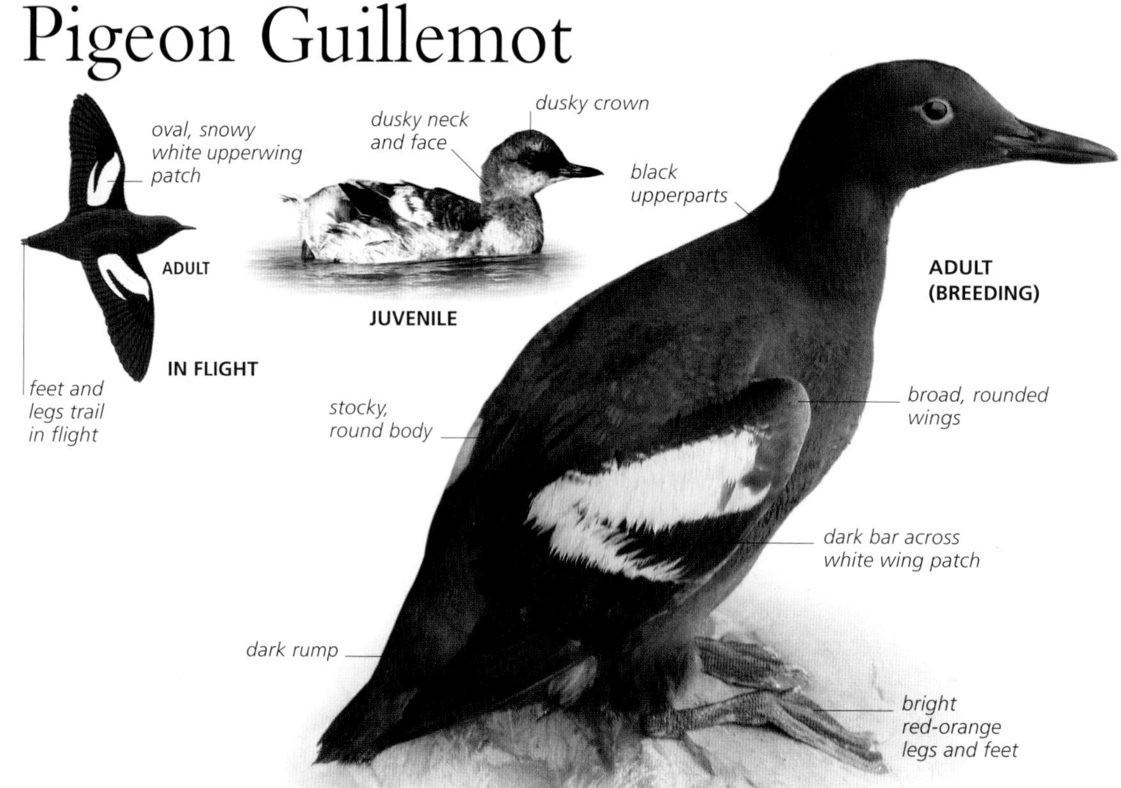
oval, snowy white upperwing patch
ADULT
IN FLIGHT
feet and legs trail in flight
dusky neck and face
dusky crown
JUVENILE
black upperparts
ADULT (BREEDING)
stocky, round body
broad, rounded wings
dark bar across white wing patch
dark rump
bright red-orange legs and feet

The Pigeon Guillemot, a North Pacific seabird, is found along rocky shores in small colonies or isolated pairs. This auk nests in burrows or under rocks, often on small islands that provide protection from land-bound predators. The male excavates a burrow, or chooses an abandoned burrow or crevice, to build a nest. During the breeding season, the bird's striking red-orange legs and mouth lining are used in courtship displays to attract a mate.

VOICE Excited, squeaky whistles, and twitters; nesting birds give a weak whistle *peeeee*.

NESTING Shallow scrape in burrow or crevice; 2 eggs; 1 brood; May–August.

FEEDING Feeds near shore; dives to seabed, then uses bill to forage for small rock eels, sculpin, crabs, shrimp, marine worms, and mollusks; carries food for chicks in beak.

FLIGHT: flies close to water surface with very rapid, fluttering wing beats.

PREDATOR BECOMES PREY
Predatory gulls can kill adult Pigeon Guillemots and sometimes eat their chicks and eggs.

SIMILAR SPECIES

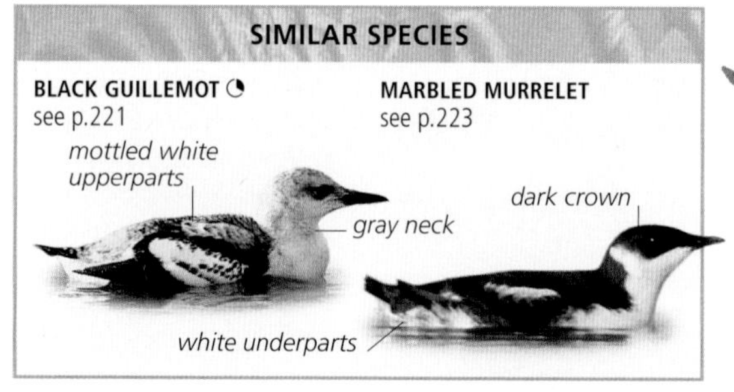
BLACK GUILLEMOT
see p.221
mottled white upperparts
gray neck
MARBLED MURRELET
see p.223
dark crown
white underparts

OCCURRENCE
Breeds on rocky islands, coastlines, and cliffs where it is less accessible to predators. At sea, it generally remains close to rocky coasts, except in the Bering Sea, where it is found further out along the edges of the pack ice. In winter, some populations are forced south by sea ice.

Length **13½in (34cm)**	Wingspan **23in (58cm)**	Weight **18oz (500g)**
Social **Colonies**	Lifespan **Up to 14 years**	Status **Localized**

Order **Charadriiformes**	Family **Alcidae**	Species ***Brachyramphus marmoratus***

Marbled Murrelet

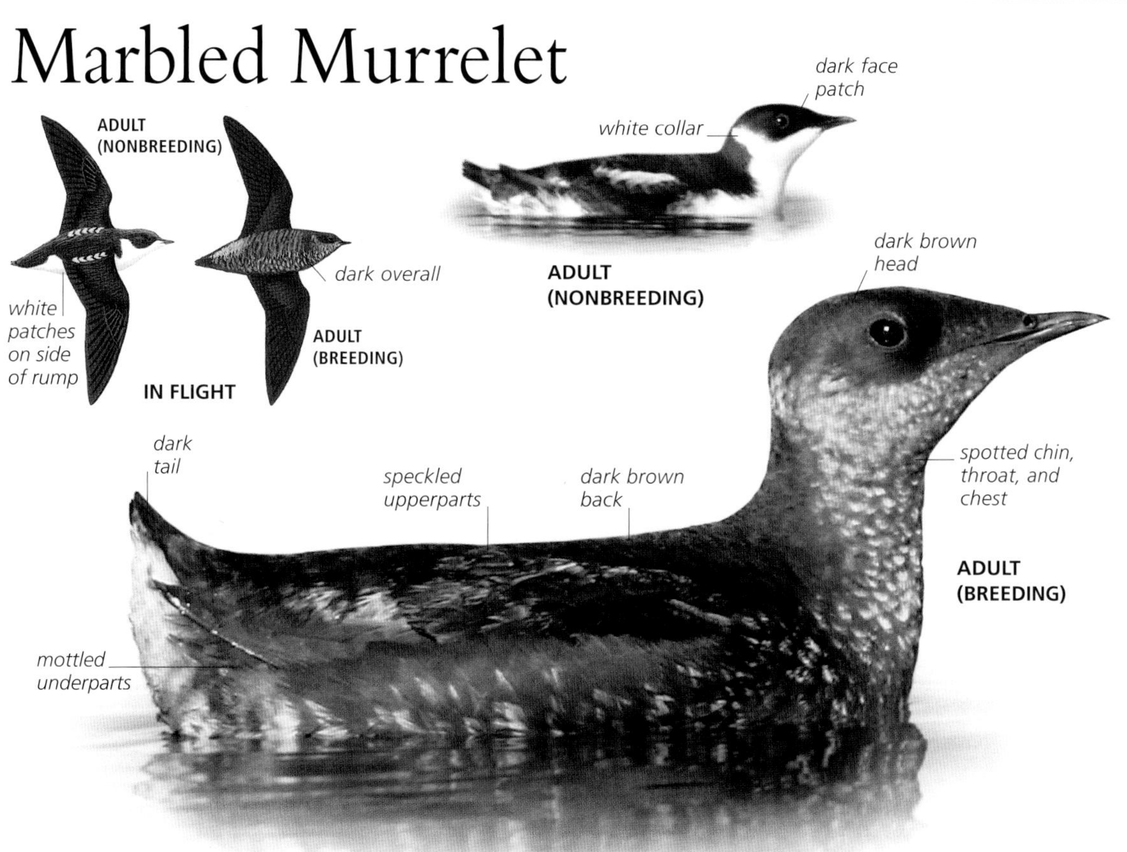
ADULT
(NONBREEDING)
white patches on side of rump
dark overall
ADULT
(BREEDING)
IN FLIGHT
dark face patch
white collar
ADULT
(NONBREEDING)
dark brown head
dark tail
speckled upperparts
dark brown back
spotted chin, throat, and chest
ADULT
(BREEDING)
mottled underparts

The breeding habits of the Marbled Murrelet, a bird of both sea and forest, remained a mystery until 1974, when the first nest was discovered high in a Douglas Fir in a California park. Unlike most auks and their relatives, which have black and white breeding plumage, the Marbled Murrelet's breeding plumage is brown, to camouflage the bird on its nest in the branches of trees or, in places, on the ground. Ornithologists are eager to learn more about this secretive seabird, even as its numbers decline due to clear-cutting of old-growth conifer forests, where it nests, entanglement of the bird in fishing gear, and oil pollution out at sea, where it feeds.

VOICE Flight call series of high-pitched, squealing, slightly descending *kleeer* notes.

NESTING In northern part of its range, on island mountainsides; in the south, on tree limbs in old-growth forests; 1 egg; 1 brood; April–September.

FEEDING Short dives to catch small fish and crustaceans in shallow offshore waters, "flying" underwater; feeds at night, in pairs.

FLIGHT: straight, fast, and low over water, with extremely rapid wing beats.

RUNNING ON WATER
The Marbled Murrelet flaps its wings energetically and runs across the surface to become airborne.

SIMILAR SPECIES

KITTLITZ'S MURRELET
see p.494

white above eyes
white undertail

OCCURRENCE
Relies on marine and forested habitats for both feeding and breeding, on Pacific coasts from Alaska to California; at sea, usually found near coast, in relatively shallow waters. In the breeding season, travels back and forth between the sea and inland breeding grounds.

Length **10in (26cm)**	Wingspan **16in (41cm)**	Weight **8oz (225g)**
Social **Pairs/Small groups**	Lifespan **Unknown**	Status **Vulnerable**

Order **Charadriiformes**	Family **Alcidae**	Species ***Synthliboramphus antiquus***

Ancient Murrelet

ADULT (BREEDING)
white under wing
white underparts with gray sides
IN FLIGHT
lacks distinctive white plumes behind eyes
lacks black throat
ADULT (NONBREEDING)
uniform gray upperparts
distinctive white plumes behind eyes
black face and throat
pale bill tip
distinctive white collar on side of neck
ADULT (BREEDING)

Of the five murrelets that occur regularly in North America, this little species is the most numerous. Like its close relatives, Xantus's Murrelet and Craveri's Murrelet, the Ancient Murrelet usually raises two chicks, and takes them out to sea when they are just a few days old, usually under the cover of darkness. The Ancient Murrelet can also leap straight out of the sea and into flight. White eyebrow-like plumes on the head, combined with a shawl-like gray back, give the bird its supposedly "ancient" appearance.

VOICE Short, high-pitched trills and rattles given by nesting birds while perched in trees.

NESTING Burrow in soft soil, often among forest tree roots; 2 eggs; 1 brood; June-August.

FEEDING Dives for prey in groups, often at the same time, driving schools of small fish to the surface; Euphansiid shrimps, which are about 1in (2.5cm) long, are its primary diet.

FLIGHT: flies fast, low, and straight with rapid wing beats; capable of quick take-off from water.

GROUP FEEDER
The Ancient Murrelet flies low to the water in flocks on the lookout for food.

SIMILAR SPECIES

XANTUS'S MURRELET see p.494

CRAVERI'S MURRELET

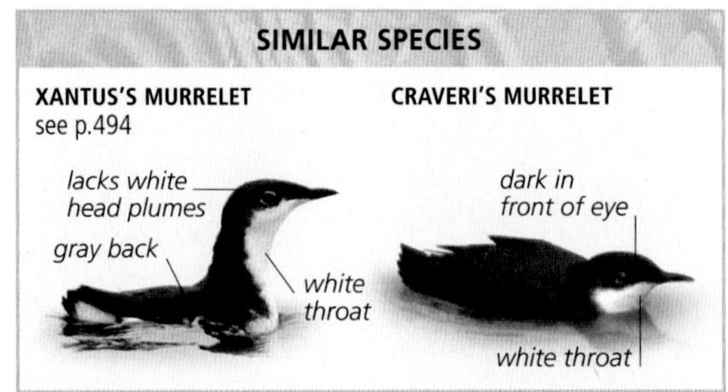
lacks white head plumes
gray back
white throat
dark in front of eye
white throat

OCCURRENCE
Lives in the north Pacific, and Bering Sea. Concentrates where food is abundant—most often in straits, sounds, and coastal waters—where it often feeds quite close to shore. Nests on coastal islands, mainly on forest floor but also where there is proper cover and sufficient peaty soil to dig burrows.

Length **10in (26cm)**	Wingspan **17in (43cm)**	Weight **7oz (200g)**
Social **Colonies**	Lifespan **At least 4 years**	Status **Localized**

Order **Charadriiformes**	Family **Alcidae**	Species ***Ptychoramphus aleuticus***

Cassin's Auklet

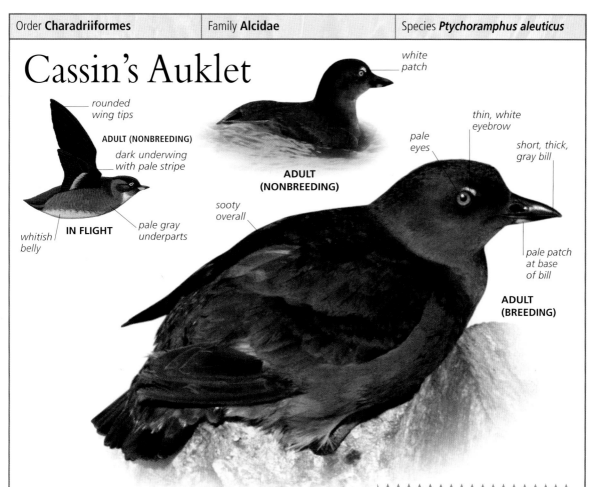

rounded wing tips

ADULT (NONBREEDING)

dark underwing with pale stripe

whitish belly

IN FLIGHT

pale gray underparts

white patch

ADULT (NONBREEDING)

sooty overall

pale eyes

thin, white eyebrow

short, thick, gray bill

pale patch at base of bill

ADULT (BREEDING)

This secretive little seabird usually nests in an underground burrow, which can take a breeding pair many weeks to scratch out. Parent birds fish by day, returning to the nest in the safety of darkness to avoid gulls and other predators. Nestlings encourage regurgitation by nibbling at a white spot at the base of the parent's lower mandible. Uniquely for a member of the alcid family, Cassin's Auklet has been known to raise more than one brood in a season.

VOICE Hoarse, rhythmic night calls in colonies; squeals and peeps when in burrow; silent at sea.

NESTING On offshore islands, in crevices or burrows; 1 egg; 1–2 broods; March–September.

FEEDING Dives and swims underwater using wings to pursue small crustaceans, fish, and squid.

FLIGHT: low over the surface of the sea, with rapid wing beats.

RUNNING ON WATER
After a long run and some energetic wing beating, Cassin's Auklet eventually takes off from the water.

SIMILAR SPECIES

MARBLED MURRELET (BREEDING)
see p.223
paler head
reddish brown upperparts

KITTLITZ'S MURRELET (BREEDING)
lacks white stripe on underwing; see p.494
mottled brown-and-white feathers

OCCURRENCE
Pacific distribution; breeds on cliffs, grassy plains, or slopes on coastal islands. During the nonbreeding season, northern birds found in deep waters beyond the continental shelf, where upwelling currents bring food from the depths. Southern birds remain near their colonies year-round.

Length **9in (23cm)**	Wingspan **15in (38cm)**	Weight **6oz (175g)**
Social **Colonies**	Lifespan **At least 6 years**	Status **Localized**

Order **Charadriiformes**	Family **Alcidae**	Species ***Cerorhinca monocerata***

Rhinoceros Auklet

dark wings
ADULT (NONBREEDING)
white belly
IN FLIGHT
lacks facial plumes
smaller bill
ADULT (NONBREEDING)
horny structure at base of upper bill
dark upperparts
thin, white plumes curving back
ADULT (BREEDING)

This robust bird is closely related to puffins, and is the only auk with a prominent "horn" on top of its bill; it is this structure that gives the bird its common name. The Rhinoceros Auklet forages closer to shore than its puffin relatives, and usually returns to its nesting colonies at night. This trusting seabird often allows boats to approach very closely. It became locally extinct, but re-established its population on California's Farallon Islands in the 1970s when non-native rabbits that were competing for nesting burrows were removed. When fishing, it carries its catch in its beak, rather than in a throat pouch like other auks.

VOICE Adults give series of low, mooing calls, as well as short barks and groans.

NESTING Cup of moss or twigs on islands, under vegetation, in crevice or long, soil burrow; 1 egg; 1 brood; April–September.

FEEDING Forages underwater during breeding season, looks for small schooling fish for nestlings; also eats crustaceans; powerful diver and swimmer.

FLIGHT: swift, direct with quick wing beats; takeoff appears labored.

SUBMARINE-LIKE
Its body nearly submerged and its head looking behind, this Rhinoceros Auklet is ready to dive.

SIMILAR SPECIES

PARAKEET AUKLET ♂
see p.494

paler breast

OCCURRENCE
Throughout temperate North Pacific waters, generally south of puffin habitat. Typically lives far out at sea, but may feed near shore where currents concentrate food; usually forages and returns to nesting colonies by night.

Length **15in (38cm)**	Wingspan **22in (56cm)**	Weight **16oz (450g)**
Social **Colonies**	Lifespan **Unknown**	Status **Localized**

Order **Charadriiformes**	Family **Alcidae**	Species ***Fratercula arctica***

Atlantic Puffin

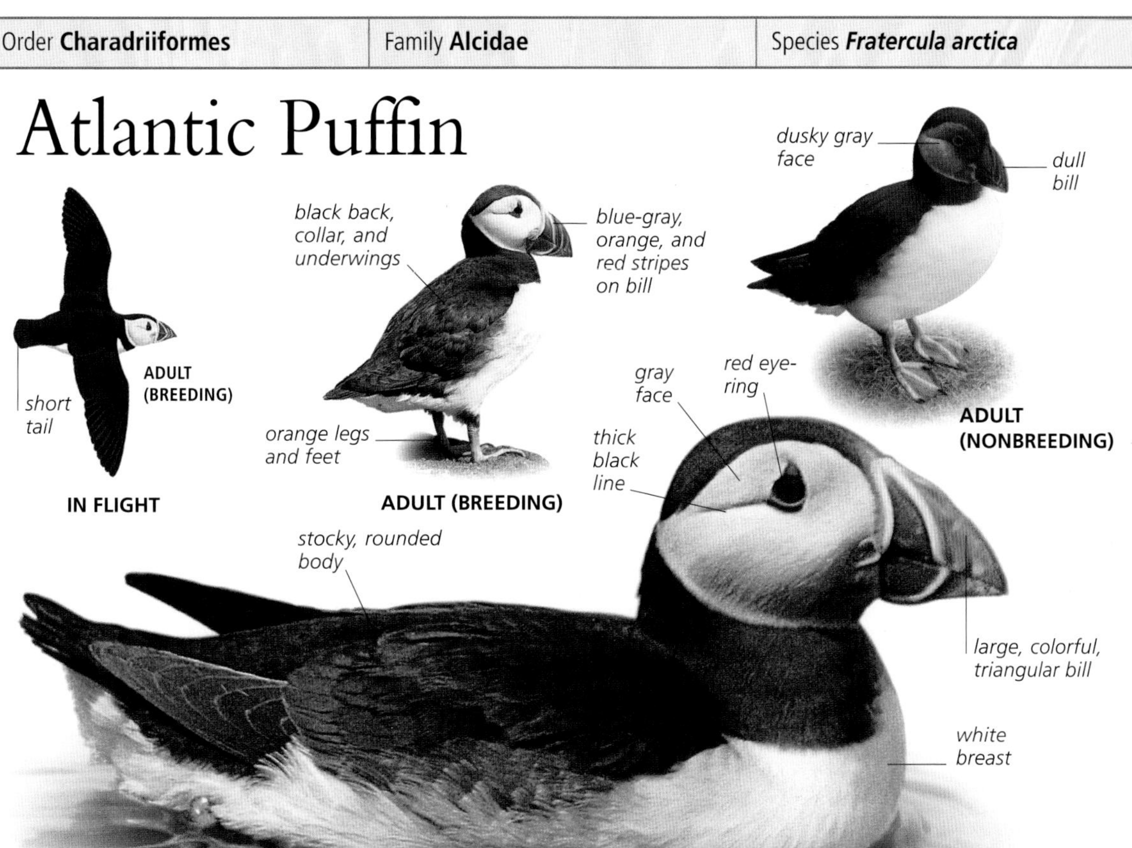
short tail
ADULT (BREEDING)
IN FLIGHT
black back, collar, and underwings
blue-gray, orange, and red stripes on bill
orange legs and feet
ADULT (BREEDING)
dusky gray face
dull bill
ADULT (NONBREEDING)
gray face
red eye-ring
thick black line
stocky, rounded body
large, colorful, triangular bill
white breast
ADULT (BREEDING)

With its black-and-white "tuxedo," ungainly upright posture, and enormous, colorful bill, the Atlantic Puffin is often known as the "clown of the sea." It is seen in summer, when large breeding colonies gather on remote, rocky islands. To feed itself and its young, it can dive down to 200ft (60m) with partly folded wings, essentially "flying" underwater in pursuit of small schooling fish. The Atlantic Puffin is the provincial bird of Newfoundland.

VOICE Rising and falling buzzy growl, resembling a chainsaw.

NESTING Underground burrow or deep rock crevice lined with grass and feathers; 1 egg; 1 brood; June–August.

FEEDING Dives deep for capelin, herring, hake, sand lance, and other small fish, which it swallows underwater, or stores crossways in its bill to take back to its chicks.

FLIGHT: swift and direct, with rapid wing beats; often circles breeding islands.

CATCH AND CARRY
When returning to breeding colonies to feed chicks, most birds carry more than one fish in their bill.

SIMILAR SPECIES

LONG-TAILED DUCK ♂ ☼
see p.68

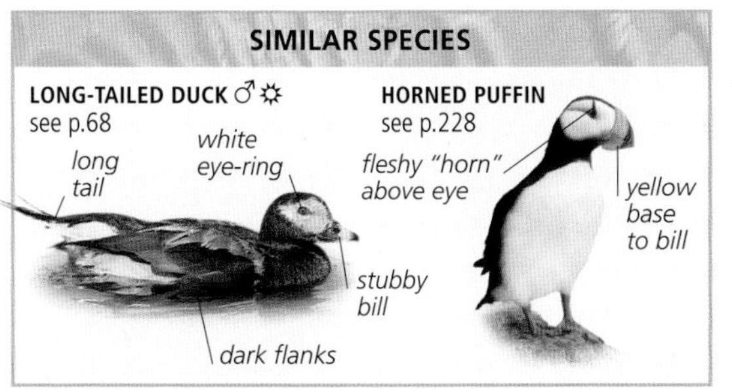
long tail
white eye-ring
stubby bill
dark flanks

HORNED PUFFIN
see p.228

fleshy "horn" above eye
yellow base to bill

OCCURRENCE
This northern North Atlantic seabird (found on both sides of the ocean) breeds in colonies on small, rocky, offshore islands, where it excavates nesting burrows or nests under boulders. Between breeding seasons, it heads for the high seas and remains far offshore, favoring cold, open waters.

Length **12½in (32cm)**	Wingspan **21in (53cm)**	Weight **12oz (350g)**
Social **Colonies**	Lifespan **At least 30 years**	Status **Localized**

Order **Charadriiformes**	Family **Alcidae**	Species ***Fratercula corniculata***

Horned Puffin

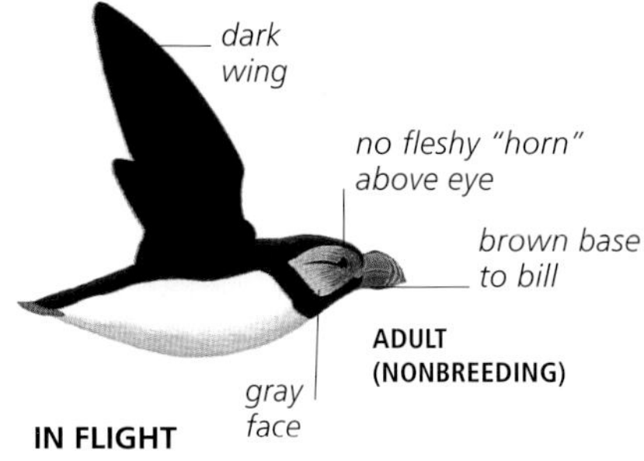
dark wing
no fleshy "horn" above eye
brown base to bill
ADULT (NONBREEDING)
gray face
IN FLIGHT

fleshy "horn" above eye
white face
black neck collar
large, yellow bill, with orange tip
dark upperparts
white underparts
ADULT (BREEDING)
bright orange legs and toes

FLIGHT: swift and direct, with rapid wing beats; usually near the water's surface.

This hardy alcid is similar to the Atlantic Puffin in appearance and behavior, but the Horned Puffin is larger and lives on the other side of North America, in the northern Pacific and Bering Sea. Here it nests on even more remote rocky offshore islands than its Atlantic relative. Outside the breeding season, Horned Puffins spend month after month far out at sea, hundreds of miles from the nearest land. When the birds return to their breeding grounds, pairs often head straight for the same rock crevice they nested in the year before.

VOICE Low-pitched, rumbling growls in rhythmic phrases.

NESTING Deep rock crevices lined with grass and feathers; 1 egg; 1 brood; May–August.

FEEDING Dives for herring, sand lance, capelin, smelt, and other small fishes to feed to chicks; adults consume squid, crustaceans, and marine worms underwater.

SIMILAR SPECIES

LONG-TAILED DUCK ♂ ☼ see p.68

ATLANTIC PUFFIN ♂ ☼ see p.227

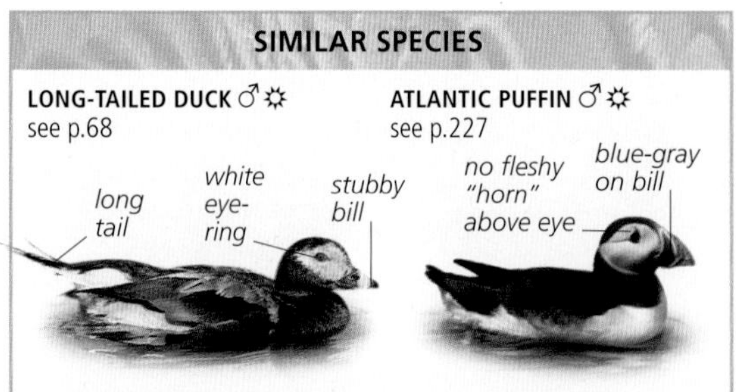
long tail
white eye-ring
stubby bill
no fleshy "horn" above eye
blue-gray on bill

BACK AND FORTH
Parent birds fly repeatedly to and from the nest to catch fish for their chicks.

OCCURRENCE
Breeds on rocky islands off Alaskan and North Pacific coast (where crevices for nesting are plentiful); feeds close to these shores. Often found with Tufted Puffins, but generally farther north. Rarely wanders as far south as California in the nonbreeding season. Winters on ocean waters far from land.

Length **15in (38cm)**	Wingspan **23in (59cm)**	Weight **23oz (650g)**
Social **Colonies**	Lifespan **At least 20 years**	Status **Localized**

Order **Charadriiformes**	Family **Alcidae**	Species ***Fratercula cirrhata***

Tufted Puffin

ADULT (NONBREEDING)
lacks long golden head plumes
dark face
IN FLIGHT
no plumes
yellow bill
ADULT (POSTBREEDING)
large, rounded head
white face
long golden plumes on back of head and nape
orange bill
stocky black body
rounded wings
dark underparts
ADULT (BREEDING)
orange legs and feet

FLIGHT: just above the ocean with strong, rapid wing beats.

Tufted Puffins, found along the northern Pacific coast, may be spotted hopping over rocky ledges, sitting alone on the sea, paddling along the surface before taking off, or flying only a couple of feet above the water. Like other puffin species, they partially open their wings underwater as they pursue prey, keeping their tail and feet spread to aid propulsion and steering. This bird's name arises from the curly golden plumes of feathers that adorn its head during the breeding season. It is the largest of the three puffin species, and can be distinguished from the Horned Puffin by its dark underparts, and from the Atlantic Puffin by its distribution.

VOICE Low, moaning growl given from burrow.

NESTING Chamber, lined with grass or feathers, at end of tunnel, under rocks, or in burrow; 1 egg; 1 brood; May–August.

FEEDING Dives deep to capture small fish, especially sand lance, juvenile pollock, and capelin; adults consume prey underwater, or take it ashore to feed their chicks.

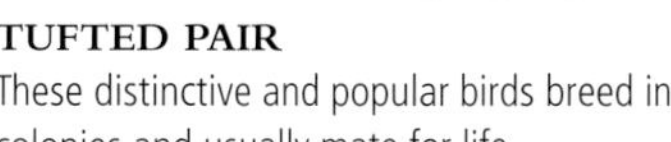

TUFTED PAIR
These distinctive and popular birds breed in colonies and usually mate for life.

SIMILAR SPECIES

RHINOCEROS AUKLET
see p.226 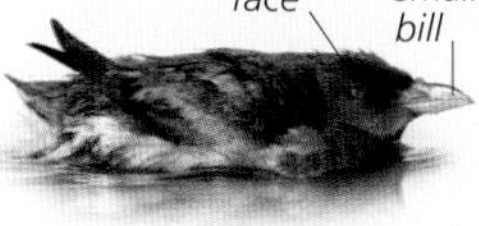
darker face
smaller bill
RHINOCEROS AUKLET
see p.226
slimmer build
no white on face

OCCURRENCE
Breeds on rocky islands, and coastal cliffs of the North Pacific, especially treeless offshore islands with sea cliffs or grassy slopes; elevation may help them take flight. Found over unusually wide geographic and climatic range. Winters at sea, usually over deep waters of the central North Pacific.

Length **15in (38cm)**	Wingspan **25in (64cm)**	Weight **27oz (775g)**
Social **Colonies**	Lifespan **Up to 30 years**	Status **Localized**

Family **Columbidae**

PIGEONS & DOVES

THE LARGER SPECIES WITHIN the family Columbidae are known as pigeons, and the smaller ones as doves, although there is no actual scientific basis for the distinction. They are all fairly heavy, plump birds with relatively small heads and short necks. They also possess slender bills with their nostrils positioned in a bumpy mound at the base. Among other things, members of this family have strong wing muscles, making them powerful and agile fliers. When alarmed, they burst into flight with their wings emitting a distinctive clapping or swishing sound. Pigeons and doves produce a nutritious "crop-milk," which they secrete to feed their young. Despite human activity having severely affected members of this family in the past (the leading cause of the Passenger Pigeon's extinction in the 19th century is thought to be overhunting), the introduced Rock Pigeon has adapted and proliferated worldwide, as has the recently introduced Eurasian Collared-Dove, albeit on a smaller scale. The introduced Spotted Dove has not shown a similar tendency for explosive expansion, however, and remains limited to southern California and the islands of Hawaii. Among the species native to North America, only the elegant Mourning Dove is as widespread as the various species of introduced birds.

NATIVE PIGEON
A native species, the Band-tailed Pigeon is sadly declining through much of its range.

DOVE IN THE SUN
The Mourning Dove sun bathes each side of its body in turn, its wings and tail outspread.

Order **Columbiformes**	Family **Columbidae**	Species ***Columba livia***

Rock Pigeon

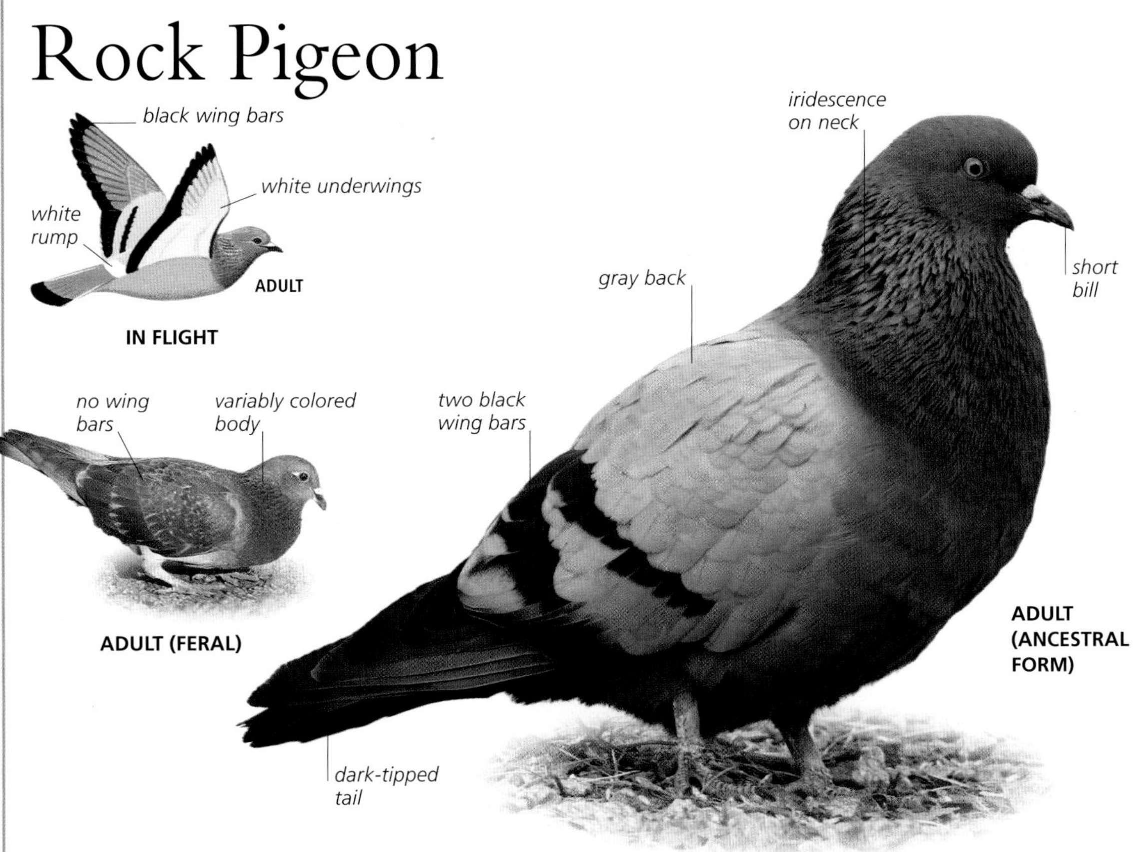
black wing bars
white underwings
white rump
ADULT
IN FLIGHT
no wing bars
variably colored body
ADULT (FERAL)
two black wing bars
gray back
iridescence on neck
short bill
ADULT (ANCESTRAL FORM)
dark-tipped tail

The Rock Pigeon was introduced to the Atlantic coast of North America by 17th century colonists. Now feral, this species is found all over the continent, especially around farms, cities, and towns. This medium-sized pigeon comes in a wide variety of plumage colors and patterns, including bluish gray, checkered, rusty red, and nearly all-white. Its wings usually have two dark bars on them—unique among North American pigeons. The variability of the Rock Pigeon influenced Charles Darwin as he developed his theory of natural selection.

VOICE Soft, gurgling *coo*, *roo-c'too-coo*, for courtship and threat.

NESTING Twig nest on flat, sheltered surface, such as caves, rocky outcrops, and buildings; 2 eggs; several broods; year-round.

FEEDING Eats seeds, fruit, and rarely insects; human foods such as popcorn, bread, peanuts; various farm crops in rural areas.

FLIGHT: strong, direct; can reach speeds up to around 60mph (95kph.)

CITY PIGEONS
Most Rock Pigeons in North America descend from domesticated forms and exhibit many colors.

SIMILAR SPECIES

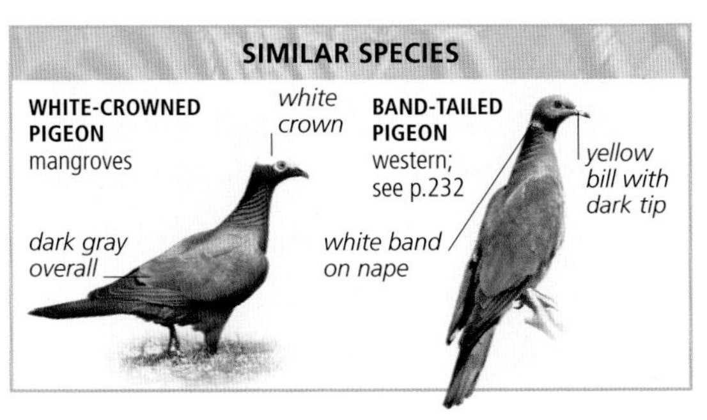
WHITE-CROWNED PIGEON
mangroves
white crown
dark gray overall
BAND-TAILED PIGEON
western;
see p.232
white band on nape
yellow bill with dark tip

OCCURRENCE
Across southern Canada and North America; nests in human structures of all sorts; resident. Original habitat in the Old World was (and still is) sea cliffs and inland canyons; found wild in some places, such as dry regions of North Africa, but feral in much of the world.

Length **11–14in (28–36cm)**	Wingspan **20–26in (51–67cm)**	Weight **9–14oz (250–400g)**
Social **Solitary/Flocks**	Lifespan **Up to 6 years**	Status **Secure**

Order **Columbiformes**	Family **Columbidae**	Species ***Columba fasciata***

Band-tailed Pigeon

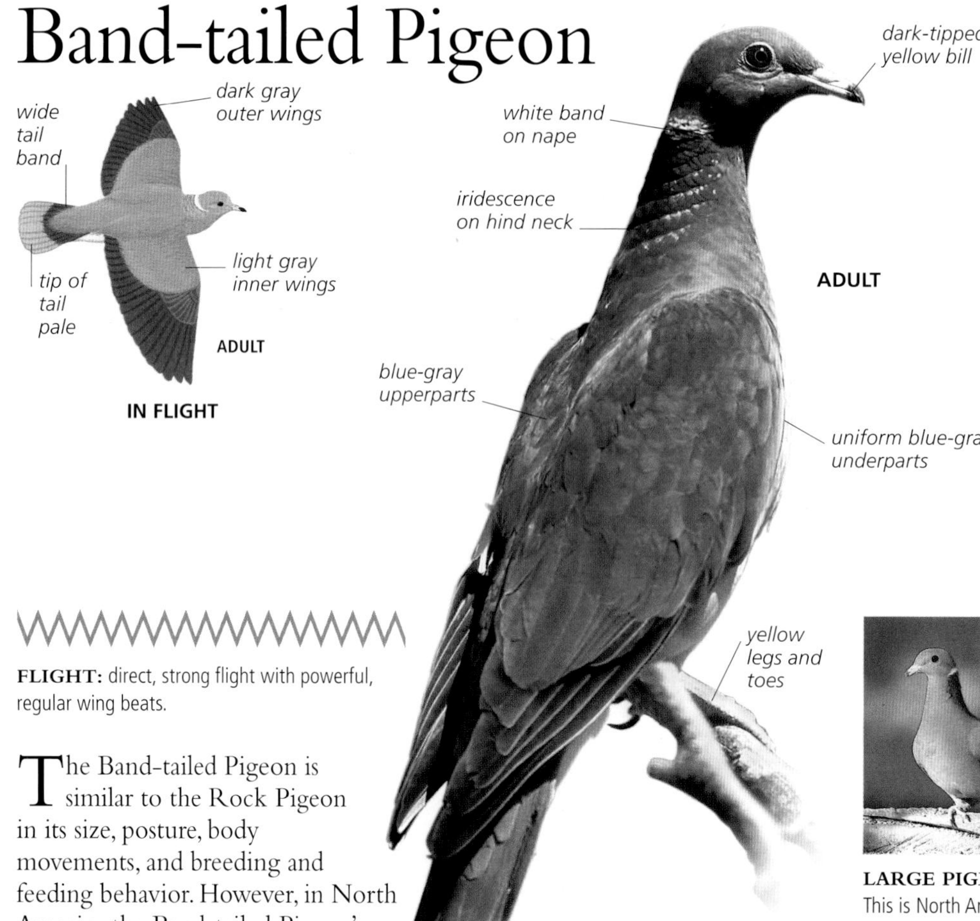
wide tail band
dark gray outer wings
tip of tail pale
light gray inner wings
ADULT
IN FLIGHT
dark-tipped yellow bill
white band on nape
iridescence on hind neck
ADULT
blue-gray upperparts
uniform blue-gray underparts
yellow legs and toes
gray tail

FLIGHT: direct, strong flight with powerful, regular wing beats.

The Band-tailed Pigeon is similar to the Rock Pigeon in its size, posture, body movements, and breeding and feeding behavior. However, in North America the Band-tailed Pigeon's distribution is limited to the dry, mountainous forests of four southwestern states, and the wet coastal forests of the West Coast, from the southeastern tip of Alaska south to Baja California. The distinguishing features of the Band-tailed Pigeon are its yellow bill and legs, a white band just above the iridescent green patch on the back of its neck—and its eponymous banded tail.

VOICE Often silent, but emits series of two-noted, low-frequency *whooos* punctuated with a pause.

NESTING Flat, saucer-shaped, rather flimsy platform of twigs, needles, and moss in a variety of trees; 1 egg; 1 brood; April–October.

FEEDING Forages on the ground for grain, seeds, fruit, acorns, and pine nuts; hangs upside down by its toes from the branches of shrubs and trees to eat dangling nuts and flowers that are otherwise out of reach.

LARGE PIGEON
This is North America's largest pigeon, bigger than the Rock Pigeon by some 10 percent.

UNIFORMITY
Unlike flocks of Rock Pigeons, Band-tailed Pigeon flocks have very uniform plumage.

SIMILAR SPECIES

ROCK PIGEON
see p.231
two wing bars
dark bill

OCCURRENCE
Breeds and winters in temperate conifer rainforest along the Pacific coast, and in mountain conifer and mixed-species forests in the interior. Lives in urban and rural areas where there are evergreen trees and access to grains, fruit, and feeders. Some populations are resident, others migratory.

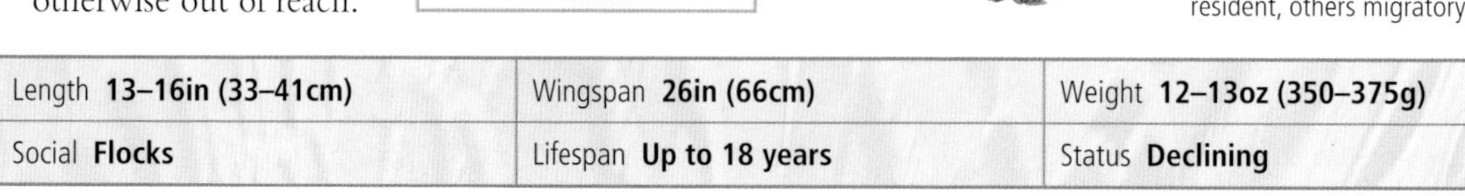

Length **13–16in (33–41cm)**	Wingspan **26in (66cm)**	Weight **12–13oz (350–375g)**
Social **Flocks**	Lifespan **Up to 18 years**	Status **Declining**

Order **Columbiformes**	Family **Columbidae**	Species ***Streptopelia decaocto***

Eurasian Collared-Dove

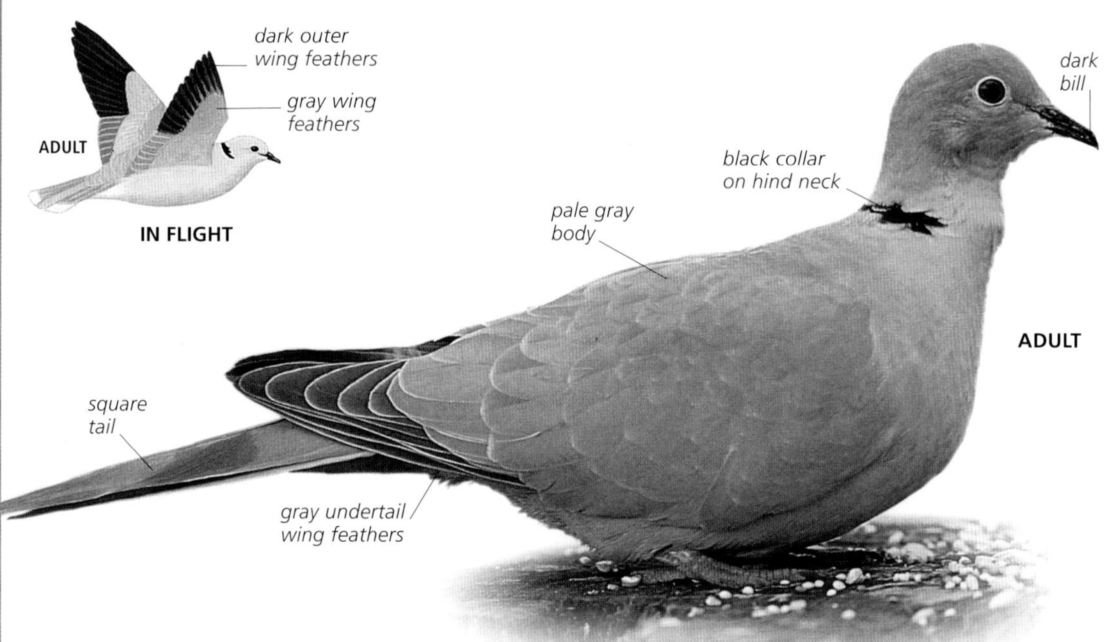
dark outer wing feathers
gray wing feathers
ADULT
IN FLIGHT
dark bill
black collar on hind neck
pale gray body
ADULT
square tail
gray undertail wing feathers

A stocky bird, the Eurasian Collared-Dove is easily recognized by the black collar on the back of its neck and its square tail. First released at New Providence, Bahamas, in the mid-1970s, this species is spreading rapidly across the continental mainland, thanks to multiple local releases, the planting of trees in urban and suburban habitats, the popularity of bird feeders making food readily available, and the bird's extraordinarily high reproductive rate. This species soon becomes very confiding and tolerant of humans, regularly nesting and feeding in urban areas. One consequence of this is that it often falls prey to domestic cats, but this has little effect on the expanding population. Based on sightings from locations all over North America—and on the evidence from Europe, throughout which it has spread since only the 1940s—it is highly likely that the Eurasian Collared-Dove will soon become a common species in North America.

VOICE Repeated four-note *coo-hoo-HOO-cook* that is quick and low-pitched; also harsh, nasal *krreeew* in flight.

NESTING Platform of twigs, stems, and grasses in trees or on buildings; 2 eggs; multiple broods; March–November.

FEEDING Eats seed and grain, plant stems and leaves, berries, and some invertebrates; feeds on the ground for seed, but also visits elevated feeders.

FLIGHT: strong, stiff flight reminiscent of hawks; occasional swoops and dives.

COLLARED COLONIZER
The Eurasian Collared-Dove has spread throughout Europe in just a few decades, and now looks set to do the same in North America.

SIMILAR SPECIES

MOURNING DOVE
see p.234

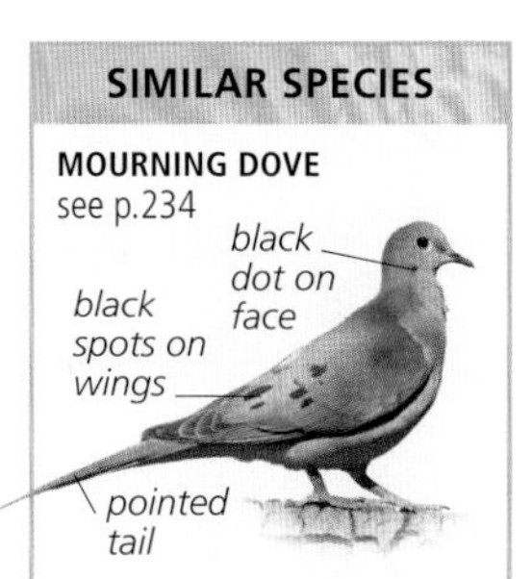
black dot on face
black spots on wings
pointed tail

OCCURRENCE
Can be seen almost anywhere in North America south of the northern forest zone, but occurs mainly in suburban and urban areas (though not large cities) and agricultural areas with seeds and grain for food and deciduous trees for nesting and roosting. May roost in man-made structures such as barns.

Length **11½–12in (29–30cm)**	Wingspan **14in (35cm)**	Weight **5–6oz (150–175g)**
Social **Large flocks**	Lifespan **Up to 13 years**	Status **Localized**

Order **Columbiformes**	Family **Columbidae**	Species ***Zenaida macroura***

Mourning Dove

mostly uniform gray wings
pointed tail
ADULT
IN FLIGHT
faint mottling on neck and underparts
JUVENILE
blue eye-ring
thin, dark bill
black dot on side of face
dark spots on wings
plump, gray body
long, pointed tail
ADULT
pink legs and toes

One of the most familiar, abundant, and widespread of North American birds, the Mourning Dove is a long, plump, medium-sized dove with an undersized head. It has a grayish tan body with a pale, rosy breast and black spots on folded wings. While coveted by hunters—as many as 70 million are shot annually—the Mourning Dove is also well known to those who live on farms and in suburbia. Found all across North America, the species is divided into two subspecies—the larger grayish brown *Z. m. carolinensis*, east of the Mississippi River, and the smaller, paler *Z. m. marginella* in the west.

VOICE Mellow, owl-like call: *hoO-Oo-oo, hoo-hoo-hoo.*

NESTING Flat, flimsy twig platform, mostly in trees, sometimes on the ground; 2 eggs; 2 broods; February–October.

FEEDING Forages mainly for seeds on the ground; obtains food quickly and digests it later at roost.

FLIGHT: swift, direct flight, with fairly quick wing beats; twists and turns sometimes.

SIMILAR SPECIES

EURASIAN COLLARED DOVE see p.233

WHITE-WINGED DOVE ♂ see p.487

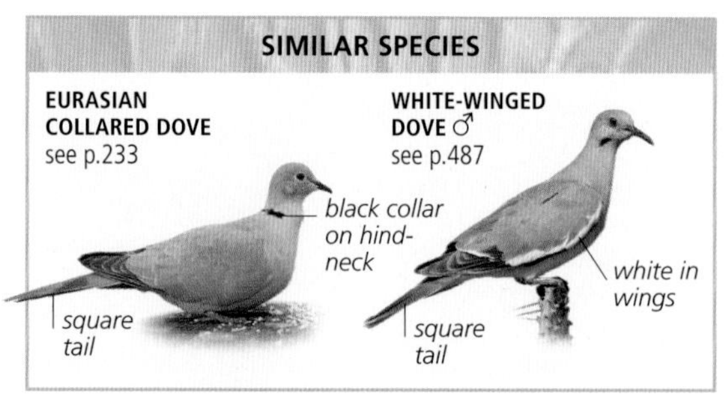
black collar on hind-neck
square tail
white in wings
square tail

FAMILIAR SIGHT The Mourning Dove is North America's most widespread member of this family.

OCCURRENCE Breeds in a wide variety of habitats but shuns extensive forests; human-altered vegetation favored for feeding, including farmland and suburbia. Winters in small to medium sheltered woodland while feeding in grain fields; winters in southern Mexico and Central America.

Length **9–13½in (23–34cm)**	Wingspan **14½–17½in (37–45cm)**	Weight **3–6oz (85–175g)**
Social **Pairs/Winter flocks**	Lifespan **Up to 19 years**	Status **Secure**

CUCKOOS

CUCKOOS ARE NOTORIOUS for laying eggs in other birds' nests, but the two species found in Canada seldom do so. Their close relatives on the continent are the Greater Roadrunner, and two species of Ani. The Groove-billed Ani sometimes shows up in Ontario.

Generally shy and reclusive, the Black-billed Cuckoo and Yellow-billed Cuckoo favor dense, forested habitats. They are more often heard than seen. Both species usually build a nest and raise their own offspring. However, sometimes the Black-billed Cuckoo and the Yellow-billed Cuckoo lay their eggs in other birds' nest, including each other's, and even the nests of their own kind. In flight, cuckoos are often mistaken for small birds of prey. They do sometimes pounce on lizards, frogs, and other small animals—even small birds—but mostly they glean insects from the foliage of trees. Both cuckoos regularly feed on caterpillars; the Black-billed Cuckoo especially relishes tent caterpillars and gypsy moth larvae. The numbers of both species vary from year to year in a given locale in response to prey abundance. Besides their slender bodies and long tails, cuckoos have zygodactyl feet, with the two inner toes pointing forward and the two outer toes pointing backward. Cuckoos in North America are vulnerable to pollutants, and the Yellow-billed Cuckoo is declining rapidly to the point of arousing serious concerns over its future.

STRONG STOMACH
The Black-billed Cuckoo can safely eat caterpillars that are poisonous to other birds.

WEATHER BIRD
Folklore has it that the Yellow-billed Cuckoo, or "Raincrow," calls most on cloudy days.

NIGHT SINGER
During the breeding season, the Black-billed Cuckoo will often call throughout the night.

Order **Cuculiformes**	Family **Cuculidae**	Species ***Coccyzus erythropthalmus***

Black-billed Cuckoo

long tail
small white spots on tips of tail feathers
ADULT
long wings
IN FLIGHT

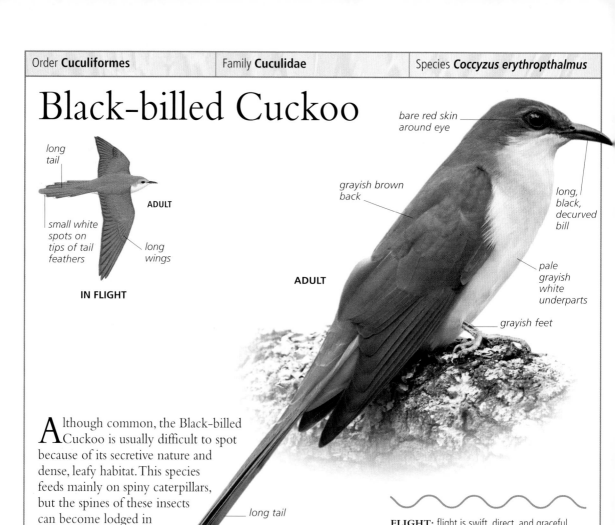

bare red skin around eye
grayish brown back
long, black, decurved bill
ADULT
pale grayish white underparts
grayish feet
long tail

Although common, the Black-billed Cuckoo is usually difficult to spot because of its secretive nature and dense, leafy habitat. This species feeds mainly on spiny caterpillars, but the spines of these insects can become lodged in the cuckoo's stomach, obstructing digestion, so the bird periodically empties its stomach to clear any such blockage. The decline of this species is probably an indirect result of the chemical control of caterpillar outbreaks in forests throughout their range. During the breeding season, the birds call throughout the night, which leads some to believe erroneously that the cuckoo is nocturnal.

VOICE Series of 2–5 repeatedly whistled notes, *coo-coo-coo-coo*, with short breaks between series.

NESTING Shallow cup of sticks lined with moss, leaves, grass, and feathers; 2–4 eggs; 1 brood; May–July.

FEEDING Almost exclusively eats caterpillars, especially tent caterpillars and gypsy moths.

FLIGHT: flight is swift, direct, and graceful, with long, smooth wing beats.

SEARCHING FOR FOOD
These cuckoos spend a lot of their time in trees as they search for their favorite hairy caterpillars.

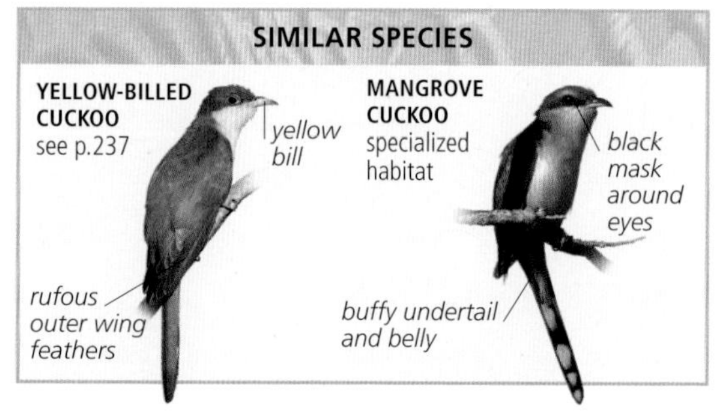
SIMILAR SPECIES
YELLOW-BILLED CUCKOO
see p.237
yellow bill
rufous outer wing feathers
MANGROVE CUCKOO
specialized habitat
black mask around eyes
buffy undertail and belly

OCCURRENCE
Widespread northern and eastern North American species, lives in thickly wooded areas close to water, but can also be found in brushy forest edges and evergreen woods. Winters in South America in evergreen woodlands, scrub, and humid forests.

Length **11–12in (28–31cm)**	Wingspan **16–19in (41–48cm)**	Weight **1 9/16–2oz (45–55g)**
Social **Solitary**	Lifespan **Up to 5 years**	Status **Secure (p)**

Order **Cuculiformes**	Family **Cuculidae**	Species ***Coccyzus americanus***

Yellow-billed Cuckoo

ADULT

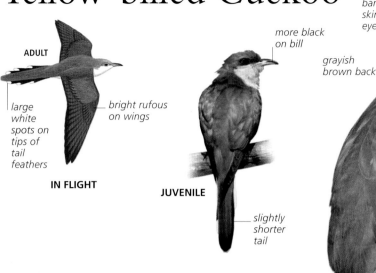

large white spots on tips of tail feathers

bright rufous on wings

IN FLIGHT

more black on bill

JUVENILE

slightly shorter tail

bare yellow skin around eye

grayish brown back

mostly yellow bill

ADULT

rufous outer wing feathers

long tail

FLIGHT: flight is swift using long strokes to maintain level pattern.

The Yellow-billed Cuckoo is a shy, slow-moving bird, with a reputation for fairly odd behaviors, including its habit of calling more often on cloudy days. This tendency has earned it the nickname "rain crow" in some areas. In addition to raising young in its own nest, females often lay eggs in the nests of more than a dozen other species, especially during years with abundant food. The host species may be chosen on the basis of how closely the color of its eggs matches those of the cuckoo's. This brood parasitism is the rule in the Yellow-billed Cuckoo, which is an Old World species, and occurs in North America as a widespread vagrant.

VOICE Call a series of 10–12 low notes that slow down as it progresses, *ca ca ca ca coo coo coo cowl cowl cowl.*

NESTING Flimsy oval-shaped platform of small sticks and branches, often lined with leaves and strips of plants; 2–4 eggs; 1–2 broods; May–August.

FEEDING Mostly consumes insects such as grasshoppers, crickets, katydids, and caterpillars of several moth species; also eats seeds.

RARE SIGHT

Given the habitat they prefer and their skittish nature, a clear view of a Yellow-billed Cuckoo is rare.

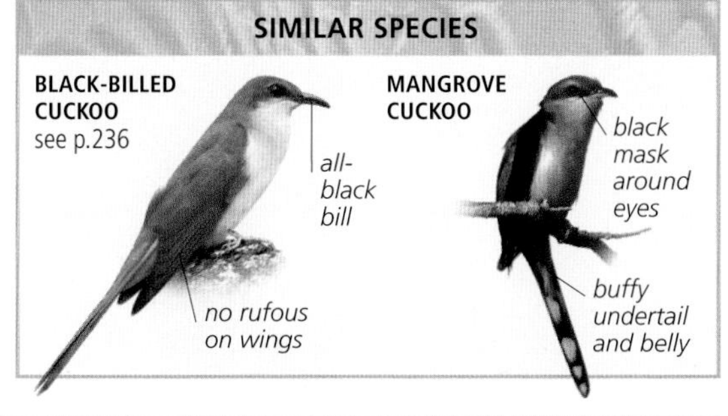
SIMILAR SPECIES
BLACK-BILLED CUCKOO
see p.236
all-black bill
no rufous on wings
MANGROVE CUCKOO
black mask around eyes
buffy undertail and belly

OCCURRENCE

Has a wide range in the US; extends into southeastern Canada. Found primarily in open forests with a mix of openings and thick understory cover, especially those near water. Winters in similar habitats in Central and South America.

Length **10–12in (26–30cm)**	Wingspan **17–20in (43–51cm)**	Weight **2–2¼oz (55–65g)**
Social **Small winter flocks**	Lifespan **Up to 4 years**	Status **Secure (p)**

Family **Tytonidae, Strigidae**

OWLS

PARTLY BECAUSE OF THEIR nocturnal habits and eerie cries, owls have fascinated humans throughout history. They are placed in the order Strigiformes, and two families are represented in North America: the Barn Owl is classified in Tytonidae, while the rest of the owl species are the Strigidae. Most owls are active primarily at night and have developed adaptations for living in low-light environments. Their large eyes are sensitive enough to see in the dark and face forward to maximize binocular vision. Since the eyes are fixed in their sockets, a flexible neck helps owls turn the head almost 180° toward a direction of interest. Ears are offset on each side of the head to help identify the source of a sound; "ear tufts" on some species, however, are for visual effect and unrelated to hearing. Many owls have serrations on the forward edges of their flight feathers to cushion airflow, so their flight is silent while stalking prey. All North American owls are predatory to some degree and they inhabit most areas of the continent. The Burrowing Owl is unique in that it hunts during the day and nests underground.

OWL IN DAYLIGHT
The habits of the Barn Owl remain secretive, because it is not often seen in daylight.

BIG HORNS
The "ear" tufts of the Great Horned Owl are taller than those of other "tufted" owls.

SNOW SWOOP
The Great Gray Owl can hunt by sound alone, allowing it to locate and capture prey hidden even beneath a thick snow cover.

Order **Strigiformes**	Family **Tytonidae**	Species ***Tyto alba***

Barn Owl

barring on wings and tail

ADULT

IN FLIGHT

head lacks "ear" tufts

long wings

ADULT

relatively small eyes

rounded, heart-shaped facial disc

pale buff upperparts

white underparts

gray and black spots

feathered legs

dark eyes

ruff surrounds facial disk

ADULT

FLIGHT: irregular bursts of flapping, interspersed with short glides, banking, doubling back, fluttering.

Aptly named, the Barn Owl inhabits old sheds, sheltered rafters, and empty buildings in rural fields. With its affinity for human settlement, and 32 subspecies, this owl has an extensive range covering every continent except Antarctica. Although widespread, the Barn Owl is secretive. Primarily nocturnal, it can fly undetected until its screeching call pierces the air. The Barn Owl is endangered in several Midwestern states due to modern farming practices, which have decimated prey populations and reduced the number of barns for nesting.

VOICE Typical call loud, raspy, screeching shriek, *shkreee,* often given in flight; also clicking sounds associated with courtship.

NESTING Unlined cavity in tree, cave, building, hay bale, or nest box; 5–7 eggs; 1–2 broods; March–September.

FEEDING Hunts on the wing for small rodents such as mice; research reveals it can detect the slightest rustle made by prey even in total darkness.

NOCTURNAL HUNTER
The Barn Owl hunts at night for small rodents, but may be seen before sunset feeding its young.

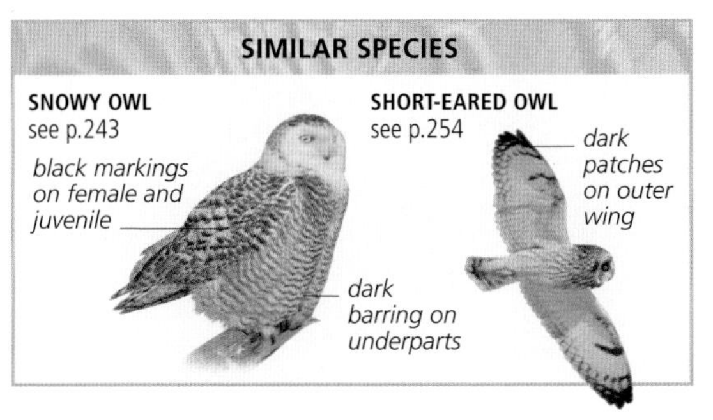
SIMILAR SPECIES
SNOWY OWL
see p.243
black markings on female and juvenile
dark barring on underparts
SHORT-EARED OWL
see p.254
dark patches on outer wing

OCCURRENCE
In North America breeds from northwestern and northeastern US south to Mexico. Small Canadian range in southern Ontario and British Columbia. Resident in all except very north of range. Prefers open habitats, such as desert, grassland, and fields, wherever prey and suitable nest sites are available.

Length **12½–15½in (32–40cm)**	Wingspan **3ft 3in (100cm)**	Weight **14–25oz (400–700g)**
Social **Solitary**	Lifespan **Up to 8 years**	Status **Declining**

Order **Strigiformes**	Family **Strigidae**	Species ***Otus flammeolus***

Flammulated Owl

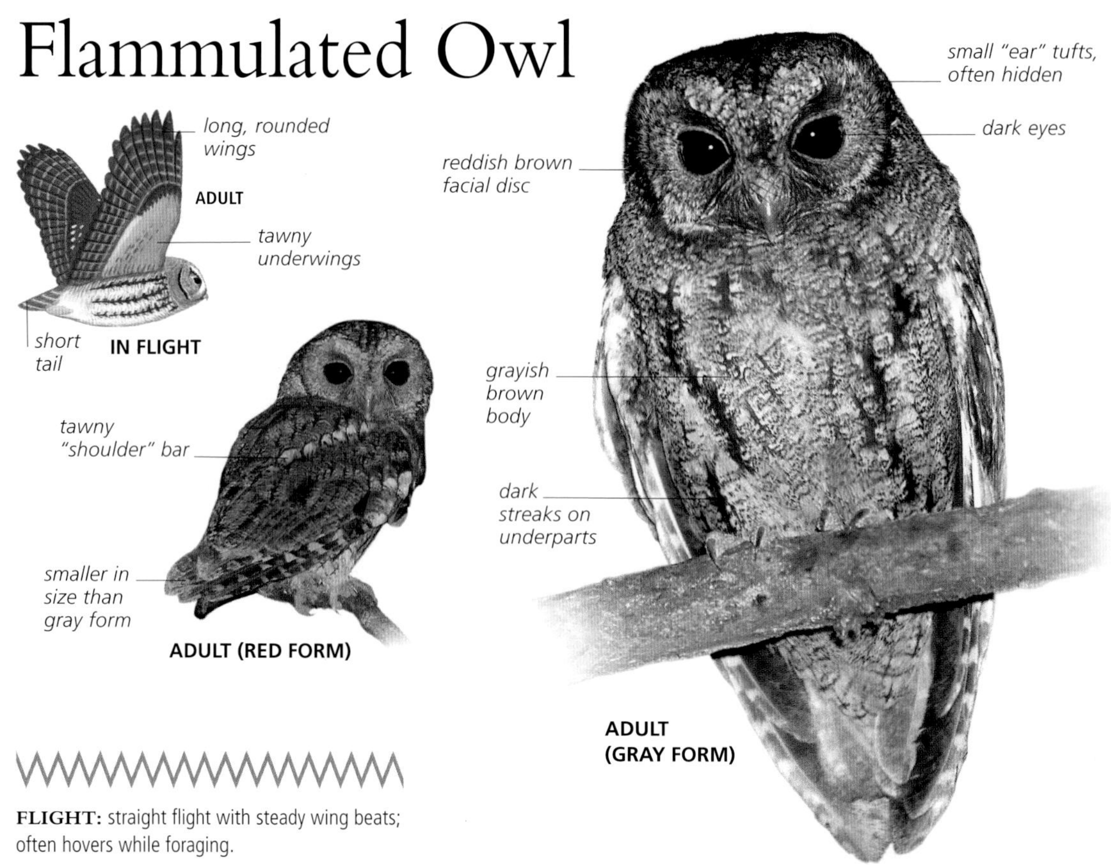
long, rounded wings
ADULT
tawny underwings
short tail
IN FLIGHT
tawny "shoulder" bar
smaller in size than gray form
ADULT (RED FORM)
small "ear" tufts, often hidden
dark eyes
reddish brown facial disc
grayish brown body
dark streaks on underparts
ADULT (GRAY FORM)

FLIGHT: straight flight with steady wing beats; often hovers while foraging.

The tiny Flammulated Owl nests in dry mountain pine forests from British Columbia to Mexico, moving south to Central America for the winter months. Its dark, watery-looking eyes distinguish it from other species of small North American owls. Entirely nocturnal, it is heard more often than seen. When the Flammulated Owl is visible, its trademark reddish brown plumage blends quite well with the color of pine tree bark. This species appears to breed in loose colonies, although this may reflect patchiness in habitat quality. Like some other owls, it has a "red" and "gray" form.

VOICE Series of soft low-frequency toots, often difficult to locate, can continue for hours; barks and screams when disturbed at nest site.

NESTING Cavity in tree, woodpecker hole, nest box; 3–4 eggs; 1–2 broods; May–August.

FEEDING Hunts from stationary perch, from which it flies to capture insects—mostly moths, and beetles—from branches, foliage, or ground.

BLENDING IN
If this owl peeks out of a tree-hole, its plumage blends in remarkably well with the bark.

SIMILAR SPECIES

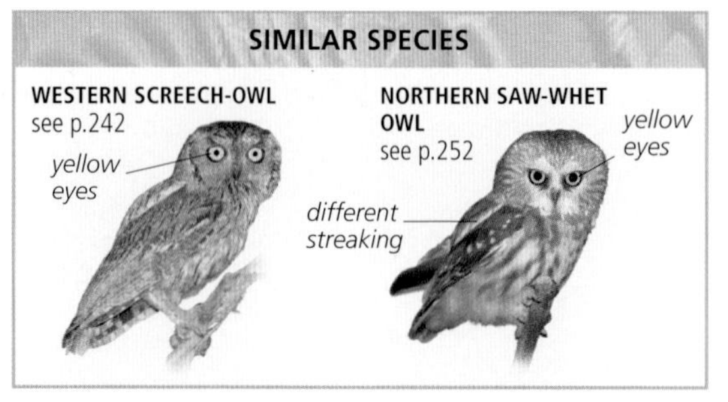
WESTERN SCREECH-OWL
see p.242
yellow eyes
NORTHERN SAW-WHET OWL
see p.252
yellow eyes
different streaking

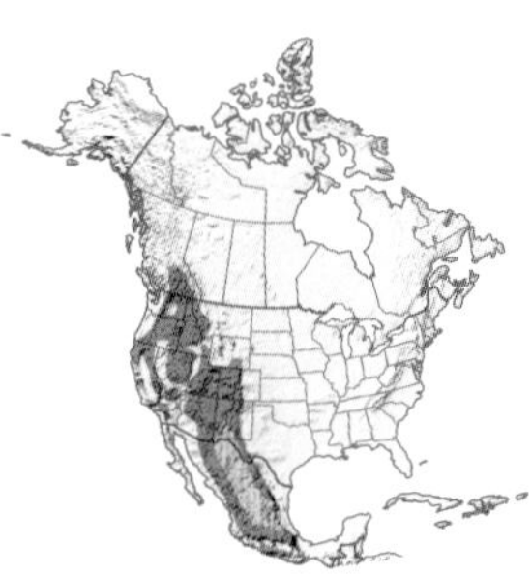

OCCURRENCE
Breeds in semiarid mountain forests, especially Ponderosa and Yellow Pine, open wooded areas at middle elevations with scattered clearings, older trees, and groves of saplings. Winters in habitat similar to breeding season, primarily in southern Mexico, Guatemala, and El Salvador.

Length **6–6¾in (15–17cm)**	Wingspan **16in (41cm)**	Weight **1⁹⁄₁₆–2¼oz (45–65g)**
Social **Solitary**	Lifespan **Up to 8 years**	Status **Secure**

Order **Strigiformes**	Family **Strigidae**	Species ***Megascops asio***

Eastern Screech-Owl

dark gray bars on short, rounded wings

ADULT

streaked underparts

short tail

IN FLIGHT

"ear" tufts

yellow eyes

white spots on inner wing feathers

ADULT (GRAY FORM)

feathered legs

FLIGHT: direct, purposeful flight; straight with steady wing beats, typically below tree cover.

This widespread little owl has adapted to suburban areas, and its distinctive call is a familiar sound across the eastern US and southern Canada at almost any time of the year. Although it is an entirely nocturnal species, it may be found roosting during the day in a birdhouse or tree cavity. With gray and red color forms, this species shows more plumage variation than the Western Screech-Owl. The relatively high mortality rate of Eastern Screech-Owls, especially juveniles, is caused in part by predation by Great Horned Owls and collisions with motor vehicles.

VOICE Most familiar call a descending whinny and often used in movie soundtracks; also an even trill; occasional barks and screeches; female higher-pitched than male.

NESTING No nest; lays eggs in cavity in tree, woodpecker hole, rotted snag, nest box; 2–6 eggs; 1 brood; March–August.

FEEDING Captures prey with toes; eats insects, earthworms, rodents, songbirds, crayfish, small fish, tadpoles, snakes, and lizards.

STANDING OUT
The striking red color form of the Eastern Screech-Owl is less common than the gray.

SIMILAR SPECIES

BOREAL OWL see p.251
no ear tufts
brown back
white spots

NORTHERN SAW-WHET OWL see p.252
long brown streaks

OCCURRENCE
In the US and south Canada, breeds in a variety of different lowland wooded areas east of the Rockies. Also breeds south to northeast Mexico. Can be found in suburban and urban parks and gardens; usually avoids mountain forests.

Length **6½–10in (16–25cm)**	Wingspan **19–24in (48–61cm)**	Weight **5–7oz (150–200g)**
Social **Solitary**	Lifespan **Up to 13 years**	Status **Secure**

Order **Strigiformes**	Family **Strigidae**	Species ***Megascops kennicottii***

Western Screech-Owl

dark gray bars on rounded wings

ADULT

short tail

IN FLIGHT

yellow eyes

small "ear" tufts

gray to brown upperparts

heavily streaked underparts

ADULT

feathered legs and feet

The Western Screech-Owl is tolerant of human presence, and lives in a wide variety of wooded areas, including suburban habitats. Because of its nocturnal habits, the Western Screech-Owl is heard more often than it is seen; its "bouncing ball" call, sometimes repeated for hours, is a familiar sound in much of western North America. This species exhibits significant differences in plumage color, and size, depending on its geographical location.

VOICE Series of toots accelerating and descending in pitch; also occasional trills, barks, chirps; female higher-pitched.

NESTING Hole in a tree, nest box, woodpecker cavity; 2–5 eggs; 1 brood; March–July.

FEEDING Sits quietly under canopy waiting to spot small prey below, then pounces; eats small birds and mammals, insects, crayfish, and worms.

FLIGHT: straight, steady flight, seldom over long distances; rarely hovers or glides.

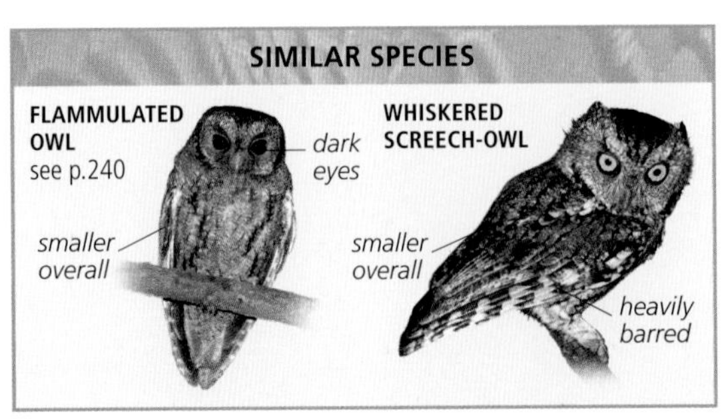
SIMILAR SPECIES
FLAMMULATED OWL
see p.240
dark eyes
smaller overall
WHISKERED SCREECH-OWL
smaller overall
heavily barred

GOOD CAMOUFLAGE
This roosting Western Screech-Owl blends in perfectly with the bark color of a tree.

OCCURRENCE
Breeds from British Columbia southward to Baja California and continental Mexico. Favors riverside and mixed deciduous woodlands, but uses many types of woodlands, parks, and gardens in residential areas; most common at lower elevations. Nonmigratory.

Length **7½–10in (19–25cm)**	Wingspan **21–22in (53–56cm)**	Weight **3½–11oz (100–300g)**
Social **Family groups**	Lifespan **Up to 13 years**	Status **Secure**

Order **Strigiformes**	Family **Strigidae**	Species ***Bubo scandiacus***

Snowy Owl

IMMATURE
IN FLIGHT
variably barred underparts
JUVENILE
flecked gray-brown
white face
dusky barring
variable barring on wings
large round head
yellow eyes
nearly all-white breast
feathered legs
ADULT

FLIGHT: slow, steady flight with strong, deep wing beats; flaps interspersed with glides.

An icon of the far north, the Snowy Owl is a bird of the open tundra, where it hunts from headlands or hummocks and nests on the ground. In such a harsh environment, the Snowy Owl largely depends on lemmings for prey. It is fiercely territorial, and will valiantly defend its young in the nest even against larger animals, such as the Arctic Fox. The Snowy Owl is the provincial bird of Quebec.

VOICE Deep hoots, doubled or given in a short series, usually by male; also rattles, whistles, and hisses.

NESTING Scrape in ground vegetation or dirt, with no lining; 3–12 eggs; 1 brood; May–September.

FEEDING Mostly hunts lemmings, but takes whatever other small mammals, birds, and occasionally fish, it can find.

SNOWY MALE
Some adult males display no barring at all and have entirely pure white plumage.

SIMILAR SPECIES
BARN OWL
see p.239
black eyes
golden brown
SHORT-EARED OWL
see p.254
mottled brown markings
larger overall

OCCURRENCE
Breeds in the tundra of Eurasia and northern North America, north to Ellesmere Island; North American birds winter south to the Great Plains. In some years, many North American birds winter south of their normal range, including in dunes, marshes, and airfields, as far south as Idaho and New Jersey.

Length **20–27in (51–68cm)**	Wingspan **4¼–5¼ft 1.3–1.6m)**	Weight **3½–6½lb (1.6–2.9kg)**
Social **Solitary**	Lifespan **Up to 9 years**	Status **Vulnerable**

Order **Strigiformes**	Family **Strigidae**	Species ***Bubo virginianus***

Great Horned Owl

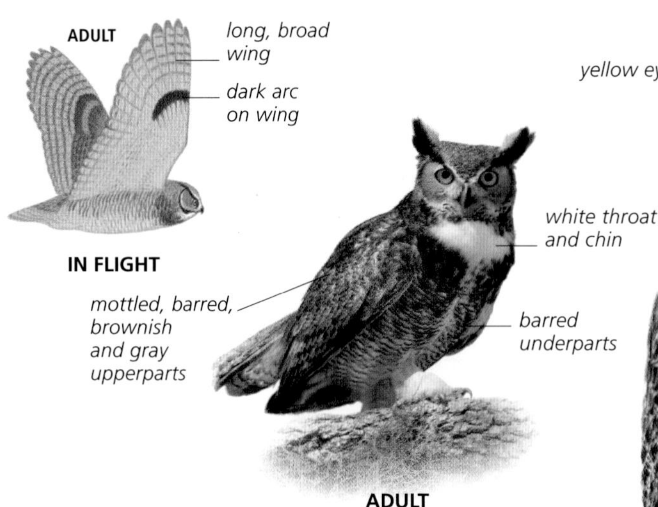
ADULT
long, broad wing
dark arc on wing
IN FLIGHT
white throat and chin
mottled, barred, brownish and gray upperparts
barred underparts
ADULT

large "ears"
yellow eye
rusty facial disk
ADULT
heavy barring of underparts
barring on undertail

FLIGHT: fairly slow with heavy wing beats alternating with short glides; swoops when hunting.

The Great Horned Owl is perhaps the archetypal owl. Large and adaptable, it is resident from Alaska to Tierra del Fuego and is the provincial bird of Alberta. With such a big range, geographical variation occurs; at least 13 subspecies have been described. The southernmost populations—*B. v. magellanicus*, from Peru to Patagonia—are often considered a distinct species. The Great Horned Owl's deep hoots are easily recognized, and can often be heard in movie soundtracks. The bird is the top predator in its food chain, often killing and eating other owls, and even skunks. An early breeder, it starts hooting in the middle of winter, and often lays its eggs in January.

VOICE Series of hoots *whoo-hoo-oo-o*; also screams, barks, and hisses; female higher-pitched.

NESTING Old stick nest, in tree, exposed cavity, cliff, human structure, or on the ground; 1–5 eggs; 1 brood; January–April.

FEEDING Hunts mammals, reptiles, amphibians, birds, and insects; mostly nocturnal.

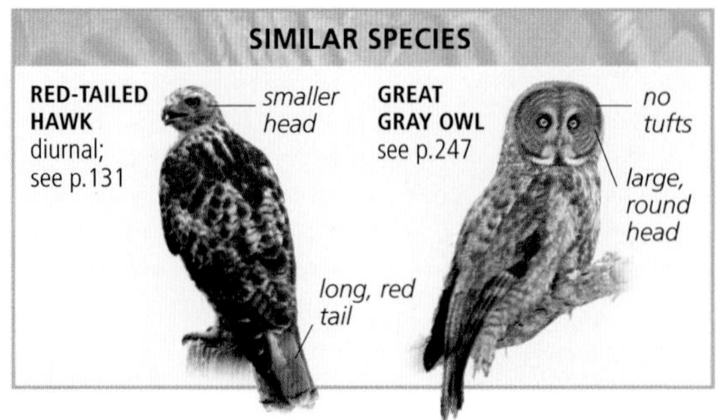
SIMILAR SPECIES
RED-TAILED HAWK
diurnal;
see p.131
smaller head
long, red tail
GREAT GRAY OWL
see p.247
no tufts
large, round head

RECYCLING
The Great Horned Owl breeds in old stick nests constructed by other large birds, like crows.

OCCURRENCE
In North America, found in nearly every type of habitat, except Arctic tundra. Prefers fragmented landscapes: desert, swamp, prairie, woodland, and urban areas. Rare only in the Appalachian Mountains in the East and in the Sonoran and Mohave Deserts in the West.

Length **18–25in (46–63cm)**	Wingspan **3–5ft (0.9–1.6m)**	Weight **1⅞–5½lb (0.9–2.5kg)**
Social **Solitary**	Lifespan **Up to 28 years**	Status **Secure**

Order **Strigiformes**	Family **Strigidae**	Species ***Strix occidentalis***

Spotted Owl

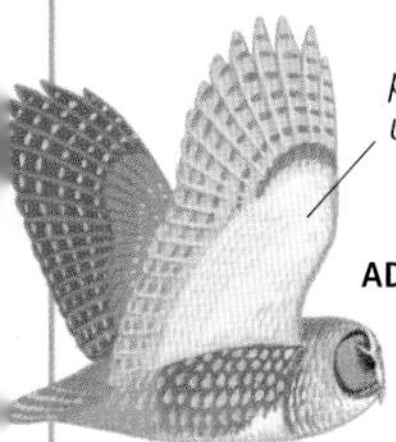

large, puffy head, without ear tufts

down feathers around head

dark eye

pale underwings

ADULT

IN FLIGHT

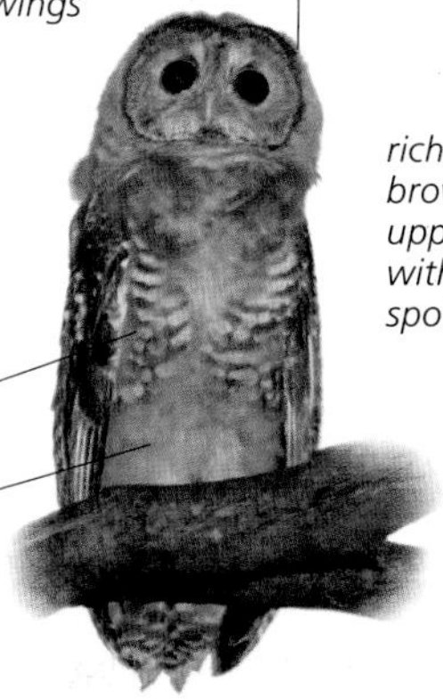

pale bill

rich, dark brown upperparts with white spots

barred flanks

rusty belly

JUVENILE (SOUTHWEST US, CENTRAL MEXICO)

pale oval bars on underparts

ADULT (NORTHWEST US, CANADA)

FLIGHT: short flights; quick flaps interspersed with short glides; heavier flaps when flying upward.

Threatened by competition from expanding Barred Owl populations, and especially habitat loss by clearcutting of old-growth forests, the Spotted Owl has entered the political arena and is a topic of hot debate between conservationists and forest managers. As a result, the Spotted Owl has been the subject of intensive research. It has been divided into four subspecies: *S. o. caurina*, in British Columbia, the Pacific Northwest, and northern California; *S. o. occidentalis*, in southern California; *S. o. lucida*, in the Rocky Mountains south to Mexico; and *S. o. juanaphillipsae*, locally in central Mexico. *S. o. occidentalis* and *S. o. lucida* may form two species of Spotted Owl. To complcate matters, Spotted and Barred Owls interbreed, producing hybrids.

VOICE Typical call of four notes, *whoo hoo-hoo hooo*, with emphasis on the last syllable; also whistles and barks.

NESTING No nest; lays eggs in broken-off snags, cavities, and platforms, occasionally cliffs; 1–4 eggs; 1 brood; March–July.

FEEDING Sits, waits and pounces on prey; eats small rodents.

FLUFFY FLEDGLINGS
Juveniles can be recognized by lingering down feathers, especially around the head.

SIMILAR SPECIES
GREAT HORNED OWL
see p.244
tufts
yellow eyes
larger overall
BARRED OWL
see p.246
streaked underparts

OCCURRENCE
In two or three geographically separated populations, lives in old-growth and mature stands of fir, hemlock, redwood, pine, cedar, oak, and mixed riverside woodlands. Occasionally seen elsewhere, but breeding only occurs in forested areas.

Length **18–19in (46–48cm)**	Wingspan **3½ft (1.1m)**	Weight **17–28oz (475–800g)**
Social **Solitary**	Lifespan **Up to 17 years**	Status **Declining**

Order **Strigiformes**	Family **Strigidae**	Species ***Strix varia***

Barred Owl

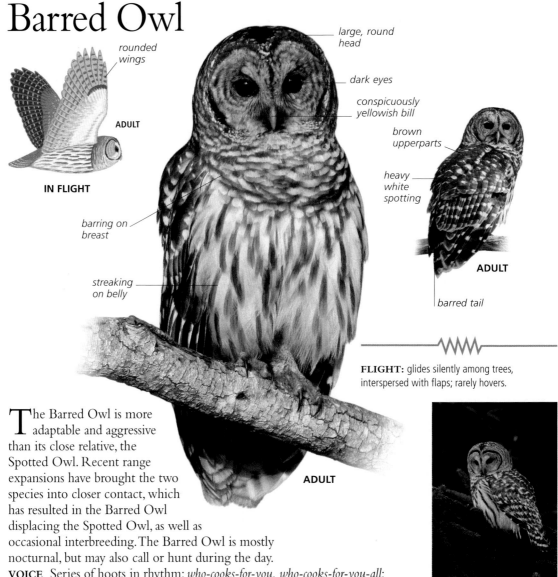

rounded wings

ADULT

IN FLIGHT

large, round head

dark eyes

conspicuously yellowish bill

barring on breast

streaking on belly

ADULT

brown upperparts

heavy white spotting

ADULT

barred tail

FLIGHT: glides silently among trees, interspersed with flaps; rarely hovers.

The Barred Owl is more adaptable and aggressive than its close relative, the Spotted Owl. Recent range expansions have brought the two species into closer contact, which has resulted in the Barred Owl displacing the Spotted Owl, as well as occasional interbreeding. The Barred Owl is mostly nocturnal, but may also call or hunt during the day.

VOICE Series of hoots in rhythm: *who-cooks-for-you, who-cooks-for-you-all*; also pair duetting (at different pitches), cawing, cackling, and guttural sounds.

NESTING No nest; lays eggs in broken-off branches, cavities, old stick nests; 1–5 eggs; 1 brood; January–September.

FEEDING Perches quietly and waits to spot prey below, then pounces; eats small mammals, birds, amphibians, reptiles, insects, and spiders.

WOODED HABITATS
The Barred Owl is very much at home in deep woodlands, including conifer forests.

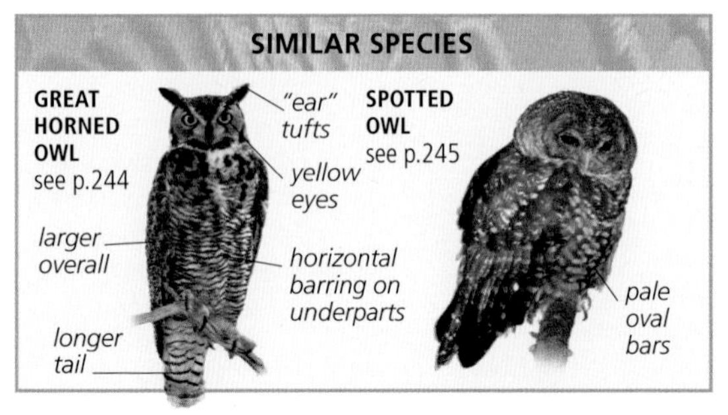
SIMILAR SPECIES
GREAT HORNED OWL
see p.244
"ear" tufts
yellow eyes
larger overall
horizontal barring on underparts
longer tail
SPOTTED OWL
see p.245
pale oval bars

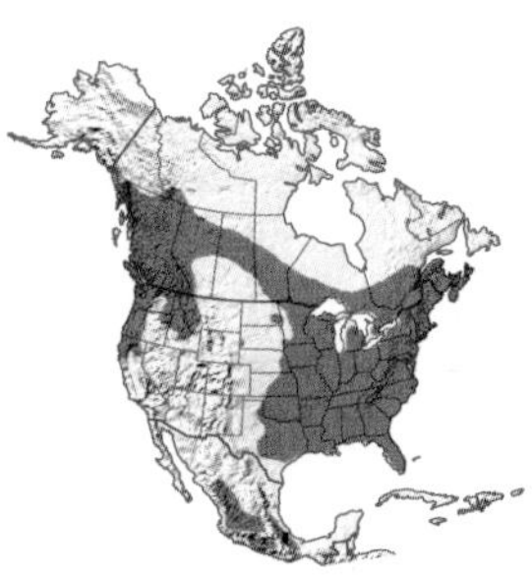

OCCURRENCE
Widespread, though not evenly so, across North America from British Columbia across to the Maritimes and much of the eastern US. Found in a variety of wooded habitats—from cypress swamps in the south to conifer rainforest in the northwest—and in mixed hardwoods.

Length **17–19½in (43–50cm)**	Wingspan **3½ft (1.1m)**	Weight **17–37oz (475–1,050g)**
Social **Solitary**	Lifespan **Up to 18 years**	Status **Secure**

Order **Strigiformes**	Family **Strigidae**	Species ***Strix nebulosa***

Great Gray Owl

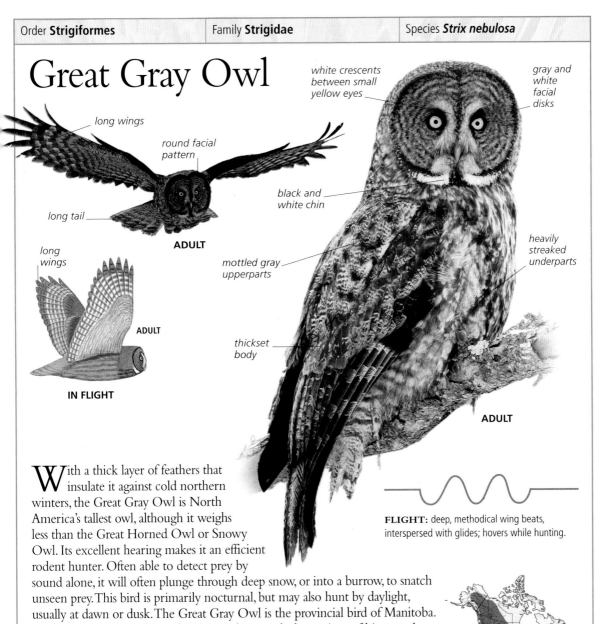

long wings
round facial pattern
long tail
ADULT
long wings
ADULT
IN FLIGHT
white crescents between small yellow eyes
gray and white facial disks
black and white chin
mottled gray upperparts
heavily streaked underparts
thickset body
ADULT

With a thick layer of feathers that insulate it against cold northern winters, the Great Gray Owl is North America's tallest owl, although it weighs less than the Great Horned Owl or Snowy Owl. Its excellent hearing makes it an efficient rodent hunter. Often able to detect prey by sound alone, it will often plunge through deep snow, or into a burrow, to snatch unseen prey. This bird is primarily nocturnal, but may also hunt by daylight, usually at dawn or dusk. The Great Gray Owl is the provincial bird of Manitoba.

VOICE Slow series of deep hoots, evenly spaced; also variety of hisses and chattering noises around nest site.

NESTING Reuses old eagle or hawk nests, broken-off trees; 2–5 eggs; 1 brood; March–July.

FEEDING Eats rodents and other small mammals; waits to pounce from perch or hunts in flight.

FLIGHT: deep, methodical wing beats, interspersed with glides; hovers while hunting.

SIMILAR SPECIES
GREAT HORNED OWL
see p.244
"ear" tufts
barring on belly
BARRED OWL
see p.246
dark eyes
barring on breast

MAKESHIFT NEST
The Great Gray Owl often utilizes hollow snags as nesting sites, besides reusing deserted nests.

OCCURRENCE
In North America, resident across northern forests from Alaska to Quebec, south to Montana and Wyoming. Also resident in Eurasia from Scandinavia to the Russian Far East. Found in taiga, and muskeg (peat bogs), in fir, spruce, and pine forests.

Length **24–33in (61–84cm)**	Wingspan **4½ft (1.4m)**	Weight **1½–3¾lb (0.7–1.7kg)**
Social **Solitary**	Lifespan **Up to 14 years**	Status **Secure**

Order **Strigiformes**	Family **Strigidae**	Species ***Surnia ulula***

Northern Hawk Owl

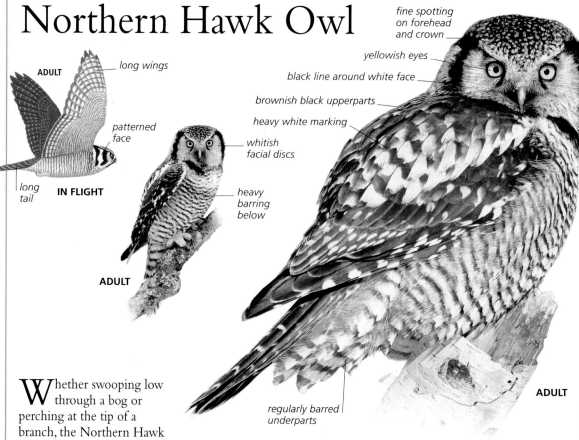

fine spotting on forehead and crown

yellowish eyes

black line around white face

brownish black upperparts

heavy white marking

ADULT

long wings

patterned face

long tail

IN FLIGHT

whitish facial discs

heavy barring below

ADULT

regularly barred underparts

ADULT

Whether swooping low through a bog or perching at the tip of a branch, the Northern Hawk Owl is as falcon-like as it is owl-like, being streamlined, a powerful flier, and an active daytime hunter. It is patchily distributed across the northern North American forests, far from most human settlements, so is seldom seen—and is not well studied—on its breeding grounds. In winter, though, the bird is somewhat nomadic, and is occasionally seen south of its breeding range for a few days or weeks in southern Canada and the northern US.

VOICE Ascending, whistled, drawn-out trill; also chirps, screeches, and yelps.

NESTING Cavities, hollows, broken-off branches, old stick nests, nest boxes; 3–13 eggs; 1 brood; April–August.

FEEDING Swoops like a falcon, from an elevated perch, to pounce on prey; preys mainly on rodents in summer, and on grouse, ptarmigan, and other birds in summer.

FLIGHT: powerful, deep wing beats; glides; highly maneuverable, occasionally soars.

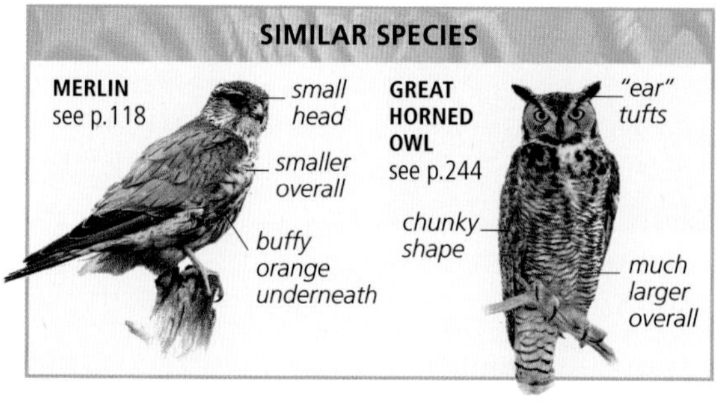
SIMILAR SPECIES
MERLIN
see p.118
small head
smaller overall
buffy orange underneath
GREAT HORNED OWL
see p.244
"ear" tufts
chunky shape
much larger overall

KEEN-EYED OWL
The Northern Owl hunts mainly by sight, swooping on prey spotted from a high perch.

OCCURRENCE
Breeds across the forests of northern Canada, from Alaska to Québec and Newfoundland, in sparse woodland or mixed conifer forest with swamps, bogs, burnt areas, or storm damage. In winter occasionally moves south to southern Canada, Great Lakes region and New England.

Length **14–17½in (36–44cm)**	Wingspan **31in (80cm)**	Weight **11–12oz (300–350g)**
Social **Family groups**	Lifespan **Up to 10 years**	Status **Secure**

Order **Strigiformes**	Family **Strigidae**	Species ***Glaucidium gnoma***

Northern Pygmy-Owl

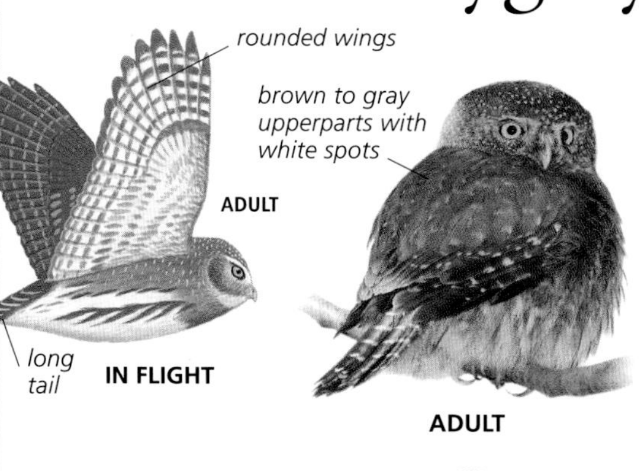
rounded wings
brown to gray upperparts with white spots
ADULT
long tail
IN FLIGHT
ADULT
spotted crown
round head
yellow eye
yellowish bill
heavily streaked whitish underparts
ADULT
long tail, with brown and white barring

FLIGHT: undulating, rapid series of flaps, followed by glide with wings tucked.

In spite of its small size, the Northern Pygmy-Owl is a fierce hunter. It regularly preys on other birds, including relatively large ones such as bobwhites. When hunting, it gradually moves closer to its prey by making short, zigzagging flights from tree to tree before pouncing. It is often active during the day, most frequently around dawn and dusk, and in winter is frequently seen in gardens, pouncing on birds at feeders. The Northern Pygmy-Owl is one of two *Glaucidium* pygmy-owls in North America. Like the rare Ferruginous Pygmy-Owl (*G. brasilianum*), it has "false eyes"—a pair of black-feathered spots on the back of its head. These may act as a deterrent to potential attackers, especially when the owl is sleeping.

VOICE Hollow *poot, poot, poot* calls, 1–2 seconds apart, continuing in series for minutes or more; also excited trill.

NESTING Usually unlined cavity in tree; 2–7 eggs; 1 brood; April–July.

FEEDING Pounces from perch, pinning prey to the ground; eats, insects, reptiles, birds, and mammals.

SIMILAR SPECIES

NORTHERN SAW-WHET OWL
see p.252
thick brown streaks
short tail
FERRUGINOUS PYGMY-OWL
streaked crown

DAYTIME HUNTER
Unlike most other species of owl, the Northern Pygmy-Owl is often active during the day.

OCCURRENCE
Breeds in western North American mountains from British Columbia to California, Arizona, and New Mexico, and from Mexico to Honduras; can be found in mixed spruce, fir, pine, hemlock, cedar, and oak woodlands; nests at higher elevations, and often winters lower down.

Length **6½–7in (16–18cm)**	Wingspan **15in (38cm)**	Weight **2⅛–2½oz (60–70g)**
Social **Family groups**	Lifespan **Unknown**	Status **Secure**

Order **Strigiformes**	Family **Strigidae**	Species ***Athene cunicularia***

Burrowing Owl

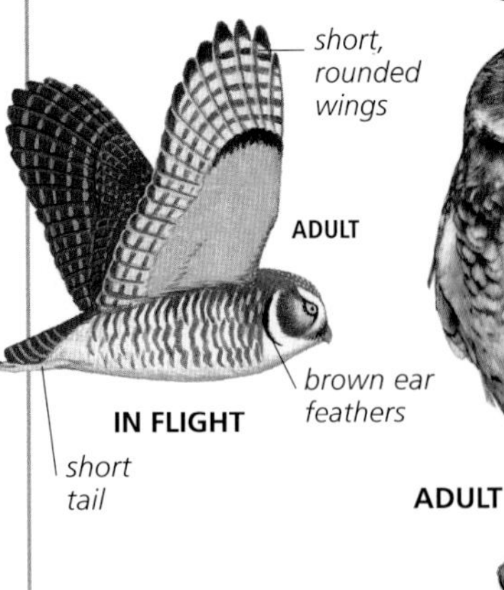
short, rounded wings
ADULT
brown ear feathers
IN FLIGHT
short tail
white streaking on forehead and crown
chest spotted with white
ADULT
short tail
yellow eyes
white contrasting with dark brown band below
brown upper-parts with white spotting
white spots
brown streaks on lower belly
ADULT
short tail
long, feathered legs

FLIGHT: buoyant, often undulating; close to ground; sometimes hovers while hunting.

The Burrowing Owl is unique among North American owls in nesting underground. Usually it uses the abandoned burrows of prairie dogs, ground squirrels, armadillos, badgers, and other mammals. Where such burrows are scarce, however—in built-up areas of Florida, notably—it excavates its own burrow, digging out the soil with its bill and scraping it away with its feet. Usually it nests in loose colonies, too. Active by day or night, the Burrowing Owl hunts prey on foot or on the wing. Populations of the bird in southern areas of North America tend to stay there year-round, but those farther north move south to Mexico for the winter.

ON THE ALERT
A Burrowing Owl keeps watch from the entrance of its burrow, which can be 10ft (3m) long.

VOICE *Coo-cooo*, or *ha-haaa*, with accent on second syllable; also clucks, chatters, warbles, and screams.

NESTING Cavity lined with grass, feathers, sometimes animal dung, at end of burrow; 8–10 eggs; 1 brood; March–August.

FEEDING Walks, hops, runs, hovers, or flies from perch to capture mainly insects, and occasionally small mammals, birds, reptiles, and amphibians.

SIMILAR SPECIES

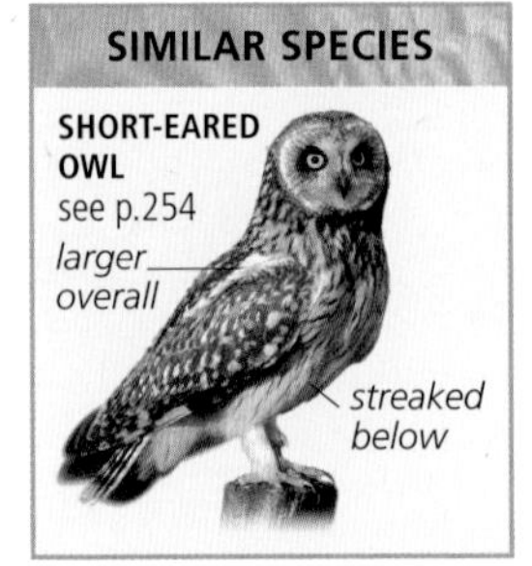
SHORT-EARED OWL
see p.254
larger overall
streaked below

OCCURRENCE
Breeds in Florida, the western US, and southwestern Canada, in a wide range of open, well-drained habitats not prone to flooding, including pastures, plains, deserts, grasslands, and steppes, but also developed area, up to about 6,500ft (2,000m). Partial migrant.

Length **7½–10in (19–25cm)**	Wingspan **21½in (55cm)**	Weight **5oz (150g)**
Social **Loose colonies**	Lifespan **Up to 9 years**	Status **Declining**

Order **Strigiformes**	Family **Strigidae**	Species ***Aegolius funereus***

Boreal Owl

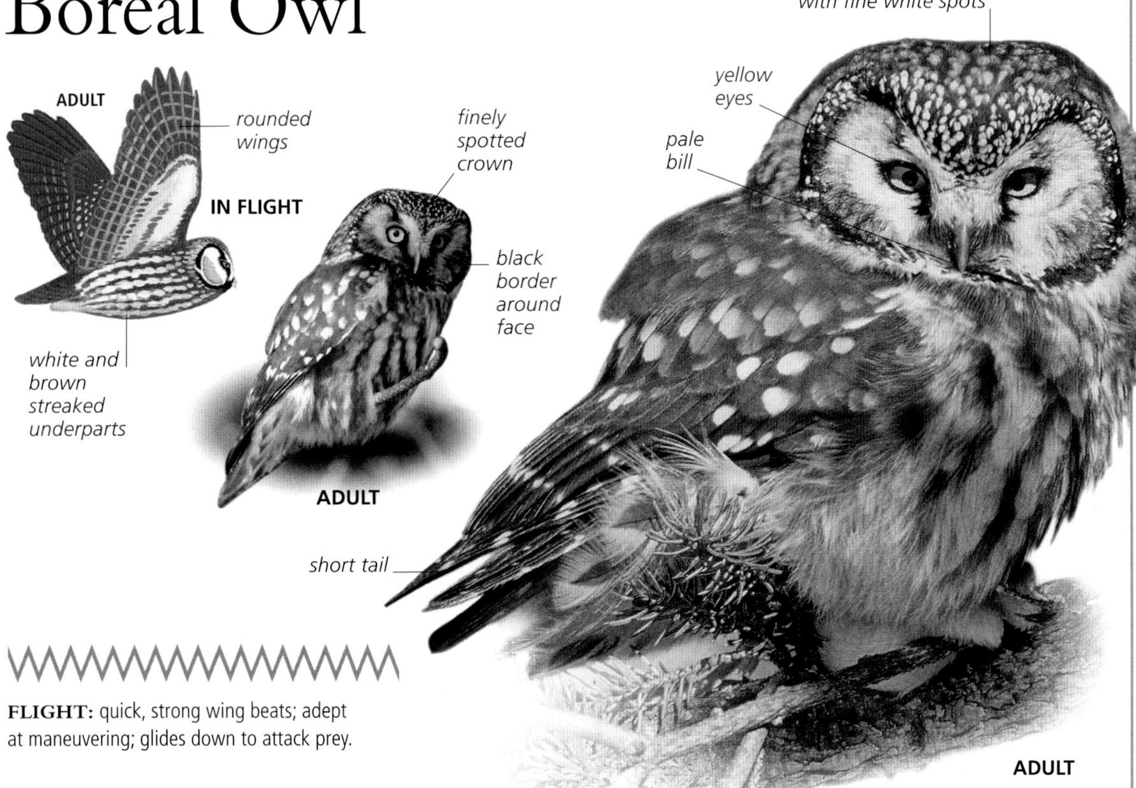
usually flat-topped head, with fine white spots
yellow eyes
pale bill
ADULT
rounded wings
IN FLIGHT
finely spotted crown
black border around face
white and brown streaked underparts
ADULT
short tail
ADULT

FLIGHT: quick, strong wing beats; adept at maneuvering; glides down to attack prey.

Unusually, the female Boreal Owl is much bigger than the male. Males will mate with two or three females in years when voles and other small rodents are abundant. The Boreal Owl roosts on an inconspicuous perch by day and hunts at night, detecting its prey by sound. In the US and Canada it is elusive and rarely seen, since it breeds at high elevations in isolated western mountain ranges. White spotting on the crown, a grayish bill, and a black facial disk distinguish the Boreal Owl from the Northern Saw-whet Owl.

VOICE Prolonged series of whistles, usually increasing in volume and intensity toward the end; also screeches and hisses; can be heard from afar.

NESTING Natural and woodpecker-built tree cavities, also nest boxes; 3–6 eggs; 1 brood; March–July.

FEEDING Mainly eats small mammals, occasionally birds and insects; pounces from elevated perch; sometimes stores prey.

DAYTIME ROOSTING
The Boreal Owl roosts in dense vegetation by day, even when the branches are laden with snow.

SIMILAR SPECIES

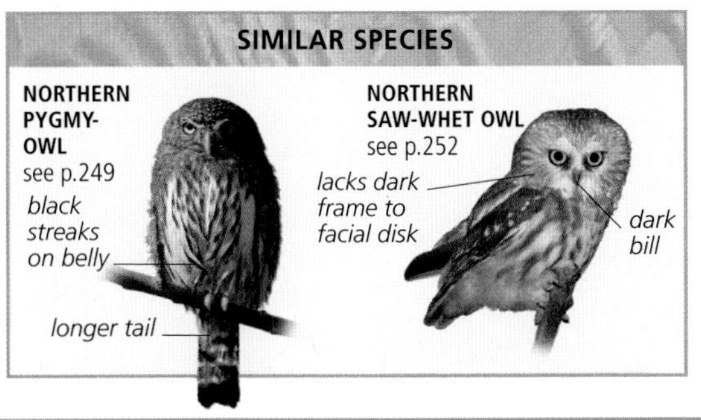
NORTHERN PYGMY-OWL
see p.249
black streaks on belly
longer tail
NORTHERN SAW-WHET OWL
see p.252
lacks dark frame to facial disk
dark bill

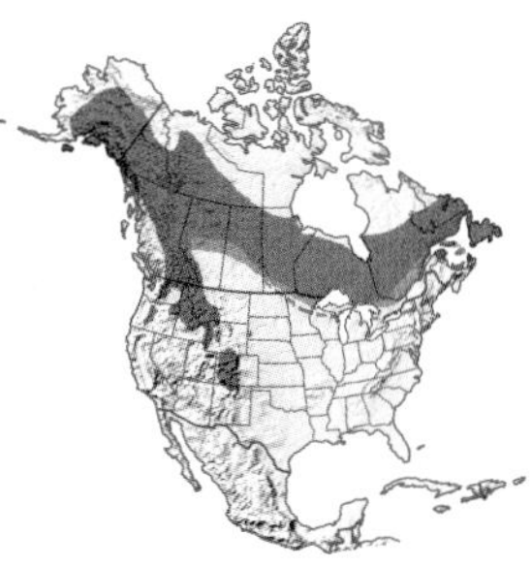

OCCURRENCE
Breeds in northern forests from Alaska to Newfoundland and Québec, south into the Rockies to Colorado and New Mexico. Largely sedentary, but irregular movements take place south of the breeding range, southward to New England and New York.

Length **8½–11in (21–28cm)**	Wingspan **21½–24in (54–62cm)**	Weight **3⅜–8oz (90–225g)**
Social **Solitary**	Lifespan **Up to 11 years**	Status **Secure**

Order **Strigiformes**	Family **Strigidae**	Species ***Aegolius acadicus***

Northern Saw-whet Owl

ADULT
rounded wings
short tail
IN FLIGHT
thin white streaks on forehead and crown
yellow eyes
dark bill
brown streaks
ADULT
whitish eyebrows
white patch between eyes
chestnut-brown upperparts with white spots
unmarked white undertail feathers
ADULT

FLIGHT: swift and direct; low to ground with quick wing beats; swoops up to perch.

One of the most secretive yet common and widespread owls in North America, the Northern Saw-whet Owl is much more often heard than seen. Strictly nocturnal, it is concealed as it sleeps by day in thick vegetation, usually in conifers. Although the same site may be used for months if it remains undisturbed, it is never an easy bird to locate and, like most owls, it is elusive, even though it sometimes roosts in large garden trees. When it is discovered, the Northern Saw-whet Owl "freezes," and relies on its camouflage rather than flying off. At night it watches intently from a perch, before swooping down to snatch its prey.

VOICE Series of rapid whistled notes, on constant pitch; can continue for minutes on end; also whines and squeaks.

NESTING Unlined cavity in tree, usually old woodpecker hole or nest box; 4–7 eggs; 1 brood; March–July.

FEEDING Hunts from elevated perch; eats small mammals, including mice and voles; also eats insects and small birds.

RARE SIGHT
Despite being abundant in its range, this species is quite shy and is rarely seen by humans.

SIMILAR SPECIES

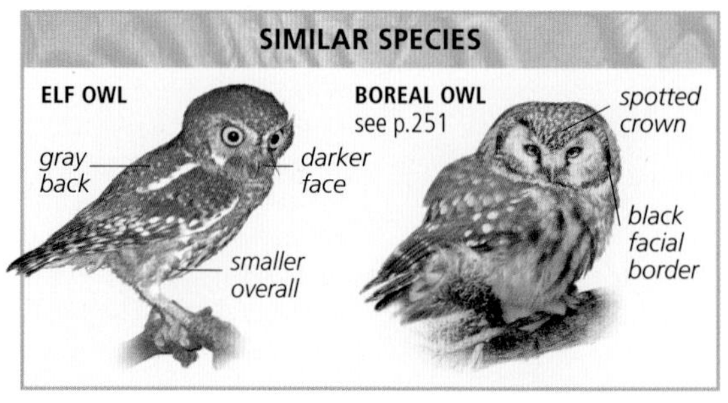
ELF OWL
gray back
darker face
smaller overall
BOREAL OWL
see p.251
spotted crown
black facial border

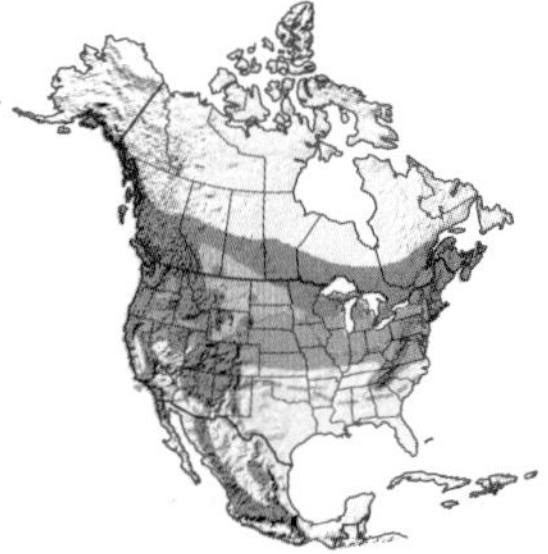

OCCURRENCE
Breeds from Alaska and British Columbia to Maritimes; in west, south to Mexico; in east, south to Appalachians; coniferous and mixed deciduous forests, swampy forests, wooded wetlands, bogs. Winters in south to central states, in open woodlands, pine plantations, shrubby areas.

Length **7–8½in (18–21cm)**	Wingspan **16½–19in (42–48cm)**	Weight **3½oz (100g)**
Social **Solitary**	Lifespan **Up to 10 years**	Status **Secure**

Order **Strigiformes**	Family **Strigidae**	Species ***Asio otus***

Long-eared Owl

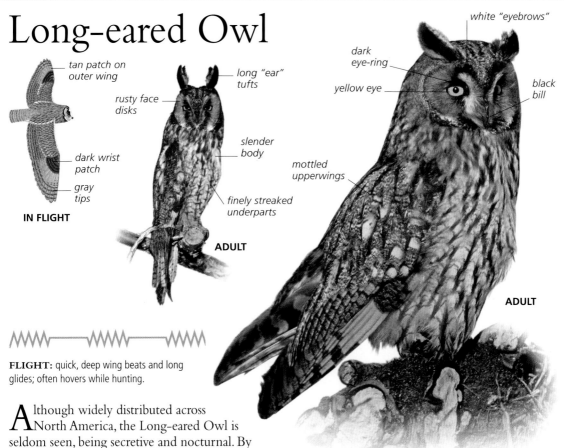

tan patch on outer wing

dark wrist patch

gray tips

IN FLIGHT

long "ear" tufts

rusty face disks

slender body

finely streaked underparts

ADULT

white "eyebrows"

dark eye-ring

yellow eye

black bill

mottled upperwings

ADULT

FLIGHT: quick, deep wing beats and long glides; often hovers while hunting.

Although widely distributed across North America, the Long-eared Owl is seldom seen, being secretive and nocturnal. By day it roosts high up and out of sight in thick cover. Only at nightfall does it fly out to hunt on the wing over open areas, patrolling for small mammals. Its wing feathers, like those of many other owls, have sound-suppressing structures that allow it to fly almost silently, so it can hear the slightest rustle on the ground below.

VOICE Evenly spaced *hooo* notes, continuously repeated, about 3 seconds apart, typically 10–50 per series, sometimes more; barks when alarmed.

NESTING Old stick nests of ravens, crows, magpies, and hawks; 2–7 eggs; 1 brood; March–July.

FEEDING Preys mainly on mice and other small rodents, occasionally small birds.

OWL ON THE WING

In flight this bird's "ear" tufts are flattened back and not visible, but the face and underwing markings are clearly revealed.

SIMILAR SPECIES
GREAT HORNED OWL
see p.244
tufts farther apart
much larger overall
horizontal barring on underparts
SHORT-EARED OWL
see p.254
patterned buffy above
pale below
larger overall

OCCURRENCE

Breeds in old nests, especially in dense stands of cottonwood, willow, juniper, and conifers by open areas suitable for hunting. Occasionally uses old nests in tree holes, cliffs, or on ground in dense vegetation; in winter, up to 100 birds in roosts. Northern birds move south for winter; some western birds resident.

Length **14–15½in (35–40cm)**	Wingspan **34–39in (86–98cm)**	Weight **8–15oz (225–425g)**
Social **Solitary/Winter flocks**	Lifespan **Up to 27 years**	Status **Secure**

Order **Strigiformes**	Family **Strigidae**	Species ***Asio flammeus***

Short-eared Owl

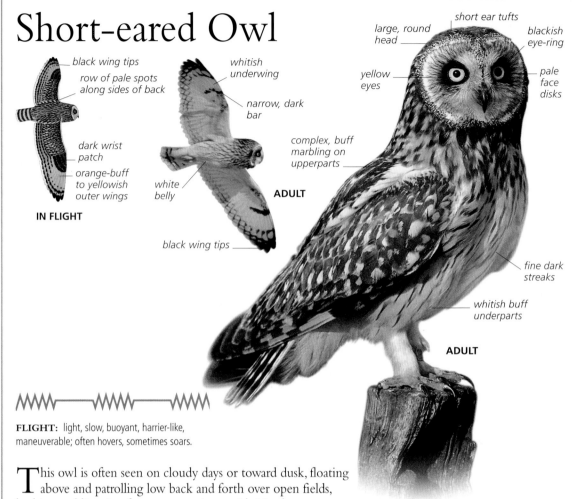

black wing tips
row of pale spots along sides of back
dark wrist patch
orange-buff to yellowish outer wings
IN FLIGHT

whitish underwing
narrow, dark bar
white belly
black wing tips
ADULT

short ear tufts
large, round head
blackish eye-ring
yellow eyes
pale face disks
complex, buff marbling on upperparts
fine dark streaks
whitish buff underparts
ADULT

FLIGHT: light, slow, buoyant, harrier-like, maneuverable; often hovers, sometimes soars.

This owl is often seen on cloudy days or toward dusk, floating above and patrolling low back and forth over open fields, looking and listening for prey, sometimes with Northern Harriers. Although territorial in the breeding season, it sometimes winters in communal roosts of up to 200 birds, occasionally alongside Long-eared Owls. About 10 subspecies are widely distributed across five continents and numerous islands, including the Greater Antilles, Galápagos, the Falklands and Hawaii. Unlike other North American owls, the Short-eared Owl builds its own nest.

VOICE Usually silent; male courtship call a rapid *hoo hoo hoo*, often given during display flights; about 16 notes in 3 seconds; also barking, *chee-oww*.

NESTING Scrape lined with grass and feathers on ground; 4–7 eggs; 1–2 broods; March–June.

FEEDING Eats small mammals and some birds.

SIMILAR SPECIES

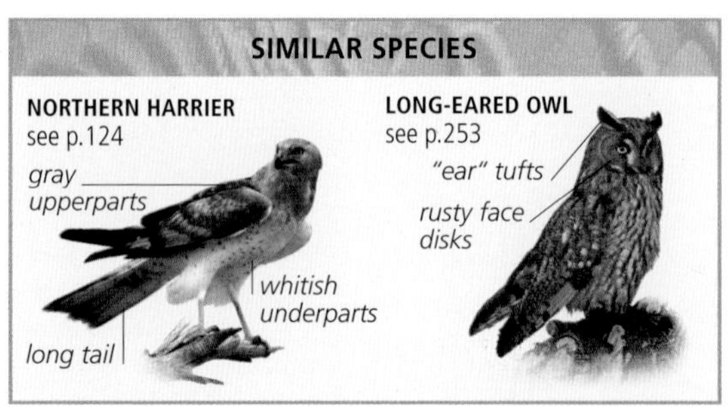
NORTHERN HARRIER
see p.124
gray upperparts
whitish underparts
long tail
LONG-EARED OWL
see p.253
"ear" tufts
rusty face disks

LOOKOUT POST
Perched on a branch, a Short-eared Owl keeps a wary eye on any intruder on its territory.

OCCURRENCE
Breeds in open areas, including prairie, grasslands, tundra, fields, and marshes, across northern North America, from Alaska, the Yukon, and British Columbia to Québec, and Newfoundland, south to the western and central prairies, and east to New England. Partial migrant.

Length **13½–16in (34–41cm)**	Wingspan **2¾–3½ft (0.9–1.1m)**	Weight **11–13oz (325–375g)**
Social **Solitary/Winter flocks**	Lifespan **Up to 13 years**	Status **Vulnerable**

NIGHTJARS

ALTHOUGH WIDESPREAD and common throughout North America, species of the family Caprimulgidae are heard more often than they are seen. The exceptions to this rule are the two species of Common Nighthawks that regularly forage for insects at dawn and dusk. All members of this group are medium-sized birds that use their long wings and wide tails to make rapid and graceful turns to capture their insect prey in the air. They feed predominantly on large flying insects such as moths. Their wide, gaping mouths are surrounded by bristles that greatly aid in foraging efforts. They have very small legs and toes. Both nightjars and nighthawks are similar in coloration and pattern, having a mottled mixture of various browns, grays, and blacks that provides impeccable camouflage when they remain hidden during daylight hours. This ability to hide in plain sight is useful during the nesting season when all nightjars lay their patterned eggs directly on the ground, without any nest material. The nature of the camouflage pattern of their feathers makes it difficult to distinguish between species when they rest in trees or on the ground. The most reliable means of telling species apart is their voice. If seen, the placement and nature of white markings, combined with the style of flight are the best means of identification. Most members of the family migrate and move southward as insects become dormant in the North. Nightjars are also known as "Goatsuckers," because it was believed in ancient Greece that these birds sucked blood from goats.

NIGHT HUNTER
The nocturnal Common Poorwill hunts from the ground, looking up to spot its flying insect prey.

SITTING PRETTY
Unusually for birds, members of the nightjar family, such as this Common Nighthawk, often perch lengthwise on branches.

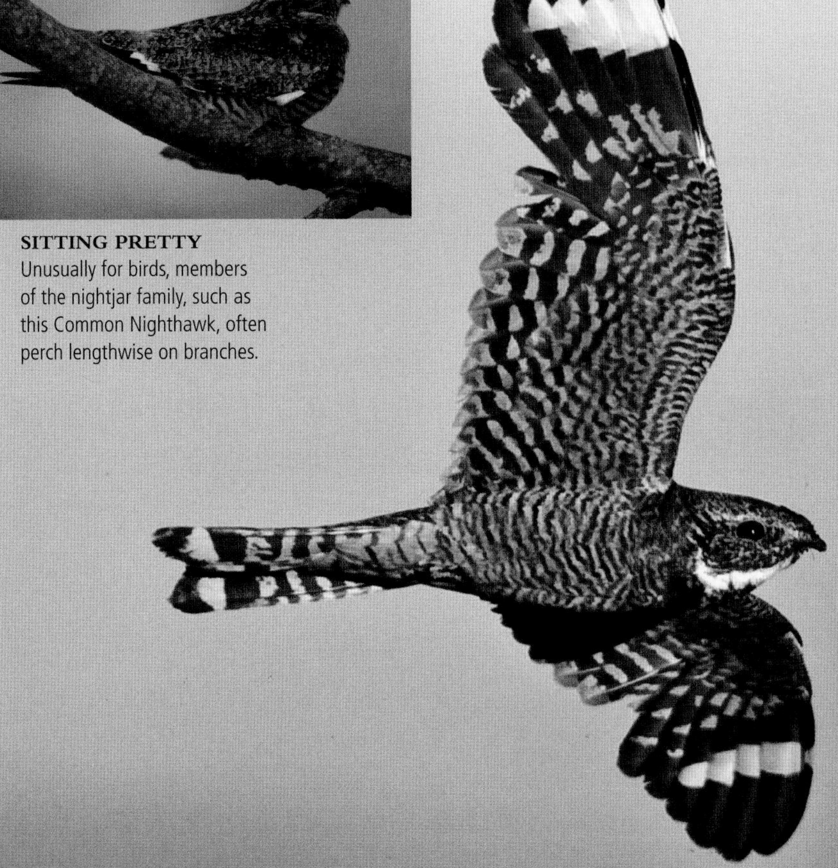

ELEGANT HUNTER
This male Lesser Nighthawk, a rare bird in Canada, soars through the air, hunting for insects.

Order **Caprimulgiformes**	Family **Caprimulgidae**	Species ***Chordeiles minor***

Common Nighthawk

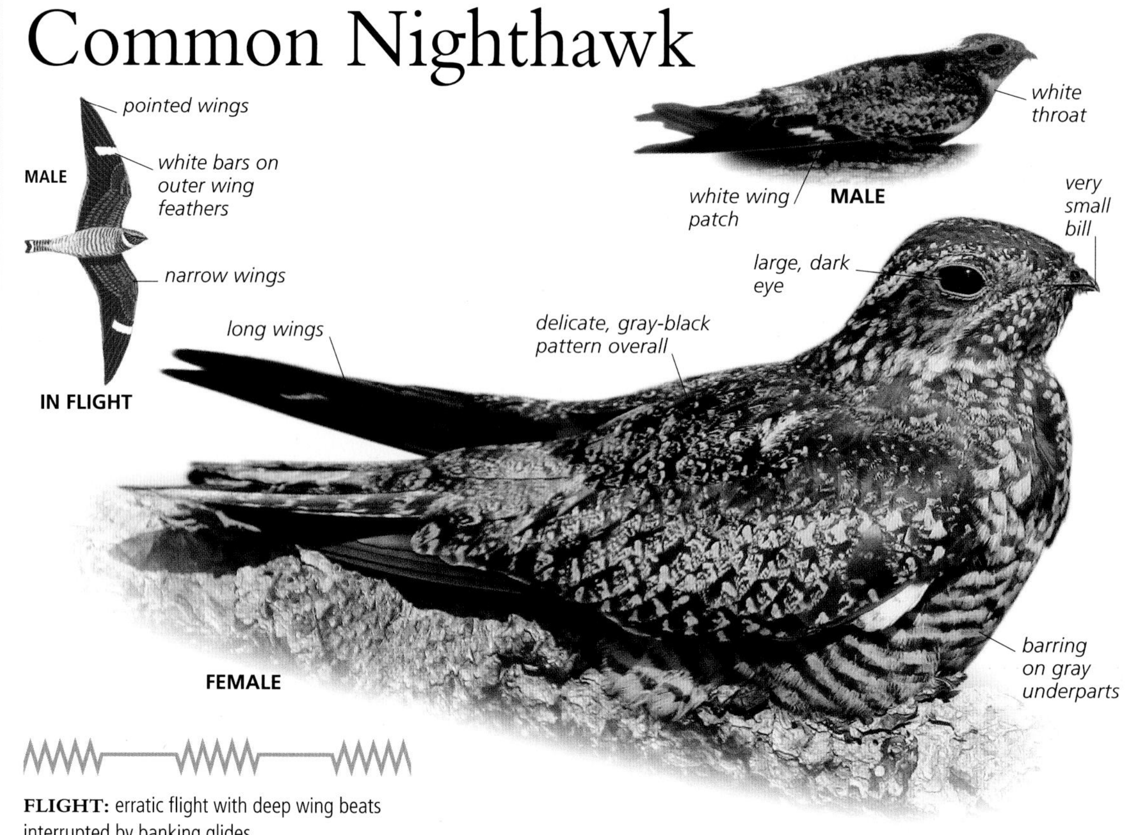
pointed wings
MALE
white bars on outer wing feathers
narrow wings
IN FLIGHT
long wings
white throat
white wing patch
MALE
very small bill
large, dark eye
delicate, gray-black pattern overall
barring on gray underparts
FEMALE

FLIGHT: erratic flight with deep wing beats interrupted by banking glides.

Common Nighthawks are easy to spot as they swoop over parking lots, city streets, and athletics fields during the warm summer months. They are more active at dawn and dusk than at night, pursuing insect prey up to 250ft (76m) in the air. The species once took the name Booming Nighthawk, a reference to the remarkable flight display of the male birds, during which they dive rapidly towards the ground, causing their feathers to vibrate and produce a characteristic "booming" sound.

VOICE Nasal *peeent*; also soft clucking noises from both sexes.

NESTING Nests on ground on rocks, wood, leaves, or sand, also on gravel-covered rooftops in urban areas; 2 eggs; 1 brood; May–July.

FEEDING Catches airborne insects, especially moths, mayflies, and beetles, also ants; predominantly active at dusk and dawn.

A RARE SIGHT
Common Nighthawks are seen in flight more often than other caprimulgids, and it is a rare treat to see one resting on a perch.

SIMILAR SPECIES

LESSER NIGHTHAWK
more buffy barring on underside of wings; see p.488

COMMON PAURAQUE
longer, rounded tail with white patches

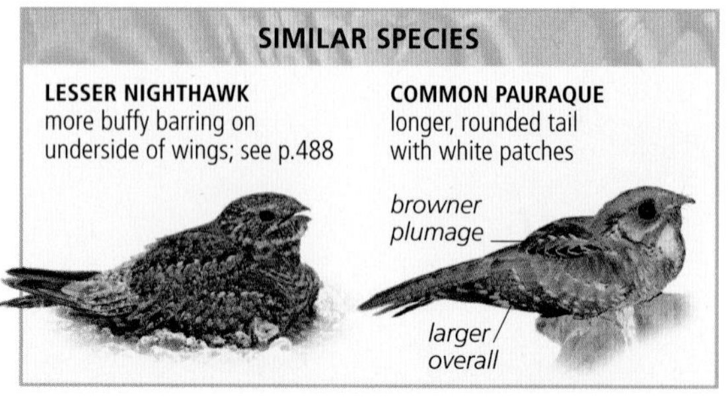
browner plumage
larger overall

OCCURRENCE
Wide variety of open habitats such as cleared forests, fields, grassland, beaches, and sand dunes; also common in urban areas, including cities. The most common and widespread North American nighthawk, this species also occurs in Central and South America.

Length **9–10in (23–26cm)**	Wingspan **22–24in (56–61cm)**	Weight **2⅞oz (80g)**
Social **Solitary/Flocks**	Lifespan **Up to 9 years**	Status **Declining**

Order **Caprimulgiformes**	Family **Caprimulgidae**	Species ***Phalaenoptilus nuttallii***

Common Poorwill

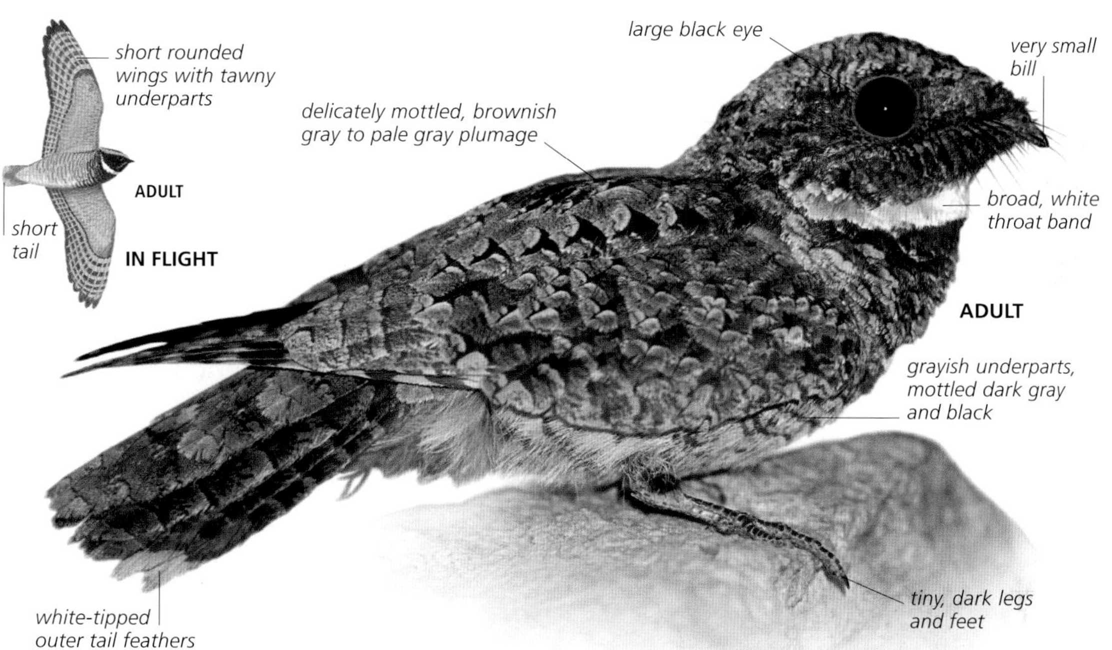
short rounded wings with tawny underparts
ADULT
short tail
IN FLIGHT
large black eye
delicately mottled, brownish gray to pale gray plumage
very small bill
broad, white throat band
ADULT
grayish underparts, mottled dark gray and black
white-tipped outer tail feathers
tiny, dark legs and feet

This noctural bird is the smallest North American nightjar, with much shorter wings than its relatives, and a stubbier tail, but a comparatively large head. In 1946 scientists discovered that it was able to go into a state of torpor, similar to mammalian hibernation. During "hibernation" its body temperature is about 64°F (18°C) instead of the usual 106°F (41°C), and it may remain in this state for several weeks during cold weather when food is unavailable. This may account for its colloquial name, "sleeping one," among the Hopi of the Southwest. Males and females are similar in appearance, but the male has whitish corners to its tail, while the female's are more buffy.

VOICE Call low *purr-WHEEOO* or *pooor-WEELLUP*, whistled at night when perched in the open.

NESTING Eggs laid on the ground among rocks, sometimes under shrubs; 2 eggs; 2 broods; May–August.

FEEDING Jumps up from the ground and flies briefly to capture night-flying insects, such as moths and beetles.

FLIGHT: brief, erratic; with slow and deep wing beats.

GRAVEL ROADS
The Common Poorwill uses gravel roads as a convenient place from which to jump at flying insects.

SIMILAR SPECIES

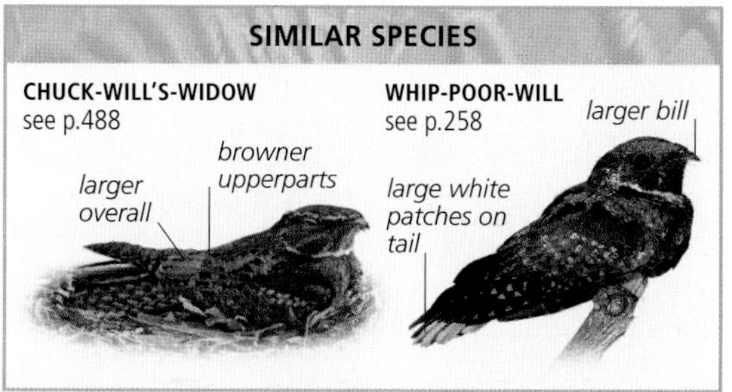
CHUCK-WILL'S-WIDOW
see p.488
larger overall
browner upperparts
WHIP-POOR-WILL
see p.258
larger bill
large white patches on tail

OCCURRENCE
Breeds from southwestern Canada and the western US southwards into Mexico, in arid habitats with much bare ground and sparse vegetation, such as grasses, shrubs, and cacti. Winters in northern Mexico.

Length **7½–8½in (19–21cm)**	Wingspan **15½–19in (40–48cm)**	Weight **1¼–2oz (35–55g)**
Social **Solitary**	Lifespan **Up to 3 years**	Status **Secure**

Order **Caprimulgiformes**	Family **Caprimulgidae**	Species ***Caprimulgus vociferus***

Whip-poor-will

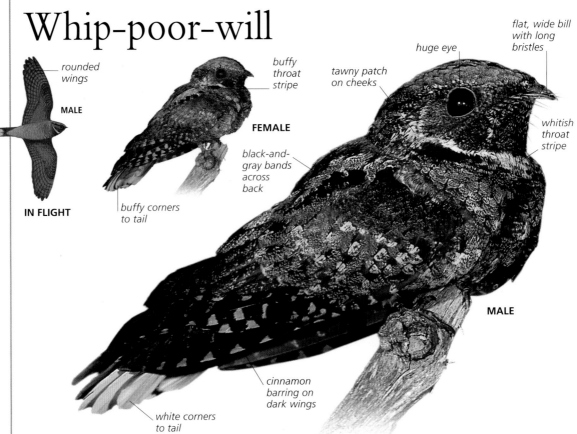

rounded wings

MALE

IN FLIGHT

buffy throat stripe

FEMALE

buffy corners to tail

tawny patch on cheeks

huge eye

flat, wide bill with long bristles

whitish throat stripe

black-and-gray bands across back

MALE

cinnamon barring on dark wings

white corners to tail

As with many of the nightjars, the Whip-poor-will is heard more often than seen. Its camouflage makes it extremely difficult to spot on the forest floor and it usually flies away only when an intruder is very close—sometimes within a few feet. This species apparently has an unusual breeding pattern—while the male feeds the first brood until fledging, the female lays eggs for a second brood. The two eggs from each brood may hatch simultaneously during full moon, when there is most light at night, allowing the parents more time to forage for their young.

VOICE Loud, three-syllable whistle *WHIP-perrr-WIIL*.

NESTING Lays eggs on leaf litter on forest floor, often near overhead plant cover; 2 eggs; 2 broods; April–July.

FEEDING Flies upward quickly from perch to capture passing moths and other insects, such as mosquitoes.

FLIGHT: slow, erratic flight, with alternating bouts of flapping and gliding.

WAITING IN AMBUSH
Like other nightjars, this species waits in ambush for its prey from a perch on the forest floor.

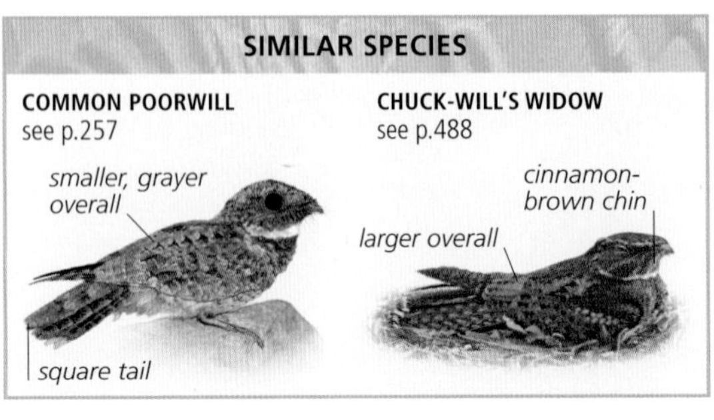

SIMILAR SPECIES

COMMON POORWILL
see p.257

CHUCK-WILL'S WIDOW
see p.488

smaller, grayer overall
square tail
cinnamon-brown chin
larger overall

OCCURRENCE
Mixed mature forests with open understory, especially oak and pine forests on dry upland sites. Breeds north to southern Canada and south to El Salvador. Eastern and southwestern populations are widely separated.

Length **9–10in (23–26cm)**	Wingspan **17–20in (43–51cm)**	Weight **1 9/16–2 1/4oz (45–65g)**
Social **Solitary**	Lifespan **Up to 15 years**	Status **Secure**

Family **Apodidae**

SWIFTS

SWIFTS SPEND VIRTUALLY ALL their daylight hours and many night hours as well, plying the skies. The most aerial birds in North America—if not the world—swifts eat, drink, court, mate, and even sleep on the wing. Unsurprisingly, swifts also are some of the fastest and most acrobatic flyers of the bird world. Several species have been clocked at over 100mph (160kph). They feed on insects caught in zooming, zigzagging and dashing pursuits. The family name, based on the Greek *apous*, which means "without feet," originates from the ancient belief that swifts had no feet and lived their entire lives in the air.

ACROBATIC FLOCKS White-throated Swifts are usually seen in groups of a handful to hundreds of birds.

Family **Trochilidae**

HUMMINGBIRDS

FOUND ONLY IN THE AMERICAS, hummingbirds are sometimes referred to as the crown jewels of the bird world. The first sight of a glittering hummingbird can be a life-changing experience. The amount of iridescence in their plumages varies from almost none to seemingly every feather. Most North American male hummingbirds have a colorful throat patch called a gorget, but most females lack this gorgeous attribute. Because iridescent colors are structural and not pigment-based, a gorget can often appear blackish until seen at the correct angle towards the light. Hummingbirds are the only birds that can fly backwards, an adaptation that allows them to move easily between flowers. Flying sideways, up, down, and hovering are also within hummingbirds' abilities, and all are achieved by their unique figure-eight, rapid wing strokes and reduced wing bone structure. Their long, thin bills allow them access to nectar in tubular flowers.

AGGRESSIVE MALES This male Ruby-throated Hummingbird defends his territory from a perch.

NECTAR FEEDERS All North American hummingbirds, such as this Blacked-chinned, subsist on nectar from wildflowers.

Order **Apodiformes**	Family **Apodidae**	Species ***Cypseloides niger***

Black Swift

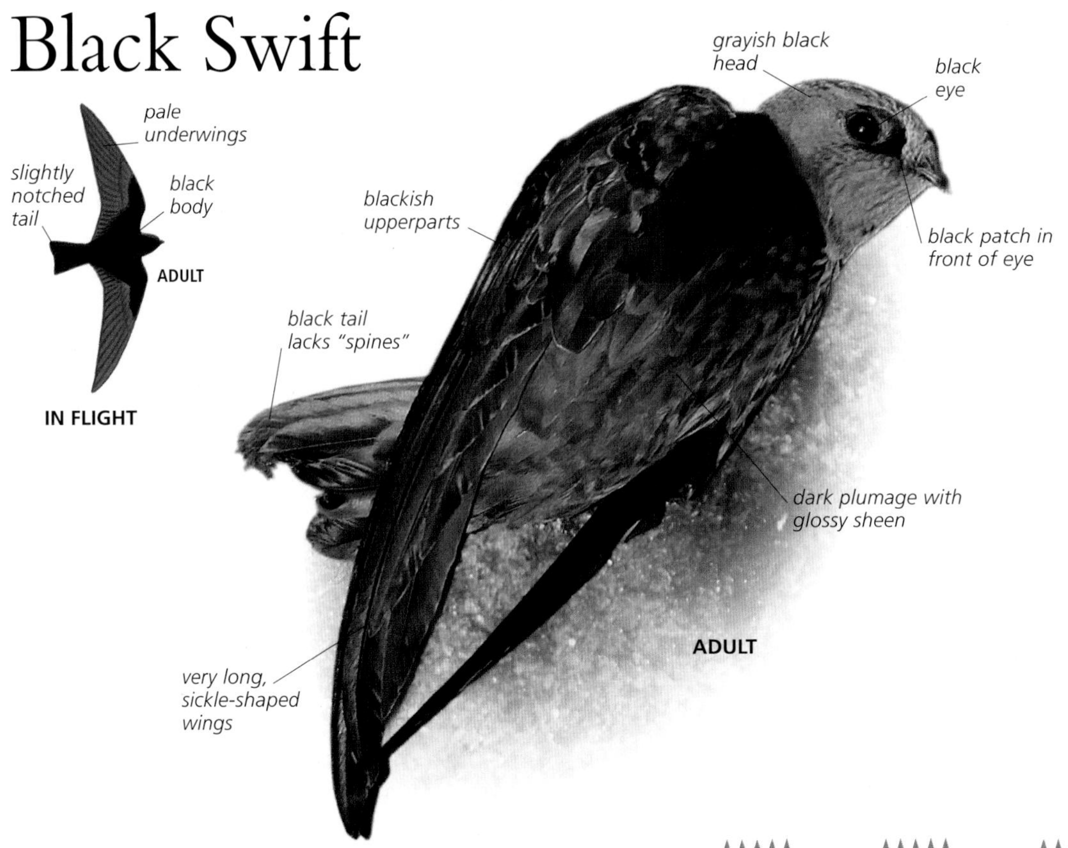
pale underwings
slightly notched tail
black body
ADULT
IN FLIGHT
blackish upperparts
grayish black head
black eye
black patch in front of eye
black tail lacks "spines"
dark plumage with glossy sheen
ADULT
very long, sickle-shaped wings

The largest of the North American swifts, the Black Swift is also the most enigmatic. It forages at high altitudes and nests on sea cliffs or behind waterfalls in mountainous terrains, and therefore can be difficult to observe. On cold and cloudy days, when their aerial insect prey occurs closer to the ground, Black Swifts also forage lower, and are easier to see. Like other swifts, the Black Swift often forms large feeding flocks, particularly in areas where swarms of winged ants occur.

VOICE Generally silent, but gives twittering chips, sometimes in fast series, during interactions with other swifts; sharp *cheep* when approaching nest.

NESTING Shallow cup of moss and mud on ledge or in rocky niche, often behind waterfalls; 1 egg; 1 brood; June–September.

FEEDING Catches airborne flies, beetles, bees, spiders, and other arthropods on the wing.

FLIGHT: shallow, rapid wing beats; often soars; acrobatic, looping flight when feeding.

TOTAL COMMITMENT
The female incubates her egg for up to a month, then both parents feed the nestling for seven weeks.

SIMILAR SPECIES

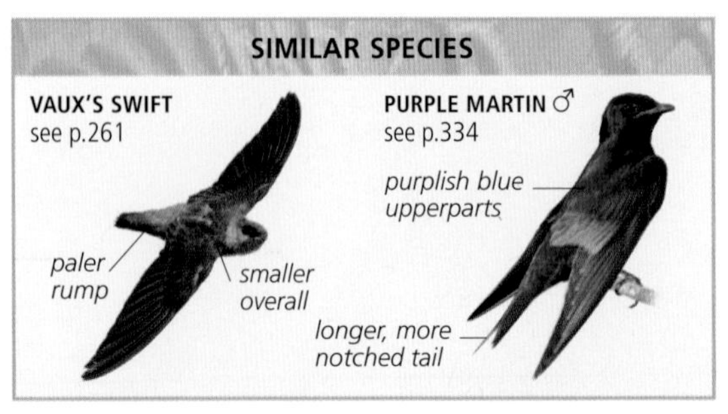
VAUX'S SWIFT
see p.261
paler rump
smaller overall
PURPLE MARTIN ♂
see p.334
purplish blue upperparts
longer, more notched tail

OCCURRENCE
Breeds from British Columbia in Canada, south to Mexico, Costa Rica, and the West Indies. Found in mountains from May or June to early October, feeding high over any habitat near nesting sites. Occasionally seen elsewhere during migration, often in flocks. Wintering areas still largely unknown.

Length **7in (18cm)**	Wingspan **18in (46cm)**	Weight **1$\frac{7}{16}$–2oz (40–55g)**
Social **Flocks**	Lifespan **Up to 16 years**	Status **Localized**

Order **Apodiformes**	Family **Apodidae**	Species ***Chaetura vauxi***

Vaux's Swift

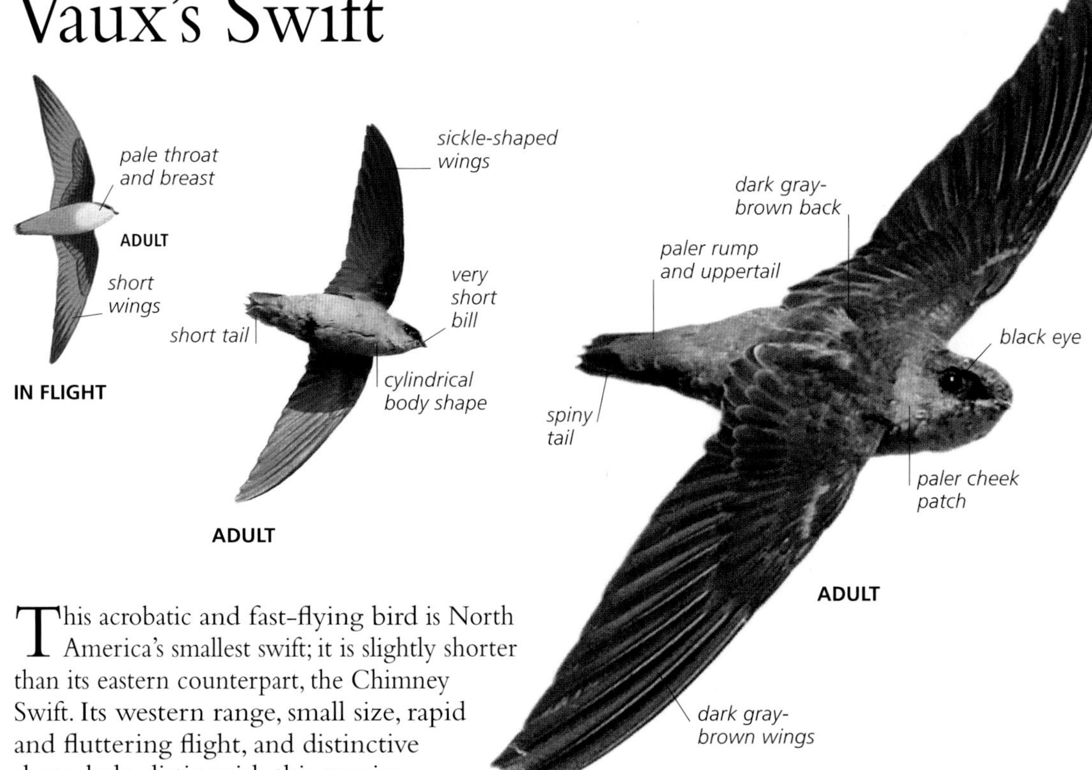
pale throat and breast
ADULT
short wings
IN FLIGHT
sickle-shaped wings
very short bill
short tail
cylindrical body shape
ADULT
dark gray-brown back
paler rump and uppertail
black eye
spiny tail
paler cheek patch
ADULT
dark gray-brown wings

This acrobatic and fast-flying bird is North America's smallest swift; it is slightly shorter than its eastern counterpart, the Chimney Swift. Its western range, small size, rapid and fluttering flight, and distinctive shape help distinguish this species from others. Vaux's Swifts are typically found foraging in flocks over mature forest and can be easily spotted on cold, cloudy days, often mixed with other swifts. Very large flocks are also sighted seemingly "pouring" into communal roost sites at dusk. It is fairly reliant on mature forest, and areas where this habitat has diminished have seen a corresponding decline in populations of Vaux's Swift. They may wander more widely in search of food in poor weather, even over towns.

VOICE High, insect-like chips and twittering in flight, often ending in buzzy trill.

NESTING Shallow cup of twigs, needles, and saliva attached to inside of hollow tree, rarely on chimneys; 4–6 eggs; 1 brood; June–September.

FEEDING Catches a wide variety of flying insects on the wing, including flies, moths, bees, beetles, and many others.

FLIGHT: swift, erratic flight; shallow, fluttering wing beats; acrobatic and bat-like when feeding.

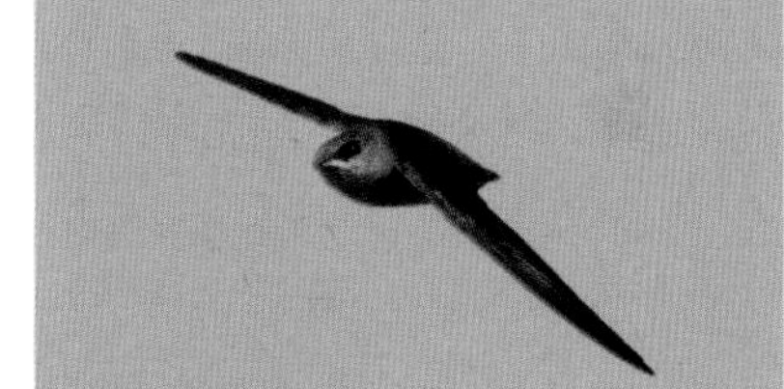

AERIAL ACROBAT
Vaux's Swifts rarely land, spending all day hawking insects and even mating in flight.

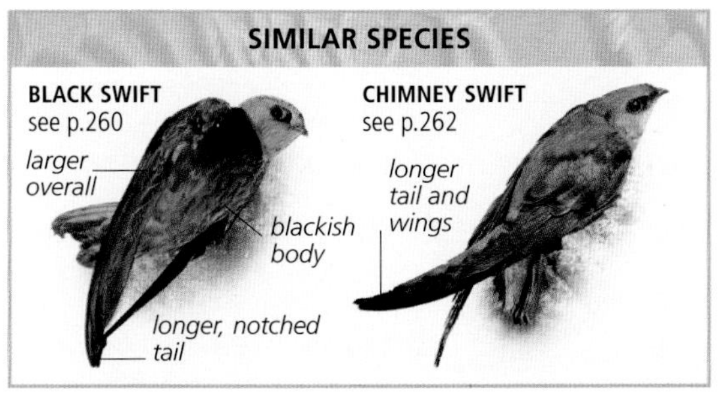
SIMILAR SPECIES
BLACK SWIFT
see p.260
larger overall
blackish body
longer, notched tail
CHIMNEY SWIFT
see p.262
longer tail and wings

OCCURRENCE
Occurs in North America from southeastern Alaska to California, where it breeds primarily in coniferous forests, nesting in large, hollow trunks; forages widely in many habitats. Resident population in Mexico, North American migrants move to Central America.

Length **4¾in (12cm)**	Wingspan **12in (30cm)**	Weight **½–⅞oz (15–25g)**
Social **Migrant flocks**	Lifespan **Up to 7 years**	Status **Declining**

Order **Apodiformes**	Family **Apodidae**	Species ***Chaetura pelagica***

Chimney Swift

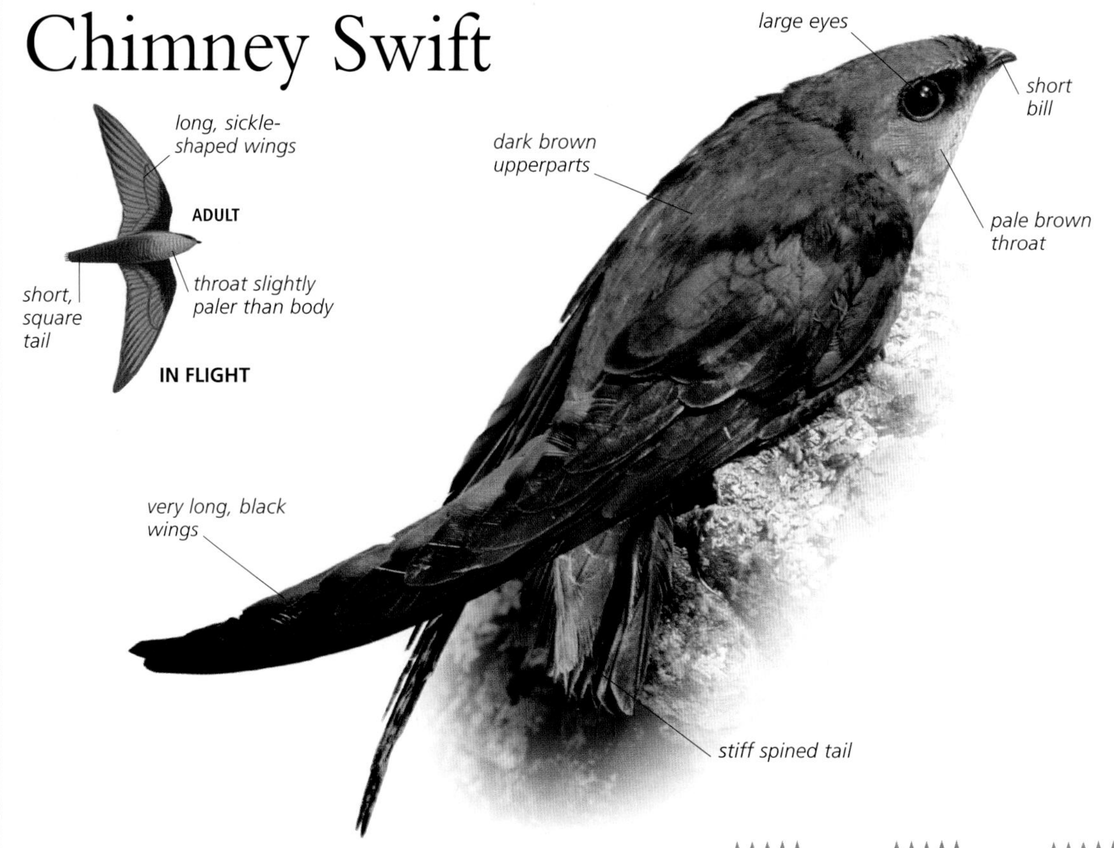
long, sickle-shaped wings
ADULT
short, square tail
throat slightly paler than body
IN FLIGHT
dark brown upperparts
large eyes
short bill
pale brown throat
very long, black wings
stiff spined tail

Nicknamed "spine-tailed," the Chimney Swift is a familiar summer sight and sound, racing through the skies east of the Rockies, its rolling twitters often heard. These birds do almost everything on the wing—feeding, drinking, and even bathing. Chimney Swifts have adapted to nest in human structures, including chimneys, although they once nested in tree holes. It remains a common bird, although local populations have declined; and it has expanded its range west and south.

VOICE High, rapid chips and twittering; notes from individuals in a flock run together into a rapid, descending chatter.

NESTING Shallow cup of twigs and saliva attached to inside of chimney or other artificial structure, rarely hollow tree; 4–5 eggs; 1 brood; April–August.

FEEDING Pursues a large variety of small aerial insects.

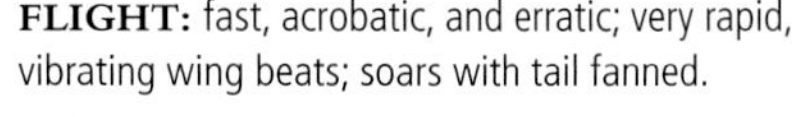

FLIGHT: fast, acrobatic, and erratic; very rapid, vibrating wing beats; soars with tail fanned.

HIGH FLYER
Swifts feed at heights on sunny days, and only feed near the ground when it is cold and cloudy.

SIMILAR SPECIES

BLACK SWIFT see p.260
larger overall
broader wings

VAUX'S SWIFT see p.261
paler rump
shorter wings and tail
paler throat

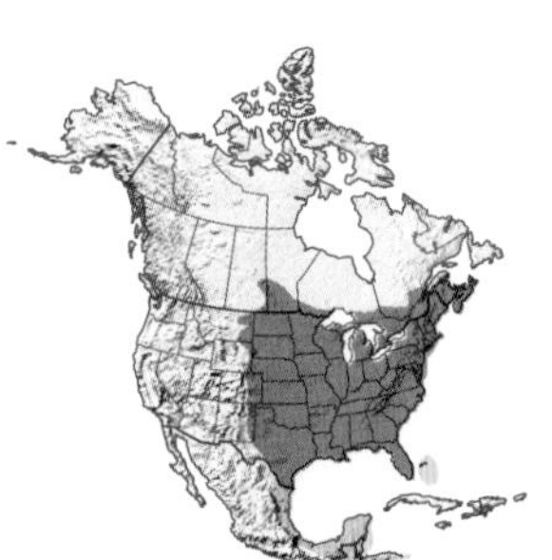

OCCURRENCE
Widespread in eastern North America, over many habitats: urban and suburban areas, small towns; in sparsely populated areas nests in hollow trees and caves; regular in summer in southern California, present late March to early November. Winters in Amazonian South America.

Length **5in (13cm)**	Wingspan **14in (36cm)**	Weight **$\frac{5}{8}$–$1\frac{1}{16}$oz (17–30g)**
Social **Flocks**	Lifespan **Up to 15 years**	Status **Secure**

Order **Apodiformes**	Family **Apodidae**	Species ***Aeronautes saxatalis***

White-throated Swift

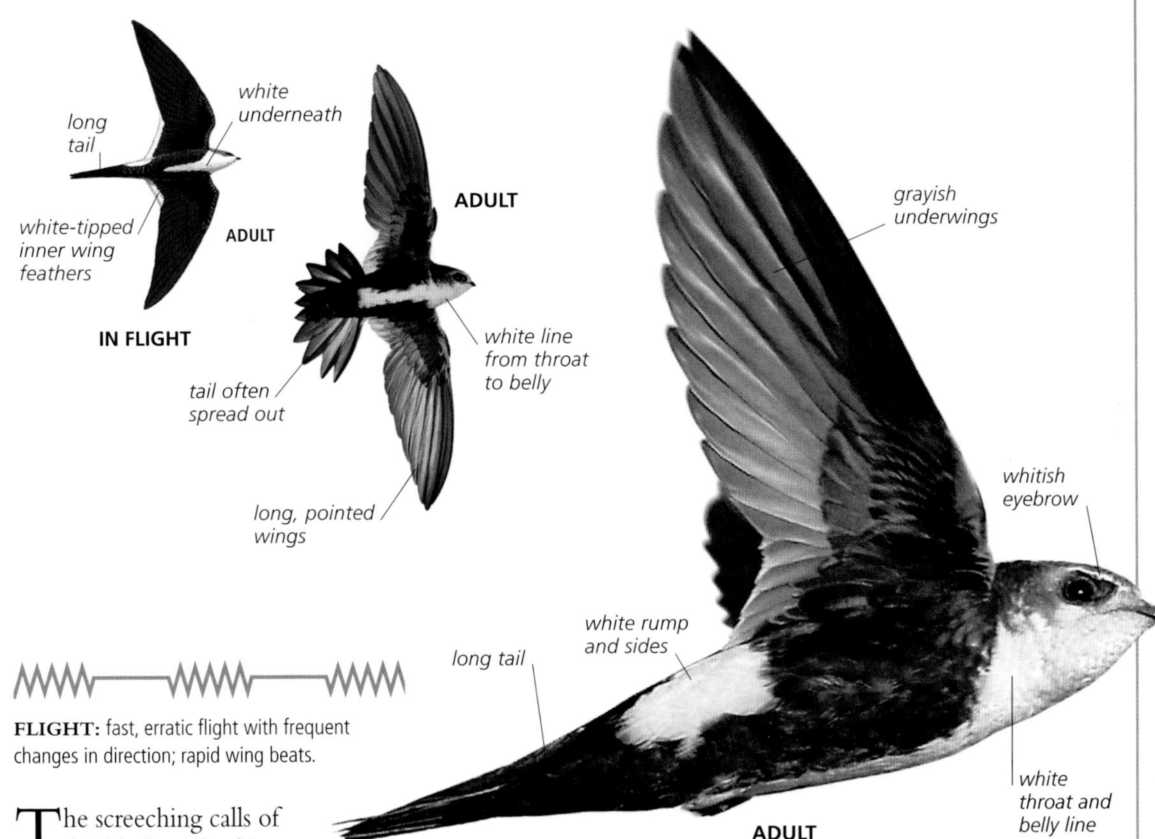

long tail
white underneath
white-tipped inner wing feathers
ADULT
IN FLIGHT
ADULT
tail often spread out
white line from throat to belly
long, pointed wings
grayish underwings
whitish eyebrow
white rump and sides
long tail
white throat and belly line
ADULT

FLIGHT: fast, erratic flight with frequent changes in direction; rapid wing beats.

The screeching calls of this black-and-white swift is a familiar sound in canyon country. Often seen racing around the cliffs on which they nest, White-throated Swifts are distinguished from other North American swifts by their black-and-white plumage and longer tail. This is also the only swift that winters in North America in large numbers. This species has become increasingly common in urban areas, as it has adapted to nesting in human structures that resemble its natural nest sites, such as bridges and quarries. As with other swifts, huge flocks of White-throated Swifts can be seen rushing into communal roosts at dusk, particularly outside the breeding season.

VOICE Drawn-out, descending, shrill twitter, *tee-tee-tee-ter-ter-ter-trr-trr-trr*, commonly given by flocks; occasionally gives two-note call in flight or sharp single note.

NESTING Shallow cup of feathers and saliva in rock, wall, crevice, or human structure; 3–6 eggs; 1 brood; March–August.

FEEDING Forages on a variety of aerial insects.

"AIR SAILOR"
These swifts—the aeronauts—were named to emphasize their mastery of the air.

SIMILAR SPECIES

VIOLET-GREEN SWALLOW ♂ slower flight and wing beats; see p.333

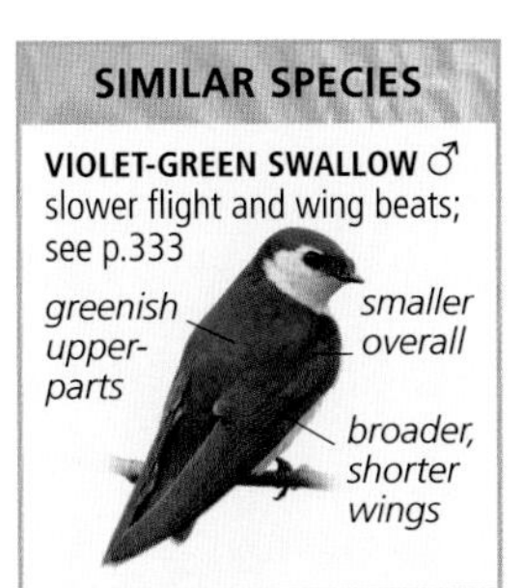

greenish upper-parts
smaller overall
broader, shorter wings

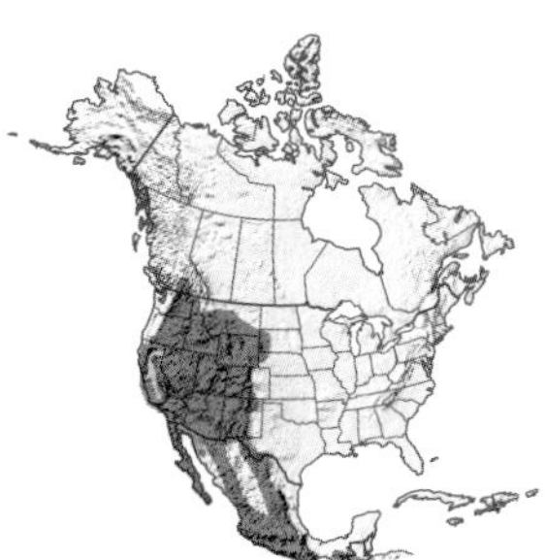

OCCURRENCE
Breeds in western North America, from British Columbia to California, eastward to the Dakotas, and south to New Mexico. Prefers hilly and mountainous areas; forages over wide variety of habitats winters in the extreme southwest of North America, in communal roosts in canyons.

Length **6¾in (17cm)**	Wingspan **15in (38cm)**	Weight **1¹⁄₁₆–1⁹⁄₁₆oz (30–45g)**
Social **Flocks**	Lifespan **Unknown**	Status **Secure**

Order **Apodiformes**	Family **Trochilidae**	Species ***Archilochus colubris***

Ruby-throated Hummingbird

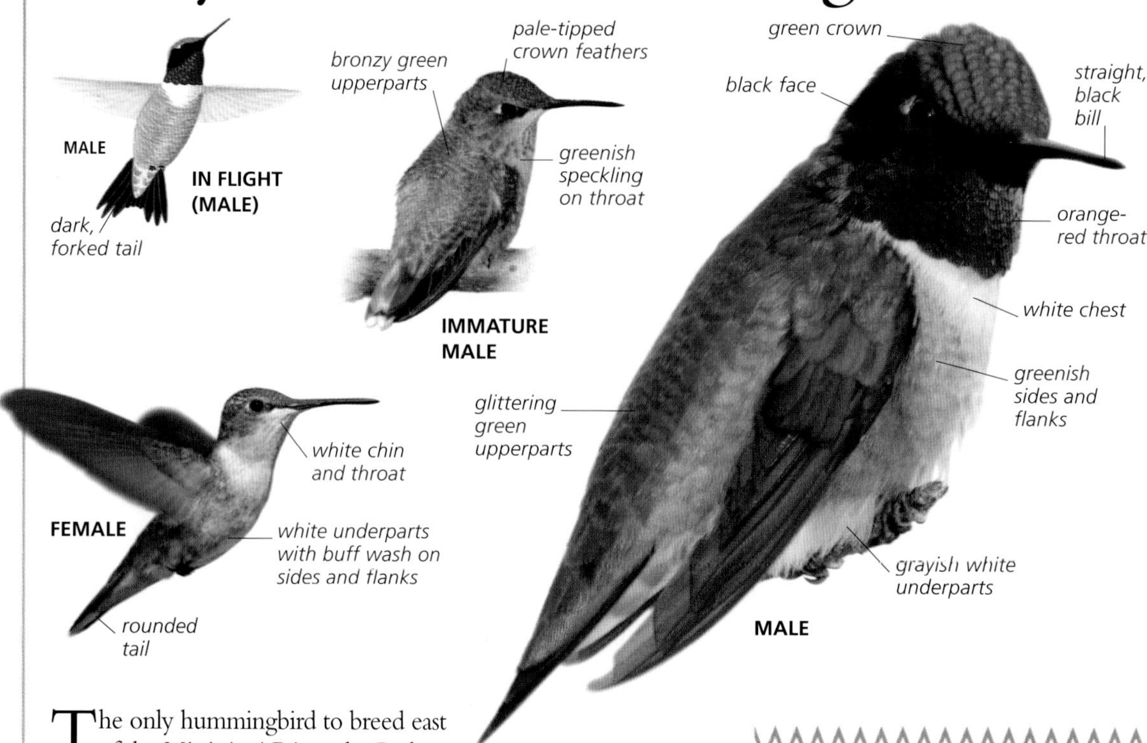
MALE
IN FLIGHT (MALE)
dark, forked tail
bronzy green upperparts
pale-tipped crown feathers
greenish speckling on throat
IMMATURE MALE
green crown
black face
straight, black bill
orange-red throat
white chest
greenish sides and flanks
glittering green upperparts
white chin and throat
FEMALE
white underparts with buff wash on sides and flanks
rounded tail
grayish white underparts
MALE

The only hummingbird to breed east of the Mississippi River, the Ruby-throated Hummingbird is a welcome addition to gardens throughout its range. It is easily identified in most of its range, though more difficult to distinguish in areas where other species are found, particularly during migration. Males perform a deep diving display for females. Before migration, these birds add about 1⁄16oz (2g) of fat to their weight to provide enough fuel for their nonstop 800-mile (1,300km) flight across the Gulf of Mexico.

VOICE Call a soft, thick *chic*, sometimes doubled; twittered notes in interactions; chase call a fast, slightly buzzy *tsi-tsi-tsi-tsi-tsi-tsi-tsi-tsi*; soft, rattling song very rarely heard.

NESTING Tiny cup of plant down, with bud scales and lichen on the exterior, bound with spider's silk, usually in deciduous trees; 2 eggs; 1–2 broods; April–September.

FEEDING Drinks nectar from many species of flowers; feeds on small insects and spiders, caught aerially or gleaned from foliage.

FLIGHT: swift, forward flight with very fast wing beats; hovers at flowers and darts after insects.

CATCHING THE LIGHT
Although the throat patch often appears all black, the right lighting sets it afire with color.

SIMILAR SPECIES

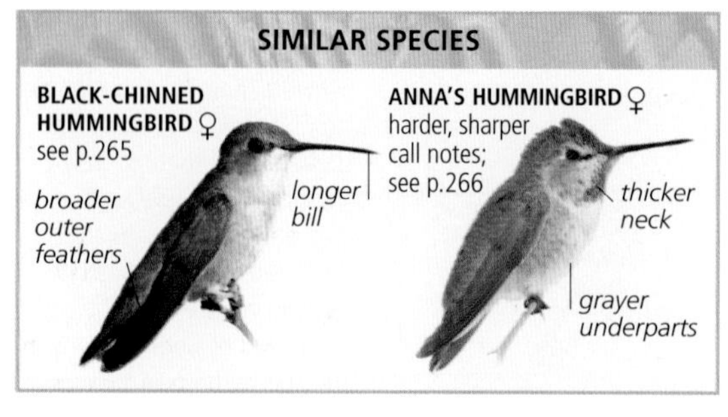
BLACK-CHINNED HUMMINGBIRD ♀
see p.265
broader outer feathers
longer bill
ANNA'S HUMMINGBIRD ♀
harder, sharper call notes;
see p.266
thicker neck
grayer underparts

OCCURRENCE
Favors a variety of woodlands, and gardens; earliest migrants appear in the South as early as late February; most leave by November; regular in winter in south Florida; small numbers winter elsewhere on the Gulf Coast; vagrant to the West. The bulk of the population migrates to Central America in winter.

Length **3½in (9cm)**	Wingspan **4¼in (11cm)**	Weight **1⁄16–7⁄32oz (2–6g)**
Social **Solitary**	Lifespan **Up to 9 years**	Status **Secure**

Order **Apodiformes**	Family **Trochilidae**	Species ***Archilochus alexandri***

Black-chinned Hummingbird

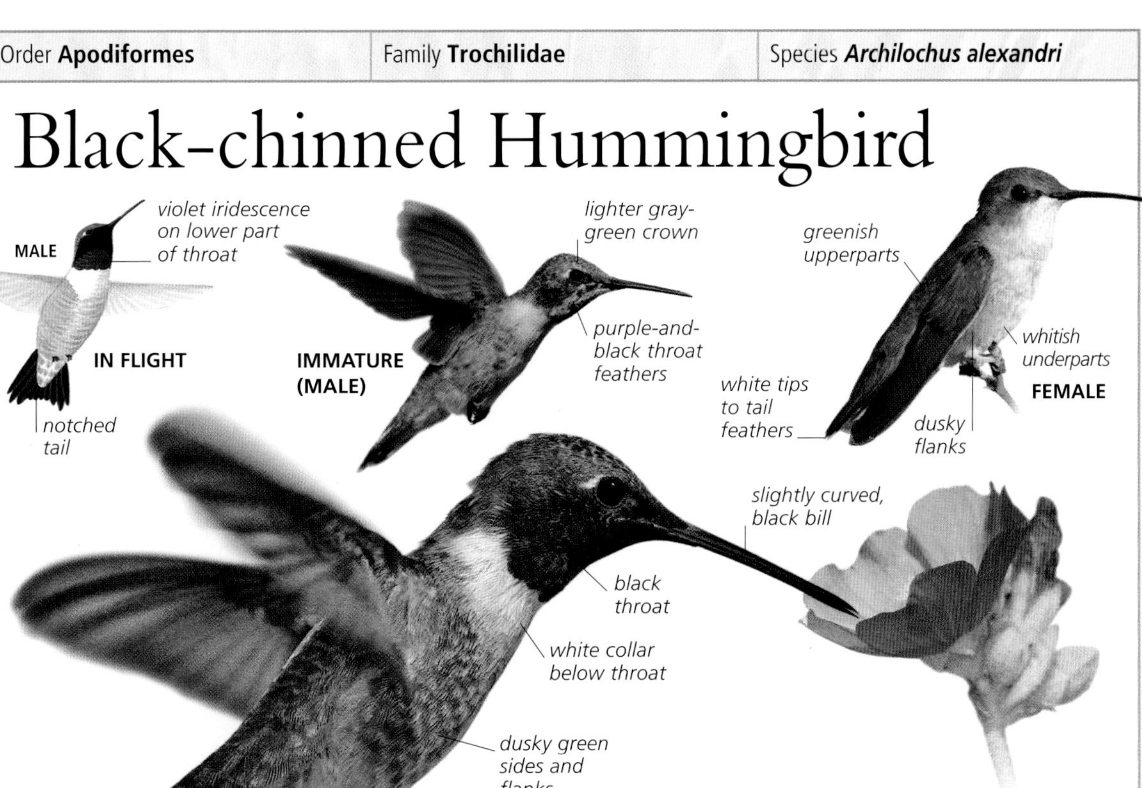

MALE
violet iridescence on lower part of throat
IN FLIGHT
notched tail
IMMATURE (MALE)
lighter gray-green crown
purple-and-black throat feathers
greenish upperparts
whitish underparts
FEMALE
white tips to tail feathers
dusky flanks
slightly curved, black bill
black throat
white collar below throat
dusky green sides and flanks
MALE
notched greenish tail with darker outer feathers

The Black-chinned Hummingbird is found in southern British Columbia and is widespread across the western US, mainly due to its adaptability. It readily accepts offerings of sugar water from birdfeeders. During courtship, the males perform a distinctive dive display comprising several broad arcs in addition to a short, back-and-forth shuttle display. The latter is accompanied by a droning noise produced by the bird's wings.

VOICE Call a soft, thick *chic*; fast, buzzy *tsi-tsi-tsi-tsi-tsi-tsi-tsi-tsi* is used to chase off other birds; song soft, warbling, very rarely heard.

NESTING Tiny cup of plant down, with leaves or lichen on the exterior, bound with spider's silk; usually built in a deciduous tree; 2 eggs; 1–2 broods; April–August.

FEEDING Drinks nectar from flowers; eats small insects and spiders, caught aerially or gleaned from foliage.

FLIGHT: rapid with very fast wing beats; hovers at flowers and darts after insects.

TAIL WAGGER
Black-chinned Hummingbirds regularly wag their tails from side to side while feeding.

SIMILAR SPECIES

RUBY-THROATED HUMMINGBIRD ♀ see p.264

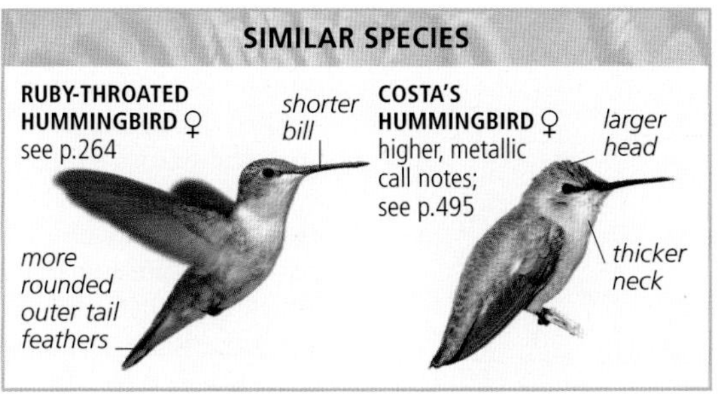

shorter bill
more rounded outer tail feathers

COSTA'S HUMMINGBIRD ♀ higher, metallic call notes; see p.495

larger head
thicker neck

OCCURRENCE
Widespread in a variety of habitats, particularly scrub and woodlands close to rivers and streams, and irrigated urban areas; also found in drier habitats; forages away from breeding habitat where nectar sources are found. Winters on the Pacific Coast of Mexico.

Length **3½in (9cm)**	Wingspan **4¾in (12cm)**	Weight **1/16–3/16oz (2–5g)**
Social **Solitary**	Lifespan **Up to 8 years**	Status **Secure**

Order **Apodiformes**	Family **Trochilidae**	Species ***Calypte anna***

Anna's Hummingbird

pale throat
MALE
square tail
IN FLIGHT
rose-red head, sides of neck, and throat
iridescent green upperparts
short, straight, black bill
green upperparts
green crown and nape
reddish spots or flecks on throat
pale gray underparts
FEMALE
rounded, green tail
slightly notched, dark green tail
grayish underparts
MALE
greenish sides and flanks
mottled rosy crown
IMMATURE (MALE)

The most common garden hummingbird along the Pacific Coast from British Columbia to Baja California, the iridescent rose-red helmet of a male Anna's Hummingbird is spectacular and distinctive. The females are rather drab by comparison. This adaptable hummingbird has expanded its range dramatically in the last century because of the availability of garden flowers and feeders. It previously bred only in areas of dense evergreen shrubs along the coast of southern California. The males perform an impressive diving display to court females.

VOICE Call a hard, sharp *tsit*, often doubled or given in series when perched; fast, buzzy chatter used to chase off other birds; song variable series of thin, high, buzzing, warbled notes.

NESTING Tiny cup of mostly plant down, with lichen on the exterior, bound with spider's silk, built in trees or shrubs; 2 eggs; 2 broods; December–July.

FEEDING Drinks nectar from flowers; eats small insects and spiders, caught aerially or gleaned from foliage.

FLIGHT: rapid flight with very fast wing beats; hovers at flowers and darts after insects.

VARIABLE THROAT
Mature female Anna's Hummingbirds often show small iridescent patches on their throats.

SIMILAR SPECIES

BLACK-CHINNED HUMMINGBIRD ♀ see p.265

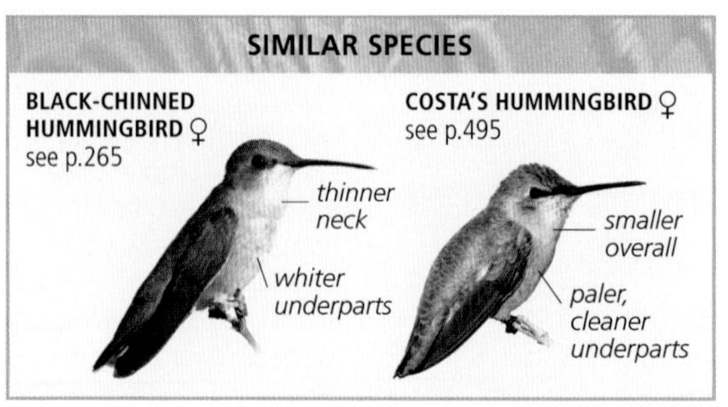
thinner neck
whiter underparts

COSTA'S HUMMINGBIRD ♀ see p.495

smaller overall
paler, cleaner underparts

OCCURRENCE
Primary breeding habitat is coastal dense shrubs and open woodland; also utilizes human areas. Habitat during migration and in winter largely dependent on available nectar sources; range expands northward and eastward during this time. Some birds winter in northwest Mexico; vagrant in the East.

Length **4in (10cm)**	Wingspan **5in (13cm)**	Weight **3/32–7/32oz (3–6g)**
Social **Solitary**	Lifespan **Up to 8 years**	Status **Secure**

Order **Apodiformes**	Family **Trochilidae**	Species ***Selasphorus rufus***

Rufous Hummingbird

MALE
rufous tail base with dark tips
IN FLIGHT
white spot near eye
green to bronze-green crown
straight, smooth bill
rufous upperparts
white patch on breast
wrinkled top bill
mostly green back
rufous uppertail feathers
IMMATURE
rich, rufous underparts
buff face coloration
whitish underparts
MALE
FEMALE

One of the most aggressive hummingbirds, the Rufous Hummingbird packs quite a punch, despite its small size; it often chases other hummingbirds away from nectar sources. This bird also breeds farther north than any other North American species of hummingbird and undertakes a lengthy migration. Males are recognizable by their overall fiery orange-rufous color, but females and immature birds are difficult to distinguish from Allen's Hummingbirds.

VOICE Call a hard *chuk*, sometimes in steady series or doubled; also short, buzzy warning call, *tssrr*; chase call a fast, raspy twitter, *tzzerr tichupy tichupy*.

NESTING Tiny cup of plant down, lichen, and other plant matter on exterior, bound with spider's silk, in shrubs or trees; 2 eggs; 1–2 broods; April–July.

FEEDING Drinks nectar from flowers and sap from trees; catches small insects and other arthropods in the air or gleans them off foliage.

FLIGHT: fast flight with extremely rapid wing beats; hovers at flowers; darts after insects.

SIMILAR SPECIES
BROAD-TAILED HUMMINGBIRD ♀
higher-pitched call; see p.495
dull pinkish flanks
broad tail
ALLEN'S HUMMINGBIRD ♂
entirely green back

FIERY MALE
With temperaments matching their bold, flame-like color, males aggressively defend territories.

OCCURRENCE
Breeds in old-growth forest clearings, bushy country, as well as urban gardens; early migrants appear in March; most leave by August; it has become a regular winter inhabitant along the Gulf Coast and southern California; fall or winter vagrants are becoming more common in the East.

Length **3½in (9cm)**	Wingspan **5in (13cm)**	Weight **3/32–7/32oz (3–6g)**
Social **Solitary**	Lifespan **Up to 12 years**	Status **Secure**

Order **Apodiformes**	Family **Trochilidae**	Species ***Stellula calliope***

Calliope Hummingbird

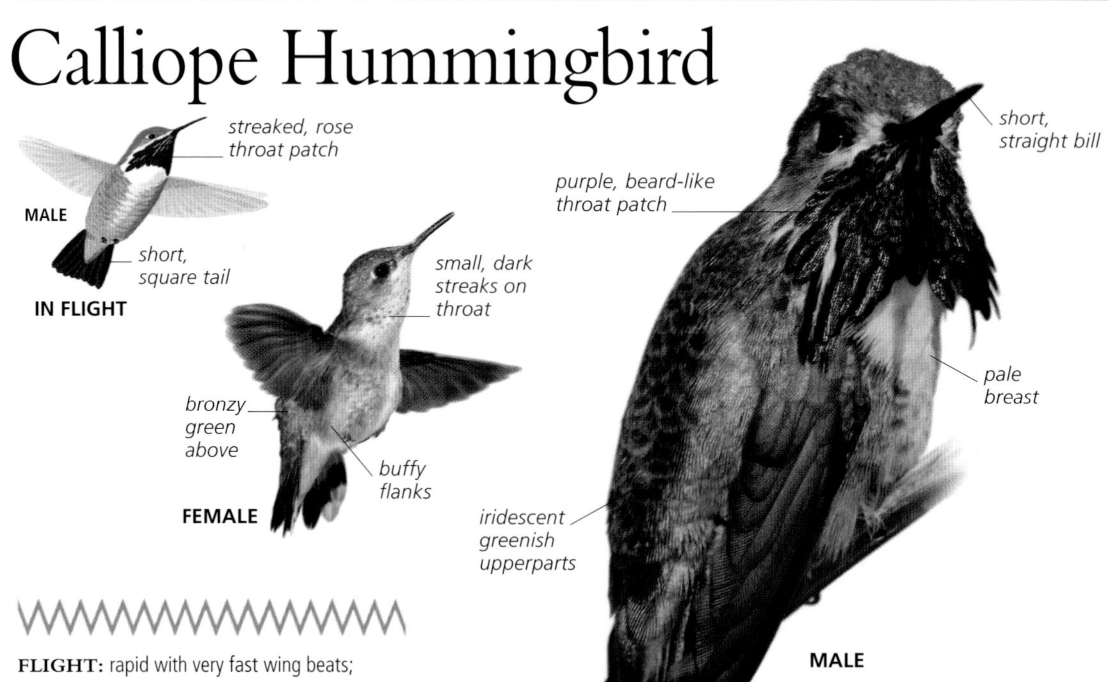
streaked, rose throat patch
MALE
short, square tail
IN FLIGHT
small, dark streaks on throat
bronzy green above
buffy flanks
FEMALE
short, straight bill
purple, beard-like throat patch
pale breast
iridescent greenish upperparts
MALE
short tail

FLIGHT: rapid with very fast wing beats; hovers at flowers and darts after insects.

The Calliope Hummingbird is North America's smallest bird. Despite its diminutive size, it is just as territorial as other hummingbird species; the females even attack squirrels trying to rob their nests. The streaky, purplish throat patch of the males is unique, but the plainer females can be confused with other hummingbird species when their small size is not evident in a direct comparison. The male courtship display includes a number of J-shaped dives, which are accompanied by a high *tzzt-zing* at the bottom, in addition to a buzzing hover display in front of a female.

VOICE Relatively silent for a hummingbird; call a soft, high *chip*, sometimes doubled or repeated; series of high buzzes and chips used to chase off other birds.

NESTING Tiny cup of plant material and lichen, bound with spider's silk and lined with plant down, usually under an overhanging conifer branch; 2 eggs; 1 brood; May–August.

FEEDING Catches small insects aerially or gleans insects and spiders from foliage; also drinks nectar.

ATTRACTED TO SAP
The Calliope Hummingbird commonly feeds on sap and the insects attracted to it.

MOUNTAIN GEM
Like other hummingbirds, this mountain dweller hovers to take nectar from flowers.

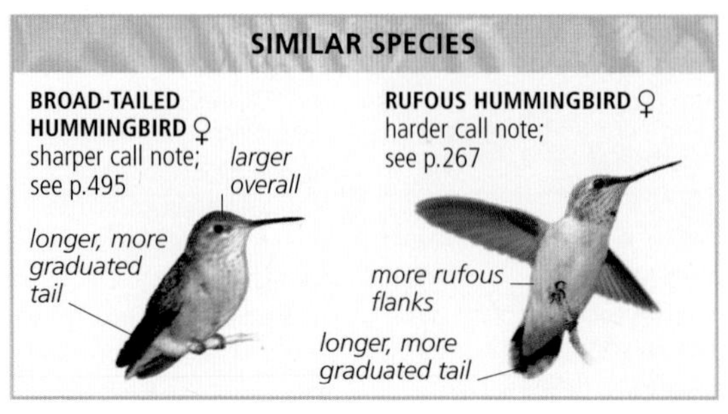
SIMILAR SPECIES
BROAD-TAILED HUMMINGBIRD ♀
sharper call note;
see p.495
larger overall
longer, more graduated tail
RUFOUS HUMMINGBIRD ♀
harder call note;
see p.267
more rufous flanks
longer, more graduated tail

OCCURRENCE
Present in western mountains primarily March–September; breeds mostly in coniferous mountainous forests, meadows, and thickets; spring migrants found in a variety of lower elevation habitats; fall migrants are found at higher elevations; very rare in winter along the Gulf Coast.

Length **3¼in (8cm)**	Wingspan **4¼in (10.5cm)**	Weight **1/16–5/32oz (2–4g)**
Social **Solitary**	Lifespan **Up to 12 years**	Status **Secure**

KINGFISHERS

KINGFISHERS ARE PRIMARILY a tropical family that apparently originated in the Australasian region. There are approximately 90 species of kingfisher in the world, and most have large heads with long pointed bills, short legs, stubby tails, and bright plumage. Three species of Alcedinidae are found in North America, but only one, the Belted Kingfisher, is widespread and found in Canada. Like most species of kingfishers, these birds are large-headed and large-billed but have comparatively short legs and toes. Although lacking the array of bright blues, greens, and reds associated with their tropical and European counterparts, Belted Kingfishers are striking birds, distinguished by shaggy head crests, breastbands, and white underparts. The females of the species are more brightly colored than the males, sporting chestnut-colored breastbands. While they also eat amphibians, reptiles, insects, and crustaceans, Belted Kingfishers are primarily fish-eaters. They will frequent a favorite perch along a waterway for hunting, or hover if no perch is available, and will plunge headfirst into the water to catch their prey. After catching a fish, they routinely stun their prey by beating it against a perch before turning the fish around so that it can be eaten head first. Mating pairs dig a burrow in a bank about 3–6ft (1–2m) long. The female lays 6–7 eggs; both adults share the task of incubating the eggs and feeding the young. Parents entice the young to leave the burrow by perching outside with a fish in their bill and calling to them. A week usually passes before the fledglings are able to capture live fish.

Migration depends on the availability of open water—kingfishers will stay in an area year round if they have access to fishing grounds.

FISH DINNER
A Belted Kingfisher uses its large bill to catch and hold slippery prey.

SEDATE MALE
Unlike many birds, the male Belted Kingfisher is not as colorful as the female.

Order **Coraciiformes**	Family **Alcedinidae**	Species ***Megaceryle alcyon***

Belted Kingfisher

MALE
large head
single blue breastband
barred tail
IN FLIGHT
bluish gray head with shaggy crest
long, thick, powerful bill
white collar
bluish slate upperparts
white belly
MALE
prominent crest
chestnut band across breast
chestnut flanks
FEMALE
double crest
white collar
single dark breastband
IMMATURE MALE

Its stocky body, double-pointed crest, large head, and contrasting white collar distinguish the Belted Kingfisher from other species in its range. This kingfisher's loud and far-carrying rattles are heard more often than the bird is seen. Interestingly, it is one of the few birds in North America in which the female is more colorful than the male. The Belted Kingfisher can be found in a large variety of aquatic habitats, both coastal and inland, vigorously defending its territory, all year round.

VOICE Harsh mechanical rattle given in flight or from a perch; sometimes emits screams or trill-like warble during breeding.

NESTING Unlined chamber in subterranean burrow 3–6ft (1–2m) deep, excavated in earthen bank usually over water, but sometimes in ditches, sand, or gravel pits; 6–7 eggs; 1 brood; March–July.

FEEDING Plunge-dives from branches or wires to catch a wide variety of fish near the surface, including sticklebacks and trout; also takes crustaceans, such as crayfish.

FLIGHT: strongly flaps its wings and then glides after two or three beats; frequently hovers.

CATCH OF THE DAY
The female's chestnut belly band and flanks are clearly visible here as she perches with her catch.

OCCURRENCE
Breeds and winters around clear, open waters of streams, rivers, lakes, estuaries, and protected marine shorelines, where perches are available and prey is visible. Avoids water with emergent vegetation. Northern populations migrate south to Mexico, Central America, and the West Indies.

SIMILAR SPECIES

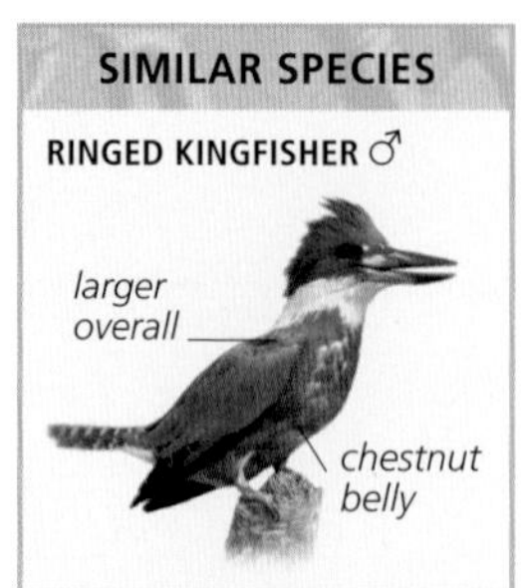
RINGED KINGFISHER ♂
larger overall
chestnut belly

Length **11–14in (28–35cm)**	Wingspan **19–23in (48–58cm)**	Weight **5–6oz (150–175g)**
Social **Solitary**	Lifespan **Unknown**	Status **Secure**

WOODPECKERS

THE THREE GROUPS of closely related species that constitute the family Picidae are found throughout North America. They are a physically striking group adapted to living on tree trunks.

WOODPECKERS

The species that constitute the typical woodpeckers of North America share a distinct set of physical characteristics and behaviors. Their pecking and drumming, which they use for purposes of constructing nest cavities and communication, is made possible by a very thick skull, adapted to withstand the shock that results from continual pecking on wood. Woodpeckers nest in cavities in dead trees, and they are vulnerable to the loss of their specialized habitats as well as forest clearing.

RED ALERT
With its crimson head, the Red-headed Woodpecker is an instantly recognizable bird in North America.

SAPSUCKERS

This group of bird feed on tree sap as a primary source of nourishment for both adults and their young. Sapsuckers have tongues tipped with stiff hairs to allow sap that stick to them. The holes the birds create in trees in order to extract the sap also attract insects, which make up the main protein source in the sapsucker diet. Because they damage living trees, some orchard growers consider sapsuckers to be pests.

BALANCING ACT
The Yellow-bellied Sapsucker rests its stiff tail against a tree to maintain its balance.

FLICKERS

Flickers are relatively large members of the family Picidae and spend more time feeding on the ground than other woodpeckers, consuming ants and other insects. Flickers often forage in open areas around human habitation. They are notable for their colorful underwing feather plumages and their distinctive white rump.

COMMON FLICKER
The Northern Flicker can be found across the entire North American continent.

Order **Piciformes**	Family **Picidae**	Species ***Melanerpes lewis***

Lewis' Woodpecker

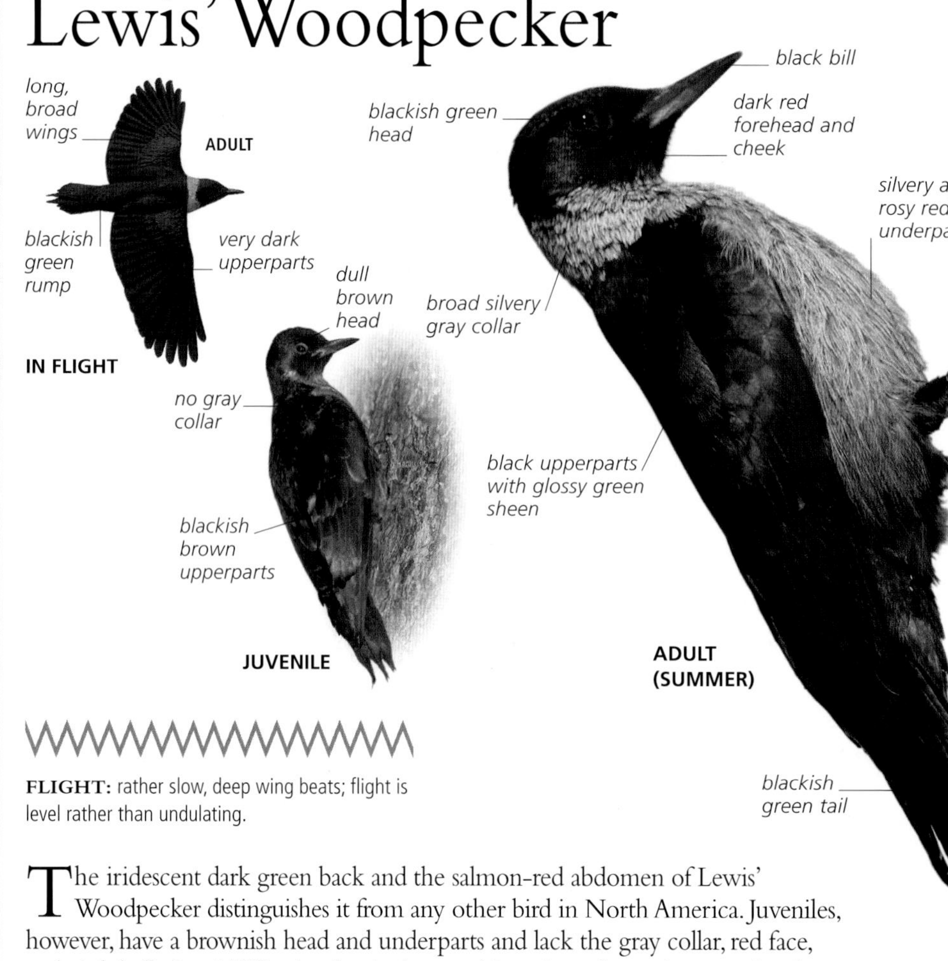
long, broad wings
ADULT
blackish green rump
very dark upperparts
IN FLIGHT
dull brown head
no gray collar
blackish brown upperparts
JUVENILE
blackish green head
broad silvery gray collar
black bill
dark red forehead and cheek
silvery and rosy red underparts
black upperparts with glossy green sheen
ADULT (SUMMER)
blackish green tail

FLIGHT: rather slow, deep wing beats; flight is level rather than undulating.

The iridescent dark green back and the salmon-red abdomen of Lewis' Woodpecker distinguishes it from any other bird in North America. Juveniles, however, have a brownish head and underparts and lack the gray collar, red face, and pink belly. Lewis' Woodpecker is also notably quieter than other woodpeckers, but it aggressively defends its food sources from other woodpeckers, especially in the winter. During flight, the bird accomplishes acrobatic maneuvers in pursuit of flying insects, sallying out from a perch in order to catch them. Alexander Wilson, the founder of North American ornithology, named this species in 1811, to honor Meriwether Lewis, because it was collected during the Lewis and Clark expedition.

VOICE *Churrs* sound; drumming not loud.

NESTING Cavity nester, usually in dead tree trunks, with preference for natural cavities and previously used nest holes; 6–7 eggs; 1 brood; May–August.

FEEDING Eats a variety of flying insects during breeding season; acorns, other nuts, and fruits, at other times.

FAVORITE HANGOUT
This bird is found in a variety of habitats, but is most common in Ponderosa pine forests.

LOVE NEST
Lewis' Woodpecker excavates cavities in dead trees for nesting purposes.

OCCURRENCE
Prefers open Ponderosa pine forests for breeding, especially old growth stands that have been modified by burning. Also found in riverside woodlands with cottonwood trees. Gravitates to open canopy; in winter, oak woodlands and nut and fruit orchards.

Length **10–11in (25–28cm)**	Wingspan **19–20in (48–51cm)**	Weight **3¼–5oz (90–150g)**
Social **Solitary**	Lifespan **Unknown**	Status **Localized**

Order **Piciformes**	Family **Picidae**	Species ***Melanerpes erythrocephalus***

Red-headed Woodpecker

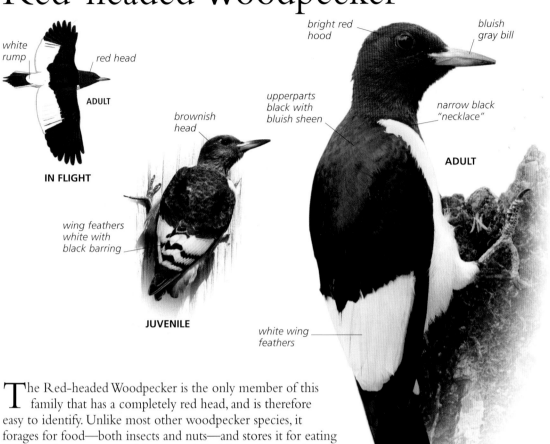

white rump

red head

ADULT

IN FLIGHT

brownish head

wing feathers white with black barring

JUVENILE

bright red hood

bluish gray bill

upperparts black with bluish sheen

narrow black "necklace"

ADULT

white wing feathers

The Red-headed Woodpecker is the only member of this family that has a completely red head, and is therefore easy to identify. Unlike most other woodpecker species, it forages for food—both insects and nuts—and stores it for eating at a later time. It is one of the most skilled flycatchers in the woodpecker family. Its numbers have declined, largely because of the destruction of its habitat, especially the removal of dead trees in urban and rural areas, and clearing and cutting of trees for firewood in rural areas. The Red-headed Woodpecker is a truly North American bird, not extending south of the Rio Grande.

VOICE Primary call an extremely harsh and loud *churr*, also produces breeding call and alarm; no song; active drummer.

NESTING Excavates cavity in dead wood; 3–5 eggs; 1–2 broods; May–August.

FEEDING Forages in flight, on ground, and in trees; feeds on a variety of insects, spiders, nuts seeds, berries, and fruit, and, in rare cases, small mammals such as mice.

WORK IN PROGRESS The Red-headed Woodpecker excavates its breeding cavities in tree trunks and stumps.

FLIGHT: strong flapping; undulation not as marked as in other woodpecker species.

OCCURRENCE
Breeds in a variety of habitats, especially open deciduous woodlands, including riverine areas, orchards, municipal parks, agricultural areas, forest edges, and forests affected by fire. Uses the same habitats during the winter as in the breeding season.

Length **8½–9½in (22–24cm)**	Wingspan **16–18in (41–46cm)**	Weight **2–3oz (55–85g)**
Social **Solitary**	Lifespan **At least 10 years**	Status **Declining**

Order **Piciformes**	Family **Picidae**	Species ***Melanerpes carolinus***

Red-bellied Woodpecker

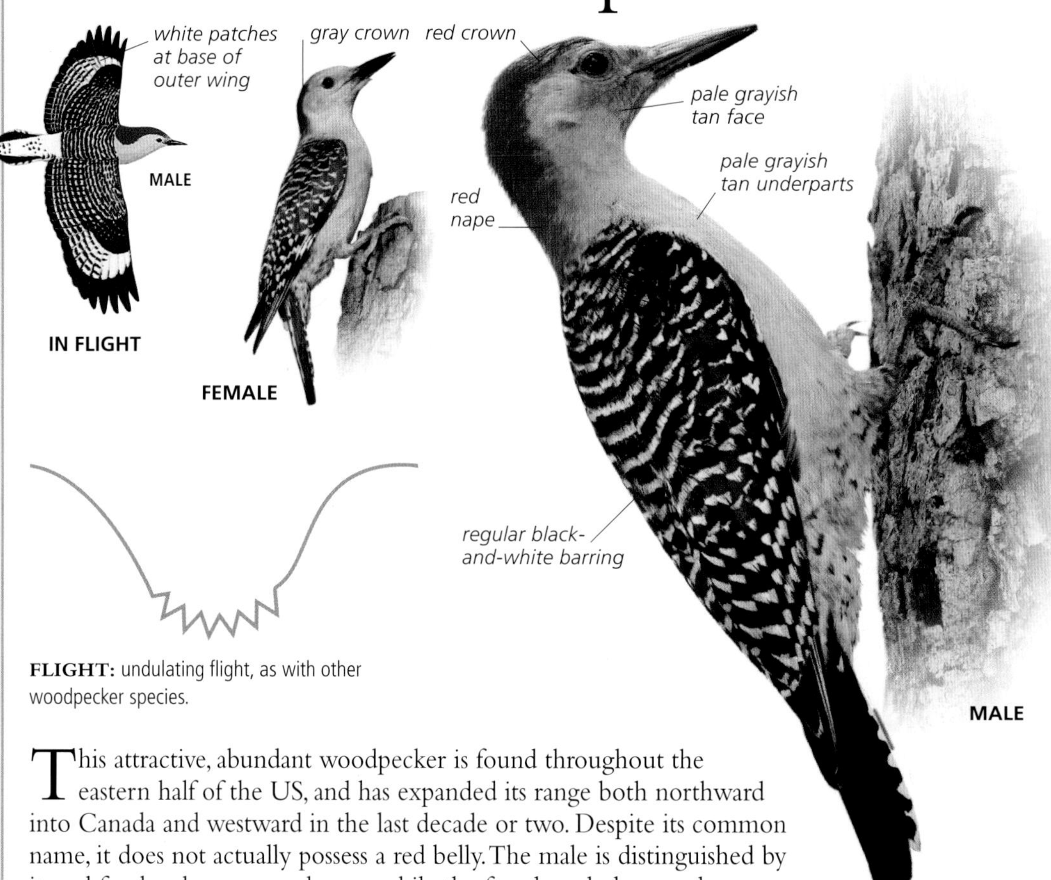
white patches at base of outer wing
MALE
IN FLIGHT
gray crown
FEMALE
red crown
pale grayish tan face
pale grayish tan underparts
red nape
regular black-and-white barring
MALE

FLIGHT: undulating flight, as with other woodpecker species.

This attractive, abundant woodpecker is found throughout the eastern half of the US, and has expanded its range both northward into Canada and westward in the last decade or two. Despite its common name, it does not actually possess a red belly. The male is distinguished by its red forehead, crown, and nape, while the female only has a red nape; both have pale-colored underparts and regularly barred upperparts. Male Red-bellied Woodpeckers excavate several holes in trees, one of which the female chooses. They also use previously available cavities, but often lose them to aggressive starlings. Unlike many woodpecker species, although the Red-bellied eats insects, it does not excavate trees to find them.

VOICE Rather soft, clearly rolling, slightly quivering *krrurrr* call.

NESTING Cavity nester; 4–5 eggs; 1–3 broods; May–August.

FEEDING Eats insects, fruit, seeds, acorns, and other nuts; in winter, eats mainly vegetable matter.

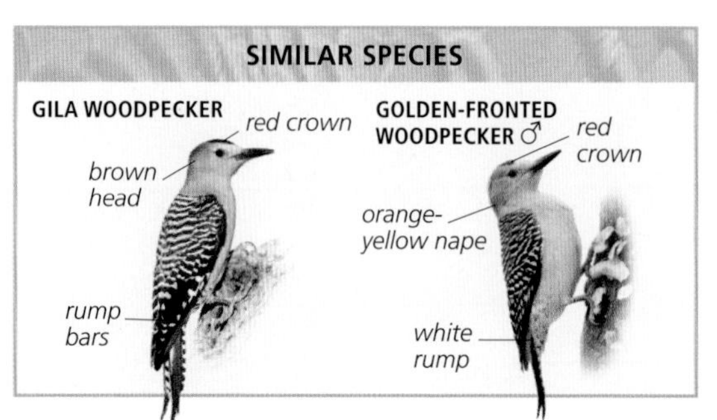
SIMILAR SPECIES
GILA WOODPECKER
red crown
brown head
rump bars
GOLDEN-FRONTED WOODPECKER ♂
red crown
orange-yellow nape
white rump

SUBURBAN SPECIES
These birds can be seen and heard on tree trunks in suburban and urban woods.

OCCURRENCE
Resident in southeastern Canada and eastern and southeastern US, where it breeds in a wide range of habitats; found in forests, swamps, suburban wooded areas, open woodlands, and parks. Winter habitats resemble the breeding areas.

Length **9–10½in (23–27cm)**	Wingspan **16in (41cm)**	Weight **2½ oz (70g)**
Social **Solitary/Pairs**	Lifespan **Up to 12 years**	Status **Secure**

Order **Piciformes**	Family **Picidae**	Species ***Sphyrapicus thyroideus***

Williamson's Sapsucker

white rump

black wings with white patches

black tail

FEMALE

IN FLIGHT

MALE

dark bill

red throat

white head stripe

brown head

black back

barred flanks

brown overall with barred plumage

dark back

white wing patch

FEMALE

JUVENILE MALE

MALE

The Williamson's Sapsucker is one of the four sapsucker species occurring in North America. Unlike other sapsuckers, the male and female plumages are so dissimilar that it is difficult to believe they belong to the same species. The species has very specific habitat needs, partly because of its dependence on the sap and phloem, the innermost bark layer of trees. This secretive sapsucker can be located in the breeding season by its rather hesitant drumming, which occurs in an uneven series. With its white rump the female looks like a flicker in flight.

VOICE Primary call nasal *churr;* also a mewing call.

NESTING Excavates cavity in dead wood; 5–6 eggs; 1 brood; May–July.

FEEDING Mainly eats tree sap and ants during the breeding season; nonbreeding birds feed on the sap, phloem, and fruit of trees.

DRILLING FOR FOOD
These birds drill holes in tree barks and then eat the sap and insects that emerge.

FLIGHT: undulating flight pattern, similar to other sapsuckers

OCCURRENCE
A species of the Intermountain West, breeding in coniferous forest. Winters at lower elevations, where it mainly occupies pine-oak woodlands, in the southeastern US and in Mexico.

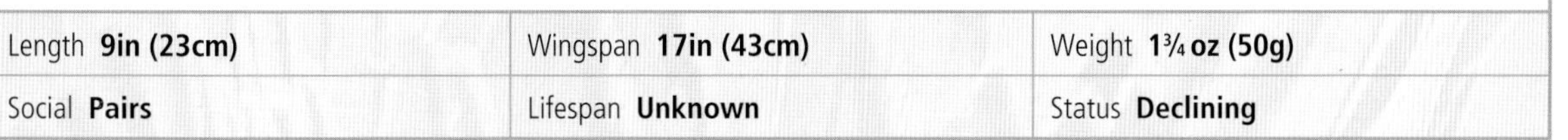

Length **9in (23cm)**	Wingspan **17in (43cm)**	Weight **1¾oz (50g)**
Social **Pairs**	Lifespan **Unknown**	Status **Declining**

Order **Piciformes**	Family **Picidae**	Species ***Sphyrapicus varius***

Yellow-bellied Sapsucker

MALE

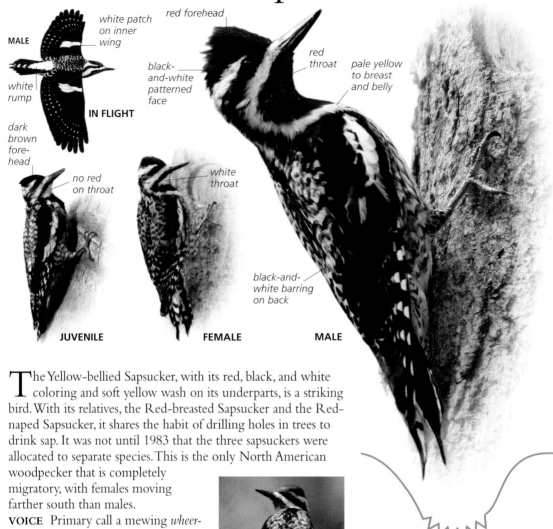

white patch on inner wing

white rump

IN FLIGHT

dark brown forehead

no red on throat

JUVENILE

white throat

FEMALE

red forehead

black-and-white patterned face

red throat

pale yellow to breast and belly

black-and-white barring on back

MALE

The Yellow-bellied Sapsucker, with its red, black, and white coloring and soft yellow wash on its underparts, is a striking bird. With its relatives, the Red-breasted Sapsucker and the Red-naped Sapsucker, it shares the habit of drilling holes in trees to drink sap. It was not until 1983 that the three sapsuckers were allocated to separate species. This is the only North American woodpecker that is completely migratory, with females moving farther south than males.

VOICE Primary call a mewing *wheer-wheer-wheer.*

NESTING Cavities in dead trees; 5–6 eggs; 1 brood; May–June.

FEEDING Drinks sap; eats ants and other small insects; feeds on the inner bark of trees, also a variety of fruit.

FLIGHT: typical woodpecker, undulating flight pattern with intermittent flapping and gliding.

STRIKING SPECIES
The Yellow-bellied Sapsucker's white rump and black-and-white forked tail are clearly evident here.

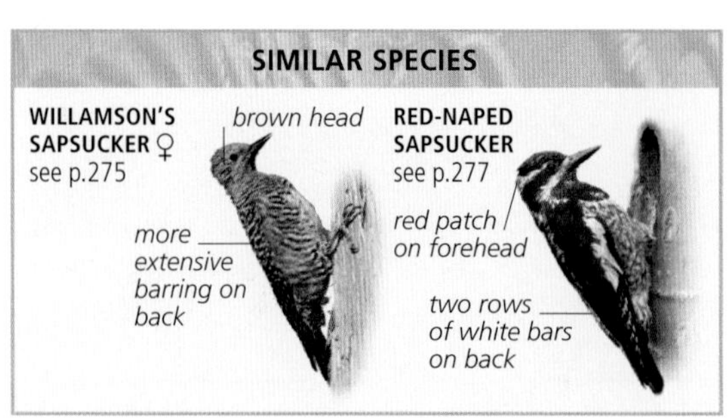
SIMILAR SPECIES
WILLAMSON'S SAPSUCKER ♀
see p.275
brown head
more extensive barring on back
RED-NAPED SAPSUCKER
see p.277
red patch on forehead
two rows of white bars on back

OCCURRENCE
Breeds in eastern Alaska, Canada, and south to the Appalachians. Prefers either deciduous forests or mixed deciduous-coniferous forests; prefers young forests. In winter, it is found in open wooded areas in southeastern states, Caribbean islands, and Central America.

Length **8–9in (20–23cm)**	Wingspan **16–18in (41–46cm)**	Weight **1¾oz (50g)**
Social **Solitary/Pairs**	Lifespan **Up to 7 years**	Status **Secure**

Order **Piciformes**	Family **Picidae**	Species ***Sphyrapicus nuchalis***

Red-naped Sapsucker

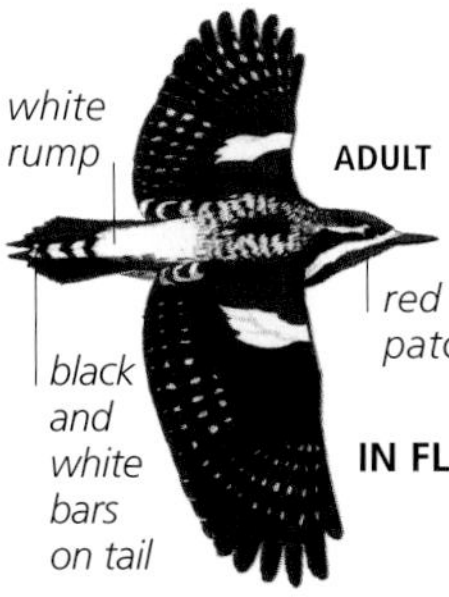

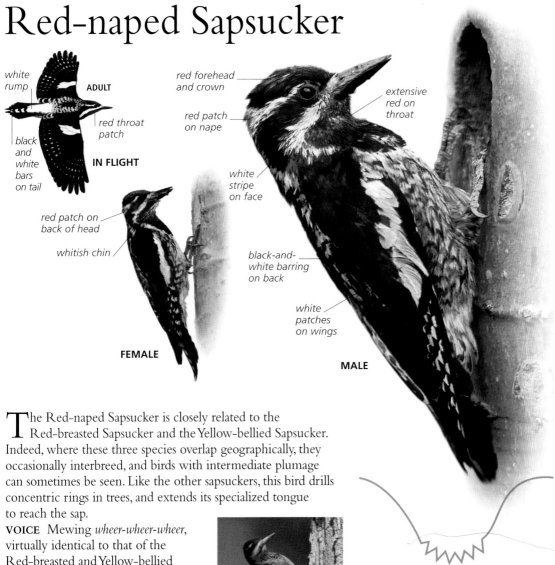

white rump
ADULT
red throat patch
black and white bars on tail
IN FLIGHT
red patch on back of head
whitish chin
FEMALE
red forehead and crown
red patch on nape
extensive red on throat
white stripe on face
black-and-white barring on back
white patches on wings
MALE

The Red-naped Sapsucker is closely related to the Red-breasted Sapsucker and the Yellow-bellied Sapsucker. Indeed, where these three species overlap geographically, they occasionally interbreed, and birds with intermediate plumage can sometimes be seen. Like the other sapsuckers, this bird drills concentric rings in trees, and extends its specialized tongue to reach the sap.

VOICE Mewing *wheer-wheer-wheer*, virtually identical to that of the Red-breasted and Yellow-bellied sapsuckers.

NESTING Cavity nester; 4–5 eggs; 1 brood; May–August.

FEEDING Feeds on sap and seeds; fruit and other vegetable matter; also insects and spiders.

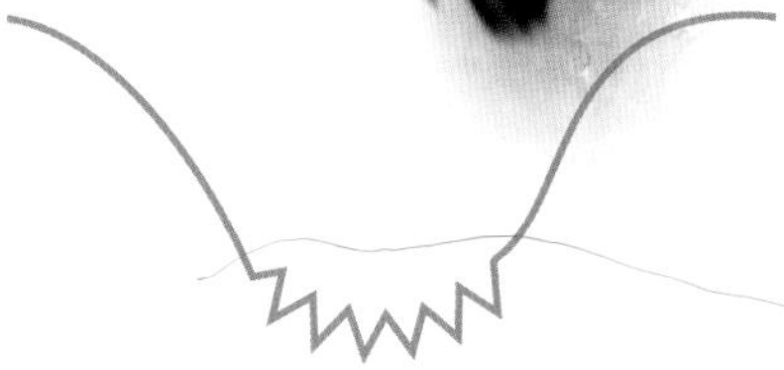

FLIGHT: typical woodpecker, undulating flight pattern, with intermittent flapping and gliding.

ASPEN DWELLER
The Red-naped Sapsucker excavates its nest cavities in live aspens.

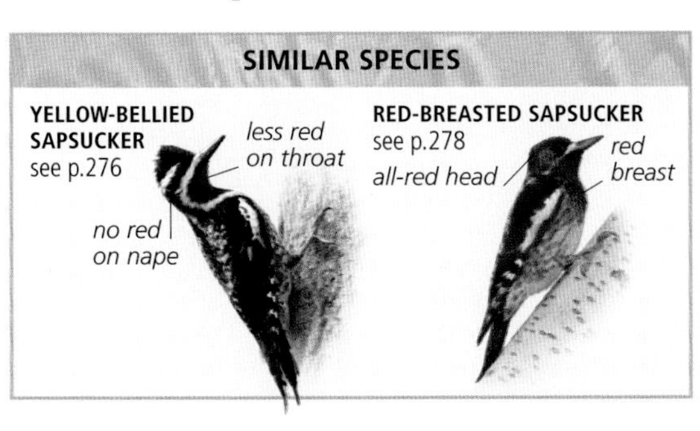
SIMILAR SPECIES
YELLOW-BELLIED SAPSUCKER
see p.276
less red on throat
no red on nape
RED-BREASTED SAPSUCKER
see p.278
all-red head
red breast

OCCURRENCE
Breeds in coniferous forest, intermixed with aspen, in the Rocky Mountains from Canada to California; but also riverside woodlands. Winter habitats include forests, open woodlands, parks, and orchards in the Southeast.

Length **8–9in (20–23cm)**	Wingspan **17in (43cm)**	Weight **2⅛oz (60g)**
Social **Solitary/Migrant flocks**	Lifespan **Up to 3 years**	Status **Localized**

Order **Piciformes**	Family **Picidae**	Species ***Sphyrapicus ruber***

Red-breasted Sapsucker

yellowish spots on back
white rump
MALE (S. r. ruber)
IN FLIGHT
duller head
deep red head
heavy white markings on upperparts
ADULT (S. r. ruber)
ADULT (S. r. daggetti)
red head
thick bill
large white patch on wing
red breast
pale yellowish belly
black back with white feathers
ADULT (S. r. daggetti)

FLIGHT: undulating flight pattern with intermittent flapping and gliding.

Apart from its distinctive red head and breast, the Red-breasted Sapsucker resembles other sapsuckers—so much so that the interrelated Red-breasted, Red-naped, and Yellow-bellied Sapsuckers were once all considered to belong to the same species. Like its relatives, the Red-breasted Sapsucker drills holes in tree trunks to extract sap. Other birds and mammals, such as squirrels and bats, obtain food from these holes. The northern form, *S. r. ruber,* occurs from Alaska to Oregon, and has a back lightly marked with gold spots and a brightly colored head. It's southern counterpart, *S. r. daggetti*, has a back more heavily marked with white.

VOICE Call reminiscent of a mewing cat; normally does not vocalize outside the breeding season.

NESTING Excavates cavity in deciduous trees such as aspen and willow, but will also nest in conifers if deciduous trees are not available; 4–5 eggs; 1 brood; May–July.

FEEDING Mainly drills for sap from a number of plants; also eats the insects that have become trapped in the sap.

SIMILAR SPECIES

RED-NAPED SAPSUCKER see p.277

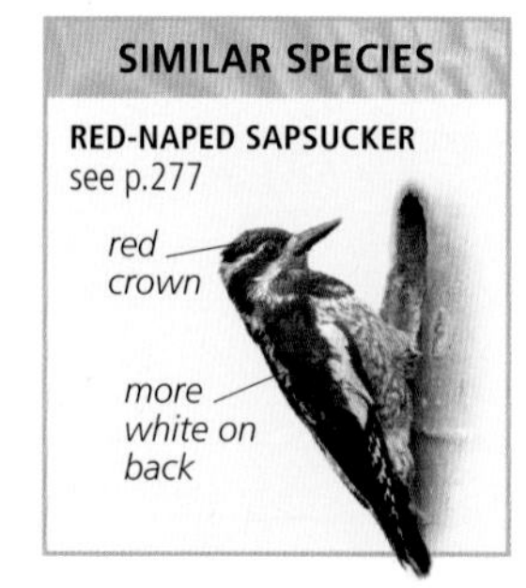

red crown
more white on back

RED-HEADED DRILLER
Red-breasted Sapsuckers drill holes in trees to drink sap and eat the insects attracted to it.

OCCURRENCE
Breeds in a wide range of habitats, including coniferous forests, but may also select deciduous forests and habitats along rivers. Prefers areas with dead trees. A partial migrant, it winters within its breeding range, but also moves south, as far as northern Baja California.

Length **8–9in (20–23cm)**	Wingspan **15–16in (38–41cm)**	Weight **2oz (55g)**
Social **Solitary**	Lifespan **2–3 years**	Status **Localized**

Order **Piciformes**	Family **Picidae**	Species ***Picoides pubescens***

Downy Woodpecker

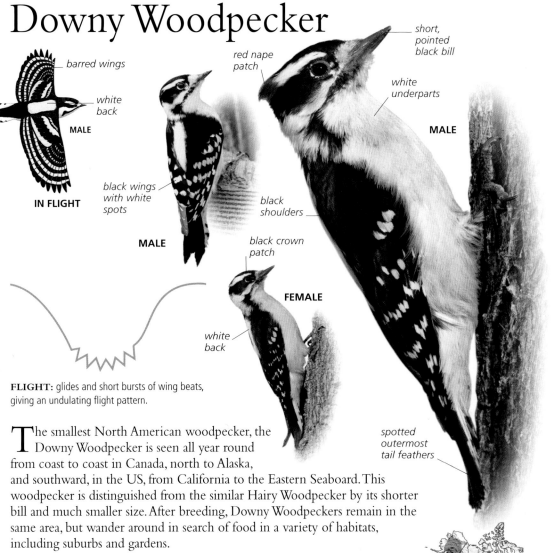

barred wings
white back
MALE
IN FLIGHT
black wings with white spots
MALE
red nape patch
short, pointed black bill
white underparts
MALE
black shoulders
black crown patch
FEMALE
white back
spotted outermost tail feathers

FLIGHT: glides and short bursts of wing beats, giving an undulating flight pattern.

The smallest North American woodpecker, the Downy Woodpecker is seen all year round from coast to coast in Canada, north to Alaska, and southward, in the US, from California to the Eastern Seaboard. This woodpecker is distinguished from the similar Hairy Woodpecker by its shorter bill and much smaller size. After breeding, Downy Woodpeckers remain in the same area, but wander around in search of food in a variety of habitats, including suburbs and gardens.

VOICE Two main calls—a high-pitched *pik*, and an even higher-pitched whinny; also rattles and chirps.

NESTING Excavates cavity in dead wood; 4–5 eggs; 1 brood; May–July.

FEEDING Forages for insects and spiders from the surfaces and bark crevices of live and dead trees, but also eats fruits, seeds, and other vegetable matter, depending on the season.

SIMILAR SPECIES

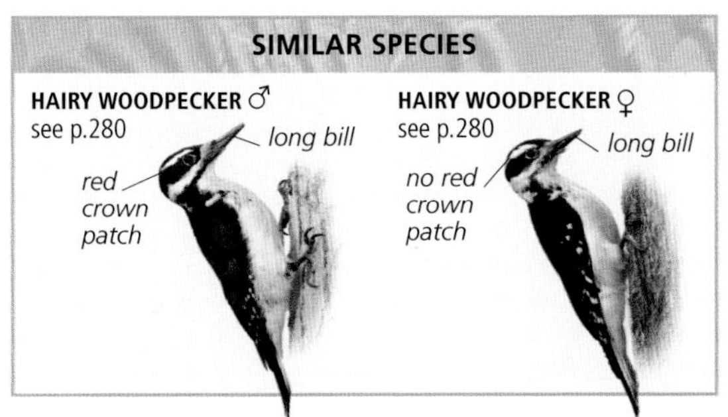
HAIRY WOODPECKER ♂
see p.280
long bill
red crown patch
HAIRY WOODPECKER ♀
see p.280
long bill
no red crown patch

SUET LOVERS
Downy Woodpeckers will feed on suet provided in feeders during the winter.

OCCURRENCE
Breeds in a wide variety of habitats, including deciduous and mixed deciduous-coniferous woodlands, parks, wooded suburban areas, and areas near rivers. While using nature's bounty of dead trees, it will also use man-made objects such as fence posts. Resident, but local movements occur.

Length **6–7in (15–18cm)**	Wingspan **10–12in (25–30cm)**	Weight **1¹⁄₁₆oz (30g)**
Social **Solitary/Flocks**	Lifespan **Up to 11 years**	Status **Secure**

Order **Piciformes**	Family **Picidae**	Species ***Plcoides villosus***

Hairy Woodpecker

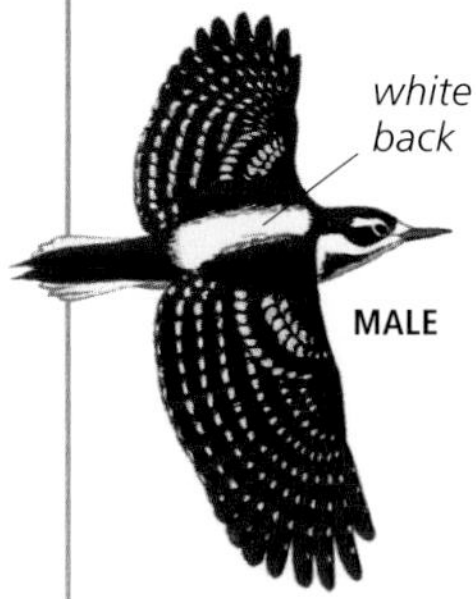

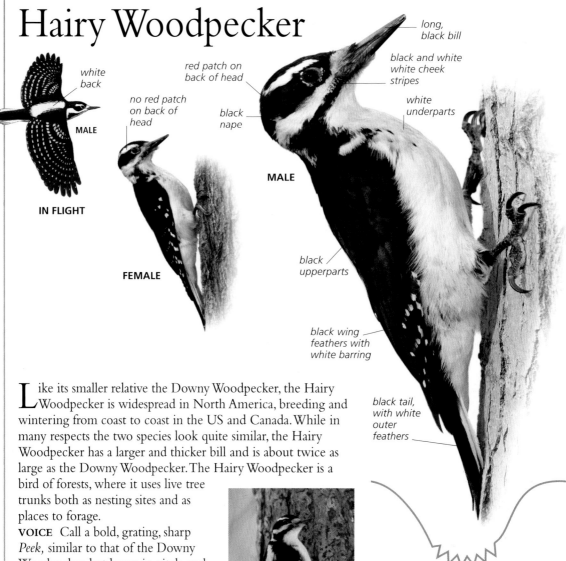

white back

MALE

IN FLIGHT

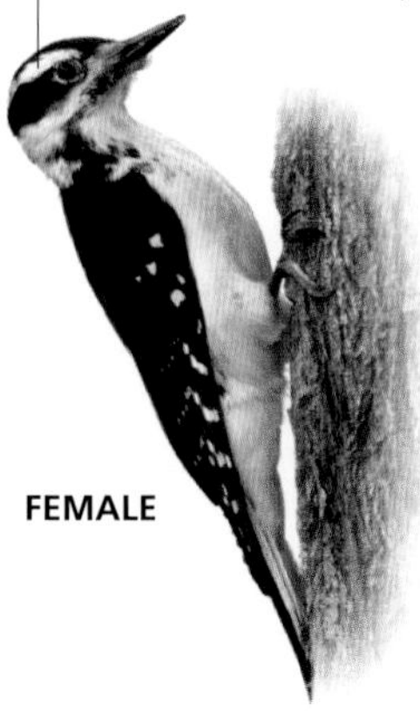

no red patch on back of head

FEMALE

red patch on back of head

black nape

long, black bill

black and white white cheek stripes

white underparts

MALE

black upperparts

black wing feathers with white barring

black tail, with white outer feathers

Like its smaller relative the Downy Woodpecker, the Hairy Woodpecker is widespread in North America, breeding and wintering from coast to coast in the US and Canada. While in many respects the two species look quite similar, the Hairy Woodpecker has a larger and thicker bill and is about twice as large as the Downy Woodpecker. The Hairy Woodpecker is a bird of forests, where it uses live tree trunks both as nesting sites and as places to forage.

VOICE Call a bold, grating, sharp *Peek,* similar to that of the Downy Woodpecker, but lower in pitch, and louder. Drumming a rather loud, even series of taps.

NESTING Excavates cavity in live trees; 4 eggs; 1 brood; May–July.

FEEDING Eats mainly insects and their larvae; also nuts and seeds.

FLIGHT: undulating; short glides alternating with wing beats.

HOME SWEET HOME
The Hairy Woodpecker is generally found in forests and prefers mature woodland areas, using both deciduous and coniferous trees.

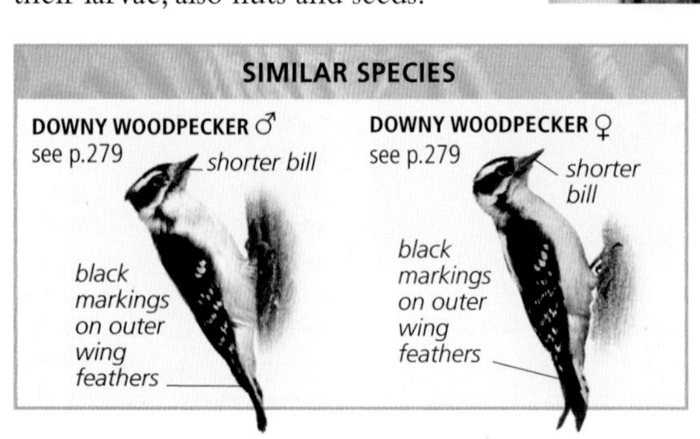
SIMILAR SPECIES
DOWNY WOODPECKER ♂
see p.279
shorter bill
black markings on outer wing feathers
DOWNY WOODPECKER ♀
see p.279
shorter bill
black markings on outer wing feathers

OCCURRENCE
Breeds primarily in forests, both deciduous and coniferous, but also in more open woodlands, swamps, suburban parks, and wooded areas. Resident in North America all the year-round, though in the far north of its range it may move south for the winter.

Length **9–9½in (23–24cm)**	Wingspan **15–16in (38–41cm)**	Weight **2½oz (70g)**
Social **Solitary/Winter flocks**	Lifespan **At least 16 years**	Status **Secure**

Order **Piciformes**	Family **Picidae**	Species ***Picoides albolarvatus***

White-headed Woodpecker

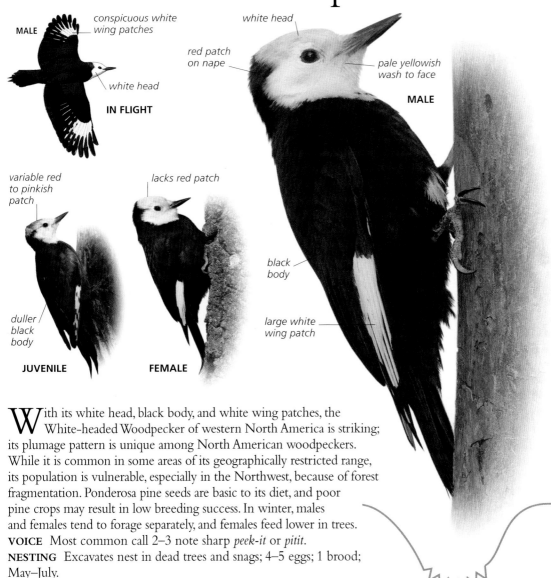

MALE
conspicuous white wing patches
white head
IN FLIGHT

white head
red patch on nape
pale yellowish wash to face
MALE

variable red to pinkish patch
duller black body
JUVENILE

lacks red patch
FEMALE

black body
large white wing patch

With its white head, black body, and white wing patches, the White-headed Woodpecker of western North America is striking; its plumage pattern is unique among North American woodpeckers. While it is common in some areas of its geographically restricted range, its population is vulnerable, especially in the Northwest, because of forest fragmentation. Ponderosa pine seeds are basic to its diet, and poor pine crops may result in low breeding success. In winter, males and females tend to forage separately, and females feed lower in trees.

VOICE Most common call 2–3 note sharp *peek-it* or *pitit*.

NESTING Excavates nest in dead trees and snags; 4–5 eggs; 1 brood; May–July.

FEEDING Eats arthropods, including ants, beetles, and spiders; also berries, and seeds, particularly pine seeds.

FLIGHT: undulating flight pattern typical of woodpeckers.

SIMILAR SPECIES

ACORN WOODPECKER see p.495
white forehead patch
red crown

PARENTING CHORES
This bird is carrying food back to the nest to feed its young.

OCCURRENCE
A strictly western North American bird, occurs from British Columbia to California in mountainous pine forests, especially with Ponderosa pines. Habitat specialist, but many birds move to lower elevations in winter, can be seen in deserts of Montana, Wyoming, and California.

Length **9–9½in (23–24cm)**	Wingspan **16–17in (41–43cm)**	Weight **2oz (55g)**
Social **Solitary**	Lifespan **Unknown**	Status **Localized**

Order **Piciformes**	Family **Picidae**	Species ***Picoides dorsalis***

American Three-toed Woodpecker

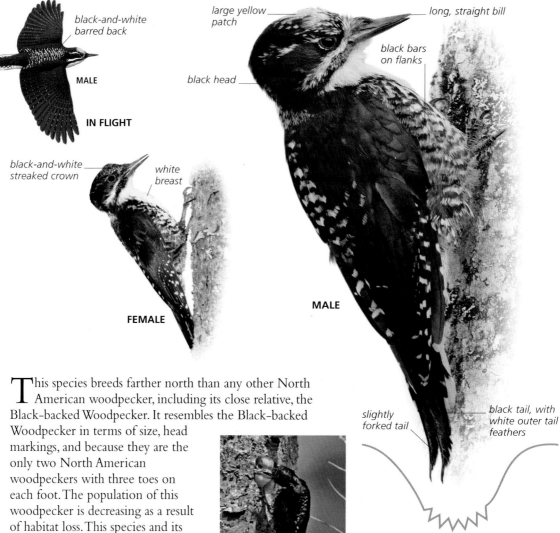

black-and-white barred back

MALE

IN FLIGHT

large yellow patch

long, straight bill

black bars on flanks

black head

black-and-white streaked crown

white breast

FEMALE

MALE

slightly forked tail

black tail, with white outer tail feathers

This species breeds farther north than any other North American woodpecker, including its close relative, the Black-backed Woodpecker. It resembles the Black-backed Woodpecker in terms of size, head markings, and because they are the only two North American woodpeckers with three toes on each foot. The population of this woodpecker is decreasing as a result of habitat loss. This species and its relative require matures forests with old or dead trees.

VOICE Call notes *queep*, *quip*, or *pik*; generally quiet, likened to the Yellow-bellied Sapsucker.

NESTING Excavates cavity mainly in dead or dying wood, sometimes in live wood; 4 eggs; 1 brood; May–July.

FEEDING Flakes off bark and eats insects underneath, mainly the larvae of Bark Beetles.

FLIGHT: undulating flight with rapid wing beats typical of other woodpeckers.

COLOR VARIATION

The streaks on this species' back are highly variable; some populations have nearly all-white backs.

SIMILAR SPECIES

BLACK-BACKED WOODPECKER
shorter call;
see p.283

solid black back

OCCURRENCE

Breeds in mature northerly coniferous forests across Canada and through the Rockies. Since it is largely nonmigratory, this is also the winter habitat for most populations, although it is found in more open areas in winter.

Length **8–9in (20–23cm)**	Wingspan **15in (38cm)**	Weight **2¼–2½oz (65–70g)**
Social **Solitary/Pairs**	Lifespan **Unknown**	Status **Vulnerable**

Order **Piciformes**	Family **Picidae**	Species ***Picoides arcticus***

Black-backed Woodpecker

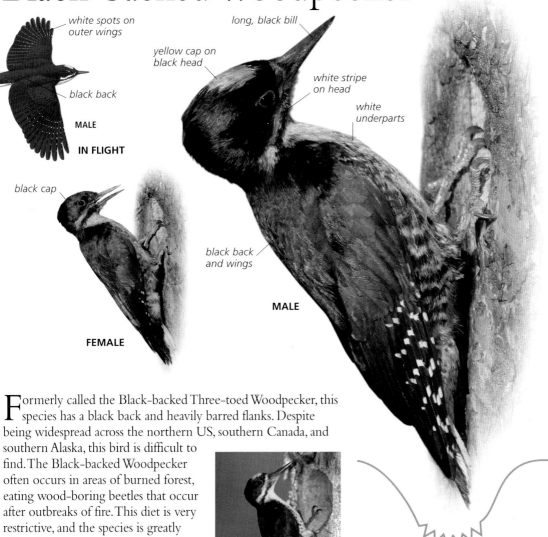

white spots on outer wings

black back

MALE

IN FLIGHT

long, black bill

yellow cap on black head

white stripe on head

white underparts

black cap

black back and wings

MALE

FEMALE

Formerly called the Black-backed Three-toed Woodpecker, this species has a black back and heavily barred flanks. Despite being widespread across the northern US, southern Canada, and southern Alaska, this bird is difficult to find. The Black-backed Woodpecker often occurs in areas of burned forest, eating wood-boring beetles that occur after outbreaks of fire. This diet is very restrictive, and the species is greatly affected by forestry programs, which prevent the spread of fire. Although it overlaps geographically with the American Three-toed Woodpecker, the two are rarely found together in the same locality.

VOICE Main call a single *pik*.
NESTING Cavity excavated in tree; 3–4 eggs; 1 brood; May–July.
FEEDING Eats beetles, especially larvae of wood-boring beetles, by flaking off bark.

FLIGHT: typical undulating flight of woodpeckers.

FREQUENT MOVING
This bird excavates a new nest cavity each year, rarely returning in subsequent years.

SIMILAR SPECIES

AMERICAN THREE-TOED WOODPECKER
see p.282

black-and-white barred upperparts

OCCURRENCE
Inhabitant of northerly and mountainous coniferous forests that require fire for renewal. Breeding occurs soon after sites are burned as new colonies are attracted to the habitat. In Michigan's Upper Peninsula, the bird uses trees similar to those in its northern habitat.

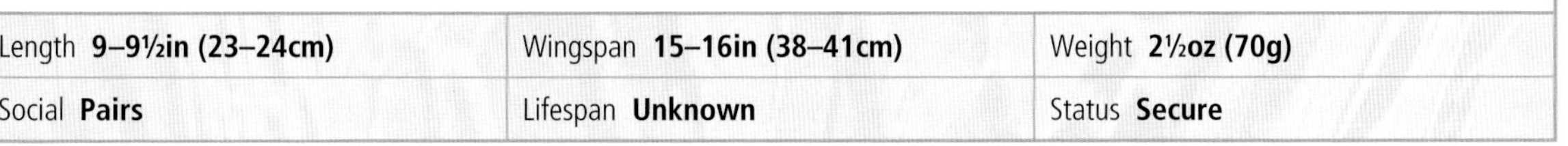

Length **9–9½in (23–24cm)**	Wingspan **15–16in (38–41cm)**	Weight **2½oz (70g)**
Social **Pairs**	Lifespan **Unknown**	Status **Secure**

Order **Piciformes**	Family **Picidae**	Species ***Colaptes auratus***

Northern Flicker

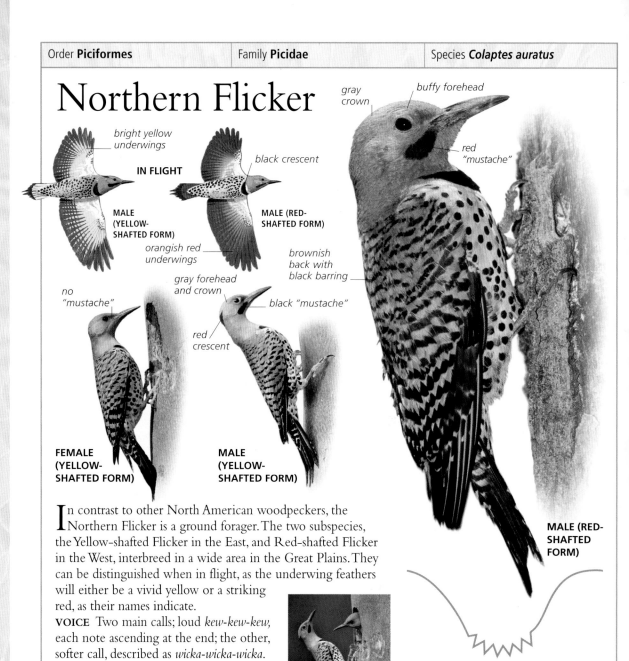

gray crown
buffy forehead
red "mustache"
bright yellow underwings
IN FLIGHT
black crescent
MALE (YELLOW-SHAFTED FORM)
MALE (RED-SHAFTED FORM)
orangish red underwings
brownish back with black barring
gray forehead and crown
no "mustache"
black "mustache"
red crescent
FEMALE (YELLOW-SHAFTED FORM)
MALE (YELLOW-SHAFTED FORM)
MALE (RED-SHAFTED FORM)

In contrast to other North American woodpeckers, the Northern Flicker is a ground forager. The two subspecies, the Yellow-shafted Flicker in the East, and Red-shafted Flicker in the West, interbreed in a wide area in the Great Plains. They can be distinguished when in flight, as the underwing feathers will either be a vivid yellow or a striking red, as their names indicate.

VOICE Two main calls; loud *kew-kew-kew,* each note ascending at the end; the other, softer call, described as *wicka-wicka-wicka*.

NESTING Cavity usually in dead wood, but sometimes in live wood; 6–8 eggs; 1 brood; May–June.

FEEDING Feeds mainly on ants in breeding season; also fruits in winter.

FLIGHT: rapid wing beats followed by glides; fewer undulations than most woodpeckers.

SHARING CHORES
The Northern Flicker nests in tree cavities, where parents take turns incubating eggs.

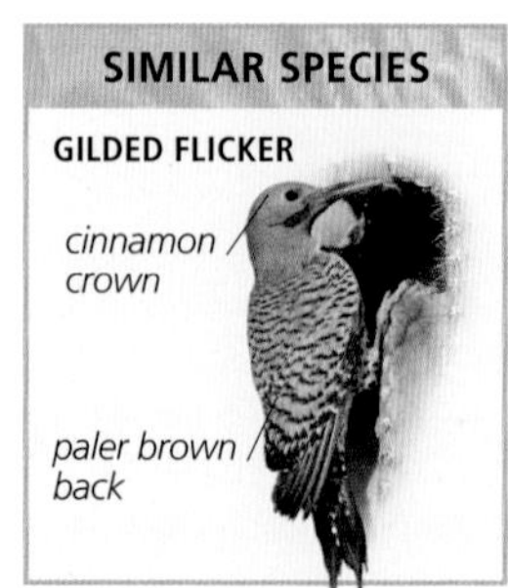
SIMILAR SPECIES
GILDED FLICKER
cinnamon crown
paler brown back

FEET ON THE GROUND
Unlike other woodpeckers, flickers can be found foraging for ants on the ground.

OCCURRENCE
A common species found in woodland in every part of the US, the southern half of Canada, and north into Alaska. During breeding season, prefers open woodlands and forest edge; also suburbs. Little is known about this bird's winter habitat.

Length **12–13in (31–33cm)**	Wingspan **19–21in (48–53cm)**	Weight **4oz (125g)**
Social **Solitary**	Lifespan **9 years**	Status **Secure**

Order **Piciformes**	Family **Picidae**	Species ***Dryocopus pileatus***

Pileated Woodpecker

large overall
MALE
large white patch
long tail
IN FLIGHT
black forehead
black "mustache"
red crest
FEMALE
red forehead
red crest
large black bill
white chin
scarlet "mustache"
black back
white patch on wing
MALE

The largest woodpecker in North America, the Pileated Woodpecker is instantly recognizable by its spectacular large, tapering, bright-red crest. A mated pair of Pileated Woodpeckers defends their breeding territory all year—even if one bird dies, the other does not desert the territory. Indeed, a pair may live in the same old, dead tree every year, but will hammer out a new nest cavity with their powerful bills each season. The abandoned nest cavities created by the Pileated Woodpecker are sometimes reused by other birds, and occasionally inhabited by mammals.

VOICE Two primary calls, both high-pitched and quite loud—*yuck-yuck-yuck*, and *yuka-yuka-yuka*.

NESTING Excavates cavity, usually in dead tree; 3–5 eggs; 1 brood; May–July.

FEEDING Bores deep into trees and peels off large strips of bark to extract carpenter ants and beetle larvae; also digs on ground and on fallen logs, and opportunistically eats fruit and nuts.

EASY PICKINGS
This Pileated Woodpecker readily visits feeders to supplement its natural diet.

FLIGHT: slow, deep wing beats, with occasional undulation when wings briefly folded.

OCCURRENCE
Breeds and lives year-round in northwestern North America and throughout the eastern half of the US, in deciduous and coniferous forest and woodlands; also found in swampy areas. In some areas, chooses young forests with dead trees but in other places, old-growth conifers.

Length **16–18in (41–46cm)**	Wingspan **26–30in (66–76cm)**	Weight **10oz (275g)**
Social **Pairs**	Lifespan **Up to 9 years**	Status **Secure**

FLYCATCHERS

BIRDS POPULARLY KNOWN AS "flycatchers" occur in many parts of the world, but several different families of songbird have this name. With the exception of some Old World species that may stray into Alaska, the North American species are all members of a single family—the Tyrant Flycatchers (Tyrannidae). With about 400 species, this is the largest bird family in the New World. The North American species are uniform in appearance with only a hint of the family's diversity found in Central and South America. Most are drab colored, olive-green or gray birds, sometimes with yellow on the underparts, but two exceptions are the Vermilion Flycatcher and the Scissor-tailed Flycatcher, both species seen on rare occasions in Canada. The members of the genus *Empidonax* include some of the most difficult birds to identify in North America; they are best distinguished by their songs. Typical flycatcher feeding behavior is to sit on a branch or exposed perch sallying forth to catch flying insects. Tyrannid flycatchers are found across North America, except in Arctic regions. Many live in wooded habitats, though the kingbirds (genus *Tyrannus*) prefer woodland edges and deserts. Nearly all flycatchers are long distance migrants and spend the winter in Central and South America.

ERECT STANCE
A large headed look and erect posture are typical of this Eastern Phoebe.

KEEPING WATCH
This Alder Flycatcher is on the alert to spot a potential meal.

BIG MOUTHS
Young Dusky Flycatchers display the wide bills that help them to catch flying insects as adults.

Order **Passeriformes**	Family **Tyrannidae**	Species ***Sayornis phoebe***

Eastern Phoebe

ADULT
rounded wings with two faint wing bars
white throat
IN FLIGHT
yellowish tint on lower belly
ADULT (FALL)
round, dark-capped head
dark eye
olive tint to sides and breast
long, dark tail
ADULT (BREEDING)

The Eastern Phoebe is an early spring migrant that tends to nest under bridges, culverts, and on buildings, in addition to rocky outcroppings. Not shy, it is also familiar because of its *fee-bee* vocalization and constant tail wagging. By tying a thread on the leg of several Eastern Phoebes, ornithologist John James Audubon established that individuals return from the south to a previously used nest site. Although difficult to tell apart, males tend to be slightly larger and darker than females.

VOICE Common call a clear, weak *chip*; song an emphatic *fee-bee* or fee-*b-be-bee*.

NESTING Open cup of mud, moss, and leaves, almost exclusively on manmade structures; 3–5 eggs; 2 broods; April–July.

FEEDING Feeds mainly on flying insects; also consumes small fruits from fall through winter.

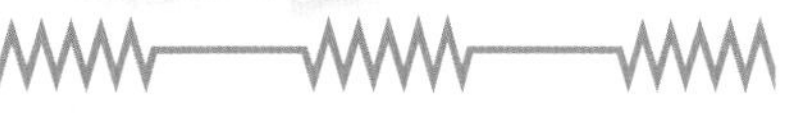

FLIGHT: direct, with steady wing beats; hovers occasionally; approaches nest with a low swoop.

PALE EDGES
Perched on a twig, a male shows off the pale margins of his wing feathers.

LIGHTER FEMALE
They are difficult to distinguish, but the female is slightly lighter overall than the male.

SIMILAR SPECIES

EASTERN WOOD-PEWEE
lacks tail-wag; see p.291
distinct wing bars
WILLOW FLYCATCHER
flicks tail upwards; see p.294
often has eye-ring
more distinct wing bars
smaller overall

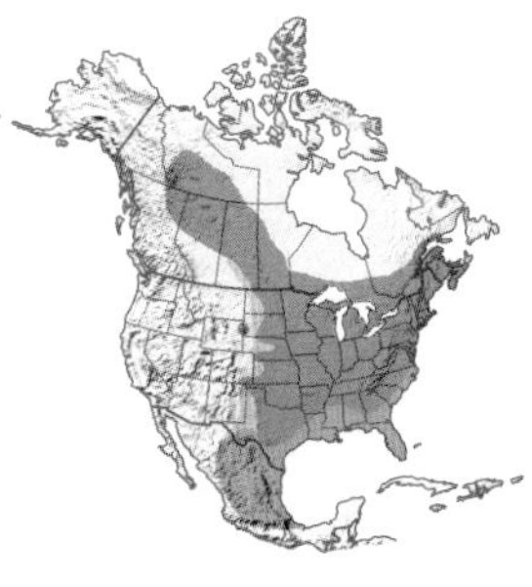

OCCURRENCE
Found in open woodland and along deciduous or mixed forest edges, in gardens and parks, near water. Breeds across Canada from the Northwest Territories south of the tundra belt and in the eastern half of the US. Winters in the southeast US and Mexico.

Length **5½–7in (14–17cm)**	Wingspan **10½in (27cm)**	Weight **11/16oz (20g)**
Social **Solitary**	Lifespan **Up to 9 years**	Status **Secure**

Order **Passeriformes**	Family **Tyrannidae**	Species ***Sayornis saya***

Say's Phoebe

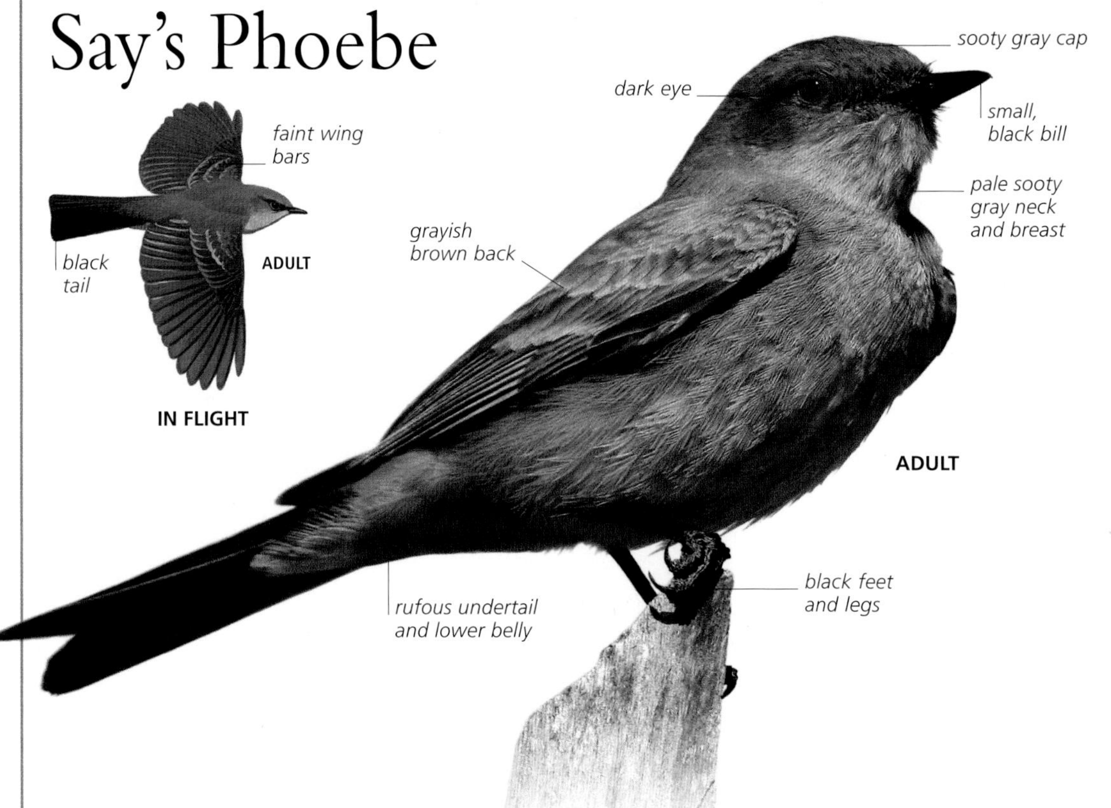
faint wing bars
black tail
ADULT
IN FLIGHT
dark eye
sooty gray cap
small, black bill
pale sooty gray neck and breast
grayish brown back
ADULT
rufous undertail and lower belly
black feet and legs

Say's Phoebe breeds farther north than any other flycatcher in its family. Although it is a bird of open country, it is not particularly shy around people, and from early spring to late fall is a common sight on ranches and farms. Its contrasting dark cap is conspicuous even at a distance as it perches on bushes, boulders, or power lines, often wagging its tail. Shortly after a pair is formed on the breeding grounds, the male will hover in front of potential nest sites, in a manner similar to the Black Phoebe. The pair bond among Say's Phoebes is relatively weak, though, and does not last through the summer.

VOICE Call a *pee-ee* or *pee-ur*; also a whistled *churr-eep*, which may be integrated with a chatter; primary song a *pit-see-eur* and *pit-eet*.

NESTING Shallow cup of twigs, moss, or stems on ledge or in rocky crevice; 3–7 eggs; 1–2 broods; April–July.

FEEDING Catches insects in flight, such as beetles, wasps, grasshoppers, and crickets; also eats berries.

FLIGHT: direct, with regular wing beats; chases may be erratic; hovers while foraging.

PALE WING FEATHERS
Say's Phoebe's pale underwings are clearly visible from below as it hovers.

SIMILAR SPECIES

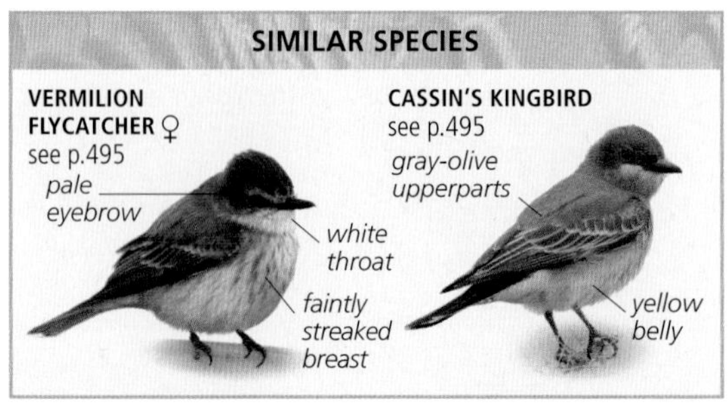
VERMILION FLYCATCHER ♀
see p.495
pale eyebrow
white throat
faintly streaked breast
CASSIN'S KINGBIRD
see p.495
gray-olive upperparts
yellow belly

OCCURRENCE
Breeds in dry, open, or semi-open country, such as desert canyons, sagebrush ranch, and agricultural areas; generally avoids watercourses. Birds in the southwestern US are resident year-round, but those breeding farther north fly south for the winter.

Length **7in (17.5cm)**	Wingspan **13in (33cm)**	Weight **$^{11}/_{16}$oz (20g)**
Social **Solitary**	Lifespan **At least 3–4 years**	Status **Secure**

Order **Passeriformes**	Family **Tyrannidae**	Species ***Contopus cooperi***

Olive-sided Flycatcher

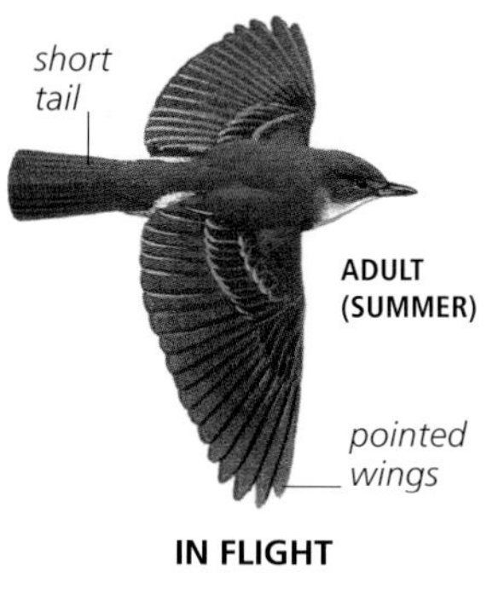
short tail
ADULT (SUMMER)
pointed wings
IN FLIGHT

large, dark head
lower base of bill often dull orange
brownish gray back
dull white throat
brownish olive flanks
white belly
ADULT (SUMMER)

FLIGHT: fast and direct, with deep, rapid wing beats; turns sharply to chase prey.

The Olive-sided Flycatcher is identified by its distinctive song, large size, and contrasting belly and flank colors, which make its underside appear like a vest with the buttons undone. Both members of a breeding pair are known to aggressively defend their territory. This flycatcher undertakes a long journey from northern parts of North America to winter in Panama and the Andes.

VOICE Call an evenly spaced *pip-pip-pip*; song a loud 3-note whistle: *quick-THREE-BEERS* or *whip-WEE-DEER.*

NESTING Open cup of twigs, rootlets, lichens; 2–5 eggs; 1 brood; May–August.

FEEDING Sits and waits for prey to fly past its perch before swooping after it; eats flying insects, such as bees, wasps, and flying ants.

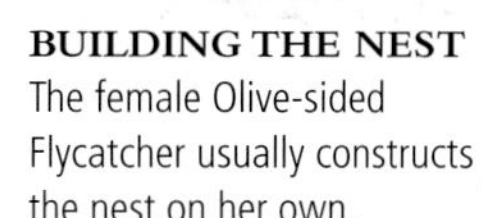

BUILDING THE NEST
The female Olive-sided Flycatcher usually constructs the nest on her own.

EXPOSED PERCH
This species can often be found singing from an exposed twig emerging from the canopy.

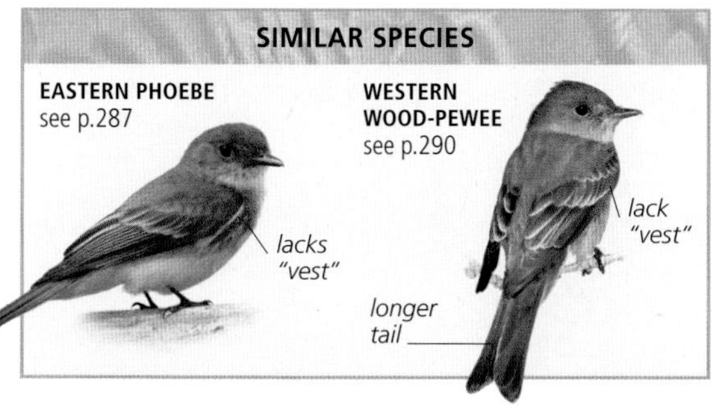
SIMILAR SPECIES
EASTERN PHOEBE
see p.287
lacks "vest"
WESTERN WOOD-PEWEE
see p.290
lack "vest"
longer tail

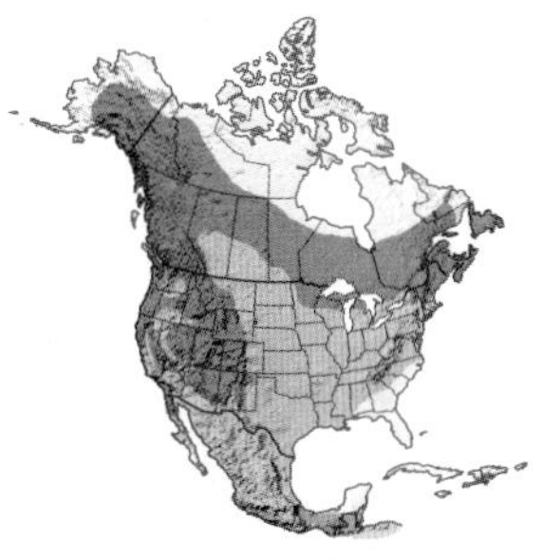

OCCURRENCE
Breeds in mountainous, northern coniferous forests at edges or openings around ponds, bogs, meadows where standing dead trees occur. Also found in post-fire forests with abundant stumps. Winters in forest edges with tall trees and stumps.

Length **7–8in (18–20cm)**	Wingspan **13in (33cm)**	Weight **$1\frac{1}{16}$–$1\frac{1}{4}$oz (30–35g)**
Social **Solitary**	Lifespan **Up to 7 years**	Status **Declining**

Order **Passeriformes**	Family **Tyrannidae**	Species ***Contopus sordidulus***

Western Wood-pewee

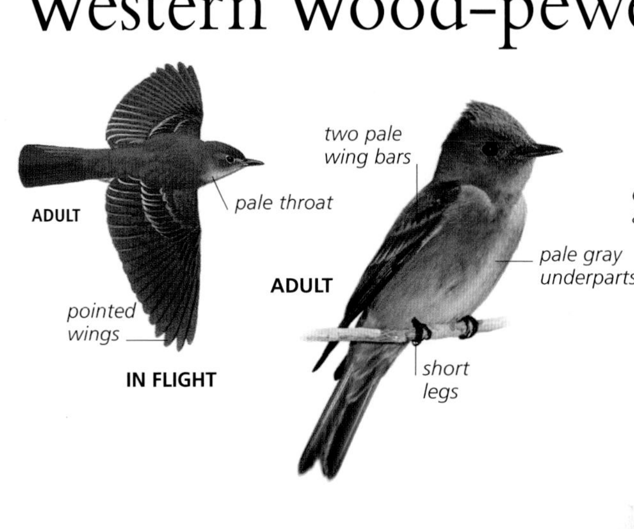
ADULT
pale throat
pointed wings
IN FLIGHT
two pale wing bars
ADULT
pale gray underparts
short legs

slight crest
dark brown eye
dark gray back and head
ADULT

FLIGHT: flurries of rapid wing beats; returns to open perch with quivering wings.

This species is a widespread breeder in many forested habitats of western North America. Where its range overlaps that of the Eastern Wood-pewee, it shows no evidence of interbreeding. It vocalizes from high perches, principally during the breeding season, but also during winter and while on migration. The Western Wood-pewee forages aerially on insects in much the same way as swallows do. Adults are very aggressive toward laying parasitic intruders, however, they accept Brown-headed Cowbird eggs, though few fledge successfully from their nests. The Western Wood-pewee is a migrant that winters in the Andes from Colombia to Bolivia.

VOICE Calls burry *bzew* and infrequent *chip*; male's dawn song *pee-pip-pip* or *tswee-tee-teet*, given alternately with *pee-er*.

NESTING Shallow cup of woven grasses in fork of horizontal branch; 2–4 eggs; 1 brood; May–August.

FEEDING Sit-and-wait hunter; primarily eats flies, bees, wasps, ants, beetles, and moths; also forages for flying insects.

PERCHED AND ALERT
The crest is apparent in this alert bird probably on the look-out for prey.

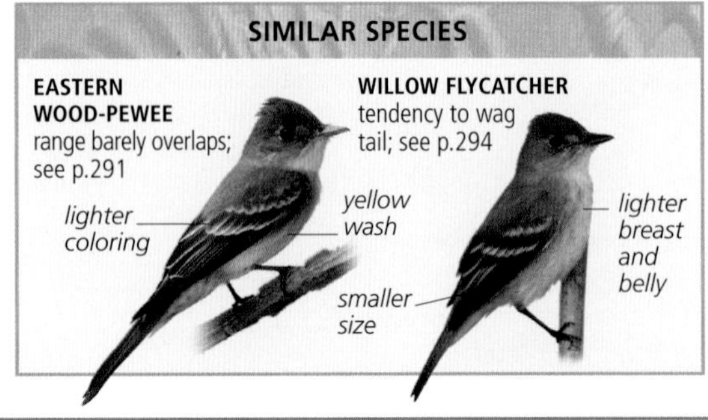
SIMILAR SPECIES
EASTERN WOOD-PEWEE
range barely overlaps; see p.291
lighter coloring
yellow wash
WILLOW FLYCATCHER
tendency to wag tail; see p.294
smaller size
lighter breast and belly

OCCURRENCE
Open woodlands, forest edges and beside rivers and other water bodies; also in dry forests. Absent from dense forests. Large-diameter trees, open understory, stumps, and woodland edges are important. Winters in mature tropical forests. Breeds in Mexico and Central America to Nicaragua.

Length **6¼in (16cm)**	Wingspan **10½in (27cm)**	Weight **⅜–½oz (11–14g)**
Social **Solitary**	Lifespan **Up to 6 years**	Status **Secure**

Order **Passeriformes**	Family **Tyrannidae**	Species ***Contopus virens***

Eastern Wood-pewee

slightly ragged crest

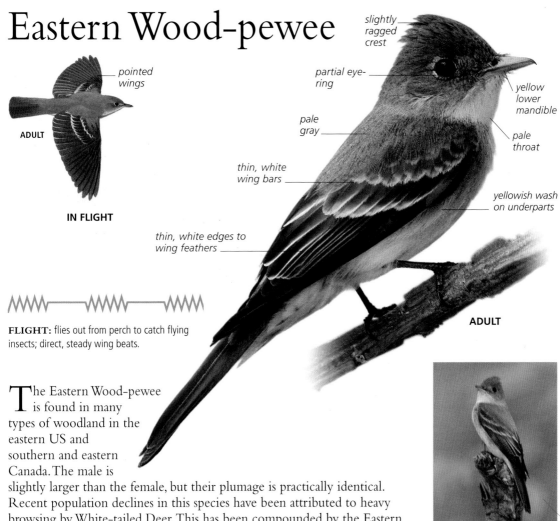

pointed wings

partial eye-ring

yellow lower mandible

ADULT

pale gray

pale throat

thin, white wing bars

yellowish wash on underparts

IN FLIGHT

thin, white edges to wing feathers

ADULT

FLIGHT: flies out from perch to catch flying insects; direct, steady wing beats.

The Eastern Wood-pewee is found in many types of woodland in the eastern US and southern and eastern Canada. The male is slightly larger than the female, but their plumage is practically identical. Recent population declines in this species have been attributed to heavy browsing by White-tailed Deer. This has been compounded by the Eastern Wood-pewee's susceptibility to brood parasitism by Brown-headed Cowbirds.

VOICE Call terse *chip*; song slurred *pee-ah-wee*, plaintive *wee-ooo*, or *wee-ur*, and slurred *ah di dee*.

NESTING Shallow cup of grass, lichens on horizontal limb; 2–4 eggs; 1 brood; May–September.

FEEDING Consumes mainly flying insects, such as flies, beetles, and bees; occasionally forages for insects on foliage on the ground.

SEARCHING FOR PREY
Holding its tail perfectly still, this Wood-pewee is perched upright, scanning for prey.

COLORATION
The Eastern Wood-pewee has yellowish underparts and a yellow lower mandible.

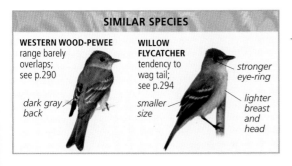

SIMILAR SPECIES

WESTERN WOOD-PEWEE range barely overlaps; see p.290
dark gray back

WILLOW FLYCATCHER tendency to wag tail; see p.294
stronger eye-ring
smaller size
lighter breast and head

OCCURRENCE
Widely distributed in eastern US and adjacent Canadian provinces. Breeds in deciduous and coniferous forests, often near clearings or edges; uses waterside areas in Midwest, less so in the East. Late-arriving migrant. Winters in shrubby, second-growth forests of South America.

Length **6in (15cm)**	Wingspan **9–10in (23–26cm)**	Weight **3/8–11/16oz (10–19g)**
Social **Solitary**	Lifespan **Up to 7 years**	Status **Secure**

Order **Passeriformes**	Family **Tyrannidae**	Species ***Empidonax flaviventris***

Yellow-bellied Flycatcher

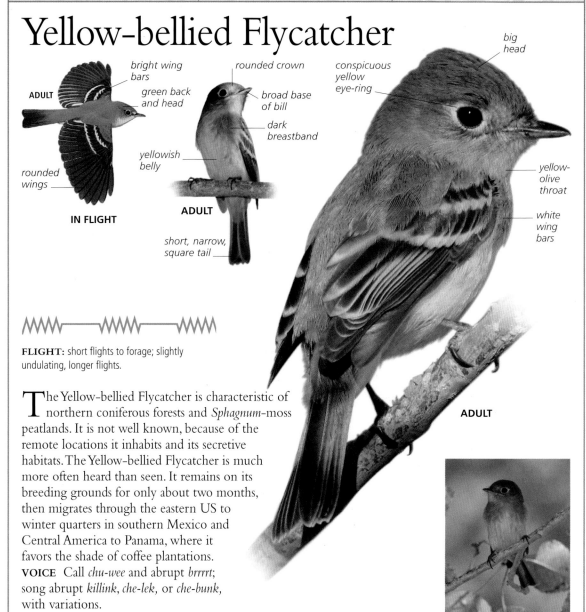

ADULT
bright wing bars
green back and head
rounded wings
IN FLIGHT

rounded crown
broad base of bill
dark breastband
yellowish belly
ADULT
short, narrow, square tail

big head
conspicuous yellow eye-ring
yellow-olive throat
white wing bars
ADULT

FLIGHT: short flights to forage; slightly undulating, longer flights.

The Yellow-bellied Flycatcher is characteristic of northern coniferous forests and *Sphagnum*-moss peatlands. It is not well known, because of the remote locations it inhabits and its secretive habitats. The Yellow-bellied Flycatcher is much more often heard than seen. It remains on its breeding grounds for only about two months, then migrates through the eastern US to winter quarters in southern Mexico and Central America to Panama, where it favors the shade of coffee plantations.

VOICE Call *chu-wee* and abrupt *brrrrt*; song abrupt *killink*, *che-lek*, or *che-bunk*, with variations.

NESTING Cup of moss, twigs, and needles on or near ground, often in a bog; 3–5 eggs; 1 brood; June–July.

FEEDING Catches insects in the air or gleans mosquitoes, midges, and flies from foliage; sometimes eats berries and seeds.

ANISODACTYL FOOT
Note the bird's foot arrangement—three toes point forward and one backward.

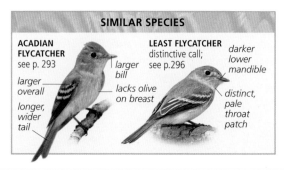

SIMILAR SPECIES

ACADIAN FLYCATCHER see p. 293
larger bill
larger overall
lacks olive on breast
longer, wider tail

LEAST FLYCATCHER distinctive call; see p.296
darker lower mandible
distinct, pale throat patch

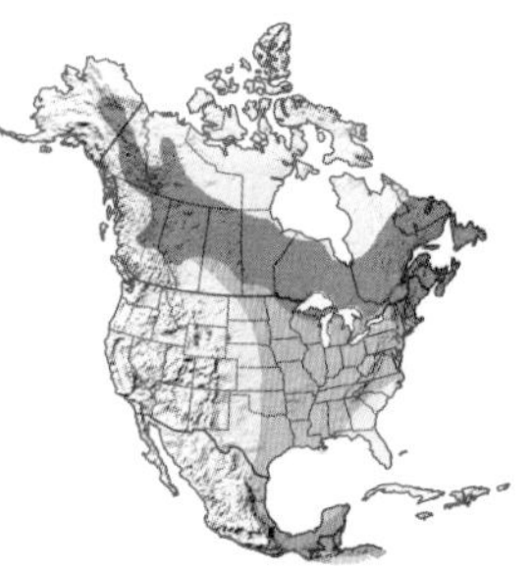

OCCURRENCE
Breeds from Alaska to Quebec, Newfoundland, and the northeast US (New England) in boreal forests and bogs dominated by spruce trees. Winters in Mexico and Central America to Panama, in lowland forests, second-growth, and riverside habitats.

Length **5½in (14cm)**	Wingspan **8in (20cm)**	Weight **9/32–½oz (8–15g)**
Social **Solitary**	Lifespan **At least 4 years**	Status **Secure**

Order **Passeriformes**	Family **Tyrannidae**	Species ***Empidonax virescens***

Acadian Flycatcher

ADULT

prominent wing bars

IN FLIGHT

slight crest

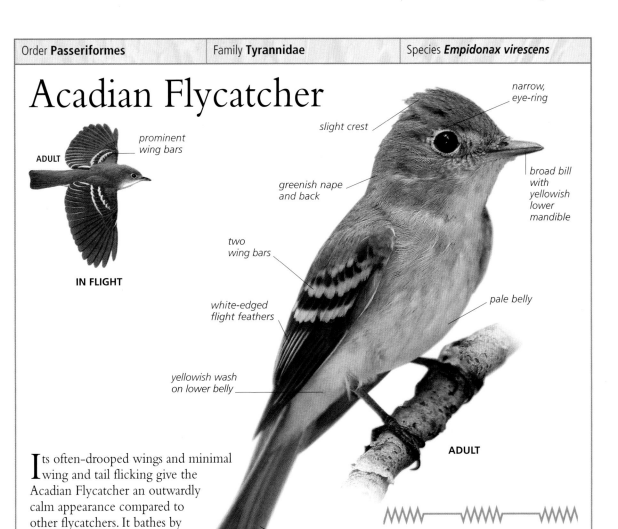

narrow, eye-ring

broad bill with yellowish lower mandible

greenish nape and back

two wing bars

white-edged flight feathers

pale belly

yellowish wash on lower belly

broad tail

ADULT

Its often-drooped wings and minimal wing and tail flicking give the Acadian Flycatcher an outwardly calm appearance compared to other flycatchers. It bathes by diving into water, then preens on a perch. It suffers more parasitism from Brown-headed Cowbirds in small woodlots than in large forests. Where Cowbirds lay their eggs in the flycatcher's nest, they displace the flycatcher's young.

FLIGHT: direct, fast with quick wing beats; short flights to and from perches; hovers while foraging.

VOICE Contact call soft *peet,* one of many calls; territorial song *tee-chup*, *peet-sah* or *flee-sick*, loud and "explosive" sounding.

NESTING Shallow, open cup in tree fork or shrub near water; 3 eggs; 2 broods; May–August.

FEEDING Takes insects from undersides of leaves, also catches them in the air and occasionally on the ground; eats berries.

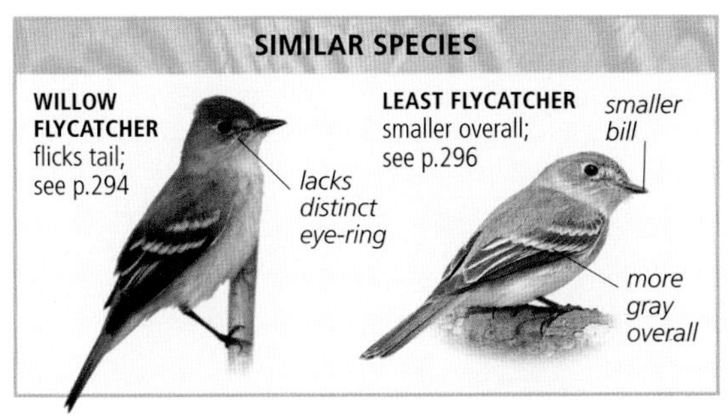
SIMILAR SPECIES
WILLOW FLYCATCHER
flicks tail;
see p.294
lacks distinct eye-ring
LEAST FLYCATCHER
smaller overall;
see p.296
smaller bill
more gray overall

TOP PERFORMER
This flycatcher is seen typically perched on a treetop from where it sings forcefully.

OCCURRENCE
Breeds in eastern US and southern Ontario in mature deciduous forests associated with water; prefers large undisturbed tracts. Winters in Nicaragua, Costa Rica, and Panama, and in South America along the Andes from Venezuela and Colombia to Ecuador, in tropical forests and woodlands with evergreen trees.

Length **6in (15cm)**	Wingspan **9in (23cm)**	Weight **3/8–1/2oz (11–14g)**
Social **Solitary**	Lifespan **Up to 10 years**	Status **Secure**

Order **Passeriformes**	Family **Tyrannidae**	Species ***Empidonax traillii***

Willow Flycatcher

square tail

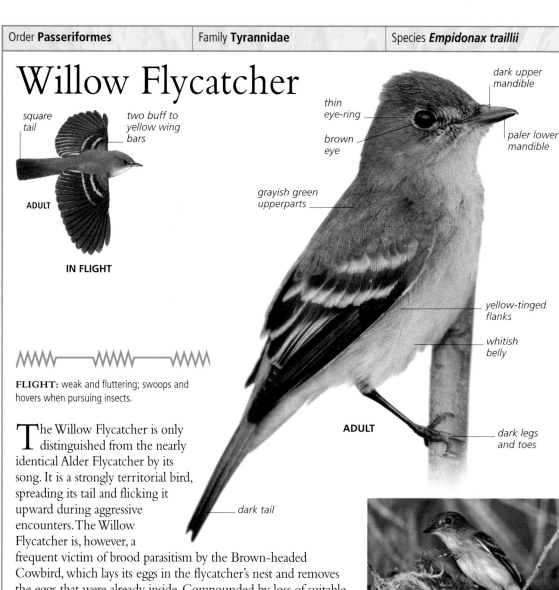

two buff to yellow wing bars

ADULT

IN FLIGHT

dark upper mandible

thin eye-ring

brown eye

paler lower mandible

grayish green upperparts

yellow-tinged flanks

whitish belly

ADULT

dark legs and toes

dark tail

FLIGHT: weak and fluttering; swoops and hovers when pursuing insects.

The Willow Flycatcher is only distinguished from the nearly identical Alder Flycatcher by its song. It is a strongly territorial bird, spreading its tail and flicking it upward during aggressive encounters. The Willow Flycatcher is, however, a frequent victim of brood parasitism by the Brown-headed Cowbird, which lays its eggs in the flycatcher's nest and removes the eggs that were already inside. Compounded by loss of suitable breeding habitat, this may be a major reason for the Willow Flycatcher's decline, especially in the case of the southwestern subspecies, *E. t. extimus*, which is now considered endangered.

VOICE Calls include soft, dry *whit* and several buzzy notes; song sharp *fitz-bew* with accent on the first syllable; also *creet*.

NESTING Rather loose and untidy cup in base of shrub near water; 3–4 eggs; 1 brood; May–August.

FEEDING Eats insects, mostly caught in flight; eats fruit in winter.

UNEVEN WORKLOAD
Although both parents feed their young, the female Willow Flycatcher does so the most.

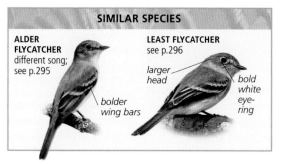

SIMILAR SPECIES

ALDER FLYCATCHER different song; see p.295

bolder wing bars

LEAST FLYCATCHER see p.296

larger head

bold white eye-ring

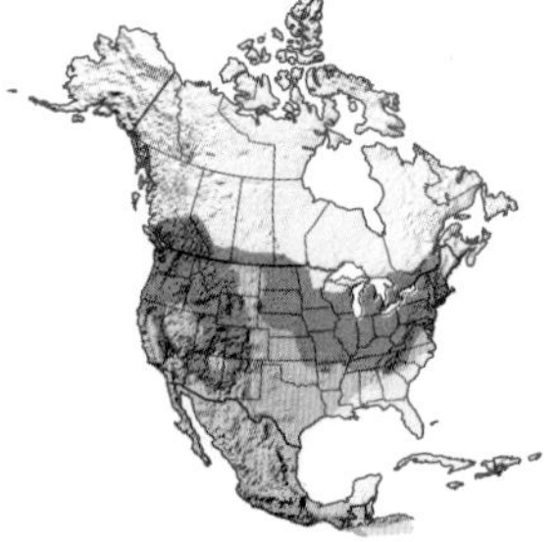

OCCURRENCE
Breeds from southern Canada to eastern and southwestern US, mainly in willow thickets and other moist shrubby areas along watercourses. On winter grounds, it favors lighter woodland, shrubby clearings, and brush near water in coastal areas.

Length **5–6¾in (13–17cm)**	Wingspan **7½–9½in (19–24cm)**	Weight **⅜–9/16oz (11–16g)**
Social **Solitary**	Lifespan **Up to 11 years**	Status **Declining**

Order **Passeriformes**	Family **Tyrannidae**	Species ***Empidonax alnorum***

Alder Flycatcher

ADULT
two white wing bars
rounded wings
IN FLIGHT

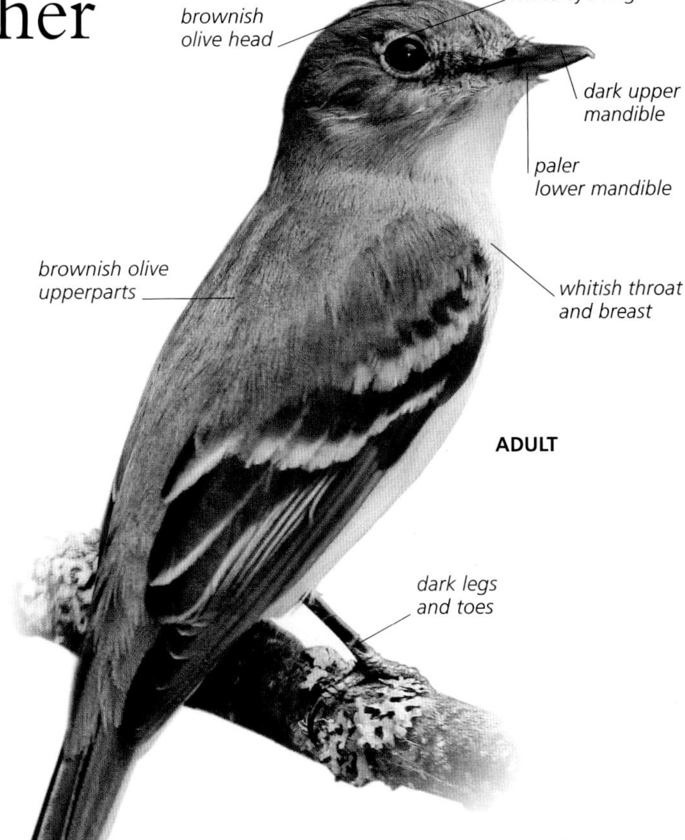
brownish olive head
white eye-ring
dark upper mandible
paler lower mandible
brownish olive upperparts
whitish throat and breast
ADULT
dark legs and toes
long, dark tail

FLIGHT: weak with shallow wing beats; swoops and hovers when pursuing prey.

Until 1973 the Alder Flycatcher and the Willow Flycatcher were considered to be one species called Traill's Flycatcher. The two species cannot be reliably identified by sight, but they do have distinctive songs. The Alder Flycatcher also breeds farther north than the Willow Flycatcher, arriving late in spring and leaving early in fall. Its nests are extremely hard to locate, and much remains to be learned about this bird's breeding habits.

VOICE Calls include flat *pit* or *pip-peep-tip*, also *wee-oo* and *churr*; male sings characteristic *fee-bee-o* song while breeding, and occasionally during spring migration.

NESTING Coarse and loosely structured nest low in fork of deciduous shrub; 3–4 eggs; 1 brood; June–July.

FEEDING Mostly eats insects, caught mainly in flight, but some gleaned from foliage; eats fruit in winter.

ON THE ALERT
Attentive to potential meals, an Alder Flycatcher will swiftly pursue prey as soon as it flies by.

SIMILAR SPECIES

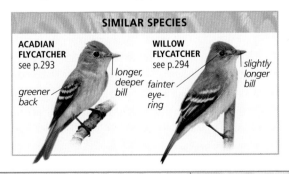

ACADIAN FLYCATCHER see p.293
greener back; longer, deeper bill

WILLOW FLYCATCHER see p.294
fainter eye-ring; slightly longer bill

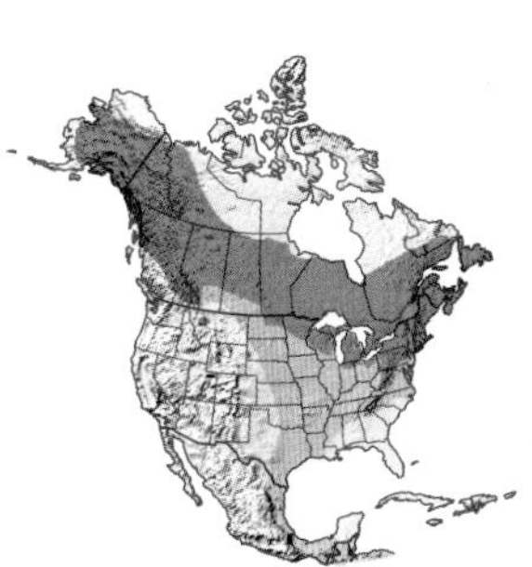

OCCURRENCE
Breeds at low density across northern North America, in wet shrubby habitats with alder or willow thickets, often close to streams. Winters at low elevations in South America in tropical second-growth forest and forest edges.

Length **5¾in (14.5cm)**	Wingspan **8½in (22cm)**	Weight **½oz (14g)**
Social **Solitary**	Lifespan **At least 3 years**	Status **Secure**

Order **Passeriformes**	Family **Tyrannidae**	Species ***Empidonax minimus***

Least Flycatcher

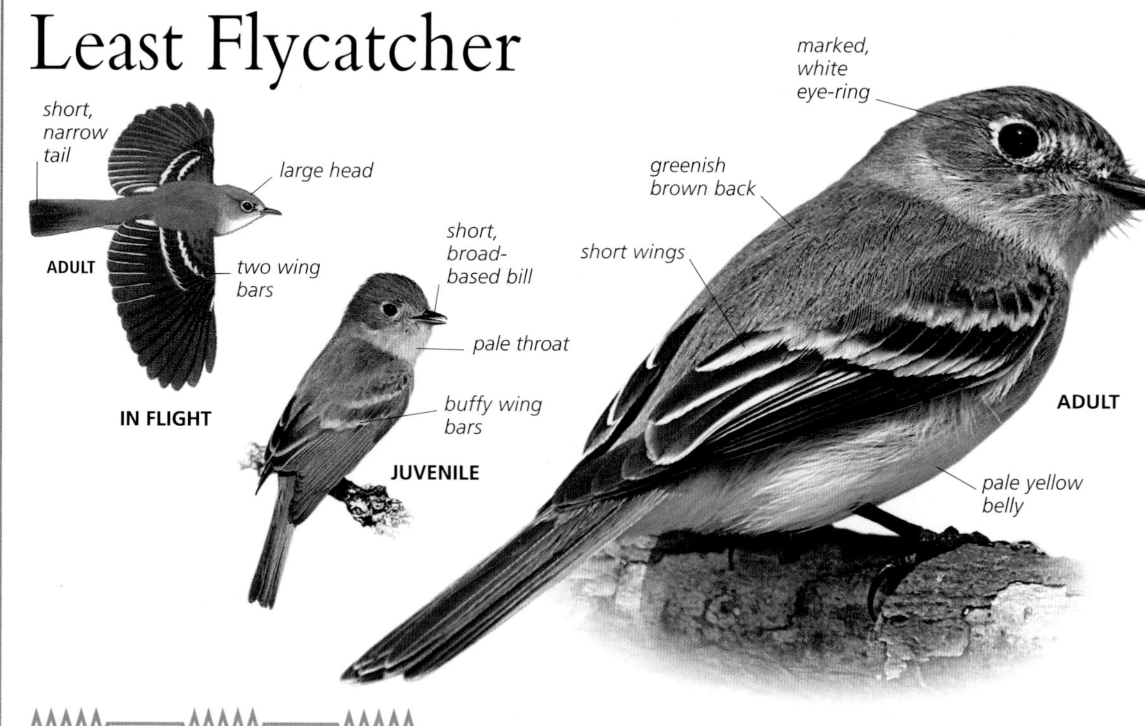
short, narrow tail
large head
ADULT
two wing bars
IN FLIGHT
short, broad-based bill
pale throat
buffy wing bars
JUVENILE
marked, white eye-ring
greenish brown back
short wings
ADULT
pale yellow belly

FLIGHT: direct, short forays with rapid wing beats to catch prey; sometimes hovers briefly.

The smallest eastern member of the *Empidonax* genus is a solitary bird and is very aggressive towards intruders encroaching upon its breeding territory. This combative behavior reduces the likelihood of acting as unwitting host parents to eggs laid by the Brown-headed Cowbird. The Least Flycatcher is very active, and frequently flicks its wings and tail upward. Common in the eastern US and across Canada in mixed and deciduous woodland, especially at the edges, it spends a short time—up to only two months—on its northern breeding grounds before migrating south. Adults molt in winter, while young molt before and during fall migration.

VOICE Call soft, short *whit*; song frequent, persistent, characteristic *tchebeck*, sings during spring migration and breeding season.

NESTING Compact cup of tightly woven bark strips and plant fibers in fork of deciduous tree; 3–5 eggs; 1 brood; May–July.

FEEDING Feeds principally on insects, such as flies, midges, beetles, ants, butterflies, and larvae; occasionally eats berries and seeds.

YELLOW TINGE
The subtle yellow tinge to its underparts and white undertail feathers are evident here.

SIMILAR SPECIES

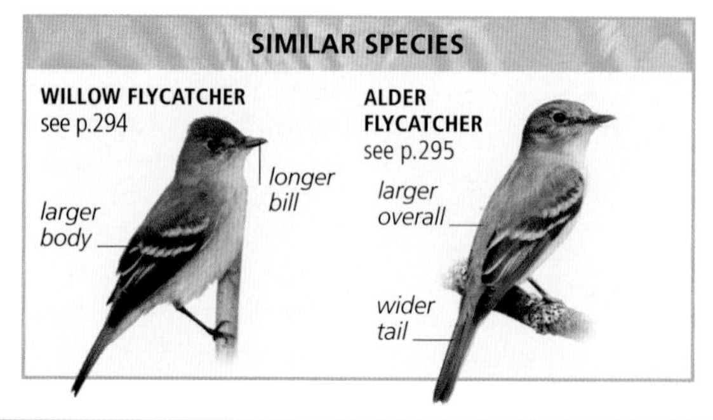
WILLOW FLYCATCHER
see p.294
larger body
longer bill
ALDER FLYCATCHER
see p.295
larger overall
wider tail

OCCURRENCE
Breeds in coniferous and mixed deciduous forests across North America, east of Rockies to East Coast; occasionally in conifer groves or wooded wetlands, often near openings or edges. Winters in Central America in varied habitat from second-growth evergreen woodland to arid scrub.

Length **5¼in (13.5cm)**	Wingspan **7¾in (19.5cm)**	Weight **9/32–7/16oz (8–13g)**
Social **Solitary**	Lifespan **Up to 6 years**	Status **Secure**

Order **Passeriformes**	Family **Tyrannidae**	Species ***Empidonax hammondii***

Hammond's Flycatcher

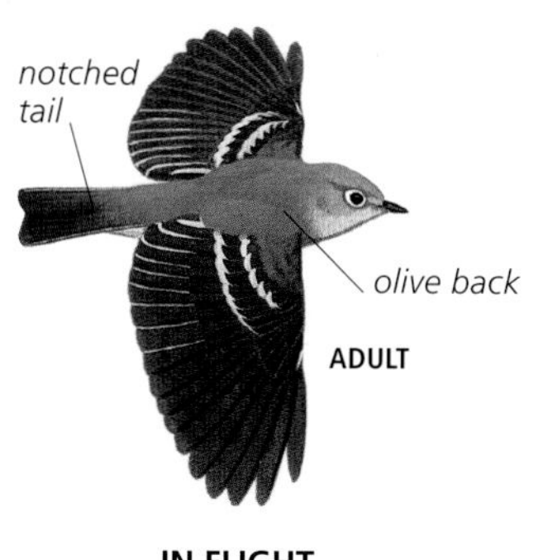
notched tail
olive back
ADULT
IN FLIGHT

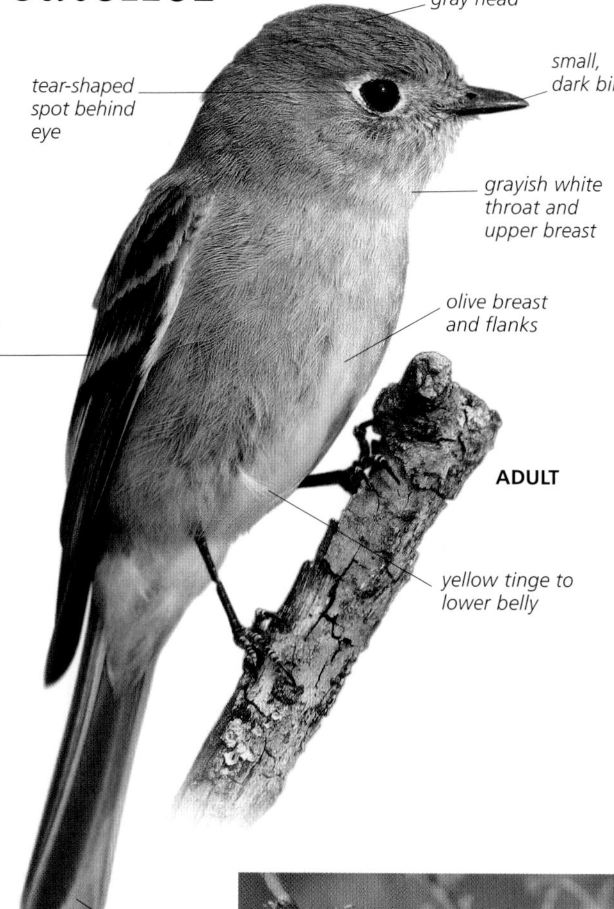
gray head
small, dark bill
tear-shaped spot behind eye
grayish white throat and upper breast
olive breast and flanks
two white wing bars
ADULT
yellow tinge to lower belly
notched tail

FLIGHT: short, direct flights to pursue prey; occasionally hovers.

Hammond's Flycatcher is a small, gray migrant from Central and South America. It is generally silent on its wintering grounds, but starts performing its distinctive song shortly after arriving on its breeding grounds. In the breeding season, males are competitive and aggressive, and are known to lock together in mid-air to resolve their territorial squabbles. Since this species is dependent on mature old-growth forest, logging is thought to be adversely affecting its numbers.

VOICE Calls *peek* or *wheep*; song of 3 elements—dry, brisk *se-put*, low, burry *tsurrt*, or *greep*, and drawn-out *chu-lup*.

NESTING Compact open cup of plant fibers and fine grass saddled on large branch; 3–4 eggs; 1 brood; May–August.

FEEDING Sit-and-wait predator; pursues flying insects from perch.

DISTINCTIVE EYE-RING
Hammond's Flycatcher's white tear-shaped spot behind the eye is only visible in good lighting.

SIMILAR SPECIES

DUSKY FLYCATCHER distinctive "whit" call; see p.298
mouse gray overall
wider, longer bill

GRAY FLYCATCHER wags tail; see p.495
smaller body
paler overall

OCCURRENCE
Breeds in mature coniferous and mixed woodland in from Alaska to California. Inhabits primarily dense firs or conifers, but also occurs in aspen and other broadleaf mixed forests. Winters in oak-pine forests and dry shrubbery in the highlands of Mexico and Central America.

Length **5–6in (12.5–15cm)**	Wingspan **9in (22cm)**	Weight **9/32–7/16oz (8–12g)**
Social **Solitary**	Lifespan **Up to 7 years**	Status **Secure**

Order **Passeriformes**	Family **Tyrannidae**	Species ***Empidonax oberholseri***

Dusky Flycatcher

ADULT

wing bars

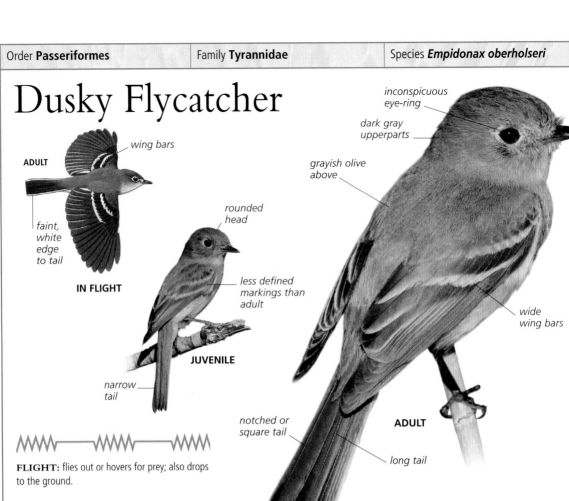

faint, white edge to tail

IN FLIGHT

rounded head

less defined markings than adult

JUVENILE

narrow tail

inconspicuous eye-ring

dark gray upperparts

grayish olive above

wide wing bars

notched or square tail

long tail

ADULT

FLIGHT: flies out or hovers for prey; also drops to the ground.

The Dusky Flycatcher waits on a perch to locate a flying insect, flies out to catch it, and then returns to its position to consume it, often wiping its bill on the perch after completing its meal. It lives in mountainous areas of the western US and Canada, where it is vulnerable to storms that can severely impact a local breeding population by flattening the trees. The Dusky Flycatcher prefers shrubby habitats, and can benefit from forestry practices that open up dense stands of conifers.

VOICE Call a soft *whit*, vocal in early morning; song a two-syllabled rising *prll-it*, rough, low-pitched *prrdrrt*, high, clear *pseet*.

NESTING Tight, open grass cup in upright fork of shrub or low tree; 3–5 eggs; 1 brood; May–August.

FEEDING Catches insects in flight; sometimes from bark, rarely from ground; also eats caterpillars, wasps, bees, moths, butterflies.

FEEDING TIME
This adult Dusky Flycatcher is feeding three hungry nestlings in an open cupped nest.

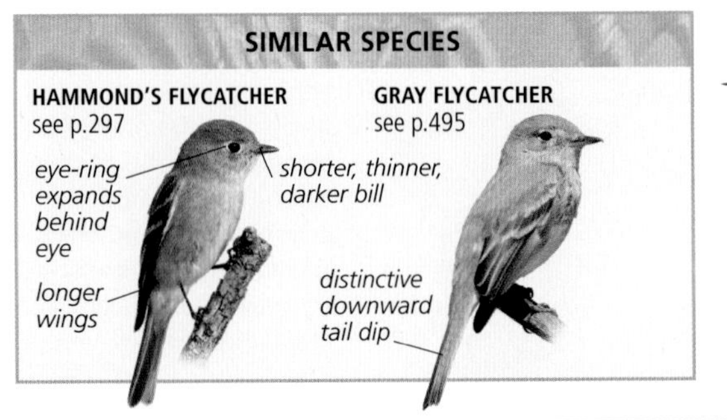
SIMILAR SPECIES
HAMMOND'S FLYCATCHER
see p.297
eye-ring expands behind eye
shorter, thinner, darker bill
longer wings
GRAY FLYCATCHER
see p.495
distinctive downward tail dip

OCCURRENCE
Breeds in west North America, through west US into Mexico, in open coniferous forest, mountain thickets, aspen groves, water-side thickets, open brush, and chaparral. Winters in the highlands of Mexico, south to Oaxaca, in oak scrub and pine-oak; also in open riverside woods, and semi-arid scrub.

Length **5–6in (13–15cm)**	Wingspan **8–9in (20–23cm)**	Weight **$\frac{5}{16}$–$\frac{3}{8}$oz (9–11g)**
Social **Solitary**	Lifespan **Up to 8 years**	Status **Secure**

Order **Passeriformes**	Family **Tyrannidae**	Species ***Empidonax difficilis***

Pacific-slope Flycatcher

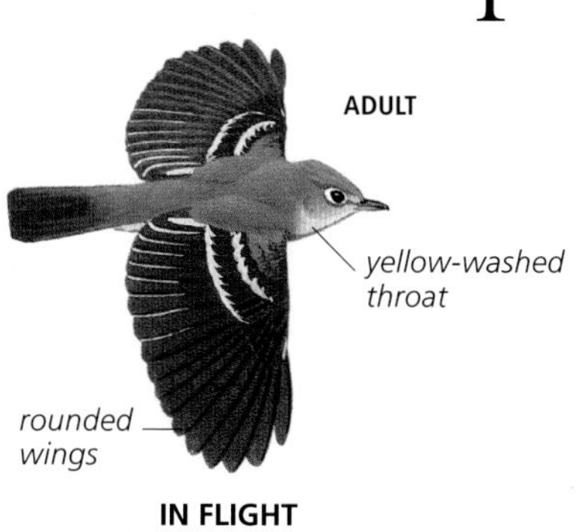
ADULT
yellow-washed throat
rounded wings
IN FLIGHT

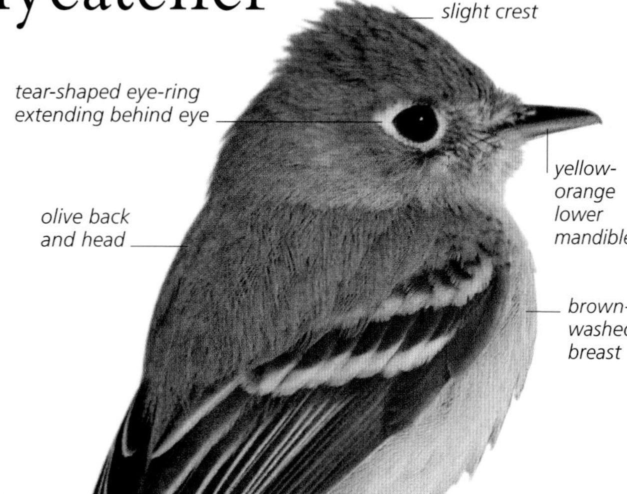
slight crest
tear-shaped eye-ring extending behind eye
yellow-orange lower mandible
olive back and head
brown-washed breast
ADULT

FLIGHT: sallies forth from a perch to hawk or glean insects.

The Pacific-slope Flycatcher is virtually identical to the Cordilleran Flycatcher—both were formerly considered to be one species called the Western Flycatcher. Differences in song led researchers to find genetic and behavioral differences between the two species. A population of Pacific-slope Flycatchers found on the Channel Islands off California may also be a distinct species, larger than mainland forms. The Pacific-slope Flycatcher is a short-distance migrant that winters in Mexico. The female is active during nest-building and incubation, but the male provides food for nestlings.

VOICE Call *chrrip, seet, zeet*; song 3 squeaky, repeated syllables *ps-SEET, ptsick, seet*, or *TSEE-wee, pttuck, tseep*.

NESTING Open cup, often with shelter above, in fork of tree or shelf on bank or bridge; 2–4 eggs; 2 broods; April–July.

FEEDING Feeds on insects caught in air or gleaned from foliage: beetles, wasps, bees, flies, moths, caterpillars, spiders; rarely berries.

DISTINCT MARKINGS
The Pacific-slope Flycatcher has distinct buffy wing bars and a streaked breast and belly.

SIMILAR SPECIES

YELLOW-BELLIED FLYCATCHER see p.292

blacker wings; *shorter tail*

CORDILLERAN FLYCATCHER see p.300

bolder wing bars; *yellowish underparts*

OCCURRENCE
Breeds to west of mountains from northern British Columbia to southern California in humid coastal coniferous forest, Pine Oak forest, and dense second-growth forest. Resides in well-shaded woods, along stream bottoms, and steep-walled ravines.

Length **6–7in (15–17.5cm)**	Wingspan **8–9in (20–23cm)**	Weight **$^9/_{32}$–$^7/_{16}$oz (8–12g)**
Social **Solitary**	Lifespan **Up to 6 years**	Status **Declining**

Order **Passeriformes**	Family **Tyrannidae**	Species ***Empidonax occidentalis***

Cordilleran Flycatcher

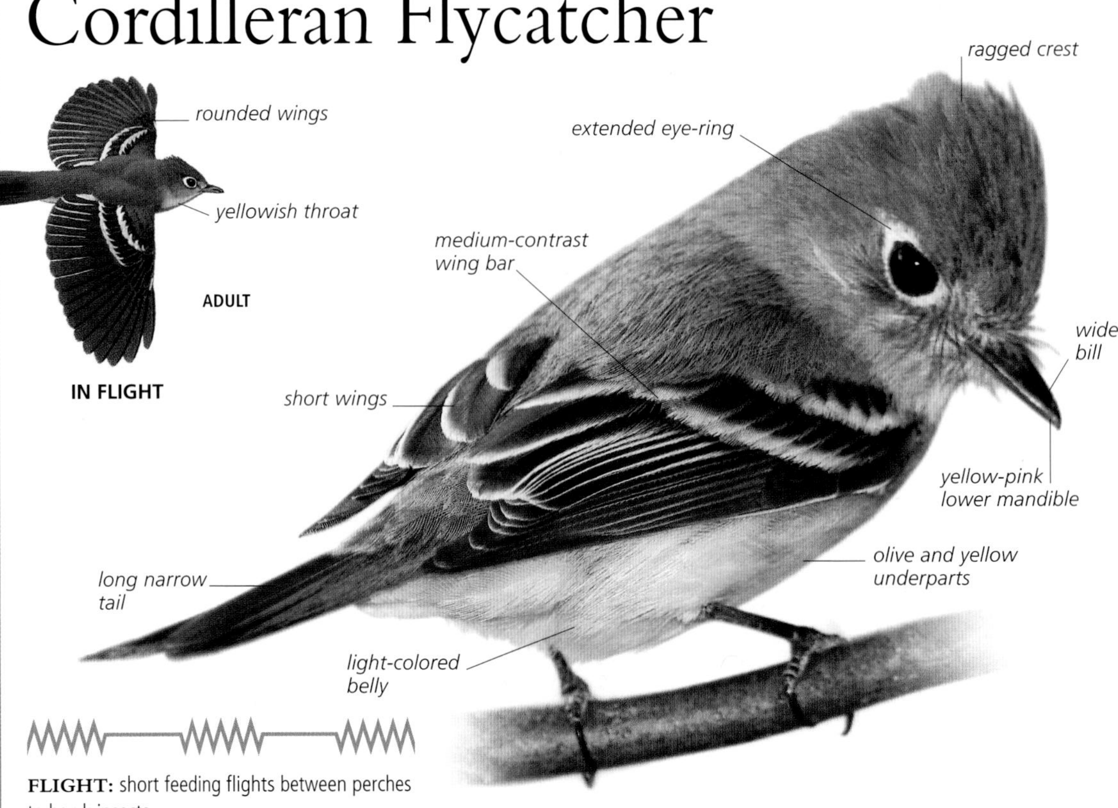

rounded wings
yellowish throat
ADULT
IN FLIGHT
ragged crest
extended eye-ring
medium-contrast wing bar
wide bill
short wings
yellow-pink lower mandible
olive and yellow underparts
long narrow tail
light-colored belly

FLIGHT: short feeding flights between perches to hawk insects.

The Cordilleran Flycatcher is almost indistinguishable from the Pacific-slope Flycatcher; even their songs are difficult to differentiate. The Cordilleran, however, has slightly larger and darker upperparts and more olive and yellow underparts than its Pacific-slope cousin. This bird is found east of the Rocky Mountains, barely reaching southeastern British Columbia and southwestern Alberta, south to the Arizona border. The sexes look alike and are monogamous, behaving territorially during the breeding season. Most molting occurs when the birds are wintering.

VOICE Call *seet*, vocalizes principally on breeding grounds, with occasional calls at other times; song *ps-SEET, ptsick, seet*.

NESTING Cup on rocky outcrop, in natural cavity or root mass; 2–5 eggs; 2 broods; April–July.

FEEDING Feeds on insects; waits on perch to fly out for hunt.

READY TO HUNT
The Cordilleran Flycatcher often adopts a sit-and-wait hunting posture before chasing insects.

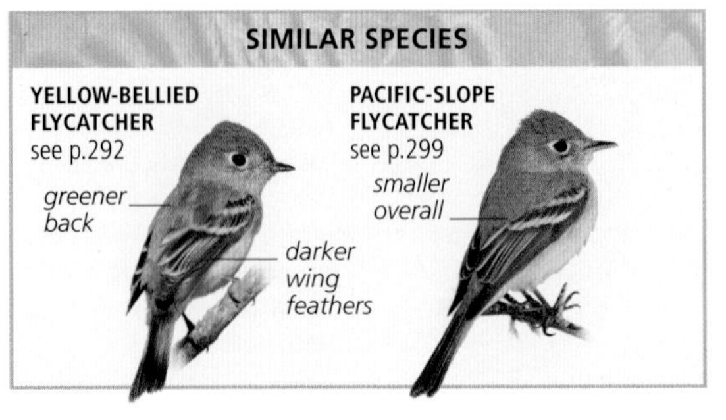

SIMILAR SPECIES
YELLOW-BELLIED FLYCATCHER
see p.292
greener back
darker wing feathers
PACIFIC-SLOPE FLYCATCHER
see p.299
smaller overall

OCCURRENCE
Breeds in cool, arid, relatively dense forests of pine, fir, and spruce, at mid- to high elevation, often associated with watercourses and openings. Winters in the mountains of Mexico.

Length **6–7in (15–17.5cm)**	Wingspan **9in (23cm)**	Weight **3/8–7/16oz (11–13g)**
Social **Solitary**	Lifespan **Unknown**	Status **Secure**

Order **Passeriformes**	Family **Tyrannidae**	Species ***Tyrannus verticalis***

Western Kingbird

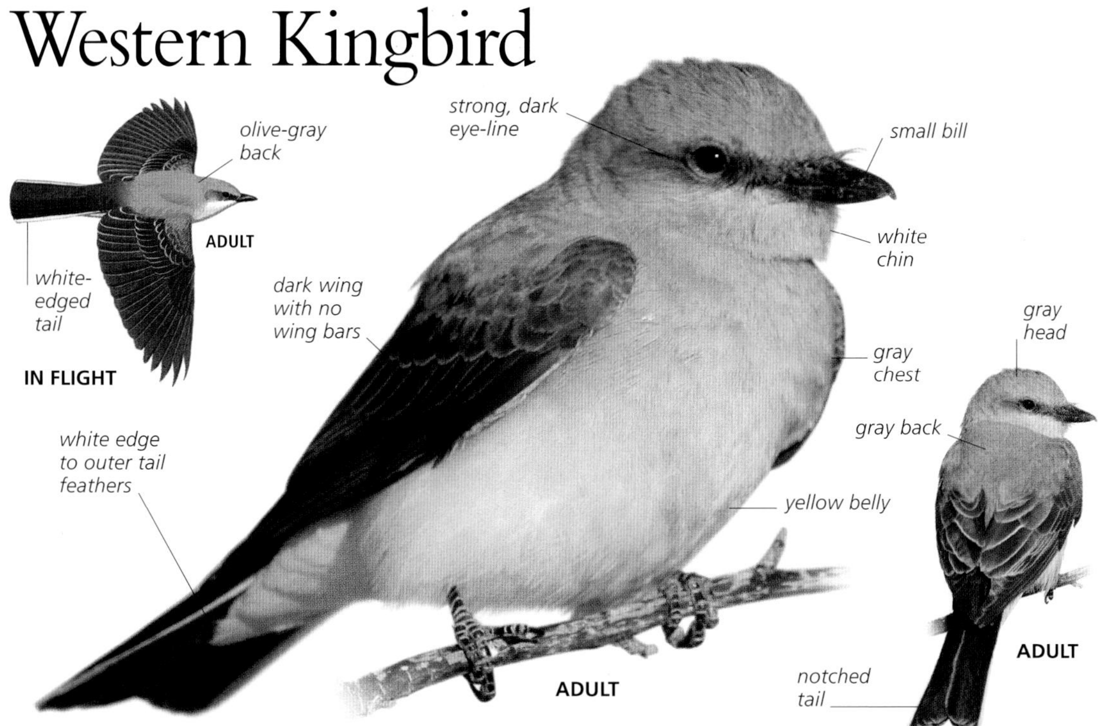
olive-gray back
ADULT
white-edged tail
IN FLIGHT
strong, dark eye-line
small bill
white chin
dark wing with no wing bars
gray head
gray chest
gray back
white edge to outer tail feathers
yellow belly
ADULT
notched tail
ADULT

A conspicuous summer breeder in the US and lower parts of the western provinces, the Western Kingbird occurs in open habitats in much of western North America. The white outer edges on its outer tail feathers distinguish it from other kingbirds. Its population has expanded eastward over the last 100 years. A large, loosely defined territory is defended against other kingbirds when breeding begins in spring; a smaller core area is defended as the season progresses.

VOICE Calls include *whit*, *pwee-t*, and chatter; song, regularly repeated sharp *kip* notes and high-pitched notes.

NESTING Open, bulky cup of grass, rootlets, and twigs in tree, shrub, utility pole; 2–7 eggs; 1 brood; April–July.

FEEDING Feeds on insects and fruit.

FLIGHT: agile, fast, direct, flapping flight; flies to catch insects; hovers to pick bugs on vegetation.

FENCE POST
A favorite place for the Western Kingbird to perch, and look around, is on fenceposts.

QUENCHING THIRST
A juvenile Western Kingbird drinks at the edge of a shallow pools of water.

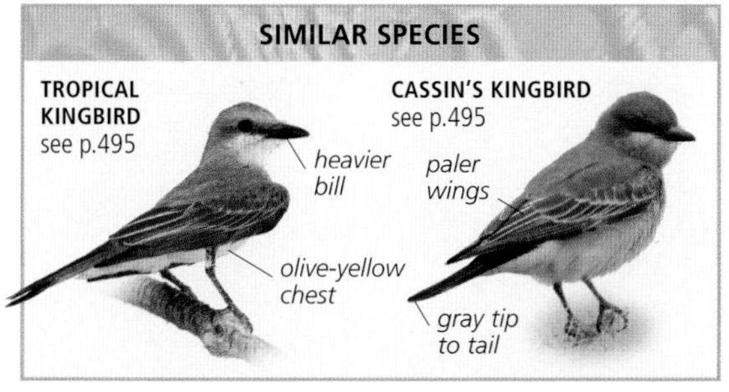
SIMILAR SPECIES
TROPICAL KINGBIRD
see p.495
heavier bill
olive-yellow chest
CASSIN'S KINGBIRD
see p.495
paler wings
gray tip to tail

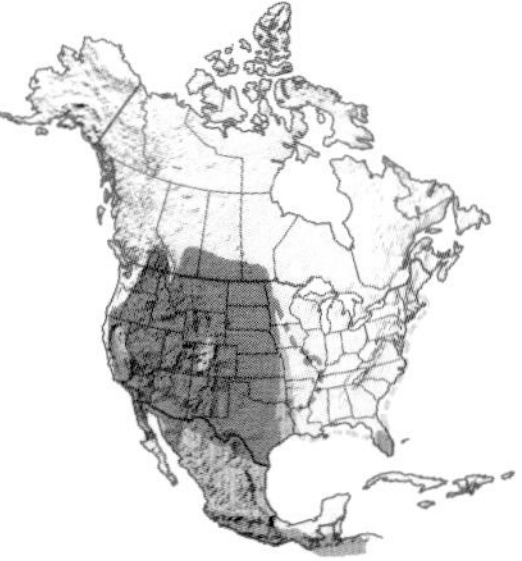

OCCURRENCE
Widespread in southwestern Canada and the western US, in open habitats such as grasslands, savannah, desert shrub, pastures, and cropland, near elevated perches; particularly near water. Winters in similar habitats and in tropical forest and shrubbery from Mexico to Costa Rica.

Length **8–9in (20–23cm)**	Wingspan **15–16in (38–41cm)**	Weight **1¼–1$^{9}/_{16}$oz (35–45g)**
Social **Solitary**	Lifespan **Up to 6 years**	Status **Secure**

Order **Passeriformes**	Family **Tyrannidae**	Species ***Tyrannus tyrannus***

Eastern Kingbird

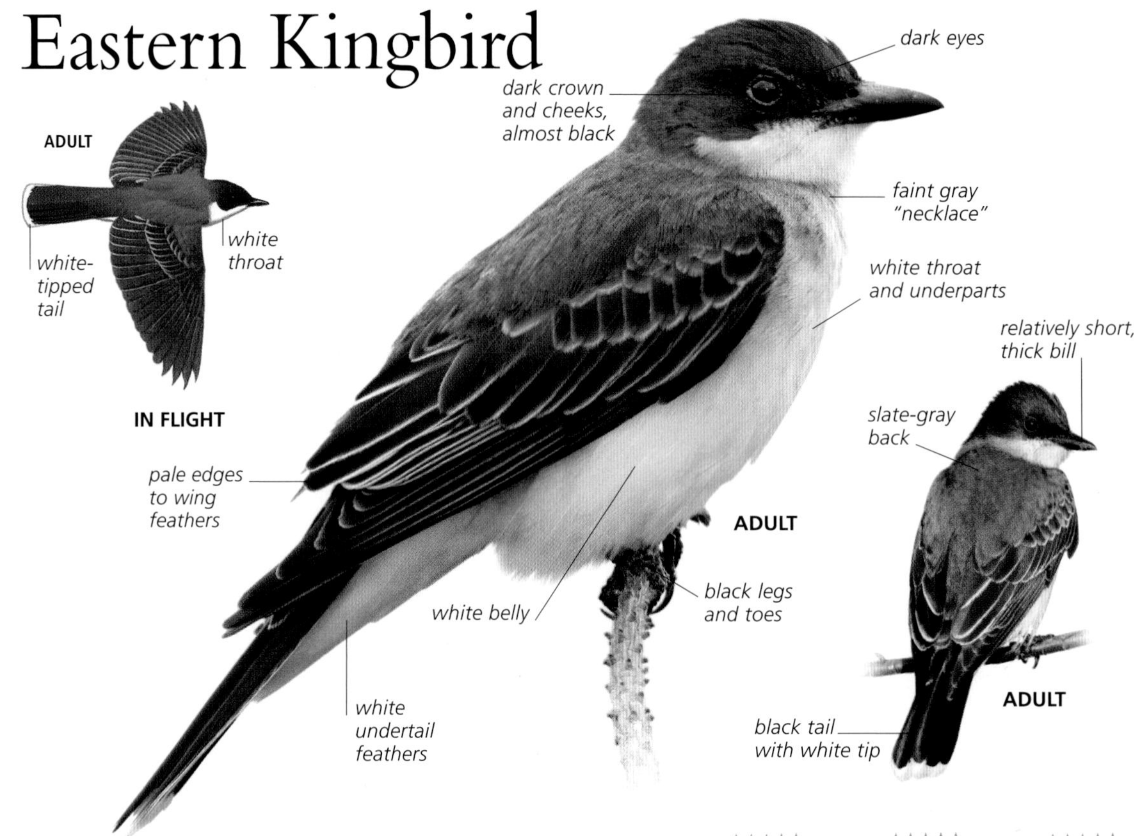
ADULT
white-tipped tail
white throat
IN FLIGHT
dark crown and cheeks, almost black
dark eyes
faint gray "necklace"
white throat and underparts
relatively short, thick bill
slate-gray back
pale edges to wing feathers
ADULT
white belly
black legs and toes
white undertail feathers
ADULT
black tail with white tip

The Eastern Kingbird is a tame and widely distributed bird. It is a highly territorial species and is known for its aggressive behavior toward potential predators, particularly crows and hawks, which it pursues relentlessly. It is able to identify and remove the eggs of the Brown-headed Cowbird when they are laid in its nest. The Eastern Kingbird is generally monogamous and pairs will return to the same territory in subsequent years. This species winters in tropical South America, where it forages for fruit in the treetops of evergreen forests.

VOICE Principal call is loud, metallic *chatter-zeer*; song rapid, electric *kdik-kdik-kdik-pika-pika-pika-kzeeeer.*

NESTING Open cup of twigs, roots, stems in hawthorn, elm, stump, fence, or post; 2–5 eggs; 1 brood; May–August.

FEEDING Catches flying insects from elevated perch or gleans insects from foliage; eats berries and fruit, except in spring.

FLIGHT: strong, direct, and very agile with vigorous, rapid wing beats; hovers and sails.

WHITE-TIPPED
The white-tipped tails of these two Eastern Kingbirds are conspicuous as they sit on a budding twig.

SIMILAR SPECIES

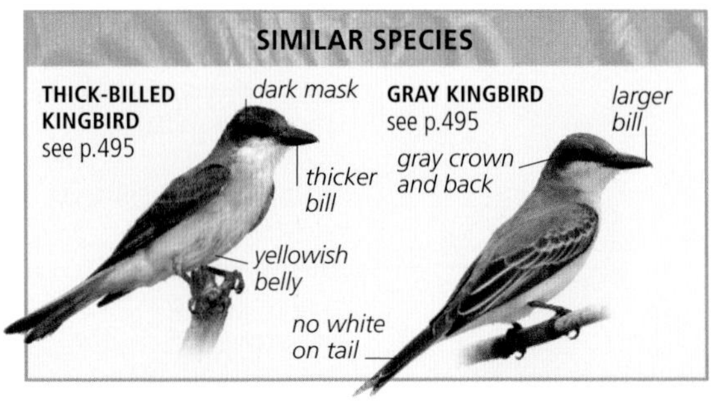
THICK-BILLED KINGBIRD
see p.495
dark mask
thicker bill
yellowish belly
GRAY KINGBIRD
see p.495
larger bill
gray crown and back
no white on tail

OCCURRENCE
Breeds across much of North America in a variety of open habitats, including urban areas, parks, golf courses, fields with scattered shrubs, beaver ponds, and along forest edges. Long distance migrant; winters in South America, south to Argentina.

Length **7–9in (18–23cm)**	Wingspan **13–15in (33–38cm)**	Weight **1 1/16–2oz (30–55g)**
Social **Solitary/Pairs**	Lifespan **Up to 7 years**	Status **Secure**

Order **Passeriformes**	Family **Tyrannidae**	Species ***Myiarchus crinitus***

Great Crested Flycatcher

ADULT

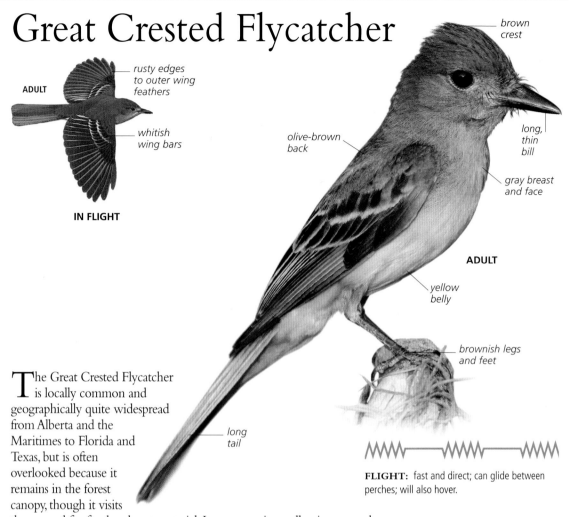

rusty edges to outer wing feathers

whitish wing bars

IN FLIGHT

brown crest

long, thin bill

olive-brown back

gray breast and face

ADULT

yellow belly

brownish legs and feet

long tail

FLIGHT: fast and direct; can glide between perches; will also hover.

The Great Crested Flycatcher is locally common and geographically quite widespread from Alberta and the Maritimes to Florida and Texas, but is often overlooked because it remains in the forest canopy, though it visits the ground for food and nest material. Its presence is usually given away by its loud, sharp, double-syllabled notes. It lines its nest with shed snakeskins like other *Myiarchus* flycatchers.

VOICE Principal call a loud, abrupt *purr-it* given by both sexes; male song repeated *whee-eep*, occasionally *wheeyer*.

NESTING In deep cavity, usually woodpecker hole, lined with leaves, bark, trash, and snakeskins; 4–6 eggs; 1 brood; May–July.

FEEDING Picks flying insects, moths, and caterpillars mainly from leaves and branches in the canopy; also small berries and fruits.

OCCURRENCE
Widespread in eastern North America, from Alberta to the Maritimes in Canada, and, in the US, south to Texas and Florida. Migrates to Mexico, Central America, and northern South America. Breeds in deciduous and mixed woodlands with clearings.

TRICOLORED SPECIES
Viewed from the front, the eastern Great Crested Flycatcher is tricolored.

SIMILAR SPECIES

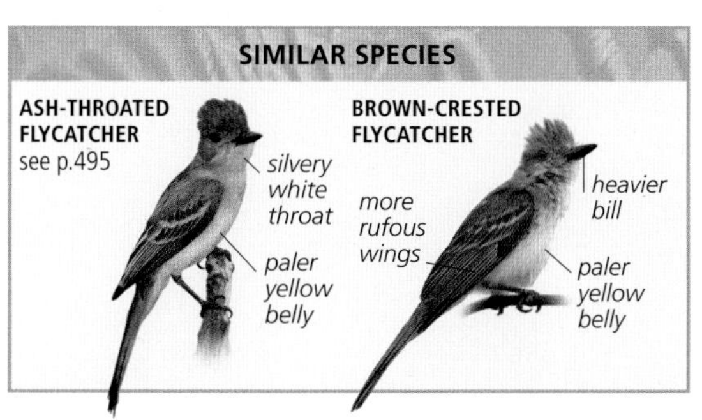
ASH-THROATED FLYCATCHER
see p.495
silvery white throat
paler yellow belly
BROWN-CRESTED FLYCATCHER
more rufous wings
heavier bill
paler yellow belly

Length **7–8in (18–20cm)**	Wingspan **13in (33cm)**	Weight **⅞–1⁷⁄₁₆oz (25–40g)**
Social **Solitary**	Lifespan **Up to 13 years**	Status **Secure**

Family **Vireonidae**

VIREOS

VIREOS ARE A FAMILY of songbirds restricted to the New World, with 15 species occurring in Canada and the United States. The classification of vireos has long been problematic—traditionally they were associated with warblers, but recent molecular studies suggest that they are actually related to crow-like birds. Vireo plumage is drab, often predominantly greenish or grayish above and whitish below, augmented by eye-rings, "spectacles," eyestripes, and wing bars. Most vireos have a preference for broadleaved habitats, where they move about deliberately, hopping and climbing as they slowly forage for their prey. Because they are mainly insect-eaters, most are mid- to long-distance migrants, retreating to warmer climes in winter, when insects are dormant. Vireos are most often detected by the male's loud and clear territorial song, which is repetitive and persistent.

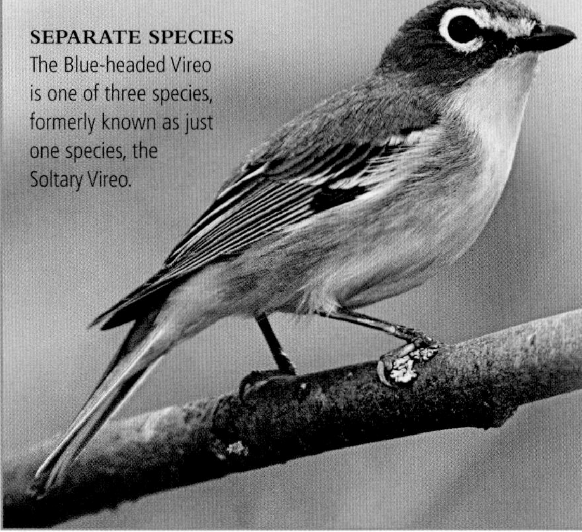

SEPARATE SPECIES
The Blue-headed Vireo is one of three species, formerly known as just one species, the Soltary Vireo.

KEEN SONGSTER
The White-eyed Vireo sings almost continuously, even on the hottest of summer days.

Family **Corvidae**

JAYS & CROWS

ALTHOUGH JAYS AND CROWS belong to a highly diverse family, the corvids, most members share some important characteristics. They are remarkably social, some species even breeding cooperatively, but at the same time they can be quiet and stealthy. Always the opportunists, corvids use strong bills and toes to obtain a varied, omnivorous diet. Ornithologists have shown that ravens, magpies, and crows are among the most intelligent birds. They exhibit self-awareness when looking into mirrors, can make tools, and successfully tackle difficult counting and problem-solving. As a rule, most corvid plumage comes in shades of blue, black, and white. The plumage of adult corvids does not vary by season. Corvidae are part of an ancient bird lineage (Corvoidea) that originated in Australasia. Crows and jays were among the birds most affected by the spread of West Nile virus in the early 2000s, but most populations seem to have recovered quickly.

BLACK AND BLUE
Many corvids (especially jays such as this Steller's Jay) have plumage in shades of black, blue, and gray.

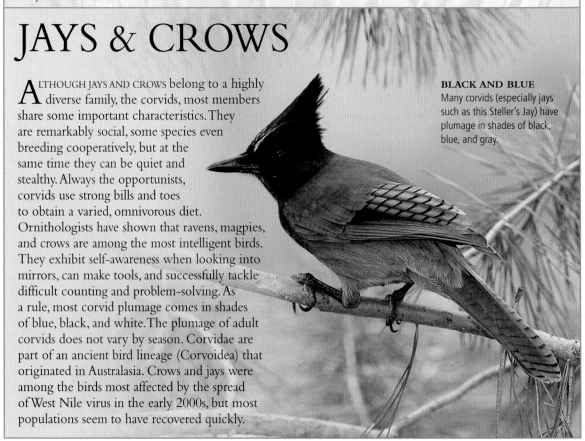

Order **Passeriformes**	Family **Laniidae**	Species ***Lanius ludovicianus***

Loggerhead Shrike

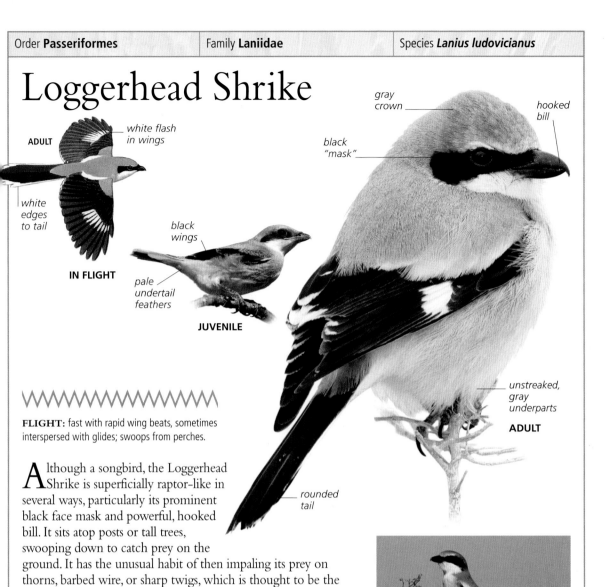

ADULT
white flash in wings
white edges to tail
IN FLIGHT
black wings
pale undertail feathers
JUVENILE
gray crown
hooked bill
black "mask"
unstreaked, gray underparts
ADULT
rounded tail

FLIGHT: fast with rapid wing beats, sometimes interspersed with glides; swoops from perches.

Although a songbird, the Loggerhead Shrike is superficially raptor-like in several ways, particularly its prominent black face mask and powerful, hooked bill. It sits atop posts or tall trees, swooping down to catch prey on the ground. It has the unusual habit of then impaling its prey on thorns, barbed wire, or sharp twigs, which is thought to be the reason for the nickname "butcher bird." Unfortunately, the Loggerhead Shrike is declining, principally because of human alteration of its habitat.

VOICE Quiet warbles, trills, and harsh notes; song harsh notes singly or in series: *chaa chaa chaa*.

NESTING Open cup of vegetation, placed in thorny tree; 5 eggs; 1 brood; March–June.

FEEDING Kills large insects and small vertebrates—rodents, birds, reptiles—with powerful bill.

GEARED FOR HUNTING
The Loggerhead Shrike perches upright on tall shrubs or small trees, where it scans for prey.

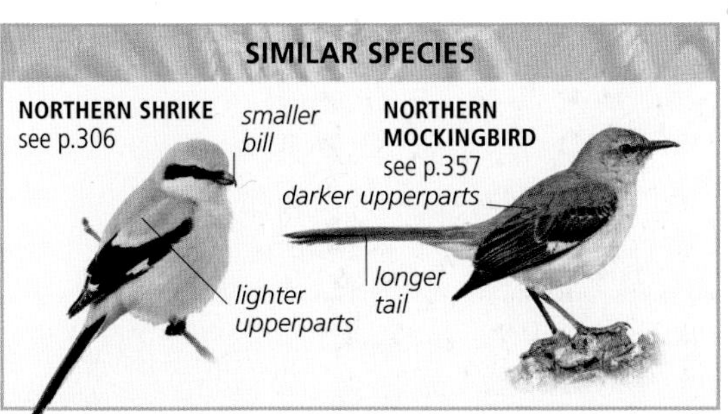
SIMILAR SPECIES
NORTHERN SHRIKE
see p.306
smaller bill
lighter upperparts
NORTHERN MOCKINGBIRD
see p.357
darker upperparts
longer tail

OCCURRENCE
Found in semi-open country with scattered perches, but its distribution is erratic, occurring in relatively high densities in certain areas, but absent from seemingly suitable habitat. Occurs in congested residential areas in some regions (south Florida), but generally favors fairly remote habitats.

Length **9in (23cm)**	Wingspan **12in (31cm)**	Weight **1¼–2⅛oz (35–60g)**
Social **Solitary**	Lifespan **Unknown**	Status **Declining**

Order **Passeriformes**	Family **Laniidae**	Species ***Lanius excubitor***

Northern Shrike

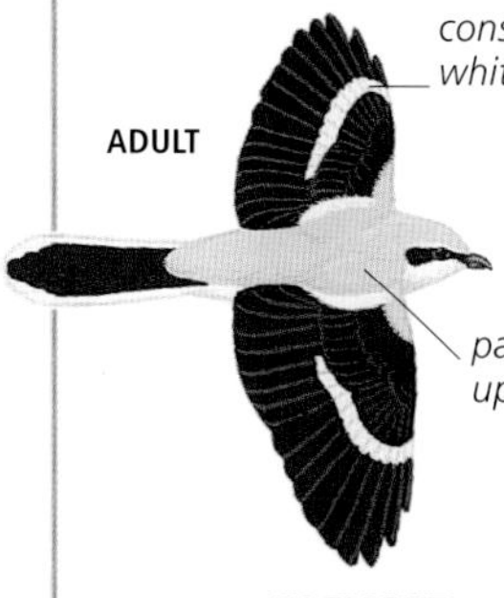

ADULT — conspicuous white wing bar; pale gray upperparts

IN FLIGHT

IMMATURE — strongly hooked bill; delicately barred breast; brownish underparts; long tail

ADULT — large head; narrow black mask; pale gray upperparts; black wings; gray-white underparts; black tail, with white outer tail feathers

FLIGHT: short flights between hunting perches; pounces on prey.

This northern version of the familiar Loggerhead Shrike is an uncommon winter visitor to the northern US and southern Canada. In some winters, this species is widespread across the mid-latitudes of North America, in other winters it is nearly absent. The Northern Shrike is paler, larger bodied, and larger billed than the Loggerhead Shrike, which enables it to attack and subdue larger prey than the Loggerhead. Many Northern Shrike populations worldwide are in decline, but to date there is no sign of a similar decline in North America.

VOICE Variety of short warbles, trills, and harsh notes; generally silent on wintering grounds.

NESTING Open, bulky cup in low tree or large shrub, lined with feathers and hair; 4–6 eggs; 1 brood; May–June.

FEEDING Swoops down on prey, such as rodents, small birds, and insects, which it impales on thorns or pointed branches.

BLACK-AND-WHITE DISPLAY
The Northern Shrike flashes its distinctive black-and-white markings while in flight.

SIMILAR SPECIES

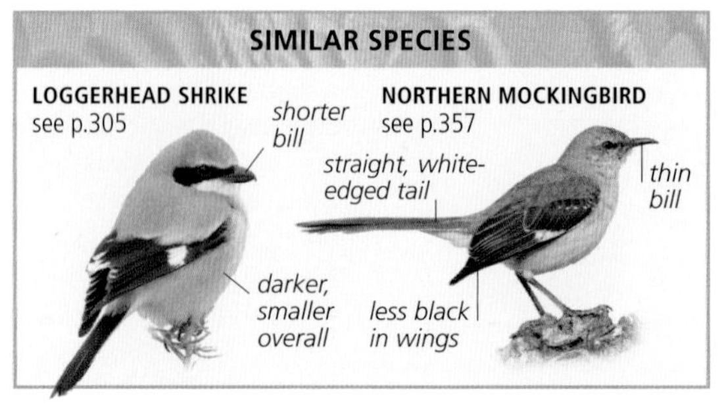
LOGGERHEAD SHRIKE
see p.305
shorter bill
darker, smaller overall
NORTHERN MOCKINGBIRD
see p.357
straight, white-edged tail
thin bill
less black in wings

OCCURRENCE
Breeds in sub-Arctic coniferous forests, across Canada and Alaska. Winters in more southerly open country with sufficient perches. Avoids built-up and residential districts, but spends much time perching on fence posts and roadside signs.

Length **10in (25cm)**	Wingspan **14in (35cm)**	Weight **1¾–2⅝oz (50–75g)**
Social **Solitary**	Lifespan **Unknown**	Status **Vulnerable**

Order **Passeriformes**	Family **Vireonidae**	Species ***Vireo griseus***

White-eyed Vireo

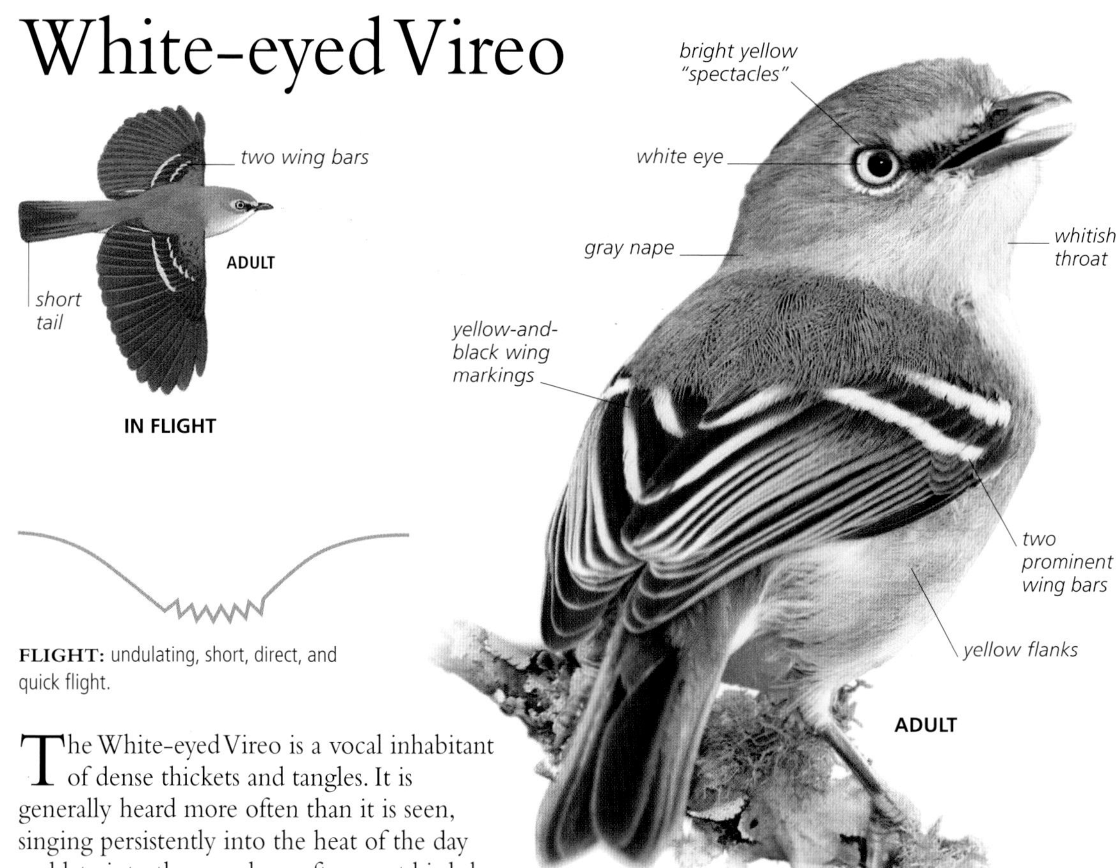
two wing bars
ADULT
short tail
IN FLIGHT
bright yellow "spectacles"
white eye
gray nape
whitish throat
yellow-and-black wing markings
two prominent wing bars
yellow flanks
ADULT

FLIGHT: undulating, short, direct, and quick flight.

The White-eyed Vireo is a vocal inhabitant of dense thickets and tangles. It is generally heard more often than it is seen, singing persistently into the heat of the day and late into the year, long after most birds have become silent. A small-bodied but large-headed vireo, it looks and behaves like a plump warbler as it forages actively in shrubbery. It is heavily parasitized by the Brown-headed Cowbird, and as many as half of the White-eyed Vireo's offsprings do not survive.

VOICE Call a raspy, angry scold; male's song a highly variable and complex repertoire of over a dozen distinct songs.

NESTING Deep cup in dense vegetation, outer layer composed of coarse material, lined with finer fibers, often near water, suspended from twigs by the rim; 3–5 eggs; 2 broods; March–July.

FEEDING Hops from branch to branch pursuing bees, flies, beetles, and bugs, plucking them from leaves or sallying out to snatch them in the air; feeds primarily on fruit in winter.

WHITE EYE, WHITE WING BARS
The White-eyed Vireo's distinctive markings ensure that it is highly conspicuous.

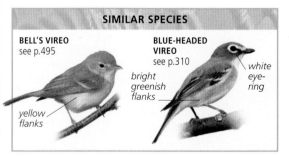

SIMILAR SPECIES

BELL'S VIREO
see p.495
yellow flanks

BLUE-HEADED VIREO
see p.310
bright greenish flanks
white eye-ring

OCCURRENCE
A common breeder in dense brush and scrub across the eastern US and southern Ontario, from Texas to the Great Lakes region and southern New England. Retreats to southern states of the US, the Atlantic slope of Mexico, Cuba, and the Bahamas in winter.

Length **5in (13cm)**	Wingspan **7½in (19cm)**	Weight **⅜oz (10g)**
Social **Solitary**	Lifespan **Up to 7 years**	Status **Secure**

Order **Passeriformes**	Family **Vireonidae**	Species ***Vireo flavifrons***

Yellow-throated Vireo

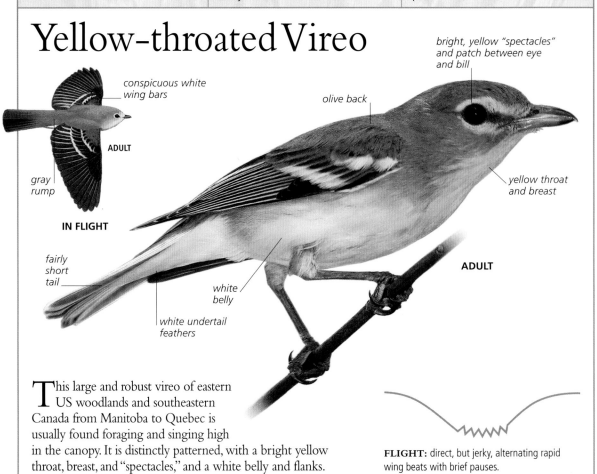

conspicuous white wing bars
ADULT
gray rump
IN FLIGHT
bright, yellow "spectacles" and patch between eye and bill
olive back
yellow throat and breast
ADULT
fairly short tail
white belly
white undertail feathers

This large and robust vireo of eastern US woodlands and southeastern Canada from Manitoba to Quebec is usually found foraging and singing high in the canopy. It is distinctly patterned, with a bright yellow throat, breast, and "spectacles," and a white belly and flanks. The fragmentation of forests, spraying of insecticides, and cowbird parasitism have led to regional declines in Yellow-throated Vireo populations, but the bird's range, as a whole, has actually expanded.

VOICE Scolding, hoarse, rapid calls; male song a slow, repetitive, two- or three-note phrase, separated by long pauses.

NESTING Rounded cup of plant and animal fibers bound with spider webs, usually located towards the top of a large tree and hung by the rim; 3–5 eggs; 1 brood; April–July.

FEEDING Forages high in trees, picking insects from the branches; also eats fruit when available.

FLIGHT: direct, but jerky, alternating rapid wing beats with brief pauses.

CANOPY SINGER
The Yellow-throated Vireo sings from the very tops of tall trees.

HIGH FORAGER
This bird finds much of its food in the peeling bark of mature trees.

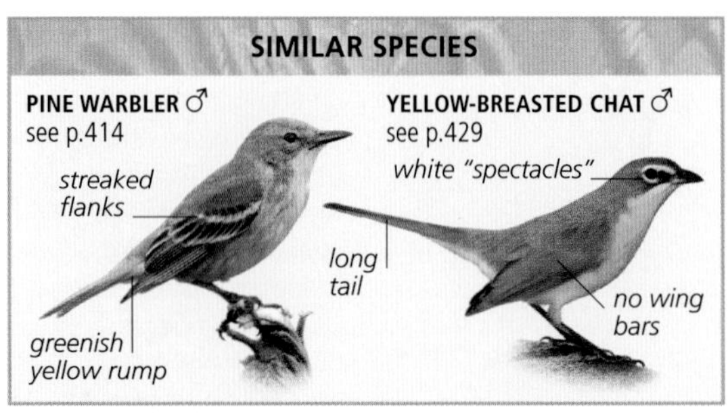
SIMILAR SPECIES
PINE WARBLER ♂
see p.414
streaked flanks
greenish yellow rump
YELLOW-BREASTED CHAT ♂
see p.429
white "spectacles"
long tail
no wing bars

OCCURRENCE
Breeds in extensive, mature deciduous, and mixed woodlands in the eastern half of the US, and extreme southern Canada. Winters mainly from southern Mexico to northern South America, primarily in wooded areas.

Length **5½in (14cm)**	Wingspan **9½in (24cm)**	Weight **⅝oz (18g)**
Social **Solitary/Pairs**	Lifespan **Up to 6 years**	Status **Secure**

Order **Passeriformes**	Family **Vireonidae**	Species ***Vireo cassinii***

Cassin's Vireo

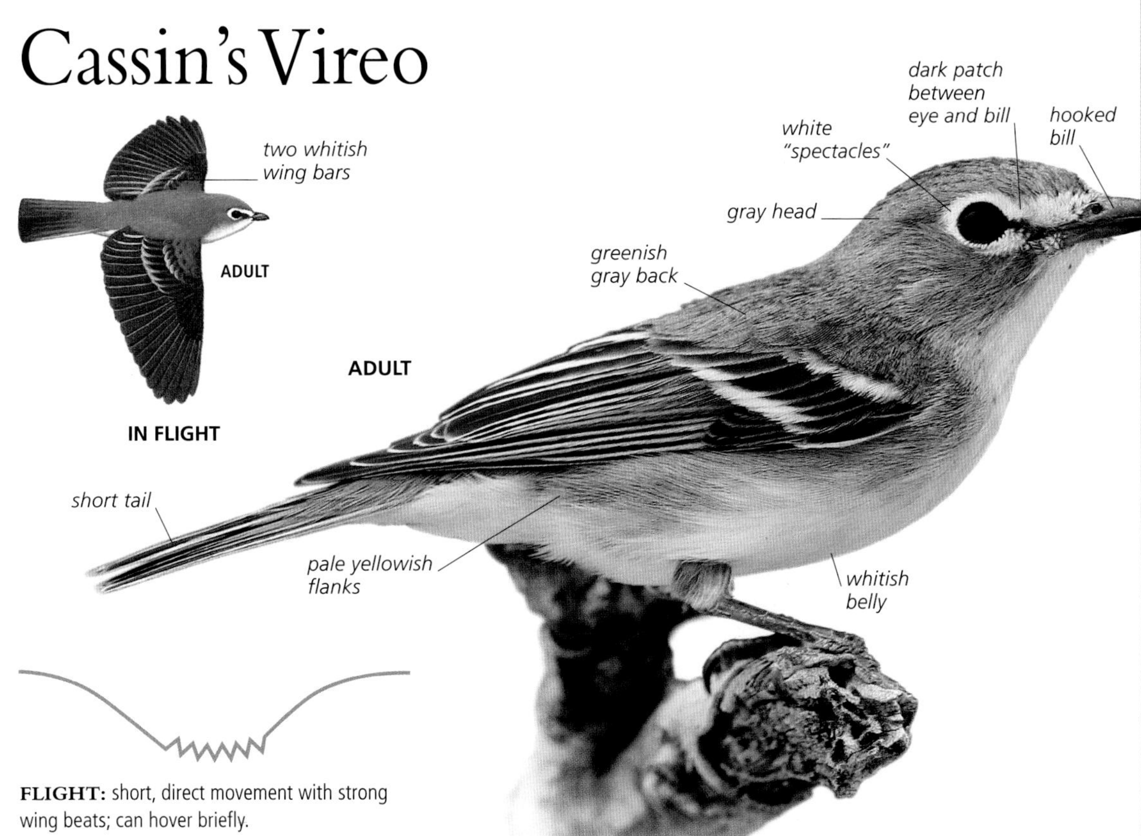

two whitish wing bars
ADULT
IN FLIGHT
ADULT
dark patch between eye and bill
hooked bill
white "spectacles"
gray head
greenish gray back
short tail
pale yellowish flanks
whitish belly

FLIGHT: short, direct movement with strong wing beats; can hover briefly.

Cassin's Vireo is similar to the closely related Plumbeous and Blue-headed Vireos in appearance and song. It is conspicuous and vocal throughout its breeding grounds in the far west of the US and north into southwest Canada. In winter, virtually the entire population migrates to Mexico. Cassin's Vireo was named in honor of John Cassin, who published the first comprehensive study of North American birds in 1865.

VOICE Call a harsh, scolding chatter; male's song a broken series of whistles, which ascend then descend; lower in tone than Blue-headed Vireo and higher than the Plumbeous.

NESTING Cup of fibers, lined with fine plant down; suspended from twigs; 2–5 eggs; 1–2 broods; April–July.

FEEDING Picks insects and spiders from leaves and twigs as it hops from branch to branch; occasionally sallies out or hovers.

TIRELESS SINGER
Cassin's Vireo is well known for its loud and incessant singing throughout the spring and into the summer.

SIMILAR SPECIES

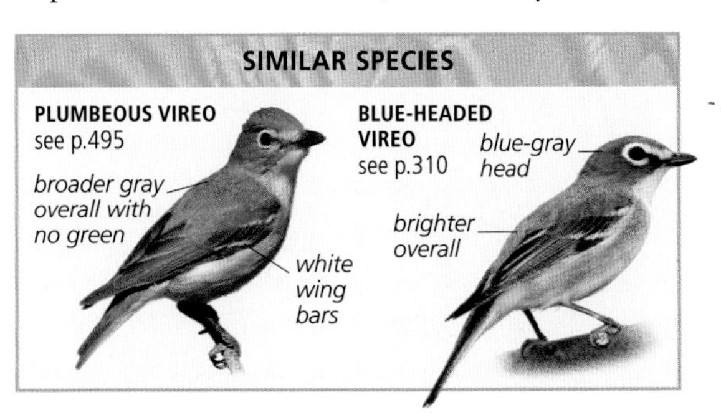

PLUMBEOUS VIREO
see p.495
broader gray overall with no green
white wing bars
BLUE-HEADED VIREO
see p.310
blue-gray head
brighter overall

OCCURRENCE
Breeds in coniferous and mixed forests in the hills and mountains of British Columbia, Alberta, and, in the US, the Pacific Northwest through to southern California. Winters in western Mexico.

Length **5½in (14cm)**	Wingspan **9½in (24cm)**	Weight **9/16oz (16g)**
Social **Solitary/Pairs**	Lifespan **Unknown**	Status **Secure**

Order **Passeriformes**	Family **Vireonidae**	Species ***Vireo solitarius***

Blue-headed Vireo

gray head
conspicuous white "spectacles"
two wing bars
looks "big-headed"
contrasting white throat
greenish back
ADULT
ADULT
IN FLIGHT
white belly
bright greenish flanks
relatively short tail

Closely related to the Cassin's Vireo and Plumbeous Vireo, the fairly common Blue-headed Vireo is the brightest and most colorful of the three. Its blue-gray, helmeted head, adorned with striking white "spectacles" around its dark eyes also helps to distinguish it from other vireos in its range. This stocky and slow moving bird is heard more often than it is seen in its forest breeding habitat. However, during migration it can be more conspicuous and, is the first vireo to return in spring.

VOICE Call a harsh, scolding chatter; male's song a series of rich, sweet, high phrases of two to six notes slurred together.

NESTING Shallow, rounded cup loosely constructed of animal and plant fibers, lined with finer material and suspended from twigs by the rim; 3–5 eggs; 2 broods; May–July.

FEEDING Gleans insects from branches and leaves, usually high in shrubs and trees; often makes short sallies after prey.

FLIGHT: slow, heavy, undulating flight with a series of deep wing beats followed by short pauses.

SPECTACLED VIREO
Its rather thick head with conspicuous "spectacles" and gray color are distinctive field marks.

SIMILAR SPECIES

BLACK-CAPPED VIREO ◔
see p.495

CASSIN'S VIREO
see p.309

smaller overall
thin bill
duller overall

OCCURRENCE
Breeds in large tracts of undisturbed coniferous and mixed forests with a rich understory, largely across eastern North America. It winters in woodlands across the southeastern US from Virginia to Texas, as well as in Mexico and northern Central America to Costa Rica.

Length **5½in (14in)**	Wingspan **9½in (24cm)**	Weight **⁹⁄₁₆oz (16g)**
Social **Solitary/Pairs**	Lifespan **Up to 7 years**	Status **Secure**

Order **Passeriformes** | Family **Vireonidae** | Species ***Vireo huttoni***

Hutton's Vireo

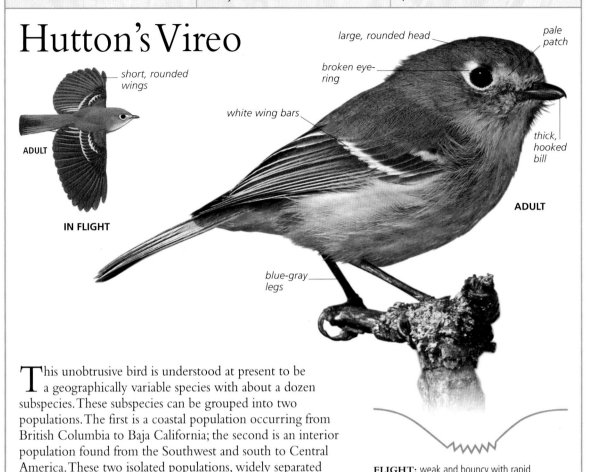

short, rounded wings

ADULT

IN FLIGHT

large, rounded head

pale patch

broken eye-ring

white wing bars

thick, hooked bill

ADULT

blue-gray legs

This unobtrusive bird is understood at present to be a geographically variable species with about a dozen subspecies. These subspecies can be grouped into two populations. The first is a coastal population occurring from British Columbia to Baja California; the second is an interior population found from the Southwest and south to Central America. These two isolated populations, widely separated by desert, may actually represent different species. Very similar in appearance to the Ruby-crowned Kinglet with which it flocks in winter, Hutton's Vireo is distinguishable by its larger size and thicker bill. Unlike other vireos, this bird is largely nonmigratory.

VOICE Varied calls include harsh mewing and nasal, raspy *spit*; male's song a repetition of a simple phrase.

NESTING Deep cup constructed from plant and animal fibers, lined with finer materials, often incorporating lichens, suspended from twigs by the rim; 3–5 eggs; 1–2 broods; February–May.

FEEDING Hops diligently from branch to branch searching for caterpillars, spiders, and flies; also eats berries; gleans from leaves usually while perched, but occasionally sallies or hovers.

FLIGHT: weak and bouncy with rapid wing beats.

FOLLOW THE SONG
This kinglet-sized vireo is easily overlooked and is often detected by its song.

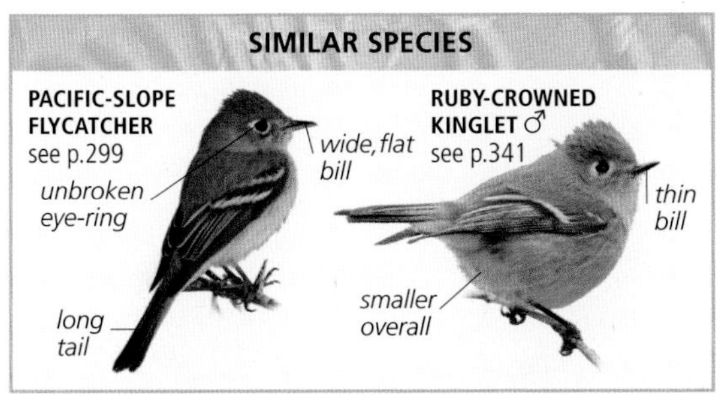
SIMILAR SPECIES
PACIFIC-SLOPE FLYCATCHER
see p.299
unbroken eye-ring
wide, flat bill
long tail
RUBY-CROWNED KINGLET ♂
see p.341
thin bill
smaller overall

OCCURRENCE
Year-round resident in mixed evergreen forests; particularly common in live oak woods. Breeds in mixed oak-pine woodlands along the Pacific coast from British Columbia southward to northern Baja California, and from southwest California and New Mexico to Mexico and Guatemala.

Length **5in (13cm)**	Wingspan **8in (20cm)**	Weight **3/8oz (11g)**
Social **Solitary/Pairs**	Lifespan **Up to 13 years**	Status **Secure**

Order **Passeriformes**	Family **Vireonidae**	Species ***Vireo gilvus***

Warbling Vireo

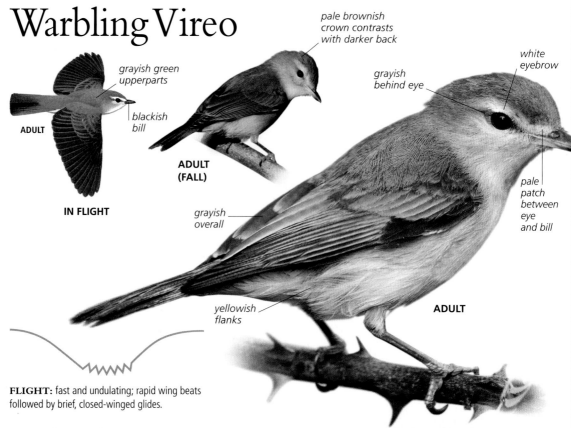

grayish green upperparts
blackish bill
ADULT
IN FLIGHT
pale brownish crown contrasts with darker back
ADULT (FALL)
white eyebrow
grayish behind eye
pale patch between eye and bill
grayish overall
yellowish flanks
ADULT

FLIGHT: fast and undulating; rapid wing beats followed by brief, closed-winged glides.

Widely distributed across North America, this rather drab vireo is better known for its cheerful warbling song than for its plumage, and coincidentally, its thin bill and longish tail give this rather active vireo a somewhat warbler-like appearance. The eastern subspecies (*V. g. gilvus*), which is heavier and has a larger bill, and the western subspecies (*V. g. swainsonii*) are quite different and may in fact be separate species. Out of all the vireos, the Warbling Vireo is most likely to breed in human developments, such as city parks, suburbs, and orchards.

VOICE Harsh, raspy scold call; male's persistent song a high, rapid, and highly variable warble.

NESTING Rough cup placed high in a deciduous tree, hung from the rim between forked twigs; 3–5 eggs; 2 broods; March–July.

FEEDING Gleans a variety of insects, including grasshoppers, aphids, and beetles from leaves; eats fruit in winter.

PLAIN-LOOKING SONGSTER
The Warbling Vireo makes up for its plain appearance by its colorful voice, full of rounded notes and melodious warbles.

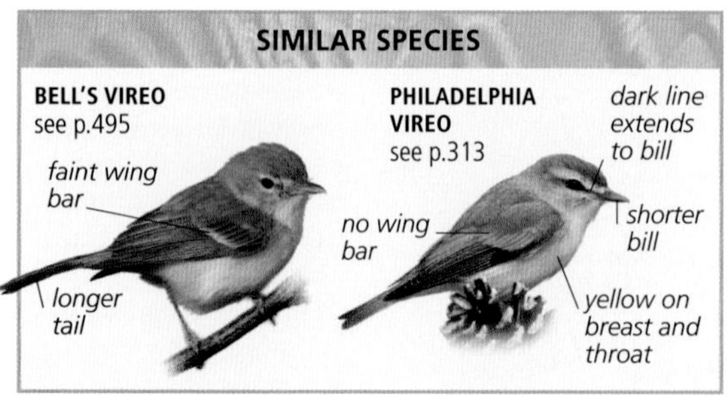
SIMILAR SPECIES
BELL'S VIREO
see p.495
faint wing bar
longer tail
PHILADELPHIA VIREO
see p.313
dark line extends to bill
no wing bar
shorter bill
yellow on breast and throat

OCCURRENCE
Extensive distribution across most of temperate North America, from Alaska, around the northern limit of the northerly zone, and through western, central, and eastern North America. Breeds in deciduous and mixed forests, particularly near water. Winters in southern Mexico and Central America.

Length **5½in (14cm)**	Wingspan **8½in (21cm)**	Weight **7/16oz (12g)**
Social **Solitary/Pairs**	Lifespan **Up to 13 years**	Status **Secure**

Order **Passeriformes**	Family **Vireonidae**	Species ***Vireo philadelphicus***

Philadelphia Vireo

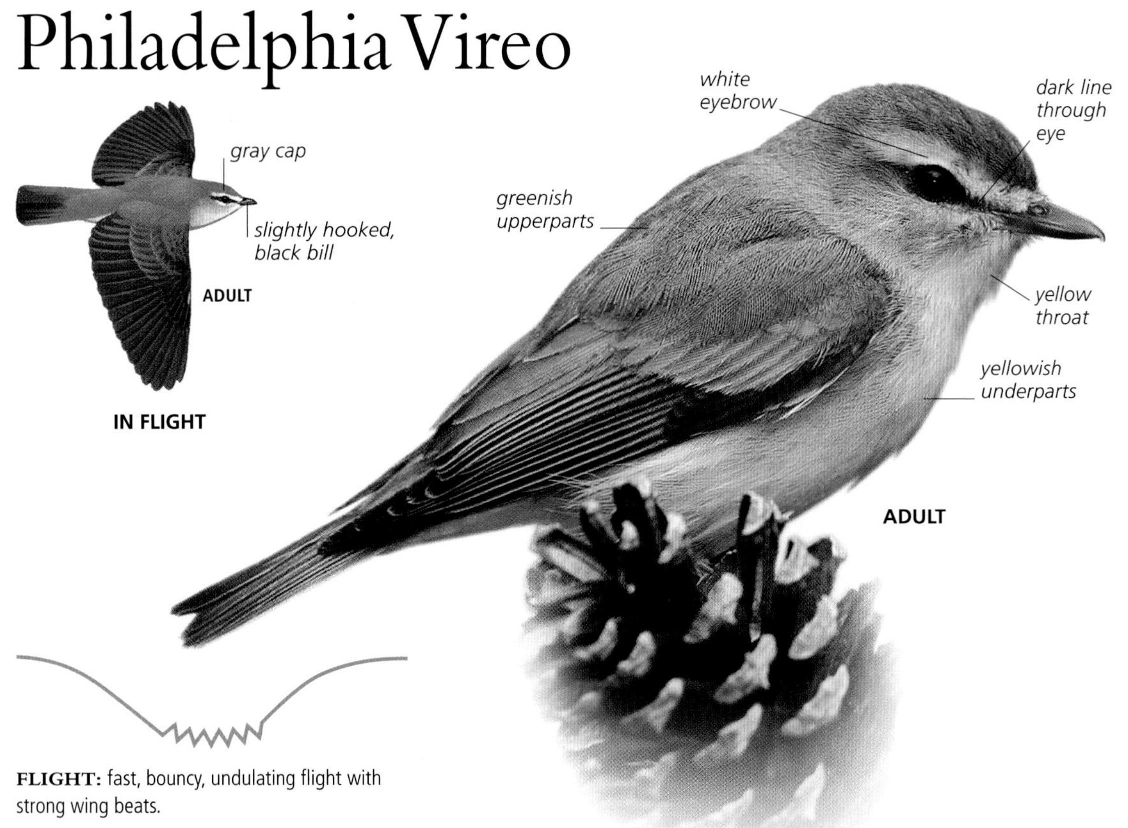
gray cap
slightly hooked, black bill
ADULT
IN FLIGHT
white eyebrow
dark line through eye
greenish upperparts
yellow throat
yellowish underparts
ADULT

FLIGHT: fast, bouncy, undulating flight with strong wing beats.

Despite being widespread, the Philadelphia Vireo remains rather poorly studied. It shares its breeding habitat with the similar looking, but larger and more numerous, Red-eyed Vireo, and, interestingly, it modifies its behavior to avoid competition. It is the most northerly breeding vireo, with its southernmost breeding range barely reaching the US. Its scientific and English names derive from the fact that the bird was first discovered near Philadelphia in the mid-19th century.

VOICE Song a series of two and four note phrases, remarkably similar to the song of the Red-eyed Vireo.

NESTING Rounded cup of plant fibers bound by spider webs, hanging between forked twigs that narrows at the rim; 3–5 eggs; 1–2 broods; June–August.

FEEDING Gleans caterpillars, bees, flies, and bugs from leaves; usually forages high in trees, moving with short hops and flights.

DISTINGUISHED APPEARANCE
The Philadelphia Vireo's gentle expression and pudgy appearance help separate it from its neighbor, the Red-eyed Vireo.

SIMILAR SPECIES

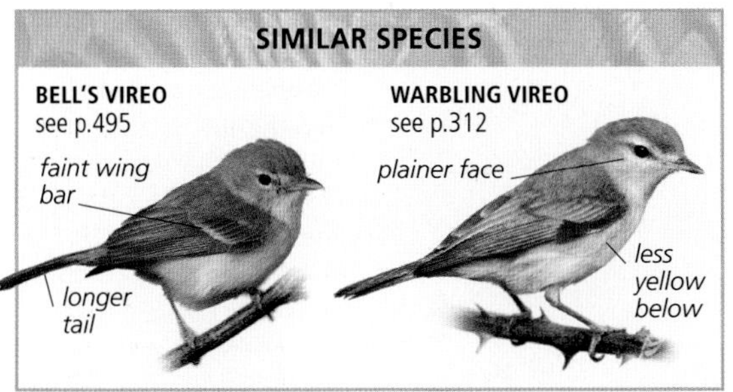
BELL'S VIREO
see p.495
faint wing bar
longer tail
WARBLING VIREO
see p.312
plainer face
less yellow below

OCCURRENCE
Breeds in deciduous woodlands, mixed woodlands, and woodland edges, in a wide belt across Canada, reaching the Great Lakes and northern New England. The Philadelphia Vireo winters from Mexico to Panama and northern Colombia.

Length **5¼in (13.5cm)**	Wingspan **8in (20cm)**	Weight **7/16oz (12g)**
Social **Solitary/Pairs**	Lifespan **Up to 8 years**	Status **Secure**

Order **Passeriformes**	Family **Vireonidae**	Species ***Vireo olivaceus***

Red-eyed Vireo

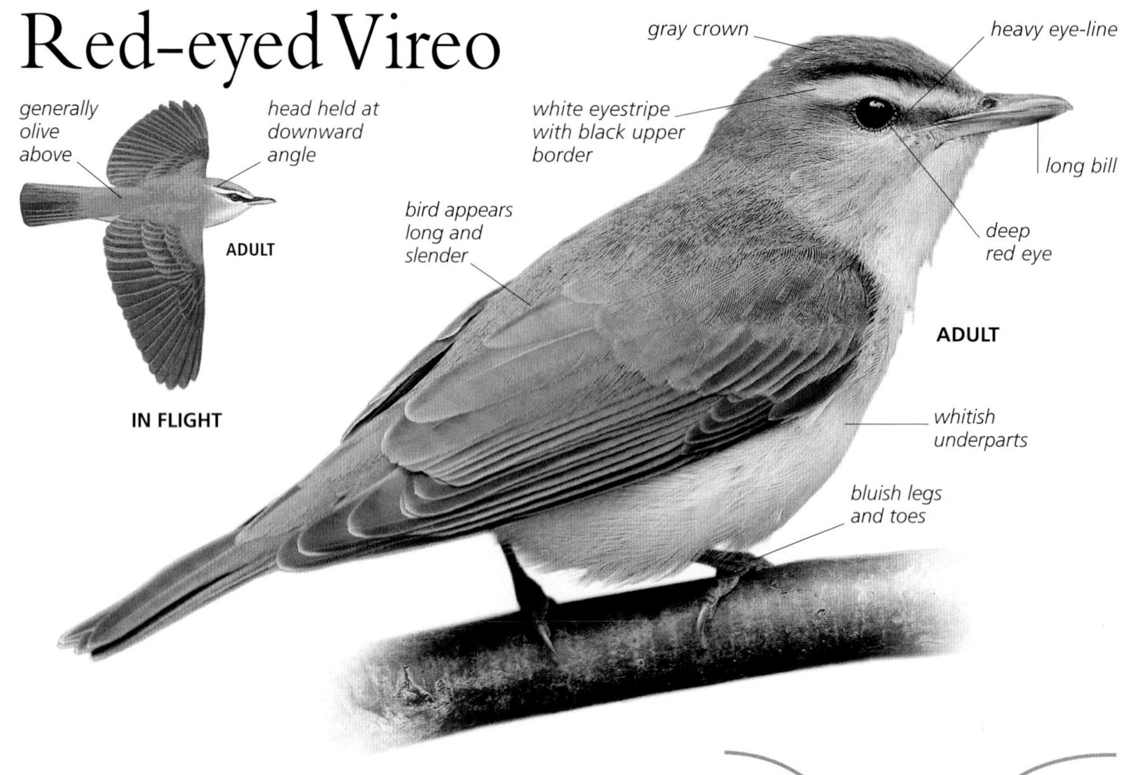
generally olive above
head held at downward angle
ADULT
IN FLIGHT
gray crown
heavy eye-line
white eyestripe with black upper border
long bill
bird appears long and slender
deep red eye
ADULT
whitish underparts
bluish legs and toes

Probably the most common songbird of northern and eastern North America, the Red-eyed Vireo is perhaps the quintessential North American vireo, although it is heard far more often than it is seen. It sings persistently and monotonously all day long and late into the season, long after other species have stopped singing. It generally stays high in the canopy of the deciduous and mixed woodlands where it breeds. The entire population migrates to central South America in winter. To reach their Amazonian winter habitats, Red-eyed Vireos migrate in fall (August–October) through Central America, Caribbean Islands, and northern South America to Educador, Peru, and Brazil.

VOICE Nasal mewing call; male song consists of slurred three-note phrases.

NESTING Open cup nest hanging on horizontal fork of tree branch; built with plant fibers bound with spider's web; exterior is sometimes decorated with lichen; 3–5 eggs; 1 brood; May–July.

FEEDING Gleans insects from leaves, hopping methodically in the canopy and sub-canopy of deciduous trees; during fall and winter, primarily feeds on fruit.

FLIGHT: fast, strong, and undulating with the body angled upwards.

HOPPING BIRD
The Red-eyed Vireo's primary form of locomotion is hopping; at ground level and in trees.

SIMILAR SPECIES

BLACK-WHISKERED VIREO
faint black "mustache"
duller green upperparts

BROWN EYES
Immature Red-eyed Vireos have brown eyes, but those of the adult birds are red.

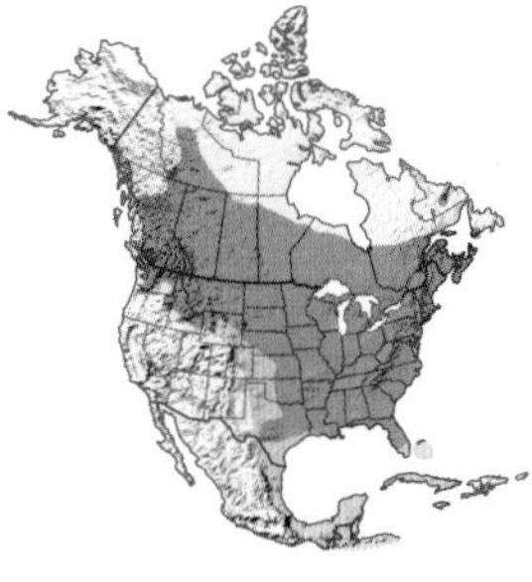

OCCURRENCE
Breeds across North America from the Yukon and British Columbia east to the Canadian maritimes, southward from Washington to south central Texas, and west to Canada in central and northern states. Inhabits the canopy of deciduous forests and pine hardwood forests.

Length **6in (15cm)**	Wingspan **10in (25cm)**	Weight **⅝oz (17g)**
Social **Solitary/Pairs**	Lifespan **Up to 10 years**	Status **Secure**

Order **Passeriformes**	Family **Corvidae**	Species ***Perisoreus canadensis***

Gray Jay

ADULT

IN FLIGHT

long, tail with white corners

dark gray upperparts

brownish back with white streaks

***P. c. obscurus* (NORTHWESTERN)**

whitish "mustache"

uniform medium to dark gray

JUVENILE

dark crown

white forehead

white collar

short bill

gray overall, darker upperparts

***P. c. canadensis* (NORTHERN)**

dark, smoky gray tail and wings

black legs and toes

Fearless and cunning, the Gray Jay can often be a nuisance to campers due to its inquisitive behavior. It is particularly adept at stealing food and shiny metal objects, which has earned it the colloquial name of "Camp Robber." One of the interesting aspects of its behavior is the way it stores food for later use, by sticking it to trees with its viscous saliva. This is thought to be one of the reasons that enable it to survive the long northern winters. Gray Jays can often collect in noisy groups of three to six birds in order to investigate intruders encroaching upon their territory.

VOICE Mostly silent, but also produces variety of odd clucks and screeches; sometimes Blue Jay-like *jay!* and eerie whistles, including bisyllabic *whee-oo* or *ew*.

NESTING Bulky platform of sticks with cocoons on south side of coniferous tree; 2–5 eggs; 1 brood; February–May.

FEEDING Forages for insects and berries; also raids birds' nests.

FLIGHT: hollow-sounding wing beats followed by slow, seemingly awkward, rocking glides.

BUILT FOR COLD
The Gray Jay's short extremities and dense, fluffy plumage are perfect for long, harsh winters.

SIMILAR SPECIES

CLARK'S NUTCRACKER
see p.319
white wing patch
longer bill

NORTHERN MOCKINGBIRD
see p.357
no dark crown
longer tail
white wing patch

OCCURRENCE
Northerly forests, especially lichen-festooned areas with firs and spruces. Found in coniferous forests across northern North America from Alaska to Newfoundland, the Maritimes, and north New York and New England; south to the western mountains; an isolated population in the Black Hills.

Length **10–11½in (25–29cm)**	Wingspan **18in (46cm)**	Weight **2⅛–2⅞oz (60–80g)**
Social **Family groups**	Lifespan **Up to 10 years**	Status **Secure**

Order **Passeriformes**	Family **Corvidae**	Species ***Cyanocitta cristata***

Blue Jay

long tail with white corners
white streak in blue wings
ADULT
white trailing edge feathers
IN FLIGHT
blue crest
black patch between eye and bill
black collar
plain blue mantle
blue wings and tail
long, black bill
whitish throat
ADULT
grayish underparts
black legs and feet
black bars on tail

The Blue Jay is common in rural and suburban backyards across Canada and the eastern US. Beautiful as it is, the Blue Jay has a darker side. It often raids the nests of smaller birds for eggs and nestlings. Although usually thought of as a nonmigratory species, some Blue Jays undergo impressive migrations, with loose flocks sometimes numbering in the hundreds visible overhead in spring and fall. The Blue Jay is the provincial bird of Prince Edward Island.

VOICE Harsh, screaming *jay! jay!;* other common call an odd ethereal, chortling *queedle-ee-dee;* soft clucks when feeding.

NESTING Cup of strong twigs at variable height in trees or shrubs; 3–6 eggs; 1 brood; March–July.

FEEDING Eats insects, acorns, small vertebrates, such as lizards, rodents, bird eggs, birds, tree frogs; fruits and seeds.

FLIGHT: bursts of flapping followed by long glides on flat wings.

UNIQUE FEATURES
The Blue Jay is unique among Americans jays, in having white patches on its wings and tail.

VERSATILE BIRD
Blue Jays are true omnivores, eating almost anything they can find. They are also excellent imitators of other bird calls.

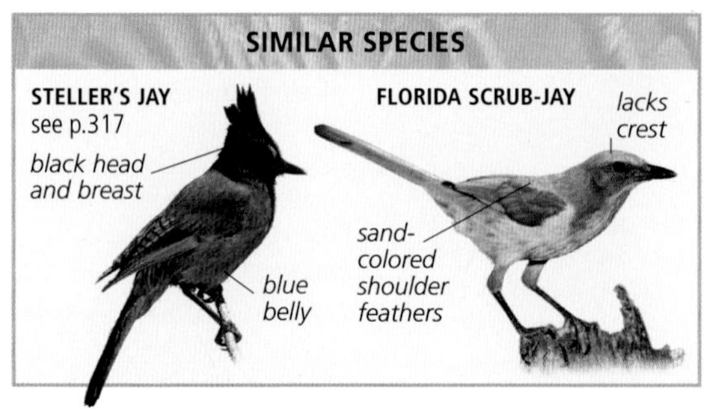
SIMILAR SPECIES
STELLER'S JAY
see p.317
black head and breast
blue belly
FLORIDA SCRUB-JAY
lacks crest
sand-colored shoulder feathers

OCCURRENCE
Native to eastern deciduous, coniferous, and mixed woodlands, but also at home in suburban vegetation; found extensively in backyards. The Blue Jay is especially fond of oak trees and their acorns.

Length **9½–12in (24–30cm)**	Wingspan **16in (41cm)**	Weight **2¼–3½oz (65–100g)**
Social **Small flocks**	Lifespan **Up to 7 years**	Status **Secure**

Order **Passeriformes**	Family **Corvidae**	Species ***Cyanocitta stelleri***

Steller's Jay

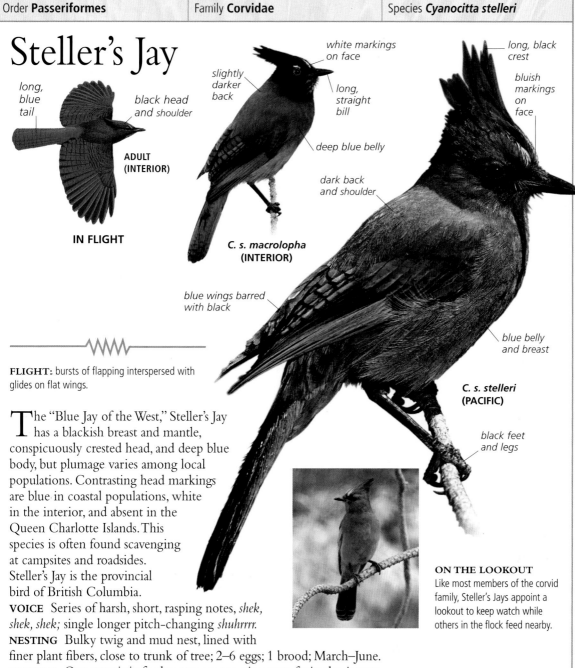

long, blue tail

black head and shoulder

ADULT (INTERIOR)

IN FLIGHT

slightly darker back

white markings on face

long, straight bill

deep blue belly

***C. s. macrolopha* (INTERIOR)**

long, black crest

bluish markings on face

dark back and shoulder

blue wings barred with black

blue belly and breast

***C. s. stelleri* (PACIFIC)**

black feet and legs

FLIGHT: bursts of flapping interspersed with glides on flat wings.

The "Blue Jay of the West," Steller's Jay has a blackish breast and mantle, conspicuously crested head, and deep blue body, but plumage varies among local populations. Contrasting head markings are blue in coastal populations, white in the interior, and absent in the Queen Charlotte Islands. This species is often found scavenging at campsites and roadsides. Steller's Jay is the provincial bird of British Columbia.

VOICE Series of harsh, short, rasping notes, *shek, shek, shek;* single longer pitch-changing *shuhrrrr.*

NESTING Bulky twig and mud nest, lined with finer plant fibers, close to trunk of tree; 2–6 eggs; 1 brood; March–June.

FEEDING Opportunistic feeder, eats acorns, pine nuts, fruit; also insects and spiders; small vertebrates such as lizards and rodents; also raids birds' nests.

ON THE LOOKOUT

Like most members of the corvid family, Steller's Jays appoint a lookout to keep watch while others in the flock feed nearby.

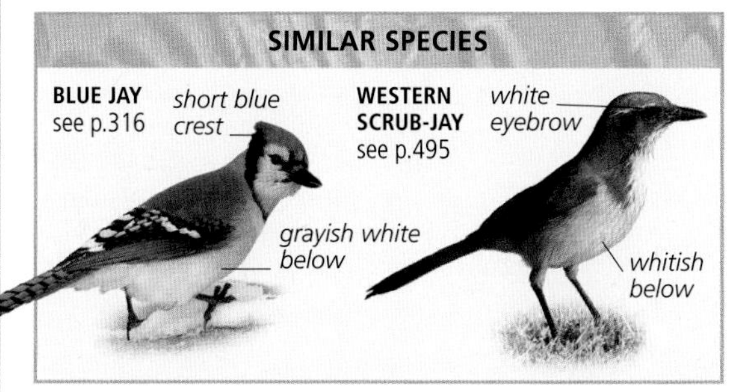
SIMILAR SPECIES
BLUE JAY
see p.316
short blue crest
grayish white below
WESTERN SCRUB-JAY
see p.495
white eyebrow
whitish below

OCCURRENCE

Found mainly in montane coniferous and mixed forests; but also in adjacent broad-leafed habitats; and occasionally, in winter, makes sudden migrations to lower elevations, east onto the Great Plains. Interbreeds locally with the Blue Jay where their ranges overlap the Rockies.

Length **11–12½in (28–32cm)**	Wingspan **19in (48cm)**	Weight **3½–5oz (100–150g)**
Social **Small flocks**	Lifespan **Up to 15 years**	Status **Secure**

Order **Passeriformes**	Family **Corvidae**	Species ***Pica hudsonia***

Black-billed Magpie

large, white patches on outer wings
white shoulder feathers
ADULT
blue-green iridescence to wings and tail
IN FLIGHT
black back and head
thick, black bill
black breast
ADULT
white belly
long, dark tail

Loud, flashy, and conspicuous, the Black-billed Magpie is abundant in the northwestern quarter of the continent, from Alaska to the interior of the US. It has adapted to suburbia, confidently strutting across front lawns in some places. Until recently, it was considered the same species as the Eurasian Magpie (*P. pica*), and even though they look nearly identical, scientific evidence points instead to a close relationship with the other North American magpie, the Yellow-billed Magpie. Its long tail enables it to make rapid changes in direction in flight. The male will also use his tail to perform a variety of displays while courting a female. Black-billed Magpies are rarely found in large flocks; but they form sometimes in fall.

VOICE Common call a questioning, nasal *ehnk*; also raspy *shenk, shenk, shenk*, usually in series.

NESTING Large, domed, often made of thorny sticks; 5–8 eggs; 1 brood; March–June.

FEEDING Omnivorous; forages on ground, mainly for insects, worms, seeds and carrion; even picks ticks from mammals.

FLIGHT: direct, with slow, steady, and often shallow wing beats; occasional shallow glides.

IRIDESCENT SHEEN
In bright sunlight, beautiful iridescent blues, greens, golds, and purples appear on the wings and tail.

SIMILAR SPECIES

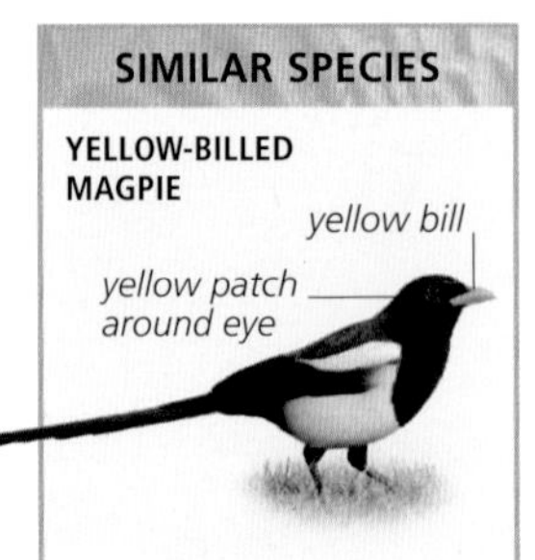
YELLOW-BILLED MAGPIE
yellow bill
yellow patch around eye

OCCURRENCE
Found in open habitats, foothills, and plains of the western US and Canada; nests in streamside vegetation; persecution has made it wary and restricted to wilderness in some areas, but in others it has adapted to suburbs of towns and cities.

Length **17–19½in (43–50cm)**	Wingspan **25in (63cm)**	Weight **6–7oz (175–200g)**
Social **Small flocks**	Lifespan **Up to 15 years**	Status **Secure**

Order **Passeriformes**	Family **Corvidae**	Species ***Nucifraga columbiana***

Clark's Nutcracker

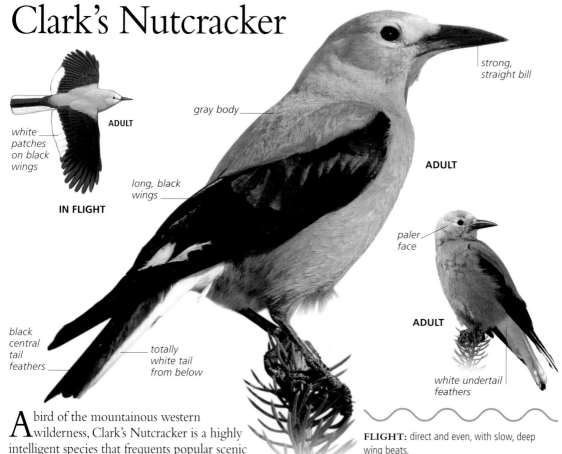

white patches on black wings

ADULT

IN FLIGHT

gray body

strong, straight bill

long, black wings

ADULT

paler face

ADULT

black central tail feathers

totally white tail from below

white undertail feathers

A bird of the mountainous western wilderness, Clark's Nutcracker is a highly intelligent species that frequents popular scenic overlooks, where it begs for food from visitors. This species gets its name from its dependence on pine nuts, which it forcefully extracts using its powerful feet and chisel-like bill. When food is abundant, nutcrackers hide it in caches—a special throat pouch enables them to carry up to 100 pine nuts per trip. The species was discovered by the explorers Lewis and Clark on their early 19th-century journey across the Louisiana Purchase.

VOICE Call a harsh, nasal, rolling rattle, often paired *kraaaa, kraaaa;* also mellower down-slurred *weee-uh,* and frog-like rattle.

NESTING Fine inner cup on stick platform on the side of tree away from trunk; 2–5 eggs; 1 brood; March–June.

FEEDING Hawks insects and raids nests; eats insects, spiders, and carrion.

FLIGHT: direct and even, with slow, deep wing beats.

CRACKING NUTS
Nutcrackers, such as Pinyon Jays, specialize in eating the seeds from pine cones.

SIMILAR SPECIES

GRAY JAY
see p.315
white forehead
longer tail
shorter bill
PINYON JAY
see p.495
blue body
lacks black and white on tail

OCCURRENCE
Restricted to coniferous forests, especially those dominated by large-seeded pines in southwest Canada and US mountains; found higher up in summer; sudden journeys in massive flocks periodically into lower elevations and Great Plains when cone crops fail, otherwise resident.

Length **12in (31cm)**	Wingspan **24in (62cm)**	Weight **4–5oz (125–150g)**
Social **Pairs/Flocks**	Lifespan **Up to 17 years**	Status **Secure**

Order **Passeriformes**	Family **Corvidae**	Species ***Corvus brachyrhynchos***

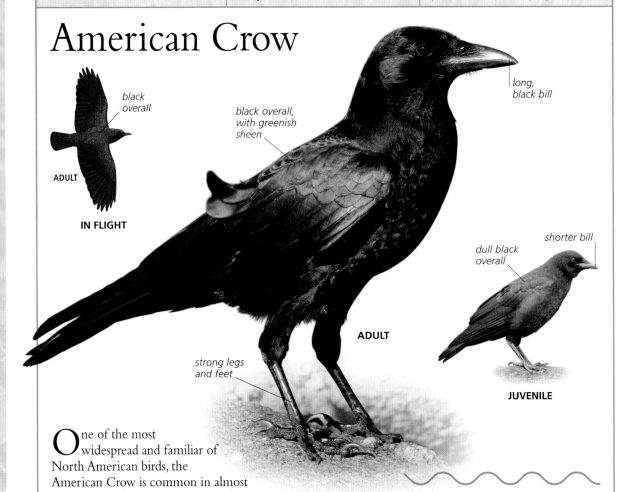

American Crow

black overall

ADULT

IN FLIGHT

black overall, with greenish sheen

long, black bill

strong legs and feet

ADULT

dull black overall

shorter bill

JUVENILE

One of the most widespread and familiar of North American birds, the American Crow is common in almost all habitats—from wilderness to urban centers. Like most birds with large ranges, there is substantial geographical variation in this species. Birds are black across the whole continent, but size and bill shape vary from region to region. The birds of the coastal Pacific Northwest (*C. b. hesperis*), are on average smaller and have a lower-pitched voice; Floridian birds (*C. b. pascuus*) are more solitary and warier than most.

VOICE Call a loud, familiar *caw!*; juveniles' call higher-pitched.

NESTING Stick base with finer inner cup; 3–7 eggs; 1 brood; April–June.

FEEDING Feeds omnivorously on fruit, carrion, garbage, insects, spiders; raids nests.

FLIGHT: direct and level with slow, steady flapping; does not soar.

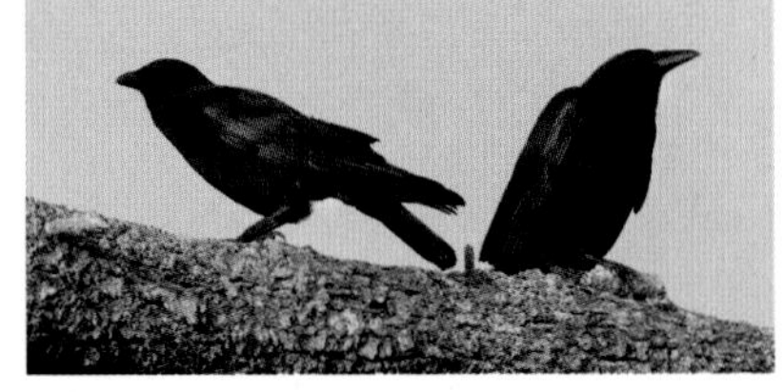

LOOKING AROUND
Extremely inquisitive, American Crows are always on the look-out for food or something of interest.

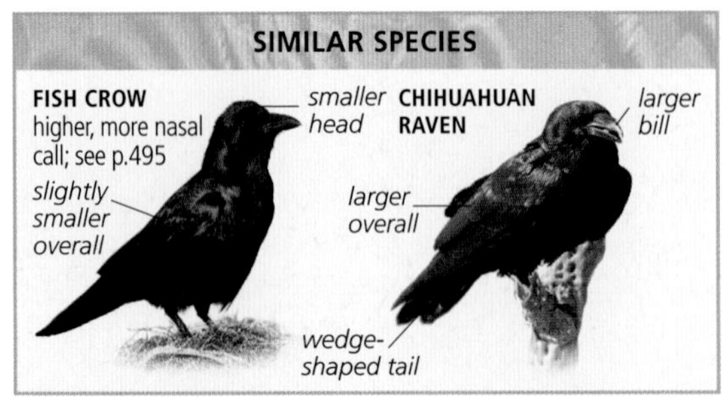
SIMILAR SPECIES
FISH CROW
higher, more nasal call; see p.495
slightly smaller overall
smaller head
CHIHUAHUAN RAVEN
larger bill
larger overall
wedge-shaped tail

OCCURRENCE
Often seen converging on favored roosting areas; most numerous in relatively open areas with widely spaced, large trees; has become abundant in some cities; a partial migrant, some populations are more migratory than others.

Length **15½–19½in (39–49cm)**	Wingspan **3ft (1m)**	Weight **15–22oz (425–625g)**
Social **Social**	Lifespan **Up to 15 years**	Status **Secure**

Order **Passeriformes**	Family **Corvidae**	Species ***Corvus caurinus***

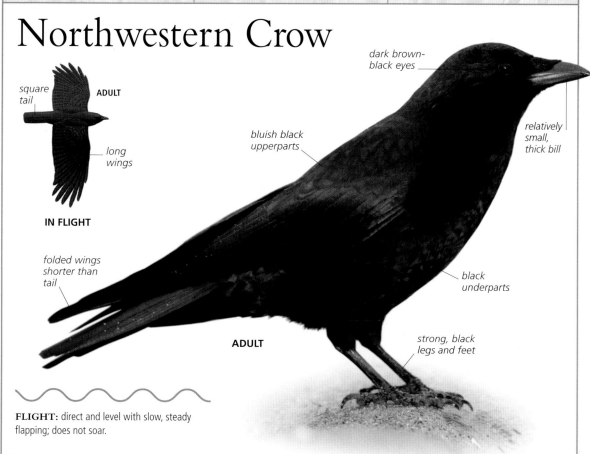

Northwestern Crow

square tail

ADULT

long wings

IN FLIGHT

dark brown-black eyes

relatively small, thick bill

bluish black upperparts

folded wings shorter than tail

black underparts

strong, black legs and feet

ADULT

FLIGHT: direct and level with slow, steady flapping; does not soar.

Although smaller, with a lower-pitched voice than the American Crow, the Northwestern Crow is very similar to one American Crow subspecies, *C. b. hesperis*. In fact, ornithologists are still debating how closely related the Northwestern and American Crows actually are. Among its feeding habits, the Northwestern Crow is known to dig for clams, pry open barnacles, chase crabs, and catch small fish. It often feeds and roosts in large flocks.

VOICE Varied, but most common call a loud, familiar *caw*! lower, raspier, and more rapid than most American Crows.

NESTING Stick base with fine inner cup, placed on ground or in trees; 3–6 eggs; 1 brood; April–June.

FEEDING Raids nests; eats fruit, carrion, garbage, mollusks, and stranded sea life from areas between the high- and low-tide marks.

BEACHCOMBER
The Northwestern Crow searches for prey items along coastlines.

SIMILAR SPECIES

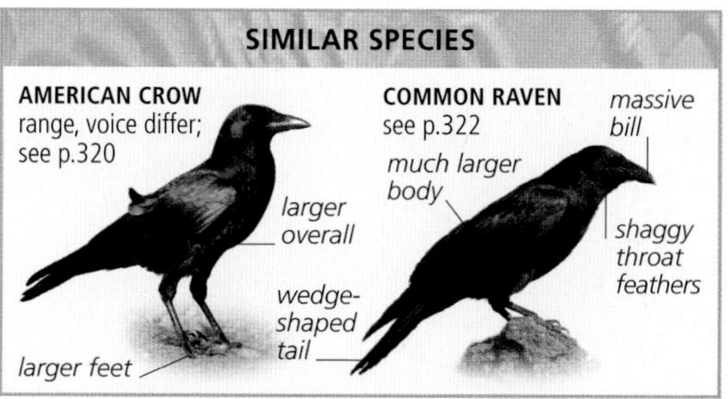
AMERICAN CROW
range, voice differ;
see p.320
larger overall
wedge-shaped tail
larger feet
COMMON RAVEN
see p.322
massive bill
much larger body
shaggy throat feathers

OCCURRENCE
Restricted to coastal areas from Alaska to Washington state, where it is found in tidal pools, refuse dumps, towns, and urban areas; avoids dense forest. It can be found along rivers at higher elevation inland.

Length **13–16in (33–41cm)**	Wingspan **34in (86cm)**	Weight **11–16oz (325–450g)**
Social **Flocks**	Lifespan **Up to 15 years**	Status **Secure**

Order **Passeriformes**	Family **Corvidae**	Species ***Corvus corax***

Common Raven

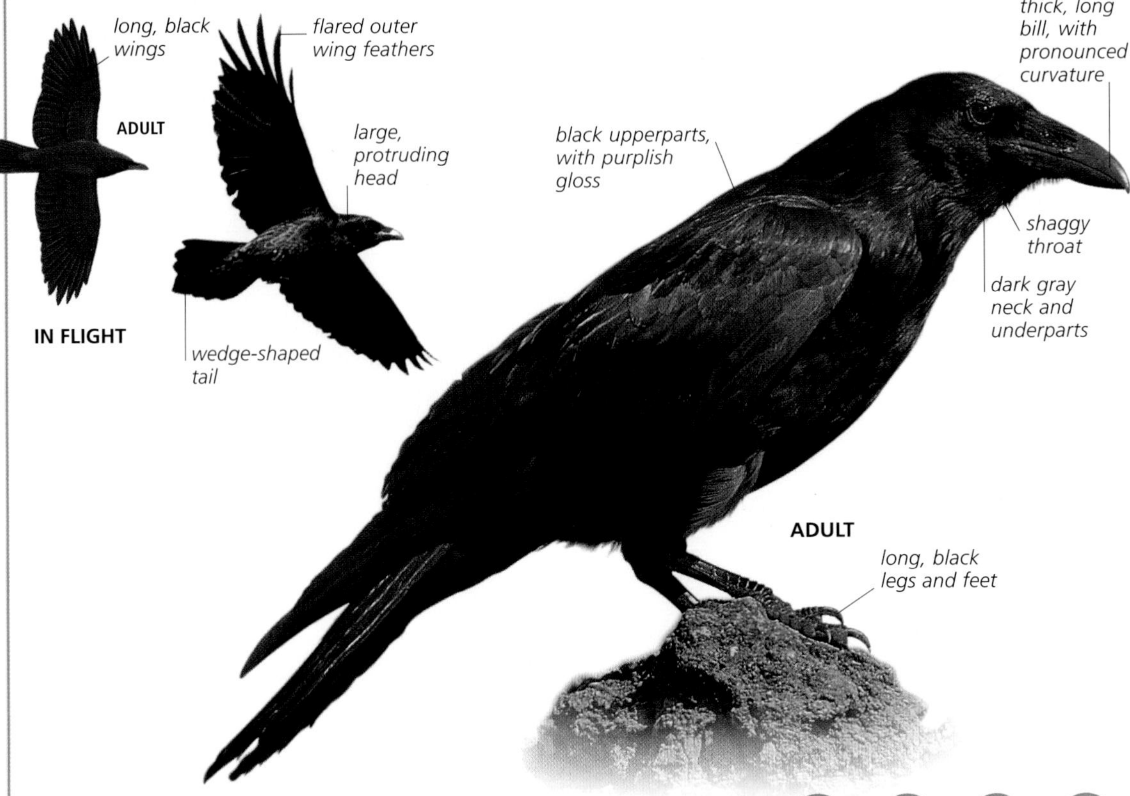

long, black wings
flared outer wing feathers
ADULT
large, protruding head
IN FLIGHT
wedge-shaped tail
black upperparts, with purplish gloss
thick, long bill, with pronounced curvature
shaggy throat
dark gray neck and underparts
ADULT
long, black legs and feet

The Common Raven is twice the size of the American Crow, a bird of Viking legend, literature, and scientific wonder. Its Latin name, *Corvux corax*, means "crow of crows." Ravens are perhaps the most brilliant of all birds: they learn quickly, adapt to new circumstances with remarkable mental agility, and communicate with each other through an array of vocal and motional behaviors. The Common Raven is the official bird of the Yukon Territory.

VOICE Varied vocalizations, including hoarse, rolling *krruuk*, twangy peals, guttural clicks, and resonant *bonks*.

NESTING Platform of sticks with fine inner material on trees, cliffs, or man-made structure; 4–5 eggs; 1 brood; March–June.

FEEDING Feeds omnivorously on carrion, small crustaceans, fish, rodents, fruit, grain, and garbage; also raids nests.

FLIGHT: slow, steady, and direct; can also be quite acrobatic; commonly soars.

SHARING INFORMATION
Ravens in flocks can communicate information about food sources.

SIMILAR SPECIES

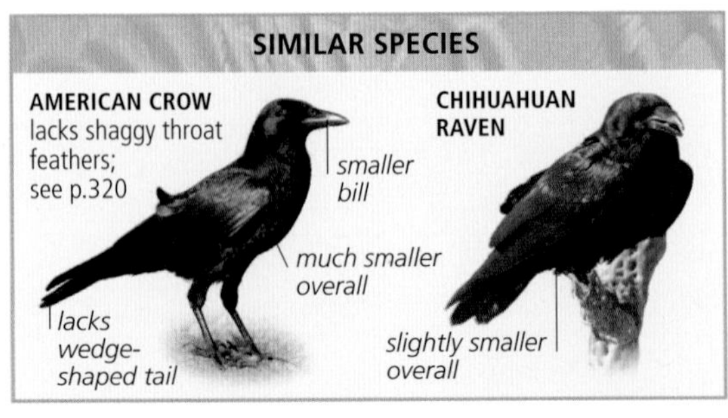

AMERICAN CROW
lacks shaggy throat feathers;
see p.320
smaller bill
much smaller overall
lacks wedge-shaped tail
CHIHUAHUAN RAVEN
slightly smaller overall

OCCURRENCE
Found in almost every kind of habitat, including tundra, mountainous areas, northern forest, woodlands, prairies, arid regions, coasts, and around human settlements; has recently recolonized areas on southern edge of range, from which it was once expelled by humans.

Length **23½–27in (60–69cm)**	Wingspan **4½ft (1.4m)**	Weight **2½–3¼lb (1–1.5kg)**
Social **Solitary/Pairs/Small flocks**	Lifespan **Up to 15 years**	Status **Secure**

Family **Paridae**

CHICKADEES & TITMICE

CHICKADEES AND TITMICE may be some of the most well-known and widespread birds in North America. Scientific studies have shown that more than one genus exists, despite the bird's plumage similarities.

CHICKADEES

Regardless of their genus, chickadees are frequent visitors to backyards and are readily distinguished from titmice by their smooth-looking, dark caps and black bibs. The name "chickadee" is derived from the common calls of several species. Highly social outside the breeding season and generally tolerant of people, these energetic little birds form flocks in winter. Some species, such as the Black-capped Chickadee, can lower their body temperature to survive the cold, but others, like the similar-looking Carolina Chickadee (a vagrant species in Canada), have a high winter mortality rate. Most species eat a combination of insects and plant material.

TITMICE

Titmice are distinguished from chickadees by their crests; most, like the familiar Tufted Titmouse, also have plain throats. Like chickadees, titmice are highly territorial and insectivorous during the breeding season, then become gregarious seed-eaters afterwards. At that time they often form mixed-species flocks with other small birds, like Kinglets, as they move through woodlands searching for food. Titmice are nonmigratory.

TAME BIRDS
Black-capped Chickadees have distinctive black-and-white markings and are often very tame.

Family **Hirundinidae**

SWALLOWS

SWALLOWS ARE A COSMOPOLITAN family of birds with species found nearly everywhere, except in the polar regions and some of the largest deserts, although during migration the fly over the some of the world's harshest deserts, including the Sahara and Atacama. Ornithologists usually call the short-tailed species martins and the long-tailed ones swallows. For example, the bird known as a Bank Swallow in most of North America is called Sand Martin in southern states such as Mississippi and Alabama, as well as in the UK. The Bank Swallow and the Barn Swallow, which is also found across Eurasia, are the most widespread. All North American swallows are migratory, and most of them winter in Central and South America, where they feed on flying insects that occur year-round. They are all superb fliers, and skilled at aerial pursuit and capture of flying insects. They are sometimes confused with swifts, which belong to a different group, and have a different style of flight. Swallows have relatively shorter, broader wings and less stiff wing beats.

SURFACE SKIMMER
This Tree Swallow flies low over fresh water to catch insects as they emerge into the air.

Order **Passeriformes**	Family **Bombycillidae**	Species ***Bombycilla garrulus***

Bohemian Waxwing

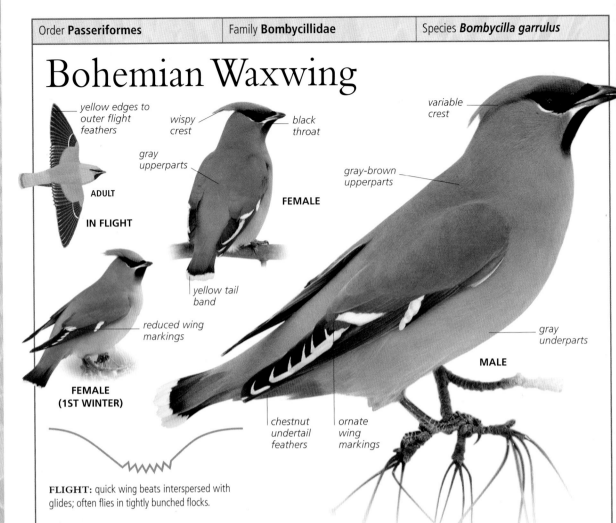

yellow edges to outer flight feathers

ADULT

IN FLIGHT

wispy crest

black throat

gray upperparts

FEMALE

yellow tail band

reduced wing markings

FEMALE (1ST WINTER)

variable crest

gray-brown upperparts

gray underparts

MALE

chestnut undertail feathers

ornate wing markings

FLIGHT: quick wing beats interspersed with glides; often flies in tightly bunched flocks.

The Bohemian Waxwing is the wilder and rarer of the two waxwing species in North America. It breeds mainly in Alaska and western Canada. The species is migratory, but the extent of its wintertime movement is notoriously variable, depending on the availability of wild fruits. In most winters, relatively few Bohemian Waxwings visit the lower 48 states, but in special "irruption" years, tens of thousands may reach as far south as Colorado.

VOICE Call actually a dull trill, but effect of hundreds of birds calling at the same time is remarkable; flocks vocalize constantly.

NESTING Dishevelled cup of sticks and grasses, placed in tree; 4–6 eggs; number of broods unknown; June–July.

FEEDING Catches insects on the wing in summer; flocks devour berries of native and exotic trees and shrubs throughout the year.

STRIKING TAIL
The Bohemian Waxwing's yellow tail band and chestnut undertail are evident here.

SIMILAR SPECIES
CEDAR WAXWING
see p.325
plainer wing markings
warmer tones overall
CEDAR WAXWING ◔
see p.325
unmarked wings
smaller overall

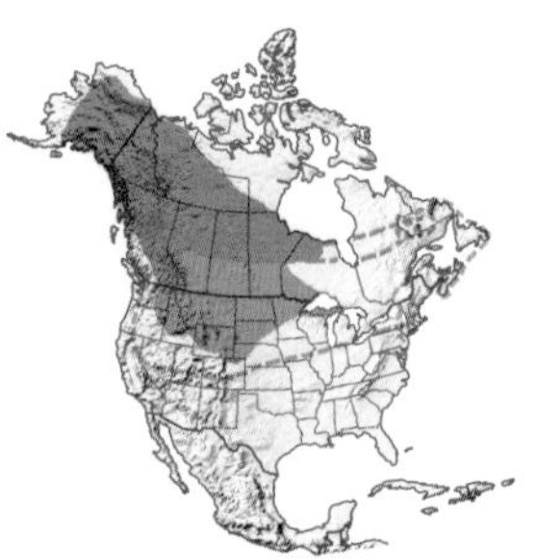

OCCURRENCE
Breeds in sub-Arctic coniferous forest, favoring disturbed areas such as beaver ponds and logging sites. Flocks gather at forest edges, hedges, and residential areas in winter. Hundreds or thousands of birds appear in an area, then disappear once food is depleted.

Length **8½in (21cm)**	Wingspan **14½in (37cm)**	Weight **1⁹⁄₁₆–2½oz (45–70g)**
Social **Flocks**	Lifespan **Up to 12 years**	Status **Localized**

Order **Passeriformes**	Family **Bombycillidae**	Species ***Bombycilla cedrorum***

Cedar Waxwing

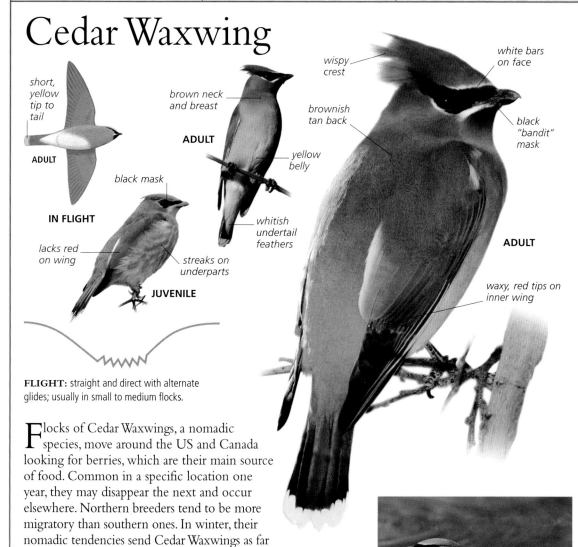

short, yellow tip to tail

ADULT

IN FLIGHT

brown neck and breast

ADULT

yellow belly

whitish undertail feathers

black mask

lacks red on wing

streaks on underparts

JUVENILE

wispy crest

white bars on face

brownish tan back

black "bandit" mask

ADULT

waxy, red tips on inner wing

FLIGHT: straight and direct with alternate glides; usually in small to medium flocks.

Flocks of Cedar Waxwings, a nomadic species, move around the US and Canada looking for berries, which are their main source of food. Common in a specific location one year, they may disappear the next and occur elsewhere. Northern breeders tend to be more migratory than southern ones. In winter, their nomadic tendencies send Cedar Waxwings as far south as South America. They can often be heard and identified by their calls, long before the flock settles to feed.

VOICE Basic vocalization a shrill trill: *shr-r-r-r-r-r* or *tre-e-e-e-e-e*, which appears to serve the function of both call note and song.

NESTING Open cup placed in fork of tree, often lined with grasses, plant fibers; 3–5 eggs; 1–2 broods; June–August.

FEEDING Eats in flocks at trees and shrubs with ripe berries throughout the year; also catches flying insects in summer.

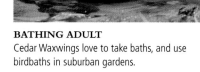

BATHING ADULT
Cedar Waxwings love to take baths, and use birdbaths in suburban gardens.

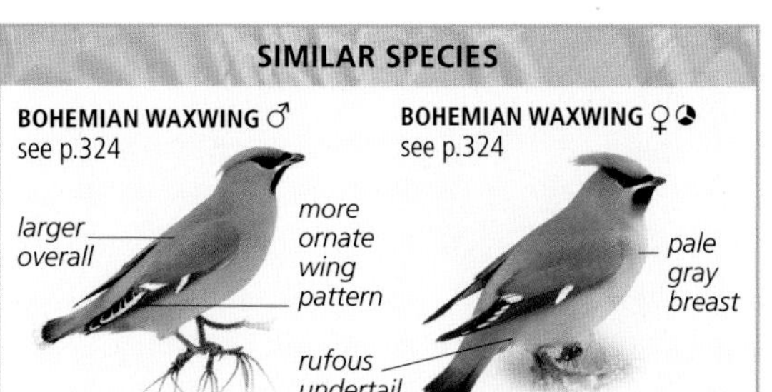
SIMILAR SPECIES
BOHEMIAN WAXWING ♂
see p.324
larger overall
more ornate wing pattern
rufous undertail
BOHEMIAN WAXWING ♀
see p.324
pale gray breast

OCCURRENCE
Across northern US and southern Canada, in wooded areas. Breeds in woodlands, especially near streams and clearings. Winters anywhere where trees and shrubs have ripe fruits, especially in Mexico and South America. Spends a lot of time in treetops, but sometimes comes down to shrub level.

Length **7½in (19cm)**	Wingspan **12in (30cm)**	Weight **1 1/16–1 1/4oz (30–35g)**
Social **Flocks**	Lifespan **Up to 7 years**	Status **Secure**

Order **Passeriformes**	Family **Paridae**	Species ***Poecile atricapillus***

Black-capped Chickadee

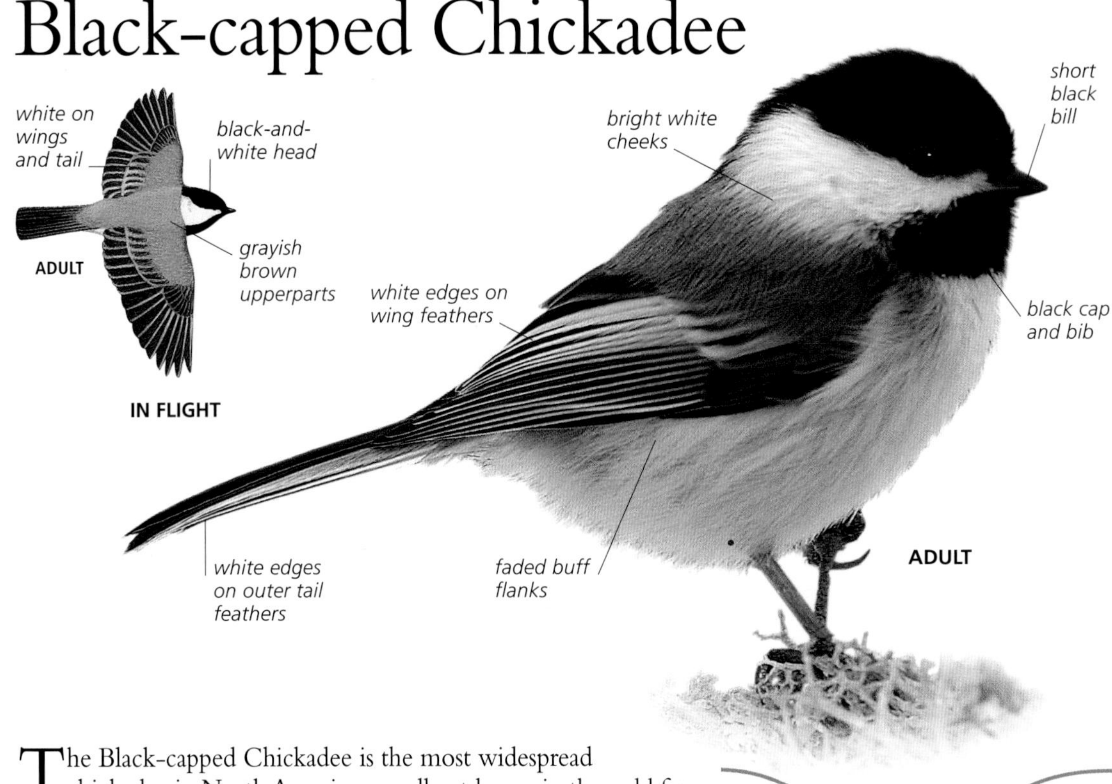
white on wings and tail
black-and-white head
grayish brown upperparts
ADULT
IN FLIGHT
bright white cheeks
short black bill
white edges on wing feathers
black cap and bib
white edges on outer tail feathers
faded buff flanks
ADULT

The Black-capped Chickadee is the most widespread chickadee in North America, equally at home in the cold far north and in warm Appalachian valleys. To cope with the harsh northern winters, this species can decrease its body temperature, entering a controlled hypothermia to conserve energy. There is some variation in appearance according to geographical location, with northern birds being slightly larger and possessing brighter white wing edgings than southern birds. Although it is a nonmigratory species, in winter flocks occasionally travel south of their traditional range in large numbers. The Black-capped Chickadee is the provincial bird of New Brunswick.

VOICE Raspy *tsick-a-dee-dee-dee* call*;* song loud, clear whistle *bee-bee* or *bee-bee-be*, first note higher in pitch.

NESTING Cavity in rotting tree stump, lined with hair, fur, feathers, plant fibers; 6–8 eggs; 1 brood; April–June.

FEEDING Forages for insects and their eggs, and spiders in trees and bushes; mainly seeds in winter; may take seeds from an outstretched hand.

FLIGHT: swift and undulating, with fast wing beats.

ROUGH-EDGED BIB
The Black-capped Chickadee has a less well-defined lower bib margin than the Carolina Chickadee.

SIMILAR SPECIES

CAROLINA CHICKADEE
see p.496
lacks white wing edges
no white tail edges
MEXICAN CHICKADEE
large bib extends to upper breast

OCCURRENCE
Variety of wooded habitats, from vast forests in the far north to small woodlands in urban parks and suburbs. In years of poor seed crops in northern parts of the range, large numbers migrate sometimes as far south as Texas.

Length **5¼in (13.5cm)**	Wingspan **8½in (22cm)**	Weight **⅜oz (11g)**
Social **Mixed flocks**	Lifespan **Up to 12 years**	Status **Secure**

Order **Passeriformes**	Family **Paridae**	Species ***Poecile gambeli***

Mountain Chickadee

ADULT (EASTERN)

black crown

black bib

IN FLIGHT

short, black bill

buff-tinged flanks

ADULT (EASTERN)

white eyebrow

white cheeks

dull gray upperparts

gray flanks

pale gray underparts

ADULT (WESTERN)

FLIGHT: bouncy, with fast wing beats; interrupted by brief glides.

The Mountain Chickadee is aptly named as it is found at elevations—of up to 12,000ft (3,600m). Like other chickadees, it stores pine and spruce seeds for harsh mountain winters. Social groups defend their winter territories and food resources, migrating to lower elevations when seeds are scarce. Birds in the Rocky Mountains have a conspicuous white eyebrow and buff-tinged flanks; those in the California mountains have grayish flanks and a fainter eyebrow.

VOICE Call raspy *tsick-jee-jee-jee*; whistle song of descending notes *bee-bee-bay*.

NESTING Natural tree cavity or old woodpecker hole, lined with moss and fur; 7–9 eggs; 1–2 broods; May–June.

FEEDING Forages high in trees for insects and spiders; eats seeds and berries; stores seeds in fall in preparation for winter.

VARIABLE EYEBROW
The white eyebrow is evident, but it may become duller in worn spring and summer plumage.

TYPICAL PERCH
The species spends much time perched in conifer trees, where it feeds.

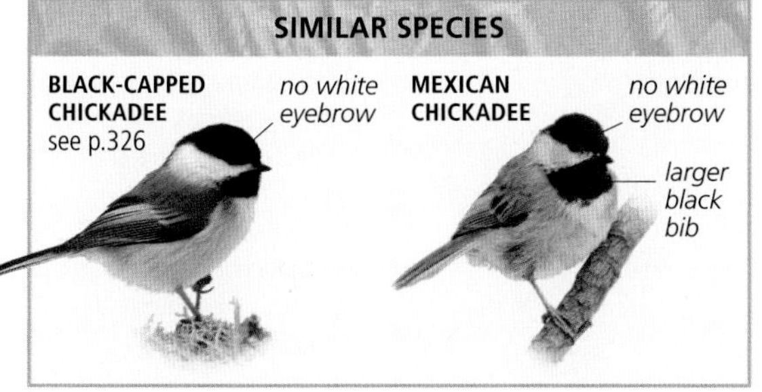
SIMILAR SPECIES
BLACK-CAPPED CHICKADEE
see p.326
no white eyebrow
MEXICAN CHICKADEE
no white eyebrow
larger black bib

OCCURRENCE
High elevations, preferring coniferous forests. May even be seen higher than the limit of tree growth. Some birds, especially the young, move down to foothills and valleys in winter and may visit feeders. Some also wander away from the mountains and out onto the Great Plains.

Length **5¼in (13.5cm)**	Wingspan **8½in (22cm)**	Weight **⅜oz (11g)**
Social **Winter flocks**	Lifespan **Up to 10 years**	Status **Secure**

Order **Passeriformes**	Family **Paridae**	Species ***Poecile hudsonicus***

Boreal Chickadee

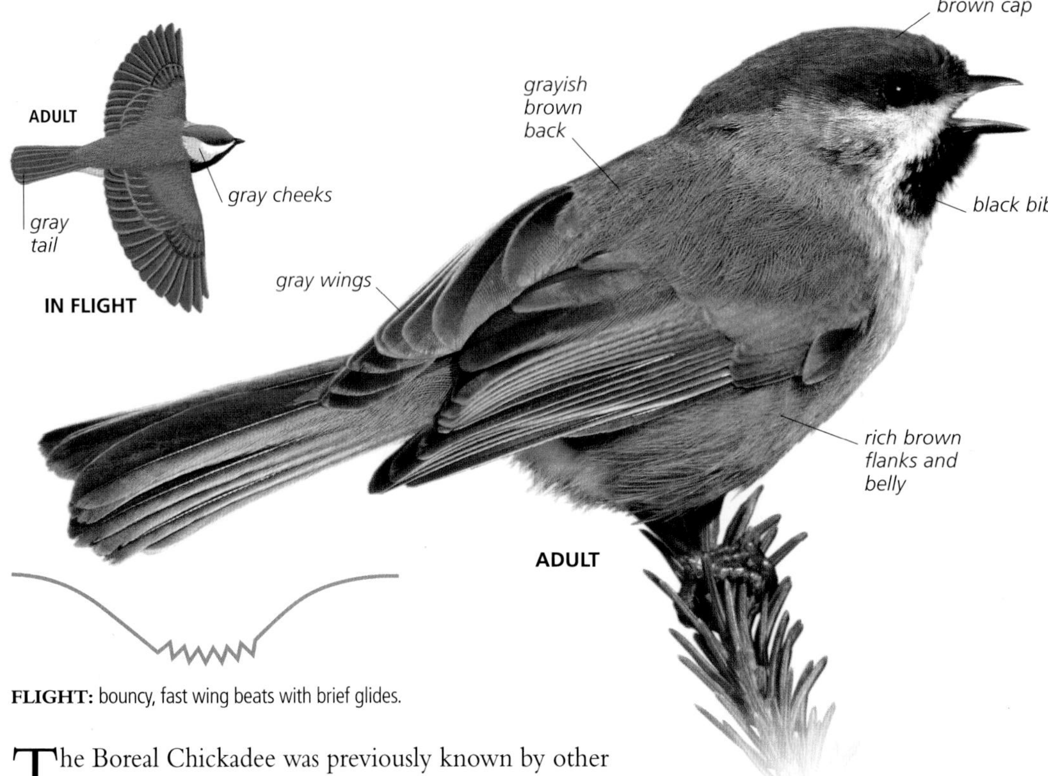
ADULT
gray tail
gray cheeks
IN FLIGHT
gray wings
grayish brown back
brown cap
black bib
rich brown flanks and belly
ADULT

FLIGHT: bouncy, fast wing beats with brief glides.

The Boreal Chickadee was previously known by other names, including Hudsonian Chickadee, referring to its northern range, and the Brown-capped Chickadee, due to its appearance. In the past, this species made large, irregular journeys south of its usual range during winters of food shortage, but this pattern of invasions has not occurred in recent decades. Its back color is an interesting example of geographic variation—grayish in the West and brown in the central and eastern portions of its range.

VOICE Call a low-pitched, buzzy, lazy *tsee-day-day*; also a high-pitched trill, *dididididididi*; no whistled song.

NESTING Cavity lined with fur, hair, plant down; in natural, excavated, or old woodpecker hole; 4–9 eggs; 1 brood; May–June.

FEEDING Gleans insects, conifer seeds; hoards larvae and seeds in bark crevices in fall in preparation for winter.

IDENTIFICATION TIP
A brown back or flank help distinguish a Boreal Chickadee from a Black-capped Chickadee.

SIMILAR SPECIES

CHESTNUT-BACKED CHICKADEE see p.329

narrow, white cheeks
chestnut sides

ACROBATIC FORAGER
This acrobatic feeder is able to cling on to conifer needles as it searches for insects and spiders.

OCCURRENCE
Found across the vast northern spruce-fir forests, from Alaska to Newfoundland, and from the treeline at the tundra south to the northeastern and northwestern states. The southern edge of the range appears to be retracting for unknown reasons.

Length **5½in (14cm)**	Wingspan **8½in (21cm)**	Weight **⅜oz (10g)**
Social **Flocks**	Lifespan **Up to 5 years**	Status **Secure**

Order **Passeriformes**	Family **Paridae**	Species ***Poecile rufescens***

Chestnut-backed Chickadee

chestnut back and rump
ADULT
dark gray wings
IN FLIGHT
paler gray wings
gray sides and flanks
P. r. barlowi
white edges on outer wing feathers
rich chestnut back
narrow white cheeks
dark brown cap
black bib extends to sides of neck and breast
chestnut sides
ADULT

FLIGHT: bouncy, fast wing beats with brief glides.

The Chestnut-backed is the smallest of all chickadees and possesses the shortest tail. Northern populations have the most brightly colored sides and flanks of all North American chickadees—rich chestnut or rufous, matching the bright back and rump. Birds found southward into California have paler and less extensive rufous underparts. Further south still, in California, the sides and flanks are dull olive-brown or gray. The Chestnut-backed Chickadee may nest in loose colonies, unlike any other chickadee species.

VOICE A fast, high-pitched *sic-zee-zee, seet-seet-seet*, sharp *chek-chek*, crisp *twit-twit-twit*, and many variations; no whistled song.

NESTING Excavates hole, or uses natural cavity or old woodpecker hole; lined with moss, hair, fur; 5–8 eggs; 1 brood; April–June.

FEEDING Forages high in conifers for caterpillars and other insects; eats seeds and berries in winter.

A DASH OF WHITE
Bright white edges on the wing feathers are often a conspicuous field mark of this species.

SIMILAR SPECIES

BOREAL CHICKADEE
see p.328

grayish brown back
gray cheeks
rich brown flanks and belly

DARK CAP
In good light, this chickadee's brown cap is apparent; in poor light, the cap may look black.

OCCURRENCE
Year-round resident in humid coniferous forests of the Pacific Northwest; in drier mixed and deciduous woodlands, and even in urban and suburban habitats south of San Francisco, California. Northern coastal populations have one of the most specialized habitats of all chickadee species.

Length **4¾in (12cm)**	Wingspan **7½in (19cm)**	Weight **⅜oz (10g)**
Social **Flocks**	Lifespan **Up to 9 years**	Status **Secure**

Order **Passeriformes**	Family **Paridae**	Species ***Baeolophus bicolor***

Tufted Titmouse

ADULT

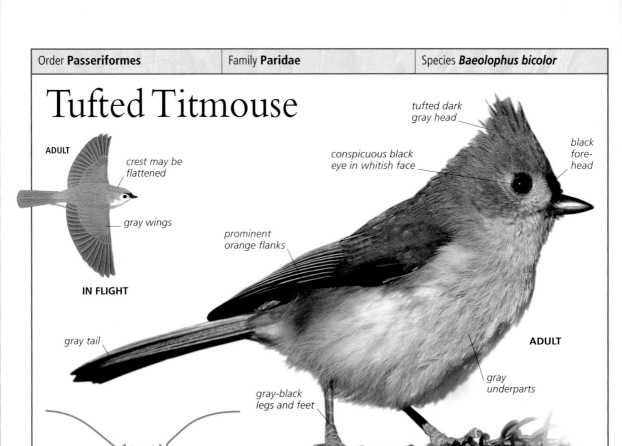

crest may be flattened

gray wings

IN FLIGHT

tufted dark gray head

black forehead

conspicuous black eye in whitish face

prominent orange flanks

gray tail

ADULT

gray underparts

gray-black legs and feet

FLIGHT: swift and undulating, with irregular wing beats; usually across short distances.

A familiar and friendly sight, the Tufted Titmouse is the most widespread of the North American titmice, and one of the two largest and most fearless; this lack of fear, particularly around people, has enabled it to adapt very well to human habitations. In the last century, its range has expanded significantly northward up to southern Canada, probably due to the increased numbers of birdfeeders, which allow the Tufted Titmouse to survive the cold northern winters.

VOICE Call a loud, harsh *pshurr, pshurr, pshurr,* song a ringing, far-carrying *peto peto peto,* sometimes shortened to *peer peer peer.*

NESTING Tree cavities, old woodpecker holes, and nest boxes, lined with damp leaves, moss, grass, hair; 5–6 eggs; 1 brood; March–May.

FEEDING Forages actively in trees and shrubs for insects, spiders, and their eggs; in winter, corn kernels, seeds, and small fruits, can split an acorn by hammering it with its bill.

COLOR VARIATION

The orange on the flanks varies between bright on freshly molted feathers and dull on worn adults.

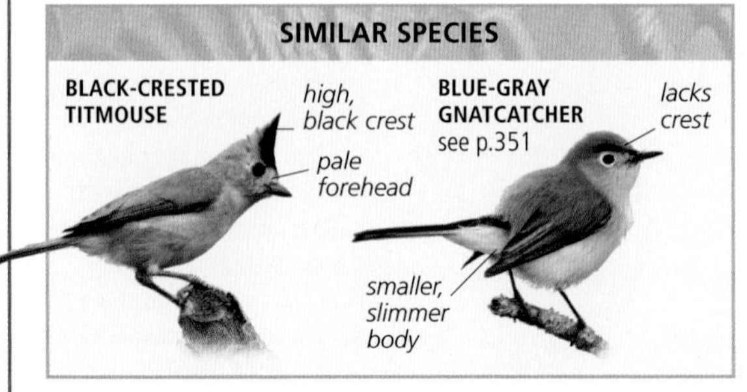
SIMILAR SPECIES
BLACK-CRESTED TITMOUSE
high, black crest
pale forehead
BLUE-GRAY GNATCATCHER
see p.351
lacks crest
smaller, slimmer body

OCCURRENCE

Lives year-round in areas of large and small deciduous and coniferous woodlands in the eastern half of the US and southeastern Canada. It has flourished in parks and gardens and can often be found using nest boxes in suburban backyards.

Length **6½in (16cm)**	Wingspan **10in (25cm)**	Weight **$^{11}/_{16}$oz (20g)**
Social **Mixed flocks**	Lifespan **Up to 13 years**	Status **Secure**

Order **Passeriformes**	Family **Hirundinidae**	Species ***Riparia riparia***

Bank Swallow

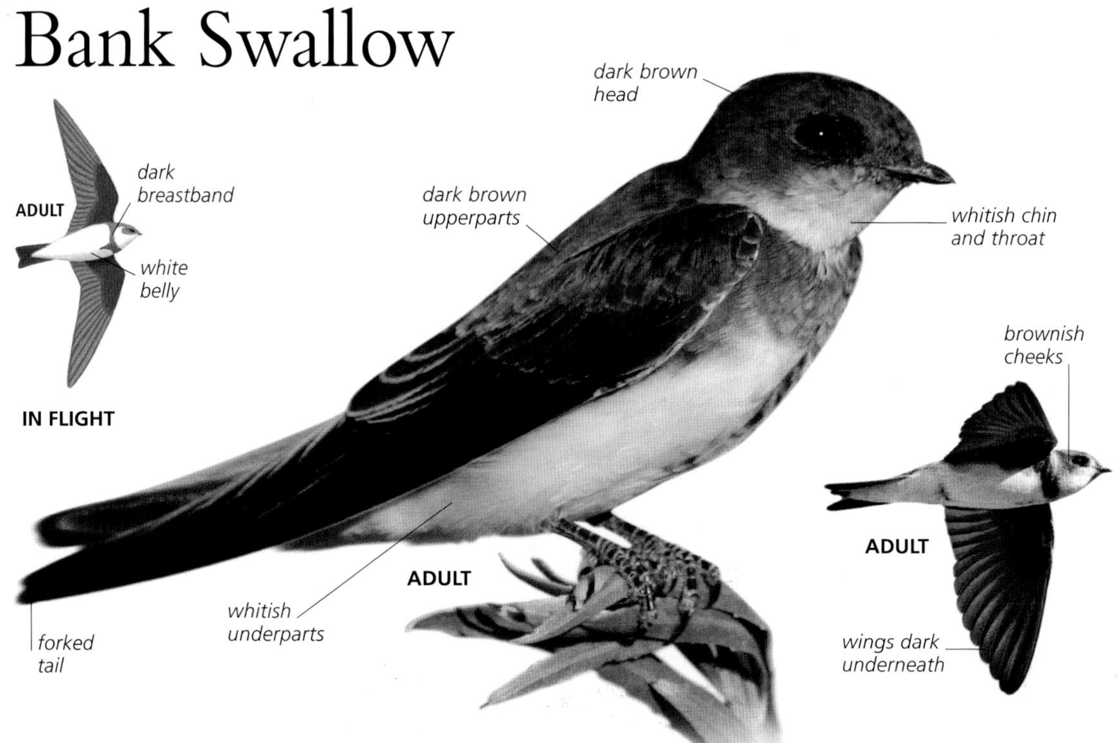

ADULT
dark breastband
white belly
IN FLIGHT
dark brown head
dark brown upperparts
whitish chin and throat
brownish cheeks
ADULT
forked tail
whitish underparts
ADULT
wings dark underneath

The Bank Swallow, known in the UK as the Sand Martin, is the slimmest and smallest of North American swallows. As its scientific name *riparia* (meaning "riverbanks") and common names suggest, the Bank Swallow nests in the banks and bluffs of rivers, streams, and lakes. It also favors sand and gravel quarries in the East. It is widely distributed across North America, breeding from south of the tundra–taiga line down to the central US. The nesting colonies can range from as few as 10 pairs to as many as 2,000, which are quite noisy when all the birds are calling or coming in to feed the young.

VOICE Call a soft *brrrrr* or *breee* often issued in pairs; song a harsh twittering or continuous chatter.

NESTING Burrow in soft, sandy bank containing a flat platform of grass, feathers, and twigs; 2–6 eggs; 1 brood; April–August.

FEEDING Catches insects, such as flies, moths, dragonflies, and bees in flight, but occasionally skims aquatic insects or their larvae off the water or terrestrial insects from the ground.

FLIGHT: fast, frantic, butterfly-like flight with glides, twists, and turns; shallow, rapid wing beats.

WAITING FOR MOM
Hungry youngsters still expect to be fed, even when they're ready to fledge.

SIMILAR SPECIES

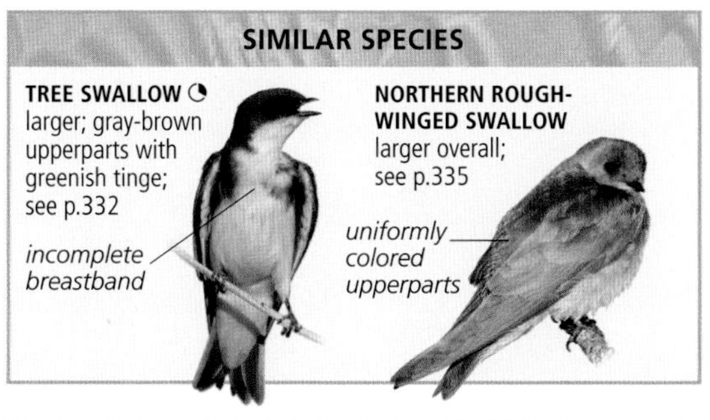

TREE SWALLOW
larger; gray-brown upperparts with greenish tinge;
see p.332
incomplete breastband
NORTHERN ROUGH-WINGED SWALLOW
larger overall;
see p.335
uniformly colored upperparts

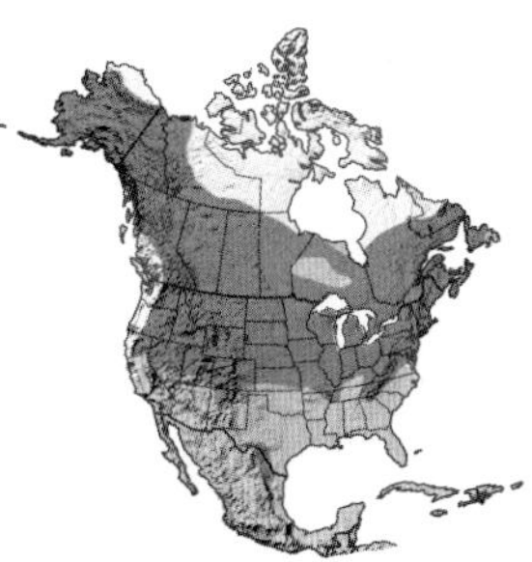

OCCURRENCE
Widespread in North America. Breeds in lowland habitats associated with rivers, streams, lakes, reservoirs, and coasts, as well as in sand and gravel quarries. Often prefers manmade sites; winters in grasslands, open farm habitat, and freshwater areas in South America.

Length **4¾–5½in (12–14cm)**	Wingspan **10–11in (25–28cm)**	Weight **⅜–¹¹⁄₁₆oz (10–19g)**
Social **Colonies**	Lifespan **Up to 9 years**	Status **Secure**

Order **Passeriformes**	Family **Hirundinidae**	Species ***Tachycineta bicolor***

Tree Swallow

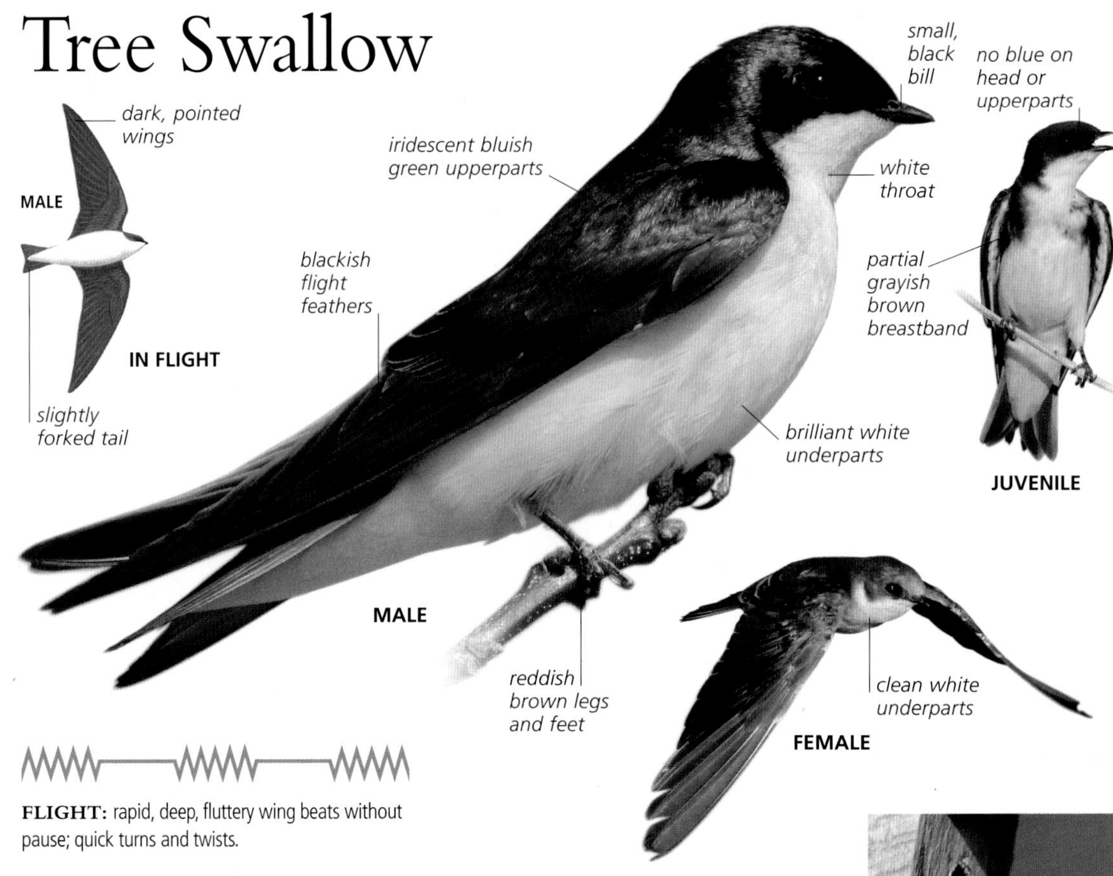
dark, pointed wings
MALE
IN FLIGHT
slightly forked tail
iridescent bluish green upperparts
blackish flight feathers
small, black bill
no blue on head or upperparts
white throat
partial grayish brown breastband
brilliant white underparts
JUVENILE
MALE
reddish brown legs and feet
clean white underparts
FEMALE

FLIGHT: rapid, deep, fluttery wing beats without pause; quick turns and twists.

One of the most common North American swallows, the Tree Swallow is found from coast to coast in the upper half of the continent all the way up to Alaska. As its Latin name *bicolor* suggests, it has iridescent bluish green upperparts and white underparts. Juveniles can be confused with the smaller Bank Swallow, which has a more complete breastband. The Tree Swallow lives in a variety of habitats, but its hole-nesting habit makes it completely dependent on abandoned woodpecker cavities in dead trees and on artificial "housing" such as nestboxes. The size of the population fluctuates according to the availability of the nesting sites.

VOICE Ranges from variable high, chirping notes to chatters and soft trills; also complex high and clear two-note whistle phrases.

NESTING Layer of fine plant matter in abandoned woodpecker hole or nest box, lined with feathers; 4–6 eggs; 1 brood; May–July.

FEEDING Swoops after flying insects from dawn to dusk; also takes bayberries.

KEEPING LOOKOUT
This species uses artificial nestboxes, which the males defend as soon as they arrive.

SIMILAR SPECIES

BANK SWALLOW
paler brown rump; see p.331
distinct dusky breastband

VIOLET-GREEN SWALLOW
white flank patch; see p.333
white eye patch
violet-green upperparts

OCCURRENCE
Typically breeds close to water in open habitat such as fields, marshes, lakes, and swamps, especially those with standing dead wood for cavity-nesting. Winters in large roosts in hundreds of thousands of birds in tall marsh vegetation.

Length **5–6in (13–15cm)**	Wingspan **12–14in (30–35cm)**	Weight **⅝–⅞oz (17–25g)**
Social **Large flocks**	Lifespan **Up to 11 years**	Status **Secure**

Order **Passeriformes**	Family **Hirundinidae**	Species ***Tachycineta thalassina***

Violet-green Swallow

long wings
ADULT
white underparts
IN FLIGHT

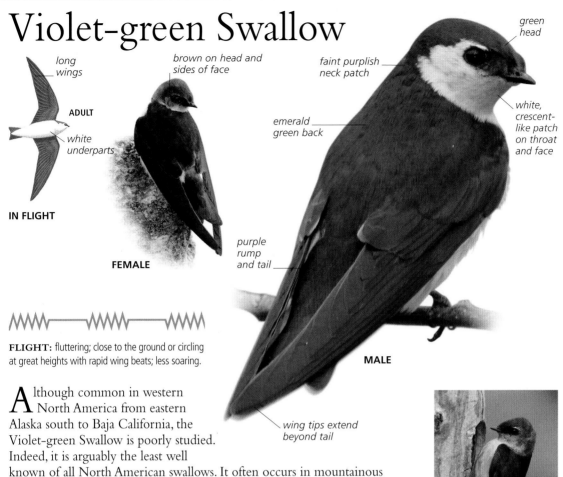

brown on head and sides of face
FEMALE

faint purplish neck patch
green head
white, crescent-like patch on throat and face
emerald green back
purple rump and tail
wing tips extend beyond tail
MALE

FLIGHT: fluttering; close to the ground or circling at great heights with rapid wing beats; less soaring.

Although common in western North America from eastern Alaska south to Baja California, the Violet-green Swallow is poorly studied. Indeed, it is arguably the least well known of all North American swallows. It often occurs in mountainous conifer forests where it breeds in woodpecker holes in dead trees, or in cliff crevices, but it will also use birdhouses. A distinguishing feature of this swallow is the white patch that covers its throat and forms a line over its eyes. Its Latin name *thalassina* means "sea-green," while its common name refers to the same color, along with the violet of its rump. In its mountain habitat, the Violet-green Swallow can be encountered together with the White-throated Swift.

VOICE Primary call a twittering *chee-chee* of brief duration; alarm call a dry, brief *zwrack*.

NESTING Nest of grass, twigs, straw, and feathers in a natural or woodpecker cavity in a tree, also cliff or nesting box; 4–6 eggs; 2 broods; March–August.

FEEDING Catches flying insects, such as bees, wasps, moths, and flies; usually at higher levels than other species of swallows.

AT THE NEST HOLE
The female of this species can be distinguished from the male by her darker face.

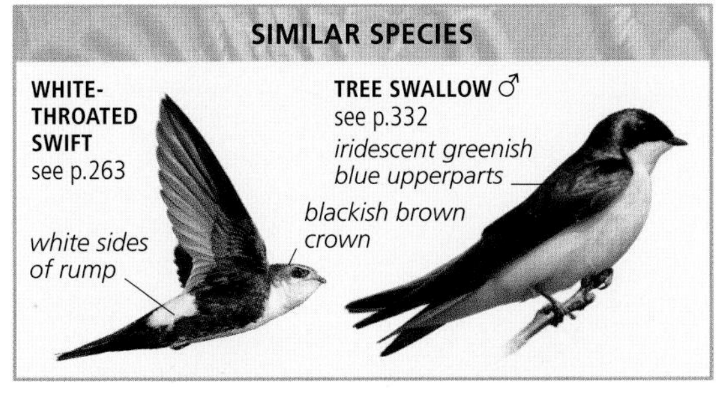
SIMILAR SPECIES
WHITE-THROATED SWIFT
see p.263
white sides of rump
TREE SWALLOW ♂
see p.332
iridescent greenish blue upperparts
blackish brown crown

OCCURRENCE
In US and Canada, breeds in open deciduous, coniferous, and mixed woodlands, especially Ponderosa and Monterey Pine and Quaking Aspen; also wooded canyons. Frequents waterways during migration; prefers higher elevations in general. Breeds south of the US, in Mexico.

Length **5in (13cm)**	Wingspan **11in (28cm)**	Weight **½oz (14g)**
Social **Solitary/Colonies**	Lifespan **Unknown**	Status **Secure**

Order **Passeriformes**	Family **Hirundinidae**	Species ***Progne subis***

Purple Martin

wings lighter in color than in male

FEMALE

pale collar

bluish gray upperparts

whitish gray underparts

FEMALE

MALE

blue-black underparts

IN FLIGHT

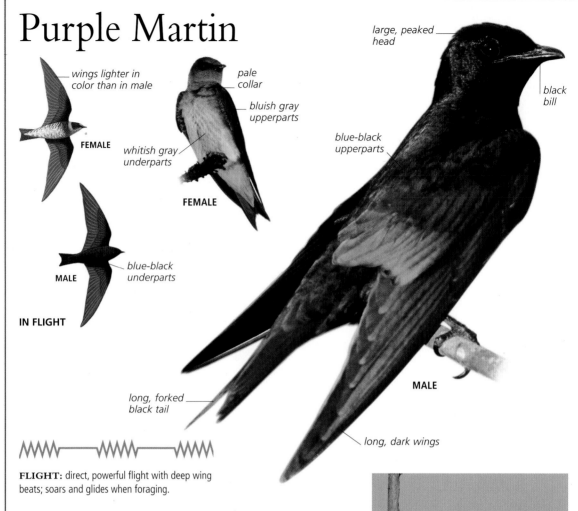

large, peaked head

black bill

blue-black upperparts

MALE

long, forked black tail

long, dark wings

FLIGHT: direct, powerful flight with deep wing beats; soars and glides when foraging.

The Purple Martin, the largest of all North American swallows, is one of the most popular of all backyard birds. Thousands of devoted Purple Martin-lovers belong to two national organizations that publish magazines and newsletters devoted to the species. Found mostly in the eastern half of the continent, with local populations scattered across the West, this glossy-blue swallow is common in some areas and yet quite scarce in others. In the West it nests in abandoned woodpecker holes, but in the East the Purple Martin now depends almost entirely on the provisioning of "apartment-type" birdhouses for breeding.

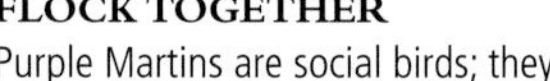

FLOCK TOGETHER
Purple Martins are social birds; they breed in colonies and roost in flocks, as shown.

VOICE Alarm call a *zwrack* or *zweet*; other calls are a variety of rolling, bubbling sounds; song a series of gurgles, chortles, and croaking phrases.

NESTING Loose mat of vegetation and mud in birdhouse compartments, rarely in natural cavities; 4 eggs; 1 brood; April–August.

FEEDING Captures flying insects at 150–500ft (45–150m) in the air; sometimes gleans insects from foliage or the ground.

OCCURRENCE
In North America, eastern birds found almost exclusively in towns and cities where nestboxes are provided; western populations occur in more rural areas such as mountain and coastal forests where woodpecker holes are abundant; also uses Saguaro cactus for nesting in the Southwest.

Length **7–8in (18–20cm)**	Wingspan **15–16in (38–41cm)**	Weight **1 7/16–2 1/8oz (40–60g)**
Social **Large flocks/Colonies**	Lifespan **Up to 13 years**	Status **Secure**

Order **Passeriformes**	Family **Hirundinidae**	Species ***Stelgidopteryx serripennis***

Northern Rough-winged Swallow

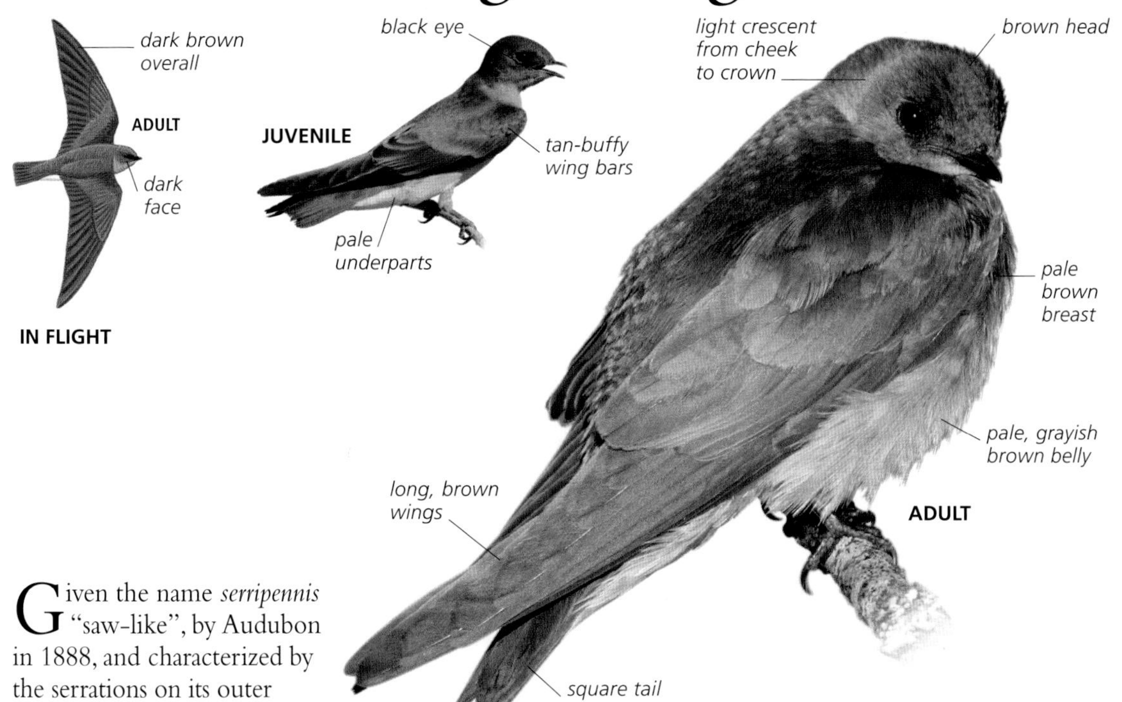

dark brown overall
ADULT
dark face
IN FLIGHT
black eye
JUVENILE
tan-buffy wing bars
pale underparts
light crescent from cheek to crown
brown head
pale brown breast
pale, grayish brown belly
ADULT
long, brown wings
square tail

Given the name *serripennis* "saw-like", by Audubon in 1888, and characterized by the serrations on its outer wing feathers, this species is otherwise somewhat drab in color and aspect. The Northern Rough-winged Swallow has a broad distribution in North America, being found across southern Canada and throughout the US. Often overlooked by birdwatchers, this brown-backed, dusky-throated swallow can be spotted hunting insects over water. In size and habit, the Northern Rough-winged Swallow shares many similarities with the Bank Swallow, including breeding habits and color, but the latter's notched tail and smaller size makes it easy to tell them apart.

VOICE Steady repetition of short, rapid *brrrt* notes inflected upward; sometimes a buzzy *jee-jee-jee* or high-pitched *brzzzzzt.*

NESTING Loose cup of twigs and straw in a cavity or burrow in a bank, such as road cuts; 4–7 eggs; 1 brood; May–July.

FEEDING Captures flying insects, including flies, wasps, bees, damselflies, and beetles in the air; more likely to feed over water and at lower altitudes than other swallows.

FLIGHT: slow, deliberate wing beats; short to long glides; long, straight flight, ends in steep climb.

BROWN BIRD
This swallow is brownish above and pale grayish below, with just a brown smudge on its neck.

SIMILAR SPECIES

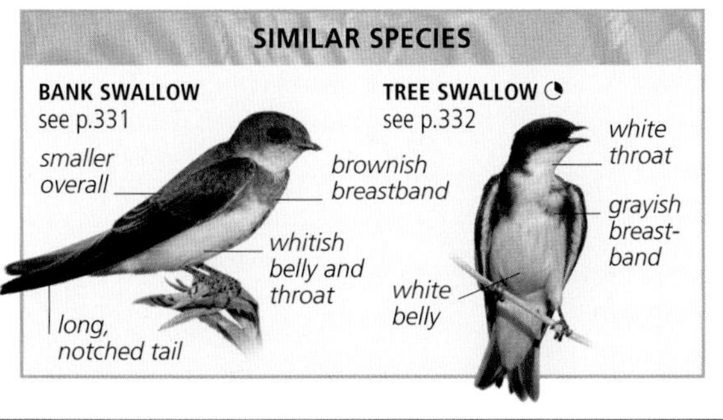

BANK SWALLOW
see p.331
smaller overall
brownish breastband
whitish belly and throat
long, notched tail
TREE SWALLOW
see p.332
white throat
grayish breast-band
white belly

OCCURRENCE
In North America, widespread from coast to coast. Nests at a wide variety of altitudes, prefers exposed banks of clay, sand, or gravel such as gorges, shale banks, and gravel pits. Forages along watercourses where aerial insects are plentiful. Breeds south to Costa Rica. Winters in Central America.

Length **4¾–6in (12–15cm)**	Wingspan **11–12in (28–30cm)**	Weight **⅜–⅝oz (10–18g)**
Social **Solitary**	Lifespan **Unknown**	Status **Secure**

Order **Passeriformes**	Family **Hirundinidae**	Species ***Hirundo rustica***

Barn Swallow

long, pointed wings

ADULT

IN FLIGHT

reddish orange underparts

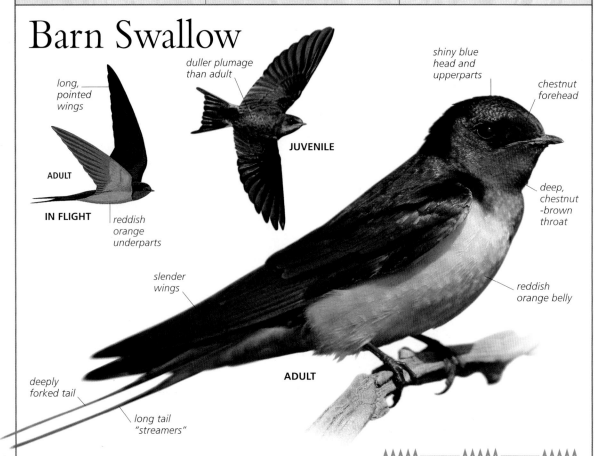

duller plumage than adult

JUVENILE

shiny blue head and upperparts

chestnut forehead

deep, chestnut -brown throat

reddish orange belly

slender wings

ADULT

deeply forked tail

long tail "streamers"

The most widely distributed and abundant swallow in the world, the Barn Swallow is found just about everywhere in North America south of the Arctic timberline. Originally a cave-nester before Europeans settlers came to the New World, the Barn Swallow readily adapted to nesting under the eaves of houses, under bridges, and inside buildings such as barns. It is now rare to find this elegant swallow breeding in a natural site. Steely blue upperparts, reddish underparts, and a deeply forked tail identify the Barn Swallow. North American breeders have deep, reddish orange underparts, but birds from Eurasia are white-bellied.

VOICE High-pitched, squeaky *chee-chee* call; song a long series of chatty, pleasant churrs, squeaks, chitterings, and buzzes.

NESTING Deep cup of mud and grass-stems attached to vertical surfaces or on ledges; 4–6 eggs; 1–2 broods; May–September.

FEEDING Snatches flying insects, such as flies, mosquitoes, wasps, and beetles in the air at lower altitudes than other swallows; sometimes eats wild berries and seeds.

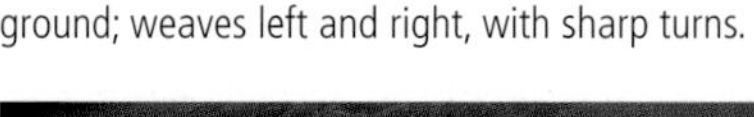

FLIGHT: bursts of straight flight; close to the ground; weaves left and right, with sharp turns.

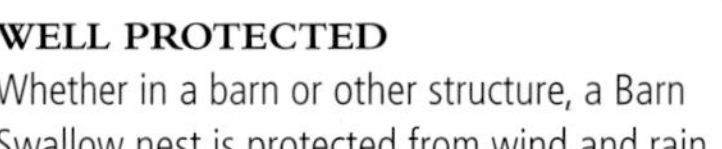

WELL PROTECTED
Whether in a barn or other structure, a Barn Swallow nest is protected from wind and rain.

SIMILAR SPECIES

TREE SWALLOW ♂
see p.332

lacks forked tail and dark breast band
white under-parts

OCCURRENCE
Breeds across North America, except in the tundra zone; south as far as central Mexico. Found in most habitats, but prefers agricultural regions, towns, and highway overpasses; migrates over coastal marshes; winters near sugarcane fields, grain fields, and marshes.

Length **6–7½in (15–19cm)**	Wingspan **11½–13in (29–33cm)**	Weight **⅝–¹¹⁄₁₆oz (17–20g)**
Social **Small colonies/flocks**	Lifespan **Up to 8 years**	Status **Secure**

Order **Passeriformes**	Family **Hirundinidae**	Species ***Petrochelidon pyrrhonota***

Cliff Swallow

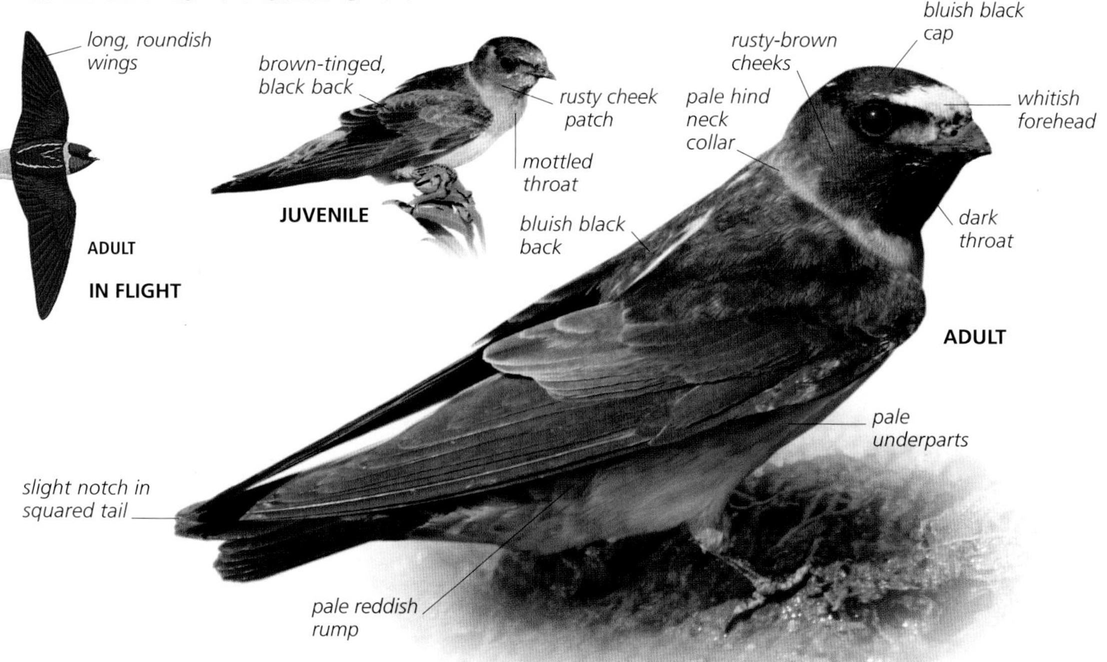
long, roundish wings
ADULT
IN FLIGHT
brown-tinged, black back
rusty cheek patch
mottled throat
JUVENILE
rusty-brown cheeks
bluish black cap
pale hind neck collar
whitish forehead
bluish black back
dark throat
ADULT
pale underparts
slight notch in squared tail
pale reddish rump

The Cliff Swallow is one of North America's most social land birds, sometimes nesting in colonies of over 3,500 pairs, especially in the western US. It is more locally distributed across the east. It can be distinguished from other North American swallows by its square tail and orange rump, but it resembles its close relative, the Cave Swallow, in color, pattern, and in affixing its mud nests to the sides of highway culverts, bridges, and buildings. The considerable increase in such structures has allowed the species to expand its range from the west to breed almost everywhere on the continent, south of the tundra forest.

VOICE Gives *purr* and *churr* calls when alarmed; song a low, squeaky, 6-second twitter given in flight and near nests.

NESTING Domed nests of mud pellets on cave walls, buildings, culverts, bridges, and dams; 3–5 eggs; 1–2 broods; April–August.

FEEDING Catches flying insects (often swarming varieties) while on the wing; sometimes forages on the ground; ingests grit to aid digestion.

FLIGHT: strong, fast wing beats; glides more often but less acrobatically than other swallows.

GATHERING MUD
The Cliff Swallow gathers wet mud from puddles, pond edges, and streamsides to build its nests.

SIMILAR SPECIES

CAVE SWALLOW
see p.496
brighter orange cheek
paler overall

INDIVIDUAL HOMES
In a Cliff Swallow colony, each nest has a single opening.

OCCURRENCE
Breeds almost anywhere in North America from Alaska to Mexico, except deserts, tundra, and unbroken forest; prefers concrete or cliff walls, culverts, buildings, cliffs, and undersides of piers on which to affix mud nests; feeds over grasslands, marshes, lakes, and reservoirs. Migrates to South America.

Length **5in (13cm)**	Wingspan **11–12in (28–30cm)**	Weight **$1^{1}/_{16}$–$1^{1}/_{4}$oz (20–35g)**
Social **Colonies**	Lifespan **Up to 11 years**	Status **Secure**

Order **Passeriformes**	Family **Aegithalidae**	Species ***Psaltriparus minimus***

Bushtit

brownish cap
yellow eye
FEMALE (PACIFIC; BREEDING)

pale ear patch
FEMALE (INTERIOR; BREEDING)

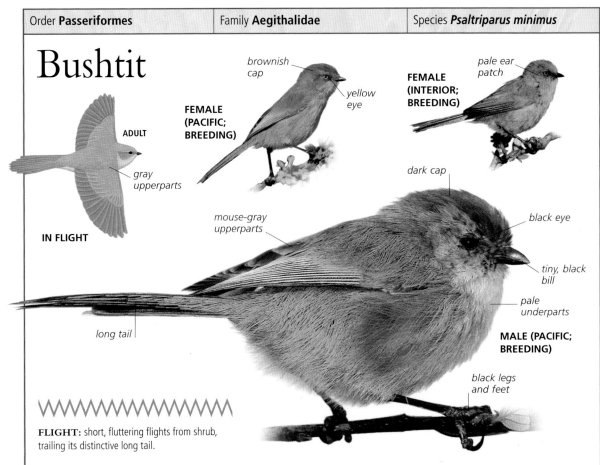

ADULT
gray upperparts
IN FLIGHT

dark cap
mouse-gray upperparts
black eye
tiny, black bill
pale underparts
long tail
MALE (PACIFIC; BREEDING)
black legs and feet

FLIGHT: short, fluttering flights from shrub, trailing its distinctive long tail.

For much of the year, the Bushtit roams the foothills and valleys of the western US and southwestern British Columbia, in flocks that usually number just a handful, but occasionally total many hundreds. This little bird is constantly on the move, foraging busily in the foliage of shrubs and small trees. Even during the breeding season, when most other perching birds become territorial, the Bushtit retains something of its social nature—raising the young is often a communal affair, with both siblings and single adults helping in the rearing of a pair's chicks.

VOICE Basic call a 2–3-part soft lisp, *ps psss pit*, interspersed with hard spit and spick notes, like little sparks.

NESTING Enormous pendant structure of cobwebs and leaves, hung from branch; 4–10 eggs; 2 broods; April–July.

FEEDING Gleans spiders and insects from vegetation; acrobatic while feeding, often hangs upside-down.

FORAGING
Constantly aflutter, the Bushtit flits through foliage, looking for insects and other small arthropods.

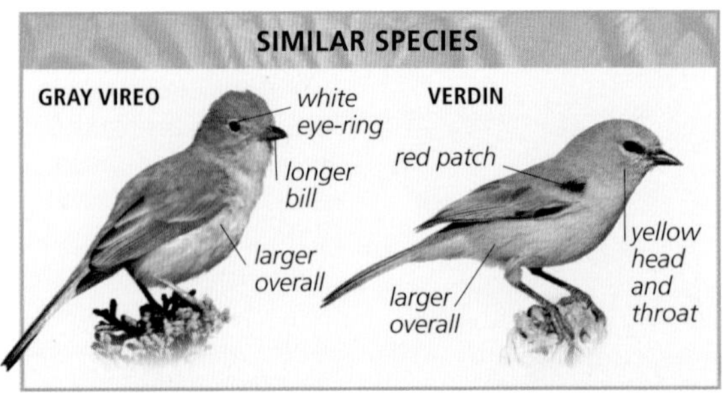
SIMILAR SPECIES
GRAY VIREO
white eye-ring
longer bill
larger overall
VERDIN
red patch
yellow head and throat
larger overall

OCCURRENCE
Away from the coast, common in open woodlands and areas of shrubs, mainly on hillsides in summer, some birds move down to low-elevation valleys in the fall. Coastal populations, commonly seen in cities and gardens as well as on hillsides, live in native and non-native plant communities.

Length **4½in (11.5cm)**	Wingspan **6in (15.5cm)**	Weight **3/16–7/32oz (4.5–6g)**
Social **Flocks**	Lifespan **Up to 8 years**	Status **Secure**

Order **Passeriformes**	Family **Alaudidae**	Species ***Eremophila alpestris***

Horned Lark

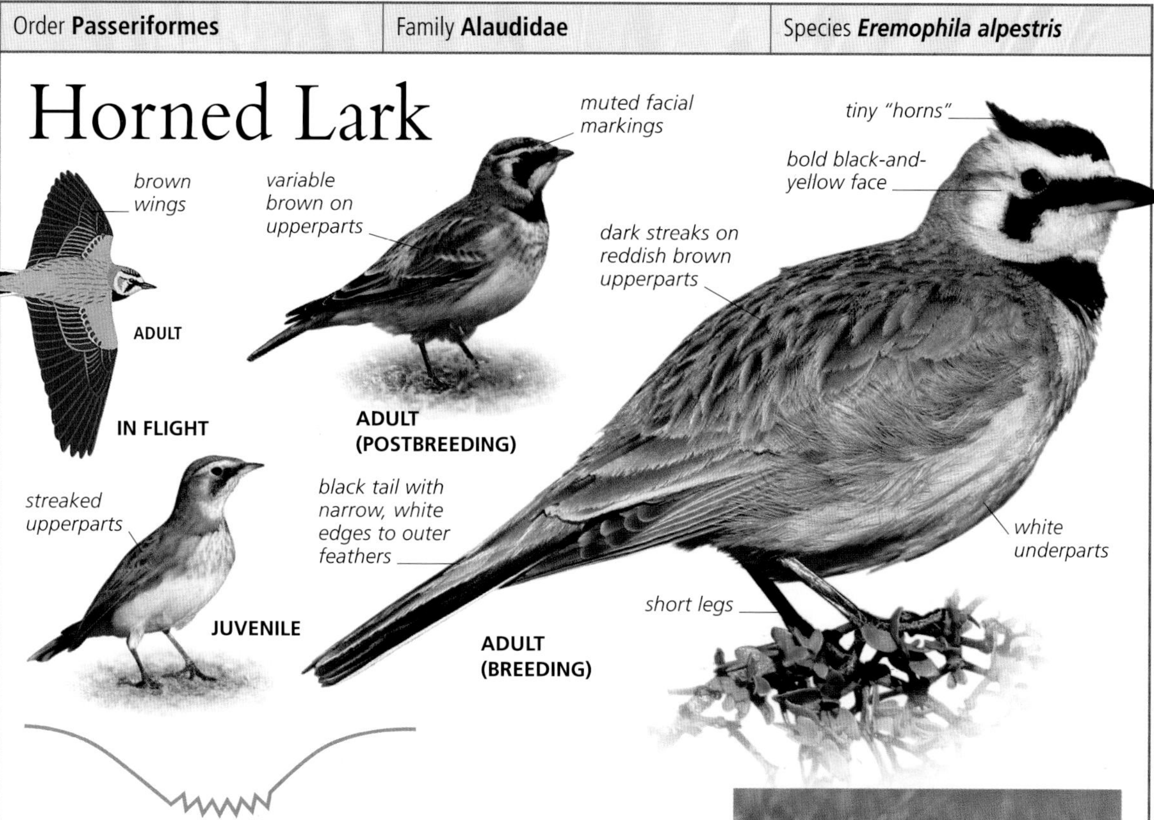
brown wings
ADULT
IN FLIGHT
variable brown on upperparts
muted facial markings
ADULT (POSTBREEDING)
tiny "horns"
bold black-and-yellow face
dark streaks on reddish brown upperparts
streaked upperparts
JUVENILE
black tail with narrow, white edges to outer feathers
white underparts
short legs
ADULT (BREEDING)

FLIGHT: undulating, with wings folded in after every few beats.

GROUND FORAGER
With its short legs bent under its body, an adult looks for insects and seeds.

The Horned Lark is a bird of open country, especially places with extensive bare ground. The species is characteristic of arid, alpine, and Arctic regions; in these areas, it flourishes in the bleakest of habitats imaginable, from sun-scorched, arid lakes in the Great Basin, to windswept tundra above the timberline. In some places, the only breeding bird species are the Horned Lark and the equally resilient Common Raven. In Europe and Asia, this species is known as the Shore Lark.

VOICE Flight call a sharp *sweet* or *soo-weet*; song, either in flight or from the ground, pleasant, musical tinkling series, followed by *sweet... swit... sweet... s'sweea'weea'witta'swit.*

NESTING In depression in bare ground, somewhat sheltered by grass or low shrubs, lined with plant matter; 2–5 eggs; 1–3 broods; March–July.

FEEDING Survives exclusively on seeds of grasses and sedges in winter; eats mostly insects in summer.

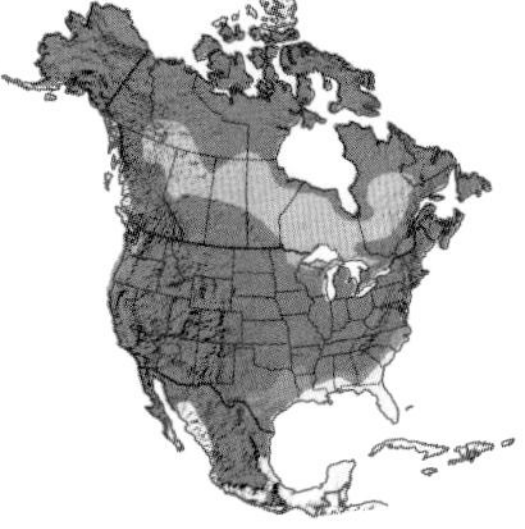

SIMILAR SPECIES

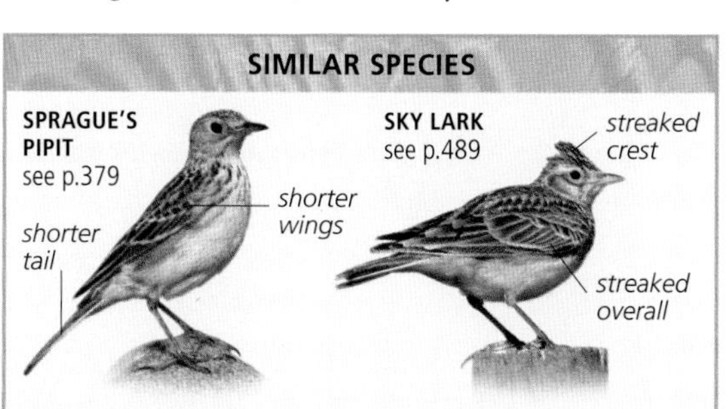
SPRAGUE'S PIPIT
see p.379
shorter wings
shorter tail
SKY LARK
see p.489
streaked crest
streaked overall

VERY VOCAL
The Horned Lark is a highly vocal bird, singing from the air, the ground, or low shrubs.

OCCURRENCE
Breeds widely, in any sort of open, even barren habitat with extensive bare ground, especially short-grass prairies and deserts. Winters wherever there are snow-free openings, including places along beaches and roads. Winters from southern Canada southward to Florida and Mexico.

Length **7in (18cm)**	Wingspan **12in (30cm)**	Weight **1¹⁄₁₆oz (30g)**
Social **Winter flocks**	Lifespan **Up to 8 years**	Status **Secure**

Order **Passeriformes**	Family **Muscicapidae**	Species ***Regulus satrapa***

Golden-crowned Kinglet

whitish
wing bars
MALE
IN FLIGHT
yellow crown patch,
with black border
FEMALE
orange-and-yellow
patch on crown,
with black border
broad whitish
stripe above eye
olive-green
upperparts
short,
straight
bill
MALE
white
wing bar
notched
tail
pale buff
to whitish
underparts

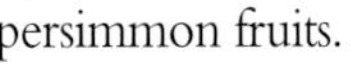

FLIGHT: quick and erratic, but not direct; high in the air; can hover while foraging.

This hardy little bird, barely more than a ball of feathers, breeds in northern and mountainous coniferous forests in Canada and the US, after a considerable hiatus in mountain forests of Mexico and Guatemala. Planting of spruce trees in parts of the US Midwest has allowed this species to increase its range in recent years to Ohio, Indiana, Illinois, and Pennsylvania.

VOICE Call a thin, high-pitched and thread-like *tsee* or *see see*; song a series of high-pitched ascending notes for 2 seconds; complex song *tsee-tsee-tsee-tsee-teet-leetle*, followed by brief trill.

NESTING Deep, cup-shaped nest with rims arching inward, made of moss, lichen, and bark, and lined with finer strips of the same; 8–9 eggs; 1–2 broods; May–August.

FEEDING Gleans flies, beetles, mites, spiders, and their eggs from tips of branches, under bark, tufts of conifer needles; eats seeds, and persimmon fruits.

EXPANDING RANGE
This bird has expanded its range southward following spruce forestation.

SIMILAR SPECIES

RUBY-CROWNED KINGLET
see p.341
white
eye-ring
no eye-
stripe
olive
underparts

HIGHER VOICE
The Golden-crowned has a higher-pitched and less musical song than the Ruby-crowned.

OCCURRENCE
Breeds in remote northern and subalpine spruce or fir forests, mixed coniferous–deciduous forests, single-species stands, and pine plantations; winters in a wide variety of habitats—coniferous and deciduous forests, pine groves, low-lying hardwood forests, swamps, and urban and suburban habitats.

Length **3¼–4¼in (8–11cm)**	Wingspan **5½–7in (14–18cm)**	Weight **5/32–9/32oz (4–8g)**
Social **Solitary/Pairs**	Lifespan **Up to 5 years**	Status **Secure**

Order **Passeriformes**	Family **Muscicapidae**	Species ***Regulus calendula***

Ruby-crowned Kinglet

red patch on crown

white wing bars

ADULT

patch on crown often concealed

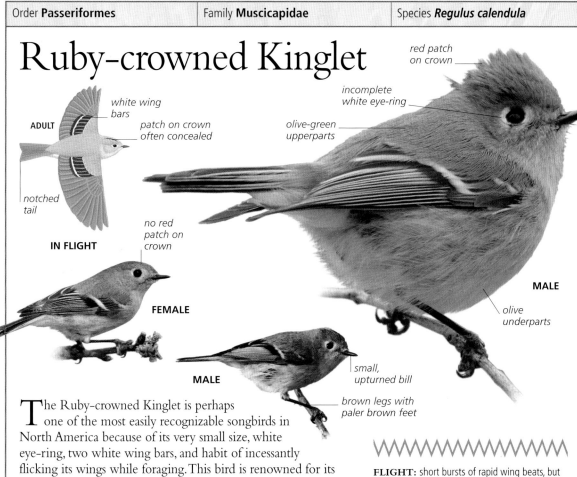

incomplete white eye-ring

olive-green upperparts

notched tail

IN FLIGHT

no red patch on crown

FEMALE

MALE

olive underparts

MALE

small, upturned bill

brown legs with paler brown feet

The Ruby-crowned Kinglet is perhaps one of the most easily recognizable songbirds in North America because of its very small size, white eye-ring, two white wing bars, and habit of incessantly flicking its wings while foraging. This bird is renowned for its loud, complex song and for laying up to 12 eggs in a clutch—probably the highest of any North American songbird. Despite local declines resulting from logging and forest fires, the Ruby-crowned Kinglet is common across the continent. It will sometimes join mixed-species flocks in winter with nuthatches and titmice.

VOICE Call a low, husky *jidit*; song, remarkably loud for such a small bird, begins with 2–3 high, clear notes *tee* or *zee* followed by 5–6 lower *tu* or *turr* notes, and ends with ringing galloping notes *tee-da-leet, tee-da-leet, tee-da-leet.*

NESTING Globular or elongated nest hanging from or on large branch with an enclosed or open cup, made of mosses, feathers, lichens, spider's silk, bark, hair, and fur; 5–12 eggs; 1 brood; May–October.

FEEDING Gleans a wide variety of insects, spiders, and their eggs among the leaves on the outer tips of higher, smaller branches; eats fruit and seeds; often hovers to catch prey.

FLIGHT: short bursts of rapid wing beats, but overall quick and direct flight.

CONCEALED COLOR
This bird's red patch is often concealed unless the bird is agitated or excited.

SIMILAR SPECIES

HUTTON'S VIREO
see p.311
larger head
stouter bill
heavier overall

ALWAYS FLICKING
Ruby-crowned Kinglets are easily identified by their habit of constantly flicking their wings.

OCCURRENCE
Within the northerly forest zone, breeds near water in Black Spruce and tamarack forests, muskegs, forests with mixed conifers and northern hardwoods; in the mountainous West, spruce-fir, Lodgepole Pine, and Douglas Fir forests. Winters in a broad range of forests, thickets, and borders.

Length **3½–4¼in (9–11cm)**	Wingspan **6–7in (15–18cm)**	Weight **³⁄₁₆–³⁄₈oz (5–10g)**
Social **Winter flocks**	Lifespan **Up to 5 years**	Status **Secure**

Family **Troglodytidae**

WRENS

WITH ONE EXCEPTION, the Eurasian Winter Wren, wrens are all small North American songbirds. Generally dull-colored, most species are shades of brown with light and dark streaking. The scientific family name, which derives from a Greek word for "cave-dweller," seems apt in light of the furtive habits of some wren species. Wrens are also renowned in the avian world for their remarkable songs, and, in some species, for singing precisely synchronized duets.

COCKED TAIL
As they sing, Winter Wrens often hold their tails upward in a near-vertical position.

Family **Sittidae**

NUTHATCHES

EASILY RECOGNIZED BY their distinctive shape and characteristic feeding technique, nuthatches are common woodland birds. They are plump-bodied, short-tailed birds with blue-gray backs and often a contrasting darker crown. Nuthatches use their straight, pointed bills to probe for insects and spiders in crevices in tree trunks and branches. Strong feet and long claws allow these birds to move downwards, upwards, upside-down along the underside of branches in search of food. This contrasts with many other similar birds, which only move upward on a tree trunk.

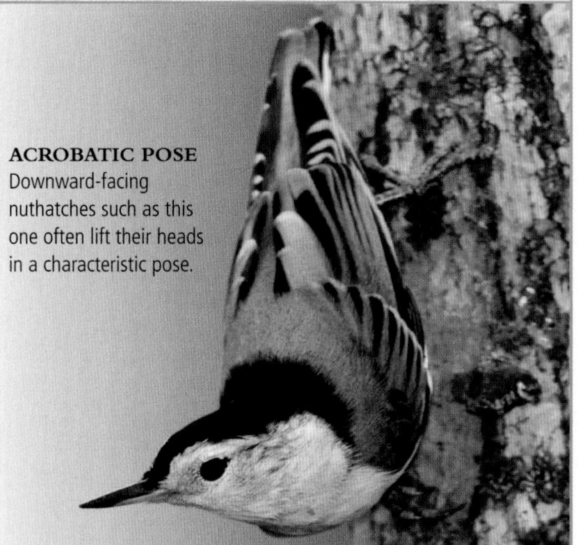

ACROBATIC POSE
Downward-facing nuthatches such as this one often lift their heads in a characteristic pose.

Family **Mimidae**

THRASHERS

THE FAMILY NAME for thrashers is derived from the Latin for "to imitate," and perhaps no other word better represents the dozen or so species or subspecies found in North America. They are well known for their ability to mimic the songs of other species in their own song sequences. Members of this group are characterized by their long, curved bill and somewhat reclusive habits, though some, like the Northern Mockingbird, are as brash and conspicuous as any other species on the continent, and sport a short, somewhat straight bill.

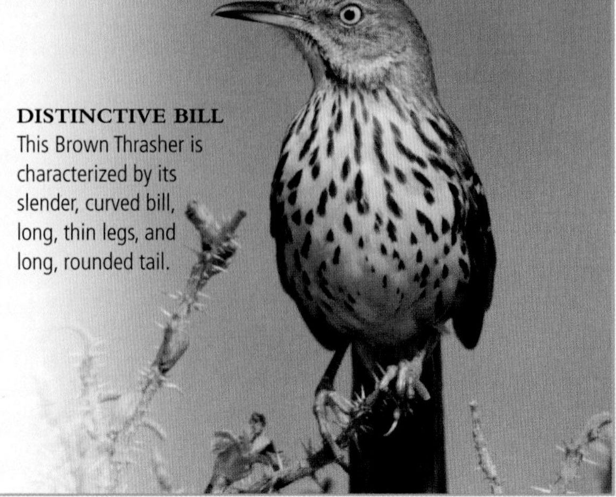

DISTINCTIVE BILL
This Brown Thrasher is characterized by its slender, curved bill, long, thin legs, and long, rounded tail.

Order **Passeriformes**	Family **Troglodytidae**	Species ***Salpinctes obsoletus***

Rock Wren

rusty rump
ADULT
bright buff feather tips
IN FLIGHT

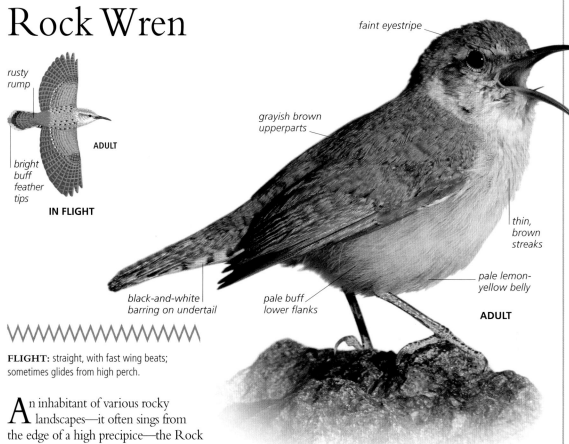

faint eyestripe
grayish brown upperparts
thin, brown streaks
pale lemon-yellow belly
black-and-white barring on undertail
pale buff lower flanks
ADULT

FLIGHT: straight, with fast wing beats; sometimes glides from high perch.

An inhabitant of various rocky landscapes—it often sings from the edge of a high precipice—the Rock Wren's voice, while not particularly loud, carries surprisingly far through the dry air of the West. It is perpetually busy running, fluttering, and darting in and out of crevices in search of food. A well-known behavioral quirk of the Rock Wren is to bob and sway conspicuously when a human approaches. However, its oddest habit is to "pave" the area in front of its nest entrance with a walkway of pebbles—the purpose of this is unknown.

VOICE Call a sharp *ch'keer*; varied series of warbles, trills, chatters, and repeated musical phrases such as *chuwee chuwee, teedee teedee*, reminiscent of a mockingbird or a thrasher; sings at all elevations.

NESTING Cup of various grasses lined with soft materials, in rock crevice or under overhang; 4–8 eggs; 1–2 broods; April–August.

FEEDING Probes in rock crevices on ground and in dirt banks for a variety of insects and spiders.

A CHANGE OF SCENERY
Rock Wrens occasionally venture out into open grasslands and perch on manmade structures, well away from their usual surroundings.

SIMILAR SPECIES

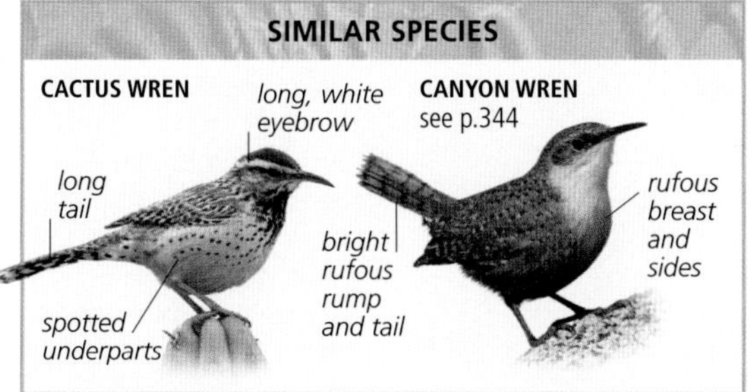
CACTUS WREN
long, white eyebrow
long tail
spotted underparts
CANYON WREN
see p.344
bright rufous rump and tail
rufous breast and sides

OCCURRENCE
Inhabits arid country with rocky cliffs and canyons, as well as manmade quarries and gravel piles; a wide variety of elevations from hot, low deserts to windswept mountain tops as high as 10,000ft (3,000m). Northern birds migrate to southern states for winter.

Length **6in (15cm)**	Wingspan **9in (23cm)**	Weight **⅝oz (17g)**
Social **Solitary/Pairs**	Lifespan **Unknown**	Status **Secure**

Order **Passeriformes**	Family **Troglodytidae**	Species ***Catherpes mexicanus***

Canyon Wren

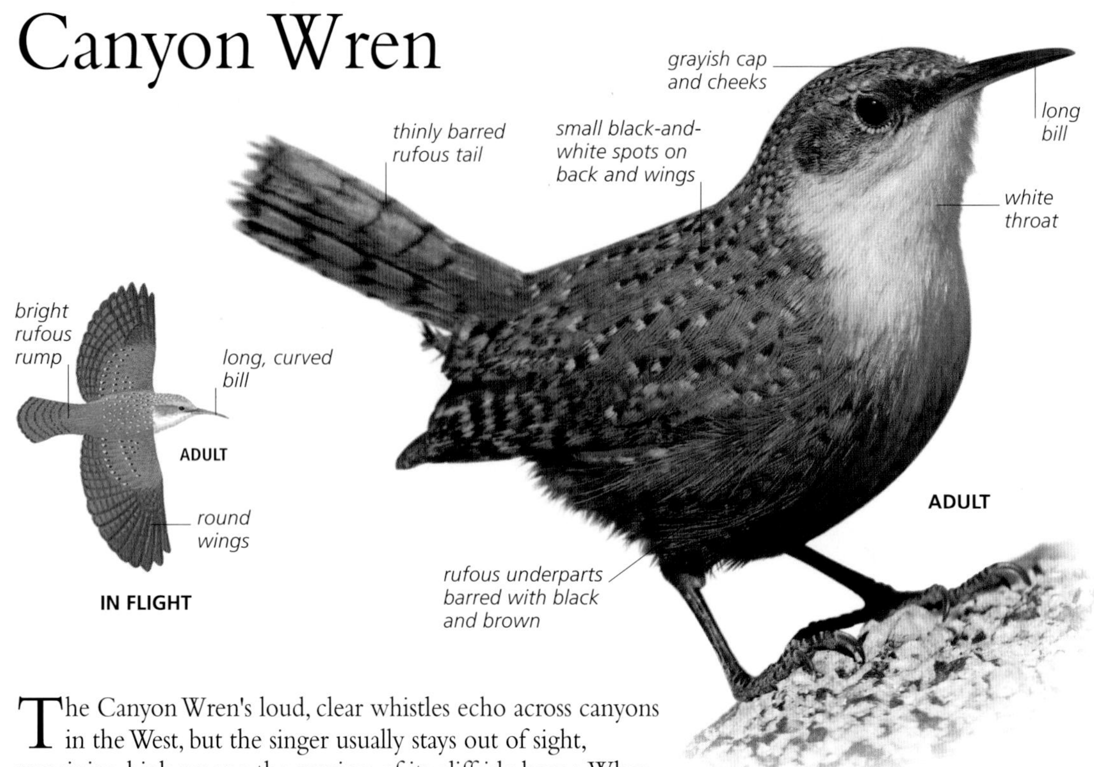
grayish cap and cheeks
long bill
thinly barred rufous tail
small black-and-white spots on back and wings
white throat
bright rufous rump
long, curved bill
ADULT
round wings
IN FLIGHT
rufous underparts barred with black and brown
ADULT

The Canyon Wren's loud, clear whistles echo across canyons in the West, but the singer usually stays out of sight, remaining high among the crevices of its cliffside home. When it can be observed, the most striking aspect of its behavior is its extraordinary ability to walk up, down, and sideways on vertical rock walls. This remarkable agility is achieved through its strong toes and long claws; these features enable Canyon Wrens to find a grip in the tiniest of depressions and fissures in the rock.

VOICE Series of 10–15 loud, ringing whistles, descending in pitch, gradually slowing, and ending with several thin buzzes.

NESTING Cup of sticks lined with soft material like plant down, in crevice or hole; 4–6 eggs; 1–2 broods; April–August.

FEEDING Uses extremely long bill to probe crevices for insects and spiders; can flatten itself by spreading legs to enter low overhangs.

FLIGHT: steady, straight, and fluttery; broad, rounded wings let it glide to a lower perch.

BLENDING IN
Except for the white throat, the Canyon Wren's plumage matches its rocky habitat.

CLIFF-HOPPER
This bird can half-fly and half-hop up steep cliffs by flapping its broad wings for extra lift.

SIMILAR SPECIES

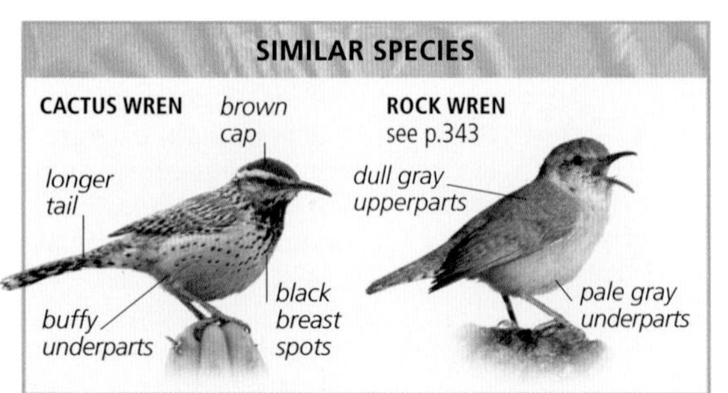
CACTUS WREN
brown cap
longer tail
buffy underparts
black breast spots
ROCK WREN
see p.343
dull gray upperparts
pale gray underparts

OCCURRENCE
Maintains year-round territory on rocky hillsides, outcroppings, and vertical rock-walled canyons through much of the west of the continent and southward to Mexico. Sometimes nests in holes in stone buildings, old sheds, and other structures, apparently unconcerned by nearby human activity.

Length **5¾in (14.5cm)**	Wingspan **7½in (19cm)**	Weight **⅜oz (11g)**
Social **Solitary/Pairs**	Lifespan **Unknown**	Status **Secure**

Order **Passeriformes**	Family **Troglodytidae**	Species ***Cistothorus platensis***

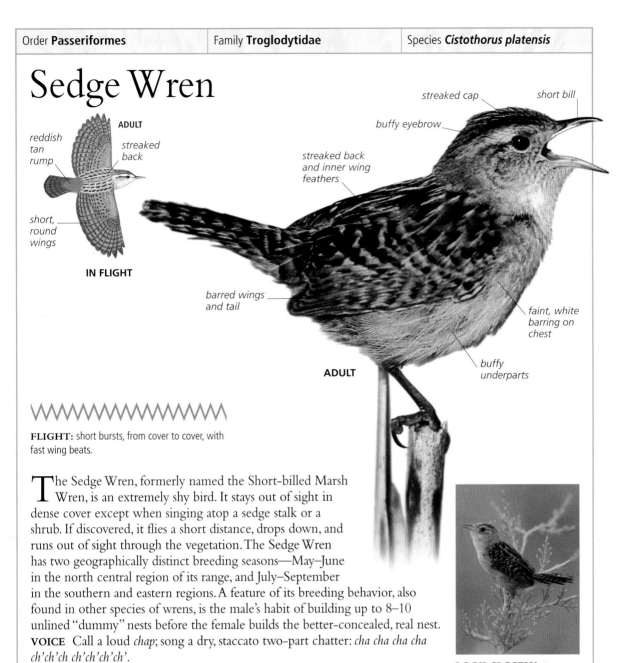

Sedge Wren

ADULT

reddish tan rump

streaked back

short, round wings

IN FLIGHT

streaked cap

short bill

buffy eyebrow

streaked back and inner wing feathers

barred wings and tail

faint, white barring on chest

buffy underparts

ADULT

FLIGHT: short bursts, from cover to cover, with fast wing beats.

The Sedge Wren, formerly named the Short-billed Marsh Wren, is an extremely shy bird. It stays out of sight in dense cover except when singing atop a sedge stalk or a shrub. If discovered, it flies a short distance, drops down, and runs out of sight through the vegetation. The Sedge Wren has two geographically distinct breeding seasons—May–June in the north central region of its range, and July–September in the southern and eastern regions. A feature of its breeding behavior, also found in other species of wrens, is the male's habit of building up to 8–10 unlined "dummy" nests before the female builds the better-concealed, real nest.

VOICE Call a loud *chap*; song a dry, staccato two-part chatter: *cha cha cha cha ch'ch'ch ch'ch'ch'ch'*.

NESTING Globular, woven structure of sedges with side entrance; lined with plant matter, down, and hair; 4–8 eggs; 1–2 broods; May–August.

FEEDING Forages for spiders and insects, such as grasshoppers, flies, mosquitoes, and bugs, close to or on ground in cover of sedges and grass.

LOOK CLOSELY
Close study is necessary to appreciate the Sedge Wren's subtle patterning, which is plainer than the Marsh Wren's.

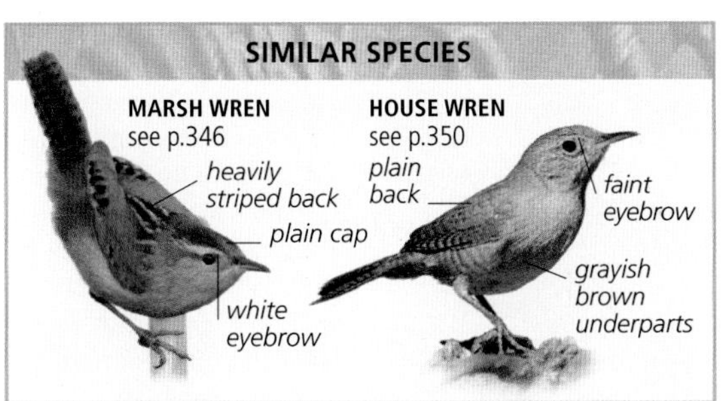
SIMILAR SPECIES
MARSH WREN
see p.346
heavily striped back
plain cap
white eyebrow
HOUSE WREN
see p.350
plain back
faint eyebrow
grayish brown underparts

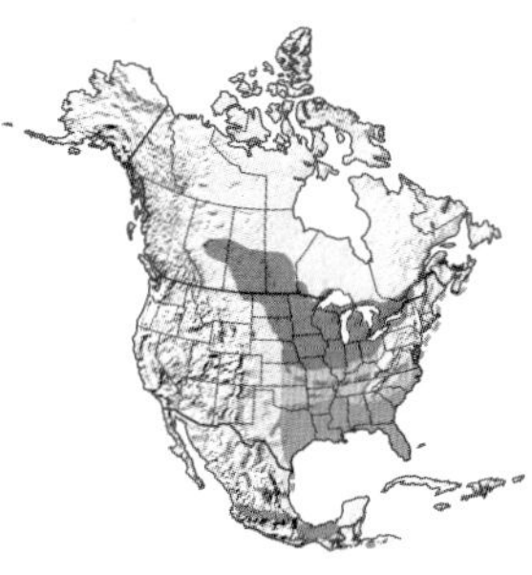

OCCURRENCE
In North America, breeds in wet meadows and sedge marshes with low water levels. Widely distributed in the Americas from the Canadian prairies, east to Quebec and from northern US, to the south central states. Winters from Texas to Florida in drier habitats including grassy fields and coastal-plain prairies.

Length **4½in (11.5cm)**	Wingspan **5½–6in (14–15.5cm)**	Weight **5/16oz (9g)**
Social **Loose colonies**	Lifespan **Unknown**	Status **Secure**

Order **Passeriformes**	Family **Troglodytidae**	Species ***Cistothorus palustris***

Marsh Wren

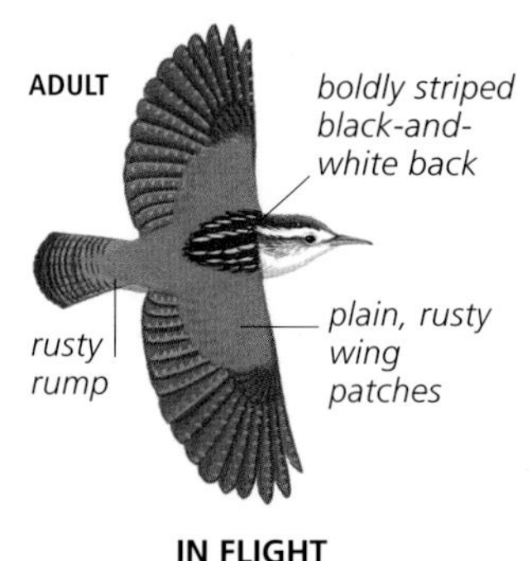
ADULT
boldly striped black-and-white back
rusty rump
plain, rusty wing patches
IN FLIGHT

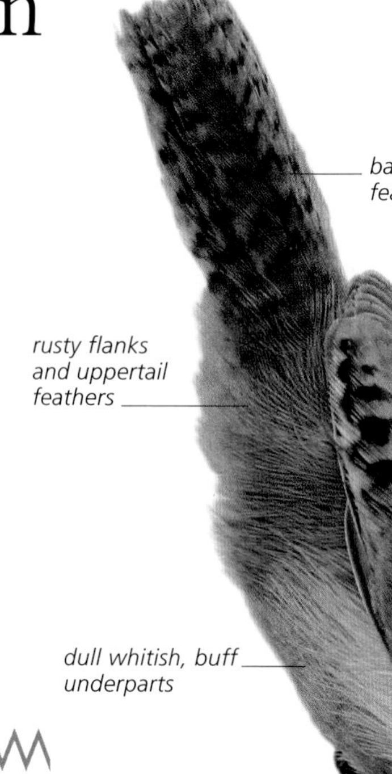
barred tail feathers
rusty flanks and uppertail feathers
heavily streaked, black-and-white back
whitish eyebrow
brown cap
dull whitish, buff underparts
long bill
ADULT

FLIGHT: straight, with rapid wing beats over short distances, from one reed patch to another.

The Marsh Wren, a common resident of saltwater and freshwater marshes, is known for singing loudly through both day and night. The males perform fluttery, aerial courtship flights while singing, and are polygamous, mating with two or more females. Like the Sedge Wren, the male builds several dummy nests before his mate constructs one herself. The Marsh Wren nests in taller vegetation than the Sedge Wren and over deeper water. Eastern (*C. p. palustris*) and Western (*C. p. paludicola*) Marsh Wrens differ in voice and behavior, and some ornithologists classify them as separate species.

VOICE Calls a low *chek* and a raspy *churr*; song a loud *chuk chuk chuk*, then fast *tih-tih-tih-rih-tih-tih*, an enthusiastic singer.

NESTING Oblong structure with side entrance, woven of reeds and lined with soft materials; 4–5 eggs; 2 broods; March–July.

FEEDING Forages acrobatically for insects, such as mosquitoes, dragonflies, and beetles, within dense clusters of cattails and reeds.

DELICATELY PERCHED
This wren perches on vertical reeds and often holds itself up by spreading its legs across two stalks.

SIMILAR SPECIES

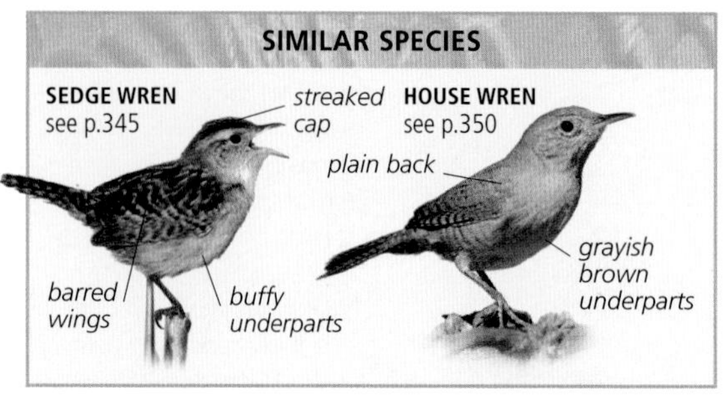
SEDGE WREN
see p.345
streaked cap
barred wings
buffy underparts
HOUSE WREN
see p.350
plain back
grayish brown underparts

OCCURRENCE
Breeds across North America from Canada to the mountains of the western and central northern states. Inhabits freshwater and saltwater marshes with tall vegetation, above water, sometimes more than 3ft (1m) deep. It is irregularly distributed in its range. Winters in grassy marshes and wetlands.

Length **5in (13cm)**	Wingspan **6in (15cm)**	Weight **3/8oz (11g)**
Social **Loose colonies**	Lifespan **Unknown**	Status **Localized**

Order **Passeriformes**	Family **Troglodytidae**	Species ***Thryomanes bewickii***

Bewick's Wren

black-and-white outer tail tips

long, rounded tail

ADULT

dark brown flight feathers

IN FLIGHT

brown cheeks

white eyebrow

long, slightly curved bill

largely unmarked, dull brown upperparts

whitish throat and breast

ADULT
T. b. drymoecus
(PACIFIC COAST)

plain gray upperparts

pale gray underparts

ADULT
T. b. eremophilus
(WESTERN)

FLIGHT: fast and straight; over short distances.

Like the House Wren, but less common and occupying a smaller range, Bewick's Wren is also familiar around human habitations. It is known to nest in any sort of hole or crevice in barns, houses, abandoned machinery, woodpiles, and even trash heaps in farms and towns. Bewick's Wren has undergone large-scale changes in geographic distribution: in the 19th century its range expanded northward to the eastern and midwestern US, but it gradually disappeared from those regions in the 20th century. It has been suggested that the more aggressive House Wren slowly replaced Bewick's Wren in these areas.

VOICE Loud, complex, and varied mixture of cheeps, buzzes, and clear notes; vocalizations differ according to geographic location; also mimics other birds.

NESTING Cup of sticks lined with leaves, and other soft materials, in natural or human-made cavity, including nest boxes; 5–10 eggs; 2 broods; March–June.

FEEDING Forages for insects in brush, shrubs, crannies of buildings, and leaf litter on ground.

TALENTED MIMIC
Bewick's is sometimes known as the "Mocking Wren," due to its imitations of other species' songs.

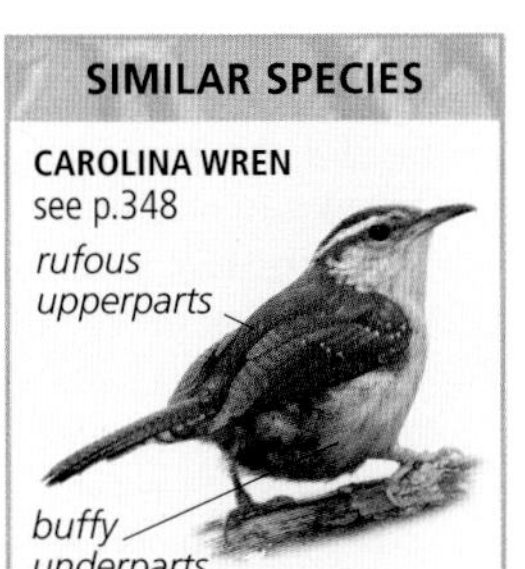
SIMILAR SPECIES
CAROLINA WREN
see p.348
rufous upperparts
buffy underparts

TYPICAL POSTURE
Bewick's Wren may often be spotted with its distinctive tail cocked vertically.

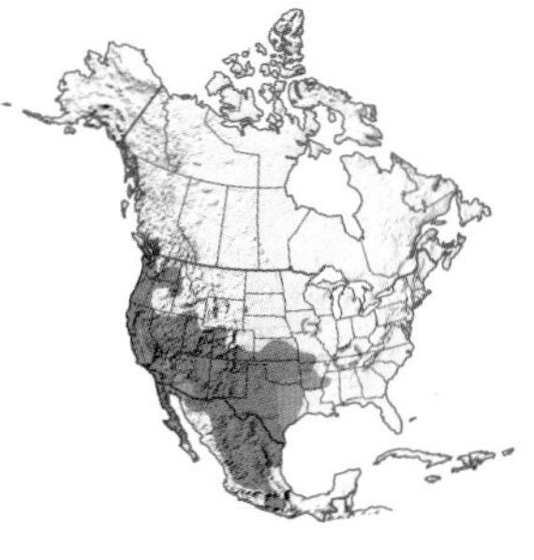

OCCURRENCE
Year-round resident in brushy areas, open woodlands, and around human structures; from southern British Columbia southward to Baja California, east to Arkansas, and as far south as Oaxaca in Mexico. May withdraw slightly southward from northernmost portions of range in winter.

Length **5in (13cm)**	Wingspan **7in (18cm)**	Weight **3/8oz (11g)**
Social **Solitary/Pairs**	Lifespan **At least 8 years**	Status **Secure**

Order **Passeriformes**	Family **Troglodytidae**	Species ***Thryothorus ludovicianus***

Carolina Wren

white eyebrow bordered by black above
huge head
tiny tail
ADULT
powerful-looking, bluish bill
rufous upperparts
duller overall
white wing spots
thin, black barring on tail
white spots on wing
FLEDGLING
IN FLIGHT
ADULT
buffy underparts
pinkish legs and toes

The Carolina Wren is a popular and common backyard bird in most of its range. It is rarely still, often flicking its tail and looking around nervously. Extremely harsh winters at the northernmost fringe of the Carolina Wren's range in New England and southeastern Canada can cause a sudden decline in numbers, as food resources are covered for long periods by ice and heavy snow. At such times, survival may depend on human help for food and shelter.

VOICE Calls variable; often a sharp *chlip* or long, harsh chatter; song a loud, long, fast *whee'dle-dee whee'dle-dee whee'dle-dee*.

NESTING Cup of weeds, twigs, leaves in natural or human-made cavity; 4–8 eggs; 2–3 broods; April–July.

FEEDING Forages for insects in shrubs and on ground; in winter, favorite foods are peanut butter or suet at a feeder.

FLIGHT: fast and straight over short distances, with rapid wing beats.

DISTINCTIVE BORDER
A unique feature of this wren, not always noticed but visible here, is the black border on the eyebrow.

SIMILAR SPECIES

BEWICK'S WREN
see p.347
dull brown or gray upperparts
longer tail

TIRELESS SINGER
Unlike many birds, the male Carolina Wren sings all year long, even on cold winter days.

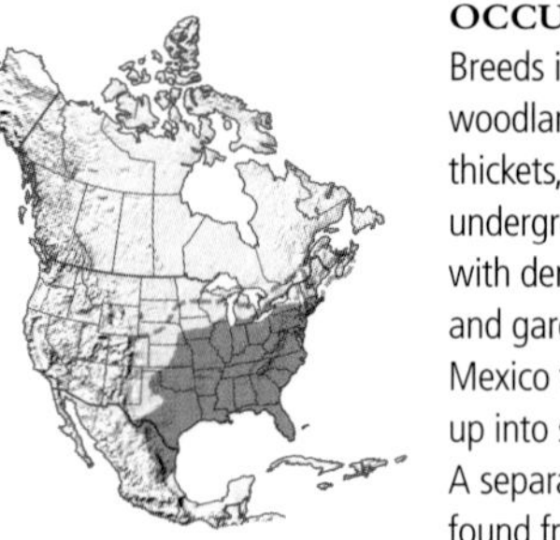

OCCURRENCE
Breeds in a variety of bushy woodland habitats, such as thickets, parks with shrubby undergrowth, suburban yards with dense, low trees or bushes, and gardens; from northeastern Mexico to the Great Lakes and up into southeastern Canada. A separate population can be found from Mexico to Nicaragua.

Length **5¼in (13.5cm)**	Wingspan **7½in (19cm)**	Weight **11/16oz (19g)**
Social **Pairs/Family groups**	Lifespan **At least 9 years**	Status **Secure**

Order **Passeriformes**	Family **Troglodytidae**	Species ***Troglodytes troglodytes***

Winter Wren

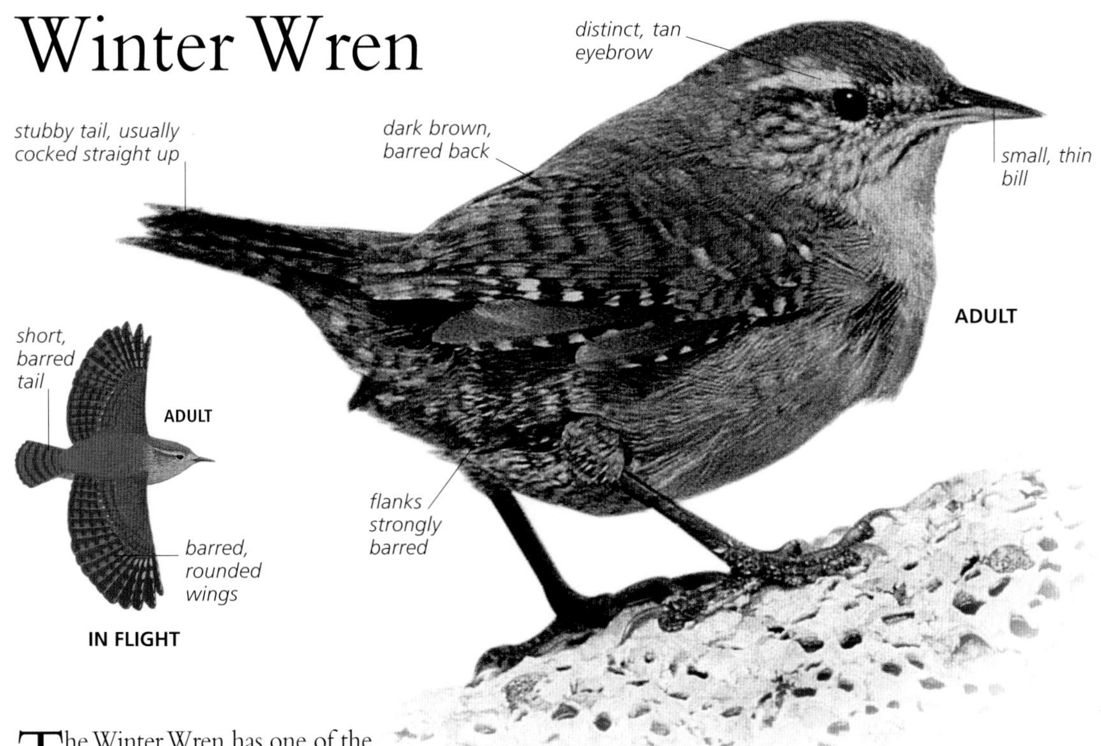
distinct, tan eyebrow
stubby tail, usually cocked straight up
dark brown, barred back
small, thin bill
ADULT
short, barred tail
ADULT
flanks strongly barred
barred, rounded wings
IN FLIGHT

The Winter Wren has one of the loudest songs of any North American bird of a similar size: the male's song carries far through its forest haunts. It is a widespread breeder, found from the Aleutians and Alaska eastward to Newfoundland, and as far south as California in the West and the Appalachians in the East, where the subspecies *T. t. pullus* resides. Its winter range is also western (to California) and eastern (to Texas), with a wide hiatus in between. This species spends its time foraging in tangles of fallen trees and shrubs, appearing mouse-like as it creeps amid the shadows. In Europe, as its family's sole species, it is simply called "the Wren."

VOICE Call a double *chek-chek* or *chimp-chimp*; song a loud, extremely long, complex series of warbles, trills, and single notes.

NESTING Well-hidden in a cavity near ground with dead wood and crevices; nest a messy mound lined with feathers; 4–7 eggs; 1–2 broods; April–July.

FEEDING Forages for insects in low, dense undergrowth, often in wet areas along streams; sometimes thrusts its head into water to capture prey.

FLIGHT: fast and direct, with rapid beats of its short, broad wings.

VOCAL VIRTUOSO
The Winter Wren is a skulker, but in the breeding season singing males show up on lower perches.

SIMILAR SPECIES

HOUSE WREN
see p.350

pale brown back
long tail
plain, unbarred flanks

NERVOUS REACTION
When alarmed, this wren cocks its tail almost vertically, before escaping into a mossy thicket.

OCCURRENCE
Breeds in northerly and mountain forests dominated by evergreen trees with a dense understory, fallen trees, and banks of streams. In the Appalachians, breeds in treeless areas with grass near cliffs. Northernmost birds migrate south to winter in woodlands, brush piles, tangles, and secluded spots.

Length **4in (10cm)**	Wingspan **5½in (14cm)**	Weight **5/16oz (9g)**
Social **Solitary/Family groups**	Lifespan **At least 4 years**	Status **Secure**

Order **Passeriformes**	Family **Troglodytidae**	Species ***Troglodytes aedon***

House Wren

faintly barred wings

ADULT (EASTERN)

IN FLIGHT

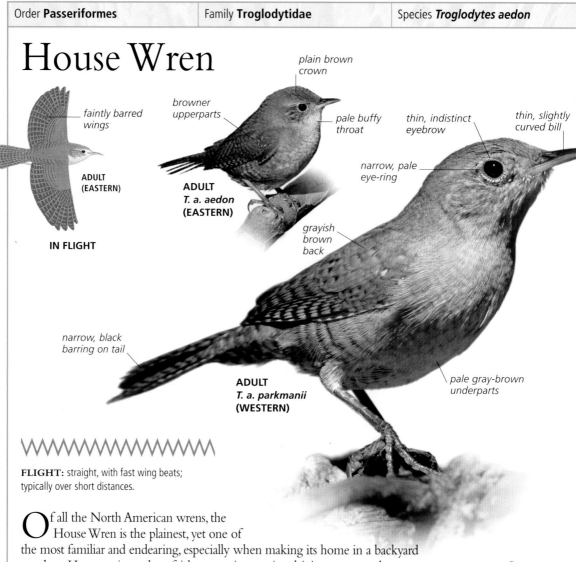

plain brown crown

browner upperparts

pale buffy throat

ADULT
T. a. aedon
(EASTERN)

thin, indistinct eyebrow

thin, slightly curved bill

narrow, pale eye-ring

grayish brown back

narrow, black barring on tail

pale gray-brown underparts

ADULT
T. a. parkmanii
(WESTERN)

FLIGHT: straight, with fast wing beats; typically over short distances.

Of all the North American wrens, the House Wren is the plainest, yet one of the most familiar and endearing, especially when making its home in a backyard nest box. However, it can be a fairly aggressive species, driving away nearby nesting birds of its own species and others by destroying nests, puncturing eggs, and even killing young. In the 1920s, distraught bird lovers mounted a campaign calling for the eradication of House Wrens, though the campaign did not last long as most were in favor of letting nature take its course.

VOICE Call a sharp *chep* or *cherr*; song opens with several short notes, followed by bubbly explosion of spluttering notes.

NESTING Cup lined with soft material on stick platform in natural, manmade cavities, such as nest boxes; 5–8 eggs; 2–3 broods; April–July.

FEEDING Forages for insects and spiders in trees and shrubs, gardens, and yards.

SIMILAR SPECIES

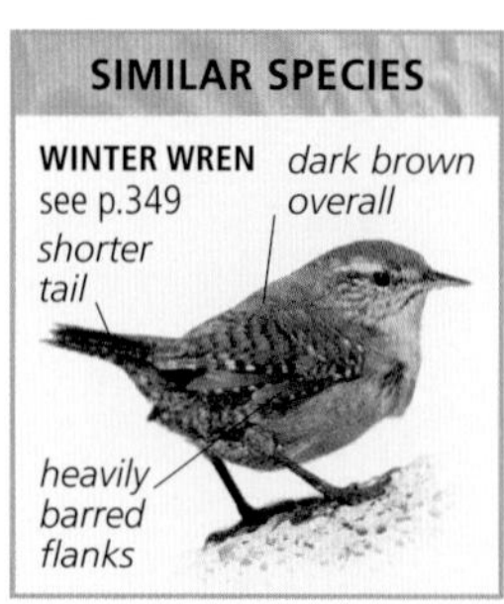
WINTER WREN
see p.349
dark brown overall
shorter tail
heavily barred flanks

NESTING MATERIAL
This small bird has brought an unusually large twig to its nest inside an old woodpecker hole.

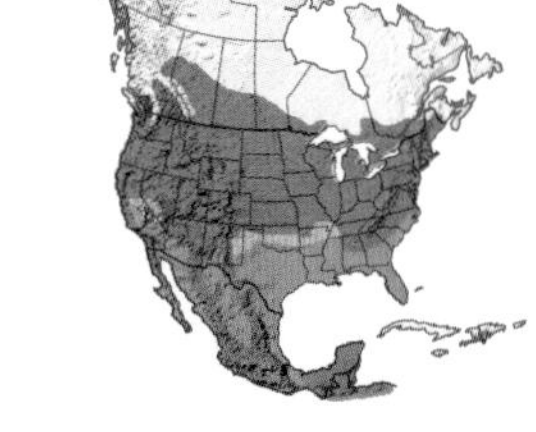

OCCURRENCE
Breeds in cities, towns, parks, farms, yards, gardens, and woodland edges. Rarely seen during migration period (late July to early October). Winters south of its breeding range, from southern US to Mexico, in woodlands, shrubby areas, and weedy fields. Nests, or is resident as far south as Tierra del Fuego.

Length **4½in (11.5cm)**	Wingspan **6in (15cm)**	Weight **⅜oz (11g)**
Social **Solitary**	Lifespan **Up to 9 years**	Status **Secure**

Order **Passeriformes**	Family **Sylviidae**	Species ***Polioptila caerulea***

Blue-gray Gnatcatcher

MALE

IN FLIGHT

white outer tail feathers

pale gray overall

paler upperparts

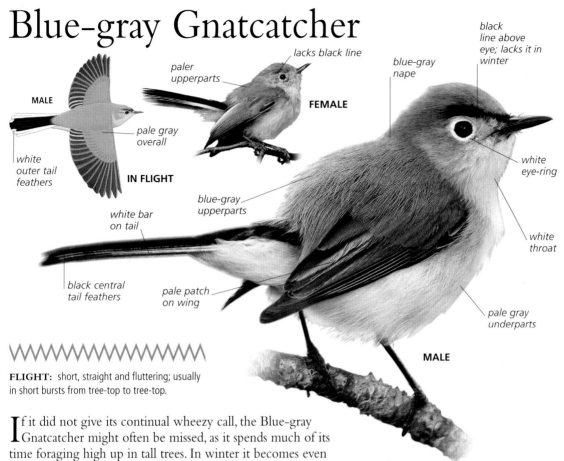

lacks black line

FEMALE

blue-gray nape

black line above eye; lacks it in winter

white eye-ring

white throat

blue-gray upperparts

white bar on tail

black central tail feathers

pale patch on wing

pale gray underparts

MALE

FLIGHT: short, straight and fluttering; usually in short bursts from tree-top to tree-top.

If it did not give its continual wheezy call, the Blue-gray Gnatcatcher might often be missed, as it spends much of its time foraging high up in tall trees. In winter it becomes even harder to find as it is generally silent. This species is the most northerly of the North American gnatcatchers and is also the only one to migrate. It can exhibit aggressive behavior and is capable of driving off considerably larger birds than itself. The range of the Blue-gray Gnatcatcher appears to be expanding and populations are increasing.

VOICE Call soft, irregular *zhee, zhee*, uttered constantly while foraging; song soft combination of short notes and nasal wheezes.

NESTING Cup of plant fibers, spider webs, mosses; usually high on branch; lined with soft plant material; 4–5 eggs; 1–2 broods; April–June.

FEEDING Forages for small insects and spiders by acrobatically flitting from twig to twig, while twitching long tail.

LISTEN CLOSELY
The complex song is rather faint; it is heard best when the bird is singing on a low perch.

SIMILAR SPECIES

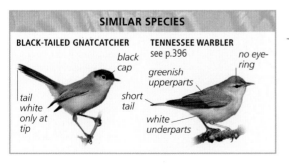

BLACK-TAILED GNATCATCHER

black cap

tail white only at tip

TENNESSEE WARBLER
see p.396

no eye-ring

greenish upperparts

short tail

white underparts

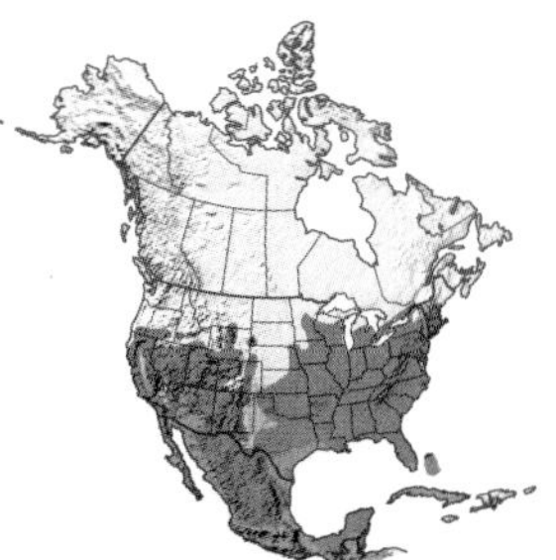

OCCURRENCE
In eastern North America, breeds in deciduous or pine woodlands; in the West, in scrubby habitats, often near water. Winters in brushy habitats in southern US, Mexico, and Central America. Also breeds in Mexico, Belize, and the Bahamas.

Length **4¼in (11cm)**	Wingspan **6in (15cm)**	Weight **7/32oz (6g)**
Social **Solitary/Flocks**	Lifespan **At least 4 years**	Status **Secure**

Order **Passeriformes**	Family **Sittidae**	Species ***Sitta pygmaea***

Pygmy Nuthatch

rounded wings
ADULT
IN FLIGHT
grayish brown cap
pointed, chisel-like bill
blue-gray upperparts
black eyestripe
dusky underparts
very short tail
grayish flanks
ADULT
sharp claws

Pygmy Nuthatches are found in noisy and busy flocks throughout the year in their pine forest home of western North America. They are cooperative breeders, with young birds from the previous year's brood often helping adult birds raise the next year's young. They have a particular preference for Ponderosa and Jeffery Pines and are often absent from mountain ranges that lack their favourite trees. Pygmy Nuthatches are heard more often than they are seen, probably because they like to stick to the treetops.

VOICE Highly vocal species; calls piercing *peep* and *pip* notes, given singly or in frenzied series; in series, call resembles vocalizations of some Red Crossbills; calls of birds in flocks are somewhat bell-like.

NESTING Excavates cavity in pine tree; nest is a mass of plant material and feathers; 5–9 eggs; 1–2 broods; April–July.

FEEDING Forages on pine trees; mainly eats insects, caterpillars, moths, and grubs.

FLIGHT: jerky, undulating motion; appears bobtailed and rotund in flight.

SQUEEZING OUT OF A NEST
All nuthatches nest in tree cavities, which they wholly or partially excavate themselves.

SIMILAR SPECIES

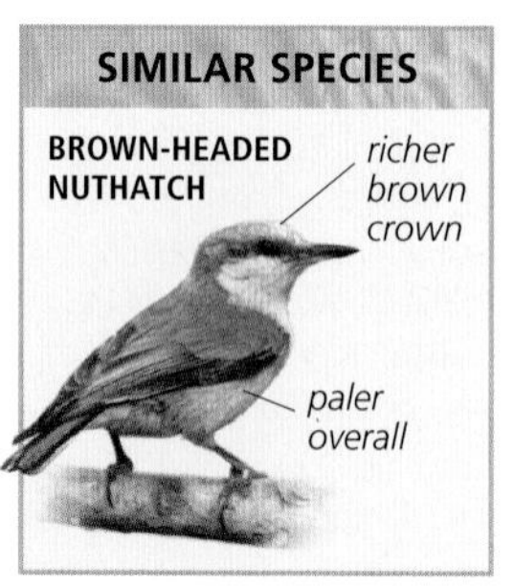
BROWN-HEADED NUTHATCH
richer brown crown
paler overall

PINE FORAGER
A Pygmy Nuthatch hangs upside down, carrying a tiny piece of food.

OCCURRENCE
Patchily distributed in pine forests of western North America, from British Columbia south to California, Arizona, New Mexico, and Texas; also in Mexico. Most numerous in dry mountain forests up to 650ft (2,000m), but in California ranges down to sea level.

Length **4¼in (11cm)**	Wingspan **8in (20cm)**	Weight **⅜oz (11g)**
Social **Small flocks**	Lifespan **Up to 2 years**	Status **Secure**

Order **Passeriformes**	Family **Sittidae**	Species ***Sitta canadensis***

Red-breasted Nuthatch

rounded wings
slightly muted head pattern
dark blue-gray crown and eyestripe
bold black-and-white head pattern
pointed, chisel-like bill
black eyestripe
MALE
pale orange underparts
white bands on tail
FEMALE
blue-gray upperparts
IN FLIGHT
white cheeks
blue-gray, short tail, with black side feathers
rusty underparts
compact body shape
MALE

FLIGHT: short, swift dashes across forest clearings; irregular, undulating motion.

This aggressive, inquisitive nuthatch, with its distinctive black eyestripe, breeds in conifer forests across North America. The bird inhabits mountains in the West; in the East, it is found in lowlands and hills. However, sometimes it breeds in conifer groves away from its core range. Each fall, birds move from their main breeding grounds, but the extent of this exodus varies from year to year, depending on population cycles and food availability.

VOICE Call a one-note tooting sound, often repeated, with strong nasal yet musical quality: *aaank, enk, ink*, rather like a horn.

NESTING Excavates cavity in pine tree; nest of grass lined with feathers, with sticky pine resin applied to entrance; 5–7 eggs, 1 brood; May–July.

FEEDING Probes bark for beetle grubs; also eats insect larvae found on conifer needles; seeds in winter.

TASTY GRUB
This nuthatch has just extracted its dinner from the bark of a tree, a favorite foraging habitat.

SIMILAR SPECIES

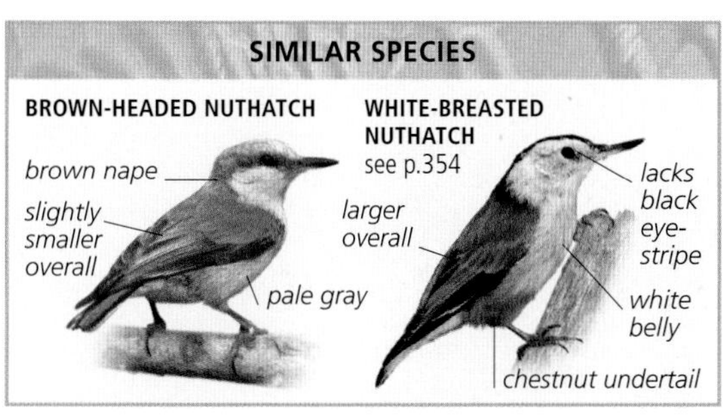
BROWN-HEADED NUTHATCH
brown nape
slightly smaller overall
pale gray
WHITE-BREASTED NUTHATCH
see p.354
larger overall
lacks black eye-stripe
white belly
chestnut undertail

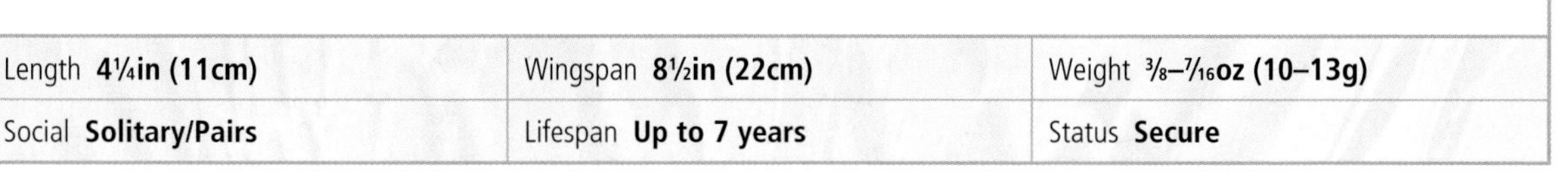

OCCURRENCE
Found year-round in coniferous and mixed hardwood forests. During breeding season, absent from southeastern pine forests, except in the Appalachians. In the west, shares its habitat with Pygmy Nuthatch, but ranges to higher elevations.

Length **4¼in (11cm)**	Wingspan **8½in (22cm)**	Weight **3/8–7/16oz (10–13g)**
Social **Solitary/Pairs**	Lifespan **Up to 7 years**	Status **Secure**

Order **Passeriformes**	Family **Sittidae**	Species ***Sitta carolinensis***

White-breasted Nuthatch

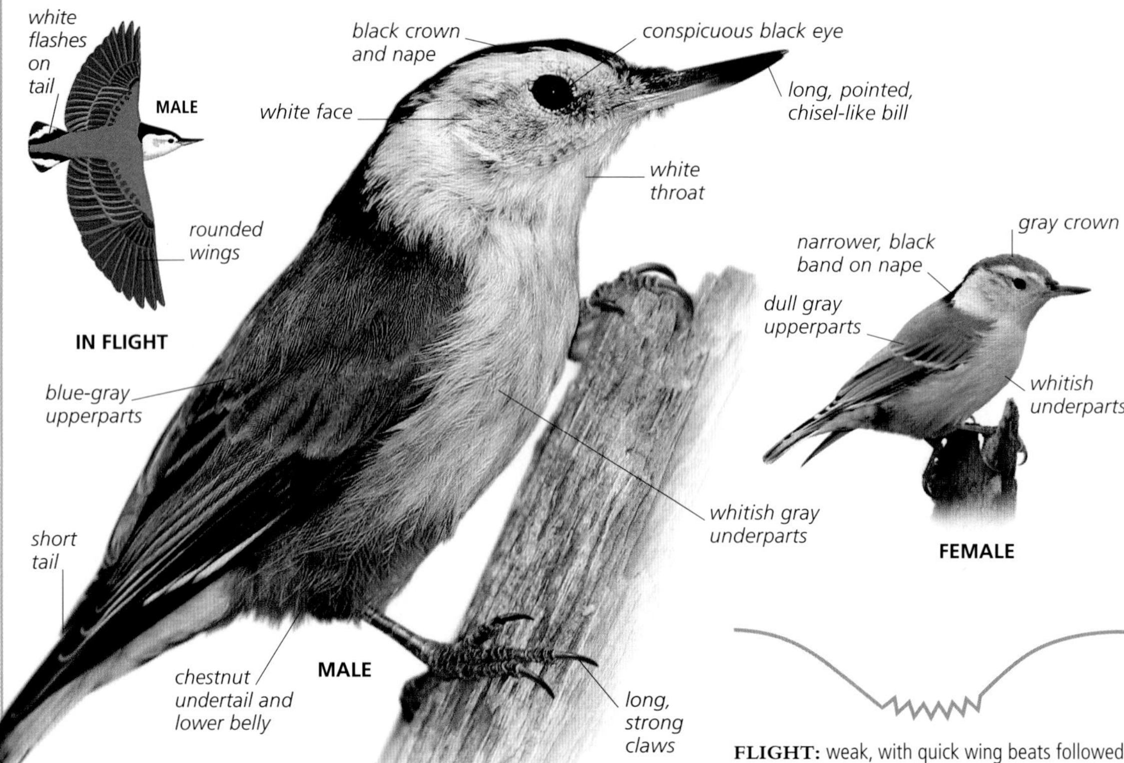
white flashes on tail
MALE
rounded wings
IN FLIGHT
black crown and nape
conspicuous black eye
white face
long, pointed, chisel-like bill
white throat
blue-gray upperparts
short tail
chestnut undertail and lower belly
MALE
long, strong claws
whitish gray underparts
gray crown
narrower, black band on nape
dull gray upperparts
whitish underparts
FEMALE

FLIGHT: weak, with quick wing beats followed by glide; often short, from tree to tree.

The amiable White-breasted Nuthatch inhabits residential neighborhoods across the US and southern Canada, and often visits birdfeeders in winter. The largest of our nuthatches, it spends more time probing furrows and crevices on trunks and boughs than other nuthatches do. It walks irregularly on trees: forward, backward, upside-down, or horizontally. Of the eleven subspecies in its Canada-to-Mexico range, five occur in Canada and in the US. They differ in call notes and, to a lesser extent, in plumage.

VOICE Calls vary geographically: eastern birds nasal *yank yank*; interior birds stuttering *st't't't't*; Pacific slope birds tremulous *yiiiirk*; song of all populations a mellow *tu tu tu tu*, like a flicker, but softer.

NESTING Tree cavity, once used by woodpeckers, lined with grass and hair, adds mud to cavity opening; 5–9 eggs, 1 brood; April–June.

FEEDING Scours bark methodically for insects such as beetle larvae.

UNUSUAL DESCENT
Nuthatches are unusual in that they routinely descend branches and trunks head-first.

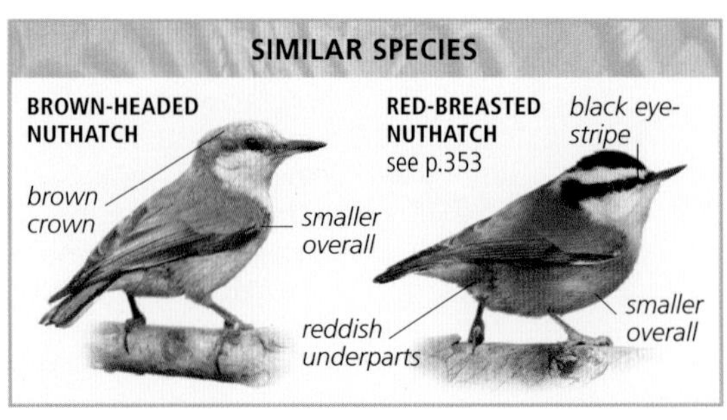
SIMILAR SPECIES
BROWN-HEADED NUTHATCH
brown crown
smaller overall
RED-BREASTED NUTHATCH
see p.353
black eye-stripe
reddish underparts
smaller overall

OCCURRENCE
More liberal than other nuthatches in use of forest types; overlaps with the smaller species in coniferous forest ranges, but also common in broadleaf deciduous or mixed forests; weakly migratory: little movement in most falls, but moderate departures from breeding grounds in some years.

Length **5¾in (14.5cm)**	Wingspan **11in (28cm)**	Weight **11/16–7/8oz (19–25g)**
Social **Solitary/Pairs**	Lifespan **Up to 9 years**	Status **Secure**

Order **Passeriformes**	Family **Certhiidae**	Species ***Certhia americana***

Brown Creeper

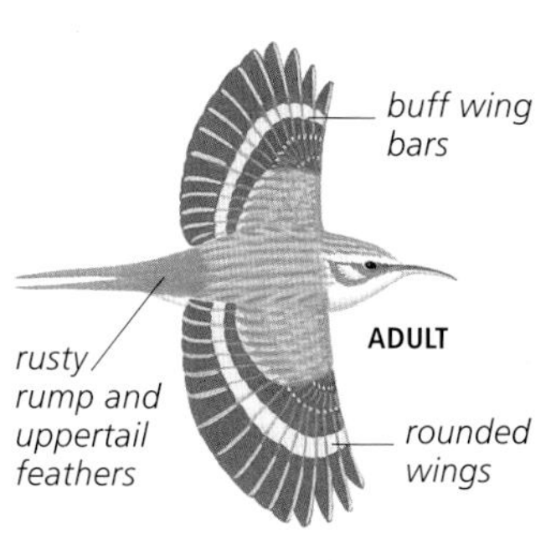
buff wing bars
ADULT
rusty rump and uppertail feathers
rounded wings

IN FLIGHT

thin, downward-curving bill

whitish streak above eye

white chin, throat, and breast

finely streaked crown

mottled brown above

pale streaks on brown background

rusty tint to belly and undertail

long, forked tail

ADULT (SUMMER)

FLIGHT: short, floppy flights from one tree to another; also capable of sustained migration.

Although distinctive, widespread, and fairly common, the Brown Creeper is one of the most understated of the forest birds, with its soft vocalizations and cryptic plumage. As it forages, it hops up a tree trunk, then flies down to another tree, starts again from near the ground, hops up, and so on. These birds have adapted to habitat changes in the Northeast and their numbers have increased in regenerating forests. Mid- and southwestern populations, by contrast, have declined because forest cutting has reduced their breeding habitat. The Brown Creeper is a partial migrant—some individuals move south in the fall, and head north in the spring; others remain close to their breeding grounds.

VOICE High-pitched and easily overlooked call a buzzy *zwisss*, flight call an abrupt *tswit*; song a wheezy jumble of thin whistles and short buzzes.

NESTING Unique hammock-shaped nest, behind piece of peeling bark; 5–6 eggs, 1 brood; May–July.

FEEDING Probes bark for insects, especially larvae, eggs, pupae, and aphids.

SIMILAR SPECIES

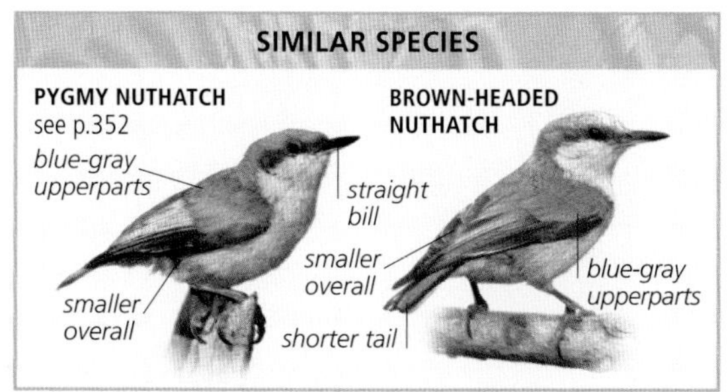
PYGMY NUTHATCH
see p.352
blue-gray upperparts
straight bill
smaller overall
BROWN-HEADED NUTHATCH
smaller overall
shorter tail
blue-gray upperparts

STRONG TAIL
The Brown Creeper uses its forked tail to prop it against the trunk of this tree.

OCCURRENCE
The only North American creeper, it breeds in a variety of forests, particularly fairly moist coniferous or mixed hardwood forests, also large stands with snags and standing dead trees. In winter, seen in small groves without coniferous trees; also in residential districts or suburbs.

Length **5¼in (13.5cm)**	Wingspan **8in (20cm)**	Weight **¼–⅜oz (7–10g)**
Social **Solitary**	Lifespan **Up to 4 years**	Status **Secure**

Order **Passeriformes**	Family **Mimidae**	Species ***Dumetella carolinensis***

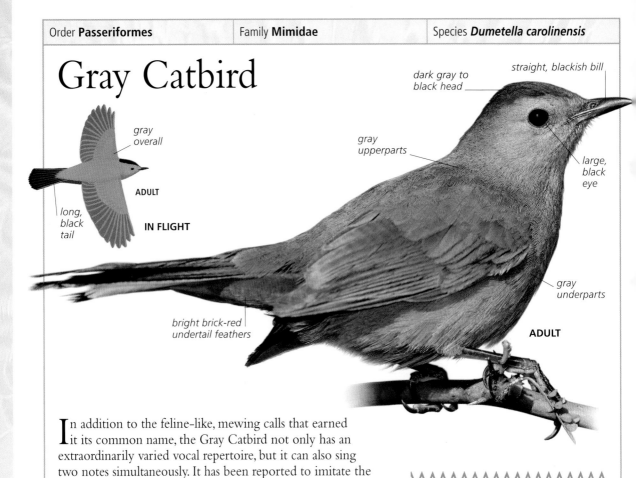

Gray Catbird

gray overall
long, black tail
ADULT
IN FLIGHT

dark gray to black head
straight, blackish bill
gray upperparts
large, black eye
gray underparts
bright brick-red undertail feathers
ADULT

In addition to the feline-like, mewing calls that earned it its common name, the Gray Catbird not only has an extraordinarily varied vocal repertoire, but it can also sing two notes simultaneously. It has been reported to imitate the vocalizations of over 40 bird species, at least one frog species, and several sounds produced by machines and electronic devices. Despite their shy, retiring nature, Gray Catbirds tolerate human presence and will rest in shrubs in suburban and urban lots. Another fascinating skill is the Gray Catbird's ability to recognize and remove eggs of the brood parasite, the Brown-headed Cowbird.

VOICE *Mew* call, like a young kitten; song a long, complex series of unhurried, often grouped notes, sometimes interspersed with whistles and squeaks.

NESTING Large, untidy cup of woven twigs, grass, and hair lined with finer material; 3–4 eggs; 1–2 broods; May–August.

FEEDING Feeds on a wide variety of berries and insects, usually whatever is most abundant in season.

FLIGHT: short flights between habitat patches with constant, medium-speed wing beats.

ANGLED ATTITUDE
Between bouts of feeding, a Gray Catbird often rests with its body and tail at a 50 degree angle.

LARGE BLACK EYES
Peering from the foliage, a Gray Catbird investigates its surroundings.

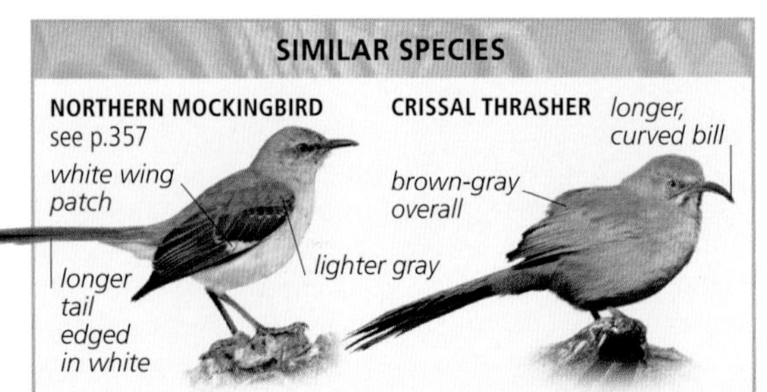
SIMILAR SPECIES
NORTHERN MOCKINGBIRD
see p.357
white wing patch
longer tail edged in white
lighter gray
CRISSAL THRASHER
longer, curved bill
brown-gray overall

OCCURRENCE
Breeds in mixed young to mid-aged forests with abundant undergrowth, from British Columbia east to Maritimes and Newfoundland, and in the US diagonally west-east from Washington State to New Mexico, east to the Gulf Coast, north to New England. Northern population migratory.

Length **8–9½in (20–24cm)**	Wingspan **10–12in (25–30cm)**	Weight **1¼–2⅛oz (35–60g)**
Social **Solitary/Pairs**	Lifespan **Up to 11 years**	Status **Secure**

Order **Passeriformes**	Family **Mimidae**	Species ***Mimus polyglottos***

Northern Mockingbird

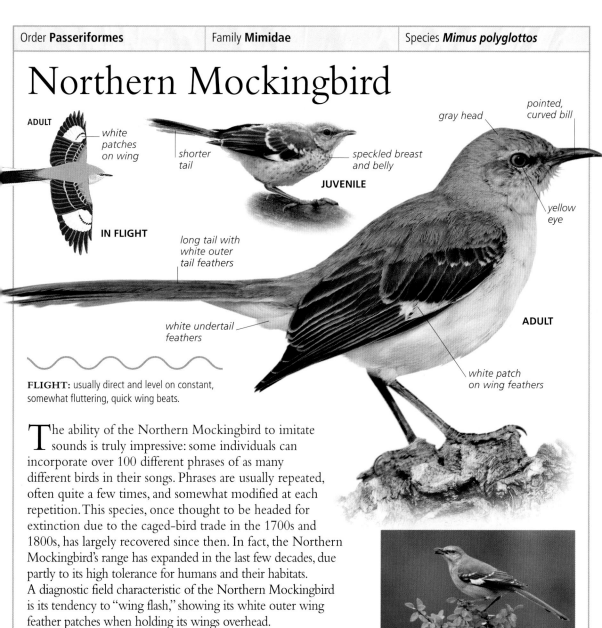

ADULT
white patches on wing
IN FLIGHT

shorter tail
speckled breast and belly
JUVENILE

gray head
pointed, curved bill
yellow eye
long tail with white outer tail feathers
white undertail feathers
white patch on wing feathers
ADULT

FLIGHT: usually direct and level on constant, somewhat fluttering, quick wing beats.

The ability of the Northern Mockingbird to imitate sounds is truly impressive: some individuals can incorporate over 100 different phrases of as many different birds in their songs. Phrases are usually repeated, often quite a few times, and somewhat modified at each repetition. This species, once thought to be headed for extinction due to the caged-bird trade in the 1700s and 1800s, has largely recovered since then. In fact, the Northern Mockingbird's range has expanded in the last few decades, due partly to its high tolerance for humans and their habitats. A diagnostic field characteristic of the Northern Mockingbird is its tendency to "wing flash," showing its white outer wing feather patches when holding its wings overhead.

VOICE Long, complex repertoire often imitating other birds, non-bird noises, and the sounds of mechanical devices.

NESTING Bulky cup of twigs, lined, in shrub or tree; 3–5 eggs; 1–3 broods; March–August.

FEEDING Eats a wide variety of fruit, berries, and insects, including ants, beetles, and grasshoppers.

BERRY PICKER
Northern Mockingbirds love berries, and make good use of them during the fall.

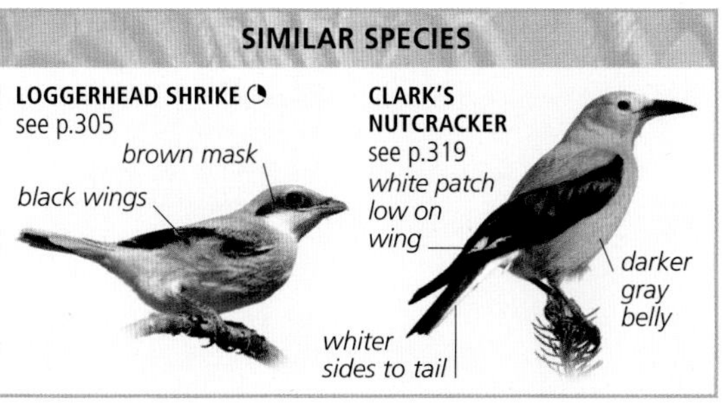
SIMILAR SPECIES
LOGGERHEAD SHRIKE
see p.305
brown mask
black wings
CLARK'S NUTCRACKER
see p.319
white patch low on wing
darker gray belly
whiter sides to tail

OCCURRENCE
Widespread in the US from coast to coast south of the timberline, primarily along edges of disturbed habitats, including young forests and especially suburban and urban areas with shrubs or hedges. Breeding range has extended into southern Canada.

Length **8½–10in (22–25cm)**	Wingspan **13–15in (33–38cm)**	Weight **1⁹⁄₁₆–2oz (45–55g)**
Social **Pairs**	Lifespan **Up to 20 years**	Status **Secure**

Order **Passeriformes**	Family **Mimidae**	Species ***Oreoscoptes montanus***

Sage Thrasher

ADULT

thin, white wing bars

gray overall

white corners on wedge-shaped tail

IN FLIGHT

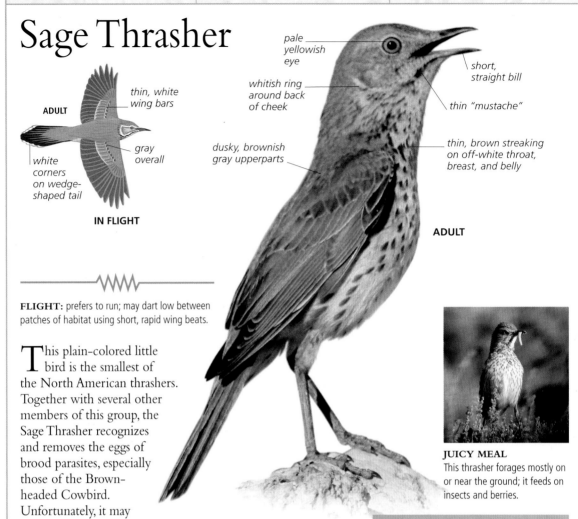

pale yellowish eye

whitish ring around back of cheek

short, straight bill

thin "mustache"

dusky, brownish gray upperparts

thin, brown streaking on off-white throat, breast, and belly

ADULT

FLIGHT: prefers to run; may dart low between patches of habitat using short, rapid wing beats.

This plain-colored little bird is the smallest of the North American thrashers. Together with several other members of this group, the Sage Thrasher recognizes and removes the eggs of brood parasites, especially those of the Brown-headed Cowbird. Unfortunately, it may also be the least studied of the thrasher group, perhaps because the dense nature of its habitat makes study difficult. The English name, "Sage Thrasher," truly describes this bird's western habitat.

VOICE Song varies in duration: low, repeated, very musical notes or phrases that may blend together in a melodious song.

NESTING Large cup with stick frame lined with grass, horse hair, sheep's wool, and fur; 3–6 eggs; 1-2 broods; April–July.

FEEDING Eats insects, especially ants and beetles, on the ground; will also consume berries when seasonally available.

JUICY MEAL
This thrasher forages mostly on or near the ground; it feeds on insects and berries.

SHOW-OFF TENDENCIES
Males attract mates and defend their territory with raised wings, in a fluttering display.

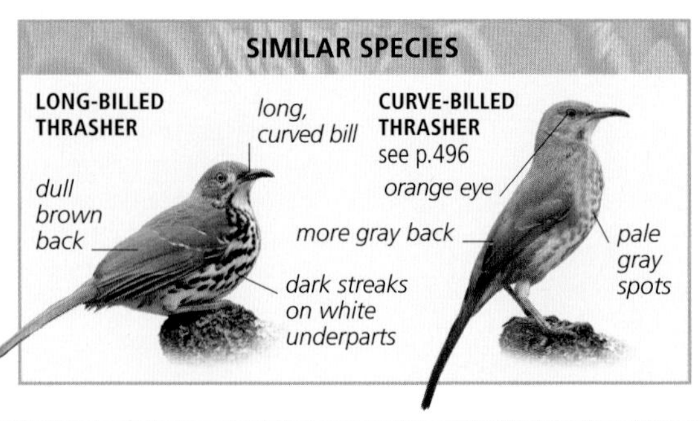
SIMILAR SPECIES
LONG-BILLED THRASHER
long, curved bill
dull brown back
dark streaks on white underparts
CURVE-BILLED THRASHER
see p.496
orange eye
more gray back
pale gray spots

OCCURRENCE
Very closely associated with sagebrush habitat in low-elevation, semi-arid valleys of the western US and southwestern Canada. Winters from southwestern US to Baja California and continental Mexico, southwards to Sonora and Coquila.

Length **8–9in (20–23cm)**	Wingspan **10–13in (25–33cm)**	Weight **1 7/16–1 3/4oz (40–50g)**
Social **Solitary/Pairs**	Lifespan **Unknown**	Status **Localized**

Order **Passeriformes**	Family **Mimidae**	Species ***Toxostoma rufum***

Brown Thrasher

rufous wings and upperparts
ADULT
long tail with pale outer tips
IN FLIGHT

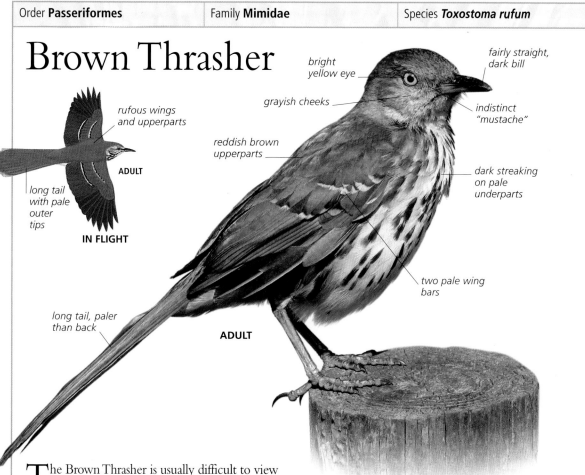

bright yellow eye
fairly straight, dark bill
grayish cheeks
indistinct "mustache"
reddish brown upperparts
dark streaking on pale underparts
two pale wing bars
long tail, paler than back
ADULT

The Brown Thrasher is usually difficult to view clearly because it keeps to dense underbrush. Like most other thrashers, this species prefers running or hopping to flying. When nesting, it can recognize and remove the eggs of brood parasites like the Brown-headed Cowbird. The current population decline is most likely the result of fragmentation of large, wooded habitats into patches, which lack the forest interior habitat this species needs.

VOICE Calls varied, including rasping sounds; song a long series of musical notes, sometimes imitating other species; repeats phrase twice before moving onto the next one.

NESTING Bulky cup of twigs, close to ground, lined with leaves, grass, bark; 3–5 eggs; 1 brood; April–July.

FEEDING Mainly insects (especially beetles) and worms gathered from leaf litter on the forest floor; will peck at cultivated grains, nuts, berries, and fruit.

FLIGHT: slow and heavy with deep wing beats; below treetops, especially in and around ground.

STREAKED BREAST
Displaying its heavily streaked underparts, this Brown Thrasher is perched and ready to sing.

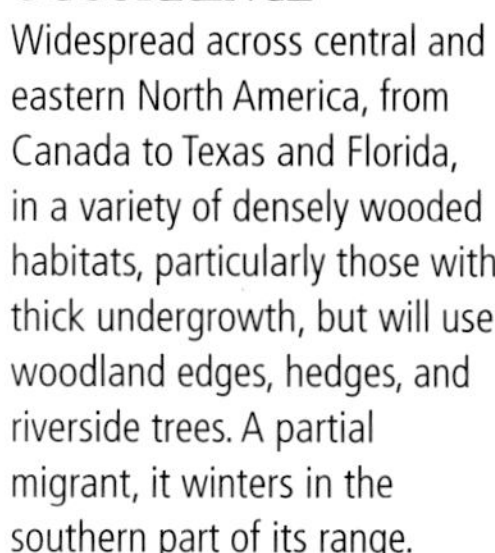

OCCURRENCE
Widespread across central and eastern North America, from Canada to Texas and Florida, in a variety of densely wooded habitats, particularly those with thick undergrowth, but will use woodland edges, hedges, and riverside trees. A partial migrant, it winters in the southern part of its range.

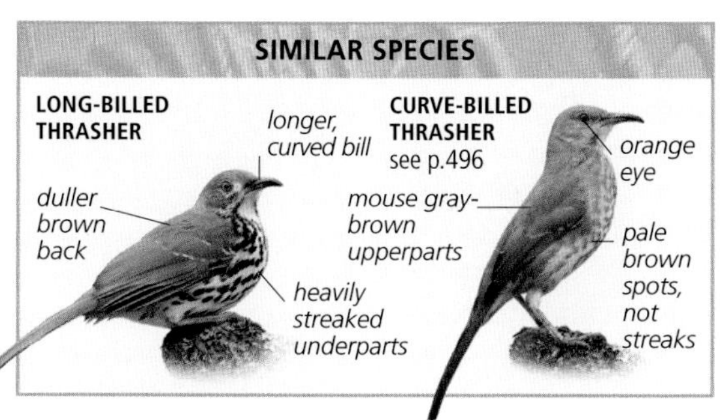
SIMILAR SPECIES
LONG-BILLED THRASHER
longer, curved bill
duller brown back
heavily streaked underparts
CURVE-BILLED THRASHER
see p.496
orange eye
mouse gray-brown upperparts
pale brown spots, not streaks

Length **10–12in (25–30cm)**	Wingspan **11–14in (28–36cm)**	Weight **2⅛–2⅞oz (60–80g)**
Social **Solitary/Flocks**	Lifespan **Up to 13 years**	Status **Declining**

Order **Passeriformes**	Family **Sturnidae**	Species ***Sturnus vulgaris***

European Starling

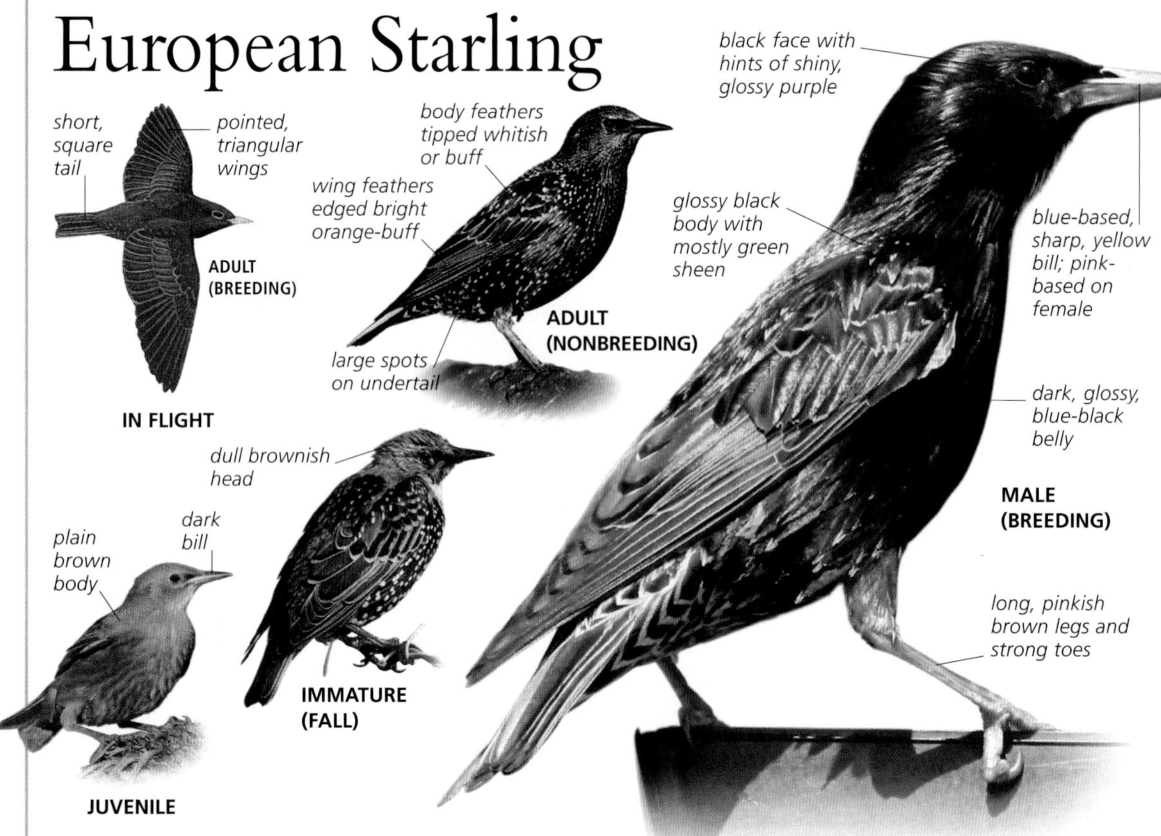
short, square tail
pointed, triangular wings
ADULT (BREEDING)
IN FLIGHT
body feathers tipped whitish or buff
wing feathers edged bright orange-buff
large spots on undertail
ADULT (NONBREEDING)
black face with hints of shiny, glossy purple
glossy black body with mostly green sheen
blue-based, sharp, yellow bill; pink-based on female
dark, glossy, blue-black belly
MALE (BREEDING)
long, pinkish brown legs and strong toes
dull brownish head
plain brown body
dark bill
IMMATURE (FALL)
JUVENILE

This distinctive non-native species is perhaps the most successful bird in North America—and probably the most maligned. In the 1890s, 100 European Starlings were released in New York City's Central Park; these were the ancestors of the many millions of birds that now live all across the US and Canada. This adaptable and aggressive bird competes with native species for nest sites, and usually wins—even against larger species such as the Northern Flicker.

VOICE Highly varied; gives whooshing *sssssheer*, often in flight; also whistled *wheeeooo*; song an elaborate pulsing series with slurred whistles and clicking notes; imitates other species' vocalizations.

NESTING Natural or artificial cavity of any sort; 4–6 eggs; 1–2 broods; March–July.

FEEDING Omnivorous; picks at anything that might be edible; insects and berries are common food items; also visits birdfeeders and trashcans; often feeds on grubs in lawns.

FLIGHT: individuals fly in direct, buzzy manner; flocks bunch up tightly in flight.

INSECT EATER
Despite its parents' omnivorous diet, the nestlings are fed almost exclusively on insects and larvae.

SIMILAR SPECIES

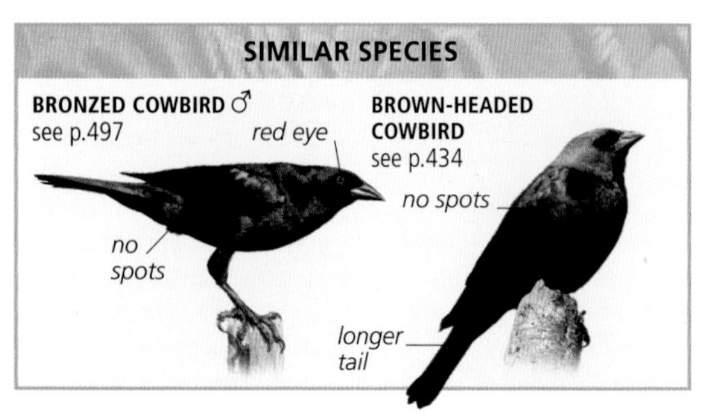
BRONZED COWBIRD ♂
see p.497
red eye
no spots
BROWN-HEADED COWBIRD
see p.434
no spots
longer tail

OCCURRENCE
In North America from southern Canada to the US–Mexico border; also Puerto Rico and other Caribbean islands. Common to abundant in cities, towns, and farmlands; also occurs in relatively "wild" settings far from human habitation. Forms flocks at all times, huge in winter.

Length **8½in (21cm)**	Wingspan **16in (41cm)**	Weight **2⅝– 3⅜oz (75–95g)**
Social **Colonies**	Lifespan **Up to 17 years**	Status **Secure**

Family **Turdidae**

THRUSHES

MOST THRUSHES ARE medium-sized brown- or olive-brown-backed birds with varying amounts of spotting or speckling underneath. Although undistinguished in color, they more than make up for their drab plumage with beautiful flutelike songs. By contrast, the Varied Thrush, which is the sole member of the *Ixoreus* genus, differs dramatically from many other thrushes with its bold black-and-rust pattern, and is one of the most distinctive thrushes in Canada and the US. Similarly, the brightly colored bluebirds, which have been the target of many successful conservation efforts, and the duller Townsend's Solitaire, are both striking enough to stand out from other thrushes, although juvenile birds have markings that are similar to other species.

ORCHARD DWELLER
Bluebirds, for example this Mountain Bluebird, favor orchards far more than other thrushes.

GROUND BIRDS
Though they perch to sing, thrushes, including this Varied Thrush, spend a lot of their time on or near the ground.

Family **Motacillidae**

WAGTAILS & PIPITS

THESE TWO GROUPS OF ground-dwelling songbirds are represented by more than 50 species worldwide. Only four of these, however, are found regularly in North America.

WAGTAILS

Named for their habit of constantly bobbing their long, slender tails up and down, wagtails' plumage contrasts bright colors with black. Although primarily a European genus, one species is considered a regular breeder in Canada, and two others are routinely sighted along the Bering Sea coast and Aleutian Islands.

PIPITS

Unlike wagtails, the two species of pipit that breed in North America also winter there. Very much birds of open, treeless country, both pipit species are likely to be seen on their widespread wintering grounds more often than in their breeding range.

COUNTRY-LOVERS
Pipits, such as this female American Pipit, like to live in open countryside.

Order **Passeriformes**	Family **Turdidae**	Species ***Ixoreus naevius***

Varied Thrush

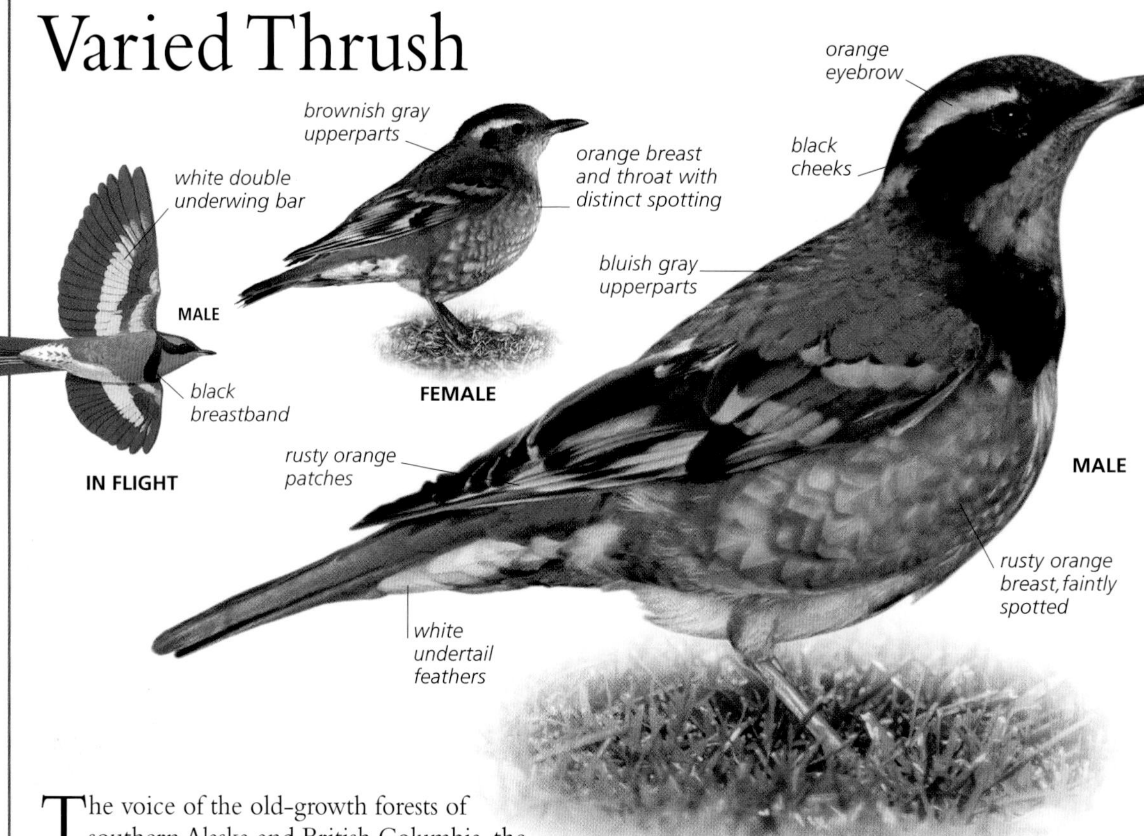

white double underwing bar
MALE
black breastband
IN FLIGHT
brownish gray upperparts
orange breast and throat with distinct spotting
FEMALE
orange eyebrow
black cheeks
bluish gray upperparts
rusty orange patches
MALE
rusty orange breast, faintly spotted
white undertail feathers

The voice of the old-growth forests of southern Alaska and British Columbia, the Varied Thrush is also the most beautiful of the thrushes. Its song is so haunting and ethereal that to hear it can give the listener goosebumps. To see the bird is another matter, as it is often rather shy, except when bringing food to its nestlings. The Varied Thrush's orange and black head, deep bluish black back, and its two rusty wing bars are an unmistakable combination of markings.

VOICE Song is a single note that rises or falls in tone; repeats its song after about 10 seconds; sings for long periods of time from one perch, then moves to another to start anew.

NESTING Bulky cup of twigs, dead leaves, pieces of bark, stems of grass and weeds, lined with fine grass stems, mainly in conifer trees, against trunk; 3–4 eggs; 1–2 broods; April–August.

FEEDING Feeds on insects and caterpillars while breeding; fruit and berries in winter.

FLIGHT: rapid wing beats; fast and direct.

SUMMER DIET
During its breeding season, this thrush forages for insects, often outside the forest interior.

SIMILAR SPECIES

AMERICAN ROBIN
see p.373
dark back
yellow bill
brick-red breast

FOREST DWELLER
The Varied Thrush is often difficult to find, because it inhabits dark forests.

OCCURRENCE
Breeds from Alaska south to Montana; prefers moist coniferous forests throughout breeding range; likely to be found in mature forests. Winters south of its breeding range; habitat varies between ravines and thickets to suburban lawns. Habitat in migration much like winter choices.

Length **7–10in (18–25cm)**	Wingspan **13–15in (33–38cm)**	Weight **2¼–3½oz (65–100g)**
Social **Solitary/Flocks**	Lifespan **At least 5 years**	Status **Declining**

Order **Passeriformes**	Family **Turdidae**	Species ***Sialia sialis***

Eastern Bluebird

MALE
bluish gray underwings
white belly
rufous breast and throat
IN FLIGHT

bright blue upperparts
chestnut brown chin, throat, breast, and flanks
white belly
white undertail
MALE

spotted throat and breast
gray-brown upperparts
JUVENILE

pale chestnut throat
gray upperparts
blue wings, rump, and tail
FEMALE

The Eastern Bluebird's vibrant blue and chestnut body is a beloved sight in eastern North America, especially after the remarkable comeback of the species in the past 30 years. After much of the bird's habitat was eliminated by agriculture in the mid-1900s, volunteers offered the bluebirds nest boxes as alternatives to their tree cavities, and they took to these like ducks to water. The Eastern Bluebird's mating system involves males seeking (or not minding) multiple partners.

VOICE Main song a melodious series of soft, whistled notes; *churr-wi* or *churr-li*; songs for mating and asserting territoriality.

NESTING Cavity nester, in trees or man-made boxes; nest of grass lined with grass, weeds, and twigs; uses old nests of other species; 3–7 eggs; 2 broods; February–September.

FEEDING Feeds on insects, like grasshoppers, and caterpillars in breeding season; in winter, also takes fruits and plants.

FLIGHT: shallow wing beats; slow and easy.

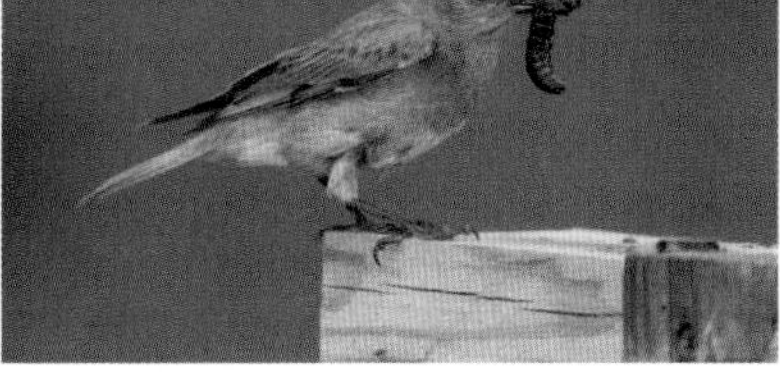

HOME DELIVERY
A female bluebird delivers food to a nest box.

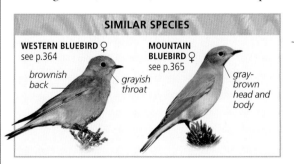

SIMILAR SPECIES

WESTERN BLUEBIRD ♀ see p.364
brownish back
grayish throat

MOUNTAIN BLUEBIRD ♀ see p.365
gray-brown head and body

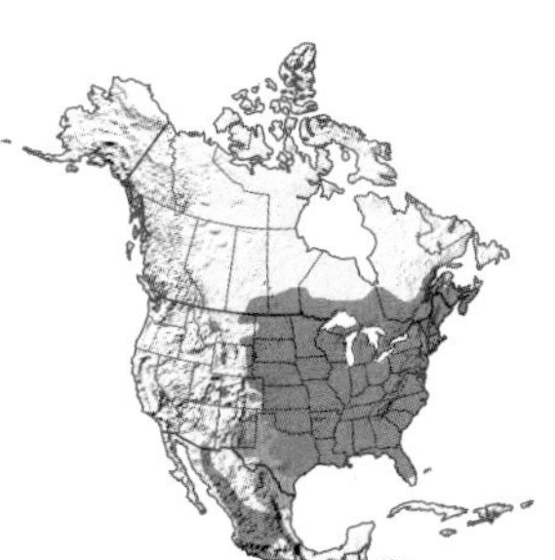

OCCURRENCE
Found in eastern Canada and the eastern US, where it lives in clearings and woodland edges; occupies multiple open habitats in rural, urban, and suburban areas: woodlands, plains, orchards, parks, and spacious lawns. Breeds and winters across the eastern half of the US.

Length **6–8in (15–20cm)**	Wingspan **10–13in (25–33cm)**	Weight **1¹⁄₁₆ oz (30g)**
Social **Flocks**	Lifespan **8–10 years**	Status **Vulnerable**

Order **Passeriformes**	Family **Turdidae**	Species ***Sialia mexicana***

Western Bluebird

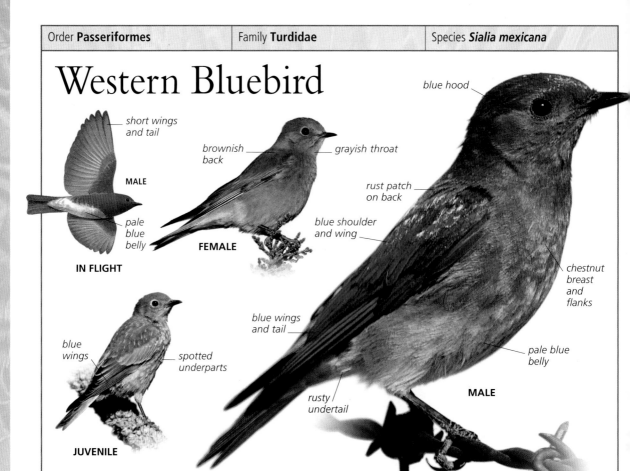

short wings and tail
MALE
pale blue belly
IN FLIGHT

brownish back
grayish throat
FEMALE

blue wings
spotted underparts
JUVENILE

blue hood
rust patch on back
blue shoulder and wing
chestnut breast and flanks
blue wings and tail
pale blue belly
rusty undertail
MALE

Very similar to its close relative, the Eastern Bluebird, but with a distribution restricted to the western part of the continent, the male Western Bluebird is endowed with a spectacular plumage—brilliant blue upperparts and deep chestnut-orange underparts. Unlike the Eastern Bluebird, the Western Bluebird has a brown back and a complete blue hood. Females and juveniles are harder to distinguish, but their ranges are quite different.

VOICE Vocalizations similar to those of the Eastern Bluebird; calls soft *few, few* or *fewrr-fewrr*; song a pleasant, soft series of churring notes, all strung together, often given at dawn.

NESTING Shallow cup of dry grass and feathers in natural tree cavity or old woodpecker cavity; 4–6 eggs; 1–2 broods; March–July.

FEEDING Feeds mainly on insects in breeding season; eats berries, such as juniper, in winter.

FLIGHT: slow and easy-looking, with shallow wing beats.

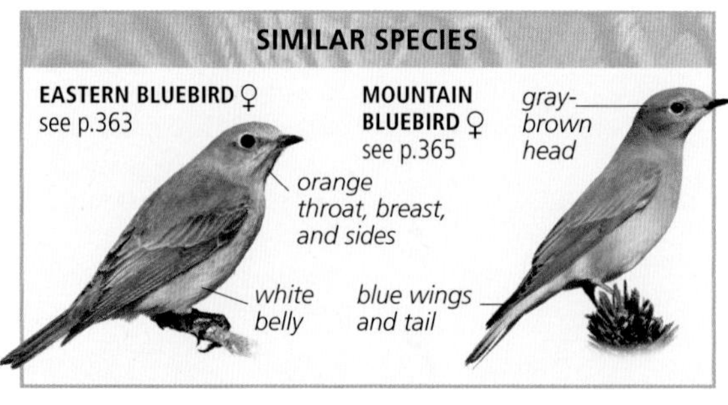
SIMILAR SPECIES
EASTERN BLUEBIRD ♀
see p.363
orange throat, breast, and sides
white belly
MOUNTAIN BLUEBIRD ♀
see p.365
gray-brown head
blue wings and tail

PERCHED MALE
The Western Bluebird hunts from low perches, from which it takes insects from the ground or air.

OCCURRENCE
During breeding season, open woodlands (coniferous and deciduous) and forest edges. In winter, moves to lower elevations and occupies open and semi-open areas such as pinyon-juniper forests and deserts. Partial migrant; northern birds move south where southern breeders reside.

Length **6–7in (15–18cm)**	Wingspan **11½–13in (29–33cm)**	Weight **⅞–1$\frac{1}{16}$oz (25–30g)**
Social **Winter flocks**	Lifespan **Up to 7 years**	Status **Secure**

Order **Passeriformes**	Family **Turdidae**	Species ***Sialia currucoides***

Mountain Bluebird

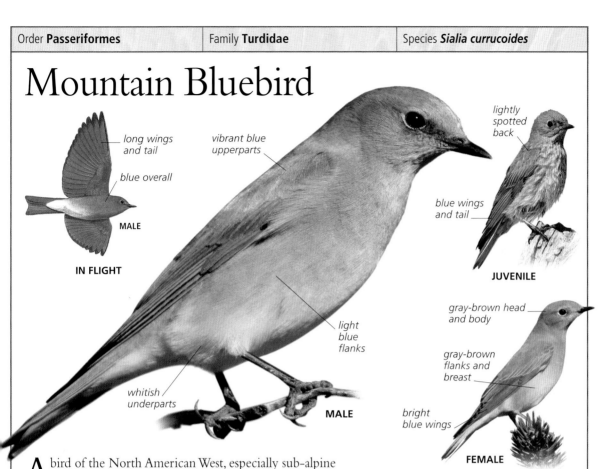

long wings and tail
blue overall
MALE
IN FLIGHT

vibrant blue upperparts
light blue flanks
whitish underparts
MALE

lightly spotted back
blue wings and tail
JUVENILE

gray-brown head and body
gray-brown flanks and breast
bright blue wings
FEMALE

A bird of the North American West, especially sub-alpine meadows, the Mountain Bluebird is as striking as the other two *Sialia* species, but, unlike them, lacks any reddish chestnut in its plumage. It is also more slender-looking, and flies in an almost lazy manner. More often than its two relatives, it feeds by hovering, kestrel-like, over meadows, before pouncing on insects. Males guard their mates from pair-bond time to egg-hatching time.

VOICE Calls rolled, soft churring; one song, loud but infrequent, similar to the American Robin's song—*sing-song cheerily cheer-up cheerio*; the other, soft and repetitive whistle.

NESTING Cavity nest of grass, weeds, and bark; 5–6 eggs; 2 broods; May–July.

FEEDING Insects, including crickets, grasshoppers, bees, and caterpillars, dominate its diet year round; also berries.

FLIGHT: slow unhurried, almost leisurely, with shallow wing beats.

BERRY LOVER
Berries are an important part of the bird's diet along with insects and caterpillars.

OCCURRENCE
Breeds in western North America, in grassland or open canyons with scattered trees, or alpine parklands. In winter, prefers open habitats and avoids dry areas. Winter habitat includes juniper forest and Ponderosa Pine in the south of its territory.

SIMILAR SPECIES
EASTERN BLUEBIRD ♀
see p.363
brownish back
white belly
WESTERN BLUEBIRD ♀
see p.364
grayish throat
pale orange on breast and flanks
TOWNSEND'S SOLITAIRE
see p.366
white eye-ring
gray overall
longer tail

Length **6–8in (15–20cm)**	Wingspan **11–12½in (28–32cm)**	Weight **1 1/16oz (30g)**
Social **Flocks**	Lifespan **At least 5 years**	Status **Secure**

Order **Passeriformes**	Family **Muscicapidae**	Species ***Myadestes townsendi***

Townsend's Solitaire

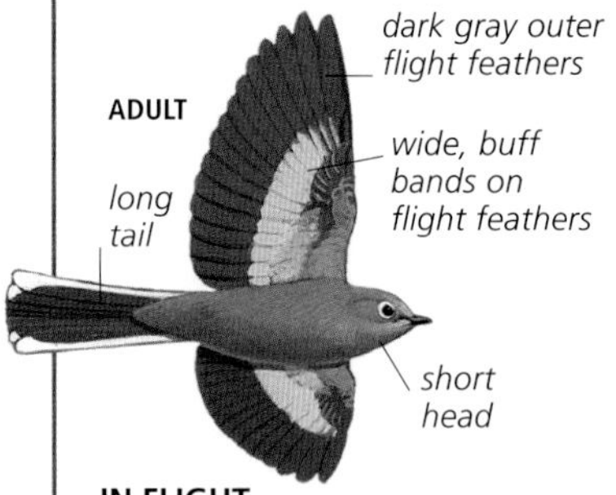

ADULT

dark gray outer flight feathers

wide, buff bands on flight feathers

long tail

short head

IN FLIGHT

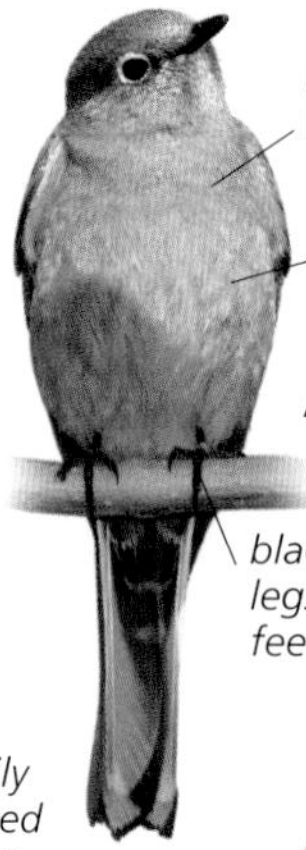

plain gray

upright posture

ADULT

black legs and feet

spotted back

heavily spotted breast

JUVENILE

long tail

large, black eye

white eye-ring

gray upperparts and head

short, black bill

paler underparts

ADULT

pale chestnut-tan patches

long, dark tail with white outer feathers

The rather shy Townsend's Solitaire inhabits most of western North America, especially high-elevation coniferous forests of the Sierras and Rockies. Its drab gray plumage, with a chestnut-tan wing pattern, remains the same throughout the year, and the sexes look alike. From a perch high on a branch, Townsend's Solitaire darts after flying insects and snaps its bill shut after catching its prey, unlike other thrush-like birds.

VOICE Calls are single-note, high-pitched whistles; sings all year, but especially when establishing territories; main song robin-like, full of rolled or trilled sounds, interspersed with squeaky notes.

NESTING Cup of pine needles, dry grass, weed stems, and bark on ground or under overhang; 4 eggs; 1–2 broods; May–August.

FEEDING Forages for a wide variety of insects and spiders during breeding season; feeds on fruits and berries after breeding, particularly junipers.

FLIGHT: unhurried motion, usually over short distances, with slow, steady wing beats.

JUNIPER LOVER
Solitaires love the berry-like cones of junipers, which they eat to supplement their winter diet.

SIMILAR SPECIES

MOUNTAIN BLUEBIRD ♀
see p.365
dull bluish back
blue in wings and tail
short tail

GRAY PLUMAGE
Townsend's Solitaire is a drab gray overall, but a conspicuous white eye-ring.

OCCURRENCE
During breeding season, found in open conifer forests along steep slopes or areas with landslides; during winter, at lower elevations, in open woodlands where junipers are abundant. Partial-migrant northern populations move south in winter, as far as central Mexico.

Length **8–8½in (20–22cm)**	Wingspan **13–14½in (33–37cm)**	Weight **1¹⁄₁₆–1¼oz (30–35g)**
Social **Solitary**	Lifespan **Up to 5 years**	Status **Secure**

Order **Passeriformes**	Family **Turdidae**	Species ***Catharus fuscescens***

Veery

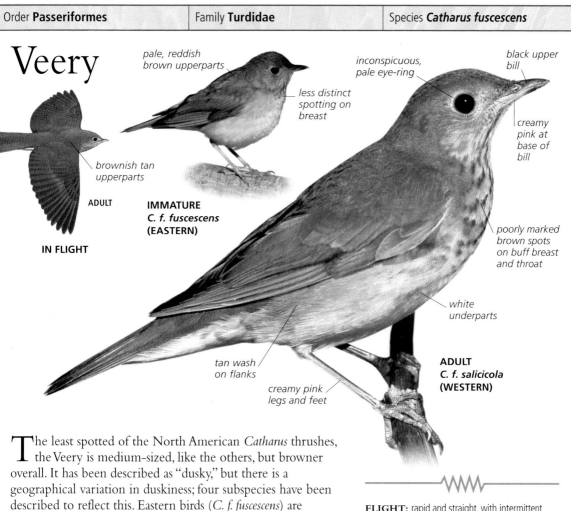

pale, reddish brown upperparts
less distinct spotting on breast
brownish tan upperparts
ADULT
IMMATURE
C. f. fuscescens
(EASTERN)
IN FLIGHT
inconspicuous, pale eye-ring
black upper bill
creamy pink at base of bill
poorly marked brown spots on buff breast and throat
white underparts
tan wash on flanks
creamy pink legs and feet
ADULT
C. f. salicicola
(WESTERN)

The least spotted of the North American *Catharus* thrushes, the Veery is medium-sized, like the others, but browner overall. It has been described as "dusky," but there is a geographical variation in duskiness; four subspecies have been described to reflect this. Eastern birds (*C. f. fuscescens*) are ruddier than their western relations (*C. f. salicicola*). The Veery is a long-distance migrant, spending the northern winter months in central Brazil, in a variety of tropical habitats.

VOICE A series of descending *da-vee-ur, vee-ur, veer, veer,* somewhat bi-tonal, sounding like the name Veery; call a rather soft *veer.*

NESTING Cup of dead leaves, bark, weed stems, and moss on or near ground; 4 eggs; 1–2 broods; May–July.

FEEDING Forages on the ground for insects, spiders, snails; eats fruit and berries after breeding.

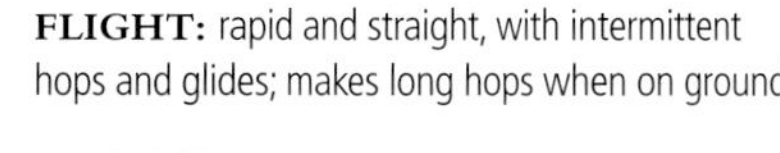

FLIGHT: rapid and straight, with intermittent hops and glides; makes long hops when on ground.

DAMP DWELLINGS
The Veery breeds in damp habitats such as moist wooded areas or in trees near or in swamps.

OCCURRENCE
In summer, mainly found in damp deciduous forests, but in some places habitat near rivers preferred. In winter, choice of habitat flexible; found in tropical broadleaf evergreen forest, on forest edges, in open woodlands, and in second-growth areas regenerating after fires or clearing.

SIMILAR SPECIES
GRAY-CHEEKED THRUSH
see p.368
gray face
bold black-brown breast spots
BICKNELL'S THRUSH
see p.369
bold brown breast spots
grayish brown upperparts
SWAINSON'S THRUSH
see p.370
buffy-colored face
bold brown-black breast spots

Length **7in (18cm)**	Wingspan **11–11½in (28–29cm)**	Weight **1¹⁄₁₆–2oz (28–54g)**
Social **Pairs**	Lifespan **Up to 10 years**	Status **Declining**

Order **Passeriformes**	Family **Turdidae**	Species ***Catharus minimus***

Gray-cheeked Thrush

ADULT

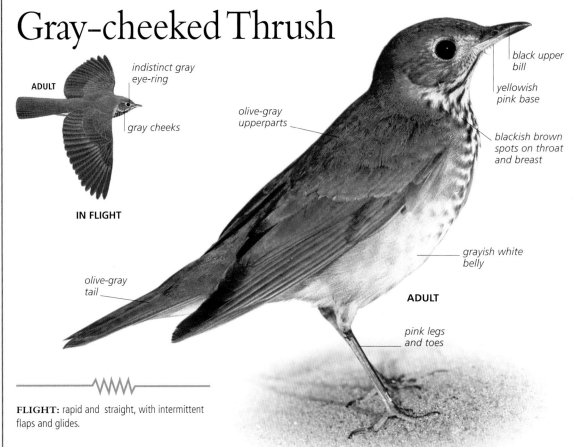

indistinct gray eye-ring

gray cheeks

IN FLIGHT

olive-gray upperparts

black upper bill

yellowish pink base

blackish brown spots on throat and breast

grayish white belly

olive-gray tail

ADULT

pink legs and toes

FLIGHT: rapid and straight, with intermittent flaps and glides.

The Gray-cheeked Thrush is the least known of the four North American *Catharus* thrushes because it breeds in remote areas of Canada and Alaska. In fact, most of the existing information on this species is a result of research on the Bicknell's Thrush, which was considered to be a subspecies of the Gray-cheeked Thrush until 1993. During migration, the Gray-cheeked Thrush is more likely to be heard in flight at night than seen on the ground by birdwatchers.

VOICE Call a thin *kweer*, sometimes two notes; song flute-like, somewhat nasal, several notes ending on a lower pitch.

NESTING Cup of grass, twigs, moss, dead leaves, and mud, placed near ground in shrubbery; 4 eggs; 1 brood; May–July.

FEEDING Forages insects, including beetles, ants, spiders, earthworms, and fruits.

FEEDING HABITAT
A Gray-cheeked Thrush hops across the forest floor looking for prey.

SIMILAR SPECIES

BICKNELL'S THRUSH
olive-brown upperparts
brownish spots
see p.369

MIGRATION PATTERN
During migration, this bird can be seen near a variety of sites with trees or shrubs.

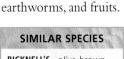

OCCURRENCE
On breeding grounds, occupies densely vegetated areas with small shrubs; preference for spruce forests in northern Canada and Alaska. During migration, favors wooded areas with dense understory. In winter, prefers forested areas and secondary succession woodlands.

Length **6½–7in (16–18cm)**	Wingspan **11½–13½in (29–34cm)**	Weight **7/8–1 1/16 oz (26–30g)**
Social **Mixed flocks**	Lifespan **Up to 7 years**	Status **Secure**

Order **Passeriformes**	Family **Turdidae**	Species ***Catharus bicknelli***

Bicknell's Thrush

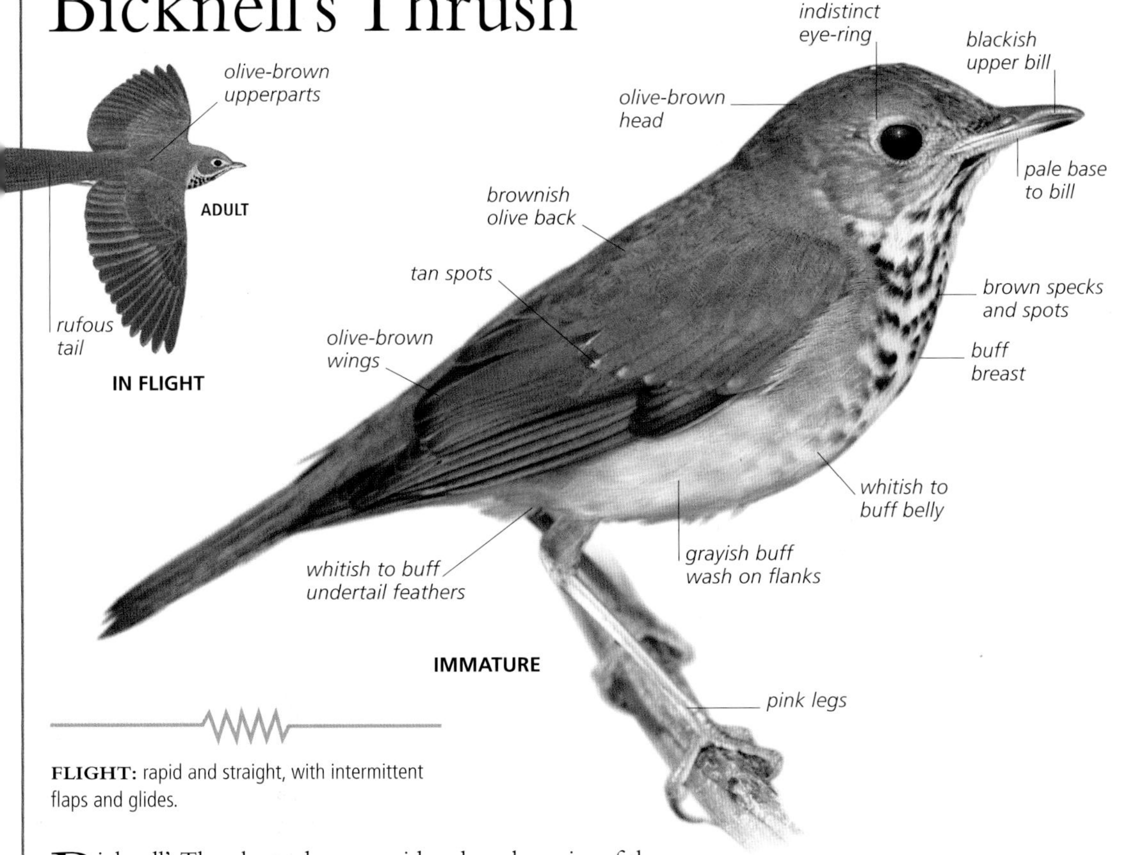

olive-brown upperparts

ADULT

rufous tail

IN FLIGHT

indistinct eye-ring
blackish upper bill
olive-brown head
pale base to bill
brownish olive back
tan spots
brown specks and spots
olive-brown wings
buff breast
whitish to buff belly
grayish buff wash on flanks
whitish to buff undertail feathers

IMMATURE

pink legs

FLIGHT: rapid and straight, with intermittent flaps and glides.

Bicknell's Thrush was long considered a subspecies of the Gray-cheeked Thrush, until 1993 when it was shown to be a distinct species with a slight difference in color, song, habitat, and migration. In the field, it is best distinguished from the Gray-cheeked Thrush by its song, which is less full and lower in pitch. Bicknell's Thrush breeds only in dwarf conifer forests on mountain tops in the northeastern US and adjacent Canada, usually above 3,000ft (1,000m). Habitat loss threatens this species on its wintering grounds in Cuba, Hispaniola, and Puerto Rico. Males and females mate with multiple partners in a single season; because of this, males may care for young in multiple nests.

VOICE Call *pheeuw*, one or two notes; complicated flute-like song of about four parts, ending with rising pitch; males sing, especially during flight; females rarely sing; song varies among populations.

NESTING Cup of moss and evergreen twigs, near ground; 3–4 eggs; 1 brood; June–August.

FEEDING Feeds mainly on caterpillars and insects; in addition, fruit during migration and possibly in winter.

MOUNTAIN-TOP BREEDING
This species breeds in high-elevation woodland areas, especially in conifers.

SIMILAR SPECIES

GRAY-CHEEKED THRUSH
see p.368

olive-gray brown
grayish face

OCCURRENCE
Restricted to dense spruce or fir forest at or near the treeline, at 3,000ft (1,000m), often in disturbed areas undergoing successional changes. During migration, found in a variety of habitats, such as woodlots and beaches. In winter, strong preference for wet mountainous Caribbean forests.

Length **6½–7in (16–18cm)**	Wingspan **12in (30cm)**	Weight **⅞–1¹⁄₁₆ oz (26–30g)**
Social **Solitary/Small flocks**	Lifespan **Up to 8 years**	Status **Vulnerable**

Order **Passeriformes**	Family **Turdidae**	Species ***Catharus ustulatus***

Swainson's Thrush

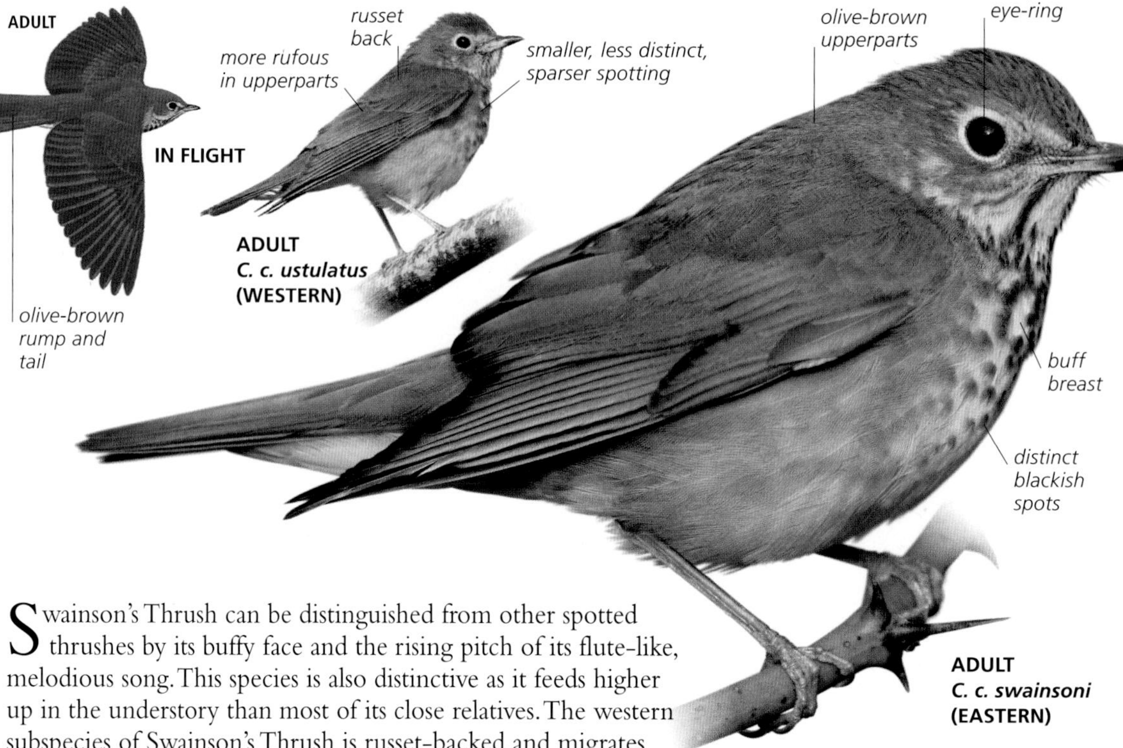
ADULT
IN FLIGHT
olive-brown rump and tail
russet back
more rufous in upperparts
smaller, less distinct, sparser spotting
ADULT
C. c. ustulatus
(WESTERN)
olive-brown upperparts
buffy eye-ring
buff breast
distinct blackish spots
ADULT
C. c. swainsoni
(EASTERN)

Swainson's Thrush can be distinguished from other spotted thrushes by its buffy face and the rising pitch of its flute-like, melodious song. This species is also distinctive as it feeds higher up in the understory than most of its close relatives. The western subspecies of Swainson's Thrush is russet-backed and migrates to Central America for the winter, while the other populations are olive-backed and winter in South America.

VOICE Single-note call *whit* or *whooit*; main song delivered by males, several phrases, each one spiraling upward; flute-like song is given during breeding and migration.

NESTING Open cup of twigs, moss, dead leaves, bark, and mud, on branches near trunks of small trees or in shrubs; 3–4 eggs; 1–2 broods; April–July.

FEEDING Forages in the air, using fly-catching methods to capture a wide range of insects during breeding season; berries during migration and in winter.

DISTINCTIVE SONG
This bird's song distinguishes it from other thrushes.

FLIGHT: rapid and straight, with intermittent flaps and glides.

TREE DWELLER
Shy and retiring, Swainson's Thrush feeds in trees more than other *Catharus* thrushes.

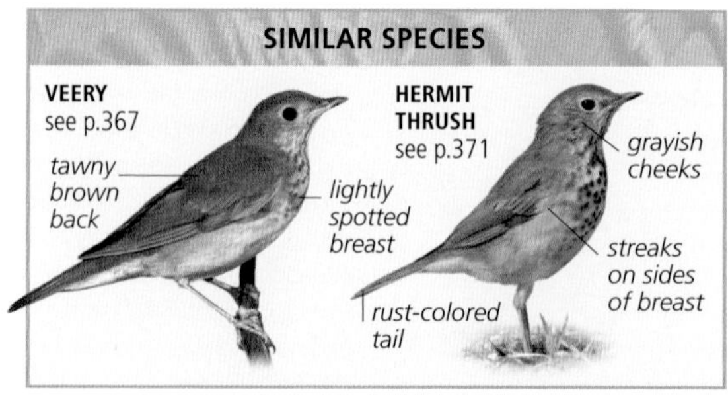
SIMILAR SPECIES
VEERY
see p.367
tawny brown back
lightly spotted breast
HERMIT THRUSH
see p.371
grayish cheeks
streaks on sides of breast
rust-colored tail

OCCURRENCE
Breeds mainly in coniferous forests, especially spruce and fir, except in California, where it prefers deciduous riverside woodlands and damp meadows with shrubbery. During spring and fall migrations, dense understory is preferred. Winter habitat is mainly old growth forest.

Length **6½–7½in (16–19cm)**	Wingspan **11½–12in (29–31cm)**	Weight **7/8–1 9/16oz (25–45g)**
Social **Pairs/Flocks**	Lifespan **Up to 11 years**	Status **Declining**

Order **Passeriformes**	Family **Turdidae**	Species ***Catharus guttatus***

Hermit Thrush

gray-brown upperparts

ADULT
C. g. faxoni
(EASTERN)

IN FLIGHT

darker brown upperparts

dark spots on whitish breast

paler gray flanks

ADULT
C. g. guttatus
(NORTHWESTERN)

gray-brown upperparts

more extensive breast spotting

ADULT
C. g. audoboni
(ROCKIES)

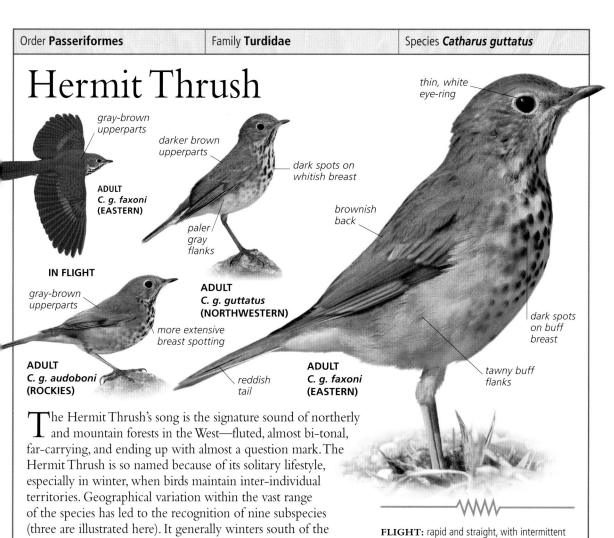

thin, white eye-ring

brownish back

dark spots on buff breast

tawny buff flanks

reddish tail

ADULT
C. g. faxoni
(EASTERN)

The Hermit Thrush's song is the signature sound of northerly and mountain forests in the West—fluted, almost bi-tonal, far-carrying, and ending up with almost a question mark. The Hermit Thrush is so named because of its solitary lifestyle, especially in winter, when birds maintain inter-individual territories. Geographical variation within the vast range of the species has led to the recognition of nine subspecies (three are illustrated here). It generally winters south of the US, in Mexico, Guatemala, and El Salvador.

FLIGHT: rapid and straight, with intermittent flaps and glides.

VOICE Calls *tchek*, soft, dry; song flute-like, ethereal, falling, repetitive, and varied; several phrases delivered on a different pitch.

NESTING Cup of grasses, mosses, twigs, leaves, mud, hair, on ground or in low tree branches; 4 eggs; 1–2 broods; May–July.

FEEDING Mainly forages on ground for insects, larvae, earthworms, and snails; in winter, also eats fruit.

URBAN VISITOR
This thrush is frequently seen in wooded areas in urban and suburban parks.

SIMILAR SPECIES
VEERY
see p.367
tawny brown back
lightly spotted breast
BICKNELL'S TRUSH
see p.369
olive-brown back
yellow base of bill
SWAINSON'S THRUSH
see p.370
olive-brown upperparts

OCCURRENCE
Occurs in coniferous forests and mixed conifer–deciduous woodlands; prefers to nest along the edges of a forest interior, like a bog location. Found in forest and other open woodlands during winter. During migration, found in many wooded habitats.

Length **6–7in (15–18cm)**	Wingspan **10–11in (25–28cm)**	Weight **7/8–1 1/16 oz (25–30g)**
Social **Solitary**	Lifespan **Up to 9 years**	Status **Secure**

Order **Passeriformes**	Family **Turdidae**	Species ***Hylocichla mustelina***

Wood Thrush

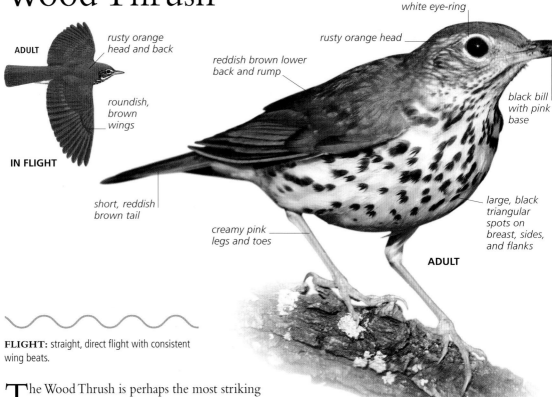

ADULT
rusty orange head and back
roundish, brown wings
IN FLIGHT
white eye-ring
rusty orange head
reddish brown lower back and rump
black bill with pink base
short, reddish brown tail
large, black triangular spots on breast, sides, and flanks
creamy pink legs and toes
ADULT

FLIGHT: straight, direct flight with consistent wing beats.

The Wood Thrush is perhaps the most striking of the small North American thrushes, due to the black spots that cover its underparts, and its rufous head and back. In the breeding season, its flute-like song echoes through the Northeastern hardwood forests and suburban forested areas. Wood Thrush populations have fallen over the past 30 years, largely due to forest destruction and fragmentation. Sadly, this decline has been exacerbated by the Wood Thrush's susceptibility to parasitism by the Brown-headed Cowbird.

VOICE Rapid *pip-pippipip* or *rhuu-rhuu*; a three-part flute-like song—first part indistinct, second part loudest, third part trilled; males have variations of all three parts; mainly before sunrise.

NESTING Cup-shaped nest made with dried grass and weeds in trees or shrubs; 3–4 eggs; 1–2 broods; May–July.

FEEDING Forages in leaf litter, mainly for worms, beetles, moths, caterpillars; eats fruits after breeding season.

STUNNING SOLOIST
The Wood Thrush can often be seen singing its melodious songs from a conspicuous perch.

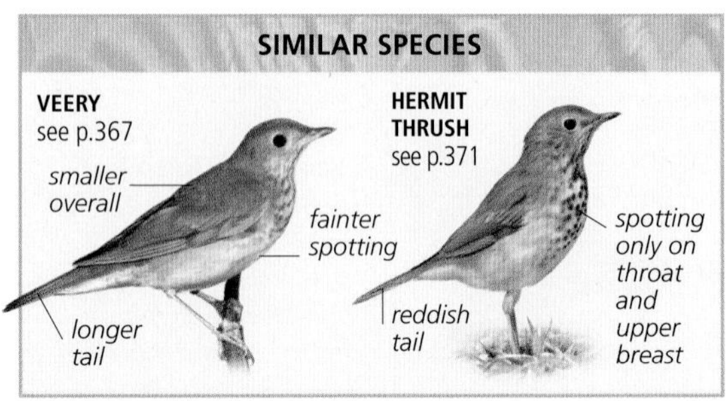
SIMILAR SPECIES
VEERY
see p.367
smaller overall
longer tail
fainter spotting
HERMIT THRUSH
see p.371
reddish tail
spotting only on throat and upper breast

OCCURRENCE
Hardwood forests in the East, from Texas and Florida to Minnesota and the Canadian Maritimes. Breeds in interior and at edges of deciduous and mixed forests; needs dense understory, shrubbery, and moist soil. Winters in Texas, Louisiana, Florida, and south through Central America to Panama.

Length **7½–8½in (19–21cm)**	Wingspan **12–13½in (30–34cm)**	Weight **1$\frac{7}{16}$–1¾oz (40–50g)**
Social **Pairs/Flocks**	Lifespan **Up to 9 years**	Status **Declining**

Order **Passeriformes**	Family **Turdidae**	Species ***Turdus migratorius***

American Robin

MALE

dark head

IN FLIGHT

gray back

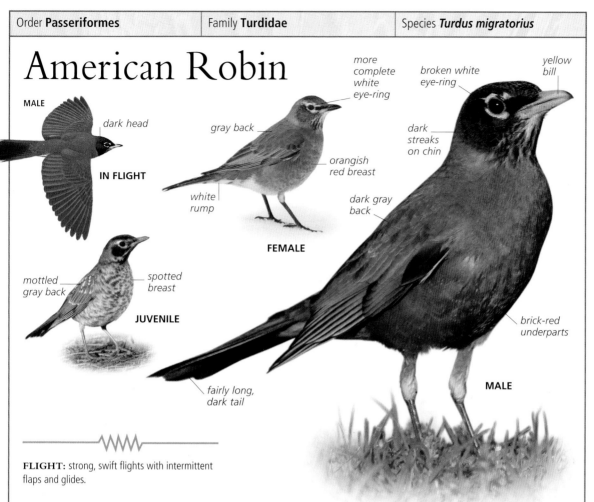

more complete white eye-ring

orangish red breast

white rump

FEMALE

broken white eye-ring

yellow bill

dark streaks on chin

dark gray back

mottled gray back

spotted breast

JUVENILE

brick-red underparts

fairly long, dark tail

MALE

FLIGHT: strong, swift flights with intermittent flaps and glides.

The American Robin, the largest and most abundant of the North American thrushes, is probably the most familiar bird on the continent, and its presence on suburban lawns is an early sign of spring. Unlike other species, it has adapted and prospered in human-altered habitats. It breeds across the entire US and Canada and also winters across the US, migrating out of most of Canada in fall. The decision to migrate is largely governed by changes in the availablity of food. As the breeding season approaches, it is the males that sing first, either late in winter or early spring. The bird's brick-red breast—more vivid in males than in females—is its most distinguishing feature.

VOICE Calls a high pitch *tjip* and a multi-note, throaty *tjuj-tjuk*; primary song a melodious *cheer-up*, *cheer-up*, *cheer-wee*, one of the first birds to be heard during dawn chorus, and one of the last to cease singing in the evening.

NESTING Substantial cup of grass, weeds, twigs, occasional garbage in tree or shrub, in fork of tree, or on branch on tree; 4 eggs; 2–3 broods; April–July.

FEEDING Forages in leaf litter, mainly for earthworms and small insects; mostly consumes fruit in the winter season.

SIMILAR SPECIES

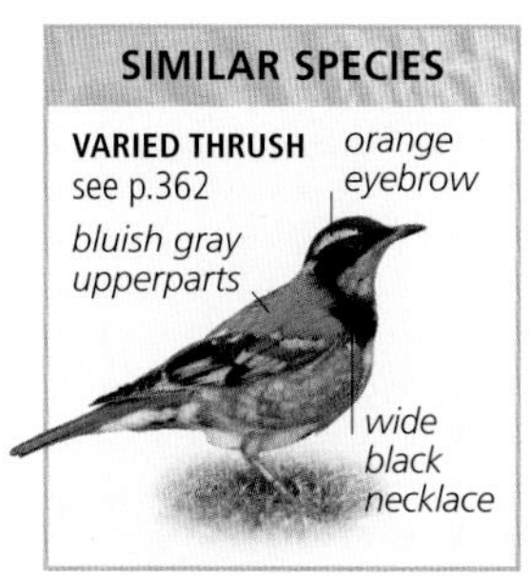
VARIED THRUSH
orange eyebrow
bluish gray upperparts
wide black necklace
see p.362

SEASONAL DIET
Robins are particularly dependent on the availability of fruit during the winter months.

OCCURRENCE
Breeding habitat a mix of forest, woodland, suburban gardens, lawns, municipal parks, and farms. A partial migrant, these robins tend to be found in woodlands where berry-bearing trees are present. Nonmigrating populations' winter habitat is similar to breeding habitat.

Length **8–11in (20–28cm)**	Wingspan **12–16in (30–41cm)**	Weight **2⁵⁄₈oz (75g)**
Social **Flocks**	Lifespan **Up to 13 years**	Status **Secure**

Order **Passeriformes**	Family **Muscicapidae**	Species ***Oenanthe oenanthe***

Northern Wheatear

MALE (BREEDING)

tail has a black "T"

black mask

IN FLIGHT

long, black wings

FEMALE (BREEDING)

mouse-brown back

tan eyebrow

tan throat and breast

FEMALE (BREEDING)

white forehead and eyebrow

black bill

gray back

white underparts

MALE (BREEDING)

long, thin, black legs

similar to female, but duller

JUVENILE

Although widely distributed in Europe, the Middle East and Africa, the Northern Wheatear is present in North America only during its brief breeding season, where it is confined to Alaska and northeastern Canada. The two subspecies that breed in North America, the larger *O. o. leucorhoa* in the Northeast and *O. o. oenanthe* in the Northwest, migrate to wintering grounds in sub-Saharan Africa. The Northern Wheatear can be distinguished by its black-and-white tail, which bobs when the bird walks.

VOICE Multiple calls, a sharp *tuc* or *tek* common; three types of songs—territorial, conversational, and perched—consisting of mixtures of sweet and harsh notes; imitates other species.

NESTING Under rocks or in abandoned burrows; nests have coarse outer foundation, with cradle and cup within of finer material; 5–6 eggs; 1 brood; June–July.

FEEDING Eats insects, but also takes berries; diet in North America not well known.

KEEP YOUR DISTANCE
Northern Wheatears are highly territorial, so neighbors get yelled at if they come too close.

FLIGHT: undulating when flying long distances; fluttering from perch to perch.

OCCURRENCE
Breeds in rocky tundra of Alaska and northern Canada, including the Yukon (*O. o. oenanthe*) and the Arctic archipelago (*O. o. leucorhoa*). Both subspecies winter in Africa, *O. o. oenanthe* by flying across Asia, *O. o. leucorhoa* by flying across the Atlantic.

Length **5½–6in (14–15cm)**	Wingspan **10¾in (27cm)**	Weight **½oz (14g)**
Social **Solitary/Flocks**	Lifespan **Up to 7 years**	Status **Secure**

Order **Passeriformes**	Family **Cinclidae**	Species ***Cinclus mexicanus***

American Dipper

white eyelid

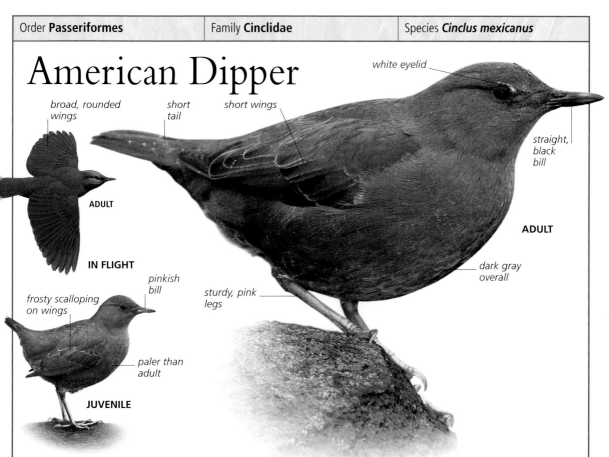

broad, rounded wings

short tail

short wings

straight, black bill

ADULT

IN FLIGHT

ADULT

dark gray overall

pinkish bill

frosty scalloping on wings

sturdy, pink legs

paler than adult

JUVENILE

The most aquatic North American songbird, the American Dipper is at home in the cold, rushing streams of western North America. It is known for its feeding technique of plunging into streams for insect larvae under stones or in the streambed. When it is not foraging, it watches from a rock or log, bobbing up and down, constantly flashing its nictating membrane (the transparent third eyelid that protects the eye when the bird is underwater). Susceptible to changes in water chemistry and turbulence, which alters the abundance of its main food, caddisfly larvae, this bird has been proposed as an indicator for stream quality.

VOICE Call a harsh *bzzt*, given singly or in rapid series; song a loud, disorganized series of pleasing warbles, whistles, and trills.

NESTING Domed nest with side entrance, placed underneath bridge or behind waterfall; 4–5 eggs; 1–2 broods; March–August.

FEEDING Forages for insects and insect larvae, especially caddisflies; sometimes eats small fish and fish eggs.

FLIGHT: low over water, twisting and turning with the stream with rapid, buzzy wing beats.

BOBBING MOTION
The American Dipper often pauses on rocks in streams, where it bobs up and down.

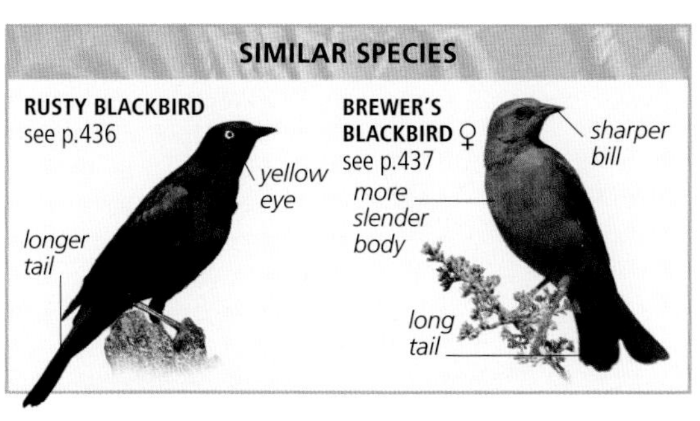
SIMILAR SPECIES
RUSTY BLACKBIRD
see p.436
yellow eye
longer tail
BREWER'S BLACKBIRD ♀
see p.437
sharper bill
more slender body
long tail

OCCURRENCE
Found from Alaska, the Yukon, and British Columbia, south to California, Arizona, New Mexico, Mexico, and Panama. On Pacific slope, breeds down to sea level; in Interior West, breeds mainly in mountains and foothills; retreats to lower elevations in winter.

Length **7½in (19cm)**	Wingspan **11in (28cm)**	Weight **1¾–2¼oz (50–65g)**
Social **Solitary**	Lifespan **Up to 7 years**	Status **Secure**

Order **Passeriformes**	Family **Passeridae**	Species ***Passer domesticus***

House Sparrow

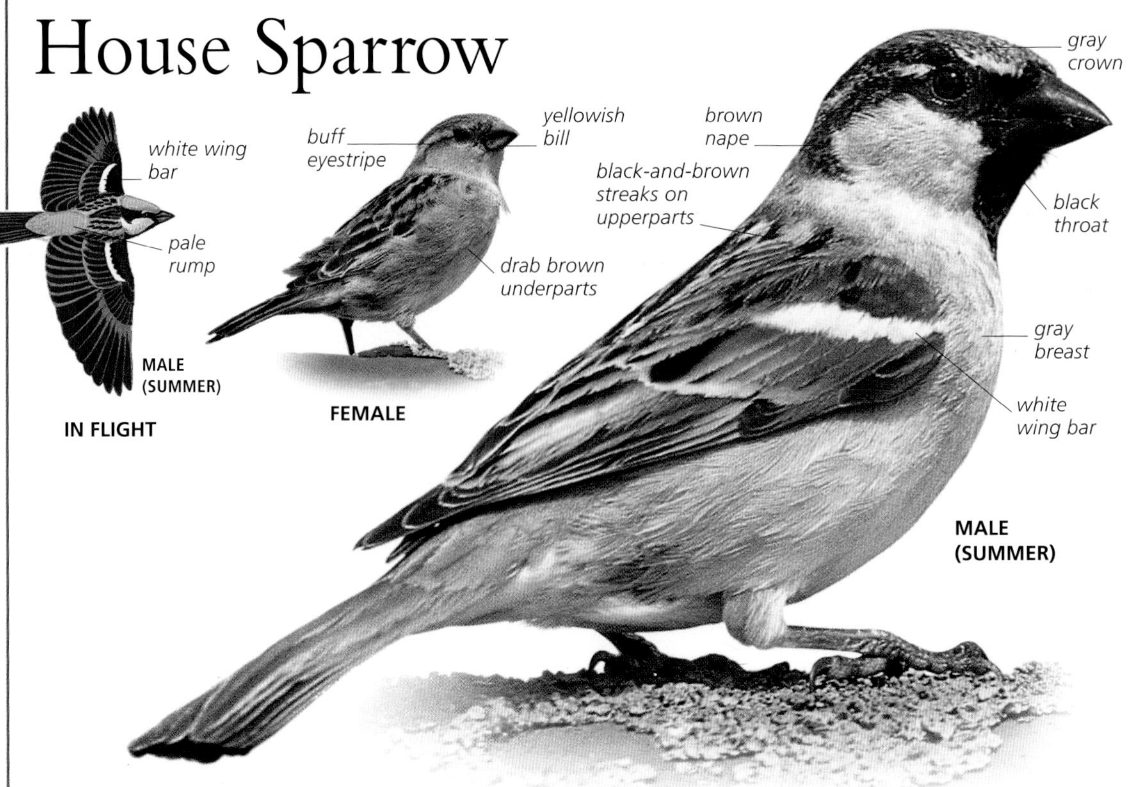
white wing bar
pale rump
MALE (SUMMER)
IN FLIGHT
buff eyestripe
yellowish bill
drab brown underparts
FEMALE
brown nape
black-and-brown streaks on upperparts
gray crown
black throat
gray breast
white wing bar
MALE (SUMMER)

This is the familiar "sparrow" of towns, cities, suburbs, and farms. The House Sparrow is not actually a sparrow as understood in North America, but rather a member of a Eurasian family called the weaver-finches. It was first introduced in Brooklyn, New York, in 1850. From this modest beginning, and with the help of several other introductions up until the late 1860s, this hardy, and aggressive bird eventually spread right through the North American continent. In a little more than 150 years, the House Sparrow has evolved and shows the same sort of geographic variation as some widespread native birds. It is pale in the arid southwest US, and darker in wetter regions.

VOICE Variety of calls, including a *cheery chirp*, a dull *jurv* and a rough *jigga*; song consists of *chirp* notes repeated endlessly.

NESTING Untidy mass of dried vegetable material in either natural or artificial cavities; 3–5 eggs; 2–3 broods; April–August.

FEEDING Mostly seeds; sometimes gleans insects and fruits.

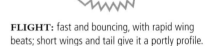

FLIGHT: fast and bouncing, with rapid wing beats; short wings and tail give it a portly profile.

APTLY NAMED
This sparrow is seen near human structures—roofs, outbuildings, loading docks, curbs, and streetlights.

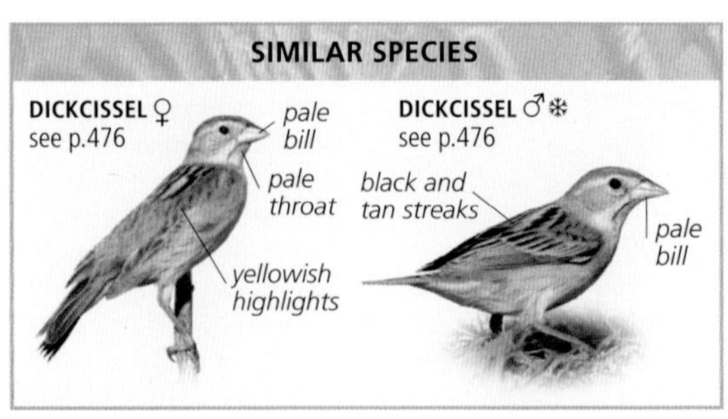
SIMILAR SPECIES
DICKCISSEL ♀
see p.476
pale bill
pale throat
yellowish highlights
DICKCISSEL ♂ ❄
see p.476
black and tan streaks
pale bill

OCCURRENCE
Flourishes in the downtown sections of cities and anywhere near human habitations, including agricultural outbuildings in remote areas of the continent. Found also in Mexico, Central and South America, and the West Indies.

Length **6in (15.5cm)**	Wingspan **9½in (24cm)**	Weight **⅝–1¹⁄₁₆oz (18–30g)**
Social **Flocks**	Lifespan **Up to 7 years**	Status **Declining**

Order **Passeriformes**	Family **Motacillidae**	Species ***Motacilla flava***

Yellow Wagtail

MALE
long black tail with white outer tail feathers
IN FLIGHT
light gray-blue head
light grayish back
pale yellow underparts
white undertail feathers
FEMALE
ashy blue-gray head
bold, white eyebrow
dark cheeks
dark greenish gray back
bright yellow throat
inconspicuous wing bar
grayish brown head, with white eyebrow
dark brown markings on breast
whitish underparts
JUVENILE
yellow undertail feathers
bright yellow belly
MALE
long, thin, dark legs

FLIGHT: direct, alternating strong wing beats on upswing and glide on the downswing.

The Yellow Wagtail, like several other songbird species, is a widely distributed Eurasian breeder with a nesting foothold in Alaska and the Yukon. An extroadinarily variable species, the Yellow Wagtail has about 17 subspecies. The Alaskan-Canadian population belongs to the subspecies *tschutschensis*, which was described as long ago as 1789. It likes to perch on exposed low shrubs and mossy mounds in the tundra, persistently wagging its tail and calling its insistent *tzeep*. Other than the North American tundra, its breeding grounds include the Kamchatka Peninsula in eastern Russia.

VOICE Call is a short, "outgoing" *tzeep!*; song a thin, musical, *tzee-ouee-sir*.

NESTING Small cup of woven plant matter including grass, moss, and bark, lined with hair and feathers; often positioned near clump of grass; 4–5 eggs; 1 brood; June–July.

FEEDING Forages, mainly for land- and water-based insects, especially mosquitoes on or near the ground, especially along the water's edge; sometimes makes short flights to catch insects in flight.

EYE-CATCHING
This conspicuous bird with bright yellow underparts perches in the open and constantly wags its tail.

SIMILAR SPECIES

YELLOW-BREASTED CHAT
see p.429

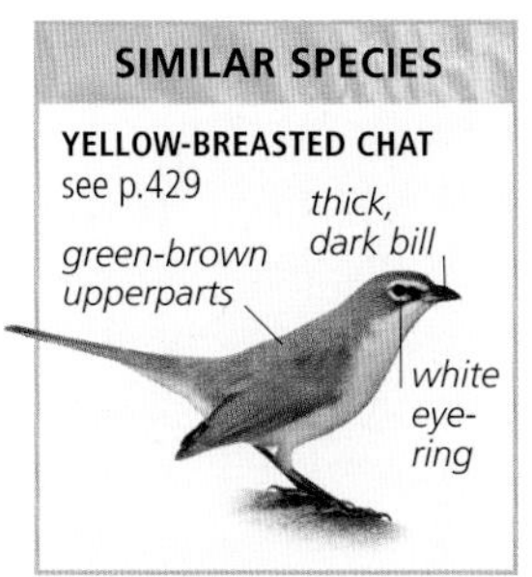
thick, dark bill
green-brown upperparts
white eye-ring

OCCURRENCE
Its North American range is restricted to western Alaska and extreme western Yukon, where it is found in tundra with scattered shrub, especially along watercourses. It winters in eastern Asia, south to Indonesia.

Length **5–7in (13–18cm)**	Wingspan **7–9in (18–23cm)**	Weight **½–¹¹⁄₁₆oz (15–20g)**
Social **Flocks**	Lifespan **Up to 9 years**	Status **Localized**

Order **Passeriformes**	Family **Motacillidae**	Species ***Anthus rubescens***

American Pipit

ADULT

gray cheek with buffy eyestripes

white outer tail feathers

IN FLIGHT

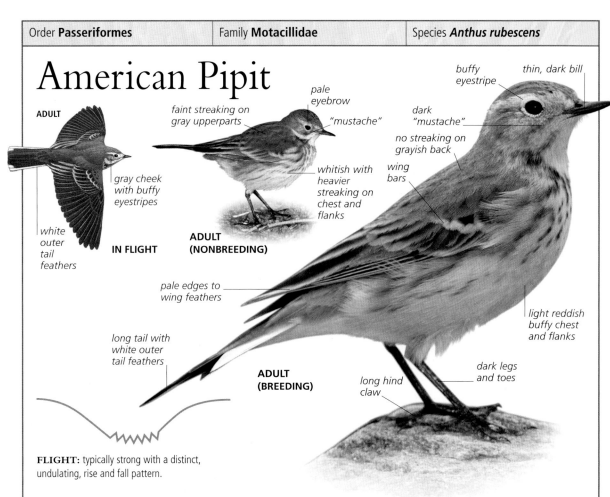

faint streaking on gray upperparts

pale eyebrow

"mustache"

whitish with heavier streaking on chest and flanks

ADULT (NONBREEDING)

buffy eyestripe

thin, dark bill

dark "mustache"

no streaking on grayish back

wing bars

pale edges to wing feathers

light reddish buffy chest and flanks

long tail with white outer tail feathers

ADULT (BREEDING)

long hind claw

dark legs and toes

FLIGHT: typically strong with a distinct, undulating, rise and fall pattern.

The American Pipit is divided into four subspecies, three of which breed in North America, and the fourth in Siberia. In nonbreeding plumage, the American Pipit is a drab-looking, brownish gray bird that forages for insects along water and shores, or in cultivated fields with short stems. In the breeding season, molting transforms it into a beauty—with gray upperparts and reddish underparts. American Pipits are known for pumping their tails up and down. When breeding, males display by rising into the air, then flying down with wings open and singing. Its migration takes the American Pipit as far south as Guatemala.

VOICE Alarm call a *tzeeep*; song repeated *tzwee-tzooo* from the air.

NESTING Cup in shallow depression on ground, outer frame of grass, lined with fine grass and hair; 4–6 eggs; 1 brood; June–July.

FEEDING Picks insects; also eats seeds during migration.

WINTER DRAB
Foraging in short vegetation, this bird is almost the same color as its surroundings.

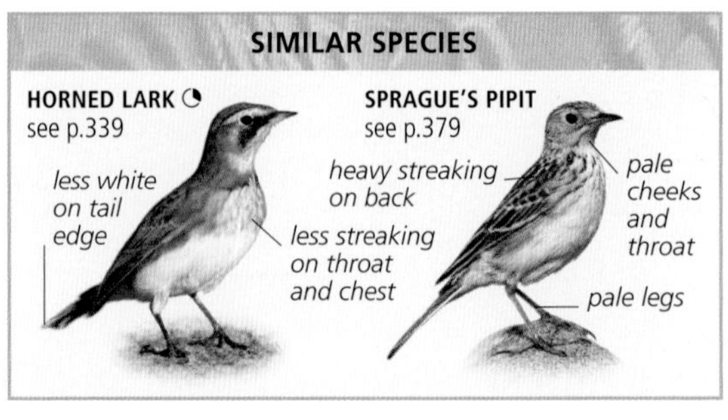
SIMILAR SPECIES
HORNED LARK
see p.339
less white on tail edge
less streaking on throat and chest
SPRAGUE'S PIPIT
see p.379
heavy streaking on back
pale cheeks and throat
pale legs

OCCURRENCE
Breeds in Arctic tundra in the north, and alpine tundra in the Rockies; also breeds on treeless mountain tops in Maine and New Hampshire. Winters in open coastal areas and harvested agricultural fields across the US. Some North American migrants fly to Asia for the winter.

Length **6–8in (15–20cm)**	Wingspan **10–11in (25–28cm)**	Weight **¹¹⁄₁₆oz (20g)**
Social **Flocks**	Lifespan **Up to 6 years**	Status **Secure**

Order **Passeriformes**	Family **Motacillidae**	Species ***Anthus spragueii***

Sprague's Pipit

ADULT

broken "collar"

white outer tail feathers

IN FLIGHT

eyes appear large

pale cheeks

thin "mustache"

thick, two-tone bill

heavily streaked back

two pale wing bars

buffy wash on flanks

pale whitish belly

ADULT

long, pale pink legs and toes

white outer tail feathers

long, dark hind claw

FLIGHT: strong with distinct up and down bobbing; prefers running to escape predators.

Sprague's is the only wholly North American pipit. Males perform a very extraordinary fluttering display flight, circling high above the earth while singing an unending series of high-pitched calls, for periods up to an hour. The current decline in the population of the Sprague's Pipit is quite likely the result of the conversion of tall-grass native prairie to extensive farmland. Interestingly, the Chaco Pipit of Argentina now breeds almost exclusively in wheat fields, offering some hope for this species.

VOICE Call a high *squeeek*; song a high, repetitive series of *szee- szee-szee*, usually given during lengthy aerial displays.

NESTING Small cup of loose woven grass on the ground and level with it, often attached to standing vegetation to form a sort of dome; 4–5 eggs; 1–2 broods; May–August.

FEEDING Feeds almost exclusively on insects when breeding, especially crickets and grasshoppers; eats seeds occasionally.

SONG PERCH
This Sprague's Pipit sings from a perch in its vanishing tall-grass prairie habitat.

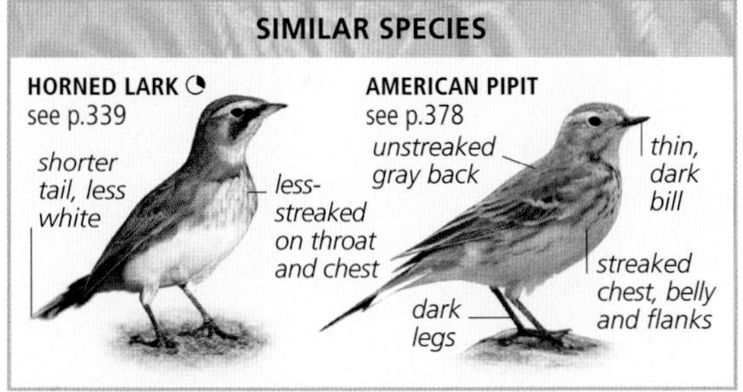
SIMILAR SPECIES
HORNED LARK
see p.339
shorter tail, less white
less-streaked on throat and chest
AMERICAN PIPIT
see p.378
unstreaked gray back
thin, dark bill
streaked chest, belly and flanks
dark legs

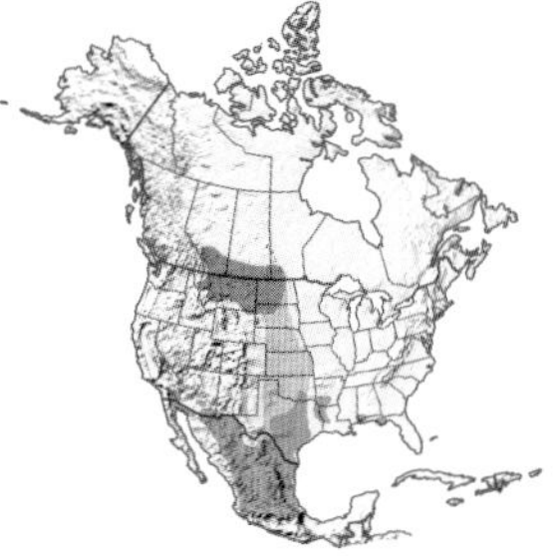

OCCURRENCE
Sprague's Pipit is truly North American, it breeds along the border of Canada with the US, in dry, open, tall-grass upland habitat, especially native prairie systems in the northern part of the Great Plains; most migrate to Mexico in winter, where habitat is similar to breeding grounds.

Length **4–6in (10–15cm)**	Wingspan **6–8in (15–20cm)**	Weight **11/16–7/8oz (20–25g)**
Social **Solitary**	Lifespan **Unknown**	Status **Vulnerable**

Family **Fringillidae**

FINCHES

THE NAME "FINCHES" applies to the Fringillidae, a family of seed-eating songbirds that includes sixteen species in North America. They vary in size and shape from the small and fragile-looking redpolls to the robust and chunky Evening Grosbeak. Finch colors range from whitish with some pink (redpolls) to gold (American Goldfinch), bright red (crossbills), and yellow, white, and black (Evening grosbeak). However, irrespective of body shape, size, and color, all have conical bills with razor-sharp edges. Finches do not crush seeds. Instead, they cut open the hard hull, then seize the seed inside with their tongue and swallow it. The bills of conifer loving crossbills are crossed at the tip, a unique arrangement that permits them to open tough-hulled pine cones. Roughly 50 percent of crossbills are "left-billed" and 50 percent "right-billed"—lefties are right-footed, and vice versa. Most finches are social. Although they breed in pairs, after nesting finches form flocks, some of which are huge. Most finch populations fluctuate in size, synchronized with seed production and abundance. All finches are vocal, calling constantly while flying, and singing in the spring. Calls are usually sharp, somewhat metallic sounds, although the American Goldfinch's tinkling calls are sweeter. Songs can be quite musical, clear-sounding melodies, like that of the Cassin's Finch. Finches make open cup-shaped nests of grasses and lichens, in trees or shrubs, and are remarkably adept at hiding them.

CROSSBILL
Perched on a pine tree branch, a female Red Crossbill grinds a seed in her bill to break open the hull and reach the fat-rich kernel inside.

NOT REALLY PURPLE
The inaccurately named Purple Finch actually has a lovely wine-red coloration.

GARDEN GLOW
Even pink flower buds cannot compete with the yellow of a male American Goldfinch.

Order **Passeriformes**	Family **Fringillidae**	Species ***Spinus pinus***

Pine Siskin

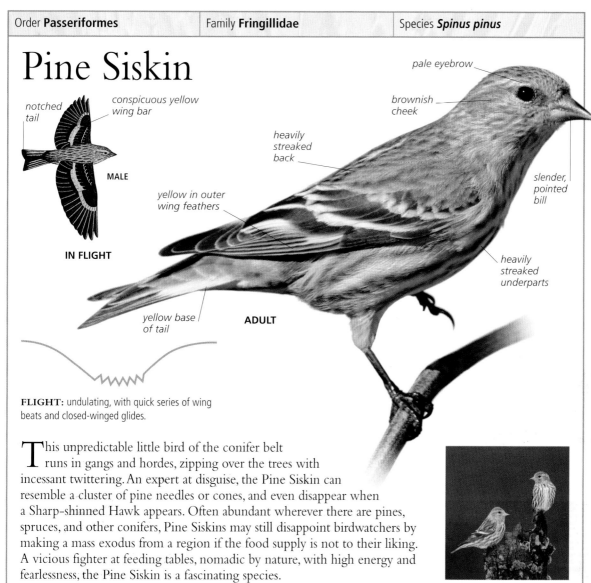

notched tail
conspicuous yellow wing bar
MALE
IN FLIGHT

pale eyebrow
brownish cheek
heavily streaked back
slender, pointed bill
yellow in outer wing feathers
heavily streaked underparts
yellow base of tail
ADULT

FLIGHT: undulating, with quick series of wing beats and closed-winged glides.

This unpredictable little bird of the conifer belt runs in gangs and hordes, zipping over the trees with incessant twittering. An expert at disguise, the Pine Siskin can resemble a cluster of pine needles or cones, and even disappear when a Sharp-shinned Hawk appears. Often abundant wherever there are pines, spruces, and other conifers, Pine Siskins may still disappoint birdwatchers by making a mass exodus from a region if the food supply is not to their liking. A vicious fighter at feeding tables, nomadic by nature, with high energy and fearlessness, the Pine Siskin is a fascinating species.

VOICE Rising *toooeeo*, mostly when perched; also raspy *chit-chit-chit* in flight.

NESTING Shallow cup of grass and lichens near the end of a conifer branch; 3–4 eggs; 1–2 broods; February–August.

FEEDING Eats conifer seeds; gleans insects and spiders; also seen feeding on roadsides, lawns, and weed fields.

FOREST DWELLER
The streaked Pine Siskin inhabits northern and western coniferous forests.

QUARRELSOME
A bird warns off a neighbor at a food source, displaying its yellow wing stripe.

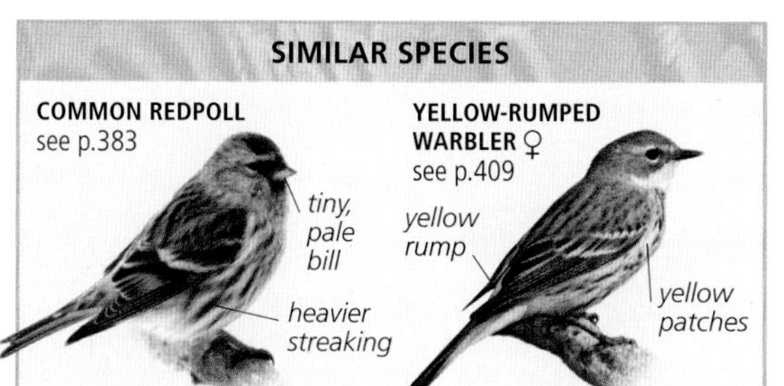
SIMILAR SPECIES
COMMON REDPOLL
see p.383
tiny, pale bill
heavier streaking
YELLOW-RUMPED WARBLER ♀
see p.409
yellow rump
yellow patches

OCCURRENCE
Widespread across North America; occurs in coniferous and mixed coniferous forests, but also seen in parkland and suburbs. In some winters may appear south of regular breeding range to Missouri and Tennessee, also Mexico. Prefers open areas to continuous forest.

Length **4¼–5½in (11–14cm)**	Wingspan **7–9in (18–23cm)**	Weight **7/16–5/8oz (12–18g)**
Social **Flocks**	Lifespan **Up to 10 years**	Status **Secure**

Order **Passeriformes**	Family **Fringillidae**	Species ***Spinus tristis***

American Goldfinch

MALE (NONBREEDING)
bright yellow back
IN FLIGHT

tan back
brownish bill
yellow throat and collar
pale tan underparts
MALE (NONBREEDING)

brownish olive back
pinkish bill
FEMALE (BREEDING)

black forehead and crown
short conical pinkish bill
black tail
white rump
white wing bar
bright yellow underparts
pinkish legs and feet
MALE (BREEDING)

brownish overall
dull yellow throat
FEMALE (NONBREEDING)

Often described as a giant yellow-and-black bumblebee, a male American Goldfinch in full breeding plumage is a common summer sight. Even when not seen, the presence of goldfinches in an area is quickly given away by the sound of the birds calling in flight. If there are weed seeds around, goldfinches will find them, whether they are out in the fields or on the feeding table. When a male performs his courtship songs, often singing them while circling his female, he does justice to the nickname "American canary."

FLIGHT: deeply undulating; wing beats alternating with closed-wing dips.

VOICE Loud, rising *pter-yee* by males; 3–5-note *tit-tse-tew-tew* by both sexes, usually in flight; song complex warbling.

NESTING Open cup nest of grass, usually shaded from above; 4–5 eggs; 1–2 broods; July–September.

FEEDING Feeds mainly on seeds from annual plants, birch, and alder; some insects; prefers sunflower and thistle seed at feeders.

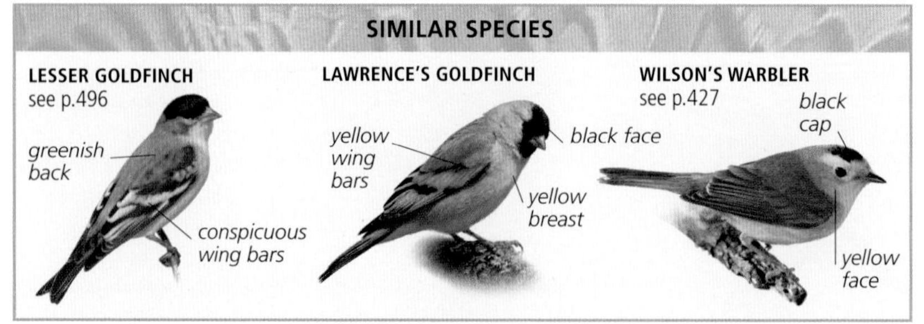
SIMILAR SPECIES
LESSER GOLDFINCH
see p.496
greenish back
conspicuous wing bars
LAWRENCE'S GOLDFINCH
yellow wing bars
black face
yellow breast
WILSON'S WARBLER
see p.427
black cap
yellow face

OCCURRENCE
In low shrubs, deciduous woodlands, farmlands, orchards, suburbs, and gardens across much of North America, from southern Canada to California and Georgia; in winter south to Northern Mexico and Florida; winter habitats similar to those used at other times.

Length **4¼–5in (11–13cm)**	Wingspan **7–9in (18–23cm)**	Weight **⅜–¹¹⁄₁₆oz (11–20g)**
Social **Small flocks**	Lifespan **Up to 11 years**	Status **Secure**

Order **Passeriformes**	Family **Fringillidae**	Species ***Acanthis flammea***

Common Redpoll

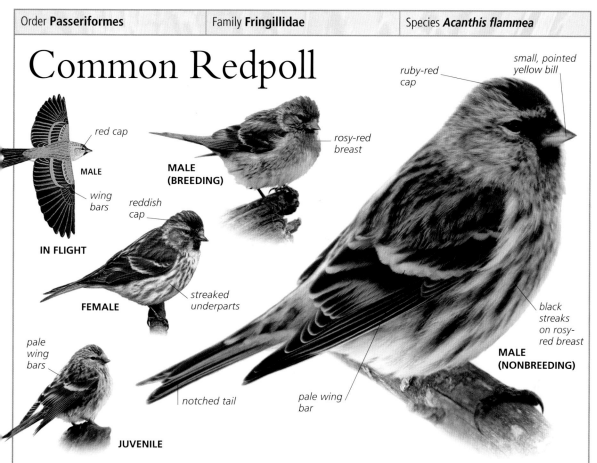

red cap
MALE
wing bars
IN FLIGHT
MALE (BREEDING)
rosy-red breast
reddish cap
FEMALE
streaked underparts
pale wing bars
JUVENILE
ruby-red cap
small, pointed yellow bill
black streaks on rosy-red breast
MALE (NONBREEDING)
notched tail
pale wing bar

Every other year, spruce, birch, and other trees in the northern forest zone fail to produce a good crop of seeds, forcing the Common Redpoll to look for food farther south than usual—as far south as the northern US states. The common Redpoll is oddly tame around people and is easily attracted to winter feeders. The degree of whiteness in its plumage varies greatly among individuals, due to sex and age. The taxonomy of the Common Redpoll includes four subspecies around the world, and there are suggestions that some may be distinct species.

VOICE Flight call dry *zit-zit-zit-zit* and rattling *chirr*; also high *too-ee* call while perched; song series of rapid trills.

NESTING Cup of small twigs in spruces, larches, willows, alders; 4–6 eggs; 1–2 broods; May–June.

FEEDING Feeds on small seeds from conifers, sedge, birch, willow, alder; also insects and spiders.

FLIGHT: deeply undulating, with dips between bouts of wing beats.

SIMILAR SPECIES

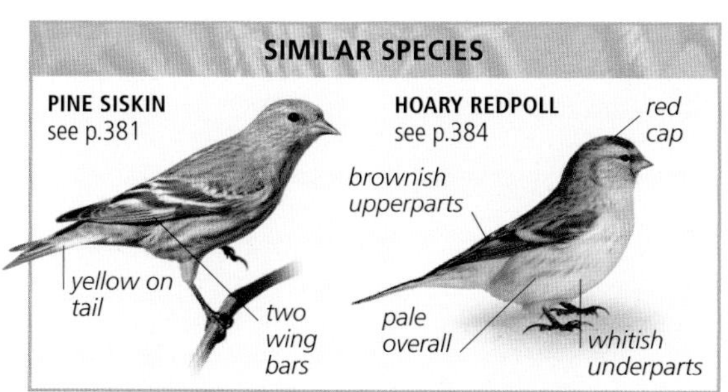
PINE SISKIN
see p.381
yellow on tail
two wing bars
HOARY REDPOLL
see p.384
red cap
brownish upperparts
pale overall
whitish underparts

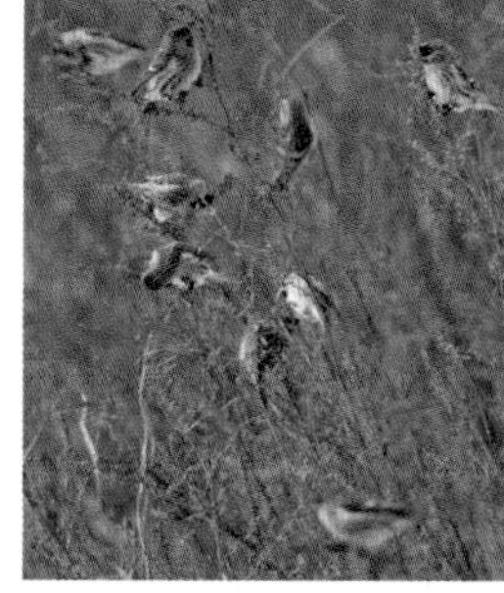

FRIENDLY FLOCK
Common Redpolls are only weakly territorial, sometimes even nesting close together.

OCCURRENCE
Mainly in extreme northern North America from Alaska to Quebec and Labrador, in low forest, subarctic, and shrubby tundra habitats. More southerly winter appearances typically occur every other year, rarely south of northern US states, from Dakota east to New York City and New England.

Length **4¾–5½in (12–14cm)**	Wingspan **6½–6¾in (16–17cm)**	Weight **⅜–11/16oz (11–19g)**
Social **Flocks**	Lifespan **Up to 10 years**	Status **Secure**

Order **Passeriformes**	Family **Fringillidae**	Species ***Acanthis hornemanni***

Hoary Redpoll

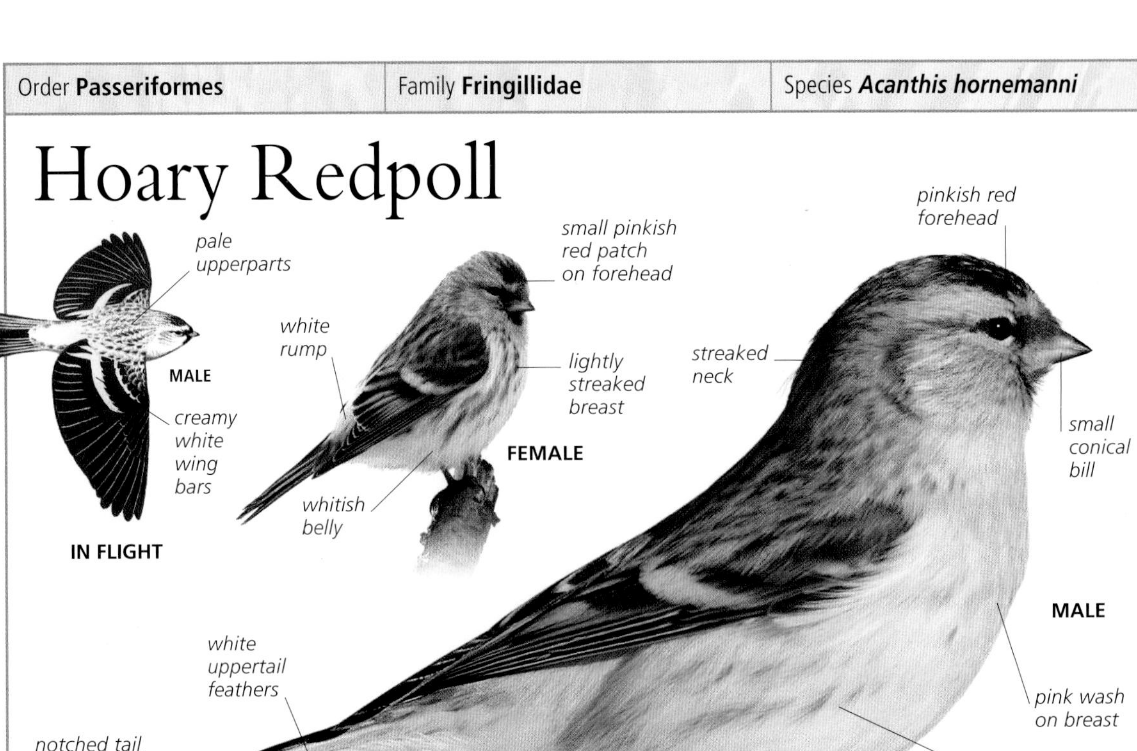
pale upperparts
MALE
creamy white wing bars
IN FLIGHT
small pinkish red patch on forehead
white rump
lightly streaked breast
FEMALE
whitish belly
pinkish red forehead
streaked neck
small conical bill
MALE
white uppertail feathers
notched tail
pink wash on breast
faint streaks
creamy white undertail feathers

When a flock of redpolls settles at a feeding station, one or more may stand out as exceptionally white, somewhat fluffier, and with a stubbier bill. These may be Hoary Redpolls, a distinct species from the rest of the redpoll group. This bird of the high Arctic has two recognized subspecies—*A. h. exilipes* and *A. h. hornemanni*. These close relatives of the Common Redpoll often breed in the same areas, but do not interbreed. Like Common Redpolls, chattering flocks of Hoary Redpolls buzz rapidly over trees and fields and are tame around humans, but this species is less well known because of its more limited contact with people.

VOICE Flight calls dry *zit-zit-zit-zit* and rattling *chirr*; also high *too-ee* call while perched; song series of rapid trills.

NESTING Lined cup of twigs, grasses in scrubby trees; 4–6 eggs; 1–2 broods; May–July.

FEEDING Eats seeds, insects, and spiders; in winter, prefers niger thistle seed.

FLIGHT: flurries of energetic wing beats alternating with glides.

GROUND FEEDER
Seeds that fall from trees onto the snow provide a good meal for the Hoary Redpoll.

SIMILAR SPECIES

COMMON REDPOLL
see p.383
more slender shape
more heavily streaked
SNOW BUNTING
see p.448
larger overall
band across chest

OCCURRENCE
Breeds in the High Arctic, including the Canadian Arctic Archipelago; prefers low trees of the open tundra; winters within the boreal forest belt from the Canadian Maritimes and northern New England eastward to Alaska.

Length **5–5½in (12.5–14cm)**	Wingspan **8½–9¼in (21–23.5cm)**	Weight **7/16–11/16oz (12–20g)**
Social **Flocks**	Lifespan **Unknown**	Status **Secure**

Order **Passeriformes**	Family **Fringillidae**	Species ***Leucosticte tephrocotis***

Gray-crowned Rosy-Finch

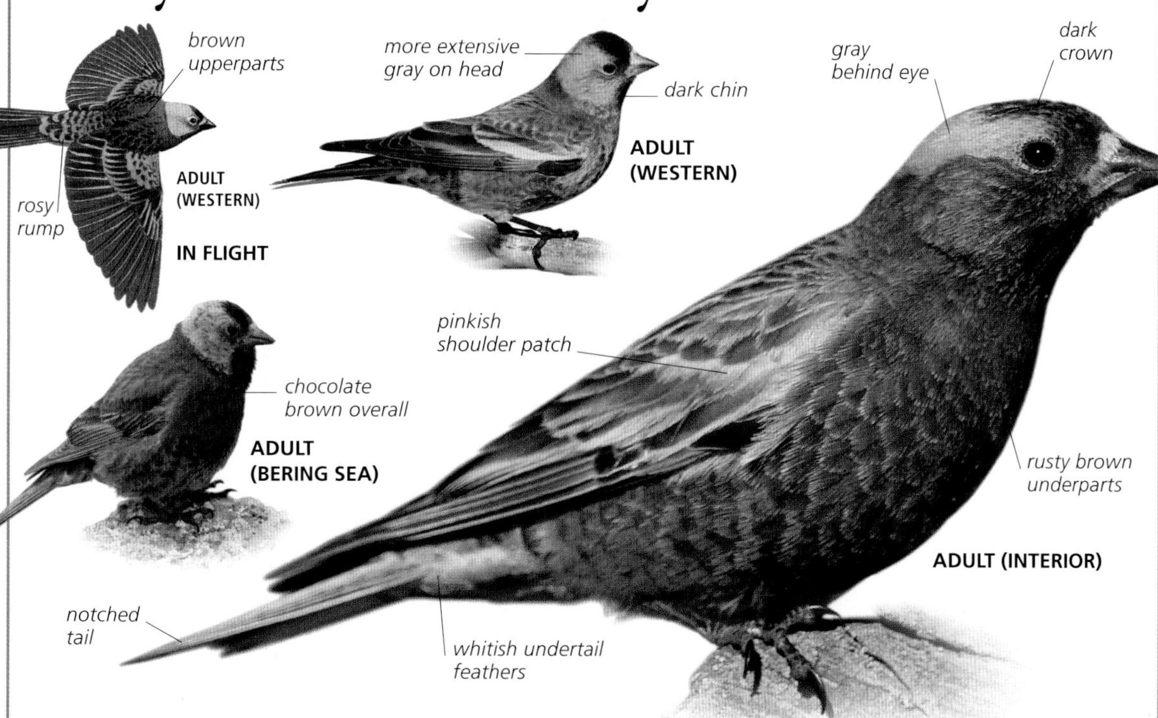

brown upperparts
rosy rump
ADULT (WESTERN)
IN FLIGHT
more extensive gray on head
dark chin
ADULT (WESTERN)
gray behind eye
dark crown
chocolate brown overall
ADULT (BERING SEA)
pinkish shoulder patch
rusty brown underparts
ADULT (INTERIOR)
notched tail
whitish undertail feathers

The often lifeless and windswept rocks and crags of high western mountains are the domain of these brown-and-pink birds, which are seldom in contact with humanity. The Gray-crowned Rosy-Finch is one of several mountain finch species that extend across the Bering Strait into eastern Asia. Geographically variable in size and coloration, with exceptionally large forms occurring on the Pribilof and Aleutian Islands, the Gray-crowned Rosy-Finch is the most abundant of the North American rosy-finches.

VOICE High-pitched *peew*, given singly or in short series; song repetitive series of *twee* notes.

NESTING Bulky assemblage of grasses, lichens, and twigs in cracks or under rock overhangs; 3–5 eggs; 1–2 broods; May–June.

FEEDING Feeds on the ground on a variety of seeds, with insects and their larvae comprising a larger part of the diet in summer.

FLIGHT: undulating but often irregular with glides.

ROCK LOVER
This dark rusty-brown species watches its surroundings from a rocky perch near an icy field.

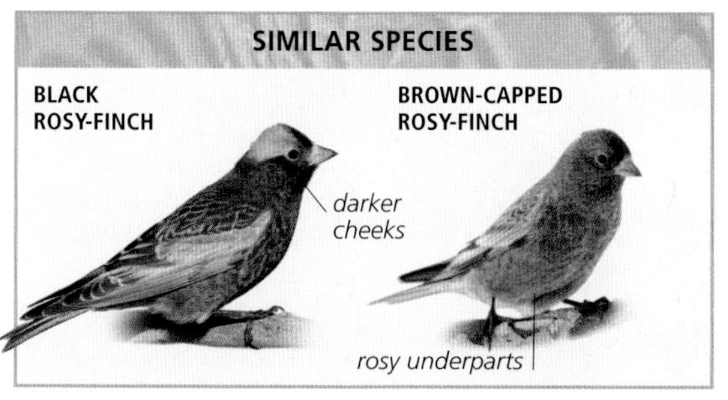

SIMILAR SPECIES
BLACK ROSY-FINCH
darker cheeks
BROWN-CAPPED ROSY-FINCH
rosy underparts

OCCURRENCE
Most widely distributed of the three North American rosy-finch species, occurring from Alaska south to the Rockies; breeds in alpine habitats like rocky screes above snow line and Arctic tundra; in winter also occurs at lower elevations; sometimes at feeders.

Length **5½–8½in (14–21cm)**	Wingspan **13in (33cm)**	Weight **⅞–2⅛oz (25–60g)**
Social **Flocks**	Lifespan **Unknown**	Status **Localized**

Order **Passeriformes**	Family **Fringillidae**	Species ***Carpodacus purpureus***

Purple Finch

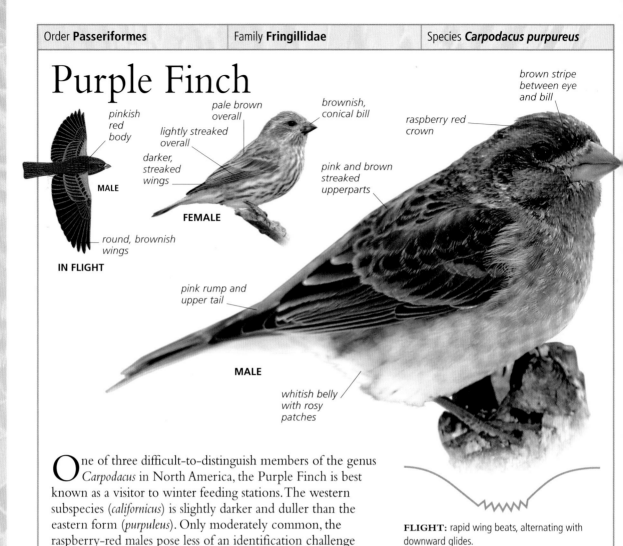

pinkish red body
MALE
round, brownish wings
IN FLIGHT
pale brown overall
lightly streaked overall
darker, streaked wings
FEMALE
brownish, conical bill
brown stripe between eye and bill
raspberry red crown
pink and brown streaked upperparts
pink rump and upper tail
MALE
whitish belly with rosy patches

One of three difficult-to-distinguish members of the genus *Carpodacus* in North America, the Purple Finch is best known as a visitor to winter feeding stations. The western subspecies (*californicus*) is slightly darker and duller than the eastern form (*purpuleus*). Only moderately common, the raspberry-red males pose less of an identification challenge than the brown-streaked females. Even on their breeding grounds in open and mixed coniferous forest, Purple Finches are more often heard than seen.

VOICE Flight call single, rough *pikh*; songs rich series of notes, up and down in pitch.

NESTING Cup of sticks and grasses on a conifer branch; 4 eggs; 2 broods; May–July.

FEEDING Eats buds, seeds, flowers of deciduous trees; insects and caterpillars in summer; also seeds and berries.

FLIGHT: rapid wing beats, alternating with downward glides.

RASPBERRY TINTED
On a lichen-covered branch this male's delicate coloring is quite striking.

OCCURRENCE
Breeds in northern mixed conifer and hardwood forests in all Canadian provinces, the Yukon and Northwest Territories, where it is partially migratory. Resident from Baja California north along the Pacific coast up to Yukon Territory.

SIMILAR SPECIES

HOUSE FINCH ♀ western; see p.388

CASSIN'S FINCH ♀ see p.387

RED-WINGED BLACKBIRD ♀ see p.435

thinner streaks
more marked facial patterning
larger overall
heavily streaked
darker overall

Length **4¾–6in (12–15cm)**	Wingspan **8½–10in (22–26cm)**	Weight **11/16–1 1/16oz (20–30g)**
Social **Flocks**	Lifespan **Unknown**	Status **Declining**

Order **Passeriformes**	Family **Fringillidae**	Species ***Carpodacus cassinii***

Cassin's Finch

notched tail
red face
MALE
IN FLIGHT
streaked all over
FEMALE
bright rose-red crown
dark reddish cheeks
grayish bill
streaked upperparts
rosy red neck
reddish rump
whitish underparts
streaked undertail feathers
MALE

Named after the 19th-century ornithologist John Cassin, this finch has a rich, melodious song that incorporates phrases from the songs of several different Rocky Mountain species. From below, the male Cassin's Finch resembles a sparrow, but when it alights on a tree stump, its full, purple-red plumage is immediately evident. This species closely resembles the other two species in the genus *Carpodacus*, the Purple and House finches, whose ranges it overlaps, so it may take time and practice to be certain of this species' identity in the field. The female Cassin's Finch is not distinctive—it resembles a generic fledgling or a sparrow.

VOICE Call *tee-uhh* or *piddlit*; song rich and warbling; may include high-frequency whistles and imitations of other species.

NESTING Open cup on lateral branch of conifer, also in aspen or sagebrush; 4–5 eggs; 1 brood; May–July.

FEEDING Eats berries, pine seeds, aspen buds, insects, larvae; feeds mainly on ground but frequents feeding stations in winter.

FLIGHT: rapid wing beats, then a glide, in a regular sequence.

ARBOREAL FINCH
Cassin's Finch likes to perch on an elevated twig or branch, often in coniferous forests.

SIMILAR SPECIES

PURPLE FINCH see p.386

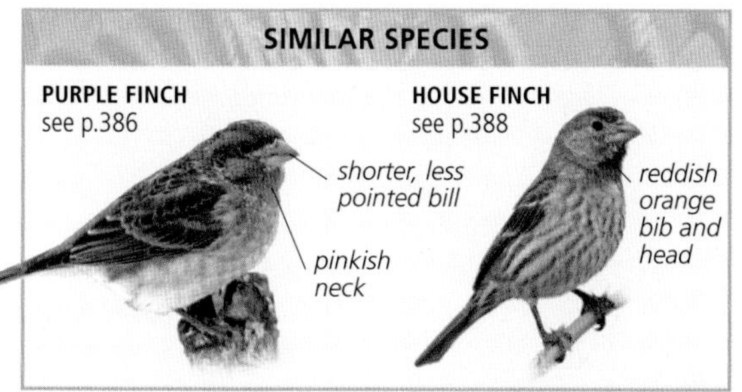
shorter, less pointed bill
pinkish neck

HOUSE FINCH see p.388

reddish orange bib and head

OCCURRENCE
Found in coniferous forests in mountains of western US and southwestern Canada; may occur in sagebrush–juniper plains or open areas with Ponderosa or Lodgepole pine. Migratory both toward lower elevations and southward. Winters throughout its breeding range.

Length **5½–6½in (14–16cm)**	Wingspan **10–10½in (25–27cm)**	Weight **⅞–1¼oz (25–35g)**
Social **Flocks**	Lifespan **Up to 10 years**	Status **Secure**

Order **Passeriformes**	Family **Fringillidae**	Species ***Carpodacus mexicanus***

House Finch

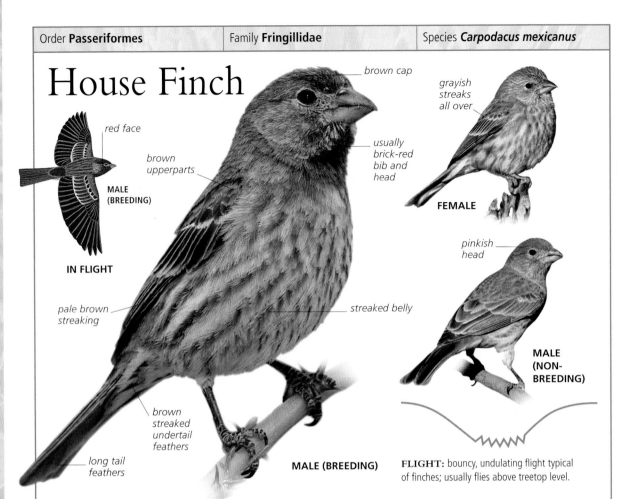

red face
MALE (BREEDING)
IN FLIGHT
brown cap
brown upperparts
usually brick-red bib and head
pale brown streaking
streaked belly
brown streaked undertail feathers
long tail feathers
MALE (BREEDING)
grayish streaks all over
FEMALE
pinkish head
MALE (NON-BREEDING)

FLIGHT: bouncy, undulating flight typical of finches; usually flies above treetop level.

Historically, the House Finch was a western bird, and was first reported in the eastern side of the US on Long Island, New York City in 1941. These birds are said to have originated from the illegal bird trade. The population of the eastern birds started expanding in the 1960s, by the late 1990s, their population had expanded westward to link up with the original western population. The male House Finch is distinguished from the Purple and Cassin's finches by its brown streaked underparts, while the females have plainer faces and generally blurrier streaking.

VOICE Call note *queet*; varied jumble of notes, often starting with husky notes to whistled and burry notes, and ending with a long *wheeerr*.

NESTING Females build nests from grass stems, thin twigs, and thin weeds in trees and on man-made structures; 1–6 eggs; 2–3 broods; March–August.

FEEDING Eats, almost exclusively, vegetable matter, such as buds, fruits, and seeds; readily comes to feeders.

RED IN THE FACE
The breeding male House-Finch can be identified by its stunning brick-red plumage.

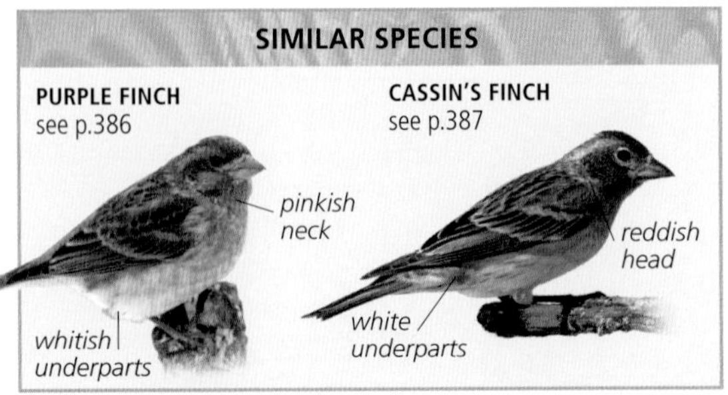
SIMILAR SPECIES
PURPLE FINCH
see p.386
pinkish neck
whitish underparts
CASSIN'S FINCH
see p.387
reddish head
white underparts

OCCURRENCE
Found in urban, suburban, and settled areas; in the West also in wilder areas such as savannas, desert grasslands, and chaparral, particularly near people; in the East almost exclusively in settled areas, including the centers of large cities. Resident, some birds move after breeding.

Length **5–6in (12.5–15cm)**	Wingspan **8–10in (20–25cm)**	Weight **9/16–1oz (16–27g)**
Social **Flocks**	Lifespan **Up to 12 years**	Status **Secure**

Order **Passeriformes**	Family **Fringillidae**	Species ***Pinicola enucleator***

Pine Grosbeak

two white wing bars
MALE
IN FLIGHT
greenish head
pale patch under eye
greenish rump
gray belly
FEMALE
stubby, curved, blackish bill
pinkish-red head
short neck
pinkish rump
long, blackish tail
IMMATURE MALE
pinkish red underparts (but regionally variable)
MALE

FLIGHT: undulating, buoyant, calm wing beats interrupted by glides.

The largest member of the family Fringillidae in North America, and easily distinguished by the male's unmistakable thick, stubby bill, the Pine Grosbeak is a resident of high elevations in the Rocky Mountains in the West. The bird is also found across northern Eurasia, where nine subspecies have been identified, four of which are found in North America. Due to extensive color variation of individual plumages, the age and sex of the bird are not always easily determined.

VOICE Contact calls of eastern birds *tee-tew*, or *tee-tee-tew*; western forms give more complex *tweedle*; warbling song.

NESTING Well-hidden, open cup nest usually in spruce or larch trees; 2–5 eggs, 1 brood; June–July.

FEEDING Eats spruce buds, maple seeds, and mountain ash berries throughout the year; consumes insects in summer.

FRUIT LOVER
This species can often be seen hanging from branches, gorging on ripe fruit.

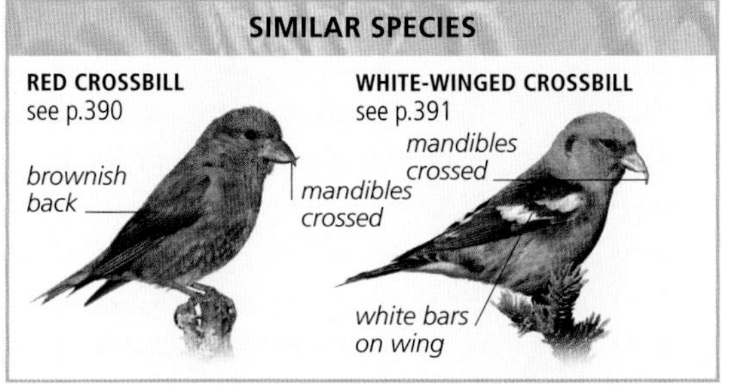
SIMILAR SPECIES
RED CROSSBILL
see p.390
brownish back
mandibles crossed
WHITE-WINGED CROSSBILL
see p.391
mandibles crossed
white bars on wing

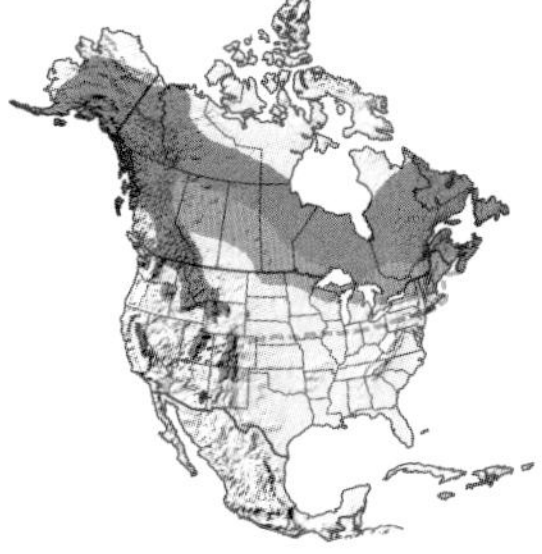

OCCURRENCE
Found in the boreal zone from Alaska to Quebec and Newfoundland, in open, northerly coniferous forests of North America in summer, usually near fresh water. Winters throughout its breeding range, but may move southward to southern Canada and the northeastern US.

Length **8–10in (20–25cm)**	Wingspan **13in (33cm)**	Weight **2–2½oz (55–70g)**
Social **Flocks**	Lifespan **Up to 10 years**	Status **Secure**

Order **Passeriformes**	Family **Fringillidae**	Species ***Loxia curvirostra***

Red Crossbill

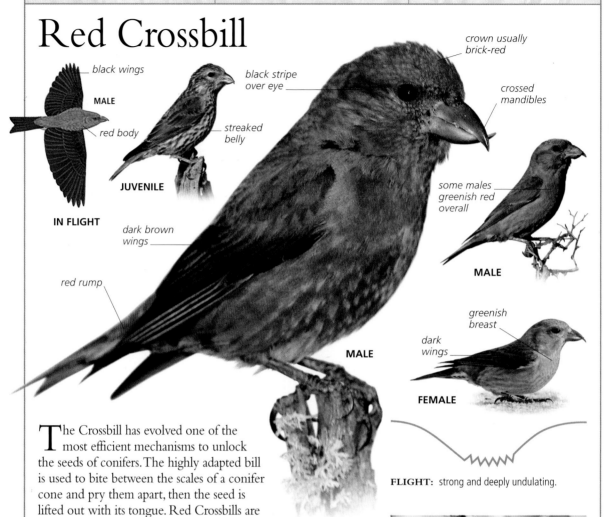

black wings
MALE
red body
IN FLIGHT
black stripe over eye
streaked belly
JUVENILE
crown usually brick-red
crossed mandibles
dark brown wings
red rump
MALE
some males greenish red overall
MALE
greenish breast
dark wings
FEMALE

FLIGHT: strong and deeply undulating.

The Crossbill has evolved one of the most efficient mechanisms to unlock the seeds of conifers. The highly adapted bill is used to bite between the scales of a conifer cone and pry them apart, then the seed is lifted out with its tongue. Red Crossbills are further specialized to harvest types of conifer seeds; eight different forms have been recognized, all the same color but different in body size, bill shape and size. Each form has a different flight call and rarely interbreeds with other forms even where they overlap.

VOICE Common call *jit* repeated 2–5 times; song complex, continuous warbling of notes, whistles, and buzzes.

NESTING Cup nest on lateral conifer branch; 3–5 eggs; 2 broods; can breed year-round.

FEEDING Feeds on pine seeds; also insects and larvae, particularly aphids; also other seeds.

PROCESSING SEEDS
The Red Crossbill manipulates seeds with its tongue before swallowing them.

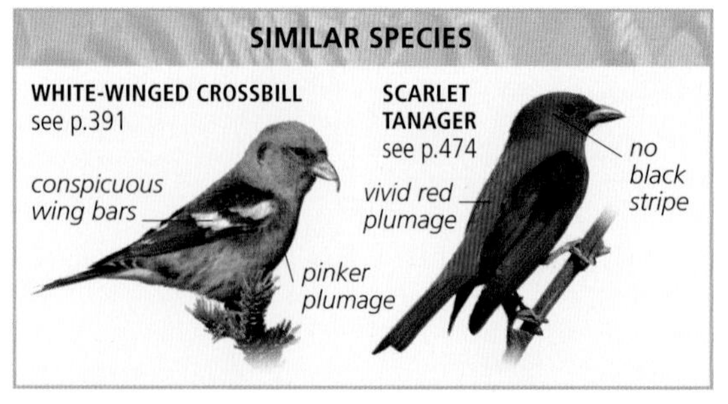
SIMILAR SPECIES
WHITE-WINGED CROSSBILL
see p.391
conspicuous wing bars
pinker plumage
SCARLET TANAGER
see p.474
vivid red plumage
no black stripe

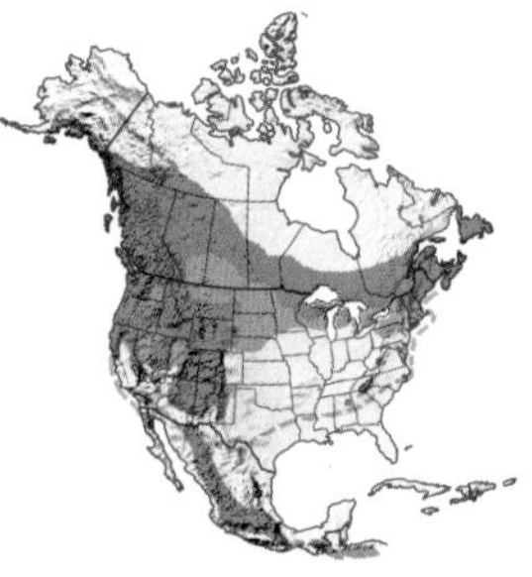

OCCURRENCE
Range covers coniferous or mixed-coniferous, and deciduous forests from Newfoundland to British Columbia and southern Alaska; also mountain forests in the Rockies, south to Mexico; irregular movements, depending on the availability of pine cones.

Length **5–6¾in (13–17cm)**	Wingspan **10–10½in (25–27cm)**	Weight **⅞–1¼oz (25–35g)**
Social **Flocks**	Lifespan **Up to 10 years**	Status **Secure**

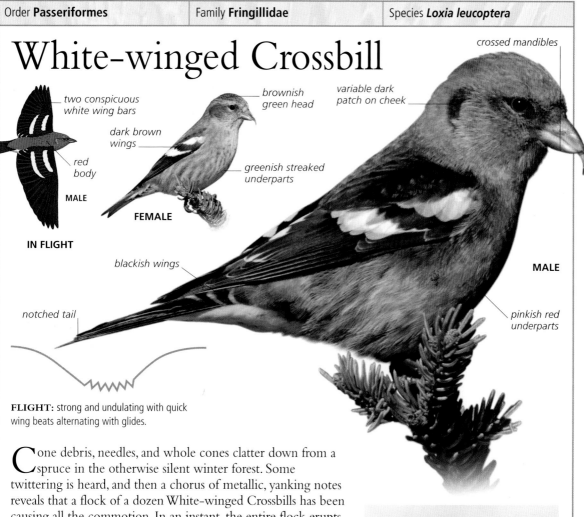

Order **Passeriformes**	Family **Fringillidae**	Species ***Loxia leucoptera***

White-winged Crossbill

two conspicuous white wing bars
red body
MALE
IN FLIGHT
dark brown wings
brownish green head
greenish streaked underparts
FEMALE
variable dark patch on cheek
crossed mandibles
blackish wings
MALE
notched tail
pinkish red underparts

FLIGHT: strong and undulating with quick wing beats alternating with glides.

Cone debris, needles, and whole cones clatter down from a spruce in the otherwise silent winter forest. Some twittering is heard, and then a chorus of metallic, yanking notes reveals that a flock of a dozen White-winged Crossbills has been causing all the commotion. In an instant, the entire flock erupts into the air, calling loudly in flight, only to disappear completely in the distance. Few other creatures of the northerly forest go about their business with such determined energy, and no others accent a winter woodland with hot pink and magenta—the colors of the White-winged Crossbill's head and breast.

VOICE Calls are sharp, chattering *plik*, or deeper *tyoop*, repeated in series of 3–7 notes; song melodious trilling.

NESTING Open cup nest, usually high on end of a spruce branch; eggs 3–5; 2 broods; July, January–February.

FEEDING Eats seeds from small-coned conifers; spruces, firs, larches; feeds on insects when available.

EATING SNOW
The White-winged Crossbill frequently eats snow to provide essential moisture.

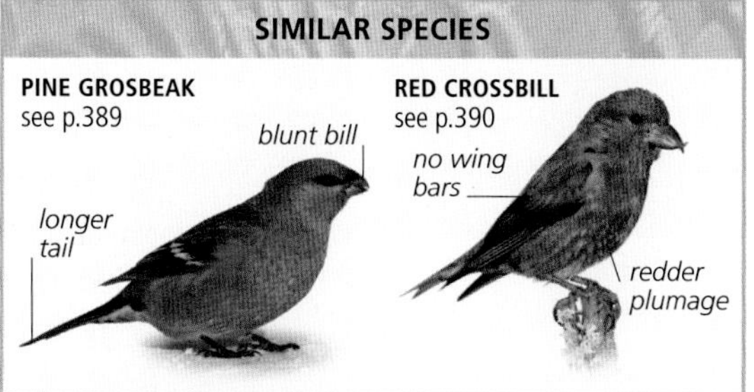
SIMILAR SPECIES
PINE GROSBEAK
see p.389
blunt bill
longer tail
RED CROSSBILL
see p.390
no wing bars
redder plumage

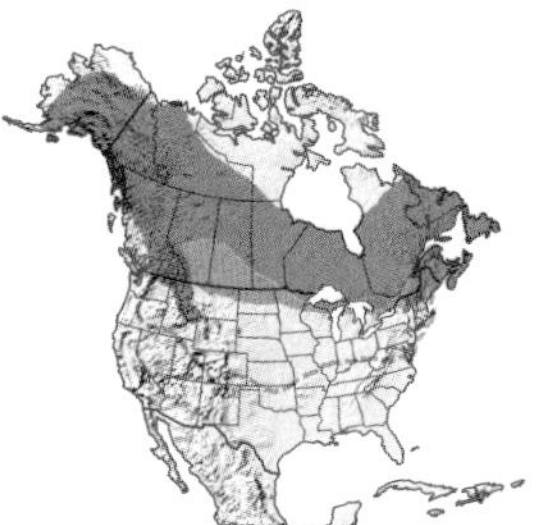

OCCURRENCE
Nomadic; most common in the spruce zone of Alaska and Canada but has bred as far south as Colorado in the West; in the East, from Quebec and Newfoundland southward to New York City and New England.

Length **5½–6in (14–15cm)**	Wingspan **10–10½in (26–27cm)**	Weight **11/16–1 1/16oz (20–30g)**
Social **Flocks**	Lifespan **Up to 10 years**	Status **Secure**

Order **Passeriformes**	Family **Fringillidae**	Species ***Coccothraustes vespertinus***

Evening Grosbeak

black wing tips
MALE
large white wing patches
IN FLIGHT
black outer wing feathers
very dark gray head and shoulders
yellow rump
large white wing patch
short, square tail
conspicuous yellow eyebrow
huge, yellowish bill
MALE
mustard yellow underparts
large, grayish bill
grayish wing patch
FEMALE

There is no mistaking a noisy, boisterous winter flock of husky gold-and-black Evening Grosbeaks when they descend on a bird feeder. The bird's outsize yellow bill seems to be made as much for threatening would-be rivals as it is designed for efficiently cracking sunflower seeds. In the breeding season, by contrast, the Evening Grosbeak is secretive and seldom seen, neither singing loudly nor displaying ostentatiously and nesting high in a tree. Once a bird of western North America, it has extended its range eastward in the past 200 years, and now nests as far as Newfoundland. This may be due to the planting of ornamental box elder, which carries its abundant seeds winter-long, ensuring a ready food supply for the bird.

VOICE Call descending *feeew*; also buzzy notes and beeping chatter.

NESTING Loose, grass-lined twig cup, usually on conifer branch; 3–4 eggs; 1–2 broods; May–July.

FEEDING Eats seeds of pines and other conifers, maple, and box elder seeds; also insects, and their larvae, particularly spruce budworm.

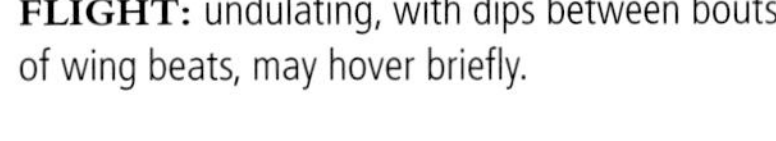

FLIGHT: undulating, with dips between bouts of wing beats, may hover briefly.

SIMILAR SPECIES

PINE GROSBEAK ♀
see p.389
stubby bill
wing bars
gray underparts
BALTIMORE ORIOLE ♀
see p.432
slender aspect
mottled head
pale orange underparts

CAPABLE BILL
This bird's extremely robust bill can deal with all kinds of winter fruits and seeds.

OCCURRENCE
Breeds in mixed conifer and spruce forest from Rocky Mountain region to eastern Canada, and on mountain ranges south to Mexico. Winters in coniferous or deciduous woodlands, often in suburban locations; may move south from northern range, depending on food supply.

Length **6½–7in (16–18cm)**	Wingspan **12–14in (30–36cm)**	Weight **2–2½oz (55–70g)**
Social **Flocks**	Lifespan **Up to 15 years**	Status **Secure**

WOOD-WARBLERS

THE FAMILY PARULIDAE IS REMARKABLE for its diversity: in plumage, song, feeding, breeding biology, and sexual dimorphism. In general, though, warblers share similar shapes: all are smallish birds with longish, thin bills (unlike thick vireo bills) used mostly for snapping up invertebrates. The odd, chunky, thick-billed Yellow-breasted Chat is a notable exception, but genetic data suggest what many birders have long suspected: it's not a warbler at all. Ground-dwelling warblers tend to be larger and clad in olives, browns, and yellows, while many arboreal species are small and sport bright oranges, cool blues, and even ruby reds. The color, location, and presence or absence of paler wingbars and tail spots is often a good identification aid. Warblers recently underwent an explosion of speciation in the East, and over 30 species may be seen there in a morning of spring birding. The spring arrival of beautiful singing males is the birding highlight of the year for many birdwatchers. Eastern-breeding species utilize three different migration strategies to deal with the obstacle of the Gulf of Mexico when coming from and going to their Neotropical wintering grounds. Circum-Gulf migrants fly through Mexico, along the western shore of the Gulf of Mexico. Caribbean migrants travel through Florida and island hop through the Caribbean. And finally, trans-Gulf migrants fly directly across the Gulf of Mexico between the Yucatan Peninsula and the northern Gulf Coast. Birds flying this last and most deadly route are subject to abrupt weather changes over the Gulf which sometimes yield spectacular fallout events at famed locations like High Island, Texas. The family is restricted to the Americas.

PLASTIC PLUMAGE
Many male Dendroica warblers (like this Blackburnian) are only brightly-colored when breeding.

FEEDING STRATEGIES
Some warblers, such as this Black-and-white, probe the cracks in tree trunks for food.

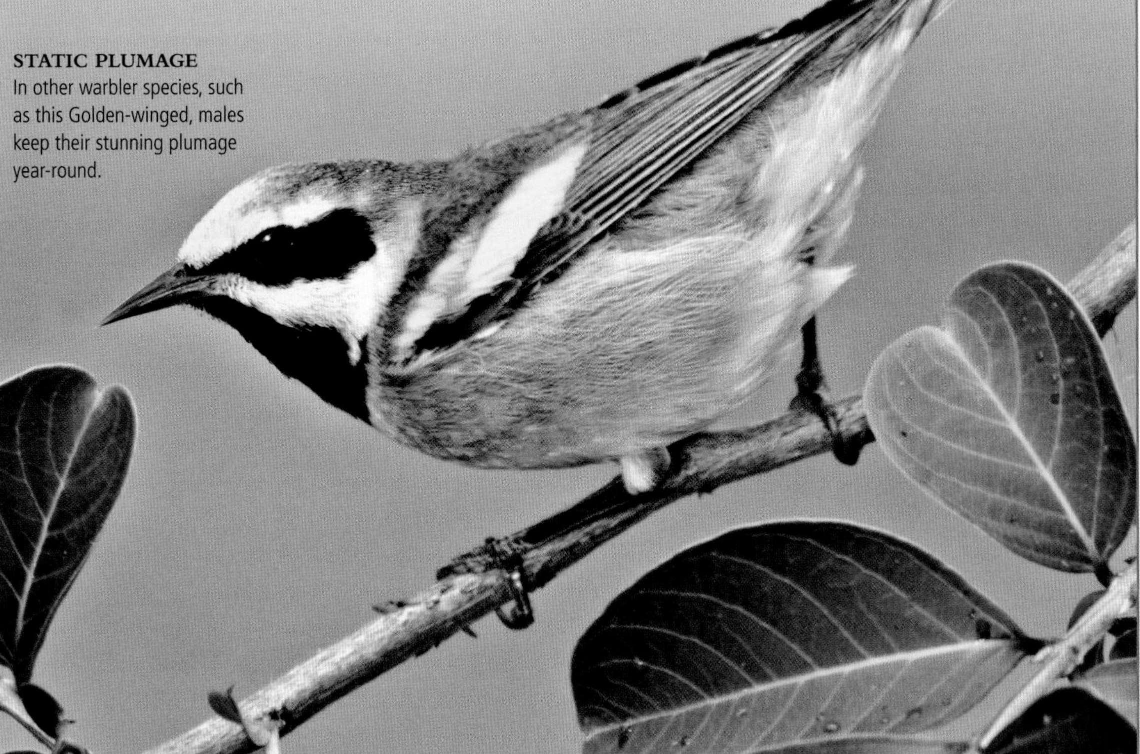

STATIC PLUMAGE
In other warbler species, such as this Golden-winged, males keep their stunning plumage year-round.

Order **Passeriformes**	Family **Parulidae**	Species ***Vermivora chrysoptera***

Golden-winged Warbler

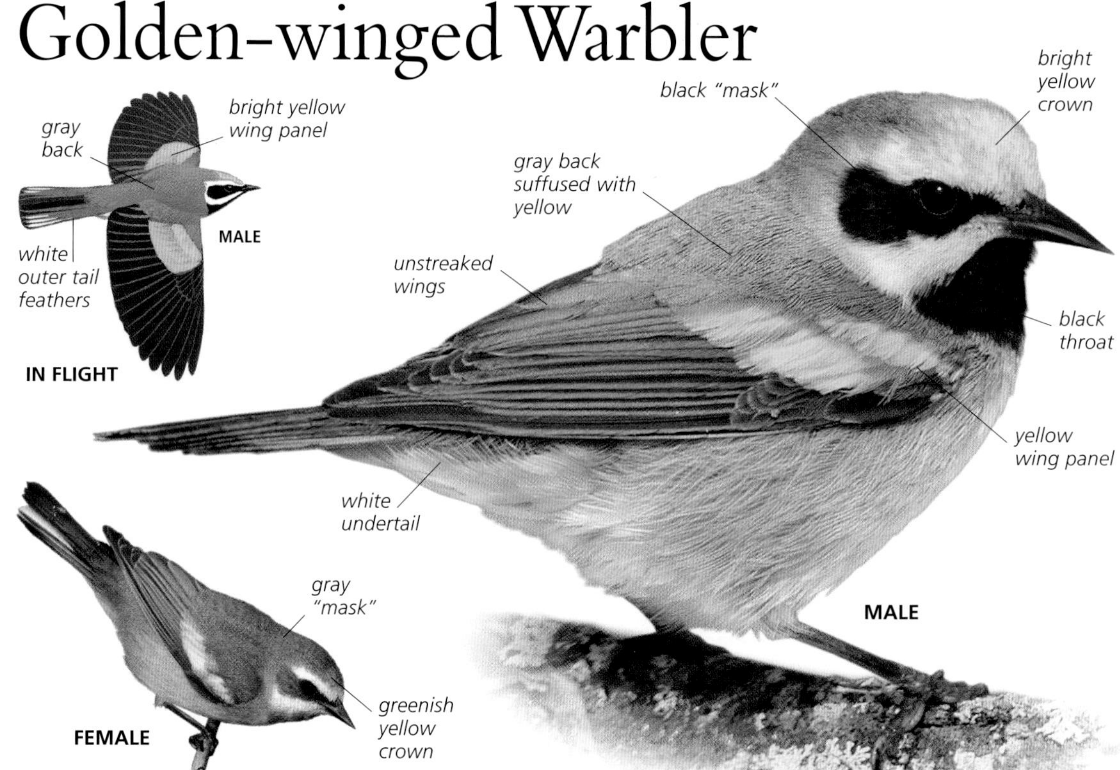
gray back
bright yellow wing panel
white outer tail feathers
MALE
IN FLIGHT
black "mask"
bright yellow crown
gray back suffused with yellow
unstreaked wings
black throat
yellow wing panel
white undertail
MALE
gray "mask"
greenish yellow crown
FEMALE

One of the continent's most beautiful warblers, this species is unfortunately being genetically swamped by the more southerly Blue-winged Warbler. This situation is worsening as more habitat is cleared and climate changes take place. It commonly interbreeds with the Blue-winged, resulting in two more frequently seen hybrid forms: Brewster's Warbler, which resembles the Blue-winged Warbler, and Lawrence's Warbler, which looks like a Blue-winged Warbler with the mask and black throat of a Golden-winged.

VOICE Call a sharp *tsip*; flight call high, slightly buzzy *ziiih;* song buzzy *zee zuu zuu zuu*, first note higher; birds that deviate from this song pattern may be hybrids.

NESTING Shallow bulky cup, on or just above ground; 4–6 eggs; 1 brood; May–July.

FEEDING Hangs upside-down at clusters of curled-up dead leaves; feeds on moth larvae, other winged insects, and spiders.

FLIGHT: typical warbler flight: fast, slightly undulating, and direct with rapid wing beats.

SMALL TREES REQUIRED
Golden-winged Warblers breed in shrubby habitats created by clearance and re-growth.

SIMILAR SPECIES

CAROLINA CHICKADEE see p.496
black cap
yellowish wash on underparts

BLACK-CAPPED CHICKADEE see p.326
black cap
white cheek
buffy underparts

OCCURRENCE
Breeds in the northeastern US and southeastern Canada in short secondary growth habitat with dense patches of deciduous shrubs or tangles, or in marshes with a forest edge; uses any wooded habitat on migration; winters in Central America from Guatemala to north Colombia; mostly on the Caribbean side.

Length **4¾in (12cm)**	Wingspan **7½in (19cm)**	Weight **9/32–3/8oz (8–11g)**
Social **Migrant/Winter flocks**	Lifespan **Unknown**	Status **Declining**

Order **Passeriformes**	Family **Parulidae**	Species ***Vermivora pinus***

Blue-winged Warbler

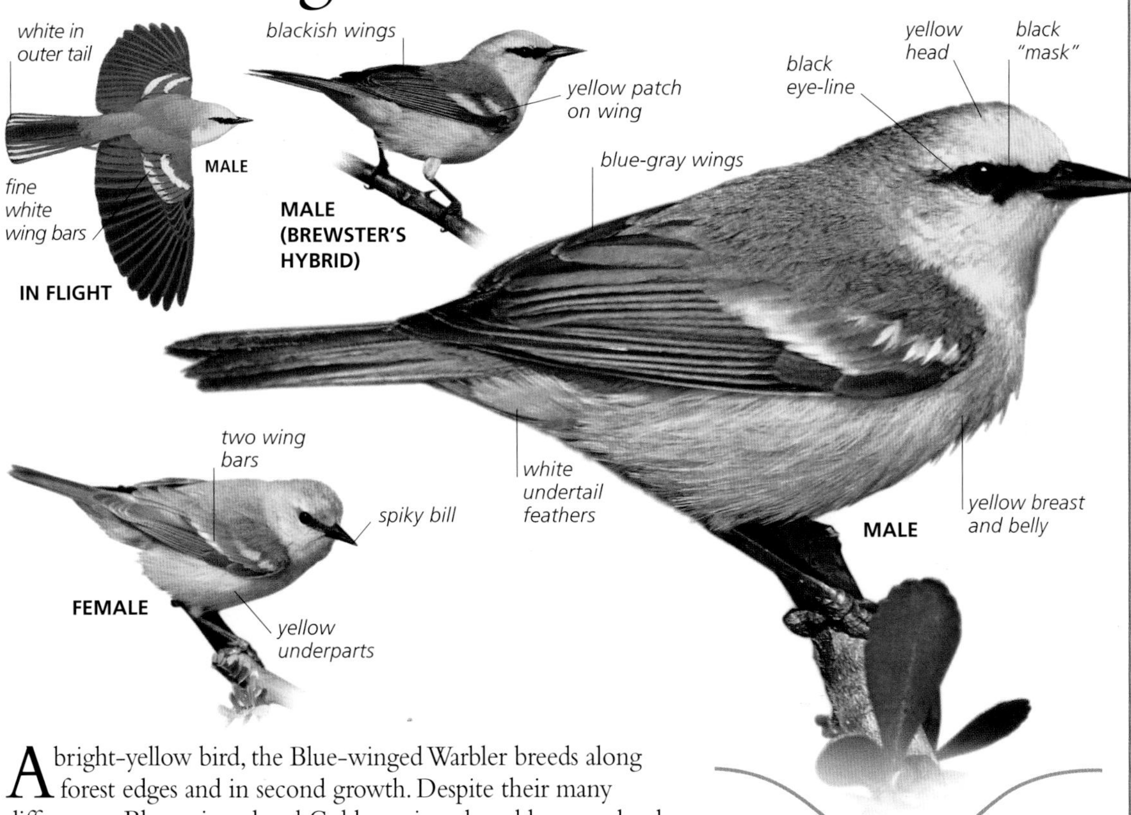
white in outer tail
fine white wing bars
MALE
IN FLIGHT
blackish wings
yellow patch on wing
MALE (BREWSTER'S HYBRID)
black eye-line
yellow head
black "mask"
blue-gray wings
two wing bars
spiky bill
white undertail feathers
yellow breast and belly
MALE
FEMALE
yellow underparts

A bright-yellow bird, the Blue-winged Warbler breeds along forest edges and in second growth. Despite their many differences, Blue-winged and Golden-winged warblers are closely related and interbreed freely, producing a variety of fertile combinations. The most frequently produced hybrid, Brewster's Warbler, named in 1874, was once believed to be a different species. It is similar to the Golden-winged Warbler (yellowish breast, two yellow wing bars), but has the Blue-winged's facial pattern, minus the black mask and throat.

FLIGHT: typical warbler flight: fast, slightly undulating, and direct with rapid wing beats.

VOICE Sharp *tsip* call, like *Spizella* sparrows; flight call: a high, slightly buzzy *ziiih;* song is a low, harsh, buzzy *beee-burrrrr,* second note very low in pitch and rattling; deviation from this song pattern may hint at hybrid origin.

NESTING Deep, bulky cup of vegetation, just off the ground in grasses; 4–5 eggs; 1 brood; May–June.

FEEDING Hangs upside-down at clusters of dead leaves; probes for moth larvae and small insects.

OCCURRENCE
Breeds in areas of second-growth forest, but is less picky than the Golden-winged Warbler and can use older and taller stands. Occurs in any wooded habitat on migration. Migrates across the Gulf of Mexico to winter in southeastern Mexico and central Panama.

DECEPTIVE HYBRID
The black border to this bird's ear patch indicates a Blue- or Golden-winged ancestry.

SIMILAR SPECIES

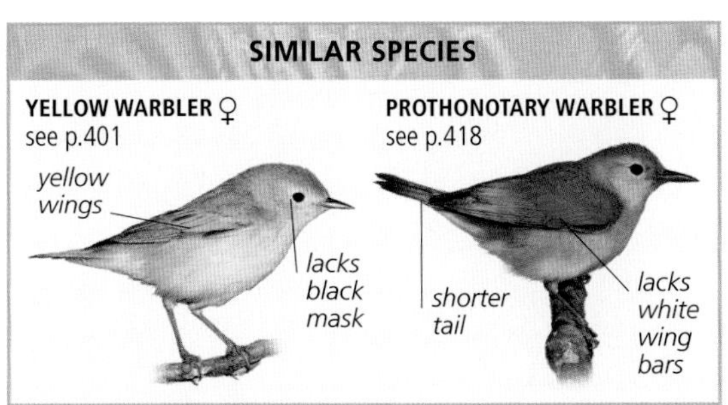
YELLOW WARBLER ♀
see p.401
yellow wings
lacks black mask
PROTHONOTARY WARBLER ♀
see p.418
shorter tail
lacks white wing bars

Length **4¾in (12cm)**	Wingspan **7½in (19cm)**	Weight **9⁄32–3⁄8oz (8–11g)**
Social **Loose flocks**	Lifespan **Up to 7 years**	Status **Secure**

Order **Passeriformes**	Family **Parulidae**	Species ***Vermivora peregrina***

Tennessee Warbler

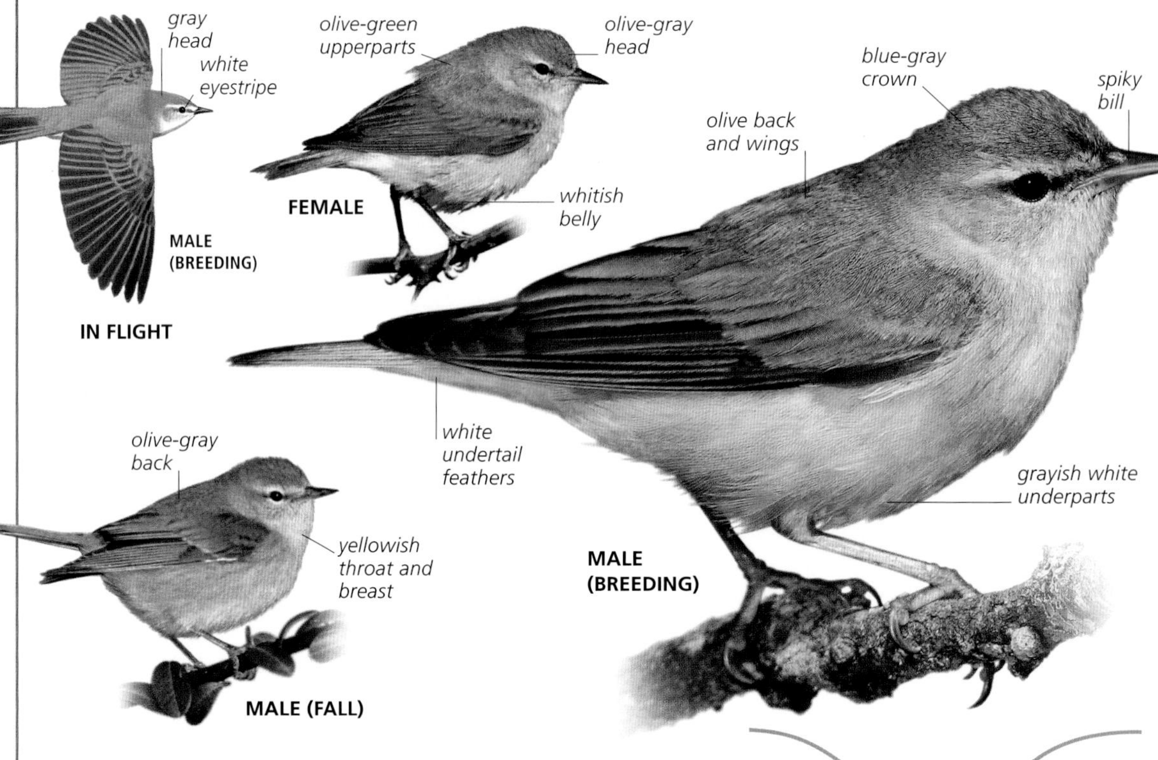
gray head
white eyestripe
MALE (BREEDING)
IN FLIGHT
olive-green upperparts
olive-gray head
FEMALE
whitish belly
blue-gray crown
spiky bill
olive back and wings
white undertail feathers
grayish white underparts
MALE (BREEDING)
olive-gray back
yellowish throat and breast
MALE (FALL)

The Tennessee Warbler was named after its place of discovery, but this bird would have been on migration, as it breeds almost entirely in Canada and winters in Central America. These warblers inhabit fairly remote areas, and their nests are difficult to find. It is one of a number of species that takes advantage of outbreaks of spruce budworm; the population of Tennessee Warblers tends to increase in years when budworms are abundant.

VOICE Call a sharp *tzit*; flight call a thin slightly rolling *seet*; song usually three-part staccato series, *chip-chip-chip*, each series increasing in pitch and usually in tempo.

NESTING Nest woven of fine plant matter, in ground depression, concealed from above by shrubbery; 4–7 eggs; 1 brood; June.

FEEDING Searches outer branches of trees for caterpillars, bees, wasps, beetles, and spiders; also eats fruits in winter and drinks nectar by piercing base of flowers.

FLIGHT: fast, slightly undulating, and direct with rapid wing beats.

UNIQUE UNDERPARTS
The breeding male is the only North American warbler with unmarked grayish white underparts.

SIMILAR SPECIES

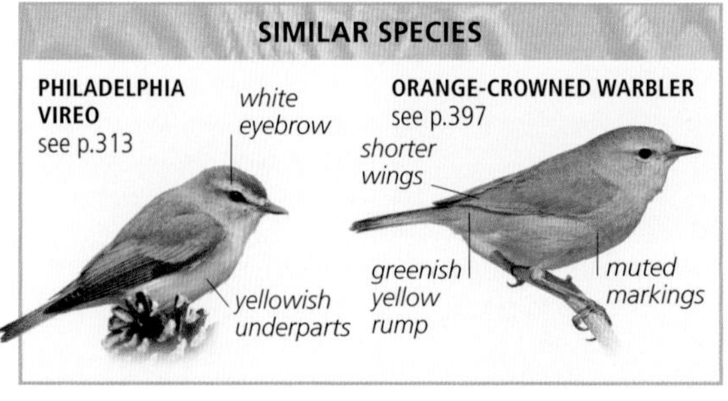
PHILADELPHIA VIREO
see p.313
white eyebrow
yellowish underparts
ORANGE-CROWNED WARBLER
see p.397
shorter wings
greenish yellow rump
muted markings

OCCURRENCE
Breeds in a variety of habitats, especially woodlands with dense understory and thickets of willows and alders. Very common in suburban parks and gardens during migration, particularly in the Midwest. Winters from southern Mexico to northern Ecuador and northern Venezuela.

Length **4¾in (12cm)**	Wingspan **7¾in (19.5cm)**	Weight **9/32–5/8oz (8–17g)**
Social **Flocks**	Lifespan **Up to 6 years**	Status **Secure**

Order **Passeriformes**	Family **Parulidae**	Species ***Vermivora celata***

Orange-crowned Warbler

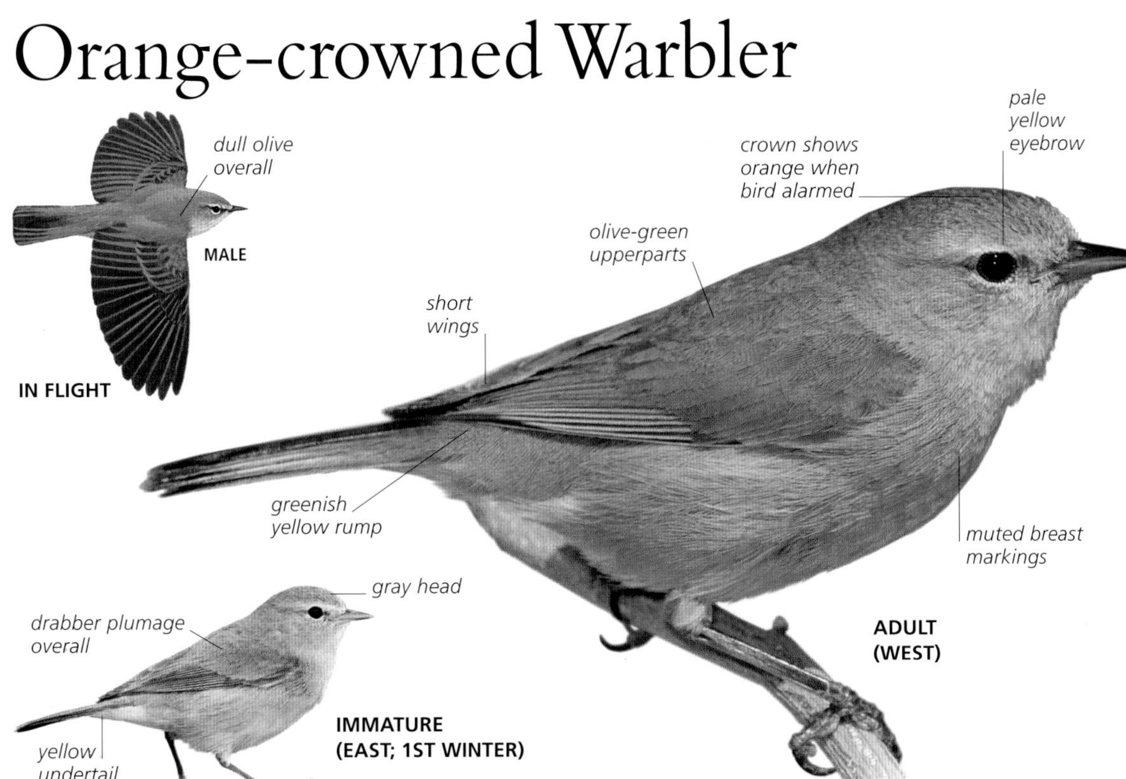
dull olive overall
MALE
IN FLIGHT
crown shows orange when bird alarmed
pale yellow eyebrow
olive-green upperparts
short wings
greenish yellow rump
muted breast markings
ADULT (WEST)
gray head
drabber plumage overall
yellow undertail feathers
IMMATURE (EAST; 1ST WINTER)

Common and relatively brightly colored in the West but uncommon and duller in the East, the Orange-crowned Warbler has a large breeding range. The 19th-century American naturalist Thomas Say described this species on the basis of specimens collected in Nebraska. He was struck by the tiny orange cap, but because it was so concealed in the plumage of the crown, he named it *celata*, which is Latin for "hidden." The orange cap is not usually visible in the field.

VOICE Call a clean, sharp *tsik*; flight call a high, short *seet*; song a loose, lazy trill; eastern birds lazier, western birds more emphatic.

NESTING Cup of grasses, fibers, and down, usually on ground under bush; 4–5 eggs; 1 brood; March–July.

FEEDING Gleans mostly arthropods such as beetles, ants, spiders, and their larvae; also eats fruits; collects nectar by piercing base of flower.

FLIGHT: fast, slightly undulating, and direct with rapid wing beats.

FACE MARKINGS

In eastern populations of this warbler, the birds have whitish facial markings during their first winter.

SIMILAR SPECIES

TENNESSEE WARBLER ♂ see p.396

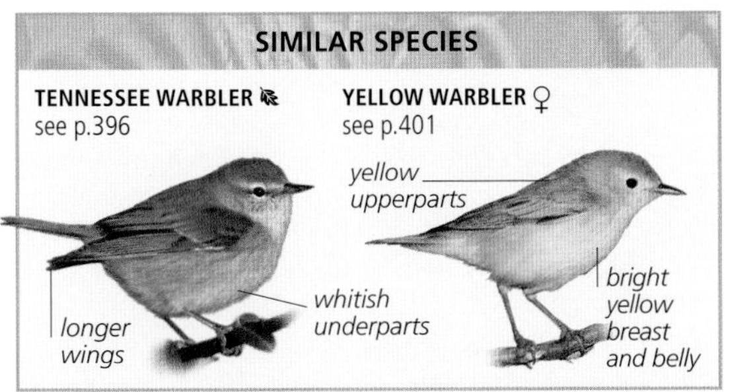
longer wings
whitish underparts

YELLOW WARBLER ♀ see p.401

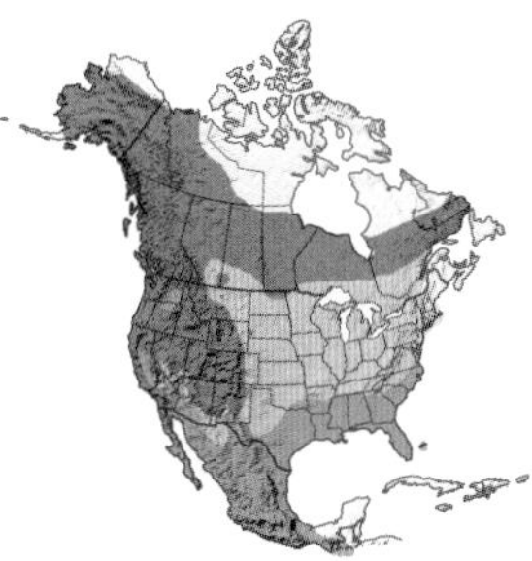
yellow upperparts
bright yellow breast and belly

OCCURRENCE

Breeds in varied habitats across North America from Alaska eastward to Newfoundland, and in the West from British Columbia southward to California, New Mexico, and western Texas. Prefers streamside thickets. Some winter in the West, while others go to Mexico and Guatemala.

Length **5in (13cm)**	Wingspan **7¼in (18.5cm)**	Weight **¼–⅜oz (7–11g)**
Social **Winter flocks**	Lifespan **Up to 6 years**	Status **Secure**

Order **Passeriformes**	Family **Parulidae**	Species ***Vermivora ruficapilla***

Nashville Warbler

MALE
V. r. ruficapilla
(EASTERN)

olive-green upperparts

IN FLIGHT

rounded wings

rufous crown patch

conspicuous white eye-ring

blue-gray helmet

grayish green back

olive wings

yellow undertail feathers

white patch on belly

MALE
V. r. ridgwayi
(WESTERN)

duller olive back

less contrast between gray and yellow

FEMALE
V. r. ruficapilla
(EASTERN)

FLIGHT: fast, slightly undulating, and direct, with rapid wing beats.

Although often confused with the ground-walking, chunky Connecticut Warbler, the Nashville Warbler is much smaller, hops about up in trees, and has a yellow throat. Nashville has two subspecies: *V. r. ruficapilla* in the East and *V. r. ridgwayi* in the West. Differences in voice, habitat, behavior, and plumage hint that they may in fact be separate species. *V. r. ridgwayi* can be distinguished as it has more extensive white on its belly and a grayish green back.

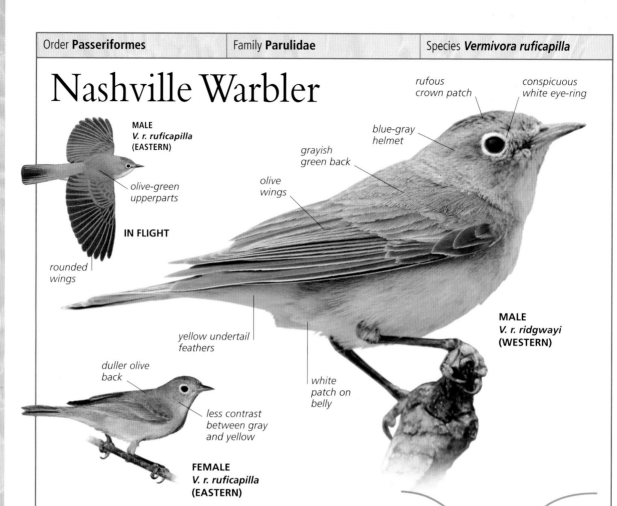

VOICE Call sharp *tik*, sharper in West; flight call high, thin *siit*; eastern song two parts: first part lazy, second faster trill *tee-tsee tee-tsee tee-tsee tititititi*; western song slightly lower and fuller with lazier second part, a seldom trilled *tee-tsee tee-tsee tee-tsee weesay weesay way*.

NESTING Cup hidden on ground in dense cover; 3–6 eggs; 1 brood; May–July.

FEEDING Gleans insects and spiders from trees.

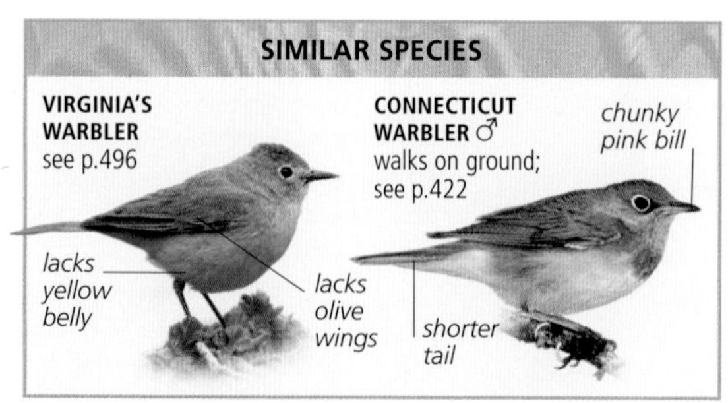
SIMILAR SPECIES
VIRGINIA'S WARBLER
see p.496
lacks yellow belly
lacks olive wings
CONNECTICUT WARBLER ♂
walks on ground; see p.422
chunky pink bill
shorter tail

FIELD MARKS
The white eye-ring and belly are evident on this singing male.

OCCURRENCE
Ruficapilla breeds in wet habitats of Saskatchewan east to Newfoundland and south to West Virginia; *ridgwayi* in brushy montane areas in Sierras and northern Rockies; *ridgwayi* winters in coastal California and south Texas to Guatemala; *ruficapilla* migrates to winter mainly in Mexico.

Length **4¾in (12cm)**	Wingspan **7½in (19cm)**	Weight **¼–7/16oz (7–13g)**
Social **Migrant/Winter flocks**	Lifespan **Up to 7 years**	Status **Secure**

Order **Passeriformes**	Family **Parulidae**	Species ***Parula americana***

Northern Parula

MALE

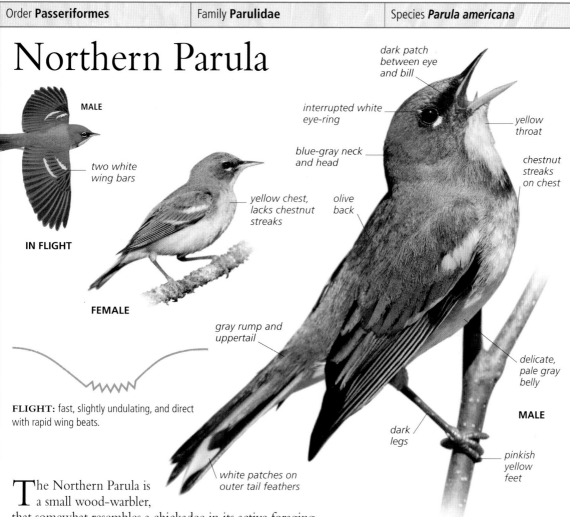

two white wing bars

IN FLIGHT

yellow chest, lacks chestnut streaks

FEMALE

dark patch between eye and bill

interrupted white eye-ring

blue-gray neck and head

olive back

yellow throat

chestnut streaks on chest

gray rump and uppertail

delicate, pale gray belly

MALE

dark legs

pinkish yellow feet

white patches on outer tail feathers

FLIGHT: fast, slightly undulating, and direct with rapid wing beats.

The Northern Parula is a small wood-warbler, that somewhat resembles a chickadee in its active foraging behavior. This bird depends on very specific nesting materials—*Ushea* lichens, or "Old Man's Beard," in the north, and *Tillandsia*, or Spanish Moss, in the South. The presence of these parasitic plants on trees greatly limits the geographical range of this species. The Northern Parula interbreeds with the Tropical Parula in southern Texas where their ranges cross, producing hybrid birds.

VOICE Call a very sharp *tsip*; flight call a thin, weak, descending *tsiif*; song a variable, most common buzzy upslurred trill, variably continuous or in steps, ending very high, but then dropping off in an emphatic *zip*.

NESTING Hanging pouch in clump of lichens; 4–5 eggs; 1 brood; May–July (south) or April–August (north).

FEEDING Gleans for caterpillars, flies, moths, beetles,wasps, ants, spiders; also eats berries, nectar, some seeds.

THE AMERICAN TIT

This small yellow-and chestnut-breasted bird was named by Carl Linnaeus in 1758.

SIMILAR SPECIES

TROPICAL PARULA
dark face
more yellow

OCCURRENCE

Nests in almost any kind of wooded area with its preferred nesting material; migrants (some of which cross the Gulf of Mexico) occur in almost any habitat; winters in varied habitats from southern Texas and Florida across Caribbean and Mexico south to Panama.

Length **4¼in (11cm)**	Wingspan **7in (18cm)**	Weight **¼–⅜oz (7–10g)**
Social **Winter flocks**	Lifespan **Up to 7 years**	Status **Secure**

Order **Passeriformes**	Family **Parulidae**	Species ***Dendroica pensylvanica***

Chestnut-sided Warbler

MALE (BREEDING)
two yellow wing bars
IN FLIGHT
white outer tail feathers
yellow cap
black "mustache"
chestnut band along flanks
FEMALE (BREEDING)
yellow-and-black streaks on upperparts
conspicuous white cheeks
yellow crown
white throat
white tail spots
two wing bars
rich chestnut flanks
MALE (BREEDING)
olive crown
bright lime-green above
plain face with white eye-ring
FEMALE (1ST FALL)
plain gray underside

The Chestnut-sided Warbler is one of the few wood-warbler species that has benefited from deforestation, because it depends on deciduous second-growth and forest edges for breeding. Once a rare bird, it is more common now than it was in the early 19th century. These birds vary in appearance, immature females looking quite unlike adult males in breeding. In all plumages, yellowish wing bars and whitish belly are the most distinguishing characteristics. Its pleasant song has long been transcribed as *pleased pleased pleased to MEET'cha*.

VOICE Call a sweet *chip*; flight call a low, burry *brrrt;* song a series of fast, sweet notes, usually ending with emphatic *WEET-chew*.

NESTING Open, easy-to-find cup just off ground in small deciduous tree or shrub; 3–5 eggs; 1 brood; May–August.

FEEDING Eats insects, especially larvae; also berries and seeds.

FLIGHT: fast, slightly undulating, and direct with rapid wing beats.

MALE TERRITORY
This singing, territorial male prefers second-growth thickets as its habitat.

SIMILAR SPECIES

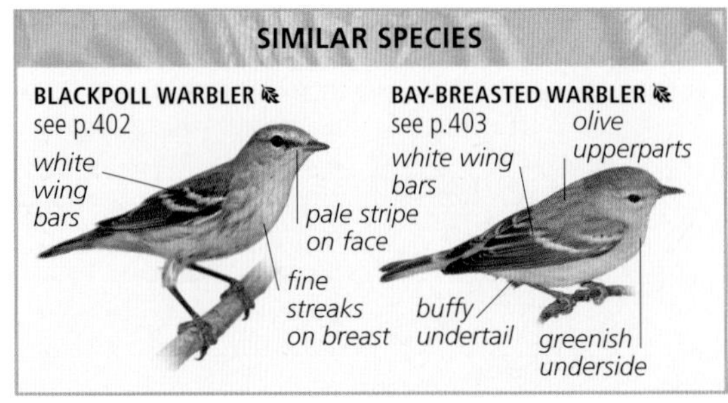
BLACKPOLL WARBLER
see p.402
white wing bars
pale stripe on face
fine streaks on breast
BAY-BREASTED WARBLER
see p.403
white wing bars
olive upperparts
buffy undertail
greenish underside

OCCURRENCE
Breeds in successive stages of regrowth in deciduous forests, from Alberta to the Great Lakes, New England, and the Appalachians; isolated populations in the Midwest. Winters in the West Indies, Mexico, and Central America, south to Venezuela and northern Colombia.

Length **5in (13cm)**	Wingspan **8in (20cm)**	Weight **9/32–7/16oz (8–13g)**
Social **Winter flocks**	Lifespan **Up to 7 years**	Status **Secure**

Order **Passeriformes**	Family **Parulidae**	Species ***Dendroica petechia***

Yellow Warbler

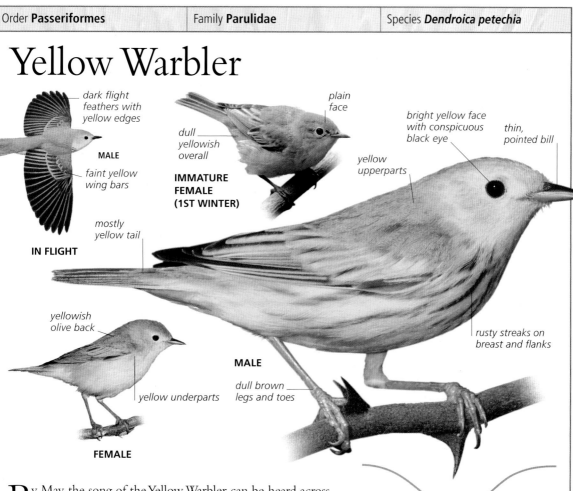

dark flight feathers with yellow edges

MALE

faint yellow wing bars

IN FLIGHT

mostly yellow tail

dull yellowish overall

plain face

IMMATURE FEMALE (1ST WINTER)

bright yellow face with conspicuous black eye

thin, pointed bill

yellow upperparts

rusty streaks on breast and flanks

MALE

dull brown legs and toes

yellowish olive back

yellow underparts

FEMALE

FLIGHT: fast, slightly undulating, and direct, with rapid wing beats.

By May, the song of the Yellow Warbler can be heard across North America as the birds arrive for the summer. This species is extremely variable geographically, with about 40 subspecies, especially on its tropical range (West Indies and Central and South America). The Yellow Warbler is known to build another nest on top of an old one when cowbird eggs appear in it, which can result in up to six different tiers. The Yellow Warbler does not walk, but rather hops from branch to branch.

VOICE Call a variable *chip*, sometimes given in series; flight call buzzy *zeep*; song variable series of fast, sweet notes; western birds often add an emphatic ending.

NESTING Deep cup of plant material, grasses in vertical fork of deciduous tree or shrub; 4–5 eggs; 1 brood; May–July.

FEEDING Eats mostly insects and insect larvae, plus some fruit.

ONE OF A KIND
This species has more yellow in its plumage than any other North American wood-warbler.

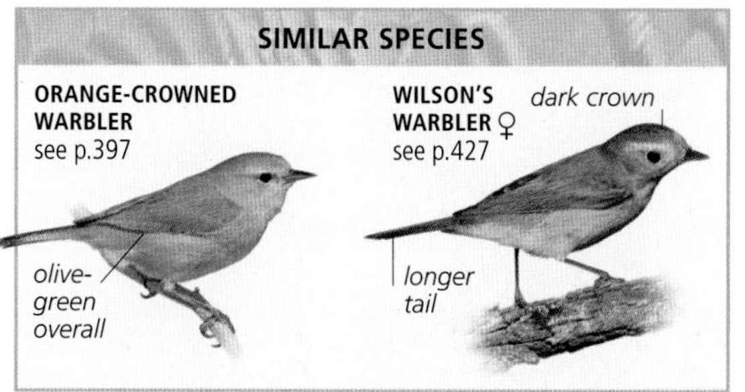
SIMILAR SPECIES
ORANGE-CROWNED WARBLER
see p.397
olive-green overall
WILSON'S WARBLER ♀
see p.427
dark crown
longer tail

OCCURRENCE
Widespread in most shrubby and second-growth habitats of North America. Migrates to southern US and southward to Mexico, Central America, and South America. Resident populations live in Florida and the West Indies.

Length **5in (13cm)**	Wingspan **8in (20cm)**	Weight **⁹⁄₃₂–½oz (8–14g)**
Social **Flocks**	Lifespan **Up to 9 years**	Status **Secure**

Order **Passeriformes**	Family **Parulidae**	Species ***Dendroica striata***

Blackpoll Warbler

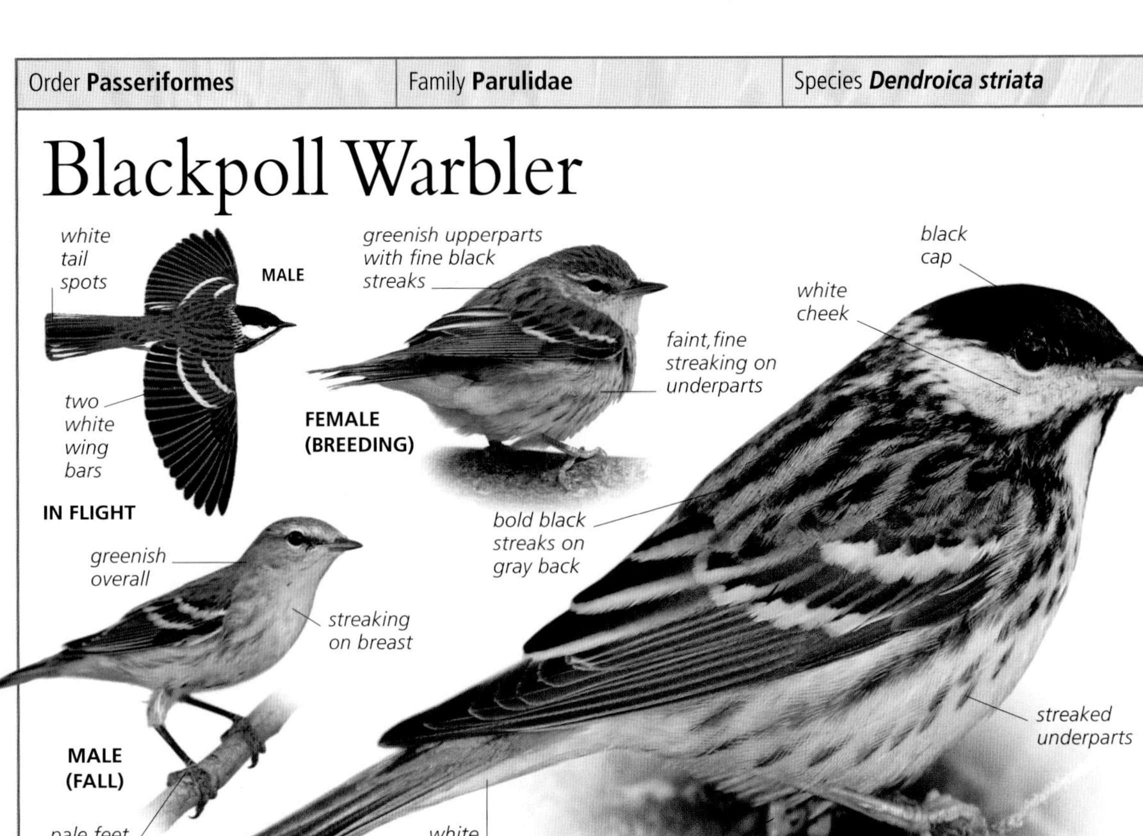
white tail spots
MALE
two white wing bars
IN FLIGHT
greenish upperparts with fine black streaks
faint, fine streaking on underparts
FEMALE (BREEDING)
black cap
white cheek
greenish overall
streaking on breast
bold black streaks on gray back
MALE (FALL)
pale feet contrasting with darker legs
white undertail feathers
MALE (BREEDING)
orange legs
streaked underparts

FLIGHT: fast, slightly undulating, and direct, with rapid wing beats.

The Blackpoll Warbler is well known for undergoing a remarkable fall migration that takes it over the Atlantic Ocean from southern Canada and the northeastern US to northern Venezuela. Before departing, it almost doubles its body weight with fat to serve as fuel for the nonstop journey. In spring, most of these birds travel the shorter Caribbean route back north.

VOICE Call piercing *chip*; flight call high, buzzy yet sharp *tzzzt*; common song crescendo of fast, extremely high-pitched ticks, ending with a decrescendo *tsst tsst TSST TSST TSST tsst tsst;* less commonly, ticks run into even faster trill.

NESTING Well-hidden cup placed low against conifer trunk; 3–5 eggs; 1–2 broods; May–July.

FEEDING Gleans arthropods, such as worms and beetles, but will take small fruit in fall and winter.

REACHING THE HIGH NOTES
The song of the male Blackpoll is so high-pitched that it is inaudible to many people.

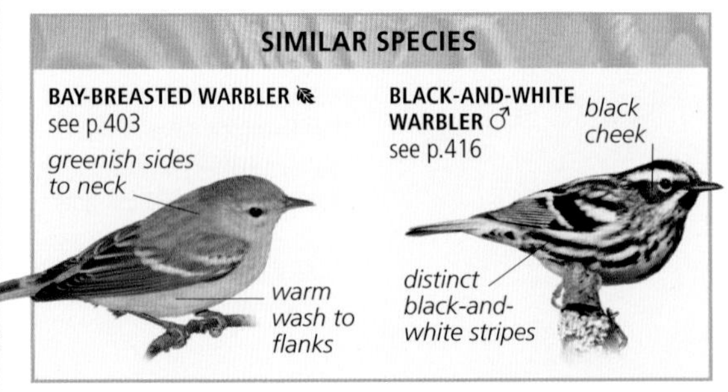
SIMILAR SPECIES
BAY-BREASTED WARBLER
see p.403
greenish sides to neck
warm wash to flanks
BLACK-AND-WHITE WARBLER ♂
see p.416
black cheek
distinct black-and-white stripes

OCCURRENCE
Breeds in spruce-fir forests across the northern boreal forest zone from Alaska eastward to Newfoundland, southward to coastal coniferous forests in the Maritimes and northern New England. Migrants gather in the Atlantic Ocean to landfall in the Caribbean and northern South America.

Length **5½in (14cm)**	Wingspan **9in (23cm)**	Weight **3/8–5/8oz (10–18g)**
Social **Flocks**	Lifespan **Up to 8 years**	Status **Secure**

Order **Passeriformes**	Family **Parulidae**	Species ***Dendroica castanea***

Bay-breasted Warbler

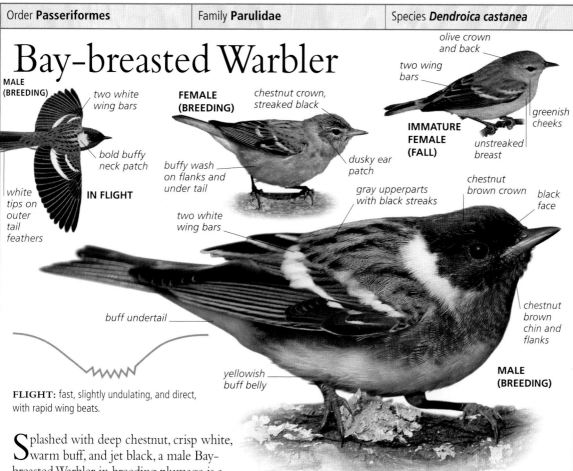

MALE (BREEDING)
two white wing bars
bold buffy neck patch
white tips on outer tail feathers
IN FLIGHT

FEMALE (BREEDING)
chestnut crown, streaked black
buffy wash on flanks and under tail
dusky ear patch

olive crown and back
two wing bars
greenish cheeks
IMMATURE FEMALE (FALL)
unstreaked breast

gray upperparts with black streaks
chestnut brown crown
black face
two white wing bars
buff undertail
chestnut brown chin and flanks
yellowish buff belly
MALE (BREEDING)

FLIGHT: fast, slightly undulating, and direct, with rapid wing beats.

Splashed with deep chestnut, crisp white, warm buff, and jet black, a male Bay-breasted Warbler in breeding plumage is a particularly striking bird, but fall females are very different with their dull, greenish plumage. Like the Tennessee Warbler, this species depends largely on outbreaks of spruce budworms (a major food source), so its numbers rise and fall according to those outbreaks. Overall, the Bay-breasted Warbler population has decreased because of the increased use of pesticide sprays.

VOICE Call a somewhat upslurred *tsip*; flight call a high, buzzy, short, and sharp *tzzzt*; song of very high, thin notes, often ending on lower pitch: *wee-si wee-si wee-si wee*.

NESTING Fragile-looking cup of grass and lichens on horizontal branch at mid-level in forest; 4–5 eggs; 1 brood; May–July.

FEEDING Mostly eats moths, smaller insects, worms, spiders, and caterpillars during migration and on breeding grounds; eats mainly fruit in winter.

SINGING IN THE FOREST
A brilliantly colored breeding male sings its high-pitched song on a spruce branch.

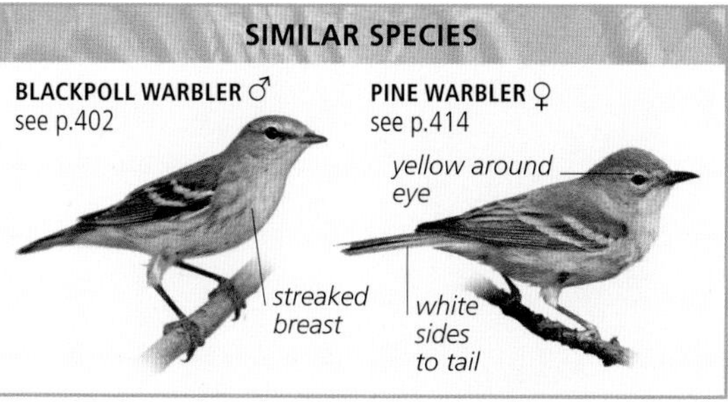
SIMILAR SPECIES
BLACKPOLL WARBLER ♂
see p.402
streaked breast
PINE WARBLER ♀
see p.414
yellow around eye
white sides to tail

OCCURRENCE
Breeds in mature spruce-fir-balsam forest across the forest belt from Yukon to the Maritimes, and south to the Great Lakes area and northern New England. Migrants occur in varied habitat, but especially woodland edges. Winters in wet forest in central America.

Length **5½in (14cm)**	Wingspan **9in (23cm)**	Weight **⅜–½oz (11–15g)**
Social **Migratory/Winter flocks**	Lifespan **Up to 4 years**	Status **Vulnerable**

Order **Passeriformes**	Family **Parulidae**	Species ***Dendroica fusca***

Blackburnian Warbler

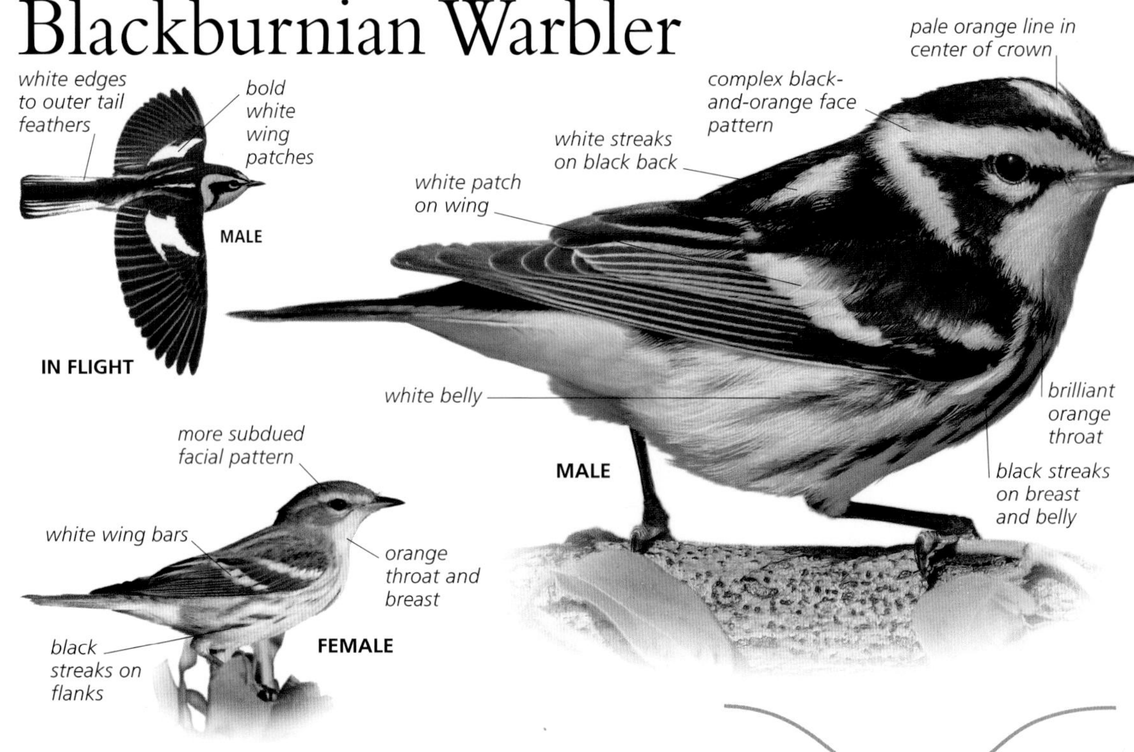

white edges to outer tail feathers
bold white wing patches
MALE
IN FLIGHT
pale orange line in center of crown
complex black-and-orange face pattern
white streaks on black back
white patch on wing
white belly
brilliant orange throat
black streaks on breast and belly
MALE
more subdued facial pattern
white wing bars
orange throat and breast
black streaks on flanks
FEMALE

FLIGHT: fast, slightly undulating, and direct with rapid wing beats.

This fiery beacon of the treetops is considered one of the most beautiful members of its family; its orange throat is unique among the North American warblers. The Blackburnian Warbler co-exists with many other *Dendroica* warblers in the coniferous and mixed woods of the north and east, but is able to do so by exploiting a slightly different niche for foraging—in this case the treetops. It also seeks the highest trees for nesting.

VOICE Call a slightly husky *chik*; flight-call a high, thin *zzee;* song variable, but always high-pitched; swirling series of lisps, spiraling upward to end in an almost inaudible *trill.*

NESTING Fine cup in conifer on horizontal branch away from trunk, usually high in tree; 4–5 eggs; 1 brood; May–July.

FEEDING Gleans arthropods, such as spiders, worms, and beetles; also fruit.

DISTINGUISHING FEATURES
The female is like a dull adult male, but with two wing bars and no black on the face.

AVIAN FIREFLY
This male in breeding plumage glows when seen against a dark forest background.

SIMILAR SPECIES

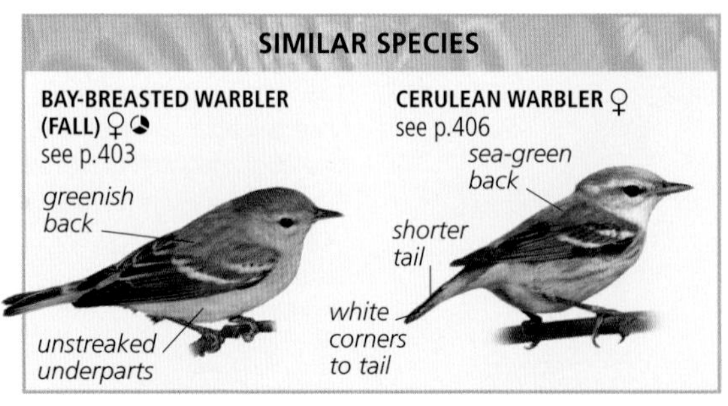

BAY-BREASTED WARBLER (FALL) ♀
see p.403
greenish back
unstreaked underparts
CERULEAN WARBLER ♀
see p.406
sea-green back
shorter tail
white corners to tail

OCCURRENCE
Breeds in coniferous and mixed forests from Alberta east through the North Great Lakes to Newfoundland and south into the Appalachians of Georgia; migrants found in wooded, shrubby, or forest edge habitats. Winters in wet forests in Costa Rica and Panama, and southward as far as Peru.

Length **5in (13cm)**	Wingspan **8½in (21cm)**	Weight **5⁄16–7⁄16oz (9–12g)**
Social **Winter flocks**	Lifespan **Up to 8 years**	Status **Secure**

Order **Passeriformes**	Family **Parulidae**	Species ***Dendroica magnolia***

Magnolia Warbler

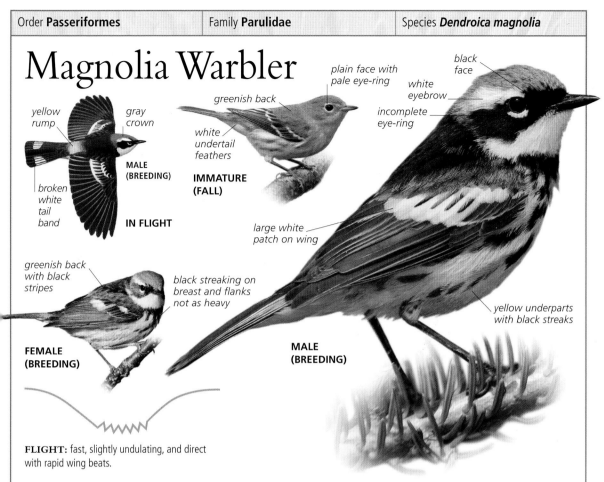

yellow rump
gray crown
MALE (BREEDING)
broken white tail band
IN FLIGHT

greenish back
plain face with pale eye-ring
white undertail feathers
IMMATURE (FALL)

black face
white eyebrow
incomplete eye-ring
large white patch on wing
yellow underparts with black streaks
MALE (BREEDING)

greenish back with black stripes
black streaking on breast and flanks not as heavy
FEMALE (BREEDING)

FLIGHT: fast, slightly undulating, and direct with rapid wing beats.

The bold, flashy, and common Magnolia Warbler is hard to miss as it flits around at eye level, fanning its uniquely marked tail. This species nests in young forests and winters in almost any habitat, so its numbers have not suffered in recent decades, unlike some of its relatives. Although it really has no preference for its namesake plant, the 19th-century ornithologist Alexander Wilson discovered a Magnolia Warbler feeding in a magnolia tree during migration, which is how it got its name.

VOICE Call a tinny *jeinf*, not particularly warbler-like; also short, simple whistled series *wee'-sa wee'-sa WEET-a-chew*; short, distinctive, flight call a high, trilled *zeep*.

NESTING Flimsy cup of black rootlets placed low in dense conifer against trunk; 3–5 eggs; 1 brood; June–August.

FEEDING Gleans mostly caterpillars, beetles, and spiders.

SPRUCE WARBLER
The conspicuous male Magnolia Warbler can be found singing its distinctive, loud song throughout the day often in a spruce tree.

SIMILAR SPECIES

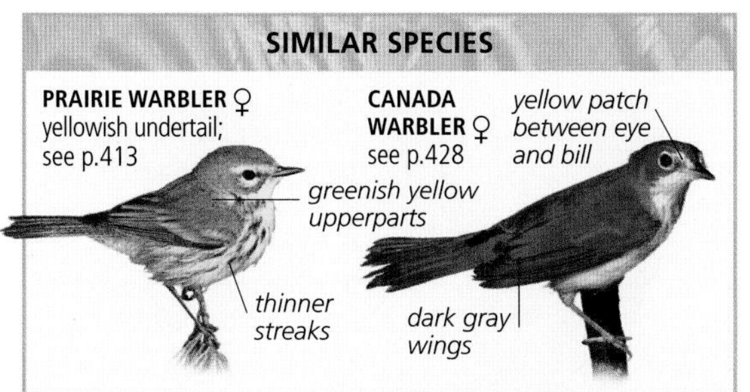
PRAIRIE WARBLER ♀
yellowish undertail;
see p.413
greenish yellow upperparts
thinner streaks
CANADA WARBLER ♀
see p.428
yellow patch between eye and bill
dark gray wings

OCCURRENCE
Breeds in dense, young mixed and coniferous forests from Yukon east to Newfoundland and south into Appalachians of Tennessee; migrates across the Gulf and Caribbean; winters in varied habitats in Caribbean and from southeast Mexico to Panama; rare vagrant in the West.

Length **5in (13cm)**	Wingspan **7½in (19cm)**	Weight **7/32–7/16oz (6–12g)**
Social **Migrant/Winter flocks**	Lifespan **Up to 6 years**	Status **Secure**

Order **Passeriformes**	Family **Parulidae**	Species ***Dendroica cerulea***

Cerulean Warbler

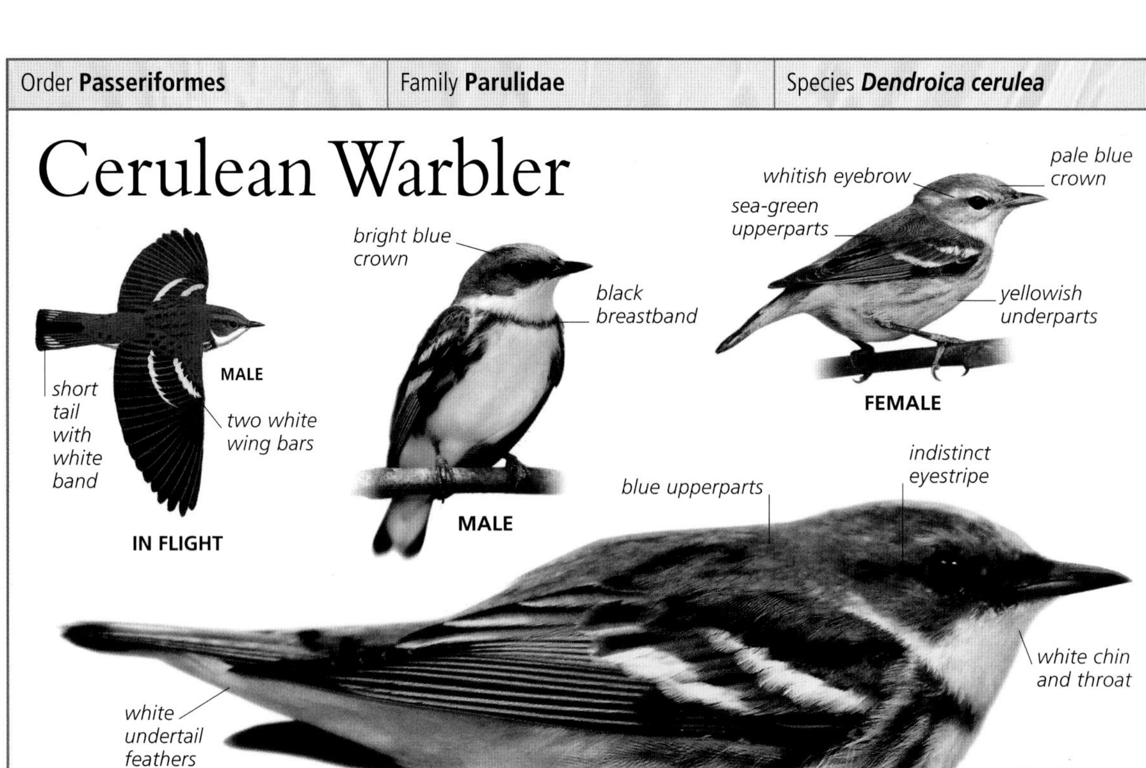
short tail with white band
MALE
two white wing bars
IN FLIGHT
bright blue crown
black breastband
MALE
whitish eyebrow
pale blue crown
sea-green upperparts
yellowish underparts
FEMALE
indistinct eyestripe
blue upperparts
white chin and throat
white undertail feathers
MALE
black streaks on flanks
white belly

FLIGHT: fast, slightly undulating, and direct with rapid wing beats.

This unusually colored species is difficult to spot, as it spends the majority of its time foraging in the canopy of deciduous forests. It was once common across the Midwest and the Ohio River Valley, but its habitat is being cleared for agriculture and fragmented by development. In winter, this bird lives high in the canopy of the Andean foothills, but sadly this habitat is threatened by coffee cultivation.

VOICE Call a slurred *chip*; flight call a buzzy *zeet*; three-part, buzzy song consisting of a short series of low paired notes followed by a mid-range trill and upslurred high-pitched *zhree*.

NESTING Compact cup high on fork in deciduous tree, far from trunk; 2–5 eggs; 1 brood; May–July.

FEEDING Gleans insects high in canopy, especially from leaf bases.

UNIQUE COLOR
Female Cerulean Warblers have a unique blue color on their head and upperparts.

SIMILAR SPECIES

BLACKBURNIAN WARBLER ♀ see p.404

BLACK-AND-WHITE WARBLER ♀ see p.416

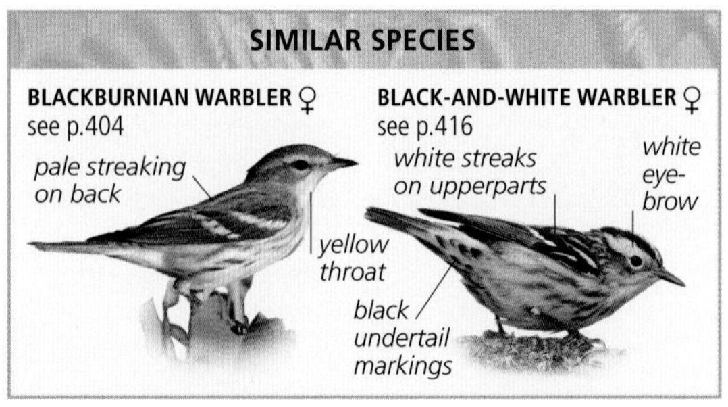
pale streaking on back
yellow throat
white streaks on upperparts
white eye-brow
black undertail markings

OCCURRENCE
Mainly breeds in mature deciduous forests across the northeastern US and southeastern Canada; tends to prefer dense woodlands during migration. Winters in evergreen forests in the Andes, principally from Columbia to Peru.

Length **4¾in (12cm)**	Wingspan **7¾in (19.5cm)**	Weight **9/32–3/8oz (8–10g)**
Social **Migrant/Winter flocks**	Lifespan **Up to 6 years**	Status **Vulnerable**

Order **Passeriformes**	Family **Parulidae**	Species ***Dendroica tigrina***

Cape May Warbler

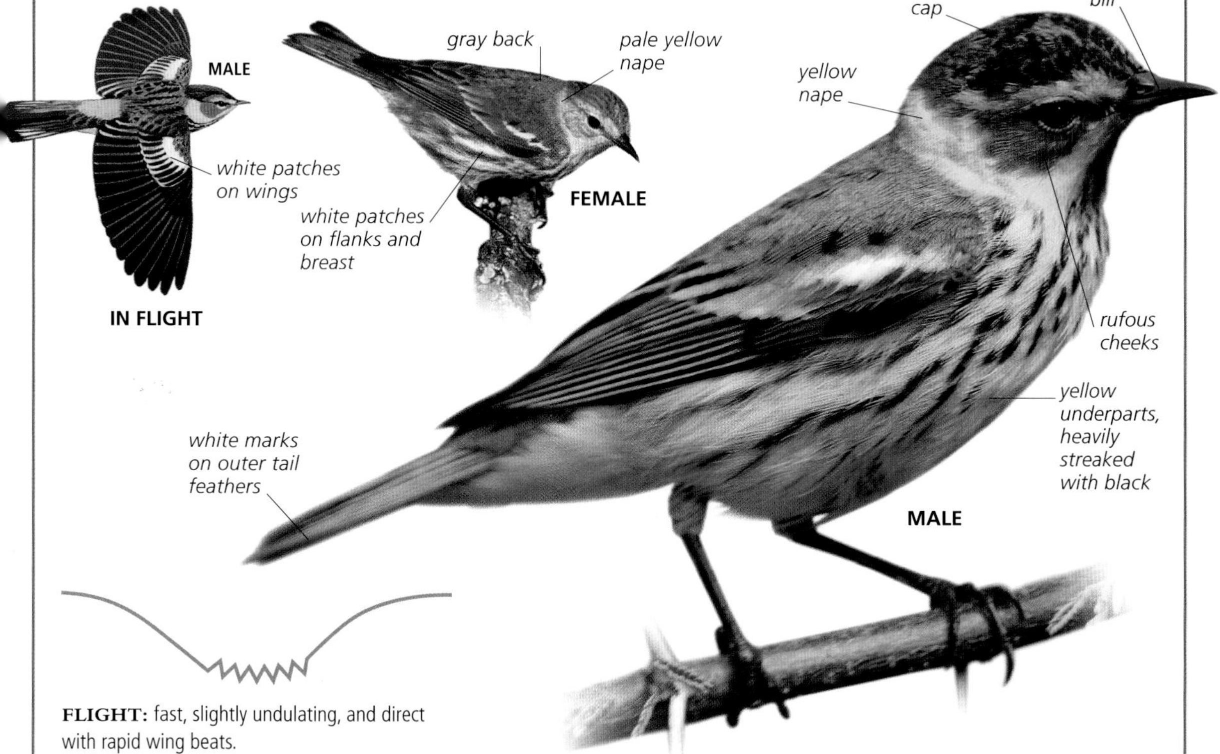

MALE
white patches on wings
IN FLIGHT
gray back
pale yellow nape
white patches on flanks and breast
FEMALE
black cap
thin, pointed bill
yellow nape
rufous cheeks
yellow underparts, heavily streaked with black
white marks on outer tail feathers
MALE

FLIGHT: fast, slightly undulating, and direct with rapid wing beats.

The Cape May Warbler is a spruce budworm specialist, and so the populations of this bird increase during outbreaks of that insect. These birds often chase other birds aggressively from flowering trees, where they use their especially thin and pointed bills and semitubular tongues to suck the nectar from blossoms. In its summer forest habitat, the Cape May Warbler uses its bill to feed on insects by plucking them from clumps of conifer needles.

VOICE Song a high, even-pitched series of whistles *see see see see.*
NESTING Cup placed near trunk, high in spruce or fir near top; 4–9 eggs; 1 brood; June–July.
FEEDING Gleans arthropods, especially spruce budworms, but also flies, moths, and beetles from mid-high levels in canopy; also fruit and nectar during the nonbreeding season.

SPRING FLASH
Magnificently colored, a male warbler displays its chestnut cheek, yellow necklace, and yellow rump.

SIMILAR SPECIES

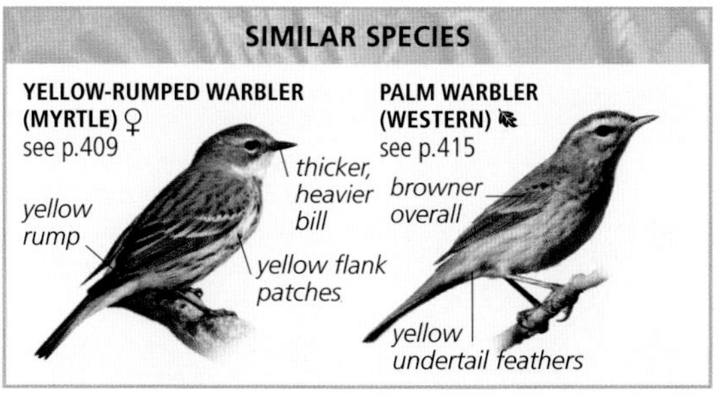
YELLOW-RUMPED WARBLER (MYRTLE) ♀
see p.409
thicker, heavier bill
yellow rump
yellow flank patches
PALM WARBLER (WESTERN)
see p.415
browner overall
yellow undertail feathers

OCCURRENCE
Breeds from the Yukon and British Columbia to the Great Lakes, the Maritimes, and New England in mature spruce–fir forests. Migrants found in varied habitats. Winters in varied habitats, especially backyard gardens, in Central America, as far south as Honduras.

Length **5in (13cm)**	Wingspan **8in (20cm)**	Weight **5/16–7/16oz (9–13g)**
Social **Migrant flocks**	Lifespan **Up to 4 years**	Status **Secure**

Order **Passeriformes**	Family **Parulidae**	Species ***Dendroica caerulescens***

Black-throated Blue Warbler

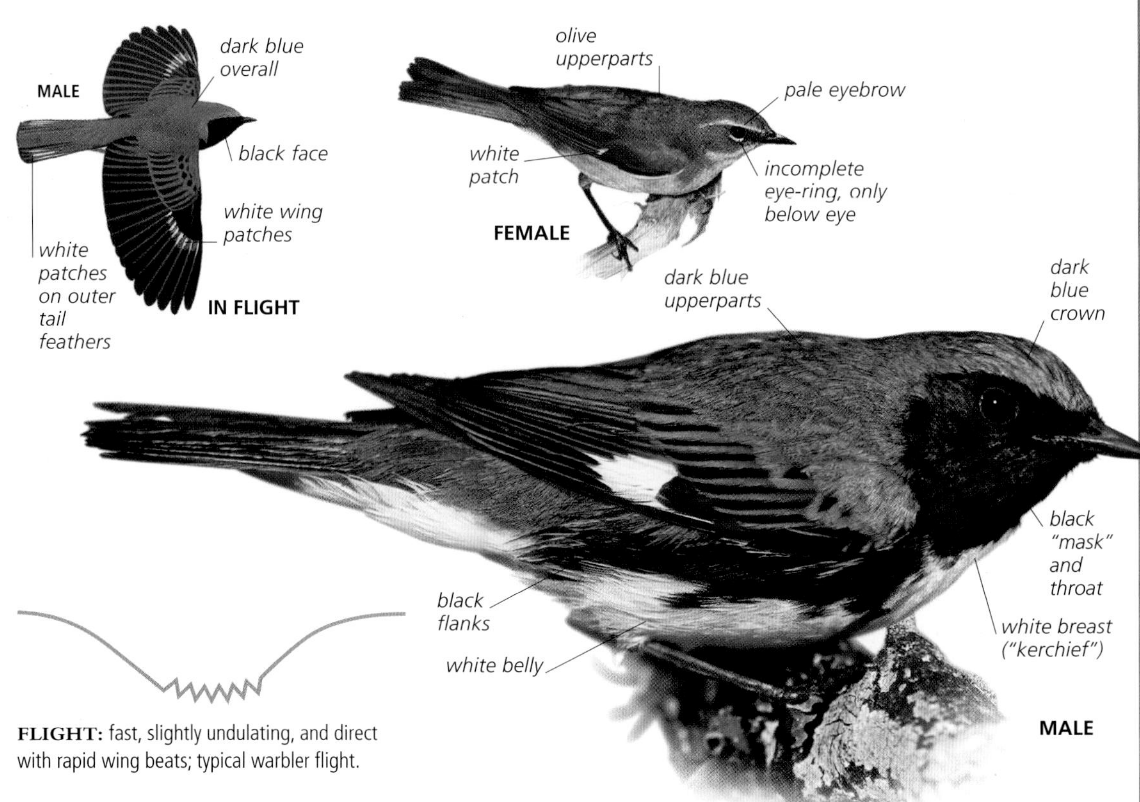
MALE
dark blue overall
black face
white wing patches
white patches on outer tail feathers
IN FLIGHT
olive upperparts
pale eyebrow
white patch
incomplete eye-ring, only below eye
FEMALE
dark blue upperparts
dark blue crown
black "mask" and throat
white breast ("kerchief")
black flanks
white belly
MALE

FLIGHT: fast, slightly undulating, and direct with rapid wing beats; typical warbler flight.

Male and female Black-throated Blue Warblers look so dissimilar that early ornithologists thought they were different species. Many of the females have a blue wash to their wings and tail, and almost all have a subdued version of the male's white "kerchief," so identification is not difficult. This beautiful eastern North American species migrates northward in spring, along the eastern flank of the Appalachians, but a small number of birds fly, along an imaginary line, northwestward to the Great Lakes. This "line" is so clearly defined that this bird is common in Chicago but extremely rare in St. Louis.

VOICE Call a husky junco-like *tchunk*; flight call a distinctive, drawn-out, metallic *ssiiink,* reminiscent of some Northern Cardinal calls; song a relatively low-pitched series of upslurred buzzes *zu zu zo zhray zhree*, or slower *zhray zhray zhreee.*

NESTING Bulky cup of plant material a meter off ground in dense forest; 3–5 eggs; 1–2 broods; May–August.

FEEDING Gleans arthropods, mainly caterpillars, from mid-low level in forest; takes small fruit and nectar.

BLACK, WHITE, AND BLUE
Males are gorgeous year-round, especially when viewed against contrasting, fall foliage.

SIMILAR SPECIES

YELLOW-RUMPED WARBLER (MYRTLE) ♀
see p.409

yellow rump
two wing bars

OCCURRENCE
Breeds in relatively undisturbed deciduous and mixed hardwood forests from southern Ontario and northern Minnesota to Nova Scotia and into the Appalachians of Georgia. Fall migration through wooded habitats; a Caribbean migrant. Winters in Central and South America.

Length **5in (13cm)**	Wingspan **7½in (19cm)**	Weight **9/32–7/16oz (8–12g)**
Social **Migrant flocks**	Lifespan **Up to 10 years**	Status **Secure**

Order **Passeriformes**	Family **Parulidae**	Species ***Dendroica coronata***

Yellow-rumped Warbler

white wing bars
dark cheeks
MALE (MYRTLE)
black streaks on gray back
IN FLIGHT
bright yellow rump
white corners on outer tail feathers
white throat
black streaks across breast
MALE
D. c. coronata
(MYRTLE)
same pattern as male, but duller
whitish eyebrow
whitish throat
yellow flanks
FEMALE
D. c. coronata
(MYRTLE)
lacks white eyebrow
large, white wing patch
solid black breast
unmarked undertail
MALE
D. c. auduboni
(AUDUBON'S)
yellowish throat
grayish overall
FEMALE
D. c. auduboni
(AUDUBON'S)

The abundant and widespread Yellow-rumped Warbler is not choosy about its wintering habitats. It was often considered to consist of two species, "Myrtle" (*D. c. coronata*) in the East, and "Audubon's" (*D. c. auduboni*) in the West. Because they interbreed freely in a narrow zone of contact in British Columbia and Alberta, the American Ornithologists Union merged them. The two forms differ in plumage and voice, and their hybrid zone appears stable.

VOICE Myrtle's call a flat, husky *tchik*; Audubon's a higher-pitched, relatively musical, rising *jip*; flight call of both a clear, upslurred *sviiit*; song loose, warbled trill with an inflected ending; Myrtle's song higher and faster, Audubon's lower and slower.

NESTING Bulky cup of plant matter in conifer; 4–5 eggs; 1 brood; March–August.

FEEDING Feeds mostly on flies, beetles, wasps, and spiders during breeding; takes fruit and berries at other times of the year, often sallies to catch prey.

FLIGHT: fast, slightly undulating, and direct with rapid wing beats.

WIDESPREAD WARBLER
Yellow-rumped Warblers are widespread and are likely to be spotted often.

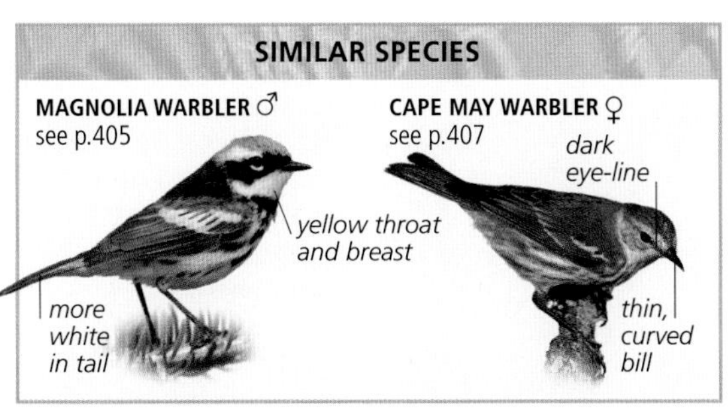
SIMILAR SPECIES
MAGNOLIA WARBLER ♂
see p.405
yellow throat and breast
more white in tail
CAPE MAY WARBLER ♀
see p.407
dark eye-line
thin, curved bill

OCCURRENCE
Both eastern and western populations are widespread across the continent from Alaska eastward to Quebec and Labrador, and westward in the mountains south to Arizona, New Mexico, and Northern Mexico. Prefers coniferous and mixed hardwood coniferous forests.

Length **5in (13cm)**	Wingspan **9in (23cm)**	Weight **⅜–⅝oz (10–17g)**
Social **Flocks**	Lifespan **Up to 7 years**	Status **Secure**

Order **Passeriformes**	Family **Parulidae**	Species ***Dendroica nigrescens***

Black-throated Gray Warbler

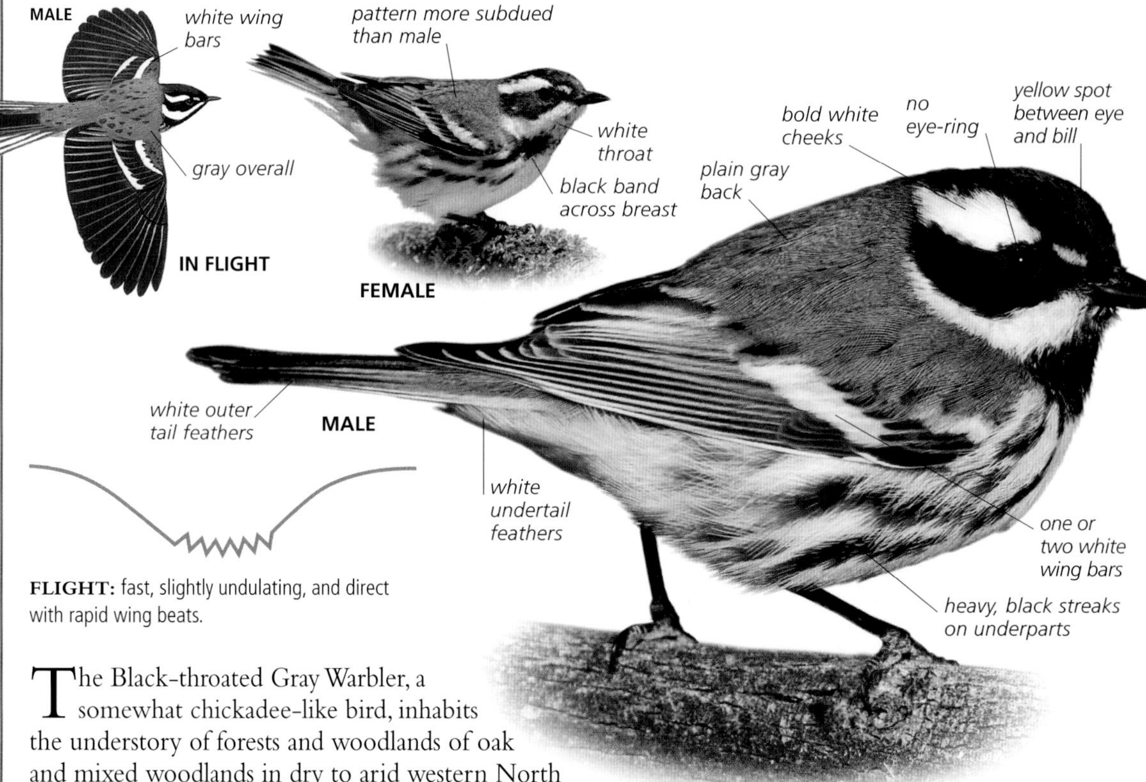
MALE
white wing bars
gray overall
IN FLIGHT
pattern more subdued than male
white throat
black band across breast
FEMALE
bold white cheeks
no eye-ring
yellow spot between eye and bill
plain gray back
white outer tail feathers
MALE
white undertail feathers
one or two white wing bars
heavy, black streaks on underparts

FLIGHT: fast, slightly undulating, and direct with rapid wing beats.

The Black-throated Gray Warbler, a somewhat chickadee-like bird, inhabits the understory of forests and woodlands of oak and mixed woodlands in dry to arid western North America. Remarkably, considering that it is fairly common, not much is known about its life history, except that it has a rather leisurely foraging style, that its nest is built by both males and females, placed only a feet few away from the ground, and that it lingers in its range until late fall, sometimes even wintering in California and Arizona.

VOICE Call a hard, flat *chep*; flight call a rising *siiit*; song a series of mid-range, paired, buzzy notes, slightly rising then dropping in pitch with the last note, *buzz-zu buzz-zu buzz-zu buzz-zo buzz-zo buzz-zee BEE-chu!*

NESTING Deep and compact cup of grass, lined with feathers, in brush; 3–5 eggs; 2 broods; May–July.

FEEDING A rather deliberate forager, gleans insects, especially caterpillars, from foliage at mid-levels.

LIVELY SONG
The buzzy song of this species is typical of the "black-throated" warbler group.

SIMILAR SPECIES

BLACK-AND-WHITE WARBLER ♂ see p.416

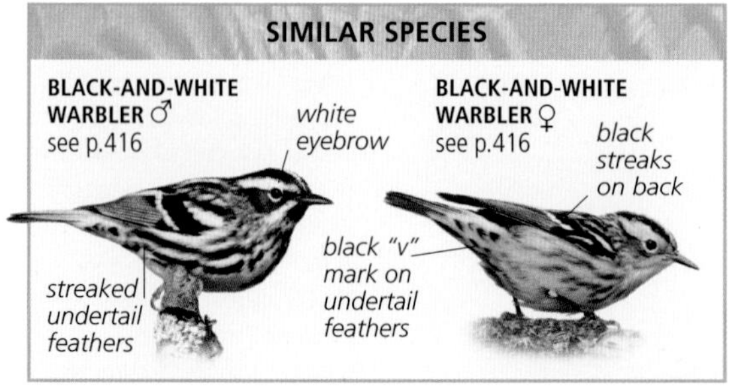
white eyebrow
streaked undertail feathers
black "v" mark on undertail feathers

BLACK-AND-WHITE WARBLER ♀ see p.416

black streaks on back

OCCURRENCE
Ranges from British Columbia south to California. Breeds in open coniferous and mixed woodlands with dense scrubby understory of pinyon, juniper, and/or oak; migrants use a greater variety of habitats; winters in dry scrub and woodlands southward away from its breeding range.

Length **5in (13cm)**	Wingspan **7½in (19cm)**	Weight **¼–⅜oz (7–10g)**
Social **Flocks**	Lifespan **Unknown**	Status **Secure**

Order **Passeriformes**	Family **Parulidae**	Species ***Dendroica virens***

Black-throated Green Warbler

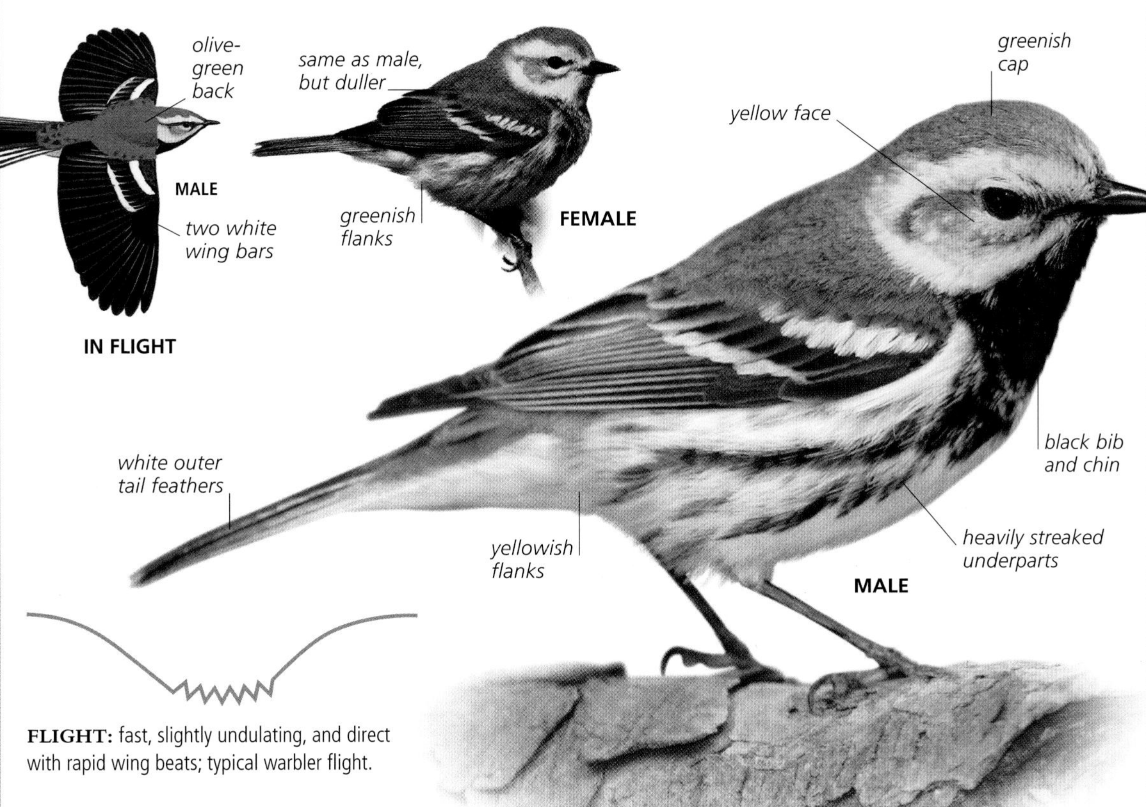

olive-green back
MALE
two white wing bars
IN FLIGHT
same as male, but duller
greenish flanks
FEMALE
greenish cap
yellow face
black bib and chin
heavily streaked underparts
MALE
yellowish flanks
white outer tail feathers

FLIGHT: fast, slightly undulating, and direct with rapid wing beats; typical warbler flight.

This species is easy to distinguish as its bright yellow face is unique among birds inhabiting northeastern North America. It is a member of the *virens* "superspecies," a group of non-overlapping species that are similar in plumage and vocalizations—the Black-throated Green, Golden-cheeked, Townsend's, and Hermit Warblers. Sadly, this species is vulnerable to habitat loss in parts of its wintering range.

VOICE Flat *tchip* call; flight call a rising *siii*; two high-pitched, buzzy songs, fast *zee zee zee zee zoo zee*; and lower, slower *zu zee zu-zu zee.*

NESTING Cup of twigs and grasses around 10–65ft (3–20m) on horizontal branch near trunk in the North, away from trunk in the South; 3–5 eggs; 1 brood; May–July.

FEEDING Gleans arthropods, especially caterpillars; also takes small fruit, including poison ivy berries, in nonbreeding season.

YELLOW-AND-BLACK GEM
From a high perch on a spruce tree, a male bird advertises his territory with a song.

SIMILAR SPECIES

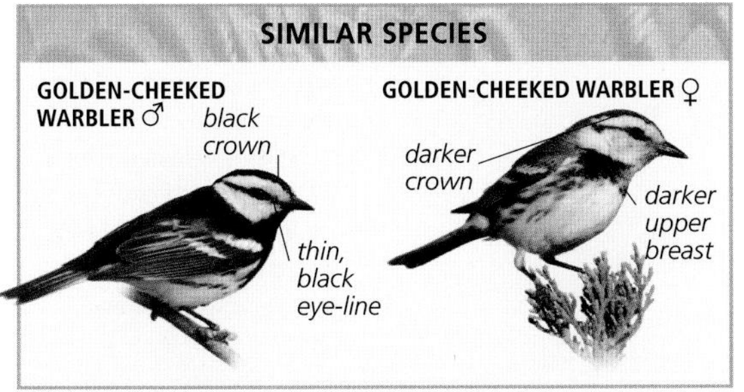

GOLDEN-CHEEKED WARBLER ♂
black crown
thin, black eye-line
GOLDEN-CHEEKED WARBLER ♀
darker crown
darker upper breast

OCCURRENCE
Breeds in many forest types, especially a mix of conifers and hardwood, from British Columbia east to Newfoundland and into southeast US along the Appalachians. Migrants and wintering birds use a variety of habitats. Winters from southern Texas into Venezuela; small numbers in Caribbean.

Length **5in (13cm)**	Wingspan **8in (20cm)**	Weight **9/32–3/8oz (8–11g)**
Social **Migrant/Winter flocks**	Lifespan **Up to 6 years**	Status **Secure**

Order **Passeriformes**	Family **Parulidae**	Species ***Dendroica townsendi***

Townsend's Warbler

MALE

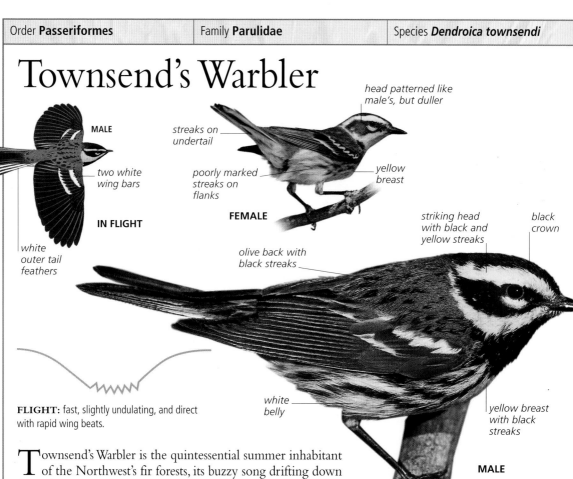

two white wing bars

white outer tail feathers

IN FLIGHT

streaks on undertail

head patterned like male's, but duller

poorly marked streaks on flanks

yellow breast

FEMALE

striking head with black and yellow streaks

black crown

olive back with black streaks

white belly

yellow breast with black streaks

MALE

FLIGHT: fast, slightly undulating, and direct with rapid wing beats.

Townsend's Warbler is the quintessential summer inhabitant of the Northwest's fir forests, its buzzy song drifting down from the treetops between May and July. The species has an interesting winter distribution—birds from the Pacific Northwest winter along the Pacific coast, while mainland breeders winter in the mountain forests of Mexico and Central America. The Townsend's Warbler interbreeds with the closely related Hermit Warbler in Washington and Oregon, resulting in varied-looking hybrids.

VOICE Song a series of buzzy notes that accelerate and increase in pitch; two examples are *wheezy wheezy wheezy zeee* and *zuuu dit-dit-dit zuuu dit-dit-dit zo ZEE zu ZAY.*

NESTING Bulky shallow cup of plant matter, hidden by needles on branch far from trunk, high in conifer trees; 3–7 eggs; 1 brood; May–July.

FEEDING Gleans insects, spiders, and caterpillars; will also take honeydew secreted by aphids and other insects.

PALER JUVENILE
Young Townsend's Warblers are paler than adults but show the same color pattern as adult females.

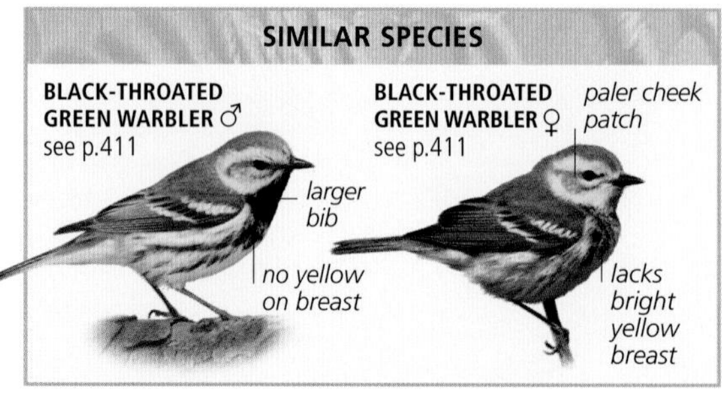
SIMILAR SPECIES
BLACK-THROATED GREEN WARBLER ♂
see p.411
larger bib
no yellow on breast
BLACK-THROATED GREEN WARBLER ♀
see p.411
paler cheek patch
lacks bright yellow breast

OCCURRENCE
Breeds from southern Alaska to Wyoming in mature fir, coniferous, and mixed coniferous–deciduous forests; elevations range from sea level to subalpine. Winters in Mexico and Central America in different habitats including coastal, woodland, and suburban parks and gardens.

Length **5in (13cm)**	Wingspan **8in (20cm)**	Weight **¼–⅜oz (7–11g)**
Social **Flocks**	Lifespan **Up to 4 years**	Status **Secure**

Order **Passeriformes**	Family **Parulidae**	Species ***Dendroica discolor***

Prairie Warbler

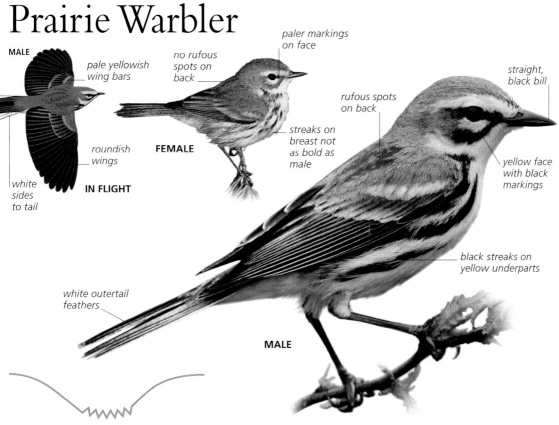

MALE
pale yellowish wing bars
roundish wings
white sides to tail
IN FLIGHT
no rufous spots on back
paler markings on face
FEMALE
streaks on breast not as bold as male
rufous spots on back
straight, black bill
yellow face with black markings
black streaks on yellow underparts
white outertail feathers
MALE

FLIGHT: fast, slightly undulating, and direct, with rapid wing beats.

Contrary to its common name, the Prairie Warbler does not live on the "prairie." Its distinctive song is a quintessential sound of scrubby areas across the eastern US. Although the population of this bird increased in the 19th century due to the widespread clearing of forests, the maturation of this habitat, along with human development, is having a negative impact on local populations.

VOICE Call a thick *tsik* or *tchip*, flight call a high, thin *sssip*; song variable in tempo, but always series of husky, buzzy notes that increase in pitch: *zzu zzu zzu zzo zzo zzo zzee zzee.*

NESTING Cup of plant material in fork of sapling or low trees, often within human reach; 3–5 eggs; 1 brood; May–July.

FEEDING Eats various insects, such as flies and crickets; also berries.

HIGH AND LOUD
Males sing from preferred elevated perches, producing their characteristic buzzy song that increases in pitch and tempo.

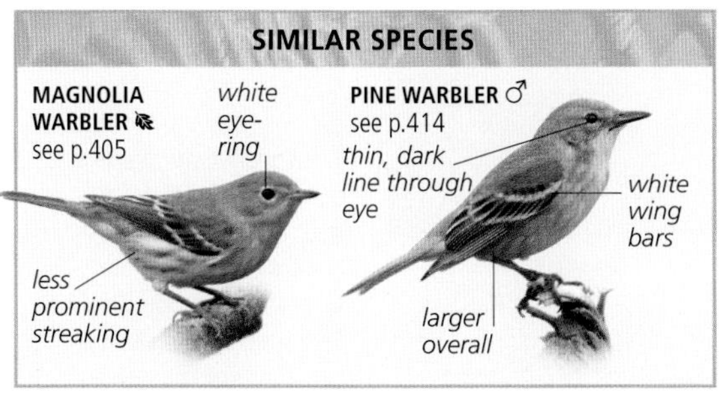
SIMILAR SPECIES
MAGNOLIA WARBLER
see p.405
white eye-ring
less prominent streaking
PINE WARBLER ♂
see p.414
thin, dark line through eye
white wing bars
larger overall

OCCURRENCE
Breeds in shrubby, open-canopied, second-growth habitats, and mangroves; migrant and wintering birds prefer similar brushy habitats. Breeds in parts of southern Ontario. Winters in the Bahamas, Greater and Lesser Antilles, and coasts of southern Mexico to El Salvador.

Length **4¾in (12cm)**	Wingspan **9in (23cm)**	Weight **7/32–5/16oz (6–9g)**
Social **Solitary/Winter flocks**	Lifespan **Up to 10 years**	Status **Declining**

Order **Passeriformes**	Family **Parulidae**	Species ***Dendroica pinus***

Pine Warbler

round wings

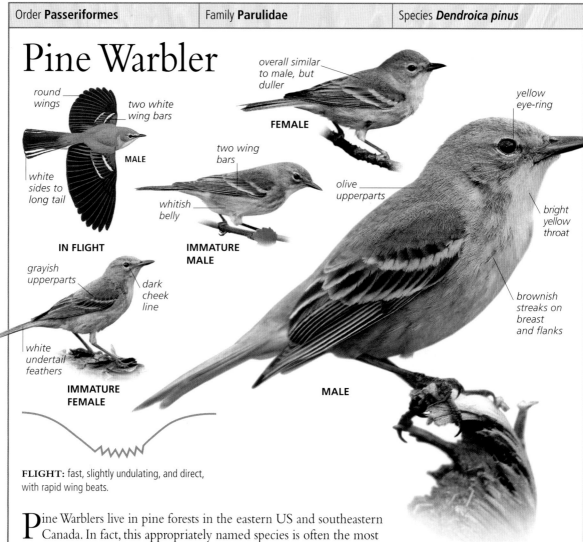

two white wing bars

white sides to long tail

MALE

IN FLIGHT

overall similar to male, but duller

FEMALE

two wing bars

whitish belly

IMMATURE MALE

grayish upperparts

dark cheek line

white undertail feathers

IMMATURE FEMALE

yellow eye-ring

olive upperparts

bright yellow throat

brownish streaks on breast and flanks

MALE

FLIGHT: fast, slightly undulating, and direct, with rapid wing beats.

Pine Warblers live in pine forests in the eastern US and southeastern Canada. In fact, this appropriately named species is often the most common bird in its namesake habitat and its distinctive song can be heard from several birds at once. One of the few warblers that uses birdfeeders, the Pine Warbler is a hardy bird, staying within the US throughout the winter.

VOICE Call a soft *tsip*, flight call a high, thin, slightly rolling, descending *ziit*; song a lazy, musical *trill*, variably of round or sharper notes.

NESTING Cup of grass high up, far out on horizontal branch, concealed by pine needles; 3–5 eggs; 1–2 broods; March–July.

FEEDING Gleans arthropods, especially caterpillars, from pine needles; will also eat seeds and fruit in nonbreeding season.

SIMILAR SPECIES
BLACKPOLL WARBLER
see p.402
streaks on flanks
larger overall
BAY-BREASTED WARBLER
see p.403
greenish cheeks
buff underparts

WELL NAMED
In many areas, Pine Warblers are the most common breeding birds in mature pine woods.

OCCURRENCE
Pine and mixed forests from southern Canada and the eastern US, south to eastern Texas and Florida. Nests in deciduous forests if individual trees or small stands of pine are present. Resident in southern half of its US range. Breeds and winters in the Bahamas and Hispaniola.

Length **5in (13cm)**	Wingspan **9in (23cm)**	Weight **5/16–1/2oz (9–15g)**
Social **Migrant/Winter flocks**	Lifespan **Up to 7 years**	Status **Secure**

Order **Passeriformes**	Family **Parulidae**	Species ***Dendroica palmarum***

Palm Warbler

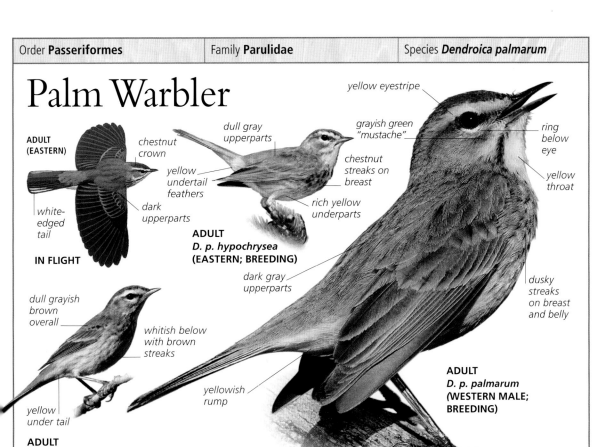

ADULT (EASTERN)

chestnut crown

white-edged tail

dark upperparts

IN FLIGHT

dull gray upperparts

yellow undertail feathers

chestnut streaks on breast

rich yellow underparts

ADULT *D. p. hypochrysea* (EASTERN; BREEDING)

yellow eyestripe

grayish green "mustache"

ring below eye

yellow throat

dark gray upperparts

dusky streaks on breast and belly

yellowish rump

ADULT *D. p. palmarum* (WESTERN MALE; BREEDING)

dull grayish brown overall

whitish below with brown streaks

yellow under tail

ADULT *D. p. palmarum* (WESTERN; NONBREEDING)

The Palm Warbler is one of North America's most abundant warblers. Its tail-pumping habits make it easy to identify in any plumage. It was named *palmarum* (meaning "palm") in 1789 because it was first recorded among palm thickets on the Caribbean island of Hispaniola. The western subspecies (*D. p. palmarum*) is found in Western and Central Canada. It is grayish brown above and lacks the chestnut streaks of the eastern subspecies (*D. p. hypochrysea*), which has a yellower face, and breeds in southeastern Canada and northeastern US.

VOICE Call a husky *chik* or *tsip*; flight call a light *ziint*; slow, loose, buzzy trill: *zwi zwi zwi zwi zwi zwi zwi zwi*.

NESTING Cup of grasses on or near ground in open area of conifers at forest edge of a bog; 4–5 eggs; 1 brood; May–July.

FEEDING Eats insects, sometimes caught in flight; also takes seeds and berries.

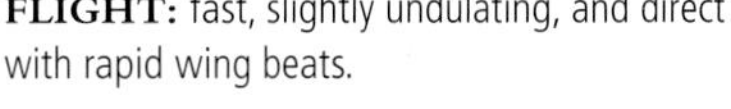

FLIGHT: fast, slightly undulating, and direct with rapid wing beats.

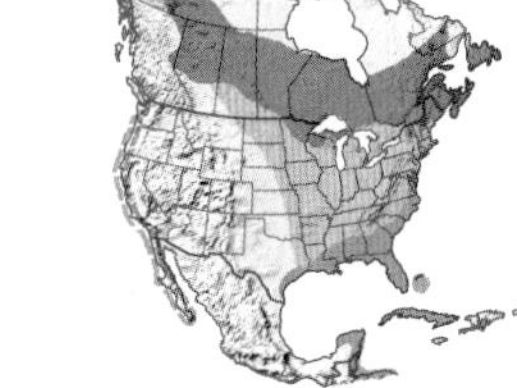

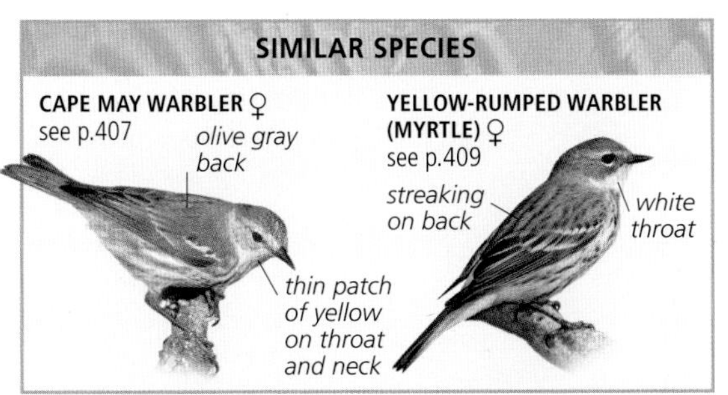
SIMILAR SPECIES
CAPE MAY WARBLER ♀
see p.407
olive gray back
thin patch of yellow on throat and neck
YELLOW-RUMPED WARBLER (MYRTLE) ♀
see p.409
streaking on back
white throat

FAR FROM THE PALMS
This male Palm Warbler is far north of the coastal palms where its kin spend the winter.

OCCURRENCE
In North America, breeds in spruce bogs within the northerly forest zone, across Canada from Yukon to the Maritimes and Labrador, and in the US from Minnesota to Maine. Often migrates through central portions of eastern US; winters in southeastern US, Florida, and Central America.

Length **5½in (14cm)**	Wingspan **8in (20cm)**	Weight **¼–7⁄16oz (7–13g)**
Social **Flocks**	Lifespan **Up to 6 years**	Status **Secure**

Order **Passeriformes**	Family **Parulidae**	Species ***Mniotilta varia***

Black-and-white Warbler

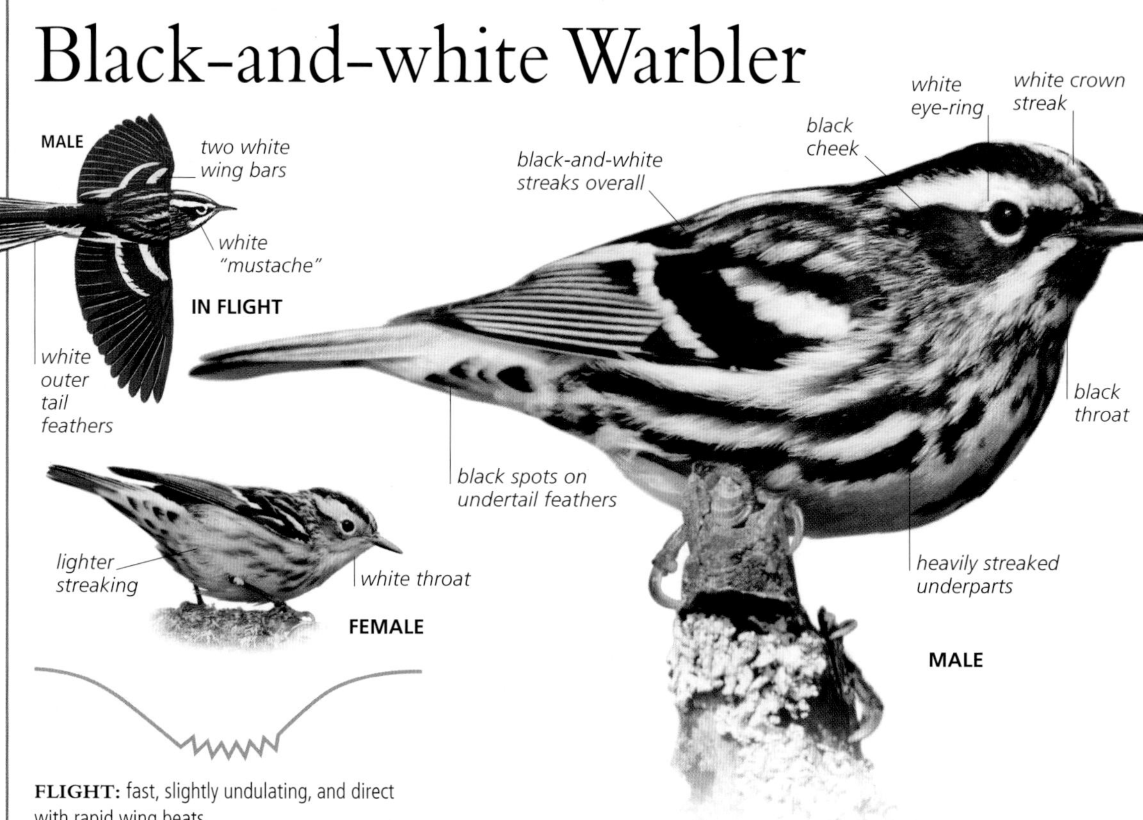
MALE
two white wing bars
white "mustache"
IN FLIGHT
white outer tail feathers
lighter streaking
white throat
FEMALE
black-and-white streaks overall
black cheek
white eye-ring
white crown streak
black throat
black spots on undertail feathers
heavily streaked underparts
MALE

FLIGHT: fast, slightly undulating, and direct with rapid wing beats.

The Black-and-white Warbler is best known for its creeper-like habit of feeding in vertical and upside-down positions as it pries into bark crevices, where its relatively long, curved bill allows it to reach tiny nooks and crannies. These habits, combined with streaked plumage, make this bird one of the most distinctive warblers in North America. It is a long-distance migrant, with some birds wintering in parts of northern South America.

VOICE Sharp *stik* call; flight call a very high, thin *ssiit*, often doubled; song a thin, high-pitched, wheezy series *wheesy wheesy wheesy wheesy wheesy wheesy*.

NESTING Cup on ground against stump, fallen logs, or roots; 4–6 eggs; 1 brood; April–August.

FEEDING Creeps along branches and trunks, probing into bark for insects and insect larvae.

SQUEAKY WHEEL
The high-pitched, wheezy song of this warbler is said to be reminiscent of a squeaky wheel.

UPSIDE-DOWN
Black-and-white Warblers often creep head-first along trunks and branches of trees.

SIMILAR SPECIES

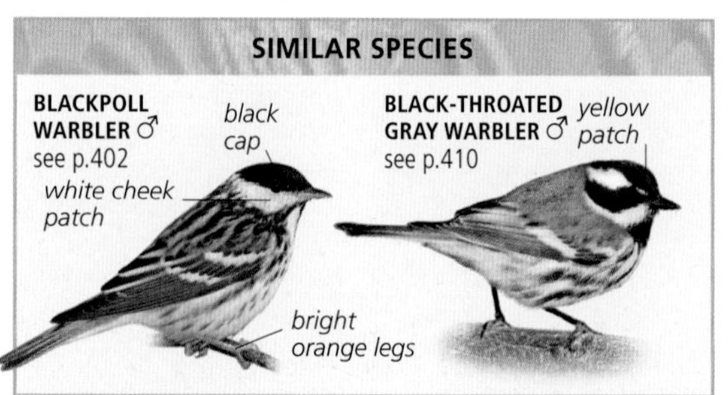
BLACKPOLL WARBLER ♂
see p.402
black cap
white cheek patch
bright orange legs
BLACK-THROATED GRAY WARBLER ♂
see p.410
yellow patch

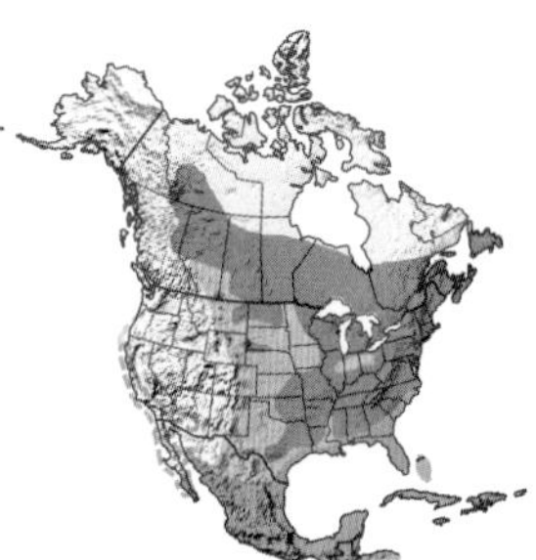

OCCURRENCE
Breeds in deciduous and mixed mature and second-growth woodlands; migrants occur on a greater variety of habitats; winters in a wide range of wooded habitats in southern US, Mexico and into Central and South America.

Length **5in (13cm)**	Wingspan **8in (20cm)**	Weight **$^5/_{16}$–½oz (9–14g)**
Social **Migrant/Winter flocks**	Lifespan **Up to 11 years**	Status **Secure**

Order **Passeriformes**	Family **Parulidae**	Species ***Setophaga ruticilla***

American Redstart

MALE

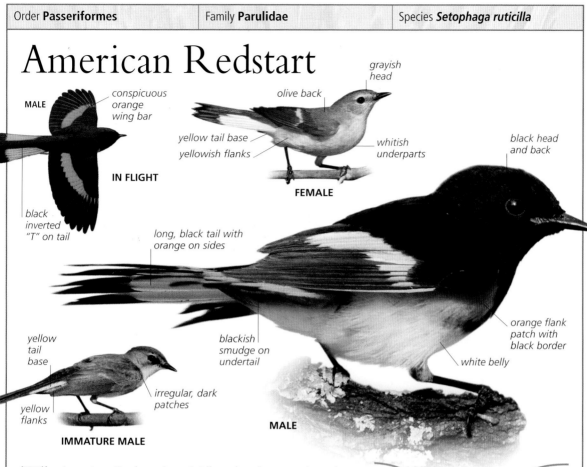

conspicuous orange wing bar

black inverted "T" on tail

IN FLIGHT

grayish head

olive back

yellow tail base

yellowish flanks

whitish underparts

FEMALE

black head and back

long, black tail with orange on sides

orange flank patch with black border

blackish smudge on undertail

white belly

yellow tail base

irregular, dark patches

yellow flanks

IMMATURE MALE

MALE

The American Redstart is a vividly colored, energetic and acrobatic warbler with a reasonably broad range across North America. One of its behavioral quirks is to fan its tail and wings while foraging, supposedly using the flashes of bold color to scare insects into moving, making them easy prey. It possesses well-developed rictal bristles, hair-like feathers extending from the corners of the mouth, which help it to detect insects.

VOICE Harsh *tsiip* call; flight call a high, thin *sveep*; song a confusingly variable, high, thin, yet penetrating series of notes; one version burry, emphatic, and downslurred *see-a see-a see-a see-a ZEE-urrrr.*

NESTING Cup of grasses and rootlets, lined with feathers; placed low in deciduous tree; 2–5 eggs; 1–2 broods; May–July.

FEEDING Gleans insects and spiders from leaves at mid-levels in trees; also catches moths, flies in flight; will also eat fruit.

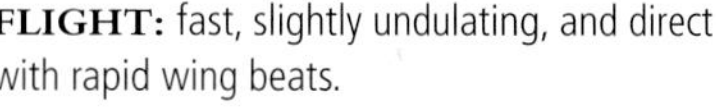

FLIGHT: fast, slightly undulating, and direct with rapid wing beats.

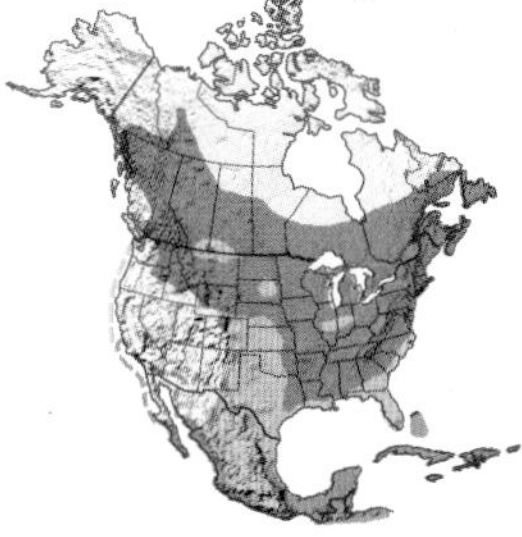

COMMON SONG
This bird's short, ringing song is a common sound in the moist deciduous woods of the East and North.

MALE CARER
As with most warblers, male Redstarts help raise the young, though they may be polygamous.

OCCURRENCE
Breeds in moist deciduous and mixed woodlands across North America; migrants and wintering birds use a wide range of habitats. Winters from Baja California and south Florida through Middle America and the Caribbean to northern South America.

Length **5in (13cm)**	Wingspan **8in (20cm)**	Weight **$\frac{7}{32}$–$\frac{3}{8}$oz (6–11g)**
Social **Flocks**	Lifespan **Up to 10 years**	Status **Secure**

Order **Passeriformes**	Family **Parulidae**	Species ***Protonotaria citrea***

Prothonotary Warbler

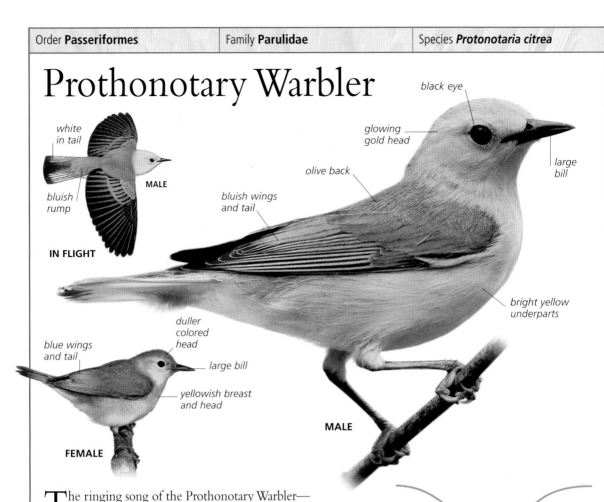

white in tail
bluish rump
MALE
IN FLIGHT
black eye
glowing gold head
large bill
olive back
bluish wings and tail
bright yellow underparts
duller colored head
blue wings and tail
large bill
yellowish breast and head
MALE
FEMALE

The ringing song of the Prothonotary Warbler—once known as the Golden Swamp Warbler—echoes through the swamps of the southeastern US and southern Ontario every summer. This is one of the few cavity-nesting warbler species; it will use manmade bird houses placed close to still water. Prothonotary Warblers also tend to stay fairly low over the water, making them easy to spot. This warbler's yellow head and breast reminded an early naturalist of the bright yellow robes worn by Prothonotaries (high ranking papal clerks), and he passed the name to this colorful bird.

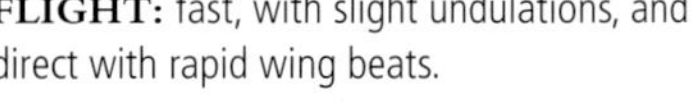

FLIGHT: fast, with slight undulations, and direct with rapid wing beats.

VOICE Flight call a loud, high *sviit*; call note a loud *chip*; song a loud series of penetrating and internally rising notes *tsveet tsveet tsveet tsveet tsveet tsveet tsveet.*

NESTING Over or near still water; woodpecker holes often used; 3–8 eggs; 1–2 broods; April–July.

FEEDING Mostly eats insects and small mollusks; also seeds, fruit, and nectar.

SIMILAR SPECIES

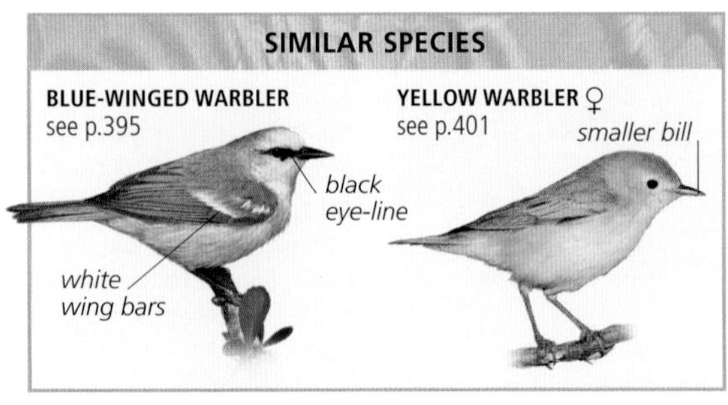
BLUE-WINGED WARBLER
see p.395
black eye-line
white wing bars
YELLOW WARBLER ♀
see p.401
smaller bill

GOLDEN SONGBIRD
Visible in the darkness of a southern swamp, a Prothonotary Warbler sings its ringing song.

OCCURRENCE
Breeds in wooded areas over or near still water, especially in cypress swamps and bottomlands across the southeastern US and up into southern Ontario. Winters in mangroves and dry forests in Southern Mexico.

Length **5½in (14cm)**	Wingspan **9in (23cm)**	Weight **½–⅝oz (14–18g)**
Social **Winter flocks**	Lifespan **Up to 8 years**	Status **Endangered**

Order **Passeriformes**	Family **Parulidae**	Species ***Seiurus aurocapilla***

Ovenbird

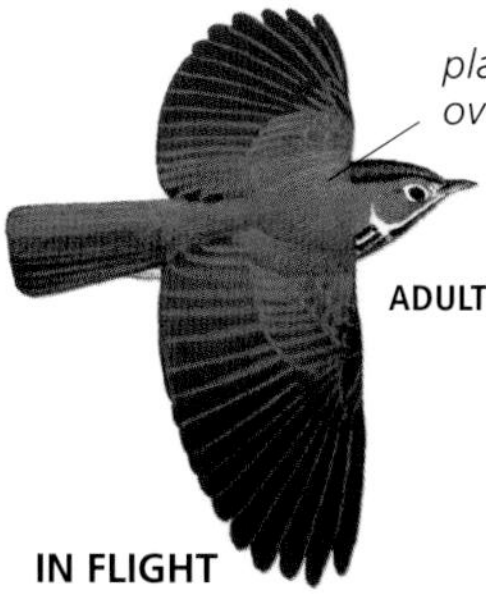

plain olive overall

ADULT

IN FLIGHT

orange-and-black striped crown

bold white eye-ring

olive upperparts

white throat

black streaked underparts

ADULT

FLIGHT: fast, slightly undulating, and direct with rapid wing beats.

Like members of the unrelated, tropical ovenbird family (Furnariidae), this little bird is so-called for the domed, oven-like nests it builds on the ground; unique structures for a North American bird. The Ovenbird is also noted for its singing. Males flit about boisterously, often at night, incorporating portions of their main song into a jumble of spluttering notes. In the forest, one male singing loudly to declare his territory can set off a whole chain of responses from his neighbors, until the whole forest rings.

VOICE Call variably pitched, sharp *chik* in series; flight call high, rising *siiii*; song loud, ringing crescendo of paired notes *chur-tee' chur-tee' chur-tee' chur-tee' chur-TEE chur-TEE chur-TEE.*

NESTING Domed structure of leaves and grass on ground with side entrance; 3–6 eggs; 1 brood; May–July.

FEEDING Forages mainly on the forest floor for insects and other invertebrates.

STRUTTING ITS STUFF
The Ovenbird is noted for the way it struts across the forest floor like a tiny chicken.

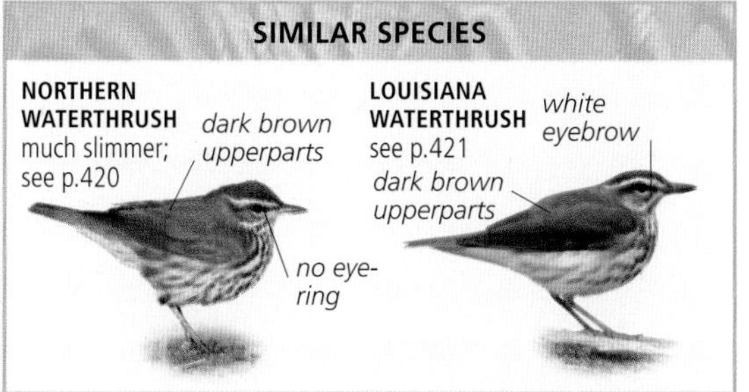
SIMILAR SPECIES
NORTHERN WATERTHRUSH
much slimmer;
see p.420
dark brown upperparts
no eye-ring
LOUISIANA WATERTHRUSH
see p.421
white eyebrow
dark brown upperparts

OCCURRENCE
Breeds in closed-canopy mixed and deciduous forests with suitable amount of fallen plant material for nest building and foraging; migrants and wintering birds use similar habitats.

Length **6in (15cm)**	Wingspan **9½in (24cm)**	Weight **9/16–7/8oz (16–25g)**
Social **Solitary/Flocks**	Lifespan **Up to 7 years**	Status **Declining**

Order **Passeriformes**	Family **Parulidae**	Species ***Seiurus noveboracensis***

Northern Waterthrush

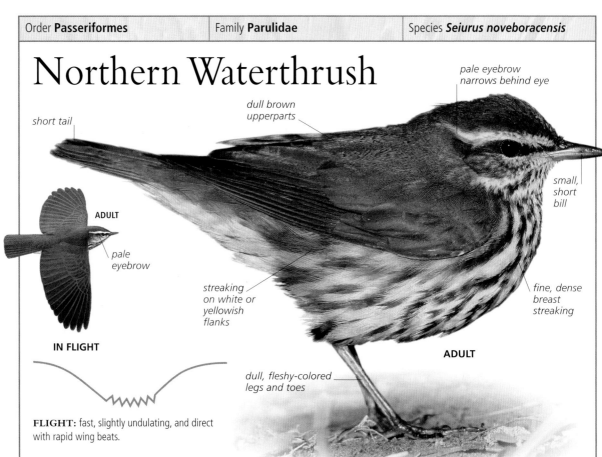

pale eyebrow narrows behind eye

dull brown upperparts

short tail

small, short bill

ADULT

pale eyebrow

streaking on white or yellowish flanks

fine, dense breast streaking

IN FLIGHT

ADULT

dull, fleshy-colored legs and toes

FLIGHT: fast, slightly undulating, and direct with rapid wing beats.

The tail-bobbing Northern Waterthrush is often heard giving a *spink!* call as it swiftly flees from observers. Although this species may be mistaken for the closely related Louisiana Waterthrush, there are clues that are helpful in its identification. While the Northern Waterthrush prefers still water, its relative greatly prefers running water; in addition, its song is quite unlike that of the Louisiana Waterthrush.

VOICE Call a sharp, rising, ringing *spink!*; flight call a rising, buzzy *ziiiit*; song a loud series of rich, accelerating, staccato notes, usually decreasing in pitch *teet, teet, toh-toh toh-toh tyew-tyew!*

NESTING Hair-lined, mossy cup placed on or near ground, hidden in roots of fallen or standing tree or in riverbank; 4–5 eggs; 1 brood; May–August.

FEEDING Mostly eats insects such as ants, mosquitoes, moths, and beetles, both larvae and adult, plus slugs, and snails; when migrating, also eats small crustaceans, and even tiny fish.

YELLOW FORM
Many Northern Waterthrushes have yellow underparts, like this one, while others have white.

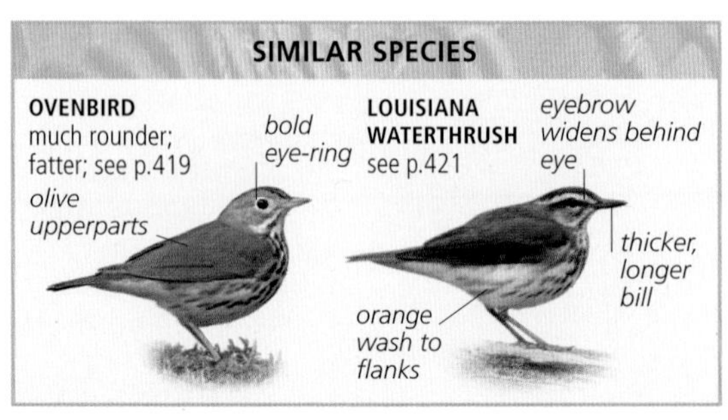
SIMILAR SPECIES
OVENBIRD
much rounder; fatter; see p.419
bold eye-ring
olive upperparts
LOUISIANA WATERTHRUSH
see p.421
eyebrow widens behind eye
thicker, longer bill
orange wash to flanks

OCCURRENCE
Breeds right across northern North America in dark, still-water swamps and bogs; also in the still edges of rivers and lakes; migrant birds use wet habitats; winters in shrubby marshes, mangroves, and occasionally in crops, such as rice fields and citrus groves.

Length **6in (15cm)**	Wingspan **9½in (24cm)**	Weight **½–⅞oz (14–23g)**
Social **Solitary**	Lifespan **Up to 9 years**	Status **Secure**

Order **Passeriformes**	Family **Parulidae**	Species ***Seiurus motacilla***

Louisiana Waterthrush

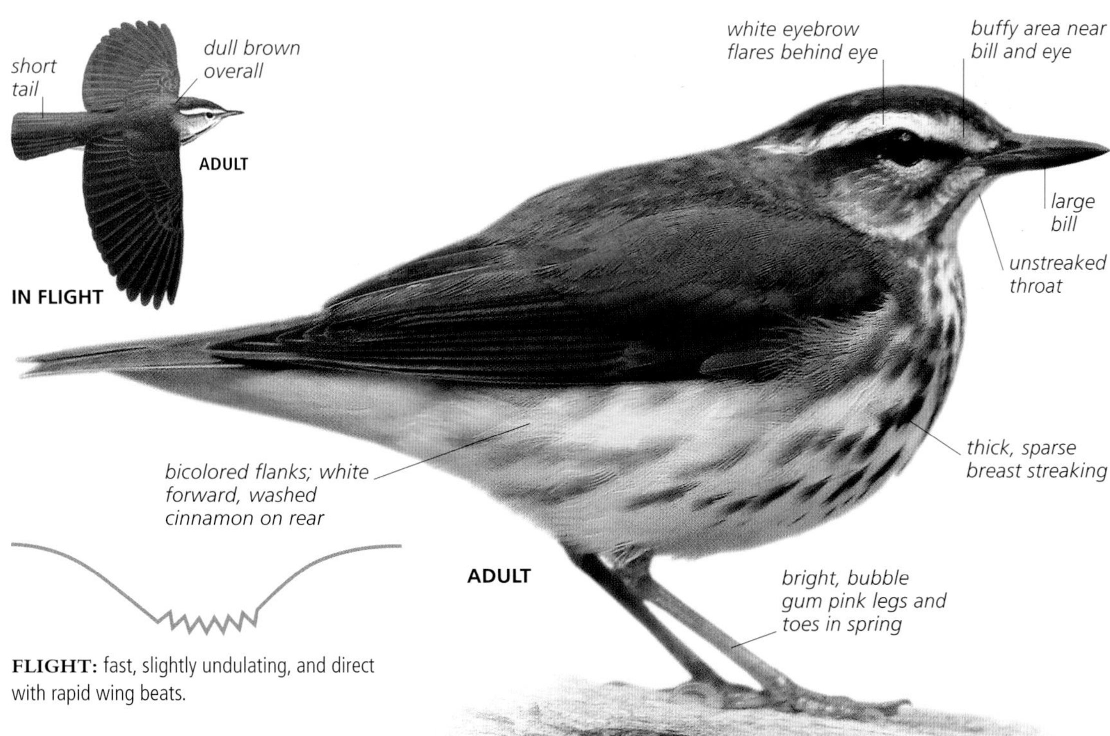
short tail
dull brown overall
ADULT
IN FLIGHT
white eyebrow flares behind eye
buffy area near bill and eye
large bill
unstreaked throat
thick, sparse breast streaking
bicolored flanks; white forward, washed cinnamon on rear
ADULT
bright, bubble gum pink legs and toes in spring

FLIGHT: fast, slightly undulating, and direct with rapid wing beats.

The Louisiana Waterthrush is one of the earliest warblers to return north in the spring; as early as March, eastern ravines are filled with cascades of its song. Both the stream-loving Louisiana Waterthrush and its still-water cousin, the Northern Waterthrush, bob their tails as they walk (the genus name, *Seiurus*, means "tail-bobber"), but the Louisiana Waterthrush arcs its entire body at the same time. In spring, this species shows brighter pink legs than the Northern Waterthrush.

VOICE Call a round *spink*; flight call a rising, buzzy *ziiiit*; song a loud, descending, ringing, whistled cascade, ending with sputtering *see'-oh see'-oh see'-uh see'-uh tip-uh-tik-uh-tip-whee'ur-tik*.

NESTING Bulky mass of leaves, moss, and twigs, under steep stream bank over water; 4–6 eggs; 1 brood; May–August.

FEEDING Forages in streams for insect larvae, snails, and small fish; also catches flying insects such as dragonflies and stoneflies.

TAKING A LITTLE DIP
In many ways, this species is the "dipper of the East," picking invertebrates from shallow streams.

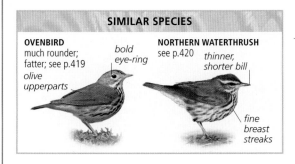

SIMILAR SPECIES

OVENBIRD much rounder; fatter; see p.419
olive upperparts; *bold eye-ring*

NORTHERN WATERTHRUSH see p.420
thinner, shorter bill; *fine breast streaks*

OCCURRENCE
Breeds along fast-moving streams in deciduous forests in the eastern US and southern Ontario; migrants stop over near running water, including gardens; winters along wooded streams and rivers in mountains and hills in the Caribbean, Mexico, Central America, and northern parts of South America.

Length **6in (15cm)**	Wingspan **10in (25cm)**	Weight **⅝–⅞oz (18–25g)**
Social **Solitary**	Lifespan **Up to 8 years**	Status **Secure**

Order **Passeriformes**	Family **Parulidae**	Species ***Oporornis agilis***

Connecticut Warbler

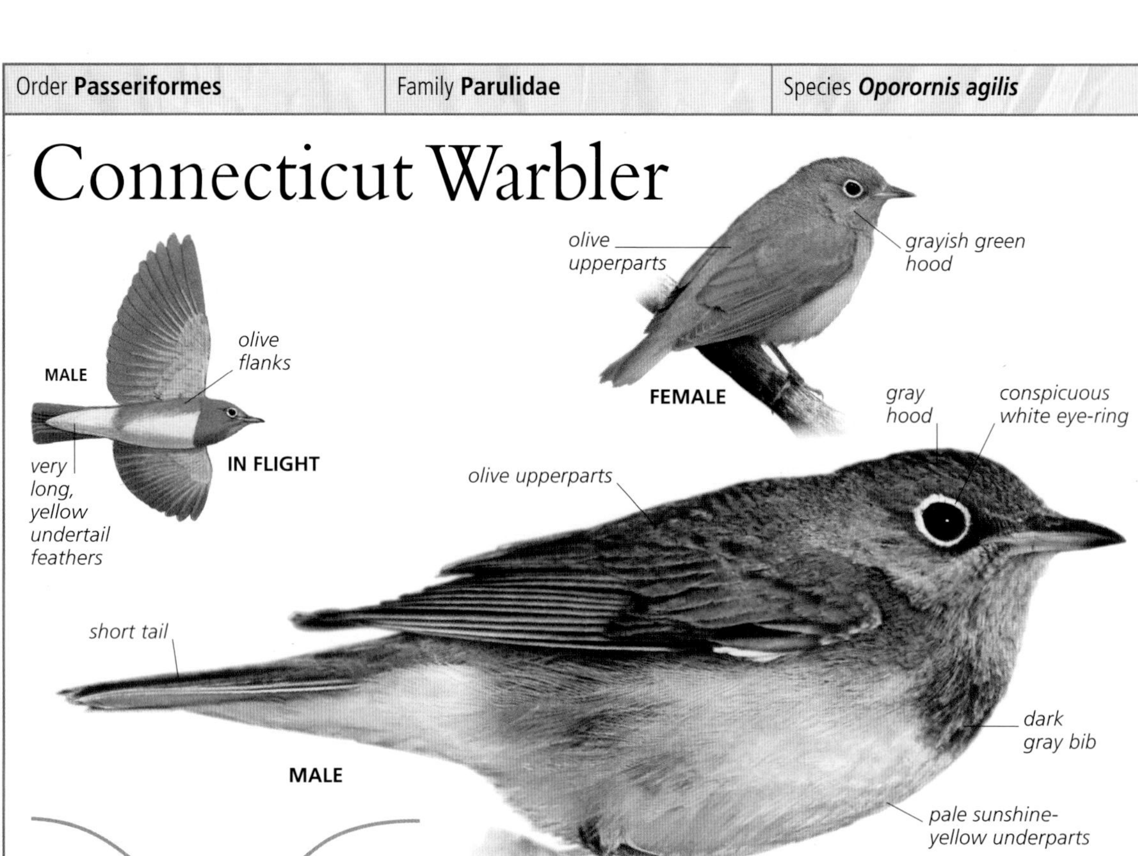
olive
upperparts
grayish green
hood
FEMALE
olive
flanks
MALE
IN FLIGHT
very long, yellow undertail feathers
gray
hood
conspicuous
white eye-ring
olive upperparts
short tail
MALE
dark
gray bib
pale sunshine-
yellow underparts
pink legs
and feet

FLIGHT: fast, slightly undulating, and direct with rapid wing beats.

The shy Connecticut Warbler, which incidentally does not breed in this state, breeds in remote, boggy habitats in Canada and is hard to spot during its spring and fall migrations. It arrives in the US in late May and leaves its breeding grounds in August. It is the only warbler that walks along the ground in a bouncy manner, with its tail bobbing up and down.

VOICE Seldom-heard call a nasal *champ*, flight call a buzzy *ziiiit*; song a loud "whippy," accelerating series, often ending with upward inflection *tweet, chuh WHIP-uh chee-uh-WHIP-uh chee-uh-WAY.*

NESTING Concealed cup of grass or leaves, lined with fine plant matter and hair; placed near or on ground in damp moss or grass clump; 3–5 eggs; 1 brood; June–July.

FEEDING Gleans a variety of adult insects, insect larvae, and spiders from under leaves; also eats small fruits.

EXCEPTIONAL UNDERTAIL
The yellow undertail feathers nearly reach the tip of the Connecticut Warbler's tail.

SIMILAR SPECIES

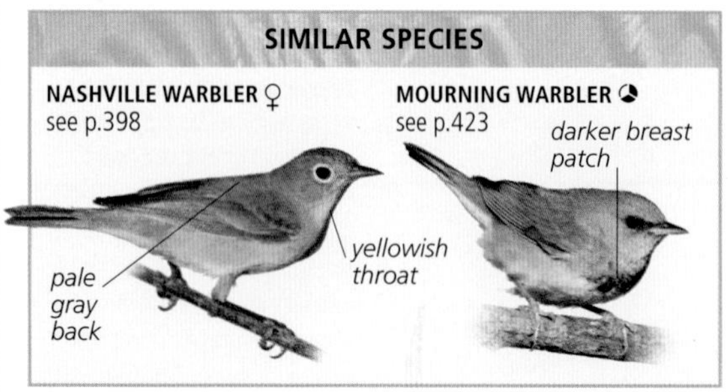
NASHVILLE WARBLER ♀
see p.398
MOURNING WARBLER
see p.423
darker breast
patch
yellowish
throat
pale
gray
back

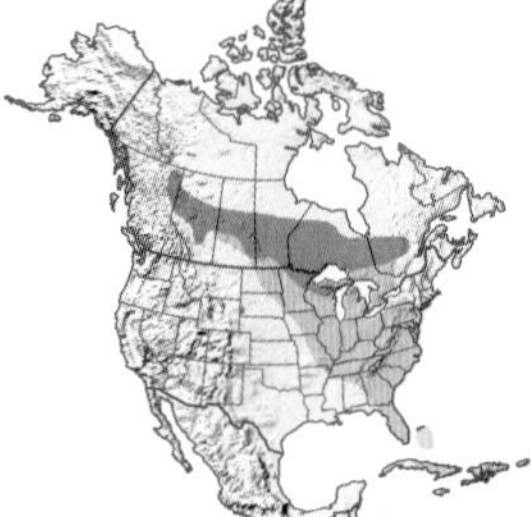

OCCURRENCE
Breeds across Canada from British Columbia to Quebec and in the US in Minnesota and the Great Lakes region, in bogs and pine forests. Winters in forest habitats of Amazonian Peru and Brazil.

Length **6in (15cm)**	Wingspan **9in (23cm)**	Weight **$^{7}/_{16}$–$^{11}/_{16}$oz (13–20g)**
Social **Solitary**	Lifespan **Up to 4 years**	Status **Secure (p)**

Order **Passeriformes**	Family **Parulidae**	Species ***Oporornis philadelphia***

Mourning Warbler

MALE (BREEDING)

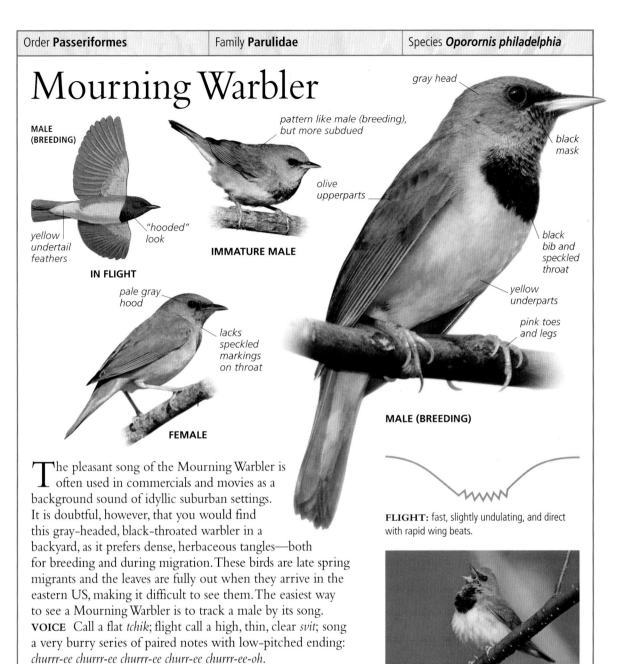

yellow undertail feathers

"hooded" look

IN FLIGHT

pattern like male (breeding), but more subdued

IMMATURE MALE

pale gray hood

lacks speckled markings on throat

FEMALE

gray head

black mask

olive upperparts

black bib and speckled throat

yellow underparts

pink toes and legs

MALE (BREEDING)

The pleasant song of the Mourning Warbler is often used in commercials and movies as a background sound of idyllic suburban settings. It is doubtful, however, that you would find this gray-headed, black-throated warbler in a backyard, as it prefers dense, herbaceous tangles—both for breeding and during migration. These birds are late spring migrants and the leaves are fully out when they arrive in the eastern US, making it difficult to see them. The easiest way to see a Mourning Warbler is to track a male by its song.

VOICE Call a flat *tchik*; flight call a high, thin, clear *svit*; song a very burry series of paired notes with low-pitched ending: *churrr-ee churrr-ee churrr-ee churr-ee churrr-ee-oh.*

NESTING Well-concealed cup of leaves, lined with grass, on or near ground in dense tangle; 2–5 eggs; 1 brood; June–August.

FEEDING Mainly gleans insects and spiders in low foliage; eats some plant material in winter.

FLIGHT: fast, slightly undulating, and direct with rapid wing beats.

FOLLOW THAT BIRD
Tracking down a singing male is the easiest way to find this skulking species.

SIMILAR SPECIES

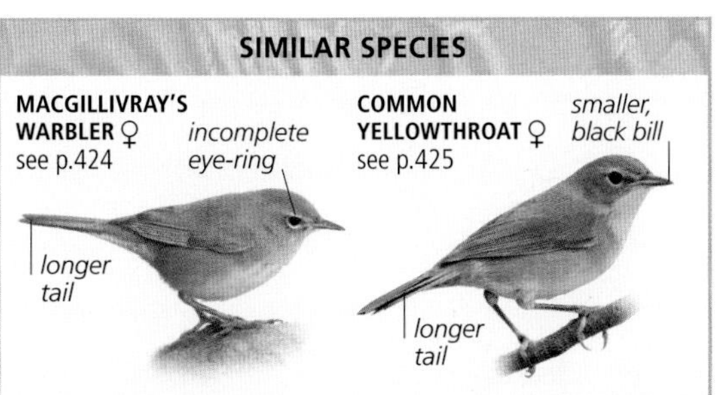

MACGILLIVRAY'S WARBLER ♀
see p.424
incomplete eye-ring
longer tail
COMMON YELLOWTHROAT ♀
see p.425
smaller, black bill
longer tail

OCCURRENCE
Breeds in dense thickets of disturbed woodlands from the Yukon and British Columbia, east to Quebec and Newfoundland, south to the Great Lakes, New England, New York, and the Appalachians. Winters in dense thickets in Central and South America.

Length **5in (13cm)**	Wingspan **7.5in (19cm)**	Weight **⅜–⁷⁄₁₆oz (10–13g)**
Social **Solitary**	Lifespan **Up to 8 years**	Status **Secure**

Order **Passeriformes**	Family **Parulidae**	Species ***Oporornis tolmiei***

MacGillivray's Warbler

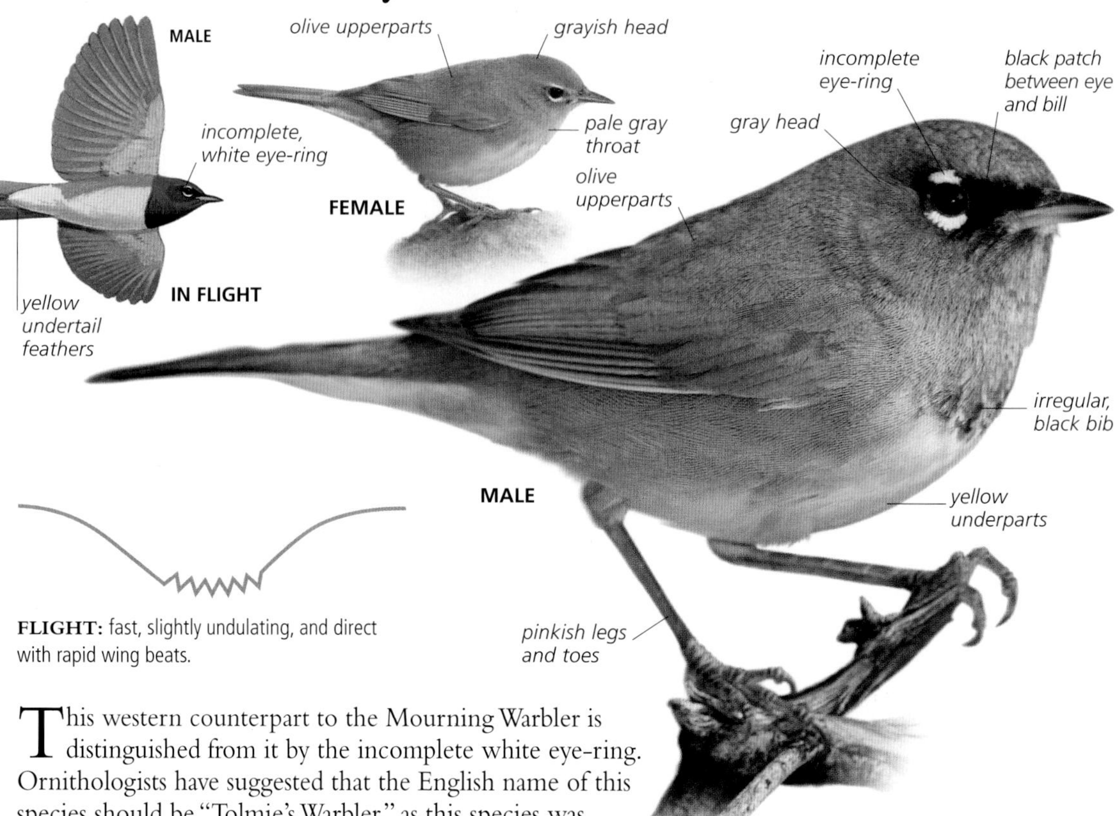
MALE
olive upperparts
grayish head
incomplete, white eye-ring
pale gray throat
FEMALE
yellow undertail feathers
IN FLIGHT
incomplete eye-ring
black patch between eye and bill
gray head
olive upperparts
irregular, black bib
MALE
yellow underparts
pinkish legs and toes

FLIGHT: fast, slightly undulating, and direct with rapid wing beats.

This western counterpart to the Mourning Warbler is distinguished from it by the incomplete white eye-ring. Ornithologists have suggested that the English name of this species should be "Tolmie's Warbler," as this species was described and given its Latin species name, *tolmiei*, in April 1839, to honor the Scottish-born physician W. F. Tolmie. But a month later, John James Audubon, apparently unaware of the name *tolmiei*, named the same species *macgillivrayi*, to honor the naturalist William MacGillivray. This problem was easily solved, as the rule of priority establishes the earliest scientific name as the valid one, so the name *tolmiei* was retained. However, the English name, MacGillivray, has also stuck.

VOICE Call a sharp *tssik*; flight call a high, thin, clear *svit*; song a loud, staccato, rolling series; ends lower or higher than rest of song.

NESTING Cup of plant material just off the ground in deciduous shrubs and thickets; 3–5 eggs; 1 brood; May–August.

FEEDING Gleans beetles, flies, bees, caterpillars from low foliage.

FAIRLY EASY TO FIND
This species is easy to spot, often popping up onto a branch in response to some disturbance.

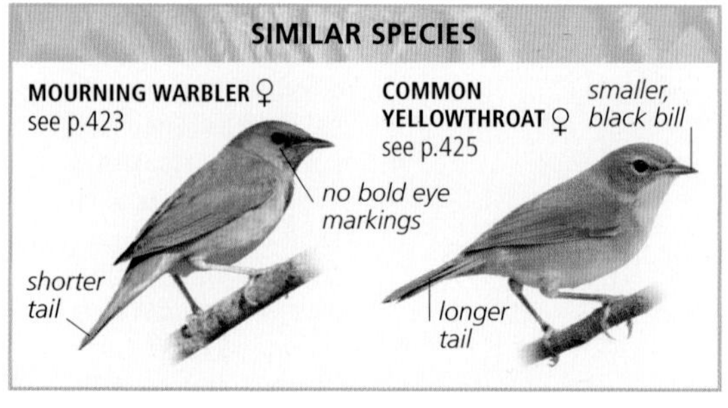
SIMILAR SPECIES
MOURNING WARBLER ♀
see p.423
no bold eye markings
shorter tail
COMMON YELLOWTHROAT ♀
see p.425
smaller, black bill
longer tail

OCCURRENCE
Breeds in thickets within mixed and coniferous forests, often along streams from southeast Alaska and British Columbia south to California and Baja California, and across the western states. Winters in varied habitats with sufficient thickets in Mexico and in Central America.

Length **5in (13cm)**	Wingspan **7.5in (19cm)**	Weight **5/16–7/16oz (9–12g)**
Social **Solitary**	Lifespan **Up to 4 years**	Status **Secure**

Order **Passeriformes**	Family **Parulidae**	Species ***Geothlypis trichas***

Common Yellowthroat

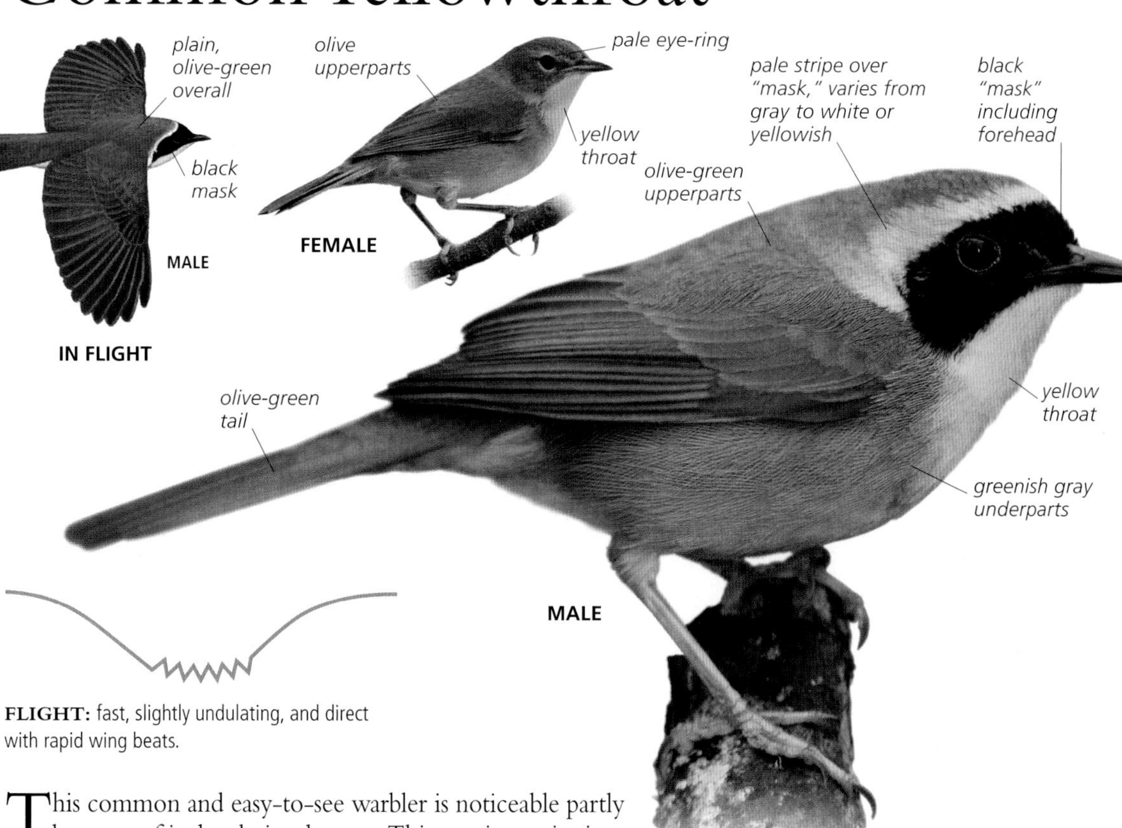
plain, olive-green overall
black mask
MALE
IN FLIGHT
olive upperparts
pale eye-ring
yellow throat
FEMALE
pale stripe over "mask," varies from gray to white or yellowish
black "mask" including forehead
olive-green upperparts
yellow throat
greenish gray underparts
olive-green tail
MALE

FLIGHT: fast, slightly undulating, and direct with rapid wing beats.

This common and easy-to-see warbler is noticeable partly because of its loud, simple song. This species varies in voice and plumage across its range and 14 subspecies have been described. In the western US, the birds have yellower underparts, brighter white head stripes, and louder, simpler songs than the eastern birds. The male often flies upwards rapidly, delivering a more complex version of its song.

VOICE Call a harsh, buzzy *tchak*, repeated into chatter when agitated; flight call a low, flat, buzzy *dzzzit*; song a variable but distinctive series of rich (often three-note) phrases: *WITCH-uh-tee WITCH-uh-tee WITCH-uh-tee WHICH*; more complex flight song.

NESTING Concealed, bulky cup of grasses just above ground or water; 3–5 eggs; 1 brood; May–August.

FEEDING Eats insects and spiders in low vegetation; also seeds.

UNFORGETABLE CALL
The song of the male Common Yellowthroat is an extremely helpful aid in its identification.

SIMILAR SPECIES

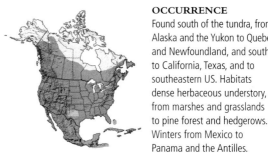

KENTUCKY WARBLER ♂ much larger; see p.496

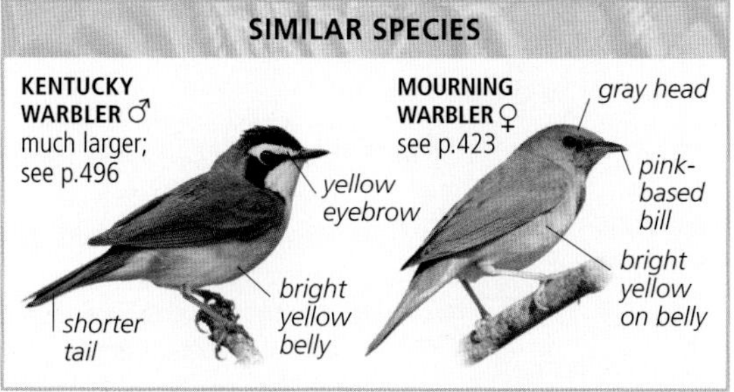
yellow eyebrow
bright yellow belly
shorter tail

MOURNING WARBLER ♀ see p.423

gray head
pink-based bill
bright yellow on belly

OCCURRENCE
Found south of the tundra, from Alaska and the Yukon to Quebec and Newfoundland, and south to California, Texas, and to southeastern US. Habitats dense herbaceous understory, from marshes and grasslands to pine forest and hedgerows. Winters from Mexico to Panama and the Antilles.

Length **5in (13cm)**	Wingspan **6¾in (17cm)**	Weight **29oz (825g)**
Social **Migrant/Winter flocks**	Lifespan **Up to 11 years**	Status **Secure**

Order **Passeriformes**	Family **Parulidae**	Species ***Wilsonia citrina***

Hooded Warbler

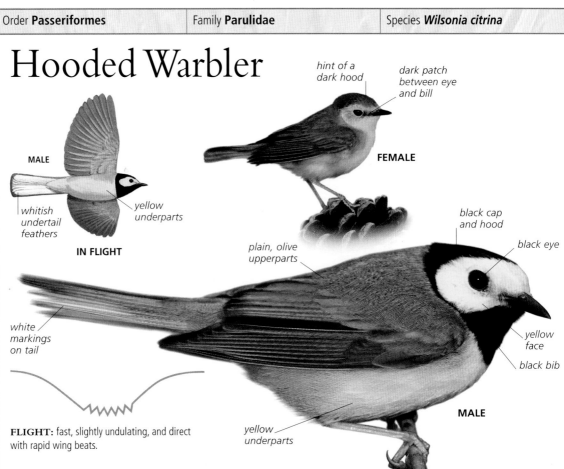

hint of a dark hood

dark patch between eye and bill

FEMALE

MALE

whitish undertail feathers

yellow underparts

IN FLIGHT

black cap and hood

black eye

plain, olive upperparts

white markings on tail

yellow face

black bib

MALE

yellow underparts

FLIGHT: fast, slightly undulating, and direct with rapid wing beats.

The Hooded Warbler is a strikingly patterned and loud warbler, and is often particularly conspicuous over its eastern US breeding range. Both male and females frequently flash the white markings hidden on the inner webs of their tails. The extent of the black hood varies in female Hooded Warblers; it ranges from none in first fall birds to almost as extensive as males in some adult females. Genetic (DNA) and vocal information point to a close relationship with *Dendroica* warblers.

VOICE Call a metallic *tsink*; flight call a high, thin *sveep*; song a rich, whistled series, ending loudly and emphatically: *tu-wee' tu-wee' tu-wee-TEE-tee-yu*.

NESTING Bulky cup of leaves lined with hair, in shrub near eye level; 3–5 eggs; 1–2 broods; May–July.

FEEDING Eats many different kinds of insects found low in vegetation.

STRIKING MASK
The black and yellow face of the Hooded Warbler makes the male an unmistakable bird.

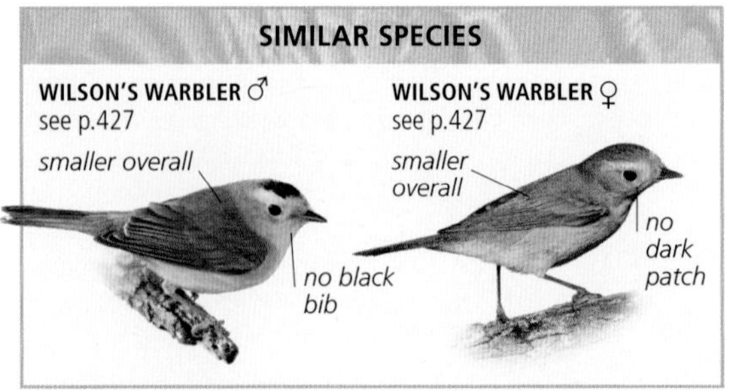
SIMILAR SPECIES
WILSON'S WARBLER ♂
see p.427
smaller overall
no black bib
WILSON'S WARBLER ♀
see p.427
smaller overall
no dark patch

OCCURRENCE
Breeds in moist deciduous forests with dense understory in eastern US and southern Ontario; has bred in some moist mountain canyons. Migrants like similar habitat. Winters in moist woodlands with good understory, especially lowland rainforest, from eastern Mexico to Panama and the West Indies.

Length **5¼in (13.5cm)**	Wingspan **7in (17.5cm)**	Weight **5⁄16oz–7⁄16oz (9–12g)**
Social **Migrant/Winter flocks**	Lifespan **Up to 8 years**	Status **Secure (p)**

Order **Passeriformes**	Family **Parulidae**	Species ***Wilsonia pusilla***

Wilson's Warbler

MALE

IN FLIGHT

long, narrow tail

FEMALE

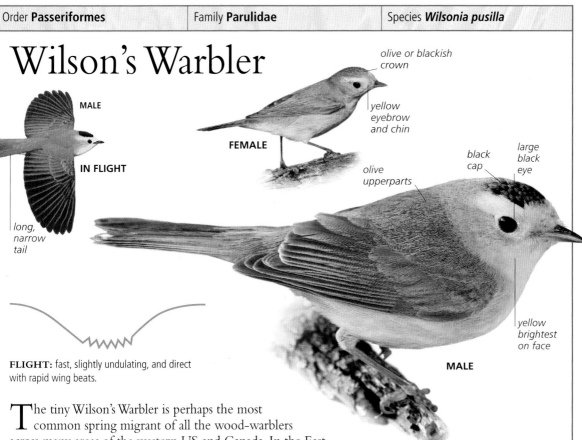

olive or blackish crown

yellow eyebrow and chin

olive upperparts

black cap

large black eye

yellow brightest on face

MALE

FLIGHT: fast, slightly undulating, and direct with rapid wing beats.

The tiny Wilson's Warbler is perhaps the most common spring migrant of all the wood-warblers across many areas of the western US and Canada. In the East, however, it is much scarcer in spring. Wilson's Warblers have a wide range of habitats, yet their numbers are declining, especially in the West, as its riverside breeding habitats are gradually being destroyed by development. This species and the entire genus are named after the renowned early 19th-century ornithologist, Alexander Wilson.

VOICE Call a rich *chimp* or *champ;* flight call a sharp, liquid *tsik;* song a variable, chattering trill, often increases in speed *che che che che chi-chi-chi-chit.*

NESTING Cup of leaves and grass placed on or near ground in mosses or grass, higher along Pacific coast; 4–6 eggs; 1 brood; April–June.

FEEDING Captures insects in foliage, leaf litter, or during flight; also takes berries and honeydew.

BRIGHT WESTERN BIRD
In its western range, male Wilson's Warblers have a glowing yellow-orange face; eastern birds are duller.

EASY IDENTIFICATION
The black cap and yellow face of the otherwise olive-colored Wilson's Warbler are good field marks.

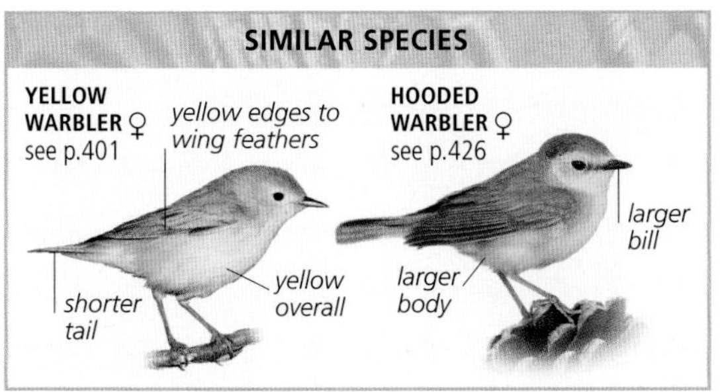
SIMILAR SPECIES
YELLOW WARBLER ♀
see p.401
yellow edges to wing feathers
shorter tail
yellow overall
HOODED WARBLER ♀
see p.426
larger bill
larger body

OCCURRENCE
Breeds in wet shrubby thickets with no canopy, often along streams and lakes; Pacific slope birds use more varied habitats, including moist forests. Widespread in forests south of tundra, from Newfoundland, the Great Lakes, and northern New England; British Columbia to California and New Mexico.

Length **$4\frac{3}{4}$in (12cm)**	Wingspan **7in (17.5cm)**	Weight **$\frac{7}{32}$–$\frac{5}{16}$oz (6–9g)**
Social **Flocks**	Lifespan **Up to 6 years**	Status **Declining**

Order **Passeriformes**	Family **Parulidae**	Species ***Wilsonia canadensis***

Canada Warbler

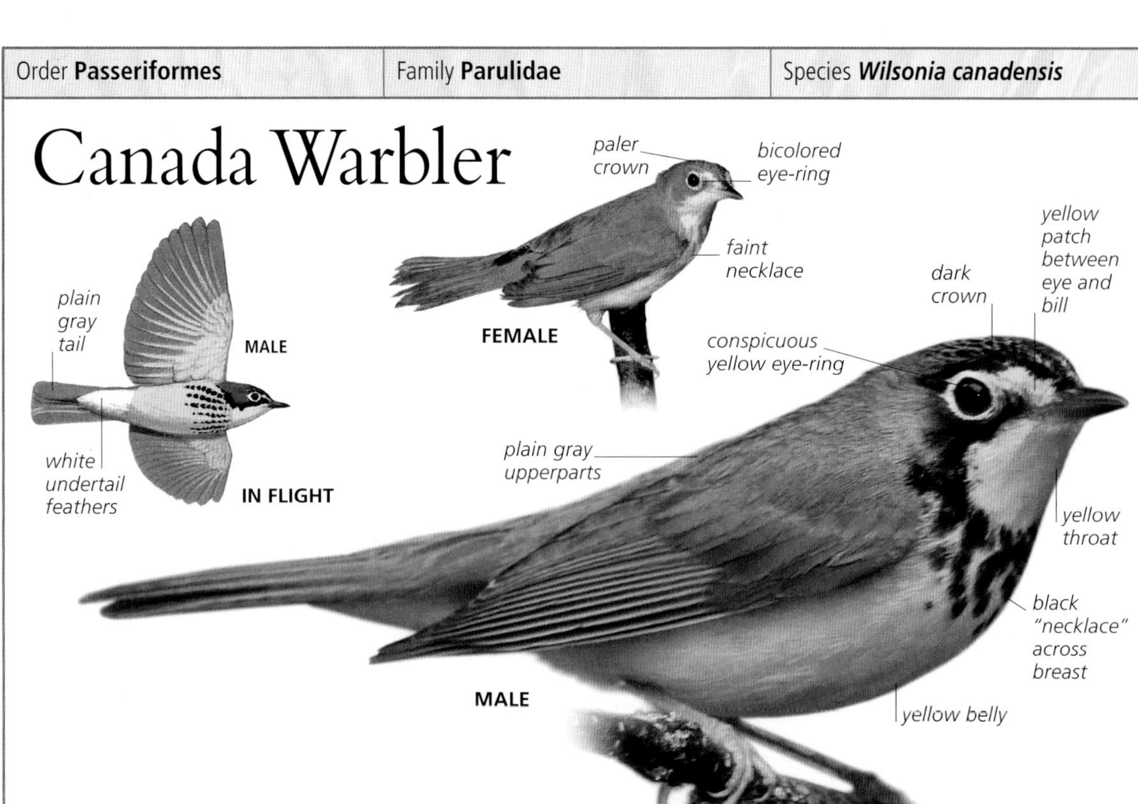
paler crown
bicolored eye-ring
faint necklace
FEMALE
yellow patch between eye and bill
dark crown
conspicuous yellow eye-ring
plain gray tail
MALE
white undertail feathers
IN FLIGHT
plain gray upperparts
yellow throat
black "necklace" across breast
MALE
yellow belly

One of the last species of wood-warblers to arrive in the US and Canada in the spring, and among the first to leave in the fall, the Canada Warbler is sometimes called the "Necklaced Warbler," for the conspicuous black markings on its chest. This uncommon bird is sadly declining, probably because of the maturation and draining of its preferred breeding habitat, consisting of old mixed hardwood forests with moist undergrowth.

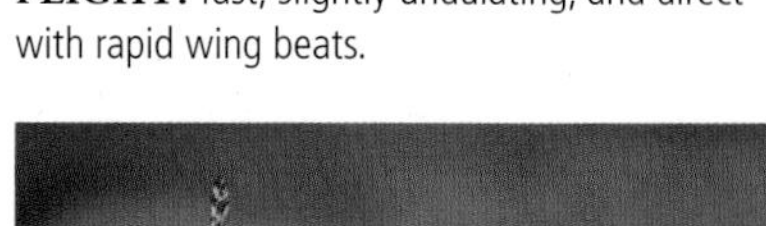

FLIGHT: fast, slightly undulating, and direct with rapid wing beats.

VOICE Call a thick *tchip;* flight call a variable, clear *plip;* song a haphazard jumble of sweet notes, often beginning with or interspersed with *tchip,* followed by a pause.

NESTING Concealed cup of leaves, in moss or grass, on or near ground; 4–5 eggs; 1 brood; May–June.

FEEDING Gleans at mid-levels for many species of insects; also flycatches and forages on ground.

TAKING FLIGHT
This species often waits for prey to fly by, before launching into flight to pursue it.

FAMILIAR MEAL
Flying insects, including crane flies, make up the bulk of the Canada Warbler's diet.

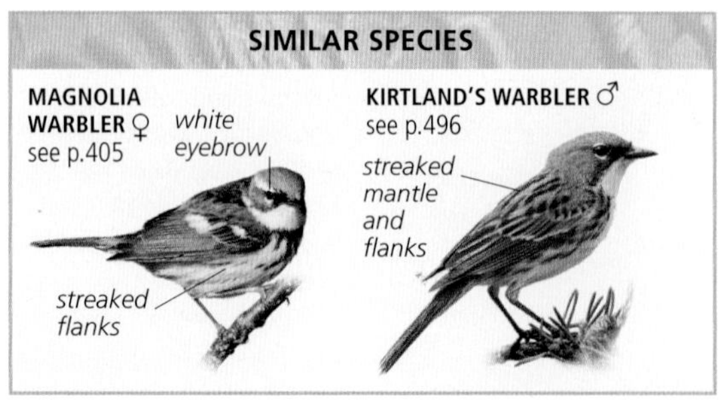
SIMILAR SPECIES
MAGNOLIA WARBLER ♀
see p.405
white eyebrow
streaked flanks
KIRTLAND'S WARBLER ♂
see p.496
streaked mantle and flanks

OCCURRENCE
Breeds in moist deciduous, mixed, and coniferous forests with well-developed understory, especially swampy woods; migrants use well-vegetated habitats; winters in dense, wet thickets and a variety of tropical woodlands in South America.

Length **5in (13cm)**	Wingspan **8in (20cm)**	Weight **⁹⁄₃₂–½oz (8–15g)**
Social **Flocks**	Lifespan **Up to 8 years**	Status **Declining**

Order **Passeriformes**	Family **Parulidae**	Species ***Icteria virens***

Yellow-breasted Chat

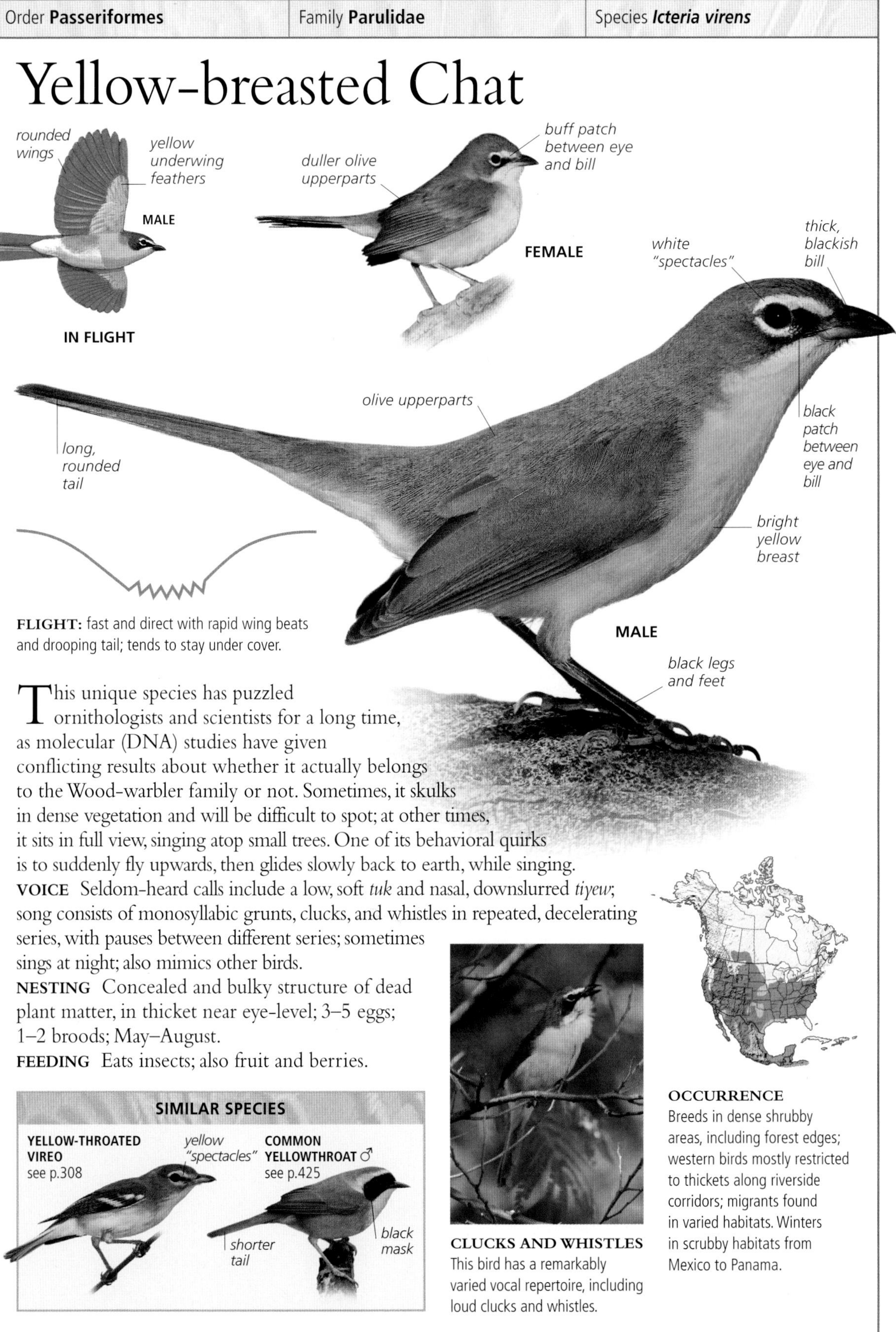
rounded wings
yellow underwing feathers
MALE
IN FLIGHT
duller olive upperparts
buff patch between eye and bill
FEMALE
white "spectacles"
thick, blackish bill
olive upperparts
long, rounded tail
black patch between eye and bill
bright yellow breast
MALE
black legs and feet

FLIGHT: fast and direct with rapid wing beats and drooping tail; tends to stay under cover.

This unique species has puzzled ornithologists and scientists for a long time, as molecular (DNA) studies have given conflicting results about whether it actually belongs to the Wood-warbler family or not. Sometimes, it skulks in dense vegetation and will be difficult to spot; at other times, it sits in full view, singing atop small trees. One of its behavioral quirks is to suddenly fly upwards, then glides slowly back to earth, while singing.

VOICE Seldom-heard calls include a low, soft *tuk* and nasal, downslurred *tiyew*; song consists of monosyllabic grunts, clucks, and whistles in repeated, decelerating series, with pauses between different series; sometimes sings at night; also mimics other birds.

NESTING Concealed and bulky structure of dead plant matter, in thicket near eye-level; 3–5 eggs; 1–2 broods; May–August.

FEEDING Eats insects; also fruit and berries.

CLUCKS AND WHISTLES
This bird has a remarkably varied vocal repertoire, including loud clucks and whistles.

OCCURRENCE
Breeds in dense shrubby areas, including forest edges; western birds mostly restricted to thickets along riverside corridors; migrants found in varied habitats. Winters in scrubby habitats from Mexico to Panama.

SIMILAR SPECIES

YELLOW-THROATED VIREO see p.308
yellow "spectacles"

COMMON YELLOWTHROAT ♂ see p.425
shorter tail
black mask

Length **7½in (19cm)**	Wingspan **9½in (24cm)**	Weight **11/16–1 1/16oz (20–30g)**
Social **Solitary**	Lifespan **Up to 9 years**	Status **Declining**

Family **Iceteridae**

ORIOLES & BLACKBIRDS

THE ICTERIDS exemplify the wonderful diversity that exists among birds. Its members are common and widespread, occurring from coast to coast in nearly every habitat in North America. The species reveal extremes of color, nesting, and social behavior—from the vibrant, solitary orioles to the vast nesting colonies of comparatively drab blackbirds.

ORIOLES

Generally recognized by their contrasting black and orange plumage, although some species tend more toward yellow or chestnut shades, Orioles are common tropical to subtropical seasonal migrants to North America. Their intricate hanging nests are an impressive combination of engineering and weaving. Most species boast a melodious song and tolerance for humans, a combination that makes them popular throughout their range.

COWBIRDS

These strictly parasitic birds have been known to lay eggs in the nests of close to 300 different species in North and South America. The species found in Canada is readily identified by its thick bill and dark, iridescent body contrasting with a brown head.

BLACKBIRDS

As their name suggests, this group of birds is largely covered in dark feathers, and their long, pointed bills and tails add to their streamlined appearance. Not as brilliantly colored as some other Icterids, these are among the most numerous birds on the continent after the breeding season, and form an impressive sight during migration.

SUBTLE BRILLIANCE
Although its plumage is dark, the Common Grackle displays a beautiful iridescence.

MEADOWLARKS

There are just two species in this group, the Eastern and Western Meadowlark, but they are nevertheless distinctive (although difficult to tell apart). Birds of open country, both species have a characteristic bright-yellow chest with a black bib and a sweet singing voice.

BIG VOICE
A Meadowlark's melodious voice is a defining feature in many rural landscapes.

NECTAR LOVER
The magnificently colored Baltimore Oriole inserts its bill into the base of a flower, taking the nectar, but playing no part in pollination.

Order **Passeriformes**	Family **Icteridae**	Species ***Icterus spurius***

Orchard Oriole

black back

IN FLIGHT

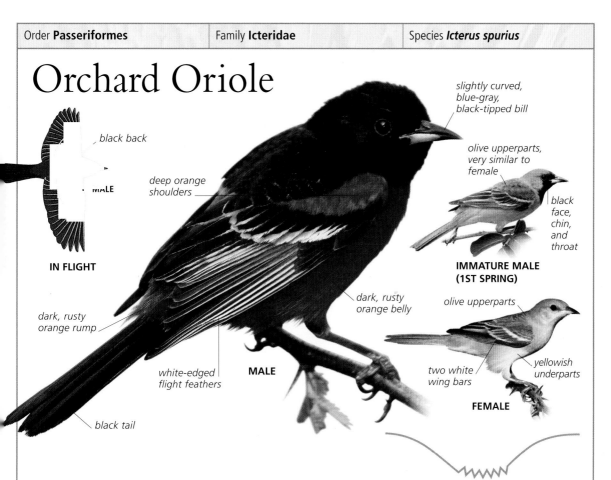

deep orange shoulders

slightly curved, blue-gray, black-tipped bill

olive upperparts, very similar to female

black face, chin, and throat

IMMATURE MALE (1ST SPRING)

dark, rusty orange rump

dark, rusty orange belly

olive upperparts

white-edged flight feathers

MALE

two white wing bars

yellowish underparts

FEMALE

black tail

FLIGHT: quite bouncy flight due to shallow, quick wing beats; interrupted by glides.

A small bird, the Orchard Oriole resembles a large warbler in size, color, and the way it flits among leaves while foraging for insects. It flutters its tail, unlike other orioles. It spends less time on the breeding grounds than other migrant orioles, often arriving there as late as mid-May and leaving as early as late-July. The Orchard Oriole tolerates humans and can be found breeding in suburban parks and gardens. In recent years, its numbers have increased in the eastern part of its range.

VOICE Fast, not very melodious, series of high warbling notes mixed with occasional shorter notes ending in slurred *shheere*.

NESTING Woven nest of grass suspended in fork between branches; 4–5 eggs; 1 brood; April–July.

FEEDING Mainly eats insects during breeding season, but will also feed on seeds, fruit, and occasionally, nectar; in winter, mostly fruit and nectar, and some insects.

RUSTY ORANGE SPLASH

The male Orchard Oriole has distinctive black upperparts and dark, rusty orange underparts.

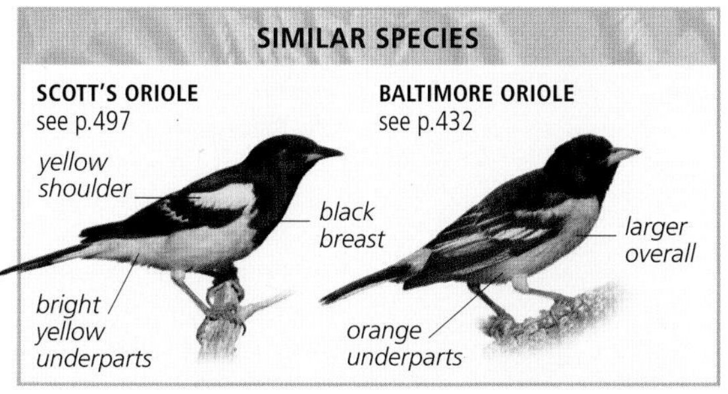
SIMILAR SPECIES
SCOTT'S ORIOLE
see p.497
yellow shoulder
black breast
bright yellow underparts
BALTIMORE ORIOLE
see p.432
larger overall
orange underparts

OCCURRENCE

Breeds in the eastern US and south-central Canada, in open forest and woodland edges with a mixture of evergreen and deciduous trees, especially along river bottoms and in shelter belts surrounding agricultural land. Winters in Mexico, Central America, and South America.

Length **7–8in (18–20cm)**	Wingspan **9in (23cm)**	Weight **11/16oz (20g)**
Social **Pairs**	Lifespan **Up to 9 years**	Status **Secure**

Order **Passeriformes**	Family **Icteridae**	Species ***Icterus galbula***

Baltimore Oriole

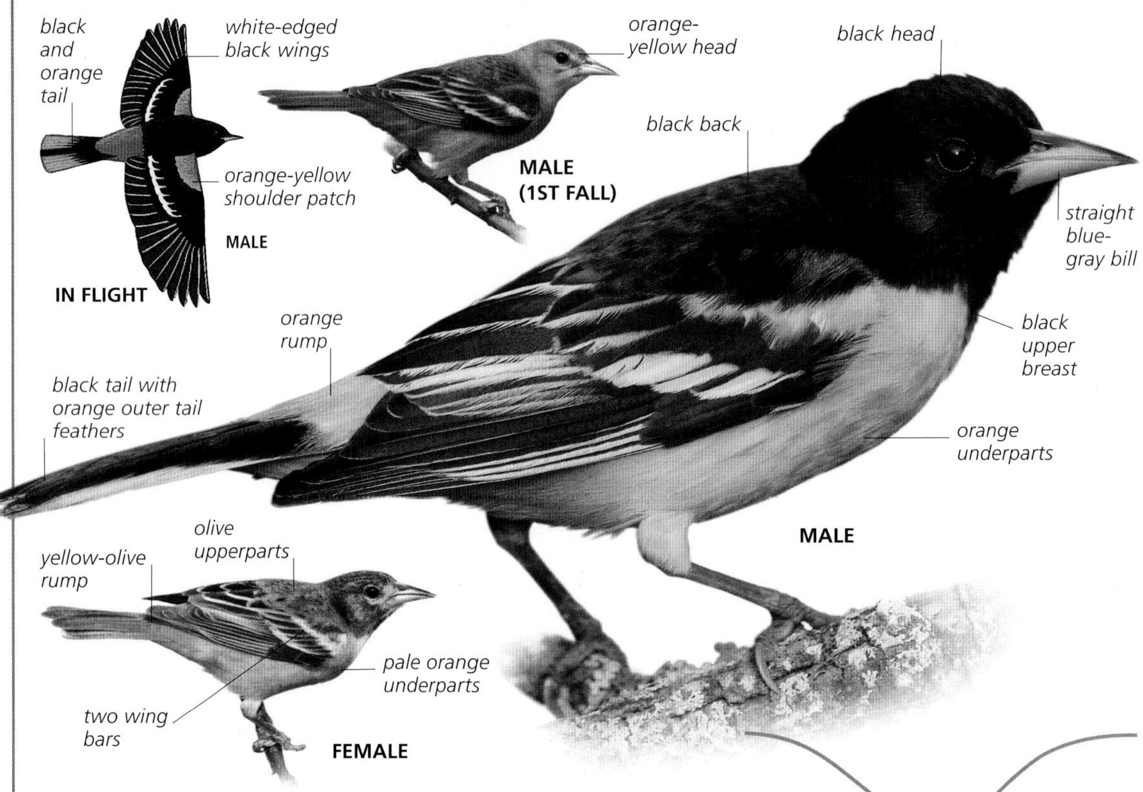

black and orange tail
white-edged black wings
orange-yellow shoulder patch
MALE
IN FLIGHT
orange-yellow head
MALE (1ST FALL)
black head
black back
straight blue-gray bill
orange rump
black upper breast
black tail with orange outer tail feathers
orange underparts
MALE
olive upperparts
yellow-olive rump
pale orange underparts
two wing bars
FEMALE

The Baltimore Oriole's brilliant colors are familiar to many in eastern North America because this bird is so tolerant of humans. This species originally favored the American Elm for nesting, but Dutch Elm disease decimated these trees. The oriole has since adapted to using sycamores, cottonwoods, and other tall trees as nesting sites. Its ability to use suburban gardens and parks has helped expand its range to incorporate areas densely occupied by humans.

VOICE Loud, clear, melodious song comprising several short notes in series, often of varying lengths.

NESTING Round-bottomed basket usually woven of grass, hung toward the end of branches; 4–5 eggs; 1 brood; May–July.

FEEDING Hops or flits among leaves and branches picking insects and spiders; fond of caterpillars; also eats fruits and sips nectar.

FLIGHT: strong with rapid wing beats; full downstrokes during flight provide great power.

PERFECT FOR FORAGING
The Baltimore Oriole forages alone in dense foliage of trees and bushes or on the ground.

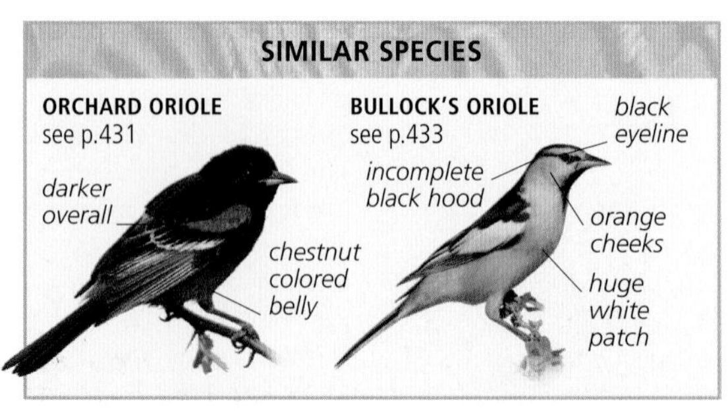

SIMILAR SPECIES
ORCHARD ORIOLE
see p.431
darker overall
chestnut colored belly
BULLOCK'S ORIOLE
see p.433
black eyeline
incomplete black hood
orange cheeks
huge white patch

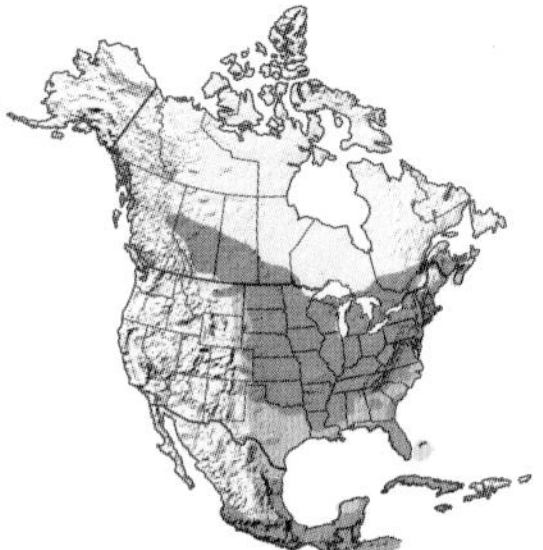

OCCURRENCE
Forest edges and tall, open mixed hardwoods, especially close to rivers; regularly uses forested parks, suburban and urban areas with abundant tall trees. Small numbers winter in southeastern US and Florida, but most birds move to Mexico, Colombia, and Venezuela.

Length **8–10in (20–26cm)**	Wingspan **10–12in (26–30cm)**	Weight **1¹⁄₁₆–1¼oz (30–35g)**
Social **Solitary/Pairs**	Lifespan **Up to 11 years**	Status **Secure**

Order **Passeriformes**	Family **Icteridae**	Species ***Icterus bullockii***

Bullock's Oriole

black eye stripe

black cap and nape

orange face

black bib

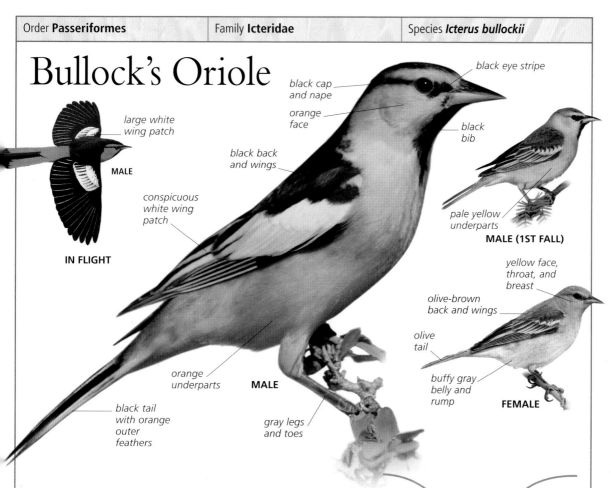

large white wing patch

black back and wings

MALE

conspicuous white wing patch

pale yellow underparts

MALE (1ST FALL)

IN FLIGHT

yellow face, throat, and breast

olive-brown back and wings

olive tail

orange underparts

MALE

buffy gray belly and rump

FEMALE

black tail with orange outer feathers

gray legs and toes

The Bullock's Oriole is the western counterpart of the Baltimore in both behavior and habitat. The two were thought to belong to a single species, the Northern Oriole (*I. galbula*), because they interbreed where they overlap in the Great Plains. Recent studies, however, suggest that they are separate species. Unlike many other orioles, the Bullock's is more resistant to brood parasites and punctures and removes cowbird eggs from its nest.

FLIGHT: full, powerful wing beats, resulting in a "heavier" flight aspect than similar species.

VOICE Varied string of one- and two-part notes often mumbled or slurred at the end; similar to, but less melodious, than the Baltimore Oriole's song.

NESTING Hanging basket of woven plant strips located at the tips of branches; 4–5 eggs; 1 brood; March–June.

FEEDING Forages for insects, in particular grasshoppers and caterpillars, but also ants, beetles, and spiders; nectar and fruit when available.

OBLIVIOUS TO THORNS
This male Bullock's Oriole perches on a branch with long thorns, but it is not perturbed.

OCCURRENCE
Found especially in riverside woodlands with willows and cottonwoods; also mixed hardwood forests, mesquite woodland, and groves of fruit trees. Breeds in open mixed hardwood forests, especially those surrounding waterways and containing stands of oak, cottonwood, and willow.

SIMILAR SPECIES

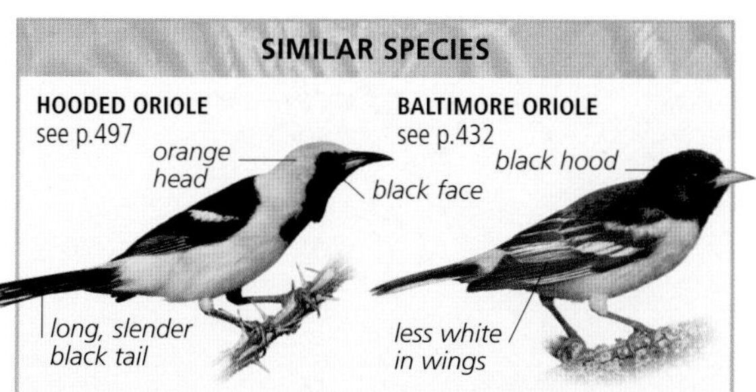
HOODED ORIOLE
see p.497
orange head
black face
long, slender black tail
BALTIMORE ORIOLE
see p.432
black hood
less white in wings

Length **6½–7½in (16–19cm)**	Wingspan **10–12in (25–30cm)**	Weight **1¹⁄₁₆–1⁹⁄₁₆oz (30–45g)**
Social **Pairs/Flocks**	Lifespan **Up to 8 years**	Status **Secure**

Order **Passeriformes**	Family **Icteridae**	Species ***Molothrus ater***

Brown-headed Cowbird

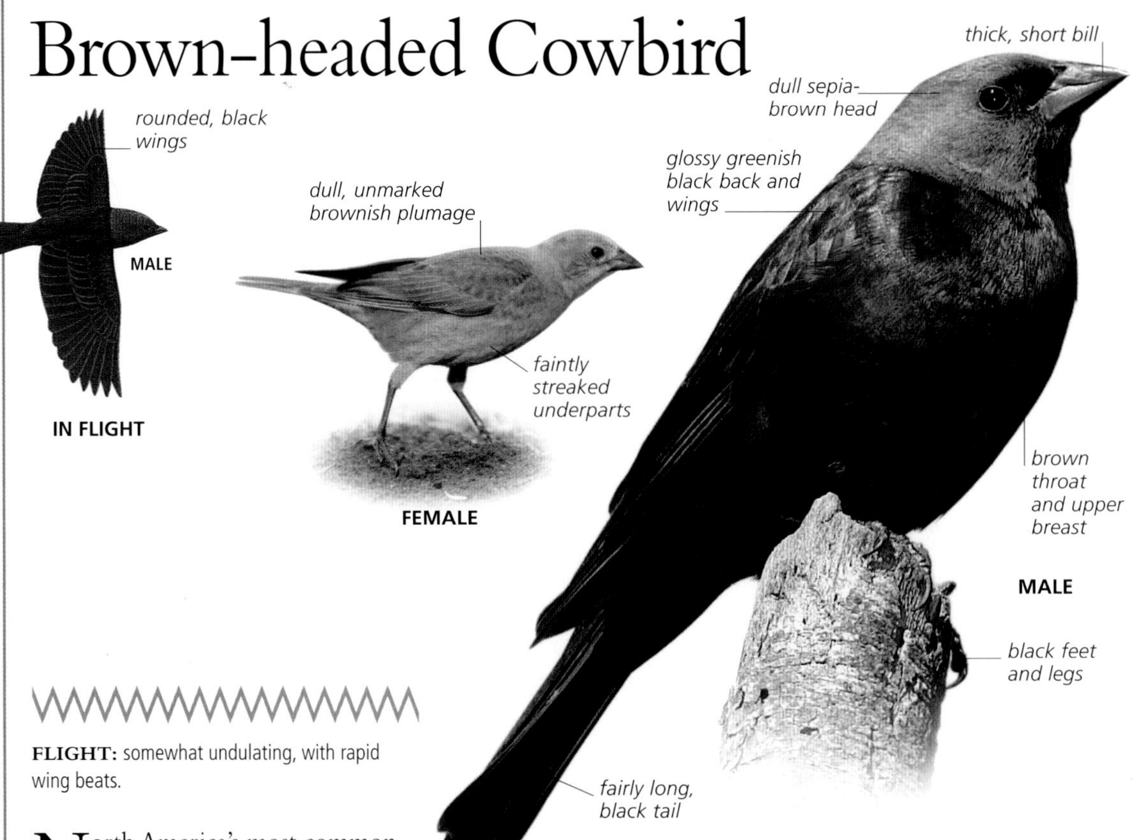
rounded, black wings
MALE
IN FLIGHT
dull, unmarked brownish plumage
faintly streaked underparts
FEMALE
thick, short bill
dull sepia-brown head
glossy greenish black back and wings
brown throat and upper breast
MALE
black feet and legs
fairly long, black tail

FLIGHT: somewhat undulating, with rapid wing beats.

North America's most common and best-known brood parasite, the Brown-headed Cowbird was once a bird of the Great Plains, following vast herds of bison to prey on insects kicked up by their hooves. Now, due to forest clearance and suburban development, it is found continent-wide. It has recently become a serious threat to North American songbirds, laying its eggs in the nests of more than 220 different species, and having its young raised to fledglings by more than 140 species, including the highly endangered Kirtland's Warbler.

VOICE High-pitched, squeaky whistles and bubbling notes, *dub-dub-come-tzeee*; also various clucks and *cheks*.

NESTING No nest, lays eggs in nests of other species; a single female may lay 25–55 (or more) eggs per season; April–August.

FEEDING Primarily eats grass seeds and cereal grains, but also insects when available, especially grasshoppers and beetles.

AT A FEEDER
A female Brown-headed Cowbird enjoys a snack of seeds at a suburban feeder.

SIMILAR SPECIES

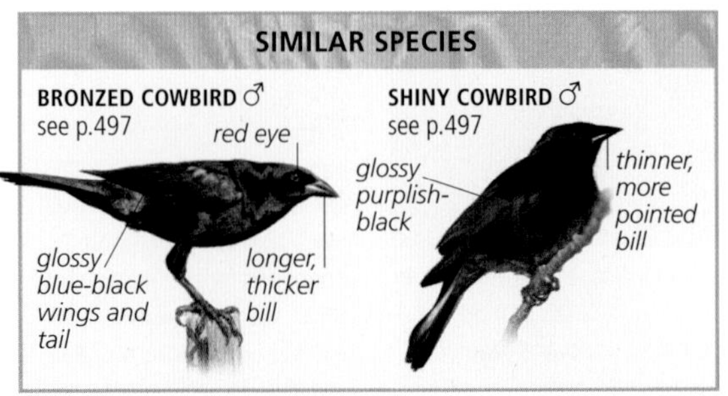
BRONZED COWBIRD ♂
see p.497
red eye
glossy blue-black wings and tail
longer, thicker bill
SHINY COWBIRD ♂
see p.497
glossy purplish-black
thinner, more pointed bill

OCCURRENCE
Favors habitats modified by human activity, such as open wooded patches, low grass fields, fruit orchards, agricultural pastures with livestock, and gardens and residential areas. Widespread across North America.

Length **6–8in (15–20cm)**	Wingspan **11–13in (28–33cm)**	Weight **1⁷⁄₁₆–1¾oz (40–50g)**
Social **Large flocks**	Lifespan **Up to 16 years**	Status **Secure**

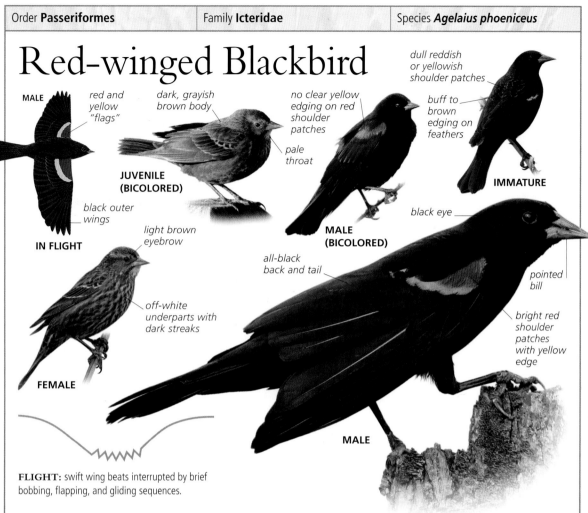

Order **Passeriformes**	Family **Icteridae**	Species ***Agelaius phoeniceus***

Red-winged Blackbird

MALE IN FLIGHT
red and yellow "flags"
black outer wings

JUVENILE (BICOLORED)
dark, grayish brown body
pale throat

MALE (BICOLORED)
no clear yellow edging on red shoulder patches

IMMATURE
dull reddish or yellowish shoulder patches
buff to brown edging on feathers

FEMALE
light brown eyebrow
off-white underparts with dark streaks

MALE
black eye
all-black back and tail
pointed bill
bright red shoulder patches with yellow edge

FLIGHT: swift wing beats interrupted by brief bobbing, flapping, and gliding sequences.

One of the most abundant native bird species in North America, the Red-winged Blackbird is also one of the most conspicuous in wetland habitats. The sight and sound of males singing from the tops of cattails is a sure sign that spring is near. This adaptable species migrates and roosts in flocks that may number in the millions. There are numerous subspecies, one of the most distinctive being the "Bicolored" Blackbird (*A. p. gubernator.*)

VOICE Various brusk *chek*, *chit*, or *chet* calls; male song a *kronk-a-rhee* with a characteristic nasal, rolling and metallic "undulating" ending.

NESTING Cup of grasses and mud woven into dense standing reeds or cattails; 3–4 eggs; 1–2 broods; March–June.

FEEDING Forages for seeds and grains; largely insects when breeding.

DENSE FLOCKS
The huge flocks of Red-winged Blackbirds seen in migration are quite an amazing sight.

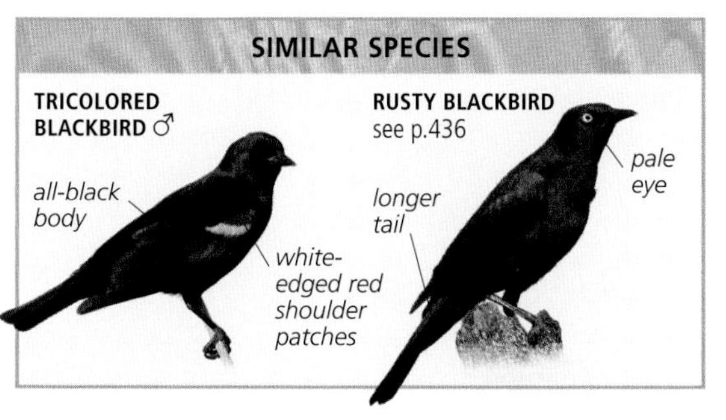
SIMILAR SPECIES
TRICOLORED BLACKBIRD ♂
all-black body
white-edged red shoulder patches
RUSTY BLACKBIRD
see p.436
longer tail
pale eye

OCCURRENCE
Widespread across Canada and the US from Alaska to the Maritimes, and south to Mexico, Central America, and the Bahamas. Lives in wetlands, especially freshwater marshes but also saltwater; wet meadows with tall grass cover and open woodlands with reedy vegetation.

Length **7–10in (18–25cm)**	Wingspan **11–14in (28–35cm)**	Weight **1⁹⁄₁₆–2½oz (45–70g)**
Social **Flocks**	Lifespan **At least 14 years**	Status **Secure**

Order **Passeriformes**	Family **Icteridae**	Species ***Euphagus carolinus***

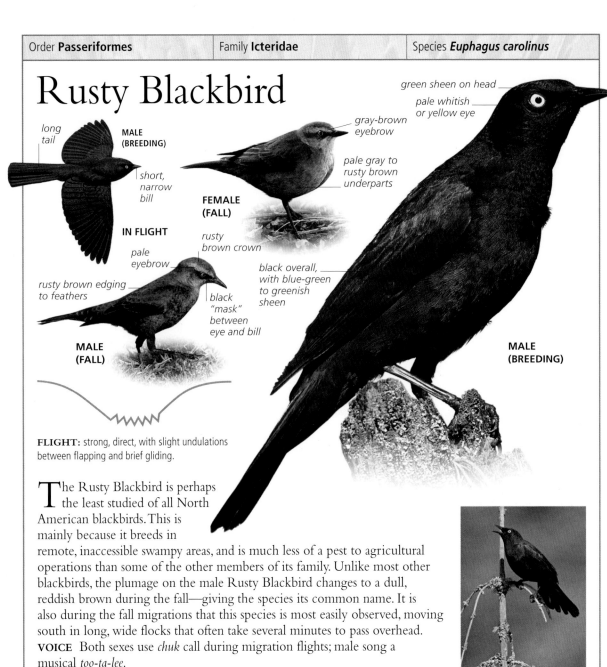

Rusty Blackbird

long tail

MALE (BREEDING)

short, narrow bill

IN FLIGHT

gray-brown eyebrow

pale gray to rusty brown underparts

FEMALE (FALL)

rusty brown crown

pale eyebrow

rusty brown edging to feathers

black "mask" between eye and bill

MALE (FALL)

green sheen on head

pale whitish or yellow eye

black overall, with blue-green to greenish sheen

MALE (BREEDING)

FLIGHT: strong, direct, with slight undulations between flapping and brief gliding.

The Rusty Blackbird is perhaps the least studied of all North American blackbirds. This is mainly because it breeds in remote, inaccessible swampy areas, and is much less of a pest to agricultural operations than some of the other members of its family. Unlike most other blackbirds, the plumage on the male Rusty Blackbird changes to a dull, reddish brown during the fall—giving the species its common name. It is also during the fall migrations that this species is most easily observed, moving south in long, wide flocks that often take several minutes to pass overhead.

VOICE Both sexes use *chuk* call during migration flights; male song a musical *too-ta-lee*.

NESTING Small bowl of branches and sticks, lined with wet plants and dry grass, usually near water; 3–5 eggs; 1 brood; May–July.

FEEDING Eats seasonally available insects, spiders, grains, seeds of trees, and fleshy fruits or berries.

OPEN WIDE
Seldom seen, the male's courtship display includes gaping and tail-spreading.

SIMILAR SPECIES
BREWER'S BLACKBIRD
see p.437
purplish sheen on head
longer tail
COMMON GRACKLE
see p.438
bluish sheen on head
bill thicker at base
large tail
glossy bronze body

OCCURRENCE
Breeds in moist to wet forests up to the timberline in the far north (farther north than any other species of North American blackbird); winters in eastern US, in various swampy forests.

Length **8–10in (20–25cm)**	Wingspan **12–15in (30–38cm)**	Weight **$1\frac{9}{16}$–$2\frac{7}{8}$oz (45–80g)**
Social **Pairs/Winter flocks**	Lifespan **At least 9 years**	Status **Secure**

Order **Passeriformes**	Family **Icteridae**	Species ***Euphagus cyanocephalus***

Brewer's Blackbird

stout bill

long, dark tail

MALE

IN FLIGHT

brown eyes

gray brown overall

FEMALE

purplish sheen on head

yellow eyes

black body with greenish blue sheen

MALE

black legs and feet

FLIGHT: several wing beats followed by short glides with shallow rise and fall pattern.

The Brewer's Blackbird, unlike the swamp-loving Rusty Blackbird, seems to prefer areas disturbed by humans to natural ones throughout much of its range. It is likely that the relatively recent eastward range expansion of Brewer's Blackbird has been aided by changes in land practices. Interestingly, when the Brewer's Blackbird range overlaps with that of the Common Grackle, it wins out in rural areas, but loses out in urban areas. This species can be found feasting on waste grains left behind after the harvest.

VOICE Buzzy *tshrrep* song ascending in tone.

NESTING Bulky cup of dry grass, stem and twig framework lined with soft grasses and animal hair; 3–6 eggs; 1–2 broods; April–July.

FEEDING Forages on the ground for many species of insects during breeding season, also snails; seeds, grain, and occasional fruit in fall and winter.

BROWN-EYED BIRD
Brown eyes distinguish the female Brewer's from the yellow-eyed, female Rusty Blackbird.

SIMILAR SPECIES

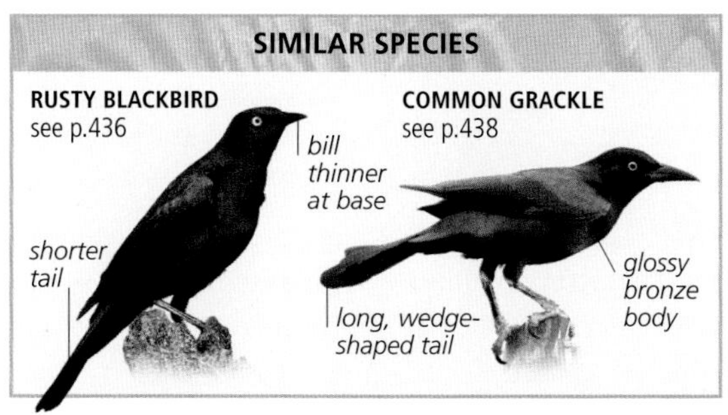
RUSTY BLACKBIRD
see p.436
bill thinner at base
shorter tail
COMMON GRACKLE
see p.438
glossy bronze body
long, wedge-shaped tail

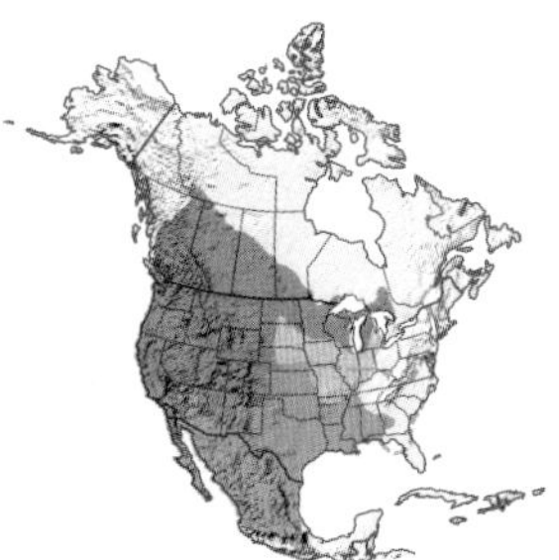

OCCURRENCE
Breeds and winters in open areas, readily adapting to, and preferring, disturbed areas and human developments such as parks, gardens, clear-felled forests, and fallow fields edged with dense trees or shrubs.

Length **10–12in (25–30cm)**	Wingspan **13–16in (33–41cm)**	Weight **1¾–2½oz (50–70g)**
Social **Flocks/Colonies**	Lifespan **Up to 13 years**	Status **Secure**

Order **Passeriformes**	Family **Icteridae**	Species ***Quiscalus quiscula***

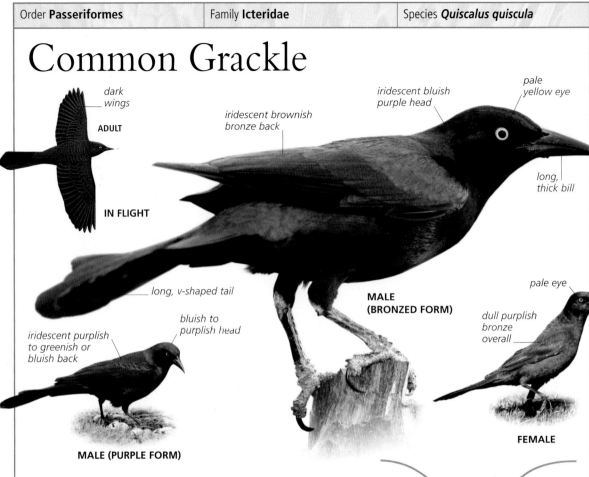

Common Grackle

dark wings

ADULT

IN FLIGHT

iridescent brownish bronze back

iridescent bluish purple head

pale yellow eye

long, thick bill

long, v-shaped tail

MALE (BRONZED FORM)

iridescent purplish to greenish or bluish back

bluish to purplish head

MALE (PURPLE FORM)

pale eye

dull purplish bronze overall

FEMALE

This adaptable species has expanded its range rapidly in the recent past, thanks to human land clearing practices. The Common Grackle is so well suited to urban and suburban habitats that it successfully excludes other species from them. During migration and winter, Common Grackles form immense flocks, some of which may be made up of more than 1 million individuals. This tendency, combined with its preference for cultivated areas, has made this species an agricultural pest in some regions.

VOICE Call a low, harsh *chek*; loud song series of odd squeaks and whistles.

NESTING Small bowl in trees, with a frame of sticks filled with mud and grasses; 4–6 eggs; 1–2 broods; April–July.

FEEDING Eats beetles, flies, spiders, and worms, as well as small vertebrates; also seeds and grain, especially in nonbreeding season; an omnivore.

FLIGHT: straight, level, and direct without the up and down undulation of blackbird species.

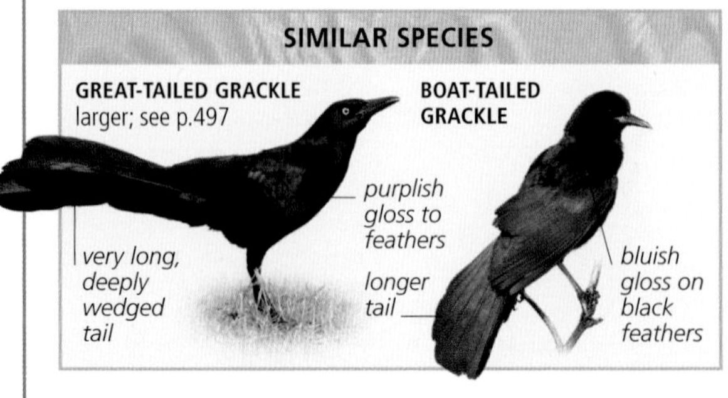
SIMILAR SPECIES
GREAT-TAILED GRACKLE
larger; see p.497
very long, deeply wedged tail
purplish gloss to feathers
BOAT-TAILED GRACKLE
longer tail
bluish gloss on black feathers

HIGHLY ADAPTABLE
This grackle is comfortable near human developments, resulting in the expansion of its range.

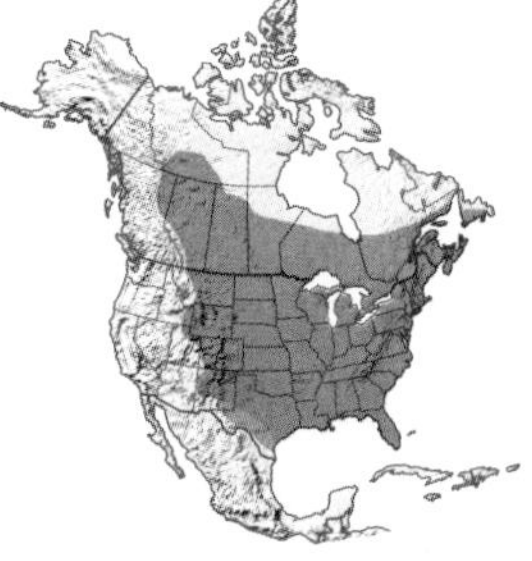

OCCURRENCE
The Common Grackle lives in a wide variety of open woodlands, suburban woodlots, city parks, gardens, and hedgerows. It is absent west of the Great Plains. Wintering range extends south to the Gulf Coast.

Length **11–13½in (28–34cm)**	Wingspan **15–18in (38–46cm)**	Weight **3⅛–4oz (90–125g)**
Social **Flocks**	Lifespan **Up to 20 years**	Status **Secure**

Order **Passeriformes**	Family **Icteridae**	Species ***Sturnella magna***

Eastern Meadowlark

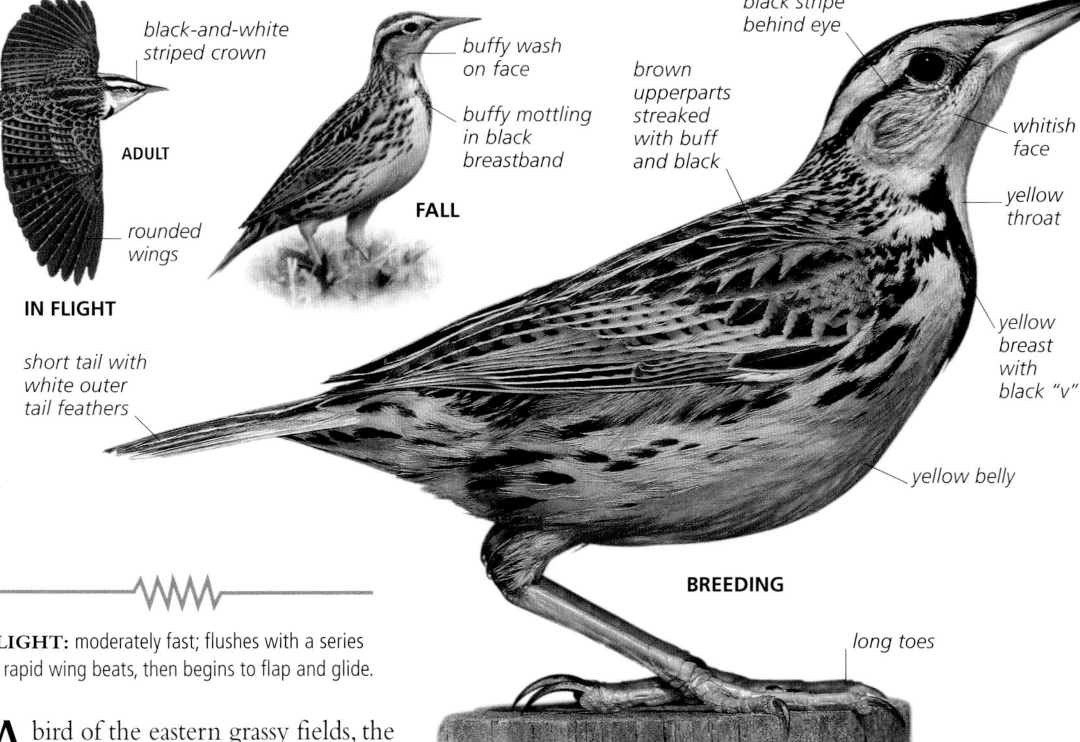
black-and-white striped crown
ADULT
rounded wings
IN FLIGHT
buffy wash on face
buffy mottling in black breastband
FALL
short tail with white outer tail feathers
long, pointed bill
black stripe behind eye
brown upperparts streaked with buff and black
whitish face
yellow throat
yellow breast with black "v"
yellow belly
BREEDING
long toes

FLIGHT: moderately fast; flushes with a series of rapid wing beats, then begins to flap and glide.

A bird of the eastern grassy fields, the colorful Eastern Meadowlark is well known for its plaintive sounding song. During courtship, the male sings enthusiastically from the highest available perch. This species overlaps with the very similar looking Western Meadowlark in the western Great Plains, but is the only meadowlark further east. Where they overlap, these birds are most easily distinguished by their different calls and songs. Throughout its range, numbers of the Eastern Meadowlark have fallen due to human encroachment on its habitat, although in the last decade or so, the species has made a slow (and local) comeback.

VOICE Call a sharp *dzzeer*; song a series of clear, descending whistles consisting of 3–8 notes, *tseeeooou tseeeeou*.

NESTING Loosely woven, usually domed, cup of grasses and other plants, located on the ground in tall grass fields; 3–8 eggs; 1 brood; March–May.

FEEDING Forages on ground, mainly for insects, especially grasshoppers, but also caterpillars and grubs; seeds and grain in winter.

FAVORITE PERCH
Eastern Meadowlarks are partial to fenceposts as a favorite perch for singing.

SIMILAR SPECIES

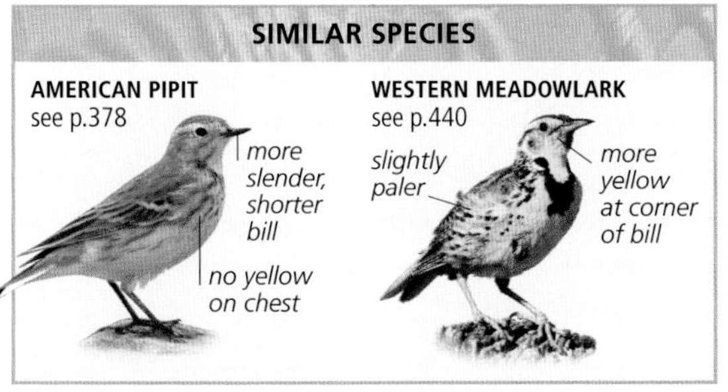
AMERICAN PIPIT
see p.378
more slender, shorter bill
no yellow on chest
WESTERN MEADOWLARK
see p.440
slightly paler
more yellow at corner of bill

OCCURRENCE
Breeds in native tallgrass openings, pastures, and overgrown roadsides. Widespread in eastern North America, from Quebec to New Mexico and Arizona; also in Mexico and Cuba, and locally in South America. Partial migrant in the US, resident in Mexico and South America.

Length **7–10in (18–25cm)**	Wingspan **13–15in (33–38cm)**	Weight **2⅛–4oz (60–125g)**
Social **Pairs/Winter flocks**	Lifespan **Up to 9 years**	Status **Declining**

Order **Passeriformes**	Family **Icteridae**	Species ***Sturnella neglecta***

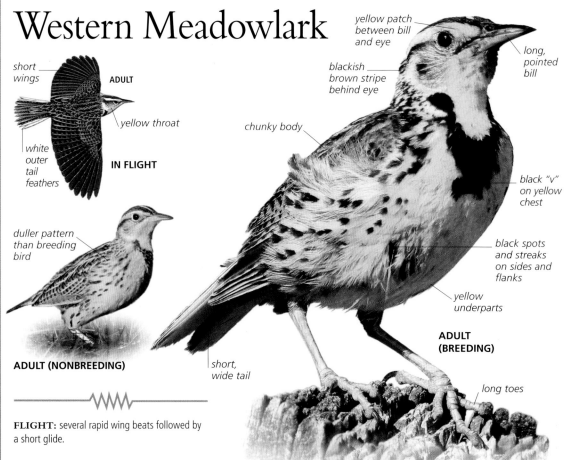

Western Meadowlark

short wings

ADULT

yellow throat

white outer tail feathers

IN FLIGHT

duller pattern than breeding bird

ADULT (NONBREEDING)

yellow patch between bill and eye

long, pointed bill

blackish brown stripe behind eye

chunky body

black "v" on yellow chest

black spots and streaks on sides and flanks

yellow underparts

ADULT (BREEDING)

short, wide tail

long toes

FLIGHT: several rapid wing beats followed by a short glide.

Although the range of the Western Meadowlark overlaps widely with that of its Eastern counterpart, hybrids between the two species are very rare and usually sterile. The large numbers of Western Meadowlarks in the western Great Plains, the Great Basin, and the Central Valley of California, combined with the male's tendency to sing conspicuously from the tops of shrubs, when fence posts are not available, make this species attractive to birdwatchers. Where the two meadowlarks overlap they are best identified by their song.

VOICE Series of complex, bubbling, whistled notes descending in pitch.

NESTING Domed grass cup, well hidden in tall grasses; 3–7 eggs; 1 brood; March–August.

FEEDING Feeds mostly on insects, including beetles, grubs, and grasshoppers; also grains and grass seeds.

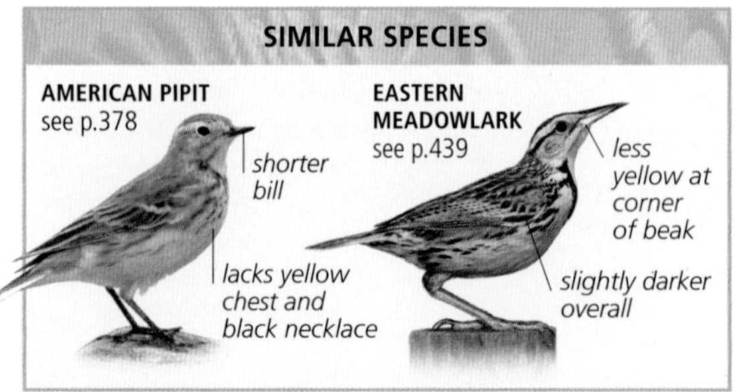
SIMILAR SPECIES
AMERICAN PIPIT
see p.378
shorter bill
lacks yellow chest and black necklace
EASTERN MEADOWLARK
see p.439
less yellow at corner of beak
slightly darker overall

A SHRUB WILL DO
With few fenceposts in the Western Meadowlark's habitat, it perches on a shrub to sing.

OCCURRENCE
Common in western North America, across much of southern Canada and the western US, south to Mexico. Breeds primarily in open grassy plains, but also uses agricultural fields with overgrown edges and hayfields. Partial migrant in US, winters south to Mexico.

Length **7–10in (18–26cm)**	Wingspan **13–15in (33–38cm)**	Weight **2⅞–4oz (80–125g)**
Social **Pairs/Winter flocks**	Lifespan **Up to 10 years**	Status **Secure**

Order **Passeriformes**	Family **Icteridae**	Species ***Xanthocephalus xanthocephalus***

Yellow-headed Blackbird

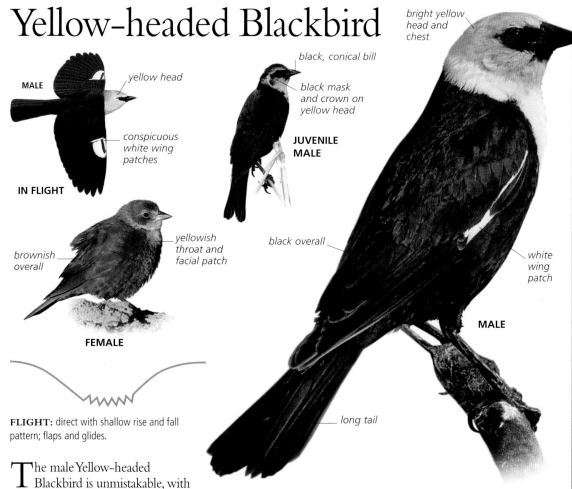

MALE
yellow head
conspicuous white wing patches
IN FLIGHT

black, conical bill
black mask and crown on yellow head
JUVENILE MALE

bright yellow head and chest
black overall
white wing patch
MALE
long tail

brownish overall
yellowish throat and facial patch
FEMALE

FLIGHT: direct with shallow rise and fall pattern; flaps and glides.

The male Yellow-headed Blackbird is unmistakable, with its conspicuous bright yellow head. Females, however, are more drab. Populations of this species fluctuate widely, but locally, according to available rainfall, which controls the availability, and quality, of its breeding marshland habitat. In some wetlands, the Yellow-headed Blackbird can be extremely abundant, and is easily noticeable due to its amazing song.

VOICE Call a nasal *whaah*; song a series of harsh, cackling noises, followed by a brief pause, and a high, long, wailing trill.

NESTING Cup of plant strips woven into standing aquatic vegetation; 3–4 eggs; 1 brood; May–June.

FEEDING Eats insects while breeding; agricultural grains and grass seeds in winter.

OCCURRENCE
Widely distributed in western Canada and the central and western US, this species breeds in marshes with cattail and bullrush vegetation, and also, locally, in wetlands within wooded areas. Winters in Mexico; resident in Baja California.

YELLOW GARLAND
Five evenly spaced yellow-headed males watch over their wetland habitat from a twig.

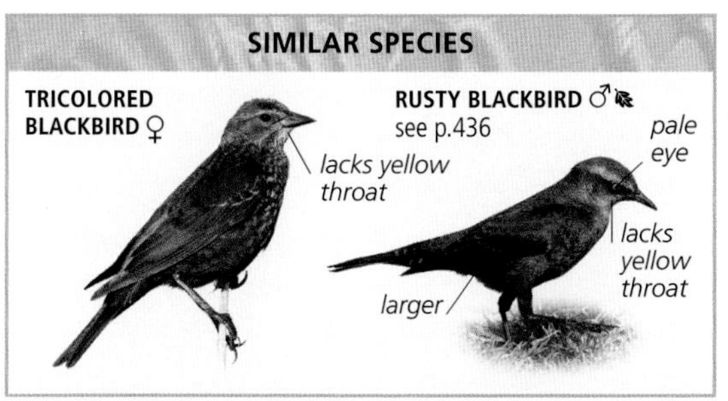
SIMILAR SPECIES
TRICOLORED BLACKBIRD ♀
lacks yellow throat
RUSTY BLACKBIRD ♂
see p.436
pale eye
lacks yellow throat
larger

Length **8½–10½in (21–27cm)**	Wingspan **15in (38cm)**	Weight **2⅛–3½oz (60–100g)**
Social **Flocks/Colonies**	Lifespan **Up to 9 years**	Status **Localized**

Order **Passeriformes**	Family **Icteridae**	Species ***Dolichonyx oryzivorus***

Bobolink

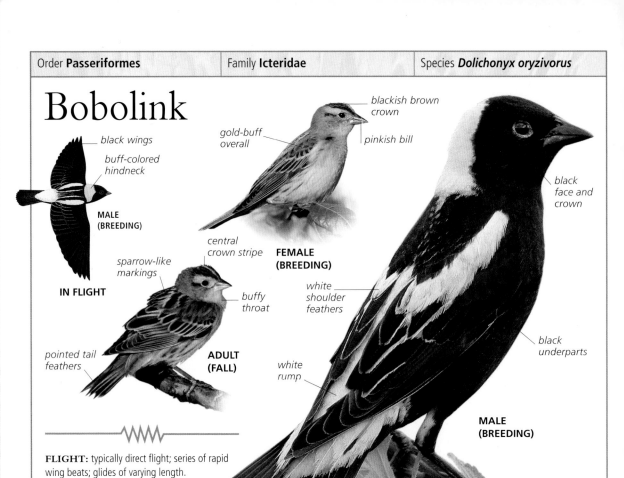

black wings
buff-colored hindneck
MALE (BREEDING)
IN FLIGHT

blackish brown crown
gold-buff overall
pinkish bill
FEMALE (BREEDING)

central crown stripe
sparrow-like markings
buffy throat
pointed tail feathers
ADULT (FALL)

black face and crown
white shoulder feathers
black underparts
white rump
black tail with pointed feathers
MALE (BREEDING)

FLIGHT: typically direct flight; series of rapid wing beats; glides of varying length.

The Bobolink is a common summer resident of open fallow fields through much of the northern US and southern Canada. In spring, the males perform a conspicuous circling or "helicoptering" display, which includes singing, to establish territory and to attract females. Bobolink populations have declined on its breeding grounds and in wintering areas because of habitat loss and changing agricultural practices.

VOICE Calls like the end of its name *link*; song a long, complex babbling series of musical notes varying in length and pitch.

NESTING Woven cup of grass close to or on the ground, well hidden in tall grass; 3–7 eggs; 1 brood; May–July.

FEEDING Feeds mostly on insects, spiders, grubs in breeding season, but seasonally variable; also cereal grains and grass seeds.

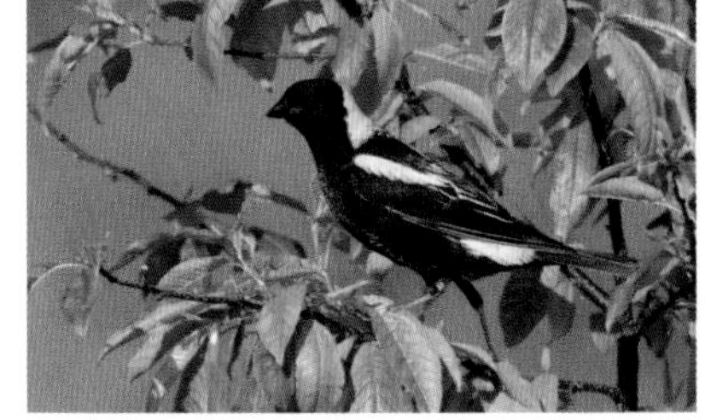

TAKING A BREAK
This male has fled the sun of the open fields to seek shelter in the shade of a tree.

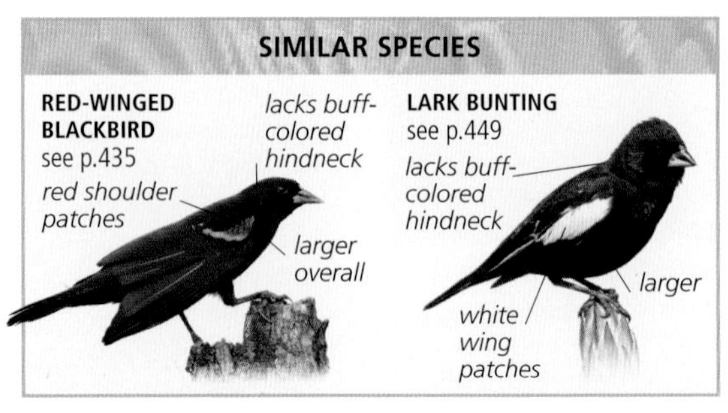
SIMILAR SPECIES
RED-WINGED BLACKBIRD
see p.435
lacks buff-colored hindneck
red shoulder patches
larger overall
LARK BUNTING
see p.449
lacks buff-colored hindneck
larger
white wing patches

OCCURRENCE
Breeds in open fields with a mixture of tall grasses and other herbaceous vegetation, especially old hayfields. In Canada from British Columbia to the East Coast; in the US from Idaho to New England. Migrates through the southern US and the Caribbean; winters in northern South America.

Length **6–8in (15–20cm)**	Wingspan **10–12in (25–30cm)**	Weight **1¹⁄₁₆–2oz (30–55g)**
Social **Winter flocks**	Lifespan **Up to 10 years**	Status **Declining**

Family **Emberizidae**

AMERICAN SPARROWS

THE EMBERIZIDS ARE A DIVERSE group, with an almost worldwide distribution; only Australasia and Antarctica are without them. In Europe, emberizids are called buntings. North American emberizids tend to be duller than their Eurasian relatives, with most in shades of brown. Early settlers in North America thought they resembled European sparrows, so most North American emberizids are named as sparrows, despite having no close relationship with European sparrows, which are really weavers. Species of emberizids not called sparrows are the longspurs and the Snow Bunting, which are shared with Eurasia. All members of the family Emberizidae tend to forage on or near the ground. Their stout, conical bills are used for eating seeds. Most species of American sparrows show little difference between the sexes. While identifying sparrows can be daunting, clues such as habitat, behavior, voice, and body shape make the task easier.

TYPICAL SPARROW
A White-crowned Sparrow shows the typical stout emberizid beak.

BEST VIEW
Singing males, like this Chestnut-collared Longspur, are easily seen in summer.

Family **Thraupidae**

TANAGERS

THE TANAGERS COMPRISE a large and diverse family of songbirds found only in the Western Hemisphere. Some are dull and feed on insects from the forest floor, others are rainbow-colored, fruit-eating, and dart through the high canopy. North American species of tanagers of the genus *Piranga*, have brightly colored males and dull, olive-colored females. They are relatively sluggish birds that feed mostly on insects such as bees, wasps, and fruit. While their songs are very similar, each species has a distinctive call.

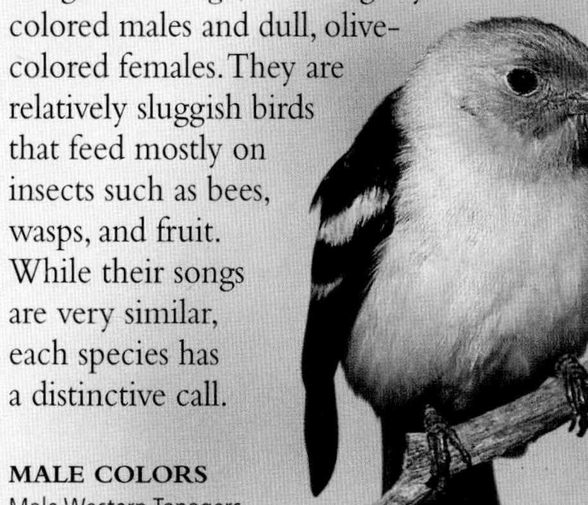

MALE COLORS
Male Western Tanagers are some of North America's most colorful birds.

Family **Cardinalidae**

CARDINALS

VISUALLY STUNNING AND VOCALLY conspicuous, male cardinalids are among best known birds in North America. The smaller members of the family are called buntings, but they are unrelated to the Eurasian buntings, members of the family Emberizidae. Cardinalidae range in color from the red of the Northern Cardinal to the electric-blue Indigo Bunting and the multicolored Painted Bunting, a vagrant in Canada.

STRONG BILLS
Male Northern Cardinals have impressive bills, perfect for cutting open seed hulls.

Order **Passeriformes**	Family **Emberizidae**	Species ***Calcarius mccownii***

McCown's Longspur

MALE (BREEDING)

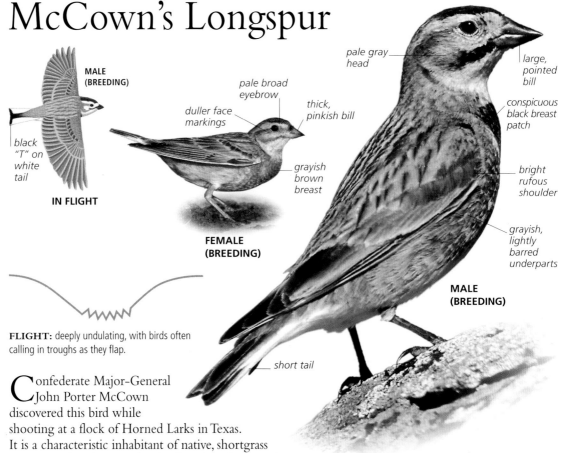

black "T" on white tail

IN FLIGHT

pale broad eyebrow

duller face markings

thick, pinkish bill

grayish brown breast

FEMALE (BREEDING)

pale gray head

large, pointed bill

conspicuous black breast patch

bright rufous shoulder

grayish, lightly barred underparts

MALE (BREEDING)

short tail

FLIGHT: deeply undulating, with birds often calling in troughs as they flap.

Confederate Major-General John Porter McCown discovered this bird while shooting at a flock of Horned Larks in Texas. It is a characteristic inhabitant of native, shortgrass prairies, and males can often be found performing their spectacular flight displays over this barren, windswept habitat. Flying high, these birds sing as they hover and float downward on wings held in a V position, similar to that of a Monarch butterfly. With their black chest patches and gray underparts, males look surprisingly dark against the pale sky. A dull female could be potentially confused with a female House Sparrow, but the former can be distinguished by the white patches on its tail. Recent genetic (DNA) evidence suggests that McCown's Longspur may actually be more closely related to the Snow Bunting than to the other species of longspurs.

IN THE OPEN
This species favors open habitats such as heavily grazed fields and other areas with very short grass.

VOICE Flight call a short, liquid *rit-up*; also an abrupt *poink* and metallic *tink*; song melodious; high-pitched tinklings in flight.

NESTING Cup of dried grass placed in depression on the ground, often against a clump of grass; 3–4 eggs; 1–2 broods; April–July.

FEEDING Eats insects while breeding; seeds in winter.

SIMILAR SPECIES
CHESTNUT-COLLARED LONGSPUR ♀ ❄
see p.447
dark cheek patch
longer tail

OCCURRENCE
Breeds in the shortgrass prairie of the the High Plains, from Alberta and Saskatchewan, southward to northwest Nebraska and northeast Colorado. Winters in grasslands and barren ground from southeast Colorado southward into Texas and westward into southeast Arizona.

Length **6in (15cm)**	Wingspan **10–11in (25–28cm)**	Weight **7/8–1 1/16oz (25–30g)**
Social **Large flocks**	Lifespan **Unknown**	Status **Declining**

Order **Passeriformes**	Family **Emberizidae**	Species ***Calcarius lapponicus***

Lapland Longspur

thin, white edge to tail
MALE (BREEDING)
black face
IN FLIGHT

streaked crown
black streak on throat
FEMALE (BREEDING)

rich buffy hood
thick streaking on flanks
ADULT (NONBREEDING)

white eye-line
thick, yellowish bill
bright rufous nape
rusty wing panel
black flanks
white underparts
MALE (BREEDING)

FLIGHT: deeply undulating, with birds often calling in troughs as they flap.

One of the most numerous breeding birds of the Arctic tundra, the Lapland Longspur is found in huge flocks over open habitats of the US in the winter. They can be seen on gravel roads and in barren countryside immediately following heavy snowfalls. Genetic (DNA) evidence suggests that the four longspur species and the two *Plectrophenax* buntings do not belong to the Emberizidae family, but rather form a distinct group of their own. This species is known as the Lapland Bunting in Great Britain and Ireland.

VOICE Flight call a dry rattle, *tyew*, unlike other longspurs; song a series of thin tinklings and whistles, often in flight.

NESTING Cup of grass and sedges placed in depression on ground next to a clump of vegetation; 4–6 eggs; 1 brood; May–July.

FEEDING Eats insects during breeding season; seeds in winter.

CONSPICUOUS SPECIES
This longspur is one of the most conspicuous breeding birds on the Arctic tundra.

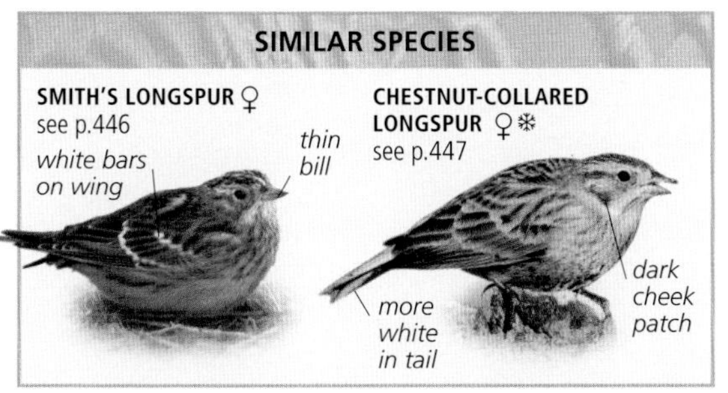
SIMILAR SPECIES
SMITH'S LONGSPUR ♀
see p.446
white bars on wing
thin bill
CHESTNUT-COLLARED LONGSPUR ♀❄
see p.447
dark cheek patch
more white in tail

OCCURRENCE
Breeds in tundra right across Arctic North America and Eurasia. Winters in open grasslands and barren fields, and on beaches across the northern and central US and parts of southern Canada.

Length **6½in (16cm)**	Wingspan **10½–11½in (27–29cm)**	Weight **⅞–1¹⁄₁₆oz (25–30g)**
Social **Large flocks**	Lifespan **Up to 5 years**	Status **Secure**

Order **Passeriformes**	Family **Emberizidae**	Species ***Calcarius pictus***

Smith's Longspur

MALE
(BREEDING)
white cheek patch
white outer tail feathers
relatively long wings
IN FLIGHT
rich, buffy overall
fine breast streaks
wings extend past tail
FEMALE (FALL)
black-and-white "helmet"
thin bill
orange collar
white shoulder
rich pumpkin colored underparts
MALE
(BREEDING)
white undertail feathers

With its pumpkin colored breast and black-and-white "helmet," Smith's Longspur in its breeding colors contrasts strongly with its drab winter plumage. On both its remote breeding grounds in the Arctic, and its restricted shortgrass range in winter, this bird hides on the ground at all times, making it very hard to spot. Smith's Longspur migrates through the Great Plains to reach its wintering grounds, but on the return journey it swings east, giving it an elliptical migration path. This species breeds communally: males mate with several females who, in turn, mate with other males.

VOICE Flight call a mechanical, dry, sharp rattle; also a nasal *nief* when squabbling; song a series of thin, sweet whistles.

NESTING Concealed cup of sedges, lined with feathers, placed in hummock on ground; 3–5 eggs; 1 brood; June–July.

FEEDING Eats mainly seeds and insects; migrants may rely heavily upon introduced foxtail grass.

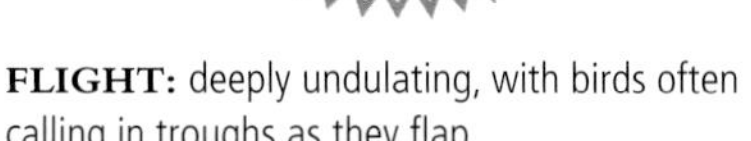

FLIGHT: deeply undulating, with birds often calling in troughs as they flap.

LINEBACK LONGSPUR
On his breeding or spring staging grounds, the male sports a striking black-and-white "helmet."

SIMILAR SPECIES

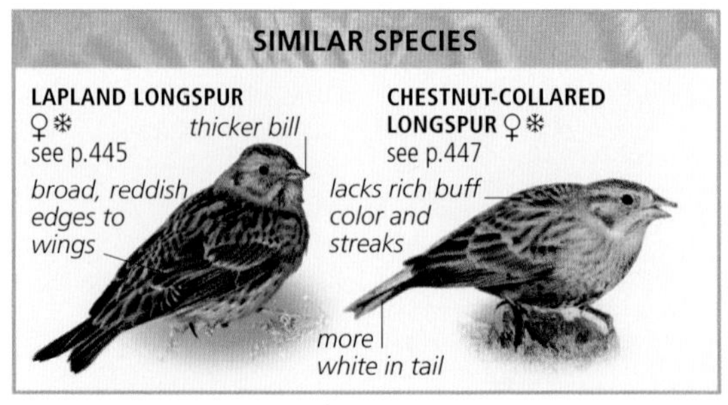
LAPLAND LONGSPUR
♀ ❄
see p.445
thicker bill
broad, reddish edges to wings
CHESTNUT-COLLARED LONGSPUR ♀ ❄
see p.447
lacks rich buff color and streaks
more white in tail

OCCURRENCE
Breeds along the tundra-taiga timberline from northern Alaska southeast to northern Ontario; also mountainous southeastern Alaska and southwestern Yukon. Migrant birds are found in shortgrass prairie. Winters in various open areas with shortgrass in Kansas, Texas, and Arkansas.

Length **6–6½in (15–16cm)**	Wingspan **10–11½in (25–29cm)**	Weight **⅞–1¹⁄₁₆oz (25–30g)**
Social **Large flocks**	Lifespan **Up to 5 years**	Status **Secure**

Order **Passeriformes**	Family **Emberizidae**	Species ***Calcarius ornatus***

Chestnut-collared Longspur

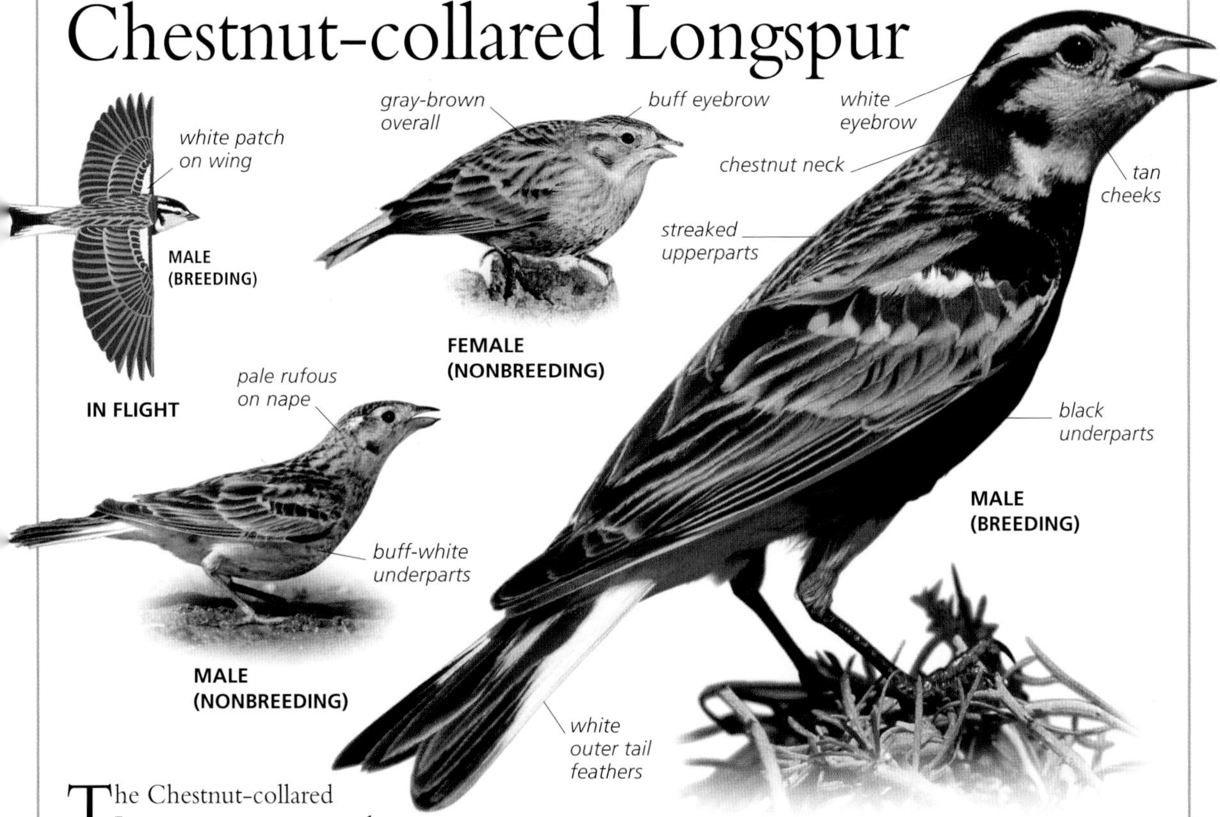

white patch on wing
MALE (BREEDING)
IN FLIGHT

gray-brown overall
buff eyebrow
FEMALE (NONBREEDING)

pale rufous on nape
buff-white underparts
MALE (NONBREEDING)

white eyebrow
chestnut neck
tan cheeks
streaked upperparts
black underparts
white outer tail feathers
MALE (BREEDING)

The Chestnut-collared Longspur was once much more widespread and numerous than today. This is because it traditionally bred in areas of the western prairies that had been recently disturbed by huge, roaming herds of bison, or by wild fires. After the elimination of the bison, however, and the "taming" of the plains, such areas were hard to find, and so the bird declined. One of the Chestnut-collared Longspur's distinguishing features is the triangular black patch on its tail. The breeding male's black belly is also unique among the North American longspurs.

VOICE Flight call a chortling *KTI-uhl-uh*, often in series; also a soft rattle and short buzz; song a sweet, rich, whistled series, in fluttering, circular flights over the prairies.

NESTING Grassy cup on ground, in grass clump or next to rock; 3–5 eggs; 1–2 broods; May–August.

FEEDING Eats seeds year-round; also feeds on insects when breeding.

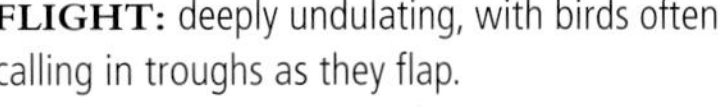

FLIGHT: deeply undulating, with birds often calling in troughs as they flap.

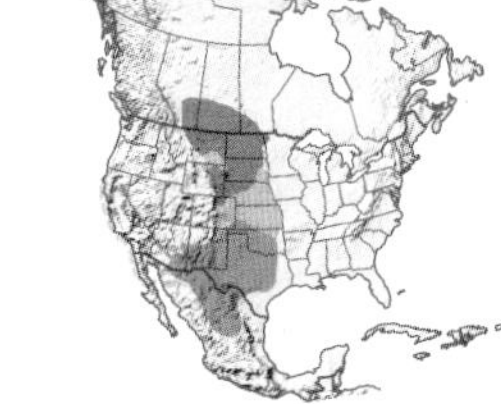

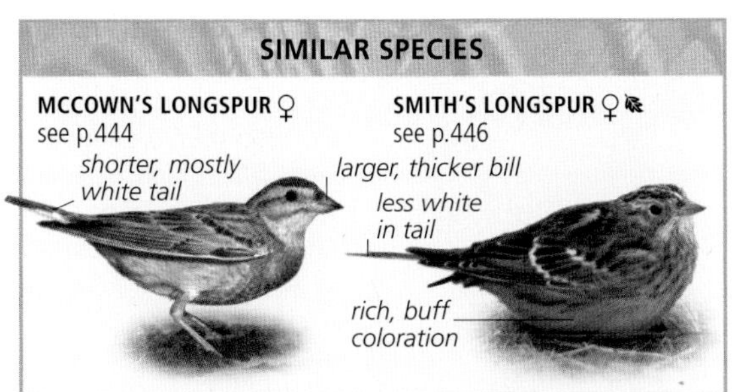
SIMILAR SPECIES
MCCOWN'S LONGSPUR ♀
see p.444
shorter, mostly white tail
SMITH'S LONGSPUR ♀
see p.446
larger, thicker bill
less white in tail
rich, buff coloration

NOW AND THEN
The male bird usually sings from the air, but occasionally from a prominent perch.

OCCURRENCE
Breeds in shortgrass prairie from Alberta east to Minnesota, south to northeastern Colorado and northwestern Nebraska; on migration, grasslands and cultivated fields. Winters in grasslands and other barren areas in the southern Great Plains west to southeastern Arizona and south to Mexico.

Length **5½–6in (14–15cm)**	Wingspan **10–10½in (25–27cm)**	Weight **⅜–¹¹⁄₁₆oz (11–20g)**
Social **Large flocks**	Lifespan **Up to 4 years**	Status **Declining**

Order **Passeriformes**	Family **Emberizidae**	Species ***Plectrophenax nivalis***

Snow Bunting

less white in wings
white outer tail feathers
MALE (NONBREEDING)
yellow bill
IN FLIGHT
large white patches on black wings
FEMALE (NONBREEDING)
white head and underparts
black back
black bill
MALE (BREEDING)
pale rufous crown
white underparts
dark brown eyes
FEMALE (BREEDING)
rusty orange cheek patch
black peeks through buffy feather edgings
rusty orange breast patch
white underparts
MALE (NONBREEDING)
gray body
white eye-ring
JUVENILE

The bold white wing patches of the Snow Bunting make it immediately recognizable in a whirling winter flock of dark-winged longspurs and larks. In winter, heavy snowfall forces flocks onto roadsides, where they can be seen more easily. To secure and defend the best territories, some of the males of this remarkably hardy species arrive as early as April in their barren high-Arctic breeding grounds. The Snow Bunting is very similar in appearance to the rare and localized McKay's Bunting. Although McKay's Bunting generally has less black on the back, in the wings, and on the tail, the two species cannot always be conclusively identified. This is especially true since Snow and McKay's Buntings sometimes interbreed, producing hybrids.

VOICE Flight a call musical, liquid rattle, also *tyew* notes and short buzz; song a pleasant series of squeaky and whistled notes.

NESTING Bulky cup of grass and moss, lined with feathers, and placed in sheltered rock crevice; 3–6 eggs; 1 brood; June–August.

FEEDING Eats seeds (sedge in Arctic), flies and other insects, and buds on migration.

FLIGHT: deeply undulating; flocks "roll" along as birds at back overtake those in front.

ROCKY GROUND
About the only perches in the Snow Bunting's barren breeding grounds are large boulders.

SIMILAR SPECIES

McKAY'S BUNTING
see p.497
mostly white tail, back, and wings

OCCURRENCE
Breeds in rocky areas, usually near sparsely vegetated tundra, right across the Arctic. North American birds winters in open country and on shores across the whole of southern Canada and the northern US, and in southern and western coastal areas of Alaska.

Length **6½–7in (16–18cm)**	Wingspan **12½–14in (32–35cm)**	Weight **1¼–2oz (35–55g)**
Social **Large flocks**	Lifespan **Unknown**	Status **Secure**

Order **Passeriformes**	Family **Emberizidae**	Species ***Calamospiza melanocorys***

Lark Bunting

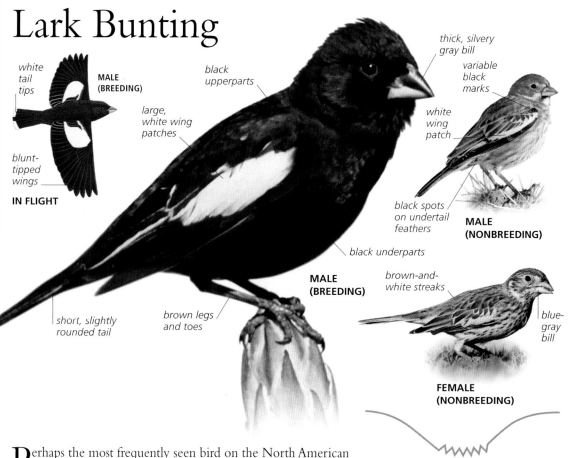

white tail tips
MALE (BREEDING)
blunt-tipped wings
IN FLIGHT

black upperparts
large, white wing patches
thick, silvery gray bill
black underparts
short, slightly rounded tail
brown legs and toes
MALE (BREEDING)

variable black marks
white wing patch
black spots on undertail feathers
MALE (NONBREEDING)

brown-and-white streaks
blue-gray bill
FEMALE (NONBREEDING)

FLIGHT: low and undulating, short glides alternating with stiff wing beats.

Perhaps the most frequently seen bird on the North American High Plains, the stocky Lark Bunting—unlike the Chestnut-collared Longspur, which lives alongside it—has been able to cope with the changes wrought on its habitat by humans, and occurs in extraordinary density throughout its range. Nomadic flocks of thousands scour the high deserts, open grasslands, and sage bush for seeds. Breeding-plumaged males are unmistakable: black with large white wing patches. Females and immature birds are duller, with more subdued wing patches.

VOICE Call a low, soft, whistled *hwoik*; song a partly melodious, partly "scratchy," with repetitions of phrases, then whistles.

NESTING Open cup of grass, lined with fine plant material, in depression in ground; 4–5 eggs; 1 brood; May–August.

FEEDING Mainly seeds in winter, insects in summer.

CAUGHT BY ANY MEANS
The Lark Bunting hawks, gleans, and forages insect prey throughout the breeding season.

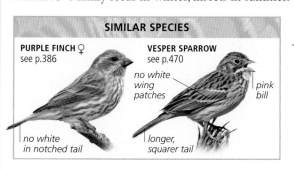

SIMILAR SPECIES

PURPLE FINCH ♀
see p.386
no white in notched tail

VESPER SPARROW
see p.470
no white wing patches
pink bill
longer, squarer tail

OCCURRENCE
Breeds in grasslands and sage flats on High Plains from Alberta south to the Texas panhandle. Winters in similar habitats—and also in desert, cultivated plains, and open shrub–steppe—across interior southwestern US and northern Mexico. Migrants use similar open-country habitats.

Length **7in (18cm)**	Wingspan **10½–11in (27–28cm)**	Weight **1¹⁄₁₆–1³⁄₄oz (30–50g)**
Social **Large flocks**	Lifespan **Unknown**	Status **Secure**

Order **Passeriformes**	Family **Emberizidae**	Species ***Passerella iliaca***

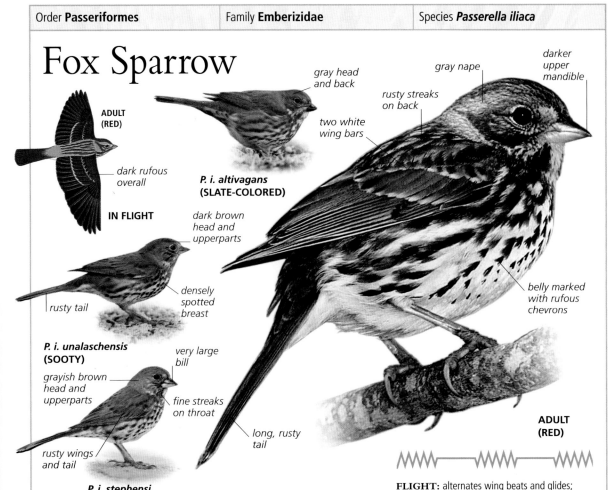

Fox Sparrow

ADULT (RED)

dark rufous overall

IN FLIGHT

gray head and back

***P. i. altivagans* (SLATE-COLORED)**

dark brown head and upperparts

rusty tail

densely spotted breast

***P. i. unalaschensis* (SOOTY)**

very large bill

grayish brown head and upperparts

fine streaks on throat

rusty wings and tail

***P. i. stephensi* (THICK-BILLED)**

gray nape

darker upper mandible

rusty streaks on back

two white wing bars

belly marked with rufous chevrons

long, rusty tail

ADULT (RED)

FLIGHT: alternates wing beats and glides; straight and fluttery, from cover to cover.

Larger, more robust, and more colorful than its close relatives, the Fox Sparrow is a beautiful species. When it appears in backyards, its presence can be detected by its foraging habits; it crouches low in leaf littter, and hops to disturb leaves, under which it finds seeds or insects. It varies considerably over its huge range, from thick-billed birds in the Sierras to dark ones in the Northwest, and distinctive reds in the East.

VOICE Call is sharp, dry *tshak* or *tshuk;* flight call a high-pitched *tzeep!;* song is complex and musical with trills and whistles.

NESTING Dense cup of grasses or moss lined with fine material; usually placed low in shrub; 2–5 eggs; 1 brood; April–July.

FEEDING Forages for insects, seeds, and fruit.

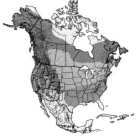

FOXY RED

The Fox Sparrow gets its name from the rusty coloration of the eastern "Red" birds.

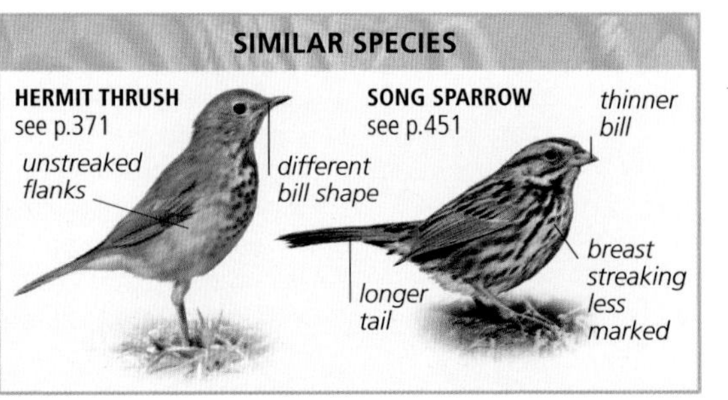
SIMILAR SPECIES
HERMIT THRUSH
see p.371
unstreaked flanks
different bill shape
SONG SPARROW
see p.451
thinner bill
breast streaking less marked
longer tail

OCCURRENCE

Encompasses the entire boreal forest zone, from Alaska in the West to Quebec, Labrador, and Newfoundland in the East. In the West, it occurs in coastal and near-coast thickets within coniferous or mixed woodlands. Winters in the Pacific West, south to Baja California; also from Texas to Massachusetts.

Length **6–7½in (15–19cm)**	Wingspan **10½–11½in (27–29cm)**	Weight **⅞–1⁹⁄₁₆oz (25–45g)**
Social **Solitary/Small flocks**	Lifespan **Up to 9 years**	Status **Secure**

Order **Passeriformes**	Family **Emberizidae**	Species ***Melospiza melodia***

Song Sparrow

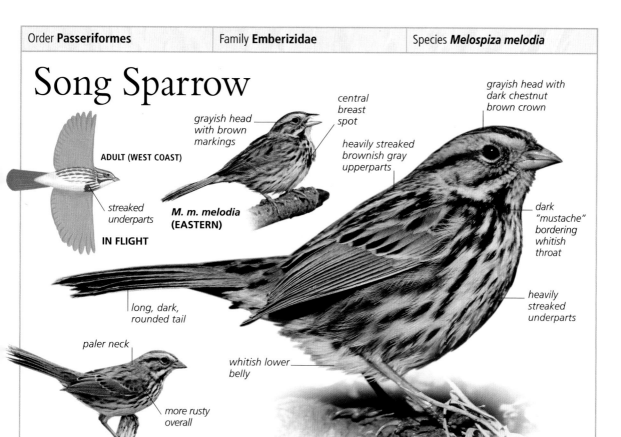

ADULT (WEST COAST)
streaked underparts
IN FLIGHT

grayish head with brown markings
central breast spot
M. m. melodia (EASTERN)

grayish head with dark chestnut brown crown
heavily streaked brownish gray upperparts
dark "mustache" bordering whitish throat
long, dark, rounded tail
heavily streaked underparts
whitish lower belly
ADULT (WEST COAST)

paler neck
more rusty overall
M. m. saltonis (SOUTHWEST)

The familiar song of this species can be heard in backyards across the continent, including in winter, although it varies both individually and geographically. In the southeastern US, where it does not breed, migrant birds start singing in early spring before departing for northern areas. The Song Sparrow may be the North American champion of geographical variation—about 30 subspecies have been described. These vary from the large, dark birds of the Aleutian Islands (*M. m. maxima*) to the smaller, paler birds of southern Arizona (*M. m. saltonis*). Eastern birds, such as *M. m. melodia*, fall between the two in size.

VOICE A dry *tchip* call; flight call a clear *siiiti*; song a jumble of variable whistles and trills, *deeep deeep deep-deep chrrrr tiiiiiiiiiiii tyeeur* most common.

NESTING Bulky cup on or near ground, in brush or marsh vegetation; 3–5 eggs; 1–3 broods; March–August.

FEEDING In summer, feeds mainly on insects; in winter, eats mainly seeds, but also fruit.

FLIGHT: low and direct, staying within cover whenever possible.

OCCURRENCE
Widespread in a range of habitats (although not in dense forests) across Canada and the US, from the Atlantic to the Pacific Coasts and north to Alaska. Some populations move south of their breeding range in winter.

BREAST SPOT
The Song Sparrow often sings from exposed perches, showing off its characteristic breast spot.

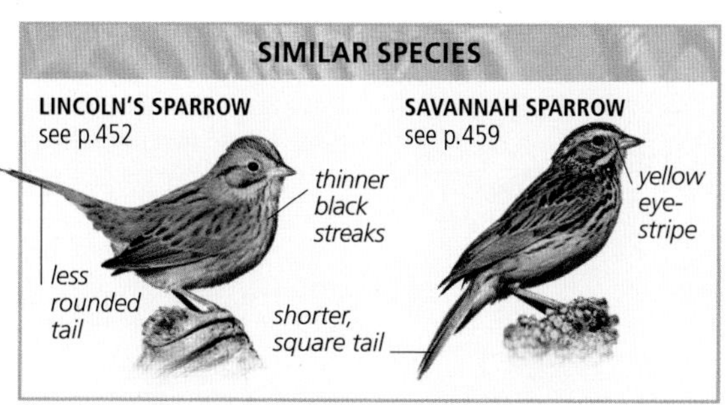
SIMILAR SPECIES
LINCOLN'S SPARROW
see p.452
thinner black streaks
less rounded tail
SAVANNAH SPARROW
see p.459
yellow eye-stripe
shorter, square tail

Length **5–7½in (13–19cm)**	Wingspan **8½–12in (21–31cm)**	Weight **7/16–1¾oz (13–50g)**
Social **Solitary/Flocks**	Lifespan **Up to 9 years**	Status **Secure**

Order **Passeriformes**	Family **Emberizidae**	Species ***Melospiza lincolnii***

Lincoln's Sparrow

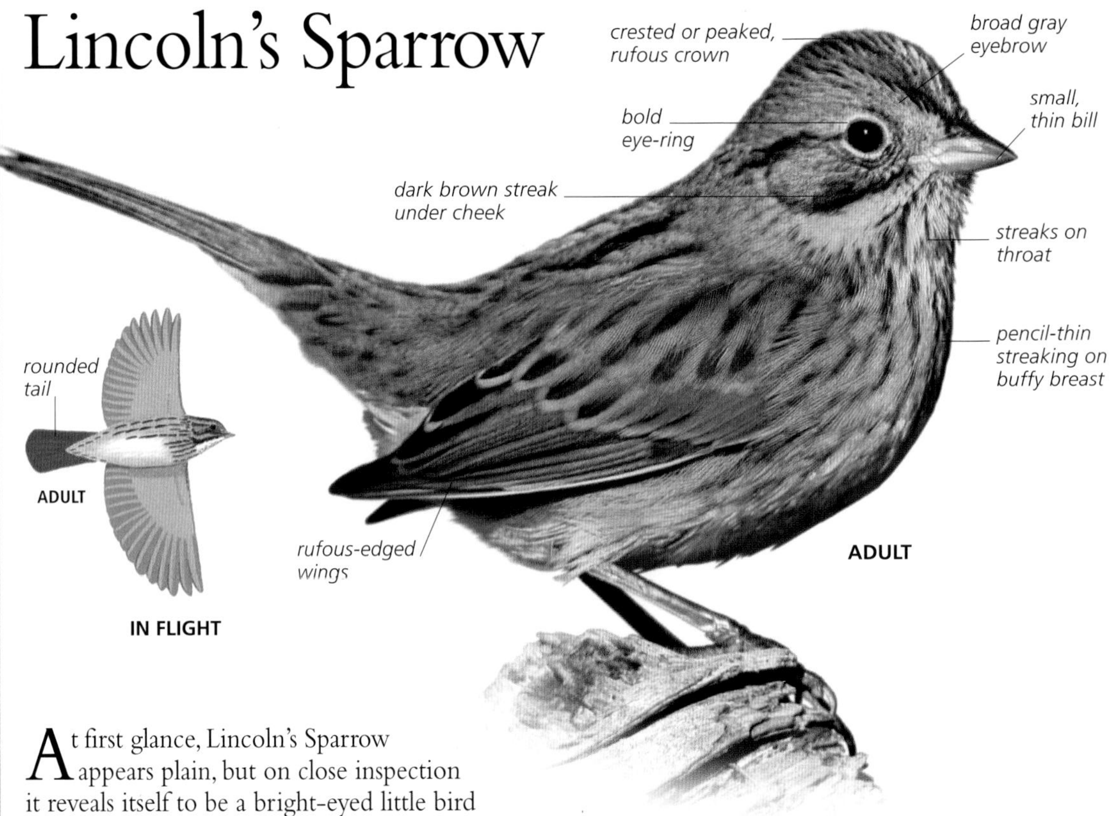
crested or peaked, rufous crown
broad gray eyebrow
small, thin bill
bold eye-ring
dark brown streak under cheek
streaks on throat
pencil-thin streaking on buffy breast
rounded tail
ADULT
rufous-edged wings
ADULT
IN FLIGHT

At first glance, Lincoln's Sparrow appears plain, but on close inspection it reveals itself to be a bright-eyed little bird with subtly varying, but crisply outlined, markings. In the breeding season, it seeks out predominantly moist willow scrub at the tundra–taiga timberline; outside the breeding season, Lincoln's Sparrow can be found in scrubby habitats right across North America. It will occasionally visit backyard feeders in winter, but it is generally a secretive bird that stays within fairly dense cover wherever it can. However, Lincoln's Sparrow's rich, musical song is unmistakable, and it varies remarkably little from region to region.

VOICE Call a variable, loud *tchip*, flight call a rolling *ziiiit*; song series of rich, musical trills, *ju-ju-ju dododo didididi whrrrrr.*

NESTING Grass cup, lined with fine grass, and hidden in depression in ground under overhanging sedges or grasses; 3–5 eggs;1 brood; June–August.

FEEDING Mainly seeds in winter; in summer, mostly insects, such as beetles, mosquitoes, and moths.

FLIGHT: low and direct, staying within cover whenever possible.

RAISE THE ALARM
When disturbed, Lincoln's Sparrow often raises its central crown feathers, which form a crest.

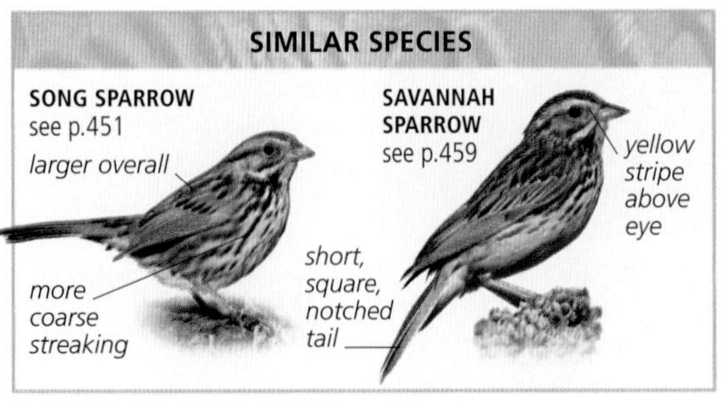
SIMILAR SPECIES
SONG SPARROW
see p.451
larger overall
more coarse streaking
SAVANNAH SPARROW
see p.459
yellow stripe above eye
short, square, notched tail

OCCURRENCE
Breeds in muskeg and wet thickets across northern North America, also south into the western ranges of California and Arizona. Migrants and wintering birds use a variety of scrubby habitats. Winters in southern US (and farther south), and on Pacific Coast north to British Columbia.

Length **5¼–6in (13.5–15cm)**	Wingspan **7½–8½in (19–22cm)**	Weight **½–⅞oz (15–25g)**
Social **Solitary/Small flocks**	Lifespan **Up to 7 years**	Status **Secure**

Order **Passeriformes**	Family **Emberizidae**	Species ***Melospiza georgiana***

Swamp Sparrow

rufous flanks

ADULT (BREEDING)

IN FLIGHT

dark, rounded tail

unstreaked gray nape

tawny flanks

ADULT (NON-BREEDING)

rufous crown

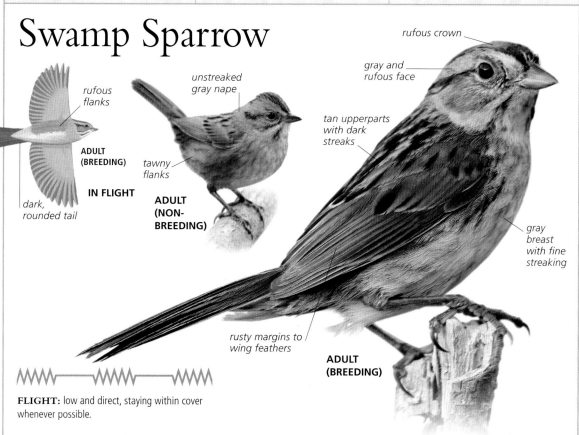

gray and rufous face

tan upperparts with dark streaks

gray breast with fine streaking

rusty margins to wing feathers

ADULT (BREEDING)

FLIGHT: low and direct, staying within cover whenever possible.

The Swamp Sparrow is a common breeder in wet habitats across eastern North America and Canada west to the Yukon and British Columbia. It is especially abundant in its preferred habitat of tall reed marshes. A somewhat skittish bird, the Swamp Sparrow is often seen darting rapidly into cover, but usually repays the patient observer with a reappearance, giving its characteristic *chimp* call. Though often confused with both the Song Sparrow and Lincoln's Sparrow, the Swamp Sparrow never shows more than a very faint, blurry streaking on its gray breast, and sports conspicuous rusty-edged wing feathers.

VOICE Call a slightly nasal, forceful *chimp*, flight call a high, buzzy *ziiiiii*; song a slow, monotonous, loose trill of chirps.

NESTING Bulky cup of dry plants placed 1–4ft (30–120cm) above water in marsh vegetation; 3–5 eggs; 1–2 broods; May–July.

FEEDING Mostly insects in the breeding season, especially grasshoppers; seeds in winter; occasionally fruit.

WATCH TOWER
This male Swamp Sparrow is perusing his territory from atop a seeding cattail flower.

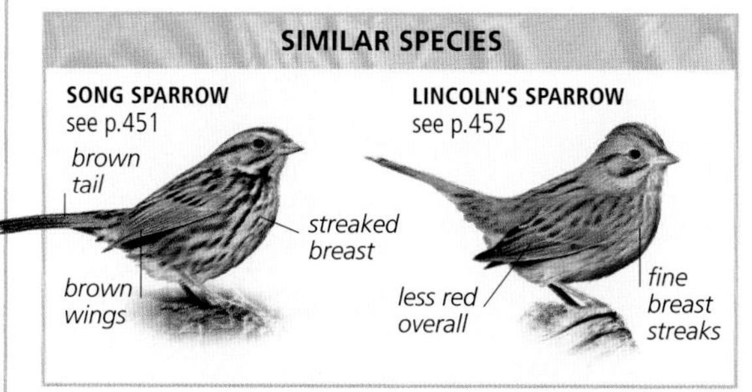
SIMILAR SPECIES
SONG SPARROW
see p.451
brown tail
streaked breast
brown wings
LINCOLN'S SPARROW
see p.452
less red overall
fine breast streaks

OCCURRENCE
Breeds in marshes, cedar bogs, damp meadows, and wet hayfields, from Yukon east to Newfoundland and south to Nebraska and the Delmarva Peninsula; winters in marshes in eastern US and south through Mexico; rare but regular on Pacific coast.

Length **5–6in (12.5–15cm)**	Wingspan **7–7½in (18–19cm)**	Weight **½–⅞oz (15–25g)**
Social **Solitary/Small flocks**	Lifespan **Up to 6 years**	Status **Secure**

Order **Passeriformes**	Family **Emberizidae**	Species ***Zonotrichia querula***

Harris's Sparrow

ADULT (NONBREEDING)
indistinct facial markings
IN FLIGHT
two wing bars
pinkish bill
ADULT (NONBREEDING)
black crown
pinkish or yellow bill
gray cheeks
black cheek patch
black chin and throat
gray rump and undertail feathers
tan cheek
white chin
concentration of streaks on chest
JUVENILE
ADULT (BREEDING)

An unmistakable black-faced, pink-billed bird, Harris's Sparrow is the only breeding bird endemic to Canada. It can be seen in the US during migration or in winter on the Great Plains. This species is occasionally found in large flocks of White-throated and White-crowned Sparrows. Harris's Sparrow is the largest sparrow in the US, approaching the Northern Cardinal in size. Its scientific name, *querula*, comes from the plaintive quality of its whistled song. The First Harris's Sparrow nest was found in 1907 in the Northwest Territories.

VOICE Call a sharp *weeek*; song a melancholy series of 2–4 whistles on the same pitch.

NESTING Bulky cup placed on ground among vegetation or near ground in brush; 3–5 eggs; 1 brood; June–August.

FEEDING Eats seeds, insects, buds, and even young conifer needles in summer.

FLIGHT: low and direct, staying within cover whenever possible.

NORTHERN ACROBAT
This nonbreeding Harris's Sparrow grips two different weeds, one in each foot.

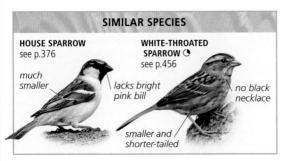

SIMILAR SPECIES

HOUSE SPARROW see p.376
much smaller
lacks bright pink bill

WHITE-THROATED SPARROW see p.456
no black necklace
smaller and shorter-tailed

OCCURRENCE
Breeds in scrub-tundra along Canadian taiga–tundra timberline from northern Northwest Territories to north Ontario. Winters in US Great Plains from South Dakota and Iowa south to northern Texas. Nonbreeders found in thickets, hedges. Casual to rare in East and West.

Length **6 3/4–7 1/2in (17–19cm)**	Wingspan **10 1/2–11in (27–28cm)**	Weight **1 1/16–1 7/16oz (30–40g)**
Social **Flocks**	Lifespan **Up to 12 years**	Status **Secure**

Order **Passeriformes**	Family **Emberizidae**	Species ***Zonotrichia leucophrys***

White-crowned Sparrow

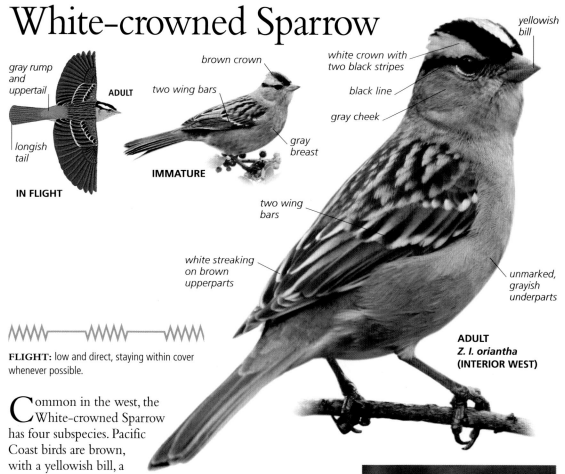

gray rump and uppertail
longish tail
ADULT
IN FLIGHT

brown crown
two wing bars
gray breast
IMMATURE

yellowish bill
white crown with two black stripes
black line
gray cheek
two wing bars
white streaking on brown upperparts
unmarked, grayish underparts

ADULT
Z. l. oriantha
(INTERIOR WEST)

FLIGHT: low and direct, staying within cover whenever possible.

Common in the west, the White-crowned Sparrow has four subspecies. Pacific Coast birds are brown, with a yellowish bill, a gray patch between the eye and bill, and a gray-washed head stripe; western and northwestern birds are gray below, with a gray patch between the eye and bill, an orange bill, and a white head stripe. Eastern and Rocky Mountain birds have a pink bill, a black patch between the eye and bill, and a bright white head stripe; while birds in southwest Canada are darker.

VOICE Call a sharp *tink*; flight call a thin *seep*; song a buzzy whistle followed by buzzes, trills, and whistles.

NESTING Bulky cup of grass placed on or near the ground in bushes; 4–6 eggs; 1–3 broods; March–August.

FEEDING Forages for seeds, insects, fruit, buds, and even grass.

LOOKING RESTED
Perched on a shrub, this sparrow's white eyestreak is highly visible.

SIMILAR SPECIES

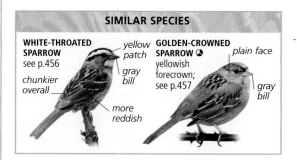

WHITE-THROATED SPARROW see p.456
yellow patch
gray bill
chunkier overall
more reddish

GOLDEN-CROWNED SPARROW ◔
yellowish forecrown; see p.457
plain face
gray bill

OCCURRENCE
Widespread across the boreal forest and tundra limit, from Alaska eastward to Quebec and Labrador, and southward from British Columbia to coastal California and the interior mountainous west. In the North, breeds in willow thickets, wet forest; in the west, varied habitats include suburbs.

Length **6½–7in (16–18cm)**	Wingspan **9½–10in (24–26cm)**	Weight **1¹⁄₁₆–1¼oz (20–35g)**
Social **Flocks**	Lifespan **Up to 13 years**	Status **Secure**

Order **Passeriformes**	Family **Emberizidae**	Species ***Zonotrichia albicollis***

White-throated Sparrow

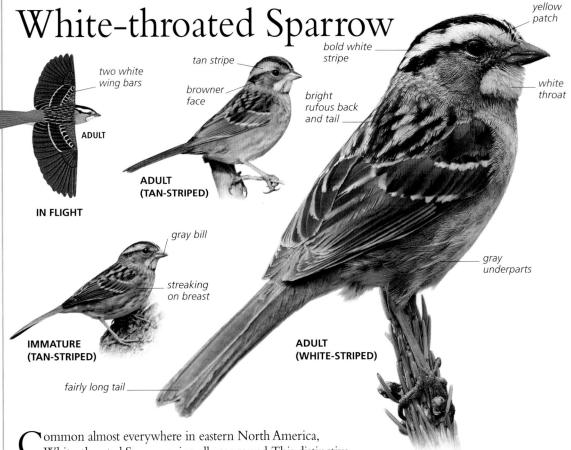

two white wing bars

ADULT

IN FLIGHT

tan stripe

browner face

ADULT (TAN-STRIPED)

bold white stripe

yellow patch

white throat

bright rufous back and tail

gray bill

streaking on breast

IMMATURE (TAN-STRIPED)

gray underparts

ADULT (WHITE-STRIPED)

fairly long tail

Common almost everywhere in eastern North America, White-throated Sparrows sing all year round. This distinctive, whistled, rhythmic song can be remembered with the popular mnemonics *Oh sweet Canada Canada Canada*, or the less accurate *Old Sam Peabody*. This species has two different color forms, one with a white stripe above its eye, and one with a tan stripe. In the nonbreeding season, large flocks roam the leaf litter of woodlands in search of food. Often the only indication of their presence is the occasional moving leaf or thin, lisping flight call.

VOICE Call loud, sharp *jink*; flight call lisping *tssssst!*; song clear whistle comprising 1–2 higher notes, then three triplets.

NESTING Cup placed on or near ground in dense shrubbery; 2–6 eggs; 1 brood; May–August.

FEEDING Mainly forages on the ground for seeds, fruit, insects, buds, and various grasses.

FLIGHT: low and direct, staying within cover whenever possible.

DIFFERENT COLOR FORMS
The presence of white or tan stripes on White-throated Sparrows is not related to their sex.

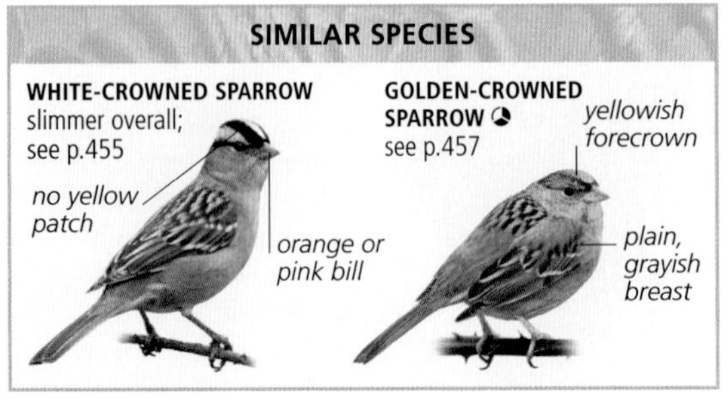
SIMILAR SPECIES
WHITE-CROWNED SPARROW
slimmer overall;
see p.455
no yellow patch
orange or pink bill
GOLDEN-CROWNED SPARROW
see p.457
yellowish forecrown
plain, grayish breast

OCCURRENCE
Breeds in forests from eastern Yukon to Newfoundland, south into Great Lakes and northern Appalachians. Nonbreeders prefer wooded thickets and hedges. Winters across the eastern US and extreme south of the Southwest. Rare but regular along the Pacific Coast.

Length **6½–7½in (16–17.5cm)**	Wingspan **9–10in (23–26cm)**	Weight **11/16–1¼oz (20–35g)**
Social **Flocks**	Lifespan **Up to 10 years**	Status **Secure**

Order **Passeriformes**	Family **Emberizidae**	Species ***Zonotrichia atricapilla***

Golden-crowned Sparrow

white wing bars

ADULT (BREEDING)

IN FLIGHT

streaks on head

dull yellow crown

IMMATURE

duller yellow on crown

much less black on face

ADULT (NONBREEDING)

bright yellow crown

thick black eyebrow

long tail

light grayish brown underparts

ADULT (BREEDING)

The Golden-crowned Sparrow is in many respects the western counterpart of the White-throated Sparrow. It sings in a minor key and, as a result, has a reputation for sounding melancholy. Many late 19th-century Klondike gold prospectors called this bird "Weary Willie"—to them, its song sounded remarkably like *I'm so tired* or *No gold here*. It has been regarded as a pest in the past because of its habit of consuming crops in agricultural fields and gardens. Nonbreeding adults retain their distinctive golden crown in the winter, but it appears duller.

VOICE Call loud *tsik*; flight call soft, short *seeep*; song variable series of melancholy whistles, sometimes slurred or trilled.

NESTING Concealed bulky cup placed on ground at base of bush; 3–5 eggs; 1–2 broods; June–August.

FEEDING Predominantly forages on the ground for seeds, insects, fruit, flowers, and buds.

FLIGHT: low and direct, staying within cover whenever possible.

GROUND FORAGER
This sparrow can be found by listening for the noise it makes as it roots around in the leaf litter.

SIMILAR SPECIES
WHITE-CROWNED SPARROW
see p.455
white eyebrow
orange bill
WHITE-THROATED SPARROW (TAN-STRIPED)
see p.456
lacks yellowish fore-crown
white throat

OCCURRENCE
Breeds in shrubby habitat along the tree line and open, boggy forests from Alaska east to southwest Northwest Territories, south to British Columbia and southwest Alberta. Winters in dense thickets from south coastal British Columbia to north Baja California.

Length **7in (18cm)**	Wingspan **9–10in (23–25cm)**	Weight **11/16–1¼oz (20–35g)**
Social **Flocks**	Lifespan **Up to 10 years**	Status **Secure**

Order **Passeriformes**	Family **Emberizidae**	Species ***Junco hyemalis***

Dark-eyed Junco

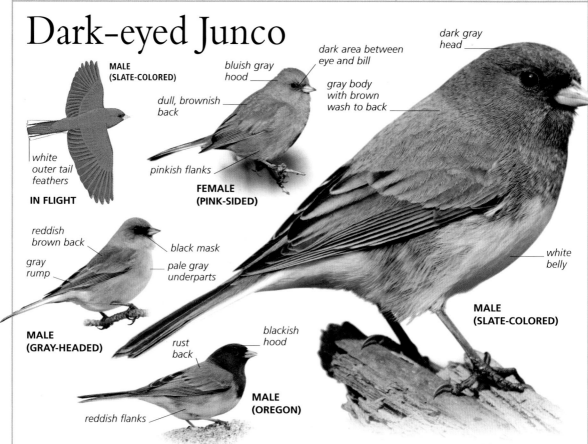

MALE
(SLATE-COLORED)
white
outer tail
feathers
IN FLIGHT
bluish gray
hood
dull, brownish
back
pinkish flanks
FEMALE
(PINK-SIDED)
dark area between
eye and bill
gray body
with brown
wash to back
dark gray
head
reddish
brown back
black mask
gray
rump
pale gray
underparts
MALE
(GRAY-HEADED)
white
belly
MALE
(SLATE-COLORED)
blackish
hood
rust
back
MALE
(OREGON)
reddish flanks

The Dark-eyed Junco's appearance at birdfeeders during snowstorms has earned it the colloquial name of "snowbird." The name "Dark-eyed Junco" is actually used to describe a group of birds that vary geographically in an incredibly diverse way. Sixteen subspecies have been described. "Slate-colored" populations are widespread across Canada and the northeastern US, the "White-winged" nests in the Black Hills, "Pink-sided" birds breed in Idaho, Montana, and Wyoming, and "Oregon" birds breed in the Pacific West, from Alaska to British Columbia and the mountainous western US in the Sierras south to Mexico. "Red-backed" populations reside in the mountains of Arizona and New Mexico, while "Gray-headed" birds range between the "Red-backed" and "Pink-sided" populations.

VOICE Loud, smacking *tick* and soft *dyew* calls; flight call a rapid, twittering, and buzzy *zzeet*; song a simple, liquid, 1-pitch trill.

NESTING Cup placed on ground hidden under vegetation or next to rocks; 3–5 eggs; 1–2 broods; May–August.

FEEDING Eats insects and seeds; also berries.

FLIGHT: low and direct, staying within cover whenever possible.

PINK-SIDED MALE
Like most juncos, this male is brighter with greater contrasts, darker eye areas, and more vivid colors.

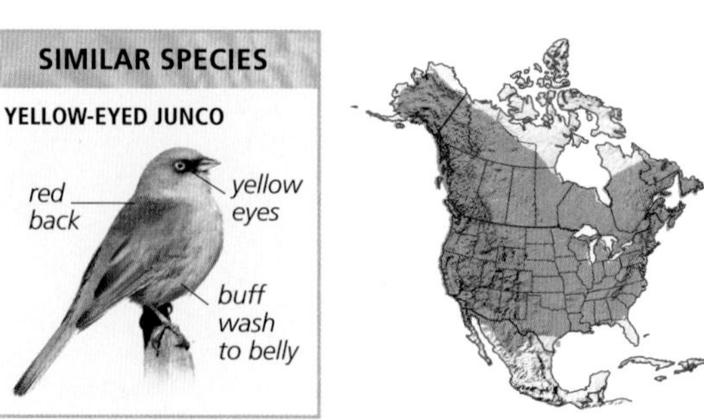
SIMILAR SPECIES
YELLOW-EYED JUNCO
red
back
yellow
eyes
buff
wash
to belly

OCCURRENCE
Breeds in coniferous and mixed forests across Canada and the southern US, south in the east Appalachians to Georgia, and in the west, in mountains from Alaska and British Columbia to New Mexico and northern Baja California. Winters from southern Canada to northern Mexico.

Length **6–6¾in (15–17cm)**	Wingspan **8–10in (20–26cm)**	Weight **⅝–1¹⁄₁₆oz (18–30g)**
Social **Flocks**	Lifespan **Up to 11 years**	Status **Secure**

Order **Passeriformes**	Family **Emberizidae**	Species ***Passerculus sandwichensis***

Savannah Sparrow

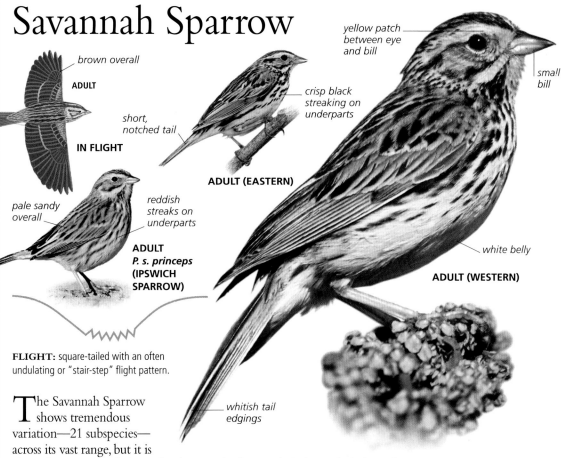

brown overall

ADULT

IN FLIGHT

short, notched tail

crisp black streaking on underparts

ADULT (EASTERN)

yellow patch between eye and bill

small bill

pale sandy overall

reddish streaks on underparts

ADULT *P. s. princeps* (IPSWICH SPARROW)

white belly

ADULT (WESTERN)

whitish tail edgings

FLIGHT: square-tailed with an often undulating or "stair-step" flight pattern.

The Savannah Sparrow shows tremendous variation—21 subspecies—across its vast range, but it is always brown, with dark streaks above and white with dark streaks below. The pale "Ipswich Sparrow" (*P. s. princeps*), originally described as a species, breeds on Sable Island, Nova Scotia, and winters along the East Coast. The "Large-billed Sparrow" (*P. s. rostratus* and *P. s. atratus*) breeds in Baja, California, and Sonora, Mexico. The most distinct of all populations, these birds occur as nonbreeders, near California's Salton Sea. Their distinct song consists of three buzzy trills, and their flight calls are lower and more metallic than other populations.

VOICE Call a sharp, but full *stip*; flight call a thin, weak, down-slurred *tseew*; song a *sit sit sit sit suh-EEEEE say*, from perch or in display flight with legs dangling.

NESTING Concealed cup of grass placed in depression on ground, protected by overhanging grass or sedges; 2–6 eggs; 1–2 broods; June–August.

FEEDING Forages on the ground, mostly for insects; in summer also eats seeds; in winter berries and fruit when available; also small snails and crustaceans.

BELDING'S SPARROW
This darker, more heavily streaked subspecies inhabits coastal marshes in southern California.

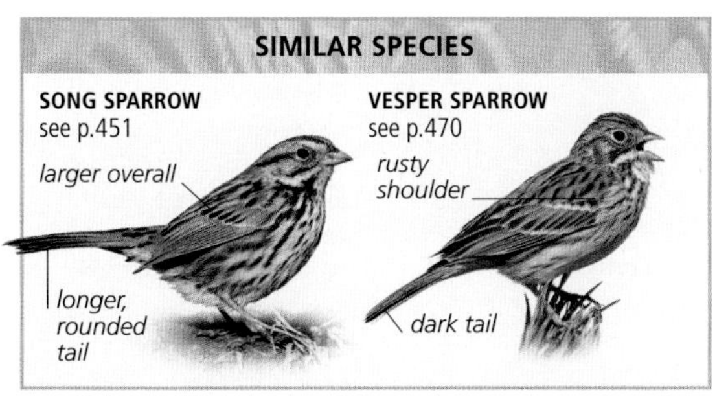
SIMILAR SPECIES
SONG SPARROW
see p.451
larger overall
longer, rounded tail
VESPER SPARROW
see p.470
rusty shoulder
dark tail

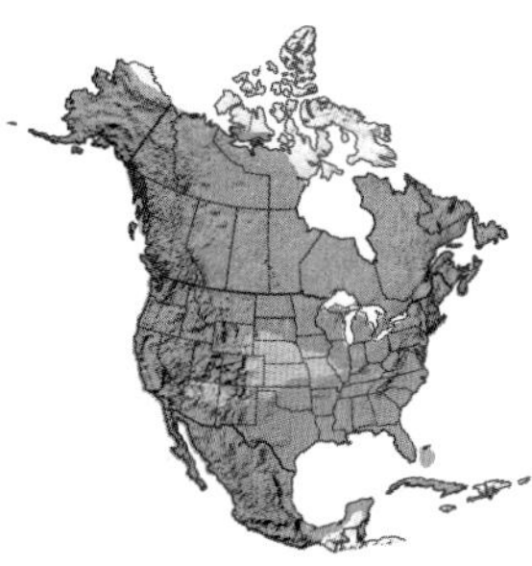

OCCURRENCE
Breeds in meadows, grasslands, pastures, bushy tundra, and some cultivated land across northern North America. Also along Pacific Coast and in Mexican interior. Nonbreeders use varied open habitats. Winters across southern US to Honduras, also Cuba, the Bahamas, and Cayman Islands.

Length **5½–6in (14–15cm)**	Wingspan **6¾in (17cm)**	Weight **½–1¹⁄₁₆oz (15–30g)**
Social **Solitary/Loose flocks**	Lifespan **Unknown**	Status **Secure**

Order **Passeriformes**	Family **Emberizidae**	Species ***Ammodramus nelsoni***

Nelson's Sharp-tailed Sparrow

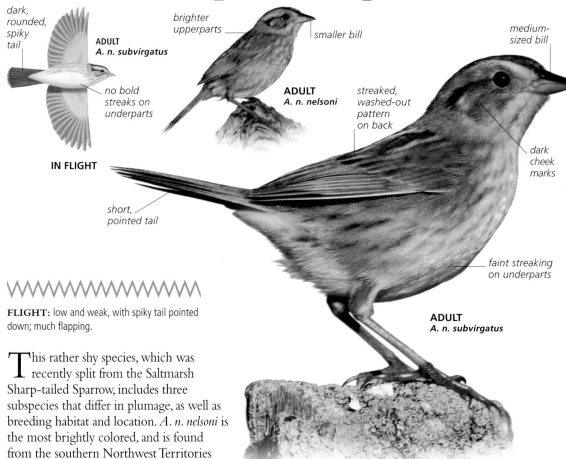

dark, rounded, spiky tail

ADULT
A. n. subvirgatus

no bold streaks on underparts

IN FLIGHT

brighter upperparts

smaller bill

ADULT
A. n. nelsoni

streaked, washed-out pattern on back

medium-sized bill

dark cheek marks

short, pointed tail

faint streaking on underparts

ADULT
A. n. subvirgatus

FLIGHT: low and weak, with spiky tail pointed down; much flapping.

This rather shy species, which was recently split from the Saltmarsh Sharp-tailed Sparrow, includes three subspecies that differ in plumage, as well as breeding habitat and location. *A. n. nelsoni* is the most brightly colored, and is found from the southern Northwest Territories south to northwest Wisconsin. *A. n. subvirgatus* breeds in coastal Maine and the Maritimes, and along the St. Lawrence River. It is visually duller than *A. n. nelsoni*, with a longer bill and flatter head. The intermediate-looking *A. n. alterus* breeds along the southern and western coasts of Hudson Bay.

VOICE Sharp *tik* call; song a husky *t-SHHHHEE-uhrr*.

NESTING Cup of grass placed on or just above ground; 4–5 eggs; 1 brood; May–July.

FEEDING Forages on the ground mainly for insects, spiders, and seeds.

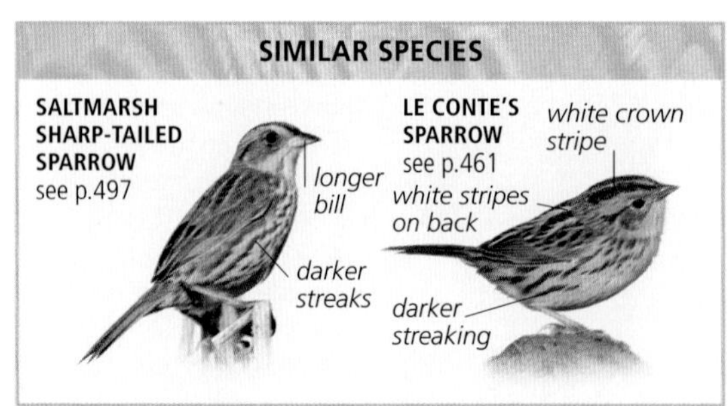
SIMILAR SPECIES
SALTMARSH SHARP-TAILED SPARROW
see p.497
longer bill
darker streaks
LE CONTE'S SPARROW
see p.461
white crown stripe
white stripes on back
darker streaking

IDENTIFYING MARKS
The orange-and-gray facial pattern and streaks on the breast are clearly visible.

OCCURRENCE
Breeds in a variety of marsh habitats across Canada and extreme north central North America. Nonbreeders found in marshes and wet, weedy fields. *A. n. nelsoni* and *A. n. alterus* winter on coast from Texas northeast to New Jersey; *A. n. subvirgatus* from eastern Florida to New Jersey.

Length **4¾in (12cm)**	Wingspan **7in (17.5cm)**	Weight **7/16–11/16oz (13–20g)**
Social **Solitary/Flocks**	Lifespan **Unknown**	Status **Secure**

Order **Passeriformes**	Family **Emberizidae**	Species ***Ammodramus leconteii***

Le Conte's Sparrow

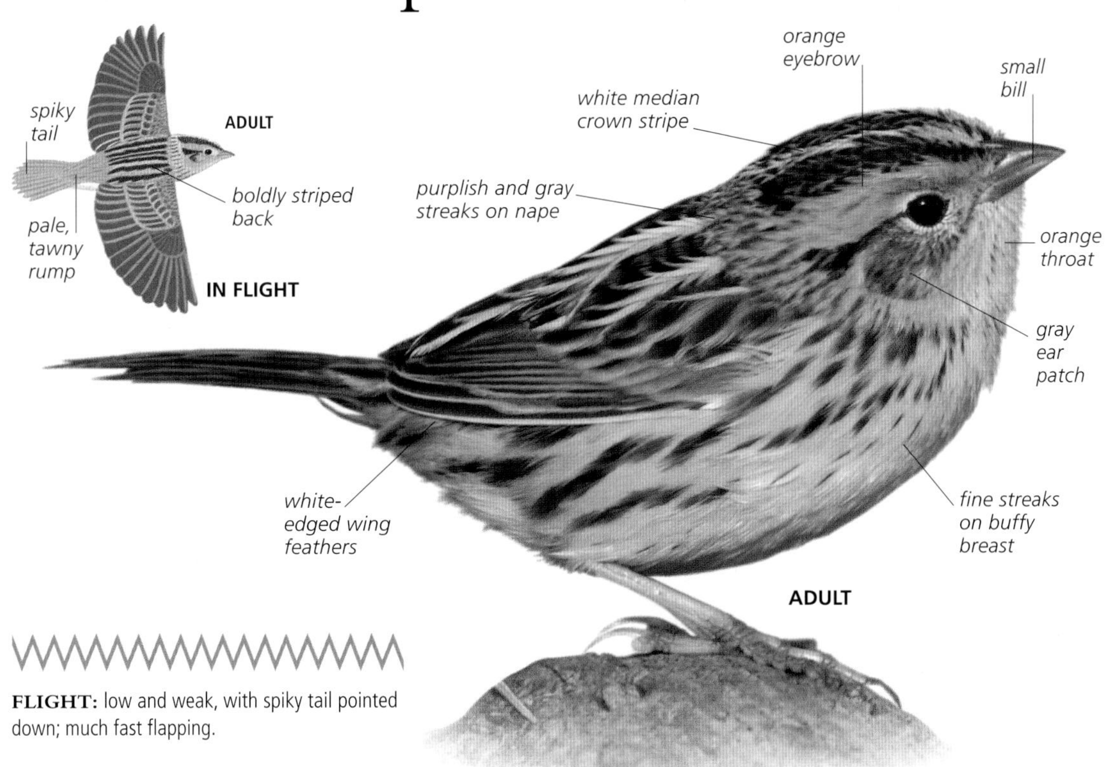
spiky tail
ADULT
boldly striped back
pale, tawny rump
IN FLIGHT
orange eyebrow
small bill
white median crown stripe
purplish and gray streaks on nape
orange throat
gray ear patch
white-edged wing feathers
fine streaks on buffy breast
ADULT

FLIGHT: low and weak, with spiky tail pointed down; much fast flapping.

Although intricately patterned in glowing colors, Le Conte's Sparrow is usually very difficult to see. Not only is it tiny—one of the smallest of all sparrows—but in the grasslands and marshes of interior North America where it lives it prefers to dart for cover under grasses instead of flushing when disturbed. Meanwhile the flight call and song of this elusive little bird are remarkably insect-like. Many people who hear it often then pass off the unseen bird as a grasshopper. Its nest is even harder to find, making this bird a real challenge to study as well as observe.

VOICE Call long, down-slurred *zheeep*; flight call similar to grasshopper; song insect-like, buzzy *tik'-uht-tizz-ZHEEEEEE-k*.

NESTING Concealed little cup placed on or near ground; 3–5 eggs; 1 brood; June–August.

FEEDING Forages on the ground and in grasses for insects, insect larvae, spiders, and seeds.

HIDEAWAY BIRD
Le Conte's Sparrow is usually found skulking in medium-to-tall grass in all seasons.

SIMILAR SPECIES

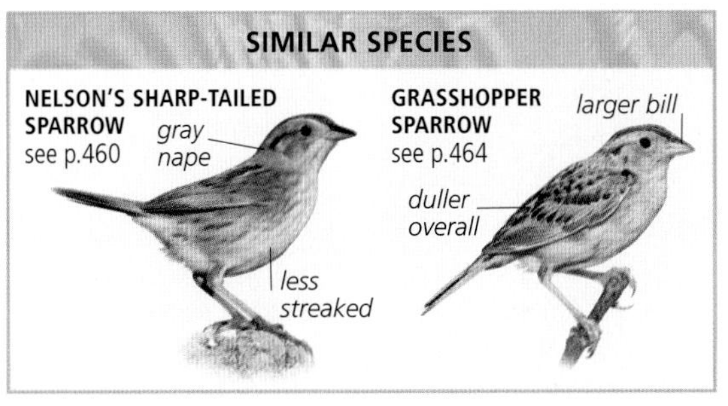
NELSON'S SHARP-TAILED SPARROW
see p.460
gray nape
less streaked
GRASSHOPPER SPARROW
see p.464
larger bill
duller overall

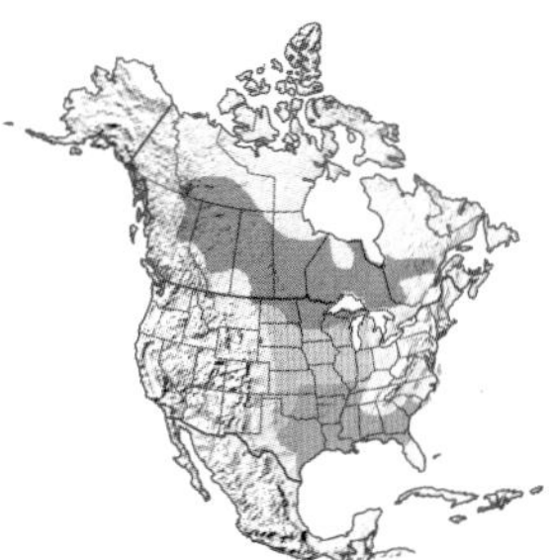

OCCURRENCE
Breeds in marshes, wet meadows, and bogs from southwest Yukon to Lake Superior and west Quebec. Migrants or wintering birds found in tall grass and marshes in southwest Kansas to south Indiana, and central Texas to coastal Carolinas.

Length **4½–5in (11.5–13cm)**	Wingspan **6½–7in (16–18cm)**	Weight **7/16–9/16oz (12–16g)**
Social **Solitary/Loose flocks**	Lifespan **Unknown**	Status **Secure**

Order **Passeriformes**	Family **Emberizidae**	Species ***Ammodramus bairdii***

Baird's Sparrow

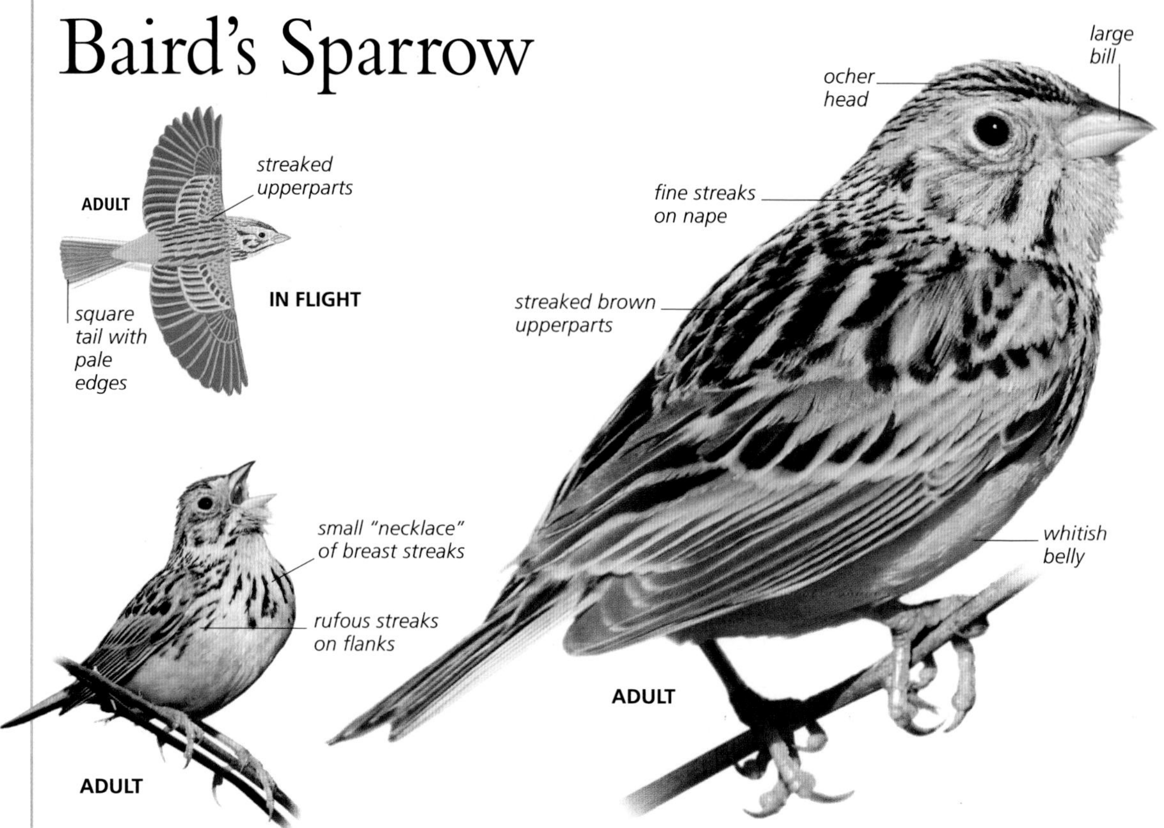

ADULT
streaked upperparts
IN FLIGHT
square tail with pale edges
ocher head
large bill
fine streaks on nape
streaked brown upperparts
small "necklace" of breast streaks
rufous streaks on flanks
whitish belly
ADULT
ADULT

The sweet, tinkling song of Baird's Sparrow is a sure sign of high-quality mixed-grass prairie on the Northern Plains. This sparrow's musical song is quite different to the buzzy songs of the other *Ammodramus* sparrows. Its square, pale-edged tail is also unique within its genus. Baird's Sparrow is usually seen only on its breeding grounds, for it is very difficult to find elsewhere, scurrying out of sight if disturbed. Like other birds that depend on native grasslands, it has not coped well with the intensive agriculture that has swept across the Northern Plains in the last century or so.

VOICE Call soft, metallic *tsink*; flight call insect-like *tisk*; song *tsk tsk tsuck tsooweeeeee.*

NESTING Well-concealed grass cup placed on ground in depression or in grass clump or shrub; 4–5 eggs; 1–2 broods; May–August.

FEEDING Forages for seeds and insects.

FLIGHT: low and weak, short in duration, much flapping.

OCCURRENCE
Breeds in light mixed-grass prairie, from south Alberta southeast to northern South Dakota and northern Wyoming. Migrates through the High Plains. Winters in diverse, patchy grasslands, in Chihuahua, northern Sonora in Mexico, and in adjacent US.

SIMILAR SPECIES

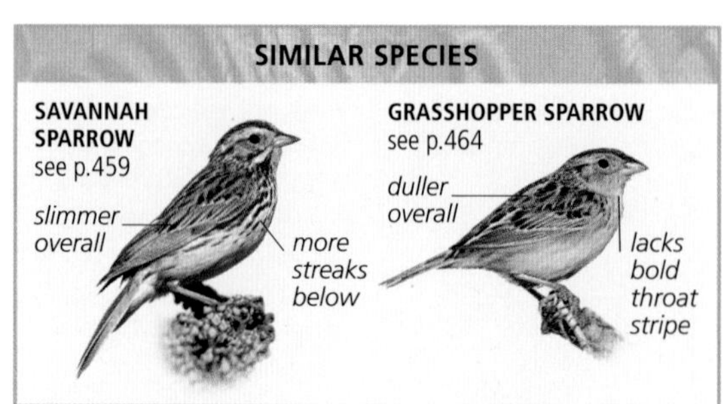

SAVANNAH SPARROW
see p.459
slimmer overall
more streaks below
GRASSHOPPER SPARROW
see p.464
duller overall
lacks bold throat stripe

HABITAT SPECIALIST
Baird's Sparrow needs the previous year's dead grass as suitable breeding habitat.

Length **5½in (14cm)**	Wingspan **8½–8¾in (21–22.5cm)**	Weight **½–$^{11}/_{16}$oz (15–20g)**
Social **Solitary/Loose flocks**	Lifespan **Unknown**	Status **Declining**

Order **Passeriformes** | Family **Emberizidae** | Species ***Ammodramus henslowii***

Henslow's Sparrow

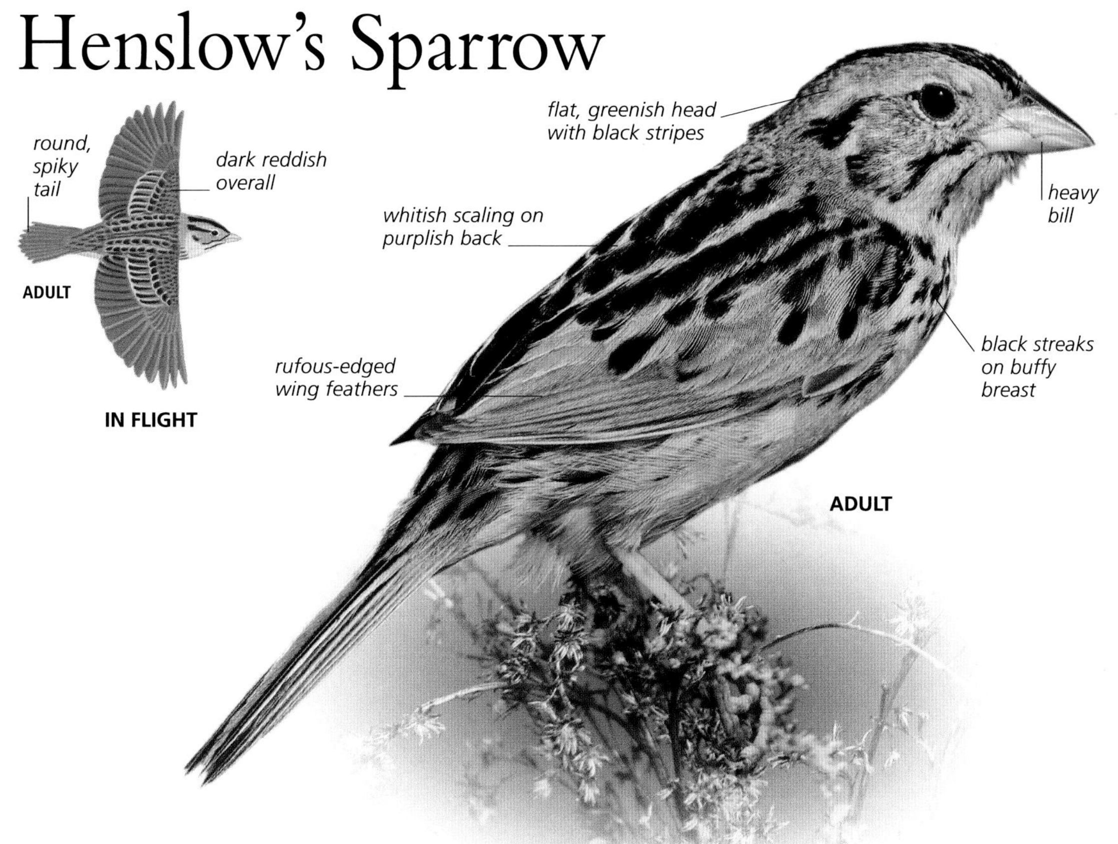
round, spiky tail
dark reddish overall
ADULT
IN FLIGHT
flat, greenish head with black stripes
whitish scaling on purplish back
heavy bill
rufous-edged wing feathers
black streaks on buffy breast
ADULT

The combination of a large, flat, greenish head, and purplish back are unique to Henslow's Sparrow. A bird of the tallgrass prairies and wet grasslands, the breeding range of this sparrow closely mirrors the extent of its habitat. While it has suffered greatly from the drainage, cultivation, and urbanization of much of its preferred breeding grounds, the Henslow's Sparrow has also recently started to use reclaimed strip mines in northwest Missouri and Iowa for breeding.

VOICE Call a sharp *tsik*, flight call a long, high, shrill *tseeeeee*; song a hiccupping sputter with second note higher *tsih-LIK!*

NESTING Cup of grass placed on or near ground; 2–5 eggs; 1–2 broods; May–August.

FEEDING Eats seed that forages for insects, insect larvae, and spiders in the summer.

FLIGHT: low and weak, with spiky tail pointed down; much flapping.

OCCURRENCE
Breeds predominantly in tallgrass prairie and wet grasslands from Oklahoma eastward to New York and up into southeastern Canada, and southward to North Carolina. Winters in weedy, brushy fields, grassy pine woods, and undergrowth along Gulf Coastal Plain from Texas to North Carolina.

INTO THE AIR
The male puts considerable effort into his short, but surprisingly far-carrying song.

SIMILAR SPECIES

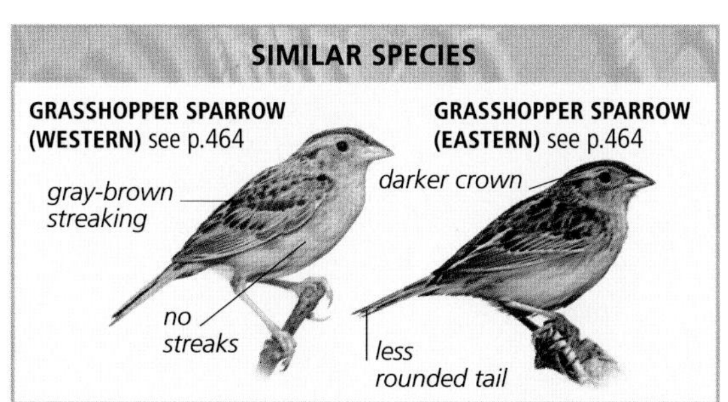
GRASSHOPPER SPARROW (WESTERN) see p.464
gray-brown streaking
no streaks
GRASSHOPPER SPARROW (EASTERN) see p.464
darker crown
less rounded tail

Length **4¾–5in (12–13cm)**	Wingspan **6½in (16cm)**	Weight **⅜–½oz (11–15g)**
Social **Solitary/Loose flocks**	Lifespan **Unknown**	Status **Declining**

Order **Passeriformes**	Family **Emberizidae**	Species ***Ammodramus savannarum***

Grasshopper Sparrow

short, spiky tail
buff overall
ADULT
IN FLIGHT

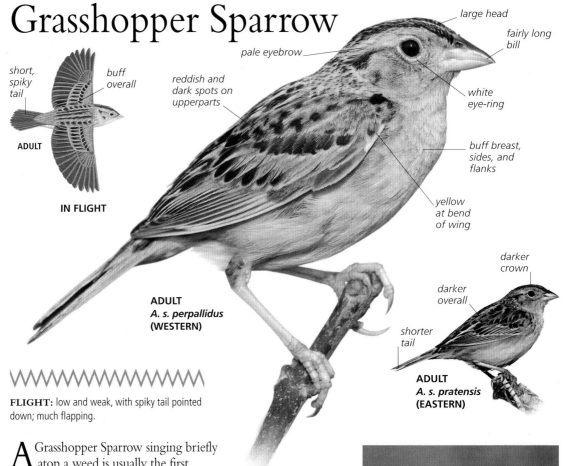

pale eyebrow
large head
fairly long bill
reddish and dark spots on upperparts
white eye-ring
buff breast, sides, and flanks
yellow at bend of wing
ADULT
A. s. perpallidus
(WESTERN)

darker crown
darker overall
shorter tail
ADULT
A. s. pratensis
(EASTERN)

FLIGHT: low and weak, with spiky tail pointed down; much flapping.

A Grasshopper Sparrow singing briefly atop a weed is usually the first glimpse people get of a member of the secretive *Ammodramus* genus. Although its large head and spiky tail are typical of its genus, the Grasshopper Sparrow is the only *Ammodramus* sparrow to have a plain breast and two completely different songs. While it does eat grasshoppers, its common name derives from its song, which resembles the sounds grasshoppers make. It varies geographically, with about 12 subspecies.

VOICE Sharp *tik* call; flight call a long, high *tseeee*; song an insect-like trill *tik'-tok-TREEEE*, or series of quick buzzes.

NESTING Cup of grass placed in clump of grass; 3–6 eggs; 1–2 broods; April–August.

FEEDING Forages on ground for seeds and insects.

YELLOW PATCH
The pale crown stripe and small yellow patch at the bend of its wings are visible here.

SIMILAR SPECIES

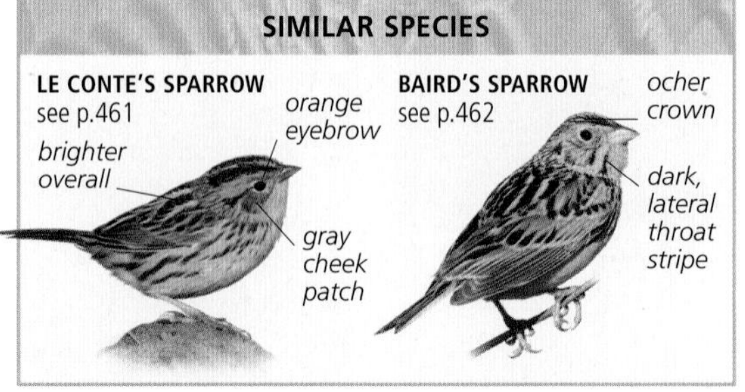
LE CONTE'S SPARROW
see p.461
orange eyebrow
brighter overall
gray cheek patch
BAIRD'S SPARROW
see p.462
ocher crown
dark, lateral throat stripe

OCCURRENCE
Breeds in short grassland, pastures, and even mown areas across much of the US and southern Canada. Locally distributed in the Southwest, also patchily through central US. Winters in similar habitats from southern US to Colombia; also found in the West Indies.

Length **5in (13cm)**	Wingspan **8in (20cm)**	Weight **1/2–11/16oz (15–20g)**
Social **Solitary/Flocks**	Lifespan **Up to 7 years**	Status **Declining**

Order **Passeriformes**	Family **Emberizidae**	Species ***Spizella arborea***

American Tree Sparrow

rufous crown

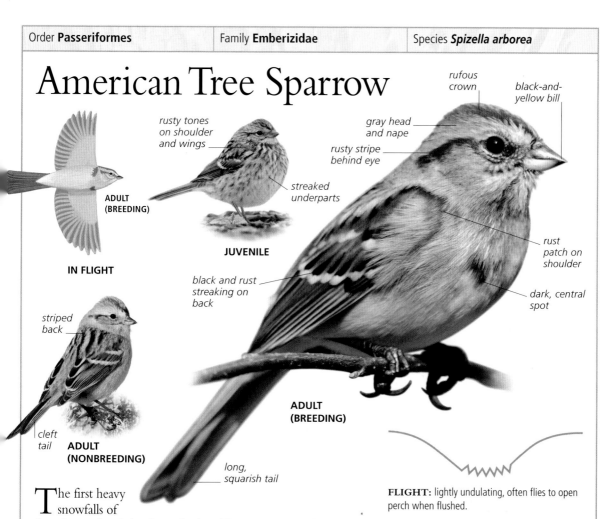

black-and-yellow bill

gray head and nape

rusty stripe behind eye

rusty tones on shoulder and wings

streaked underparts

ADULT (BREEDING)

IN FLIGHT

JUVENILE

rust patch on shoulder

black and rust streaking on back

dark, central spot

striped back

ADULT (BREEDING)

cleft tail

ADULT (NONBREEDING)

long, squarish tail

The first heavy snowfalls of the winter often bring large flocks of American Tree Sparrows to birdfeeders. This bird is commonly mistaken for the smaller Chipping Sparrow, but the two species look quite dissimilar in the winter. The American Tree Sparrow's central breast spot, bicolored bill, and large size are unique among the *Spizella*. A highly social, vocal, and misnamed species, noisy winter flocks numbering in the hundreds can be found feeding in weedy fields and along the roadsides of the northern US and southern Canada.

VOICE Call a bell-like *teedle-ee*; flight call a thin, slightly descending *tsiiiu*; song *seee seee di-di-di di-di-di dyew dyew.*

NESTING Neat cup on ground concealed within thicket; 4–6 eggs; 1 brood; June–July.

FEEDING Feeds on seeds, berries, and a variety of insects.

FLIGHT: lightly undulating, often flies to open perch when flushed.

WINTER HABITATS
In winter, this species frequents barren habitats, like old fields and roadsides, as well as feeders.

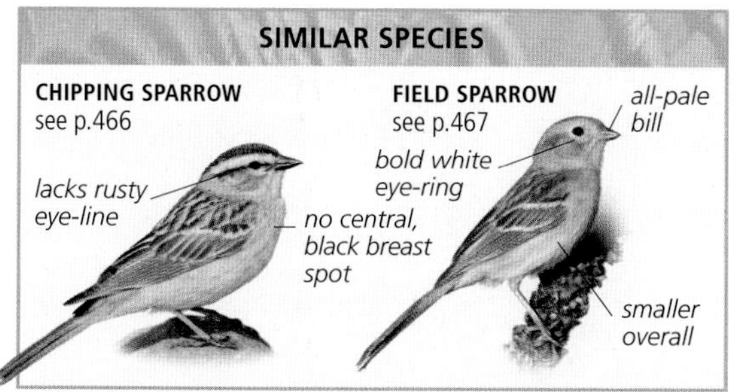
SIMILAR SPECIES
CHIPPING SPARROW
see p.466
lacks rusty eye-line
no central, black breast spot
FIELD SPARROW
see p.467
all-pale bill
bold white eye-ring
smaller overall

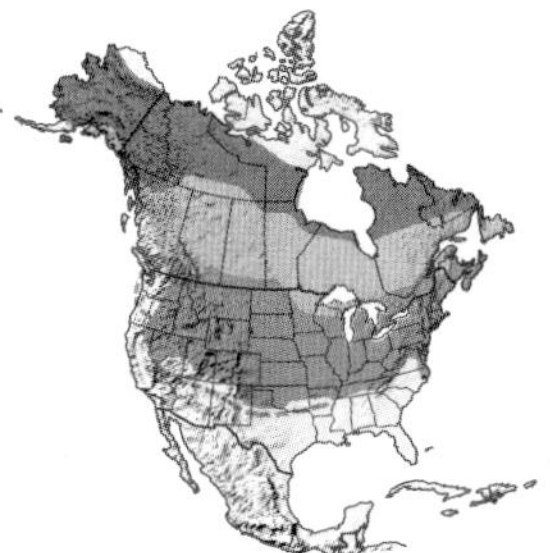

OCCURRENCE
Breeds in scrubby thickets of birch and willows in the area between taiga and tundra across Alaska and north Canada. Nonbreeders choose open, grassy, brushy habitats. Winters across south Canada and the northern US. Casual to Pacific coast and southern US.

Length **6¼in (16cm)**	Wingspan **9½in (24cm)**	Weight **7/16–7/8oz (13–25g)**
Social **Flocks**	Lifespan **Up to 11 years**	Status **Secure**

Order **Passeriformes**	Family **Emberizidae**	Species ***Spizella passerina***

Chipping Sparrow

pale underparts
ADULT
IN FLIGHT
rusty cast to crown
pinkish bill
ADULT (WINTER)
heavily streaked, especially on breast
JUVENILE
bright rufous crown
blackish bill
white eyebrow
black eye line
ADULT (BREEDING)
gray underparts
cleft tail

The Chipping Sparrow is a common, trusting bird, which breeds in backyards across most of North America. While they are easily identifiable in the summer, "Chippers" molt into a drab, nonbreeding plumage during fall, at which point they are easily confused with the Clay-colored and Brewer's Sparrows they flock with. Most reports of this species across the north in winter are actually of the larger American Tree Sparrow. In the winter, Chipping Sparrows can be easily recognized as they lack their bright, rusty crown and are restricted to the south.

VOICE Call a sharp *tsip*; flight call a sharp, thin *tsiiit*; song an insect-like trill of *chip* notes, variable in duration and quality.

NESTING Neat cup usually placed well off the ground in tree or shrub; 3–5 eggs; 1–2 broods; April–August.

FEEDING Eats seeds of grasses and annuals, plus some fruits; when breeding, also eats insects and other invertebrates.

FLIGHT: lightly undulating, often to open perch when flushed.

BACKYARD BIRD
Chipping Sparrows are a very common sight in gardens and backyards all across the continent.

SIMILAR SPECIES

CLAY-COLORED SPARROW
see p.468
heavy streaks
BREWER'S SPARROW
see p.469
partial "necklace"
streaked crown
pale underparts

OCCURRENCE
Found in a wide variety of habitats: open forest, woodlands, grassy, park-like areas, shorelines, and backyards. Breeds in North America south of the Arctic timberline and in Mexico, and in Central America, as far south as Nicaragua. Winters from southern states to Nicaragua.

Length **5½in (14cm)**	Wingspan **8½in (21cm)**	Weight **⅜–½oz (10–15g)**
Social **Large flocks**	Lifespan **Up to 9 years**	Status **Secure**

Order **Passeriformes**	Family **Emberizidae**	Species ***Spizella pusilla***

Field Sparrow

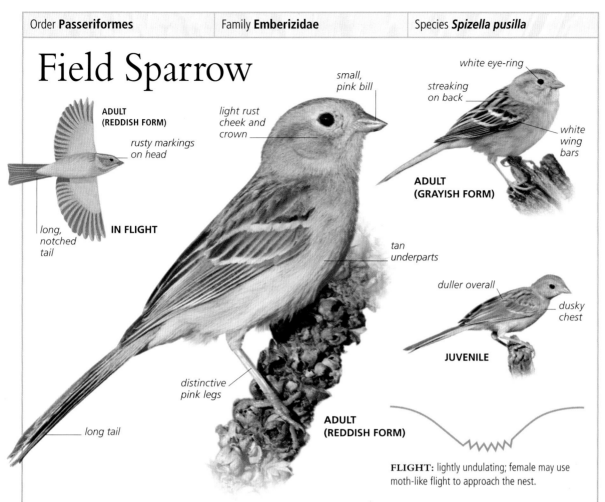

ADULT (REDDISH FORM)
rusty markings on head
long, notched tail
IN FLIGHT

light rust cheek and crown
small, pink bill
tan underparts
distinctive pink legs
long tail
ADULT (REDDISH FORM)

white eye-ring
streaking on back
white wing bars
ADULT (GRAYISH FORM)

duller overall
dusky chest
JUVENILE

FLIGHT: lightly undulating; female may use moth-like flight to approach the nest.

The distinctive accelerating trill song of the Field Sparrow is a characteristic sound of shrubby fields and scrubby areas in the eastern US and southeastern Canada. The bird's bright-pink bill, plain "baby face," and white eye-ring make this sparrow one of the easiest to identify. The Field Sparrow has brighter plumage in the East, and drabber plumage in the interior part of its range. Although quite dissimilar at first glance, the Black-chinned Sparrow may in fact be the Field Sparrow's closest relative, sharing its pink bill, relatively unpatterned plumage, and its song.

VOICE Call a sharp *tsik*; flight call a strongly descending *tsiiiu*; song a series of sweet, down-slurred whistles accelerating to a rapid trill.

NESTING Grass cup placed on or just above ground in grass or bush; 3–5 eggs; 1–3 broods; March–August.

FEEDING Eats seeds; also insects, insect larvae, and spiders in the summer.

FAMILIAR SONG
Male Field Sparrows sing their familiar and distinctive song throughout the summer.

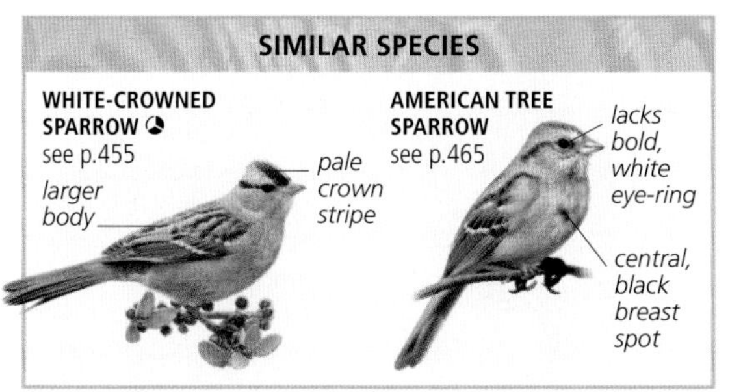
SIMILAR SPECIES
WHITE-CROWNED SPARROW
see p.455
larger body
pale crown stripe
AMERICAN TREE SPARROW
see p.465
lacks bold, white eye-ring
central, black breast spot

OCCURRENCE
Breeds in overgrown fields, woodland edges, roadsides, and other shrubby, overgrown areas; occasionally in orchards and parks in the eastern US, west to Dakota, east to New England. Winters in similar habitats in the southern US. Casual in Atlantic Canada and on the Pacific Coast.

Length **5½in (14cm)**	Wingspan **8in (20cm)**	Weight **⅜–½oz (11–15g)**
Social **Solitary/Flocks**	Lifespan **Up to 6 years**	Status **Declining**

Order **Passeriformes**	Family **Emberizidae**	Species ***Spizella pallida***

Clay-colored Sparrow

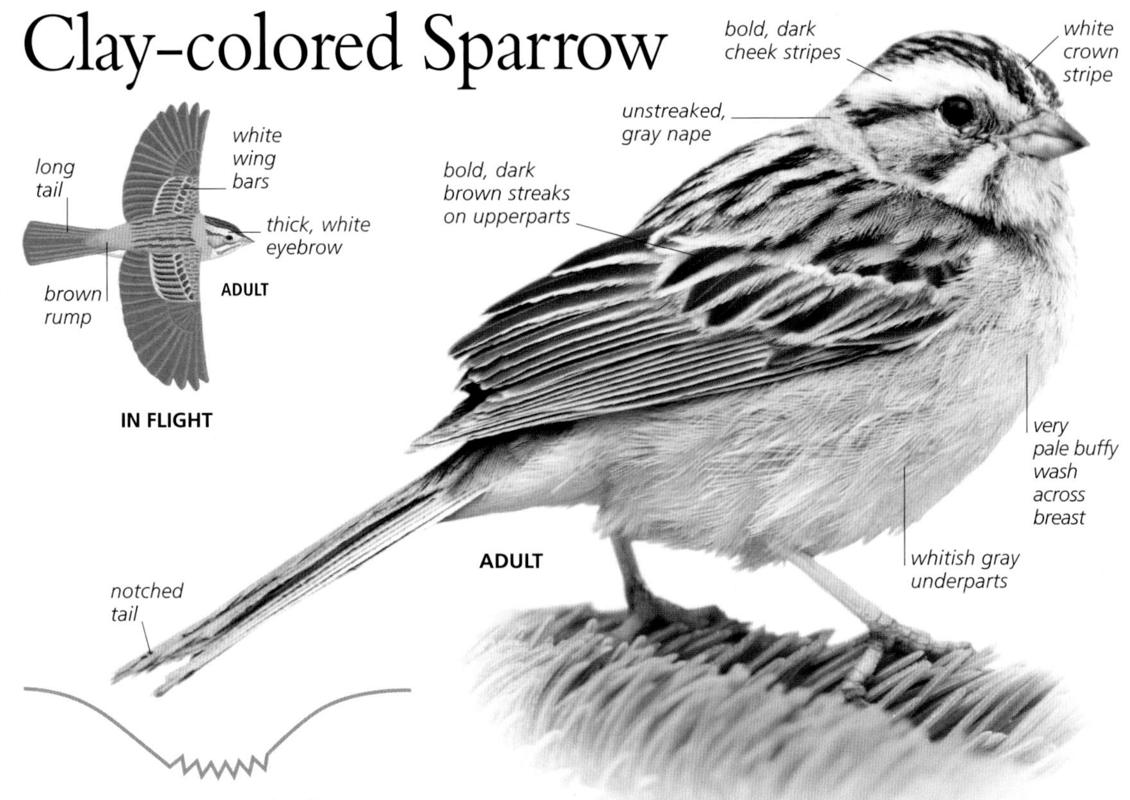
bold, dark
cheek stripes
white
crown
stripe
unstreaked,
gray nape
white
wing
bars
long
tail
thick, white
eyebrow
bold, dark
brown streaks
on upperparts
brown
rump
ADULT
IN FLIGHT
very
pale buffy
wash
across
breast
ADULT
whitish gray
underparts
notched
tail

FLIGHT: lightly undulating, often flies to open perch when flushed.

The little Clay-colored Sparrow is best known for its mechanical, buzzy song. This bird spends much of its foraging time away from the breeding habitat; consequently, males' territories are quite small, allowing for dense breeding populations. Clay-colored Sparrows have shifted their breeding range eastward and northward over the last century, most likely because of changes in land practices. During the nonbreeding season, they form large flocks in open country, associating with other *Spizella* sparrows, especially Chippings and Brewer's.

VOICE Call a sharp *tsip*; flight a call short, rising *sip*; song a series of 2–7 mechanical buzzes on one pitch.

NESTING Cup of grass placed just off the ground in shrub or small tree; 3–5 eggs; 1–2 broods; May–August.

FEEDING Forages on or low to the ground for seeds and insects.

CHRISTMAS PRESENT
The Clay-colored Sparrow is fond of short conifers for breeding, so Christmas tree farms form a perfect habitat.

SIMILAR SPECIES
CHIPPING SPARROW ❄
see p.466
grayish
rump
dark stripe
through
eye
grayer
breast
BREWER'S SPARROW
see p.469
streaked
nape
lacks
bold,
crown
stripe

OCCURRENCE
Breeds in open habitats: prairies, shrubland, forest edges, and Christmas tree farms along the US/Canadian border and northward to the southern Northwest Territory. Winters in a large variety of brushy, weedy areas from south Texas to Mexico. Migration takes it to the Great Plains.

Length **5½in (14cm)**	Wingspan **7½in (19cm)**	Weight **⅜–½oz (10–15g)**
Social **Large flocks**	Lifespan **Up to 5 years**	Status **Secure**

Order **Passeriformes**	Family **Emberizidae**	Species ***Spizella breweri***

Brewer's Sparrow

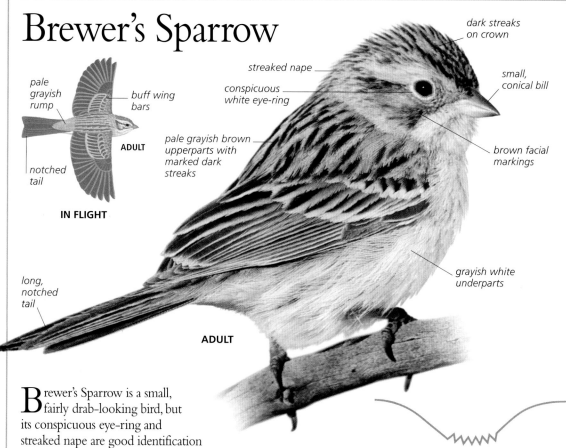

pale grayish rump
buff wing bars
ADULT
notched tail
IN FLIGHT

dark streaks on crown
streaked nape
conspicuous white eye-ring
small, conical bill
pale grayish brown upperparts with marked dark streaks
brown facial markings
grayish white underparts
long, notched tail
ADULT

Brewer's Sparrow is a small, fairly drab-looking bird, but its conspicuous eye-ring and streaked nape are good identification features. In addition, its varied, loud, trilling and chattering song is a memorable sound of the West. Most Brewer's Sparrows nest on arid sagebrush in the western US, but there is an isolated population, subspecies "Timberline," which breeds in the Canadian Rockies and into Alaska. It is usually darker, more boldly marked, and longer-billed with a lower, slower, more musical song than its relative.

VOICE Call a sharp *tsip*; flight call a short, rising *sip*; song a series of descending trills, rattles, and buzzes on different pitches.

NESTING Compact cup on or near ground in small bush; 3–4 eggs; 1–2 broods; May–August.

FEEDING Forages on ground for insects and seeds.

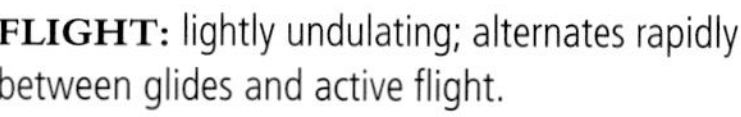

FLIGHT: lightly undulating; alternates rapidly between glides and active flight.

CONTINUOUS CHORUS
Across its range in spring, the male Brewer's Sparrow sings continuously to attract a mate.

HIGH AND DRY
These sparrows are fond of the arid brushland and deserts of the High Plains and Great Basin.

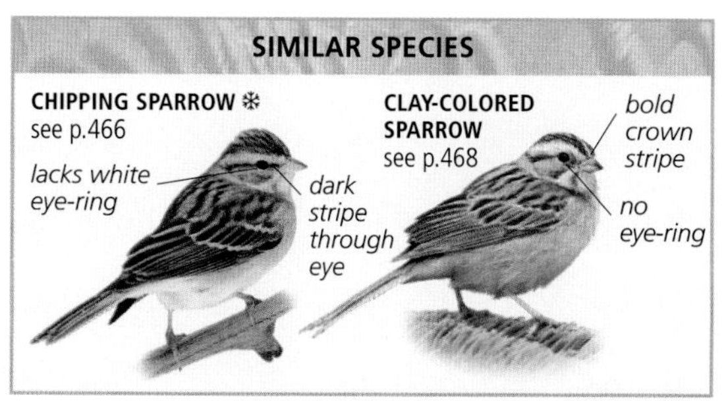
SIMILAR SPECIES
CHIPPING SPARROW ❄
see p.466
lacks white eye-ring
dark stripe through eye
CLAY-COLORED SPARROW
see p.468
bold crown stripe
no eye-ring

OCCURRENCE
Timberline subspecies breeds in valleys in eastern Alaska through Yukon to northwestern British Columbia. Brewer's subspecies breed in brushland, shrubland, thickets, and mountain basins of the western US. Winters in desert scrub and weedy fields in the Southwest and northwestern Mexico.

Length **5½in (14cm)**	Wingspan **7½in (19cm)**	Weight **5/16–½oz (9–14g)**
Social **Solitary/Flocks**	Lifespan **Unknown**	Status **Declining**

Order **Passeriformes**	Family **Emberizidae**	Species ***Pooecetes gramineus***

Vesper Sparrow

rusty shoulders
ADULT
IN FLIGHT

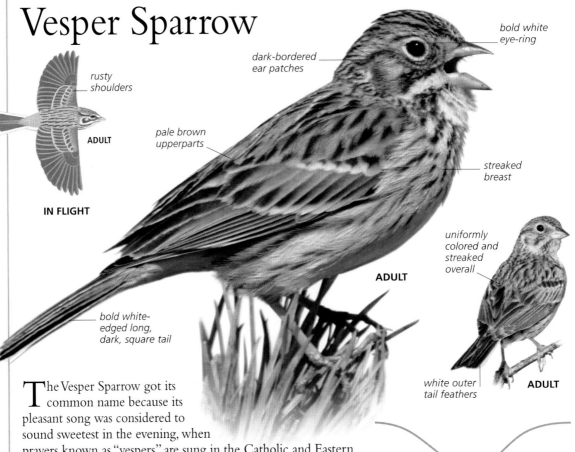

dark-bordered ear patches
bold white eye-ring
pale brown upperparts
streaked breast
ADULT
bold white-edged long, dark, square tail

uniformly colored and streaked overall
white outer tail feathers
ADULT

The Vesper Sparrow got its common name because its pleasant song was considered to sound sweetest in the evening, when prayers known as "vespers" are sung in the Catholic and Eastern Orthodox churches. When Henry David Thoreau wrote of this species, he called it the "Bay-winged Bunting," because of its (sometimes concealed) rusty shoulder patches and its relation to the Old World *Emberizidae* buntings. The Vesper Sparrow needs areas with bare ground to breed, so it is one of the few species that can successfully nest in areas of intense agriculture; the bird's numbers seem to be declining in spite of this.

VOICE Full *tchup* call, flight call thin *tseent*; song consists of 2 whistles of same pitch, followed by 2 higher-pitched ones, then trills, ends lazily.

NESTING Cup placed on patch of bare ground, against grass, bush, or rock; 3–5 eggs; 1 brood; April–August.

FEEDING Eats insects and seeds.

FLIGHT: strong, often perches when flushed; often moves on ground.

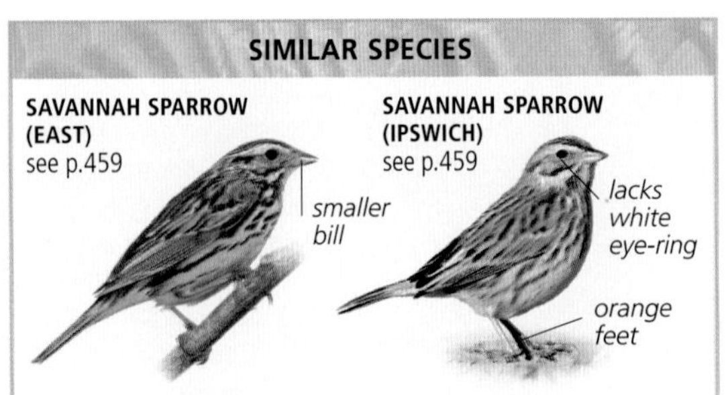
SIMILAR SPECIES
SAVANNAH SPARROW (EAST)
see p.459
smaller bill
SAVANNAH SPARROW (IPSWICH)
see p.459
lacks white eye-ring
orange feet

GIFTED SONGSTER
The sweet song of the Vesper Sparrow is a characteristic sound of more northerly open areas.

OCCURRENCE
Breeds in sparse grassland, cultivated fields, recently burned areas, and mountain parks across south Canada and the northern US. Winters in sparsely vegetated, open habitats from southern US to southwest Mexico. Found in patches of bare earth in all seasons.

Length **6¼in (16cm)**	Wingspan **10in (25cm)**	Weight **11/16–1 1/16oz (20–30g)**
Social **Flocks**	Lifespan **Up to 7 years**	Status **Declining**

Order **Passeriformes**	Family **Emberizidae**	Species ***Chondestes grammacus***

Lark Sparrow

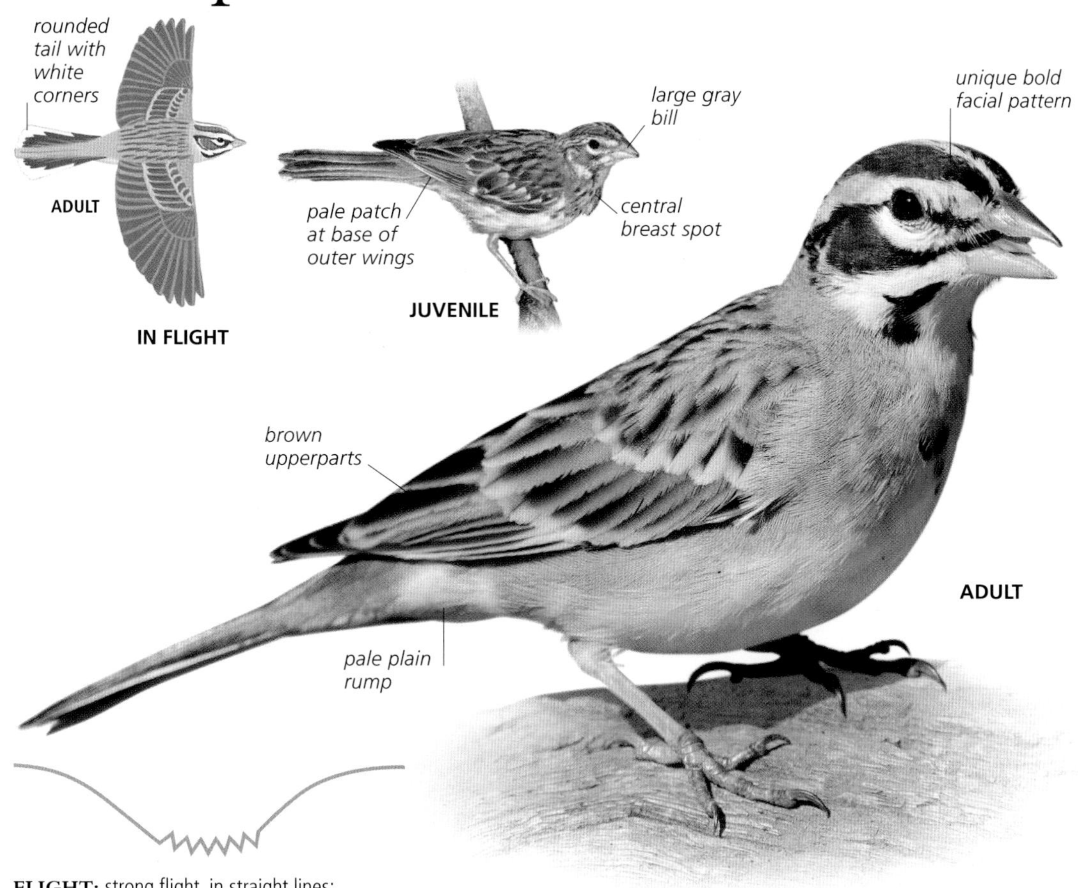
rounded tail with white corners
ADULT
IN FLIGHT
large gray bill
pale patch at base of outer wings
central breast spot
JUVENILE
unique bold facial pattern
brown upperparts
ADULT
pale plain rump

FLIGHT: strong flight, in straight lines; often perches when flushed.

The bold harlequin face pattern, single central breast spot, and long, rounded, black tail with white corners make the Lark Sparrow one of the most easily identifiable of all sparrows. It is commonly found singing from the top of a fencepost or small tree in the western US and southern Canadian prairies. Conversely, Lark Sparrow numbers have declined precipitously in the East, where the species is mostly associated with western-like sandy soils. It is likely that its presence in the East was only possible because of the clearing of forests, so the species may in fact simply be retreating to its natural range. Male birds are strongly territorial of their nesting sites, though this does not extend as a wider area to other species.

VOICE Thin, up-slurred *tseep* call, flight call sharp *tink*; song series of trills, whistles, and rattles on varying pitches.

NESTING Cup usually placed on ground at base of plant, or off-ground in tree or bush; 3–5 eggs; 1–2 broods; April–August.

FEEDING Eats seeds and insects.

ON THE FENCE
The Lark Sparrow is a common roadside bird, often found perching on barbed wire fences.

OCCURRENCE
Breeds in varied open habitats such as sage flats and grassland from British Columbia and Saskatchewan to Baja California and central Mexico, east to Ohio; localized breeder in East, associated with well-drained, poor soils. Winters from southern US to southwest Mexico.

Length **6–6¾in (15–17cm)**	Wingspan **11in (28cm)**	Weight **11⁄16–1 1⁄16oz (20–30g)**
Social **Large flocks**	Lifespan **Up to 8 years**	Status **Secure**

Order **Passeriformes**	Family **Emberizidae**	Species ***Pipilo maculatus***

Spotted Towhee

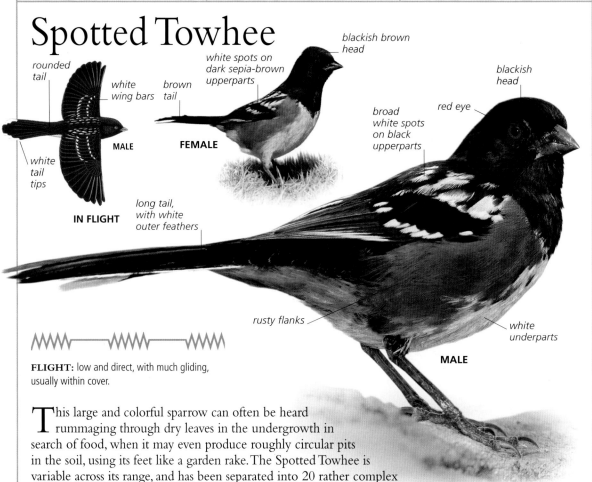

rounded tail
white wing bars
white tail tips
MALE
IN FLIGHT
brown tail
white spots on dark sepia-brown upperparts
blackish brown head
FEMALE
long tail, with white outer feathers
blackish head
red eye
broad white spots on black upperparts
rusty flanks
white underparts
MALE

FLIGHT: low and direct, with much gliding, usually within cover.

This large and colorful sparrow can often be heard rummaging through dry leaves in the undergrowth in search of food, when it may even produce roughly circular pits in the soil, using its feet like a garden rake. The Spotted Towhee is variable across its range, and has been separated into 20 rather complex subspecies, but all are distinguished from the Eastern Towhee by the presence of white spots and bars on their upperwings.

VOICE Depending on geographical location, call *zhreee* or a buzzy, nasal, descending *reeeer*; song ends with a trill.

NESTING Large cup in depression on ground, under cover, also low in thicket; 3–5 eggs; 1–2 broods; April–June.

FEEDING Scratches for food, including insects, fruits, seeds, and acorns; sometimes eats small snakes and lizards.

RUFOUS SIDES
The Spotted Towhee was once grouped with the Eastern Towhee under the name "Rufous-sided Towhee."

DIVERGENT DIALECTS
The vocalizations of the Spotted Towhees vary according to geographical location.

SIMILAR SPECIES

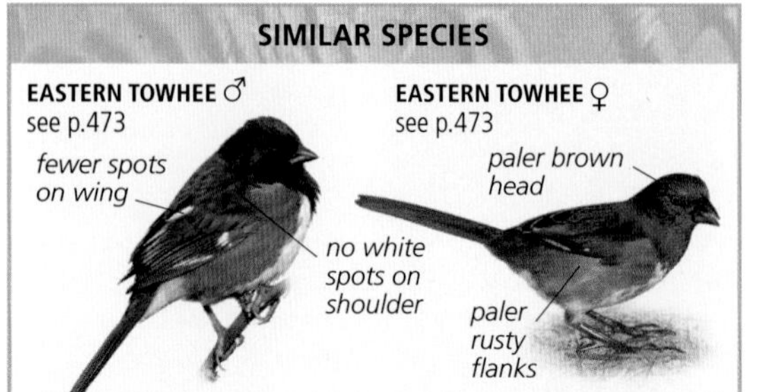
EASTERN TOWHEE ♂
see p.473
fewer spots on wing
no white spots on shoulder
EASTERN TOWHEE ♀
see p.473
paler brown head
paler rusty flanks

OCCURRENCE
Breeds mainly in thickets, shrubby hillsides, and disturbed forests, from south British Columbia and Saskatchewan across the western US, southward to south Oaxaca, Mexico. Winters in the south-central US and western Midwest.

Length **8in (20cm)**	Wingspan **10½in (27cm)**	Weight **1¼–1 9/16oz (35–45g)**
Social **Solitary/Small flocks**	Lifespan **Up to 11 years**	Status **Secure**

Order **Passeriformes**	Family **Emberizidae**	Species ***Pipilo erythrophthalmus***

Eastern Towhee

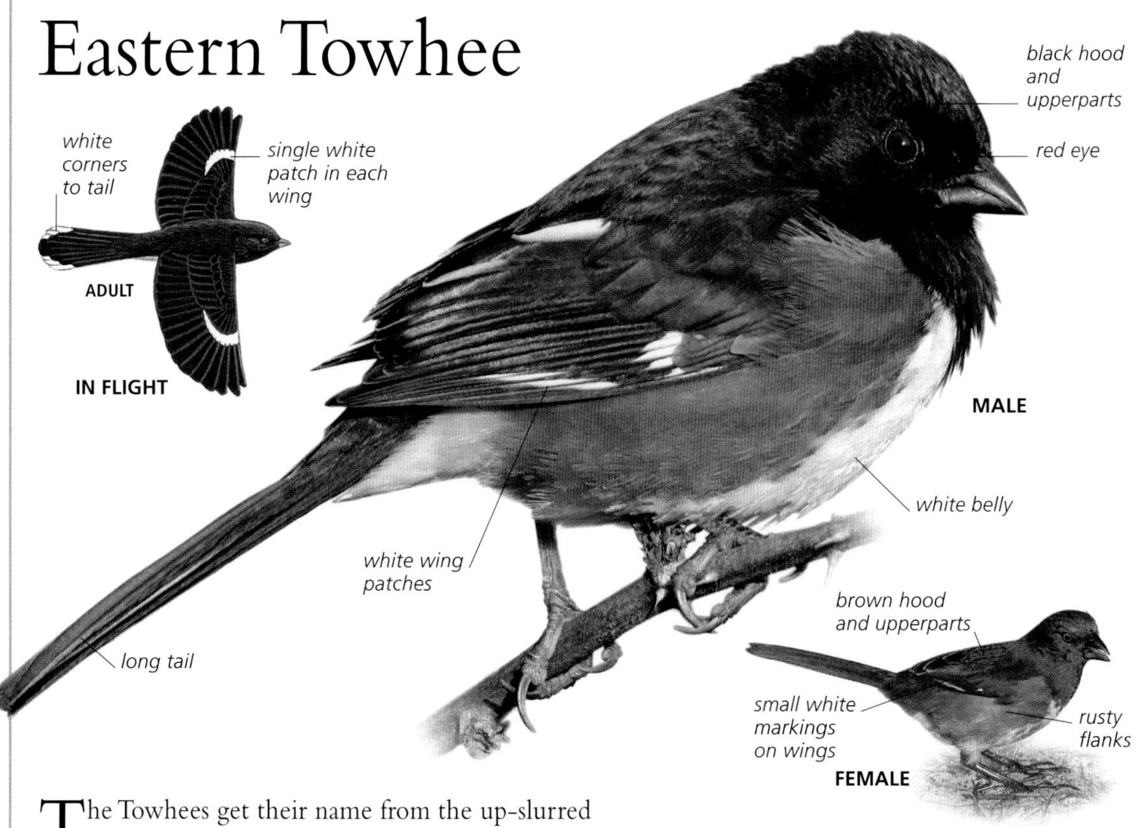

white corners to tail
single white patch in each wing
ADULT
IN FLIGHT
black hood and upperparts
red eye
MALE
white belly
white wing patches
long tail
brown hood and upperparts
small white markings on wings
rusty flanks
FEMALE

The Towhees get their name from the up-slurred *chew-eee* (or *to-whee*) call they make. The Eastern Towhee is famous for its vocalizations and has one of the best-known mnemonics for its song: "drink your tea." The Eastern Towhee was once lumped with Spotted Towhees under the name "Rufous-sided Towhee," because they interbreed in the Great Plains. In the southeastern US, Eastern Towhees have paler eyes the further south they are located; individuals with nearly white eyes are found in Florida. Like all towhees, the Eastern Towhee feeds noisily by jumping backwards with both feet at once to move leaves and reveal the insects and seeds that may be hidden underneath.

VOICE Call a nasal, up-slurred *chew-eee*; flight call *zeeeooooweeet*; song sounds like *dweee, dyooo di-i-i-i-i-i-i-i-i-i-i-i*.

NESTING Large cup in depression on ground under cover, also low in thicket; 3–5 eggs; 1–2 broods; May–August.

FEEDING Eats seeds, fruits, insects, and buds.

FLIGHT: low and direct with much gliding, usually within cover.

TERRESTRIAL LIFE
The bird stays close to the ground, and is usually found not more than a few yards off it.

SIMILAR SPECIES

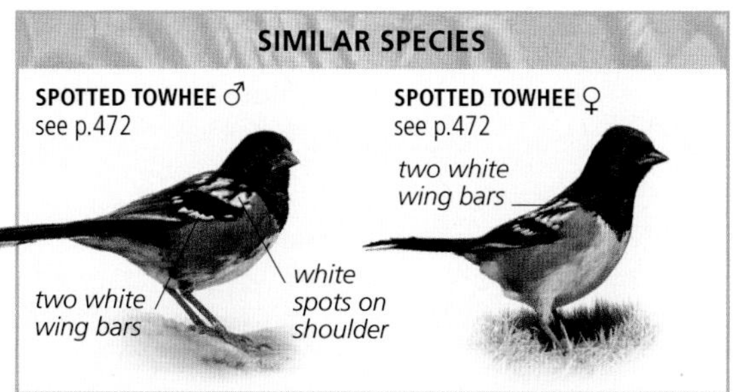

SPOTTED TOWHEE ♂
see p.472
two white wing bars
white spots on shoulder
SPOTTED TOWHEE ♀
see p.472
two white wing bars

OCCURRENCE
Found in dense thickets, woodland, dense shrubbery, forest edges and disturbed forests from southeast Saskatchewan, east Nebraska, west Louisiana, east to south Quebec, south Maine, and south Florida. Retreats from areas north of Chicago to winter in east Texas.

Length **7½–8in (19–20cm)**	Wingspan **10½in (27cm)**	Weight **1¹⁄₁₆–1¾oz (30–50g)**
Social **Solitary/Small flocks**	Lifespan **Up to 12 years**	Status **Declining**

Order **Passeriformes**	Family **Thraupidae**	Species ***Piranga olivacea***

Scarlet Tanager

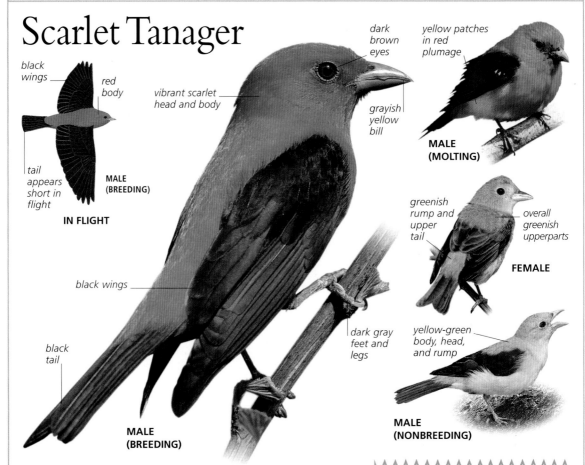

black wings
red body
tail appears short in flight
MALE (BREEDING)
IN FLIGHT

vibrant scarlet head and body
dark brown eyes
grayish yellow bill
black wings
black tail
dark gray feet and legs
MALE (BREEDING)

yellow patches in red plumage
MALE (MOLTING)

greenish rump and upper tail
overall greenish upperparts
FEMALE

yellow-green body, head, and rump
MALE (NONBREEDING)

Although the male Scarlet Tanager, in its breeding plumage, is one of the brightest and most easily identified North American birds, its secretive nature and preference for the canopies of well-shaded oak woodlands makes it difficult to spot. The male is most easily located by its distinctive and easily recognizable song. Male Scarlet Tanagers can vary in appearance—some are orange, not scarlet, and others have a faint reddish wing bar.

VOICE Call a hoarse, drawn out *CHIK-breeer*, often shortened to *CHIK*; flight call an upslurred, whistled *pwee*; song a burry, slurred *querit-queer-query-querit-queer.*

NESTING Loosely woven cup of grass, lined with fine material, high up in tree; 3–5 eggs; 1 brood; May–July.

FEEDING Gleans insects, larvae, fruit, buds, and berries.

FLIGHT: strong and direct; rapid wing beats.

STUNNING MALE
Taking a bath away from the treetops, a male Scarlet Tanager can be seen in all its glory.

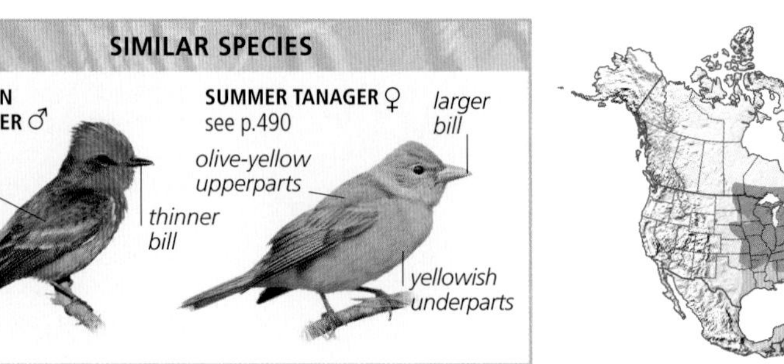
SIMILAR SPECIES
VERMILION FLYCATCHER ♂
see p.495
brown wings and tail
thinner bill
SUMMER TANAGER ♀
see p.490
larger bill
olive-yellow upperparts
yellowish underparts

OCCURRENCE
Breeds in mature deciduous and mixed forests (especially with large oaks) from southern Manitoba and eastern Oklahoma east to the Maritime Provinces and the Carolinas. Trans-Gulf migrant. Winters in varied habitats along the eastern slope of the Andes from eastern Panama to Bolivia.

Length **7in (18cm)**	Wingspan **11½in (29cm)**	Weight **11⁄16–1¼oz (20–35g)**
Social **Solitary/Small flocks**	Lifespan **At least 10 years**	Status **Secure**

Order **Passeriformes**	Family **Thraupidae**	Species ***Piranga ludoviciana***

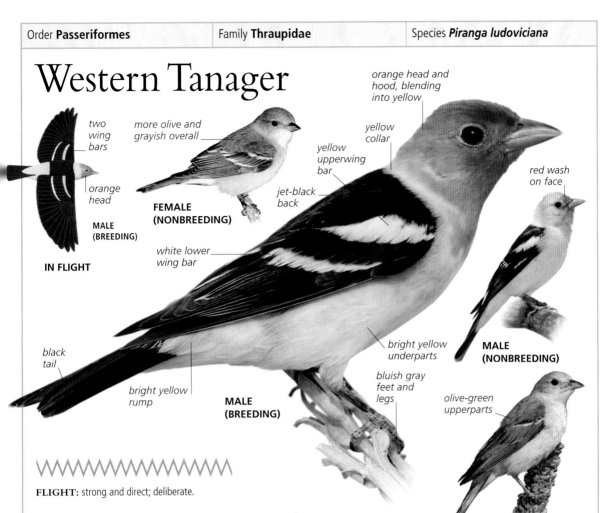

Western Tanager

two wing bars

orange head

MALE (BREEDING)

IN FLIGHT

more olive and grayish overall

FEMALE (NONBREEDING)

orange head and hood, blending into yellow

yellow collar

yellow upperwing bar

jet-black back

white lower wing bar

red wash on face

MALE (NONBREEDING)

black tail

bright yellow rump

MALE (BREEDING)

bright yellow underparts

bluish gray feet and legs

olive-green upperparts

FEMALE (BREEDING)

FLIGHT: strong and direct; deliberate.

The hoarse song of the exquisitely plumaged male Western Tanager is a characteristic sound of coniferous forests in western North America. All *Piranga* tanagers have songs and whistled flight calls that closely resemble those of the *Pheucticus* grosbeaks. Recent studies hint that this is not a coincidence and that *Piranga* tanagers are actually part of the family Cardinalidae, not Thraupidae (tanagers).

VOICE Distinctive call, a rolled *pruh-DHIT!* or *pur-duh-RIT!*; flight call a *hweee*; song similar to Scarlet Tanager, but less burry.

NESTING Loosely woven cup of grasses, lined with rootlets, high in tree; 3–5 eggs; 1 brood; May–August.

FEEDING Forages for insects such as termites, flies, moths, and bees in breeding season; eats berries in nonbreeding season.

ORANGE AND YELLOW
Two Western Tanagers proudly display their bright fall-colored plumage.

SIMILAR SPECIES
SCARLET TANAGER ♀
see p.474
greener overall
lacks bold wing bars

BRIGHT BLEND
This colorful bird blends into its surroundings surprisingly well.

OCCURRENCE
Breeds farther north than any other tanager, in open coniferous and mixed forests of the West, from southeastern Alaska and southwestern Northwest Territories to north Baja California and western Texas. Winters from southern California and northeastern Mexico.

Length **7½in (19cm)**	Wingspan **11½in (29cm)**	Weight **⅞–1¼ oz (25–35g)**
Social **Solitary**	Lifespan **Up to 8 years**	Status **Secure**

Order **Passeriformes**	Family **Cardinalidae**	Species ***Spiza americana***

Dickcissel

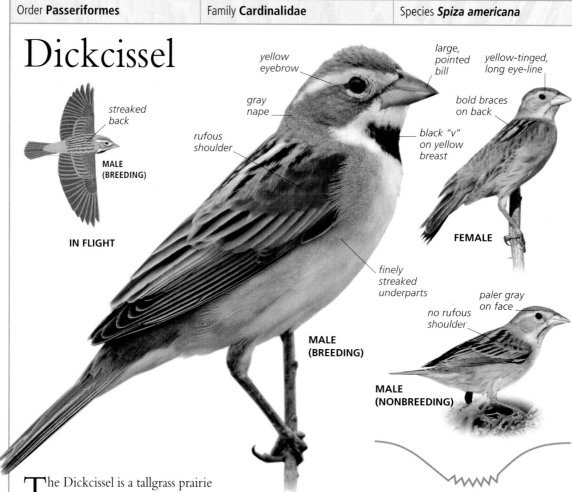

streaked back
MALE (BREEDING)
IN FLIGHT

yellow eyebrow
gray nape
rufous shoulder
large, pointed bill
black "v" on yellow breast
finely streaked underparts
MALE (BREEDING)

yellow-tinged, long eye-line
bold braces on back
FEMALE

paler gray on face
no rufous shoulder
MALE (NONBREEDING)

FLIGHT: strong, direct, and slightly undulating; flocks in tight balls.

The Dickcissel is a tallgrass prairie specialist and seldom breeds outside this core range. Known for its dramatic seasonal movements, the Dickcissel winters in Venezuela, with flocks in tens of thousands ravaging rice fields and damaging seed crops, making it a notorious pest. Immature birds, without yellow and rusty plumage, are very similar to female House Sparrows—vagrant and wintering Dickcissels in North America are often mistaken for sparrows.

VOICE Call a flat *chik*; flight call a distinctive, low, electric buzz *frrrrrrt*; song a short series of sharp, insect-like stutters followed by few longer chirps or trill *dick-dick-dick-SISS-SISS-suhl.*

NESTING Bulky cup placed near ground in dense vegetation; 3–6 eggs; 1–2 broods; May–August.

FEEDING Forages on ground for insects, spiders, and seeds.

UNIQUE SONG
The Dickcissel's onomatopoetic song is the classic sound of a healthy tallgrass prairie.

SIMILAR SPECIES

HOUSE SPARROW ♀ see p.376
shorter bill
no streaking on underparts

EASTERN MEADOWLARK see p.439
longer bill
shorter tail
bright yellow underparts

OCCURRENCE
Breeds in tallgrass prairie, grassland, hayfields, unmown roadsides, and untilled cropfields across eastern central US. Barely reaches southernmost Canada and northeast Mexico. Winters in huge flocks in Venezuela, in open areas with tall grass-like vegetation, including rice fields.

Length **6½in (16cm)**	Wingspan **9½in (24cm)**	Weight **⅞–1¼oz (25–35g)**
Social **Large flocks**	Lifespan **Up to 5 years**	Status **Declining**

Order **Passeriformes**	Family **Cardinalidae**	Species ***Pheucticus ludovicianus***

Rose-breasted Grosbeak

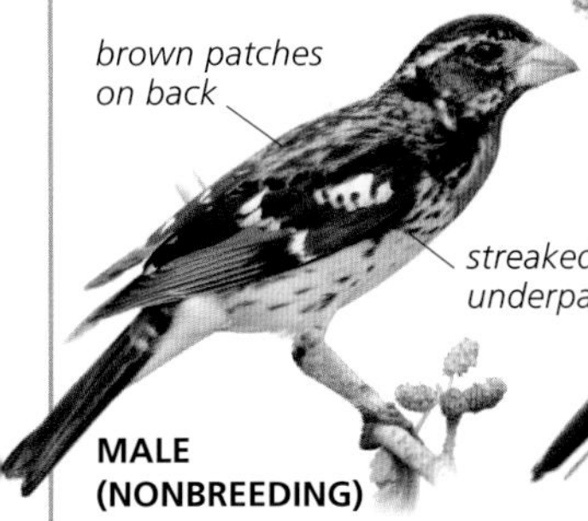

white rump
MALE (BREEDING)
IN FLIGHT
short tail with white corners
IMMATURE MALE (1ST FALL)
rosy or orange breast
white marks on head
white wing bars
large, pinkish bill
thick streaks on underparts
FEMALE
brown patches on back
streaked underparts
MALE (NONBREEDING)
black head and back
bold, white wing patches
rose-red breast
white belly
MALE (BREEDING)

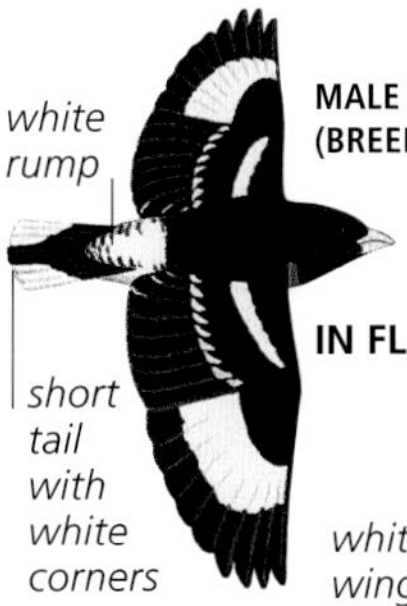

For many birdwatchers in the East, the appearance of a flock of dazzling male Rose-breasted Grosbeaks in early May signals the peak of spring songbird migration. Adult males in their tuxedo attire, with rose-red ties, are unmistakable, but females and immature males are more somber. In the fall, immature male Rose-breasted Grosbeaks often have orange breasts, and are commonly mistaken for female Black-headed Grosbeaks. The difference is in the pink wing lining usually visible on perched birds, pink bill, and streaking across the center of the breast.

VOICE Call a high, sharp, explosive *sink* or *eeuk*, reminiscent of the squeak of sneakers on floor tiles, flight call an airy *vreee*; song a liquid, flute-like warble, rather slow in delivery, almost relaxed.

NESTING Loose, open cup or platform, usually in deciduous saplings, mid to high level; 2–5 eggs; 1–2 broods; May–July.

FEEDING Eats arthropods, fruit, seeds, and buds.

FLIGHT: undulating but powerful flight with bursts of wing beats.

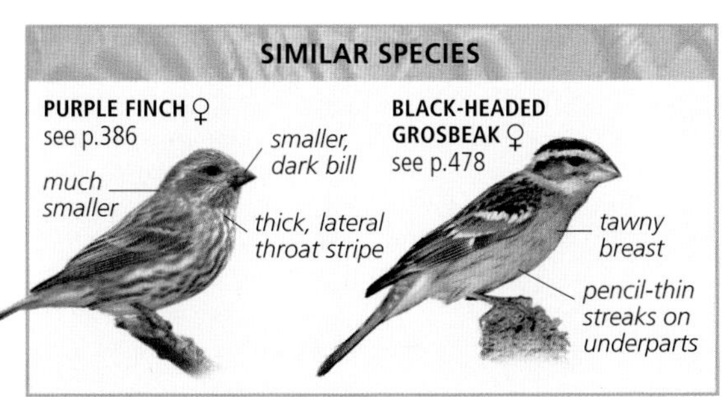
SIMILAR SPECIES
PURPLE FINCH ♀
see p.386
much smaller
smaller, dark bill
thick, lateral throat stripe
BLACK-HEADED GROSBEAK ♀
see p.478
tawny breast
pencil-thin streaks on underparts

STUNNING MALE
A striking male Rose-breasted Grosbeak in springtime is quite unmistakable on a tree.

OCCURRENCE
Breeds in deciduous and mixed woods, parks, and orchards across the northeastern quarter of the US, and across Canada westward from Newfoundland through Ontario to southeast Yukon. Winters from Mexico and the Caribbean, south to Guyana and Peru. Rare in the West.

Length **8in (20cm)**	Wingspan **12½in (32cm)**	Weight **1¼–2oz (35–55g)**
Social **Solitary/Small flocks**	Lifespan **Up to 13 years**	Status **Secure**

Order **Passeriformes**	Family **Cardinalidae**	Species ***Pheucticus melanocephalus***

Black-headed Grosbeak

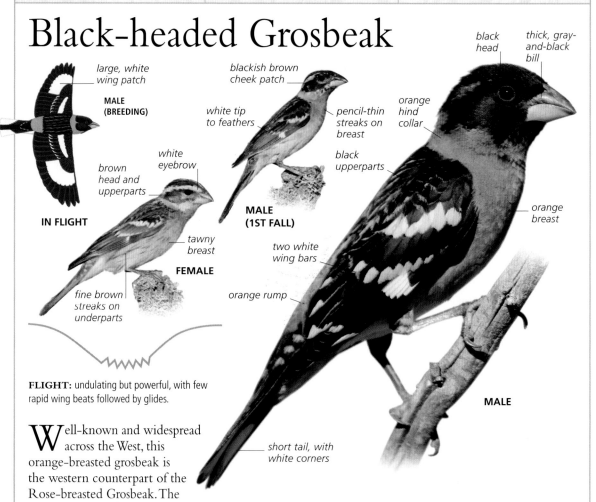

large, white wing patch

MALE (BREEDING)

IN FLIGHT

blackish brown cheek patch

white tip to feathers

pencil-thin streaks on breast

MALE (1ST FALL)

white eyebrow

brown head and upperparts

tawny breast

FEMALE

fine brown streaks on underparts

black head

thick, gray-and-black bill

orange hind collar

black upperparts

orange breast

two white wing bars

orange rump

short tail, with white corners

MALE

FLIGHT: undulating but powerful, with few rapid wing beats followed by glides.

Well-known and widespread across the West, this orange-breasted grosbeak is the western counterpart of the Rose-breasted Grosbeak. The two species are closely related, despite their color differences, and interbreed where their ranges meet in the Great Plains. The Black-headed Grosbeak is aggressive on its breeding grounds, with both sexes fighting off intruders.

VOICE Call a *hwik*, similar to Rose-breasted Grosbeak, but flatter, "hollow," and less squeaky; song generally higher, faster, less fluid, and harsher.

NESTING Loose, open cup or platform, usually in deciduous sapling, not far above eye level; 3–5 eggs; 1–2 broods; May–September.

FEEDING Gleans insects and spiders; also eats seeds and fruit.

STREAMSIDE SONGSTER
Through much of its range, this species is common along riverside corridors containing a variety of trees.

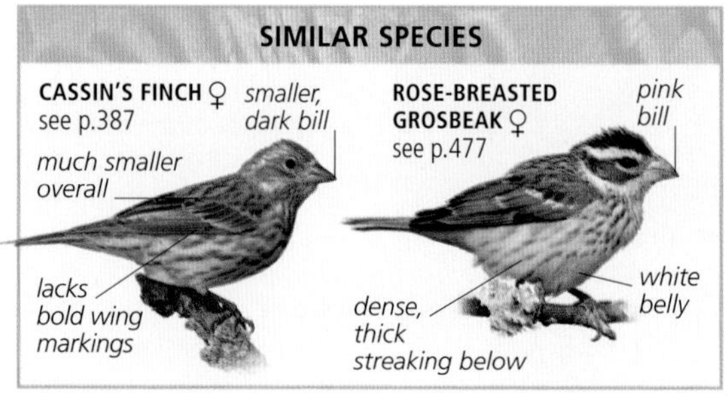
SIMILAR SPECIES
CASSIN'S FINCH ♀
see p.387
smaller, dark bill
much smaller overall
lacks bold wing markings
ROSE-BREASTED GROSBEAK ♀
see p.477
pink bill
white belly
dense, thick streaking below

OCCURRENCE
Breeds in dense deciduous growth—old fields, hedgerows, next to waterways, disturbed forests, and hillside thickets—from British Columbia and Saskatchewan, south to Baja California, and central Mexico. Winters in interior, highlands, and Pacific slope of Mexico.

Length **8½in (21cm)**	Wingspan **12½in (32cm)**	Weight **1$\frac{7}{16}$–2oz (40–55g)**
Social **Solitary/Small flocks**	Lifespan **Up to 9 years**	Status **Secure**

Order **Passeriformes**	Family **Cardinalidae**	Species ***Cardinalis cardinalis***

Northern Cardinal

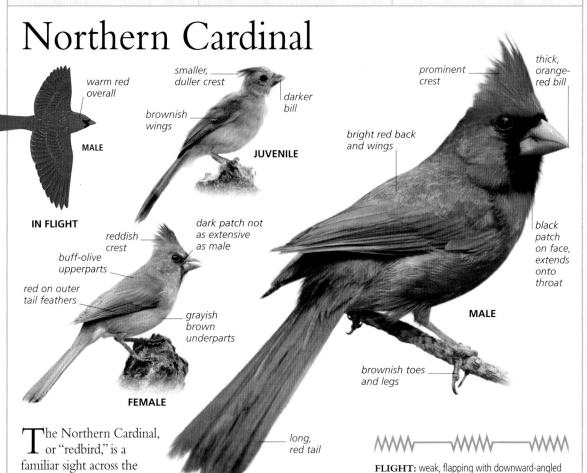

warm red overall
MALE
IN FLIGHT
smaller, duller crest
darker bill
brownish wings
JUVENILE
reddish crest
dark patch not as extensive as male
buff-olive upperparts
red on outer tail feathers
grayish brown underparts
FEMALE
prominent crest
thick, orange-red bill
bright red back and wings
black patch on face, extends onto throat
MALE
brownish toes and legs
long, red tail

The Northern Cardinal, or "redbird," is a familiar sight across the eastern US and southeastern Canada. Its range was expanding in the early- to mid-20th century, when state birds were being chosen, and was considered a novelty at the time; as a result, it is the state bird of seven different states. The male aggressively repels intruders and will occasionally attack his reflection in windows and various shiny surfaces.

VOICE Sharp, metallic *tik* call, also bubbly chatters; song a loud, variable, sweet, slurred whistle, *tsee-ew-tsee-ew-whoit-whoit-whoit-whoit-whoit.*

NESTING Loose, flimsy cup of grass, bark, and leaves, in deciduous thicket; 2–4 eggs; 1–3 broods; April–September.

FEEDING Eats seeds and insects, such as beetles and caterpillars; also buds and fruit.

FLIGHT: weak, flapping with downward-angled tail; interrupted by short glides; low within cover.

CONSPICUOUS COLOR
This Northern Cardinal's vivid plumage means that it is often easy to spot on snowy winter days.

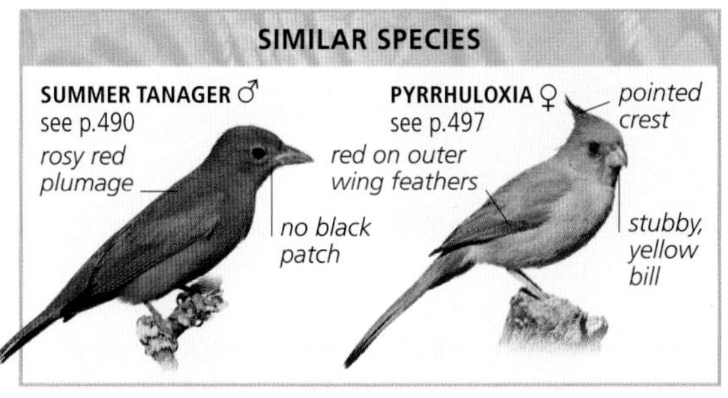
SIMILAR SPECIES
SUMMER TANAGER ♂
see p.490
rosy red plumage
no black patch
PYRRHULOXIA ♀
see p.497
pointed crest
red on outer wing feathers
stubby, yellow bill

OCCURRENCE
Resident in thickets of various relatively moist habitats, such as deciduous woodland, scrub, desert washes, and backyards. Range spans across the eastern US, southernmost Canada, the extreme Southwest, and south into Mexico, northern Guatemala, and northern Belize.

Length **8½in (22cm)**	Wingspan **12in (30cm)**	Weight **$1\frac{7}{16}$–$1\frac{3}{4}$oz (40–50g)**
Social **Solitary**	Lifespan **Up to 16 years**	Status **Secure**

Order **Passeriformes**	Family **Cardinalidae**	Species ***Passerina cyanea***

Indigo Bunting

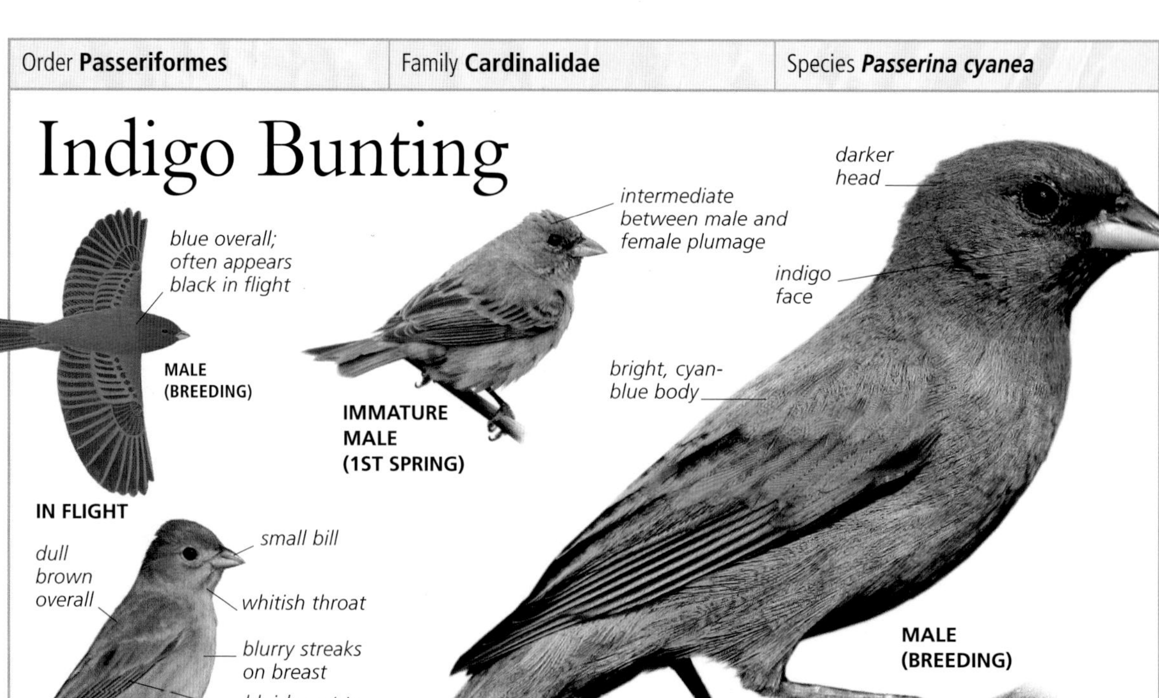
blue overall; often appears black in flight
MALE (BREEDING)
IN FLIGHT
intermediate between male and female plumage
IMMATURE MALE (1ST SPRING)
darker head
indigo face
bright, cyan-blue body
MALE (BREEDING)
small bill
dull brown overall
whitish throat
blurry streaks on breast
bluish cast to wings and tail
FEMALE

Few North American birds are more brilliantly colored than the Indigo Bunting. However, it is not particularly well named, because the bird is really not indigo but rather a vibrant, almost cyan-blue. The color only turns to indigo on the male's head before finally becoming a rich violet on the face. Indigo Buntings are specialists of disturbed habitats, originally depending on tree-falls within forests and the grassland-forest edge. Human activity, however, has radically increased suitable breeding habitats. As a result, Indigo Buntings are much more common and widespread than they were a hundred years ago. This adaptable species has even learned to nest in cornfields.

FLIGHT: lightly undulating, fast, and direct; gliding and fluttering in territorial encounters.

VOICE Call a sharp, dry, rattling *pik*!; flight a call long buzz; song series of simple, high-pitched, paired whistles, often described as "*fire!-fire*!, *where*?-*where*?, *there*!-*there*!, *put-it-out*!, *put-it-out*!"

NESTING Open cup above ground in dense tangle or shrub; 3–4 eggs; 1–3 broods; May–September.

FEEDING Eats seeds, insects, fruits, and buds.

SOUND OF SUMMER
This is one of the most common and cheerful songbirds found in eastern North America.

OCCURRENCE
Breeds in moist disturbed habitats—weedy fields, forest edges, and areas of heavy cultivation across the eastern US, southeastern Canada, and also locally in the Southwest. Winters from Mexico and the Caribbean south to Panama, and in small numbers along the Gulf Coast and in Florida.

SIMILAR SPECIES

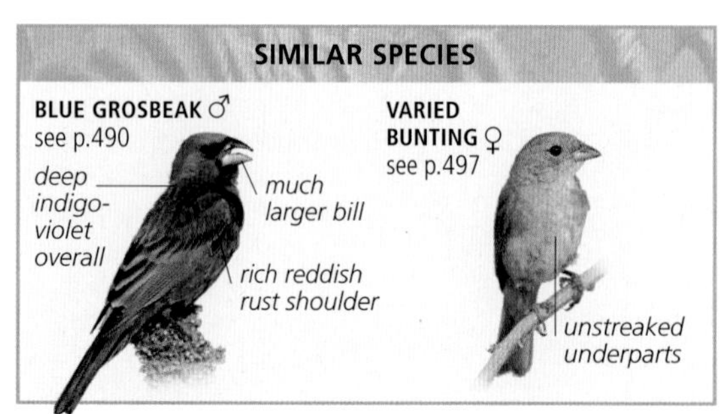
BLUE GROSBEAK ♂
see p.490
deep indigo-violet overall
much larger bill
rich reddish rust shoulder
VARIED BUNTING ♀
see p.497
unstreaked underparts

Length **5½in (14cm)**	Wingspan **8in (20cm)**	Weight **7/16–11/16oz (12–19g)**
Social **Large flocks**	Lifespan **Up to 11 years**	Status **Secure**

Order **Passeriformes**	Family **Cardinalidae**	Species ***Passerina amoena***

Lazuli Bunting

bold, white wing bars

MALE (BREEDING)

IN FLIGHT

blue tinge to wings and tail

tawny breast

unstreaked underparts

FEMALE

sky-blue head

mantle tinged with brown

dull orange breast

conspicuous white shoulder

white belly

MALE

sky-blue rump

white shoulder

bluish rump

whitish belly

IMMATURE MALE (1ST SPRING)

Resembling a small bluebird, the dazzling Lazuli Bunting is the Indigo Bunting's western counterpart. The two species are closely related and hybrids are locally common where the two species meet on the Great Plains. Male hybrids are of two main types—the first resembles an Indigo Bunting with a white belly and wing bars, and the second resembles a dull Indigo Bunting with a brownish smudged back. Females may be impossible to identify. The Lazuli Bunting's common name is taken from the blue, semiprecious gemstone, lapis lazuli.

VOICE Call a sharp, dry, rattling *pik!* similar to Indigo Bunting; song a higher, faster, thinner, and with less repetition than Indigo Bunting.

NESTING Open cup above ground in dense tangle or shrub; 3–4 eggs; 1–2 broods; April–August.

FEEDING Eats seeds and fruits; insects if breeding.

FLIGHT: lightly undulating, fast, and direct; erratic flights during territorial encounters.

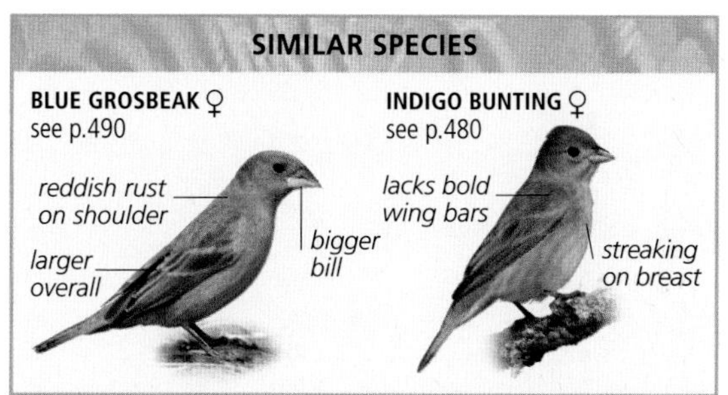
SIMILAR SPECIES
BLUE GROSBEAK ♀
see p.490
reddish rust on shoulder
larger overall
bigger bill
INDIGO BUNTING ♀
see p.480
lacks bold wing bars
streaking on breast

DAPPLED AND DAPPER
Brightly colored males blend into their surroundings surprisingly well in dappled sunlight.

OCCURRENCE
Breeds in various open, disturbed habitats, especially alongside waterways and in thickets from southern British Columbia and southern Saskatchewan to northern Baja California and northern New Mexico. Winters from southern Arizona to southwestern Mexico. Casual in the East.

Length **5½in (14cm)**	Wingspan **8½in (22cm)**	Weight **7/16–5/8oz (13–18g)**
Social **Large flocks**	Lifespan **Up to 10 years**	Status **Secure**

RARE SPECIES

Family **Anatidae** | Species ***Anas penelope***

Eurasian Wigeon

The adult male Eurasian Wigeon is distinctive with its bright chestnut head and broad, creamy yellow forehead. Its bold white forewing, with a green patch bordered in black, is conspicuous in flight. In recent decades, the number of Eurasian Wigeons recorded has increased, particularly in the Pacific Northwest.

OCCURRENCE Winters regularly on both Atlantic and Pacific coasts, with small numbers found inland.

VOICE Males a high-pitched, whistled *wheeeo*; females a low, growling *krrr* or *karr*.

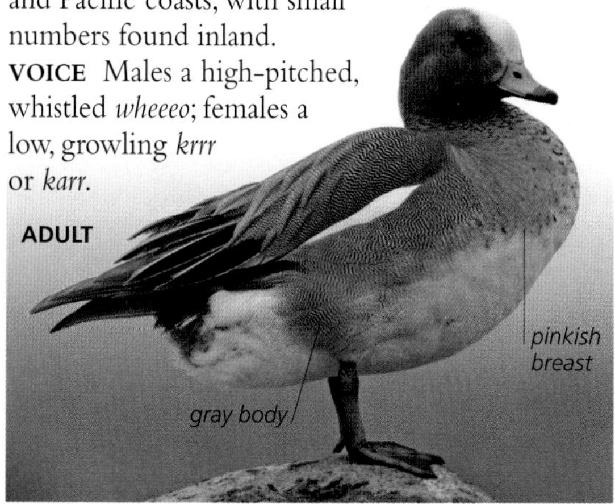
ADULT
pinkish breast
gray body

Length **17½–20in (45–51cm)** | Wingspan **30–34in (75–86cm)**

Family **Anatidae** | Species ***Anas querquedula***

Garganey

The Garganey is a small dabbling duck, the same size and shape as the Blue-winged Teal. A male in breeding plumage is unmistakable, its bold white eyebrow contrasting sharply with its dark brown head. In flight, it has a silver-gray forewing with a broad, white trailing edge.

OCCURRENCE Native to Eurasia, records span North America; prefers wetland habitats with emergent vegetation.

VOICE Male a low, dry rattling *knerek* or *kerrek* call; female a high-pitched quack.

gray sides contrast with brown breast
bold white eyebrow extends to nape
MALE

Length **14½–16in (37–41cm)** | Wingspan **23½–25in (60–64cm)**

Family **Anatidae** | Species ***Polysticta stelleri***

Steller's Eider

The smallest of the four species of eiders, Steller's Eider resembles a dabbling duck, with its steeper forehead, flatter crown, and the way that it floats higher on the water. In late winter, large groups dive in unison to feed, creating a spray.

OCCURRENCE Pacific population breeds mainly in Russia's far northeast; small numbers breed in Alaska. Can winter as far south as Queen Charlotte Islands.

VOICE Female a rapid, harsh growling call; also loud *qua-haaa* or *cooay*; males growl but are mostly silent.

flat crown
rufous-cream belly and breast
ADULT

Length **17–18in (43–46cm)** | Wingspan **28–30in (70–76cm)**

Family **Procellariidae** | Species ***Puffinus bulleri***

Buller's Shearwater

Like other species of tubenoses that occur occasionally off the west coast of North America, this migrant breeds on islands off New Zealand. Abundant, yet threatened by long-line fishing operations, Buller's Shearwater is the only silvery gray *Puffinus* species to show a black zigzag wing pattern that is found in North American waters.

OCCURRENCE Breeds at Poor Knights Island, New Zealand. Uncommon but regular in open ocean off British Columbia during the late summer and fall.

VOICE Silent at sea; strange wailing calls at colonies.

dark zigzag pattern
dark-gray cap
long, dark, wedge-shaped tail
ADULT

Length **18–18½in (46–47cm)** | Wingspan **38–39in (97–99cm)**

Family **Procellariidae** | Species ***Puffinus carneipes***

Flesh-footed Shearwater

The Flesh-footed Shearwater, an uncommon visitor to the nutrient-rich marine waters off the Pacific coast of North America, can be found in large numbers with other tubenoses. It is distinguished from the Sooty and Short-tailed shearwaters by its dark color and pink bill and legs.

OCCURRENCE Two breeding populations: one in the southwest Pacific Ocean, the other in the Indian Ocean; occasional summer visitor to open ocean off British Columbia northward to Alaska.

VOICE Silent at sea; mewing calls at the breeding sites at night.

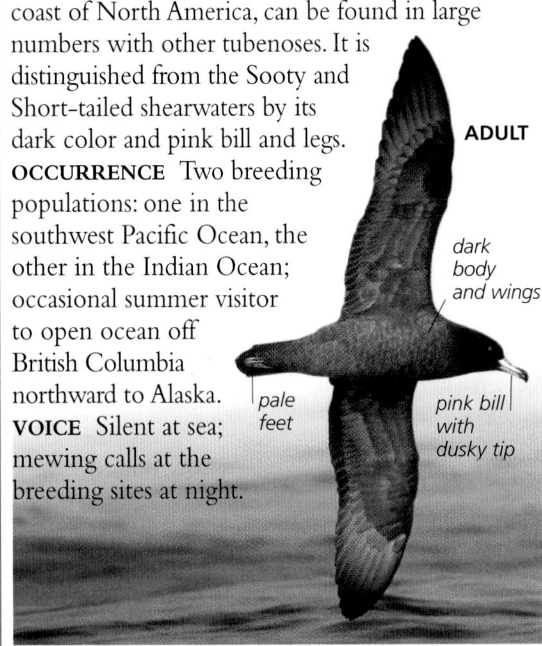
ADULT
dark body and wings
pale feet
pink bill with dusky tip

Length **18in (46cm)** | Wingspan **4½ft (1.4m)**

Family **Ardeidae** | Species ***Nyctanassa violacea***

Yellow-crowned Night-Heron

The Yellow-crowned Night-Heron was unaffected by the 19th century plume hunting trade. It then expanded northward in the 20th century, but has since retreated slightly from the northern edge of its range. It can be seen in wooded areas.

OCCURRENCE Breeds near wetlands in southeastern US and along coast up to Canadian Maritimes; also likes being near houses in wooded habitat.

VOICE Call an abrupt *quark* or *wok*, higher pitched than Black-crowned Night Heron; most vocal in the mornings, and after dusk.

ADULT
thick, black bill

Length **19½–28in (50–70cm)** | Wingspan **3¼–3½ft (1–1.1m)**

Family **Rallidae** | Species ***Porphyrio martinica***

Purple Gallinule

The Purple Gallinue is conspicuous due to its vibrant coloring. Well known for long distance vagrancy far outside its normal breeding range, it has been found in Labrador, Switzerland, and South Africa.

OCCURRENCE Breeds and winters in freshwater marshes in the southeastern US; occasionally shows up in southern Ontario east to the Maritimes.

VOICE Call a chicken-like clucking; also grunts and higher-pitched single notes.

ADULT (BREEDING)
dark blue breast and belly

Length **13in (33cm)** | Wingspan **22in (56cm)**

Family **Charadridae** | Species ***Charadrius hiaticula***

Ringed Plover

The Ringed Plover is widespread in Eurasia. It also breeds in North America, where it only overlaps with the closely related Semipalmated Plover locally on Baffin Island. This species does not have toe webbing, and usually has a wider black breastband than its Semipalmated cousin.

OCCURRENCE Breeds on St. Lawrence and St. Matthew Islands in Alaska, and in the Canadian Arctic Archipelago (Baffin, Bylot, Ellesmere).

VOICE Soft, mellow two-note *poo-eep* from the ground or in flight.

brown upperparts

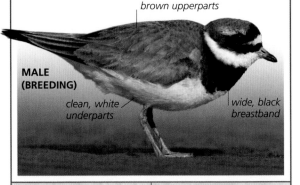

MALE (BREEDING)

clean, white underparts

wide, black breastband

Length **7–8in (18–20cm)** | Wingspan **19–22½in (48–57cm)**

Family **Charadriidae**	Species ***Charadrius wilsonia***

Wilson's Plover

Wilson's Plover is the largest of the North American *Charadrius* species. Its distinctive habit of running horizontally, low to the ground, is a familiar sight on beaches. Wilson's Plover was listed as a species of "high concern" in 2000.

OCCURRENCE Found primarily in coastal habitats (beaches, sand dunes), mostly in the southeast, but sometimes up into Nova Scotia.

VOICE Flight call a short *pip*, or *pi-dit*; alarm calls include slurred whistle *tweet*, and short whistled *peet*.

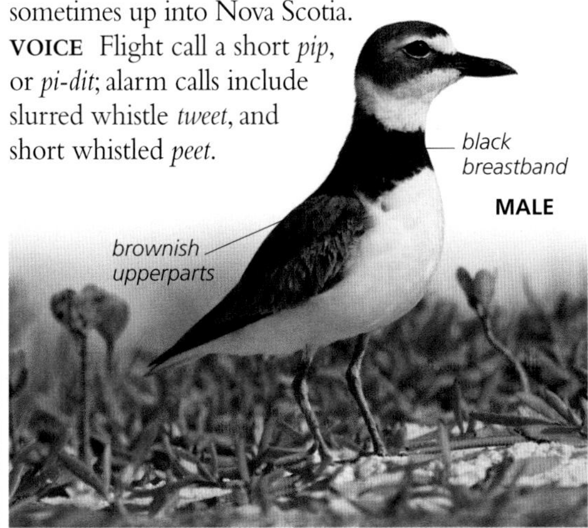
black breastband
MALE
brownish upperparts

Length **6½–8in (16–20cm)**	Wingspan **15½–19½in (39–49cm)**

Family **Charadriidae**	Species ***Charadrius alexandrinus***

Snowy Plover

The smallest and palest of all North American plovers, the Snowy Plover's cryptic coloration blends in well with its beach and dune habitat. The species is designated as threatened, due to habitat destruction

OCCURRENCE Breeds on open beach and dune habitats on the Pacific and Gulf coasts; occasionally shows up in western Canada.

VOICE Repeated *tow-heet*; *purrt* and single *churr* during breeding, tinkling *ti* at roosts or before flight.

short, stubby bill
MALE (BREEDING)
grayish to pinkish legs

Length **6–6½in (15–17cm)**	Wingspan **16–18in (41–46cm)**

Family **Scolopacidae**	Species ***Calidris ruficollis***

Red-necked Stint

This small Siberian stint or peep is very similar to nonbreeding and juvenile Semipalmated Sandpipers. However, it has a more slim and tapered body; slimmer, finer-tipped bill; and unwebbed toes. Breeding birds have a rich, rufous-orange face, throat, and upper breast, with spotted breast sides.

OCCURRENCE Uncommon migrant and rare breeder in western Alaska; rare, but annual migrant along Pacific coast.

VOICE Flight call rough *kiirp*, similar to Semipalmated Sandpiper but usually higher pitched.

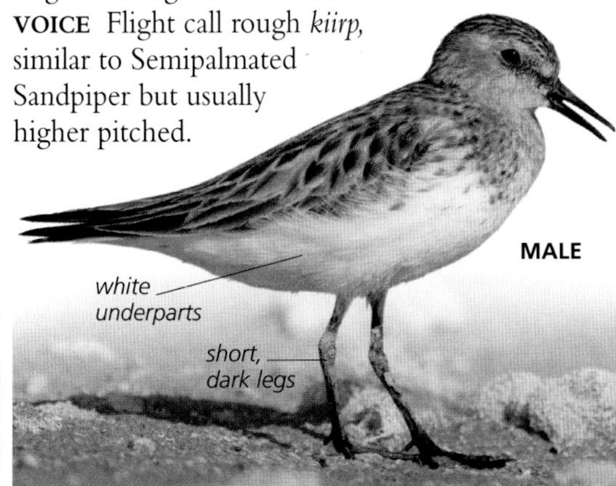
MALE
white underparts
short, dark legs

Length **5–6½in (13–16cm)**	Wingspan **14–15in (35–38cm)**

Family **Scolopacidae**	Species ***Calidris acuminata***

Sharp-tailed Sandpiper

This intermediate-sized sandpiper is similar to the Pectoral Sandpiper, but breeds only in Siberia. It is slightly rounder in body shape than the Pectoral Sandpiper with longer legs and a shorter, slimmer bill. Breeding birds have rufous caps, a buff wash on the face and breast, and V-shaped breast markings.

OCCURRENCE Accidental in spring but common in fall in western Alaska; rare fall migrant along Pacific Coast; accidental in fall elsewhere in North America.

VOICE Call a rolled, soft *prrrt*.

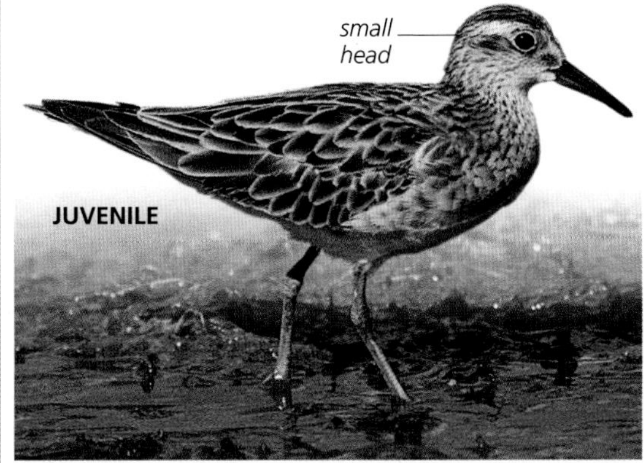
small head
JUVENILE

Length **6¾–8in (17–20cm)**	Wingspan **16½–19in (42–48cm)**

Family **Scolopacidae** | Species ***Calidris ferruginea***

Curlew Sandpiper

The Curlew Sandpiper is a medium-sized sandpiper that breeds in northern Siberia. It resembles the Dunlin and Stilt Sandpiper in nonbreeding plumage. It is slimmer than the Dunlin, with longer wings, neck, legs, and bill, and differs from the nonbreeding Stilt Sandpiper by its shorter legs and faint white eyebrow.
OCCURRENCE Rare, but regular migrant on Pacific Coast; accidental elsewhere.
VOICE Flight call musical, trilled, or rolled *chrreep,* dropping in the middle.

JUVENILE
black legs
long decurved bill

Length **7–7½in (18–19cm)** | Wingspan **16½–18in (42–46cm)**

Family **Scolopacidae** | Species ***Philomachus pugnax***

Ruff

The Ruff is well known for the elaborately colored head ruffs and tufts of breeding male birds. Males are 20 percent larger than the females (known as Reeves), which are more muted in appearance.
OCCURRENCE Rare migrant along Pacific coast, occasional in St. Lawrence River and Great Lakes.
VOICE Mostly silent; occasionally gives a soft *krruk.*

short, slightly drooped bill
JUVENILE (FALL)

Length **8–12in (20–30cm)** | Wingspan **19–23in (48–58cm)**

Family **Laridae** | Species ***Larus schistisagus***

Slaty-backed Gull

This rare visitor from eastern Russia and Japan is most likely to be confused with the Western Gull. Adults have a series of white spots on the outer wing feather tips, referred to as "a string of pearls." Winter adults have heavily streaked heads with white linings to their underwings that contrast with the gray outer and inner wing feathers.
OCCURRENCE Occurs occasionally in northern and southwestern British Columbia; accidental in winter across Canada and US.
VOICE Slow *aah-aah-aah.*

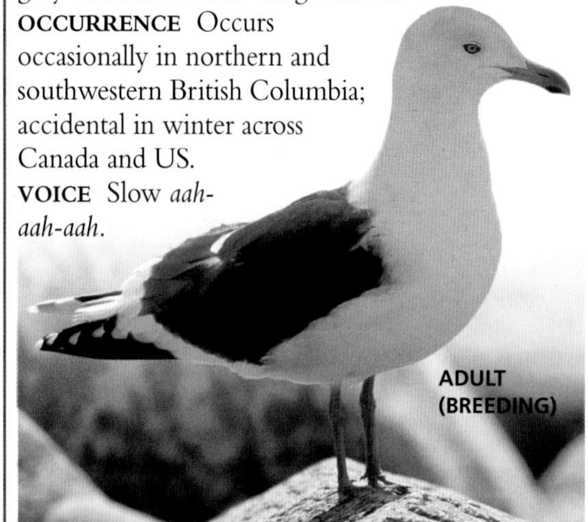
ADULT (BREEDING)

Length **24–26in (61–66cm)** | Wingspan **4½–5ft (1.4–1.5m)**

Family **Laridae** | Species ***Rhodostethia rosea***

Ross's Gull

In adult breeding plumage, this small, delicate gull is unmistakable. Dove-gray upperparts, pale-pink underparts, red legs, and a black collar, make it an elegant and beautiful-looking bird.
OCCURRENCE Siberian breeder found only along Alaskan north coast in fall; expanded as a breeding bird into Arctic Canada; winter strays found across Canada and to northeast and northwest US.
VOICE Rarely heard in winter; tern-like *kik-kik-kik.*

black "necklace"
wedge-shaped tail
ADULT (BREEDING)

Length **11½–12in (29–31cm)** | Wingspan **35–39in (90–100cm)**

Family **Laridae** | Species ***Pagophila eburnea***

Ivory Gull

The Ivory Gull, all white with black legs, is unlikely to be confused with any other gull. Adults are pure white in summer and winter. Juveniles are patterned to varying degrees with black spots on the tips of their flight feathers, and tail and wing outer feathers, and they have a smudgy black face.

OCCURRENCE High Arctic breeder; rarely strays far south of the pack ice, even in winter; casual in winter to British Columbia and Maritime Provinces; accidental elsewhere.

VOICE Tern-like, harsh *keeuur*; rarely heard away from breeding grounds.

pure white plumage
yellow-tipped slate-blue bill
ADULT
black legs

Length **15½–17in (40–43cm)** | Wingspan **3½–4ft (1.1–1.2m)**

Family **Laridae** | Species ***Sternula antillarum***

Least Tern

The Least Tern is the smallest of the North American terns and, in summer, its distinctive black cap and white forehead distinguish it from other members of its family. In the 19th century their numbers declined. They have rebounded but are now threatened by ongoing habitat loss.

OCCURRENCE Breeds along both coasts, major rivers, lakes, reservoirs; favors sandy areas such as beaches and sandbars. Scattered sightings across Canada.

VOICE Extremely vocal during breeding; a high-pitched *ki-deek, ki-deek*; also a rapid, almost non-stop chatter.

ADULT (BREEDING)
yellow bill
two dark outer wing feathers

Length **8½–9in (21–23cm)** | Wingspan **19–21in (48–53cm)**

Family **Stercorariidae** | Species ***Stercorarius skua***

Great Skua

Similar to the South Polar Skua, this large and aggressive predator and scavenger can be differentiated by its heavier streaking and more reddish tones to its brown body. Known in Scotland as the "bonxie," a name with nordic origins, the Great Skua is closely related to several species of southern skuas including the Falkland Skua.

OCCURRENCE Rare visitor, mostly in fall through spring, to pelagic waters off the Atlantic Coast of North America.

VOICE Rough, cackling *rah-rah-rah*.

dark nape
mottled gray to warm brown plumage
hooked, dark bill
ADULT

Length **19½–23in (50–58cm)** | Wingspan **4–4½ft (1.2–1.4m)**

Family **Columbidae** | Species ***Zenaida asiatica***

White-winged Dove

This large gray-colored dove is best identified in flight by the conspicuous white bands on its wings. Perched birds display bright blue skin around orange eyes and longish, square tails with white tips. This species has been expanding its population northwards into Canada in recent decades.

OCCURRENCE Breeds and winters in dense, thorny woodlands, deserts, orchards, and residential areas. It is now expanding north into Canada.

VOICE Distinctive, drawn-out cooing: *who-cooks-for-you*; also makes five-note variation from the nest: *la-coo-kla-coo-kla*.

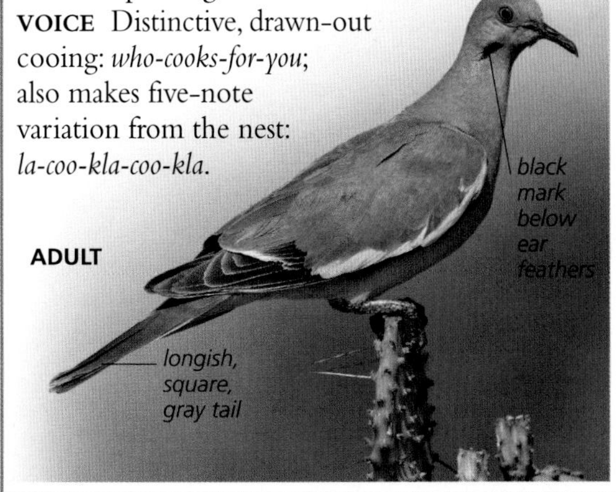
black mark below ear feathers
ADULT
longish, square, gray tail

Length **11½in (29cm)** | Wingspan **19in (48cm)**

Family **Caprimulgidae** | Species ***Chordeiles acutipennis***

Lesser Nighthawk

Well camouflaged while resting on the ground during daytime, the Lesser Nighthawk is a wide-ranging airborne forager, most active at dusk and dawn, sweeping low in pursuit of insect prey. Its distinctive trill distinguishes it from the Common Nighthawk.

OCCURRENCE Breeds in desert or open scrub and along watercourses. Occurs from the southern US down to South America; is spreading northward to Canada.

VOICE Low, trilled whistle lasting up to 12 seconds and resembling calling toad.

huge eye
tiny bill
MALE

Length **8–9in (20–23cm)** | Wingspan **21–23in (53–58cm)**

Family **Caprimulgidae** | Species ***Caprimulgus carolinensis***

Chuck-will's-widow

The larger of the two species of North American nightjar and least known, the Chuck-will's-widow is very tolerant of human development and nests in suburban and urban areas. It often feeds by flying continuously and catching its prey in the air, hunting mostly at dawn and dusk but also during a full moon.

OCCURRENCE Breeds in mixed forests and in open fields. Found mainly in the eastern US; sometimes seen in Ontario and the Maritimes.

VOICE Whistled *chuck-will's-wid-ow*; begins softly, then increases in volume with emphasis on the two middle syllables.

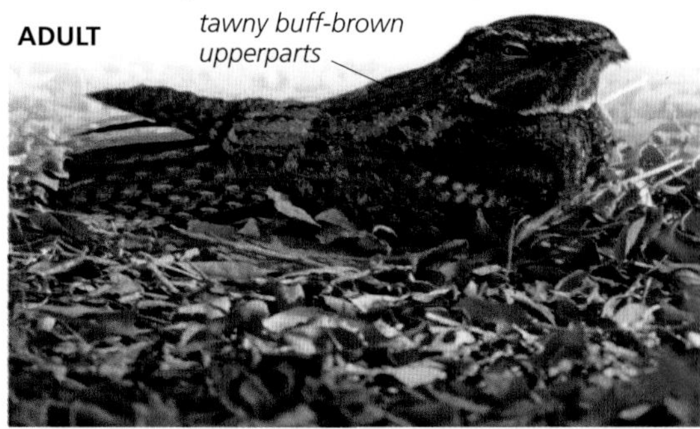
ADULT
tawny buff-brown upperparts

Length **11–12½in (28–32cm)** | Wingspan **25–28in (63–70cm)**

Family **Tyrannidae** | Species ***Tyrannus forficatus***

Scissor-tailed Flycatcher

Often perched on a wire or fence, the Scissor-tailed Flycatcher also has a spectacular aerial courtship display, with its long tail streaming behind it. Its nest incorporates many human products, such as string, cloth, and paper. Pre-migratory roosting flocks during late summer consist of 100 to 1,000 birds.

OCCURRENCE Breeds in southern states and into Mexico; savanna, open grasslands, pastures, and golf courses. Sporadically appears from coast to coast in Canada.

VOICE Male song variable number of *pups* followed by *perleep* or *peroo* in breeding territories and communal roots.

pale gray head
ADULT
black rump and inner wing feathers

Length **9–15in (23–38cm)** | Wingspan **15in (38cm)**

Family **Paridae** | Species ***Poecile cinctus***

Gray-headed Chickadee

The Gray-headed Chickadee, which is a little larger than the Boreal Chickadee, is not found in the same coniferous habitat as the latter, but favors willows. It looks unkempt—not neat like other chickadees—and its voice is burrier and slower. In Eurasia, it is known as a Siberian Tit.

OCCURRENCE Willows and stunted spruce, and thickets and woodlands along gravelly waterways, in scattered localities in northern Alaska and northwestern Canada.

VOICE Call a low-pitched, nasal, slow, deep *jeer jeer jeer*; song is a series of repeated double notes: *tchee-rrr, tcheee-rrrh*.

grayish brown upperparts
white wing edges
buffy flanks
ADULT

Length **5½in (14cm)** | Wingspan **8½in (22cm)**

Family **Alaudidae** | Species ***Alauda arvensis***

Sky Lark

The Sky Lark's streaked brown plumage recalls pipits and sparrows, but its slightly raised crest is distinctive. It stays close to the ground and is hard to see unless flushed, displaying its fluttery flight.
OCCURRENCE Introduced to North America in the Seattle and Vancouver area; occurs as a vagrant from Eurasia in the Bering Sea region of Alaska, where it breeds. Likes windswept, hilly, and grassy areas near the ocean.
VOICE Flight call a sudden *jeerup;* famous aerial song consists of endless trills and buzzes.

prominent crest
ADULT
short tail with white outer feathers

Length **7¼in (18.5cm)** | Wingspan **12–14in (30–36cm)**

Family **Fringillidae** | Species ***Fringilla montifringilla***

Brambling

Widespread in northern Eurasia, from Scandinavia to the far east of Russia, the Brambling is unlike any native North American finch. In all seasons, males and females have a conspicuous white rump and orange outer wing feathers.
OCCURRENCE Regular migrant to the Aleutian and Pribilof Islands, and mainland western Alaska. Occasionally seen elsewhere in Canada and the US.
VOICE Call a characteristic, mewing *jee-eek*; song a trilled *zhreeeee*.

head blackish, with white spots
MALE
bill yellow with black tip
white rump and uppertail feathers
orange chin and breast

Length **5¾in (14.5cm)** | Wingspan **10–11in (25–28cm)**

Family **Parulidae** | Species ***Dendroica dominica***

Yellow-throated Warbler

The Yellow-throated Warbler is perhaps best known for its habit of creeping along branches, much like the Black-and-white Warbler. The species occasionally interbreeds with the Northern Parula, creating the so-called "Sutton's Warbler."
OCCURRENCE Breeds in the eastern half of North America, in woods with cypress, sycamore, or live oak. Its range has extended northwards in recent years with occasional sightings in Canada.
VOICE Flight call high, thin *siit*; song long, descending cascade of clear whistles, sometimes jumbled.

ADULT
unmarked white undertail feathers
white line from bill to nape

Length **5in (13cm)** | Wingspan **8in (20cm)**

Family **Parulidae** | Species ***Helmitheros vermivorum***

Worm-eating Warbler

The Worm-eating Warbler often hangs upside down, searching suspended dead leaves for inchworms and other caterpillars. Although this bird nests on the ground and tends to forage fairly low, singing males may perch quite high in trees.
OCCURRENCE Breeds in mature, deciduous forests with abundant leaf litter and dense undergrowth; mostly in eastern US but occasionally up into Ontario.
VOICE Thick chip call; flight call an upslurred, thin, rolling *ziiit*; song a thin, dry trill.

ADULT
blurry pattern on undertail feathers
tawny wash on breast

Length **5in (13cm)** | Wingspan **8½in (21cm)**

Family **Thraupidae**	Species ***Piranga Rubra***

Summer Tanager

The stunning male Summer Tanager is the only North American bird that is entirely bright red. Immature males in their first spring plumage wear a patchwork of bright yellow-and-red plumage. Of the two subspecies, *P. r. rubra* breeds in the East while *P. r. cooperi* breeds in the West.

OCCURRENCE *P. r. rubra* breeds in deciduous and mixed woodlands in the east up into Canada; *P. r. cooperi* in cottonwood-willow habitats near streams in the west.

VOICE Call an explosive *PIT-tuck!* or *PIT-a TUK*; flight call a muffled, airy *vreee.*

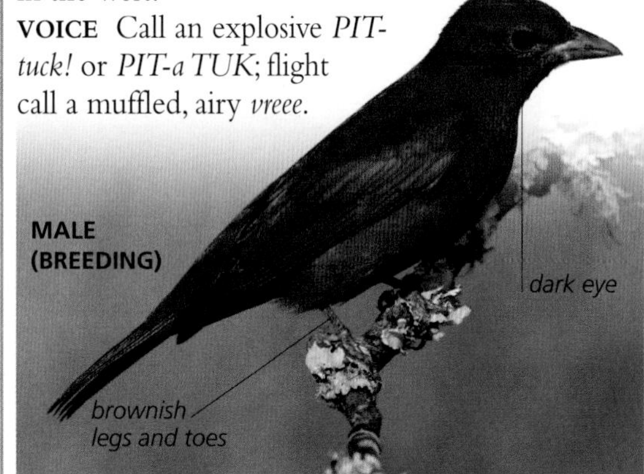
MALE
(BREEDING)
dark eye
brownish
legs and toes

Length **8in (20cm)**	Wingspan **12in (31cm)**

Family **Cardinalidae**	Species ***Passerina caerulea***

Blue Grosbeak

Blue Grosbeaks have expanded their range northward in recent years, especially in the Great Plains. However, they are still a rare find. Features that can help identification are the Grosbeak's huge bill, uniformly dark plumage, black face, and reddish shoulder.

OCCURRENCE Breeds in dense undergrowth of disturbed habitats: old fields, hedgerows, and desert scrub across all of southern US and expanding north into eastern Canada.

VOICE Call a loud, sharp, metallic *tchink*; similar to Indigo Bunting; song rambling, husky.

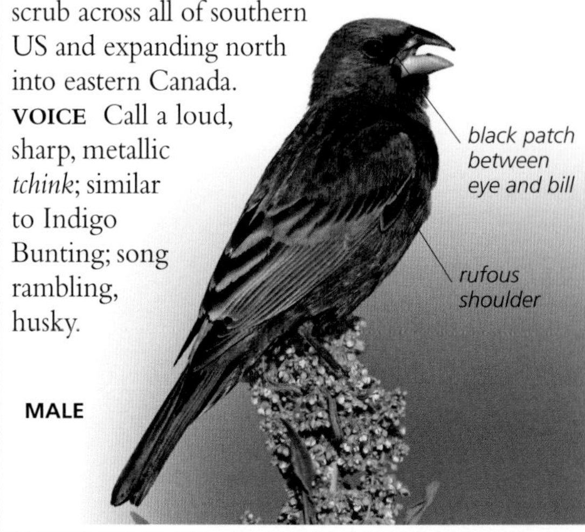
black patch
between
eye and bill
rufous
shoulder
MALE

Length **6¾in (17cm)**	Wingspan **11in (28cm)**

VAGRANTS

THE LIST THAT FOLLOWS, ALTHOUGH not exhaustive, consists of species that occur only very rarely in Canada. Vagrants to Canada arrive from both the Northern and Southern Hemispheres—Europe, Russia, and eastern Asia as well as South America, Africa, and Oceania. The US and Canada are well placed to receive birds that drift off course from eastern Asia and Siberia, crossing the Pacific, and from Europe, crossing the Atlantic. Western Alaska has a particularly high concentration of vagrants because the western tip forms a series of islands, the Aleutians, that reach almost all the way across the Bering Sea to Russia. Some of these birds find their way to Canada's west coast.

The occurrence of vagrant species is classified by the American Birding Association as rare, casual, or accidental depending on how often they have been seen, and this terminology is used in the comment section on each species. Rare species are seen every year, but in low numbers. Casual visitors have been seen in Canada at least half a dozen times, including three sightings in the last 30 years. Accidental species have been recorded in Canada no more than five times.

COMMON NAME	SCIENTIFIC NAME	SCIENTIFIC/FAMILY NAME	DESCRIPTION
Waterfowl			
Black-bellied Whistling Duck	*Dendrocygna autumnalis*	Anatidae/Waterfowl	Casual visitor to Ontario
Fulvous Whistling Duck	*Dendrocygna bicolor*	Anatidae/Waterfowl	Casual visitor across Canada
Taiga Bean-Goose	*Anser fabalis*	Anatidae/Waterfowl	Rare visitor to Maritimes
Pink-footed Goose	*Anser brachyrhynchus*	Anatidae/Waterfowl	Accidental in southern Quebec
Emperor Goose	*Chen canagica*	Anatidae/Waterfowl	Accidental on southern British Columbia coast
Barnacle Goose	*Branta leucopsis*	Anatidae/Waterfowl	Accidental in southern Quebec, Baffin Island, Ontario, and Maritimes
Graylag Goose	*Anser anser*	Anatidae/Waterfowl	Accidental off the coast of Newfoundland and Labrador
Common Pochard	*Aythya ferina*	Anatidae/Waterfowl	Accidental in southern Quebec
Tufted Duck	*Aythya fuligula*	Anatidae/Waterfowl	Accidental in British Columbia, southern Ontario, and southern Quebec
Spectacled Eider	*Somateria fischeri*	Anatidae/Waterfowl	Accidental in northern British Columbia
Smew	*Mergellus albellus*	Anatidae/Waterfowl	Accidental in British Columbia, Ontario, and Quebec
Albatrosses, Petrels, and Shearwaters			
Laysan Albatross	*Phoebastria immutabilis*	Diomedeidae/Albatrosses	Rare visitor to Pacific coast
Short-tailed Albatross	*Phoebastria albatrus*	Diomedeidae/Albatrosses	Accidental in northern British Columbia
Yellow-nosed Albatross	*Thalassarche chlororhynchos*	Diomedeidae/Albatrosses	Casual visitor off Maritime coast
Black-browed Albatross	*Thalassarche melanophris*	Diomedeidae/Albatrosses	Casual visitor off Maritime coast
Fea's Petrel	*Pterodroma feae*	Procellariidae/Petrels and Shearwaters	Accidental off Nova Scotia coast

COMMON NAME	SCIENTIFIC NAME	SCIENTIFIC/FAMILY NAME	DESCRIPTION
Albatrosses, Petrels, and Shearwaters *continued*			
Black-capped Petrel	*Pterodroma hasitata*	Procellariidae/Petrels and Shearwaters	Accidental off Nova Scotia coast
Mottled Petrel	*Pterodroma inexpectata*	Procellariidae/Petrels and Shearwaters	Accidental off British Columbia coast
Black-vented Shearwater	*Puffinus opisthomelas*	Procellariidae/Petrels and Shearwaters	Rare visitor to southern British Columbia
Bulwer's Petrel	*Bulweria bulwerii*	Procellariidae/Petrels and Shearwaters	Accidental off coast of South Carolina up to Nova Scotia and Newfoundland
Audubon's Shearwater	*Puffinus lherminieri*	Procellariidae/Petrels and Shearwaters	Accidental in Ontario and Nova Scotia
Short-tailed Shearwater	*Puffinus tenuirostris*	Procellariidae/Petrels and Shearwaters	Rare visitor off the Pacific coast
Flamingos			
Greater Flamingo	*Phoenicopterus ruber*	Phoenicopteridae/Flamingos	Accidental in Ontario, Quebec, and Maritimes
Ibises and Herons			
Wood Stork	*Mycteria americana*	Ciconiidae/Storks	Accidental in British Columbia, Ontario, and New Brunswick
White Ibis	*Eudocimus albus*	Threskiornithidae/Ibises and Spoonbills	Accidental in southern Canada
White-faced Ibis	*Plegadis chihi*	Threskiornithidae/Ibises and Spoonbills	Accidental in southern Canada
Gray Heron	*Ardea cinerea*	Ardeidae/Herons	Accidental in Newfoundland recently
Tricolored Heron	*Egretta tricolor*	Ardeidae/Herons	Accidental in Ontario and New Brunswick
Little Blue Heron	*Egretta caerulea*	Ardeidae/Herons	Rare visitor to southern Canada
Snowy Egret	*Egretta thula*	Ardeidae/Herons	Accidental in southern Canada
Little Egret	*Egretta garzetta*	Ardeidae/Herons	Accidental in Nova Scotia
Pelicans and Relatives			
Red-tailed Tropicbird	*Phaethon rubricauda*	Phaethontidae/Tropicbirds	Accidental on Vancouver Island
White-tailed Tropicbird	*Phaethon lepturus*	Phaethontidae/Tropicbirds	Accidental in Nova Scotia
Magnificent Frigatebird	*Fregata magnificens*	Fregatidae/Frigatebirds	Accidental in Newfoundland
Brown Pelican	*Pelecanus occidentalis*	Pelecanidae/Pelicans	Accidental in British Columbia and Nova Scotia
Brown Booby	*Sula leucogaster*	Sulidae/Gannets and Boobies	Accidental in southern British Columbia and Nova Scotia
Red-faced Cormorant	*Phalacrocorax urile*	Phalacrocoracidae/ Cormorants	Accidental off British Columbia coast
Anhinga	*Anhinga anhinga*	Anhingidae/Pelicans and Relatives	Casual visitor to southern Ontario
Birds of Prey			
Black Vulture	*Coragyps atratus*	Cathartidae/Birds of Prey	Rare visitor across Canada; recently in British Columbia and Ontario

COMMON NAME	SCIENTIFIC NAME	SCIENTIFIC/FAMILY NAME	DESCRIPTION
Birds of Prey *continued*			
Crested Caracara	*Caracara cheriway*	Falconidae/Birds of Prey	Accidental in southern Ontario
Eurasian Kestrel	*Falco tinnunculus*	Falconidae/Birds of Prey	Accidental in southern British Columbia
White-tailed Kite	*Elanus leucurus*	Accipitridae/Birds of Prey	Casual visitor to British Columbia
Mississippi Kite	*Ictinia mississippiensis*	Accipitridae/Birds of Prey	Accidental in Newfoundland
Zone-tailed Hawk	*Buteo albonotatus*	Accipitridae/Birds of Prey	Accidental in Nova Scotia
Rails and Cranes			
Black Rail	*Laterallus jamaicensis*	Rallidae/Rails	Accidental in Ontario and Quebec
Clapper Rail	*Rallus longirostris*	Rallidae/Rails	Casual visitor to Maritimes
Corn Crake	*Crex crex*	Rallidae/Rails	Accidental in eastern Canada; recently in Newfoundland and Nova Scotia
Eurasian Coot	*Fulica atra*	Rallidae/Rails	Accidental in Newfoundland and Labrador
Common Crane	*Grus grus*	Gruidae/Cranes	Accidental in Alberta and Quebec
Limpkin	*Aramus guarauna*	Aramidae/Cranes	Accidental in Nova Scotia
Shorebirds			
American Oystercatcher	*Haematopus palliatus*	Haematopodidae/Shorebirds	Accidental in Ontario, Quebec, and Maritimes
Eurasian Oystercatcher	*Haematopus ostralegus*	Haematopodidae/Shorebirds	Accidental in Newfoundland
Northern Lapwing	*Vanellus vanellus*	Charadriidae/Plovers	Accidental in Baffin Island, Maritimes west to Quebec
European Golden-Plover	*Pluvialis apricaria*	Charadriidae/Plovers	Accidental in Newfoundland and St. Lawrence River, Quebec
Lesser Sand-Plover/ Mongolian Plover	*Charadrius mongolus*	Charadriidae/Plovers	Accidental in British Columbia
Eurasian Dotterel	*Charadrius morinellus*	Charadriidae/Plovers	Accidental in Northwest Territories
Mountain Plover	*Charadrius montanus*	Charadriidae/Plovers	Casual breeder in Alberta and Saskatchewan
Eurasian Woodcock	*Scolopax rusticola*	Scolopacidae/Sandpipers	Accidental from Eurasia to northeastern North America
Jack Snipe	*Lymnocryptes minimus*	Scolopacidae/Sandpipers	Accidental in Labrador
Black-tailed Godwit	*Limosa limosa*	Scolopacidae/Sandpipers	Casual migrant on Atlantic coast and inland to Ontario
Bar-tailed Godwit	*Limosa lapponica*	Scolopacidae/Sandpipers	Rare visitor to both coasts
Bristle-thighed Curlew	*Numenius tahitiensis*	Scolopacidae/Sandpipers	Accidental in Yukon Delta
Eurasian Curlew	*Numenius arquata*	Scolopacidae/Sandpipers	Accidental in Newfoundland and Nunavut

COMMON NAME	SCIENTIFIC NAME	SCIENTIFIC/FAMILY NAME	DESCRIPTION
Shorebirds *continued*			
Far Eastern Curlew	*Numenius madagascariensis*	Scolopacidae/Sandpipers	Accidental in British Columbia
Spotted Redshank	*Tringa erythropus*	Scolopacidae/Sandpipers	Casual visitor to both coasts
Common Redshank	*Tringa totanus*	Scolopacidae/Sandpipers	Casual visitor to Newfoundland
Common Greenshank	*Tringa nebularia*	Scolopacidae/Sandpipers	Casual visitor to eastern Canada
Wood Sandpiper	*Tringa glareola*	Scolopacidae/Sandpipers	Casual visitor to British Columbia
Terek Sandpiper	*Xenus cinereus*	Scolopacidae/Sandpipers	Accidental to coastal British Columbia
Little Stint	*Calidris minuta*	Scolopacidae/Sandpipers	Accidental across Canada, especially British Columbia, Ontario, New Brunswick, and Nova Scotia
Temminck's Stint	*Calidris temminckii*	Scolopacidae/Sandpipers	Accidental in British Columbia
Spoon-billed Sandpiper	*Eurynorhynchus pygmeus*	Scolopacidae/Sandpipers	Accidental in British Columbia
Gulls and Terns			
Black-tailed Gull	*Larus crassirostris*	Laridae/Gulls	Accidental on British Columbia coast
Yellow-legged Gull	*Larus michahellis*	Laridae/Gulls	Casual visitor to Quebec and Newfoundland
Red-legged Kittiwake	*Rissa brevirostris*	Laridae/Gulls	Accidental on northern British Columbia coast
Elegant Tern	*Thalasseus elegans*	Laridae/Gulls	Casual visitor to Vancouver area
Royal Tern	*Thalasseus maximus*	Laridae/Gulls	Accidental in Ontario and Maritimes
Black Skimmer	*Rynchops niger*	Laridae/Gulls	Accidental in Newfoundland
Auks			
Kittlitz's Murrelet	*Brachyramphus brevirostris*	Alcidae/Auks	Rare visitor to northern British Columbia coast
Xantus's Murrelet	*Synthliboramphus hypoleucus*	Alcidae/Auks	Rare visitor to southern British Columbia coast
Parakeet Auklet	*Aethia psittacula*	Alcidae/Auks	Rare visitor to northern British Columbia coast
Least Auklet	*Aethia pusilla*	Alcidae/Auks	Rare visitor to northern British Columbia
Crested Auklet	*Aethia cristatella*	Alcidae/Auks	Accidental in northern British Columbia
Pigeons and Doves			
Common Ground-Dove	*Columbina passerina*	Columbidae/Pigeons and Doves	Casual visitor to Nova Scotia
Cuckoos			
Groove-billed Ani	*Crotophaga sulcirostris*	Cuculidae/Cuckoos	Accidental in Ontario
Hummingbirds			
Green Violetear	*Colibri thalassinus*	Hummingbird/Trochilidae	Accidental in Alberta and Ontario
Xantus's Hummingbird	*Hylocharis xantusii*	Hummingbird/Trochilidae	Accidental in British Columbia

COMMON NAME	SCIENTIFIC NAME	SCIENTIFIC/FAMILY NAME	DESCRIPTION
Hummingbirds *continued*			
Costa's Hummingbird	*Calypte costae*	Hummingbird/Trochilidae	Accidental to the coast of British Columbia
Broad-billed Hummingbird	*Cynanthus latirostris*	Hummingbird/Trochilidae	Accidental in New Brunswick
Broad-tailed Hummingbird	*Selasphorus platycerus*	Hummingbird/Trochilidae	Accidental in southern Manitoba
Woodpeckers			
Acorn Woodpecker	*Melanerpes formicivorus*	Picidae/Woodpeckers	Accidental in British Columbia
Tyrant Flycatchers			
Gray Flycatcher	*Empidomax wrightii*	Tyrannidae/Tyrant Flycatchers	Casual visitor to southern British Columbia
Vermilion Flycatcher	*Pyrocephalus rubinus*	Tyrannidae/Tyrant Flycatchers	Accidental in Ontario and Quebec
Sulphur-bellied Flycatcher	*Myiodynastes luteiventris*	Tyrannidae/Tyrant Flycatchers	Casual visitor to Ontario and New Brunswick
Variegated Flycatcher	*Empidonomus varius*	Tyrannidae/Tyrant Flycatchers	Accidental in southern Canada
Tropical Kingbird	*Tyrannus melancholicus*	Tyrannidae/Tyrant Flycatchers	Accidental on Vancouver Island
Cassin's Kingbird	*Tyrannus vociferans*	Tyrannidae/Tyrant Flycatchers	Accidental in eastern Canada, mostly Ontario
Thick-billed Kingbird	*Tyrannus crassirostris*	Tyrannidae/Tyrant Flycatchers	Accidental in southwestern British Columbia
Fork-tailed Flycatcher	*Tyrannus savana*	Tyrannidae/Tyrant Flycatchers	Accidental from Quebec to Maritimes
Gray Kingbird	*Tyrannus dominicensis*	Tyrannidae/Tyrant Flycatchers	Accidental in British Columbia, Ontario, and Maritimes
Ash-throated Flycatcher	*Myiarchus cinerascens*	Tyrannidae/Tyrant Flycatchers	Accidental in British Columbia, Ontario, and Quebec
Black Phoebe	*Sayornis nigricans*	Tyrannidae/Tyrant Flycatchers	Accidental in southwestern British Columbia
Shrikes			
Brown Shrike	*Lanius cristatus*	Laniidae/Shrikes	Accidental in Nova Scotia
Vireos, Jays, and Crows			
Bell's Vireo	*Vireo bellii*	Vireonidae/Vireos	Casual visitor to Ontario
Black-capped Vireo	*Vireo atricapilla*	Vireonidae/Vireos	Accidental in southern Ontario
Plumbeous Vireo	*Vireo plumbeus*	Vireonidae/Vireos	Accidental in Alberta, Ontario, and Nova Scotia
Western Scrub-jay	*Aphelocoma californica*	Corvidae/Jays and crows	Accidental in southern British Columbia
Pinyon Jay	*Gymnorhinus cyanocephalus*	Corvidae/Jays and crows	Accidental in southwestern Saskatchewan
Eurasian Jackdaw	*Corvus monedula*	Corvidae/Jays and crows	Accidental in Quebec and Maritimes
Fish Crow	*Corvus ossifragus*	Corvidae/Jays and crows	Casual visitor to Ontario

COMMON NAME	SCIENTIFIC NAME	SCIENTIFIC/FAMILY NAME	DESCRIPTION
Chickadees and Titmice			
Phainopepla	*Phainopepla nitens*	Ptilogonatidae/Phainopepla	Accidental in Ontario
Carolina Chickadee	*Poecile carolinensis*	Paridae/Chickadees and Titmice	Accidental in southeastern Ontario
Swallows			
Cave Swallow	*Petrochelidon fulva*	Hirundinidae/Swallows	Accidental in southern Ontario and Nova Scotia
Wrens and Thrashers			
Curve-billed Thrasher	*Toxostoma curvirostre*	Mimidae/Thrashers	Accidental in south-central Saskatchewan
Thrushes and Old World Sparrows			
Eurasian Blackbird	*Turdus merula*	Turdidae/Thrushes	Accidental in Ontario, southern Quebec, and Newfoundland
Dusky Thrush	*Turdus naumanni*	Turdidae/Thrushes	Accidental in Yukon and coastal British Columbia
Fieldfare	*Turdus pilaris*	Turdidae/Thrushes	Casual visitor to Northwest Territories, Ontario, Quebec, and Maritimes
Redwing	*Turdus iliacus*	Turdidae/Thrushes	Accidental in Newfoundland
Song Thrush	*Turdus philomelos*	Turdidae/Thrushes	Accidental in Quebec
Bluethroat	*Luscinia svecica*	Turdidae/Thrushes	Accidental in Yukon
Siberian Accentor	*Prunella montanella*	Turdidae/Thrushes	Accidental in northern British Columbia
Wagtails and Pipits			
Gray Wagtail	*Motacilla cinerea*	Motacillidae/Wagtails and Pipits	Accidental in British Columbia
Red-throated Pipit	*Anthus cervinus*	Motacillidae/Wagtails and Pipits	Rare visitor to British Columbia coast
Cardueline Finches			
Common Chaffinch	*Fringilla coelebs*	Fringillidae/ Cardueline Finches	Accidental in Nova Scotia
Lesser Goldfinch	*Spinus psaltria*	Fringillidae/ Cardueline Finches	Accidental to southern British Columbia and Ontario
Wood-warblers			
Virginia's Warbler	*Vermivora virginiae*	Parulidae/Wood-warblers	Rare visitor to Maritimes
Hermit Warbler	*Dendroica occidentalis*	Parulidae/Wood-warblers	Accidental in British Columbia, Ontario, Quebec, and Nova Scotia
Kirtland's Warbler	*Dendroica kirtlandii*	Parulidae/Wood-warblers	Rare visitor to Ontario and Quebec
Swainson's Warbler	*Limnothlypis swainsonii*	Parulidae/Wood-warblers	Accidental in southern Manitoba, Ontario, and Nova Scotia
Kentucky Warbler	*Oporornis formosus*	Parulidae/Wood-warblers	Casual visitor to Ontario, Quebec, and Maritimes
Painted Redstart	*Myioborus pictus*	Parulidae/Wood-warblers	Accidental in Ontario

COMMON NAME	SCIENTIFIC NAME	SCIENTIFIC/FAMILY NAME	DESCRIPTION
Orioles and Blackbirds			
Hooded Oriole	*Icterus cucullatus*	Icteridae/Orioles and Blackbirds	Casual visitor to British Columbia; accidental in Ontario
Scott's Oriole	*Icterus parisorum*	Icteridae/Orioles and Blackbirds	Accidental in Ontario
Bronzed Cowbird	*Molothrus aeneus*	Icteridae/Orioles and Blackbirds	Accidental in Nova Scotia
Shiny Cowbird	*Molothrus bonariensis*	Icteridae/Orioles and Blackbirds	Accidental in New Brunswick
Great-tailed Grackle	*Quiscalus mexicanus*	Icteridae/Orioles and Blackbirds	Accidental in southern British Columbia
Sparrows and Buntings			
Rustic bunting	*Emberiza rustica*	Emberizidae/ American Sparrows	Accidental on British Columbia coast
McKay's Bunting	*Plectrophenax hyperboreus*	Emberizidae/ American Sparrows	Accidental on British Columbia coast
Seaside Sparrow	*Ammodramus maritimus*	Emberizidae/ American Sparrows	Casual visitor to Maritimes
Saltmarsh Sharp-tailed Sparrow	*Ammodramus caudacutus*	Emberizidae/ American Sparrows	Accidental in southern Quebec
Black-throated Sparrow	*Amphispiza bilineata*	Emberizidae/ American Sparrows	Accidental in southern British Columbia
Sage Sparrow	*Amphispiza belli*	Emberizidae/ American Sparrows	Accidental in southern British Columbia
Bachman's Sparrow	*Aimophila aestivalis*	Emberizidae/ American Sparrows	Rare visitor to southern Ontario
Green-tailed Towhee	*Pipilo chlorurus*	Emberizidae/ American Sparrows	Accidental across Canada
Cardinals			
Pyrrhuloxia	*Cardinalis sinuatus*	Cardinalidae/Cardinals	Accidental in Ontario
Varied Bunting	*Passerina versicolor*	Cardinalidae/Cardinals	Accidental in Ontario
Painted Bunting	*Passerina ciris*	Cardinalidae/Cardinals	Accidental in Ontario and Maritimes

GLOSSARY

Many terms defined here are illustrated in the general introduction (pp.8—19).

adult A fully developed, sexually mature bird. It is in its final plumage, which no longer changes pattern with age and remains the same after yearly molt, although it may change with season. *See also* **immature**, **juvenile**.

aerie The nest of birds of prey, like eagles or peregrine falcons, usually on a cliff, and often used by the same pair of adult birds in successive years.

alarm call A call made by a bird to signal danger. Alarm calls are often short and urgent in tone, and a few species use different calls to signify the precise nature of the threat. *See also* **call**.

allopreening Mutual preening between two birds, the main purpose of which is to reduce the instinctive aggression when birds come into close contact. In the breeding season, allopreening helps to strengthen the pair bond between the male and female. *See also* **preening**.

altitudinal migrant *see* **vertical migrant**

alula A small group of two to six feathers projecting from a bird's "thumb," at the bend of its wing that reduces turbulence when raised.

Audubon, John James (1785—1851) American naturalist and wildlife illustrator, whose best known work was his remarkable collection of prints, *Birds of North America*.

axillary A term describing feathers at the base of the underwing. Axillary feathers often form small patches, with coloration differing from the rest of the underwing.

barred With marks crossing the body, wing, or tail; the opposite of streaked. *See also* **streaks**.

bastard wing *see* **alula**

beak *see* **bill**

bill A bird's jaws. A bill is made of bone, with a hornlike outer covering of keratin.

bird of prey Any of the predatory birds in the orders Falconiformes (eagles, hawks, falcons, kites, buzzards, ospreys, and vultures) and Strigiformes (owls). They are characterised by their acute eyesight, powerful legs, strongly hooked bill, and sharp talons. These birds, particularly the Falconiformes, are also known as raptors. *See also* **talon**, **raptor**.

body feather *see* **contour feather**

booming A sound produced by bitterns and some species of grouse. The booming of male bitterns is a deep, resonant, hollow sound that can carry for several miles. The booming of male grouse is produced by wind from air pouches in the sides of the bird's neck.

brackish Containing a mixture of saltwater and freshwater.

breeding plumage A general term for the plumage worn by adult birds when they display and form breeding pairs. It is usually (but not always) worn in the spring and summer. *See also* **nonbreeding plumage**.

brood (noun) The young birds produced from a single clutch of eggs and incubated together. *See also* **clutch**. **(verb)** In birds, to sit on nestlings to keep them warm. Brooding is usually carried out by the adult female. *See also* **incubate**.

brood parasite A bird that lays its eggs in the nest of other birds. Some brood parasites always breed this way, while others do so only occasionally.

brood patch An area of bare skin on the belly of a parent bird, usually the female, that is richly supplied with blood vessels and thus helps keep the eggs warm during incubation. This area loses its feathers in readiness for the breeding season and is fully feathered at other times.

caged-bird A species of bird commonly kept in captivity.

call A sound produced by the vocal apparatus of a bird to communicate a variety of messages to other birds. Calls are often highly characteristic of individual species and can help to locate and identify birds in the field. Most bird calls are shorter and simpler than songs. *See also* **alarm call**, **booming**, **contact call**, **song**.

casque A bony extension on a bird's head.

cere A leathery patch of skin that covers the base of a bird's bill. It is found only in a few groups, including birds of prey, pigeons, and parrots.

claw In birds, the nail that prolongs their toes.

cloaca An opening toward the rear of a bird's belly. It is present in both sexes and is used in reproduction and excretion.

clutch The group of eggs in a single nest, usually laid by one female and incubated together.

cock A term sometimes used to describe the adult male in gamebirds and songbirds. *See also* **hen**.

collar The area around a bird's neck, which in some species is a prominent feature of its plumage pattern and can be used for identification.

color form One of two or more clearly defined plumage variations found in the same species. Also known as a color morph or phase, a color form may be restricted to part of a species's range or occur side by side with other color forms over the entire range. Adults of different color forms are able to interbreed, and these mixed pairings can produce young of either form.

comb A fleshy growth of bare skin usually above the eyes.

contact call A call made by a bird to give its location as a means of staying in touch with others of the same species. Contact calls are used by birds in flocks and by breeding pairs. Contact calls are crucial for nocturnal migrants. *See also* **call**.

contour feather A general term for any feather that covers the outer surface of a bird, including its wings and tail. Contour feathers are also known as body feathers, and help streamline the bird.

cooperative breeding A breeding system in which a pair of parent birds are helped in raising their young by several other birds, which are often related to them and may be young birds from previous broods.

courtship display Ritualized, showy behavior used in courtship by the male, and sometimes by the female, involving plumage, sound (vocal and non-vocal), and movements.

covert A small feather covering the base of a bird's flight feather. Together, coverts form a well-defined feather tract on the wing or at the base of the tail. *See also* **feather tract**.

creche A group of young birds of about the same age, produced by different parents but tightly packed together. One or more adults guards the entire creche.

crepuscular Relating to the period just before dawn, when many birds are active, especially during courtship. When used in connection with birds, the term is often used to refer to both dawn and twilight.

crest A group of elongated feathers on top of a bird's head, which may be raised during courtship or to indicate alarm.

crown The area on top of a bird's head. It is often a prominent plumage feature, with a different color from the feathers on the rest of the head.

dabble To feed in shallow water by sieving water and obtain food through comblike filters in the bill; used mostly for ducks (dabbling ducks or dabblers).

decurved A term describing a bird's bill that curves downward from the forehead toward the tip.

dimorphism *see* **sexual dimorphism**

display *see* **courtship display**, **distraction display**, **threat display**

distraction display A display in which a bird deliberately attempts to attract a predator's attention in order to lure it away from its nest or nestlings.

diurnal Active during the day.

down feather A soft, fluffy feather, lacking the system of barbs of contour or flight feathers, that provides good insulation. Young birds are covered by down feathers until they molt into their first juvenile plumage. Adult birds have a layer of down feathers under their contour feathers. *See also* **contour feather**, **juvenile**.

drake An adult male duck. The adult female is known as the duck.

drift The diversion of migrating birds from their normal migration route by strong winds.

dynamic soaring *see* **soaring**

ear tuft A distinct tuft of feathers on each side of a bird's forehead, with no connection to the true ears, which can be raised as a visual signal. Many owls have ear tufts.

echolocation A method of sensing nearby objects using pulses of high-frequency sound. Echoes bounce back from obstacles, enabling the sender to build up a "picture" of its surroundings.

eclipse plumage A female-like plumage worn in some birds, especially waterfowl, by adult males for a short period after the breeding season is over. The eclipse plumage helps camouflage them during their molt, when they are flightless.
elevational migrant *see* **vertical migrant**
endemic A species (or subspecies) native to a particular geographic area—such as an island, a forest patch, a mountain, or state, or country—and found nowhere else.
escape An individual bird that has escaped from a zoo or other collection to live in the wild. *See also* **exotic**
eye-ring A ring of color, usually narrow and well defined, around the eye of a bird.
eyestripe A stripe of color running as a line through the eye of a bird.
eyrie *see* **aerie**
exotic A bird found in a region from which it is not native. Some of these are escapes, or were originally, but now live as wild birds.

feather tract A well-defined area on a bird's skin where feathers grow, leaving patches of bare skin inbetween.
fledge In young birds, to leave the nest or acquire the first complete set of flight feathers. Known as fledglings, these birds may still remain dependent on their parents for some time. *See also* **flight feather**.
fledging period The average time taken by the young of a species to fledge, timed from the moment they hatch. Fledging periods in birds range from 11 days in some small songbirds to as long as 280 days in the Wandering Albatross.
fledgling *see* **fledge**
flight feather A collective term for a bird's wing and tail feathers, used in flight. More specifically, it refers to the largest feathers on the outer part of the wing, the primaries and secondaries.
forewing The front section of a bird's wing, including the primary coverts and secondary coverts. *See also* **hindwing**.

gamebird Generally, any bird that is legally hunted, including some doves and waterfowl. This name is generally used for members of the order Galliformes.
gular sac Also known as a gular pouch, it is a large, fleshy, extendable sac just below the bill of some birds, especially fish-eaters such as pelicans. It forms part of the throat.

habitat The geographical and ecological area where a particular organism usually lives.
hen A term sometimes used to describe the adult female in gamebirds, especially grouse and songbirds. *See also* **cock**.
hindwing The rear section of a bird's spread wing, including the secondary feathers, especially when it has a distinctive color or pattern. *See also* **forewing**.
hybrid The offspring produced when two species, sometimes from different genera, interbreed. Hybrids are usually rare in the wild. Among birds, they are most frequent in gamebirds and waterfowl, especially ducks. Hybrid progeny may or may not be fertile.
immature In birds, an individual that is not yet sexually mature or able to breed. Some birds pass through a series of immature plumages over several years before adopting their first adult plumage and sexual maturity. *See also* **adult, juvenile**.
incubate In birds, to sit on eggs to keep them warm, allowing the embryo inside to grow. Incubation is often carried out by the female. *See also* **brood**.
incubation period In birds, the period when a parent incubates its eggs. It may not start until the clutch is completed.
injury feigning *see* **distraction display**.
inner wing The inner part of the wing, comprising the secondaries and rows of coverts (typically marginal, lesser, median, and greater coverts).
introduced species A species that humans have accidentally or deliberately brought into an area where it does not normally occur.
iridescent plumage Plumage that shows brilliant, luminous colors, which seem to sparkle and change color when seen from different angles.
irruption A sporadic mass movement of animals outside their normal range. Irruptions are usually short-lived and occur in response to food shortage. Also called irruptive migration.

juvenile A term referring to the plumage worn by a young bird at the time it makes its first flight and until it begins its first molt. *See also* **adult, immature**.

keratin A tough but lightweight protein. In birds, keratin is found in the claws, feathers, and outer part of the bill.
kleptoparasite A bird that gets much of its food by stealing it from other birds, usually by following them in flight and forcing them to disgorge their food.

lamellae Delicate, comblike structures on the sides of the bill of some birds used for filtering tiny food particles out of water.
leap-frog migration A pattern of migration in which some populations of a species travel much further than the other populations, by "leap-frogging" over the area where these sedentary (nonmigratory) birds are found. *See also* **migration**.
lek An area, often small, used by males as a communal display arena, where they show off special plumage features accompanied by vocal and non-vocal sounds, to attract females. Females wait along the lek and select the male or males that they will mate with.
lobed feet Feet with loose, fleshy lobes on the toes, adapted for swimming.
lore A small area between a bird's eye and the base of its upper bill.

mandible The upper or lower part of a bird's bill, known as the upper or lower mandible respectively.
mantle The loose term used to define the back of a bird, between its neck and rump.
migrant A species that regularly moves between geographical areas. Most migrants move on an annual basis between a breeding area and a wintering area. *See also* **partial migrant, sedentary**.
migration A journey to a different region, following a well-defined route. *See also* **leap-frog migration, partial migrant, reverse migration, sedentary, vertical migrant**.
mobbing A type of defensive behavior in which a group of birds gang up to harass a predator, such as a bird of prey or an owl, swooping repeatedly to drive it away.
molt In birds, to shed old feathers so that they can be replaced. Molting enables birds to keep their plumage in good condition, change their level of insulation, and change their coloration or markings so that they are ready to breed or display.
monogamous Mating with a single partner, either in a single breeding season or for life. *See also* **polygamous**.
morph *see* **color form**

nape The back of the neck.
nestling A young bird still in the nest.
New World The Americas, from Alaska to Cape Horn, including the Caribbean and offshore islands in the Pacific and Atlantic oceans. *See also* **Old World**.
nictitating membrane A transparent or semiopaque "third eyelid," which moves sideways across the eye. Waterbirds often use the membrane as an aid to vision when swimming underwater.
nocturnal Active at night.
nomadic Being almost constantly on the move. Birds of deserts, grasslands, and the coniferous forests of the far north are commonly nomadic.
nonbreeding plumage The plumage worn by adult birds outside the breeding season. In many species, particularly in temperate regions, it is also known as winter plumage. *See also* **breeding plumage**.
nonmigrant *see* **sedentary**
nonpasserine Any bird that is not a member of the order Passeriformes (or passerines). *See also* **passerine**.

oil gland Also called the preen gland, a gland at the base of a bird's tail that secretes oils that are spread over the feathers for waterproofing them during preening.
Old World Europe, Asia, Africa, and Australasia. *See also* **New World**.
orbital ring A thin, bare, fleshy ring around the eye, sometimes with a distinctive color. *See also* **eye-ring**.
outer wing The outer half of the wing, comprising the primaries, their coverts, and the alula (the "thumb").

partial migrant A species in which some populations migrate while others are sedentary. This situation is common in broadly distributed species that experience a wide range of climatic conditions. *See also* **migration, sedentary**.
passerine A bird belonging to the vast order Passeriformes (the passerines). This group contains more species than all other orders of birds combined. Passerines are also called songbirds or perching birds. *See also* **nonpasserine**.
pelagic Relating to the open ocean. Pelagic birds spend most of their life at sea and only come to land to nest.
phase *see* **color form**

polygamous Mating with two or more partners during the course of a single breeding season. *See also* **monogamous**.
population A group of individual birds of the same species living in a geographically and ecologically circumscribed area.
preening Routine behavior by which birds keep their feathers in good condition. A bird grasps a feather at its base and then "nibbles" upward toward the tip, and repeats the process with different feathers. This helps smooth and clean the plumage. Birds often also smear oil from their preen gland onto their feathers at the same time.
see also **allopreening**.
primary feather One of the large outer wing feathers, growing from the digits of a bird's "hand." *See also* **secondary feather**.

race *see* **subspecies**
range A term to indicate the geographical distribution of a species or population.
raptor A general name for birds belonging to the order Falconiformes, often used interchangeablely with bird of prey. *See also* **bird of prey**.
ratite A member of an ancient group of flightless birds that includes the ostrich, cassowaries, emus, rheas, and kiwis. In the past, the group was larger and more diverse.
resident *see* **sedentary**
reverse migration A phenomenon that occurs when birds from a migratory species mistakenly travel in the opposite direction from normal, causing birds to turn up in places far outside their normal range. *See also* **migration**.
roost A place where birds sleep, either at night or by day.
rump The area between a bird's back and the base of its upper tail coverts. In many species, the rump is a different color from the rest of the plumage and can be a useful diagnostic character for identification.

sally A feeding technique (sallying), used especially by tyrant flycatchers, in which a bird makes a short flight from a perch to catch an insect, often in midair, followed by a return to a perch, often the same one.
salt gland A gland located in a depression of the skull, just above the eye of some birds, particularly seabirds. This enables them to extract the fluids they need from saltwater and then expel the excess salts through the nostrils.
scapular Any one of a group of feathers on the "shoulder," forming a more or less oval patch on each side of the back, at the base of the wing.
scrape A simple nest that consists of a shallow depression in the ground, which may be unlined or lined with material such as feathers, bits of grass, or pebbles.
secondary feather One of the row of long, stiff feathers along the rear edge of a bird's wing, between the body and the primary feathers at the wingtip. *See also* **primary feather**.
sedentary Having a settled lifestyle that involves little or no geographic movement. Sedentary birds are also said to be resident or nonmigratory. *See also* **migration**.
semipalmated The condition in which two or more of the toes are partially joined by an incomplete membrane at their base.
sexual dimorphism The occurrence of physical differences between males and females. In birds, the most common differences are in size and plumage.
shield In birds, a hard structure on the forehead that joins the bill and often appears to be an extension of it.
shorebird Also known as a wader, any member of several families in the order Charadriiformes, including plovers, sandpipers, godwits, snipe, avocets, stilts, oystercatchers, and curlews. Not all species actually wade in water and some live in dry habitats.
soaring In birds, flight without flapping of the wings. A soaring bird stays at the same height or gains height. Updraft soaring is a type of soaring in which a bird benefits from rising currents that form at cliffs or along mountain ridges. Seabirds are expert at dynamic soaring, repeatedly diving into the troughs between waves and then using the rising air deflected off the waves to wheel back up into the air.
song A vocal performance by a bird, usually the adult male, to attract and impress a potential mate, advertise ownership of a territory, or drive away rival birds. Songs are often highly characteristic of individual species and can be a major aid in locating and identifying birds in the field. *See also* **call**.
songbird A general term used to describe a member of the suborder Passeri (or oscines), a subdivision of the largest order of birds, the Passeriformes (passerines).
species A group of similar organisms that are capable of breeding among themselves in the wild and producing fertile offspring that resemble themselves, but that do not interbreed in the wild with individuals of another similar group, are called a species. *See also* **subspecies**.
speculum A colorful patch on the wing of a duck, formed by the secondary feathers. *See also* **secondary feather**.
spur A sharply pointed, clawlike structure at the back of the leg of some birds, like the Wild Turkey.
staging ground A stopover area where migrant birds regularly pause while on migration, to rest and feed.
stoop A near-vertical and often very fast dive made by falcons and some other birds of prey when chasing prey in the air or on the ground.
streaks Marks that run lengthwise on feathers; opposite of bars.
subspecies When species show geographical variation in color, voice, or other characters, these differentiated populations are recognized by ornithologists as subspecies (formerly also called races). *See also* **species**.
syrinx A modified section of a bird's trachea (windpipe), equivalent to the voicebox in humans, that enables birds to call and sing.
talon One of the sharp, hooked claws of a bird of prey.
territory An area that is defended by an animal, or a group of animals, against other members of the same species. Territories often include useful resources, such as good breeding sites or feeding areas, which help a male attract a mate.
tertial Any one of a small group of feathers, sometimes long and obvious, at the base of the wing adjacent to the inner secondaries.
thermal A rising bubble or column of warm air over land that soaring birds can use to gain height with little effort. *See also* **soaring**.
threat display A form of defense in which a bird adopts certain postures, sometimes accompanied by loud calls, to drive away a rival or a potential predator.
trachea The breathing tube in animals, also known as the windpipe.
tubenose A general term used to describe members of the order Procellariiformes, including albatrosses, petrels, and shearwaters; their nostrils form two tubes on the upper mandible.

underwing The underside of a bird's wing, usually visible only in flight or when a bird is preening, displaying, or swimming.
upperwing The upper surface of a bird's wing clearly exposed in flight but often mostly hidden when the bird is perched.

vagrant A bird that has strayed far from its normal range. Usually, vagrants are long-distance migrants that have been blown off course by storms, have overshot their intended destination due to strong winds, or have become disoriented.
vent Also called the crissum, the undertail feathers between the lower belly feathers and tail feathers, which in some species are differently colored from either belly or tail feathers. Can be helpful in identification.
vertical migrant A species that migrates up and down mountains, usually in response to changes in the weather or food supply. *See also* **migration**.

wader *see* **shorebird**.
waterfowl A collective term for members of the family Anatidae, including ducks, geese, and swans.
wattle A bare, fleshy growth that hangs loosely below the bill in some birds. It is often brightly colored, and may play a part in courtship.
wildfowl *see* **waterfowl**
Wilson, Alexander (1766–1813) A contempory of J.J. Audubon, Wilson's seminal *American Ornithology* marks the start of scientific ornithology in the US.
wingbar A line or bar of color across the upper surface of a bird's wing. Wingbars can often be seen when a bird is on the ground or perched and its wings are in the closed position, but they are normally much more obvious in flight. Wingbars may be single or in groups of two or more.
wingspan The distance across a bird's outstretched wings and back, from one wingtip to the other.

INDEX

R

S

X

Y

Z

Acknowledgments

Dorling Kindersley would like to thank the following people for their help in compiling this book: Lucy Baker, Rachel Booth, Kim Bryan, Arti Finn, Peter Frances, Lynn Hassett, Riccie Janus, Maxine Lea, Megan Jones, Ruth O'Rourke, Yen-Mai Tsang.

Producing such a comprehensive book would be impossible without the research and observations of hundreds of field and museum ornithologists and birdwatchers. The Editor-in-Chief would like to name four who have been especially inspirational and supportive over the years: the late Paul Géroudet, the late Ernst Mayr, Patricia Stryker Joseph, and Helen Hays. In addition, we acknowledge *Birds of North America Online*, edited by Alan Poole, a joint project of the American Ornithologists' Union and Cornell's Laboratory of Ornithology, and The Howard Moore *Complete Checklist of the Birds of the World*, 3rd edition.

The publisher would like to thank the following for their kind permission to reproduce their photographs:

Almost without exception, the birds featured in the profiles in this book were photographed in the wild.

(Key: a-above; b-below/bottom; c-centre; f-far; l-left; r-right; t-top)

Alamy Images: AfriPics.com 9cra; Derrick Alderman 16cl; All Canada Photos 224tr; Blickwinkel 17cr; Rick & Nora Bowers, 262t; Bruce Coleman Inc. 12tr, 17crb; Gay Bumgarner 16cb; Nancy Camel 17clb; Redmond Durrell 13cb; Elvele Images Ltd 16-17c; David Hosking 11fcrb; Juniors Bildachiv 11tr; Don Kates 14cla; Charles Melton 27fbl; Renee Morris 482; Rolf Nussbaumer 14clb; Peter Arnold, Inc. 14cl; Stock Connection Blue 11clb; © tbkmedia.de 14-15c.
Ardea: Ian Beames 9cr; Peter Steyn 89ca.
Doug Backlund: 10-11ca, 25cb, 42crb, 119cra, 119tc, 125crb, 131cra, 139tr, 197crb, 358cr, 366cla, 366cra, 366crb, 462bc.
The Barn Owl Centre, UK: 238cla.
Giff Beaton: 403tr.
Corbis: Tim Davis 2-3; Joe McDonald 12cla, 115cla.
Mike Danzenbaker: 78tc, 88ca, 90cra, 91crb, 143bc, 218cla, 223ca, 223crb, 223tc, 224crb, 226ca, 226crb, 226tc, 229tc, 258ca, 258tl, 261ca, 261crb, 261tc, 263cra, 263crb, 263tc, 289cb, 408tc, 436tc, 446tc, 484tl, 483br.
DK Images: Robin Chittenden 73tr; Chris Gomersall Photography 32crb, 32tr, 51ca, 51crb, 51tr, 54crb, 70crb, 85ca, 85tr, 107crb, 110crb, 118ca, 118crb, 122cra, 122tc, 169crb, 172crb, 180bc, 198cra, 200ca, 208ca, 208crb, 210cb, 219cla, 219cra, 220cra, 221crb, 227crb, 227tc, 231cra, 322cla, 360tc, 376cra, 376tc; David Cottridge 374cla; David Tipling Photo Library 52ca, 60cr, 60cra, 73tc, 75tc, 94tc, 122crb, 149cla, 182cla, 192cl, 192cra, 198cla, 199cra, 204cla, 231cla, 339tc; Mark Hamblin 55ca, 60cla, 77c, 113cra, 239cra, 254cra, 374tc; Chris Knights 74crb; Mike Lane 32cla, 32cra, 36tc, 48ca, 60tr, 68cla, 75tr, 95ca, 110cra, 173cla, 179tc, 180tr, 189tc, 200cra, 208tc, 209ca, 216cra, 216crb, 220crb, 221ca, 227ca, 322ca, 487bl, 488bl; Gordon Langsbury 105cla, 110tr, 151cra, 162tc, 166cla, 183tr; Tim Loseby 55crb, 187crb, 383cla; George McCarthy 33crb, 36tr, 103ca, 105cra, 169cla, 199bc, 210tc, 215ca; Natural History Museum, London 8cla, 10cl; Kim Taylor 306tr; Roger Tidman 44ca, 44tc, 47ca, 56tr, 64ca, 70ca, 75ca, 77tr, 100ca, 110cla, 169tr, 174tc, 180tc, 186ca, 187ca, 187tr, 192tc, 209crb, 214cra, 217ca, 221tc, 233ca, 360cla, 374cra, 448cla, 448tc, 486tr; Ray Tipper 148tr; Steve Young 48tc, 56cr, 60crb, 60tc, 68cra, 68tr, 70tc, 70tr, 74ca, 74tc, 85tc, 90crb, 90tc, 113tc, 182tc, 189cla, 192crb, 199fcla, 200cla, 264cla, 266cra, 204crb, 204fcla, 209tc, 209tr, 214tc, 216cla, 349ca, 448cra.
Dudley Edmondson: 21cra, 25tc, 30tr, 33cla, 39b, 39cra, 39tl, 96ca, 96tc, 101cb, 109cla, 120ca, 123ca, 123cb, 123cla, 123tc, 125cla, 125cra, 125tc, 127crb, 130cla, 130cra, 131crb, 139crb, 142crb, 144tc, 145crb, 146ca, 147crb, 168crb, 171cra, 178tc, 188cr, 190tr, 194cla, 194cr, 203crb, 212crb, 247tl, 248cb, 251cla, 251cra, 256crb, 279bc, 302crb, 316ca, 345crb, 363crb, 364bc, 418bc, 435crb, 449ca, 450cra, 466cra.
Tom Ennis: 184ca.
Hanne & Jens Eriksen: 148cla, 160crb, 207tc, 213bc, 217crb, 217tc, 486bl.
Neil Fletcher: 38bc, 38cla, 39cla, 41tc, 46ca, 46cra, 48tr, 55tr, 57tc, 58crb, 58tr, 233crb, 360cra, 376crb.
FLPA: Tui De Roy/Minden Pictures 15ca; Goetz Eichhorn/ Foto Natura 79fbl, 80ca; John Hawkins 15cla; David Hosking, 84bl; S Jonasson 81cra; Daphne Kinzler 15tr; S & D & K Maslowski 16clb; Geoff Moon; Roger Tidman 81tr; Winfried Wisniewski/Foto Natura 15cr.
Joe Fuhrman: 112cra, 160ca, 299crb, 362bc, 399crb.
Getty Images: Marc Moritsch 12-13c; Brad Sharp 16c.
Bob Glover: 192fcra, 204fcra.
Melvin Grey: 52crb, 99bc, 99cra, 102ca, 102tr, 104crb, 105crb, 106cla, 119cla, 141cra, 150tr, 172ca, 173cra, 213tr, 330crb, 483tr; Tom Grey: 86cr, 98crb, 101cra, 116crb, 118cra, 126crb, 131cla, 141crb, 189cl, 207crb, 222ca, 222crb, 234ca, 242bc, 275bc, 320cra, 325tc, 329tc, 343crb, 435fcla, 435fcra, 440cla, 440cra, 457crb, 484tr, 484bl, 485tl. 485tr.
Martin Hale: 91ca.
Josef Hlasek: 186crb.
Barry Hughes: 143cr, 219crb.
Arto Juvonen: 35tc, 84ca, 84crb, 84tc, 113crb, 133cra.
Kevin T. Karlson: 25cla, 26tc, 67ca, 67crb, 78ca, 119crb, 129cla, 129tc, 156cr, 156cra, 156crb, 156fcla, 158ca, 158cra, 184tc, 220ca, 413tc, 459cla.
Garth McElroy: 13cl, 26tc, 43cla, 50crb, 62tr, 66tc, 67tc, 68ca, 69tc, 71cla, 72crb, 79tc, 95tc, 96cla, 100crb, 103tr, 104cla, 106tc, 107ca, 108tr, 112crb, 112tc, 112tl, 114crb, 135tr, 138cra, 138crb, 145ca, 150cra, 151cla, 151crb, 152ca, 153cla, 153crb, 154ca, 155cr, 155tc, 156ca, 157tr, 158crb, 158tc, 162crb, 163ca, 163cra, 163crb, 164cra, 165crb, 166cra, 168ca, 168cra, 170ca, 170crb, 171crb, 173crb, 173tr, 174cb, 176tc, 177crb, 177tc, 178ca, 187tc, 188crb, 190ca, 195crb, 195tc, 195tl, 196ca, 196cla, 196cra, 196crb, 201cra, 202crb, 235cra, 236crb, 246cr, 250crb, 252crb, 253cla, 254bc, 254tc, 264cla, 264tc, 268cra, 282cb, 282cla, 282cra, 287crb, 287tc, 290crb, 296cla, 296crb, 302ca, 311crb, 314bc, 315cla, 315cra, 315crb, 324cla, 324cra, 324tc, 325cla, 326crb, 328bc, 328ca, 328crb, 330ca, 332ca, 332crb, 335cra, 337bc, 337ca, 337crb, 339cr, 340crb, 342c, 342t, , 344tr, 348crb, 349bc, 351tc, 352crb, 354cra, 354crb, 355bc, 355cra, 356cb, 356crb, 359bc, 361b, 363ca, 363cra, 367cb, 367tc, 369ca, 369crb, 370cb, 370crb, 371cb, 371cra, 373crb, 373tc, 375crb, 378cra, 380tr, 381crb, 382cra, 382tc, 383bc, 384crb, 386cb, 386cra, 386tc, 389cra, 389crb, 390cr, 391cra, 391crb, 391tc, 392bc, 392ca, 398bc, 399cra, 400cra, 400crb, 400tc, 402cra, 402tc, 403crb, 404cla, 405cla, 405crb, 405tc, 408crb, 411cra, 413cra, 414bc, 416cb, 416cra, 417bl, 419ca, 419crb, 420crb, 421crb, 423crb, 425cra, 425crb, 428cb, 432crb, 436crb, 436tr, 438bc, 442crb, 442tc, 450crb, 451bc, 451tc, 452ca, 453tc, 456cla, 456crb, 456tc, 458cra, 460bc, 460tc, 464cra, 465cra, 466crb, 466tc, 467crb, 468ca, 470ca, 472cb, 472tc, 473ca, 473crb, 475cra, 477cra, 479crb, 480bc, 481tr, 484tr.
Arthur Morris/Birds As Art: 208tr.
Bob Moul: 95cla, 152crb, 307crb, 372crb, 425tc, 438cla.
Alan Murphy: 21cl, 93ca, 230b, 235cl, 237crb, 259b, 259cl, 269bl, 269br, 270ca, 270cb, 271l, 275cla, 293crb, 308cb, 308crb, 311crb, 323ca, 326ca, 393b, 401cla, 430b, 467cra, 467tr, 474cra, 474crb.
Tomi Muukonen: 48crb, 76cl, 94tr, 124tr, 133cla, 198fcla, 200crb, 206cla, 206crb, 210ca, 374bc, 445crb, 448crb, 488tl.
naturepl.com: Barry Mansell 37c; Vincent Munier 8-9c; Nigel Marven 224ca; Tom Vezo 15crb.
NHPA/Photoshot: Bill Coster 92bc, 144bc; Dhritiman Mukherjee; Kevin Schafer 81cb.

Wayne Nicholas: 143c, 143tr.
Judd Patterson: 20, 29cra, 29tc, 108bc, 129bc, 129cra, 240cla, 433ca.
E. J. Peiker: 24cra, 40cra, 44fcra, 44tr, 47tc, 49cb, 50ca, 52tc, 53ca, 53tr, 56cla, 56cra, 57ca, 57crb, 57tr, 58ca, 58cb, 58tc, 59cb, 59crb, 61ca, 61crb, 71crb, 72tc, 76tr, 78crb, 79crb, 97crb, 99cl, 100tc, 106cra, 107cra, 112fcra, 117ca, 117cla, 128cra, 132cla, 132crb, 135t, 140tc, 144cr, 146crb, 147ca, 147cra, 149cra, 149crb, 153cra, 157tc, 161ca, 166crb, 167cla, 167crb, 169cr, 183cr, 188ca, 193crb, 206cra, 211tr, 218cb, 229cra, 229crb, 234bc, 239cla, 239tc, 244cra, 264crb, 265tr, 266tr, 271br, 276cb, 286cl, 300ca, 300crb, 301cb, 307cra, 316cb, 317tc, 318crb, 325cra, 327crb, 327tc, 329bc, 333cla, 341c, 341crb, 350bc, 382tr, 388crb, 388tr, 397cla, 401crb, 409tr, 429bc, 430tr, 431crb, 433bc, 434tr, 439fcla, 441bc, 443cla, 469crb, 471ca, 474tr, 477bc, 481cla, 488bl.
Jari Peltomäki: 1c, 33tc, 35cra, 38ca, 62crb, 68crb, 76bc, 115bc, 134ca, 134cra, 134crb, 140cla, 140cra, 140crb, 210crb, 231crb, 238b, 247cb, 306crb, 331cra, 331crb, 380cla, 445cra, 484br, 486tl.
Mike Read: 34bc, 83crb, 121crb.
George Reszeter: 487tl.
Robert Royse: 26cla, 28cla, 33cra, 41crb, 66ca, 97ca, 137ca, 137crb, 148cra, 160cra, 163cla, 164ca, 172tr, 177ca, 195cra, 207ca, 207tr, 235bc, 236cra, 267ca, 296cra, 347cra, 350tc, 358crb, 361ca, 415cra, 422crb, 422tr, 423cla, 444crb, 446cra, 446crb, 448tr, 449crb, 461ca, 461crb, 462cla, 462cra, 467ca, 468crb, 474ca, 486br.
Chris Schenk: 68fcla.
Bill Schmoker: 28crb, 42ca, 43cra, 46tc, 80cla, 80tc, 83cr, 86ca, 86crb, 86tr, 87ca, 87crb, 87tr, 88crb, 89crb, 89tc, 96crb, 101ca, 120crb, 131tc, 132cr, 132cra, 184crb, 232crb, 260ca, 260crb, 305ca.
Brian E. Small: 9fcra, 22tc, 22tr, 23tc, 23tr, 24cr, 26cra, 28tr, 30crb, 31cla, 31cra, 31crb, 41ca, 45ca, 45tc, 49ca, 49tc, 55tc, 59ca, 59tc, 61tc, 65tc, 66tr, 69ca, 72ca, 77ca, 78cla, 82cla, 82cra, 92tr, 102tc, 109cra, 111cla, 111crb, 116ca, 116tc, 123cra, 124ca, 126cra, 128bc, 136ca, 136crb, 142c, 142cla, 149tc, 150tc, 153tc, 159ca, 159tc, 161cra, 164cla, 165ca, 166ca, 171ca, 171tr, 172tc, 174ca, 175ca, 175cra, 176tr, 181tc, 186fcla, 190cra, 191cra, 194ca, 194tr, 197ca, 197cla, 197cra, 202ca, 202cra, 203tr, 205ca, 211ca, 212ca, 232ca, 234tc, 237ca, 237cra, 240cra, 240crb, 241cra, 242ca, 244cla, 246ca, 246cra, 247cra, 248cla, 248cra, 249cb, 250cra, 255cl, 257ca, 258crb, 262crb, 265cla, 265crb, 266cra, 267bc, 268cla, 270cra, 270tr, 271cra, 272cla, 273bc, 273cra, 274bc, 274tc, 276cla, 276cra, 277cb, 277cla, 277cra, 278tc, 280cb, 280cla, 280cra, 283cb, 284ca, 284cb, 284cra, 284fcla, 285cla, 285cra, 286tr, 287cb, 288ca, 289ca, 290cra, 290tc, 291cb, 291cra, 293ca, 294cra, 295ca, 295crb, 297ca, 297crb, 298crb, 299cra, 302cra, 303bc, 303ca, 304cla, 305crb, 308ca, 309ca, 309crb, 310ca, 310crb, 311tr, 311cra, 313ca, 313crb, 314ca, 315tc, 317cra, 319ca, 319cra, 325crb, 330crb, 331ca, 334cra, 335crb, 336ca, 338ca, 339tr, 340bc, 340cra, 341cla, 345cra, 346crb, 347crb, 348bc, 348cra, 351ca, 352bc, 352ca, 353cra, 353tc, 354cla, 356ca, 357ca, 357crb, 357tc, 362cra, 362tc, 363tr, 364tc, 365ca, 365cra, 365tr, 367ca, 368bc, 368ca, 370cra, 370tc, 371cla, 371tc, 372cra, 377tc, 378tc, 379cra, 379crb, 381ca, 382cla, 383cra, 385tc, 387ca, 387crb, 389cla, 389tc, 390ca, 390cra, 390tl, 393tr, 394cla, 394cra, 394crb, 395bc, 395cla, 395cra, 396cra, 396tc, 397crb, 398tr, 399cla, 401cra, 402crb, 403ca, 403tc, 404tr, 405tr, 406ca, 406crb, 406tc, 406tr, 407cra, 407crb, 407tc, 408ca, 409cla, 410cra, 410crb, 410tc, 411tc, 412cra, 412tc, 413crb, 414ca, 414cla, 414cra, 414tc, 415bc, 415cla, 415tc, 416cla, 417cra, 417tc, 418cla, 418cra, 420ca, 421ca, 422ca, 423tc, 423tr, 424cra, 424crb, 426ca, 427ca, 427tc, 428tc, 429ca, 429tc, 431cla, 431cra, 431tr, 432cla, 432cra, 432tc, 434tc, 435cra, 437crb, 438ca, 438cra, 439ca, 439crb, 440bc, 441cra, 441tc, 442cla, 442cra, 443tr, 443br, 444cla, 444cra, 447bc, 447cla, 447cra, 449tr, 450cl, 451cra, 452crb, 453cra, 453crb, 454cra, 455cra, 455crb, 455tc, 456cra, 457cla, 458cl, 458crb, 458fcla, 458tc, 459tr, 460cra, 463bc, 463ca, 464ca, 466cla, 470cra, 471tc, 472ca, 473cra, 475cr, 475tc, 476cla, 476cr, 476crb, 476tr, 477cl, 477cla, 477tc, 478cla, 478cra, 478crb, 478tc, 479cla, 479cra, 479tc, 480cla, 480tc, 480tr, 481bc, 481tc, 487br, 489bl, 489br, 490tl, 490tr.
Michelle Lynn St.Sauveur: 154crb.
Bob Steele: 11cb, 21cla, 22cla, 22crb, 24tr, 25ca, 27ca, 27crb, 27tc, 29cla, 31tc, 34ca, 38cra, 39tc, 40cla, 40crb, 42tc, 42tr, 43crb, 45crb, 46crb, 47tr, 49crb, 51tc, 52tr, 53crb, 61tr, 65crb, 65tr, 69crb, 71tc, 72tr, 79tr, 82cb, 82tr, 83ca, 93crb, 93tc, 97tc, 98ca, 98cb, 102cb, 103crb, 105tc, 109tc, 111cra, 114cra, 114tc, 117crb, 117tr, 124cra, 126ca, 128cla, 128tc, 130bc, 130ca, 130tr, 132tr, 133crb, 135b, 138cla, 139ca, 139tc, 141cla, 142cra, 145cra, 146bl, 146cra, 146tc, 147cla, 148tc, 150ca, 151tc, 157ca, 157crb, 159crb, 161crb, 162ca, 164crb, 165tc, 167ca, 168tc, 170cra, 175crb, 175tr, 176ca, 176crb, 178crb, 179bc, 179ca, 181cla, 181cra, 181crb, 181tr, 182cra, 183bc, 183ca, 185ca, 185crb, 185tc, 185tr, 186fcra, 188tr, 189cra, 189crb, 190cla, 190crb, 190tc, 191cla, 191cr, 191crb, 191tr, 193cla, 193cra, 193tc, 193tr, 194cra, 194crb, 198crb, 198tc, 201cla, 201tc, 203ca, 205cla, 205crb, 211crb, 211tc, 212tc, 213tc, 214bc, 214fcla, 216tc, 218cra, 222tc, 228bc, 228cra, 238tr, 243cra, 243tc, 244cb, 245cla, 245cra, 245crb, 249cra, 249tc, 250cla, 252cra, 252tc, 253crb, 255tr, 255b, 256ca, 257crb, 259t, 264cra, 265tc, 266ca, 266crb, 267cla, 267cr, 268cb, 268crb, 272cra, 272fclb, 272fcrb, 274cra, 275ca, 275cra, 278cla, 278cra, 278crb, 279ca, 279tr, 281bc, 281ca, 281cla, 281cra, 283cla, 283cra, 286b, 287cra, 288crb, 289crb, 291cr, 292cra, 292crb, 292tc, 294crb, 298cla, 298cra, 301ca, 301cra, 301crb, 304b, 305cra, 306tc, 311tc, 314crb, 316crb, 317cb, 318ca, 319crb, 320ca, 320crb, 321ca, 321crb, 322crb, 323b, 327cb, 327cra, 329cra, 329crb, 332cra, 332tr, 333cra, 333crb, 334crb, 334tc, 335tc, 336crb, 336tc, 337tc, 338crb, 338tc, 338tr, 339bc, 339cla, 340tc, 341bc, 341tr, 343cra, 344crb, 346cra, 347bc, 347ca, 348tc, 350cra, 351crb, 353crb, 354ca, 358ca, 359ca, 360fcla, 361cra, 362crb, 364cla, 364cra, 365cb, 366tc, 368crb, 373cla, 373cra, 375cla, 375tr, 377cla, 377cra, 377crb, 378crb, 380b, 381cb, 383cl, 383tc, 385cla, 385cra, 385crb, 387tc, 388cla, 388cra, 392cra, 393cl, 396cla, 396crb, 397cra, 398cla, 400cla, 401tc, 402cla, 404cb, 404crb, 409c, 409cra, 409crb, 411crb, 412crb, 416crb, 417bc, 417cla, 424tc, 426crb, 426tc, 427cb, 427crb, 428ca, 428crb, 430cr, 433ca, 433cra, 433tr, 434crb, 435cla, 435tr, 436cla, 437cra, 437tc, 441cla, 443bl, 447tc, 449cra, 450cla, 450tc, 451cl, 454cla, 454crb, 454tc, 457cra, 457tc, 459crb, 459tc, 464crb, 465cla, 465crb, 465tc, 469ca, 469cb, 470bc, 471bc, 472crb, 475bc, 475ca, 475crb, 488tl, 488tr.
Matthew Studebaker: 395tc.
Andy & Gill Swash: 83tr, 104cra, 109crb, 344cb.
Glen Tepke: 225tc.
Markus Varesvuo: 4-5, 10-11bc, 21cb, 32ca, 35crb, 36cra, 36fbr, 37cra, 38crb, 44crb, 54ca, 54cb, 54tr, 62ca, 62tc, 64cb, 64crb, 64tc, 66crb, 71ca, 73ca, 73crb, 77crb, 79ca, 79cb, 92cl, 94ca, 94crb, 95crb, 121cla, 124crb, 127cra, 127tr, 133ca, 133tr, 180ca, 182crb, 187cb, 215crb, 215tc, 219tc, 243crb, 253cra, 306cra, 324crb, 349crb, 360crb, 384cra, 384tc, 390crb, 445cla, 445tc, 483tl, 483bl, 488br;Vireo: Dr.Yuri Artukhin, Rick and Nora Bowers 337fbl; Herbert Clarke, 91bc; Robert L. Pitman 85bc, 225ca; Don Roberson 224bc; Harold Stiver, 88fbl; Glen Tepke 224fbl, 225crb.
Cal Vornberger: 474cr.
Peter S Weber: 23crb, 24crb, 29crb, 40tc, 65ca, 104tr, 106ca, 230cla, 232cr, 241crb, 251crb, 256tr, 353crb, 273cla, 276fcla, 279tc, 285clb.
Ian Whetton: 85crb.
Roger Wilmshurst: 121cra.
Jacket images: *Front*: Brian E. Small. *Back*: DK Images: Mike Lane fcl; George McCarthy cl; Dudley Edmondson: fbr; Garth McElroy: fclb; Tomi Muukonen: cb (Kittiwake); E. J. Peiker: bl, c, fbl, tl; Brian E. Small: ca, cb (Junco), cla, clb, cra, crb (Bluebird), crb (Painted Bunting), fcra, ftl, ftr; Bob Steele: tc; Markus Varesvuo: fcr. *Spine*: Alan Murphy. *Front and Back Endpapers*: Corbis: Stephen G. Maka/Photex.